Recent Developments in the Economics of International Migration
Volume I

The International Library of Critical Writings in Economics

Founding Editor: Mark Blaug

Late Professor Emeritus, University of London, UK
Late Professor Emeritus, University of Buckingham, UK

This series is an essential reference source for students, researchers and lecturers in economics. It presents by theme a selection of the most important articles across the entire spectrum of economics. Each volume has been prepared by a leading specialist who has written an authoritative introduction to the literature included.

Wherever possible, the articles in these volumes have been reproduced as originally published using facsimile reproduction, inclusive of footnotes and pagination to facilitate ease of reference.

For a full list of published and future titles in this series and a list of all Edward Elgar published titles visit our website at www.e-elgar.com

Recent Developments in the Economics of International Migration

Volume I
Immigration: Flows and Adjustment

Edited by

Barry R. Chiswick

Professor and Department Chair
Department of Economics, George Washington University, USA

and

Paul W. Miller

Professor, School of Economics and Finance, Curtin University, Australia

THE INTERNATIONAL LIBRARY OF CRITICAL WRITINGS IN ECONOMICS

An Elgar Research Collection
Cheltenham, UK • Northampton, MA, USA

© Barry R. Chiswick and Paul W. Miller 2012. For copyright of individual articles, please refer to the Acknowledgements.

All rights reserved. No part of this publication may be reproduced, stored in a retrieval system, or transmitted in any form or by any means, electronic, mechanical, photocopying, recording, or otherwise without the prior permission of the publisher.

Published by
Edward Elgar Publishing Limited
The Lypiatts
15 Lansdown Road
Cheltenham
Glos GL50 2JA
UK

Edward Elgar Publishing, Inc.
William Pratt House
9 Dewey Court
Northampton
Massachusetts 01060
USA

A catalogue record for this book is available from the British Library

Library of Congress Control Number: 2011942548

MIX
Paper from responsible sources
FSC C018575

ISBN 978 1 84980 942 9 (two volume set)

Printed and bound by MPG Books Group, UK

To our wives and children.

Contents

Acknowledgements xi
Introduction Barry R. Chiswick and Paul W. Miller xiii

PART I   **INTERNATIONAL MIGRATION FLOWS**
1. Ximena Clark, Timothy J. Hatton, and Jeffrey G. Williamson (2007), 'Explaining U.S. Immigration, 1971–1998', *Review of Economics and Statistics*, **89** (2), May, 359–73   3
2. Timothy J. Hatton (2004), 'Emigration from the UK, 1870–1913 and 1950–1998', *European Review of Economic History*, **8**, 149–71   18
3. Timothy J. Hatton and Jeffrey G. Williamson (2002), 'Out of Africa? Using the Past to Project African Emigration Pressure in the Future', *Review of International Economics*, **10** (3), 556–73   41
4. Cynthia Feliciano (2005), 'Educational Selectivity in U.S. Immigration: How Do Immigrants Compare to Those Left Behind?', *Demography*, **42** (1), February, 131–52   59

PART II   **THE LABOR MARKET ADJUSTMENT OF IMMIGRANTS**
5. Joseph Schaafsma and Arthur Sweetman (2001), 'Immigrant Earnings: Age at Immigration Matters', *Canadian Journal of Economics*, **34** (4), November, 1066–99   83
6. Barry R. Chiswick and Paul W. Miller (2002), 'Immigrant Earnings: Language Skills, Linguistic Concentrations and the Business Cycle', *Journal of Population Economics*, **15** (1), 31–57   117
7. Rachel M. Friedberg (2000), 'You Can't Take It with You? Immigrant Assimilation and the Portability of Human Capital', *Journal of Labor Economics*, **18** (2), April, 221–51   144
8. Darren Lubotsky (2007), 'Chutes or Ladders? A Longitudinal Analysis of Immigrant Earnings', *Journal of Political Economy*, **115** (5), October, 820–67   175
9. Denise Doiron and Rochelle Guttmann (2009), 'Wealth Distributions of Migrant and Australian-born Households', *Economic Record*, **85** (268), March, 32–45   223
10. Barry R. Chiswick and Paul W. Miller (2005), 'Do Enclaves Matter in Immigrant Adjustment?', *City and Community*, **4** (1), March, 5–35   237
11. Anna Piil Damm (2009), 'Ethnic Enclaves and Immigrant Labor Market Outcomes: Quasi-Experimental Evidence', *Journal of Labor Economics*, **27** (2), April, 281–314   268

12. John M. McDowell and Larry D. Singell, Jr (2000), 'Productivity of Highly Skilled Immigrants: Economists in the Postwar Period', *Economic Inquiry*, **38** (4), October, 672–84 — 302
13. Magnus Lofstrom (2002), 'Labor Market Assimilation and the Self-employment Decision of Immigrant Entrepreneurs', *Journal of Population Economics*, **15** (1), 83–114 — 315
14. Francine D. Blau, Lawrence M. Kahn, Joan Y. Moriarty, and Andre Portela Souza (2003), 'The Role of the Family in Immigrants' Labor-Market Activity: An Evaluation of Alternative Explanations: Comment', *American Economic Review*, **93** (1), March, 429–47 — 347
15. Heather Antecol, Peter Kuhn, and Stephen J. Trejo (2006), 'Assimilation via Prices or Quantities? Sources of Immigrant Earnings Growth in Australia, Canada, and the United States', *Journal of Human Resources*, **XLI** (4), Fall, 821–40 — 366

PART III   DEMOGRAPHIC ADJUSTMENT OF IMMIGRANTS

16. Heather Antecol and Kelly Bedard (2006), 'Unhealthy Assimilation: Why do Immigrants Converge to American Health Status Levels?', *Demography*, **43** (2), May, 337–60 — 389
17. Aïda Solé-Auró and Eileen M. Crimmins (2008), 'Health of Immigrants in European Countries', *International Migration Review*, **42** (4), Winter, 861–76 — 413
18. Barry R. Chiswick and Christina Houseworth (2011), 'Ethnic Intermarriage Among Immigrants: Human Capital and Assortative Mating', *Review of Economics of the Household*, **9** (2), 149–80 — 429
19. Xin Meng and Robert G. Gregory (2005), 'Intermarriage and the Economic Assimilation of Immigrants', *Journal of Labor Economics*, **23** (1), January, 135–75 — 461
20. Guillermina Jasso, Douglas S. Massey, Mark R. Rosenzweig and James P. Smith (2000), 'Assortative Mating Among Married New Legal Immigrants to the United States: Evidence From the New Immigrant Survey Pilot', *International Migration Review*, **34** (2), Summer, 443–59 — 502
21. Jochen Mayer and Regina T. Riphahn (2000), 'Fertility Assimilation of Immigrants: Evidence from Count Data Models', *Journal of Population Economics*, **13** (2), July, 241–61 — 519
22. Neeraj Kaushal (2005), 'New Immigrants' Location Choices: Magnets without Welfare', *Journal of Labor Economics*, **23** (1), January, 59–80 — 540
23. Jorgen Hansen and Magnus Lofstrom (2003), 'Immigrant Assimilation and Welfare Participation: Do Immigrants Assimilate Into or Out of Welfare?', *Journal of Human Resources*, **XXXVIII** (1), Winter, 74–98 — 562

24. Barry R. Chiswick and Noyna DebBurman (2004), 'Educational Attainment: Analysis by Immigrant Generation', *Economics of Education Review*, **23** (4), 361–79 587
25. Carmel U. Chiswick (2009), 'The Economic Determinants of Ethnic Assimilation', *Journal of Population Economics*, **22** (4), October, 859–80 606
26. Amelie F. Constant, Liliya Gataullina and Klaus F. Zimmermann (2009), 'Ethnosizing Immigrants', *Journal of Economic Behavior and Organization*, **69** (3), 274–87 628

Acknowledgements

The editors and publishers wish to thank the authors and the following publishers who have kindly given permission for the use of copyright material.

American Economic Association for article: Francine D. Blau, Lawrence M. Kahn, Joan Y. Moriarty, and Andre Portela Souza (2003), 'The Role of the Family in Immigrants' Labor-Market Activity: An Evalution of Alternative Explanations: Comment', *American Economic Review*, **93** (1), March, 429–47.

Blackwell Publishing Ltd for articles: Guillermina Jasso, Douglas S. Massey, Mark R. Rosenzweig, and James P. Smith (2000), 'Assortative Mating Among Married New Legal Immigrants to the United States: Evidence from the New Immigrant Survey Pilot', *International Migration Review*, **34** (2), Summer, 443–59; John M. McDowell and Larry D. Singell, Jr (2000), 'Productivity of Highly Skilled Immigrants: Economists in the Postwar Period', *Economic Inquiry*, **38** (4), October, 672–84; Joseph Schaafsma and Arthur Sweetman (2001), 'Immigrant Earnings: Age at Immigration Matters', *Canadian Journal of Economics*, **34** (4), November, 1066–99; Timothy J. Hatton and Jeffrey G. Williamson (2002), 'Out of Africa? Using the Past to Project African Emigration Pressure in the Future', *Review of International Economics*, **10** (3), 556–73; Barry R. Chiswick and Paul W. Miller (2005), 'Do Enclaves Matter in Immigrant Adjustment', *City and Community*, **4** (1), March, 5–35; Aïda Solé-Auró and Eileen M. Crimmins (2008), 'Health of Immigrants in European Countries', *International Migration Review*, **42** (4), Winter, 861–76; Denise Doiron and Rochelle Guttmann (2009), 'Wealth Distributions of Migrant and Australian-born Households', *Economic Record*, **85** (268), March, 32–45.

Cambridge University Press for article: Timothy J. Hatton (2004), 'Emigration from the UK, 1870–1913 and 1950–1998', *European Review of Economic History*, **8**, 149–71.

Elsevier Ltd for articles: Barry R. Chiswick and Noyna DebBurman (2004), 'Educational Attainment: Analysis by Immigrant Generation', *Economics of Education Review*, **23**, 361–79; Amelie F. Constant, Liliya Gataullina, and Klaus F. Zimmermann (2009), 'Ethnosizing Immigrants', *Journal of Economic Behaviour and Organization*, **69**, 274–87.

MIT Press for article: Ximena Clark, Timothy J. Hatton and Jeffrey G. Williamson (2007), 'Explaining U.S. Immigration, 1971–1988', *Review of Economics and Statistics*, **89** (2), May, 359–73.

Population Association of America for articles: Cynthia Feliciano (2005), 'Educational Selectivity in U.S. Immigration: How do Immigrants Compare to Those Left Behind?',

Demography, **42** (1), February, 131–52; Heather Antecol and Kelly Bedard (2006), 'Unhealthy Assimilation: Why do Immigrants Converge to American Health Status Levels?', *Demography*, **43** (2), May, 337–60.

Springer Science and Business Media B.V. for articles: Jochen Mayer and Regina T. Riphahn (2000), 'Fertility Assimilation of Immigrants: Evidence from Count Data Models', *Journal of Population Economics*, **13** (2), July, 241–61; Barry R. Chiswick and Paul W. Miller (2002), 'Immigrant Earnings: Language Skills, Linguistic Concentrations and the Business Cycle', *Journal of Population Economics*, **15**, 31–57; Magnus Lofstrom (2002), 'Labor Market Assimilation and the Self-employment Decision of Immigrant Entrepreneurs', *Journal of Population Economics*, **15**, 83–114; Carmel U. Chiswick (2009), 'The Economic Determinants of Ethnic Assimilation', *Journal of Population Economics*, **22**, (4), October, 859–80; Barry R. Chiswick and Christina Houseworth (2011), 'Ethnic Intermarriage Among Immigrants: Human Capital and Assortative Mating', *Review of Economics of the Household*, **9** (2), 149–80.

University of Chicago Press for articles: Rachel M. Friedberg (2000), 'You Can't Take It with You? Immigrant Assimilation and the Portability of Human Capital', *Journal of Labor Economics*, **18** (2), April, 221–51; Neeraj Kaushal (2005), 'New Immigrants' Location Choices: Magnets without Welfare', *Journal of Labor Economics*, **23** (1), January, 59–80; Xin Meng and Robert G. Gregory (2005), 'Intermarriage and the Economic Assimilation of Immigrants', *Journal of Labor Economics*, **23** (1), January, 135–75; Darren Lubotsky (2007), 'Chutes or Ladders? A Longitudinal Analysis of Immigrant Earnings', *Journal of Political Economy*, **115** (5), October, 820–67; Anna Piil Damm (2009), 'Ethnic Enclaves and Immigrant Labor Market Outcomes: Quasi-Experimental Evidence', *Journal of Labor Economics*, **27** (2), April, 281–314.

University of Wisconsin Press for articles: Jorgen Hansen and Magnus Lofstrom (2003), 'Immigrant Assimilation and Welfare Participation: Do Immigrants Assimilate Into or Out of Welfare?', *Journal of Human Resources*, **XXXVIII** (1), Winter, 74–98; Heather Antecol, Peter Kuhn, and Stephen J. Trejo (2006), 'Assimilation via Prices or Quantities? Sources of Immigrant Earnings Growth in Australia, Canada, and the United States', *Journal of Human Resources*, **XLI** (4), Fall, 821–40.

Every effort has been made to trace all the copyright holders but if any have been inadvertently overlooked the publishers will be pleased to make the necessary arrangement at the first opportunity.

In addition the publishers wish to thank the Library of Indiana University at Bloomington, USA, for their assistance in obtaining these articles.

Introduction

Barry R. Chiswick and Paul W. Miller

The migration of people in search of better economic opportunities or in search of refuge has been a continuous feature of human life. From the time of hunter-gatherers, to herdsmen, to farmers, to industrial workers, and to contemporary knowledge workers, we have been a species on the move. This migration, however, did not occur at a constant rate. The size of the flows, distance traveled, and even the extent of return flows depended on climatic conditions and economic circumstances in the origin and in alternative destinations, the transportation technology, security at home, the safety of travel, and the extent to which people could leave their origins and were able to enter, whether welcomed or not, alternative destinations.

The movement of people can occur within countries (internal migration) or across countries (international migration). This distinction became of greater importance after the establishment of nation states, and especially in the past century and a half as most countries established regulations of various sorts regarding who may enter, although most did not regulate movements of people within their borders.

In the modern period, say over the past two centuries, there have been dramatic shifts in the size, origins, and destinations of immigrant flows (Chiswick and Hatton, 2003). The large trans-Atlantic and trans-Pacific migrations of the 19th century slowed dramatically with the increased danger and trauma of World War I. Their resurgence in the 1920s was cut short by the economic crisis of the Great Depression, which was followed by World War II. In the post-war period migration patterns have changed – Western Europe went from a region of out-migration to one of in-migration from Africa, the Middle East, Asia, and Eastern Europe; the primarily European/Canadian origins of migrants to the USA changed to Latin American (about half from Mexico) and Asian origins; and the contract labor brought from Asia to work in the European colonial plantations and mines in Asia and Africa ended with the independence of the colonies, to be supplanted by Asian and Middle Eastern contract workers to the oil-rich Persian Gulf states. Equally dramatic has been the high rate of growth of international migration flows in the post-war period. Nor is the migration primarily of low-skilled workers seeking agricultural, service, or industrial jobs, as high-skilled knowledge workers, or STEM (science, technology, engineering, and management) workers, have become an important component of the recent migration streams.

While most countries do not have barriers to emigration, they all have barriers of one sort or another to in-migration. Countries that try to keep immigration below the level that would prevail without regulations need a mechanism for rationing admissions. Rationing criteria include coming from a particular set of origins (e.g. ethnically similar countries or ethnic groups, or former colonies), having family members in the destination, having 'needed' skills or investment funds, humanitarian concerns (refugees), and lotteries, among other criteria.

The increased size of international migration and the changes in the major source and destination countries, as well as public policies to influence the size and characteristics of these migration flows, have raised many challenges to our understanding of these phenomena. International migration has provided ample opportunity for economics researchers to apply their theoretical models and statistical methodologies to understanding the range of its determinants and consequences.

Just as worldwide migration has increased in recent decades, so too has research on the economics of international migration.[1] In 2002, Klaus Zimmermann and Thomas Bauer edited *The Economics of Migration*, a five-volume set of the major English language research articles on the economics of migration from the earliest days of research to 2000 (Zimmermann and Bauer, 2002). The present volume extends the compilation of papers from 2000 to the present.

The selection of journal articles published since 2000 included in this collection required many difficult choices. It was decided to focus exclusively on international migration, leaving out the vast literature on internal migration. The selections were limited to English language articles published in academic economics journals. There still remained about a thousand outstanding research studies. We decided to select articles primarily based on their contribution to an understanding of the economics of international migration, rather than on their primary contributions to economic theory or statistical methodology; yet they had to be sound in their applications of both theory and statistical tools. We also sought coverage of the diverse aspects of immigration research. Although much of the research on the economics of immigration over the past few decades has focused on microdata analyses of aspects of the skills and labor market adjustment of immigrants, we sought a broader treatment of the topics. Immigration research cuts across the various sub-fields in economics, and we sought to have coverage of as wide a range of these sub-fields as possible, subject to constraints on high quality and the length of these volumes. Thus, while we believe that the articles included here are of very high quality and represent the broad range of immigration research in economics, we recognize that many other high-quality papers did not make the cut, often because we had to choose among several papers on similar topics.

Volume I   Immigration: Flows and Adjustment
Part I   International Migration Flows

Volume I, *Immigration: Flows and Adjustment*, includes 26 articles divided among three sections – International Migration Flows, The Labor Market Adjustment of Immigrants, and Demographic Adjustment of Immigrants.

While there has been extensive research on the adjustment of immigrants in the destination, typically using census or survey microdata, and to a lesser extent research on the impact of immigration on the host economy, unlike research in the early 20th century there has been far less attention devoted to the determinants of international migration flows. The section on International Migration Flows includes four papers. Clark, Hatton and Williamson (2007) study immigration to the USA (1971–1998), the largest recipient of immigrants. They consider a wide range of countries of origin and include economic, demographic, and network (family and friends) effects, and immigration policy variables, which are all found to be important determinants of migration by country of origin. Hatton (2004) examines emigration from the UK in two periods – pre-WWI, before the major destination countries imposed severe immigration restrictions (1870–1913) and post-WWII, when such restrictions were in place

(1950–1998). The decline in the favorable treatment of British immigrants in their major destinations decreased British emigration, and together with increased Third World immigration into Britain changed Britain from a country of net emigration to one of net in-migration.

There has been relatively little research on the economics of international migration regarding Africa, in part because of the small size of these migration flows to North America and Oceania, and in part because of data limitations. Hatton and Williamson (2002) use data on emigration from poor European countries in the late 19th century to predict the extent of African emigration pressures. Assuming that the analogy holds, they predict strong incentives for emigration from Africa, particularly to Europe and especially from North Africa. Because of European restrictions on immigration from Africa they predict substantial illegal migration. Although one might be skeptical regarding using migration from poor European countries over 100 years ago to 'forecast' 21st century migration from Africa, events over the past few decades have in general been consistent with their predictions.

Feliciano (2005) is concerned with the selectivity of contemporary immigrants to the USA, and in particular their educational attainment compared with those who remain in the origin. Consistent with the human capital model of migration, she finds that legal migrants are more highly educated than the stayers in the origin, even though US immigration policy places very little emphasis on the skill level of immigrants. This suggests favorable self-selection in migration to the USA.

Part II The Labor Market Adjustment of Immigrants

The section on the labor market adjustment of immigrants contains the largest number of papers because this has been the most intense area of research on the economics of international migration in the past decade.

Schaafsma and Sweetman (2001) study the earnings of immigrants in Canada. They find that in general pre-migration labor market experience has very little economic return in Canada and that the payoff to schooling falls with age at migration. They find that those who arrive in Canada in the secondary school years (age 15 to 18) achieve a lower level of educational attainment than those who came at younger or at older ages. Adjustment may be the most difficult among those who immigrate in this age group.

Chiswick and Miller (2002) study the earnings of immigrants to the USA. They find that English language proficiency has a large positive effect on immigrant earnings, that living in an ethnic enclave has a negative effect on earnings, and that arriving at a time of high unemployment has a persistent negative ('scarring') effect that does diminish but does not disappear over time. The phenomenon of ethnic enclaves emphasized in this paper has become a major theme in subsequent immigration research.

Immigrant earnings in Israel, a major immigrant-receiving country, are the subject of Friedberg's (2000) analysis. She also finds that pre-migration schooling and labor market experience provide little benefit in the Israeli labor market. Education acquired in Israel, however, has a double positive effect: it provides direct labor market returns and increases the labor market returns to schooling obtained before migration. This evidence adds to that of other studies that demonstrate complementarity between post-immigration investments, such as investment in destination language skills, and the returns to origin-country human capital.

Post-migration investments in schooling, language, and job training appear to increase the returns to pre-migration investments.

While the three previous studies relied on cross-sectional data, Lubotsky (2007) studies immigrant earnings in the USA using longitudinal data. He concludes that the higher propensity for return migration of lower wage immigrants has biased upwards the apparent economic progress of immigrants observed in cross-sectional data. Lubotsky nevertheless, reports that immigrants make solid economic progress in the USA.

Immigrant wealth acquisition in another major destination, Australia, is analyzed by Doiron and Guttmann (2009). Although immigrants have more favorable characteristics for accumulating wealth, they are consistently less wealthy than native-born Australians, even if they have lived in Australia a long time. Consistent with the evidence on immigrant earnings adjustment, however, the wealth differential between immigrants and the native born dissipates with duration of residence in Australia.

The determinants and consequences of immigrants living in ethnic/linguistic enclaves in the USA are analysed by Chiswick and Miller (2005). They base their analysis on the demand by immigrants for 'ethnic goods'. Earnings are lower among immigrants the lower their own English language proficiency and the greater the extent that they live in an ethnic/linguistic enclave. Living in the enclave also has a negative effect on acquiring English language proficiency.

Damm (2009) also considers immigrant enclaves, but in this case refugees in Denmark. She finds that refugees with unfavorable unobserved characteristics gravitate to ethnic enclaves. She concludes that the ethnic networks provide labor market information that enhances wages.

McDowell and Singell (2000) study the productivity of a subset of high-skilled immigrants in the USA. They analyze the productivity of immigrant economists in the post-war period. They report a shift in origins from Europe to Asia. However, they find no change in productivity due to this shift, and that recent cohorts of immigrants are more productive than native-born economists. This may be due to greater incentives for the more able and productive to migrate and the effects of the occupation-based visas in US immigration law.

There has been interest in the degree of self-employment among immigrants. In the USA the rate of non-farm self-employment is greater among the foreign-born than among the native-born. Lofstrom (2002) shows, using US census data, that the self-employed immigrants earn more than wage and salary immigrants, and that the earnings disadvantage of immigrants compared to the native-born appears greater if, as is done by some researchers, the self-employed are excluded from the analysis.

The immigrant family investment hypothesis implies an interdependence in the labor supply and the labor market investment behavior of husbands and wives; namely, that just after arrival wives enter the labor market to provide family income so that their husbands can afford to invest in destination, or host economy, human capital. Blau et al. (2003) use US 1980 and 1990 Census data to test this hypothesis and find that it is rejected by the data. Immigrant wives at arrival work less than native-born women, just as immigrant men work less than native-born men. In both instances, however, labor supply increases with duration. This is not consistent with the Canadian results in Baker and Benjamin (1997), where there was evidence of immigrant women working to help finance their husbands' human capital. Blau et al. (2003) speculate as to why there is this difference.

The final article in this section, by Antecol et al. (2006), is a comparative analysis of immigrant earnings adjustment in Australia, Canada, and the USA. The increase in earnings with duration can come through wage rate increases (prices) or through employment increases (quantities). The wage rate effect is greatest in the USA, which has the most flexible labor market of the three, whereas employment adjustments are most important in Australia, which has the least flexible wage system. This paper demonstrates the importance of institutions to the patterns of immigrant economic adjustment.

Part III   Demographic Adjustment of Immigrants

The section on the demographic adjustment of immigrants includes papers on health status, marriage, fertility, location, welfare participation, educational attainment, and ethnic identity. These appear to be topics where research on immigration has increased in recent years.

Antecol and Bedard (2006) analyze the health status of immigrants to the USA. Using the Body Mass Index (BMI) as the measure of health status, they find that immigrants at arrival are healthier (lower BMI) than US natives, but their BMI converges toward that of natives with duration in the USA, with female immigrants closing the gap before males. On the other hand, in a study of older (age 50 and over) immigrants in Europe, Solé-Auró and Crimmins (2008) find a poorer level of health among the immigrants.

One indicator of the integration and social acceptance of immigrants in the destination is the extent of intermarriage with members of other ethnic groups. Analyzing US Census data, Chiswick and Houseworth (2011) find that intermarriage increases with a younger age at migration, a longer duration in the USA, and a higher level of educational attainment. It also increases with a smaller 'availability' of members of one's own ethnic group. Marriage to a native (but not another immigrant) appears to accelerate the acquisition of destination human capital and thereby steepens the economic assimilation of immigrants, according to Meng and Gregory (2005).

Jasso et al. (2000) discuss the pilot sample for the US New Immigrant Survey, and use these data to study the schooling attainment of husbands and wives by US citizenship status. They report that husband–wife schooling levels are less similar when both spouses are immigrants than among immigrants married to a US citizen. Jasso et al. (2000) conclude that the criteria used for entry affect the schooling levels of the immigrants, and hence their well-being and the well-being of their children.

The fertility behavior of immigrants is studied by Mayer and Riphahn (2000) using the German Socioeconomic Panel (GSOEP). Immigrants to Germany in the period under study generally came from high-fertility countries. With the passage of time the immigrants' fertility behavior converges to that of the native-born Germans. This suggests an adjustment of immigrant fertility behavior to host country economic incentives.

Kaushal (2005) uses features of the US 1996 welfare reform that allowed for state differences in welfare benefits to test the 'welfare magnet' hypothesis, that is, to test whether the location choice of newly arrived low-skilled unmarried women with children is influenced by these differential benefits. No significant welfare effects were found, perhaps because the differential benefits were too small to influence behavior.

Hansen and Lofstrom (2003) study the use of welfare by immigrants in Sweden. Refugees have higher initial welfare participation rates and a longer length of time on benefits than other immigrants, while native-born Swedes have the lowest rates. Both immigrant groups show a decline in welfare participation with duration in Sweden, but the gap between the immigrants and the natives closes only after 20 years in the country.

Another dimension of the demographic adjustment of immigrants is their post-migration educational attainment. Using US Current Population Survey (CPS) data, Chiswick and DebBurman (2004) study the educational attainment of first-, second-, and higher-generation Americans. Second-generation American adults have the highest educational attainment. Immigrating as a teenager is associated with a lower schooling attainment than coming as a pre-teen or a post-teen. The gender gap in favor of men is greatest among the foreign born, although the native-born women are now achieving a higher educational attainment than are native-born men.

The final two articles in Volume I are on dimensions of ethnic assimilation among immigrants. C. Chiswick (2009) distinguished between ethnic-specific human capital and general human capital. Groups will vary as to whether these forms of skills are complements or competitive (anti-complements), and implications are developed for a range of socio-economic outcomes. Constant et al. (2009) developed an index of the intensity of an immigrant's ethnic identity ('ethnosizer') and applied it to the German Socioeconomic Panel (GSOEP). This index is based on language use, cultural aspects, ethnic networks, migration history, and ethnic self-identification. The authors show that they can classify individuals on the basis of their attachment to their ethnic origin and their attachment to the destination (Germany).

Volume II Immigration and Language: Impacts and Policy
Part I Language Adjustment of Immigrants

Volume II, *Immigration and Language: Impacts and Policy*, includes 24 articles divided among four sections – Language Adjustment of Immigrants, Impacts of Immigrants, Citizenship, and Immigration Policy.

The five papers in this section encompass studies of the determinants of destination language proficiency among immigrants, and the consequences of this proficiency for labor market outcomes. Carliner (2000) uses the 1980 and 1990 US Censuses to study the English proficiency of the native born and immigrants. Lack of proficiency in English is rare among the native born, but not among the foreign born. English fluency among immigrants has declined over time in the post-war period because of the shift in immigrants' countries of origin away from Canada and Europe and in favor of Latin America and Asia. Carliner documents relationships between immigrants' proficiency in English and both their personal characteristics (e.g. age at migration, education, gender, years since migration) and source country. He argues that the differences in English proficiency by region of origin are more closely associated with the geographic distance from the USA than they are with the source country's per capita income or linguistic distance from English.

Chiswick and Miller (2001) develop a comprehensive model of destination language proficiency among immigrants and apply it to Canada using the 1991 Census. They use a human capital approach and an immigrant adjustment model in a dual language (English/French) destination. Destination proficiency among immigrants is found to increase with a younger age of arrival, a longer duration of residence, a higher level of education, and the 'closer' the mother tongue is to English or French, among non-refugee migrants, and among those who live in a region in which few people speak their original mother tongue.

The German language proficiency of immigrants in the German Socio-Economic Panel is analyzed by Dustmann and van Soest (2002). They are concerned primarily with unobserved heterogeneity in language skills and errors in the measurement of proficiency, which have opposite effects on the extent of bias in the partial effect of language proficiency on earnings. Their analyses suggest that measurement error is a more important source of bias than unobserved heterogeneity, and this implies that language proficiency is even more important to earnings determination than shown in conventional studies.

Several studies have attempted to address, without particular success, the potential simultaneity in the determination of earnings and language skills. Bleakley and Chin (2004) use US data in an attempt to address this issue through the analysis of young immigrants. Their correction for endogeneity is based on an Instrumental Variables (IV) strategy, and the estimated effects of English-language proficiency on wages derived using this approach were greater than those obtained in analyses which do not attempt to correct for endogeneity and measurement error.

Chiswick, Lee and Miller (2005) change the focus of the analysis of destination language proficiency from the individual immigrant to the entire nuclear family of immigrants. Using multivariate probit analyses, in addition to their earlier findings (reported in this volume), they conclude that there are large positive correlations across the unmeasured determinants of proficiency between spouses, among siblings, and between parents and their children. Mothers are shown to have a larger impact on the proficiency of their children than do the fathers. The findings imply that there is language learning among family members in the home, including older children and adults.

Part II The Impact of Immigrants

While there has been less research by economists on immigrant impact than on immigrant individual characteristics and adjustment, the impact literature has fostered many interesting and important papers.

A: Labor Markets

Grossmann and Stadelmann (2011) are interested in the effect of high-skilled migration on relative income gaps between the origin and the destination economies. Using an overlapping generations model they show that high-skilled emigration tends to harm the origin, benefit the destination, and widen income differences across countries. It is likely that similar effects emerge if capital migrates from one place to another.

The papers by Borjas (2003) and by Card (2005) focus on whether immigrants tend to widen earnings inequality among the native workers in the US labor market by depressing the wages of workers with skills similar to those of the immigrants. Borjas finds a large effect – that a 10 per cent increase in the supply of workers with a given educational level, other factors staying the same, reduces the wages of native-born workers with similar skills by 3 to 4 per cent. Card, on the other hand, concludes that the evidence is 'scant'.

B: Prices

An issue that is often referred to, but on which there has been little research, is the effect of immigration on relative prices. Cortes (2008) examines the effect across US cities and across time of low-skilled immigration on the prices of non-traded goods and services. The prices of low-skilled immigrant intensive goods (housekeeping and gardening) are significantly lower the larger the share of low-skilled immigrants in the labor market, providing support for the hypothesis that low-skilled immigrants tend to depress the wages of low-skilled native workers.

Immigrants also have an impact on housing markets. Saiz (2007) finds that immigration increases both the rental price of housing and house values, and that the impact in the housing market appears to be greater than in the labor market.

C: Other Impacts

Dixon, Johnson and Rimmer (2011) address the impact issue by analyzing the likely consequences of three alternative enforcement strategies to reduce illegal migration – tighter border enforcement, taxes on employers, and prosecution of employers. A novel feature of their paper is the use of simulations of a dynamic Computable General Equilibrium (CGE) model to determine the impact of these policy alternatives. Their analysis concludes that of the three, taxes on employers have the most beneficial effects.

Natives are, however, not passive with respect to the local impacts of immigrants on wages and prices. Borjas (2006) shows that the location of native-born workers responds to an increase in immigrants in US metropolitan areas through a lower in-migration rate and a higher out-migration rate.

Immigrants have higher non-farm self-employment rates in the US than the native born. Fairlie and Mayer (2003) are concerned with whether differences in immigrant self-employment across US metropolitan areas have an impact on self-employment among the native born. They find that greater immigrant self-employment is associated with a lower rate of native-born self-employment.

Natives apparently also respond to the presence of immigrants for the private/public school decision for their children. Using 1980 and 1990 Census data, Betts and Fairlie (2003) find a 'white flight' effect, especially with respect to the presence of non-English speaking immigrant households. The effect is larger for high school than for primary school, presumably because high school districts are larger and less homogenous than primary school districts.

There has been less research regarding the impact of international migration on the sending country than on the destination country. One important origin country impact is on the human capital investments in the origin. Beine et al. (2008) are concerned with the 'brain drain'. They show that, in principle, high-skilled emigration can lower the human capital stock in the origin, but it can also increase it if the emigration raises the rate of return on human capital, thereby stimulating investment in human capital in the origin. Using cross-sectional international data and simulations, Beine et al. (2008) conclude that countries with a low level of skills and that have low levels of outmigration of skilled workers actually increase their human capital stock due to the brain drain effect. They conclude that the brain drain from low-income to high-income countries increases the number of skilled workers, both in the aggregate and in the low income countries.

Osili (2004) is interested in a different dimension of the impact of emigrants on the origin – investing in housing. She analyzes the investments made in housing in Nigeria through remittances by emigrants living in the USA. Those migrants in the USA who are older, with higher levels of income, and who have family members in Nigeria who have experienced negative economic shocks, are more likely to be investing in housing capital in Nigeria.

Thus, in terms of labor markets and markets for goods and services, immigrants do have an effect on a variety of outcomes and behavior of the native-born population. A synthesis of the findings of these studies, and others, on the impact of immigrants on native labor markets appears to suggest that overall there are no major measurable effects. They also indicate that the positive effects of some immigrants may be offset by the negative effects of others, and that the impacts on some natives differs from those on others. Distributional effects may be the most important impact of immigrants on the native labor market. Overall, it appears that a large exogenous increase in low-skilled immigrants has a negative effect on low-skilled natives. Yet, of all of the sub-areas in immigration research, the findings on the labor market impact tend to be the least robust.

Part III Citizenship

This volume includes three articles on the issue of immigrants acquiring citizenship in the destination. Being able to retain citizenship in one's origin reduces the cost of accepting citizenship in the destination in terms of rights regarding return migration, citizenship of children, and political and economic rights in the origin. Jones-Correa (2001) documents the increase in acceptance of dual nationality on the part of emigrants from Latin American countries. Immigrants to the USA from Latin America have higher rates of naturalization if their origin allows them to have dual citizenship.

Using Canadian census data, Bloemraad (2004) analyzes the time trend and correlates of immigrants to Canada obtaining dual nationality. In Canada, as elsewhere, there has been an increase over time in dual citizenship among immigrants. It increases with the immigrants' human capital (educational attainment) and is more frequent in Quebec than in the rest of Canada. The latter suggests a stronger commitment to staying in Canada among those who go to Quebec.

Mazzolari (2009) analyzes immigrants in the US census and finds that those who acquire dual citizenship, where their origin permits this, experience greater increases in employment and earnings compared with immigrants from the same origin who do not become US citizens. This may arise from unmeasured dimensions of ability, a greater commitment to remaining in the USA, or, less likely, to greater economic opportunities afforded to naturalized immigrants. Few naturalized citizens renounce their country of origin citizenship if the origin permits dual citizenship.

Part IV Immigration Policy

Immigration policy has become a very contentious issue in all of the major immigrant-receiving countries. The policy issues concern the number of immigrants to be admitted, the criteria used for admission (ethnicity, kinship, skills, refugees, lotteries, etc.), and policies regarding enforcement of immigration law, whether at the frontier (border or airports) or in the interior.

Facchini and Mayda (2009) consider the effect of the welfare state on the attitudes of the native born toward immigrants. In countries characterized by high levels of unskilled immigration, high-skilled natives favor their entry, whereas high income among natives is associated with opposing low-skilled immigration. These findings presumably reflect natives' perception of favorable impacts on their economic well-being of the migration of a complementary factor of production (skills), tempered by concerns over the cost of low-skilled immigration in a welfare state (income).

Enforcement of immigration law appears to be sensitive to economic factors. Hanson and Spilimbergo (2001) consider US border enforcement, the primary policy instrument used by the USA to enforce immigration law. They find that border enforcement is sensitive to economic conditions. It is relaxed when the demand for labor is high in the sectors of the economy that tend to employ low-skilled illegal migrants.

Yet, the structure of the provisions for legal immigration can also influence the characteristics of the immigrant flows. Antecol et al. (2003) find that relative to the native-born population, immigrants to Australia and Canada are more highly skilled than those to the USA. The USA receives a large share (in recent years, nearly half) of its immigrants from Latin America, of whom a large proportion are from Mexico, while Canada and Australia receive relatively few from this region. The skills of immigrants from other regions are quite similar across the three destinations. The authors suggest that this similarity implies that the Australian and Canadian skill-based admission policies and the US family-based policy generate a comparable level of skill. Thus, they argue that the relatively low overall skill of immigrants in the USA is associated more with the geographical and historical ties with Mexico and other parts of Latin America rather than with the criteria used to select immigrants. In spite of this special role of Mexican and other Latin American immigrants, given that the USA is frequently the country of 'first choice', the USA could generate a more favorable immigrant skill distribution if it adopted the Australian/Canadian approach.

Further evidence that admission criteria matter is found by Chiswick et al. (2006), who use the Longitudinal Survey of Immigrants to Australia (Panel I) to study the English language proficiency among immigrants. Among other findings, language proficiency at immigration varies by visa category – it is highest for skill-tested and economic migrants, followed by family-based visa recipients, with the lowest level of English proficiency among refugees.

The USA and some of the West European countries have used amnesties to regularize the status of illegal or undocumented migrants. Orrenius and Zavodny (2003) use the experience of the US 1986 Immigration Reform and Control Act to test whether the amnesty (of nearly three million migrants) reduced future illegal immigration. While the initial effect was a decline in apprehensions along the border with Mexico, the amnesty did not stem the tide as the illegal flows quickly returned to the pre-amnesty levels.

As can be seen from these introductory comments, the papers included in this two-volume set cover a rich array of topics, and report many interesting and important findings. The immigration research field is a very exciting one, and we invite you, the reader, to experience this first-hand through the chapters that follow.

Note

1. An analysis of English language articles listed in the economics subgroup of JSTOR that include the words 'immigration' or 'international migration' somewhere in the full text of the article indicated that the number of such articles increased in the post-war period, and that their share of all articles in the JSTOR economics subgroup has increased since the 1970s.

Years	Immigration articles	Share of all economics articles (%)
1880–1889	14	11.5
1890–1899	108	7.7
1900–1909	230	12.4
1910–1919	358	11.7
1920–1929	453	11.7
1930–1939	436	9.7
1940–1949	404	5.4
1950–1959	441	4.4
1960–1969	500	3.7
1970–1979	668	3.5
1980–1989	773	3.6
1990–1999	984	4.5
2000	127	6.0
2001	113	5.6
2002	114	5.4
2003	120	5.5
2004	109	5.2

Note: For many journals JSTOR does not include issues published in the past five years.

Source: http://www.jstor.org/action/showAdvancedSearch.

Acknowledgements

This project would not have been possible without the expert research assistance of Derby Voon, Nick Larsen, and Andrew Kosek. We are also indebted to Chris Berry and Emma Cope of Edward Elgar Publishing Ltd for guiding the volume from the initial concept to publication. Miller acknowledges financial assistance from the Australian Research Council.

We appreciate the comments we received from Carmel U. Chiswick and Evelyn Lehrer.

References

Baker, Michael and Dwayne Benjamin (1997), 'The role of family in immigrants' labor-market activity: an evaluation of alternative explanations', *American Economic Review*, **87** (4), 705–27.

Chiswick, Barry R. and Timothy J. Hatton (2003), 'International migration and the integration of labor markets' in Michael Bordo, Alan Taylor, and Jeffery Williamson (eds), *Globalization in Historical Perspective*, Cambridge: National Bureau of Economic Research, pp. 65–119.

Zimmermann, Klaus and Thomas Bauer (eds) (2002), *The Economics of Migration*, Aldershot, UK: Edward Elgar.

Part I
International Migration Flows

[1]

EXPLAINING U.S. IMMIGRATION, 1971–1998

Ximena Clark, Timothy J. Hatton, and Jeffrey G. Williamson*

Abstract—In this paper we develop and estimate a model to explain variations in immigration to the United States by source country since the early 1970s. The explanatory variables include ratios to the United States of source country income and education as well as relative inequality. In addition, we incorporate the stock of previous immigrants and a variety of variables representing different dimensions of the immigration quotas set by policy. We use the results to shed light on the impact of policy by simulating the effects of the key changes in immigration policy since the late 1970s. We also examine the factors that influenced the composition of U.S. immigration by source region over the entire period.

I. Introduction

SINCE 1950 more that 25 million immigrants have been admitted to the United States, about 20 million of whom arrived after 1970. This mass influx has stimulated a lively debate about the gains from immigration and the implications for immigration policy. Much of the literature has concentrated on the economic outcomes for the immigrants themselves and on the labor market impacts on native-born labor. These effects typically depend on how U.S. immigrants are selected—both within and between countries of origin—and models of this process are at the heart of the analysis. But while the literature is long on examining the outcomes of immigration, it is surprisingly short on estimating the determinants of immigration and on testing the models of immigrant selection that underpin our understanding of those outcomes. Our goal here is to develop and test just such a model.

This paper offers new estimates of the determinants of immigration rates by source from 1971 to 1998. It isolates the economic and demographic fundamentals that determine immigration rates across source countries and over time. These are real incomes, education, demographic composition, and inequality. We also allow for persistence in the flows arising from the stock of previous immigrants from the same source—accounting for the widely acknowledged but rarely estimated "friends and relatives effect." While existing studies typically include some of these variables, they often omit one or more of the key influences suggested by migration theory. More important is their neglect of

Received for publication June 3, 2003. Revision accepted for publication February 27, 2006.

* World Bank; University of Essex and Australian National University; and Harvard University, respectively.

Earlier versions of this paper were presented at the Population Association of America Meetings, Atlanta, Georgia (May 9–11, 2002) and the LACEA meetings, Madrid (October 11–13, 2002). We are grateful for the helpful comments of Gary Chamberlain, Andy Mason, Sam Thompson, and participants at the PAA and LACEA meetings, as well as for the excellent research assistance of Rachael Wagner. We are also grateful to the editor and two anonymous referees for valuable comments. Hatton acknowledges with pleasure the financial support of the British Academy, and Williamson does the same for the National Science Foundation SES-0001362. The views expressed herein are those of the authors and not necessarily those of the World Bank.

immigration policy. Here we include policy variables that are derived directly from the quotas allocated to different visa categories. Finally, we examine more source countries over a longer period than does existing work on late twentieth century U.S. immigration.

We start in the next section by providing some background to U.S. immigration and immigration policy. We then set out a theoretical framework that is used to guide the choice of variables for regression analysis and to interpret the results. After presenting our econometric results, we evaluate the effects of major shifts in immigration policy on the total numbers and the effects of economic and demographic variables on the composition of immigration by source region.

II. Immigration and Immigration Policy

Changes in U.S. immigration over the last fifty years are well-known. As table 1 shows, the overall number legally admitted rose from a quarter of a million per year in the 1950s to nearly half a million in the 1970s and close to a million in the 1990s. The change in source composition has been even more dramatic. Europeans formed over half of the total in the 1950s, and the bulk of these were from Western Europe; by the 1990s, Western Europeans were a mere 5% of the total. The counterpart to this is the sharp rise in the proportion coming from Asia; the other notable feature is the ongoing rise in the share from Mexico. The sharpest change in the composition occurred between the 1950s and the 1970s and was associated with a major policy shift in 1965. Since then the composition of the flows has been more stable, although Western Europe has continued to decline and Mexico has continued to increase.

The most radical shift in postwar immigration policy was the 1965 Amendments to the Immigration and Nationality Act. Before this date country-of-origin quotas allocated the bulk of the visas to European countries, and two-thirds of these went to Germany and the United Kingdom. The 1965 legislation (effective 1968) abolished the quotas so that immigrants from all countries could compete more equally for the available visas. It established a maximum quota of 20,000 for each Eastern Hemisphere country, subject to an overall ceiling of 170,000. Within the quota, visas were allocated according to a seven-category preference system, which gave 64% of visas to relatives of U.S. citizens or residents, 6% to refugees, and 30% to employment-based categories. Children and spouses of U.S. citizens were exempt from the quota, reflecting a strong emphasis on family reunion.

TABLE 1.—SOURCE AREA COMPOSITION OF U.S. IMMIGRATION, 1951–2000
(PERCENT OF TOTAL FROM EACH SOURCE)

Region of Origin	1951–60	1961–70	1971–80	1981–90	1991–2000
Europe	52.7	33.8	17.8	10.4	14.9
Western	49.8	30.8	14.7	7.5	5.9
Eastern	2.9	3.0	3.1	2.9	9.0
Asia	6.1	12.9	35.3	37.3	30.7
Americas	39.6	51.7	44.1	49.3	49.3
Canada	15.0	12.4	3.8	2.1	2.1
Mexico	11.9	13.7	14.2	22.6	24.7
Caribbean	4.9	14.2	16.5	11.9	10.8
Central America	1.8	3.1	3.0	6.4	5.8
South America	3.6	7.8	6.6	6.3	5.9
Africa	0.6	0.9	1.8	2.4	3.9
Oceania	0.5	0.8	0.9	0.6	0.6
Total (000s)	2,515	3,322	4,493	7,338	9,095

Source: *Statistical Yearbook of the Immigration and Naturalization Service for 2000*, table 2.
Notes: Immigrants classified by country of last residence. Percentages exclude the category "origin not specified." Western Europe is defined as the countries of the European Union (EU-15), excluding Finland but including Norway and Switzerland. Eastern Europe includes the category "other Europe."

In addition, a ceiling of 120,000 visas was set for the Western Hemisphere, but without country quotas or a preference system.[1]

Immigration legislation was amended again by an act of 1976 (effective 1977) when quotas of 20,000 per country, together with the system of preferences, was extended to Western Hemisphere countries, and an act of 1978 (effective 1979) when the hemispheric ceilings were combined into an overall quota of 290,000. In 1980 the preference category for refugees was removed and the worldwide ceiling was reduced to 270,000 (effective 1981). In 1986 the Immigration Reform and Control Act (IRCA) provided for the legalization of illegal immigrants who had resided in the United States since before 1982. It also expanded the H-2 program for temporary foreign workers and introduced temporary visas for agricultural workers with three years' residence in the United States.

The most important amendment to the post-1965 regulations came in the 1990 Immigration Act (effective 1992). This legislation introduced an overall quota of 675,000, divided into three classes. First, a total of 480,000 visas was allocated to family immigrants, with immediate relatives of U.S. citizens coming under the quota for the first time. Within this total, a minimum of 226,000, allocated according to a four-part preference system, was given to family-sponsored nonimmediate relatives of U.S. citizens and resident aliens.[2] Second, the 1990 act increased the number of employment-based visas to 140,000 (from 60,000 previously), under a five-part preference system.[3] Third, 55,000 visas were allocated on top of the overall quota for "diversity" immigrants—those from countries with relatively low immigration since 1965.[4]

The current (and past) legislation provides different routes into the United States. Differences among source regions in levels of economic development and immigration histories are reflected in the composition of entry routes. Table 2 illustrates these differences for 1998. Overall, just 12% entered on employment-based preference categories, but the figures are substantially higher for immigrants from Western Europe and Canada. Employment-based entry is particularly low for Eastern Europe and Africa, where refugee and asylee admissions are significant, and also from Mexico and the Caribbean. It is notable also that reunion with immediate family is the entry route for more than half of Western Hemisphere immigrants except for Canada. The data suggest that the persistence effects of past immigration has waned for Western Europe and Canada, as reflected in the small share of family-sponsored preferences (a fact partly represented in the diversity category). It is also small for Africa, a source country for whom American mass immigration has only just begun. It is *very* large for the remaining regions in transition: 34% for Asia (74% when immediate relatives are included) and the Americas (86% when immediate relatives are included), reaching an enormous 42% for Mexico (88% when immediate relatives are included).

There are two important indirect routes that have affected the sources of immigration. One is illegal immigration, which has increased over time and is currently running at about 300,000 per year. Mass legalization of 2.7 million illegal immigrants took place in the decade after the Immigration Reform and Control Act of 1986. This provided an additional route to legal immigration largely for Western Hemisphere immigrants, and especially those from Mexico. The other route is that of temporary workers or trainees with H, O, and P visas, the numbers of whom soared from 75,000 in 1985 to 430,000 in 1998. This rising number originated chiefly from Europe and Asia. Although they are not part of the overall immigration total, temporary visas clearly have been used as an intermediate step before adjusting to permanent status.

III. Modeling Immigration

Immigration is determined partly by individual incentives and constraints, and partly by policy. Immigration policy can be seen as a filter though which ex ante migration

---

[1] Further details of numbers allocated to different preference categories are given in Appendix B4.
[2] The maximum number of visas allocated to nonimmediate family members is the difference between 480,000 and the actual number of visas issued to immediate relatives in the previous year, subject to a minimum of 226,000. Thus under the "flexible cap" system the total number admitted under the quota can exceed the overall cap in a particular year.
[3] The quotas for different preferences in the employment-based category are detailed in Appendix B4.
[4] In the transitional period between 1992 and 1994, the overall quota was raised to 700,000 with 465,000 visas reserved for close family immigration, but the diversity program was limited to 40,000.

EXPLAINING U.S. IMMIGRATION

TABLE 2.—CLASS OF ADMISSION BY SOURCE AREA, 1998
(PERCENT OF TOTAL FOR EACH SOURCE)

Class of Admission	Family-Sponsored Preferences	Employment-Based Preferences	Immediate Relatives of U.S. Citizens	Refugee and Asylee Adjustments	Diversity Program
All immigrants	29.0	11.7	42.9	8.3	6.9
Europe	9.6	15.0	32.0	20.8	20.9
West	12.1	27.5	46.4	2.3	11.2
East	8.4	8.5	25.3	30.3	25.8
Asia	35.5	16.9	37.9	5.3	3.9
Americas	34.2	7.3	51.9	5.1	0.9
Canada	14.3	43.8	35.4	0.1	4.8
Mexico	42.1	2.8	45.6	0.0	0.0
Caribbean	33.8	3.1	42.9	18.8	1.3
Cnt. America	26.7	11.1	58.7	2.4	0.5
Sth. America	24.5	12.6	58.9	1.6	2.1
Africa	8.2	7.2	35.8	10.8	37.7
Oceania	30.0	14.1	42.5	0.6	12.4
Total (000s)	191.5	77.5	283.4	54.6	45.5

Source: *Statistical Yearbook of the Immigration and Naturalization Service for 1998*, table 9.
Notes: Immigrants classified by country of last residence. Rows do not add to 100 because they exclude certain other classes of admission. Western Europe is defined as the countries of the European Union (EU-15), excluding Finland but including Iceland, Norway, and Switzerland.

decisions are translated into ex post migration. The economics of the migration decision has been widely studied, most notably by Larry Sjaastad (1962), George Borjas (1987), and Barry Chiswick (2000). Here we set out a heuristic framework, which follows in that tradition. It emphasizes the effects of income differentials, skill differentials, migration costs, demographic at-risk sensitivity, and immigration policy on the probability that individuals will move from one country to another.

Individual i ($i = 1, \ldots, n$) residing in source country y receives the wage $w_y(s_i)$, where s_i is the individual's skill level. The wage the individual would receive in the destination country x is $w_x(s_i)$. Thus the gains to migration for individual i are represented by the difference $w_x(s_i) - w_y(s_i)$. Migration costs depend on four elements. First, there is an individual-specific migration cost, z_i. This may be interpreted as reflecting individual preferences for migration in terms of equivalent income. This compensating differential differs across individuals, but would be expected to be positive on average. Factors such as having relatives in the destination country are likely to lower the psychic cost component of z_i. It will also reflect the lower direct cost of immigration through family reunion or family-sponsored preference categories as compared with other routes, including illegal migration.

Second, there is a direct cost, c_1, which is the same for all migrants from source country y, but which may differ across source countries according to distance from the destination. It may also reflect immigration policy: tougher immigration policy raises the cost of migration for all immigrants by raising c_1. Third, there is the cost to migrants associated with quantitative restrictions: the greater is the total quota, the lower is the cost in terms of waiting time, or the cost and effort of moving to a higher-preference category. Thus the cost-equivalent effect of quotas is represented by $c_2(q)$, which applies to all potential migrants, given their status under the quota. Finally, skill-selective immigration policy is represented by a term $\gamma(\delta - s_i)$; the higher the individual's skill level, relative to benchmark level δ, the lower the costs of migration. A rise in δ increases the overall standard for admission, while an increase in the skill selectivity of immigration policy, for a given threshold, is represented by an increase in the parameter γ.

Putting these elements together, the probability that individual i will migrate from country y to country x is

$$m_i = \text{Prob}(v_i > 0), \text{ where } v_i = w_x(s_i) - w_y(s_i) \\ - z_i - c_1 + c_2(q) - \gamma(\delta - s_i). \quad (1)$$

Across individuals in country y, $w_x(s_i)$, $w_y(s_i)$, z_i, and s_i are assumed to be normally distributed with means μ_x, μ_y, μ_z, and μ_s respectively. Summing over all n individuals in the source country y, the emigration rate to x is:

$$M = 1 - \Phi\left[\frac{-\mu_x + \mu_y + \mu_z + c_1 - c_2(q) + \gamma(\delta - \mu_s)}{\sigma_v}\right], \quad (2)$$

where Φ is the standard normal distribution function and σ_v is the standard deviation of the net benefit function v. This is simply a modified version of the Roy model advanced by Borjas (1987), among others.

Higher mean wage rates in the destination country or lower mean wage rates in the source country (for a given skill level) increase the migration rate, as does a fall in the mean of personal migration costs, μ_z, or a fall in the fixed migration cost, c_1. An increase in the average skill level in country y would increase the migration rate if there is skill-selective immigration policy in country x ($\gamma > 0$) and could increase the migration rate through the wage differential, if the function w_x is steeper than w_y. The variances will also matter, and the effect of changing wage and skill distributions will depend on their effect on σ_v, and the sign of the mean of $-v_i$, that is $-[\mu_x - \mu_y - \mu_z - c_1 + c_2(q) - \gamma(\delta - \mu_s)]$. These effects are examined further in appendix A. To take one example, if the mean of v_i is positive (the destination is relatively rich), then the migration rate will be an inverse U-shaped function of the ratio of source to destination wage inequality (as a relative proxy for the return on skills).

Immigration policy will also influence the volume of migration through several different channels represented by the terms in equation (2). Widening of family reunification policies, by reducing z_i for some potential emigrants, will lower its mean μ_z and increase migration. A reduction in the overall quota, q, would raise direct migration costs through $c_2(q)$ and therefore reduce migration. An increase in skill selectivity through raising the threshold value, δ, would be expected to reduce the migration rate, while the effect of increasing the value of γ could raise or lower the migration rate (see Appendix A).

Since migration is a forward-looking decision, it is useful to think of the gains to migration in present-value terms. Thus $w_x(s_i)$ and $w_y(s_i)$ can be thought of as discounted income streams for individual i in the destination and source, respectively. For any individual, the present value of migration as represented by the difference between these income streams, net of costs, will depend on the length of working life remaining. Hence, the net gain represented by equation (2) will be greater the younger the potential migrant is in the source country. It follows that the source-country age structure should also matter: the larger the share of young adults, the greater will be the migration rate for a given positive wage gap, net of costs.[5]

IV. Explaining Immigration

Recent studies of U.S. immigration highlight some of the economic forces that determine immigration rates across source countries. The dependent variable is typically taken as the number of immigrants to the United States relative to the source-country population, representing the propensity to emigrate to the United States. Borjas (1987) found that, for a cross section of average emigration rates from 1951 to 1980, migration was negatively related to origin-country income per capita and to distance from the United States. In addition, the emigration rate was negatively related to inequality in the origin country, implying negative within-country selection.[6] Using a cross section of source-country immigration rates for 1982–1986, Philip Yang (1995) confirmed the income effects but found the stock of previous immigrants from each source country to be the single-most important determinant of the immigration flow.

David Karemera, Victor Oguledo, and Bobby Davis (2000) used panel data on emigration rates to the United States and to Canada for the decade 1976–1986, including a wide range of explanatory variables for both the United States and countries of origin. They found that emigration rates were related negatively to distance from the United States, negatively to origin-country income, positively to U.S. income, and negatively to the U.S. unemployment rate. In addition, they found that migration was positively related to measures of political rights and individual freedom in source countries, and negatively to political instability. Thus, their results confirm the importance of economic variables, migration costs, and civil rights in determining migration. Immigration policy in the United States was modeled as a dummy variable only.

More recently, two studies have explored the determinants of migration flows using panels for multiple origin and destination countries. Anna Maria Mayda (2004) analyzed migrants to fourteen OECD destinations for 1980–1995. One of the key findings was that income and education affect migration with opposite signs and that origin-country effects are smaller than destination-country effects. One interpretation of this is that for potential migrants in poor countries, an increase in income both reduces the incentive and increases the ability to migrate. Peder Pedersen, Mariola Pytlikova, and Nina Smith (2004) studied immigration to 27 OECD countries from 129 source countries in the 1990s, also finding source-country effects to be weaker than destination-country effects. Both studies provide evidence of positive effects on migration associated with migrant networks and of negative effects associated with the economic, cultural, and geographical distance between origin and destination.

Here we focus on the United States, which has the widest range of immigration sources over the longest period. We include in our analysis a more comprehensive set of variables than previously, all of which are suggested by migration theory, but some which are often omitted from existing studies. These variables include human capital, inequality, the demographic structure of the origin country, and the stock of previous migrants living at the destination. We also derive a set of variables to capture different dimensions of U.S. immigration policy, something that has been previously modeled only by dummy variables. And finally, we use our results to see how these variables account for the

---

[5] Let the wage difference (destination minus source country) per year of working life be a constant D. If the age range of potential working-age migrants, a, runs from 20 to 65 and the discount rate is r, then the present value of the gains will be $PV(a) = Dr[1 - (1 + r)^{-(46-a)}]$, which is a decreasing function of a.

[6] This is consistent with the Roy model summarized in equation (1) above, where source countries are relatively poor and relatively unequal compared with the United States (see Appendix A).

source-country composition of immigration and to simulate the effects over time of key changes in immigration policy.

We attempt to capture the determinants of the emigration rate to the United States with the following specification:

$$\begin{aligned}(mig/pop)_{j,t} &= \beta_0 + \beta_1(y_j/y_{us})_t + \beta_2(syr_j/syr_{us})_t \\ &+ \beta_3 age_{j,t} + \beta_4(ineq_j/ineq_{us})_t + \beta_5(ineq_j/ineq_{us})^2_t \\ &+ \beta_6 pov_{j,t} + \beta_7 dist_j + \beta_8 land_j + \beta_9 eng_j \\ &+ \beta_{10}(stock_{j,t-1}/pop_{j,t}) + \beta_{11}(stock_{j,t-1}/pop_{j,t})^2 \\ &+ \beta_{12} X_{r,j,t}(stock_{j,t-1}/pop_{j,t}) + \beta_{13} X_{e,j,t}(syr_j/syr_{us})_t \\ &+ \beta_{14} X_{d,j,t} + \beta_{15} X_{a,j,t} civ_{j,t} + \beta_{16} X_{irc,j,t} + \beta_{17} X_b.\end{aligned} \quad (3)$$

The left-hand-side variable is migration to the United States from country j in year t as proportion of the origin-country population.

Economic and demographic fundamentals are reflected by the first five terms, while the others represent costs. The first term, the ratio of the average (purchasing power parity adjusted) income in j relative to the United States is expected to have a negative effect; $\beta_1 < 0$. The second term is the ratio of average years of schooling (syr) in j relative to the United States. Since the income variable reflects both the amount of human capital and the average return on human capital, it must be "deflated" by human capital stocks in order to reflect the relative return alone. Thus, relative schooling years is expected to have a positive effect on immigration; $\beta_2 > 0$. The variable age in the origin country is the share of population aged 15–29. It reflects the fact that the present value of migration is higher, for a given wage incentive, at younger ages: thus, $\beta_3 > 0$. The ratio of inequality in the origin relative to the United States ($ineq$) is entered in quadratic form. According to the Roy model, when the destination country is richer than the source (adjusted for migration costs) the effects of inequality follow an inverse U-shape. When the origin country is relatively unequal, an increase in its relative inequality will reduce the migration rate; when the source country is relatively equal, an increase in its inequality will increase the migration rate (see appendix A). Hence $\beta_4 > 0$, $\beta_5 < 0$. Here inequality is represented by the Gini coefficient of household income.

Migration costs constrain the move. The proportion of the source-country population living in poverty is represented by the inverse of its income squared. As income increases, poverty quickly evaporates, releasing constraints on migration and hence $\beta_6 < 0$.[7] As in any gravity model, costs rise with distance from the United States; hence, $\beta_7 < 0$. Such costs are also associated with whether the source country is landlocked and whether it is predominantly English speaking; $\beta_8 < 0$, $\beta_9 > 0$. Current migration costs are also represented by the stock of previous immigrants from the sending country. This is defined as the ratio of the number born in country j residing in the United States at time $t - 1$ relative to the population of country j. Since relatives (and friends) abroad reduce migration costs, $\beta_{10} > 0$, although we expect this effect to diminish with size (over the relevant range, hence $\beta_{11} < 0$) if it is accounted for by immigrants' job search and settlement costs (diminishing returns to network externalities) rather than by remittances releasing the financial constraint.

The remaining variables represent the effects of immigration policies, through the different routes of entry. These are interacted with other variables to represent the ease of access to these channels for migrants from a given country. The variables X_r, X_e, X_d, and X_a represent the number of visas available by different entry routes, divided by the total population of the countries that qualify for them. These are derived separately for each major channel of entry, and are calculated for each country, as described in Appendix B4. This reflects the scarcity of visas and hence the cost of immigration. A fall in X as a result of a reduction in the quota will therefore reduce migration; thus β_{12} through β_{15} are expected to be positive.

The variable X_r represents the quota for nonimmediate relatives, and it is interacted with the immigrant stock divided by origin-country population. Thus, the higher the stock of foreign born from a given country, the lower the average cost of migration from that country and the more migrants choose that route. X_e represents the quota of employment visas and is interacted with the ratio of schooling years to capture the element of skill selectivity. X_d reflects the quota of diversity visas available since 1992, prior to which it takes the value of 0. Since diversity visas are awarded by lottery, it is not interacted with country characteristics. X_a represents the allocation of visas to refugees, which since 1980 has been set year by year rather than coming under the legislated quota. This variable is interacted with a dummy for civil war—the main cause of refugee flights (for example, Hatton & Williamson, 2003).

The final two variables represent somewhat special circumstances. X_{irc} is intended to capture the effects of the IRCA legalization program. It is the estimated number of illegal immigrants from a given country residing in the United States preceding the legalization program divided by that country's population. It is applied only to the years 1989–1991, when the bulk of legalizations took place, and β_{16} is therefore expected to be positive. Finally, X_b is a dummy for the years 1995–1998 when, due to administrative changes in the processing of visa applications, there was a progressive rise in the backlog. As a result, recorded

---

[7] Unfortunately there are insufficient data to construct a direct measure of poverty incidence for the country/period observations in our data. Using cross-country estimates for recent years, Ravallion (2004) finds that poverty head count ratio is inversely related to the square of per capita income.

immigration for these years was lower than it would otherwise have been, and the dummy is therefore expected to be negative; $\beta_{17} < 0$. Details of the derivation of these variables are given in Appendix B4.

V. Econometric Results

We estimate our migration model on panel data for immigration to the United States by place of birth for 81 source countries across the 28 years from 1971 to 1998 (see Appendix B, sections 1 and 5). These countries form 82.5% of all U.S. immigration over this entire period. For relative income we use purchasing power parity adjusted GDP per head from the Penn World Tables; years of education is based on the series derived by Barro and Lee. Total population and population aged 15–29 come from the UN demographic database; the Gini coefficient for household income (a crude measure for the return to skills) is calculated from data collected by the World Bank and the WIDER Institute. These sources are further detailed in Appendix B3. The stock of foreign born from each source country is calculated using census and CPS data and then interpolating using gross immigration flows in order to obtain annual series. The sources and methods of calculation are discussed in Appendix B2.

Our estimating equation is based on equation (3) but, because the gross immigration rate is bounded at zero, the left-hand-side variable is transformed by taking natural logs. This constrains the predicted values to be positive in the regression and in the counterfactual predictions examined below. The right-hand-side variables are as in equation (3). Our estimating method is fixed-effects regression. The variables distance, English speaking, and landlocked are thus eliminated since they have no time variation. These effects nevertheless influence the country means and we will return to them in what follows.

The results from estimating the equation on this panel data set appear in table 3. The first column excludes all the policy-related variables. The coefficients are significant at conventional levels with the exception of relative years of schooling and the share of source-country population aged 15–29. This probably reflects the fact that these variables are interpolated between five-year benchmarks. The full model in the second column includes the policy variables; adding these has little effect on the coefficients of the economic and demographic fundamentals. We include the uninteracted policy effects as well as the interactions with other variables. All these variables are significant with the exception of the interaction between the employment-based quota and relative education years and the processing backlog. The third column omits the variables that were insignificant in column 2.

One possible concern is that the per-country numerical limits within the worldwide immigration quota may be binding on some countries and that the coefficients might be affected by the inclusion of constrained countries. That concern is partially allayed by the facts that only about half of all immigrants come under the worldwide quota and that very few countries have been at or near the per-country limit for a sustained period.[8] The exceptions are Mexico, India, China, the Philippines, the Dominican Republic, and Korea.[9] It is reassuring also that the coefficients in column 3 are changed very little when the model is estimated excluding these countries.[10]

It is worth examining the quantitative implications of some of the estimated coefficients, focusing on the third column. The relative income term implies that a 10% increase in a source country's income per capita reduces the immigration rate by 4.4%. The inverse of source-country income squared takes a negative coefficient consistent with the idea that higher absolute income releases the poverty trap. This provides an offsetting effect of about 1% when evaluated at the mean income level. However, when evaluated at the mean for the poorest region, Africa, a 10% increase in income per capita reduces the immigration rate for an individual country by 1.2% through the relative income effect, but increases the immigration rate by 2.4% through the poverty trap effect.

The coefficients on relative inequality and its square, positive and negative respectively, support the predictions of the Roy model (see Appendix A), with the maximum occurring at an inequality ratio less than 1. Evaluated at the mean, a 10% increase in source-country inequality causes immigration to fall by 7.5%, but these effects will differ by country. At the mean for South America (1.20), a 10% increase in relative inequality will cause a fall of 11.9% in immigration as the incentives for migration decline for those higher up in the income distribution. At the mean for Western Europe (0.82), a 10% increase in inequality reduces migration by only 1.3% as incentives decrease for those higher up but increase for those lower down.

---

[8] Some evidence of substitution of quota and nonquota categories is offered by Jasso, Rosenzweig, and Smith (2000). They examined immigration of husbands of U.S. citizens, finding that the numbers entering under this nonquota category are sensitive to changes in the rules governing that route of entry, but also to changes in the rules for entry under the quota.

[9] The worldwide quota excludes immediate relatives of U.S. citizens, refugees, and legalizations under IRCA. Per-country limits were 20,000 until 1991 and subsequently 7% of the worldwide quota (25,620 in 1998). In 1998 the countries with the highest number of immigrants admitted as part of the worldwide quota were Mexico (58,758), India (24,988), China (23,231), the Philippines (17,496), the Dominican Republic (9,595), and Korea (9,105). The figure for Mexico is explained by the fact that it shares with the Dominican Republic an exemption from the per-country limit for immigrants entering under category 2 of the family-sponsored preferences. The number of Mexicans admitted under the family-sponsored and employment-based preferences was 18,795. Although India and China are currently close to the limit, this was not the case before the 1990s.

[10] A Wald test for the full set of interactions between each of the variables and a dummy for the six countries yields a value 19.4, which is not significant for $\chi_{(15)}^2$ at the 5% level.

EXPLAINING U.S. IMMIGRATION

TABLE 3.— GROSS IMMIGRATION RATE REGRESSIONS
(81 COUNTRIES, 28 YEARS; DEPENDENT VARIABLE: LOG IMMIGRANTS ADMITTED/SOURCE-COUNTRY POPULATION)

	(1)	(2)	(3)
Constant	−8.74	−8.84	−9.09
	(13.4)	(26.2)	(38.8)
GDP per capita ratio (foreign/U.S.)	−1.49	−1.42	−1.41
	(7.1)	(7.0)	(7.1)
Schooling years ratio (popn. > 14) (foreign/U.S.)	−0.02	0.04	
	(0.1)	(0.2)	
Share of population aged 15–29 (foreign)	0.49	−0.56	
	(0.7)	(0.8)	
Inequality ratio (foreign/U.S.)	1.50	1.45	1.64
	(3.5)	(5.1)	(4.1)
Inequality ratio (foreign/U.S.) squared	−1.18	−0.95	−1.01
	(6.2)	(5.1)	(5.7)
Inverse of income squared (foreign)	−0.20	−0.18	−0.18
	(4.2)	(4.1)	(4.2)
Immigrant stock $(t-1)$/foreign population	8.63	6.91	6.71
	(4.2)	(3.3)	(3.2)
(Immigrant stock $(t-1)$/foreign population)^2	−47.34	−40.78	−40.38
	(4.9)	(4.3)	(4.3)
Quota X_r		−0.60	−0.59
		(3.3)	(3.0)
Quota X_r × (immigrant stock $(t-1)$/foreign population)		32.58	33.37
		(3.1)	(3.3)
Quota X_e		9.16	4.61
		(3.3)	(4.5)
Quota X_e × schooling years ratio		−8.73	
		(1.6)	
Diversity quota X_d		0.40	0.40
		(7.6)	(7.6)
Refugee quota X_a		1.27	1.27
		(6.6)	(6.7)
Refugee quota X_a × civil war		1.45	1.49
		(3.6)	(3.7)
IRCA legalization X_{irc}		0.07	0.07
		(7.9)	(8.1)
Processing backlog X_b		−0.03	
		(0.9)	
R^2 (within)	0.15	0.23	0.23
No. of observations	2,268	2,268	2,268

The coefficients on the migrant stock by itself (that is, ignoring its interaction with X_r) reflect the nonpolicy component of the "friends and relatives effect." While the linear term is positive as expected, the squared term is strongly negative, implying that the marginal effect is large when the stock is small but diminishes as the stock increases. That marginal effect eventually falls to 0 when the migrant stock in the United States reaches 8.3% of the source-country population. At the mean (1.3% of source-country population), the coefficients imply that if the immigrant stock from a given source is raised by 1,000, the annual flow from that source would be increased by 4.7 immigrants. This direct effect is augmented by an indirect effect working through the policy variable representing the quota on nonimmediate relatives (X_r). This adds a further 1.6, yielding 6.3 more immigrants per year for every 1,000 added to the existing immigrant stock. Thus, the overall friends and relatives effect is equivalent to compounding the immigrant stock by about 0.6% per year, which is somewhat less than the "depreciation" of about 1% in the immigrant stock through deaths and return migration.

The effects of immigration policy are discernible and have the expected effects. The quota for family members works through the uninteracted term, which is negative, and the positive interaction term. An increase of 10% in the family quota raises immigration from a country by 0.3%. The same proportionate increase in employment visas raises it by 1.4%. A 10% increase in the refugee allowance raises immigration by 0.5%, while the effect of the diversity quota is minimal. By contrast, the effects of the Immigration Reform and Control Act were relatively large; these are discussed further below.

VI. The Effects of Policy Changes

The impact of immigration policy on immigrant numbers is assessed by means of counterfactual simulations. These simulations provide an important check on the model as well as a gauge of the effects of policy. Dynamic simulations are made for each of the 81 countries in the data set, using the estimated equation in the third column of table 3. A counterfactual change in one of

TABLE 4.— THE EFFECTS OF IMMIGRATION POLICY
(ACTUAL/NO-POLICY-CHANGE COUNTERFACTUAL)

Merging Hemispheres

Year	1976	1977	1978	1979	1980	1981
Eastern Hemisphere	100.0	99.9	101.9	101.6	101.4	101.3
Western Hemisphere	100.0	132.5	131.2	92.6	89.1	84.7
World	100.0	113.2	111.5	97.8	96.4	93.8

Immigration Control and Reform Act

Year	1988	1989	1990	1991	1992	1993
Eastern Hemisphere	100.0	102.3	102.4	101.9	100.1	100.0
Western Hemisphere	100.0	207.4	213.6	233.0	105.5	103.9
World	100.0	148.1	158.1	169.1	102.4	101.5

1990 Immigration Act

Year	1991	1992	1993	1994	1995	1996
Eastern Hemisphere	100.0	107.5	107.3	107.2	107.4	107.2
Western Hemisphere	100.0	110.0	109.7	107.3	107.0	106.7
World	100.0	108.6	108.2	108.1	107.4	107.1

the explanatory variables (in this case policy-related variables) serves to change the level of gross immigration, which in turn alters the immigrant stock at the end of that year. The updated immigrant stock then influences the counterfactual level the following year, and so on. The effects of changes in policy can be assessed by comparing the counterfactual level of immigration with the actual level.[11]

The first case is the period in the late 1970s when the separate quotas for the Eastern and Western Hemispheres were merged into a worldwide quota. This affected the total number of visas for both nonimmediate family members and employment-based immigration. As noted earlier, the Western Hemisphere quota for nonimmediate relatives was cut by 26%, and then in 1979 the Eastern and Western Hemispheres were merged, cutting the total numbers under the quota by a further 7%. The quota for Western Hemisphere employment visas was raised from zero to 24,000 in 1977, and then in 1979, it was merged with the Eastern Hemisphere quota (of 34,000), with reductions in the total taking place in 1980 and 1981.

In the counterfactual simulation the quotas are held constant at the 1976 levels from 1977 onward, retaining the distinction between Eastern and Western Hemisphere countries. The results are displayed in the first panel of table 4. These figures are calculated as the ratio of the actual immigrant numbers to the counterfactual simulation and hence they reflect the effect of policy change in relative terms. In the years 1977–1978 the effect of the increase in employment visas outweighs that of the decline in family-based visas for the Western Hemisphere. The subsequent sharp decline in the Western Hemisphere total reflects the crowding out of Western Hemisphere immigration when the two sectors were merged. The overall decline in immigration between 1978 and the early 1980s is just a shade larger than the 5% cut in the overall quota.

The second change is the Immigration Reform and Control Act of 1986. As is well-known, the effects of IRCA were very large; this is reflected in the ratios in the second panel of table 4. The IRCA effects are especially marked for Western Hemisphere countries but only marginal for the Eastern Hemisphere. The figures can be compared with the ratio of IRCA legalizations to all other classes of admissions recorded in the INS immigration statistics. Over the years 1989 to 1991, IRCA legalizations were 126% of non-IRCA admissions, somewhat more than the figures estimated here. This suggests that the legalization program may have substituted for other admissions to some degree, particularly by reducing nonquota immigrants.

The third panel of table 4 simulates the effects of the Immigration Act of 1990, which took effect in 1992. The 1990 act increased the number of visas available to nonimmediate relatives by about a third between 1991 and 1992, a figure that was cut by 20% in 1995. In addition, the number of employment visas was more than doubled and a new category of diversity visas was introduced. Overall, these policy changes amounted to approximately a 75% increase in the number of available visas between 1991 and 1992–1994. However, the net effect on admissions would have been much less than this because some previously non quota categories, such as immediate relatives and certain employment-based immigrants, were absorbed under the quota for the first time. Our estimated effects of these changes, taken together, suggest that between 1991 and 1992–1994 the overall effect was to raise immigration by a little over 8%. This is smaller than the increase in the numbers for non-IRCA immigrants, which rose by 18% over the same period.

---

[11] These simulations include the equation errors and use the same depreciation parameter that was generated for each country/decade when calculating the immigrant stock (see appendix B2). Thus, a simulation using the actual values of the explanatory variables would exactly replicate the data.

EXPLAINING U.S. IMMIGRATION

TABLE 5.— GROSS IMMIGRATION RATE REGRESSIONS (81 COUNTRIES, 28 YEARS; DEPENDENT VARIABLE: LOG IMMIGRANTS ADMITTED/SOURCE-COUNTRY POPULATION)

	(1)	(2)	(3)
Constant	−18.31	−16.89	−16.65
	(7.3)	(8.4)	(38.8)
GDP per capita ratio (foreign/U.S.)	−2.47	−1.77	−2.76
	(3.0)	(2.6)	(4.0)
Schooling years ratio (popn. > 14) (foreign/U.S.)	4.00	3.08	3.79
	(4.2)	(4.0)	(4.2)
Share of population aged 15–29 (foreign)	12.46	10.32	
	(1.6)	(1.6)	
Inequality ratio (foreign/U.S.)	13.30	7.51	14.92
	(3.0)	(2.0)	(4.0)
Inequality ratio (foreign/U.S.) squared	−5.79	−3.07	−6.44
	(2.9)	(1.9)	(2.8)
Inverse of income squared (foreign)	−0.61	−0.33	−0.70
	(2.2)	(4.2)	(2.8)
Distance from U.S.	−0.28	−0.09	−0.20
	(7.7)	(2.1)	(5.0)
Landlocked	−0.36	−0.33	
	(1.0)	(1.1)	
English-speaking origin	1.19	0.31	1.04
	(3.8)	(1.0)	(3.5)
Immigrant stock $(t-1)$/foreign population		89.90	
		(5.9)	
(Immigrant stock $(t-1)$/foreign population)^2		−418.74	
		(8.4)	
IRCA legalization X_{irc}			1.37
			(3.4)
R^2 (between)	0.68	0.80	0.71
No. of observations	2,268	2,268	2,268

VII. The Regional Composition of U.S. Immigration

The source-country composition of U.S. immigration changed dramatically from the 1960s; this change has been widely ascribed to the effects of the 1965 amendments to the Immigration Act. Abolishing the quotas favoring European countries widened the opportunities for immigrants from a wider range of countries to compete on a more or less equal basis for the available visas. So what influence did source-country variables have on the regional composition of immigration that emerged under the post-1965 regime?

To get a feel for these magnitudes, we reestimate the model using the "between" estimator for the country means. This allows us to include the variables distance, English speaking, and landlocked, which may be important determinants of the source-country composition, but that do not vary over time. The first column of table 5 shows that the signs on the variables for economic fundamentals are similar to those in the fixed-effects regressions of table 3, although the magnitudes are larger. As expected, distance from the United States has a strong negative effect, while English speaking is strongly positive. As column 2 shows, these effects diminish in size when the immigrant stock and its square are added. Since the immigrant stock reflects past immigration, it captures much of the effect of slow-moving fundamentals over the longer term.

In order to capture the full effect of the economic fundamentals, the third equation in table 5 omits the immigrant stock terms as well as the insignificant variables for source-country population aged 15–29 and landlocked. Among the policy variables, only the IRCA legalization has a significant effect on the source-country composition, and so this is also included in column 3. We use this equation to pose the following question: What would the regional composition of immigration look like if a given variable took the same value for all source countries? To do this we first set each country's value of a given variable to the mean across all source countries for that year. We then predict a counterfactual immigration level for each country/year in the data set.[12]

Table 6 shows the differences, in percentage points, between the counterfactual composition of total immigration between 1971 and 1998 and the actual. The actual shares are given in the top line. Thus for the relative income counterfactual, the first entry in line 1 indicates that, had the income of Western European countries (relative to the United States) been the same as the mean for all sending countries, then this lower income level would have increased Western Europe's share of total immigration by 9.7 percentage points, from 7.3% to 17%. It would also raise the

[12] Setting each variable in turn to the annual mean ensures that total predicted immigration remains approximately constant—keeping the counterfactual in line with the overall immigration policy constraint. Predictions for the individual countries by year are summed to regional aggregates, adjusting to allow for different degrees of underrepresentation of the regional totals by the countries in our data set.

TABLE 6.—EFFECTS OF VARIABLES ON THE REGIONAL COMPOSITION OF U.S. IMMIGRATION, 1971–1998

Variable adjusted	Western Europe	Eastern Europe	Middle East	East Asia	Africa	Oceania	Canada	Mexico	Caribbean	Central America	South America
	\multicolumn{11}{c}{Baseline Shares: Percent of Total Immigration 1971–1998}										
	7.3	6.0	3.9	31.5	3.0	0.6	1.8	21.7	12.8	5.2	6.2
	\multicolumn{11}{c}{Deviation from Baseline Due to Changing a Variable to the All-Country Mean for Each Year}										
(1) Relative income	9.7	−1.9	−0.4	−6.9	−1.4	1.0	7.1	0.2	−3.2	−2.3	−1.9
(2) Education years	−3.0	−4.1	1.6	−1.1	3.2	−0.4	−1.5	−3.2	4.4	3.9	0.3
(3) Rel. inc. + education	3.2	−4.2	1.8	−7.4	1.1	−0.2	0.2	2.8	1.9	1.3	−0.5
(4) Inequality	3.2	6.5	−1.0	0.3	1.1	−0.1	0.8	−4.4	−3.9	−1.2	−1.2
(5) Poverty	−1.4	−0.6	−0.6	4.6	3.5	−0.1	−0.3	−3.6	−1.1	0.1	−0.4
(6) Inc. + edu. + ineq. + pov.	4.5	−2.7	−0.5	0.8	6.5	−0.3	0.6	−3.7	−3.6	0.1	−1.8
(7) Distance	−2.2	−0.1	1.2	29.4	2.0	1.0	−1.4	−15.3	−8.6	−3.5	−2.6
(8) English speaking	−0.3	1.4	0.9	−5.1	−0.7	−0.3	−1.0	5.2	−2.0	1.2	0.6
(9) Dist. + Eng.	−1.5	2.3	3.3	22.4	0.9	0.2	−1.6	−12.7	−8.8	−2.8	−1.7
(10) IRCA	0.4	2.8	0.0	13.0	1.4	0.0	−0.1	−12.4	−3.6	−2.4	0.9

shares of Oceania, Canada, and Mexico while reducing those of other regions, especially East Asia. As line 2 in the table shows, education effects often work in the opposite direction. Thus the combined effect of relative income and relative education in line 3 tends to be smaller than for income alone. The exceptions are Eastern Europe and East Asia, both of which have low income relative to their education levels, and where the combined effect boosted immigration substantially compared with other regions.

The effects of inequality are also important for some regions, as line 4 shows. Average levels of inequality slightly below the mean tended to increase immigration from Europe relative to Mexico, the Caribbean, and Central and South America, where inequality is much higher. Line 5 shows that the effect of the inverse of income squared, reflecting the poverty trap, is most important for the poorest regions, East Asia and Africa. For Africa, the effect of higher absolute income dominates the relative income effect, indicating that the poverty was a key constraining factor there. When all the economic fundamentals are adjusted to the mean values, there are offsetting influences (line 6). Thus, for Western Europe immigration was lower than otherwise because of high relative income and low inequality, whereas for Africa it was chiefly the poverty constraint that kept immigration lower than otherwise. For Mexico, the Caribbean, and South America, economic fundamentals boosted immigration compared with the counterfactual, but only modestly.

Line 7 shows that distance effects massively reduced the share of immigrants from East Asia while dramatically increasing the shares from Latin America.[13] For these two major source regions, distance effects dominate the effects of fundamentals. Those effects are somewhat offset by the English-speaking effect (line 8). Finally, the effect of IRCA (line 10) gave a major boost to (legal) immigration from Mexico, the Caribbean, and Central America compared with all other regions.

These results shed some light on the issue of differences by source region in the composition of immigration to Canada and the United States. One argument is that the Canadian points system has the effect of reducing the shares from regions that generate low-skilled immigrants (Borjas, 1993). Another view stresses the proximity of the United States to Latin America, and especially Mexico, in accounting for the lower average skill levels of its immigrants (Antecol, Cobb-Clark, & Trejo, 2003). Just as an illustration, increasing the distance from the United States of all Latin American countries by 1,500 miles (while preserving the overall mean) reduces the share from these sources by 10 percentage points. This is almost a third of the difference between the U.S. and Canadian shares.

VIII. Conclusion

Our results offer strong support for a model of U.S. immigration that stresses both individual incentives and policy constraints. Relative incomes and absolute incomes matter in a manner predicted by the theory, and the nonlinear effects of inequality support the predictions of the Roy model. But other variables matter, too—variables that are widely acknowledged to be important but that are often omitted in empirical work. The stock of previous immigrants from a given source country has substantial effect—drawing about six more immigrants annually per thousand of the stock. A part of this reflects the stance of immigration policy that encourages family reunion, but it is mostly the traditional friends and relatives effect that has been identified even in the absence of such policies (Hatton & Williamson, 1998). The effects of other policy changes are also discernible in the data, particularly changes in the size and structure of the immigration quota and the IRCA legalization program.

The effects of changes in immigration policy can be clearly discerned in the data, and we have made an effort to

---

[13] It should be noted, however, that such a massive expansion in immigration from Asia would likely be constrained by the per-country quota noted above, particularly in the cases of China and India.

incorporate not only the overall quota level, but also key elements of its structure. Our evidence confirms that different components of the quota also interact with variables like the immigrant stock in ways that are plausible but rarely implemented in studies of immigration flows. Major policy shifts such as the merging of hemispheres into a worldwide quota, the IRCA legislation, and the 1990 Act affected both the level and the source-region composition of immigration in a manner that is consistent with other evidence. This provides further support for our model as a realistic account of the factors that drive U.S. immigration.

Finally, the effects of the economic and demographic fundamentals on the composition of U.S. immigration by source region are mixed. While the effects of differences in source-country per capita income shifted the composition away from developed regions toward poorer regions, education effects generally work in the opposite direction. It is important to recognize that, both theoretically and empirically, what drives migration is income relative to education. Since these are strongly correlated across countries, the migration incentives are not as large as income gaps alone would suggest. Another key finding is the effects of variables like distance and English speaking, which do have decisive effects on the composition of U.S. immigration. As in models of international trade, gravity effects are important, even in the presence of a wide range of other variables.

REFERENCES

Antecol, Heather, Deborah A. Cobb-Clark, and Stephen J. Trejo, "Immigration Policy and the Skills of Immigrants to Australia, Canada and the United States," *Journal of Human Resources* 38 (Winter 2003), 192–218.

Borjas, George, J., "Self Selection and the Earnings of Immigrants," *American Economic Review* 77 (Sept. 1987), 531–553.

——— "Immigration Policy, National Origin, and Immigrant Skills: A Comparison of Canada and the United States" (pp. 21–43), in David Card and Richard B. Freeman (Eds.), *Small Differences that Matter: Labor Markets and Income Maintenance in Canada and the United States* (Chicago: University of Chicago Press, 1993).

Chiswick, Barry R., "Are Immigrants Favorably Self-Selected? An Economic Analysis" (pp. 61–76), in Caroline B. Brettell and James F. Hollifield (Eds.), *Migration Theory: Talking Across Disciplines* (New York: Routledge, 2000).

De Laet, Debra L., *U.S. Immigration and Politics in an Age of Rights* (Westport, CT: Praeger, 2000).

Hatton, Timothy J., and Jeffrey G. Williamson, *The Age of Mass Migration: Causes and Economic Effects* (New York: Oxford University Press, 1998).

——— "Demographic and Economic Pressure on Emigration Out of Africa," *Scandinavian Journal of Economics* 105 (September 2003), 465–486.

Jasso, Guillermina, Mark R. Rosenzweig, and James P. Smith, "The Changing Skill of New Immigrants to the United States: Recent Trends and Their Determinants" (pp. 185–225), in George J. Borjas (Ed.), *Issues in the Economics of Immigration* (Chicago: National Bureau of Economic Research, 2000).

Karemera, David, Victor I. Oguledo, and Bobby Davis, "A Gravity Model Analysis of International Migration to North America," *Applied Economics* 32 (October 2000), 1745–1755.

Mayda, Anna Maria, "International Migration: A Panel Data Analysis of Economic and Noneconomic Determinants," Georgetown University, unpublished paper (2004).

Pedersen, Peder J., Mariola Pytlikova, and Nina Smith, "Selection or Network Effects? Migration Flows into 27 OECD Countries, 1990–2000," IZA discussion paper 1104 (2004).

Ravallion, Martin, "Growth, Inequality and Poverty: Looking Beyond Averages" (pp. 62–80), in Anthony F. Shorrocks and Rolph van der Hoeven (Eds.), *Growth, Inequality and Poverty: Prospects for Pro-poor Economic Development* (Oxford: Oxford University Press, 2004).

Sjaastad, Larry, "The Costs and Returns of Human Migration," *Journal of Political Economy* 70 (October 1962), 80–93.

U.S. Immigration and Naturalization Service (INS), *Statistical Yearbook of the Immigration and Naturalization Service, 1998* (Washington, DC: U.S. Government Printing Office, 2000).

Warren, Robert, and Jeffrey S. Passel, "A Count of the Uncountable: Estimates of Undocumented Aliens Counted in the 1980 United States Census," *Demography* 24 (August 1987), 375–393.

Yang, Philip Q., *Post-1965 Immigration to the United States* (Westport, CT: Praeger, 1995).

APPENDIX A

Migration and Selection

This appendix provides a fuller derivation of equation (2) in the text, and it illustrates the effects on migration flows of changes in relative inequality between source and destination countries. Here we ignore the effect of age on the net present value of migration and examine the migration decision for individuals at a given age.

In the source country, y, skill endowments follow a normal distribution: $s \sim N(\mu_s, \sigma_s^2)$. The incomes that individual i ($i = 1, \ldots, n$) receives at home in country y, and would receive if he/she were to migrate to country x, are the following:

Income in destination: $w_{xi} = \alpha_x + \beta_x s_i$, distributed as w_x

$$\sim N(\mu_x, \sigma_x^2). \tag{A1}$$

Income in origin: $w_{yi} = \alpha_y + \beta_y s_i$; distributed as w_y

$$\sim N(\mu_y, \sigma_y^2).$$

Thus incomes, and income inequality, differ in origin and destination but incomes in x are perfectly correlated with those in y across individuals in the origin country. This simplifying assumption could be relaxed without qualitatively altering the results, provided that cov (w_x, w_y) is sufficiently positive (see Borjas, 1987, p. 533).

As discussed in the text, the cost elements are the following. Individual-specific migration costs, z_i, follow a normal distribution, $z \sim N(\mu_z, \sigma_z^2)$, with mean, μ_z, and variance σ_z^2, where z is independent of s (Cov $(s,z) = 0$). The constant cost elements, $c_1 - c_2(q)$, are the same for all potential immigrants. The cost associated with the skill-selective element of immigration policy is $\gamma(\delta - s_i)$, where δ is a threshold or benchmark skill level.

As shown in the text, the probability that an individual, i, will migrate from country y to x, m_i, is:

$$m_i = Prob(v_i > 0), \text{ where } v_i = w_{xi} - w_{yi} - z_i - c_1 + c_2(q) \tag{A2}$$
$$- \gamma(\delta - s_i).$$

Summing over all n individuals in source country y, the emigration rate to x is:

$$M = 1 - \Phi\left[\frac{-\mu_x + \mu_y + \mu_z + c_1 - c_2(q) + \gamma(\delta - \mu_s)}{\sigma_v}\right], \tag{A3}$$

where Φ is the standard normal cumulative distribution function.

The standard deviation of v can be written as

$$\sigma_v = \sqrt{\sigma_x^2 + \sigma_y^2 + \sigma_z^2 + \gamma^2 - 2\sigma_x\sigma_y + 2\sigma_x\gamma\sigma_s - 2\sigma_y\gamma\sigma_s}. \tag{A4}$$

TABLE A1.—EFFECTS OF INCOME DISTRIBUTION AND IMMIGRATION POLICY ON MIGRATION

Effect on migration rate of:	Destination is "relatively rich": $\mu_x > \mu_y + \mu_z + c_1 - c_2(q) + \gamma(\delta - \mu_s)$	Destination is "relatively poor": $\mu_x < \mu_y + \mu_z + c_1 - c_2(q) + \gamma(\delta - \mu_s)$
Income distribution in destination country	$dM/d\sigma_x > 0$ if: $\sigma_x < \sigma_y - \gamma\sigma_s$	$dM/d\sigma_x > 0$ if: $\sigma_x > \sigma_y - \gamma\sigma_s$
Income distribution in source country	$dM/d\sigma_y > 0$ if: $\sigma_y < \sigma_x + \gamma\sigma_s$	$dM/d\sigma_y > 0$ if: $\sigma_y > \sigma_x + \gamma\sigma_s$
Selective immigration policy	$dM/d\gamma > 0$ if: $\gamma > (\sigma_y - \sigma_x)\sigma_s + (\delta - \mu_s)(\sigma_v/v)$	$dM/d\gamma > 0$ if: $\gamma > (\sigma_y - \sigma_x)\sigma_s + (\delta - \mu_s)(\sigma_v/v)$

The effects of changes in income distribution and in the selectivity of immigration policy depend on the sign of the numerator in the bracketed term in (A3) as well as on the sign of the derivative of σ_v with respect to σ_x, σ_y, and γ. The following table gives the conditions for these effects to be positive on total migration, holding the underlying skill distribution constant.

We examine the case where destination-country income exceeds source-country income adjusted for migration costs ($\mu_x > \mu_y + \mu_z + c_1 - c_2(q) + \gamma(\delta - \mu_s)$), and assume γ is small. For a source country that is initially relatively equal ($\sigma_y < \sigma_x - \gamma\sigma_s$), rising inequality will increase immigration up to the point where $\frac{\sigma_y}{\sigma_x} = 1 + \frac{\gamma\sigma_s}{\sigma_x}$, beyond which immigration will decline. The effect of changing inequality in the destination is the exact opposite. Thus the immigration rate is an inverse U-shaped function of the ratio of source to destination inequality. Note also that, in the presence of skill-selective immigration policy ($\gamma > 0$), the peak immigration rate will occur at a point where the inequality ratio exceeds 1.

These effects are illustrated in Figure A1. The figure shows wage earning profile, $w(x)$, for the destination and three alternative profiles, $w(y)$, for the source country. The source country profiles are net of migration costs and they intersect at a mean income level that is lower than the mean of $w(x)$. When source and destination profiles are parallel, as in $w(x)$ and $w(y)1$, then all individuals in the source country (with sufficiently low z) have an incentive to migrate. If the source country has a more equal income distribution, as in $w(y)2$, then low-skill individuals for whom $w(y)2 > w(x)$ will not migrate and total migration will be lower than previously. In the case where the source country is more unequal than the destination, as in profile $w(y)3$, migration will also be lower than in the case of parallel profiles, and migrants will be negatively selected.

These relationships will be shifted by skill-selective immigration policy. This is equivalent to steepening the slope of $w(y)$ in Figure A1, at the same time as shifting the profile down at the median skill level. Increasingly selective policy always increases the positive selection of immi-

FIGURE A1.— EARNINGS BY SKILL PROFILES IN DESTINATION AND SOURCE COUNTRIES

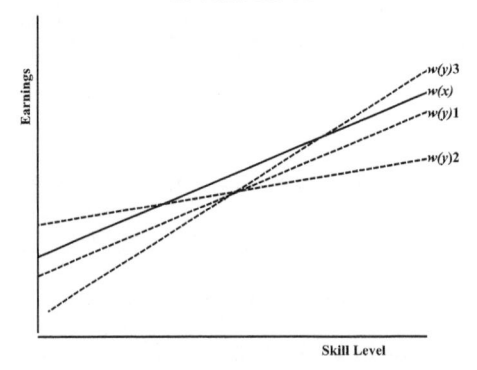

grants, and could increase migration, an effect that is more likely the lower inequality is in the source country and if $\frac{\sigma_y}{\sigma_x} > 1 + \frac{\gamma\sigma_s}{\sigma_x}$. In this case the shift effect dominates the slope effect.

APPENDIX B

Data Used in Estimation: Sources and Methods

1. The INS Gross Immigration Data

The data for the number of immigrants to the United States by country is taken from the U.S. Immigration and Naturalization Service (INS) *Statistical Yearbooks*.[14] The data cover all legal immigration, including refugees, and include those who applied from abroad and those who are already in the United States and are adjusting to permanent status. The country-of-origin classification used here is by country of birth rather than by country of last residence. Choosing country of birth rather than country of last residence allows us to gain consistency between the immigrant flow and the stock of resident immigrants, which is available only by place of birth.

Before 1976, the INS defined a fiscal year as July 1 through June 30. For example, fiscal 1974 began on July 1, 1973, and ended on June 30, 1974. In 1976, however, the INS changed its definition of a fiscal year to October 1 through September 30. Because this change occurred within our data period, the pre-1976 annual observations have been adjusted to conform to the 1976 definition of a fiscal year. The INS did not report monthly totals of immigrants admitted by country of birth, so we used data that the INS labeled as "Immigrants Admitted by Region and Country of Birth" for the third quarter (July 1 through September 30) of 1976. To convert the 1976 "June" fiscal year into a "September" fiscal year, we added the 1976 third quarter totals to the June fiscal year 1976 totals for each country. These sums represent the total immigration from each country to the United States during the fifteen-month period from July 1, 1975, to September 30, 1976. To estimate the immigration for the twelve months of the new September fiscal year 1976, we multiplied the fifteen-month totals by 0.8. This operation gives four-fifths of the fifteen-month totals, results that should be roughly equivalent to the amount of immigration that occurred during four of the five quarters represented from July 1, 1975, to September 30, 1976. This process was then repeated for the previous years. Thus, to convert the June fiscal year 1975 into a September fiscal year, we added one-fifth of the fifteen-month total we used to adjust fiscal year 1976 to the June fiscal year 1975 figures. We then took four-fifths of these sums as the data for the new September fiscal year 1975. Thus, all of the annual gross immigration figures reported in this adjusted INS database now represent October to September totals.

2. Annual U.S. Foreign-Born Stock Values

Benchmark Estimates: Foreign-born population stock data for census years 1970, 1980, and 1990 are taken from the Census Bureau, Population Division, technical working paper no. 29, *Historical Census Statistics on the Foreign-Born Population of the United States: 1850–1990* (1999). This paper by Campbell J. Gibson and Emily Lennon is available online

---

[14] Since 2002 this has become the *Yearbook of Immigration Statistics* of the Department of Homeland Security.

at http://www.census.gov/population/www/documentation/twps0029/twps0029.html. Since the 2000 Census figures were not yet available at the time of writing, the only source of post-1990 foreign-born stock values is the Census Bureau's annual Current Population Survey (CPS) March demographic supplement. These data were obtained from the online data extraction service at http://ferret.bls.census.gov/cgi-bin/ferret. A description of the survey's methodology is available online at http://www.bls.census.gov/cgi-bin/dms?Folder=657. The CPS uses a system of supplemental weights to estimate nationwide foreign-born stock values from the information it collects from its sample. Although the CPS data are useful for displaying demographic trends, the small sample size makes the estimates highly variable. Furthermore, CPS data is available only after 1994 (and up to 1998). To fill out our data set, we used the 1990 Census values and the 1994–1998 CPS data to estimate a simple source-country-specific regression against time. The regression was then used to generate predicted foreign-born by source country for 1998.

Interpolating Between-Census Years: In order to obtain annual estimates of the foreign-born stock by country, we interpolate between the benchmarks established obtained from the Census or calculated from the CPS, using the following stock adjustment equation:

$$S_{t+1} = M_t + dS_t,$$

where S_t is the stock at the beginning of year t and M_t is the flow during that year. We use the gross flow series by birthplace (as defined above) in order to update the stock. The stock observed midway through a year is updated with the flow beginning in that year but carrying through to the next year.

As noted in the text, the parameter d reflects deaths, return migration, and illegal immigration, which subtract or add to the stock independently of the additions through gross immigration and hence $1 - d$ is the rate at which the stock depreciates. This depreciation rate is calculated for each interval between Census or CPS benchmarks using an iterative procedure beginning with S_t, such that the value of S_{t+10} obtained by cumulating forward is reconciled with that of the next Census benchmark. Thus there is a different value of d for each country for each interval between benchmarks. However, in some cases no Census estimate was available for 1970; in that case the value of d calculated for the 1980–1990 interval was used, together with the gross migration series, to extrapolate back to 1970. Similarly, where it was not possible to construct a benchmark figure for 1998 using the CPS data, we use the 1980–1990 value of d to extrapolate forward to 1998.

3. Economic and Demographic Variables

The relative income variable is real GDP per capita at 1985 international prices from the Penn World Tables version 5.6 updated by the World Bank, available at http://www.worldbank.org/research/growth/GDNdata. Average years of education for the population age fifteen and over are from the database of Barro and Lee, available at http://www2.cid.harvard.edu. Since the frequency is five years, the data for each country were linearly interpolated. The share of population aged 15–19 are taken from the annual data (available on CD) underlying the United Nations, *World Population Prospects: The 2000 Revision* (Geneva: UN Population Division). Household income inequality is based on the data originally assembled by Deininger and Squire at the World Bank, now augmented and available from the WIDER Institute at http://www.wider.unu.edu/wiid/wiid.htm. The observations selected are (almost) exclusively those labeled as "high quality" with linear interpolations between these observations. Certain adjustments were made according to whether the observations were for income/expenditure, gross/net income, or individuals/households.

4. Immigration Policy Variables

Immigration policy is characterized in equation (3) in the text by a series of variables denoted by X. The Xs are variables reflecting the quota limits, which are interacted where appropriate, with different variables representing country characteristics. The derivation of the Xs for each category is detailed below:

Nonimmediate Relatives: (X_r): Nonimmediate relatives enter under the following preference categories in the post-1990 legislation (with total numbers in parentheses): (a) adult married children of U.S. citizens (23,400); (b) spouses and unmarried children of U.S. residents, 75% of whom must be minors (114,200); (c) married children of U.S. citizens (23,400); and (d) siblings of adult U.S. citizens (65,000). Before 1992 the preference categories were broadly similar (with percentages of total quota in parentheses): (a) adult married children of U.S. citizens (20%); (b) spouses and unmarried children of resident aliens (20%); (c) married children of U.S. citizens (10%); and (d) siblings of U.S. citizens (24%).

The total number of visas available for these categories is calculated as follows:

Eastern Hemisphere 1968–78: 170,000 World 1979–81: 214,600
Western Hemisphere 1968–76: 120,000 World 1981–91: 210,000
Western Hemisphere 1977–78: 88,800   World 1992–94: 281,000
                                      World 1995–98: 226,000

Note that until 1976 there were no preference categories for the Western Hemisphere, and so the entire quota is included under this heading. For 1977–1978, when a preference system was in force, the number is the total quota net of employment and refugee categories. From 1992 the figure is calculated as the total quota net of employment, diversity, and immediate family categories *plus* the floor of 226,000 for nonimmediate relatives.

The variable X_r is the total number of visas divided by world population (excluding the United States), and that value is applied to each country. Before 1978 it is calculated to produce a separate value for each hemisphere by using the respective hemispheric populations.

Employment Visas (X_e): From 1992 employment-related visas were given under the following categories (with total numbers in parentheses): (a) individuals of outstanding ability (40,000); (b) professionals with advanced degrees or with exceptional abilities (40,000); (c) skilled workers or unskilled shortage workers (40,000); (d) special occupations including religious workers (10,000); and (e) investors (10,000). Before 1992 there were just two employment categories (with percentage of quota in parentheses): (a) exceptional professionals, scientists, and artists (10%); and (b) skilled and unskilled workers in shortage occupations (10%).

The total number of visas for these categories is calculated as follows:

Eastern Hemisphere 1968–78: 34,000   World 1979: 58,000
Western Hemisphere 1968–76: 0   World 1980: 56,000
Western Hemisphere 1977–78: 24,000   World 1981–91: 54,000
                                      World 1992–98: 140,000

The variable X_e is the total number of visas divided by the world population. Before 1979, it is calculated to produce a separate value for each hemisphere by using respective hemispheric populations.

Diversity Immigrants (X_d): The diversity category was introduced for the first time in the 1990 Immigration Act. Diversity visas are a special category applied to countries that were under-represented in U.S. immigration following the 1965 amendments. Countries eligible for diversity visas are those with less than 50,000 immigrants in the preceding five years. In the period 1992–1994, 40,000 (AA-1) visas were available and these were awarded among the applicants by lottery. For those years, the list of eligible countries comprised mainly Europe (excluding the former Soviet Union), Canada, and a few other countries. Within this list there was a quota specific to Ireland, with the rest distributed among the other eligible countries. From 1995, 55,000 (DV) visas were available, and the list of eligible countries includes most of the world, with a few specific exceptions. For these years the total allocation was divided into quotas by continent, with no specific country quotas and a per-country ceiling of 7% of the worldwide total.

The variable X_d is defined only for 1992–1998 and only for those countries eligible to participate; otherwise it takes the value of 0. For 1992–1994 it is defined for each participating country as the total number of non-Irish visas available divided by the total population of countries eligible to participate, excluding Ireland. The variable for Ireland is the Irish quota divided by Irish population. For 1995–1998 it is calculated by continent and applied to each eligible country within that continent.

Refugees and Asylees (X_a): Refugees and asylees were integrated in the total quota until the 1980 Refugee Act. Since then the number, which is not part of the overall ceiling, is determined annually. The "quotas" for refugees are as follows:

Eastern Hemisphere 1968–78: 10,200
Western Hemisphere 1968–76: 0
Western Hemisphere 1977–78: 7,200
World 1979: 50,000   1986: 67,000   1993: 116,000
      1980: 213,700 1987: 70,000   1994: 117,500
      1981: 217,000 1988: 87,500   1995: 111,000
      1982: 140,000 1989: 116,500 1996: 90,000
      1983: 90,000   1990: 110,000 1997: 78,000
      1984: 72,000   1991: 116,000 1998: 83,000
      1985: 70,000   1992: 123,500

The variable X_a is defined as the refugee quota divided by the country population. Before 1979 it is calculated to produce a separate value for each hemisphere by using respective hemispheric populations. From 1980 the overall allocation was divided into regional totals. A separate value was therefore calculated for each region and applied to all countries in that region.

Immigration Reform and Control Act (X_{irc}): As regards permanent admissions, IRCA made two major provisions. The first was legalization of illegal immigrants who had resided in the United States continuously since before 1982. After first applying for temporary status (during a window in 1987–1988), these immigrants could gain permanent status after eighteen months. The second granted temporary visas to seasonal agricultural workers (SAWs), previously working illegally, with the right to become permanent immigrants after one year. Further temporary visas were made available for new agricultural workers, with the right to become permanent after two years. The IRCA provisions are relevant here only insofar as they offered a new channel for permanent immigration. Most of the illegal immigrants eligible for adjustment under IRCA were from Mexico and Central America (especially the former), and the bulk of these adjustments took place in 1989–1991.

Our variable X_{irc} is derived from the number of illegal immigrants living in the United States in 1980 estimated by Warren and Passell (1987, pp. 380–381). Estimates for 1980 are appropriate given that legalizations applied to those living in the United States since before 1982. The estimates are based on a comparison of Census data for 1980 and measures of the stock of legal immigrants based on INS data. The total number of just over two million is considered as a lower bound. Figures are given for specific countries and for continental remainders; the latter were distributed across countries using 1980 population weights. The variable X_{irc} was obtained by dividing the number of illegals, thus calculated, by the origin country population in 1990. It is applied only to the years 1989–1991.

Backlog (X_b): In 1995 the burden of dealing with adjustments shifted from consular offices to the INS, as a result of abolishing the requirement that eligible immigrants present in the United States had to leave the country and apply for immigrant visas through consular offices abroad. As a result, between the end of fiscal 1994 and fiscal 1998 the backlog of applications pending a decision increased from 121,000 to 811,000. The INS estimated that, in the absence of the increase in the pending caseload, legal immigration would have been 110,000 to 140,000 higher for each of the years 1995 to 1998 (INS, 2000, p. 15).

Our variable X_b is simply a dummy for the years 1995–1998.

5. The Balanced Panel

In our econometric work and in the simulations that follow, we use a balanced panel of 81 countries across 28 years. Although there are about twice this number of source countries separately identified in the INS immigration series, the remainder were dropped from the sample because one or more of the explanatory variables was not available for some or all of the period. In cases where countries have split or amalgamated during the period, they have been reaggregated to the combined total throughout. Thus for immigration and the foreign-born stocks, Czechoslovakia, Yugoslavia, and the Soviet Union have been reassembled. East and West Germany are together throughout as are China and Taiwan. In these cases the economic and demographic variables used to explain immigration are aggregated using current population weights.

Panel A of Table B1 lists all the countries in the data set by region. As panel B shows, these account for 82.5% of all immigration over the period. But, as reflected in panel C, under-representation is greater for some regions than others. This is especially important for Africa, the Caribbean, and the Middle East. Important countries that are omitted include Vietnam, Iraq, and Lebanon in Asia; Ethiopia, Somalia, and Nigeria in Africa; and Cuba and Haiti in the Caribbean.

EXPLAINING U.S. IMMIGRATION

TABLE B1.—THE BALANCED PANEL FOR U.S. IMMIGRATION, 1971–1998

A: Countries in the Balanced Panel

Western Europe	Austria, Belgium, Denmark, Finland, France, Germany, Greece, Ireland, Italy, Netherlands, Norway, Portugal, Spain, Sweden, Switzerland, United Kingdom (16)
Eastern Europe	Czechoslovakia (frmr.), Hungary, Poland, Romania, Soviet Union (frmr.), Yugoslavia (frmr.) (6)
East Asia	Bangladesh, China (inc. Taiwan), Hong Kong, India, Indonesia, Japan, Korea (South), Malaysia, Nepal, Pakistan, Philippines, Singapore, Sri Lanka, Thailand (14)
Middle East	Cyprus, Iran, Israel, Jordan, Turkey (5)
North America	Canada, Mexico (2)
Caribbean	Barbados, Dominican Republic, Jamaica, Trinidad and Tobago (4)
Central America	Costa Rica, El Salvador, Guatemala, Honduras, Nicaragua, Panama (6)
South America	Argentina, Bolivia, Brazil, Chile, Colombia, Ecuador, Guyana, Paraguay, Peru, Uruguay, Venezuela (11)
Africa	Algeria, Cameroon, Egypt, Ghana, Kenya, Senegal, Sierra Leone, South Africa, Sudan, Tanzania, Tunisia, Uganda, Zambia, Zimbabwe (14)
Oceania	Australia, Fiji, New Zealand (3)

B: Numbers in Balanced Panel and in Total Immigration 1971–1998, by Period

Period	Immigrants in Sample	Total Immigration	Percent in Data Set
1971–1980	3,656,107	4,389,630	83.3
1981–1990	5,913,094	7,337,806	80.6
1991–1998	6,374,841	7,597,762	83.9
1971–1998	15,944,042	19,325,630	82.5

C: Numbers in the Balanced Panel and Total Immigration, 1990–1998, by Region

Region	Immigrants in Data Set	Total Immigration	Percent in Data Set
Europe	2,507,796	2,575,018	97.4
Asia	4,959,606	6,839,410	72.5
Africa and Oceania	379,085	700,070	54.1
North America	6,923,475	8,034,314	86.2
South America	1,174,080	1,176,386	99.8

Emigration from the UK, 1870–1913 and 1950–1998

TIMOTHY J. HATTON*
*Australian National University and University of Essex.
School of Economics, Faculty of Economics and Commerce, Australian National University, Canberra ACT 0200, Australia.*

International migration is determined by both economic and political forces. This article examines the influence of economic, demographic and policy variables on British emigration to four principal destinations in two different eras. Before 1914 the economic and demographic forces that drove British emigration can be clearly identified. Had the same conditions applied in the post-Second World War period, mass emigration from Britain would have continued until the early 1990s. But from the mid-1960s these influences became less powerful as they were increasingly inhibited by immigration policies in the principal destination countries. The long-term decline in emigration is largely accounted for by shifts in policy, especially those that curtailed or abolished the preferences previously extended to settlers from the UK.

Introduction

Recent studies have suggested that rising globalisation since the Second World War in goods and capital markets has brought the developed world back to where it was a century earlier (see the studies in Bordo et al. 2003). By contrast international migration has remained highly constrained by restrictive immigration policies (Chiswick and Hatton 2003). So how much difference does policy actually make? This article focuses on one country, Britain, and it compares the factors that drove emigration to the New World before the First World War, when emigration was unimpeded by restrictions, with those that operated after the Second World War as the barriers to migration increased.

British emigrants were among the pioneers of mass migration during the nineteenth century. The chief destinations for British migrants were the United States, Canada, Australia, New Zealand and what is now South Africa. After declining sharply during the interwar period, mass emigration

---

* I am grateful to the British Academy for support through a Research Readership. I also appreciate the useful comments of Alison Booth and participants at the conference on 'The Political Economy of Globalisation: Can the Past Inform the Present?' at Trinity College, Dublin, 29–31 August 2002.

to the same destinations re-emerged in the 1950s and 1960s. Since that time British emigration has shrunk back to levels reminiscent of the interwar period. This article seeks to shed light on the following questions:

- Did the same economic variables drive British emigration in the two eras, and if so, how did the magnitude of their effects differ?
- What was the role of immigration policy in the receiving countries and can its effects on the numbers of migrants be identified?
- What combination of economic, demographic and policy variables accounts for the striking decline in British emigration since the 1960s?

The article deals with these issues in four sections. The next section looks at the overall magnitudes and trends in British emigration. This is followed by a discussion of the evolution of immigration policies in the main receiving countries. The subsequent sections present econometric estimates of the determinants of emigration before 1914 and from the mid 1960s onwards. The main conclusion is that most of the postwar fall in British emigration (and indeed much of the turnaround in net UK migration as a whole) was due to immigration policy in the traditional destination countries. In the absence of such policies, emigration of British citizens would have been substantially higher, especially between 1971 and 1991.

Two eras of mass migration

In the 60 years between 1853 and 1913 the passenger statistics record that a total of nearly 13 million British citizens left the UK bound for extra-European ports, and 10 m of these people departed after 1870. These were passengers, chiefly travelling steerage, rather than emigrants as such, and there was also a large return flow.[1] Cumulative net passenger movement after 1870 was nearly 6 m, equivalent to 13 per cent of the population in 1913. They originated from all parts of the UK, with a particularly heavy concentration from Ireland. About three-fifths of these emigrants were male, about three-fifths were single, and among the adults, more than four-fifths were aged between 18 and 45.

The annual flow plotted in Figure 1 shows an upward trend in the total numbers, and characteristic long swings with highs in the decade from 1865, in the 1880s, and in the decade immediately before the First World War. The figure also shows net passenger movements, possibly a better measure

---

[1] British citizens (as distinct from aliens) in principle included those from anywhere in the British Empire although in practice the vast bulk were from Britain and Ireland. The figures were originally recorded by the Board of Trade. In 1912 migrants were distinguished from passengers for those travelling to the USA, Canada and Australia/New Zealand. For the last three quarters of 1912, emigrants amounted to 97 per cent of total passengers (see Carrier and Jeffrey 1953, p. 96).

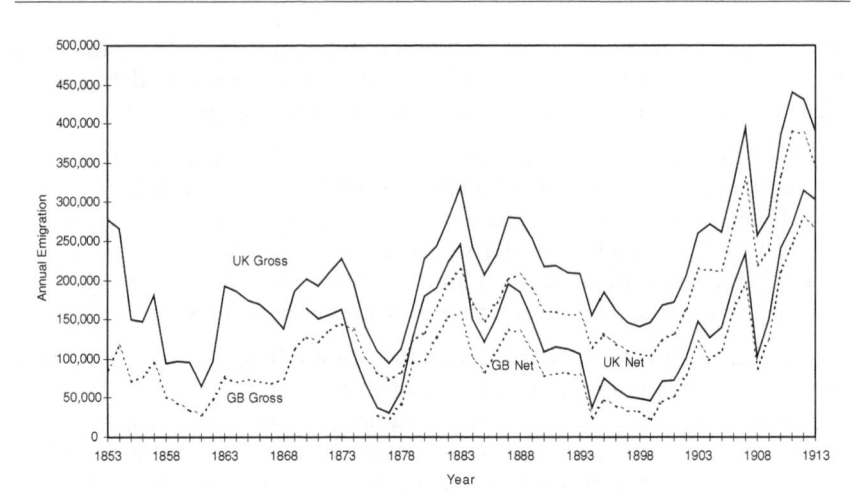

Figure 1. *Gross and net passenger movement, UK citizens 1853–1913.*

of emigration since it nets out return migrants and non-migrant travellers. The absolute numbers are lower but the profile of net migration is very similar to that of gross migration, indicating that fluctuations in the net flows are dominated by variations in the outflow rather than by return migration. Although there is an upward trend in the overall number of UK emigrants, there is no obvious long run trend in emigration per thousand of the population. Emigration rates ranged from lows of less than 4 per thousand in the late 1870s and the late 1890s to highs of around 8 per thousand in the early 1880s and in 1910–12. In the 1850s and 1860s a large share of emigrants came from Ireland, then part of the UK, but Irish emigration declined both absolutely and as a share of the Irish population. This declining Irish contribution is evident in the diminishing gap between emigration from the UK and emigration from Great Britain (England, Scotland and Wales).[2]

Most of the British emigrants travelled to one of four main destinations: the United States, Canada, Australia and New Zealand. Together these account for 88 per cent of the gross outflow of UK citizens between 1871 and 1913 and for 93 per cent of the net outflow. As Figure 2 shows, the dominant destination among these was the United States, accounting for 62 per cent of the four-country gross outflow and for 55 per cent of the overall total. Not surprisingly, emigration to the US accounts for much of the year-to-year fluctuations in total emigration observed in Figure 1. Emigration to Canada

---

[2] Many of the Irish travelled from British ports. In 1872, 39 per cent of Irish emigrants travelled from ports in England or Scotland (Carrier and Jeffrey 1953, p. 29). The data plotted for Great Britain in Figure 1 are for those leaving from ports in England, Scotland and Wales, and hence they still include some proportion of emigrants originating from Ireland.

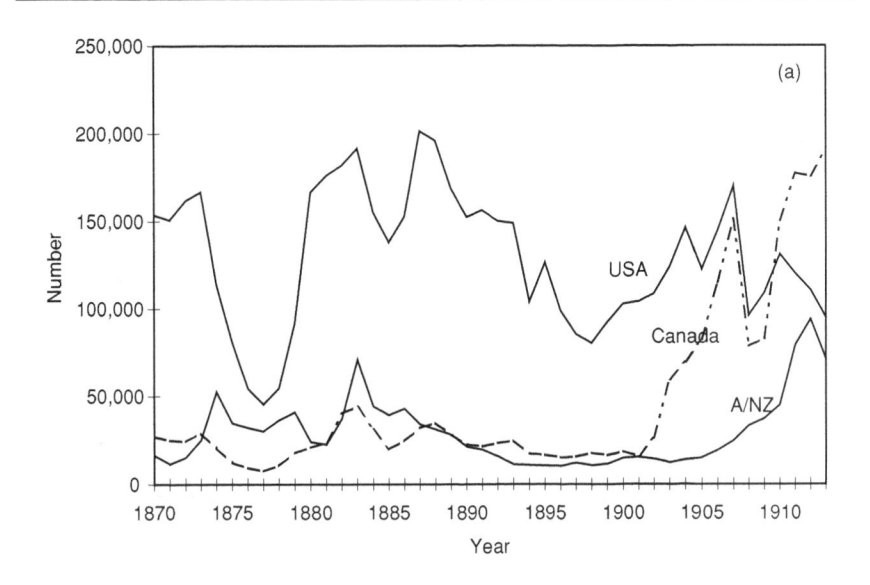

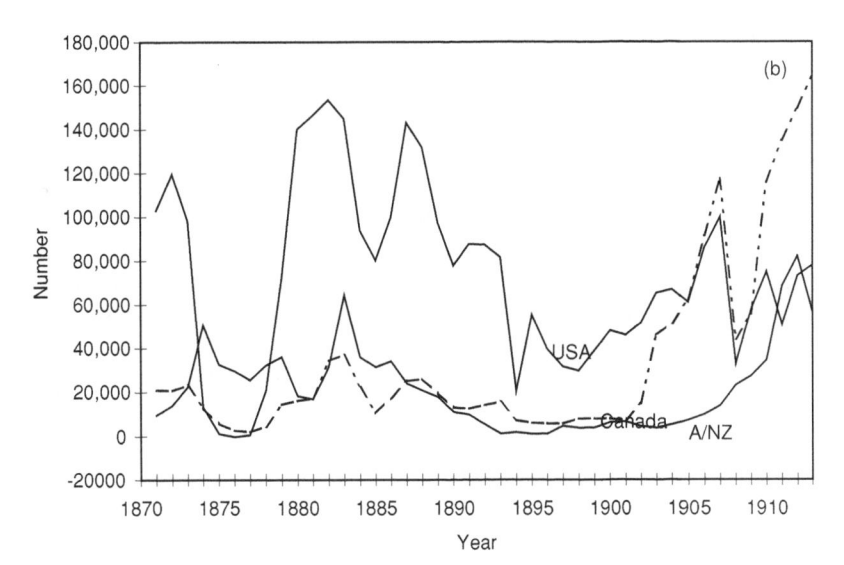

Figure 2. (a) *Gross UK migration to United States, Canada, Australia, and New Zealand, 1870–1913.* (b) *Net UK migration to United States, Canada, Australia and New Zealand, 1871–1913.*

was much smaller and followed a pattern of fluctuations somewhat similar to the US up to the turn of the century. After that there was a spectacular surge, that saw the numbers heading for Canada surpass those bound for the US in the five years before 1914. For Australia and New Zealand (which

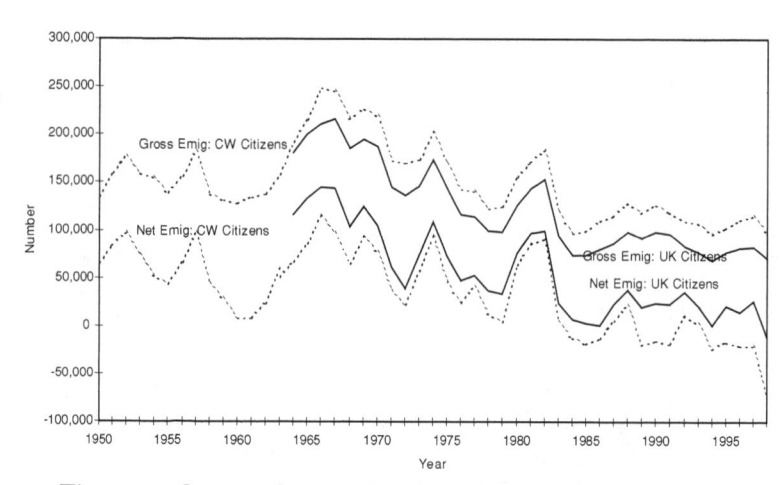

Figure 3. *Gross and net emigration, UK and Commonwealth citizens 1950–1998.*

are combined in the Board of Trade's statistics) the pattern of fluctuations was somewhat different with a notable increase in 1910–13.

After a period of very low emigration in the troubled interwar years, British emigration revived in the 1950s and 1960s. For the years up to 1963 the UK statistics record the flows of Commonwealth citizens travelling by long sea routes to ports outside Europe and the Mediterranean, after which the statistics derive from the International Passenger Survey, which also include travel by air. Both sets of statistics define migrants as those travelling for an intended stay of at least a year, having spent at least a year at the origin. In Figure 3 the gross outflow of Commonwealth citizens up to 1963 has been adjusted upwards to allow for the increasing frequency of air travel, although no adjustment has been made to the net figures.[3] These suggest a total gross outflow from 1951 to 1998 of 7.3 m to non-European destinations, or 12.2 per cent of the UK population in 1998, but a much smaller net outflow of 1.7 m or just under 3 per cent of the 1998 population. In part this reflects growing immigration of non-UK Commonwealth citizens.

From 1964 when UK citizens can be separately identified, the pattern of fluctuations is very similar to that for Commonwealth citizens. Both series show very strong downward trends in gross and net migration from the mid-1960s. Between 1966–70 and 1994–98 gross emigration of UK citizens fell

---

[3] The number travelling by air is assumed to increase linearly from 3,000 in 1949 to 50,000 in 1963. The adjustment for 1963 is based on the difference between emigration by long sea routes and an estimate for total emigration based on the pilot for the International Passenger Survey undertaken in 1963 (reported in the *Board of Trade Journal* 1964).

from an average of 199,000 per annum to 76,000 and the net figure fell from 124,000 per annum to a mere 10,000. Most of the gross emigration of UK citizens continued to be directed to the four traditional destinations. From 1966 onwards they account for 62 per cent of gross emigration and 86 per cent of net emigration to non-European destinations. They also account for most of the decline in the emigration of UK citizens between 1966–70 and 1994–98. Across these years gross emigration fell by 123,000 per annum while the four-country total fell by 100,000 per annum, and the net figures fell by 114,000 and 92,000 respectively.[4]

These figures can also be compared with the overall net migration balance that includes foreign citizens and also includes migration to and from Europe. The overall balance shifted from an average net outward flow of 75,000 per annum in 1966–70 to an average net inward flow of 73,000 in 1994–98, a turnaround of nearly 150,000.[5] Thus the decline in the emigration of UK citizens to the four traditional destinations accounts for nearly two-thirds of the change in the balance that has transformed the UK from a country of net emigration to a country of net immigration over the last forty years.

Figure 4 shows the profiles of annual gross and net emigration to the four principal destinations. Whereas in the period before 1914 the United States was the leading destination, in the early postwar period it was Australia, which from 1966 accounted for 53 per cent of the four-country gross emigration total. The steep decline in gross emigration to Australia in the mid-1970s was followed by much lower average levels, with peaks in the early 1980s and in the late 1980s and early 1990s. The profile for Canada shows a sharp rise and decline in the 1960s followed by a series of fluctuations on a downward trend. Emigration to the United States exhibits milder fluctuations in the 1960s and it is the only country for which the total numbers of emigrants (either net or gross) increased between the early 1970s and the late 1990s. By contrast the pattern of emigration to New Zealand shows an upturn in the early 1970s followed by a gradual decline that resulted in net immigration of UK citizens in the early 1990s. These patterns are closely replicated in the immigration data of the receiving countries. Many observers would argue that these profiles owe much to the changing immigration policy stance in the respective countries, a review of which follows.

---

[4] The fall in emigration to the four traditional destinations was not counterbalanced by increased emigration to Europe after Britain's accession to the European Economic Community in 1973. Annual net emigration of UK citizens to Europe fell by 12.8 thousand per annum between 1966–70 and 1994–8.
[5] The unadjusted IPS figures underestimate the net inflow of foreign citizens because they exclude movements to and from the Republic of Ireland, and because they undercount asylum seekers and other foreign citizens who overstay or switch to longer-term visas. Over time, the declining net inflow from Ireland has been offset by growth in the other categories, such that the overall trend is not greatly affected.

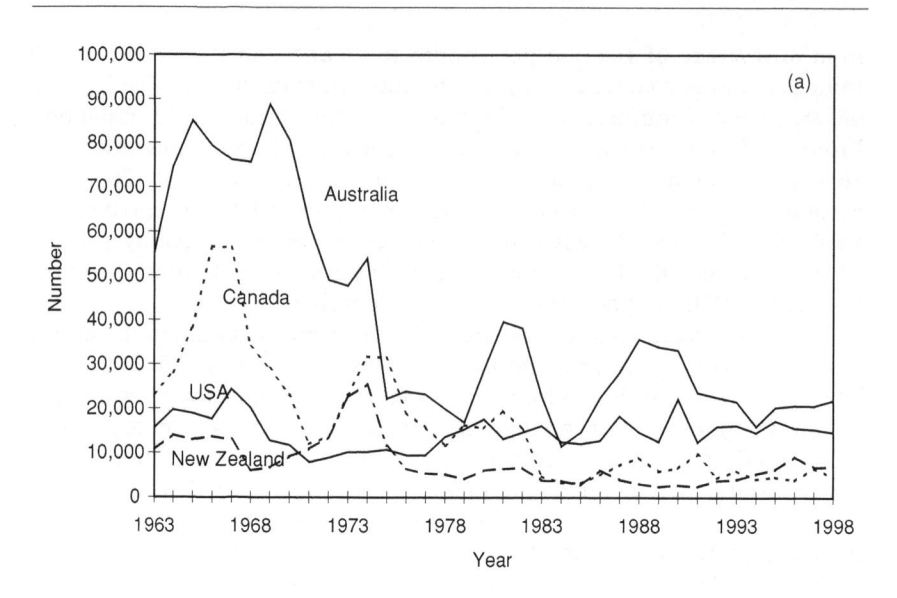

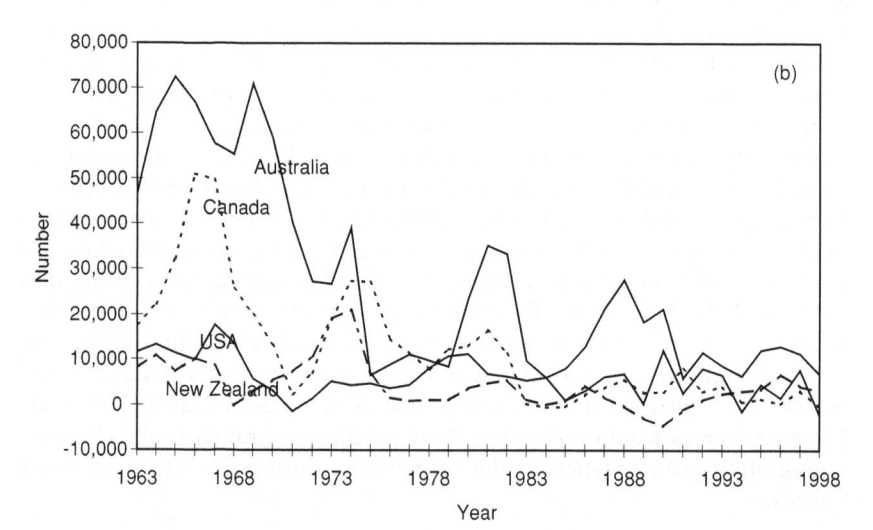

Figure 4. (a) *Gross migration to United States, Canada, Australia and New Zealand, UK citizens 1963–98.* (b) *Net emigration to United States, Canada, Australia and New Zealand, UK citizens 1963–1998.*

Immigration policy in two eras

Before the First World War there was essentially free migration for British citizens to the main New World destinations. In the British Dominions there was effectively no distinction between the native-born and those born in Britain, and there was positive encouragement for immigrants from Britain and Ireland. In Australia and New Zealand this took the form of assisted passages that were allocated to prospective emigrants by emigration agents operating in Britain. By contrast, Canadian recruitment schemes were modest (and specifically targeted at prospective farmers) and there were no subsidies for emigration to the United States.

In Australia, subsidies for free migrants to New South Wales began in 1832. Similar schemes were adopted by other Australian colonies but they were gradually abandoned between the early 1870s and the late 1880s. Subsidies were revived again from 1907 and reached new peaks in 1910–1913.[6] In New Zealand an energetic recruitment drive was initiated in 1871 following the Immigration and Public Works Act of 1870. This scheme was wound down at the end of the 1880s but revived again from 1906, and between 1908 and 1914 almost half of immigrants travelled on assisted passages (see Borrie 1991). This assistance covered only about half of the cost, which meant that a passage to the Antipodes was, for most of the period, still significantly more expensive than a passage across the Atlantic.[7]

In Canada, Australia and New Zealand the pre-war policy regime was the result of ongoing imperial ties and nation-building politics that encouraged European settlement, combined with an abundance of natural resources. From 1872 Canada's National Policy aimed to populate the prairies through immigration and to industrialise through tariff protection. In Australia, where landholders were a powerful interest group (particularly in New South Wales), policy was even more pro-immigration. These influences were less important in the United States, where from 1897 a series of votes in Congress came close to introducing restriction through a literacy test. In each of these countries immigration raised land rents and skilled wage rates relative to unskilled wage rates and this underpinned shifts towards more restrictive policies that culminated with the introduction of country-of-origin quotas in the United States in 1921 and immigration restrictions in the other countries during the early 1930s (Timmer and Williamson 1998).

The pre-1914 regime was revived in the early post-1945 years. Although restrictions on immigration had been imposed in the interim, policies that

---

[6] Assisted emigration ceased in Victoria in 1873, in South Australia in 1886 in New South Wales in 1887 and in Tasmania in 1891. Such schemes were continued on a modest scale in Queensland and Western Australia.

[7] In 1907 assisted male immigrants travelling third class to New Zealand paid £12 (2-berth cabin) or £10 (4-berth cabin) as compared with the total cost of £21 and £19 respectively. Rates charged to female domestic servants were £6.16s and £4.16s respectively. Similar rates prevailed in Australia until 1912 when minimum rates of £6 were agreed for farmers, farm hands, skilled artisans and nominated, assisted or indented male immigrants, and £3 for adult women. That compares with fares across the Atlantic that averaged £5.7s in 1910–1913 but that were mainly in the range of £2.10s –£4.10s during the previous 25 years (see Keeling 1999).

discriminated in favour of British and Irish emigrants meant that there was still essentially free migration to the three Dominions. In the United States the country-of-origin quotas, revised under the McCarran-Walter Act of 1952, made such generous visa allocations to British emigrants that the quota was never filled. But from the 1960s restrictions grew with a series of shifts in immigration policy. These policy changes can be characterised as four types: (a) the removal or reduction of subsidies to British emigrants, (b) the introduction of non-discriminatory policies that no longer favoured the British, (c) changes in global immigration targets or quotas, and (d) the introduction of points schemes or other mechanisms that shifted the balance of the selection criteria towards skills.

In the United States policy change in the 1960s was underpinned by the power of organised labour and by the civil rights movement that demanded the abolition of discrimination. The 1965 Amendments to the Immigration Act (effective 1968) abolished the country-of-origin quotas in favour of an overall quota that allocated the majority of visas to family-sponsored immigrants, with immediate relatives not subject to the quota.[8] As a result Europeans faced greater competition for visas, the proportion of low skilled immigrants increased and opposition to low-skilled immigration grew. Under the 1990 Immigration Act (effective 1992) non-immediate relatives were brought under the quota and a larger number of visas were allocated to skills-based immigration under a revised preference system.[9]

In Canada, the background to policy change was the combination of weakening links to Britain and the toughening of British policy towards immigrants from the Commonwealth.[10] The preference given to immigrants from the UK, France and the USA was abolished in 1962 and replaced with a scheme that allocated visas chiefly to sponsored dependants, nominated relatives and independent migrants. The second and third of these categories became subject to the points test that was established in 1967. In addition to having relatives in Canada, points were awarded for age, education, occupation and English or French language skills. From 1976 targets for total immigration were set administratively, depending on economic conditions– a mechanism that was used to effect a sharp reduction in immigration in 1982–5. The basic system was modified in 1988 and 1993, further increasing

---

[8] Initially there were separate quotas for immigrants from the Eastern and Western hemispheres, but these were merged into a worldwide quota in 1978.

[9] There is a large literature on US immigration policy. Among those that report the details of this evolution, see Tomasi and Keely (1975), Briggs (1984) and DeLaet (2000).

[10] The value of the Commonwealth as a strategic alliance was undermined by the Suez crisis of 1957, and its demise as a political alliance was heralded by Britain's first application to join the European Economic Community in 1961. Although the Commonwealth Immigrants Act of 1962 restricted immigration to Britain from the Commonwealth, it was aimed at those from the New Commonwealth rather than those from the White Dominions.

the degree of skill selectivity such that, by 1994, nearly half of all immigrants were admitted principally on labour market characteristics.[11]

In Australia, the weakening of British imperial protection that was demonstrated by the threat from Japan during the Second World War led to a policy of 'populate or perish', which aimed to increase the population by 2 per cent per annum.[12] The UK Assisted Passage Scheme launched in 1947 offered passages to Australia for £10 per adult and £5 for those aged 14–18. This was followed in 1957 by the 'bring out a Briton' campaign with the result that between 1961/2 and 1971/2 only 10 per cent of UK immigrants were unassisted (Appleyard 1988, p. 43). Australia's involvement in Vietnam and Britain's accession to the European Economic Community led to the demise of pro-British immigration policy. The final abolition of the so-called 'White Australia Policy' took place under the Whitlam government in 1973 and became fully effective from 1975 (Hawkins 1989, Jupp 1991). At the same time, administratively set immigration targets were reduced and new methods of selection were introduced. The first points system, somewhat similar to the Canadian system, was launched in 1979 but was replaced by a new Migrant Assessment System from 1983.[13] Over the following 15 years changes to this system involved introducing a business skills stream and increasing the proportion of immigration subject to the points test (DIMA 2001).

New Zealand was the last country to repeat the cycle in immigration policy followed by Canada and Australia. As in Australia, an Assisted Passage Scheme that offered £10 passages (but for key workers only) was introduced in 1947 and continued until 1975. The preference for British and European immigrants survived longer than in Australia because of the special concessions negotiated with the European Community, but it was eventually abolished in 1987. The points system adopted in 1991 resembles those of Canada and Australia but gives more weight to general skills rather than occupations in demand (Winkelmann 1999). As a result 65 per cent of immigrants to New Zealand in the 1990s were points-tested. Like Australia

---

[11] For detailed discussions of the evolution and impact of Canadian immigration policy, see Hawkins (1989), Green (1994) and Green and Green (1999).

[12] The slogan 'populate or perish' was coined by Arthur Calwell, Australian Immigration Minister from 1945 to 1949 and leader of the Australian Labor Party from 1960 to 1967.

[13] The Numerically Weighted Multi-Factor Assessment System (NUMAS) that was introduced in 1979 has been characterised as a 'halfway house' between the Canadian points system and the Structured Selection Assessment System (SAAS), largely based on interviews, that had existed since 1975. NUMAS came under severe criticism for giving too much weight to English language proficiency and thus undermining the shift towards non-discriminatory immigration policy (Hawkins 1989, p. 142). The down-weighting of proficiency in English under the Migrant Assessment System in 1983 aroused even more controversy from those who still favoured a white Australia—see Blainey (1984).

the minimum threshold points score is adjusted depending on conditions in the domestic labour market.

Explaining UK emigration 1872–1913

There is a large literature that concentrates on estimating the determinants of migration flows from Europe to the New World in the late nineteenth century. Those studies typically focus on bilateral flows from one origin to one destination or on aggregate emigration from a particular source country or to a particular destination. They typically specify emigration as depending on real wage rates and employment rates at the source and the destination, sometimes including a limited number of other variables.[14] Recent time series estimates for aggregate emigration from the UK, Ireland and a number of other countries follow this basic economic specification (Hatton and Williamson 1998). This model is derived for utility-maximising individuals who are risk-averse and who time their migration in order to maximise the net present value of the move (see Hatton 1995). A version of that model is adopted here with the difference that migration streams to each of the major destinations are combined in a pooled regression (rather than being combined in a single aggregate series).[15] The dependent variable is the Board of Trade's gross or net outflow of UK citizens per thousand of the UK population for the three destinations, the United States, Canada and Australia and New Zealand combined. Details of the sources for the explanatory variables can be found in the Appendix.

The result for gross emigration of UK citizens appears in Table 1. Two lags of the dependent variable were found to be statistically significant but lags of other variables, apart from those included in the table, were not found to be important. The stock of previous migrants from the UK at the destination concerned reflects the so-called friends and relatives effect that features so prominently in accounts that stress the cost-reducing and uncertainty-reducing effects that migrant networks provide.[16] Here, an addition of one thousand to the migrant stock raises the annual flow of emigrants to that destination by 48 per annum in the short run and by 94 per annum in the long run – a powerful effect consistent with those estimated

---

[14] For a survey of the earlier literature, see Gould (1979). Some of the more recent time series studies include Taylor (1994), Faini and Venturini (1994), Sanchez Alonso (2000), and Deltas et al. (2001).

[15] This model, originally applied to the late nineteenth century, has also been used to explain recent migration trends, particularly to Germany (Fertig 2001, Boeri et al. 2002, p. 95).

[16] The specific hypothesis is that the larger the stock of previous emigrants the greater the probability that an individual in the source country will have access to a network. For a discussion of migrant networks in the context of migration theories, see Massey et al. (1993). For a formal economic model of migrant stock effects, see Carrington et al. (1996).

Table 1. *Explaining British emigration, 1872–1913.*

Independent variable	UK gross (1)	GB net (2)	UK net (3)
Emigration rate, t−1	0.78	0.81	0.78
	10.0	9.9	9.7
Emigration rate, t−2	−0.29	−0.21	−0.32
	3.7	2.6	4.0
Emigrant stock/home population	0.048	0.031	0.035
	5.2	4.2	3.7
Share of population aged 15–34	12.62	9.61	4.50
	2.8	2.2	1.0
Log destination employment rate	14.72	11.46	14.62
	6.9	6.1	6.1
Log UK employment rate, t−1	−11.01	−9.87	−11.00
	5.0	5.1	4.5
Log wage ratio (destination/home)	1.50	1.45	1.30
	3.6	3.9	3.0
Dummy: Australia and NZ, 1910–13	0.47	0.49	0.41
	1.8	2.1	1.5
Canada	1.50	1.15	1.26
	3.3	2.9	2.4
Australia and New Zealand	1.08	0.89	1.00
	2.9	2.8	2.4
Constant	−6.62	−5.32	−3.64
	1.9	2.8	1.8
Adj. R^2	0.93	0.90	0.84
AR(1)	0.59	2.02	2.41
AR(2)	1.74	2.07	3.79
No. obs.	126	126	126

Notes: Pooled OLS regression with country fixed effects. Dependent variable: emigration per thousand of the UK population to the USA, Canada and Australia/New Zealand. 't' statistics in italics. AR(1) and AR(2) are Breusch-Godfrey tests for first and second order serial correlation with critical χ^2 values at the 5 per cent level of 3.84 and 5.99 respectively.

for aggregate emigration. The share of the UK population aged 15–34 is a proxy for the size of the emigration intensive cohort – those for whom the net present value of migration is largest. This effect must be multiplied by three to obtain the aggregate effect over the three emigration streams. The coefficient implies that an increase of 1 percentage point in the share of the population aged 15–34 raised emigration by 0.4 per thousand in the short run and by 0.7 per thousand in the long run.

The log of employment rates overseas and in the UK (lagged one year) have powerful effects with signs that are opposite but have similar magnitudes. These results strongly support the traditions in the literature that emphasise business cycle effects on the timing of migration. In the long run across the

Table 2. *Decomposition of trends in emigration, 1879–83 to 1909–13.*

Effect of:	1879–83 to 1894–98 Gross	1879–83 to 1894–98 Net	1894–98 to 1909–13 Gross	1894–98 to 1909–13 Net
Emigrant stock/UK population	−1.13	−0.78	−1.57	−1.08
Share of UK population 15–34	1.65	0.53	−0.14	−0.04
Foreign employment rate	−3.46	−2.76	3.17	2.98
UK employment rate	0.02	0.02	0.21	0.21
Wage ratio (UK/foreign)	−0.85	−0.70	1.06	0.86
Australia dummy	0	0	0.92	0.76
Explained total	−3.77	−3.69	3.65	3.69
Actual	−3.39	−4.26	4.20	4.29

Source: Calculated using long-run coefficients from Table 1.

three migration streams a 1 per cent increase in the destination employment rate increases the emigration rate by 0.9 per thousand in the long run while a 1 per cent increase in the UK employment rate reduces it by 0.7 per thousand. The real wage ratio has an effect that is proportionately much smaller so that a 10 per cent rise in the destination to source wage ratio raises the combined gross emigration rate by 0.9 per thousand.

A number of experiments were undertaken to capture the effects of subsidies for emigrants to Australia and New Zealand in the 1870s and 1880s and again in the years before 1914 by including dummy variables. The only one that was close to significance is for the period 1910–13, reflecting the height of assisted passages to Australia. This is consistent with Pope (1981) who finds a negative effect of passage costs on immigration to Australia after the turn of the century. That effect is somewhat more significant in the second column of the table, which is for emigration from Great Britain (excluding Ireland), a result that makes sense since subsidies were targeted mainly to Britain. In other respects the estimate for Great Britain is similar to that for the UK as a whole, suggesting that British and Irish migration streams were guided by the same forces.[17] The final column is for net UK migration and again the pattern of coefficients is similar. Thus net emigration was driven by very much the same forces as gross emigration.

The effects of the individual variables on the course of emigration can be assessed by decomposing changes over time into the effects of different variables. Table 2 offers a decomposition (for the three streams combined) using the long run coefficients to explain the fall in the emigration rate between 1879–83 and 1894–98 and its subsequent rise between 1894–98 and 1909–13. For total UK emigration, the effects of the migrant stock are negative throughout as domestic population growth outstripped that of the

---

[17] Separate estimates for emigration from Ireland, in aggregate and to the USA, are presented in Hatton and Williamson (1998), ch. 5.

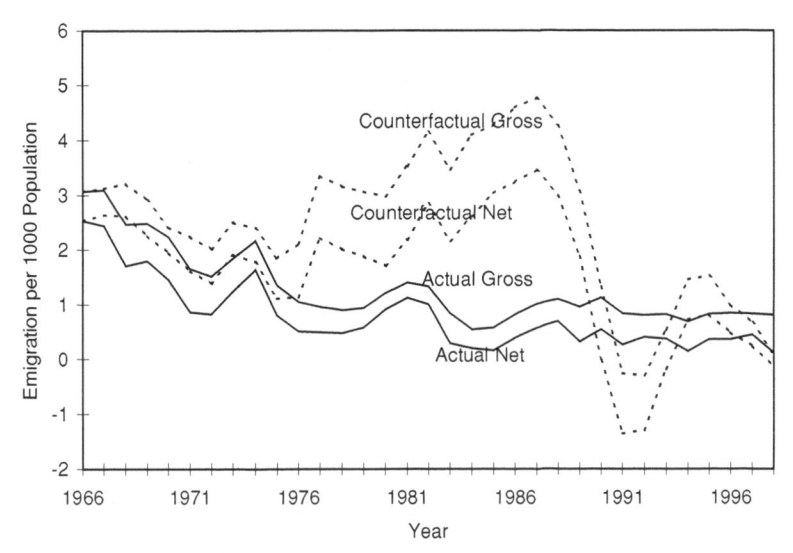

Figure 5. *Counterfactual UK emigration to US, Canada, Australia and New Zealand, 1966–98.*

stock. In the first period this was offset by the growth in the share of the population most at risk. But more important than these are the effects of destination country unemployment rates that reduced the overall emigration rate by around 3 per thousand over the first period and then raised it by about the same amount in the second period. Because these periods fall across the cycles of unemployment in Britain, the domestic unemployment effects are much smaller. The wage effects are more trended and these indicate that wage convergence reduced the emigration rate by a little less than 1 per thousand in the first period. But from the mid 1890s to 1909–13 lagging domestic wage growth boosted gross emigration by more than 1 per thousand of the population. The dummy for Australia/New Zealand also adds to the upsurge in emigration in the years before 1914.

Predicting 1966–98 from the pre-1914 experience

Given the pre-1914 experience, what should we predict for the postwar period? As we have seen, gross and net emigration to the four principal destinations fell secularly from the mid-1960s. Is that what would have been predicted on the basis of the model estimated for the pre-war period? Figure 5 shows, from 1966 onwards, total emigration of UK citizens to the four destinations per thousand of the UK population. Gross emigration declined from more than 3 per thousand in the late 1960s to around 1 per

Table 3. *Predicted emigration trends, 1966–70 to 1994–8.*

	1966–70 to 1980–4		1980–4 to 1994–8	
Effect of:	Gross	Net	Gross	Net
Immigrant stock/UK population	−0.22	−0.15	−0.59	−0.41
Share of UK population 15–34	2.32	0.78	−1.26	−0.43
Foreign employment rate	−4.33	−4.21	0.42	0.41
UK employment rate	4.44	4.19	0.40	0.38
Wage ratio (UK/foreign)	−0.19	−0.16	−2.28	−1.87
Predicted total	2.02	0.45	−3.31	−1.91
Actual	−1.60	−1.28	−0.27	−0.41

Source: Calculated using long-run coefficients from Table 1.

thousand in the 1990s. This compares with an average for the pre-1914 period of 5.3 per thousand.

The dotted lines show what would be predicted for gross and net emigration using the estimated coefficients from the pre-1914 period. These counterfactuals are obtained by applying the coefficients in Table 1 (cols 1 and 3) to comparable annual time series (detailed in the Appendix) for 1966–98, adjusting them to be equal to the actuals in 1966.[18] From that point, the predicted emigration rates fall slightly before rising strongly in the 1980s. Then there is a sharp collapse in the early 1990s such that the predicted emigration rates dip below the actuals from 1990. It is worth noting, however, that the counterfactual predictions do not allow for the endogeneity of the migrant stock.[19] With higher levels of net emigration in the 1980s the stock would have fallen by less and this would have attenuated the fall in emigration in the 1990s.

The long run coefficients estimated for the pre-1914 period are used to explain the decline in predicted emigration in terms of the individual variables. As Table 3 shows, between 1966–70 and 1980–4 the share of population aged 15–34 should have been increasing the level of emigration, especially gross emigration. The emigrant stock and the wage ratio had small negative effects while home and foreign employment rates had effects that were almost exactly offsetting. Overall, gross emigration to the four countries was predicted to rise by 2.0 per thousand whereas, in fact, it fell by 1.6 per thousand.

In the period from 1980–4 to 1994–8 both the migrant stock and the share of the UK population aged 20–34 contributed to a predicted fall in gross

---

[18] For this simulation Australia and New Zealand are combined, as they are in the data for the late nineteenth century. For each of the groups, the constant in the equation is adjusted so that the prediction is equal to the observed value for 1966.
[19] In principle the cumulative effects of higher emigration on the age structure, employment and real wages would have effects opposite to those of the migrant stock.

and net emigration. Employment rates had a small positive effect due to the slight fall in the UK employment rate and the slight rise in the average employment rate for the destination countries. But the most important factor that reduced predicted emigration was the wage ratio, largely as a result of the sharp and sustained rise in UK real hourly earnings in the early 1990s. Overall between 1966–70 and 1994–98 the prewar coefficients predict most of the decline in emigration but not its timing. As Figure 5 showed, between 1971 and 1991 both gross and net emigration are massively over-predicted. This suggests that immigration policies in the receiving countries were particularly important during those two decades.

Explaining emigration 1966–98

The model used to explain emigration rates between 1966 and 1998 is similar in spirit to that used for the pre-1914 period. The main difference is the inclusion of a range of dummy variables that are intended to capture the shifts in immigration policies outlined above. In the data for 1964–98 (see Appendix) Australia and New Zealand are separately identified so that the model is estimated over four migration streams for the years 1996–98. The model is estimated for UK citizens and for the total flow of UK and Commonwealth citizens. The more inclusive definition is arguably closer to that for the pre-1914 period when British and Dominion citizenships were not distinct. But since the estimates that include Commonwealth citizens are very similar to those for UK citizens alone, only the latter are discussed.

The results in the first two columns of Table 4 bear some similarities with those estimates for the late nineteenth century reported in Table 1. The first and second lags of the dependent variable, though somewhat smaller than those estimated earlier, suggest a similar pattern of dynamics. The effect of the stock of previous emigrants on gross emigration gives a long-run coefficient such that increasing the emigrant stock by a thousand adds a further 33 per year to gross emigration. In the presence of family reunification policies, the stock effect still matters, but the size of this effect is only one-third as large as it was in the late nineteenth century. The effect of the share aged 20–34 is also much smaller than it was in the earlier era and the coefficients are much less significant. Overall an increase in the share aged 15–34 increases emigration in the long run by less than a tenth as much as it did before 1914.[20]

The effects of economic incentives as reflected in the coefficients on the employment rates and the wage ratio are also very much smaller than those in the pre-war estimates. In the long run a rise in the employment rate

---

[20] This small effect is all the more surprising since age selectivity should be reinforced by points systems that give more weight to youth. For example the Australian system gives maximum age points to those in the age range 18–29 and does not admit those over the age of 45.

Table 4. *Explaining British and Commonwealth emigration, 1966–98.*

	UK citizens		UK and CW citizens	
Independent variable	Gross (1)	Net (2)	Gross (3)	Net (4)
Emigration rate, t−1	0.48	0.39	0.45	0.35
	6.5	5.0	6.2	4.5
Emigration rate, t−2	−0.23	−0.20	−0.24	−0.19
	3.4	2.9	3.6	2.7
Emigrant stock/home population	0.025	0.013	0.031	0.013
	2.9	1.4	1.4	1.2
Share of population aged 15–34	0.89	1.89	1.07	3.40
	1.2	2.2	1.4	3.4
Log destination employment rate	2.90	3.18	3.20	3.98
	5.4	5.0	5.6	5.5
Δlog UK employment rate	−1.53	−1.76	−1.50	−2.47
	2.3	2.3	2.2	2.8
Log wage ratio (destination/home)	−0.14	0.06	−0.15	0.19
	1.4	0.6	1.5	1.6
Australia 1966–70	0.39	0.40	0.39	0.42
	6.4	5.6	6.1	5.1
Canada 1968–98	−0.37	−0.43	−0.41	−0.48
	6.4	6.0	6.2	5.8
USA 1969–98	−0.04	−0.04	−0.04	−0.03
	0.7	0.1	0.8	0.5
Australia 1975–98	−0.35	−0.34	−0.39	−0.38
	5.7	4.8	6.1	5.1
Australia 1979–98	0.11	0.19	0.11	−0.48
	2.5	3.7	2.2	4.6
New Zealand, 1988–98	0.08	0.09	0.09	0.20
	1.5	1.6	1.8	3.5
New Zealand, 1992–98	0.05	0.10	0.06	0.11
	1.1	1.6	1.2	1.6
USA, 1992–98	0.01	0.004	0.01	0.05
	0.02	0.1	0.3	0.8
USA	−0.18	−0.23	−0.26	−0.25
	1.9	2.0	2.6	1.9
Canada	0.14	0.25	0.11	0.30
	1.9	2.7	1.4	2.8
New Zealand	−0.29	−0.29	0.32	0.30
	2.7	2.2	2.8	2.8
Adj. R^2	0.95	0.89	0.95	0.86
AR(1)	0.15	2.23	0.36	3.68
AR(2)	0.41	2.46	1.21	3.83
No. Obs.	132	132	132	132

Notes: Pooled OLS regression with country fixed effects. Dependent variable: emigration per thousand of the population to the USA, Canada, Australia and New Zealand. The 't' statistics are in italics. AR(1) and AR(2) are Breusch-Godfrey tests for first and second order serial correlation with critical χ^2 values at the 5 per cent level of 3.84 and 5.99 respectively.

across all destinations of 1 percentage point raises gross emigration by a total of 0.15 per thousand. Although this reflects the fact that immigration targets have often been responsive to employment conditions, the effect is still only about one sixth of the size of that for the late nineteenth century. For the UK employment rate, no negative effect could be found in levels, but the change in the UK employment rate does have a modest negative effect on both gross and net emigration. Finally, the log of the wage ratio produces small and insignificant effects that are negative for gross emigration and positive for net emigration. Thus, in the presence of destination country immigration policies for most of the period, the short- and long-run effects of economic variables are severely attenuated as compared to a free-migration counterfactual.

Not surprisingly, the dummies that represent country-specific policy shifts have important effects, particularly those occurring in the decade after 1966. The dummy for Australia 1966–70 reflects the peak of activity in assisted emigration, and the effect of winding down this policy was a sharp reduction in gross and net emigration to Australia. The final abolition of the White Australia Policy in 1975 had an effect that further reduced emigration from the UK by a similar order of magnitude. But surprisingly, the initial introduction of the Australian points system in 1979 had a positive effect that probably reflects the easing of the immigration quota following the clampdown of the Whitlam years.

The introduction of the points system in Canada seems to have had a large negative effect that probably reflects the tightening of immigration targets following the unusually large immigration in the two years before 1968. By contrast, the effects of the 1965 Amendments to the US Immigration Act seem to have been only a very modest reduction in emigration to the US. Changes in immigration policy in New Zealand and in the United States from the late 1980s had positive but largely insignificant effects. This probably reflects two things. First, as Figure 5 and Table 3 showed, the latent demand for emigration from Britain had largely subsided by the early 1990s. And second, the shift towards skills-based immigration policies probably favoured British immigrants on balance over those from other potential source countries.[21]

In Table 5 the trends in the emigration of UK citizens are decomposed using the long-run coefficients from equations 1 and 2 in Table 4. In the period from 1966–70 to 1980–4 the negative effects of falling employment rates overseas and the declining migrant stock were partly offset by the falling employment rate in Britain and the rising population share aged 15–34. But

---

[21] Under the New Zealand points system English language proficiency is a mandatory condition for skill-based immigration and it does not therefore contribute to the points score. For non-native speakers, minimum proficiency is measured as a score of 5 in each component of the IELTS test (Winklemann 1999, p. 26).

Table 5. Decomposition of trends in UK emigration, 1966–70 to 1994–8

Effect of:	1966–70 to 1980–4 Gross	1966–70 to 1980–4 Net	1980–4 to 1994–8 Gross	1980–4 to 1994–8 Net
Immigrant stock/UK population	−0.04	−0.02	−0.24	−0.12
Share of UK population 15–34	0.15	0.29	−0.08	−0.16
Foreign employment rate	−0.80	−0.81	−0.02	−0.02
ΔUK employment rate	0.10	0.10	−0.19	−0.20
Wage ratio (UK/foreign)	0.00	0.00	0.19	−0.08
Australia dummies	−0.84	−0.68	0.0	0.0
Canada dummy	−0.49	−0.53	0.0	0.0
USA dummies	−0.05	−0.05	0.01	0.01
New Zealand dummies	0.0	0.0	0.17	0.23
Policy effects	−1.38	−1.26	0.18	0.24
Predicted total	−1.97	−1.70	−0.16	−0.34
Actual	−1.60	−1.28	−0.27	−0.41

Source: Calculated for UK citizens using long run coefficients from Table 4.

the key effects that reduced emigration were the tightening immigration policies, especially in Canada and Australia. These shifts in immigration policy account for 68 per cent of the observed fall in gross emigration and for nearly all of the fall in net emigration. In the period from the early 1980s to 1994–98 the fall in the emigrant stock and the increasing UK employment rate added to the downward trend in emigration while the policy variables evidently had small positive effects.

Over the whole period from 1966–70 to 1994–98 policy changes accounted for two-thirds of the fall in the four-country emigration rate of UK citizens, either gross or net. These policy effects also account for about two-fifths of the change in the overall balance of net UK emigration across all citizenships and between all countries from 1.36 to −1.24 per thousand of the UK population. Allowing for the indirect effects of policy on the migrant stock would make the contribution of immigration policy larger still.

Conclusion

Economic variables are uppermost in explaining fluctuations and trends in UK emigration before the First World War. After 1945 there was another emigration boom, to the same destinations but on a slightly smaller scale. The evidence suggests that, had the postwar flows been conditioned in exactly the same way as they were before 1914, the surge of emigration would have continued until the early 1990s. Instead, net and gross emigration of UK citizens declined secularly from the late 1960s, and it made a major contribution to the shift in the overall UK balance of net migration. Shifts in immigration policy in the principal destination countries had large negative effects on British emigration in the 1970s and 1980s and, in the presence of these, the impact of economic variables on the flows was much reduced. While policy was largely responsible for falling British emigration in the 1970s and 1980s, the evidence suggests that by the 1990s the latent demand for emigration had largely evaporated.

References

APPLEYARD, R. T. (1988). *Ten Pound Immigrants*. London: Boxtree.
BLAINEY, G. (1984). *All for Australia*. Sydney: Methuen Haynes.
BORDO, M., TAYLOR, A. M. and WILLIAMSON, J. G. (eds). (2003). *Globalization in Historical Perspective*. Chicago, IL: University of Chicago Press.
BOARD OF TRADE JOURNAL (1964). London: HMSO.
BOERI, T., HANSON, G. and MCCORMICK, B. (2002). *Immigration Policy and the Welfare State*. Oxford: Oxford University Press.
BORRIE, W. D. (1991). *Immigration to New Zealand, 1854–1938*. Canberra: Highland Press.
BRIGGS, V. M. (1984). *Immigration Policy and the American Labor Force*. Baltimore, MD: Johns Hopkins University Press.
CARRIER, N. H. and JEFFREY, J. R. (1953). *External Migration: A Study of the Available Statistics, 1815–1950*. General Register Office, London: HMSO.
CARRINGTON, W. J., DETRAGIACHE, E. and VISHWANATH, T. (1996). Migration with endogenous moving costs. *American Economic Review* **86**, pp. 909–30.
CHISWICK, B. R. and HATTON, T. J. (2003). International migration and the integration of labor markets. In M. Bordo *et al.*, (eds), *Globalization in Historical Perspective*. Chicago, IL: University of Chicago Press.
DELAET, D. L. (2000). *US Immigration in An Age of Rights*. Westport, CT: Praeger.
DELTAS, G., SICOTTE, R. and TOMCZAK, P. (2001), Passenger shipping cartels and their effects on transatlantic migration. Unpublished paper, University of Calgary.
DEPARTMENT OF IMMIGRATION and MULTICULTURAL AFFAIRS (AUSTRALIA) (2001). *Immigration: Federation to Century's End*. Canberra: Commonwealth of Australia.
FAINI, R. and VENTURINI, A. (1994). Italian emigration in the pre-war period. In T. J. Hatton and J. G. Williamson (eds.), *Migration and the International Labor Market, 1850–1939*. London: Routledge.
FERTIG, M. (2001). The economic impact of EU enlargement: assessing the migration potential. *Empirical Economics* **26**, pp. 707–20.
GREEN, A. G. (1994). A comparison of Canadian and US immigration policy in the twentieth century. In D. J. DeVoretz (ed.), *Diminishing Returns: the Economics of Canada's Recent Immigration Policy*. Toronto: C. D. Howe Institute.
GREEN, A. G. and GREEN, D. A. (1999). The economic goals of Canada's immigration policy: past and present. *Canadian Public Policy–Analyse de Politiques* **25**, pp. 425–51.

GOULD, J. D. (1979). European intercontinental emigration, 1815–1914: patterns and causes. *Journal of European Economic History* **9**, pp. 41–112.
HATTON, T. J. (1995). A model of UK emigration, 1870–1913, *Review of Economics and Statistics* **77**, pp. 407–15.
HATTON, T. J. and WILLIAMSON, J. G. (eds). (1994). *Migration and the International Labor Market 1850–1939*. London: Routledge.
HATTON. T. J. and WILLIAMSON, J. G. (1998). *The Age of Mass Migration: Causes and Economic Impact*. New York: Oxford University Press.
HAWKINS, F. (1989). *Critical Years in Immigration: Canada and Australia Compared*. Sydney: McGill-Queen's University Press.
JUPP, J. (1991). *Australian Retrospectives: Immigration*. Sydney: Sydney University Press.
KEELING, D. (1999). The transport revolution and transatlantic migration, 1850–1914. *Research in Economic History* **19**, pp. 39–74.
MASSEY, D. S., ARRANGO, J., HUGO, G., KOUAOUCI, A., PELLEGRINO, A. and TAYLOR, J. E. (1993). Theories of international migration: a review and appraisal. *Population and Development Review* **19**, pp. 431–66.
POPE, D. H. (1981). Modelling the peopling of Australia, 1900–1930. *Australian Economic Papers* **20**, pp. 258–81.
SANCHEZ ALONSO, B. (2000). Emigration in the late nineteenth century: the paradoxical case of Spain. *Economic History Review* **80**, pp. 651–68.
TAYLOR, A. M. (1994). Mass migration to distant southern shores: Argentina and Australia, 1870–1939. In T. J. Hatton and J. G. Williamson (eds.), *Migration and the International Labor Market, 1850–1939*. London: Routledge.
TOMASI, S. M. and KEELY C. B. (1975). *Whom Have We Welcomed?* New York: Centre for Migration Studies.
TIMMER, A. and WILLIAMSON, J. G. (1998). Immigration policy prior to the Thirties: labor markets, policy interaction, and globalization backlash. *Population and Development Review* **24**, pp. 739–71.
WINKELMANN, R. (1999). Immigration policies and their impact: the case of Australia and New Zealand. Bonn: IZA Discussion Paper no. 169.

Appendix: Data sources

A: 1870–1913

Emigration: Gross and net passenger movements from N. H. Carrier and J. R. Jeffrey, *External Migration: A Study of the Available Statistics, 1815–1950* (General Register Office, London: HMSO, 1953), Table D/F/G (1). Inward movement for 1870–76 from I. Ferenczi and W. F. Willcox, *International Migrations*, vol. I (New York: NBER, 1929), Table XII, p. 640.

Migrant stock: Benchmarks for the population born in the UK and in Great Britain, residing in the United States and Canada in census years from Carrier and Jeffrey (1953), Table 3. Australia from D. Lucas, 'United Kingdom-born people in Australia', in *1996 Census Community Profiles* (Canberra: Department of Immigration and Multicultural Affairs, 2000), p. 3. New Zealand from *Census of Population* (Wellington: Government Printer, various dates). Annual migrant stock series were calculated by interpolating between census benchmarks using the relationship $S_t = NM + dS_{t-1}$, where S is the stock, NM is net passenger movement detailed above, and d is a parameter calculated for each interval between censuses.

Total population and share aged 15–34: For UK and Great Britain from B. R. Mitchell and P. Deane, *Abstract of British Historical Statistics* (Cambridge: Cambridge University Press, 1962), pp. 10–14. Share aged 15–34 linearly interpolated between census years.

Unemployment rates: UK from G. R. Boyer and T. J. Hatton, 'A New Index of British Unemployment, 1870–1913', *Journal of Economic History* **62** (2002), Appendix 1. United States from J. R. Vernon, 'Unemployment Rates in Post-Bellum America, 1869–1899', *Journal of Macroeconomics* **16** (1994), p. 710. For Canada an unemployment rate was constructed by regressing a non-linear transformation of the employment rate on the deviation of *per capita* real income from its logarithmic trend 1916–1926 and then extrapolating backwards. The employment rate was taken from W. Galenson and A. Zellner, 'International Comparison of Unemployment Rates', in National Bureau of Economic Research, *The Measurement and Behaviour of Unemployment* (Princeton, NJ: Princeton University Press, 1957), pp. 439–480, and real GNP *per capita* from M. C. Urquhart, 'New Estimates of Gross National Product: Canada, 1870–1926', in S. L. Engerman and L. E. Gallman (eds.), *Long Term Factors in American Economic Growth* (Chicago, IL: National Bureau of Economic Research, 1986), pp. 9–94. Australia from N. G. Butlin, 'An Index of Engineering Unemployment, 1852–1943', *Economic Record* **22** (1946), pp. 241–60. This index was transformed using the relationship between unemployment in production industries and total unemployment estimated in Boyer and Hatton (2002).

Real wage rates: Purchasing power parity adjusted unskilled wage rates for Great Britain, Ireland, USA, Canada and Australia from J. G. Williamson, 'The evolution of global labor markets since 1830: background evidence and hypotheses', *Explorations in Economic History* **32** (1995), pp. 141–96. An index for the UK is calculated by giving a weight of 0.3 to Ireland and 0.7 to Great Britain.

B: 1964–1998

Emigration: International Passenger Survey for gross and net migration; 1964–1973 from *Board of Trade Journal* (London: HMSO, various issues); 1974–1998 from *International Migration* (London: Office for National Statistics, various issues). Figures for UK citizens and Commonwealth citizens by destination for 1964–65 obtained by adjusting total migration by the shares of UK or Commonwealth citizens in total inward and outward flows for each destination country in 1966.

Migrant stock: Decennial census benchmarks for the population born in the UK residing in the United States from *Statistical Abstract of the United States* (Washington: GPO, 1997). Canada (quinquennially from 1981) from *Canada Yearbook* (Ottawa: Statistics Canada, various years). Australia (quinquennially) from Lucas (2000), *op. cit.* New Zealand (quinquennially) from *Census of Population* (Wellington: Government Printer, various dates). The annual migrant stock was calculated, as for the pre-1914 period, by using the net migrant flow to interpolate between census dates.

Total population and share aged 15–34: Annual estimates of UK population, total and by age groups, *Annual Abstract of Statistics* (London: HMSO, various issues).

Unemployment rates: OECD *Main Economic Indicators: Historical Statistics* (Paris: OECD 1993) and subsequent annual issues of *Main Economic Indicators*.

Real wage rates: 1975–98 hourly direct pay of production workers in manufacturing in national currency from US Bureau of Labor Statistics, 'International Comparisons of Hourly Compensation Costs for Production Workers in Manufacturing, 1975–2000', <ftp://bls/gov/pub/ForeignLabor/supptabitxl>. 1964–75 hourly earnings in manufacturing for UK, USA and Canada and consumer price index for UK, USA, Canada, Australia and New Zealand, 1964–98 from OECD (1993) *op cit.* and subsequent annual issues of *Main Economic Indicators*. Australia 1964–75 average minimum wage rates in manufacturing from *Yearbook of the Commonwealth of Australia* (Canberra: Australian Bureau of Statistics, various dates). New Zealand 1964–75 nominal weekly wage rates from *New Zealand Official Yearbook* (Wellington: Department of Statistics, 1982), p. 912.

[3]

Out of Africa? Using the Past to Project African Emigration Pressure in the Future

Timothy J. Hatton and Jeffrey G. Williamson*

Abstract

The paper uses analysis of the mass emigration from poor Europe in the late nineteenth century to project the future mass emigration potential from Africa, especially to the economically more mature Mediterranean economies. The economic and demographic fundamentals driving both experiences are likely to be the same, but their magnitudes are likely to be far bigger in the African case over the next few decades. Efforts to restrict the migration and to seal porous borders may be partially successful; but, if so, they are certain to create unpleasant side-effects. European restrictions will create a greater share of illegals and thus greater absorption problems in recipient nations: European restrictions will create more poverty in African sending regions. And European restrictions will create considerable diplomatic problems between the two regions.

1. Overview

Recent analysis of the late nineteenth century mass migrations from Europe has identified the underlying economic and demographic fundamentals driving those flows. The cross-border migration rates were huge during this age of "free" migration, and the pre-World War I peak hasn't been matched since. This paper uses late nineteenth century mass migration experience to guide expectations about future African mass migration potential. While the economic and demographic forces driving both experiences are likely to remain the same, their magnitudes will almost certainly be far bigger in Africa over the next few decades. Efforts to restrict the migration and to seal porous borders may be partially successful, but, if so, they are certain to create unpleasant side effects: European restrictions may choke off African emigration, but by doing so they will create bigger social problems at home; European restrictions will induce a rising share of illegals, and by so doing they will create greater social problems in recipient nations; and European restrictions will create increasing diplomatic problems between the two regions. Many young African adults will, sadly, perish in the AIDS epidemic (Collier and Gunning, 1999a), but the surviving numbers of potential emigrants will still be very great.

The next section reviews the underlying economic and demographic fundamentals responsible for the late nineteenth century mass migrations. Section 3 uses those lessons of history to explore the future demand for African emigration. We conclude that the numbers are likely to be very big even given a wide moat around Europe, and even given an AIDS epidemic at the source. Section 4 asks whether an African move to a more liberal trade policy would ease the emigration pressure; that is, it asks

---

*Hatton: Department of Economics, University of Essex, Colchester CO4 3SQ, UK. Tel: 44-1-206-872748; Fax: 872724; E-mail: hatton@essex.ac.uk. Williamson: 216 Littauer, Harvard University, Cambridge, MA 02138, USA. Tel: 617-495-2438; Fax: 496-7352; E-mail: jwilliam@kuznets.fas.harvard.edu. The authors are grateful to previous collaborators whose joint work with us has been used extensively in this paper: David Bloom, Bill Collins, Matt Higgins, Kevin O'Rourke, and Tarik Yousef. We are also grateful for useful comments from Bob Bates, Barry Chiswick, Paul Collier, Kyle Kauffman, Stephan Klasen, Andy Warner, and participants at the Delphi conference, 24–26 May 2000. In addition, Williamson acknowledges financial support from the National Science Foundation (SBR 95-05656).

whether trade and migration are substitutes. Section 5 asks whether a world savings glut—and thus more capital inflows into Africa—would keep more Africans at home. The last section offers a pessimistic conclusion.

2. Mass Migrations in the Past

The Size of the European Mass Migrations

Migration to the New World was a mere trickle in the early nineteenth century compared with what came later. It was not until after mid-century that mass migration really took hold and not until the 1880s that it became a flood. Until well into the nineteenth century, moving costs were too high relative to the perceived gains for most potential migrants. Declining costs of passage, increasing family resources at home, and the growing attractiveness of the destinations, all served to change these conditions as the century progressed. These mass migrants were typically young, single, and male (two-thirds were men). More than three-quarters of the immigrants entering the United States between 1868 and 1910 were aged 16 to 40, and over 80% of the Irish emigrants were aged 15–34.

These emigrant characteristics suggest that it was economics that moved them. Young, single males had the most to gain from the move. By emigrating as young adults, they were able to reap the gains over most of their working lives while minimizing the earnings forgone during passage and job search. By moving as single individuals, they were also able to minimize the direct costs of the move. Since they were typically unskilled, they also had less country-specific human capital invested and hence stood to lose only small rents from such acquired skills (except language). These attributes reinforce the premise that most emigrants moved to improve their living standards.

In the first three decades after 1846, European intercontinental emigration averaged about 300,000 per annum; in the next two decades the figures more than doubled; and after the turn of the century, they rose to over a million per annum. The sources also changed dramatically. In the first half of the century, the dominant emigration stream had its source in the British Isles, followed by Germany, and joined after 1870 by a rising tide from Scandinavia and elsewhere in northwest Europe. European emigration took a sharp upward trend in the 1880s as emigration surged from southern and eastern Europe; indeed, these new streams account for most of the leap in the total. They came at first from Italy and parts of Austria–Hungary, but then the flow swelled to include Poland, Russia, Spain, and Portugal.

Late nineteenth century exit rates varied enormously across Europe. Table 1 presents decade-average rates for 12 sending countries. The highest overall was recorded by Ireland with an emigration rate of 13 per thousand population between 1850 and 1913. Sweden and Norway had rates approaching 5 per thousand. Those for Germany and Belgium were under 2 per thousand, while they were close to zero for France. Furthermore, the long-run trends differed widely: rates of emigration declined in Ireland from the 1860s and they did the same in Germany and Norway from the 1880s. But the rates from Italy and Spain began a steep ascent after the 1880s, a boom that was halted only by the outbreak of war in Europe.

The Economic and Demographic Fundamentals Driving European Mass Migrations

Our recent book (Hatton and Williamson, 1998) tries to establish exactly which economic and demographic fundamentals were doing most of the work in accounting for

© Blackwell Publishers Ltd 2002

558   Timothy J. Hatton and Jeffrey G. Williamson

Table 1. Gross Emigration Rates from European Countries, 1850–1913 (emigrants per 1,000 population per annum, decade averages)

	1850–59	1860–69	1870–79	1880–89	1890–99	1900–13
Belgium	1.90	2.22	2.03	2.18	1.96	2.32
Denmark	—	—	1.97	3.74	2.60	2.80
France	—	0.12	0.16	0.29	0.18	0.15
Germany	1.80	1.61	1.35	2.91	1.18	0.43
Great Britain	4.83	2.47	3.87	5.71	3.92	7.08
Ireland	18.99	15.16	11.28	16.04	9.70	7.93
Italy	—	—	4.29	6.09	8.65	17.97
Netherlands	0.50	1.67	2.66	4.06	4.62	5.36
Norway	—	—	4.33	10.16	4.56	7.15
Portugal	—	—	2.91	3.79	5.04	5.67
Spain	—	—	—	3.91	4.63	6.70
Sweden	0.51	2.52	2.96	8.25	5.32	2.93

Notes: These figures are for gross emigration, drawn largely from Ferenczi and Willcox. Where possible the figures include emigration to other countries within Europe. Unfortunately, data on return migration are limited.
Source: Hatton and Williamson (1998, p. 33).

the mass migrations, and why. Our study of decade-average emigration rates for 12 western European countries over the period 1860–1913 uses the gross emigration rates displayed in Table 1. It also takes advantage of a new database of internationally comparable real unskilled wage rates. The database includes the major emigrant countries, making it possible to compare labor market conditions between source and destination. But these labor market variables cannot alone explain all the variation in migration across countries and over time. The other source country influences that matter are: the rate of natural increase lagged 20 years;[1] the share of the labor force in agriculture; the stock of previous emigrants living in destination countries; and the emigration rate lagged one decade.

Together these variables explain three-quarters of the variation in European emigration experience during the age of mass migration. The results in column 1 of Table 2 strongly support the view that relative wage rates were a key influence on emigration: a 10% rise in the real wage advantage of destination over source raised the long-run emigration rate by 1.27 per thousand, a substantial effect.[2] However, the coefficient on our inverse measure of industrialization—the share of the male labor force in agriculture—suggests that agricultural or rural populations were less mobile than urban or industrial ones. Insofar as industrialization increased the urban wage, it tended to reduce emigration; but this effect was offset at least in part by the falling share in agriculture, but the effect is weak. The effect of lagged natural increase strongly supports the view that the demographic transition drove emigration. The long-run estimate derived from column 1 suggests that half of excess births were manifested in emigration 20 years later. This is a very large effect and it is important to recognize that it was not the result of a labor force glut pushing down wage rates at home, since any such effect would already be captured indirectly by the wage. Rather, it had a direct impact on aggregate emigration by changing the share of the population who were most likely to move. As we shall see, this cohort size effect in Europe's past will be

© Blackwell Publishers Ltd 2002

Table 2. Determinants of European Gross Emigration Rates in the Late Nineteenth Century

	(1)	(2)
Constant	−4.66	−4.24
	(2.66)	(0.52)
Log wage ratio (destination/home)	6.86	6.80
	(3.63)	(3.10)
Share of male labor force in agriculture	−4.04	−4.08
	(1.26)	(1.23)
Natural increase lagged 20 years	0.26	0.27
	(2.61)	(2.57)
Migrant stock/home population	0.09	0.09
	(1.89)	(1.69)
Lagged emigration rate	0.52	0.52
	(3.17)	(3.13)
Real wage at home		−0.09
		(0.05)
Country dummy (Belgium, Italy, Portugal, Spain)	4.43	4.40
	(3.17)	(3.29)
R^2	0.75	0.75
RSS	194.4	194.4
RESET	0.002	0.004

Note: t-statistics in parentheses. RESET is the test for functional form using the squares of the fitted values. The 48 country/decade observations used in the analysis (with number of observations for each country) are as follows: Belgium 1860–1913 (5); Denmark 1880–1913 (3); France 1870–1913 (4); Germany 1870–1913 (4); Great Britain 1860–1913 (5); Ireland 1860–1913 (5); Italy 1880–1913 (3); Netherlands 1860–1913 (5); Norway 1880–1913 (3); Portugal 1870–1913 (4); Spain 1890–1913 (2); and Sweden 1860–1913 (5). The dependent variable is the annual average of gross emigration per 1,000 population. The variables for share in agriculture and migrant stock are measured at the beginning of the decade. Real wage rates are PPP-adjusted, and decade averages based on Great Britain in 1905 = 100.

repeated in Africa's future, implying the same underlying demographic fundamentals at work.

Both the stock of previous migrants and the lagged migration rate had a positive impact on the current decade's emigration rate, and these effects testify to the persistence in emigration streams. The migration literature has long highlighted chain migration, sometimes calling it the "friends and relatives effect." Once established, channels of migration perpetuate themselves: earlier migrants provide prepaid tickets for the passage, food and shelter to newly arrived friends and relatives, and social networks offering information on and access to job opportunities. Evidence from the United States indicates that as many as 90% of immigrant arrivals at the turn of the century were traveling to meet a friend or relative who had emigrated previously. Furthermore, a very large share of the European emigrants were traveling with prepaid tickets purchased by friends or relatives abroad. The migrant stock captures these effects and our estimate suggests that, in the long run, for each thousand previous emigrants, a further 20 were pulled abroad each year. Thus, the larger the stock of previous emigrants, the greater was the current flow. As we shall see, this effect has profound implications for Africa's future too.

One additional argument sometimes put forward is that potential emigrants are constrained by poverty in poorer preindustrial countries. The argument goes that as real incomes rise with economic development at home, more of those with the greatest incentive to escape poverty can actually afford the move. However, we do not find the predicted positive effect of the home real wage. There are two possible reasons for this. First, our sample of (relatively affluent) western European countries includes those where the poverty trap was least likely to be binding; the effect was more likely to have been binding in poorer eastern Europe. Second, emigration was well established in many of these countries so that the friends and relatives effect, by lowering the costs of emigration, served to attenuate the poverty trap. Thus, a rising migrant stock abroad may have served by itself to ease the poverty constraint on emigration. The same might have been true of Africa in recent decades.

The Stylized Life-Cycle of European Emigration

It has often been noted that as industrial and demographic revolutions take place emigration often rises—slowly at first—to a peak before declining. This life-cycle is evident for most European countries in our sample (Hatton and Williamson, 1998, p. 47). The up-side of the inverted-U is sometimes associated with the easing of the poverty constraint: as real wages increase from a low level at home, emigration rises; but with further wage growth the poverty constraint ceases to bite and the catching up between source and destination (if in fact it takes place) begins to cause emigration to decline. Industrialization and the demographic transition also made important contributions to the emigration life-cycle.

In order to explore the emigration life-cycle in late nineteenth century Europe we first identify the decade in which emigration peaked for each of our countries. We then realign emigration histories such that the peak falls in decade 5 of what we call "emigration time." We regress the actual and fitted values from column 1 of Table 2 on emigration time and its square (including country dummies). Figure 1 shows that the stylized emigration life-cycle pattern emerges. Between the first decade and the peak decade of emigration time, the rate rises by about 4 per thousand before beginning its decline. The quadratic trend which emerges from the fitted values indicates that much of this emigration life-cycle is captured by the explanatory variables in our model.

We proceed next to decompose the European emigration life-cycle into its component parts. Which variables were doing most of the work? Using the long-run coefficients derived from column 1 of Table 2, we can identify the contribution of each variable to the European emigration life-cycle (Figure 2). Rising rates of natural increase augmented emigration rates by quite a bit more than 2 per thousand by the fifth decade—a powerful effect, accounting for more than half of the surge in emigration. As the demographic transition weakened, it served to contribute to the down-side of the inverted-U. The decline in the share of the labor force in agriculture and the mounting migrant stock abroad also contributed to the upswing: these two contributed jointly to about 2 per thousand in the annual emigration rate by the fifth decade. The offsetting force was the declining wage gap, driven by the convergence of European real wages on those of the New World. In the early stages, the narrowing of the wage gap was insufficient to stem the rise in emigration: by the fifth decade, it served to lower the annual emigration rate by 1.5 per thousand; but after the fifth (peak) emigration decade the offsetting catch-up forces began to swamp the ebbing forces of demography and industrialization. Had the catching-up not taken place, the mass migration would have been even bigger, a lesson of history well worth remembering when we look at Africa's future.

© Blackwell Publishers Ltd 2002

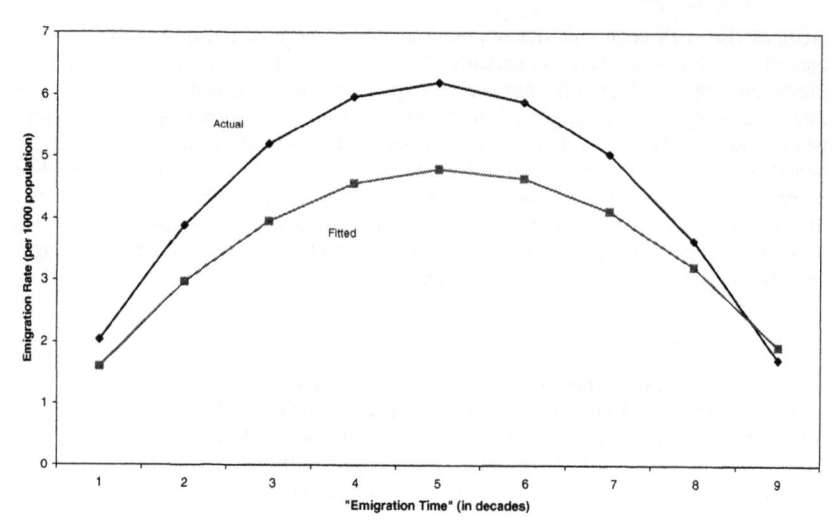

Figure 1. Stylized European Emigration Pattern

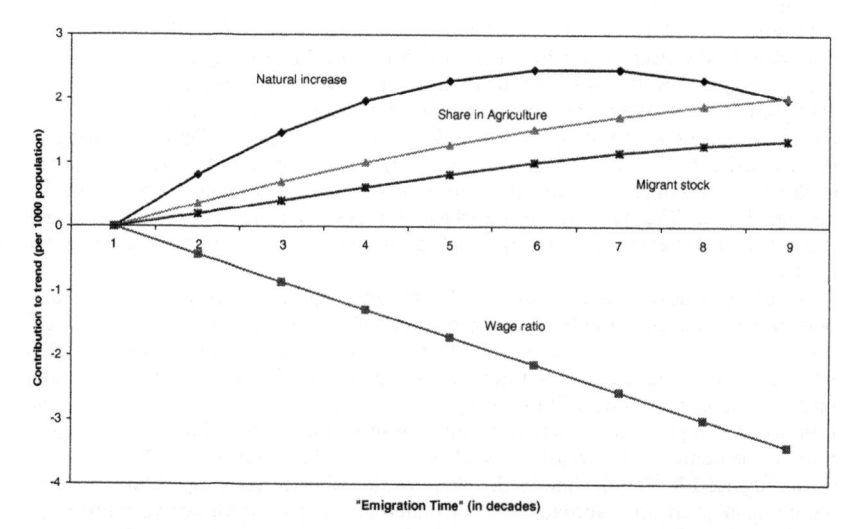

Figure 2. The Fundamentals Driving Emigration

Are There Historical Lessons for Africa?

Do the European mass emigrations a century ago, and the forces driving them, offer insights for Africa tomorrow? Or do conditions in Africa today differ so radically from those in nineteenth century Europe to undermine any useful lesson of history? We think not.

While emigration *from* Africa is still fairly modest, migration *within* Africa is not. All the evidence suggests that, given the opportunity, Africans are highly mobile. The mass movement from the countryside to the towns is one well-known confirmation of their mobility: in the last two decades the urban population in Africa has been growing at rates twice that of the total population. There have also been notable migrations between African countries. One good example is offered by the flood of Nigerians into Ghana during the 1950s and 1960s, a response to the cocoa boom. This was brought to a halt in 1969 when boom turned to bust and many of the immigrants were forced to leave. Subsequently, the migration was reversed: the oil boom in the 1970s induced a movement from Ghana to Nigeria until restrictions were imposed in the mid-1980s (Adekayne, 1998, p. 185). Much of the inter-African migrations involve exits from the more populous and/or less developed countries such as Burkina Faso, Uganda, Ghana, Lesotho, Mozambique, Mali, Rwanda, and Burundi, and Algeria and Tunisia in the north. The receiving countries have included Libya, Côte d'Ivoire, Gabon, Zaire, Zimbabwe, Equatorial Guinea, Nigeria (until recently), and, above all, the Republic of South Africa (Adepoju, 1994, p. 211). Free trade and mobility agreements such as the Economic Community of West African States and the Common Market for Eastern and Southern Africa have fostered migration and mobility within their respective regions. But such policies have followed, rather than led, growing across-border labor migration. Workers from poor southern African countries have been drawn to the mines, farms, and industries in the Republic of South Africa and have formed a quasi-permanent labor force much like guest workers in postwar Germany. Only the sputtering engines of South African growth and soaring unemployment in the townships have stemmed the flow.

Similar internal migration currents can be observed in nineteenth century Europe. Emigration to the cities and across national borders preceded and accompanied growing external migration. Italian migration across the northern border to the industrial cities of France, Germany, and Austria–Hungary was well established before mass intercontinental migration took off. There were also major migrations of Belgians to France and the Netherlands; Poles and other eastern Europeans moved to Germany; and migration within Germany from the south and east to the west took place at the same time as the exodus across the Atlantic. Similar movements can be seen both in sub-Saharan Africa, with immigrants displacing native-born workers in the smaller towns, and in North Africa, with migrants from the Sahel pushing many native-born North African emigrants into Europe.

In nineteenth century Europe, changing farm methods, low agricultural prices, land consolidation, and stunted industrial growth all added to the exodus abroad from rural regions. But there were some interesting contrasts within Europe, especially between Ireland and Italy (Hatton and Williamson, 1998, chs 5, 6). Here's one contrast: Rural poverty and lack of access to small holdings were associated with high Irish emigration. But rural poverty and *access* to smallholdings were associated with high Italian emigration. One reason for the difference is that while the Irish were almost always permanent migrants, the Italians were often temporary migrants who intended to return and become smallholders. Here's another contrast: From the 1860s emigration from Ireland declined while that from Italy (an equally poor country) increased. In Ireland, exodus induced by the Great Famine created a large migrant stock which broke the poverty trap so that, as the Irish relative wage increased, emigration declined. By contrast, in Italy demographic pressure gave rise to an accumulating migrant stock, which gradually eased the poverty trap. Thus Italian emigration increased as economic development progressed, despite the convergence of Italian wages on those of destination countries (Faini and Venturini, 1994).

While Africa shares with nineteenth century Europe the same features of agricultural backwardness, rural population pressure, and periodic famine, African emigration looks more Italian than Irish: the incidence of temporary migration is high and the stock of previous migrants is relatively low. A study of the Senegal river valley region in Senegambia and Mali (Findlay and Sow, 1998) allows some comparisons. Thousands of migrants moved in the 1980s from this region to France and the United States. They were, however, largely temporary (and often seasonal) migrants and, just as in Italy a century ago, they left extended families behind on the land. Most smallholdings generated food deficits which were offset, at least in part, by emigrant remittances. Just as in nineteenth century Italy, the emigrants were usually young males, and rural–urban emigration often preceded international migration. But poverty itself limited mobility and the poorest families were more likely to send their sons and daughters to other places in Africa rather than overseas. Accordingly, a rise in "income in the region could prompt more migrants to switch from African to French destinations" (Findlay and Sow, 1998, p. 133).

These results are likely to apply more widely. In southern and eastern Africa, there is an inverted "U"-shaped pattern between emigration and the human development index (Oucho, 1995). Nevertheless, the most notable migrations in Africa are those of refugees fleeing political instability, ethnic conflicts, and civil wars. Those forcibly ejected from countries such as Sudan, Somalia, Ethiopia, Eritrea, Angola, Mozambique, Rwanda, and Burundi have been displaced to neighboring countries, and in some cases overseas. While such migrations can hardly be characterized as market-driven, ethnic conflicts are often exacerbated by deeper fundamentals like population growth, poverty, underemployment, and competition over ever-scarcer resources.[3] As illustrated by Ghana and Nigeria, the expulsion of immigrants often coincided with the onset of economic recession (Adekayne, 1998).

It would be extreme to predict an imminent flood out of Africa: immigration policies in North America, Europe, and elsewhere in the developed world are unlikely to become more liberal. But refugees, overstayers, illegals, and special skilled workers have already established a widening African foothold in many industrial countries such that flows are likely to swell further through the forces of chain migration and family reunification. That is, emigration is likely to rise even without any change in the underlying economic and demographic fundamentals. But the underlying fundamentals *will* change, serving to raise the demand for African emigration still further.

3. African Mass Migrations in the Future

Major Fundamentals Driving Future African Mass Emigration

We no longer live in a world of unrestricted international migration, so there is little reason to expect African emigration experience in the early twenty-first century to repeat that of poor Europe in the late nineteenth century. However, the forces driving the pressure for migration are likely to be the same. A recent examination of cross-border migrations in Africa indicates that real wage gaps and bulging cohorts of 15–29-year-olds are the prime movers (Hatton and Williamson, 2001). But intercontinental wage gaps and demographic growth are far larger for Africa today than they were for Europe in the nineteenth century. These fundamentals will make the demand for exit huge and the European problem with illegals could become just as bad as it is now for the United States as it deals with Latin American and Asian illegals.

The major fundamentals driving Africa's emigration future will be three. First, the living standard gap between Africa and Europe or America is now enormous, and it is unlikely to shrink in the near future. Thus, the huge incentive to move will persist. Second, while Africa is unlikely to record significant catch-up with Europe in the near future, it will still undergo some standard-of-living improvement, which will make it easier for potential emigrants to finance their moves. Indeed, even a modest recovery from the African growth disasters of the 1970s and 1980s will serve to raise living standards at home, thus helping finance the move abroad. Third, young adults—those most vulnerable to a move—will increase their share of the African population and their numbers will rise at a rate far exceeding that of the late nineteenth century or even anywhere else in the Third World during the late twentieth century, even adjusting for the AIDS epidemic.

Motivating the Move: The Evolution of Living Standard Gaps

The highest emigration rates achieved in the nineteenth century were those for the Irish, averaging 15.4 emigrants per 1,000 per annum between 1850 and 1889 (Table 1). In the 1870s, Irish real wages were about half that of Britain and about 44% of the United States and Britain combined (Hatton and Williamson, 1998, Table 3.2); alternatively, living standards in the recipient labor markets were 2.3 times what they were at home. If the migrant response in Africa today was the same as in Europe a century ago, and if current living standard gaps were all that mattered to the potential migrant's decision, unrestricted African mass migration rates to southern Europe in 1992 would have been three or four times higher than those huge Irish nineteenth century rates.[4] But, of course, they *were* restricted.

The economic motivation for African mass migration to southern Europe was already very high in the 1970s, and it got higher by the 1990s. Between 1973 and 1992, GDP per capita in Africa stagnated, while it grew at 2% per annum in southern Europe.[5] Thus, the relative gap between southern Europe and Africa rose from 5.6 to 8.2.

Is the economic gap between Africa and southern Europe or the rest of the OECD likely to rise still further in the future? Or, is Africa likely to start catching up with southern Europe and the rest of the OECD over the next few decades? We restate the problem this way: The gap in GDP per capita growth rates between Africa and southern Europe has been about two percentage points. If the gap in growth rates evaporates in the future, relative living standard differences will remain stable and thus so will the incentive to move. If the growth rate gap switches sign favoring African catch-up (like late nineteenth century emigrating Europe), then relative living standard differences will themselves begin to erode, and thus so will the incentive to move. Which will it be?

Bloom and Williamson (1998, Table 8) use an estimated growth equation to suggest that positive demographic forces might raise African GDP per capita growth rates by almost one percentage point, while the same forces might lower European growth rates by 0.3 percentage points. Should these demographic forces have their predicted impact, they would contribute significantly to catching up by Africa on Europe, namely, they would give us 1.3 of the needed two percentage points. These demographic forces will be discussed further in the next section, where we show that they also have a nasty down-side. Furthermore, the African terms of trade deteriorated significantly after the early 1980s, perhaps by as much as 36%—an unfortunate price shock which probably cost Africa something like 0.7 percentage points in its growth rate compared with other Third World countries (Collier and Gunning, 1999b, p. 73; Deaton, 1999, p. 37). This streak of bad luck in world markets is unlikely to persist over the next two decades. Deaton shows that in the very long run the relative price of African primary products (e.g., cotton, coffee, cocoa, copper) "have been without trend or have trended gently down" (Deaton, 1999, p. 32), and recovery of those price levels late in the 1990s suggests he's right. Taking Deaton's long-run-without-trend position, future African growth rates should recover those 0.7 percentage points lost in the 1980s and 1990s. This plus the possible demographic-induced 1.3 percentage points give us the needed two percentage points, a result which would insure that the GDP per capita ratios between Africa and southern Europe would remain about the same.

There seems to be little agreement regarding the other potential influences on future African growth, the ones that would switch the sign on the growth gap and generate some catch-up. These include policy reform, more stable democratic systems, increased institutional efficiency, an acceleration in human capital deepening, and a rise in property rights protection. They will be central to whether there is any African catch-up in the future. Collier and Gunning (1999a,b) think Africa can and will exploit catch-up forces. Indeed, they see the positive effects of liberal economic reform having an influence in those precocious countries where the reforms already have had an opportunity to have their impact: Benin, Burkina Faso, Cape Verde, Côte d'Ivoire, Ethiopia, Gambia, Ghana, Guinea Bissau, Mauritania, Senegal, and Uganda (Collier and Gunning, 1999b, pp. 102–3). Ndulu and O'Connell (1999) seem to share this cautious optimism since the spread and maintenance of liberal reform is based on a rising democratization in the 1990s that they think might stick. Some are much less optimistic about democratization and policy reform, and others have pointed to how much Africa has to overcome to make serious progress on the human capital front (Schultz, 1999).

In short, the best guess seems to be that the relative living standard gap between Africa and southern Europe is likely to remain pretty stable over the next couple of decades, and any serious catch-up is likely to be postponed to the years beyond that. According to all these fundamentals driving the incentive to move, there is no reason to expect either a surge or a collapse in the African demand for exit in the near future.

Financing the Move: African Development and Migrant Pioneers

African development is likely to have two offsetting effects on emigration: if it is of the fast catching-up sort, the incentive to migrate would diminish; but if it is of the slow catching-up (or no catching-up) sort, even that slow growth will raise African living standards, making it easier for young adults to finance the move. The histories of nineteenth century latecomers to mass migration, like Italy and the eastern European countries, appear to be consistent with such speculations: this was where emigration rose with early development at home. Late nineteenth century history also confirms that pioneer migrants who moved yesterday raised significantly the probability of potential emigrants actually making the move today. This effect appears to have had its influence by reducing the income constraint on the move (via remittances) and by lowering the cost of job search.

Data documenting African emigration are scarce, but US immigration statistics indicate a significant upward trend. African immigrants to the United States were only a tiny share of the non-Canadian total in 1955–64, but their share rose to more than 9% in 1995–97. These African "pioneers" are now a significant part of US immigration. Comparisons with immigration from Europe and Asia are revealing. Economic convergence reduced the European immigration share dramatically after the 1950s. Asian immigration surged up to 1975–84 and then declined—replicating the life-cycle which the European mass migrations traced out a century ago—suggesting that the Asian economic miracle finally started doing its work in the late 1980s, after a lag. African immigration now has the same foothold that Asian immigration had in the late 1950s. Indeed, a third of the African immigrants arriving in the 1990s were classified as close relatives of US citizens and thus it seems likely that the friends-and-relatives effect is already serving to erode the poverty constraint on potential African emigrants.

Thus, here are two reasons why the demand for emigration out of Africa is likely to surge over the next two decades: slow economic growth at home and more pioneers abroad. They are both connected to financing the move rather than to the returns underlying earnings gaps.[6]

The Central Force: Soaring Numbers of Young African Adults, the Potential Movers

Over the last decade, the labor force consequences of rapid population growth have received increasing attention. At the 1994 International Conference on Population and Development in Cairo, policy documents from African governments painted a pessimistic future (Adepoju, 1998, p. 317). This intuition has not yet been translated into quantitative implications for African emigration.

Migration self-selects young adults. As we noted above, only 8% of the immigrants entering the United States between 1868 and 1910 were over 40 years old, while 76% were between 15 and 40, this during a period when the 15–40's share for the United States as a whole was about 42% (Hatton and Williamson, 1998, p. 11). The self-selection was even more apparent when viewed from the vantage point of the sending country: only 35% of the Irish who stayed home were aged 15–34, while over 80% of the Irish emigrants were. What was true of the late nineteenth century has also been true of the late twentieth century. Granted, the self-selection on age is harder to measure today since illegals are not captured in the official data and these unobserved migrants are likely to be those most sensitive to job market conditions, and are thus likely to be even more concentrated in the young adult category. Figure 3 offers an illustration of the self-selection where we plot the age distribution of all (legal) immigrants into the United States in 1997, with Nigerian immigrants offered as a comparison. The conventional young-adult spike is apparent. Furthermore, Africans, or at least Nigerians, self-selected by young-adult age more than the average US immigrant: 60.6% of the (legal) Nigerian immigrants in 1997 were aged 15–39 while 54% of all immigrants were.

Does the share of the population who are young adults change much over time and across countries? The answer is yes, especially if the countries in question are undergoing different experiences with the demographic transition. The demographic transition describes the change from preindustrial high fertility and mortality to postindustrial low fertility and mortality regimes. Declines in mortality mark the beginning of almost all demographic transitions, and changes in the age distribution are greatly exacerbated because infants and children enjoy most of the early declines in mortality. True, the improved survivor rates for children eventually induce parents to reduce their fertility. If parents adjusted completely and immediately, there would be no youth glut, no acceleration in population growth, and no transition worth talking about. But they do not: their adjustment is slow, so that the youth glut is large and persistent. After a lag, however, fertility begins to decline marking the next stage of

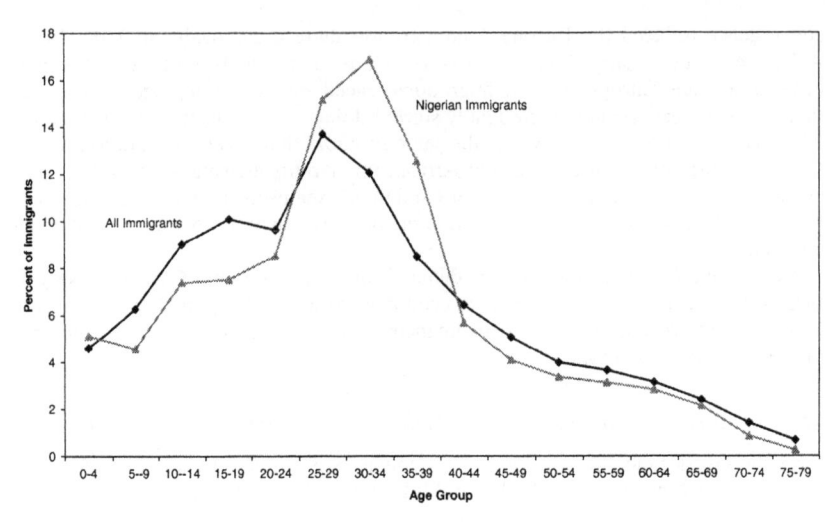

Figure 3. Age Profile of US Immigrants in 1997

the transition. In short, the demographic transition must be accompanied by a cycle in population growth *and* the age structure. In addition, the share working (and the rate of growth of the young adult population) reaches a peak later than does the rate of population growth. Furthermore, the rate of growth of the adult population undergoes far bigger swings than does the total population. These demographic differences can matter to economic performance, and, since the late 1940s, they have mattered a great deal in Asia, Africa, the Middle East, and Latin America. These demographic differences can also matter to emigration, since, as we have seen, migrants tend to be young adults.

The demographic transition in the Third World followed the stylized model by starting with a sharp decline in child mortality rates, far sharper than any European country experienced in the nineteenth century. By the late 1940s, the crude death rate had begun to decline very rapidly throughout much of the developing world. The decline was most rapid in East Asia, where the subsequent demographic impact on economic performance was also greatest (Higgins and Williamson, 1997; Bloom and Williamson, 1998), but it also was manifested in the rest of the Third World—Africa and the Middle East included (Williamson and Yousef, 1998).

The lagging fall in fertility left its mark. Africa's population grew at 2.6% per annum between 1950 and 1995, a rate of increase that is historically unprecedented anywhere in the world at any time, even for Asia (2% per annum) and Latin America (2.3%) over the past half century (Bloom and Sachs, 1998, pp. 240–7). It should be added that the Middle East and North Africa (MENA) exhibit the same demographic drama as does sub-Saharan Africa: at its peak in the 1980s, population growth rates were 3.2% per annum in MENA and 3% per annum in sub-Saharan Africa. The explanation for these unusually high rates of population growth is not hard to find. While the rest of the Third World has already undergone most of the expected lagged fall in fertility, the process has been very slow in Africa, producing both rapid population growth and a fat youth cohort.

© Blackwell Publishers Ltd 2002

Table 3. Potential Movers: Young African Adults 1955–2025

	1955	1975	1995	2005	2015	2025
African countries						
Age 15–29 (m)	63	106	195	270	364	465
Total (m)	247	413	746	1,001	1,301	1,596
[15–29]/Total (%)	25.5	25.7	26.1	27.0	28.0	29.1
More developed countries						
Age 15–29 (m)	216	269	263	257	253	249
Age 20–64 (m)	490	606	729	762	783	769
Total (m)	887	1,095	1,236	1,288	1,327	1,353
[15–29]/Total (%)	24.4	24.6	21.3	20.0	19.1	18.4
Africa, aged 15–29/ More developed, aged 20–64	0.129	0.175	0.267	0.354	0.465	0.605

Percentage growth per annum in those aged 15–29, 1995–2025
Africa   2.9
East Africa   3.4
Middle Africa   3.4
West Africa   3.3
South Africa   2.0
North Africa   1.8

Source: United Nations (1991).

The combination of high fertility rates and low child mortality rates ensures that the rate of growth of the young adult population will be huge over the near future, even adjusting for the impact of AIDS on young African adults. The 1990–2025 projected growth rate of the economically active population is 3.2% per annum for MENA and 2.8% per annum in sub-Saharan Africa (Williamson and Yousef, 1998, Table 8). More importantly, Table 3 shows that the rate of growth in the number of those Africans most likely to move, those aged 15–29, will be 2.9% per annum between 1995 and 2025, and an even bigger 3.4% per annum for a sub-Saharan Africa that excludes South Africa. The share of Africans aged 15–29 will rise from 26.1% in 1995 to 29.1% in 2025, while the same share will fall in the likely destination countries from 21.3% to 18.4%. Perhaps the most striking statistic in Table 3 is the ratio of potential African leavers (aged 15–29) relative to the total labor-market stayers (aged 20–64) in the developed economies. The ratio of potential African leavers to developed economy stayers will more than double, from 0.267 in 1995 to 0.605 in 2025. At least from the labor supply side, these facts are convenient: as the young cohorts in OECD destination labor markets get even thinner, they will get even thicker in Africa.

Demographic events accounted for about half of the surge in mass migrations during the free migrations up to World War I. The same demographic events underlying the African economies over the next 30 years are far bigger than those of a century ago. If the past is any guide to the future, African demand for entrance into protected European, North American, and other OECD labor markets will be huge over the next few decades.

Having said all of this, we would be remiss if we ignored the impact of AIDS. As Bloom and Sachs (1998, p. 234) point out, 4 million Africans died of AIDS between

1985 and 1995, and another 10 million will join them by 2005. Furthermore, it is a young-adult disease, since over 80% of AIDS deaths have occurred among 20–49 year olds. While the UN 1991 projections in Table 3 include AIDS-influenced mortality experience, the spread of the disease is so fast in sub-Saharan Africa that these projections may understate young-adult mortality and thus overstate the future size of young-adult age cohorts. Furthermore, mobile populations have higher AIDS incidence since they include so many young men (Bloom and Sachs, 1998, p. 235). Thus, rising emigration rates to Europe and North America might have a grim governing mechanism which helps limit numbers.

However, while the dreadful reality of this disease has and will leave its mark, we doubt that AIDS will eliminate the demographic–emigration connection in Africa's future.

4. Would More African Trade Suppress Future African Mass Migration?

Is Africa Less Open to Trade?

As Jeffrey Sachs and two collaborators have shown us (Sachs and Warner, 1997; Bloom and Sachs, 1998), Africa is far less open to trade than any other region of the world. Some of this economic isolation is attributable to geography. Thus, the average distance from sub-Saharan Africa to the closest core foreign market is 6,237 km, while the figure for East and Southeast Asia is 3,396 km, and for Latin America 4,651 km (Bloom and Sachs, 1998, Table 2). Alternatively, the proportion of the population landlocked is 28% in sub-Saharan Africa, while the figures are only 2% for South Asia, 3% for Latin America, and zero for East and Southeast Asia; or, the proportion of the coastal population is only 21% in Africa, but 41% in South Asia, 46% in Latin America, and 61% in East and Southeast Asia (Bloom and Sachs, 1998, Table 2). Governments can, of course, invest in transportation so as to minimize the disadvantage of poor geographic endowments, but it would require a policy switch of some magnitude to have an impact on Africa. Some of this economic isolation is also attributable to trade policy. Thus, the percentage of years during which countries were open to trade between 1965 and 1990 was only 4 in Africa while it was 45 elsewhere. Bloom and Sachs (1998, Table 7) estimate that the economic isolation of Africa helps explain about a third of their poor growth performance relative to the rest of the world.[7]

If Africa is now relatively closed to trade, the scope for various gains generated by a future (big) policy regime switch could be very great. Most relevant to the question at hand, the standard classroom version of the Heckscher–Ohlin–Samuelson (HOS) model argues that trade and international factor migration are substitutes, in which case a move in Africa away from economic isolation and towards a liberal trade policy would suppress the expected mass migration in the future. Do theoretical departures from the simple HOS model still support the view that trade and migration are substitutes? Is there any historical evidence to support the view that they are substitutes?

Are Migration and Trade Substitutes? History Says No

The elegant model associated with Eli Heckscher and Bertil Ohlin makes the unambiguous statement that trade and factor mobility are substitutes. The issue is important for the policy implications it generates: if future African mass migration threatens Europe's egalitarian distributions by creating labor abundance at the bottom of the European income pyramid, immigration quotas will simply provoke more trade and a flood of "unfair competition" from unskilled workers making labor-intensive goods using the African labor surplus which can no longer emigrate; if Europe retreats behind tariff walls, there will be far more African immigrants hammering at its gates and rowing boats across its moats since opportunities for making labor-intensive export goods at home in Africa will have dried up. The economics is so plausible that it survived with little challenge from the early post-World War I years, when Heckscher and Ohlin were writing, to the 1950s. In the four decades since, the challenges to that conventional wisdom have been so many that nothing but theoretical ambiguity remains.

The ambiguity invites empirical analysis. Collins et al. (1999) fill some of this vacuum by exploring the historical experience of the Atlantic economy between 1870 and 1940. When they look at the long swings embedded in the time-series data, they find that trade and migration were rarely substitutes and often complements. When they look at longer-run relationships in the panel data, they find that trade and migration were never substitutes. When the evolution of New World immigration policy is assessed, it appears that policymakers never acted as if they viewed trade and migration as substitutes. Thus, the history of the Atlantic economy between 1870 and 1940—a period including five decades of globalization and spectacular mass migration—rejects the thesis that trade and factor mobility were substitutes.

Coda: No Strong Trade and Mass Migration Tradeoff in Africa's Future

These theoretical and historical findings are disappointing since they suggest that even if those countries in Africa which are currently relatively "closed" to trade were to adopt the "open" trade policies which characterized so much of Asia during its miracle, the pressure on African emigration in the future would be little changed. Recent African history does *not* suggest that liberal trade policies failed to raise GDP growth: we have already argued that they *did* in the 1990s. Neither does late nineteenth century history suggest that globalization failed to raise growth rates. Rather, the economic history of the 1890s and the 1990s both suggest that these pro-growth globalization forces were swamped by demographic (and other) forces. We expect the same for Africa's future.

5. Would More African Capital Inflows Suppress Future African Mass Migration?

Simple economics argues that more capital in Africa would create more jobs, and more jobs would, in turn, help keep potential emigrants at home. However, real life is not that simple. More capital might simply serve to lower its marginal productivity and raise excess capacity.

Is Savings a Constraint on African Growth?

There is a consensus among regional specialists that capital accumulation is not the primary constraint on African growth. There is abundant evidence that points in that direction. Most persuasive is the fact that Africa has experienced more capital flight than any other region. Indeed, as of 1990, Africans placed a huge 39% of their wealth portfolios outside the region, a year when the figure was 3% for South Asia, 6% for East Asia, and 10% for Latin America (Collier and Gunning, 1999b, p. 92). This is hardly surprising given that the region has suffered negative terms-of-trade shocks, civil war, and confiscation. On the other hand, the 39% figure points out that Africa is fully integrated into global capital markets. Thus, should the fundamentals driving future African growth boom, the region is unlikely to be constrained by the availability of domestic savings, and foreign investment will be in elastic supply.

Will There Be a Global Surplus of Capital in the Near Future?

But what price will Africa have to pay for that foreign investment? Will there be a global capital surplus or scarcity?

The economic and demographic fundamentals have allowed East Asia to grow out of a dependence on foreign capital (Higgins and Williamson, 1997) so that they were not a part of the frenzy of the 1990s. While Southeast Asia was certainly part of that frenzy, the projected underlying economic and demographic fundamentals over the next few decades suggest that they too are on their way to growing out of a dependence on foreign capital. The same seems to be true of Latin America. In short, investors in the OECD are likely to be joined in the future by most of Asia and Latin America in seeking opportunities in Africa and South Asia. This implies that financial capital will be relatively cheap and plentiful in Africa's near future. The question is whether Africa will use it well, thus generating jobs which will keep young Africans at home, or whether instead it will be squandered, as it has in the recent past (Collier and Gunning, 1998b, p. 74).

6. The Bottom Line: Demography Will Probably Dominate

This paper uses the lessons of a mass migration history more than a century ago to make plausible predictions about mass migrations in the near future. History never need repeat, of course, especially when it is applied to a very different political environment. The pre-World War I mass migrations from Europe were never seriously restricted, while they have been very seriously restricted since the quotas were imposed in the United States in the 1920s. Still, the laws of motion describing any country's emigration experience seem to be pretty much the same across time and place: each obeys life-cycle patterns which seem to be driven by the same underlying economic and demographic fundamentals.

We have used this historical knowledge to explore the likely patterns of African emigration over the next quarter of a century. We think there is enough evidence to predict a mass migration out of Africa, at least enough to urge that far more research be devoted to what could become an important social problem for European and North American economies by the year 2025. We have recently attempted to estimate the pressure for emigration out of Africa up to 2025 and it confirms these predictions (Hatton and Williamson, 2001). It appears that the African demographic transition will be at the heart of the matter and, if so, it will not be easily deflected by policy responses.

References

Adekayne, J. 'Bayo, "Conflicts, Loss of State Capacities and Migration in Contemporary Africa," in R. Appleyard (ed.), *Emigration Dynamics in Developing Countries, Vol. 1: Sub-Saharan Africa*, Aldershot, UK: Ashgate (1998).

Adepoju, A., "Preliminary Analysis of Emigration Dynamics in Sub-Saharan Africa," *International Migration* 32 (1994):197–216.

———, "Linking Population Policies to International Migration in Sub-Saharan Africa," in R. Appleyard (ed.), *Emigration Dynamics in Developing Countries, Vol. 1: Sub-Saharan Africa*, Aldershot, UK: Ashgate (1998).

Bloom, D. E. and J. D. Sachs, "Geography, Demography, and Economic Growth in Africa," *Brookings Papers on Economic Activity* 2 (1998):207–73.

Bloom, D. E. and J. G. Williamson, "Demographic Transitions and Economic Miracles in Emerging Asia," *World Bank Economic Review* 12 (1998):419–55.

Collier, P. and J. W. Gunning, "Why Has Africa Grown Slowly?" *Journal of Economic Perspectives* 13 (1999a):3–22.

———, "Explaining African Economic Performance," *Journal of Economic Literature* 37 (1999b):64–111.

Collier, P. and A. Hoeffler, "On the Incidence of Civil War in Africa," unpublished, World Bank (2000).

Collins, W., K. O'Rourke, and J. G. Williamson (1998), "Were Trade and Factor Mobility Substitutes in History?" in R. Faini, J. DeMelo, and K. Zimmermann (eds.), *Migration: The Controversies and the Evidence*, Cambridge: Cambridge University Press (1998).

Deaton, A., "Commodity Prices and Growth in Africa," *Journal of Economic Perspectives* 13 (1999):23–40.

Easterly, W. and R. Levine, "Africa's Growth Tragedy: Policies and Ethnic Divisions," *Quarterly Journal of Economics* 112 (1997):1203–50.

Faini, R. and A. Venturini, "Italian Emigration in the Pre-War Period," in T. J. Hatton and J. G. Williamson (eds.), *Migration and the International Labor Market, 1850–1939*, London: Routledge (1994).

Findlay, S. and S. Sow, "From Season to Season: Poverty and Migration in the Senegal River Valley, Mali," in R. Appleyard (ed.), *Emigration Dynamics in Developing Countries, Vol. 1: Sub-Saharan Africa*, Aldershot, UK: Ashgate (1998).

Harris, J. R. and M. P. Todaro, "Migration, Unemployment, and Development: A Two-Sector Analysis," *American Economic Review* 60 (1970):126–42.

Hatton, T. J. and J. G. Williamson, *The Age of Mass Migration: An Economic Analysis*, New York: Oxford University Press (1998).

———, "Demographic and Economic Pressure on African Emigration," NBER working paper 8124 (2001).

Higgins, M. and J. G. Williamson, "Age Structure Dynamics in Asia and Dependence on Foreign Capital," *Population and Development Review* 23 (1997):261–93.

Maddison, A., *Monitoring the World Economy 1820–1992*, Paris: OECD (1995).

Ndulu, B. J. and S. A. O'Connell, "Governance and Growth in Sub-Saharan Africa," *Journal of Economic Perspectives* 13 (1999):41–66.

O'Rourke, K. and J. G. Williamson, *Globalization and History*, Cambridge, MA: MIT Press (1999).

Oucho, J., "International Migration and Sustainable Human Development in Eastern and Southern Africa," *International Migration* 31 (1995):625–45.

Sachs, J. D. and A. M. Warner, "Sources of Slow Growth in African Economies," *Journal of African Economics* 6 (1997):335–76.

Shultz, T. P., "Health and Schooling Investments in Africa," *Journal of Economic Perspectives* 13 (1999):67–88.

United Nations, *The Sex and Age Distributions of Population: The 1990 Revision*, New York: United Nations (1991).

Williamson, J. G. and T. Yousef, "Demographic Transitions and Economic Performance in the Middle East and North Africa," paper delivered to the Conference on Population Challenges in the Middle East and North Africa: Towards the 21st Century, Cairo, 2–4 November (1998).

Notes

1. Demographic information on the age and sex distribution of the population are not available for most of the countries in our sample, so lagged rates of natural increase are used as a proxy. When we turn to modern Africa, we will not have this data limitation.

2. The long-run coefficients quoted in the text are derived by taking into account the coefficient on the lagged dependent variable. Thus the coefficient on each of the independent variables in column 1 is divided by (1 − 0.52) to obtain the long-run coefficient. This takes no account of the longer-term cumulative effects working through the migrant stock.
3. Collier and Hoeffler (2000) find that the incidence of civil war starts in Africa is negatively related to per capita GDP and to GDP growth, and positively to population growth.
4. Maddison (1995, Table 1–3) reports GDP per capita in 1992 for southern Europe at $10,919, excluding Ireland (*sic*), and Africa at $1,331, so 10,919/1,331 = 8.2. As section 2 implies, the ratio of living standards abroad to those at home is the best (market incentive) predictor of late nineteenth century migration rates. Thus, 8.2/2.3 = 3.6 implies that unrestricted African emigration rates in the 1990s would have been three or four times that of the Irish in the nineteenth century, *if* current living standard gaps were all that mattered, and *if* African immigration into Europe was unrestricted.
5. See Maddison (1995, Table 1–3, pp. 23–4). We define southern Europe to include Greece, Italy, Portugal, Spain, and Turkey, while Africa includes Côte d'Ivoire, Egypt, Ethiopa, Ghana, Kenya, Morocco, Nigeria, South Africa, Tanzania, and Zaire. The regional averages are unweighted.
6. We are aware of an older literature that argues that it is job availability and the unemployment rate that matters to migration (Harris and Todaro, 1970). However, late nineteenth century history clearly shows that such variables, because they are not trended, only influenced the timing of the move, not whether to make the move at all (Hatton and Williamson, 1998, ch. 4).
7. It must be said that this estimate in Bloom and Sachs, and another like it in Sachs and Warner (1997), are the highest offered in the literature on slow African growth. Easterly and Levine (1997), for example, think the figure is about a third of the Bloom and Sachs estimate. For a survey, see Collier and Gunning (1999b).

[4]

EDUCATIONAL SELECTIVITY IN U.S. IMMIGRATION: HOW DO IMMIGRANTS COMPARE TO THOSE LEFT BEHIND?*

CYNTHIA FELICIANO

Current immigration research has revealed little about how immigrants compare to those who do not migrate. Although most scholars agree that migrants are not random samples of their home countries' populations, the direction and degree of educational selectivity is not fully understood. This study of 32 U.S. immigrant groups found that although nearly all immigrants are more educated than those who remain in their home countries, immigrants vary substantially in their degree of selectivity, depending upon the origin country and the timing of migration. Uncovering patterns of immigrant selectivity reveals the fallacy in attributing immigrants' characteristics to national groups as a whole and may help explain socioeconomic differences among immigrant groups in the United States.

Current research on immigration has not adequately addressed a basic question: how do immigrants' characteristics compare to those of persons who remain in the sending society (Gans 2000)? The seemingly simple fact that migrants are not random samples of their home countries' populations has long been uncontested (Borjas 1987, 1999; Lee 1966; Ravenstein 1885). Beyond this fact, however, little is known about immigrant selectivity or the patterns and determinants of the selection process.

In particular, immigrants' educational selectivity—how educated immigrants are relative to those who remain in the country of origin—is important for two main reasons. First, the characteristics of those who leave a country may dramatically affect the remaining population. In developing countries, "brain drain," the out-migration of highly educated professionals, deprives them of major resources, especially leadership and skills, which may hinder future progress and development (Glaser 1978; Grubel and Scott 1977; Vas-Zoltan 1976).

Second, educational selectivity may affect how well immigrants and their children adapt in the United States. The characteristics of immigrants (e.g., the education, wealth, and skills they bring with them) clearly affect their economic integration in the United States (Portes and Rumbaut 1996). However, few studies have considered the effects of immigrants' premigration characteristics, such as where they were situated in the educational distribution of their origin country.

Understanding the educational selection of immigrants may shed light on why some immigrants and their descendents are more successful in the United States than are others. It may help to explain why ethnic differences persist for a long time (Borjas 1999). Hirschman and Falcon (1985) found that the low educational attainments among some groups of immigrants are generally not overcome by successive generations. They concluded that parental schooling is the most important factor explaining educational

---

*Cynthia Feliciano, Department of Sociology, University of California, Irvine, 3151 Social Science Plaza, Irvine, CA 92697-5100; E-mail: felician@uci.edu. I gratefully acknowledge financial support from the Ford Foundation and the Social Science Research Council. I thank Rebecca Emigh, Vilma Ortiz, Meredith Phillips, Min Zhou, participants in UCLA's professional writing class, anonymous reviewers, and the *Demography* editors for their helpful comments and suggestions.

differences across groups, but that parents' education matters for social or cultural reasons, not merely for economic ones (Hirschman and Falcon 1985). Because educational opportunities differ substantially by country, immigrants who do not have high educational credentials by American standards may be selective relative to the general populations in their home countries (Lieberson 1980:214). Therefore, immigrant parents' relative premigration education may influence their children's educational outcomes as much as their formal level of schooling. In addition, differences in educational selectivity may be associated with disparities in resources among immigrant groups, affecting various socioeconomic outcomes for both immigrants and their children (Treiman et al. 1986). In short, understanding the relative position of immigrants in their country of origin is necessary to test theories of assimilation that predict upward or downward mobility in the United States among the second generation.

BACKGROUND

Theories of Immigrant Selectivity

Immigrants are selected on various characteristics in addition to education, such as occupation, skills, age, ambition, and gender. The selection process for all these characteristics occurs on several complex and interrelated levels. First, immigrants self-select, since only some people want to migrate or have the resources to do so. Second, some countries, such as China, the former Soviet Union, and the Dominican Republic, have historically had restrictive exit policies that allowed only select individuals to emigrate (Foner 2000). Third, political and economic conditions in the sending country influence the nature of migration flows (Massey 1999; Menjivar 1993; Rumbaut 1997). Fourth, the demand for certain types of workers affects the selectivity of economic migrants from different countries (Massey 1999). Fifth, the historical relationship between the United States and sending countries guides immigrant selection (Rumbaut 1995, 1997). Finally, immigrants, at least legal ones, are selected by U.S. immigration policy (Green 1999; Lobo and Salvo 1998a, 1998b; Rumbaut 1999). Although a full investigation of such causes of immigrant selection is beyond the scope of this article, the *outcome* of these selection processes itself has been understudied. Thus, the primary aim of this article is to shed light on one outcome of the selection process: how immigrants who come to the United States compare educationally to those who remain in their origin countries.

Scholars have disagreed considerably about how immigrants compare to those who are left behind. The early view, expressed as far back as the 1700s by Benjamin Franklin (1753, quoted in Abbott 1969:415–16), who maintained that the Germans were "the most stupid of their own nation," was that immigrants were the poorest of the poor and came to the United States to escape desperate poverty and unemployment (see also Portes and Rumbaut 1996). This view, which is still espoused in the popular press by those who denounce immigration, has even been expressed in some contemporary scholarly writings (Briggs 1975; Lamm and Imhoff 1985; Teitelbaum 1980).

This view has largely been replaced by newer debates. Some researchers now argue that all immigrants, whether legal or illegal, represent a positively selected group from the home country because they are more ambitious and willing to work or have higher levels of education than their counterparts who stayed behind (Portes and Rumbaut 1996; Treiman et al. 1986). Chiswick (1978) used the idea that immigrants are highly self-selected to explain why immigrants do so well in the labor force, particularly compared with natives. Portes and Rumbaut (1996) argued that migrants are the most ambitious and motivated persons of their home countries, those who experience a disjuncture between their aspirations and their means of fulfilling them in their home countries. Relative, not absolute, deprivation is what motivates individuals to migrate (Stark and Bloom 1985). Thus, poor and uneducated persons, who are often socially isolated and not aware of the possibilities of migration, are often less likely to migrate than are those who have been exposed to U.S. lifestyles or who have some education and live in cities (Portes and Rumbaut 1996). Indeed, some studies have shown that the very poor and unemployed seldom migrate, legally or illegally (Bean, Browning, and Frisbie 1985; Bray 1984; Massey 1987a; Portes 1979). Contrary to popular perception, then, even undocumented immigrants may be positively selected. Since resources are needed to migrate illegally—to pay the costs of hiring smugglers or obtaining fake documents—undocumented migrants may, in some cases, be more positively selected than authorized immigrants who can be sponsored by relatives in the United States (Bray 1984). This scholarship suggests that immigrants will be more educated than the general population who remain in their homelands.

However, in a theoretical discussion of both internal and international migration, Lee (1966) contended that only some migrant streams are positively selected, while others are negatively selected. He argued that the causes of migration are crucial: if migrants leave because of "plus factors" (or pull factors) in the destination, they will be positively selected. If they are responding to "minus factors" (or push factors) in the sending society, they will be negatively selected (Lee 1966). Obstacles are also an important factor: immigrants who face the greatest barriers in migrating will be the most positively selected (Lee 1966; Schultz 1984).

Borjas (1987, 1991) also argued that only some immigrants are positively self-selected. Expanding upon Roy's (1951) model of the impact of self-selection in occupational choice on income distributions, Borjas (1987, 1991) specified the conditions under which immigrants will be positively or negatively selected. He theorized that immigrants to the United States are positively selected only when sending countries have relatively egalitarian income distributions. If the home country's income distribution is more unequal than in the United States, immigrants will be negatively selected and will come from the lower end of that country's socioeconomic distribution. Thus, Borjas (1987, 1991) argued that skilled Mexicans do not migrate to the United States, since their skills are highly rewarded under Mexico's more unequal system. Unskilled Mexicans are the most likely to migrate because they are the most relatively disadvantaged in Mexico. Although some studies have suggested that undocumented migrants from Mexico are negatively selected on the basis of education (Borjas 1992, 1996; Massey and España 1987; Taylor 1986, 1987), Chiswick (2000:67) stated that a more-unequal source country "does not necessarily imply negative selectivity but rather only less favorable positive selectivity."

Because data on the place of origin are readily available for internal migration within the United States, most studies that have tested theories of migration have been of domestic migrants. This literature, mostly on southern blacks' migration to the North, has shown that migrants tend to be more educated than those who stay in the place of origin (Lieberson 1980; Shryock and Nam 1965; Suval and Hamilton 1965; Tolnay 1998). Long-distance migrants are especially likely to be highly selected by education (Long 1973). Several studies of the selectivity of Puerto Ricans have compared the characteristics of U.S. migrants to those who remain on the island (Landale 1994; Landale, Oropesa, and Gorman 2000; Melendez 1994; Ortiz 1986; Ramos 1992). For example, Landale et al. (2000) found that children of recent Puerto Rican migrants have lower infant mortality risks than children of nonmigrants, suggesting that migrants are positively selected on characteristics related to infants' health. Studies of education have found that Puerto Rican migrants to the U.S. mainland have about the same education as or less education than their counterparts who remain on the island (Ortiz 1986; Ramos 1992). However, since Puerto Rican and other internal migrants are U.S. citizens, it is impossible to know whether such findings are generalizable to other groups.

This literature suggests that the degree to which immigrants differ by education from nonmigrants in their homelands varies by source country. Even if immigrants are all positively selected, there may be substantial variability in the *level* of selectivity by origin country, such that immigrants from some countries are more positively selected than others. Furthermore, these theories suggest that some measurable factors are related to the degree of selection. Migrants from more-educated populations may be less positively selected, since the possibility that they have more schooling than the average person in their home country is not high. Given the greater costs associated with migrating long distances, migrants from countries that are farther from the United States should be more highly selected. According to Lee (1966), migrants who respond to push factors will be less selective; economists have also assumed that selectivity applies only to economic migrants (Chiswick 2000). Thus, political refugees who respond to push factors may not be as highly selected as others. Finally, according to Borjas (1987), migrants from countries with greater income inequality are negatively selected or, at least, less positively selected than those from more egalitarian countries.

Selectivity is also related to scholarly debates about whether the new immigration is less skilled than the old. Borjas (1999) argued that today's immigrants from developing countries in Asia and Latin America are less skilled than were immigrants who came from advanced industrial societies in Europe decades earlier. Chiswick (1986), on the other hand, noted how U.S. policies have selected certain groups of immigrants from different countries. Simply because immigrants come from less-developed countries does not mean that they themselves are drawn from the less-educated or less-skilled segments of those societies (Rumbaut 1997). Chiswick (1986) suggested that U.S. policy favoring skills has resulted in an increase in highly selected immigrants from Asia but that this policy is offset by U.S. policy favoring kinship, which has resulted in an influx of less-skilled and less-selective immigrants as well. Although selectivity and skills are not necessarily the same, they are highly correlated. Consequently, examining whether the changing national origins of immigrants are associated with a decline in educational selectivity will shed light on whether new immigrants are less skilled than were older immigrants.

Massey (1987b, 1999) contended that although migrants tend to be positively selected initially, they become less highly selected over time as successive waves migrate from a particular country. Social capital is a major force in perpetuating migration; for example, having an older sibling who migrated to the United States triples the likelihood of migration among Mexicans (Palloni et al. 2001). With each new act of migration, networks expand, such that more nonmigrants come to know someone who has migrated to the United States (Massey and Espinosa 1997). Over time, as migration that is driven by social networks continues, migration becomes less costly, and persons who are not relatively well educated or skilled begin to migrate (Massey 1987b, 1999; Massey et al. 1993). Tolnay's (1998) finding that the educational selectivity of southern black migrants to the North has declined over the past 100 years is consistent with this idea. In the case of international migration, U.S. immigration policies that are based on family reunification further increase the possibility that individuals are able to draw upon social networks to migrate. Prior research, based on data from the Mexican Migration Project, found that Mexican migrants have declined in educational selectivity over time (Durand, Massey, and Zenteno 2001). Although the Mexican case is unique and not necessarily generalizable, it is one of the few long-term immigrant streams for which data are available to answer this question. Using Mexican and U.S. census data, I examined whether successive waves of immigrants from Mexico were less educated relative to Mexican nonmigrants than were those who immigrated earlier.

Conceptual and Measurement Issues

As I mentioned earlier, immigrant selection occurs along a number of different characteristics, some of which are measurable, such as education, and others of which are not as easily measured, such as ambition, motivation, and work ethic. Such unmeasured attributes are related to conditions in the sending country and may also affect immigrants' adaptation in the United States. For example, immigrants from countries with low standards of living may be willing to work longer hours for less pay than may U.S. natives (Lieberson 1980), which can create a "split labor market," as Bonacich (1976) argued. Such attributes may be evident compared with those of U.S. natives but do not necessarily imply selectivity on measured characteristics, such as education. In the study presented here, I conceptualized selectivity as differences between immigrants and the home-country populations from which they are drawn and measured it in terms of one characteristic: education. While educational selectivity may be related to selectivity along other dimensions, such as work ethic or ambition, examining such attributes was beyond the scope of my study.

The operationalization of the concept of selectivity necessarily involves measurements relative to the population at the place of origin. However, empirical research has not adequately tested different theories on immigrant selectivity because, owing to the difficulty of obtaining data from multiple countries, most comparative studies of international migration have not included data on those who do not migrate but instead have used proxies for selectivity. For example, on the basis of theories of the factors predicting immigrant selectivity, many researchers have used readily available measures as proxies for selectivity, which even they have admitted are ad hoc, such as the gross domestic product, income inequality, and distance (Borjas 1987; Cobb-Clark 1993; Jasso and Rosenzweig 1986). Other researchers have used immigrants' premigration occupational status or absolute level of educational attainment as a proxy for immigrant selectivity (see, e.g., Lobo and Salvo 1998b; Rumbaut 1997). Using the formal level of educational attainment as a proxy for selectivity, for example, is problematic because it assumes that a high school degree in one context (say, a country where only 10% of the population earns one) has the same meaning as a high school degree earned in another context (say, where 80% of the population earns one). Thus, including information about those who remain in the homeland is critical to understanding immigrant selection.

RESEARCH QUESTIONS AND ANALYTIC STRATEGY

I directly examined the educational selectivity of multiple immigrant groups by comparing immigrants' educational profiles to those of persons in their home countries, using data on *both* the sending and receiving sides of the migration process. In doing so, I addressed several questions: (1) How do immigrants' educational attainments compare to those of nonmigrants in their home countries, and how does this educational selectivity vary by country of origin? To answer this question, I calculated a measure of selectivity for multiple immigrant groups, based on comparisons of their educational distributions to those of comparably aged persons in their home countries. (2) How do home-country characteristics, reasons for migration, and distance from the United States affect immigrant selectivity? Building upon the findings from the first question, I used the selectivity measure as an outcome and analyzed whether these country-level factors significantly predict educational selectivity. (3) Are immigrants from regions with more-recent migrant streams (Asia and Latin America) more educated or less educated than were those from European countries who migrated in the past? Here, I compared the selectivity of recent migrants from Asia and Latin America to that of older immigrant groups from Europe. (4) Does the selectivity of successive waves of migrants from the same country change over time? This analysis focused on one national-origin group (Mexicans) and compared different migrant streams from that country at different points in time.

DATA AND METHODS

Data

To compare the educational attainment of migrants and nonmigrants from the same country, age group, and period, I needed data on immigrants in the United States that contained their educational attainment, age, year of immigration, and country of origin. I also needed data on the populations of the major immigrant-sending countries to the United States, including their educational attainment, by age, from about the same period when most immigrants migrated. To assess whether the changing national-origin mix is related to changes in immigrant selectivity, I needed data on older immigrant groups from Europe who migrated in previous decades and their nonmigrant counterparts, as well as more-recent immigrant groups from Asia, Latin America, and the Caribbean. I also needed data on immigrants and nonmigrants over time from one country with a long migration history to the United States, such as Mexico.

First, I gathered published data on the sending countries' average levels of educational attainment. I searched for data from the top 38 migrant-sending countries to the United States and ended up with acceptable data (for the appropriate years for that country, by age) from 31 countries and Puerto Rico.[1] The appendix shows the data that were collected from these countries. Most of the country-of-origin data were available from UNESCO (1975–1997), which compiles census data from the various countries and presents the data in comparable ways. The UNESCO data account for the different educational systems in different countries because the data are compiled in six educational categories that are comparable across nations. For Puerto Rico, I used data published by the U.S. Census Bureau (1973). I selected the year of the data by choosing the closest year (for which data were available) to the average year of immigration of the U.S. immigrants from that country (calculated from the 1990 census).[2]

To summarize educational attainment on the receiving side of migration, I created extracts of census data on U.S. immigrants from each of the 32 countries from the Integrated Public Use Micro Samples (IPUMS; Ruggles, Sobek et al. 1997). The appendix also summarizes the data on immigrants that I used to calculate each immigrant group's educational attainment. Three main principles guided my selection of immigrants for each country's sample. First, since I wanted measures of educational attainment that would reflect those of the "average" immigrant from that country, I included only immigrants who migrated within five years (before or after) of the average year that a particular immigrant group migrated to the United States. I collected data from the IPUMS for the closest year available following the average years of immigration for that particular national-origin group, which meant that in most cases, I used IPUMS data from two decades. For example, if the average year of immigration for immigrants from a certain country was 1980–1981, I selected immigrants from that country who migrated from 1975 to 1980 using IPUMS data from 1980, and I selected immigrants from that country who migrated from 1980 to 1986 using IPUMS data from 1990.[3] Second, I limited the sample of immigrants to only those who migrated as adults. Thus, I analyzed data from those

---

1. I could not find acceptable, comparable data from Germany, England, Taiwan, Laos, Scotland, or Cambodia.

2. Although ideally, I would have used data from the year closest to the average year of migration of immigrants from that country, such data were not always available. In some cases, therefore, I had to analyze data on home-country populations that were several years removed from the data on U.S. immigrants from that country. However, I do not believe that doing so biased my results because I compared immigrants only with their home-country counterparts of the same age cohort. Since educational attainment is fairly stable among adults (that is, by early adulthood, most individuals have attained the highest level of schooling they are ever likely to attain), selectivity among immigrants can be fairly accurately assessed even if the years of the data do not correspond, since the ages of the compared groups *do* correspond. For example, an adult who responded in 1980 that he or she had completed a college degree most likely would have had the same stated educational attainment in 1990, when he or she was 10 years older.

3. I used this method because I did not want to overestimate the positive selectivity of immigrants. Positive selectivity may be overestimated by using the entire distribution of immigrants for two reasons. It is well known that migration occurs in waves and that first waves of migrants are generally thought to be more skilled and more educated than later waves (Massey 1988). What is perhaps more important is that return migration is also

who were at least 22 years old when they migrated, so that I could be reasonably sure that most of their education occurred in their home countries, rather than in the United States. Third, I selected immigrants within the same age range as the home-country populations in the published UNESCO data (see the appendix).

I then created a small data set for each immigrant group at the individual-level unit of analysis. I recoded these data on immigrants to match the educational attainment variables that were available in the UNESCO publications (1975–1997) for the countries of origin. Thus, I created an educational attainment variable for the immigrants that matched the six educational categories in the UNESCO data on the sending countries: "no schooling/illiterate," "first level incomplete," "first level completed," "second level 1st cycle," "second level, 2nd cycle," and "postsecondary schooling or higher."

For the analyses of changes in immigrant selection among migrants from Mexico, I supplemented the published UNESCO data in 1980 with data from the IPUMS-International's samples of Mexican census data from 1960, 1970, 1990, and 2000 (Sobek et al. 2002; IPUMS data for 1980 are not available) and the U.S. census from 1960 to 2000. Each is a nationally representative, 1% population sample.[4] The IPUMS-International's samples are ideal for analyses of trends over time and comparisons among countries because the variables have been recoded to allow for consistency across time and place. I combined the Mexican and U.S. census samples for 1960–2000 to create a data set for each year that consisted of a large sample of Mexicans in Mexico and Mexican immigrants in the United States.

To summarize, I collected data on educational attainment on the sending and receiving sides of the migration process for each national-origin group. I collected data on immigrants and nonmigrants from one period, whenever the migration was most frequent; in some cases, this period was the 1960s and in others, the 1990s. I also used data on Mexicans and Mexican immigrants from 1960 to 2000, so I could assess changes over time among immigrants from a single country.

Measuring Educational Selectivity

Before I compared immigrants' educational attainment to that of homeland nonmigrants, I accounted for the different age distributions of the two populations—the sending and receiving country-of-origin groups—by using direct age standardization.[5] This standardization is important because immigrants are selected by age as well as education and because age and educational attainment are related. In most cases, immigrants tend to be younger than those who remain in the home country. Since most populations are becoming

---

a common part of the migration process for many immigrants, especially those who are not successful in the United States; as many as one third of immigrants to the United States eventually return to their home countries (Massey 1987b). Donato (1993) found that those who permanently settle in the United States are more educated than those who return to their home countries. Thus, limiting my analysis to immigrants who migrated close to the average year of migration for that particular national-origin group means that my selectivity measures are conservative; that is, I underestimated the degree of positive selectivity from most countries.

4. For the United States, 1% samples were downloaded directly from the web site for IPUMS-International (Sobek et al. 2002). A 1% sample in Mexico was available for 1970 and 1990. For 1960 and 2000 (for which 1.5% and 20% samples were available from IPUMS), I randomly sampled the appropriate number of cases, so that my final sample was 1% of the original populations.

5. Direct standardization is a method for "controlling" for confounding factors—in this case, age. Thus, I adjusted the educational attainment of nonmigrants to the age distribution of immigrants to compare the educational attainments of the two populations without the contaminating influence of age. The general formula is, using percentage who are college educated as an example, age-standardized % college educated among nonmigrants = $\Sigma_i M_i^n C_i^i$, where M is the percentage college educated among nonmigrants by age and C is the proportion of immigrants in each age category. Thus, the immigrants' age distribution is used as the standard to calculate an adjusted percentage of nonmigrants who are college educated.

more educated over time, younger adults are generally more educated than older persons from the same country. Therefore, failure to account for the different age distributions would have overestimated the degree of positive selectivity, simply because immigrants tend to be younger than nonmigrants. Thus, I recalculated the educational distributions of the home-country populations on the basis of the age structure of the corresponding immigrant groups.

Once I had consolidated the appropriate age-standardized educational attainment distributions, I defined and calculated the selectivity measure—a comparative measure of immigrants' and nonmigrants' educational attainment—to be used in the analysis. The measurement of selectivity ideally involves comparisons of the entire educational distributions of immigrants and nonmigrants, rather than crude comparisons of mean or median educational attainment or comparisons that are based on any particular point on the distribution. I thus followed Lieberson (1976, 1980) in using the net difference index (NDI), which is based on the immigrants and the nonmigrants' distributions along all points of the educational range, as the measure of educational selectivity.[6] The NDI is calculated on the basis of the percentage of immigrants with the same level of educational attainment as nonmigrants, the percentage of immigrants with more education than nonmigrants, and the percentage of immigrants with less education than nonmigrants.[7] For example, an NDI of .35 indicates that an immigrant's educational attainment will exceed that of a nonmigrant from the same country 35% more often than a nonmigrant's education will exceed that of an immigrant from that country (Lieberson 1980). If all immigrants exceed all nonmigrants, the NDI will be 1. If the number of immigrants exceeding nonmigrants in educational attainment equals the number of nonmigrants exceeding immigrants in education, the value of NDI will be 0. Thus, the higher the NDI value, the more educated the immigrants are relative to the nonmigrant population in their home country. If immigrants are more often *less* educated than nonmigrants (that is, there is negative selection), the value of the NDI will be negative. I calculated the NDI for all adult immigrants from each country, as well as separately by gender, when the data were available.

Additional Variables

For my analysis, the primary data set contains the 32 countries as the units of analysis, the NDI as the measure of educational selectivity, and the original educational attainment variables used to create the selectivity measure. In addition to these measures, I added several additional measures to the data set. Using U.S. census data, I calculated, for each country-of-origin group, the percentage who migrated before 1965, the percentage of the immigrants who were female, and the average age of the immigrants. On the basis of the country-of-origin data, I calculated the average years of schooling in each home country. I also added a dummy variable to distinguish political migrants from others.[8] I added a variable indicating the distance, in thousands of miles, of each country from the United States.[9] Finally, I added the Gini coefficient for each country of origin, which is a measure

---

6. I gratefully acknowledge the suggestion of an anonymous reviewer that I calculate the NDI. Findings using a different summary measure that was based on comparisons of measures of central tendency and measures along specific points of the educational distribution were the same (and are available on request). The NDI, however, provides a simpler and more intuitive measure of educational selectivity, particularly since any immigrant group that is negatively selected would have a negative NDI value.

7. Specifically, if X is the percentage distribution of immigrants along educational attainment categories and Y is the percentage distribution of nonmigrants, $NDI_{xy} = \text{pr}(X > Y) - \text{pr}(Y > X)$ (Lieberson 1976:280).

8. I coded immigrants from Cuba, El Salvador, Guatemala, Haiti, Hungary, Iran, Nicaragua, Poland, Russia, and Vietnam as political migrants (although many of them may have also migrated for economic reasons).

9. This calculation was based on distance from the closest U.S. city that is considered a typical port of entry: New York, San Francisco, Los Angeles, or Miami.

of the degree of income inequality around the time when most immigrants arrived in the United States (taken from the data set by Deininger and Squire n.d.).

FINDINGS

How Are Immigrants Selected by Education?

Table 1 summarizes the variation in educational selectivity by country of origin for all immigrants, as well as for women and men separately. Focusing on the first column, which presents the NDI for both male and female immigrants, immigrant groups are sorted from the least selective (Puerto Ricans, who are negatively selected: –.064) to the most positively selected (Iranians: .884). The table shows that with the exception of Puerto Ricans, immigrants from all major sending countries tend to be more educated than the general populations in their home countries. This finding challenges the view that immigrants are the least desirable of their country or that immigrants are positively selected only under certain specific conditions. This finding is consistent with theories that relative, rather than absolute, deprivation is the motivation for migration and with observations that it takes a tremendous amount of resources, skills, motivation, initiative, and ambition to migrate to another country. The finding that immigrants are nearly all positively selected is also true for political refugees, even though less "choice" is often involved in their decision to migrate. Migrants from Iran, Cuba, Vietnam, Russia, and Poland (as well as those from countries such as Guatemala and El Salvador, who may flee their countries for political reasons, even though they are not granted asylum in the United States), are all more highly educated than their counterparts who remain in their home countries. These findings challenge Lee's (1966) theory that migrants who respond to push factors are negatively selected, at least as applied to international migration.

The *only* exception to the pattern of positive selectivity is Puerto Rican migrants. The Puerto Rican population in Puerto Rico is more highly educated than are Puerto Ricans who migrate to the U.S. mainland. Puerto Ricans are unique because they are U.S. citizens; therefore, other than the cost of a plane ticket, they face virtually no barriers to entry to the U.S. mainland. This finding is also consistent with several other studies on Puerto Rican selectivity that found that Puerto Rican migrants have similar or lower socioeconomic levels than nonmigrants (Melendez 1994; Ortiz 1986; Ramos 1992). However, findings from Puerto Rican case studies should not be generalized to immigrants from other countries. Ramos (1992), for example, used the findings that Puerto Ricans are negatively selected as support for Borjas's (1987, 1991) theory that immigrants from home countries with highly unequal income distributions come from the lower end of the socioeconomic distribution. But the theory may apply only in cases for which there are no major barriers to entry, such as financial costs, distance, or immigration status. My findings suggest that Borjas's theory is not applicable to most of the major immigrant-sending countries.

The findings show that even though all immigrant groups are positively selected, the degree of positive selectivity varies considerably by country of origin. Immigrants from Asia tend to be more positively selected than those from Latin America or the Caribbean. That is, the NDI for 8 out of the 13 immigrant groups from Latin America or the Caribbean (Puerto Rico, Mexico, El Salvador, Cuba, Honduras, Dominican Republic, Ecuador, and Guatemala) is below the overall median of .553 for the 32 groups, while only 2 of the 9 immigrant groups from Asia (Korea and Hong Kong) have NDIs that are slightly below the median. The variability in educational selectivity by country is striking. For example, Mexican immigrants are more educated than Mexican nonmigrants 20% more often than Mexican nonmigrants are more educated than immigrants (NDI = .200). In contrast, Indian immigrants have higher educational attainments than do Indian nonmigrants 86% more often than the converse is true (NDI = .858).

Table 1. Educational Selectivity (Net Difference Index) of U.S. Immigrants, by Country of Origin

Country of Origin	Net Difference Index	Net Difference Index, Women	Net Difference Index, Men
Puerto Rico	−0.064	−0.075	−0.050
Mexico	0.200	0.252	0.158
Portugal	0.244	0.265	0.222
Italy	0.260	0.233	0.285
El Salvador	0.342	0.365	0.322
Greece	0.402	0.373	0.426
Cuba	0.406	0.484	0.292
Honduras	0.433	0.447	0.416
Canada	0.434	0.415	0.456
Dominican Republic	0.490	N.A.	N.A.
Yugoslavia	0.502	0.511	0.493
Ecuador	0.513	0.537	0.491
Russia	0.520	0.488	0.558
Korea	0.524	0.537	0.505
Hong Kong	0.525	0.472	0.578
Guatemala	0.534	0.560	0.511
Ireland	0.572	0.542	0.617
Poland	0.573	0.605	0.540
Vietnam	0.589	0.545	0.631
Philippines	0.602	0.584	0.631
Colombia	0.617	0.606	0.630
Thailand	0.638	0.594	0.723
Peru	0.645	N.A.	N.A.
China	0.667	0.662	0.673
Nicaragua	0.669	N.A.	N.A.
Jamaica	0.670	0.649	0.693
Japan	0.670	0.631	0.722
Netherlands	0.676	0.675	0.677
Haiti	0.710	0.746	0.677
India	0.858	0.640	0.980
Hungary	0.880	0.907	0.859
Iran	0.884	0.875	0.890

Note: N.A. indicates that data on country of origin were not available by gender.

The second and third columns of Table 1 reveal that although educational selectivity often differs between male and female immigrants from the same country, these differences are generally not great. For example, among the most highly selective immigrant group, Iranians, the NDI for Iranian female immigrants is .890, compared to .875 for Indian male immigrants; likewise, the NDIs for Puerto Rican male and female immigrants are similarly low (−.075 for women and −.050 for men). Indeed, the NDIs for male and female immigrants are highly correlated (.89). Furthermore, gender differences in educational selectivity do not appear to follow any clear pattern. In over half the cases, women are less positively selected than men, but women from a substantial minority of the countries (12 out of 29) are more highly selected than men. In some cases, the gender differences are much more pronounced than in others, with the most-noticeable difference between Indian men (.980) and women (.640). Few patterns can be discerned from these gender differences, however. For example, gender differences in educational selectivity are not related to the percentage of immigrants who are female (results available on request). The only factor that is somewhat related is distance: gender differences in selectivity tend to be greater among immigrants from countries that are farther away from the United States, with these women tending to be less selective than their male counterparts. One possible explanation for this finding may be that female migrants from distant countries are less likely to migrate for their own job opportunities; rather, they migrate to accompany highly skilled husbands who are responding to particular employment opportunities in the United States. Future research is needed to explore these patterns further. However, because gender differences in educational selectivity are not substantial, the remainder of the article focuses on the overall level of educational selectivity for both male and female immigrants.

Factors Related to Immigrants' Educational Selectivity

Factors such as the relationship between the sending country and the United States, the contexts of exit, U.S. immigration policy, and economic conditions in the sending and receiving countries likely affect the selection of immigrants from any particular country. Although a full-scale investigation of all such dynamics is beyond the scope of this article, I consider several possible determinants of immigrant selection that can be straightforwardly operationalized. Possible factors that influence the selectivity of any given group of immigrants that I was able to analyze include the average years of schooling in the home country, the distance of the home country from the United States, the average year of migration, the level of income inequality in the home country, and whether most migrants left for political reasons. I also considered whether the different age or gender compositions across immigrant groups influence educational selectivity.

Table 2 presents correlations between the included variables and immigrant selectivity (NDI), bivariate regression coefficients for the NDI regressed on each variable, and multivariate regression coefficients for a model including all significant bivariate relationships. The table shows that the average years of schooling in the home population is negatively correlated with selectivity (−.353) and that this relationship is significant; thus, immigrants from highly educated populations are less likely to be as highly positively selected as those from less-educated populations. Greater distance from the United States is associated with greater positive selectivity (.421, .029). The negative correlation for the percentage of immigrants who migrated before 1965 (−.123) suggests that immigrants from countries who only recently began migrating to the United States tend to be more positively selected than those who came primarily in the 1960s or 1970s; however, this relationship is not statistically significant in the bivariate model. Thus, these findings challenge the popular perception that immigrants' skills have declined as the regional origins of immigrants have changed over time. There is a negative association (−.302) between home-country inequality and positive selectivity. While this finding provides some support for Borjas's (1987, 1991) and Chiswick's (2000) claims that immigrants from more-egalitarian countries are more positively selected, income inequality is not a statistically significant predictor of selectivity in the bivariate model. This finding contradicts the theory that immigrants from highly unequal societies are less likely to be positively selected. Furthermore, although there is a positive relationship between political reasons for

Table 2. Relationships Between Select Factors and Immigrants' Educational Selectivity (Net Difference Indexes)

Factors	Correlation Coefficient	Bivariate Regression Coefficient	Multivariate Regression Coefficient
Average Years of Schooling in Home Country	−.353	−.041*	−.043*
Distance (in thousands of miles) from the United States	.421	.029*	.030*
Percentage Who Migrated Before 1965	−.123	−.001	
Gini Coefficient (inequality level in home country)	−.302	−.007	
Political Reasons for Migration (dummy variable = 1 if political)	.240	.107	
Average Age of Immigrants	−.098	−.004	
Percentage of Immigrants Who Are Female	−.087	−.358	
Constant for Multivariate Model			.665***
R^2 for Multivariate Model			.308
N for Multivariate Model			32

*$p < .05$; ***$p < .001$

migration and positive selectivity (.240), it also is not significant. This finding conflicts with the economic view, which assumes that only economic migrants are positively selected. Finally, the correlations show that the average age and the percentage of women in the immigrant group are both negatively correlated with the level of selectivity; however, neither variable significantly predicts educational selectivity. These insignificant results are important because they suggest that the results for selectivity are not biased by the different age and gender compositions across immigrant groups.[10]

The multivariate model includes only the significant bivariate predictors of selectivity: average years of schooling in the home country and distance from the United States.[11] When included in the same model, immigrant groups from highly educated home populations are still significantly less positively selected, net of distance. While this finding seems counterintuitive, it is logical if one considers the ceiling effect: among highly educated populations, immigrants' education could not possibly be much higher than average.[12] This finding also suggests that in less-developed countries, the few individuals who have attained a higher education may have substantial incentives to migrate to a more developed country, such as the United States. This phenomenon, known as "brain drain," has been identified as a problem in developing countries (Glaser 1978; Grubel and Scott 1977; Vas-Zoltan 1976). Distance significantly increases the likelihood of a group being more positively selected, net of average home-country educational attainment. This finding suggests one reason why Asians tend to be more highly selected than most Latin

---

10. Although I was able to account for differences in the age compositions between home-country populations and their immigrant counterparts, because of data limitations, I was not able to account for differences in the age structures among immigrant groups in calculating the selectivity measure. However, this analysis suggests that differences in the age compositions across immigrant groups do not affect my results.

11. The variables that were not significant predictors of selectivity in the bivariate models are also not significant when included in multivariate models and do not add any explanatory power to the multivariate model (results available on request).

12. One way to think about this point is similar to questions of socioeconomic mobility. If a child's parents are physicians, substantial upward mobility is simply not possible.

American or Caribbean groups. Asian countries are much farther away geographically than most Latin American or Caribbean countries. For example, India is almost 8,000 miles away from the nearest major U.S. immigrant gateway city, while Mexico shares a border with the United States. Distance creates greater travel costs and perhaps psychological costs in moving to another country. Greater distance means that there is less possibility of simply returning to the homeland. Therefore, it is likely that Asians who migrate to the United States are the most highly selective because only a select few can bear the costs associated with such a drastic move.

Although it was not possible to operationalize in this analysis, U.S. immigration policies may also account for differences in educational selectivity by country of origin. With the 1965 Immigration Act, the two main criteria that are used to allow migrants to enter the United States became family reunification and occupational qualifications. On the one hand, because few Asians were allowed to enter the United States before 1965, few had family members in the United States, so most could enter only under the formal credentials criteria. On the other hand, because Mexico has a long immigration history to the United States, many Mexicans could legally migrate for family-reunification purposes. Studies have shown that immigrants who enter under family reunification have lower occupational statuses than do those who enter under employment preferences (Lobo and Salvo 1998a, 1998b); these immigrants are therefore likely to be less highly selected by education as well.

Selectivity and Changes in the Regional Origins of Immigrants

Figure 1 shows the selectivity of each immigrant group sorted by the region of origin and average decade of migration, to address whether immigrants from Asia and Latin America (currently the largest sending areas) are less selective than those from Europe (previously the largest sending area). The figure clearly illustrates how the regional origins of immigrants have changed over the past few decades. Most immigrant groups whose major waves arrived in the 1960s and 1970s are from Europe, whereas most immigrant groups who arrived more recently are from Asia, Latin America, and the Caribbean. The figure shows no clear pattern in terms of the selectivity of recent immigrant groups compared to older immigrant groups. Indeed, if anything, immigrant groups who arrived in the 1960s appear to be less positively selected than those who arrived in the 1980s. The average NDI of immigrants in the 1960s, who came mainly from Europe, was .44, compared with .58 among Asian and Latin American/Caribbean immigrants in the 1980s. Even when the average NDI is weighted by the size of the immigrant group, which accounts, for example, for the fact that over one fourth of the immigrants who arrived in the 1980s were from Mexico, immigrant groups who arrived in the 1980s are not less positively selected (.44) compared with immigrant groups who arrived in the 1960s (.26). This figure suggests that immigrant groups today, especially those from Asia, are actually more likely than were earlier immigrants to come from the top of the educational distribution in their countries of origin. Thus, any suggestions that immigrants are currently less selective than in the past owing to their changing regional origins are overstated.

Changes in the Selectivity of Mexican Immigrants Over Time

In this section, I address the question of how selectivity changes over successive waves of migrants from the same country. I examine the hypothesis that positive selectivity declines over successive waves of migrants using data on immigrants from Mexico, the largest immigrant group in the United States with one of the longest migration histories (Massey 1988) and the least positively selected group in Figure 1. It is important to note that the Mexican case is unique compared with most other immigrant-sending countries in that Mexico shares a border with the United States, has a long and substantial history

Figure 1. Educational Selectivity of Migrants to the United States, by Average Decade of Migration and Region

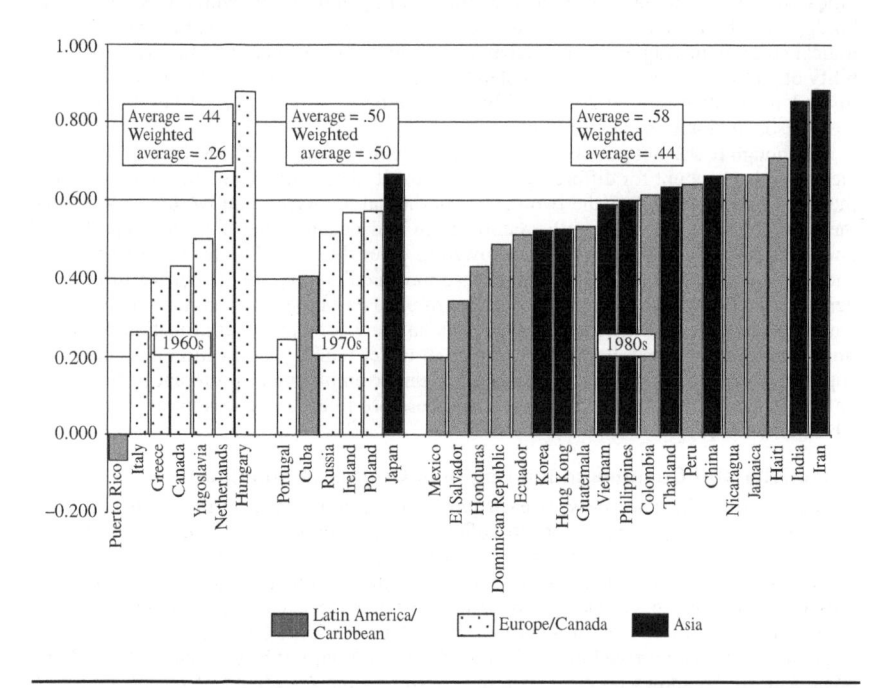

Notes: Average = average NDI for all immigrant groups with this average decade of arrival. Weighted average = average NDI weighted by the size of the immigrant groups.

of labor migration, and includes a large number of undocumented migrants.[13] Although ideally I would have liked to compare the selectivity of Mexican immigrants over time to the patterns for other groups, I was unable to locate appropriate data over time for any other group.

Table 3 presents a series of multivariate, ordinary least-squares (OLS) regression analyses to examine differences in years of schooling by migrant status among Mexicans, from 1960 to 2000, controlling for age and gender.[14] With regard to the coefficients for recent U.S. migrants,[15] those who migrated within the past five years, there is a pattern of

---

13. Unfortunately, I was unable to distinguish between documented and undocumented immigrants with the available data. These data are based on census data that include all U.S. residents, regardless of legal status; however, undocumented immigrants are most likely underrepresented in the data. Therefore, readers should be cautious in generalizing these results to undocumented immigrants, since there may be differences in selectivity by legal status.

14. The analyses presented in this section are based on all Mexican immigrants because the patterns did not differ for men and women (separate analyses for men and women are available on request).

15. I focus the discussion only on recent migrants because prior migrants are likely to be a biased sample of the most successful immigrants who have remained in the United States over a long period. The comparison group is Mexican nonmigrants, excluding those who ever lived abroad in 1960 and 1970, and those who were

Table 3. Coefficients of the Determinants of Years of Schooling Among Mexicans in the United States and Mexico, Aged 25–64

Determinants of Years of Schooling	1960	1970	1990	2000
Recent U.S. Migrant	1.178***	2.156***	1.872***	1.614***
Prior U.S. Migrant (reference = nonmigrants in Mexico)	1.569***	2.504***	2.208***	2.146***
Female	−0.177***	−0.392***	−0.803***	−0.467***
Age	−0.012***	−0.025***	−0.111***	−0.113***
Constant	3.891***	4.897***	10.751***	11.571***
R^2	0.020	0.037	0.117	0.116
N	111,662	154,416	307,728	411,006

Source: IPUMS International (Mexican and U.S. censuses).

***$p < .001$

strong positive selection from 1960 to 2000. Migrants consistently averaged more than one additional year of schooling than nonmigrants. The migrant advantage was the greatest in 1970, when migrants had more than two additional years of schooling than nonmigrants, but declined in 1990 and 2000 (although migrants in the later years still appear to have had a greater advantage over nonmigrants than was true in 1960).

Figure 2 depicts the trends in educational selectivity among Mexican immigrants over time, using two different methods. The first panel is based on the OLS regression results in Table 3. It plots the regression coefficients for recent migrant status, standardized by the mean years of schooling of all Mexicans (migrant and nonmigrant), to facilitate the interpretation of comparisons over time. This method follows Tolnay's (1998) and takes into account the rising educational attainments over the past few decades in Mexico and thus the fact that a one-year advantage in 1960, when Mexicans averaged 3.4 years of schooling, may be relatively larger than a one-year advantage in 2000, when the Mexican average was more than 7 years of schooling. The trend line indicates a sharp rise in educational selectivity among recent migrants from 1960 to 1970, perhaps because of the ending of the Bracero program in 1964, which directly recruited low-skilled laborers. From 1970 to 2000, however, educational selectivity appears to have declined (although data are not available for 1980).

The second panel in Figure 2, based on comparisons of age-standardized NDIs from 1960 to 2000, presents a slightly different picture. One still sees a sharp increase in educational selectivity from 1960 to 1970, but the pattern after 1970 is less clear. Educational selectivity among Mexican migrants declined from 1970 to 1980, increased from 1980 to 1990, and then declined slightly again from 1990 to 2000. Thus, instead of a pattern of declining selectivity from 1970 to 2000, as was shown when the comparison was based on mean years of schooling, a comparison based on the entire educational distribution shows little difference in the educational selectivity of recent migrants in 1970, 1990, and 2000, but lower levels of selection in 1960 and 1980. On the basis of these analyses, it is difficult to draw firm conclusions about the educational selectivity of Mexican immigrants over time. While the general trend is clearly *not* one of *increasing* educational selectivity over time, whether selectivity has declined since 1970 (Panel A) or has remained relatively

---

living abroad five years earlier in 1990 and 2000 (changes in the survey question do not allow for exact consistency across decades).

Figure 2. Educational Selectivity of Mexican Immigrants in the United States, 1960–2000

a. Adjusted Differentials Between Recent Mexican Immigrants and Mexican Nonmigrants, Based on OLS Regressions of Years of Schooling Completed[a]

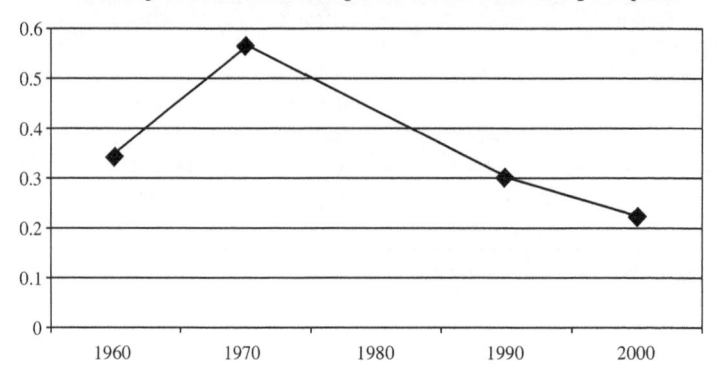

b. Age-Standardized Net Difference Indexes: Comparisons of the Educational Distributions of Recent Mexican Immigrants and Mexican Nonimmigrants

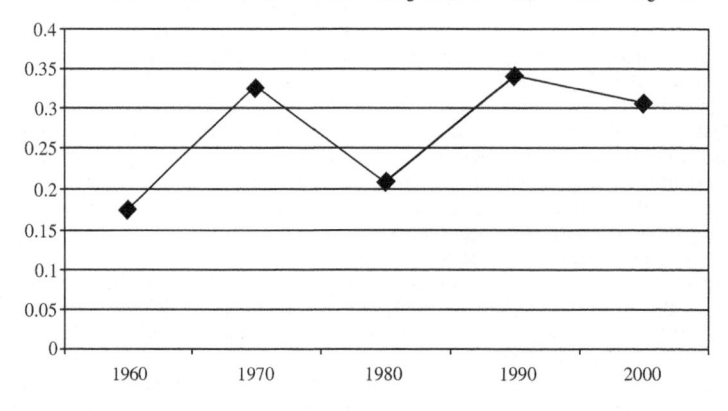

[a]The adjusted differential is the ratio of the regression coefficient of recent migrant status (see Table 3) to the mean for all Mexican-born adults aged 25-64.

stable (Panel B) depends upon how education is measured. Nevertheless, it is clear that regardless of the decade of migration, Mexican immigrants are positively selected, but the level of positive selectivity (NDI ranging from about .17 to .35) is low relative to other immigrant groups (see Table 1).

These findings lend mixed support to Massey's (1988) hypothesis that the selectivity of immigrants declines over successive waves of immigrants from the same country. Although the average years of schooling of immigrants relative to Mexican nonmigrants declined from 1970 to 2000, comparisons of the entire educational distribution reveal a pattern of lower selectivity in 1960 and 1980 but similar levels of selectivity among recent migrants in 1970, 1990, and 2000. Overall, the findings do not indicate substantial changes in selectivity. These mixed results may have to do with the changing nature of migration from Mexico. While migration from Mexico has historically been dominated by migrants from rural Mexico, in recent years, a growing number have come from urban areas (Durand et al. 2001; Fussell 2004; Marcelli and Cornelius 2001; Roberts, Frank, and Lozano-Ascencio 1999). Unfortunately, U.S. census data do not allow for distinctions between rural- and urban-origin Mexican immigrants. Thus, it may be possible that selectivity is declining among migrants from rural areas, where social capital mechanisms operate most strongly in reducing the costs of migration, whereas urban-origin migrants, who are more educated, may be responding to a different set of factors (Fussell and Massey 2004). Indeed, recent research has suggested that the mechanisms of cumulative causation that may lead to declining selectivity among rural Mexican migrants do not operate similarly among urban migrants (Fussell 2004; Fussell and Massey 2004). These findings suggest that future research should examine the factors that influence the changing characteristics over time of migrants from different regions in Mexico and other countries.

CONCLUSION

In response to Gans's (2000) appeal for more research on who immigrants are and how they differ from those who do not migrate, this article has examined how immigrants' educational attainments compare to those of their nonmigrant counterparts. Although scholars have agreed that migrants are not random samples of their home countries' populations, they have disagreed about how immigrants' characteristics compare to those of persons who remain in the sending society. Some scholars have contended that immigrants are consistently the most educated and ambitious of their home countries, while others have argued that only some immigrant groups are positively selected or that positive selectivity declines over time. This article has taken the first step toward resolving this debate by focusing on one aspect of immigrants' selectivity—how their educational attainments compare to those of nonmigrants.

I found that there is substantial variation in the degree of educational selectivity depending on the country of origin and the timing of migration from a particular country, but that nearly all immigrant groups are more educated than their nonmigrant counterparts. This finding challenges theories that have proposed that immigrants are positively selected only under certain conditions. Of the 32 immigrant groups I studied, 31 are positively selected on education. Only Puerto Ricans are negatively selected; that is, Puerto Rican migrants to the United States mainland tend to be less educated than Puerto Rican nonmigrants. However, this finding can probably be attributed to their status as U.S. citizens, which makes migration much less costly for Puerto Ricans than for other migrant groups.

Distance from the United States and the average educational attainment in the home country help determine immigrants' educational selectivity. Specifically, immigrants from countries that are farther from the United States (such as those in Asia) are more positively selected, which is consistent with the idea that immigrant groups that face greater barriers to or costs of migration will be more highly educated relative to their home countries' populations. In general, immigrants from countries with high levels of schooling are less positively selected than those from countries with low levels of schooling. This finding may be partly due to a ceiling effect created by the inclusion of countries, such as Canada and Korea, with highly educated populations. Conversely, the finding may also be due to the inclusion of brain-drain societies, such as India, where the general population has little education. In such countries, those with higher educational levels may have strong incentives to migrate to more-developed countries, such as the United States; they also may be the only ones with the resources to migrate. Future research is needed to assess these different explanations. I also found that some factors that are often thought to be predictors of selectivity, such as the level of income inequality in the origin country and whether migrants left primarily for political reasons, have no significant effect.

The changing regional origins of U.S. immigrants in the past few decades do not appear to be associated with major changes in immigrant selectivity. While previous research has suggested that recent immigrants from Asia and Latin America are less positively selected than were immigrants from Europe decades ago (Borjas 1999), my findings suggest that contemporary immigrants are not less selected, and may be more positively selected, than were those who came from Europe in the 1960s.

Finally, I found limited support for the idea that successive waves of immigrants from Mexico are less educated relative to the population in Mexico than were those who immigrated earlier. Mexican immigrants who arrived in the 1980s and 1990s are less positively selected than were their counterparts who came earlier in terms of average level of education, but their overall educational distribution is not lower. This mixed finding suggests that future research that takes into account the regional origins of immigrants within sending countries is needed to discern patterns of changing selectivity over time.

Understanding the selectivity of migrants is crucial to understanding who immigrants are in general. Although scholars have agreed that immigrants do not represent a random sample of their home countries' populations, from the vantage point of the average U.S. native, who sees only immigrants and not those who remain in the homeland, it is easy to attribute immigrants' characteristics to an entire national group. For example, Mexicans are generally seen as an uneducated group by American standards, while Indians are seen as highly educated. A look at the educational distributions of Mexico and India, however, challenges these common perceptions because *most* Indians in India have little formal schooling compared with less than one third of Mexicans in Mexico. The fact that Indians who migrate to the United States are much more highly educated than those who remain in India, while Mexicans who migrate to the United States are not much more educated than those who remain in Mexico, drives the perceptions of these groups in the United States. Future research should address the selection of immigrants in other sending and receiving contexts; the reasons why male immigrants are more highly selected than female immigrants from some countries, but not others; how social networks affect the selectivity of different types of immigrants; and whether patterns of immigrant selection are an important component for understanding differences in the socioeconomic outcomes of immigrants and their children in the United States.

REFERENCES

Abbott, E. 1969. *Historical Aspects of the Immigration Problem: Select Documents*. New York: Arno Press.

Bean, F., H. Browning, and W.P. Frisbie. 1985. "What the 1980 Census Tells Us About the Character of Illegal and Legal Mexican Immigrants." Working Paper, Series 6, No. 10. Population Research Center, University of Texas at Austin.

Bonacich, E. 1976. "Advanced Capitalism and Black/White Race Relations in the United States: A Split Labor Market Interpretation." *American Sociological Review* 41:34–51.

Borjas, G.J. 1987. "Self-Selection and the Earnings of Immigrants." *American Economic Review* 77:531–53.

———. 1991. "Immigration and Self-Selection." Pp. 29–76 in *Immigration, Trade, and the Labor Market*, edited by J.M. Abowd. Chicago: University of Chicago Press.

———. 1992. "National Origin and the Skills of Immigrants in the Postwar Period." Pp. 17–47 in *Immigration and the Workforce: Economic Consequences for the United States and Source Areas*, edited by G. Borjas and R.B. Freeman. Chicago: University of Chicago Press.

———. 1996. "The Earnings of Mexican Immigrants in the United States." *Journal of Development Economics* 51(1):69–98.

Educational Selectivity in U.S. Immigration

Appendix Table A1. Data Sources and Data Collected on Immigrants and Home Country Populations

Country of Origin	Year of Country Data	Average Year of Migration	IPUMS Data Year	Immigrants Selected[a]
Italy	1961	1960–1964	1970, 1960	Migrated 1955–1965, ages 25+ in 1961
Canada	1961	1965–1969	1970	Migrated 1960–1970, ages 25+ in 1961
Hungary	1963	1960–1964	1970	Migrated 1955–1970, ages 25+ in 1963
Ireland	1966	1965–1974	1970, 1980	Migrated 1960–1974, ages 25+ in 1966
Iran	1966	1980–1981	1980, 1990	Migrated 1970–1990, ages 25+ in 1966
Puerto Rico	1970	1965–1969	1970	Migrated 1965–1969, ages 25+ in 1970
Poland	1970	1970–1974	1970, 1980	Migrated 1965–1979, ages 20+ in 1970
Russia	1970	1970–1974	1980, 1990	Migrated 1970–1984, ages 25+ in 1970
Japan	1970	1975–1979	1980, 1990	Migrated 1970–1984, ages 25+ in 1970
Dominican Republic	1970	1980–1981	1980, 1990	Migrated 1975–1986, ages 20+ in 1970
Greece	1971	1965–1969	1970, 1980	Migrated 1960–1974, ages 25+ in 1971
Yugoslavia	1971	1965–1969	1970, 1980	Migrated 1960–1975, ages 18+ in 1971
Netherlands	1971	1965–1969	1970, 1980	Migrated 1960–1975, ages 18+ in 1971
Nicaragua	1971	1982–1984	1980, 1990	Migrated 1975–1990, ages 20+ in 1971
Columbia	1973	1980–1981	1980, 1990	Migrated 1970–1986, ages 20+ in 1973
Mexico	1980	1980–1981	1980, 1990	Migrated 1975–1984, ages 20+ in 1980
Philippines	1980	1980–1981	1980, 1990	Migrated 1975–1984, ages 20+ in 1980
Thailand	1980	1980–1981	1980, 1990	Migrated 1975–1990, ages 20+ in 1980
Korea	1980	1982–1984	1980, 1990	Migrated 1975–1986, ages 20+ in 1980
Cuba	1981	1965–1974	1970, 1980	Migrated 1965–1974, ages 25–49 in 1981
Portugal	1981	1975–1979	1980, 1990	Migrated 1970–1984, ages 20+ in 1981
Hong Kong	1981	1980–1981	1980, 1990	Migrated 1975–1986, ages 20+ in 1981
India	1981	1982–1984	1980, 1990	Migrated 1975–1986, ages 20+ in 1982
Guatemala	1981	1982–1984	1980, 1990	Migrated 1975–1990, ages 20+ in 1982
Peru	1981	1982–1984	1980, 1990	Migrated 1975–1990, ages 20+ in 1981
China	1982	1980–1981	1980, 1990	Migrated 1975–1986, ages 20+ in 1982
Ecuador	1982	1980–1981	1980, 1990	Migrated 1975–1990, ages 18+ in 1980
Jamaica	1982	1980–1981	1980, 1990	Migrated 1975–1986, ages 25+ in 1989
Haiti	1982	1980–1981	1980, 1990	Migrated 1975–1986, ages 20+ in 1982
Honduras	1983	1980–1981	1980, 1990	Migrated 1975–1990, ages 18+ in 1980
Vietnam	1989	1982–1984	1980, 1990	Migrated 1975–1986, ages 25+ in 1989
El Salvador	1992	1982–1984	1990	Migrated 1980–1990, ages 25+ in 1992

Note: The data source for all countries of origin, except Puerto Rico, is UNESCO; the data source for Puerto Rico is the census.

[a] All immigrants selected were at least 22 years old when they migrated to the United States.

———. 1999. *Heaven's Door: Immigration Policy and the American Economy*. Princeton, NJ: Princeton University Press.
Bray, D. 1984. "Economic Development: The Middle Class and International Migration in the Dominican Republic." *International Migration Review* 18:217–36.
Briggs, V.M. 1975. "The Need for a More Restrictive Border Policy." *Social Science Quarterly* 56:477–84.
Chiswick, B.R. 1978. "The Effect of Americanization on the Earnings of Foreign-born Men." *Journal of Political Economy* 86:897–921.
———. 1986. "Is the New Immigration Less Skilled Than the Old?" *Journal of Labor Economics* 4:168–92.
———. 2000. "Are Immigrants Favorably Self-Selected?" Pp. 61–76 in *Migration Theory: Talking Across Disciplines*, edited by C.B. Brettell and J.F. Hollifield. New York: Routledge.
Cobb-Clark, D.A. 1993. "Immigrant Selectivity and Wages—The Evidence for Women." *American Economic Review* 83:986–93.
Deininger, K. and L. Squire. n.d. "Deininger and Squire Data Set: A New Data Set Measuring Income Inequality." *World Bank Group, Economic Growth Research*. Available on-line at http://www.worldbank.org/research/growth/dddeisqu.htm
Donato, K.M. 1993. "Current Trends and Patterns of Female Migration: Evidence From Mexico." *International Migration Review* 27:748–71.
Durand, J., D.S. Massey, and R.M. Zenteno. 2001. "Mexican Immigration to the United States: Continuities and Changes." *Latin American Research Review* 36:107–27.
Foner, N. 2000. *From Ellis Island to JFK: New York's Two Great Waves of Immigration*. New Haven, CT: Yale University Press.
Fussell, E. 2004. "Sources of Mexico's Migration Stream: Rural, Urban, and Border Migrants to the United States." *Social Forces* 82:937–67.
Fussell, E. and D.S. Massey. 2004. "The Limits to Cumulative Causation: International Migration From Mexican Urban Areas." *Demography* 41:151–71.
Gans, H.J. 2000. "Filling in Some Holes: Six Areas of Needed Immigration Research." Pp. 76–89 in *Immigration Research for a New Century*, edited by N. Foner, R.G. Rumbaut, and S.J. Gold. New York: Russell Sage Foundation.
Glaser, W.A. 1978. *The Brain Drain: Emigration and Return*. Oxford, England: Pergamon Press.
Green, D.A. 1999. "Immigrant Occupational Attainment: Assimilation and Mobility Over Time." *Journal of Labor Economics* 17(1):49–79.
Grubel, H.G. and A. Scott. 1977. *The Brain Drain: Determinants, Measurement and Welfare Effects*. Waterloo, Ontario: Wilfrid Laurier University Press.
Hirschman, C. and L.M. Falcon. 1985. "The Educational Attainment of Religio-Ethnic Groups in the United States." *Research in Sociology of Education and Socialization* 5:83–120.
Jasso, G. and M.R. Rosenzweig. 1986. "What's in a Name? Country-of-Origin Influences on the Earnings of Immigrants in the Untied States." *Research in Human Capital and Development* 4:75–106.
Lamm, R.D. and G. Imhoff. 1985. *The Immigration Time Bomb: The Fragmenting of America*. New York: Truman Talley Books.
Landale, N.S. 1994. "Migration and the Latino Family—The Union Formation Behavior of Puerto-Rican Women." *Demography* 31:133–57.
Landale, N.S., R.S. Oropesa, and B.K. Gorman. 2000. "Migration and Infant Death: Assimilation or Selective Migration Among Puerto Ricans?" *American Sociological Review* 65:888–909.
Lee, E.S. 1966. "A Theory of Migration." *Demography* 3:47–57.
Lieberson, S. 1976. "Rank-Sum Comparisons Between Groups." *Sociological Methodology* 7:276–91.
———. 1980. *A Piece of the Pie: Blacks and White Immigrants Since 1880*. Berkeley: University of California Press.
Lobo, A.P. and J.J. Salvo. 1998a. "Changing U.S. Immigration Law and the Occupational Selectiv-

ity of Asian Immigrants." *International Migration Review* 32:737–60.

———. 1998b. "Resurgent Irish Immigration to the US in the 1980s and Early 1990s—A Socio-Demographic Profile." *International Migration Review* 36:257–80.

Long, L.H. 1973. "Migration Differentials by Education and Occupation—Trends and Variations." *Demography* 10:243–58.

Marcelli, E.A. and W.A. Cornelius. 2001. "The Changing Profile of Mexican Migrants to the United States: New Evidence From California and Mexico." *Latin American Research Review* 36: 105–31.

Massey, D.S. 1987a. "Do Undocumented Immigrants Earn Lower Wages Than Legal Immigrants?" *International Migration Review* 21:236–74.

———. 1987b. "Understanding Mexican Migration to the United States." *American Journal of Sociology* 92:1372–403.

———. 1988. "Economic Development and International Migration in Comparative Perspective." *Population and Development Review* 14:383–413.

——— 1999. "Why Does Immigration Occur? A Theoretical Synthesis." Pp. 34–52 in *Handbook of International Migration,* edited by C. Hirschman, P. Kasinitz, and J. DeWind. New York: Russell Sage Foundation.

Massey, D.S., J. Arango, G. Hugo, A. Kouaouci, A. Pellegrino, and J.E. Taylor. 1993. "Theories of International Migration—A Review and Appraisal." *Population and Development Review* 19:431–66.

Massey, D.S. and F.G. España. 1987. "The Social Process of International Migration." *Science* 237:733–38.

Massey, D.S. and K.E. Espinosa. 1997. "What's Driving Mexico-U.S. Migration? A Theoretical, Empirical, and Policy Analysis." *American Journal of Sociology* 102:939–99.

Melendez, E. 1994. "Puerto-Rican Migration and Occupational Selectivity, 1982–1988." *International Migration Review* 28:49–67.

Menjivar, C. 1993. "History, Economy and Politics: Macro and Micro-Level Factors in Recent Salvadorean Migration to the U.S." *Journal of Refugee Studies* 6:350–71.

Ortiz, V. 1986. "Changes in the Characteristics of Puerto Rican Migrants from 1955 to 1980." *International Migration Review* 20:612–28.

Palloni, A., D.S. Massey, M. Ceballos, K. Espinosa, and M. Spittel. 2001. "Social Capital and International Migration: A Test Using Information on Family Networks." *American Journal of Sociology* 106:1262–98.

Portes, A. 1979. "Illegal Immigrants and the International System: Lessons From Recent Legal Mexican Immigrants to the United States." *Social Problems* 26:425–38.

Portes, A. and R.G. Rumbaut. 1996. *Immigrant America: A Portrait.* Berkeley: University of California Press.

Ramos, F. 1992. "Out-Migration and Return Migration of Puerto Ricans." Pp. 49–66 in *Immigration and the Work Force: Economic Consequences for the United States and Source Areas,* edited by G.J. Borjas and R.B. Freeman. Chicago: University of Chicago Press.

Ravenstein, E.G. 1885. "The Laws of Migration." *Journal of the Royal Statistical Society* 48(2):167–227.

Roberts, B.R., R. Frank, and F. Lozano-Ascencio. 1999. "Transnational Migrant Communities and Mexican Migration to the US." *Ethnic and Racial Studies* 22:238–66.

Roy, A.D. 1951. "Some Thoughts on the Distribution of Earnings." *Oxford Economic Papers* 3:135–46.

Ruggles, S., M. Sobek et al. 1997. *Integrated Public Use Microdata Series: Version 2.0.* Minneapolis: Historical Census Projects, University of Minnesota. Available on-line at http://www.ipums.umn.edu

Rumbaut, R.G. 1995. "The New Californians: Comparative Research Findings on the Educational Progress of Immigrant Children." Pp. 17–69 in *California's Immigrant Children: Theory Research, and Implications for Educational Policy,* edited by R.G. Rumbaut and W.A. Cornelius.

San Diego: Center for U.S.-Mexican Studies, U.C. San Diego.

———. 1997. "Ties That Bind: Immigration and Immigrant Families in the United States." Pp. 3–46 in *Immigration and the Family: Research and Policy on U.S. Immigrants,* edited by A. Booth, A.C. Crouter, and N. Landale. Mahwah, NJ: Lawrence Erlbaum.

———. 1999. "Assimilation and Its Discontents: Ironies and Paradoxes." Pp. 172–95 in *The Handbook of International Migration: The American Experience,* edited by C. Hirschman, P. Kasinitz, and J. DeWind. New York: Russell Sage Foundation.

Schultz, T.P. 1984. "The Schooling and Health of Children of U.S. Immigrants and Natives." *Research in Population Economics* 5:251–88.

Shryock, H.S. and C.B. Nam. 1965. "Educational Selectivity of Interregional Migration." *Social Forces* 43(3):299–310.

Sobek, M., S. Ruggles, R. McCaa, M. King, and D. Levinson. 2002. *Integrated Public Use Microdata Series (IPUMS)-International: Preliminary Version 1.0.* Minneapolis: Minnesota Population Center, University of Minnesota. Available on-line at http://www.ipums.umn.edu/international/index.html

Stark, O. and D.E. Bloom. 1985. "The New Economics of Labor Migration." *American Economic Review, Papers and Proceedings of the Ninety-Seventh Annual Meeting of the American Economic Association* 75:173–78.

Suval, E.M. and C.H. Hamilton. 1965. "Some New Evidence on Educational Selectivity in Migration to and From the South." *Social Forces* 43:536–47.

Taylor, J.E. 1986. "Differential Migration, Networks, Information, and Risk." Pp. 141–71 in *Research in Human Capital and Development,* edited by O. Stark. Greenwich, CT: JAI Press.

———. 1987. "Undocumented Mexico-U.S. Migration and the Return to Households in Rural Mexico." *American Journal of Agricultural Economics* 69:626–38.

Teitelbaum, M. 1980. "Right Versus Right: Immigration and Refugee Policy in the United States." *Foreign Affairs* 59:21–59.

Tolnay, S.E. 1998. "Educational Selection in the Migration of Southern Blacks, 1880–1990." *Social Forces* 77:487–514.

Treiman, D.J., V. Lew, H. Lee, and T.A. Brown. 1986. "Occupational Status Attainment Among Ethnic Groups in Los Angeles." Working Paper. UCLA Institute for Social Science Research.

UNESCO. 1975. *United Nations Educational, Scientific and Cultural Organization Statistical Yearbook.* Paris: UNESCO Publishing and Berman Press.

———. 1978–79. *United Nations Educational, Scientific and Cultural Organization Statistical Yearbook.* Paris: UNESCO Publishing and Berman Press.

———. 1989. *United Nations Educational, Scientific and Cultural Organization Statistical Yearbook.* Paris: UNESCO Publishing and Berman Press.

———. 1992. *United Nations Educational, Scientific and Cultural Organization Statistical Yearbook.* Paris: UNESCO Publishing and Berman Press.

———. 1993. *United Nations Educational, Scientific and Cultural Organization Statistical Yearbook.* Paris: UNESCO Publishing and Berman Press.

———. 1995. *United Nations Educational, Scientific and Cultural Organization Statistical Yearbook.* Paris: UNESCO Publishing and Berman Press.

———. 1997. *United Nations Educational, Scientific and Cultural Organization Statistical Yearbook.* Paris: UNESCO Publishing and Berman Press.

U.S. Census Bureau. 1973. *1970 Census of the Population, Characteristics of the Population, Vol. 1, Part 53, Puerto Rico.* Washington, DC: U.S. Department of Commerce, Social and Economic Statistics Administration, U.S. Census Bureau.

Vas-Zoltan, P. 1976. *The Brain Drain: An Anomaly of International Relations.* Budapest: A.W. Sijthoff, Leyden.

Part II
The Labor Market Adjustment of Immigrants

Part II.

[5]

Immigrant earnings: age at immigration matters

Joseph Schaafsma *Department of Economics, University of Victoria*
Arthur Sweetman *School of Policy Studies, Queen's University*

Abstract. A correlation between age at immigration and earnings is observed in Canadian census data. The evidence supports three underlying sources of the effect; first, work experience in the source country yields virtually no return in the host country; second, the return to education varies with age at immigration, and, finally, an 'acculturation' effect is observed for immigrants who are visible minorities or whose mother tongue is not English. Further, it is found that educational attainment, and relatedly earnings, vary systematically across age at immigration with those arriving around age 15 to 18 obtaining fewer years of education. JEL Classification: J61, J31

Revenus des immigrants: l'âge auquel on immigre porte à conséquence. On observe une corrélation entre l'âge auquel on immigre et les niveaux de revenu dans les données de recensement au Canada. Les résultats soulignent trois sources d'explication pour cette relation: d'abord, l'expérience de travail dans le pays d'origine semble engendrer des rendements presque nuls dans le pays d'accueil; ensuite, les rendements sur l'investissement en éducation varient avec l'âge auquel on émigré; et enfin, on observe un effet d'acculturation chez les immigrants qui sont membres de minorités visibles ou pour lesquels l'anglais n'est pas la langue maternelle. On montre aussi que le niveau d'éducation et les niveaux de revenus qui en découlent varient systématiquement selon l'âge auquel on immigre, et que ceux qui immigrent autour de 15 à 18 ans sont ceux qui atteignent le niveau d'éducation le moins grand.

Research funding from the Vancouver Centre of Excellence for Research on Immigration and Integration in the Metropolis (RIIM), a SSHRC and CIC initiative, is gratefully acknowledged. We also thank Barry Chiswick, Tom Crossley, Don DeVoretz, Chris Worswick, and two anonymous referees for their helpful comments. Earlier drafts of this paper were presented at the Third National Metropolis Conference, Vancouver, B.C., and at the 33rd annual meeting of the Canadian Economics Association, Toronto, Ont. All opinions and conclusions are our responsibility. Email: schaafsm@uvic.ca; sweetman@qsilver.queensu.ca

1. Introduction

A small number of studies exploring the labour market impact of age at immigration have been conducted in the United States, but the issue has almost always been addressed tangentially in studies looking at the rate of immigrant economic 'assimilation' or integration.[1] The topic itself does not appear to have been given much attention, and it appears to have received almost no attention in the Canadian context.[2] This is particularly striking, since the economic implications may be sizable and, unlike the large negative coefficients observed for recent entry cohorts in assimilation studies such as Borjas (1985, 1995), Baker and Benjamin (1994), Bloom, Grenier, and Gunderson (1995), and Grant (1999) do not attenuate with time in the host country but leave permanent legacies. Further, since 1967 Canada has employed a 'points system' to determine the eligibility of applicants to immigrate, and one of the variables for which points are awarded is age, which makes age at immigration an important variable to understand.[3] Using Canadian census data, in this study we look at the impact of age at immigration on men's employment earnings and finds large effects.

There are a variety of reasons why one would expect that age at immigration might matter, either directly or indirectly, for labour market outcomes. For example, schooling obtained in the source country may not be (recognized as) equivalent to schooling in the host country and thus yield a lower return. The same may be true for labour market experience. Older immigrants may also be less able to adjust to the linguistic and cultural challenges associated with entering a new country, and this may make it difficult for them to generate earnings commensurate with their formal educational and occupational skills. Each of these factors suggests that age at immigration may be an important determinant of an immigrant's earnings. Further, the examples above suggest that immigrant earnings, relative to an equivalent Canadian-born person, will decline as age at immigration increases.

The seminal work of Chiswick (1978) and Borjas (1985) on the economic assimilation of immigrants does not include any specific consideration of the impact of age at immigration on earnings profiles. However, in a number of subsequent American studies aspects of the issue are addressed. Kossoudji (1989) allows the returns to experience and schooling to vary by whether the experience and schooling were

---

1 See Smith (1992), Friedberg (1993), Borjas (1995), Funkhouser and Trejo (1995). Addressing age at immigration in cohort studies is important because the normal procedure for constructing a sample for analysis from (repeated) cross-sectional data induces a correlation between the year of immigration (arrival cohort) and age at immigration. To be of working age and therefore in the sample, the earliest cohorts must have immigrated as children, and the most recent cohorts must have arrived as adults.
2 See Borjas (1993, 1994) for a survey of the economics of immigration and a comparison of Canada and the United States.
3 The points system, analysed in Green and Green (1995), applies only to the principal applicants in the 'skilled' (also called 'independent') class of immigrants, not to their spouses and dependants nor to refugees. Immigrants arriving as part of a family reunification have been subject to the points system only in certain policy regimes. An immigrant's entry category cannot be identified in the available data.

obtained abroad or in the United States. Her results indicate near zero returns to labour market experience acquired abroad and very little difference in the returns to pre- and post-immigration schooling. While we can replicate her results in our data, we extend the analysis to allow for parameter heterogeneity and observe that the interpretation of the results changes substantially. Friedberg (1993) extends the analysis of Chiswick (1978) and Borjas (1985) by adding an age at immigration variable to the economic assimilation model. Using 1970 and 1980 United States census data, she finds that age at immigration exerts a statistically significant negative effect on male immigrant earnings after controlling for education, experience, ethnicity, and years since immigration. Borjas (1995), using 1970, 1980, and 1990 census data, obtains similar results. Neither author seeks to determine why age at immigration matters, which is the focus of this paper. Schoeni (1998) uses the same data to examine the labour force participation of immigrant women. His results show that female immigrants who attended schools in the United States (i.e., women who immigrated at an early age) had higher labour force participation rates. Thus, if labour force participation is a measure of economic integration, the degree of integration varies inversely with age at immigration.

Kee's (1995) study of male immigrants living in the Netherlands also focuses on the returns to pre- and post-immigration labour market experience and schooling for a number of ethnic groups. His results indicate that the return to pre-immigration measures is higher for immigrants from school systems and implicitly the cultural contexts, that are more similar to the Dutch context. Using Australian data, Chiswick and Miller (1985) find that schooling obtained abroad yields a lower return than schooling obtained by the Canadian born, and that this difference is larger if the schooling was received in a non-English-speaking country. Their results also show that foreign labour market experience yields a much lower return than Australian labour market experience. Friedberg (2000) looks at foreign and native-born returns to education and experience in Israel and finds that the return to foreign experience is generally insignificant, and that in many cases foreign education is valued less than that obtained domestically.

Analysis of the effect of age at immigration on subsequent earnings in Canada has been limited to sensitivity analyses as part of studies concerned with other issues, and the results have been mixed. In their study of immigrant assimilation, Baker and Benjamin (1994) estimate a model for the subset of immigrants who were at least 16 years old at the time of immigration and find that their return to education is statistically insignificantly lower than that for all immigrants. Their return to labour market experience is about half of what it is for all immigrants, which is about two-thirds of that of the Canadian born. Grant (1999) updates Baker and Benjamin (1994) using 1991 census data and also splits the male immigrant sample on the basis of whether immigration occurred before age 16, or later. No regression results are shown, but it is reported that they do not differ from those for the full sample. Bloom, Grenier, and Gunderson (1995) report average age at immigration in their table of descriptive statistics but do not include this variable in their regression analysis of changes in the pattern of immigrant assimilation. In their analysis of the effect of macroeconomic conditions on male immigrant earnings,

McDonald and Worswick (1998) specify separate models for all male immigrants and for those who immigrated as adults, and they conclude that there is very little difference in the parameter estimates.

In the current paper we investigate the impact of age at immigration and find a sizable correlation with earnings even after controlling for cohort effects and a range of demographics. The different mechanisms that might underlie this correlation are also explored. Work experience in the source country is found to yield virtually no return in the host country. Ascertaining the relative value in the labour market of education received in Canada compared with elsewhere is more complicated. Immigrants who arrive as young children have a return to education similar to that of the Canadian born, but the return to education declines as age at immigration increases until those who arrive as older adults have quite low returns. If the parameter heterogeneity across age at immigration groups is ignored and education is measured as either Canadian or foreign, however, then immigrants' return to education from foreign and Canadian schools appears to be quite similar, with returns slightly below the return to education for the Canadian born; these results are similar to the findings of Chiswick and Miller (1985) and Kossoudji (1989). Further, we find evidence that suggests, at least for visible minorities and for those whose mother tongue is not English, that age at arrival has an economic impact that may be thought of as 'acculturation.' Finally, and very interestingly, we observe that immigrants who arrive around age 15 to 18 complete fewer years of schooling than those who arrive either earlier or later. Arriving near the transition out of high school appears to be associated with a permanent reduction in educational attainment, and this leaves a permanent scar on earnings.

We begin by outlining our methodology for estimating the effect of age at immigration on the immigrant age-earnings profile. Next, we present the data and provide descriptive statistics of the characteristics of Canadian-born and immigrant males and of the labour market outcomes for these two groups. Three sets of regression results are then presented: in the first we explore and quantify the effect of age at immigration on subsequent earnings; in the last two we focus on why age at immigration matters. The paper ends with a brief summary and conclusion.

2. Methodology and data

Unlike previous studies, this paper is not focused on identifying assimilation profiles and cohort fixed effects, and we therefore do not use a quasi-panel method like that employed in the immigration context by, for example, Borjas (1985, 1995).[4]

---

[4] Note that pooling the data across censuses is not required for a quasi-panel (time series of cross-sections) analysis (as in Baker and Benjamin 1994). Although not the focus of the paper, we did perform such an analysis to see if the addition of age-at-immigration variables affected the cohort assimilation profiles. We find that while their addition has a large effect on the cross-sectional profiles in each year, the effect is similar for the three years and the change in the assimilation profile (across censuses) is negligible. Interested readers can construct assimilation profiles from the coefficients presented in the appendix tables. Borjas (1995) and Funkhouser and Trejo (1995) report the introduction of age at immigration as having a similar negligible effect on the assimilation profile.

1070   J. Schaafsma and A. Sweetman

Further, an initial specification test rejects pooling the data, since differences in the coefficient estimates across the census years are statistically significant. Baker and Benjamin (1994) obtain a similar result for the same test, and like them, we therefore treat each census year as a separate cross-section. Borjas (1995) does not report performing such a test, but he does interact many variables of interest with the period effects, which has a similar effect to running separate regressions. Throughout the analysis we present results for the three census years and consider stability, or changes, in coefficient estimates across years as being informative.

2.1. Identification and estimation

An identification problem occurs when age at immigration, year of immigration (or equivalently, in cross-sectional data, years since migration), and age enter a regression equation as a set, since age is equal to age at immigration plus years since migration.[5] A common approach to this type of problem is to drop one of the three perfectly collinear variables, but that is not a satisfactory option in this case. Age at immigration is the focus of our paper, and although the rate of economic assimilation and cohort fixed effects are not, we believe that they are important and omitting them may bias our results. Similarly, we cannot ignore the age-earnings process, especially given that there is a substantial difference in the average age of immigrants and Canadian-born individuals in our sample, without potentially biasing our coefficient estimates.

We employ multiple distinct empirical strategies. They are not nested in the sense that one is a restricted version of another, but are conceptually distinct approaches to closely related issues. Further, each employs its own identification strategy, and, as pointed out by Borjas (1999, 1720–1), each gives a different perspective on the data and has an interpretation that is a function of the restriction imposed. Identification in the later approaches is straightforward, however, and we do not discuss it in this section; rather, we focus on the first approach here, which requires a more detailed explanation. We address this identification problem with an empirical strategy consistent with the substantive economic question: are the observed differences in outcomes between immigrant and Canadian-born workers of the same age (and in some cases other observable characteristics as well) associated with age at immigration? Fundamental to the method is that it takes the Canadian born as a comparison group.[6] A portion of Borjas's (1995) paper faces the same identification question. He identifies his model by assuming that the age effect is 'the same' (227) for both groups. That is, in a single regression containing both the immigrant and the host country born observations, he estimates a single age-earnings profile. The immigrant age-at-immigration coefficients can be interpreted, therefore, as deviations from this common profile, which is (in the presence of non-linearities) a mixture of the immigrant and Canadian-born profiles.

---

5   Note that, if years of schooling is a regressor, then the same problem occurs if age is replaced by potential experience.
6   Baker and Benjamin (1994) explore the implications of using different comparison groups in a fairly standard specification. They find that the choice does not substantially alter their results.

We are reluctant to impose this common age-earnings profile on both groups. Our approach provides an analysis that we believe to be 'cleaner.' What defines an immigrant is not age, but age at immigration and year of immigration, and we want all of the immigrant/Canadian-born differences to be assigned to those immigrant-specific characteristics. Borjas (1999, 1720) recognizes the problem inherent in imposing the 'same' age-earnings profile, arguing that it 'contradicts the notion of specific human capital.' Our approach, in general, requires a two-step procedure. This is less efficient than Borjas's single equation, but given the sample size available, the loss in precision does not appear to be important. Further, we believe that the potential gain in interpretive clarity is worth the cost.

We first estimate – as an auxiliary regression – the age-earnings profile for the Canadian-born sample. The bs are coefficients to be estimated, age measures years since birth and is modelled as a fourth-order polynomial to allow a high degree of flexibility,[7] and ϵ is a classical random error term. The Xs are additional regressors; they are in parentheses in equation (1) to indicate that they are included in some, but not all, of the models estimated.

$$\ln w^{cb} = b_0^{cb} + \sum_{j=1}^{4} \text{Age}^j b_j^{cb} (+ X b_x^{cb}) + \epsilon^{cb}. \tag{1}$$

Then, equation (2) – the equation of interest – is estimated using only the immigrant sample. The dependent variable is the difference between each immigrant's (ln) earnings and the predicted earnings that the worker would earn were he (our sample is limited to male wage earners) Canadian born and the same age (and in some models having the same Xs); the regression explains this difference as a function of immigrant characteristics.

$$\ln w^I - \left[b_0^{cb} + \sum_{j=1}^{4} \text{Age}^j b_j^{cb} (+ X b_x^{cb}) \right]$$
$$= b_0^I + \text{AgeImm} b_{\text{AgeImm}}^I + \text{ImmCohort} b_{\text{ImmCohort}}^I (+ X b_x^I) + \epsilon^I. \tag{2}$$

Equation (2) contains the immigrant-specific variables age at immigration and immigrant cohort, and a set of other observable characteristics (X) that are employed in some, but not all of the models estimated. Both immigrant-specific variables are specified as sets of indicator variables to maximize the flexibility of the functional form and to accord with the grouped census data employed. The superscript cb indicates Canadian born, and I represents immigrants. In this specification the immigration cohort coefficients in each cross-section do not have a well-defined interpretation, since they are a mixture of assimilation and cohort fixed effects. In conjunction with similar coefficients and the intercepts from additional cross-sections they can be used, however, to identify both. The coefficients are presented in appendices for those who wish to pursue this issue. A further complication arises

---

7 Murphy and Welch (1990) explore shape of the age-earnings profile and argue for a quartic.

1072   J. Schaafsma and A. Sweetman

for the two-step procedure, since OLS standard errors are not appropriate in the second stage. We bootstrap (resampling the data 500 times in all cases) the standard errors in all the models estimated.

Note that, as mentioned, in equation (2) the effect of age on earnings for immigrants is specified to be the same as that for the Canadian born. This restriction serves to identify the model, since it assigns each immigrant to the position we would expect him to have on the Canadian-born age-earnings profile. This projection onto the Canadian-born age-earnings profile poses the economic question we wish to address: Are the deviations between immigrant and Canadian-born earnings for similar people a function of immigrants' age at immigration (controlling for cohort effects)?

It is worth highlighting the key source of the difference between Borjas's (1995) identifying assumption and our own. If all variables entered the model linearly, then the coefficient estimates from the two procedures would be, in large samples, essentially identical, but our two-stage approach would be less efficient. The coefficients would be the same, since, in a single equation like Borjas's, the identity would cause the immigrant portion of the combined sample to identify only two of the three variables in question in accord with the Frisch-Waugh-Lovell theorem. Intuitively, the Canadian born portion of the sample would identify the age profile but obviously not the immigrant-specific coefficients, and the immigrant portion of the sample would take the Canadian-born age coefficients as given and then identify the age-at-immigration and year-of-migration coefficients. This is exactly what the two-stage procedure accomplishes.

If even one of these variables has a non-linear functional form, however, then the equivalence of the two approaches breaks down. The identity is linear, and does not apply to the higher-order terms: for example, age squared does not equal years since migration squared plus age at migration squared. If the model is estimated in one step, then the age-earnings profile becomes a mixture of that of the two groups, and the immigrant-specific variables measure differences from the mixture. In contrast, the two-stage approach continues to impose the Canadian-born age-earnings profile (which is non-linear) on the immigrant sample. Of course, if the 'true' profiles are not very different, or if the immigrant sample is very small relative to the Canadian-born one, then the coefficients estimated by the two procedures will be similar, but it is difficult to assert their similarity beforehand. For comparison, we estimate a version of Borjas's model in addition to our own.

2.2. Data

We estimate the effect of age at immigration in the context of a set of distinct models fitted separately to data from the public use 1986, 1991, and 1996 Canadian census microdata files. In some models the (natural logarithm of paid and positive self-employment) earnings are expressed as a function of years of schooling, potential labour market experience, marital status, visible minority status (as defined by Statistics Canada), a binary variable for 40 to 48 weeks of work in the reference year, a set of binary variables for weekly hours worked in the census reference week, whether the person was living in one of the 1986 census metropolitan areas, region of residence,[8] and whether mother tongue is English, French, or both (neither English nor French being the omitted group). In other models we include far fewer covariates. As will be seen, the changes in coefficient values as regressors are added to successive models point to interesting economic phenomena.

As in Baker and Benjamin (1994), the sample is limited to males who were 16 to 64 years old on the relevant survey date and who worked more than 40 weeks in the year before the census was taken. Some regressors, such as visible minority status and mother tongue, which have not been included in most economic assimilation studies, are employed to address issues not previously explored in the Canadian context. Not all the regressors are measured consistently across the three censuses. In the 1996 data those who immigrated before age 20 are grouped into three age-at-immigration categories: 1 to 4, 5 to 12, and 13 to 19; whereas in 1986 and 1991 four categories are used: 1 to 4, 5 to 9, 10 to 14, and 15 to 19. Identification of visible minority status also changed. In 1996 the variable in the public use file is self-reported, whereas that in the 1986 and 1991 files is imputed by Statistics Canada on the basis of a number of variables, such as ethnic origin and language.

3. Empirical results

3.1. Summary descriptive statistics

Comparative descriptive statistics for the 16 to 64 year-old Canadian-born and immigrant males are summarized in the upper part of table 1 for the 1996, 1991, and 1986 samples. A comparison of these sample statistics shows some interesting patterns. Immigrants on average are older than the Canadian born, but with the aging of the Canadian male labour force this differential has declined from 5.2 years in 1986 to 4.2 years in 1996. At the same time, the differential in labour market experience between immigrants and Canadian born dropped from 4.9 years in 1986 to 3.9 years in 1996. The years of schooling reported by people born in Canada and immigrants increased by the same amount (0.9) from 1986 to 1996, so that immigrants continue to have more formal schooling (0.3 years). Immigrant annual earnings in 1986 and 1991 (converted everywhere into $1,995 using the CPI) on average exceeded the earnings of Canadian born by some $2,000 but fell short of Canadian-born earnings by $442 in 1996 as a result of a much larger drop in the average real earnings for immigrants than for Canadian born. The proportion married is higher for immigrants than for Canadian born and appears to be trending down for both groups.

Three substantial differences between the Canadian-born and immigrant populations that have not previously been addressed adequately are urbanization, visible minority status, and mother tongue. In 1996 immigrants, at about 80 per cent, were

---

8 Quebec, Ontario, Prairies, Alberta, and British Columbia; the Atlantic provinces and the Territories are excluded from the sample, since their immigrant characteristics are severely grouped by Statistics Canada.

TABLE 1
Descriptive sample statistics

	1996 Census				1991 Census				1986 Census			
	Cdn. Born		Immigrants		Cdn. Born		Immigrants		Cdn. Born		Immigrants	
	mean	s.e.	mean	s.e.	mean	s.e.	mean	s.e.	mean	s.e.	mean	s.e.
Earnings	39534	81.10	39092	163.6	42150	80.15	44194	167.0	40440	93.04	42523	191.0
Age	38.78	0.032	42.98	0.062	37.75	0.032	42.68	0.061	37.40	0.042	42.56	0.079
Experience	20.34	0.034	24.18	0.067	19.71	0.034	24.24	0.067	19.80	0.046	24.67	0.088
Yrs of school	13.46	0.009	13.81	0.022	13.05	0.009	13.44	0.022	12.60	0.012	12.90	0.029
Married	0.705	0.001	0.790	0.002	0.712	0.001	0.803	0.002	0.723	0.002	0.819	0.003
Urban	0.509	0.001	0.807	0.002	0.511	0.001	0.796	0.002	0.513	0.002	0.784	0.003
Visible minority	0.014	0.000	0.424	0.003	0.013	0.000	0.361	0.003	0.009	0.000	0.262	0.003
English	0.656	0.001	0.318	0.003	0.643	0.001	0.339	0.003	0.639	0.002	0.358	0.003
French	0.295	0.001	0.030	0.001	0.304	0.001	0.033	0.001	0.299	0.002	0.032	0.001
Bilingual	0.003	0.000	0.001	0.000	0.003	0.000	0.001	0.000	0.013	0.000	0.004	0.000
Age-Adjusted means (predicted at age 40)												
(ln) earnings												
All	10.49	0.004	10.37	0.006	10.60	0.003	10.55	0.005	10.60	0.004	10.56	0.006
Visible minority	10.46	0.022	10.21	0.009	10.58	0.020	10.42	0.008	10.58	0.027	10.41	0.011
Not vis. min.	10.49	0.004	10.49	0.007	10.61	0.003	10.63	0.006	10.61	0.004	10.61	0.007
Schooling												
All	13.72	0.014	14.24	0.024	13.50	0.014	14.10	0.023	13.04	0.020	13.59	0.031
Visible minority	14.98	0.067	14.40	0.034	14.70	0.071	14.51	0.035	14.32	0.110	14.23	0.054
Not vis. min.	13.71	0.014	14.12	0.031	13.49	0.014	13.86	0.029	13.03	0.202	13.35	0.036
N	114922		29986		126187		32407		76128		20252	

NOTE: Age adjustment derives from predictions from a regression with a fourth order polynomial in age that is common to all observations and indicator variables for the visible minority, immigrant categories.

about 58.5 per cent more likely to live in an urban area than the Canadian born, an increase from 52.8 per cent in 1986. Over the same period the urbanization of the Canadian born stayed roughly constant at about 51 per cent. One of the more notable differences between the Canadian-born and immigrant samples, shown in table 1, is that an immigrant is much more likely (thirty times in 1996) to belong to a visible minority. It is also interesting to note that for both Canadian born and immigrants there is a substantial percentage increase from 1986 to 1996 in the proportion that belongs to a visible minority. This increase occurs despite a change in the definition that, as can be seen in table 2, appears to marginally decrease the observed fraction that is a visible minority in each and every immigrant cohort. The increase has two sources. First, as seen in table 2, the most recent cohort comprised a very high fraction of visible minorities, and second, there is attrition across the censuses as people near age 65, who are concentrated in the cohorts that arrived many years ago and had low proportions of visible minority, are more likely to leave the sample (retire). Similarly, the proportion of immigrants for whom neither English nor French is the mother tongue rose from 60.6 to 65.1 per cent.

Given the large difference in the age and visible minority distributions of immigrants and Canadian born, age adjusted (ln) earnings and schooling levels are presented by visible minority status in the lower portion of table 1. Four conclusions can be drawn from these results. First, for both immigrants and Canadian born, the visible minority group has on average more years of schooling than those who are not members of a visible minority, but in both cases the average earnings of the visible minority groups are less. (Although for non-immigrants the earnings differences are extremely small.) Second, the Canadian-born visible minority group has more years of schooling than visible minority immigrants and also earns more. Third, of those who are not a member of a visible minority, immigrants have more years of schooling than the Canadian born but earn about the same. Fourth, age-adjusted schooling rose for each group from one census year to the next except for visible-minority immigrants, where it declined from 1991 to 1996.

Average age at immigration by immigrant cohort is shown in table 2 for the three census years. These averages are based on the midpoints of the age ranges available in the census data. Since fewer ranges are used in the 1996 census, the 1996 averages are not comparable with those for 1986 and 1991. Nevertheless, the data clearly show that, as expected given the data selection procedure, the average age at immigration rises the more recent the year of immigration. Thus, if age at immigration affects assimilation, not including it in empirical models will result in omitted variable bias in the estimated assimilation pattern. It is also interesting to note that age at immigration declined in the first half of the 1990s.[9]

The proportion of the immigrants in each cohort of our sample that belongs to a visible minority is also shown in table 2. From 1945 to 1960 members of visible minorities comprised at most 5 per cent of newly arriving immigrants. This proportion rose dramatically over the next thirty-five years to 70 per cent, and this trend

---

9 We explored this in some detail to ensure that it did not result from the revision of the age-at-immigration ranges in the 1996 census.

TABLE 2
Selected descriptive statistics by immigrant cohort

Arrival cohort	Age at immigration			Visible minority			Years of school			Neither official language		
	1996	1991	1986	1996	1991	1986	1996	1991	1986	1996	1991	1986
Cdn born	–	–	–	0.01	0.01	0.01	13.46	13.05	12.61	0.05	0.05	0.05
pre 1946	4.46	4.91	5.16	0.02	0.03	0.02	12.76	12.26	11.86	0.27	0.39	0.36
1946–55	8.80	12.91	15.70	0.03	0.05	0.04	13.38	12.55	12.20	0.63	0.67	0.66
1956–60	13.18	16.36	18.40	0.03	0.05	0.05	13.04	12.65	12.36	0.65	0.66	0.65
1961–65	16.27	18.38	19.88	0.11	0.12	0.12	12.99	12.85	12.38	0.60	0.61	0.61
1966–70	19.01	20.90	22.70	0.25	0.26	0.26	13.96	13.80	13.40	0.53	0.52	0.55
1971–75	20.57	22.97	25.20	0.49	0.50	0.52	14.14	13.84	13.50	0.57	0.57	0.56
1976–80	22.18	25.20	28.12	0.56	0.57	0.57	13.94	13.72	13.42	0.63	0.64	0.62
1981–85	25.25	28.51	30.45	0.58	0.62	0.57	14.08	13.94	13.65	0.70	0.72	0.65
1986–90	29.29	31.82	–	0.66	0.69	–	13.91	13.81	–	0.77	0.74	–
1991–95	32.02	–	–	0.70	–	–	13.98	–	–	0.80	–	–

should not be ignored.[10] Table 2 also shows that, whereas in 1986 the most recent arrival cohort averaged 1.04 more years of education than the Canadian born, this differential had fallen to 0.52 years for the most recent cohort in 1996. Nevertheless, the average years of schooling for the most recently arrived cohort of immigrants rose steadily from 1986 to 1991 to 1996. While recent immigrants have more years of schooling than in the past, a smaller proportion than in the past have one, or both, of Canada's official languages as their mother tongue. As shown in table 2, 65.0 per cent of the most recent immigrant cohort did not report either English or French as their mother tongue in 1986. This proportion increased to 80 per cent in 1996.

3.2. The age-at-immigration effect

Our first set of regressions using the two-stage estimation strategy, in table 3, focuses on the relative earnings of immigrants across age-at-immigration categories.[11] As discussed above, the dependent variable is the difference between observed earnings and those predicted from the Canadian-born age-earnings profile. This dependent variable is regressed, in columns 1, 4, and 7, only on the immigrant's age at immigration and year of immigration. Both explanatory variables enter as sets of dummy variables defined over age intervals and immigrant cohorts, respectively, in accord with the information available in the Canadian census microdata files. Additional controls are added in subsequent models. The immigrant cohort dummy variables (in appendix table A1) capture the combined impact on earnings from assimilation and cohort fixed effects – neither effect is independently identified in cross-section.

The 1996, 1991, and 1986 estimates for these base cases (columns 1, 4, and 7) show that immigrants' age-earnings profile generally shifts down when their age at immigration exceeds 35, and that those who immigrated between 45 and 64 years earn substantially less than those who immigrated before age 5 (the omitted group). Quantitatively, the negative effect appears be quite substantial for those who arrive at an older age; from column 1 of table 4, in 1996 an average immigrant who arrived between the ages of 45 and 64 received about [(exp (−0.300) − 1) ∗ 100 =] 32 per cent less than an immigrant who arrived between the ages of 0 and 4. This gap appears to have increased dramatically since 1991. Further, the profile is not

---

10 Before 1962 immigration was tightly controlled by country of origin (primarily the United Kingdom, the United States, France, and northwestern European countries). Between 1962 and 1967 these restrictions were removed, and a point system was introduced to limit the entry of principal independent applicants on the basis of skills needed in Canada. This point system exists today in a revised form but has never included country of origin as a category. The point system does not apply to sponsored immigrants and refugees. Green and Green (1995) contains a good summary of Canadian immigration policy in the post-war period, as well as an analysis of its impact on the composition of the inflow of immigrants. They conclude that over time the independent immigrant has become the residual immigrant, and that the initial positive impact of the point system on the skill set of new immigrants has subsequently been swamped by an inflow of immigrants to whom the point system does not apply.
11 Since immigrants are more concentrated in urban areas, and there may be substantial parameter heterogeneity across urban and rural regions, this and all our subsequent models were also fitted to the data for the urban population only. The conclusions are very similar and the results are not reported in this paper.

TABLE 3
The impact of age at immigration – two-stage approach

	1996			1991			1986		
	Without controls (1)	Cdn-born returns (2)	Own returns (3)	Without controls (4)	Cdn-born returns (5)	Own returns (6)	Without controls (7)	Cdn-born returns (8)	Own returns (9)
Age at Immigration									
5–9	0.025 (0.022)	0.035 (0.018)	0.051*** (0.019)	0.035 (0.021)	0.028 (0.021)	0.038 (0.020)	0.027 (0.023)	0.033 (0.022)	0.038 (0.023)
(5–12)	–	–	–	–0.005 (0.021)	0.018 (0.020)	0.030 (0.022)	–0.004 (0.025)	0.030 (0.023)	0.035 (0.025)
10–14									
15–19	–0.047** (0.022)	–0.004 (0.021)	0.032 (0.021)	–0.057*** (0.020)	0.013 (0.020)	0.029 (0.020)	–0.050** (0.022)	0.023 (0.022)	0.035 (0.021)
(13–19)	–0.009 (0.022)	–0.009 (0.020)	–0.040** (0.020)	–0.005 (0.019)	–0.007 (0.018)	0.020 (0.019)	–0.045** (0.020)	–0.032 (0.019)	–0.018 (0.020)
20–24	–0.010 (0.023)	–0.056*** (0.021)	–0.001 (0.022)	0.012 (0.020)	–0.037** (0.019)	–0.004 (0.020)	–0.014 (0.021)	–0.035 (0.020)	–0.020 (0.021)
25–29	–0.019 (0.025)	–0.097*** (0.023)	–0.035*** (0.023)	–0.022 (0.023)	–0.093*** (0.023)	–0.058*** (0.022)	0.008 (0.023)	–0.043 (0.024)	–0.031 (0.024)
30–34	–0.106*** (0.028)	–0.204*** (0.026)	–0.136*** (0.026)	–0.065*** (0.027)	–0.157*** (0.026)	–0.126*** (0.025)	–0.039 (0.027)	–0.113*** (0.027)	–0.103*** (0.027)
35–44	–0.300*** (0.045)	–0.351*** (0.043)	–0.282*** (0.045)	–0.134*** (0.039)	–0.211*** (0.037)	–0.181*** (0.036)	–0.176*** (0.044)	–0.219*** (0.044)	–0.210*** (0.043)
45–64									

(continued overleaf)

Yrs of school	0.057***	−0.006***	0.055***	−0.007***	0.053***	−0.006***
	(0.001)	(0.002)	(0.001)	(0.001)	(0.001)	(0.002)
Visible minority	−0.093***	−0.085***	−0.087***	−0.070***	−0.080***	−0.087***
	(0.021)	(0.024)	(0.019)	(0.022)	(0.026)	(0.013)
Married	0.224***	−0.006***	0.227***	−0.061***	0.234***	−0.032**
	(0.006)	(0.014)	(0.005)	(0.014)	(0.007)	(0.016)
Urban	0.106***	−0.064***	0.020***	−0.035***	0.105***	−0.042***
	(0.005)	(0.013)	(0.004)	(0.012)	(0.005)	(0.014)
Bilingual	0.027	0.065	−0.064	0.067	0.032	−0.040
	(0.046)	(0.216)	(0.050)	(0.103)	(0.028)	(0.078)
English	0.066***	0.053***	0.066***	−0.017	0.073***	−0.013
	(0.012)	(0.016)	(0.010)	(0.014)	(0.013)	(0.017)
French	0.087***	0.007	0.078***	−0.012	0.084***	−0.086**
	(0.015)	(0.031)	(0.012)	(0.027)	(0.015)	(0.035)
Immig.	0.001	0.128***	0.044***	0.136***	0.030**	0.098***
	(0.021)	(0.040)	(0.017)	(0.032)	(0.017)	(0.038)
	0.087***				0.070***	
	(0.023)		0.093***		(0.018)	
			(0.017)			

NOTES

Standard errors are in parentheses; ** statistically significant at 5 per cent level; *** statistically significant at 1 per cent level. The dependent variable is the individual-specific deviation from the Canadian born age-earnings profile; first-stage standard errors are heteroscedasticity consistent, second-stage are bootstrapped; see the discussion in the text. Also included in the regressions are the immigration cohort dummy variables associated with the coefficients presented in appendix table A1, 7 indicators for hours worked, an indicator for 40–48 weeks worked in the year, and five regional indicators. Sample sizes are as in table 1. Age at immigration in parentheses is for the 1996 census when the grouping does not correspond to that in 1986 and 1991.

TABLE 4
The impact of age at immigration – one-stage approach

	1996			1991			1986		
	Without controls (1)	Cdn-born returns (2)	Own returns (3)	Without controls (4)	Cdn-born returns (5)	Own returns (6)	Without controls (7)	Cdn-born returns (8)	Own returns (9)
Age at Immigration									
5–9	0.023	0.038**	0.049***	0.036	0.032	0.039**	0.026	0.033	0.038
	(0.020)	(0.019)	(0.019)	(0.021)	(0.020)	(0.020)	(0.023)	(0.022)	(0.022)
(5–12)	–	–	–	–0.004	0.022	0.031	–0.003	0.033	0.037
10–14				(0.022)	(0.021)	(0.021)	(0.026)	(0.024)	(0.024)
15–19	–0.054***	0.004	0.027	–0.057***	0.019	0.030	–0.048**	0.032	0.038
	(0.022)	(0.021)	(0.021)	(0.021)	(0.020)	(0.020)	(0.023)	(0.022)	(0.022)
(13–19)	–0.018	–0.002	–0.034	–0.008	–0.002	0.018	–0.043**	–0.026	–0.015
20–24	(0.022)	(0.020)	(0.021)	(0.019)	(0.018)	(0.018)	(0.020)	(0.019)	(0.020)
25–29	–0.020	–0.051**	–0.006	0.008	–0.032	–0.006	–0.015	–0.032	–0.020
	(0.023)	(0.022)	(0.022)	(0.020)	(0.019)	(0.020)	(0.021)	(0.020)	(0.021)
30–34	–0.032	–0.095***	–0.044	–0.026	–0.089***	–0.060***	0.007	–0.041	–0.031
	(0.025)	(0.024)	(0.024)	(0.023)	(0.022)	(0.022)	(0.024)	(0.023)	(0.024)
35–44	–0.121***	–0.203***	–0.146***	–0.072***	–0.157***	–0.129***	–0.037	–0.110***	–0.100***
	(0.028)	(0.026)	(0.027)	(0.026)	(0.024)	(0.025)	(0.029)	(0.027)	(0.028)
45–64	–0.326***	–0.357***	–0.299***	–0.147***	–0.215***	–0.189***	–0.181***	–0.223***	–0.216***
	(0.046)	(0.044)	(0.044)	(0.039)	(0.037)	(0.038)	(0.046)	(0.042)	(0.043)

(continued overleaf)

Yrs of school	0.056***	−0.006***		0.054***	−0.007***	0.051***	−0.006***
	(0.001)	(0.002)		(0.001)	(0.001)	(0.001)	(0.002)
Visible minority	−0.169***	−0.084***		−0.149***	−0.070***	−0.157***	−0.086***
	(0.010)	(0.024)		(0.009)	(0.021)	(0.012)	(0.030)
Married	0.206***	−0.104***		0.217***	−0.060***	0.229***	−0.033**
	(0.006)	(0.014)		(0.005)	(0.013)	(0.006)	(0.016)
Urban	0.099***	−0.064***		0.117***	−0.036***	0.100***	−0.043***
	(0.004)	(0.013)		(0.004)	(0.012)	(0.005)	(0.013)
Bilingual	0.053	0.064		0.053	0.063	0.030	−0.040
	(0.044)	(0.202)		(0.046)	(0.097)	(0.025)	(0.077)
English	0.096***	0.052***		0.072***	0.017	0.072***	0.014
	(0.008)	(0.016)		(0.007)	(0.014)	(0.008)	(0.017)
French	0.110***	0.005		0.093***	0.011	0.087***	−0.085**
	(0.011)	(0.033)		(0.009)	(0.028)	(0.011)	(0.039)
Immig	0.012	0.128***		0.043***	0.135***	0.027	0.095***
	(0.021)	(0.039)		(0.017)	(0.032)	(0.017)	(0.038)
	0.083***	0.089***			0.067***		
	(0.021)	(0.017)			(0.018)		
N	144908			158594		96380	

NOTES

Heteroscedasticity-consistent standard errors are in parentheses; ** statistically significant at 5 per cent level; *** statistically significant at 1 per cent level. The dependent variable is the (ln) earnings in the year; see the discussion in the text. Also included in the regressions are nine immigration cohort indicators, seven indicators for hours worked in the survey week, an indicator for 40–48 weeks worked in the year, and five regional indicators. Age at immigration in parentheses is for the 1996 census when the grouping does not correspond to that in 1986 and 1991.

1082   J. Schaafsma and A. Sweetman

monotonic. Across all three census years, those who immigrated in their late teens (13 to 19 in 1996; 15 to 19 in 1986 and 1991) have consistently lower earnings than both those who immigrated at a slightly younger and those who were slightly older.

Our second set of regressions, in columns 2, 5, and 8 of table 3, add controls for a number of observable differences between Canadian born and immigrants that may account for differences in age-adjusted earnings across the two groups and within each group. The dependent variable is now the difference between each immigrant's observed earnings and that predicted with an expanded earnings function for Canadian born that includes all the variables unrelated to immigration. These variables capture the effect on earnings of key socio-economic characteristics that may be correlated with age at immigration and/or immigration cohort. The returns to these variables for immigrants are for now constrained to be the same as those for the Canadian born, as estimated in the first-stage regressions, and the Canadian-born return to these characteristics from the first stage are presented in the lower part of each column.

Adding the additional control variables has two distinct impacts on the coefficients for the age-at-immigration dummy variables. First, in contrast to the previous regressions, starting at age 5, relative earnings now decline close to monotonically as age at immigration rises. In particular, the sizable, statistically significant negative coefficient in the base case for those who immigrated at the ages of 15 to 19 (13 to 19 for 1996) is now close to zero and is not statistically significant. Second, for those older than 24 years at the time of immigration, it results in lower earnings relative to Canadian born than indicated in the base case. This suggests that the earnings of immigrants who migrate as adults are not commensurate with their human capital as valued by the Canadian born regression coefficients. Explanations for both of these effects are pursued below.

Next, we allow the returns to observed characteristics, other than age, to be different for the Canadian born and immigrants by adding these variables to both the Canadian born (first-stage) and immigrant (second-stage) regression equations. The dependent variable remains the difference between the immigrants' observed (ln) earnings and the predicted (ln) earnings if the immigrant had been Canadian born. The results are shown in columns 3, 6, and 9 of table 3 for the 1996, 1991, and 1986 census years, respectively. Note that the estimated coefficients for the control variables have the interpretation of deviations from the Canadian-born coefficients, and the latter are identical to the Canadian-born estimates in the lower part of columns 2, 5, and 8. Allowing for heterogeneity across immigrants and Canadian born in the return to observable characteristics, other than age, has only a small impact on the estimated effect of age at immigration on earnings. In particular, the noticeable deterioration from 1986 and/or 1991 to 1996 in the relative earnings of those who were more than 24 years old at the time they immigrated persists, although the profile is slightly less steep.[12]

---

12 The substantial increase from 1991 to 1996 in the earnings deficit for immigrants may be partly due to the sharp recession of the early 1990s, when recent immigrants probably had relatively more difficulty in finding employment. We are indebted to an anonymous referee for this point.

Looking at the differences in the other observed characteristics, we see that the parameter estimates indicate that the return to a year of schooling is 0.6 or 0.7 of a percentage point less for immigrants than for the Canadian born. The reduction in earnings as a result of belonging to a visible minority is about 9 percentage points greater for immigrants than for the Canadian born, and the return to living in an urban area is about 4 to 6 percentage points less for immigrants. The return to being married is less for immigrants than for the Canadian born. Having English as mother tongue yielded the same return for the Canadian born and immigrants in 1986 and 1991, but a 5 percentage point higher return for immigrants in 1996, relative to the omitted category of having neither English nor French as mother tongue. The return to French as mother tongue is 12 percentage points lower for immigrants than for the Canadian born in 1986, but this negative differential disappeared in 1991 and 1996. In each of the three census years there is no statistically significant difference across Canadian born and immigrants in the return to having both English and French as mother tongues.

To allow comparability with previous work, in table 4 we estimate the coefficients using an approach that is comparable to Borjas's (1995) paper, but we estimate each cross-section independently, which can be interpreted as fully interacting the census year indicator with the regressors. There are substantive changes neither in the regression coefficients nor in their standard errors relative to table 3. One interpretation is that the two groups' 'true' age-earnings profiles, conditional on the other regressors, are sufficiently similar that the two methods produce the same substantive results. Further, the Canadian born sample is much larger than the immigrant one, so that it dominates the combined profile.

4. Sources of the age-at-immigration effect on earnings

4.1. Educational attainment

The explanation for the non-monotonic age-at-immigration earnings profile appears to be that the formal schooling of those who immigrated in their late teens ended prematurely. To explore the importance of the education variable in isolation, we performed an analysis where we introduced only schooling in addition to the age-at-immigration and cohort variables in regressions for each census year like those in columns 2 and 3 of table 3, and the negative deviation was similarly eliminated. Thus, in the absence of controls for education, immigrants arriving in their late teens are observed to earn lower incomes than expected, but when we control for years of schooling, the earnings of this cohort conform to the expected, monotonic or smooth, pattern. The education deficit explanation is explored further in tables 5 and 6.

The upper panel of table 5 presents the unadjusted years of schooling and shows that those who immigrated between the ages of 15 and 19 (or 13 and 19 for 1996) have fewer years of schooling than those who immigrated at somewhat younger and older ages. To formalize this and allow for limited confounding effects, the lower panel presents regression coefficients that explore the same issue. These regres-

TABLE 5
Average number of years of schooling by age-at-immigration: 1986, 1991 and 1996 Census data

Age at immigration	1996	1991	1986
Panel A: Unadjusted means			
0–4	14.31	13.89	13.50
5–9 (5–12)	14.00	13.95	13.40
10–14	–	13.33	12.92
15–19 (13–19)	**12.92**	**12.22**	**12.03**
20–24	13.45	13.11	12.65
25–29	14.17	13.83	12.96
30–34	14.29	13.97	13.27
35–44	14.16	13.81	13.09
45–64	13.03	12.49	12.18
Panel B: Regression results			
5–9 (5–12)	−0.178**	0.069	−0.190
	(0.074)	(0.079)	(0.101)
10–14	–	−0.408***	−0.585***
		(0.086)	(0.114)
15–19(13–19)	**−0.921*** **	**−1.288*** **	**−1.288*** **
	(0.079)	(0.082)	(0.105)
20–24	−0.297***	−0.263***	−0.457***
	(0.080)	(0.075)	(0.093)
25–29	0.476***	0.531***	0.092
	(0.086)	(0.080)	(0.100)
30–34	0.793***	0.807***	0.572***
	(0.095)	(0.093)	(0.120)
35–44	1.026***	1.047***	0.868***
	(0.104)	(1.104)	(0.140)
45–64	0.714***	0.687***	0.640***
	(0.179)	(0.179)	(0.234)
Intercept	0.977***	0.696***	0.775***
	(0.084)	(0.072)	(0.080)

NOTES
Age at immigration is in parentheses for the 1996 census when the grouping does not correspond to that in 1986 and 1991. Panel B employs the same methodology as used in table 3, but the second stage includes only year of immigration indicators; the dependent variable is years of school. Bootstrapped standard errors are in parentheses; ** statistically significant at 5 per cent level; *** statistically significant at 1 per cent level. Sample sizes in table 1.

sions use the two-stage approach described in the methodology section (and column 1, 4, and 7 of table 3) without X variables. The intercept indicates that the omitted group (those who immigrated between ages 0 and 4 in 1946–55) had between two-thirds and almost a full year more education than their Canadian-born counterparts. Yet the age-at-immigration coefficients suggest that those who immigrated in their prime working years had even more schooling than their counterparts who

TABLE 6
Educational attainment as a function of age at immigration

	1996					1991				
Age at immigration	High school graduate	Coll. grad. among HS grads	Coll. grad among incomplete HS	University graduate	Univ. grad. among HS grads	High school graduate	Coll. grad. among HS grads.	Coll. grad. among incomplete HS	University graduate	Univ. grad. among HS grads
Panel A: Unadjusted means										
0–4	0.767	0.407	0.355	0.266	0.346	0.732	0.372	0.285	0.240	0.327
5–9 (5–12)	0.717	0.369	0.364	0.256	0.358	0.718	0.367	0.324	0.257	0.358
10–14	—	—	—	—	—	0.640	0.373	0.285	0.216	0.338
15–19(13–19)	**0.557**	**0.380**	**0.313**	**0.174**	**0.314**	**0.487**	**0.384**	**0.268**	**0.136**	**0.279**
20–24	0.618	0.426	0.331	0.209	0.338	0.567	0.429	0.328	0.176	0.311
25–29	0.678	0.372	0.315	0.303	0.447	0.637	0.388	0.324	0.268	0.421
30–34	0.696	0.359	0.345	0.316	0.454	0.648	0.357	0.315	0.275	0.425
35–44	0.697	0.349	0.289	0.318	0.456	0.638	0.362	0.273	0.272	0.427
45–64	0.511	0.277	0.151	0.234	0.458	0.519	0.280	0.178	0.202	0.390
Panel B: Regression results (linear probability models)										
5–9 (5–12)	−0.036***	−0.031***	0.056**	−0.018	−0.006	−0.010	−0.009	0.030	0.017	0.029
	(0.011)	(0.014)	(0.023)	(0.011)	(0.014)	(0.013)	(0.017)	(0.026)	(0.013)	(0.016)
10–14	—	—	—	—	—	−0.072***	−0.008	−0.011	−0.017	0.012
						(0.013)	(0.017)	(0.024)	(0.012)	(0.017)
15–19(13–19)	−0.175***	−0.022	0.003	−0.094***	−0.052***	−0.196***	−0.005	−0.029	−0.087***	−0.046***
	(0.011)	(0.015)	(0.021)	(0.010)	(0.014)	(0.013)	(0.017)	(0.021)	(0.011)	(0.016)
20–24	−0.108***	0.018	0.023	−0.060***	−0.034	−0.100***	0.036**	0.033	−0.043***	−0.022
	(0.010)	(0.014)	(0.020)	(0.010)	(0.013)	(0.011)	(0.015)	(0.021)	(0.010)	(0.014)
25–29	−0.047***	−0.040***	0.003	0.034***	0.075***	−0.027**	−0.008	0.024	0.048***	0.087***
	(0.010)	(0.014)	(0.021)	(0.011)	(0.013)	(0.011)	(0.014)	(0.021)	(0.011)	(0.014)
30–34	−0.019	−0.059***	0.027	0.048***	0.078***	−0.006	−0.048***	0.008	0.056***	0.088***
	(0.011)	(0.015)	(0.023)	(0.012)	(0.015)	(0.012)	(0.016)	(0.023)	(0.012)	(0.016)
35–44	−0.005	−0.075***	−0.038	0.050***	0.072***	0.019	−0.046***	−0.034	0.067***	0.093***
	(0.012)	(0.015)	(0.023)	(0.012)	(0.015)	(0.013)	(0.017)	(0.024)	(0.013)	(0.017)
45–64	−0.087***	−0.161***	−0.164***	0.005	0.068	−0.009	−0.141***	−0.111***	0.044***	0.081***
	(0.029)	(0.037)	(0.035)	(0.025)	(0.041)	(0.021)	(0.026)	(0.028)	(0.018)	(0.028)
N	29068	19284	9784	29068	19284	30737	18951	11786	30737	18951
R^2	0.04	0.01	0.01	0.02	0.02	0.06	0.01	0.01	0.02	0.02

NOTES

Heteroscedasticity-consistent standard errors are in parentheses; ** statistically significant at 5 per cent level; *** statistically significant at 1 per cent level. Regressions also contain a quartic polynomial in age. The sample is restricted to those age 25–64 in the survey year. The dependent variables are indicators for having completed the indicated level of education.

1086   J. Schaafsma and A. Sweetman

arrived at a younger age. Those who arrived in their late teen years, and to a lesser extent those who arrived in their early 20s, however, have substantial education deficits relative to those around them.

In table 6 the selected sample is further restricted to immigrants older than age 25, to focus more on completed education, and we try to understand the process by which this deficit occurs. Only data for 1991 and 1996 are presented, since the 1986 census has a slightly different set of education questions, but our informal analysis suggests very similar results. In the top panel the unadjusted proportion of males in each age-at-immigration group with various educational credentials is presented. The bottom panel presents regression coefficients from linear probability models using the immigrant subsample with controls for age at immigration and a quartic in age.[13]

Columns 1 and 6 present the fraction that had graduated from high school in the 1991 and 1996 samples. A substantial dip is obvious for those who immigrated in their late teens, which is the group that also has the earnings deficit. Interestingly, immigrants who arrived as adults, especially over age 45, report lower levels of high school completion than those who arrived as young children. Columns 2 and 7 show the proportion who graduate from college among those with a high school degree, and columns 3 and 8 present college graduation rates for those without a high school degree.[14] A substantial fraction of both immigrant high school completers and non-completers obtain some type of college degree, but, perhaps surprisingly, in both cases and for both census years no obvious dip exists for the group in question. Conditional on high school graduation, college graduation by immigrants from the age-at-immigration group in question does not appear to deviate from other age-at-immigration groups.

University graduation is explored in columns 4 and 5 and 9 and 10. Columns 4 and 9 document the incidence of obtaining a bachelor's degree for the entire sample of immigrants. In both censuses a dip is obvious for the age-at-immigration group that arrived in the late teens. In contrast to the college graduates, however, when (in columns 5 and 10) the sample is restricted to high school graduates, the probability of completing university is less for the group of interest than for those who arrived older or younger ages. Even among high school graduates, transitions to university appear to be less common for those who immigrated in their late teens.

4.2. Education and labour market experience split into foreign and Canadian components

We next turn to the reasons for the decline in earnings with increasing age at immigration. Our analysis thus far has established that age at immigration matters for subsequent earnings, even after years since migration and cohort fixed effects, human capital and labour market activity variables, and differences across Canadian born

---

13 We use linear probability models, given the sample size and our restricted set of variables; see Moffitt (1999) for a discussion of the rationale for using the linear probability model.
14 There is a wide variety of college programs in Canada, some of which do not require a high school diploma. We cannot distinguish between types in the census data.

and immigrants in the returns to these latter variables are controlled for. In 1996, 1991, and 1986 the annual earnings of someone who immigrated between the ages of 44 and 65 were [exp(b) ∗ 100 per cent =] 75, 83, and 81 per cent, respectively (columns 3, 6, and 9, table 3), of the annual earnings of an otherwise observationally equivalent immigrant who immigrated before age 5. Earlier we suggested three possible reasons: schooling received in the source country may yield a lower return than schooling obtained in Canada, pre-immigration labour market experience may yield a lower return than Canadian labour market experience, and the younger the age at immigration the more easily the person acculturates. In this section, the results for which are presented in table 7, we examine the relative importance of the first two factors by estimating earnings functions that allow for different returns to foreign and Canadian education and experience. These regressions are not directly comparable with those in tables 3 and 4, but they explore a closely related issue. Rather than seeing age at immigration as being a variable of direct interest, they deal with what immediately follows: What difference does it make that immigrants who arrive at different ages obtain different portions of their human capital (schooling and/or job experience) in Canada? Chiswick and Miller (1985) and Kossoudji (1989) used this technique on Australian and U.S. data, respectively.

The years of labour market experience are partitioned into three: those acquired in a foreign country, in Canada, and, because of Statistics Canada's groupings, in an 'unknown' location. Years of schooling are similarly split into Canadian, foreign, and unknown education.[15] Since we know only total years of schooling, partitionings are predicated on the commonly used assumptions that there are no interruptions in school attendance, and that experience is the difference between age and years of schooling plus 5. Since not all immigrants arrive as adults, years of Canadian labour market experience is not equivalent to years since arrival, and perfect multicollinearity, therefore, does not exist when immigrant cohort dummies and Canadian labour market experience enter a model fitted to a single cross-section of census data. Thus the identification issues are straightforward, since age at immigration does not enter the regressions, and we do not employ the earlier two-stage identification strategy. The regression results are shown in columns 3, 6, and 9 of table 7 for 1996, 1991, and 1986, respectively. For comparison purposes, the regression results for the Canadian-born earnings function are shown in columns 1, 4, and 7, and the regression results for immigrant earnings without splitting experience and education are shown in columns 2, 5, and 8.

---

15 The category 'unknown education' exists because age at immigration is not known exactly, but known only by age intervals. Thus, minimally, the amount of post-immigration schooling is years of schooling plus five minus the upper limit of the age-at-immigration category if this sum is positive, and zero otherwise. At most, the amount of post-immigration schooling is years of schooling plus five minus the lower limit of the age-at-immigration category if this sum is positive, and zero otherwise. The lower estimate of post-immigration schooling is used for Canadian education. The years of foreign education is the years of schooling minus the upper estimate of post-immigration schooling. The years of schooling in the 'unknown' category is the positive difference between total years of schooling and the sum of our estimates of Canadian and foreign years of schooling. The treatment of experience is essentially identical.

TABLE 7
Controlling for where education and experience were obtained

	1996			1991			1986		
	Cdn born (1)	Immigrants (2)	(3)	Cdn born (4)	Immigrants (5)	(6)	Cdn born (7)	Immigrants (8)	(9)
Total experience	0.061*** (0.001)	0.036*** (0.002)		0.060*** (0.001)	0.040*** (0.002)		0.062*** (0.001)	0.043*** (0.002)	
Total exp^2/10	−0.009*** (0.000)	−0.006*** (0.000)		−0.009*** (0.000)	−0.006*** (0.000)		−0.010*** (0.000)	−0.007*** (0.000)	
Canadian experience			0.044*** (0.003)			0.046*** (0.003)			0.051*** (0.003)
Canadian exp.^{2}/10			−0.008*** (0.001)			−0.009*** (0.001)			−0.011*** (0.001)
Foreign experience			0.009*** (0.003)			0.008*** (0.002)			0.009*** (0.003)
Foreign exp.^{2}/10			0.001 (0.001)			−0.001 (0.001)			−0.002** (0.001)
Unknown experience			0.073*** (0.011)			0.058*** (0.012)			0.030** (0.014)
Unknown exp.^{2}/10			−0.061*** (0.010)			−0.050*** (0.010)			−0.023 (0.012)
Total years of school	0.077*** (0.001)	0.058*** (0.002)		0.076*** (0.001)	0.054*** (0.001)		0.073*** (0.001)	0.052*** (0.002)	

(continued overleaf)

Years school Canadian			0.070***		0.063***	
			(0.003)		(0.003)	
Years school foreign			0.063***		0.059***	0.055***
			(0.002)		(0.002)	(0.003)
						0.057***
						(0.002)
Years school unknown			0.079***		0.084***	0.071***
			(0.004)		(0.006)	(0.007)
Married	0.254***	0.170***	0.186***	0.267***	0.218***	0.239***	0.285***	0.261***	0.284***
	(0.006)	(0.013)	(0.013)	(0.005)	(0.012)	(0.012)	(0.007)	(0.015)	(0.015)
Visible minority	−0.086***	−0.173***	−0.174***	−0.081***	−0.151***	−0.159***	−0.087***	−0.157***	−0.160***
	(0.021)	(0.012)	(0.012)	(0.019)	(0.011)	(0.011)	(0.027)	(0.014)	(0.014)
Urban	0.114***	0.048***	0.047***	0.128***	0.089***	0.084***	0.111***	0.070***	0.062***
	(0.005)	(0.013)	(0.013)	(0.004)	(0.012)	(0.012)	(0.005)	(0.013)	(0.013)
English	0.053***	0.106***	0.114***	0.051***	0.063***	0.070***	0.059***	0.066***	0.075***
	(0.012)	(0.011)	(0.011)	(0.011)	(0.010)	(0.010)	(0.013)	(0.011)	(0.011)
French	0.082***	0.095***	0.096***	0.073***	0.080***	0.086***	0.088***	−0.010	−0.002
	(0.015)	(0.030)	(0.030)	(0.013)	(0.026)	(0.026)	(0.015)	(0.036)	(0.036)
Bilingual	0.019	0.065	0.068	−0.064	−0.050	−0.071	0.028	−0.033	−0.022
	(0.047)	(0.215)	(0.211)	(0.050)	(0.092)	(0.094)	(0.028)	(0.073)	(0.074)
Intercept	8.404***	9.091***	8.852***	8.530***	9.150***	8.955***	8.582***	9.128***	9.013***
	(0.020)	(0.042)	(0.099)	(0.080)	(0.034)	(0.081)	(0.022)	(0.039)	(0.080)
N	114922	29986	29986	126187	32407	32407	76128	20252	20252
R^2	0.27	0.20	0.20	0.28	0.19	0.19	0.28	0.21	0.21

NOTES

Heteroscedasticity-consistent standard errors are in parentheses; ** statistically significant at 5 per cent level; *** statistically significant at 1 per cent level. The dependent variable is natural logarithm of annual earnings. Also included in the regressions are the same variables as used in tables 3 and 4.

Regression results for immigrants are very similar across the three census years. Foreign experience has a negligible impact on earnings, whereas the return to an additional year of Canadian experience is positive, statistically significant, but only about 75 to 80 per cent of the return for the Canadian born. Experience of unknown origin can have a sizable return. The return to pre- and post-immigration schooling are very similar and this specification suggests that it does not matter much where schooling was obtained. To the extent that it does matter, the return to post-immigration schooling is marginally the highest, but this return is only about 80 per cent of the return to schooling for the Canadian born. These results for the returns to foreign and Canadian experience and schooling are consistent with those obtained by Chiswick and Miller (1985), Kossoudji (1989), and Grant (1999). One phenomenon consistently observed in our results is that when education and experience are partitioned by source, each component of education yields a higher return than when experience and education are not split.[16]

Appendix table A2 presents the cohort coefficients from the table 7 immigrant regressions. There is, perhaps not unexpectedly, a substantial change in the slopes of the cross-sectional profiles (recall that they have different intercepts), depending upon whether the regression accounts for where immigrant education and labour market experience are obtained. Although it is beyond the topic of this paper, these results suggest that it may be worthwhile to think about the problems inherent in controlling for years since migration and generating labour market earnings 'assimilation' profiles. To say that assimilation is achieved after, say, fifteen years does not make much sense when the sample contains child immigrants. Canadian education and labour market experience may have much more economic content.

4.3. Stratifying on age at immigration
An alternative empirical strategy for analysing why age at immigration affects subsequent earnings allows for parameter heterogeneity between Canadian born and immigrants and among immigrants who arrived at different ages. As seen in equation (3), the approach consists of pooling immigrant and Canadian-born data and fitting an earnings function with separate coefficients for Canadian born and each of three age-at-immigration groups: less than 10 years old (1986/91) or less than 13 years old (1996), 20 to 29 years old, and 35 to 64 years old. The remaining regressions elements are defined as in equations (1) and (2), and ImmCohort is a vector of immigrant cohort indicator variables with the same groupings as seen in the appendix tables. Note that the cohort variables are common across the age-at-immigration

---

16 We also estimate a version of the model where all years of education are assigned as Canadian, foreign, or unknown based upon where we estimate that the education was *completed*. The results are substantially similar. Further, we estimated models in which schooling and experience were split in turn. Both sets of variables have effects that are in the same direction as those presented, but the experience effect is larger when schooling is not split.

groups and that the X vector does not contain an intercept.[17] The pooled data exclude immigrants who arrived at ages not used in this analysis.

$$\ln w = b_0 + Xb^{cb} + (X * \text{ImmAge0to10/13})b^{I0\text{to}10/13}$$

$$+ (X * \text{ImmAge20to29})b^{I20\text{to}29} + (X * \text{ImmAge35to64})b^{I35\text{to}64}$$

$$\text{ImmCohort} * b_{\text{ImmCohort}} + \epsilon. \qquad (3)$$

Those who arrived before age 10 (13) clearly received most or all of their schooling and all of their labour market experience in Canada. This group will also be the most acculturated upon entry into the labour force and will likely continue to acculturate comparatively easily. Those who arrived after age 34 likely received all of their formal schooling abroad and upon landing will have a substantial amount of experience in a foreign labour market. They will have looked for their first job in Canada as the process of acculturation began and will have been the most challenged by this process. Those who arrived as 20–29-year-olds likely received all, or most, of their schooling abroad, but will have had only a minimal amount of foreign labour market experience. This group likely also looked for their first job as the process of acculturation began, but will probably have been less challenged by this process than the older immigrants. A comparison of the returns to schooling and experience across these three groups therefore provides very useful additional information about why age at immigration affects earnings. By pooling Canadian-born and immigrant data, the returns earned by immigrants in the three age-at-migration groups can be readily compared with the returns earned by the Canadian born

The parameter estimates in table 8 for each immigrant group can be interpreted as deviations from the returns earned by the Canadian born. The basic patterns exhibit remarkable stability across the three census years. The results for the labour market experience variables conform to expectations, but differ qualitatively from those in table 7. For immigrants who arrived in the youngest age group the return to experience is by far the highest and is higher than for even the Canadian born (statistically significantly so in 1986 and 1991). This contrasts with the results in table 7, where even the return to Canadian experience was lower for immigrants than the Canadian born. The findings are consistent with the hypothesis that immi-

---

17 Since potential experience and years of schooling, which together implicitly define age, are included in the regression, if the age-at-immigration groupings were reduced to single years, then giving each its own intercept would cause an identification problem. In our regressions the intercepts are identified because of larger groupings (e.g., 20–29), that is, because of the functional form restrictions. Our use of a single intercept is akin to Borjas's (1995) restriction that the year effects are common to immigrants and Canadian born. We have not had to make this restriction in the regressions in tables 3 and 4, since we are not estimating assimilation profiles. An alternative approach to equation (3) is to include intercepts for each age-at-immigration grouping (e.g., 20–29) and drop the immigrant cohort variables. We did this exercise and found only very small differences in the estimated regression coefficients. Borjas (1999, sect. 4.1) discusses identification in this context and points out the importance of recalling that alternative specifications lead to different estimates of the underlying parameters and require different interpretations.

TABLE 8
Interactions with age at immigration: pooled Cdn-born and immigrant data

	1996				1991				1986			
		Immigrants (age at immigration)				Immigrants (age at immigration)				Immigrants (age at immigration)		
	Cdn born	<13	20–29	35–64	Cdn born	<10	20–29	35–64	Cdn born	<10	20–29	35–64
Exp.	0.061***	0.000	−0.048***	−0.068***	0.060***	0.009***	−0.041***	−0.061***	0.062***	0.017***	−0.047***	−0.099***
	(0.001)	(0.004)	(0.004)	(0.012)	(0.001)	(0.004)	(0.004)	(0.009)	(0.001)	(0.005)	(0.004)	(0.011)
Exp²/10	−0.009***	0.001	0.008***	0.009***	−0.009***	−0.001	0.007***	0.008***	−0.010***	−0.002	0.008***	0.014***
	(0.000)	(0.001)	(0.001)	(0.002)	(0.000)	(0.001)	(0.001)	(0.001)	(0.000)	(0.001)	(0.001)	(0.002)
Years of school	0.078***	0.011***	−0.023***	−0.040***	0.076***	0.009	−0.026***	−0.035***	0.072***	0.005	−0.022***	−0.030***
	(0.001)	(0.004)	(0.003)	(0.005)	(0.001)	(0.004)	(0.002)	(0.005)	(0.001)	(0.005)	(0.003)	(0.005)
Married	0.254***	−0.034	−0.129***	−0.140***	0.267***	−0.023	−0.125***	−0.129***	0.287***	−0.036	−0.149***	−0.133***
	(0.006)	(0.021)	(0.020)	(0.047)	(0.005)	(0.025)	(0.018)	(0.041)	(0.007)	(0.026)	(0.022)	(0.046)
Visible minority	−0.087***	0.036	−0.063***	−0.192***	−0.079***	0.060	−0.070***	−0.125***	−0.085***	−0.004	−0.083**	−0.105***
	(0.021)	(0.033)	(0.021)	(0.038)	(0.019)	(0.037)	(0.025)	(0.035)	(0.027)	(0.059)	(0.033)	(0.045)
Urban	0.114***	−0.020	−0.100***	−0.017	0.128***	−0.027	−0.053**	0.010	0.112***	−0.001	−0.079***	−0.094***
	(0.005)	(0.022)	(0.022)	(0.041)	(0.004)	(0.024)	(0.017)	(0.042)	(0.005)	(0.026)	(0.019)	(0.045)
English	0.050***	−0.002	0.093***	0.218***	0.055***	−0.025	0.047***	0.054	0.068***	−0.021	0.011	0.087***
	(0.011)	(0.020)	(0.020)	(0.037)	(0.010)	(0.022)	(0.017)	(0.034)	(0.012)	(0.026)	(0.020)	(0.037)
French	0.079***	−0.087	0.060	0.062	0.076***	−0.014	0.044	0.083	0.096***	−0.043	−0.094	−0.116
	(0.014)	(0.068)	(0.044)	(0.107)	(0.012)	(0.057)	(0.038)	(0.081)	(0.015)	(0.064)	(0.058)	(0.127)
Bilingual	0.016	−0.241	0.176	0.360***	−0.060	−0.013	0.024	0.093	0.036	−0.005	0.039	0.054
	(0.047)	(0.499)	(0.182)	(0.085)	(0.050)	(0.126)	(0.113)	(0.342)	(0.028)	(0.126)	(0.101)	(0.198)
Intercept	10.271***				10.385***				10.373***			
	(0.013)				(0.012)				(0.014)			

NOTES
Heteroscedasticity-consistent standard errors are in parentheses; ** statistically significant at 5 per cent level; *** statistically significant at 1 per cent level. The dependent variable is natural logarithm of annual earnings. Also included in the regressions are a common set of immigrant cohort indicators, nine immigration cohort indicators, seven indicators for hours worked in the survey week, an indicator for 40–48 weeks worked in the year, and five regional indicators; and the same interacted with the age at immigration indicators. Sample sizes in table 1. Immigrant coefficients can be interpreted as deviations from those of Canadian born.

grant families are highly motivated to rebuild their lives,[18] and that this produces superior performance when acculturation barriers are minimal. The return to experience for immigrants who arrived in the middle age group is positive, but only about two-thirds of the return to experience of the group arriving at the younger age, and is lower than the Canadian born. This is partly because the average member of this group will have some foreign labour market experience, which we earlier showed yields a negligible return. It may also be due to greater difficulty with acculturation and thus not acquiring Canadian-specific human capital on the job as rapidly as the younger age group. For those who arrived as 35–64-year-olds the return to labour market experience is non-existent (in 1991, for example, both the linear and quadratic terms are almost equal and opposite to the Canadian-born returns from which they are deviations). On average, labour market experience obtained outside Canada has no economic return in Canada.

The results for the years-of-schooling variable show that the return to schooling for immigrants in the youngest age-at-arrival category (i.e., the return to post-immigration schooling) is about the same as the return earned by the Canadian born. However, the return to pre-immigration schooling (i.e., the return earned by those who immigrated after age 19) is about two-thirds of the return to post-immigration schooling. This is a much larger difference in returns than shown in columns 3, 6, and 9 of table 7. The estimated difference between the returns to pre- and post-immigration education shown in table 8 is consistent with the difference between the returns to education for immigrants and Canadian born shown in columns 1 and 2, 4 and 5, and 7 and 8 of table 7. The latter differences are somewhat smaller than those shown in table 8, but this is what one would expect, since the estimated return to education for immigrants shown in columns 2, 5, and 8 of table 7 includes the return earned by immigrants educated in Canada. Overall, this stratified model suggests that important parameter heterogeneity exists that is not visible in the models in table 7.

The observed decline in the return to education as age at immigration rises conceivably could be the result of an improvement in the quality of education over time. Immigrants who are currently in the labour force and arrived at a young age will be on average younger and thus will have received their education more recently than immigrants who are currently in the labour force and arrived at a much older age. If the quality of education has been improving over time, and the market rewards this improvement, immigrants who arrived at a younger age should on average be earning a higher return to years of schooling. We checked whether this explanation is driving our return to schooling results by re-estimating the earnings function for the Canadian born with the additional specification that the return to schooling can vary by age. The model was fitted to data for Canadian born more than 19 years old and the return to education was allowed to be different for 20–39-year-olds, 40–49-year-olds, and 50–64-year-olds. The results are consistent across the three census years and indicate that the return to schooling is slightly higher, not lower, the longer the gap since the education was obtained.

---

18 Borjas (1987) examines self-selection and the earnings of immigrants in the wider context of economic and political conditions in the source and host countries.

The results for the visible minority indicator variables in table 8 show an extremely interesting pattern and provide strong evidence of the effect of acculturation on earnings. In each of the three census years, members of a visible minority who immigrated before age 10 (13 in 1996) have essentially the same reduction in their earnings as members of Canadian-born visible minorities: about 7 or 8 per cent. Visible minority immigrants who arrived as 20–29-year-olds, or as 35–64-year-olds, however, experience statistically significant, and large, additional reductions in earnings relative to visible minority Canadian born, and these reductions increase with increasing age at migration. Less acculturation may lead to discrimination, to a lower than normal rate of return to human capital, or to both. Note also that while the point estimates of the earnings deficit for Canadian-born visible minorities remained roughly constant from 1986 to 1996, it increased for visible minority immigrants who arrived as adults. The overall pattern indicates that while on average Canadian-born visible minorities have lower earnings relative to other Canadian-born individuals, the deficit is smaller than that for visible minorities in the population as a whole, since the latter includes the very large deficits of immigrant visible minorities that arrive late in life.[19]

Although bumpy, the results for the mother tongue variables in table 8 show that having English as one's mother tongue boosts the post-immigration earnings profile substantially for those who immigrated after age 35, somewhat for those who immigrated as 20–29-year-olds, and not at all for those who arrived before age 10 (13). Since the ability to learn a new language declines with age, and since acculturation in the job market is critically dependent on language skills, this pattern supports our earlier conclusion that ease of acculturation is inversely related to age at immigration and that it is an important factor in determining immigrant earnings. However, no such pattern is discernible for immigrants with French as mother tongue. These regressions include controls for province of residence, so this lack of an effect for French as a mother tongue is conditional on provincial wage effects. We ran separate regressions for those residing in Quebec and those in the rest of the country, but we did not find noteworthy differences relative to table 8.

5. Conclusions

Our analysis is the first detailed study of the effect of age at immigration on earnings based on Canadian data. The results suggest that age at immigration matters. Those who arrive later in life experience, on average, low returns to both foreign labour market experience and foreign education. Further, we present some evidence that age at immigration also matters because the young acculturate more easily. Visible minority immigrants who landed before their teen years do not have an earnings deficit rel-

---

19 The increase across the census years in the earnings differential across the age-at-immigration groups for visible minorities may be partly due to the changes that have occurred in the country of origin for visible minorities that are not completely captured by the cohort indicator variables. For a given census year, visible minority immigrants who arrived at an older age will have arrived more recently, and thus from different countries of origin, than those who arrived at a younger age. We are indebted to an anonymous referee for this point.

ative to observationally equivalent Canadian born. Visible minority immigrants who landed at an older age experience an earnings deficit relative to otherwise equivalent Canadian born, and this deficit grows with age at migration. We also find that the return to English as mother tongue is essentially the same for immigrants who arrived before their teens and the Canadian born, but is higher for immigrants who arrived at an older age. This again suggests that acculturation is an important reason why age at immigration matters for subsequent earnings. There is no statistically significant evidence that this is also true for immigrants whose mother tongue is French.

We also observe that immigrants who arrive in their late teens, near the high school to post-secondary transition, have lower earnings than those who arrive either slightly earlier or later. This deficit disappears, however, when we control for education and other variables. Further examination shows that this age-at-immigration group appears to obtain less education than surrounding groups. It is plausible that entering a new society near this crucial transition induces those involved to obtain less schooling and that this has a life-long earnings impact.

Our results can be used, in conjunction with other criteria, to assess the design of the point system currently used (in 2000) in Canada to determine the eligibility of 'skilled' applicants for immigrant status. In this system, 49 of the 100 points that can be earned are for four key variables in our analysis: age at immigration (10 points), education (16 points), work experience (8 points), and language ability (15 points). It is important to understand how these points align with immigrants' expected labour market outcomes.

For age, the system allocates the maximum number of points to applicants in the 21–44 year age group. This allocation is reduced by 2 points for each year below and above this range. Our results indicate that within the 21–44 year age group economic integration declines appreciably with age at immigration. A more appropriate allocation of points for age would take this into account, possibly by allocating 10 points to 21–24 year old applicants and lowering this amount by 2 points for each successive four-year age cohort, so that no points are assigned for age to applicants older than 44 years, as opposed to 48 years, as is currently the case.

The 16 points for education can be earned in a variety of ways, of which the basics are as follows: 5 points for completing a secondary education that does not lead to a post-secondary education, 10 points for completing a secondary education that can lead to a post-secondary education, 15 points for a first university degree, and 16 points for one or more graduate degrees. Our analysis measures education in terms of years of schooling, and thus it is not suitable to comment in detail here on this point allocation. However, our results in table 7 do indicate that age-at-immigration and education interact in their effect on the economic integration of immigrants. Of course, since education and social programs are subsidized in Canada, issues other than earnings should be examined in order to understand the economic implications of the policy parameters.

A minimum of one year of work experience in the intended occupation is an essential requirement for admission as an immigrant under the point system. A maximum of 8 points can be earned for four or more years of experience. Our results support this modest point allocation for labour market experience. Again, age at immigration is crucial. For immigrants who were more than 29 years old at entry, foreign labour market experience is not a marketable asset that yields a return in Canada (table 7). Immigrants who arrived in their twenties (i.e., few years of foreign labour market experience), however, earn about two-thirds of the Canadian-born return for their foreign labour market experience. While our results are not sufficiently disaggregated to be definitive, they do suggest that it may be worthwhile to explore whether the point system should consider foreign work experience an asset and, particularly, whether the lack of foreign work experience should bar an otherwise well-qualified candidate.

The current point system assigns a maximum of 15 points for being fluent in either of Canada's official languages. Our regression results indicate that, as age at immigration rises, having English as mother tongue greatly assists economic integration. The substantial weight for fluency in English is therefore supported by our results. However, our results did not indicate that fluency in French facilitates the economic integration of immigrants who arrive at an older age.

Revisions to the current point system have recently been proposed by the Ministry of Citizenship and Immigration Canada (2000). The most notable proposed change is the substantial increase in the weight given to foreign labour market experience, from a maximum of 8 points out of a 100 to 25 points out of 100 for four or more years of skilled labour market experience. As noted earlier, our results indicate that foreign labour market experience yields little, or no, return in Canada and thus do not support this increased emphasis. The exception would be if the negligible return to foreign labour market experience is the result of Canadian labour market imperfections, such as credential recognition, that can be corrected.

The proposed point system continues to assign a maximum of 10 points out of 100 to immigrants who are 21–44 years old upon arrival and has the same reductions as before for ages outside this range. Thus, as in the current point system, the proposal assumes that, ceteris paribus, economic integration is the same for immigrants who are 21–44 years old upon arrival. Our results do not support this assumption and, as noted earlier, suggest that points for age at immigration should decline rapidly as age at immigration rises above 30 years.

The proposed increase in the weight for language from 15 points to 20 points is supported by our finding that immigrants do substantially better if they have English as mother tongue.[20] In fact, our results suggest that points for mother tongue should vary with age at immigration, since mother tongue appears to be an especially important determinant of economic integration for those who arrive at an older age.

We believe that the findings here raise questions about the current, and proposed, allocation of points, in particular those for age and past labour market experience. Since we cannot isolate immigrants who were assessed under the points system from those who were not, however, there is a need for further research using administrative data. Additionally, there may be a need for programs to help young immigrants who arrive in their mid to late teen years in making the transition to post-secondary education.

---

20 Of course, it is probably Canadian language skills at landing that matter, but we do not have a measure of that in the census data.

Appendix: Tables A1 and A2

TABLE A1
The impact of age at immigration (from table 3)

Year immigrated	1996 Without controls (1)	1996 Cdn-born returns (2)	1996 Own returns (3)	1991 Without controls (4)	1991 Cdn-born returns (5)	1991 Own returns (6)	1986 Without controls (7)	1986 Cdn-born returns (8)	1986 Own returns (9)
Before 1946	−0.028 (0.155)	−0.047 (0.146)	−0.065 (0.144)	−0.119 (0.071)	−0.109 (0.068)	−0.113 (0.068)	0.007 (0.042)	−0.001 (0.042)	−0.009 (0.042)
1956–60	−0.022 (0.027)	−0.001 (0.025)	−0.007 (0.025)	−0.033 (0.019)	−0.024 (0.018)	−0.021 (0.017)	−0.023 (0.017)	−0.009 (0.016)	−0.004 (0.016)
1961–65	−0.040 (0.028)	0.020 (0.025)	0.011 (0.026)	−0.075*** (0.020)	−0.050** (0.020)	−0.043** (0.020)	−0.075*** (0.020)	−0.035 (0.019)	−0.020 (0.020)
1966–70	−0.042 (0.024)	−0.012 (0.024)	−0.012 (0.023)	−0.040** (0.018)	−0.042** (0.018)	−0.025 (0.018)	−0.058*** (0.017)	−0.054*** (0.018)	−0.026 (0.017)
1971–75	−0.083*** (0.024)	−0.020 (0.025)	0.002 (0.024)	−0.130*** (0.018)	−0.096*** (0.020)	−0.062*** (0.020)	−0.136*** (0.018)	−0.101*** (0.022)	−0.049*** (0.020)
1976–80	−0.181*** (0.026)	−0.074** (0.027)	−0.051** (0.025)	−0.159*** (0.020)	−0.094*** (0.022)	−0.055*** (0.021)	−0.193*** (0.021)	−0.130*** (0.024)	−0.072*** (0.023)
1981–85	−0.213*** (0.027)	−0.089*** (0.029)	−0.068*** (0.028)	−0.223*** (0.023)	−0.135*** (0.023)	−0.095*** (0.022)	−0.374*** (0.028)	−0.307*** (0.031)	−0.251*** (0.028)
1986–90	−0.329*** (0.028)	−0.165*** (0.028)	−0.140*** (0.028)	−0.385*** (0.024)	−0.265*** (0.025)	−0.226*** (0.024)			
1991–95	−0.486*** (0.030)	−0.298*** (0.031)	−0.270*** (0.032)						

NOTES
Bootstrapped standard errors are in parentheses; ** statistically significant at 5 per cent level; *** statistically significant at 1 per cent level. These coefficients complement those presented in table 3, and the notes are the same.

TABLE A2
Controlling for where education and experience were obtained (from table 6)

	1996		1991		1986	
	Immigrants		Immigrants		Immigrants	
Year immigrated	Not split (2)	Split (3)	Not split (5)	Split (6)	Not split (8)	Split (9)
Before 1946	−0.090 (0.143)	0.024 (0.146)	−0.128** (0.065)	0.069 (0.071)	−0.003 (0.041)	0.327*** (0.060)
1956–60	−0.004 (0.024)	−0.059** (0.027)	−0.018 (0.017)	−0.071*** (0.022)	−0.007 (0.016)	−0.047** (0.021)
1961–65	0.010 (0.025)	−0.074** (0.035)	−0.053*** (0.020)	−0.115*** (0.031)	−0.056*** (0.019)	−0.084*** (0.032)
1966–70	−0.033 (0.022)	−0.120*** (0.040)	−0.060*** (0.017)	−0.107*** (0.037)	−0.091*** (0.016)	−0.090** (0.037)
1971–75	−0.040 (0.022)	−0.107** (0.050)	−0.129*** (0.018)	−0.135*** (0.046)	−0.130*** (0.019)	−0.060 (0.048)
1976–80	−0.125*** (0.024)	−0.152*** (0.059)	−0.143*** (0.019)	−0.086 (0.055)	−0.162*** (0.021)	0.007 (0.057)
1981–85	−0.170*** (0.026)	−0.132** (0.068)	−0.192*** (0.021)	−0.043 (0.063)	−0.355*** (0.026)	−0.103 (0.067)
1986–90	−0.269*** (0.024)	−0.119 (0.077)	−0.353*** (0.022)	−0.083 (0.073)		
1991–95	−0.424*** (0.027)	−0.192** (0.085)				

NOTES
Heteroscedasticity-consistent standard errors are in parentheses; ** statistically significant at 5 per cent level; *** statistically significant at 1 per cent level. These coefficients complement those presented in table 7, and the notes are the same.

References

Baker, Michael, and Dwayne Benjamin (1994) 'The performance of immigrants in the Canadian labour market,' *Journal of Labor Economics* 12, 369–405

Bloom, D.E., G. Grenier, and M. Gunderson (1995) 'The changing labour market position of Canadian immigrants,' *Canadian Journal of Economics* 28, 987–1005

Borjas, G.J. (1985) 'Assimilation, change in cohort quality, and the earnings of immigrants,' *Journal of Labor Economics* 3, 463–89

— (1987) 'Self-selection and the earnings of immigrants,' *American Economic Review* 77, 531–53

— (1993) 'Immigration policy, national origin and immigrant skills: a comparison of Canada and the United States,' *Small Differences That Matter: Labor Markets and Income Maintenance in Canada and the United States*, ed. D. Card and R. Freeman (Chicago: University of Chicago Press)

— (1994) 'The economics of immigration,' *Journal of Economic Literature* 32, 1667–717

— (1995) 'Assimilation and changes in cohort quality revisited: what happened to immigrant earnings in the 1980s?' *Journal of Labor Economics* 13, 201–45

— (1999) 'The economic impact of immigration,' in *Handbook of Labor Economics*, 3a, ed. O. Ashenfelter and D. Card (Amsterdam: North-Holland)

Chiswick, B.R. (1978) 'The effect of Americanization on the earnings of foreign-born men,' *Journal of Political Economy* 86, 897–921

Chiswick, B.R., and P.W. Miller (1985) 'Immigrant generation and income in Australia,' *Economic Record* 61, 540–53

Citizenship and Immigration Canada (2000) 'Bill C-31 Immigration and Refugee Protection Act: explanation of the proposed regulations'

Friedberg, R. (1993) 'The labor market assimilation of immigrants in the United States: the role of age at arrival,' mimeo, Brown University

— (2000) 'You can't take it with you? Immigrant assimilation and the portability of human capital,' *Journal of Labor Economics* 18, 221–51

Funkhouser, E., and S. Trejo (1995) 'The labor market skills of recent male immigrants: evidence from the current population survey,' *Industrial and Labor Relations Review* 48, 792–811

Grant, Mary L. (1999) 'Evidence of new immigrant assimilation in Canada,' *Canadian Journal of Economics* 32, 930–55

Green, Alan G., and David E. Green. (1995) 'Canadian immigration policy: the effectiveness of the point system and other instruments,' *Canadian Journal of Economics* 38, 1006–41

Kossoudji, S. (1989) 'Immigrant worker assimilation: is it a labor market phenomenon?' *Journal of Human Resources* 24, 494–527

Kee, Peter. (1995) 'Native-immigrant wage differentials in the Netherlands: discrimination?' *Oxford Economic Papers* 47, 303–17

McDonald, J., and C. Worswick. (1998) 'The earnings of immigrant men in Canada: job tenure, cohort and macroeconomic conditions,' *Industrial and Labor Relations Review* 51, 465–82

Moffitt, Robert A. (1999) 'New developments in econometric methods for labor market analysis,' in *The Handbook of Labor Economics*, 3a, ed. Orley Ashenfelter and David Card (Amsterdam: Elsevier Science)

Murphy, Kevin M., and Finis Welch (1990) 'Empirical age-earnings profiles,' *Journal of Labor Economics* 8, 202–29

Schoeni, Robert F. (1998) 'Labor market assimilation of immigrant women,' *Industrial and Labor Relations Review* 51, 483–504

Smith, James. (1992) 'Hispanics and the American dream: an analysis of Hispanic male labor market wages, 1940–1980,' mimeo, Rand Corporation

Immigrant earnings: Language skills, linguistic concentrations and the business cycle

Barry R. Chiswick[1], Paul W. Miller[2]

[1] University of Illinois at Chicago, Department of Economics (M/C 144), S. Morgan St. 601, 60607-7121 Chicago IL, USA (Fax: +1-312-996-3344; e-mail: brchis@uic.edu)
[2] University of Western Australia, Department of Economics, 35 Stirling Highway, Crawley, Western Australia 6009, Australia (Fax: 61-8-9380-1035; e-mail: pwm@kroner.ecel.uwa.edu.au)

Received: 30 November 1999/Accepted: 6 February 2001

Abstract. This study of the determinants of earnings among adult foreign-born men using the 1990 Census of Population focuses on the effects of the respondent's own English language skills, the effects of living in a linguistic concentration area, and the effects of the stage of the business cycle at entry into the U.S. labor market. The analysis demonstrates the importance of English language fluency among the foreign born from non-English speaking countries. There is also strong evidence for the complementarity between language skills and other forms of human capital. Furthermore, there is strong evidence using selectivity correction techniques for the endogeneity between language and earnings.

JEL classification: J31, J61, J24, J15

Key words: Earnings, immigrants, language, business cycle, ethnic concentrations

---

All correspondence to Barry R. Chiswick. The research for this paper was funded in part by the Bureau of International Labor Affairs (ILAB), U.S. Department of Labor (ILAB Working Paper #31). We appreciate the comments from Shirley Smith, the ILAB Project Officer. This paper has benefited from comments received at the European Science Foundation Conference on Migration and Development, Espinoh, Portugal, April 1998, the Population Association of America Annual Meeting, New York, March 1999, the Canadian Economics Association Annual Meeting, Toronto, May 1999, the Center for Economic Policy Research Conference on Marginal Labour Markets in Metropolitan Areas, Dublin, October 1999, and the Midwest Economics Association Annual Meeting, Chicago, April 2000. Christian Dustmann's comments were especially helpful. It was written, in part, while Chiswick was the John M. Olin Visiting Professor, Center for the Study of the Economy and the State, Graduate School of Business, University of Chicago. *Responsible editor:* Alan Barrett.

1. Introduction

This paper is concerned with the analysis of the earnings of immigrants. In particular, it focuses on several inter-related and unresolved issues using data from the 1990 Census of Population of the United States.

One set of issues relates to the individual's own language skills. To what extent are the earnings of immigrants in the United States influenced by the respondent's proficiency in English?[1] Has there been a change over time in the effect of language proficiency on earnings? Are different forms of human capital complementary to language capital (language proficiency)? That is, is language capital more productive in the labor market among those with more schooling and other forms of human capital? Moreover, does it appear that investments in language capital are greater among those who expect to receive a greater economic return from English-language proficiency? That is, is language proficiency endogenous to the labor market?

A second and inter-related set of issues has to do with the linguistic characteristics of the area in which the respondent lives. Among those who speak a language other than English, does it matter whether they live in an area in which many others speak their origin language (to be referred to as linguistic concentration), as distinct from an area in which few speak this language? While linguistic concentrations have been shown to lower language proficiency (see Chiswick and Miller 1992, 1995, 1998), are they also associated with lower earnings, other things being the same? Controlling for the individual's own characteristics, the cost of "ethnic goods," broadly defined to include social networks, would be lower the greater the extent to which others speak the same origin language. Then, larger linguistic concentrations would be associated with lower reservation wages, and hence lower observed earnings.

Finally, one of the issues discussed in the literature is whether the stage of the business cycle at entry into the labor market affects the earnings of immigrants. It has been shown by Nakamura and Nakamura (1992) and Stewart and Hyclak (1984) that immigrant earnings are lower among those who enter in a period of high unemployment. Unresolved, however, is whether this is a permanent effect, perhaps due to a lower "quality" immigrant cohort in a recession, or whether this is a temporary disadvantage due to the difficulties new immigrants have in finding a high wage job or a good job match during a recession.

Section 2 presents the model of the earnings of immigrants in the labor market. Particular attention is given to the variables that are of primary focus in this study, namely, the individual's own English language proficiency, the linguistic concentration of the area, and the stage of the business cycle at entry into the labor market. This permits a separation of the effects of the immigrant's own language skills from linguistic concentration effects.

Section 3 describes the data from the 1990 Census of Population of the United States used for this study, as well as the estimating equations. The empirical estimation is presented in Section 4. Various specifications of the variable for the respondent's English language fluency are considered, as are the concentration and business cycle effects, among others. A summary and conclusion, with implications for both immigration policy and assimilation (post-migration) policy closes the paper (Sect. 5).

2. Modelling earnings in the immigrant labor market

The study of earnings in the immigrant labor market has in large part been based on the human capital earnings function (Mincer 1974), which includes schooling and labor market experience, expanded to incorporate the immigrant experience (Chiswick 1978). This equation suggests that variations in earnings across individuals (Y_i) can be explained by variations in the amount of schooling (S_i) individuals have acquired and their labor market experience, in total (T_i) and in the destination (YSM_i). Thus:

$$\text{Ln } Y_i = b_0 + b_1 S_i + b_2 T_i + b_3 T_i^2 + b_4 (YSM_i) + b_5 (YSM_i)^2 + e_i, \quad (1)$$

where Ln Y_i is the natural logarithm of the earnings of individual i, schooling (S_i) is a measure of the years of full-time equivalent schooling of the individual, experience (T_i) is the potential length of time the individual has spent in the labor market (in the origin and in the destination), and years since migration (YSM_i) is the number of years in the destination. The experience variables reflect the acquisition of skills through formal and informal training on the job, including merely living in the destination. A quadratic specification is employed as economic theory and prior empirical research have both shown that earnings tend to increase at a decreasing rate with years in the labor market and in the destination (see, for example, Ben-Porath 1967; Mincer 1974; Chiswick 1978). The stochastic error term (e_i) captures the influences of unobserved or unmeasured variables (e.g., motivation, effort, luck) on earnings.

The relationship between earnings and duration of residence is generally held to reflect learning about the institutions of the U.S. labor market, cultural adjustment factors, the development of networks for labor market contacts, and investments in U.S.-specific human capital skills that lead to labor market success (see Chiswick 1978). These effects (investments) are expected to be greatest in the first few years and to diminish with duration in the destination.

Acquisition of skills in the dominant language can be viewed as a form of human capital accumulation. Studies of immigrant language skills in the labor market have tended to treat language skills in the same way as schooling and post-school training. See, for example, McManus et al. (1981); Tainer (1988); Chiswick (1991); Chiswick and Miller (1992, 1995, 1998). Thus, the basic human capital earnings equation can be extended to:

$$\text{Ln } Y_i = b_0 + b_1 S_i + b_2 T_i + b_3 T_i^2 + b_4 (YSM_i) + b_5 (YSM_i)^2$$
$$+ b_6 LANG_i + v_i, \quad (2)$$

where $LANG_i$ is a measure of the destination language fluency of the individual and v_i is the stochastic error term.

Prior empirical analysis has confirmed that language fluency has an important effect on earnings. Chiswick and Miller (1992), for example, report that among adult foreign-born men in the U.S. 1980 Census of Population, English language fluency is associated with around 17% higher earnings. The earnings advantage associated with fluency in the dominant language in the 1981 Canadian Census is about 12%, while those fluent in English in the Australian 1986 Census have about 8% higher earnings (Chiswick and Miller 1995).[2] Fluency in the dominant language (Hebrew) in Israel (1972 and 1983 Censuses) is associated with about a 12% increase in earnings (Chiswick 1998 and Chiswick and Repetto 2001).

In competitive labor markets, the mobility of workers from low-wage areas to high-wage areas is expected to erode any regional differences in real earnings, up to a cost-of-moving wedge. If there are factors, however, that impede the mobility of individuals across regions, then real earnings variation by region of residence could be observed even beyond short-term disequilibria differentials. In the case of the foreign born, the propensity to cluster in communities formed on the basis of language and ethnicity may be important in influencing inter-regional mobility by affecting the "full cost of living" across areas.[3] These costs would be lower in areas where there are others who speak the same language and observe the same customs.

Consider a situation in which an ethnic group defined by language or some other characteristic has a market basket for goods and services that differs from other groups. These "ethnic goods" could include conventional foods and services, such as ethnic foods and ethnic-specific clothing or household items. More important may be less tangible items such as origin language media (e.g., newspapers, books, radio, television), houses of worship, social clubs, other individuals of the same background to share memories and holidays, and opportunities to interact with others of the same origin in the marriage market. The full price of "ethnic goods" would be lower the larger the size of the ethnic market because of economies of scale and lower networking costs. Then, in a competitive labor market in which internal migration equalizes regional differences in wages, group differences in linguistic and/or ethnic concentrations result in group-specific patterns of regional wage differentials. In other words, if ethnic goods are important, a high wage offer is needed to induce a member of the group to leave an area of concentration (low cost of ethnic goods) to live in an area with few others of the same origin (high cost of ethnic goods). Then, the size of the linguistic concentration is inversely related to observed earnings.

A minority language concentration measure, first introduced in Chiswick and Miller (1992), is used to measure the linguistic concentration. Concentrations of foreign language speakers may have a direct effect on the earnings of individuals through the "ethnic goods" effect. Linguistic concentration may also have an indirect influence on earnings through their negative impact on the acquisition of destination language skills (Chiswick and Miller 1992, 1995, 1998). By including variables for both linguistic concentration and the individual's own language skills in an estimating equation, the relative strengths of these direct and indirect effects may be assessed.

There may also be important interaction effects due to the limitations on internal mobility. Individuals who are not fluent in English, and who live in linguistic concentrations may have higher earnings than their counterparts who, perhaps for family reasons (tied stayers), live in predominately monolingual English-speaking regions. Those not fluent in English may have economic advantages from working in a linguistic minority enclave.

Variables for country of birth are included in the earnings equation for the foreign born to capture the unmeasured differences in the average productivity of immigrants from the various countries of origin, that is, differences in quality not measured in the other variables. Differences in average quality might be expected where the international transferability of skills varies across immigrant groups (for example, immigrants from English-speaking and non-English speaking countries), or where some immigrants are less favorably selected for migration (for example, refugees compared to economic migrants) and so have fewer skills relevant for the destination, *ceteris paribus*. Country of origin differences can also arise if the backgrounds of immigrant groups differ. For example, immigrants from Mexico are disproportionately from rural communities. The skills accumulated in the labor markets of the rural communities of developing economies may be less useful in the U.S. labor market than the pre-immigration skills of immigrant groups that are predominately from urban areas and developed countries. Moreover, expected rates of re-migration differ across origins (Ahmed and Robinson 1994), and the propensity to invest in destination-specific skills, including language skills, would decrease with a higher expected return migration or emigration propensity.[4] Finally, the birthplace, variables will also capture differences in the effects of culture and discrimination on measured earnings.

Citizenship has been shown to affect earnings (Chiswick and Miller 1992). Naturalization generally requires the demonstration of at least a minimum level of English language fluency. It also reflects a stronger commitment to the United States which would be associated with greater investment in U.S.-specific human capital, and thus higher earnings. Moreover, aliens are disadvantaged in the labor market as some jobs require citizenship status, or because of illegal discrimination against lawful resident aliens.

To measure the effect of the business cycle at entry on immigrant earnings, the analysis includes the adult male unemployment rate in the United States in the year of arrival or of entry into the U.S. labor market, whichever is later. This variable permits an examination of whether labor market entrance at a time of high unemployment has a negative effect on an immigrant's future labor market success.[5]

Interacting the unemployment rate at labor market entry with the duration in the United States will indicate whether the disadvantage due to the state of the labor market at the time of labor market entrance diminishes with duration in the destination. This will provide insights into the origins of this particular wage effect. For example, if the wage disadvantage dissipates with duration, the effect is a "temporary blemish" rather than a "permanent scar". The temporary blemish may occur if arrival in a period of high employment makes it more difficult for the new immigrant to obtain any employment or to obtain employment that makes maximum use of the new immigrant's transferable skills. The adverse effects of a poor initial placement would be expected to diminish with duration in the destination.

If the wage effect persists, however, attention needs to be focused on permanent factors for the explanation: either the initial placement in a recession results in a permanent disadvantage, or, more likely, it is the result of negative selection for immigration during recessions. Negative selection for migration during recessions might occur if factors other than economic advantage are relatively more important in the migration decision when job opportunities in the destination are scarce. In such circumstances, family reunification and refugee motivations may be relatively more prevalent in migration flows than purely economic motivations.

3. The data and methodology

The data are from the 1990 Census of Population, Public Use Microdata Sample, and are for the 5% sample of the foreign-born men from non-English speaking countries.[6] The analysis is limited to adult non-aged men to avoid the complexities of modelling labor supply in analyses for women and aged men. The variables are defined in detail and the means and standard deviations are reported in Appendix A.

The regression equation used in the empirical analysis relates the natural logarithm of annual (1989) earnings for adult (age 25 to 64) men to a set of explanatory variables. These variables (with their hypothesized partial effects in parentheses) include: years of education (+), total years of labor market experience (+), duration of residence of immigrants in the U.S. (+), English language fluency (+), U.S. citizenship (+), married (+), weeks worked (+), the adult male unemployment rate at the time of arrival or entry in the U.S. labor market (−), the interaction of this unemployment rate variable and duration of residence (+), the minority language concentration measure (−), and the interaction between the minority language concentration measure and the individual's own English language fluency (−). Country of origin dichotomous variables are also included, with Western Europe as the benchmark. Three additional dichotomous variables are unity for those living in a rural area (−), those living in a southern state (−) and those whose race is Black (−).

Separate analyses of earnings are conducted for those fluent in English and for those who lack English-language fluency, using both OLS and selectivity correction techniques.[7] In addition, the data are disaggregated by major birthplace groups, and earnings equations are estimated for each subsample.

4. The earnings of immigrants

The empirical analysis begins with the estimations for foreign-born adult men (Tables 1 and 2). Table 1 reports estimates obtained when the data are pooled across individuals fluent in English and those who lack this skill. A number of specifications of the earnings equation are reported in Table 1.[8] The first specification is a standard immigrant earnings function without the variables for English-language skills, the second includes a variable for minority language concentration, the third model adds a variable for the individual's fluency in English, the fourth considers the interaction between English language fluency and the minority language concentration measure, and the fifth augments the estimating equation with information on the unemployment rate in the year of entry into the U.S. labor market. The final model in Table 1 explores the effects on earnings of a more detailed measure of English language fluency.

The estimates presented in Table 2 are for the separate samples of individuals fluent in English (speaks only English at home or speaks English "very well" or "well") and individuals with English-language deficiencies, that is, they speak English "not well" or "not at all." The separation of the data by English language fluency is not random. Regression equations using non-random samples will result in biased and inconsistent estimates. This problem may be accommodated by employing the methodology advanced by Heckman

Table 1. Regression estimates of earnings equations, adult foreign born men, 1990

Variable	(i)	(ii)	(iii)	(iv)	(v)	(vi)
Constant	5.056	5.066	5.009	4.969	5.112	5.345
	(172.91)	(173.20)	(171.69)	(167.46)	(157.43)	(163.70)
Education	0.049	0.048	0.045	0.045	0.044	0.043
	(91.15)	(90.21)	(83.07)	(82.99)	(81.61)	(79.09)
Experience (Exp)	0.023	0.023	0.025	0.025	0.023	0.023
	(35.45)	(35.56)	(37.75)	(37.79)	(32.38)	(33.01)
$Exp^2/100$	−0.037	−0.037	−0.038	−0.038	−0.036	−0.036
	(30.90)	(31.03)	(31.82)	(31.78)	(29.36)	(29.67)
Year since migration	0.028	0.028	0.026	0.026	0.022	0.020
(YSM)	(49.79)	(50.25)	(44.81)	(44.78)	(28.30)	(25.36)
$YSM^2/100$	−0.041	−0.041	−0.038	−0.038	−0.035	−0.033
	(32.07)	(32.53)	(29.88)	(29.90)	(25.73)	(24.71)
Log weeks worked	0.968	0.968	0.964	0.964	0.966	0.965
	(135.56)	(135.51)	(134.96)	(134.99)	(134.87)	(134.76)
Married	0.214	0.214	0.210	0.210	0.209	0.210
	(55.30)	(55.57)	(54.36)	(54.52)	(54.11)	(54.36)
Citizen	0.087	0.084	0.077	0.075	0.077	0.074
	(20.66)	(20.02)	(18.19)	(17.85)	(18.14)	(17.65)
Race (black)	−0.185	−0.194	−0.200	−0.201	−0.201	−0.206
	(12.60)	(13.16)	(13.62)	(13.67)	(13.71)	(14.05)
Rural	−0.037	−0.043	−0.044	−0.045	−0.045	−0.048
	(4.68)	(5.54)	(5.59)	(5.76)	(5.77)	(6.18)
South	−0.113	−0.110	−0.111	−0.112	−0.112	−0.114
	(26.40)	(25.71)	(26.07)	(26.31)	(26.20)	(26.58)
Birthplace						
S. Europe	−0.056	−0.053	−0.051	−0.045	−0.051	−0.043
	(5.59)	(5.21)	(5.02)	(4.49)	(5.01)	(4.22)
E. Europe	−0.072	−0.072	−0.069	−0.064	−0.067	−0.057
	(5.97)	(6.03)	(5.71)	(5.32)	(5.52)	(4.69)
USSR	−0.130	−0.131	−0.123	−0.118	−0.122	−0.111
	(7.18)	(7.23)	(6.82)	(6.53)	(6.73)	(6.10)
Indochina	−0.276	−0.278	−0.266	−0.256	−0.255	−0.236
	(22.74)	(22.90)	(22.00)	(21.06)	(20.91)	(18.99)
Philippines	−0.229	−0.223	−0.233	−0.232	−0.234	−0.235
	(21.48)	(20.94)	(21.95)	(21.79)	(21.99)	(21.68)
China	−0.266	−0.263	−0.245	−0.235	−0.238	−0.223
	(23.46)	(23.19)	(21.60)	(20.68)	(20.86)	(19.28)
South Asia	−0.013	−0.015	−0.021	−0.021	−0.026	−0.032
	(1.10)	(1.32)	(1.82)	(1.79)	(2.29)	(2.73)
Other Asia	−0.195	−0.197	−0.198	−0.196	−0.202	−0.191
	(10.13)	(10.22)	(10.28)	(10.17)	(10.50)	(9.91)
Korea	−0.229	−0.230	−0.206	−0.195	−0.195	−0.177
	(14.69)	(14.73)	(13.25)	(12.51)	(12.50)	(11.30)
Japan	0.353	0.352	0.362	0.369	0.362	0.379
	(19.06)	(19.01)	(19.69)	(20.03)	(19.69)	(20.55)
Middle East	−0.089	−0.091	−0.096	−0.095	−0.100	−0.100
	(7.57)	(7.71)	(8.16)	(8.07)	(8.47)	(8.40)
Sub-Saharan Africa	−0.054	−0.051	−0.057	−0.056	−0.061	−0.066
	(2.85)	(2.68)	(3.01)	(2.98)	(3.22)	(3.48)
Mexico	−0.333	−0.238	−0.229	−0.222	−0.228	−0.224
	(36.66)	(22.46)	(21.67)	(20.94)	(21.37)	(21.07)
Cuba	−0.235	−0.173	−0.159	−0.148	−0.146	−0.146
	(20.95)	(14.70)	(13.54)	(12.45)	(12.34)	(12.36)
C. & S. America	−0.239	−0.172	−0.168	−0.158	−0.161	−0.159
(Spanish)	(25.09)	(16.71)	(16.35)	(15.28)	(15.51)	(15.39)

(continued overleaf)

Table 1 (continued)

Variable	(i)	(ii)	(iii)	(iv)	(v)	(vi)
C. & S. Amer.	−0.076	−0.070	−0.089	−0.089	−0.089	−0.099
(Non-Spanish)	(3.37)	(3.12)	(3.97)	(3.97)	(3.98)	(4.41)
Minority Language	(a)	−0.006	−0.005	−0.002	−0.002	−0.004
Concentration (CONC)		(17.54)	(14.31)	(5.09)	(5.28)	(12.32)
Fluent in English	(a)	(a)	0.144	0.186	0.183	(a)
			(30.72)	(24.71)	(24.36)	
Fluent in English* CONC	(a)	(a)	(a)	−0.004	−0.004	(a)
				(7.88)	(7.69)	
Un. Rate Yr. of Labor	(a)	(a)	(a)	(a)	−0.018	−0.021
Market Entry (U)					(10.37)	(11.87)
U*Years in US Labor	(a)	(a)	(a)	(a)	0.063	0.085
Market/100					(5.34)	(7.14)
Speaks English Very Well	(a)	(a)	(a)	(a)	(a)	0.018
						(2.62)
Speaks English Well	(a)	(a)	(a)	(a)	(a)	−0.088
						(11.53)
Speaks English Not Well	(a)	(a)	(a)	(a)	(a)	−0.186
						(22.06)
Does Not Speak English	(a)	(a)	(a)	(a)	(a)	−0.194
						(18.82)
Adjusted R^2	0.4154	0.4162	0.4186	0.4188	0.4191	0.4204
Sample size	212,384	212,384	212,384	212,384	212,384	212,384

[a] = Variable not entered.
Notes: Dependent variable: Natural logarithm of earnings in 1989.
'*t*' statistics in parentheses computed using White's (1980) heteroskedasticity-consistent covariance matrix estimator.
Source: 1990 Census of Population of the United States, Public Use Microdata Sample, 5 percent sample.

(1979) that treats the sample selectivity bias as an omitted variables problem. Hence, the equations in columns (ii) and (iv) of Table 2 include the coefficient on the sample selectivity (lambda) variable that has been constructed according to Lee (1983). In forming this variable, a reduced form model of fluency in English is estimated that has a large number of explanatory variables, including educational attainment, age, duration of residence, marital status, location, minority language concentration, veteran status, linguistic distance between English and the immigrant's mother tongue, and the geographical distance (and its square) between the major city in the immigrant's country of origin and the nearest major port of entry (New York or San Francisco) into the United States (Chiswick and Miller 1998). The latter three variables are used as the identifying instruments in the selection (English fluency) equation.[9]

The relationships between earnings and the conventional determinants of earnings will be explored first, and comparisons made between the estimated impacts among individuals who are fluent and those who are not fluent. Then the variables that are of particular interest for this study are discussed.

Additional years of education are associated with around five percent higher earnings when the focus of analysis is the total foreign-born sample (column (i) of Table 1). This impact is similar to that recorded in analyses of the 1980 Census (see Chiswick and Miller 1992). When the earnings equa-

Table 2. Regression estimates of earnings equations, by English fluency, adult foreign born men, 1990

Variable	Fluent in English OLS	Fluent in English Selectivity corrected	Not fluent in English OLS	Not fluent in English Selectivity corrected
Constant	5.001	4.752	5.091	5.706
	(125.34)	(158.04)	(62.40)	(64.38)
Education	0.056	0.067	0.017	0.010
	(83.15)	(81.85)	(18.16)	(5.69)
Experience (Exp)	0.026	0.021	0.011	0.015
	(29.51)	(24.54)	(8.60)	(9.86)
$Exp^2/100$	−0.042	−0.039	−0.020	−0.021
	(25.74)	(25.86)	(9.34)	(9.99)
Year since migration (YSM)	0.019	0.025	0.024	0.015
	(22.45)	(28.48)	(10.80)	(4.97)
$YSM^2/100$	−0.032	−0.040	−0.040	−0.034
	(21.01)	(26.84)	(11.60)	(9.55)
Log weeks worked	0.995	1.006	0.902	0.894
	(106.83)	(213.97)	(83.18)	(145.81)
Married	0.225	0.238	0.159	0.150
	(48.52)	(50.16)	(23.23)	(20.49)
Citizen	0.079	0.102	0.033	−0.002
	(16.41)	(20.33)	(3.70)	(0.18)
Race (black)	−0.214	−0.197	−0.059	−0.094
	(13.43)	(12.87)	(1.66)	(2.51)
Rural location	−0.040	−0.040	−0.073	−0.078
	(4.20)	(4.48)	(5.98)	(5.58)
South	−0.114	−0.110	−0.114	−0.122
	(22.74)	(22.04)	(14.32)	(15.14)
Birthplace				
S. Europe	−0.049	−0.067	−0.089	0.056
	(4.69)	(6.50)	(1.14)	(0.76)
E. Europe	−0.070	−0.096	−0.141	0.001
	(5.48)	(7.60)	(1.77)	(0.01)
USSR	−0.111	−0.150	−0.321	−0.169
	(5.91)	(8.21)	(3.56)	(2.09)
Indochina	−0.229	−0.285	−0.467	−0.298
	(17.33)	(21.23)	(5.95)	(3.90)
Philippines	−0.234	−0.208	−0.432	−0.398
	(21.66)	(18.62)	(5.10)	(5.37)
China	−0.194	−0.264	−0.550	−0.367
	(15.90)	(22.26)	(7.04)	(4.73)
South Asia	−0.036	−0.028	−0.380	−0.332
	(3.03)	(2.50)	(4.50)	(4.48)
Other Asia	−0.198	−0.208	−0.449	−0.349
	(9.85)	(11.00)	(4.86)	(4.06)
Korea	−0.200	−0.288	−0.293	−0.097
	(11.37)	(19.26)	(3.64)	(1.22)
Japan	0.330	0.281	0.391	0.544
	(16.52)	(15.48)	(4.58)	(6.92)
Middle East	−0.098	−0.092	−0.326	−0.264
	(8.16)	(8.52)	(3.78)	(3.64)
Sub-Saharan Africa	−0.052	−0.041	−0.345	−0.318
	(2.64)	(2.29)	(3.57)	(3.48)
Mexico	−0.208	−0.256	−0.392	−0.236
	(18.13)	(21.54)	(5.06)	(3.17)

(continued overleaf)

Table 2 (continued)

Variable	Fluent in English		Not fluent in English	
	OLS	Selectivity corrected	OLS	Selectivity corrected
Cuba	−0.127	−0.174	−0.291	−0.111
	(9.86)	(13.06)	(3.72)	(1.43)
C. & S. America (Spanish)	−0.148	−0.176	−0.323	−0.176
	(13.51)	(16.01)	(4.17)	(2.40)
C. &. S. America (Non-Spanish)	−0.055	0.004	−0.381	−0.446
	(2.40)	(0.18)	(2.63)	(2.54)
Minority Language Concentration (CONC)	−0.004	−0.007	−0.008	−0.005
	(10.35)	(16.16)	(13.29)	(5.92)
Un. Rate Yr. of Labor Market Entry (U)	−0.024	−0.028	−0.003	−0.009
	(11.89)	(13.63)	(0.58)	(1.93)
U*Years in US Labor Market/100	0.096	0.163	0.070	0.109
	(7.33)	(12.30)	(1.85)	(2.91)
Lambda	(a)	0.321	(a)	−0.158
		(21.36)		(4.51)
Adjusted R^2	0.3752	0.3770	0.3847	0.3849
Sample size	157,725	157,725	54,660	54,660

(a) = Variable not entered.
Notes: Dependent Variable: Natural logarithm of earnings in 1989.
Columns (i) and (iii) are estimated using OLS, columns (ii) and (iv) are estimated using Lee's (1983) estimator.
't' statistics in parentheses for columns (i) and (iii) computed using White's (1980) heteroskedasticity-consistent covariance matrix estimator.
Source: 1990 Census of Population of the United States, Public Use Microdata Sample, 5 percent sample.

tion is estimated separately for individuals fluent in English and for those lacking this fluency (Table 2, columns ii and iv), the coefficient of schooling is 6.6% among the fluent, but only 1.0% for those who are not fluent in English.

These findings suggest there is a considerable degree of complementarity in the labor market between English-language skills and formal education.[10] In other words, in the United States it is difficult to reap a return to human capital acquired through formal education unless one can speak English. Acquiring English language fluency therefore appears to be a means of increasing the international transferability of previously acquired forms of human capital. This provides a greater economic incentive for the better educated to become fluent in English than their less educated counterparts. The economic incentive also helps explain the very low mean educational attainment among those who are not fluent in English, only 7.9 years of schooling compared to 13.1 years among immigrants fluent in English.

The relative importance of U.S.-specific skills shows up clearly in the analysis of the effect of labor market experience on earnings. The two sets of relevant variables are years of labor market experience and years since migration. The experience variable reflects the impact of labor market experience accumulated prior to migration, while the years since migration variable reflects the premium to labor market experience accumulated after arrival in the United

States. For the total foreign-born sample, earnings increase at a decreasing rate with years of pre-immigration experience. When evaluated at 10 years of experience, the earnings growth per year of experience is 1.6% (Table 1, Column i). The earnings growth with additional years of pre-immigration experience is greater among immigrants who are fluent in English than for those that lack English-language fluency (see Table 2).[11]

The earnings premium for a longer duration of residence in the United States is 2.0% per year when evaluated at 10 years of residence for the foreign-born men (Table 1, Column i). The separate analyses for the two English-language fluency groups reveal a higher premium to U.S. labor market experience (holding total experience constant) for the group not fluent in English when the estimation is by Ordinary Least Squares (OLS), but the expected lower premium for them when the estimation is by the selectivity correction method.[12] As duration of residence lengthens, additional immigrants move from the "not fluent" to the "fluent" states, and this linguistic mobility affects the estimates of the returns to duration in the destination.

A clear pattern is evident from the comparison of the OLS and selectivity-corrected earnings regressions (Table 2). If a variable is associated with high levels of English fluency (e.g., educational attainment and years since migration) then the selectivity-corrected estimate of the wage differential is greater than the OLS estimate for the group that is fluent in English, and this pattern is reversed for the group that is not fluent in English. However, if a variable is associated with low levels of English language fluency (e.g., minority language concentration) then the selectivity-corrected estimate of the wage difference is lower than the OLS estimate for the group that is fluent in English, with this pattern being reversed for the group that is not fluent in English.

The estimates also show that married (spouse present) men earn around 20% more than their non-married counterparts.[13] The favorable effect of being married on male earnings is greater among those who are fluent in English (23%) than for the group lacking in English language fluency (15% higher earnings). Citizens have higher earnings than non-citizens (9% for the total sample), and the effect varies by level of fluency in English, 8% for immigrants fluent in English, 3% for immigrants not fluent in English.

The elasticity of earnings with respect to weeks worked also varies by English language fluency. Overall the elasticity is 0.97, which is statistically significantly lower than unity, although the difference has no economic significance. Among the fluent the elasticity is 1.00, but among the non-fluent it is 0.89. That is, a 10% increase in weeks worked in the year is associated with a 10% increase in annual earnings among those who are fluent, but only a 9% increase (i.e., weekly earning decline with weeks worked) for the non-fluent group. This difference would be consistent with the latter group having a backward bending labor supply curve or greater seasonality in their employment.

The effects of the schooling, experience, marriage, citizenship and weeks worked variables suggest that there is a complementarity between these forms of human capital and English language fluency. Those who are fluent receive larger benefits from having more of these favorable characteristics.

Earnings also differ appreciably across birthplace groups, even when account is taken of the individual skills and demographic characteristics. Compared to the benchmark group, immigrants from Western Europe, other immigrants essentially fall into four categories (see Table 1): immigrants from Japan who have earnings about 35% greater than the benchmark; immigrants from South Asia whose earnings are not significantly different from the earnings of immigrants from Western Europe; immigrants from countries with earnings 5 to 15% below the earnings of the Western Europeans (Sub-Saharan Africa, Southern Europe, Eastern Europe, the non-Spanish regions of Central and South America, Middle East, USSR); those from countries with earnings more than 15% below that of the benchmark group (Other Asia, Korea, Cuba, Philippines, the Spanish-speaking regions of Central and South America, China, Indochina, Mexico). The earnings disadvantage, *ceteris paribus*, is over 30% for immigrants from Mexico. Note also the tendency for refugee groups (e.g., Cuba, China, Indochina) to have lower earnings even when other measured variables are the same.[14]

The specification in column (ii) of Table 1 includes the variable for minority language concentration. Residence in a state that contains a larger concentration of individuals speaking the same foreign language as the respondent is associated with lower earnings. Where 10% of the population speak the same foreign language as the respondent, compared to an area where none speak this language, earnings are lower by 6%. Where 20% of the population speak the same foreign language as the respondent (as is the case of Spanish in a number of states), earnings are lower by 12%.

The addition of the minority language concentration variable reduces the earnings disadvantage of the three Spanish-speaking birthplace groups: Mexico, Cuba, and the Spanish speaking regions of Central and South America. For immigrants from Mexico, the apparent "birthplace" disadvantage is reduced by 10 percentage points to about 24%. For immigrants from Cuba and Central and South America, the reduction in the apparent birthplace effect is six percentage points. Part of the Hispanic birthplace effect on earnings, therefore, arises from Hispanics concentrating in areas where their earnings are lower because of the presence of many other Spanish speakers.

The variable for the individual's fluency in English is added to the model presented in Table 1, column (iii). Fluency in English is associated with 14% higher earnings, *ceteris paribus*. This increment in earnings is slightly lower than that recorded in study of the 1980 Census (17% higher earnings), but the difference is at the margin of statistical significance ($t = 1.75$). Hence, whereas there has been a rise in the return to language skills in the Australian labor market over the past few years, this is not the case in the United States or in Israel or Canada (Chiswick and Miller 1995, 2000; Chiswick and Repetto 2001).

Inclusion of the variable for the individual's English-speaking skills is associated with a small reduction in the estimated impact of the minority language concentration variable (from −0.006 to −0.005). Thus, about one-sixth of the effect of living in a concentration of individuals who speak the same non-English second language at home is linked directly to the individual's own lack of English skills. The greater part of the impact is due to other consequences of a labor market characterized by many minority language speakers. Where you work may be an important determinant of earnings.

In terms of its effects on earnings, fluency in English as defined in this study is the equivalent of around three years of formal education and around five years of U.S. labor market experience evaluated at 10 years of experience. Acquisition of English language skills clearly pays in the U.S. labor market. If English speaking fluency can be attained with the equivalent of between 6 months and one-year of full-time training, provided that the remaining working life is reasonably long, this implies a real rate of return to the acquisition of language skills of between 14 and 28%. There would appear to be few other investments that an immigrant could undertake that would yield such a healthy monetary return.

The inclusion of a measure of fluency in English in the estimating equation is associated with some (albeit minor) changes in the other estimated coefficients. For example, the extra earnings associated with additional years of education declines by almost one-third of one percentage point, and the income growth associated with years in the U.S. declines marginally. These changes indicate that part of the extra earnings associated with education and duration in the U.S. in analyses that do not explicitly consider language skills is in fact due to greater ability to communicate in English among the better educated and those who have resided in the U.S. for a longer period of time.

Table 1, column (iv) explores interactions between the minority language concentration measure and fluency in English. It is apparent that residence in a region with a concentration of individuals speaking the same foreign language as the immigrant has a more negative impact on earnings among those fluent in English. The impact of minority language concentration is only −0.002 for those who are not fluent in English, but is −0.006 (= −0.002 + −0.0004) for those who are fluent in English. That is, those who are fluent have a larger improvement in their earnings than their non-fluent counterparts if they move to a low concentration area.

Another perspective on these results is gained by focusing on the effect on earnings of fluency in English. This is estimated to be close to 19% for an individual who lives in an area where his origin language is not spoken. Where 20% of the population speak the immigrant's origin language, the return to English-speaking skills would only be 11%. Thus, while possession of English-speaking fluency is important, the language characteristics of the labor market also appear to matter. The favorable effect on earnings of English language fluency is greater in areas in which fewer people speak the worker's origin language. In other words, the economic penalty from not speaking English is smaller among those who live in a linguistic concentration area.

Table 1, Column (v) uses a linear interaction specification to test the hypothesis that weekly earnings are dependent on the stage of the business cycle at the time of entry into the labor market. Weekly earnings are lower when the unemployment rate is high in the year of U.S. labor market entry. In the linear specification, in the initial year (YRS = 0) the effect is nearly 1.8% lower weekly earnings for each one percentage point increase in the unemployment rate. For example, if the unemployment rate among adult men in the year of labor market entry is 8% (a deep recession), then weekly earnings are initially reduced by 9% compared to a situation where there was a 3% unemployment rate among adult men (full employment).[15] The interaction term between the unemployment rate variable and duration in the U.S. shows, however, that over time this disadvantage is gradually removed. Hence, while individuals who entered the labor market in times of 8% and 3% adult male unemployment rates would initially differ in average earnings by 9%, this earnings gap is 6% after 10 years and is closed after about 30 years of U.S. labor market activity.[16]

A linear interaction specification is arbitrary and alternative specifications were tested to see which would offer the greater explanatory power. The most successful simple specification had the squared unemployment rate in the interaction term, rather than the unemployment rate itself.[17] This increased the adjusted R-square from 0.4191 to only 0.4192. In this specification weekly earnings in the initial year (YRS = 0) are lower by 2.9% for each one percentage point increase in the adult male unemployment rate at entry into the U.S. labor market.[18] This implies that initial weekly earning would be lower by 14.5% if a male immigrant entered the United States labor market when the adult male unemployment rate was 8% compared to entry at 3%. The earnings gap as a function of the unemployment rate at entry decreases the longer the duration of residence. At ten years in the United States and a mean unemployment rate of 5.1% the partial effect of a one percentage point increase in the unemployment rate at entry is 1.3% in contrast to the 2.9% in the initial year. The effect disappears (at the mean unemployment rate) at about 18 years in the U.S. labor market.[19]

The analysis of the effect of the stage of the business cycle at entry on subsequent weekly earnings indicates that conditions at entry do matter. Earnings among adult male immigrants are substantially lower initially if they enter during a recession rather than during a period of full employment. This is not a permanent scar or disadvantage. The earnings disadvantage from entering in a recession diminishes with duration and eventually disappears. Thus, entering the U.S. labor market has two disadvantages for immigrants, one is the higher unemployment rate (lower weeks worked in the year) and the other is the lower weekly earnings.

The analyses in Table 2 show that the pattern of an initial wage disadvantage from arriving in a year of high unemployment followed by a gradual catch-up pertains only to individuals who are fluent in English. Among those who are not fluent in English, there is no initial earnings disadvantage associated with the stage of the business cycle at entry, nor does the effect of the business cycle vary with the duration of residence. This too suggests that among immigrants who are not fluent in English, there is a form of positive selection for migration during recessions. Perhaps those who are not fluent but who migrate when jobs are scarce have family ties that arrange employment.

The final column of Table 1 contains variables that record in finer detail the English-language skills of immigrants who speak a language other than English at home. The first of these variables indicates the wage differential between immigrants who are monolingual English speakers at home (the benchmark group for this analysis, whose English language proficiency is not known) and immigrants who speak a language other than English at home and report they speak English very well. The latter immigrants are assumed to be fully bilingual, and they are shown to receive a small, statistically significant wage premium, of about 2% ('t' = 2.6). The second variable identifies individuals who speak a language other than English at home and who self-report that they speak English "well". This group has earnings 9% lower than monolingual English speakers. The final two variables are for individuals who speak a language other than English at home and are not fluent in English. Immigrants in this situation have earnings almost 20% lower than the benchmark group of monolingual English speakers. Individuals who speak English "not well" earn about the same as those who do not speak English at all, and there may be little difference in the English proficiency of these two groups. These results show that the labor market is quite discerning when it comes to language skills.

The statistical significance of the lambda terms in the selectivity-corrected estimates in Table 2 indicate that the samples separated on the basis of language fluency are not random. Moreover, the sign of the coefficient on lambda is positive for the sample that is fluent in English and negative for the sample that is not fluent in English.[20] As the selection term in the "not fluent" category is constructed to be negative, a negative coefficient indicates an observed conditional mean that exceeds the population mean. That is, a negative coefficient in the "not fluent" group implies positive selection into that group. This indicates that there is positive selection into each state. In other words, the unobserved characteristics that lead to an individual having a higher than expected level of fluency in English are also associated with a higher than expected earnings in the labor market for individuals who are fluent in English. Moreover, those who have higher than expected labor market earnings for individuals who are not fluent in English are more likely to select into this state than other individuals (i.e., they have a lower than expected level of English language fluency).

This study of the correlation between the residuals in the earnings equations and the model of English-language fluency therefore suggests that English-speaking skills are endogeneously determined in the model of earnings. That is, a worker's language skills are influenced by expectations with respect to income returns.[21]

Table 3 presents selected statistics from analyses of earnings for the major birthplace regions. The first column lists the mean logarithm of earnings for each birthplace region. The second column treats immigrants from Western Europe as the reference group and reports the differences between the mean logarithm of earnings for each birthplace region and the reference group. These figures range from a high of 0.132 for Japan (14% higher earnings) to a low of −0.922 for Mexico (60% lower earnings). Other relatively low earnings origins are Indochina, Central and South America, Sub-Saharan Africa, Cuba, China and Korea. The data in the third column are the birthplace effects, other variables held constant, from column (i) of Table 1. Comparison of the data in Columns (ii) and (iii) of Table 3 reveals the extent to which factors such as differences in educational attainments, years of labor market experience, duration in the U.S., and location account for the unadjusted earnings differences measured in the Census data. In many cases the narrowing of the earnings differentials between the unadjusted and adjusted figures is pronounced. For example, in the case of immigrants from Southern Europe, the earnings differential falls by over two-thirds when adjustments are made for the impact of the determinants of earnings other than birthplace. Similarly, for immigrants from Mexico, the earnings differential falls by over two-thirds, while in the case of immigrants from Cuba, it is reduced by one-half.

Table 3, Column (iv) reports information on the mean fluency rate for each birthplace region, while Column (v) lists the partial effect of fluency on earnings for each birthplace. This is computed from an equation with the same structure as Table 1, Column (iii) estimated separately for each birthplace. It is only among immigrants from South Asia, Sub-Saharan Africa and from non-Spanish speaking parts of Central and South America that fluency in English is not associated with significantly higher earnings in the U.S. labor market. These groups have very high levels of English language fluency (96%, 97% and 99%, respectively); nearly all of the respondents are fluent in English. Among the other birthplace regions, the effect on earnings associated with fluency in English ranges from lows of 7% for Southern Europe and the Philippines, to highs of 14 to 16% for Western Europe, USSR, Indochina, Other Asia,

Table 3. Selected statistics for analyses of earnings for birthplace regions, adult foreign-born men, 1990

Birthplace region	Mean log of earnings	Unadjusted earnings difference	Adjusted earnings difference	Fluency rate	Returns to fluency	Returns to bilingualism	Impact of minority language concentration	Mean level of education	Coefficients of education	Sample size
	(i)	(ii)	(iii)	(iv)	(v)	(vi)	(vii)	(viii)	(ix)	(x)
Western Europe	10.320	—	—	0.990	0.136 (1.73)	−0.016 (0.94)	0.003 (0.65)	14.42	0.078 (25.91)	13,283
Southern Europe	10.116	−0.204 (18.01)	−0.056 (5.59)	0.849	0.071 (4.00)	−0.058 (2.95)	0.001 (0.71)	10.96	0.035 (18.01)	16,899
Eastern Europe	10.121	−0.199 (13.93)	−0.072 (5.97)	0.859	0.102 (3.82)	0.041 (1.34)	0.008 (1.09)	13.50	0.050 (15.71)	7,467
USSR	10.007	−0.313 (13.13)	−0.130 (7.18)	0.841	0.148 (2.45)	−0.050 (0.96)	0.001 (0.09)	14.43	0.058 (9.87)	2,776
Indochina	9.647	−0.673 (48.65)	−0.276 (22.74)	0.722	0.161 (7.12)	−0.032 (0.55)	−0.013 (1.13)	11.95	0.025 (9.68)	8,747
Philippines	9.949	−0.371 (30.26)	−0.229 (21.48)	0.962	0.071 (1.70)	0.047 (1.79)	−0.011 (3.60)	14.32	0.073 (14.32)	11,508
China	9.838	−0.482 (36.03)	−0.266 (23.46)	0.742	0.241 (10.24)	−0.069 (1.60)	0.005 (0.30)	14.15	0.052 (21.55)	12,763
South Asia	10.153	−0.167 (12.32)	−0.013 (1.10)	0.959	0.055 (1.36)	−0.072 (2.68)	−0.007 (1.01)	15.83	0.082 (25.27)	10,502
Other Asia	9.937	−0.383 (15.97)	−0.195 (10.13)	0.918	0.154 (2.37)	−0.041 (0.80)	0.041 (1.99)	14.80	0.079 (14.80)	2,389
Korea	9.859	−0.461 (26.42)	−0.229 (14.69)	0.695	0.188 (5.50)	0.065 (0.97)	−0.010 (0.43)	14.45	0.036 (14.45)	6,438
Japan	10.452	0.132 (6.55)	0.353 (19.06)	0.798	0.270 (6.41)	0.027 (0.46)	−0.007 (0.89)	15.14	0.064 (10.17)	3,043
Middle East	10.035	−0.265 (21.02)	−0.089 (7.57)	0.952	0.144 (3.28)	0.004 (0.15)	−0.001 (0.19)	14.72	0.074 (24.67)	12,062
Sub-Saharan Africa	9.801	−0.519 (30.08)	−0.054 (2.85)	0.971	0.072 (1.07)	−0.088 (2.85)	0.001 (0.15)	15.09	0.077 (14.81)	4,413

Mexico	9.387	−0.932 (96.17)	0.535	0.145 (23.11)	0.095 (4.86)	−0.002 (5.45)	7.90	0.025 (27.09)	61,700
Cuba	9.841	−0.479 (36.50)	0.710	0.087 (3.88)	−0.114 (2.91)	−0.004 (2.16)	12.01	0.051 (18.59)	10,859
Central & South America (Spanish)	9.647	−0.673 (62.96)	0.683	0.150 (13.15)	0.094 (4.03)	−0.009 (14.04)	11.54	0.041 (29.01)	25,926
Central & South America (non-Spanish)	9.828	−0.491 (21.10)	0.989	0.126 (1.74)	0.126 (1.74)	−0.005 (1.00)	12.56	0.034 (5.56)	1,601

't' statistics in parentheses computed using White's (1980) heteroskedasticity-consistent covariance matrix estimator.
Note: Column (i) is the mean logarithm of earnings by country of birth, Column (ii) is the difference between the country's mean log earnings and that of immigrants from Western Europe (10.320), while Column (iii) is the birthplace regression coefficient from Table (1) Column (i). Column (iv) is the observed fluency rate and Column (viii) is the mean level of education for the birthplace group. Columns (v), (vii) and (ix) are regression coefficients estimated from equations similar to Table 1 Column (iii) for each birthplace separately. Column (vi) is the partial effect of speaking English "very well" from an equation similar to Table 1, Column (vi), estimated for each birthplace separately. Column (x) is the sample size for each birthplace group.
Source: 1990 Census of Population of the United States, Public Use Microdata Sample, 5% sample.

Middle East, Mexico and the Spanish-speaking regions of Central and South America.

The data were also examined for the returns to "bilingualism." That is, do those who speak a language other than English at home and who report they speak English "very well" have higher earnings than monolingual English speakers? Table 3, Column (vi) reports the coefficient on the "very well" variable for equations with the same structure as Table 1, Column (vi), but estimated separately for each birthplace group. In only four birthplace groups is there evidence of the labor market rewarding this skill, namely the Philippines (5% higher earnings), Mexico (10% higher earnings), the Spanish-speaking regions of Central and South America (also 10% higher earnings) and the non-Spanish speaking regions of Central and South America (13% higher earnings).

The impact of the minority language concentration variable on earnings within country of birth categories is examined in the seventh column of Table 3, estimated from birthplace-specific equations. This variable has negative and significant impacts on earnings for the three Spanish-speaking birthplace groups, and also for the Philippines. The size of the estimated coefficients for the Spanish-speaking regions are interesting: the smallest partial effect is estimated for immigrants from Mexico and the largest partial effect is estimated for immigrants from the Spanish speaking regions of Central and South America. The coefficient is negative, although not statistically significant, for most of the Asian countries.[22] The coefficient is positive, although not statistically significant, for the European countries. Thus, there is a clear negative effect for Spanish and Tagalog, with weaker negative effects for most of the other Asian languages. This is consistent with the ethnic goods model as the cultural characteristics of the Hispanic and Asian immigrants differ far more from the American mainstream than that of the European immigrants.

The final two columns of estimates in Table 3 give the mean level of schooling and the estimated partial effect of schooling on earnings, estimated from birthplace-specific equations similar to Table 1, Column (iii). On the basis of the previous study of the determinants of English language fluency, the positive relationship between the mean level of education and the fluency rate is to be expected. What is surprising, however, is the lack of association between the returns to fluency and the returns to education. Examination of the correlation coefficient between the two returns shows a weak negative association (correlation coefficient −0.25). While there are obvious complementarities between the two types of skills (see in particular Table 2), they have sufficiently different impacts on earnings that separate analyses of each is required.

5. Summary, conclusions and implications

This study of the determinants of earnings among adult foreign-born men from non-English speaking countries uses the microdata files from the 1990 Census of Population (5% sample). The study focuses on the effects on earnings of the respondent's own English language skills, the extent to which others who live in the area in which the respondent lives speak the same foreign language, and the stage of the business cycle at the time of entry into the U.S. labor market.

The analysis demonstrates the importance for earnings of English language fluency. *Ceteris paribus*, the foreign born from non-English speaking countries who are fluent in English earn about 14% more than those lacking this fluency. This is about the same effect as that observed in the 1980 Census (17%). The earnings effect is found for immigrants from all non-English speaking countries of origin.

The effect of fluency varies with the extent to which others in the area where the respondent lives speak the same non-English language. Earnings are lower among the foreign born the greater is the intensity of the linguistic concentration. The adverse effect of living in an area with a greater concentration of origin-language speakers is more pronounced among those immigrants more fluent in English. That is, compared to those who are fluent, those who are not fluent in English have relatively greater earnings opportunities inside the linguistic concentration area than outside such an area.

There is strong evidence of endogeneity between language and earnings, as found in the selectivity correction analysis. Those who are fluent are found to be favorably selected for higher earnings in this sector, while the same is true for the unmeasured characteristics of those who are not fluent. Thus, as with other forms of human capital, language skills are acquired, in part, in response to the expected increment in earnings.

There is also strong evidence of complementarity among forms of human capital. The partial effects on earnings of schooling, total labor market experience, duration in the U.S., being married, being a citizen, and weeks worked in the year are greater among those more fluent in English, and are generally very low among those lacking fluency.

Among the foreign born, the stage of the business cycle on entry into the U.S. labor market does influence current earnings overall and among those who are fluent. Earnings are lower for those who enter during a period of high unemployment. Yet this effect is not a permanent scar as the adverse effect of a high unemployment rate at entry diminishes with duration in the U.S. Among those who are not fluent, however, the stage of the business cycle at entry has no effect on earnings.

This paper highlights the important relationship between earnings and English language fluency among the foreign born. English language fluency enhances earnings, and at the same time is itself, in part, a consequence of the expectation of higher earnings. Where one lives matters as earnings are higher, especially for those fluent in English, among those who do not live in a linguistic concentration area.

These findings have important implications for public policy. They emphasize the value to be had from including English language fluency, or the correlates of English language fluency, in the criteria for rationing immigration visas. They also point to the value of encouraging immigrants to participate in English-as-a-second-language programs either prior to or after arrival in the United States.

Those who live in linguistically concentrated areas have lower earnings, even after controlling for their own language skills, among other variables. This may be reflecting an "ethnic goods" effect, that is, that immigrants sort themselves across the country to equalize real incomes and that "ethnic goods", including community ties and networking, have a lower cost the greater the concentration of people speaking the same origin language. If so, the regional wage differentials may merely reflect ethnic-group specific cost of living differentials, rather than a "crowding effect".

The finding of a temporary adverse effect on earnings from entering the U.S. labor market in a period of high unemployment will add fuel to the debate on whether business cycle considerations should be explicitly included in the allocation of immigration visas. This finding may reflect the temporary negative labor market effects of an initial poor job placement of those who came in a recession, or a lesser degree of skill transferability among those who arrive in a recession as they rely more heavily on family ties. Yet the adverse effect is temporary as it diminishes and eventually disappears the longer an immigrant has lived in the United States.

Appendix A
Definitions of variables

The variables used in the statistical analyses are defined below. Mnemonic names are also listed where relevant. The means and standard deviations are reported in Appendix Table A-1 for the total sample and separately for the fluent and not fluent groups.

Data source. 1990 Census of Population, Public Use Microdata Sample, 5% sample of the foreign born, except where noted otherwise.

Definition of population. Except where otherwise stated, foreign born men aged twenty-five to sixty-four with earnings in 1989, born in countries other than the English-speaking developed economies (UK, Ireland, Canada, Australia, New Zealand).

Dependent variable

Earnings (LNEARN). The natural logarithm of the sum of wage or salary income and self-employment income (either non-farm or farm) received in 1989.

Explanatory variables

English language fluency (LANG). LANG is set equal to one for individuals who speak only English at home, or if a language other than English is spoken in the home, who speak English either "very well" or "well". The variable is set to zero where a language other than English is spoken in the home and the respondent speaks English either "not well" or "not at all". The categories "very well", "well", "not well" and "not at all" are separately identified in the more extensive specifications of language skills included in some models.

Years of education (EDUC). This variable records the total years of full-time education. It has been constructed from the Census data on educational attainment by assigning the following values to the Census categories: completed less than fifth grade (2.5 years); completed fifth through eighth grade (7 years); completed ninth grade (9); completed tenth grade (10); completed 11th grade (11); completed 12th grade or high school (12); attended or completed college

Immigrant earnings

Table A-1. Means and standard deviations of variables[a]

Variable	Total sample	Fluent in English	Not fluent in English
Annual earnings	27061	31092	15128
	(28589)	(31013)	(14110)
Log of annual earnings	9.787	9.954	9.292
	(1.03)	(1.01)	(0.94)
Education	11.79	13.10	7.926
	(4.92)	(4.20)	(4.84)
Experience	22.76	21.46	26.58
	(11.46)	(10.98)	(12.00)
Years since migration	15.43	16.95	10.92
	(10.85)	(11.22)	(8.13)
Log weeks worked	3.75	3.78	3.66
	(0.47)	(0.44)	(0.55)
Married	0.673	0.696	0.604
	(0.47)	(0.46)	(0.49)
Citizen	0.417	0.494	0.192
	(0.49)	(0.50)	(0.39)
Race (black)	0.033	0.041	0.009
	(0.18)	(0.20)	(0.09)
Rural	0.057	0.057	0.058
	(0.23)	(0.23)	(0.23)
South	0.240	0.237	0.247
	(0.43)	(0.43)	(0.43)
Southern Europe	0.078	0.089	0.047
	(0.27)	(0.28)	(0.21)
Eastern Europe	0.036	0.041	0.020
	(0.19)	(0.20)	(0.14)
USSR	0.013	0.015	0.008
	(0.12)	(0.12)	(0.09)
Indochina	0.041	0.040	0.046
	(0.20)	(0.20)	(0.21)
Philippines	0.053	0.068	0.008
	(0.22)	(0.25)	(0.09)
China	0.061	0.060	0.062
	(0.24)	(0.24)	(0.24)
South Asia	0.051	0.066	0.008
	(0.22)	(0.25)	(0.09)
Other South-East Asia	0.011	0.014	0.004
	(0.11)	(0.12)	(0.06)
Korea	0.031	0.029	0.038
	(0.17)	(0.17)	(0.19)
Japan	0.015	0.016	0.012
	(0.12)	(0.12)	(0.11)
Middle East	0.059	0.075	0.011
	(0.24)	(0.26)	(0.10)
Sub-Saharan Africa	0.024	0.032	0.003
	(0.15)	(0.18)	(0.05)
Mexico	0.279	0.200	0.514
	(0.45)	(0.40)	(0.50)
Cuba	0.050	0.048	0.057
	(0.22)	(0.21)	(0.23)
C. & S. America (Spanish)	0.127	0.116	0.160
	(0.33)	(0.32)	(0.37)
C. & S. America (non-Spanish)	0.009	0.012	0.001
	(0.09)	(0.11)	(0.01)

(*continued overleaf*)

Table A-1 (continued)

Variable	Total sample	Fluent in English	Not fluent in English
Unemployment rate at time of labor market entry	5.14 (1.59)	5.06 (1.63)	5.39 (1.43)
Minority language concentration (CONC)	7.44 (8.93)	5.65 (8.20)	12.76 (8.89)
Fluent in English	0.748 (0.43)	1.00	0.00
Speaks English very well	0.369 (0.48)	0.493 (0.50)	0.000
Speaks English well	0.268 (0.44)	0.358 (0.48)	0.000
Speaks English not well	0.191 (0.39)	0.000	0.755 (0.430)
Speaks English not at all	0.062 (0.24)	0.000	0.245 (0.430)
Sample size	212,384	157,725	54,660

[a] The data are for men who worked and had earnings in 1989, were 25 to 64 years in 1990 and were born in non-English speaking countries.
Source: 1990 Census of Population of the United States, Public Use Microdata Sample, 5 percent sample.

(14); Bachelor's degree (16); Master's degree (17.5); Professional degree (18); Doctorate (20).

Years of experience (EXP). This is computed as age minus years of education minus 5 (that is, EXP = AGE − EDUC − 5). A quadratic specification is used.

Years since migration (YSM). The categorical Census information on year of immigration is converted to a continuous measure using the following values: 1987–1990 (1.75 years); 1985–1986 (4.25 years); 1982–1984 (6.75 years); 1980–1981 (9.25 years); 1975–1979 (12.75 years); 1970–1974 (17.75 years); 1965–1969 (22.75 years); 1960–1965 (27.75 years); 1950–1959 (35.25 years); before 1950 (49.75 years).

Birthplace (BIRTH). A number of non-English speaking birthplace regions are considered in the analyses: Western Europe; Southern Europe; Eastern Europe; former Soviet Union; China; Indochina; Philippines; South Asia (which comprises the regions of British influence, for example, India, Nepal, Pakistan); Other (South-East) Asia; Korea; Japan; Middle East and North Africa; SubSaharan Africa; Mexico; Cuba; Central and South America (Spanish influence); Central and South America (non-Spanish influence). The benchmark group (omitted category) in the regression analysis for the foreign born is Western Europe.

Log of weeks worked (LNWW). The number of weeks worked in 1989 is used in natural logarithmic form.

Minority language concentration (CONC). Each respondent is assigned a measure equal to the percentage of the population aged eighteen to sixty-four in the state in which he lives who reports the same non-English language as the respondent. In the construction of this variable, only the twenty-four largest language groups nationwide are considered. In descending order there are: Spanish; French; German; Italian; Chinese; Tagalog; Polish; Korean; Vietnamese; Japanese; Portugese; Greek; Arabic; Hindi; Russian; Yiddish; Thai; Persian; French Creole; Armenian; Hebrew; Dutch; Hungarian; Mon-Khmer (Cambodian). These constitute 94 percent of all responses that a language other than English is used at home. Representation in the other language groups is so small numerically that the proportions are approximately zero, and this value is assigned. Those who reported only English are also assigned a zero value.

Marital Status (MARRIED). This is a binary variable that distinguishes individuals who are married, spouse present (equal to 1) from all other marital states.

Location. The two location variables record residence of a rural area (Rural) or of the Southern States (South). The states included in the latter are: Alabama, Arkansas, Delaware, District of Columbia, Florida, Georgia, Kentucky, Louisiana, Maryland, Mississippi, Missouri, North Carolina, Oklahoma, South Carolina, Tennessee, Texas, Virginia, West Virginia.

Race. This is a dichotomous variable, set to one if the individual is Black, and set to zero for all other racial groups (White, Asian and Pacific Islander groups, other groups, American Indian).

Unemployment rate in the year of labor market entry (U). These data are the unemployment rate of males aged 20 years and over. Year of labor force entry is obtained from the data on year of entry for the foreign born for whom duration in the U.S. is less than total labor market experience (age minus schooling minus five), and it is year of entry into the labor market (year in which age is years of schooling plus five) for other immigrants. The unemployment rate data are from the Council of Economic Advisers, *Economic Report of the President, 1996*, Washington: U.S. Government Printing Office, Table B-38, p. 324.

Appendix B
English language fluency equation

Table B-1. Logit estimates of English-language fluency, foreign-born males, United States, 1990[a]

Variable	Estimate	t-ratio
Constant	0.753	5.07
Age	−0.054	67.32
Educational attainment	0.176	113.20
Years since migration (YSM)	0.160	44.95
YSM squared/100	−0.137	23.81
Married	0.194	13.93
Veteran	0.478	10.71
Black	0.617	9.18
Citizenship	0.545	34.90
Rural	0.092	3.20
South	0.135	8.71
Log weeks worked	0.175	14.08
Minority language concentration	−0.047	39.51
Linguistic distance	−0.673	4.50
Miles of origin country from US (10 thousands)	−0.051	0.15
Miles squared (10 millions)	0.325	6.68
Birthplace		
S. Europe	−2.224	23.60
E. Europe	−2.237	22.75
USSR	−2.502	23.02
Indochina	−4.215	25.02
Philippines	−1.658	11.73
China	−3.471	27.65
S. Asia	−2.092	13.65
Other Asia	−3.247	16.90
Korea	−3.365	24.65
Japan	−2.500	18.17
Middle East	−1.445	13.11
Sub Saharan Africa	−1.494	10.14
Mexico	−2.014	20.54
Cuba	−2.305	20.40
C & S American (Spanish)	−1.875	19.24
C & S American (non-Spanish)	1.555	6.19
Un rate yr. of labor market entry	0.083	10.30
U × YSM	0.003	5.12
Sample size	212,385	
McFadden's R^2	0.3426	

[a] The data are for men who worked and had earnings in 1989, were 25 to 64 years in 1990 and were born in non-English speaking countries. The dependent variable is LANG.

Notes

[1] One of the earliest studies to consider this issue is the McManus et al. (1981) paper on Hispanics in the United States.

[2] This is greater than the 5.3% higher earnings for the fluent in the 1981 Australian Census (Chiswick and Miller 1995).

[3] For analyses of the internal migration of immigrants see, for example, Bartel and Koch (1991).

4 Chiswick and Miller (1998) find that, other variables the same, English language fluency among immigrants in the United States is lower the higher is the emigration or return migration rate of immigrants in the United States from their country of birth.
5 Nakamura and Nakamura (1992) report that a higher national unemployment rate in the year of entry into the labor market is associated with a lower current wage among the foreign born in both the U.S. (1980 Census) and Canadian (1981 Census) labor markets. Stewart and Hyclak (1984) find that a higher annual growth rate in real GNP in the period of entry is associated with higher earnings among the foreign born in the 1970 U.S. Census. These studies did not test for whether the "scarring effect" varies by duration of residence in the destination. Chiswick et al. (1996), however, find that, using the Current Population Survey, the labor market conditions at the time of entry have an adverse effect on employment shortly after arrival, but do not have an effect on the future employability (employment ratio or unemployment rate) of immigrants in the United States.
6 Immigrants from English-speaking countries are excluded as the language issues do not exist for this group, while they may exist for immigrants from non-English speaking countries.
7 To the extent that there is measurement error in the language variable, there is misclassification in the fluent/non-fluent dichotomy.
8 The analyses in Table 1 were also computed with state fixed effects, that is, state level dummy variables, with the South variable deleted from the equation. There are no substantive differences in findings among any of the variables. For the specification (Table 1, column iii) and variables of primary interest (t-ratios in parentheses):

Variable	Table 1 column iii	Same Specification State-Fixed Effects
EDUC	0.045	0.045
	(83.1)	(82.4)
LANG	0.144	0.148
	(30.7)	(31.6)
CON	−0.0048	−0.0054
	(−14.3)	(−12.4)

The coefficient on the minority language concentration index is the variable most affected since its construction is based on state level data. Even so, the coefficient and t-ratio hardly change.
9 Estimates of the logit equation used in the computation of the sample selectivity correction terms are presented in Appendix B. See Chiswick and Miller (1998) for the model of the determinants of English language proficiency that serves as the basis for the selection equation. There are three identifying variables. The veteran status variable is used because experience in the United States Armed Forces would enhance the English-language proficiency of veterans. The U.S. Armed Forces accepts immigrants (resident aliens and naturalized citizens) as volunteers and drafted immigrants during periods of conscription. "Linguistic distance" between the origin language and English reflects the difficulty immigrants would have learning English. Geographic distance is a proxy for the probability of the immigrant returning to the origin country (emigration rate) and hence their incentive to learn English. A logit selection equation is used for consistency with earlier studies of the determinants of English language fluency. As logit and probit models of language fluency with these data yield similar results, the specification of the selection equation employed will have results similar to the more familiar specification based on a probit selection specification (Heckman 1979). Estimation of both types of models confirms this.
10 Similar findings regarding the complementarity of language skills with education and labor market experience are found for Canada (Chiswick and Miller 2000).
11 Using the equations with the selectivity corrections (Table 2, columns ii and iv), the partial effect of pre-immigration experience at 10 years is 1.7% for those who are fluent in English and 1.1% for those who are not fluent.
12 Evaluated at 10 years duration it is 1.3% per year for the fluent and also 1.1% per year for those who are not fluent when the selectivity correction is applied (Table 2, Columns ii and iv).

[13] See Korenman and Neumark (1991) for a discussion of the effect of marriage on earnings among men.
[14] Chiswick (1997) shows, using data from the 1980 and 1990 U.S. Censuses, that post-World War II immigrants from the Soviet Union, predominately refugees, have very low earnings initially but their earnings rise rapidly with duration of residence.
[15] This is obtained (Table 1, Column v) from $0.018(8 - 3) = 0.09$ or 9%.
[16] The partial effect of the unemployment rate on the natural logarithm of earnings (Table 1, Column v), is:

$$\partial \ln Y / \partial U = -0.018 + 0.00063(YRS),$$

which diminishes linearly in absolute value as years in the U.S. increases, and reaches zero at about 29 years.
[17] More complex specifications are precluded by the limited number of period of immigration intervals and the small variability in the adult male unemployment rate in the post-World War II period.
[18] The partial effects and t-ratios in this specification which is otherwise the same as Table 1, Column (v) are:

Variable	Coefficient	t-ratio
UR	−.0288	−10.42
UR squared*	0.000159	6.88
Years in U.S. Labor Market		
Adjusted R square = 0.4192		

[19] The partial effect is: $\partial \ln Y / \partial U = -0.0288 + 2(0.000159)(U)(YRS)$. $\partial \ln Y / \partial U$ at the mean unemployment rate of 5.1 equals 1.26 at ten years in the U.S. labor market and equals zero at 17.8 years. The mean years in the U.S. labor market is 13 years.
[20] The selection variables in the fluent and not fluent samples are defined as f_i/F_i and $-f_i/(1 - F_i)$, where f_i and F_i are the standard normal density and standard normal distribution functions, respectively, evaluated at the level of the index of fluency for individual i computed using Lee's (1983) methodology.
[21] An alternative methodology is to estimate the specification presented in Table 1 using an Instrumental Variables (IV) estimator. Results using this procedure on 1980 Census data for the U.S. and Canada are reported in Chiswick and Miller (1992) and for several countries in Chiswick and Miller (1995). Note that identification in the selectivity-corrected estimating equation is obtained through both the identifying instruments and the non-linearity of the selection-correction term (lambda). This may account for the relatively greater reliability (robustness) of the selectivity corrected compared to the IV estimates.
[22] The variable is associated with higher earnings (at the margin of statistical significance) among the small sample of immigrants from the heterogenous Other South-East Asia ($t = 1.99$). A positive effect on earnings could arise where immigrants can work in ethnic labor markets that afford protection against discrimination experienced in the general labor market. It is not clear, however, why the estimated impact for immigrants from Other South-East Asia is so different from that estimated for other birthplace regions.

References

Ahmed B, Gregory Robinson J (1994) *Estimates of Emigration of the Foreign-Born Population: 1980–1990*. Technical Working Paper No. 9, Washington, D.C.: U.S. Bureau of the Census

Bartel A, Koch M (1991) Internal Migration of U.S. Immigrants. In: Abowd JM, Freeman RB (eds) *Immigration, Trade and the Labor Market*. University of Chicago Press, Chicago 121–134

Ben-Porath Y (1967) The Production of Human Capital and the Life Cycle of Earnings. *Journal of Political Economy* 75(4):352–365
Chiswick BR (1978) The Effect of Americanization on the Earnings of Foreign-born Men. *Journal of Political Economy* 86(5):897–921
Chiswick BR (1979) The Economic Progress of Immigrants: Some Apparently Universal Patterns. In: Fellner W (ed) *Contemporary Economic Problems*. American Enterprise Institute, Washington 357–399
Chiswick BR (1997) Soviet Jews in the United States: Language and Labour Market Adjustments Revisited. In: Lewin-Epstein N, Ro'i Y, Ritterband P (eds) *Russian Jews on Three Continents: Migration and Resettlement*. Frank Cass, London 233–260
Chiswick BR (1998) Hebrew Language Usage: Determinants and Effects on Earnings Among Immigrants in Israel. *Journal of Population Economics* 11(2):253–271
Chiswick BR, Cohen Y, Zach T (1997) The Labor Market Status of Immigrants: Effects of the Unemployment Rate at Arrival and Duration of Residence. *Industrial and Labor Relations Review* 50(2):289–303
Chiswick BR, Miller PW (1985) Immigrant Generation and Income in Australia. *Economic Record* 61(173):540–553
Chiswick BR, Miller PW (1988) Earnings in Canada: The Roles of Immigrant Generation, French Ethnicity and Language. *Research in Population Economics* 6:183–224
Chiswick BR, Miller PW (1992) Language in the Immigrant Labor Market. In: Chiswick BR (ed) *Immigration, Language, and Ethnicity: Canada and the United States*. American Enterprise Institute, Washington D.C. 229–296
Chiswick BR, Miller PW (1995) The Endogeneity between Language and Earnings: International Analyses. *Journal of Labor Economics* 13(2):246–288
Chiswick BR, Miller PW (1998) English Language Fluency Among Immigrants in the United States. *Research in Labor Economics* 17:151–200
Chiswick BR, Miller PW (2000) The Complementarity of Language and Other Human Capital: Immigrants Earnings in Canada. RIIM Working Paper No. 00-08, Vancouver, July
Chiswick BR, Repetto G (2001) Immigrant Adjustment in Israel: The Determinants of Literacy and Fluency in Hebrew and Their Effects on Earnings. In: Djajic S (ed) *International Migration: Trends, Policies and Economic Impact*. Routledge, London 204–228
Heckman JJ (1979) Sample Selection Bias as a Specification Error. *Econometrica* 47:153–162
Korenman S, Neumark D (1991) Does Marriage Really Make Men More Productive. *Journal of Human Resources* 26(2): (Spring) pp. 282–308
Lee L-F (1983) Generalized Econometric Models with Selectivity. *Econometrica* 51:507–512
Mincer J (1974) *Schooling, Experience and Earnings*. National Bureau of Economic Research, New York
Nakamura A, Nakamura M (1992) Wage Rates of Immigrant and Native Men in Canada and the United States. In: Chiswick BR (ed) *Immigration, Language and Ethnicity: Canada and the United States*. American Enterprise Institute, Washington, D.C. 145–166
Stewart JB, Hyclak T (1984) An Analyses of Earnings Profiles of Immigrants. *Review of Economics and Statistics* 66(2):292–303
Tainer E (1988) English Language Proficiency and Earnings Among Foreign-Born Men. *Journal of Human Resources* 23(1):108–122
White H (1980) A Heteroskedasticity-Consistent Covariance Matrix Estimator and a Direct Test for Heteroskedasticity. *Econometrica* 48:817–838

[7]
You Can't Take It with You? Immigrant Assimilation and the Portability of Human Capital

Rachel M. Friedberg, *Brown University and National Bureau of Economic Research*

The national origin of an individual's human capital is a crucial determinant of its value. Education and labor market experience acquired abroad are significantly less valued than human capital obtained domestically. This difference can fully explain the earnings disadvantage of immigrants relative to comparable natives in Israel. Variation in the return to foreign schooling across origin countries may reflect differences in its quality and compatibility with the host labor market. The return to foreign experience is generally insignificant. Acquiring additional education following immigration appears to confer a compound benefit by raising the return to education acquired abroad.

I. Introduction

In recent years, much attention has been devoted in the labor literature to the issue of immigrant labor market assimilation. Upon arrival in their host country, immigrants usually command lower wages than native-born workers with comparable measured characteristics. The literature

I thank Joshua Angrist, David Cutler, Henry Farber, Stanley Fischer, Lawrence Katz, and David Weil for helpful discussions; Alexander Cavallo for able research assistance; and Michal Peleg of the Social Sciences Data Archive at the Hebrew University of Jerusalem for providing access to the data. Financial support from the Falk Institute for Economic Research in Israel, the Program for the Study of the Israeli Economy at MIT, and the U.S. Department of Education is gratefully acknowledged.

has focused on quantifying the size of this initial earnings differential and the rate at which it diminishes with time since migration (see Chiswick 1978a; Borjas 1985, 1995; Friedberg 1992; LaLonde and Topel 1992; Baker and Benjamin 1994; Schoeni 1997). At issue is whether immigrants ever attain earnings parity with natives and, if so, how long this process takes. A related question is how the earnings gap differs for immigrants from different countries and different arrival cohorts (see Chiswick 1986; Jasso and Rosenzweig 1988, 1990; Borjas 1992; Funkhouser and Trejo 1995; Butcher and DiNardo 1996; Duleep and Regets 1996).[1]

The innovation of this article is to introduce to this analysis a distinction between human capital acquired abroad and human capital acquired domestically. Foreign and domestic human capital may not be very close substitutes, and considering them as a homogeneous factor may be misleading. Many immigrants complete their schooling in their countries of origin. Many, however, immigrate at young ages and obtain virtually all their human capital after immigration. A sizable number possess a combination of foreign and domestic human capital. Thus, although previous work on immigrant and native earnings has allowed the return to human capital to differ for immigrants and natives, doing so is not equivalent to distinguishing between domestic- and foreign-source human capital in the analysis of earnings determination.[2]

This study demonstrates that the most important factor determining the gap in the standard human-capital-corrected earnings of immigrants and natives is the source of their human capital. Foreign human capital often—although not always—earns a lower return than domestic human capital, and this fact alone is sufficient to fully explain the residual earnings disadvantage of immigrants.[3]

The data most commonly used to study immigrants in the United States are the series of public-use microdata samples of the U.S. Census of Population. These data do not contain adequate information to reliably determine the source of an immigrant's education. There is no direct measure of where schooling was obtained, and the information on an immigrant's year of arrival, which could be used to impute it, is reported in bracketed form. It is therefore not feasible to analyze the importance of

---

[1] For a comprehensive study, see Smith and Edmonston (1997). For reviews of the literature, see LaLonde and Topel (1996) and Borjas (1999).

[2] Chiswick (1978a) and Fishelson, Weiss, and Mark (1980) consider the difference in the return to foreign and domestic schooling, but they do not bring this directly to the question of immigrant assimilation.

[3] Eckstein and Weiss (1998) study recent immigrants to Israel from the former Soviet Union and find that the initial return to imported skills is negligible, but that it rises with time in Israel.

human capital source using the U.S. Census.[4] The Census of Population in Israel lends itself more readily to this kind of study. It is possible in this data to precisely date the timing of immigration. In addition, the lack of a systematic change in the unobserved quality of successive immigrant cohorts to Israel makes it possible to use a single cross section of data to analyze assimilation rates. The Israeli case provides a large, richly varied pool of immigrants to observe. These immigrants have come from a wide range of countries and have vastly different educational and occupational backgrounds.

This article first establishes that the national origin of an individual's human capital is a crucial determinant of its return. It shows that the gap in the residual earnings of immigrant and native workers is eliminated or even reversed once this factor is taken into account. It then goes on to show when the difference in returns is most marked and what factors mitigate it. Section II of the article presents the econometric model and highlights important restrictions implicit in the standard specification used in the immigration literature. The third section provides basic facts about immigration to Israel and describes the data used. Section IV presents the empirical results in three steps. First, it examines the effects of immigrant status and length of residence on earnings, comparing the returns to human capital obtained in the country of origin and in Israel. Second, it analyzes whether human capital acquired subsequent to immigration may raise the return to human capital obtained abroad. This is followed by an analysis of the extent to which the portability of education depends on its level or configuration, in terms of type and source. The final section of the article summarizes and discusses implications for the immigration literature and for immigration policy.

II. Immigrants' Earnings and the Returns to Human Capital

When immigrants first arrive in a new country, they are at a disadvantage in the labor market relative to natives with comparable demographic characteristics and measured skill levels. One reason is that natives have country-specific skills and information that immigrants lack. As immigrants spend time in the host country and gradually acquire this country-specific knowledge, their labor market performance may improve relative to that of their native counterparts. The rate at which the earnings gap between immigrants and natives narrows with years since migration is referred to as the assimilation rate. The standard earnings function used in the immigration literature (due to Chiswick 1978a) is

---

[4] The 1976 Survey of Income and Education (SIE) is a U.S. data set containing direct information on country of schooling, but the sample of immigrants is small. See Borjas (1982) and Friedberg (1993) for examples of papers that use the SIE.

$$y = \alpha_0 + \alpha_1 ED + \alpha_2 EXP + \alpha_3 EXP^2 + \alpha_4 M$$
$$+ \alpha_5 YSM + \alpha_6 YSM^2 + \varepsilon, \qquad (1)$$

where y is log earnings, ED is years of schooling completed, EXP is years of potential labor market experience, M is a dummy variable for immigrant status, and YSM is the number of years elapsed since an immigrant's arrival in the host country. Since years since migration is held constant in this regression, the coefficient on the immigrant status dummy measures the initial earnings disadvantage of a newly arrived immigrant relative to an otherwise comparable native. In the absence of systematic changes in the unobserved earnings potential (ε) of successive immigrant arrival cohorts, the coefficients on YSM capture the rate at which the immigrant-native earnings gap narrows as immigrants assimilate into the labor market.

There are some important restrictions implicit in estimating equation (1). To see this, consider recasting the model purely in terms of education and experience. Let ED_i and EXP_i denote years of schooling and potential labor market experience obtained in country i, where $i = 1$ for the country of origin and $i = 2$ for the destination country.[5] Thus,

$$ED = ED_1 + ED_2 \qquad (2)$$

and

$$EXP = EXP_1 + EXP_2. \qquad (3)$$

By definition, YSM = 0 for natives, while for immigrants,

$$YSM = EXP_2 + ED_2 + k, \qquad (4)$$

where $k = \max(0, 6 - \text{age} + YSM)$.[6] Ignoring quadratic terms, equation (1) can, therefore, be rewritten as

$$y = \alpha_0 + \alpha_1(ED_1 + ED_2) + \alpha_2(EXP_1 + EXP_2) + \alpha_4 M$$
$$+ \alpha_5[(ED_2 + EXP_2 + k) \times M] + \varepsilon, \qquad (5)$$

---

[5] By construction, $ED_1 = 0$ and $EXP_1 = 0$ for natives. While some native-born Israelis may have attended school or worked abroad, there is no information available on this in the census data. The return to ED_1 and EXP_1 will therefore measure the return to foreign schooling and experience for immigrants only.

[6] In the data used here, k equals 0 for the 81% of immigrants who migrated to Israel after the age of 6, and k equals between 1 and 6 for the others.

or, collecting terms, as

$$y = \alpha_0 + (\alpha_4 + \alpha_5 \times k)M + \alpha_1 ED_1 + \alpha_1 ED_2 + \alpha_5(ED_2 \times M) \\ + \alpha_2 EXP_1 + \alpha_2 EXP_2 + \alpha_5(EXP_2 \times M) + \varepsilon. \quad (6)$$

There are eight coefficients but only five underlying parameters in this model. Equation (1) is thus equivalent to a restricted version of a human capital earnings function that allows the return to human capital to vary according to its source ($i = 1, 2$) and the worker's nativity ($M = 0, 1$). Relabeling the coefficients, that is,

$$y = \beta_0 + \beta_1 M + \beta_2 ED_1 + \beta_3 ED_2 + \beta_4(ED_2 \times M) \\ + \beta_5 EXP_1 + \beta_6 EXP_2 + \beta_7(EXP_2 \times M) + \varepsilon, \quad (7)$$

we see that equation (1) imposes the following three restrictions: (1) $\beta_2 = \beta_3$, (2) $\beta_5 = \beta_6$, and (3) $\beta_4 = \beta_7$. The first restriction imposes equal returns to immigrants' foreign schooling and natives' domestic schooling. The second restriction imposes equal returns to immigrants' foreign labor market experience and natives' domestic labor market experience. Because of the first two restrictions, the third restriction has two interpretations. It constrains the relative return to immigrants' foreign and domestic human capital to be the same for both education and experience. It also constrains the immigrant-native differential in the return to domestic human capital to be the same for both education and experience.

Although equation (1) is the standard specification used in the literature, as will be seen in the empirical estimates below, the data strongly reject these restrictions. This is not surprising, considering the many reasons why the return to human capital might differ, depending on whether the schooling or experience was acquired abroad or domestically and on whether the worker is an immigrant or a native.

The degree to which the human capital that immigrants acquired in their countries of origin is transferable into earnings potential in their destination country—the "portability" of their human capital—is measured by β_2 and β_5. Differences across origin groups in the value placed on foreign human capital may stem from two factors. First, school quality varies considerably across countries. Immigrants from developed countries, for example, might receive a higher return to their foreign education than immigrants from developing countries because schooling is generally of lower quality in the latter. A second important factor is the compatibility of the human capital received abroad with the skill requirements of the host-country labor market. The more similar the origin and destination countries are in terms of their levels of economic development, industrial and occupational structures, institutional settings, and so forth, the more likely it is that education and work experience received in the origin country will be highly valued in the destination labor market. Even within country of origin, the type of education is likely to be important for its portability. For example, elementary school education might transfer well for many origin groups, while law and other professional schooling might not.

The return to domestic human capital for immigrants may differ from the return received by natives, that is, β_4 and β_7 may not equal zero. On the one hand, natives have an advantage in language and other country-specific knowledge, which may enable them to gain more productivity-enhancing skills from a given year of formal instruction or work experience. On the other hand, time spent at school or work in the host country has compound benefits for immigrants since in addition to acquiring the human capital usually associated with schooling and experience, immigrants gain language skills, learn about domestic institutions and norms, and so forth. The marginal return to a year of investment in domestic human capital could, therefore, be lower or higher for immigrants than for natives.

In addition to the direct effects of foreign and domestic human capital on immigrants' labor market success, there may well be important interactions between them. The earnings of more- and less-skilled immigrants may be compressed upon their arrival in the host country, with both groups constrained to work in low-skill jobs that require little language proficiency or other country-specific human capital. Over time, as they gain exposure to the new labor market, immigrants become better able to maximize the return to their origin-country skills through several types of learning. These include learning by doing on the job, accumulating more information about the host labor market, and engaging in search to find better earnings opportunities and job matches. As a result, immigrants may gradually sort themselves into more differentiated occupations, resulting in a rise in skill differentials (β_2 and β_5) among immigrants with labor market experience in the host country.[7] A rise with time since migration in the return to schooling obtained abroad is definitionally equivalent to a faster assimilation rate for better-educated immigrants. We also might expect earnings growth to be greater for more educated immigrants because the gap between their initial and potential occupational standing is greater.

An even more effective way for immigrants to gain the skills necessary to adapt their previously acquired training to their new country may be

---

[7] For empirical evidence documenting occupational downgrading upon arrival and subsequent upgrading with duration of residence, see Chiswick (1978*b*) and Jasso and Rosenzweig (1988) for the United States, and Sabatello (1979) and Flug, Kasir, and Ofer (1992) for Israel.

by obtaining further formal education after arrival. Attending school in the host country may aid in the transferability of an immigrant's human capital by giving him the language proficiency needed to literally translate his skills. It may also provide him with other country-specific human capital that will enable him better to apply his previously acquired skills in the new labor market setting.[8] Especially for immigrants who arrive with education or training that is not very well matched to the host country, attending school there may be invaluable in teaching them to use that human capital in ways rewarded in the host labor market. Such knowledge might be very difficult to obtain without further formal instruction. A higher return to an immigrant's foreign schooling when it has been followed by schooling in the host country is consistent with the hypothesis that domestic schooling raises the return to schooling obtained abroad. It could, however, also reflect positive self-selection on the part of individuals who choose to get further schooling after immigration. Immigrants differ in both their incentives and their capacity to acquire domestic human capital. More educated immigrants might have a higher net benefit from acquiring domestic skills than less educated immigrants, and if prior education is correlated with unobserved ability, the estimated return to domestic human capital will be higher for the more educated. Unfortunately, it is impossible to distinguish between treatment and selection effects using the available data.

To measure the importance of interaction effects, equation (7) is modified by the addition of three variables interacting foreign and domestic human capital:[9]

$$y = \beta_0 + \beta_1 M + \beta_2 ED_1 + \beta_3 ED_2 + \beta_4 (ED_2 \times M) + \beta_5 EXP_1 \\ + \beta_6 EXP_2 + \beta_7 (EXP_2 \times M) + \beta_8 (ED_1 \times ED_2) \quad (8) \\ + \beta_9 (ED_1 \times EXP_2) + \beta_{10} (EXP_1 \times EXP_2) + \varepsilon.$$

III. Immigration to Israel and the Census of Population Data

Like the United States, Israel is a country of immigrants. Israel continues to receive very large inflows, relative to its population. Most

---

[8] One example is that in Israel, as in many countries, immigrant lawyers and physicians must pass a series of licensing exams in order to practice. In the case of law, there is a "conversion" exam covering general legal principles, which is followed by the bar exam. For physicians, there is a licensing exam for general competence, which is followed by specialization exams. For all of these exams, immigrants commonly attend 6-month-long preparatory courses (often offered in their native languages). There are also required internship periods for both law and medicine, which typically last over a year.

[9] Note that if $EXP_1 > 0$, then by construction $ED_2 = 0$, so there is no interaction term for EXP_1 and ED_2.

current immigrants are from the former Soviet Union. Earlier immigrants originated in diverse parts of the world, with the largest concentrations coming from Eastern Europe and North Africa.

The data used in this study are the public-use microdata samples of the two most recent available Israeli Censuses of Population and Housing, conducted in 1972 and 1983 (Israel Central Bureau of Statistics 1974, 1985). As stated earlier, these data have the advantage that year of migration is recorded as a continuous variable, rather than in the bracketed form available in the U.S. Census. Appendix B uses both Israeli censuses to show that, in the Israeli case, one cross section is sufficient to identify the parameters of interest. This is because the coefficient on years since migration in the single 1983 cross section is found indeed to reflect assimilation rather than a decline in cohort quality over time. The analysis can therefore be conducted on the 1983 data alone.[10] This is another strength, relative to the U.S. case, in which the issue of changing cohort quality necessitates the use of multiple cross sections. All Israeli citizens—Jews, Arabs, and others—are included in the census. This covers virtually all residents of Israel proper, as well as citizens living in the West Bank and the Gaza Strip, who constitute 2% of the Israeli population. The census microdata are a one-in-five sample of the population.

In order to facilitate comparisons with results from the literature on immigration to the United States, which focuses primarily on male immigrants, the sample is restricted to men ages 25–65.[11] In addition, so as not to confound the present analysis with the issue of Arab-Jewish differences in the labor market, Arabs are not included in the sample. Kibbutz and collective members, students, and the self-employed are also excluded. Finally, only full-time, salaried, nonagricultural workers reporting earnings of between 5,000 and 500,000 Israeli shekels per month are retained.[12] After these adjustments, 54,103 individuals remain in the 1983 sample.

Only one-third of these men are native-born Israelis. The foreign-born

---

[10] Although most of the literature on immigrant assimilation uses cross-sectional data, this is primarily due to the unavailability of panel data. Panel data would be superior since one could directly track individual developments over time rather than infer them.

[11] For military security reasons, men between the ages of 18 and 24 are coded as age 21 in the public-use files of the census microdata. Such censoring generates difficulties in calculating many key variables used in the analysis, such as years since migration. Men under the age of 25 are therefore excluded from the sample. Given Israel's compulsory 3-year military service, many men in this age range would not be employed in the civilian labor market in any event.

[12] This is equal to approximately $90–$9,000 in 1983 U.S. dollars. About 10% of the sample had zero income. Another 3% had income below 5,000 shekels, and 0.1% had income over 500,000 shekels.

Table 1
Area of Origin of Immigrants to Israel

Percentage of immigrants by continent group:	
Western Hemisphere and Western Europe	9.01
Eastern Europe	29.26
USSR	12.88
Asia and Africa	48.85
Percentage of immigrants by most common countries:	
Morocco	14.65
Romania	14.29
Soviet Union	12.88
Iraq	8.79
Poland	8.72
Iran	3.72
Yemen	3.63
Turkey	3.59
Egypt and the Sudan	2.81
Tunisia	2.34
Bulgaria	2.28
Germany	2.26
Libya	1.85
India and Pakistan	1.59
Argentina	1.36
Hungary	1.31
Czechoslovakia	1.23
United States	1.04

SOURCE.—Author's tabulation of the 1983 Israeli Census of Population microdata.

are classified into four area-of-origin groups: Western (primarily from Western Europe and the Americas), Eastern European, Soviet, and those from Asia and Africa. The countries included under each of these headings are listed in appendix A. Table 1 shows the breakdown of immigrants into these four groups, as well as the major countries of origin. Roughly half of the immigrants are of African or Asian descent, and half are of European, American, or Soviet origin. Forty-two percent are from Morocco, Romania, or the Soviet Union, with the remainder distributed over a wide range of countries.

The mean characteristics of the 1983 sample are presented in table 2. The average age of immigrants is 45.6; this is 11 years older than the typical native. The mean immigrant came to Israel in 1956, at age 19, but at the time of the survey, 14.7% of Soviet immigrants had been in Israel for only 5 years or less. Mean monthly earnings for the native sample are 44,796 Israeli shekels, or about $750 in 1983 U.S. dollars. Information is available in the census on hours worked per week. However, many people appear to have reported hours per month instead. Since creating an hourly wage variable might introduce more noise than signal to the data, the monthly earnings measure is used in all of the analysis below.

Table 3 contains detailed information on schooling for the five broad origin groups. The average years of completed schooling among native Israelis is 12.4 years. Educational attainment is highest for Western im-

Table 2
Summary Statistics

	Natives	All Immigrants	Immigrants from the West	Immigrants from Eastern Europe	Immigrants from the USSR	Immigrants from Asia or Africa
Gross monthly income (1983 Israeli shekels)	44,796	41,505	55,593	48,270	41,294	34,910
	(32,056)	(29,754)	(37,737)	(33,000)	(29,014)	(23,833)
Hours worked per week	48.9	47.9	48.4	48.1	47.5	47.8
	(6.5)	(5.8)	(6.5)	(6.0)	(5.5)	(5.6)
Weeks worked per year	50.5	51.0	50.2	51.3	51.2	50.9
	(8.1)	(7.3)	(7.3)	(6.3)	(7.0)	(7.8)
Year of migration	...	1956	1958	1953	1968	1955
		(11.0)	(14.6)	(9.9)	(12.2)	(8.0)
Percentage with 5 or fewer years since migration	...	3.7	9.1	1.1	14.7	1.2
Age at migration	...	18.7	18.9	19.8	29.1	15.2
		(12.6)	(13.6)	(11.7)	(14.0)	(10.7)
Age	34.8	45.6	44.2	49.8	44.3	43.7
	(8.6)	(10.9)	(10.8)	(10.6)	(11.5)	(10.1)
Years of experience (total)	16.4	28.7	24.1	32.3	26.2	28.2
	(8.9)	(12.4)	(12.1)	(12.3)	(12.7)	(11.8)
Years of experience abroad	...	6.2	4.7	6.4	13.0	4.7
		(9.2)	(7.9)	(8.6)	(12.5)	(7.9)
Years of experience in Israel	16.4	22.5	19.3	25.9	13.2	23.5
	(8.9)	(10.5)	(12.1)	(10.3)	(9.8)	(8.7)
N	18,488	35,615	3,209	10,422	4,587	17,397

NOTE.—Figures are means for the sample of full-time, salaried, nonagricultural male workers ages 25–65 in the 1983 Israeli Census of Population. Standard deviations are in parentheses.

Table 3
Schooling Characteristics

	Natives	All Immigrants	Immigrants from the West	Immigrants from Eastern Europe	Immigrants from the USSR	Immigrants from Asia or Africa
Years of schooling:						
Total	12.4	10.8	14.1	11.5	12.0	9.4
	(3.3)	(4.2)	(3.9)	(3.9)	(4.0)	(3.9)
Abroad	...	7.0	9.2	7.9	10.3	5.2
	...	(5.4)	(6.9)	(5.0)	(5.0)	(4.6)
In Israel	12.4	3.7	4.8	3.6	1.7	4.1
	(3.3)	(5.1)	(6.1)	(5.3)	(4.0)	(4.8)
Terminated education in Israel (%)	...	46.3	51.6	42.7	21.3	54.1
Highest level attained (%):						
Elementary	12.8	27.4	7.7	24.8	18.7	34.9
Secondary	51.0	41.4	34.4	40.8	35.9	44.6
Postsecondary	35.9	27.3	57.3	33.4	43.7	13.8
Whether level attained and source (%):						
Elementary = F	...	67.9	69.2	76.7	88.0	57.1
Elementary = I	99.7	28.4	30.3	22.4	10.3	36.3
Secondary = F	...	35.2	52.6	40.1	63.8	21.5
Secondary = I	86.9	33.6	39.1	34.1	15.8	36.8
Postsecondary = F	...	13.3	31.7	14.1	33.5	4.1
Postsecondary = I	35.9	14.0	25.6	19.3	10.2	9.6
Undergraduate = F	...	14.5	34.9	15.4	34.6	4.9
Undergraduate = I	35.9	12.9	22.5	18.1	9.2	9.0
Graduate = F	...	4.4	16.8	4.6	9.2	.9
Graduate = I	11.1	4.3	11.2	6.5	3.0	2.2

NOTE.—"Elementary = I" is a dummy variable, indicating that elementary schooling was completed in Israel; "Elementary = F" indicates that elementary schooling was completed abroad. Standard errors are in parentheses.

migrants (14.1 years) and lowest for Asian/African immigrants (9.4 years). More than one-third of Asian/African immigrants have only attended elementary school, while over one-third of native Israelis and 57.3% of Western immigrants have had some postsecondary education.

The measure of education used here is the number of completed years of schooling.[13] To construct measures of the years of schooling completed in the country of origin and in Israel, it is assumed that children start school at the age of seven and attend continuously until completing their total years of schooling. Since the age at which an immigrant arrived in Israel is known, one can calculate the years of schooling that would have been completed before and after his move to Israel.[14] The resulting mean years of schooling in Israel and abroad are shown in the second and third rows of table 3. Just under half of all immigrants have attended school in Israel, with 19% of them having received all their schooling domestically and 27.5% having attended school both before and after immigrating. The average fraction of schooling acquired abroad is 65%. This fraction is lowest for Asian/African immigrants (55%) and highest for Soviet immigrants (86%), only one-fifth of whom have attended school in Israel at all.

IV. Empirical Results

A. The Return to Foreign versus Domestic Human Capital for Immigrants and Natives

The first column of table 4 presents estimates of equation (5), the standard specification that constrains the returns to schooling and experience to be invariant to the worker's nativity and to where the human

---

[13] Observations for which the last type of schooling was postsecondary yeshiva (religious academy) are excluded from the sample. This is because religious Jews often continue to study at such institutions throughout their lives. Attending a postsecondary yeshiva is better classified as a religious activity than as a program of human capital accumulation applicable in the labor market. Thus, including in the sample individuals who count years spent at a yeshiva in their total years of schooling would bias the coefficient on schooling downward. Also excluded are the small number of other people in the sample who report over 27 years of schooling.

[14] For an individual with a discontinuous schooling history who temporarily suspended his education while still in his country of origin, this method will overstate the number of years acquired abroad. The bias will be greater the longer an individual was out of school between schooling spells abroad or—if he did not return to school abroad at all following the interruption—the longer he was out of school before migrating. This will lead to an underestimate of β_2 and an overestimate of β_3. To test the accuracy of this imputation technique, I applied it to data from the U.S. Survey of Income and Education, a dataset which also contains direct information on years of schooling completed abroad. The correlation between the true and imputed measures of origin-country schooling was 0.78.

Table 4
The Return to Human Capital

	(1)	(2)	(3)
Immigrant	−.253	.040	.374
	(.008)	(.006)	(.233)
Education	.081	...	...
	(.006)	...	...
Education abroad	...	.076	.071
	...	(.001)	(.001)
Education in Israel	...	.088	.100
	...	(.001)	(.001)
Experience	.0068	...	...
	(.0002)	...	...
Experience abroad	...	.0032	.0010
	...	(.0003)	(.0003)
Experience in Israel	...	.014	.017
	...	(.0002)	(.0004)
Years since migration	.0081	...	...
	(.0003)	...	...
Education in Israel × immigrant	...	...	−.020
	...	...	(.002)
Experience in Israel × immigrant	...	...	−.0057
	...	...	(.0005)
R^2	.254	.266	.269
N	54,103	54,103	54,103

NOTE.—Dependent variable is log monthly earnings. Standard errors are in parentheses.

capital was obtained. The estimated returns to schooling and experience are 8% and 0.7%, respectively. Immigrants are found to earn approximately 25% less than natives upon arrival, with their relative earnings rising by 0.8% per year following migration.

The restrictions implicit in equation (5) are easily rejected. The second column of table 4 shows that human capital obtained abroad is of significantly less value in the Israeli labor market than human capital obtained in Israel. The return to domestic schooling is 8.8%, while the return to foreign schooling is only 7.6%.[15] The return to domestic experience is 1.4%, while the return to foreign experience is just 0.3%. F-tests of the equality of the coefficients on foreign and domestic human capital yield p-values of zero to the fourth decimal place.

Estimates of equation (7), the fully unrestricted form of equation (5), are presented in the third column. All three of the restrictions listed following equation (7) are rejected. The return to domestic human capital

---

[15] Using the 1970 U.S. Census, Chiswick (1978a) finds that the return to schooling obtained abroad is 1 percentage point higher than the return to U.S. schooling. These results may be affected by the difficulty of imputing accurate measures of premigration and postmigration schooling in this data, in which years since migration are reported in 5- and 10-year bracketed intervals.

is higher than the return to foreign human capital, and it is higher for natives than for immigrants. The native-immigrant gap is 2 percentage points for schooling and 0.6 percentage points for experience. The fact that natives receive a higher return lends support to the argument that their country-specific skills, including their superior Hebrew fluency, enable them to extract more productive potential from a year of schooling or experience than can immigrants. There is a 10.0% return to domestic schooling for natives, an 8.0% return to domestic schooling for immigrants, and a 7.1% return to foreign schooling for immigrants. The results for experience show a similar pattern: native earnings rise by 1.7% for each year of domestic experience, while immigrants gain 1.1% for each year of domestic experience and just 0.1% for years of foreign experience. F-tests of the equality of the native and immigrant coefficients yield p-values of zero to the fourth decimal place.

At first glance, the results of equations (5) and (7) might seem to contradict each other. By definition in equation (4), $ED_2 \times M$ and $EXP_2 \times M$ roughly sum to years since migration. The negative estimated coefficients β_4 and β_7 on the former variables in equation (7) might therefore seem inconsistent with the positive coefficient on the latter found in equation (5), α_5. The key to reconciling these results lies in understanding the difference in the implicit benchmark in the two specifications. The coefficients β_4 and β_7 measure the return to immigrants' domestic human capital relative to the return to natives' domestic human capital. The coefficient α_5 measures the return to immigrants' domestic human capital relative to a weighted average of the returns to natives' domestic and immigrants' foreign human capital, which are constrained in equation (5) to be equal. The estimates from the two specifications are, therefore, not inconsistent: the return to immigrants' domestic human capital is lower than the return to natives' domestic human capital, but it is higher than the return to immigrants' foreign human capital.[16]

The earnings gap between immigrants and natives can be fully explained by the lower value placed on the immigrants' human capital. In equation (5), immigrants were found to earn about one-quarter less than natives upon arrival. In equation (7), once the return to human capital is allowed to differ for immigrants and natives and for foreign and domestic human capital, newly arrived immigrants no longer earn less than natives.

---

[16] These two specifications highlight a problem with the standard interpretation of α_5 as a measure of the assimilation rate. Recall that the assimilation rate is the rate at which immigrants' earnings grow more quickly than natives' over time as both groups accumulate domestic labor market experience. In fact, the coefficient α_5 actually measures the rise in immigrants' earnings, holding total education and experience constant, as the source mix of their human capital shifts from foreign to domestic.

Table 5
The Return to Human Capital (by Area of Origin)

	Natives	All Immigrants	Immigrants from the West	Immigrants from Eastern Europe	Immigrants from the USSR	Immigrants from Asia or Africa
Education abroad		.071	.071	.067	.064	.057
		(.001)	(.003)	(.002)	(.002)	(.001)
Education in Israel	.100	.079	.081	.072	.077	.065
	(.001)	(.001)	(.003)	(.002)	(.003)	(.001)
Experience abroad		.001	.001	−.005	−.0002	−.0002
		(.0004)	(.002)	(.001)	(.0007)	(.0006)
Experience in Israel	.017	.012	.014	.008	.014	.009
	(.0004)	(.0003)	(.001)	(.001)	(.001)	(.001)
Constant	9.01	9.39	9.40	9.65	9.49	9.52
	(.018)	(.015)	(.055)	(.034)	(.035)	(.022)
R^2	.297	.250	.205	.223	.292	.176
N	18,488	35,615	3,209	10,422	4,587	17,397

NOTE.—Dependent variable is log monthly earnings. Standard errors are in parentheses.

In fact, taking into consideration that their human capital is all foreign and that foreign human capital is less valued than natives' human capital, immigrants earn roughly 37.4% more than natives. This is seen in the change in the value of the estimated coefficient on the immigrant dummy variable across the two specifications.

The results when immigrants are split into four area-of-origin groups are shown in table 5. Foreign human capital always earns a lower return than domestic human capital. The highest return to schooling obtained abroad is found among immigrants from the West (7.1%), while immigrants from Asia and Africa earn the lowest return (5.7%). While this pattern supports the idea that Western school quality is higher and better matched to the Israeli labor market than Asian/African schooling, these results could also reflect less discrimination between Western and Asian/African immigrant workers at lower levels of education than at higher levels. With respect to experience accumulated abroad, the return is actually negative for Eastern Europeans (−0.5%) and is insignificantly different from zero for Westerners, Soviets, and Asians/Africans.[17]

Comparing the return to Israeli schooling across groups, Westerners again receive the highest return (8.1%) and Asian/African immigrants the lowest (6.5%). With respect to Israeli labor market experience, Soviet and

---

[17] A negative coefficient on EXP_1 could reflect the negative effect on earnings of immigrating at an older age (see Friedberg 1992).

Western immigrants earn the highest return (1.4%, as compared to 1.7% for natives), with the other immigrant groups earning substantially less.

B. Raising the Return to Foreign Human Capital

Having established that the lower value placed on immigrants' human capital fully explains their earnings disadvantage relative to natives with the same observable characteristics, a natural question is whether this difference is fixed or whether there exist factors that can reduce or eliminate it. This section studies whether acquiring domestic labor market experience or education might raise the return to foreign human capital. Estimates of equation (8) are reported in table 6.[18]

One way immigrants may learn to adapt their previously acquired training to Israel could be by obtaining further formal education after arrival. The interaction of foreign and Israeli schooling enters positively and significantly in the regression for immigrants taken as a whole, meaning that immigrants who attend school in Israel earn a higher return on their country-of-origin human capital than immigrants who completed their education abroad. For the average immigrant, who has completed 3.7 years of schooling in Israel, this interaction raises the average return to origin-source education to 7.6%, eliminating half of the gap between the returns to foreign and Israeli schooling. For Asian/African immigrants, there is a large rise in the return to foreign schooling resulting from acquiring further education in Israel. Just 3 years of schooling in Israel completely eliminate the difference in the return to foreign schooling and the return to Israeli schooling. It is not surprising that the indirect effect of domestic schooling would be largest for immigrants from Asia and Africa since, among immigrant groups, their country-of-origin education is initially least valued in the Israeli economy. East European immigrants also experience an increase in the return to their source-country education following schooling in Israel, but the effect for this group is smaller. For Western immigrants, there is a puzzling negative effect of having attended school in Israel on the return to education acquired abroad. It is unclear what lies behind this anomaly, though it could be negative selection: the results overall are consistent with a model in which acquiring further education raises the return to schooling obtained abroad. But as pointed out above, they could also reflect self-

---

[18] In results not reported here (see Friedberg 1996), immigrants who do not speak Hebrew are found to earn 14% less than other immigrants. This effect is larger for more educated immigrants. The rise in the return to foreign schooling associated with some knowledge of Hebrew is 2.2 percentage points per year of schooling. Hebrew language ability thus considerably raises the return to schooling obtained abroad, but it cannot eliminate the gap between the returns to foreign and domestic education.

Table 6
Postimmigration Human Capital Accumulation

	All Immigrants	Immigrants from the West	Immigrants from Eastern Europe	Immigrants from the USSR	Immigrants from Asia or Africa
Education abroad	.072 (.001)	.068 (.004)	.071 (.003)	.057 (.003)	.057 (.003)
Education in Israel	.078 (.001)	.085 (.003)	.070 (.002)	.081 (.003)	.063 (.002)
Experience abroad	.0009 (.001)	−.0009 (.002)	−.005 (.002)	−.002 (.001)	−.001 (.001)
Experience in Israel	.012 (.001)	.012 (.002)	.010 (.001)	.008 (.002)	.010 (.001)
Education abroad × education in Israel	.0010 (.0002)	−.0018 (.0005)	.0008 (.0003)	.0001 (.0006)	.0023 (.0003)
Education abroad × experience in Israel	−.00003 (.0001)	.0004 (.0002)	−.0002 (.0001)	.0006 (.0002)	−.0001 (.0001)
Experience abroad × experience in Israel	.00003 (.00003)	.0001 (.0002)	−.00004 (.0001)	.0002 (.0001)	.0001 (.0001)
Constant	9.38 (.017)	9.43 (.061)	9.61 (.039)	9.56 (.038)	9.51 (.028)
R^2	.251	.210	.224	.296	.180
N	35,615	3,209	10,422	4,587	17,397

Note.—Dependent variable is log monthly earnings. Standard errors are in parentheses.

selection on the part of individuals who choose to get further schooling after immigration.

As argued earlier, accumulating labor market experience in Israel may also enable an immigrant to translate the human capital he brought with him into terms valued in the Israeli labor market. For immigrants taken as a whole, the interaction between foreign education and domestic experience is insignificant. This is because the effect exists only for certain area-of-origin groups. The return to foreign schooling rises with experience in Israel for Western and Soviet immigrants, but it is unaffected by domestic experience or even reduced for others. Even for the former groups, the effect is small, resulting only in a roughly 0.5 percentage point rise for every 10 years of experience. Finally, the interaction between foreign and domestic labor market experience is largely insignificantly different from zero, with marginally significant positive effects for Soviet and Asian/African immigrants.

C. Simulated Earnings Profiles

The empirical results thus far can usefully be summarized using simulated earnings profiles. Figures 1–3 use parameter estimates from equation (8), augmented by quadratic terms in experience, to trace out earnings profiles for hypothetical native and immigrant workers. Since the return to foreign work experience was found to be generally insignificantly different from zero in table 6, the simulations focus on new labor market entrants (i.e., immigrants with $EXP_1 = 0$).

Figure 1 charts the earnings paths of five high school graduates. One is a native, and the others are new immigrants from the four major origin groups. The figure shows how monthly earnings rise with domestic labor market experience, or, equivalently for the immigrants, with years since migration. Earnings are at similar levels and increase at roughly the same rate for natives and Ashkenazi immigrants (those from the West, Eastern Europe, and the Soviet Union), with immigrants from Asia and Africa lagging far behind. The earnings of immigrants from Asia and Africa would be even lower if their lower average years of schooling were taken into account.

Figure 2 traces out earnings profiles for another set of high school graduates, this time focusing on differences in the source of schooling. There are one native and three immigrants: one who was educated abroad ($ED_1 = 12$, $ED_2 = 0$), one who was educated in Israel ($ED_1 = 0$, $ED_2 = 12$), and one who has a mix of foreign and domestic education ($ED_1 = 6$, $ED_2 = 6$). The graph shows that earnings are generally higher for natives than for immigrants, and higher, the greater the fraction of schooling obtained in Israel rather than abroad.

Finally, figure 3 displays the earnings paths of four new immigrants. Two arrive as high school dropouts ($ED_1 = 8$), with one entering the

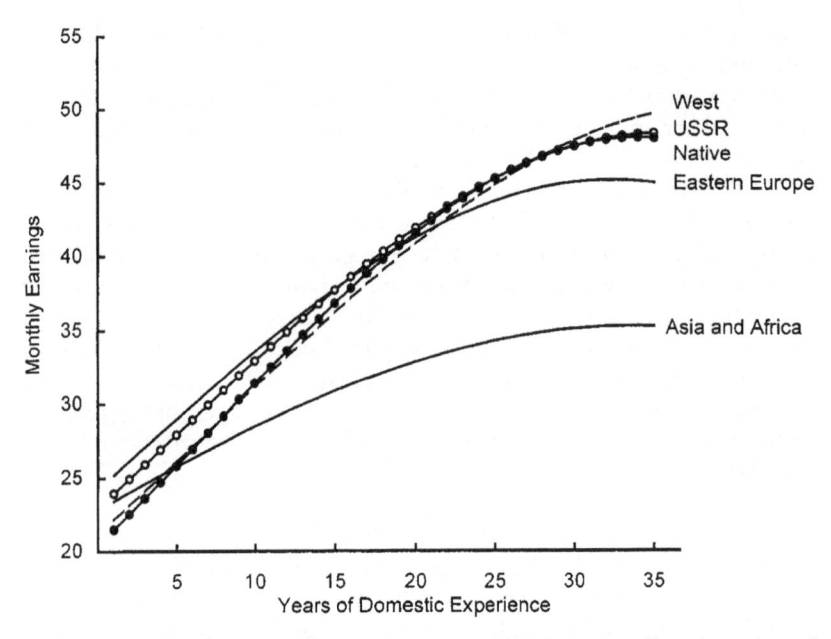

FIG. 1.—Earnings by area of origin. Figure plots simulated wage profiles using estimated parameters from equation (8), augmented by quadratic terms in experience, and assuming $EXP_1 = 0$ and $ED_1 = 12$ for immigrants and $ED_2 = 12$ for natives.

labor force immediately, while the other attends school in Israel prior to entering the labor force ($ED_2 = 4$). The other two immigrants arrive as college graduates ($ED_1 = 16$), again with one entering the labor force immediately and the other attending school in Israel prior to entering the labor force. The figure highlights that the benefit to attending school in Israel is higher for more educated immigrants, that is, $\beta_8 > 0$. Graphically, the upward shift in the earnings profile associated with attending school in Israel is proportionately higher for college graduates than for high school dropouts.

D. Variation in the Return to Schooling by Level and Source

Some of the results found in the preceding sections, such as the lower return to domestic education for immigrants compared to natives, could simply be artifacts of the assumption of linearity in the return to schooling. Since immigrants' foreign education precedes their Israeli education, their education in Israel takes place at a higher level of total years of schooling than does the natives', on average. If there are decreasing returns to schooling, the estimated return to domestic schooling for immigrants, following the methodology in the previous analysis, will be downward biased. In this section, the return to schooling is allowed to

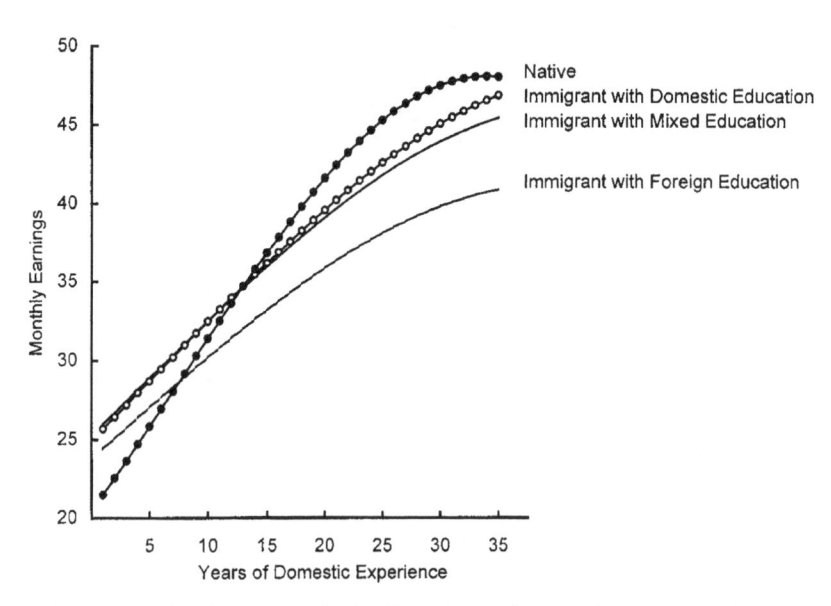

FIG. 2.—Earnings by source of schooling. Figure plots simulated wage profiles using estimated parameters from equation (8), augmented by quadratic terms in experience, and assuming $EXP_1 = 0$ and $ED = 12$. For immigrants, "foreign education" denotes $ED_1 = 12$ and $ED_2 = 0$, "domestic education" denotes $ED_1 = 0$ and $ED_2 = 12$, and "mixed education" denotes $ED_1 = 6$ and $ED_2 = 6$.

vary with its level. This will also show whether the transferability of education depends on its level. For example, higher levels of education may be more country-specific than the basic skills learned in elementary school.

To analyze this question, years of education are divided into categories: elementary school (years 1–8), secondary school (years 9–12), and post-secondary school (years 13+), which is subdivided into undergraduate (years 13–16) and graduate (years 17+) schooling.[19] The return to education is then estimated as a piecewise linear function. Equation (9) modifies equation (7) by replacing the uniform years of schooling variables, ED_i, with years of schooling in each of the four categories, ED_{ij}, where $j = e, s, u, g$ indicate elementary, secondary, undergraduate, and graduate, respectively.

$$y = \gamma_0 + \gamma_1 EXP_1 + \gamma_2 EXP_2 + \gamma_3 ED_e + \gamma_4 ED_s + \gamma_5 ED_u \\ + \gamma_6 ED_g + \gamma_7 ED_{1e} + \gamma_8 ED_{1s} + \gamma_9 ED_{1u} + \gamma_{10} ED_{1g} + \varepsilon. \quad (9)$$

[19] Although the undergraduate degree is ostensibly a 3-year program in Israel, the modal years of schooling for a bachelor's degree recipient is in fact 4 years.

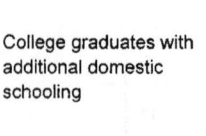

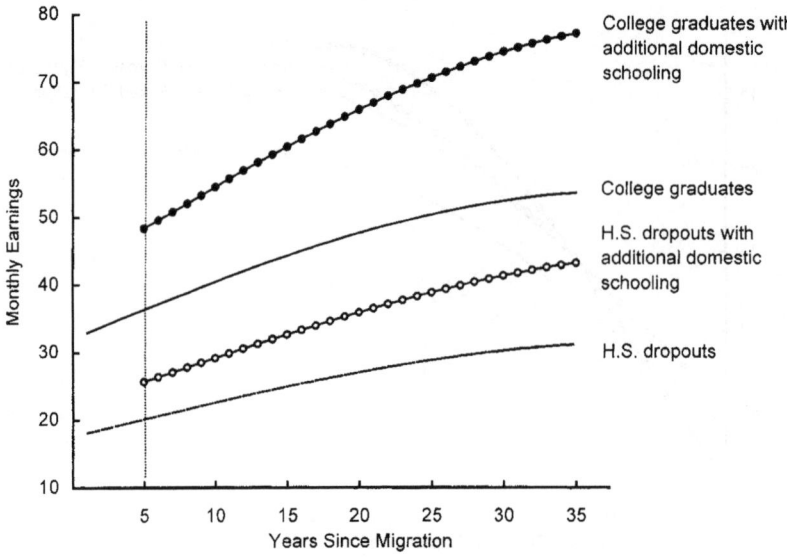

FIG. 3.—The effect of acquiring domestic human capital. Figure plots simulated wage profiles using estimated parameters from equation (8), augmented by quadratic terms in experience, and assuming $EXP_1 = 0$. "H.S. Dropouts" denotes $ED_1 = 8$, "College Graduates" denotes $ED_1 = 16$, and $ED_2 = 0$ or 4.

Estimates of equation (9) can be found in table 7. The results in the first column, for natives, reveal that the return to schooling is indeed strongly nonlinear. Secondary and undergraduate education both have high returns (12.2% and 11.5%), while elementary school and graduate school have much lower returns (6.5% and a mere 3.7%). Consistent with the results in Section IVA, immigrants receive a lower return than natives to Israeli schooling, but the ordering of coefficients across schooling levels is similar: elementary, 3.2%; secondary, 10.9%; undergraduate, 10.7%; and graduate, 2.9%.

Turning to the difference in the returns to schooling acquired abroad and in Israel by immigrants, some interesting patterns emerge. For immigrants taken as a whole, the point estimates generally show the return to foreign schooling to be lower than the return to Israeli schooling. However, because of heterogeneity across origin groups, the coefficients are mostly insignificant.

Elementary school is equally valued, regardless of whether it was acquired in Israel or abroad. This is seen in the marginally significant coefficients on the variable "elementary abroad." The one exception is the somewhat higher return for Westerners to attending elementary school in Israel. In general, the skills embodied in elementary schooling seem to be quite portable across national boundaries.

Table 7
The Return to Schooling by Level and Source

	Natives	All Immigrants	Immigrants from the West	Immigrants from Eastern Europe	Immigrants from the USSR	Immigrants from Asia or Africa
Experience abroad	...	−.0008 (.0004)	.0015 (.0015)	−.0053 (.0008)	−.0008 (.0007)	−.0042 (.0006)
Experience in Israel	.0180 (.0004)	.0119 (.0003)	.0162 (.0010)	.0089 (.0007)	.0142 (.0008)	.0089 (.0005)
Total elementary	.065 (.007)	.032 (.002)	.047 (.017)	.022 (.006)	.023 (.008)	.024 (.003)
Total secondary	.122 (.003)	.109 (.003)	.138 (.011)	.107 (.006)	.128 (.011)	.086 (.003)
Total undergraduate	.115 (.003)	.107 (.003)	.082 (.010)	.089 (.006)	.058 (.011)	.109 (.005)
Total graduate	.037 (.004)	.029 (.005)	.028 (.010)	.025 (.008)	.066 (.015)	.014 (.010)
Elementary abroad	...	−.0008 (.0012)	−.0114 (.0048)	.0043 (.0026)	.0023 (.0050)	−.0020 (.0015)
Secondary abroad	...	−.0264 (.0031)	−.0318 (.0118)	−.0297 (.0060)	−.0691 (.0107)	−.0085 (.0043)
Undergraduate abroad	...	.0015 (.0045)	.0365 (.0123)	.0065 (.0079)	.0430 (.0120)	−.0138 (.0091)
Graduate abroad	...	−.0022 (.0070)	−.0108 (.0131)	−.0001 (.0134)	−.0362 (.0183)	−.0020 (.0187)
Constant	9.21 (.055)	9.64 (.018)	9.48 (.132)	9.88 (.048)	9.75 (.055)	9.76 (.025)
R^2	.308	.269	.229	.235	.306	.200
N	18,488	35,615	3,209	10,422	4,587	17,397

NOTE.—Dependent variable is log monthly earnings. Elementary, secondary, undergraduate, and graduate indicate years of schooling completed at that level. Standard errors are in parentheses.

The results at the secondary school level are quite different. The Israeli labor market places a large premium on acquiring high school training in Israel rather than abroad. This is true for all areas of origin, with an average difference of 2.6 percentage points in the rates of return per year.

Finally, the differential associated with attending postsecondary school abroad rather than in Israel is smaller than that differential at the high school level. This is somewhat surprising given that postsecondary education is generally considered to be more specialized than secondary education, suggesting that it would be less internationally portable. Foreign graduate study receives a lower return than Israeli training, but Western and Soviet undergraduate training actually receive higher returns.

A final issue concerns the possibility that the return to schooling depends on the particular configuration of schooling obtained. For example, a year of university study in Israel may yield a different return depending on whether the high school education that preceded it was acquired in Israel or abroad. A set of indicator variables is constructed for different combinations of schooling levels and sources. For each individual, it is determined whether he attended elementary school, secondary school, and postsecondary school, and if so, whether the given school level was acquired abroad or in Israel.[20] This yields six dummy variables: (1) attended elementary school abroad, (2) attended elementary school in Israel, (3) attended secondary school abroad, (4) attended secondary school in Israel, (5) attended postsecondary school abroad, and (6) attended postsecondary school in Israel. The sample means for these attainment variables are presented in the second to bottom panel of table 3. These variables then enter into the calculation of the nine indicator variables used in the regressions below. The three letters in the variable name denote elementary school, high school, and postsecondary school, respectively. An "I" signifies that this schooling took place in Israel, an "F" signifies that it took place abroad, and "O" means that this level was not attained. The nine dummy variables are

III = elementary, secondary, and postsecondary all acquired in Israel;
IIO = elementary and secondary in Israel, no postsecondary;
IOO = elementary in Israel, no secondary or postsecondary;
FFF = elementary, secondary, and postsecondary all obtained abroad;

---

[20] For people who completed part of a schooling level in each country, three alternative methods of assigning that schooling to a country were used: according to where the majority of schooling at that level took place, as foreign if any of it took place abroad, or as Israeli if any of it took place in Israel. The results using these different measures being quite similar, results are presented only for the first method.

FFO = elementary and secondary abroad, no postsecondary;
FOO = elementary abroad, no secondary or postsecondary;
FFI = elementary and secondary abroad, postsecondary in Israel;
FII = elementary abroad, secondary and postsecondary in Israel; and
FIO = elementary abroad, secondary in Israel, no postsecondary.

Replacing the continuous years of schooling measures used in equation (9) with these nine schooling configuration dummies, we have

$$y = \gamma_0 + \gamma_1 EXP_1 + \gamma_2 EXP_2 + \gamma_3 III + \gamma_4 IIO + \gamma_5 IOO + \gamma_6 FFF \\ + \gamma_7 FFO + \gamma_8 FOO + \gamma_9 FFI + \gamma_{10} FII + \gamma_{11} FIO + \varepsilon. \quad (10)$$

Since the constant term and the returns to experience vary somewhat across groups, direct comparisons cannot be made between the returns to a given configuration for two area-of-origin groups merely by comparing their corresponding coefficients. Direct comparisons can be made, however, for the difference between two groups in the difference between two schooling configurations (i.e., comparing the difference between III and FFF for Western immigrants vs. that difference for Soviets).

These differences in differences are presented in table 8. It is instructive to focus on three comparisons: (1) the return to attending school in Israel for natives versus immigrants when both groups acquired their previous education in Israel; (2) the return to attending school in Israel for natives versus immigrants when the immigrants acquired their previous education abroad; and (3) the return to Israeli versus foreign schooling for immigrants.

The return to attending school in Israel for natives versus immigrants when both groups obtained their previous education in Israel can be seen in first two lines of table 8. The college–high school differential (III–IIO) is slightly smaller for the four immigrant groups than it is for natives. The high school–elementary school differential (IIO–IOO) varies considerably by group, with Western and Soviet immigrants gaining much more than natives and Asian/African immigrants gaining much less. Among immigrants who received no schooling abroad (i.e., those who immigrated too young), the return to college is only slightly lower than the return for natives, while for high school, some immigrant groups actually earn a higher return.

The second set of comparisons is of the return to attending school in Israel for immigrants versus natives when the immigrants obtained their previous education abroad. One case is the difference in the return to postsecondary school in Israel for a high school educated native (III–IIO) and the return for an immigrant who attended high school abroad (FFI–

Table 8
Differences in the Returns to Different Configurations of Schooling

	Natives	All Immigrants	Immigrants from the West	Immigrants from Eastern Europe	Immigrants from the USSR	Immigrants from Asia or Africa
III-IIO	.5140	.4944	.4453	.4486	.3946	.4102
	(.0080)	(.0120)	(.0367)	(.0229)	(.0470)	(.0176)
IIO-IOO	.3696	.3446	.4482	.3459	.5243	.2753
	(.0117)	(.0126)	(.0701)	(.0378)	(.0728)	(.0139)
FFF-FFO	...	.4305	.4661	.3487	.3746	.3692
	...	(.0098)	(.0318)	(.0181)	(.0184)	(.0199)
FFO-FOO	...	.2725	.7423	.2293	.1880	.2414
	...	(.0079)	(.0480)	(.0157)	(.0231)	(.0119)
III-FFF	...	.1286	.0514	.1597	.2002	.0943
	...	(.0129)	(.0324)	(.0241)	(.0373)	(.0247)
III-FFI	...	.0916	.1207	.1318	.1864	−.0240
	...	(.0193)	(.0482)	(.0332)	(.0560)	(.0325)
III-FII	...	.0501	.1351	.0685	.0424	−.0061
	...	(.0166)	(.0498)	(.0264)	(.0518)	(.0271)
FFI-FFF	...	.0370	−.0692	.0279	.0138	.1183
	...	(.0183)	(.0462)	(.0320)	(.0475)	(.0337)
FII-FFF	...	.0785	−.0836	.0912	.1579	.1004
	...	(.0157)	(.0480)	(.2259)	(.0427)	(.0288)
IIO-FFO	...	.0647	.0723	.0598	.1802	.0533
	...	(.0119)	(.0397)	(.0218)	(.0374)	(.0142)
IOO-FOO	...	−.0074	−.0998	−.0568	−.1561	.0194
	...	(.0130)	(.0790)	(.0014)	(.0702)	(.0147)
FIO-FFO	...	.0606	.1047	.0640	.0972	.0388
	...	(.0118)	(.0486)	(.0221)	(.0417)	(.0159)
FIO-FOO	...	.3331	.3808	.2929	.3264	.2798
	...	(.0123)	(.0607)	(.0242)	(.0450)	(.0156)
IIO-FIO	...	.0041	−.0324	−.0042	.0831	.0146
	...	(.0120)	(.0487)	(.0243)	(.0503)	(.0147)
FFI-FFO	...	.4676	.3969	.3766	.3884	.4874
	...	(.0182)	(.0509)	(.0312)	(.0480)	(.0303)

NOTE.—Measures are the difference in log monthly earnings for people with the specified configurations of schooling. The three-letter combinations (FIO, etc.) are dummy variables that are interpreted as follows: the first letter indicates the location of elementary school, the second the location of secondary school, and the third the location of postsecondary school. F indicates foreign, I indicates Israel, and O indicates none. OOO is the omitted category. Standard errors on the differences are in parentheses.

FFO). The difference for natives is 0.5140, or 67.2%.[21] As shown in the bottom line of the table, this increment is much lower for immigrants (0.4676 or 59.6%). The same comparison at the high school level (IIO–IOO vs. FIO–FOO) yields a similar result (44.7% and 39.5%). In both cases, immigrants receive a much lower return than do natives. Contrasting this with the previous set of comparisons suggests that one of the main reasons immigrants earn a lower return to Israeli schooling than do natives is that they are building on a base of foreign schooling, rather than

---

[21] $\ln(\text{III}) - \ln(\text{IIO}) = 0.5140$, so $\text{III}/\text{IIO} = e^{0.5140} = 1.672$.

one of Israeli schooling. It is, however, not the only reason, as immigrants earn a lower return to domestic schooling than do natives, even when they have no prior foreign schooling.

The third set of comparisons is of the return to Israeli versus origin country schooling for immigrants. The difference in earnings for someone who attended school through the postsecondary level in Israel versus abroad is (III–FFF). This difference is positive for all immigrant groups (approximately 12.9% on average). The difference for individuals who terminated their education at the high school level (IIO–FFO) is also positive in all cases (6.5% on average). Examining immigrants with foreign schooling who completed their education in Israel versus those who completed it abroad yields a similar pattern. For example, the value of attending postsecondary school in Israel versus abroad (FFI–FFF) is positive for almost all immigrant groups (3.7% on average). The exception is Westerners, whose postsecondary schooling is more highly valued. Looking at this comparison at the high school level (FIO–FFO) also shows positive values for all groups, ranging from 3.9% for African and Asian immigrants to 10.5% for Westerners, whose origin-source education is always highly valued.

V. Conclusion

This article studies the labor market assimilation of immigrants, focusing on the source of the immigrants' human capital. The national origin of an individual's education and labor market experience is found to be a crucial determinant of their value in the labor market. Human capital is imperfectly portable across countries. Estimation of standard earnings determination and immigrant assimilation equations yields patterns similar to those found in the literature on the United States, suggesting that the evidence from Israel may be used to shed light on this set of questions more generally.

Upon arrival, immigrants to Israel earn approximately one-quarter less than their native counterparts of comparable measured skill levels. This gap can be fully attributed to the significantly lower value placed on the immigrants' human capital. With few exceptions, human capital acquired abroad receives a lower return in the host labor market than human capital acquired domestically. The return to education obtained abroad is higher for immigrants from Europe and the Western Hemisphere than for immigrants from Asia and Africa. These patterns may reflect differences in school quality across continents of origin, as well as the compatibility of the education obtained abroad with the requirements of the host labor market. They may also reflect a lesser degree of discrimination against immigrant workers from Asia or Africa at low levels of education than at high levels. The return to labor market experience acquired abroad is generally insignificant.

The direct return to a year of schooling or experience obtained in the host country is also found to be higher for natives than for immigrants. One explanation for this result is that natives' superior language proficiency and other country-specific knowledge enable them to learn and train more productively than immigrants. The portability of education is found to vary significantly with its level. Elementary school education is equally valued, almost regardless of where it was acquired. The source of a high school education, however, is an important determinant of its value, with domestic high school earning the highest return. The return to postsecondary schooling obtained abroad varies greatly with area of origin.

Finally, acquiring further human capital following immigration is associated with a rise in the return to education obtained abroad. Education obtained in the destination country appears to significantly raise the return to schooling acquired abroad for Asian and African immigrants, with weaker effects for European and American immigrants. For Western and Soviet immigrants, the return to origin-country schooling also rises with the accumulation of host-country work experience. Equivalently, the more highly educated immigrants in these groups experience more earnings growth over time than do their less educated counterparts. The faster assimilation rate of the more educated immigrants somewhat offsets their larger initial earnings deficit relative to comparably educated natives. These findings are consistent with a model in which destination-country human capital enables immigrants to translate the skills they accumulated in their countries of origin into terms rewarded in the host labor market. This suggests a compound benefit to immigrants of receiving further training following immigration.

Appendix A
Area of Origin Groups

I. West

Argentina, Australia, Austria, Belgium, Bolivia, Brazil, Canada, Chile, Colombia, Cuba, Denmark, Ecuador, Finland, France, Germany, Holland, Ireland, Italy, Luxembourg, Mexico, New Zealand, Norway, Panama, Peru, Portugal, South Africa, Spain, Sweden, Switzerland, United Kingdom, United States, Uruguay, Venezuela, Zimbabwe (Rhodesia), unspecified Central America, unspecified South America, unspecified Europe, and unspecified Oceania.

II. Eastern Europe

Albania, Bulgaria, Czechoslovakia, Greece, Hungary, Poland, Romania, and Yugoslavia.

III. Soviet Union

Soviet Union.

IV. Asia and Africa

Afghanistan, Algeria, Burma, China, Cyprus, Egypt, Ethiopia, Eritrea, India, Indonesia, Iran, Iraq, Japan, Jordan, Korea, Lebanon, Libya, Mongolia, Morocco, Pakistan, Philippines, Saudi Arabia, Somalia, South Yemen, Sudan, Syria, Tangier, Tunisia, Turkey, Yemen, unspecified Africa, and unspecified Asia.

Appendix B

Assimilation versus Cohort Quality

The issue of potential "cohort quality" effects has received much attention in the literature on immigration.[22] In a single cross section of data, it is not possible to separately identify aging and cohort effects. A positive estimated effect of years since migration (YSM) on earnings in equation (1) could therefore be due either to a rise in immigrants' relative earnings with time since arrival or to earlier immigrant arrival cohorts having permanently higher earnings potential than more recent ones. In order to test the extent to which the cross-sectional return to YSM reflects assimilation versus cohort effects, two cross sections of data are needed. Equation (1) can then be estimated on the pooled data, with arrival-cohort dummies added to the equation. If the return to YSM is invariant to the addition of the cohort dummies, then it is legitimate to interpret that coefficient as a measure of assimilation in cross-sectional analysis.

Table B1 pools data from the 1972 and 1983 Israeli Censuses of Population.[23] The first column of the table presents estimates of equation (1), allowing the coefficients α_0, α_1, α_2, and α_3 to be different in the two years.[24] Note that even with two cross sections of data, in order to test for the presence of cohort effects, it is necessary to constrain the returns to immigrant status, years since migration, and arrival cohort to be the same in both years.

In the second column of table B1, a set of arrival-cohort dummy variables is added to the regression. There are 14 dummies, covering the years 1917–83 in 5-year intervals. The coefficients on YSM and its square are quite close in columns (1) and (2). If the same equations are run with

---

[22] The issue was first raised by Borjas (1985), who concludes that most of the return to years since arrival in the United States is due to a systematic decline in the quality of successive immigrant cohorts, rather than to assimilation. See Friedberg (1992) and LaLonde and Topel (1992), among others, for reexaminations of this finding.

[23] The rules used in constructing the 1972 sample are the same as those used for the 1983 sample.

[24] An F-test of the equality of these coefficients across the two years rejects at the 1% level that they are the same.

Table B1
Assimilation versus Cohort Quality

	(1)	(2)	(3)	(4)
1983	−2.56	−2.58	−2.61	−2.61
	(.015)	(.015)	(.015)	(.015)
Education (1972)	.050	.049	.043	.043
	(.001)	(.005)	(.001)	(.001)
Education (1983)	.080	.079	.075	.075
	(.001)	(.006)	(.001)	(.001)
Experience (1972)	.021	.020	.019	.020
	(.001)	(.001)	(.001)	(.001)
Experience (1983)	.027	.027	.028	.028
	(.001)	(.001)	(.001)	(.001)
Experience^2/100 (1972)	−.034	−.034	−.035	−.036
	(.001)	(.001)	(.001)	(.001)
Experience^2/100 (1983)	−.036	−.036	−.039	−.039
	(.001)	(.001)	(.001)	(.001)
All immigrants	−.317	−.447	...	...
	(.007)	(.028)		
Immigrants from the West	...	...	−.234	−.377
			(.008)	(.028)
Immigrants from Eastern Europe	...	...	−.296	−.443
			(.007)	(.028)
Immigrants from the USSR	...	...	−.292	−.426
			(.007)	(.028)
Immigrants from Asia or Africa	...	...	−.419	−.566
			(.007)	(.028)
Years since migration (YSM)	.0133	.0147	.0167	.0160
	(.0005)	(.0009)	(.0005)	(.0009)
YSM^2/100	−.0108	−.0133	−.0176	−.0157
	(.0010)	(.0016)	(.0011)	(.0016)
Constant	11.8	11.8	11.9	11.9
	(.011)	(.011)	(.011)	(.011)
Arrival-cohort dummies	No	Yes	No	Yes
R^2	.847	.847	.849	.849
N	110,285	110,285	110,285	110,285

NOTE.—This table shows pooled data from the 1972 and 1983 Censuses of Population. Dependent variable is log monthly earnings in 1983 Israeli shekels. The arrival-cohort dummies cover the years 1917–83 in 5-year intervals. The omitted dummy is the most recent one. The R^2 falls by 0.35 if the dependent variable is adjusted to have the same mean in the 2 years. Standard errors are in parentheses.

YSM entering linearly, the coefficient is 0.00836 (t-statistic of 54.4) when the arrival-cohort dummies are omitted and 0.00828 (t-statistic of 14.5) when they are included. Correcting for area of origin in columns (3) and (4) also shows the effect of YSM to be largely invariant to the inclusion of arrival-cohort effects. The linear version here yields a return to YSM of 0.00845 (t-statistic of 53.9) without cohort effects and 0.00849 (t-statistic of 14.9) with them.

These results indicate that the coefficient on YSM estimated in a single cross section of data is correctly interpreted here as a measure of immigrant earnings growth over time since arrival and does not reflect a decline in the earnings potential of more recent arrival cohorts. An F-test of the joint significance of the arrival-cohort dummies rejects the null that they do not differ from zero, although with a standard deviation of 0.04, they are rather small in size. In any case, the magnitude of the cohort effects is unimportant for the purpose of obtaining unbiased estimates of assimilation rates. All that matters is that they do not follow a systematic pattern over time. As these cohort effects do not, their omission does not bias the return to YSM. This is not surprising since, in contrast to the United States, there was no change in Israeli immigration policy analogous to the 1965 amendments to the U.S. Immigration and Nationality Act that would lead us to expect a systematic change in unobserved cohort quality over time. The analysis can therefore proceed, using the data from the 1983 Census alone to estimate the parameters of interest.

References

Baker, Michael, and Benjamin, Dwayne. "The Performance of Immigrants in the Canadian Labor Market." *Journal of Labor Economics* 12 (July 1994): 369–405.

Borjas, George. "The Earnings of Male Hispanic Immigrants in the United States." *Industrial and Labor Relations Review* 35 (April 1982): 343–53.

———. "Assimilation, Changes in Cohort Quality, and the Earnings of Immigrants." *Journal of Labor Economics* 3 (October 1985): 463–89.

———. "National Origin and the Skills of Immigrants in the Postwar Period." In *Immigration and the Workforce*, edited by George Borjas and Richard Freeman, pp. 17–47. Chicago: University of Chicago Press, 1992.

———. "Assimilation and Changes in Cohort Quality Revisited: What Happened to Immigrant Earnings in the 1980s?" *Journal of Labor Economics* 13 (April 1995): 201–45.

———. "The Economic Analysis of Immigration." In *Handbook of Labor Economics*, vol. 3, edited by Orley Ashenfelter and David Card. Amsterdam: Elsevier Science Publishing, 1999.

Butcher, Kristin, and DiNardo, John. "The Immigrant and Native-Born Wage Distributions: Evidence from United States Censuses." Unpublished manuscript. Boston: Boston College, 1996.

Chiswick, Barry. "The Effect of Americanization on the Earnings of Foreign-Born Men." *Journal of Political Economy* 86 (October 1978): 897–922. (*a*)

———. "A Longitudinal Analysis of the Occupational Mobility of Immigrants." In *Proceedings of the Thirtieth Annual Winter Meeting*, edited by Barbara Dennis, pp. 20–27. Madison, WI: Industrial Relations Research Association, 1978. (*b*)

———. "Is the New Immigration Less Skilled than the Old?" *Journal of Labor Economics* 4 (April 1986): 168–92.

Duleep, Harriet Orcutt, and Regets, Mark. "The Elusive Concept of Immigrant Quality: Evidence from 1970–1990." Discussion Paper no. PRIP-UI-41. Washington, DC: Urban Institute, 1996.

Eckstein, Zvi, and Weiss, Yoram. "The Absorption of Highly Skilled Immigrants: Israel, 1990–95." Unpublished manuscript. Tel Aviv: Tel Aviv University, 1998.

Fishelson, Gideon; Weiss, Yoram; and Mark, Nili. "Ethnic Origin and

Income Differentials among Israeli Males, 1969–1976." In *Israel: A Developing Society,* edited by Asher Arian, pp. 253–76. Assen: Van Gorcum, 1980.

Flug, Karnit; Kasir, Nitsa (Kaliner); and Ofer, Gur. "The Absorption of Soviet Immigrants into the Labor Market from 1990 Onwards: Aspects of Occupational Substitution and Retention." Discussion Paper no. 92.13. Jerusalem: Bank of Israel, 1992.

Friedberg, Rachel. "The Labor Market Assimilation of Immigrants in the United States: The Role of Age at Arrival." Unpublished manuscript. Providence, RI: Brown University, 1992.

———. "The Success of Young Immigrants in the U.S. Labor Market: An Evaluation of Competing Explanations." Unpublished manuscript. Providence, RI: Brown University, 1993.

———. "You Can't Take It with You? Immigrant Assimilation and the Portability of Human Capital." Working Paper no. 5837. Cambridge, MA: National Bureau of Economic Research, 1996.

Funkhouser, Edward, and Trejo, Stephen. "The Labor Market Skills of Recent Male Immigrants: Evidence from the Current Population Survey." *Industrial and Labor Relations Review* 48 (July 1995): 792–811.

Israel Central Bureau of Statistics. *Census of Population and Housing 1972.* Jerusalem: Central Bureau of Statistics, 1974.

———. *Census of Population and Housing, 1983.* Jerusalem: Central Bureau of Statistics, 1985.

Jasso, Guillermina, and Rosenzweig, Mark. "How Well Do U.S. Immigrants Do? Vintage Effects, Emigration Selectivity, and Occupational Mobility." In *Research in Population Economics,* vol. 6, edited by T. Paul Schultz, pp. 229–53. Greenwich, CT: JAI Press, 1988.

———. *The New Chosen People.* Census Monograph Series. New York: Russell Sage Foundation, 1990.

LaLonde, Robert, and Topel, Robert. "The Assimilation of Immigrants in the U.S. Labor Market." In *Immigration and the Workforce,* edited by George Borjas and Richard Freeman, pp. 67–92. Chicago: University of Chicago Press, 1992.

———. "Economic Impact of International Migration and the Economic Performance of Immigrants." In *Handbook of Population and Family Economics,* edited by Mark Rosenzweig and Oded Stark. Amsterdam: Elsevier Science Publishing, 1996.

Sabatello, Eitan. "Patterns of Occupational Mobility among New Immigrants to Israel." *International Migration* 17 (1979): 267–79.

Schoeni, Robert. "New Evidence on the Economic Progress of Foreign-Born Men in the 1970s and 1980s." *Journal of Human Resources* 32 (Fall 1997): 683–740.

Smith, James, and Edmonston, Barry. *The New Americans: Economic, Demographic, and Fiscal Effects of Immigration: Report of the National Research Council.* Washington, DC: National Academy Press, 1997.

[8]

Chutes or Ladders? A Longitudinal Analysis of Immigrant Earnings

Darren Lubotsky

University of Illinois at Urbana-Champaign

I use longitudinal earnings data from Social Security records to study the effect of selective emigration on the measured progress of immigrants to the United States. The immigrant-native earnings gap closes by 10–15 percent during immigrants' first 20 years in the United States, or about half as fast as typical estimates from repeated cross sections of the decennial census. The divergent results indicate that emigration by low-wage immigrants has systematically led past researchers to overestimate the wage progress of immigrants who remain in the United States. Selective back-and-forth migration also leads typical estimates to overstate the measured decline in earnings among successive immigrant arrival cohorts between 1960 and 1980.

I. Introduction

Immigration is one of the most important and most contentious policy debates in the United States. For many, support for high levels of im-

I especially wish to thank David Card for his advice and encouragement. I also thank John Abowd, Alan Auerbach, Richard Blundell, Kenneth Chay, Todd Elder, Kevin Hallock, Hilary Hoynes, Roger Koenker, Jonathan Leonard, Steven Levitt, Enrico Moretti, James Powell, two anonymous referees, and many seminar participants for their advice. I owe a special thanks to Bhashkar Mazumder, Lynn Riggs, and the staff members at the Center for Economic Studies at the U.S. Census Bureau and at the California Census Research Data Center (CCRDC) for their help in facilitating my use of the confidential data. Financial support from the Robert Burch Center for Tax Policy Analysis, the Center for Labor Economics, the Institute for Industrial Relations at the University of California, Berkeley, and the CCRDC is gratefully acknowledged. The research in this paper was conducted while I was a research associate at the CCRDC in association with the Center for Economic Studies of the U.S. Census Bureau. Research results and conclusions are my own and do not necessarily indicate concurrence by the U.S. Census Bureau, the Center for Economic Studies, or the CCRDC.

TABLE 1
IMMIGRANT-NATIVE DIFFERENCES IN LOG EARNINGS IN THE 1970–2000 DECENNIAL CENSUSES

IMMIGRANTS' PERIOD OF ENTRY	YEARS IN THE UNITED STATES 1st–5th Years	YEARS IN THE UNITED STATES 11th–15th Years
1965–69	−.377 (.013)	−.164 (.006)
1975–79	−.508 (.005)	−.249 (.007)
1985–89	−.545 (.006)	−.358 (.004)
1995–99	−.442 (.004)	. . .

NOTE.—Data are taken from the 1970–2000 decennial Censuses. The earnings gap during the first five years in the United States are computed from separate cross-sectional regressions of the log of annual wage and salary, self-employment, and farm earnings on a quartic in potential experience and an indicator for immigrants, using natives and recent immigrants, all of whom are aged 25–54. Earnings gaps during the eleventh through fifteenth years are computed from cross-sectional regressions using natives and immigrants who are aged 35–64. Immigrants who arrived before age 18 are excluded from the samples. Standard errors are in parentheses.

migration by lower-wage immigrants depends crucially on the ability of immigrants to assimilate into the U.S. workforce. Despite nearly a century of research, however, many of the basic facts about the immigrant experience in the American labor market remain in dispute, largely because of problems with the U.S. decennial census and other existing data sources. Table 1 shows tabulations from the 1970–2000 decennial Censuses of the average relative earnings of recent immigrant arrival cohorts during their first five years and during their eleventh through fifteenth years in the United States.[1] In the 1970 Census, immigrants who had been in the country for less than five years earned 38 percent less than native-born workers with similar labor market experience; in the 1990 Census, recent immigrants earned 55 percent less than natives. One area of agreement is that shifts in the national origin mix of immigrants away from developed, high-skill countries to industrializing, lower-skill countries have contributed to the decline in the average labor market earnings of immigrants over the past 30 years. Beyond this, however, there is sharp disagreement over the experience of immigrants in the U.S. labor market. In one view, immigrants quickly develop English language and other skills necessary to move up the American earnings distribution. Thus, despite their low initial earnings, immi-

---

[1] These figures are computed from cross-sectional regressions of the log of annual wage and salary, self-employment, and farm earnings on a quartic in potential experience and an indicator for immigrants. Earnings gaps among new immigrants are computed from samples of men aged 25–54, whereas the earnings gaps among immigrants who have been in the country for 11–15 years are computed from samples of men aged 35–64. Immigrants who entered before the age of 18 are excluded.

grants quickly assimilate into the U.S. labor market. Other researchers take a more pessimistic view and argue that immigrants—particularly recent arrivals—tend to earn significantly less than natives throughout their working life and, thus, do not assimilate in any meaningful way.[2] These disagreements about the degree to which immigrants assimilate into the U.S. labor market contribute to disagreements about whether or not the United States should be as welcoming to lower-skilled individuals as it traditionally has been.

Current policy initiatives and recent policy changes have largely been based on the view that immigrants increasingly enter the United States on the lower rungs of the economic ladder, feeding fears that inflows of unskilled immigrants lower the earnings and employment rate of native-born workers and impose large burdens on public transfer programs and services. For example, the Immigration Act of 1990 increased the number of visas allocated on the basis of occupational skills from 54,000 to 140,000 per year.[3] The 1996 welfare reform legislation sought to discourage immigrants from migrating in order to receive benefits by severely restricting the ability of new immigrants to obtain cash transfers, food stamps, and Medicaid during their first five years in the United States. A major policy shift currently being debated is whether the United States should adopt a point system, similar to that in Canada, that would make it easier for higher-skilled foreigners to obtain permanent residency status, perhaps at the expense of less skilled foreigners who qualify for permanent residency because they already have family in the United States.

I present evidence from new longitudinal earnings histories from Social Security records that selective out-migration by low-earning immigrants has led the evidence marshaled in favor of both the optimistic and the pessimistic views of past immigration to be overstated. As many as a third of immigrants to the United States eventually return to their home country. Since direct data on emigration are generally not available, little is known about whether it is the most successful or the least successful immigrants who return and how the selectivity of this flow

---

[2] For a statement of the former view, see, e.g., LaLonde and Topel (1992) and Duleep and Regets (1996, 1997). The latter view is expressed by Borjas (1985, 1995). Surveys of the economic literature on immigration are given in Borjas (1994, 1999), LaLonde and Topel (1997), and Smith and Edmonston (1997).

[3] By way of comparison, the Immigration Act of 1990 also provided for 480,000 visas allocated on the basis of family reunification and 55,000 "diversity visas," which were given to immigrants from countries underrepresented in the 1965 visa allocation. Jasso and Rosenzweig (1990), Bean and Fix (1992), and Smith and Edmonston (1997) provide additional summaries of U.S. immigration policies.

complicates inferences drawn from data on those who remain in the country.[4]

The earnings gap between native-born workers and a particular immigrant arrival cohort narrows sharply from one decennial census to the next. The earnings gap between natives and immigrants who arrived between 1965 and 1969 fell from 38 percent in the 1970 Census to 16 percent in the 1980 Census; the gap was eliminated in the 1990 Census, when this cohort had been in the United States for 21–25 years. The earnings gap between natives and immigrants who arrived in the late 1980s fell from 55 percent in the 1990 Census to 36 percent in the 2000 Census. Past researchers have interpreted the closing of the earnings gap from one census cross section to the next as evidence of rapid assimilation among first-generation immigrants, bolstering supporters who claim that assimilation lessens the negative fiscal and economic impacts from low-wage immigration. But the earnings gap from one census to the next could also close because of selective emigration from the United States by low-earning immigrants: If low-wage immigrants are more likely to leave the United States, then the earnings gaps measured in the censuses reflect assimilation among immigrants who stay, as well as the presence of fewer low-wage immigrants in the data over time.

Just as there may be selective permanent out-migration, there may also be selective back-and-forth migration between the United States and immigrants' home countries. The census and most other common household surveys, however, ask respondents when they arrived in the United States "to stay," and immigrants who made multiple trips are led to answer with the date of their most recent arrival rather than their initial arrival. Immigrants who report that they recently arrived are therefore disproportionately transient migrants, whereas immigrants who report that they arrived earlier are mainly permanent. If transient immigrants tend to have low earnings or slow earnings growth (which seems likely among migrant laborers or agricultural workers from Mexico), it will appear as though recent cohorts have lower earnings or slower earnings growth than earlier cohorts. The appearance of a downward trend in immigrant skills could also reflect, in part, recent U.S.

---

[4] Direct evidence is not available on the number of foreign- or American-born people who emigrate from the United States, and thus estimates of the rate of emigration have to be inferred from other data sources. Jasso and Rosenzweig (1990) use annual counts of resident aliens from the Immigration and Naturalization Service and estimate that the number of immigrants who left the United States between 1960 and 1980 was 41 percent of the number of new immigrants during that period. Borjas and Bratsberg (1996) compare INS data on immigrant inflows with population estimates from the 1980 Census and conclude that about 20 percent of immigrants who arrived in the 1970s had left the United States by 1980. Both studies find that Asian immigrants are less likely to emigrate from the United States than European and Latin American immigrants.

censuses doing a better job of finding and enumerating illegal or lower-skilled immigrants than earlier censuses had. Separating real changes in the skill or earnings level of immigrants over time from changes in census coverage and from churning among low-wage, transient immigrants is vitally important for evaluating claims that U.S. immigration policies should be adjusted to return the skill mix of immigrants back to what supposedly prevailed in earlier decades.

This paper uses a new sample of longitudinal earnings histories that helps overcome some of the limitations of the previous literature on immigrant earnings assimilation. Through a joint project of the Social Security Administration, the Internal Revenue Service, and the Census Bureau, the 1990 and 1991 Survey of Income and Program Participation (SIPP) and the 1994 March Supplement to the Current Population Survey (CPS) have been matched to annual earnings records from 1951 to 1997. The first contribution of this work is to compare the implied earnings growth of immigrants found in repeated cross sections of the decennial census with estimates from this fixed panel of individuals that is free of any bias caused by nonrandom emigration out of the United States.[5] In addition, since immigrants' reported date of arrival in the CPS and SIPP can be compared to their first year of covered earnings, the extent of temporary out-migration and its effect on measured immigrant earnings profiles can be examined.

Several important new results are found. Most important, the actual earnings growth of immigrants who remain in the United States is considerably slower than that implied by comparisons across decennial censuses. Estimates from the longitudinal earnings records indicate that immigrant earnings grow by about 10–15 percentage points more over their first 20 years in the United States than the earnings growth experienced by native-born workers. This is substantially slower than the 26-percentage-point growth implied by a comparison of immigrants and natives across decennial censuses. Selective emigration by immigrants with below-average earnings is qualitatively important and has systematically led analysts working with census data to overestimate assimilation into the U.S. labor market.

Temporary out-migration by low-wage immigrants also has significant effects on measures of the trend in earnings levels across successive immigrant arrival cohorts. In particular, the decline in the level of earnings between 1960 arrivals and 1985 arrivals is approximately one-third smaller when immigrants are classified by their initial date of arrival rather than their reported date. Thus analysis of the Social Security files

---

[5] Several previous studies have used longitudinal data to examine immigrant earnings. See Chiswick (1980), Borjas (1989), Hu (1999), and Duleep and Dowhan (2002). These and other related work are discussed below.

indicates that while immigrants do not assimilate nearly as rapidly as census-based estimates suggest, some of the concern that the United States is increasingly attracting lower-wage immigrants is perhaps misplaced.

Section II of the paper describes the matched Social Security earnings data and highlights some of their strengths and weaknesses. Section III describes the relationship between immigrant earnings measured in repeated cross sections from the decennial census and those measured in longitudinal data, in the presence of permanent and temporary selective out-migration. The main estimates are presented in Section IV. Section V presents conclusions.

II. How Comparable Are Matched Administrative Earnings Data and Household Surveys?

The centerpiece of this study is new longitudinal earnings data formed by matching individual survey records from three large household surveys to respondents' annual Social Security earnings records. Specifically, respondents in the 1990 and 1991 SIPPs are linked by Social Security number to annual Social Security earnings records from 1951 to 1993; respondents in the March Supplement to the 1994 CPS are linked to earnings records from 1951 to 1997. The annual Social Security earnings records are employer reports to the Social Security Administration for the purpose of assessing Social Security and Medicare taxes and for determining future Social Security benefits. Though approximately 96 percent of workers are covered by the system today, some groups were not covered throughout the entire sample period of this study. Most self-employed professionals and members of the uniformed services entered the Social Security system between 1954 and 1956, whereas employees of the federal government hired before 1984 had the option of participating in the system. Although self-employed individuals are covered by the system, it is unclear how much of their income goes unreported to the Social Security Administration.[6] In addition to annual earnings in each year, the Social Security records also contain information on the number of quarters of covered employment in each year,

---

[6] The earnings records are confidential and are used through an arrangement with the Center for Economic Studies of the U.S. Census Bureau. The primary groups not covered by the Social Security system today are self-employed, domestic, and farm workers who have particularly low earnings; railroad workers; and some employees of state and local governments. Statistics and short histories of key provisions of the Social Security program are given in Social Security Administration (1997, 2006). Studies by Card and Krueger (1993) and Chay (1995) used a similar match of the 1973 and 1978 March CPS to Social Security earnings records to examine black-white earnings differences. Bound and Krueger (1991) use those data to investigate the extent of measurement error in reported earnings in the CPS.

individuals' date of birth, race, and gender. Longitudinal information is not available on whether the individual was self-employed, weeks or hours worked, place of residence, schooling, and job training. Thus the focus of this study is annual earnings among workers, which capture both wage differences and labor supply choices at the intensive margin.[7]

Demographic information from the SIPP or CPS is matched to the longitudinal earnings records. The three household surveys include information on educational attainment, citizenship, and year and place of birth, among other things. Immigrants report the year they arrived in the United States "to stay," and answers are given in intervals: The 1994 CPS intervals are pre-1950, 1950–59, five-year intervals from 1960–64 to 1975–79, and then two-year intervals from 1980–81 to 1992–93. The intervals in the 1990 and 1991 SIPPs are pre-1960, five-year intervals from 1960–64 to 1975–79, 1980–81, 1982–84, and 1985–90 or 1985–91.[8] In what follows, I classify as an immigrant anyone born outside of the United States. People who were born abroad to American parents, were born in Puerto Rico or other outlying areas of the United States, or arrived in the United States prior to age 18 are dropped from the analysis. (Immigrants who arrived as children and attended school in the United States are likely to assimilate to a large extent prior to entering the labor market. Their labor market experience may be more similar to that of native-born workers than to that of immigrants who arrive in the United States as adults.)

I further restrict the sample to include only men born between 1930 and 1969. Men born before 1930 would be over 60 years old at the time of the 1990, 1991, or 1994 surveys; excluding these individuals reduces the risk that nonrandom mortality or nonrandom labor force participation decisions bias the sample of older workers in favor of the more healthy. Those born after 1969 would be under 25 years old at the time of the 1990, 1991, and 1994 cross-sectional surveys and may have not completed their schooling. I exclude women from the sample to avoid complications from selective labor force participation.

Several features of the matched data pose additional issues. The first problem is that the Social Security earnings are censored at the taxable

---

[7] Hu's (1999) analysis of longitudinal data from the Health and Retirement Study (HRS) indicates that repeated cross-sectional data may also lead to an overstatement of assimilation in employment rates among non-Hispanic white immigrants.

[8] Much of the analysis that follows consolidates some of the immigrant arrival cohorts. Except in table 2 below, where the CPS data are analyzed separately, the 1980–84 cohort used in this study includes observations from the SIPPs in which the individual reported to have arrived between 1980 and 1984, and CPS observations in which the individual reported to have arrived between 1980 and 1985. The exclusion, discussed below, of immigrants who were under 18 years of age at the time of arrival is based on their age at the midpoint of the arrival interval.

earnings ceiling in each year.[9] Figure 1 plots the real value of the top code (in 1997 dollars) and the fraction of the sample top-coded from 1951 to 1997. Average earnings increased between 1951 and 1965 and the tax ceiling remained relatively stable, which led to a steady rise in the proportion of the sample that is censored from 11 percent to 53 percent. Between 1966 and 1977 the tax ceiling increased several times and inflation eroded its real value, and the fraction of the sample top-coded increased and then decreased. Finally, between 1978 and 1997 the real value of the tax ceiling steadily increased, and thus between 1983 and 1997, about 11 percent of the sample is top-coded. The econometric procedures used below take into account the censored nature of the data.

A second problem is that the longitudinal earnings data record only an individual's earnings that were covered by the Social Security system. An earnings record of zero dollars in a given year may reflect someone who was not employed that year, who was outside of the United States for the year, or whose only earnings came from informal or other uncovered employment. Some immigrants (and natives) work entirely in the uncovered sector and thus will not have any Social Security earnings, though they may report their uncovered earnings in the census, CPS, or SIPP household surveys. It is not possible to distinguish between immigrants who are legal residents of the United States and work in jobs not covered by the Social Security system, and immigrants in the United States legally or illegally who work "under the table" and do not pay taxes on their earnings. Other workers may have earnings in both the covered and uncovered sectors, and thus their earnings in the longitudinal data set are only a portion of their total earnings.

The final issue is that not all respondents in the three household surveys are matched to earnings records. The primary reason for a nonmatch is that an individual (or the proxy respondent) refused to give his Social Security number to the survey interviewer. Social Security numbers that are provided are verified by the Social Security Administration's Enumeration Verification System, a process that ensures survey respondents are matched only to their own Social Security earnings record. The Social Security Administration is also able to look up the correct Social Security number for survey respondents who did not know

---

[9] A small number of observations from the two SIPP sources are above the tax ceiling in a few years. This may have arisen from people working two jobs during the year and the second employer overwithholding income for Social Security taxes. Since the reported earnings may still be censored, though at a higher level, earnings for these observations are replaced with the taxable maximum in that year.

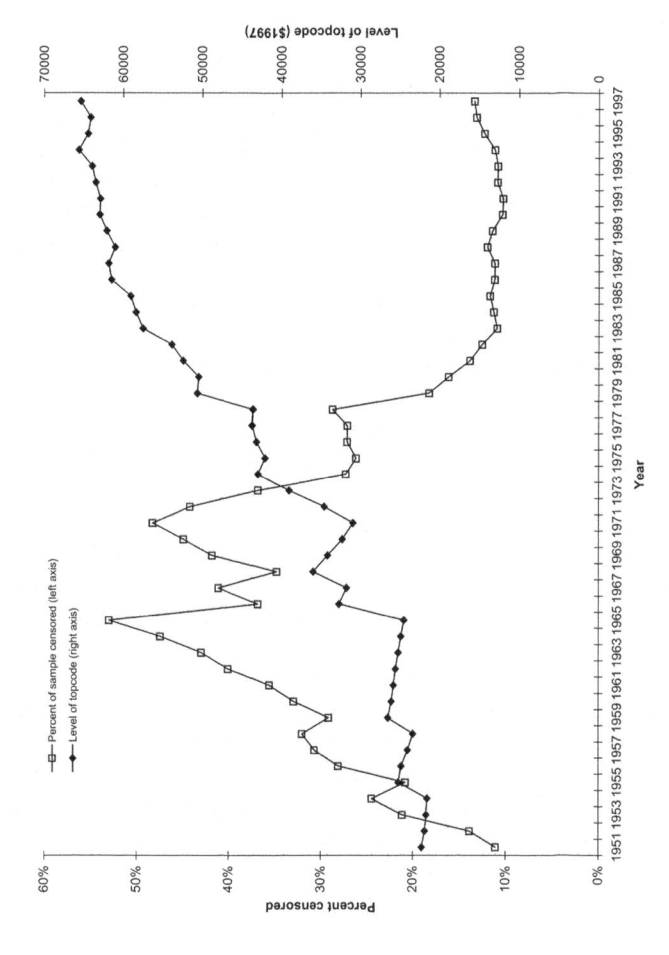

FIG. 1.—Level of top code and percentage of sample censored (Social Security earnings data, 1951–97). Data are taken from Social Security earnings records between 1951 and 1997 matched to individuals in the 1994 CPS and the 1990 and 1991 SIPPs. Only observations with positive earnings are included in the calculation of the percentage top-coded in each year. The sample includes all men aged 17–64 who had positive potential experience and were born between 1930 and 1969. The annual top code is the Social Security annual maximum taxable earnings, given in Social Security Administration (2006).

their Social Security number or who provided an incorrect number.[10] Thus it is highly unlikely that an illegal immigrant who bought a Social Security card on the black market would be in the matched sample, much less matched to someone else's earnings history. Eighty-four percent of respondents in the 1994 March CPS are matched to Social Security earnings records. The match rates are 91 percent and 87 percent in the 1990 and 1991 SIPPs. The proportion of immigrants who are matched is lower, particularly among recent arrivals. The match rates in the CPS sample are 76 percent among immigrants who report arriving in the United States between 1950 and 1964, 72 percent among those who report arriving between 1965 and 1979, and 62 percent among those who report arriving between 1980 and 1994. The match rate for immigrants in the SIPP samples is 87 percent among those who arrived before 1980 and 75 percent among those who arrived between 1980 and 1991.

To partially correct for potential selection bias induced by nonrandom matches to Social Security earnings data, population weights are computed for the matched subsample to reflect the observable characteristics of the full sample in the household surveys. Specifically, let ω_i denote the population weight provided in the household survey for individual i and $p(x_i)$ denote the probability that a person with characteristics x_i is matched to an earnings record. If that observation is matched and used in the analysis, his final weight is given by $\omega_i/\hat{p}(x_i)$, the product of ω_i and the inverse of the estimated match probability. The probability of a match is estimated with a logit model in which the match probability is a function of observables recorded in the household survey, including educational attainment; a square in potential labor market experience; weeks and hours worked; a square in reported earnings; and indicators for Hispanics, nonwhites, Hispanic nonwhites, Asians, and those who did not work in the survey year or were self-employed, worked in agriculture, worked for the government, or worked in the private sector.[11] The logit model is estimated separately for each of the three household surveys, for natives, and for five-year immigrant arrival cohorts. Note that since earnings reported in the cross-sectional survey are used to construct the match probabilities, unobservable factors, such as motivation or ability, that are correlated with earnings and

---

[10] No attempt is made by the Census Bureau or the Social Security Administration to match earnings data for individuals who refused to provide a Social Security number. I exclude from the sample a small number of additional respondents whose reported gender in the cross-sectional survey does not match that in the Social Security record or whose year of birth differed by more than two years in the two data sources.

[11] Some of the variable definitions differ in the CPS and SIPP samples. For example, the CPS model is based on earnings, weeks, and hours in the past year (i.e., 1993); the SIPP variables refer to the month prior to the interview. Nevo (2003) analyzes a more general case of using weights to adjust for selection bias.

may be more prevalent among the matched subsample are incorporated to an extent into the final weights.

To gauge how well covered Social Security earnings reflect the more familiar earnings reported in the CPS and to explore how well the final sample weights adjust for nonmatches between the household surveys and the longitudinal earnings data, table 2 compares the level of earnings and the immigrant-native earnings gaps measured in the March Supplement to the 1994 CPS (which records annual earnings from 1993) with the corresponding measures from the 1993 Social Security earnings records. Columns 1 and 2 display unconditional average reported (log) earnings among the full sample of men in the CPS and the subsample of men who are matched to Social Security earnings records, separately for the native-born and immigrant arrival cohorts (as reported in the CPS). Below the level of log earnings is the raw earnings gap between each immigrant cohort and natives, the standard error of the earnings gap, and the (unweighted) sample size.[12]

From CPS earnings data, differences in reported earnings between natives and immigrants who arrived after 1980 are eight to 13 percentage points smaller among the matched subsample than among the full CPS sample. However, when the matched immigrants are reweighted to reflect the observable characteristics of the full CPS sample (col. 3), the earnings of the matched sample are fairly similar to those of the full sample. An exception is the group of immigrants who arrived between 1970 and 1974, for whom the earnings disadvantage among the full sample is 19.7 percent and among the reweighted matched subsample is only 6.6 percent.

Column 4 reports the earnings and earnings gaps based on the 1993 Social Security earnings record for the matched subsample. About 6.5 percent fewer natives have Social Security earnings than report earnings in the CPS ($= 1 - [21{,}296/22{,}781]$), and average Social Security earnings among natives are about 11 percent lower than the reported earnings in the CPS. However, the earnings gaps between natives and immigrants based on Social Security earnings records are quite similar to those based on CPS-reported earnings (cols. 3 and 5). Indeed, for most immigrant cohorts the gaps are within two percentage points of each other, though for immigrants who arrived in 1986–89 the earnings gap differs by 11 percentage points. On the basis of these comparisons, the

---

[12] Because reported earnings in the CPS and census surveys are heavily clustered at round numbers, the comparison of medians is problematic. Table 2, therefore, reports means, after CPS earnings are censored at $57,600, the Social Security taxable maximum in 1993. Top-coded observations in both the CPS and longitudinal earnings records are multiplied by 1.38. This factor approximates the uncensored mean among the artificially top-coded observations in the 1994 CPS. Observations with annual earnings below $1,000 are dropped from this table.

TABLE 2
AVERAGE IMMIGRANT AND NATIVE EARNINGS IN THE MARCH 1994 CPS AND SOCIAL SECURITY EARNINGS DATA

	1993 CPS Reported Earnings			1993 Social Security Earnings	
	Full Sample (1)	Matched Subsample (2)	Reweighted Subsample (3)	Matched Subsample (4)	Reweighted Subsample (5)

A. Natives

	(1)	(2)	(3)	(4)	(5)
Log earnings	10.16	10.17	10.16	10.06	10.05
Sample size	27,052	22,781	22,781	21,296	21,296

B. Immigrant Cohorts

	(1)	(2)	(3)	(4)	(5)
1950–69:					
Log earnings	10.18	10.18	10.20	10.09	10.13
Earnings gap	2.4%	1.2%	4.0%	3.2%	7.7%
Standard error	(5.2)	(5.5)	(5.2)	(6.5)	(6.6)
Sample size	340	254	254	234	234
1970–74:					
Log earnings	9.96	10.13	10.09	10.06	10.02
Earnings gap	−19.7%	−3.6%	−6.6%	−.2%	−2.7%
Standard error	(6.1)	(6.6)	(6.6)	(7.1)	(7.2)
Sample size	308	204	204	193	193
1975–79:					
Log earnings	9.98	10.01	9.98	9.91	9.89
Earnings gap	−17.8%	−16.1%	−17.6%	−14.9%	−16.2%
Standard error	(5.4)	(5.8)	(5.8)	(6.3)	(6.2)
Sample size	400	284	284	265	265
1980–85:					
Log earnings	9.79	9.87	9.81	9.79	9.73
Earnings gap	−36.6%	−29.5%	−34.8%	−27.1%	−32.1%
Standard error	(3.6)	(4.3)	(4.4)	(5.0)	(5.0)
Sample size	750	517	517	462	462
1986–89:					
Log earnings	9.66	9.74	9.65	9.71	9.65
Earnings gap	−49.6%	−43.0%	−50.6%	−35.1%	−39.7%
Standard error	(4.1)	(5.8)	(5.4)	(6.3)	(5.8)
Sample size	560	320	320	286	286
1990–94:					
Log earnings	9.58	9.71	9.60	9.57	9.49
Earnings gap	−58.2%	−45.3%	−55.5%	−49.1%	−55.5%
Standard error	(5.0)	(6.5)	(6.2)	(7.5)	(7.1)
Sample size	456	254	254	203	203

NOTE.—Data in cols. 1–3 are taken from the 1994 March CPS and reflect individuals' self-reported wage and salary, self-employment, and farm income from 1993. These earnings are top-coded at the 1993 Social Security maximum of $57,600. Longitudinal data are taken from the 1993 Social Security earnings records among men matched in the 1994 March CPS. Top-coded observations in both data sets are multiplied by 1.38 to approximate the uncensored mean. Only observations with positive earnings are used. Earnings gaps are computed as the difference in log earnings between natives and each immigrant cohort. Standard errors of the earnings gaps are given in parentheses. The means given in cols. 1, 2, and 4 are weighted by the March Supplement weights. The means in cols. 3 and 5 are weighted by the probability of each individual in the public use file being matched to earnings records, as described in Sec. II. Sample sizes are unweighted. Observations with annual earnings less than $1,000 (1993 dollars) are dropped.

use of Social Security earnings data, rather than the familiar self-reported earnings in the CPS, does not systematically affect immigrant-native earnings comparisons.

III. How Out-Migration Affects Immigrant Earnings Measured in Repeated Cross-Sectional and Longitudinal Data

This section begins with a discussion of how permanent out-migration from the United States affects measurement of within- and across-cohort wage changes in repeated cross-sectional data and in longitudinal data, and then summarizes existing empirical evidence on selective out-migration. Next, I describe how temporary out-migration, or migration back and forth between the United States and a migrant's home country, complicates measurement of immigrant wage changes and how data on immigrants' first year of covered earnings in the United States can help paint a more nuanced picture of immigrant wage growth. Finally, the section concludes by comparing sample statistics from the Social Security earnings records and from repeated cross-sectional data that empirically demonstrate the potential importance of selective permanent and temporary out-migration.

A. Permanent Out-Migration

Before I turn to direct estimates of immigrant earnings growth in longitudinal data, it is important to clarify the potential sources of any differences between earnings growth rates measured from longitudinal data and those from the more traditional repeated cross sections of the decennial census. The first issue is the *permanent* out-migration of immigrants. Permanent out-migration leads to several problems in measuring earnings assimilation. Most important, the average earnings of an immigrant cohort will appear to increase from one census cross section to the next if those who leave the country tend to have below-average earnings. In the matched longitudinal sample, by contrast, earnings data are available only for workers who remain in the country until the 1990, 1991, or 1994 cross-sectional surveys are administered. To see the relationship between estimates of immigrant earnings growth from the two data sets, let $E(w_{c,t}|x)$ denote the average earnings among immigrants who arrived in the United States at time c, measured at time t, conditional on the sample criterion x. Panel A of table 3 shows the average earnings of immigrants who arrived in 1967 and 1977, measured

TABLE 3
MEASURES OF AVERAGE IMMIGRANT EARNINGS BY DATA SOURCE AND YEAR

	YEAR EARNINGS ARE MEASURED		
	1970	1980	1990
	A. Earnings Measured in the Repeated Cross Section of the Censuses		
1967 arrivals	$E(w_{67,70}\|\text{stay 3 years})$	$E(w_{67,80}\|\text{stay 13 years})$	$E(w_{67,90}\|\text{stay 23 years})$
1977 arrivals		$E(w_{77,80}\|\text{stay 3 years})$	$E(w_{77,90}\|\text{stay 13 years})$
1987 arrivals			$E(w_{87,90}\|\text{stay 3 years})$
	B. Earnings Measured from Social Security Earnings Records Matched to the 1994 CPS		
1967 arrivals	$E(w_{67,70}\|\text{stay 27 years})$	$E(w_{67,80}\|\text{stay 27 years})$	$E(w_{67,90}\|\text{stay 27 years})$
1977 arrivals		$E(w_{77,80}\|\text{stay 17 years})$	$E(w_{77,90}\|\text{stay 17 years})$
1987 arrivals			$E(w_{87,90}\|\text{stay 7 years})$

in the 1970, 1980, and 1990 decennial Censuses.[13] The longitudinal file contains data only for immigrants who remained in the United States until 1990, 1991, or 1994, depending on which of the three samples the individual appears in. The corresponding earnings measures from the longitudinal Social Security earnings records matched to the 1994 CPS are given in panel B of table 3. Thus the 1970 earnings of immigrants who arrived in 1967 and remained in the United States at least until 1970 can be estimated from the 1970 Census: $E(w_{67,70}|\text{stay 3 years})$; however, only the earnings in 1970 among members of this cohort who remained in the United States until 1994 are available in the longitudinal data: $E(w_{67,70}|\text{stay 27 years})$.

The U.S. earnings at time t of an immigrant who arrived at time c can be decomposed as $w_{ct} = \mu_{ct} + \varepsilon_{ct}$, where μ_{ct} is the average earnings that the *entire initial* arrival cohort would earn if they remained in the United States until time t, and ε_{ct} is the deviation of an immigrant's earnings from the group average. The average value of ε_{ct} is zero when the cohort arrives in the United States. Over time, however, if disproportionately less or more skilled workers leave the United States, then the average value becomes positive or negative.

---

[13] The 1970–90 Censuses, the CPS, and the SIPP record immigrants' arrival date by an interval (e.g., immigrants who arrived in 1967 would be recorded as arriving in the interval between 1965 and 1969). For simplicity, this discussion assumes that the exact year of arrival is known. Also for simplicity, the discussion that follows compares repeated cross sections of the census to the longitudinal data matched to the 1994 CPS. The actual sample used in the empirical work pools observations from the 1990 and 1991 SIPPs and the 1994 CPS that are matched to longitudinal data.

The earnings growth of the 1967 arrivals measured between the 1970 and 1980 Censuses is given by

$$\Delta_{70,80}^{\text{Census}} = E(w_{67,80}|\text{stay 13 years}) - E(w_{67,70}|\text{stay 3 years})$$

$$= (\mu_{67,80} - \mu_{67,70}) + [E(\varepsilon_{67,80}|\text{stay 13 years})$$

$$- E(\varepsilon_{67,70}|\text{stay 3 years})]$$

$$= (\mu_{67,80} - \mu_{67,70}) + E(\varepsilon_{67,80}|\text{stay 13 years})$$

$$- E(\varepsilon_{67,70}|\text{stay 13 years}) + E(\varepsilon_{67,70}|\text{stay 13 years})$$

$$- E(\varepsilon_{67,70}|\text{stay 3 years})$$

$$= E(w_{67,80}|\text{stay 13 years}) - E(w_{67,70}|\text{stay 13 years})$$

$$+ E(\varepsilon_{67,70}|\text{stay 13 years}) - E(\varepsilon_{67,70}|\text{stay 3 years}). \quad (1)$$

That is, their measured earnings growth is equal to the growth among the 1967 arrivals who remained in the United States at least until 1980, plus a bias term equal to the difference in earnings in 1970 between the immigrants who remained in the United States at least until 1970 and the subset who stayed until 1980. If emigration is concentrated among lower-earning immigrants, this last term is positive and the observed change in earnings between censuses overstates the true increase in earnings experienced by immigrants who remained in the United States until 1980. In addition, of course, the expected earnings growth of the original cohort if they all remained in the United States until 1980, $\mu_{67,80} - \mu_{67,70}$, cannot be estimated from the 1970 and 1980 Censuses.

In contrast to estimates from the census, immigrant earnings growth measured in longitudinal data provides an unbiased estimate of earnings growth *among the immigrants who are in the United States in 1994.* The growth in earnings of the 1967 arrival cohort between 1970 and 1980 in the longitudinal sample is given by

$$\Delta_{70,80}^{\text{Longitudinal}} = E(w_{67,80}|\text{stay 27 years}) - E(w_{67,70}|\text{stay 27 years})$$

$$= (\mu_{67,80} - \mu_{67,70}) + E(\varepsilon_{67,80}|\text{stay 27 years})$$

$$- E(\varepsilon_{67,70}|\text{stay 27 years}). \quad (2)$$

If out-migration is based on permanent earnings characteristics that are not related to immigrants' earnings growth over time (i.e., if $E(\varepsilon_{c,t}|\text{stay } k \text{ years}) = E(\varepsilon_{c,t'}|\text{stay } k \text{ years})$, for all t and t'), then the estimate from the longitudinal data is also equal to the potential earnings growth the initial cohort would have experienced in the absence of out-migration. In this case, only the level of earnings of the original cohort cannot be identified from longitudinal data on those who remained in the country.

The census provides meaningful comparisons of across-cohort earnings differences only if the out-migration process is constant across cohorts. In particular, the difference in average earnings three years after entry between the 1967 and 1977 arrivals, measured in the 1970 and 1980 Censuses, is

$$\Upsilon_{67,77}^{Census} = E(w_{77,80}|\text{stay 3 years}) - E(w_{67,70}|\text{stay 3 years})$$

$$= (\mu_{77,80} - \mu_{67,70})$$

$$+ E(\varepsilon_{77,80}|\text{stay 3 years}) - E(\varepsilon_{67,70}|\text{stay 3 years}). \quad (3)$$

The difference in the last line of this expression will be zero if the 1967 and 1977 cohorts have similar selective out-migration patterns during their first three years in the United States. Of course, changes in immigrant characteristics, such as the fraction of immigrants who arrive from nearby countries or arrive as refugees, will likely change the out-migration process. In this case, it is not possible to separately identify across-cohort differences in earnings—in levels or growth rates—that are due to differential selective out-migration from differences due to the labor market skills of immigrants.

Out-migration also presents problems in making comparisons across cohorts using the longitudinal data. The difference in average earnings three years after entry between the 1967 and 1977 arrivals, measured in the longitudinal sample, is

$$\Upsilon_{67,77}^{Longitudinal} = E(w_{77,80}|\text{stay 17 years}) - E(w_{67,70}|\text{stay 27 years})$$

$$= (\mu_{77,80} - \mu_{67,70})$$

$$+ E(\varepsilon_{77,80}|\text{stay 17 years}) - E(\varepsilon_{67,70}|\text{stay 27 years}). \quad (4)$$

The first term in the second line of this expression, $\mu_{77,80} - \mu_{67,70}$, is the difference in earnings three years after arrival among all immigrants in the two cohorts. The second term is the difference in earnings between the two cohorts caused by differential out-migration between the year they entered and 1994, when the CPS survey was administered. If, for example, the least successful immigrants in each year tend to leave the United States, then the additional 10 years of out-migration among the 1967 cohort mean that it will have more "successes" than the 1977 cohort will. This will give the appearance of a downward trend in earnings across successive arrival cohorts in the longitudinal data. This source of bias may be limited, however, for earlier arrival cohorts if most out-migration occurs within the first 10 years after entry.

Whether analyses based on repeated cross-sectional data over- or underestimate actual immigrant earnings growth depends crucially on whether return migrants are systematically less or more skilled than migrants who remain in the United States. A few examples indicate that, in theory, return migrants could be positively or negatively selected: Some migrants plan to remain in the United States permanently but return to their home country because their earnings in the United States were lower than what they had expected. Perhaps counterintuitively, these "unlucky" migrants could come from the top or the bottom of the immigrant earnings distribution. A standard view of Mexican migration to the United States is that lower-skilled Mexicans earn a higher wage in the United States than what they would earn in Mexico, high-skilled workers earn a higher wage in Mexico, and those on the margin of moving tend to be Mexicans from the middle of the skill distribution. Migrants who were close to the margin tend to experience the smallest gains from migrating and are therefore the most likely to return to Mexico if their experiences in the U.S. labor market turn out to be slightly worse than expected. In this scenario return migration to Mexico is positively selected. By contrast, poor luck in the U.S. labor market will tend to generate negative selection among return migrants who come from countries that tend to send their most skilled individuals to the United States.[14]

Many migrants come to the United States with a plan to return to their home country after a limited period of time. This return flow may also be positively or negatively selected: If migrants plan to return after accumulating a target level of savings, success in the U.S. labor market implies that migrants hit their target and return home sooner. On the other hand, success in the United States may increase the return to staying longer and accumulating additional assets. Emigration may also be driven by the expiration of a visa that allows an immigrant to legally work in the United States, and many of these temporary visas are allocated to higher-skilled workers. For example, the H-1B visa program grants a temporary work permit to foreigners who have the equivalent of an American bachelor's degree and work in particular "specialty occupations." Finally, migrants who face lower costs of migration may be more likely to return home; thus it should not be surprising that emigration rates tend to be quite high for migrants from Mexico, a country that supplies a large fraction of the low-earning migrants in the United States.

Although systematic data are not collected on the characteristics of emigrants from the United States, past research and tabulations in Sec-

---

[14] Self-selection and the decision to migrate from Mexico to the United States are explored in Chiquiar and Hanson (2005) and Ibarraran and Lubotsky (2007). Self-selection among return migrants is modeled more formally in Borjas and Bratsberg (1996).

tion III.C below suggest that emigration is disproportionately more common among low-earning immigrants, and hence traditional measures of immigrant assimilation estimated from repeated cross sections of the census are likely to overestimate earnings growth among migrants who remain in the United States. For example, Chiswick (1980, 1986) compares the distribution of migrants' education, by arrival cohort, in the 1960 and 1970 Censuses and finds evidence that immigrants' educational attainment increased between censuses (especially among migrants from Mexico), which is consistent with selective emigration among less educated migrants or with immigrants acquiring additional schooling after arrival. My tabulations in Section III.C show a similar pattern in more recent census data. Lindstrom and Massey (1994) compare Mexicans in the 1990 U.S. Census with Mexicans surveyed between 1989 and 1991 who live in any of 11 Mexican communities with high rates of migration to the United States. Although there are some difficulties in comparing educational attainment across data sources, Lindstrom and Massey's evidence indicates that Mexicans in the United States are more educated, have higher earnings, and have greater English language ability than the Mexicans surveyed in Mexico who reported that they had moved to the United States and then returned to Mexico.[15]

Despite this limited evidence of selective migration from the United States, previous studies of immigrant earnings growth have not clearly shown whether earnings growth measured in repeated cross sections of the census is accurate. Hu (1999) (described in Hu [2000]) compares estimates of immigrant earnings assimilation from repeated cross sections from the 1970, 1980, and 1990 decennial Censuses and from longitudinal Social Security earnings records between 1951 and 1991 matched to respondents in the HRS. The HRS is a sample of individuals born between 1931 and 1941, and Hu selects a similar birth cohort from the censuses.[16] Hu presents evidence that repeated cross sections of the census overstate assimilation among non-Hispanic white migrants, but not among Hispanic migrants, conclusions similar to those below.

Two other studies are similar in spirit to this one: Chiswick (1980) (described in Chiswick [1986]) compares the relative wage growth of immigrants in the 1970 Census with longitudinal measures of wage growth between 1965 and 1973 in the original cohort of the National Longitudinal Survey of Older Men, respondents to which were aged

---

[15] Ibarraran and Lubotsky (2007) provide evidence that Mexicans in the 2000 U.S. Census appear to overstate their educational attainment.

[16] Since the HRS sample is drawn from a narrowly defined birth cohort, it is difficult to separate the effects of immigrants' age or labor market experience at the time of migration from the effect of their period of arrival. More generally, most of the immigrants in the HRS sample arrived in the United States prior to 1970, and their experiences may be quite different from those of the more contemporary group of immigrants studied here.

45–59 in 1966. The National Longitudinal Survey contains only 98 migrants and does not record their year of arrival to the United States, making a direct comparison with census data difficult. Nevertheless, Chiswick's estimates indicate that immigrant earnings rose by about 1.1 percentage points per year between 1965 and 1973, which is similar to the rate of earnings growth he estimated in the 1970 Census. This similarity is surprising because one would think that falling cohort quality and selective migration would lead to a substantially larger estimate of immigrant wage growth in the census. Borjas (1989) studies earnings growth and emigration using a unique data set that tracked about 50,000 engineers and natural and social scientists between 1972 and 1978. Borjas's estimates indicate that sample attrition—which is most likely caused by emigration from the United States—is more common among lower-earning individuals in this interesting subpopulation of immigrants.

Finally, Duleep and Dowhan (2002) use longitudinal Social Security earnings records matched to the 1994 CPS (one of the three longitudinal files used in this study) and compare the change in the immigrant-native earnings gap at the thirtieth, fortieth, and fiftieth percentiles during the first 10 years after arrival for immigrants who arrived between 1960 and 1983. Although they find that the earnings gap decreases during the first 10 years in the United States, it is not possible to ascertain from their study which types of migrants leave the United States or how selective out-migration influences measures of immigrants' progress since the authors do not compute similar outcomes in repeated cross-sectional data.

In sum, if there is selective emigration, repeated cross sections of the decennial census do not identify wage growth among immigrants who stay in the United States. Past work indicates that low-earning immigrants are probably more likely to emigrate than higher-earning immigrants, and hence past measures of immigrant wage growth from the decennial census overstate assimilation among migrants who actually remain in the country. Previous attempts to accurately measure wage growth have generally relied on quite small samples that are not particularly representative of current immigration, an issue that is remedied in the work below.

B. Temporary Out-Migration and Alternative Arrival Cohort Definitions

While previous researchers have studied the potential effects of permanent out-migration, a less well-understood but equally important phenomenon is *temporary* out-migration. Many immigrants arrive in the United States, work for several years, return to their home country, and then reimmigrate to the United States at a later time; some migrants make this trip multiple times. Common household surveys are not designed to ascertain when a migrant first arrived in the United States: The 1970–90 decennial Censuses, the CPS, and the SIPP ask the household respondent "When did this person come to the United States to stay?" The 1990 Census respondent instructions read "If the person has entered the United States (that is, the 50 states and the District of Columbia) more than once, fill the circle for the latest year he/she came to stay." The 1980 Census instructions are somewhat different and read "If the person has entered the U.S. more than once, fill the circle for the year he or she came to stay permanently." The 1970 Census does not appear to give instructions regarding how to respond for a migrant who has made multiple trips to the United States.[17] It is clear that the year of arrival data in the census, CPS, and SIPP do not necessarily correspond to migrants' first year of arrival in the United States and potentially correspond to different concepts in different census years.

This misclassification of initial entry cohorts complicates estimation of both the earnings level and growth trajectories of immigrant cohorts derived from repeated cross-sectional data, particularly if the workers who migrate back and forth tend to be lower-skilled. For example, immigrants observed in the 1990 Census who report having arrived in the United States between 1985 and 1989 are composed of those who arrived in the United States for the first time during that period plus some of those who initially arrived earlier, left the United States, and then reentered between 1985 and 1989. The average earnings of those who report that they arrived between 1985 and 1989 may over- or underestimate the earnings of genuine new arrivals, depending on whether the return migrants tend to have higher or lower earnings than the new arrivals. Similarly, the observed earnings *growth* of an arrival cohort is a mixture of the earnings growth among immigrants who arrived for the first time and the growth among reentrants. If, as seems likely, reentrants have slower earnings growth than those who arrive for the first time, estimates of earnings growth will tend to understate the earnings growth of new arrivals, especially among recent cohorts that contain a particularly large number of reentrants. Finally, repeat migration by low-earning immigrants may also influence the trend in relative earnings across successive immigrant arrival cohorts. If the incidence of back-and-forth migration increases over time, or if it becomes more common among the least skilled immigrants, the relative earnings of successive cohorts measured in repeated cross-sectional data will tend to fall over time, all else equal.

An important benefit of using the matched longitudinal earnings data is that information is available on immigrants' first year of covered

---

[17] Decennial census enumeration forms and instructions are available for download at http://www.ipums.org/. The 2000 Census asked "When did this person come to live in the United States?"

earnings and on their reported date of arrival in the household surveys. Discrepancies between immigrants' reported arrival date in the CPS or SIPP household surveys and their first year of earnings in the longitudinal Social Security data are consistent with a substantial degree of temporary, or back-and-forth, migration. Fourteen percent of immigrants in the longitudinal data have earnings prior to the year of their reported arrival year in the CPS or SIPP household survey. Two pieces of evidence suggest that many of these immigrants had temporarily left the United States and reported their most recent date of arrival in the CPS or SIPP survey: first, the country of origin pattern is similar to the pattern of emigration rates found by Jasso and Rosenzweig (1990) and Borjas and Bratsberg (1996): 10 percent of Asian immigrants, 13 percent of Europeans, 17 percent of Latin Americans, and 19 percent of Canadians had earnings in the longitudinal data prior to their reported date of arrival. A second, more direct piece of evidence on temporary emigration is that 50 percent of the immigrants who had earnings prior to their reported date of entry had a year without any covered earnings prior to their reported date of entry, which is exactly what would occur if the immigrant left the United States for an entire calendar year before reimmigrating.[18]

These discrepancies are consistent with evidence from other studies that the census's year of arrival question does not accurately reflect immigrants' initial year of arrival. Ellis and Wright (1998) uncover additional evidence of back-and-forth migration by comparing immigrants' responses in the 1980 and 1990 Censuses to the questions "When did this person arrive in the U.S. to stay?" and "Where did this person live five years ago?" Over 16 percent of male immigrants in the 1980 Census who reported that they arrived between 1975 and 1980 also reported that they lived in the United States on April 1, 1975. This rate increased in the 1990 Census, where over 27 percent of male immigrants who reported that they arrived between 1985 and 1990 also reported that they lived in the United States on April 1, 1985. These discrepancies are most common among low-wage, less educated, and Mexican migrants. Although a small fraction of these migrants arrived between January and March of 1975 or 1985, Ellis and Wright argue that these discrepancies are largely caused by migrants who moved back and forth between their home country and the United States or by migrants who view the date they decided "to stay" in the United States as a distinct concept from when they physically arrived in the United States for the first time.

[18] Disruptions in earnings histories may not be definitive evidence of out-migration since 27 percent of native-born workers had a year without covered earnings between the ages of 25 and 35. Nevertheless, the evidence is suggestive that there may be a significant number of immigrants who leave and then reenter the United States.

Additional evidence of problems with the census arrival question comes from Redstone and Massey's (2004) analysis of the New Immigrant Survey Pilot. This data set includes 1,134 individuals who were admitted legally to the United States between July and August of 1996. The baseline survey asked respondents to report the date of their first entry, the date of their last entry, and the number of separate trips to the United States, among other things. The one-year follow-up survey asked immigrants to report the year they arrived in the United States to stay, a replica of the decennial census question. Redstone and Massey find that only 55 percent of immigrants respond to the census question with their initial date of arrival.

These discrepancies between immigrants' reported date of arrival in the household surveys and their first year of covered earnings in the longitudinal data raise the question of how to best classify immigrants into arrival cohorts in the empirical analyses. I explore three alternative measures of immigrants' arrival cohort, each of which has different strengths and weaknesses. The first cohort classification groups immigrants by their reported date of arrival, with any earnings prior to that date dropped from the analysis. This classification has the virtue that it is similar to the date of arrival measure available in the repeated cross-sectional data. One obvious drawback of this approach, however, is that for some immigrants the longitudinal data clearly establish an earlier date of initial arrival. This method of constructing arrival cohorts will tend to understate exposure to the U.S. labor market of immigrants who make multiple trips to the United States and report their most recent date of arrival in the survey.

A second drawback of classifying immigrants by their reported date of arrival is that many immigrants do not have earnings in the longitudinal data for some years after their reported arrival date. This likely reflects immigrants who initially worked in uncovered employment, attended school, or simply did not participate in the labor market when they entered the United States. A prominent example is immigrants who were legalized following the Immigration Reform and Control Act (IRCA) of 1986, which granted legal residency to about 3 million people who had been living in the United States illegally (see Bean, Edmonston, and Passel 1990; Smith and Edmonston 1997). Fourteen percent of immigrants who reported in the household surveys that they arrived as adults between 1975 and 1979 did not have covered earnings in the longitudinal data until after 1986; 27 percent of those who reported that they arrived between 1980 and 1985 did not have earnings until after 1986. A lag between the reported date of entry and the first year of covered earnings creates compositional changes in immigrant arrival cohorts over time as new immigrants enter the labor force or move from uncovered to covered work. This compositional change is likely to also be present among arrival cohorts in census data if immigrants are more likely to participate in the census when they are in the United States legally. These compositional changes in cohorts over time can lead to an underestimate or an overestimate of individual earnings trajectories, depending on whether these delayed earners have relatively high or low earnings.

A second method to form arrival cohorts is to group immigrants by the earlier of their reported date of arrival and their first year of covered earnings. In the empirical work below I refer to this classification as immigrants' "adjusted date of arrival." Although this method also suffers from the problem of compositional changes in immigrant cohorts over time, I use the comparison of average earnings across cohorts when classified by "reported date of arrival" with that estimated when classified by "adjusted date of arrival" to shed light on which immigrants report an arrival date later than their first year of covered earnings. In particular, one of the striking comparisons below is that the average earnings of the 1960s and 1970s arrival cohorts are considerably higher with the reported date of arrival definition than with the adjusted date of arrival definition. This indicates that migrants who report that they arrived in these early cohorts tend to have earnings considerably higher than migrants who had earnings back then, but for whatever reason reported themselves to be more recent arrivals, and suggests that our inferences about the magnitude of changes in cohort quality are quite sensitive to the flow and earnings of these transient, or back-and-forth, migrants.

A final method of grouping immigrants minimizes the problem of compositional changes in cohorts over time by grouping immigrants solely by their first year of covered earnings in the Social Security data. Although this method understates the length of time spent in the United States by immigrants who initially worked in uncovered employment or who invested in U.S.-specific human capital in ways other than through working, it provides perhaps the most easily interpretable picture of immigrant earnings growth because it measures wage growth from the year of entry into the formal, or covered, U.S. labor market.

C. A Descriptive Picture of Immigrant Earnings

Table 4 compares earnings and other characteristics of working immigrants and natives in the longitudinal and cross-sectional data sets in 1979, 1989, and 1995.[19] Two conclusions emerge from this table: first, the earnings and characteristics of immigrant cohorts are sensitive to

---

[19] I pool observations from a three-year window around 1979, 1989, and 1995 in the longitudinal sample to increase the precision of the estimates. Top-coded observations are multiplied by 1.38 to approximate the mean of the censored observations (see n. 12). All observations with annual earnings less than $1,000 (1997 dollars) are dropped.

the choice of arrival cohort definition. The evidence is consistent with there being a relatively large number of low-earning immigrants who made multiple trips to the United States and report their most recent date of arrival in the household surveys. The second conclusion is that it is evident in "unconditional" sample means that immigrants' measured earnings growth is faster in the repeated cross-sectional data than in the longitudinal data, consistent with selective out-migration among lower-earning immigrants.

The first three sets of columns display information from the Social Security records matched to individuals in the 1990 and 1991 SIPPs and the 1994 CPS. Columns 1–3 show characteristics of workers measured in 1979, 1989, and 1995, where immigrants are classified by their reported date of arrival in the household surveys. In columns 4–6 immigrants are grouped by their adjusted date of arrival; that is, migrants with earnings prior to their reported period of arrival are moved to the earlier cohort. This simple change in how arrival cohorts are defined increases the number of migrants classified as 1960–74 arrivals and reduces the number classified as arriving between 1975 and 1991. For example, in 1979 there are 912 working migrants who reported that they arrived in the 1960s. Of these, 62 had earnings in the longitudinal data prior to 1960, whereas 148 migrants first appear in the longitudinal data during the 1960s but reported an arrival date of 1970 or later. Once these 210 migrants—or 23 percent of the original cohort—are reclassified, the adjusted 1960–69 arrival cohort has 998 migrants. Similarly, adjusting the 1970–74 cohort increases its size from 869 to 973 migrants, as 186 new migrants are moved into the cohort and 82 migrants are removed from it. These 268 migrants represent over 31 percent of the original cohort. Immigrants who are moved into earlier arrival cohorts tend to be less educated, so changing how arrival cohorts are defined tends to increase the fraction of 1960–74 arrivals who do not have a high school diploma and decreases their measured average earnings, while improving these measures among post-1975 arrivals.

The effects of the 1986 amnesty program are also clearly visible if one compares the sample sizes and characteristics when migrants are grouped by their adjusted date of arrival, in columns 4–6, and by their first year of covered earning, in columns 7–9. Classifying immigrants solely by their first year of covered earnings increases the sample sizes of the 1985–89 and 1990–91 cohorts, at the expense of earlier cohorts, as migrants who reported that they arrived before the amnesty, but do not have Social Security earnings until after the amnesty, are moved to post-1985 cohorts. For example, there are 1,856 working immigrants in 1989 with an adjusted date of arrival of 1980–84 and another 662 with an adjusted date of arrival of 1985–89. When immigrants are classified solely by their first year of covered earnings, the 1980–84 cohort de-

TABLE 4
DESCRIPTIVE STATISTICS FOR NATIVES AND IMMIGRANTS BY DATA SOURCE AND COHORT DEFINITION

	LONGITUDINAL EARNINGS DATA									REPEATED CROSS SECTIONS		
	1979 (1)	1989 (2)	1995 (3)	1979 (4)	1989 (5)	1995 (6)	1979 (7)	1989 (8)	1995 (9)	1979 (10)	1989 (11)	1995 (12)

A. Natives

Log wage	10.30	10.23	10.19	10.30	10.23	10.19	10.30	10.23	10.19	10.35	10.32	10.24
Age	35.0	38.6	41.1	35.0	38.6	41.1	35.0	38.6	41.1	35.7	39.4	42.1
No HS	14.6%	11.8%	9.4%	14.6%	11.8%	9.4%	14.6%	11.8%	9.4%	17.6%	14.0%	9.4%
Observations	61,955	97,469	61,961	61,955	97,469	61,961	61,955	97,469	61,961	160,051	235,312	36,174

B. Immigrant Cohorts by Period of Arrival

	Reported Arrival Cohort			Adjusted Arrival Cohort			First Year of Covered Earnings			Reported Arrival Cohort		

1960–69:

Log wage	10.34	10.31	10.20	10.32	10.29	10.18	10.54	10.29	10.16	10.39	10.46	10.23
Gap	3.6%	7.8%	.6%	2.3%	5.4%	−1.4%	23.8%	6.1%	−2.8%	4.2%	13.7%	−.8%
Age	39.9	49.9	53.9	40.6	50.4	54.8	45.5	51.0	55.5	40.5	50.3	54.9
No HS	33.1%	32.9%	31.4%	35.2%	34.5%	31.4%	26.6%	36.7%	33.6%	37.1%	36.4%	27.2%
Observations	912	859	422	998	958	484	915	854	429	28,348	24,459	318

1970–74:

Log wage	10.11	10.28	10.11	10.02	10.22	10.08	10.32	10.23	10.13	10.12	10.30	10.25
Gap	−19.4%	4.4%	−8.5%	−28.4%	−.9%	−10.9%	1.7%	−.5%	−6.1%	−23.7%	−2.0%	.7%
Age	34.2	43.6	48.8	32.7	42.1	47.7	41.1	42.9	48.4	35.0	44.6	49.7
No HS	32.4%	33.7%	45.8%	35.2%	35.6%	47.4%	36.7%	34.6%	45.0%	40.5%	42.0%	30.8%
Observations	869	930	477	973	1,067	548	957	972	495	25,972	23,444	334

(continued overleaf)

	(1)	(2)	(3)	(4)	(5)	(6)	(7)	(8)	(9)	(10)	(11)	(12)
1975–79:												
Log wage	9.99	10.12	10.03	10.03	10.10	10.04	10.04	10.19	10.13	9.81	10.17	10.03
Gap	−30.8%	−10.8%	−16.5%	−27.3%	−12.9%	−15.2%	−26.1%	−4.2%	−6.3%	−53.7%	−15.3%	−21.2%
Age	32.9	38.7	44.4	33.3	38.1	43.6	33.3	39.0	44.9	33.4	40.1	45.6
No HS	25.8%	34.0%	36.6%	25.1%	34.1%	32.7%	35.7%	30.2%	25.8%	34.2%	38.5%	35.5%
Observations	551	1,266	700	436	1,261	708	561	972	504	28,533	32,729	536
1980–84:												
Log wage		9.88	9.89		9.88	9.90		9.98	10.02		9.93	9.93
Gap		−35.4%	−29.8%		−35.6%	−29.7%		−25.1%	−16.8%		−39.1%	−31.0%
Age		35.5	40.3		34.8	39.6		36.4	41.7		36.0	42.1
No HS		28.57%	34.74%		27.94%	35.79%		25.74%	28.40%		38.60%	33.00%
Observations		1,937	1,299		1,856	1,261		1,431	733		48,795	929
1985–89:												
Log wage		9.77	9.87		9.70	9.82		9.73	9.84		9.70	9.78
Gap		−46.6%	−32.6%		−53.7%	−37.1%		−50.6%	−34.9%		−62.1%	−45.4%
Age		35.5	35.3		34.4	34.1		33.9	36.0		34.7	36.9
No HS		32.1%	33.4%		29.9%	35.9%		34.9%	41.0%		34.7%	33.3%
Observations		809	847		662	897		1,599	1,344		43,661	755
1990–91:												
Log wage			9.75			9.77			9.79			9.75
Gap			−44.1%			−42.5%			−40.5%			−48.8%
Age			36.5			36.5			36.2			37.3
No HS			32.2%			28.3%			37.8%			38.0%
Observations			355			282			420			304

Note.—Data in cols. 1–9 are taken from Social Security earnings records matched to men in the 1990 and 1991 SIPPs and the 1994 March CPS. Cohort definitions are described in Secs. IIIB and C. Data in cols. 10–12 are taken from the 1980 and 1990 decennial Censuses and the 1995–97 March CPS. Observations from the longitudinal data are weighted by the inverse of the probability of being matched to earnings records, as described in Sec. II. Observations from the 1990 Census and the 1995–97 March CPS are weighted by the sample weights provided in the data. Observations with annual earnings less than $1,000 (1997 dollars) are dropped. The five statistics shown are the average of the log of annual earnings of group, the difference in log earnings between each immigrant cohort and natives (expressed as a percent), the average age, the percentage of each group without a high school diploma, and the unweighted sample count. The average is computed by first multiplying all top-coded observations by 1.38, which approximates the mean of the uncensored data.

creases to 1,431 and the 1985–89 cohort increases to 1,599. Since the migrants affected by the amnesty tend to be less educated, the fraction of the 1980–84 cohort that has less than a high school diploma falls from 28 percent to 26 percent, whereas the fraction of the 1985–89 cohort that has less than a high school education increases from 30 percent to 35 percent and the fraction of the 1990–91 cohort without a high school education increases from 28 percent to 38 percent.

Finally, columns 10–12 of table 4 show similar measures of earnings, age, and educational attainment measured in the 1980 and 1990 decennial Censuses and the pooled 1995–97 March CPS (which records annual earnings in 1994–96). These samples are described in more detail in the following section. The immigrant-native earnings gaps experienced by each cohort tend to fall over time in both the longitudinal data and the repeated cross-sectional data, but the rate of convergence is generally faster in the repeated cross-sectional data. For example, in the 1980 Census, the 1960–69 arrivals had 4.2 percent higher earnings than natives; this gap increased by 9.5 percentage points to 13.7 percent in the 1990 Census. The comparable change for this cohort in the longitudinal data was only three to four percentage points, depending on the cohort definition. Similarly, the measured earnings gap among the 1975–79 arrivals narrowed by 38 percentage points between the 1980 and 1990 Censuses, whereas the corresponding change measured in the longitudinal data was between 14 and 22 percentage points, depending on the arrival cohort definition. This faster rate of earnings growth in repeated cross sections of the census is consistent with that data source conflating selective out-migration among low-earning immigrants and earnings growth among immigrants who remain in the United States. The following section more formally compares measures of earnings growth in repeated cross-sectional and longitudinal data.

IV. Direct Estimates of Immigrant-Native Earnings Differences

This section uses a median regression framework to do three things: First, I compare the relative earnings growth of immigrants in the longitudinal data with growth measured in repeated cross-sectional data drawn from the 1970–90 decennial Censuses and the 1995–97 CPS. Subsection A establishes the two main conclusions of this study: Selective out-migration by low-earning immigrants leads repeated cross-sectional data to overstate the relative earnings growth among immigrants who remain in the United States. The presence of low-earning immigrants who move back and forth between their home country and the United States, but report their more recent dates of arrival, leads to an overestimate of the secular deterioration in the level of earnings of newly arrived immigrants. Subsection B examines earnings progress among

Hispanic immigrants to the United States. Finally, in subsection C, I separately study the earnings progress of immigrants who arrived in the 1960s, the 1970s, and between 1980 and 1994.

A. Immigrant Earnings in Repeated Cross Sections and Longitudinal Data

In this subsection I contrast estimates of immigrant-native earnings gaps using two samples. The first sample is taken from the longitudinal Social Security records matched to respondents in the 1990 and 1991 SIPPs and the 1994 CPS (described in detail in Sec. II). The second sample is taken from repeated cross-sectional data and includes men drawn from the 1970 decennial Census 5 percent 1-in-100 state sample, the 1980 decennial Census 5 percent A sample, the 1990 decennial Census 5 percent sample, and the 1995–97 March CPS.[20] To match the endpoints of the repeated cross-sectional sample, the longitudinal sample includes earnings between 1969 and 1997. Both samples include only men born between 1930 and 1969 and person-year observations with positive earnings and in which the individual was aged 25 or older. Earnings from the repeated cross-sectional files are measured as the sum of wage and salary, self-employment, and farm income and are artificially censored at the Social Security taxable maximum. Finally, immigrants who arrived after 1991 are excluded from both samples.

There is now a fairly standard human capital framework to compare immigrant and native earnings, principally associated with Chiswick's (1978) cross-sectional analysis of the 1970 Census and Borjas's (1985, 1995) cohort-based analyses of the 1970–90 Censuses. Natives' log earnings are specified as a function of potential labor market experience and calendar time effects. Immigrants' earnings are further decomposed into the effects of arrival cohort (k_c), potential experience at arrival (m_{ic}), and the length of time since arrival in the United States (y_{ct}).[21] Formally, the model of the log of annual earnings is given by

$$w_{ict} = \alpha + \beta f(\text{Experience}_{ict}) + \gamma f(\text{Year}_{ict}) + k_c + m_{ic} + y_{ct} + \varepsilon_{ict}, \quad (5)$$

where i indexes the individual, c indexes native-born workers and

---

[20] Respondents in the 1995–97 March CPS files who were in the fifth through eighth rotation groups are dropped. This simplifies inferences because in principle households are surveyed in two consecutive March supplements. I use a 25 percent random sample of the natives in the longitudinal data and a 10 percent random sample of the natives in the 1980 and 1990 Census files to reduce the computational burden of the semiparametric models in this section.

[21] Friedberg (1993) demonstrates the importance of controlling for the age at which an immigrant enters the U.S. labor market in a similar model of earnings. The sample requirement that a person be in the labor force generates a negative correlation between the age at which an immigrant arrived and the years since migration. Other examples of similar models of immigrant earnings are given by Funkhouser and Trejo (1995), Carliner (1996), Schoeni, McCarthy, and Vernez (1996), Schoeni (1997), and Hu (1999).

immigrant arrival cohorts, and t indexes time. The terms $f(\text{Experience}_{ict})$ and $f(\text{Year}_{ict})$ are quartics in potential experience and calendar time, and ε_{ict} represents unobserved influences on earnings and measurement error.[22]

The immigrant arrival cohort effects (k_c) are given by indicators for immigrants who arrived in 1950–59, 1960–64, 1965–69, 1970–74, 1975–79, 1980–84, 1985–89, and 1990–91 (the native-born are the excluded group). The effect of experience at arrival is captured by indicators for immigrants who arrived with 6–10, 11–15, 16–20, or more than 21 years of potential experience (immigrants who arrived with five or fewer years of experience are the excluded group). Finally, the effect of time in the United States is captured by indicators that an immigrant has been in the United States for 6–10, 11–15, 16–20, 21–25, 26–30, and more than 30 years (immigrants who have been in the United States fewer than five years are the excluded group).[23]

The standard interpretation of equation (5) is that the estimates capture differences in the labor market skills between immigrants and natives. This interpretation may be problematic, however, because in order to separately identify the effects on earnings of immigrants' period of arrival, experience at arrival, and time spent in the United States, the effects of experience and calendar time must be constrained to be equal among immigrants and natives. While these restrictions are somewhat standard in the literature, there are reasons to believe that they may be problematic. Most important, the assumption of common effects of calendar time is at odds with work by LaLonde and Topel (1992), Borjas (1995), and Lubotsky (2007), who demonstrate that widening wage inequality during the 1970s through 1990s reduced the relative earnings of migrants, as it did for lower-wage workers more generally. Those three studies propose alternative methods to separate immigrant-native differences in skills from differences in returns to skills. I do not make a similar adjustment in this paper since I focus on understanding differences in measured wage growth between longitudinal and repeated cross-sectional data during a common time period. An identical adjustment for changes in the structure of wages in both the longitudinal

---

[22] Potential experience is the number of years an individual has been out of school. People who did not finish high school are assumed to have entered the labor market at age 18. High school graduates, people with some college, those with a four-year college degree, and those with any postcollege education are assumed to have entered the labor market at ages 19, 20, 22, and 24. In addition, the calendar time effects for the repeated cross-sectional sample are simply a set of indicators for which cross section the observation is drawn from.

[23] Since period of arrival is reported with an interval in the household surveys, time in the United States and experience at arrival are measured from the midpoint of the arrival interval, where necessary.

and repeated cross-sectional data will not have any effect on the difference in estimates between the two samples.

The assumption of a common experience-earnings profile may also be problematic. Baker and Benjamin (1997) show that family composition affects immigrant husbands and wives' labor supply decisions. This suggests that differences in life cycle labor supply behavior may differ between immigrants and natives and thereby generate differences in their experience-earnings profiles.

In contrast to most previous studies, I do not control for individuals' educational attainment. This study focuses on accurately measuring unconditional differences in earnings between immigrants and natives and on better understanding how selective out-migration influences conclusions about immigrant assimilation. The immigrant arrival cohort fixed effects will therefore reflect differences between the native-born and successive arrival cohorts in educational attainment, as well as unobserved or unmeasured abilities (such as language skills).[24]

Because earnings are top-coded, ordinary least squares estimation of equation (5) is inappropriate. Instead, the model is estimated with Powell's (1984) semiparametric censored least absolute deviation (CLAD) estimator, which is robust to heteroscedasticity and does not require knowledge of the underlying distribution of the unobservable error component. The identifying assumption is that the median of ε_{ict} is zero conditional on the regressors.[25]

The standard errors are estimated from 50 bootstrap replications of a least absolute deviation, or median, regression using only observations not predicted to be censored using the final parameter estimates. In

---

[24] Excluding education from the model also has the virtue of avoiding several other potential difficulties. First, schooling is reported in different years in the two samples: schooling is reported in the longitudinal data at the time of the associated household survey (i.e., in 1990, 1991, or 1994), whereas it is reported contemporaneously in the repeated cross-sectional data (i.e., in 1970, 1980, 1990, or in 1995–97). Second, surveys conducted prior to 1990 asked respondents how many years of schooling they have acquired, whereas later surveys ask a degree-based question.

[25] Suppose that the true data-generating process is given by $w_{it} = x'_{it}\beta + \varepsilon_{it}$ and the observed value of earnings is $w^*_{it} = \min(w_{it}, \bar{w}_t)$, where $\bar{w}_t$ is the top code in year t. The CLAD estimator is the value of β that minimizes

$$\frac{1}{N}\sum_{i=1}^{N} |w^*_{it} - \min(x'_{it}\beta, \bar{w}_t)|.$$

This is implemented by the iterative method suggested by Buchinsky (1994). An alternative estimator is the Tobit model, which is based on the assumption that the distribution of ε_{it} is known (i.e., homoscedastic with a normal, lognormal, or Weibull distribution). Chay and Honoré (1998) investigate the relative performance of several estimators of the censored regression model and conclude that nonnormality in the distribution of log earnings may lead to significant biases in Tobit estimates. The qualitative conclusions of this section are not sensitive to whether the CLAD or Tobit model is used. Deaton (1997) also discusses the CLAD estimator, and Bilias, Chen, and Ying (2000) discuss the bootstrap standard errors.

the longitudinal data, each replication contains a 50 percent random sample of individuals drawn (with replacement) from all persons who appear in the data at any time. All longitudinal earnings records associated with these individuals are included in the bootstrapped data set. In the repeated cross-sectional data, each replication contains a simple 50 percent random sample drawn (with replacement) from all observations. Equation (5) is estimated for each of the 50 data sets, and the standard deviation of the 50 parameter estimates (divided by the square root of two) is an unbiased estimate of the standard error of the parameter values.

One of the central results in the paper is that measured immigrant earnings growth is considerably faster in the repeated cross-sectional data than in the longitudinal data, regardless of how immigrant arrival cohorts are defined in the longitudinal data. This is apparent in table 5, which reports coefficient estimates of equation (5) based first on the repeated cross-sectional data and then on the longitudinal data with the three definitions of immigrants' arrival cohort. For convenience, the time in the United States and cohort effects ($\hat{y}_{ct}$ and $\hat{k}_c$) are graphed in figures 2 and 3. The cross-sectional data suggest that immigrants' relative earnings grow by 20 percent in their first 10 years in the United States and by an additional 10–20 percent in each successive decade. By contrast, in the longitudinal data, immigrants' earnings grow by 12–15 percent during their first 15 years in the United States, but relatively little after that. The difference in earnings trajectories is consistent with low-earning immigrants being disproportionately more likely to emigrate from the United States over time. Since the repeated cross-sectional model is based on 280,411 immigrants and 598,515 natives, the coefficients in this model are quite precisely estimated, with standard errors on the order of two percentage points. Although the estimates from the longitudinal data are a bit less precise, the differences in estimates between the repeated cross-sectional data and the longitudinal data are generally statistically significant at conventional levels. For example, according to the cross-sectional data, the earnings gap between natives and immigrants closes by 33.5 percent during the first 21–25 years immigrants have been in the United States. This overestimates the gap found in longitudinal data by 15.4–20.5 percentage points, depending on the definition of the immigrant arrival cohort. The standard error of the difference is 3.9–5.1 percentage points, depending on cohort definition, and so the difference is clearly statistically significant.[26]

---

[26] The standard error of the difference in point estimates is based on the assumption that the two estimates are independent of one another. Another way to see that the estimates in the longitudinal data are statistically different from those in the repeated cross-sectional data is to note that the 95 percent confidence intervals generally do not overlap.

TABLE 5
CLAD ESTIMATES OF IMMIGRANT EARNINGS GROWTH IN REPEATED CROSS-SECTIONAL AND LONGITUDINAL DATA

	REPEATED CROSS-SECTIONAL DATA (1)	LONGITUDINAL EARNINGS DATA, BY ARRIVAL COHORT DEFINITION		
		Reported Period of Arrival (2)	Adjusted Period of Arrival (3)	First Year of Covered Earnings (4)
Years in the United States:				
6–10	.132 (.018)	.080 (.026)	.086 (.026)	.060 (.025)
11–15	.215 (.008)	.119 (.031)	.148 (.037)	.145 (.032)
16–20	.259 (.020)	.104 (.035)	.139 (.043)	.158 (.044)
21–25	.335 (.013)	.131 (.039)	.176 (.051)	.181 (.046)
26–30	.387 (.023)	.181 (.052)	.195 (.054)	.205 (.059)
31+	.534 (.027)	.308 (.095)	.284 (.131)	.128 (.119)
Experience at entry:				
6–10	−.111 (.005)	−.084 (.044)	−.076 (.044)	−.092 (.058)
11–15	−.164 (.005)	−.213 (.062)	−.213 (.071)	−.204 (.064)
16–20	−.215 (.007)	−.196 (.083)	−.160 (.090)	−.180 (.088)
21+	−.244 (.008)	−.303 (.088)	−.251 (.127)	−.314 (.106)
Period of arrival:				
1950–59	−.356 (.025)	−.140 (.076)	−.224 (.108)	−.194 (.073)
1960–64	−.257 (.020)	−.071 (.066)	−.202 (.059)	−.172 (.088)
1965–69	−.295 (.009)	−.176 (.060)	−.273 (.072)	−.265 (.060)
1970–74	−.355 (.020)	−.198 (.061)	−.282 (.056)	−.249 (.070)
1975–79	−.401 (.007)	−.276 (.057)	−.316 (.066)	−.216 (.075)
1980–84	−.492 (.019)	−.425 (.058)	−.460 (.049)	−.292 (.062)
1985–89	−.524 (.008)	−.389 (.065)	−.436 (.054)	−.407 (.046)
1990–91	−.543 (.067)	−.335 (.100)	−.378 (.176)	−.394 (.067)

NOTE.—The dependent variable is the log of annual earnings. Parameters are estimated by the method of censored least absolute deviation. In addition to the variables listed above, all models also include quartics in potential experience and calendar time. Repeated cross-sectional data are taken from the pooled 1970–90 decennial Censuses and the 1995–97 March CPS. Longitudinal data include earnings between 1969 and 1997 among men matched in the 1990 and 1991 SIPPs and the 1994 March CPS. Additional information about sample construction is given in the text. Standard errors are based on 50 bootstrap replications, as described in the text. The repeated cross-sectional model uses 280,411 immigrants and 598,515 natives; the longitudinal models use about 3,069 immigrants and 10,772 natives, depending on the specification. Observations from the longitudinal data are weighted by the inverse of the probability of being matched to earnings records, as described in Sec. II. Observations from the repeated cross-sectional data are weighted by the sample weights provided in the data.

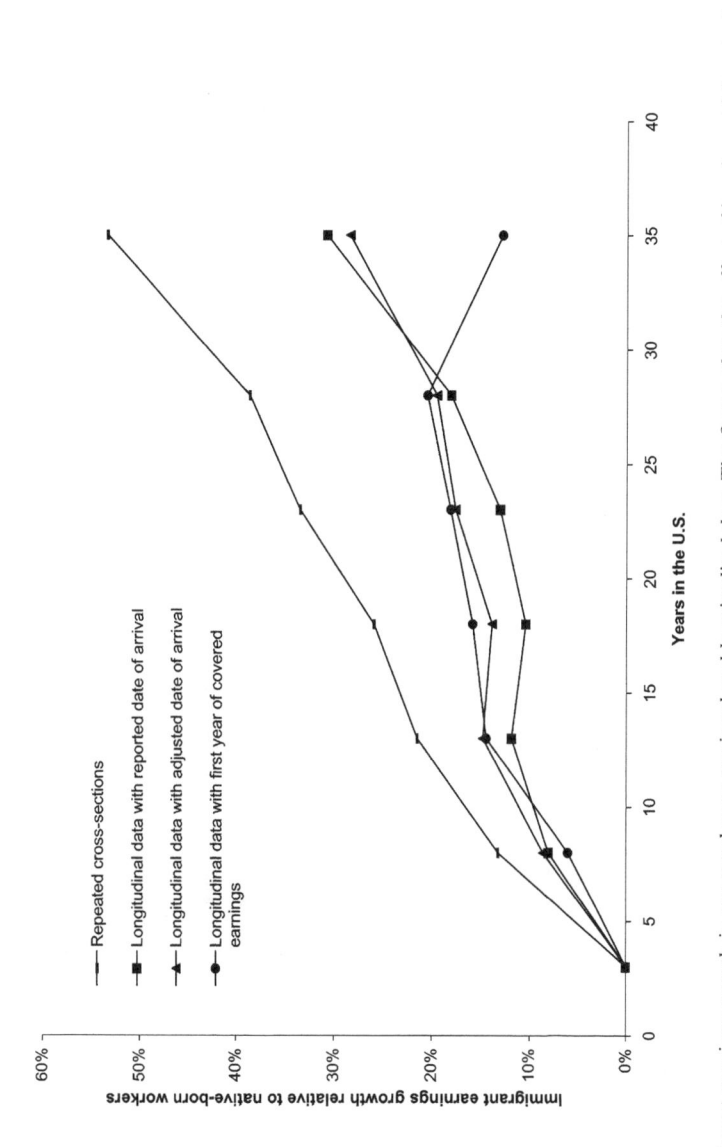

FIG. 2.—Immigrant earnings growth in repeated cross-sectional and longitudinal data. The figure plots the effect of immigrants' time in the United States on the immigrant-native earnings gap. Data are taken from estimates in table 5.

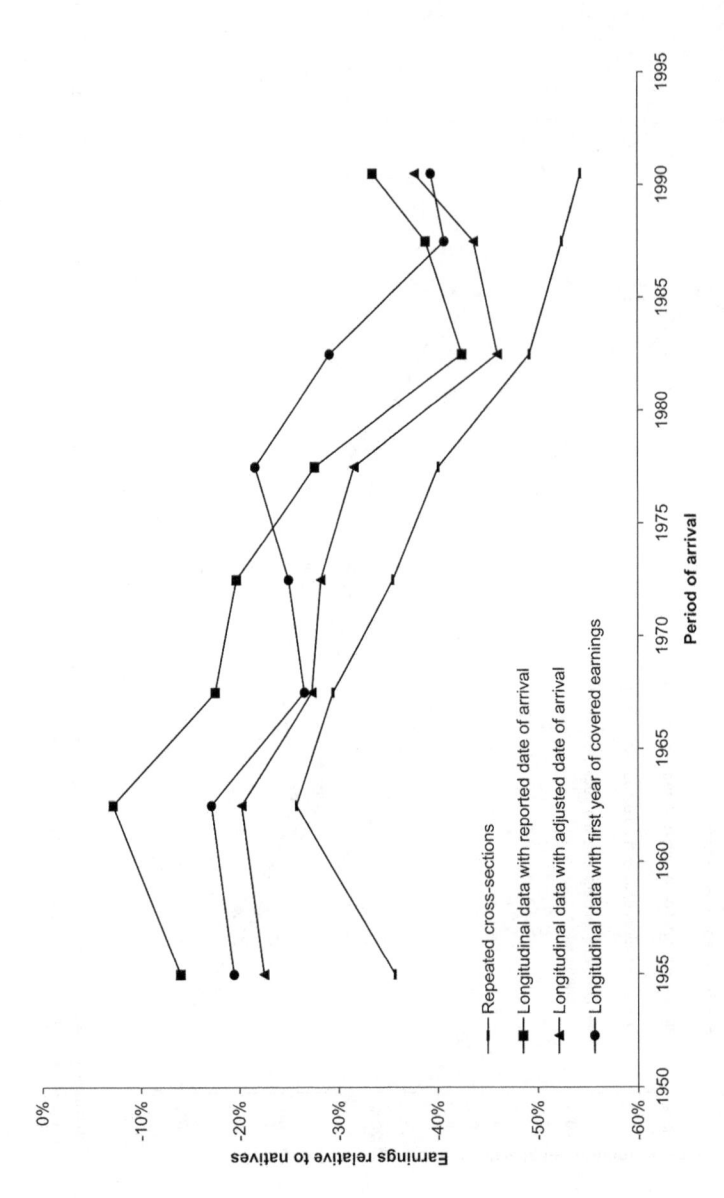

FIG. 3.—Immigrant arrival cohort fixed effects. The figure shows immigrant arrival cohort fixed effects; estimates are taken from table 5

Consistent with past research, both the repeated cross-sectional and the longitudinal earnings data indicate a marked decrease in immigrant arrival cohort fixed effects between 1960–64 and 1980–84 (see, e.g., Borjas 1985, 1995; LaLonde and Topel 1992; Funkhouser and Trejo 1995; Carliner 1996). In the repeated cross-sectional data, the level of earnings among immigrants who arrived between 1960 and 1964 was 26 percent below that of native-born workers. This gap increased to 49 percent among immigrants who arrived between 1980 and 1984. The arrival cohort fixed effects are smaller (in absolute value) in the longitudinal sample than in the repeated cross-sectional data, regardless of which cohort definition is used in the longitudinal data. This pattern is consistent with out-migration by the least successful immigrants over time. Indeed, if year of arrival were accurately measured in the repeated cross-sectional data, the divergence between the fixed-effect estimates from the longitudinal and repeated cross-sectional data would be a useful measure of the extent of nonrandom out-migration across cohorts.

Adjusting immigrants' arrival cohort for those who had earnings prior to their reported date of arrival lessens the secular decline in arrival cohort fixed effects. For example, the earnings of immigrants in the longitudinal data who report they arrived between 1960 and 1964 were 7.1 percentage points less than those of natives. If migrants who had earnings in the Social Security file prior to their reported date of arrival are reclassified into the arrival cohort of their first year of earnings (i.e., their adjusted date of arrival), the 1960–64 cohort fixed effect falls from -7.1 to -20.2. Indeed, making this adjustment reduces the secular decline in the estimated cohort fixed effects between 1960–64 and 1980–84 by about one-third. This is consistent with there being a large number of low-wage immigrants who entered in the 1960s and 1970s, left for some time, and then reentered and are recorded in the data as having arrived in the 1970s and 1980s. Once these migrants are assigned back to their first arrival cohort, the apparent labor market "quality" of earlier immigrant cohorts is lowered.

The relative earnings of immigrants who arrived in the late 1970s and early 1980s are quite sensitive to how arrival cohorts are defined. Recall that many migrants do not have earnings in the longitudinal data until substantially later than their reported date of arrival, perhaps appearing only after they begin working in the formal sector. This is especially true for migrants who reported that they arrived between 1975 and 1984, many of whom do not have earnings until the 1986 IRCA granted citizenship to many illegal migrants. Since these migrants tend to be low-skilled and have low earnings, reclassifying them as post-1986 migrants raises the measured quality of the 1975–79 and 1980–85 cohorts, as seen by a comparison of the arrival cohort fixed effects when immigrants are classified by their adjusted date of arrival and their first year of covered earnings.

The longitudinal earnings data (using the reported or adjusted arrival cohort definitions) in figure 3 also indicate a significant upsurge in the entry earnings among immigrants who arrived between 1985 and 1991. This upward trend in the earnings of very recent immigrants is also found by Funkhouser and Trejo (1995), who examine hourly earnings in several supplements to the CPS in the 1980s, and found in a slightly different form by Jasso, Rosenzweig, and Smith (1998), who use INS data to examine the occupational structure of immigrants who arrived between 1972 and 1995. Finally, Borjas and Friedberg (2006) analyze data from the 1960–2000 decennial Censuses and find an upturn among migrants who arrived in the 1990s. Borjas and Friedberg attribute the relative increase in earnings among migrants who arrived in the 1990s to the increased availability of H1-B visas, which led to an increase in the number of higher-skilled migrants, and to the relative decline in earnings among low-skilled natives.

B. Assimilation among Hispanic Migrants

There are several important reasons for measuring earnings growth and changes in cohort quality specifically for Hispanic migrants to the United States. First, Hispanic immigration to the United States has grown from 30 percent of total immigration in 1970 to 45 percent in 2000, with the large bulk coming from Mexico. Along with this rising share has come an increase in public debate over illegal immigration and calls for changes to immigration policy. Some authors argue that Hispanic immigrants, and in particular those from Mexico, are increasingly less skilled than other immigrants and are also less likely to assimilate into the U.S. labor force (see, e.g., Borjas and Katz 2007). Accurately measuring the level and growth rate of earnings for this important subset of current migration is important for setting policy, especially policy toward Mexican immigration. Second, Mexican and other Hispanic immigrants have a particularly high rate of emigration, which suggests the possibility for a particularly large bias in earnings models that use repeated cross-sectional data. It bears noting, however, that the magnitude of bias depends on both the level of emigration and the degree of selectivity of the emigrants. There would be no bias from using repeated cross-sectional data to estimate earnings growth among a group with high, but random, emigration.

Table 6 shows estimates of equation (5) that include only immigrants who identify themselves as being Hispanic or of Spanish ethnicity plus

TABLE 6
CLAD ESTIMATES OF HISPANIC IMMIGRANT EARNINGS GROWTH IN
REPEATED CROSS-SECTIONAL AND LONGITUDINAL DATA

	Repeated Cross-Sectional Data (1)	Longitudinal Data (2)
Years in the United States:		
6–10	.104 (.028)	.069 (.036)
11–15	.095 (.011)	.082 (.047)
16–20	.101 (.029)	.051 (.058)
21–25	.144 (.019)	.077 (.058)
26–30	.209 (.035)	.136 (.073)
31+	.220 (.044)	.251 (.201)
Experience at entry:		
6–10	−.113 (.007)	−.161 (.062)
11–15	−.186 (.007)	−.182 (.081)
16–20	−.235 (.010)	−.377 (.135)
21+	−.251 (.010)	−.403 (.157)
Period of arrival:		
1950–59	−.467 (.037)	−.420 (.155)
1960–64	−.364 (.031)	−.357 (.076)
1965–69	−.436 (.014)	−.447 (.093)
1970–74	−.525 (.028)	−.492 (.076)
1975–79	−.634 (.010)	−.529 (.110)
1980–84	−.712 (.029)	−.624 (.067)
1985–89	−.780 (.008)	−.496 (.067)
1990–91	−.752 (.079)	−.439 (.193)

NOTE.—The dependent variable is the log of annual earnings. Parameters are estimated by the method of censored least absolute deviation. In addition to the estimates reported above, all models also include quartics in potential experience and calendar time. Repeated cross-sectional data are taken from the pooled 1970–90 decennial Censuses and the 1995–97 March CPS. Longitudinal data include earnings between 1969 and 1997 among men matched in the 1990 and 1991 SIPPs and the 1994 March CPS. The sample of immigrants includes only men who report themselves to be of Hispanic or Spanish ethnicity. Immigrants are classified by their adjusted period of arrival. Additional information about sample construction is given in Sec. IV.A. Standard errors in the repeated cross-sectional data are based on 50 bootstrap replications; standard errors in the longitudinal data are approximated as described in this subsection. Observations from the longitudinal data are weighted by the inverse of the probability of being matched to earnings records, as described in Sec. II.

all native-born workers.[27] Migrants in the longitudinal data are grouped by their adjusted period of arrival. The longitudinal data reveal that the wage gap between Hispanic immigrants and U.S.-born workers closes by 6.9 percentage points during the first decade migrants are in the United States but does not close appreciably more during the following 15 years. The point estimates suggest some additional assimilation beyond 25 years in the United States, though these estimates are estimated quite imprecisely and are not statistically different from zero (or from the earnings level that prevailed during the first 25 years in the United

---

[27] Hispanic/Spanish ethnicity comes from respondent reports in the 1994 CPS or the 1990 or 1991 SIPP for those in the longitudinal sample and from respondent reports in the 1970, 1980, or 1990 Census or the 1995–97 CPS in the repeated cross-sectional sample. Those with imputed Hispanic/Spanish ethnicity are included in the sample.

States).[28] Earnings assimilation among Hispanics is therefore considerably slower than that of non-Hispanic migrants.

The rate of assimilation among Hispanic migrants in the longitudinal data is slightly slower than that measured in the repeated cross-sectional data. For example, Hispanic migrants in the repeated cross-sectional data who have been in the United States for six to 10 years have closed the earnings gap between themselves and natives by 10.4 percentage points, with a standard error of 2.8 percentage points. The corresponding estimate of earnings growth in the longitudinal data is 6.9 percentage points, 3.4 percentage points less than in the repeated cross-sectional data, with a standard error of 3.6 percentage points. Although the standard errors on these point estimates cannot rule out that the assimilation rates are equal in the two data sets and the difference in estimates between the two data sources is small in magnitude compared to the differences observed among all migrants, the pattern of point estimates is consistent with out-migration being more common among below-average-earning Hispanic migrants.[29]

The cohort effects in the longitudinal data indicate that the level of relative earnings of Hispanic migrants declined between 1960 and 1985, but then began to rise in the late 1980s. The cohort effect among the 1960–64 arrivals is −0.357. The cohort effect falls to a low of −0.624 for the 1980–84 arrivals, before rebounding to −0.496 among the 1985–89 arrivals. Migrants who arrived between 1990 and 1991 have relative earnings nearly equal to those of their counterparts who arrived in 1965–69. This dramatic increase in relative earnings among Hispanic migrants mirrors that found by Borjas and Friedberg (2006), though the increase appears to begin a few years earlier in the longitudinal data than in their census data.

---

[28] Restrictions on accessing the confidential data prevent me from computing bootstrap standard errors for estimates based on longitudinal data in table 6. Instead, the standard errors for Hispanics in the longitudinal data are approximated by

$$\sigma_{\text{Long,Hisp}} = \hat{\sigma}_{\text{Long,All}} \left(\frac{\hat{\sigma}_{\text{Cross,Hisp}}}{\hat{\sigma}_{\text{Cross,All}}} \right),$$

where $\hat{\sigma}_{\text{Long,All}}$ is the standard error of the parameter estimates using all immigrants in the longitudinal data (col. 3 of table 5), $\hat{\sigma}_{\text{Cross,Hisp}}$ is the standard error of the parameter estimates using Hispanic immigrants in the repeated cross-sectional data (col. 1 of table 6), and $\hat{\sigma}_{\text{Cross,All}}$ is the standard error of the parameter estimates using all immigrants in the repeated cross-sectional data (col. 1 of table 5).

Since Hispanic migrants tend to earn less than non-Hispanic migrants, further analysis of the data is required to determine whether there is selective emigration within the non-Hispanic population or whether selective emigration overall is primarily driven by greater emigration among Hispanics. Unfortunately, data access restrictions also prevent me from addressing this further.

[29] Hu (1999, 2000) also finds similar assimilation profiles among Hispanics in his longitudinal and repeated cross-sectional samples.

C. Longitudinal Estimates of Immigrant Earnings across Cohorts

This subsection examines immigrant-native earnings gaps separately for three immigrant arrival cohorts, those who arrived in the 1960s, the 1970s, and between 1980 and 1994. There are a number of reasons why it is important to examine the cohorts separately: First, previous sections have shown that immigrant-native earnings gaps are sensitive to how immigrant arrival cohorts are defined. Since the incidence of discrepancies between immigrants' reported arrival date and their first year of covered earnings differs across cohorts, adjusting for these discrepancies could have bigger effects on some cohorts than on others. Second, the model in equation (5) estimates an average rate of earnings growth across all immigrant cohorts. If earnings growth rates differ across cohorts, the fixed-effects estimates will reflect differences in both the average level of earnings and earnings growth across cohorts.[30] Thus if successive immigrant cohorts have slower rates of earnings growth, a model that imposes a constant effect of time spent in the United States will tend to yield declining estimates of cohort fixed effects. Finally, and perhaps most important, if there are differences in selective out-migration across cohorts, the accuracy of estimating immigrant assimilation in repeated cross-sectional data may be better for some cohorts than for others.

The estimates underlying figures 4–6 are derived from CLAD models that control for a quartic in the number of years in the United States, a square in the potential experience at entry, an indicator for the foreign-born, and quartics in total potential experience and calendar time. Each immigrant arrival cohort is compared to natives who had entered the labor market at the time the immigrant group arrived. That is, the 1960–69 arrivals are compared to natives who entered the labor market by 1969, the 1970–79 arrivals are compared to natives who entered the labor market by 1979, and the 1980–94 arrivals are compared

---

[30] To see this, consider a simple example in which there are two immigrant cohorts ($c = 1, 2$) and earnings are given by $w_{ict} = \alpha_c + \beta_c Y_{ict} + \varepsilon_{ict}$, where Y_{ict} is the number of years the immigrant has been in the United States. This can be written as

$$w_{ict} = \alpha_1 + \alpha_2 + \bar{\beta} Y_{ict} + (\beta_1 - \bar{\beta}) \alpha_1 Y_{i1t} + (\beta_2 - \bar{\beta}) \alpha_2 Y_{i2t} + \varepsilon_{ict}.$$

Suppose that the model given by $w_{ict} = \alpha_1 + \alpha_2 + \bar{\beta} Y_{ict} + \varepsilon_{ict}$ is estimated, and assume that the same number of years of data is available for each cohort (so $E(\alpha_c Y_{ict}) = 0$). Then the ordinary least squares estimate of $\bar{\beta}$ is $E(\hat{\bar{\beta}}) = \beta_1 E(\alpha_1) + \beta_2 E(\alpha_2)$, which is the average effect among both cohorts of time spent in the United States on earnings. The expected value of the indicator for the first cohort is $E(\hat{\alpha}_1) = \alpha_1 + E(Y_{i1t})(\beta_1 - \beta_2)$. Thus, if the first cohort has faster earnings growth than the second cohort, $\beta_1 - \beta_2$ is positive and $E(\hat{\alpha}_1) > \alpha_1$. In addition, the fixed-effect estimates cannot be interpreted as the initial earnings level for each cohort. An additional bias is present if more years of data are available for cohorts that entered earlier.

to the full sample of natives.[31] The figures show the level of the immigrant-native gap for an immigrant who arrives with five years of potential experience.

Figure 4 compares the relative earnings of immigrants in the longitudinal data based on immigrants' reported arrival date and based on their adjusted arrival date.[32] The pattern of results indicates that immigrants with earnings prior to their reported date of arrival to stay tend to have earnings above the average among their reported cohort but below the average among their original cohort. For example, immigrants who reported to have arrived between 1960 and 1969 entered the labor market with earnings 28 percent below those of natives. After 10 years the gap closed to 15 percent and was essentially stable after that point. When immigrants who reported arriving after 1969, but whose first year of earnings was during the 1960s, are included in this cohort, the earnings gap upon entry declines by five percentage points to 32 percent, and the earnings gap after 10 years is 23 percent. The level of earnings among the 1970–79 arrivals and the 1980–94 arrivals also declines when migrants are shifted to the earlier of their reported cohort or first year of earnings.

A problem documented in Section III is that many immigrants do not have earnings until some years after their reported date of arrival. If these immigrants tend to have below-average earnings, their lagged entry will tend to depress the earnings trajectory of the arrival cohort as a whole. To explore this effect, figure 5 compares the immigrant-native earnings gaps in the longitudinal data among all immigrants and then only among immigrants whose first year of earnings is within three years of their reported date of arrival. For all three arrival cohorts, the estimated rate of immigrant earnings growth is faster when immigrants whose first year of earnings is more than three years after their reported date of arrival are excluded. The immigrant-native earnings gap decreases among the 1960–69 arrivals who have been in the United States for 15 years from 24 to 20 percent. The gap after 15 years declines among the 1970–79 arrivals from 26 to 19 percent. The sample adjustment has perhaps the most noticeable effect on the 1980–94 cohort,

---

[31] The earnings history from the beginning of each immigrant cohort until 1997 is used. For example, the estimates for the 1960–69 cohort are based on earnings data for immigrants and natives from 1960 to 1997; the estimates for the 1980–94 cohort are based on data from 1980 to 1997.

[32] Immigrants' time in the United States is measured from the midpoint of the arrival interval. Earnings prior to and during the arrival interval are dropped; thus the first observed year corresponds to the third year in the United States. For example, suppose that an immigrant reports that he arrived between 1980 and 1984, but his first year of covered earnings is 1973. The adjusted cohort would then be the 1970–74 group, his time in the United States would be measured from 1972, and only his earnings beginning in 1975 would be used.

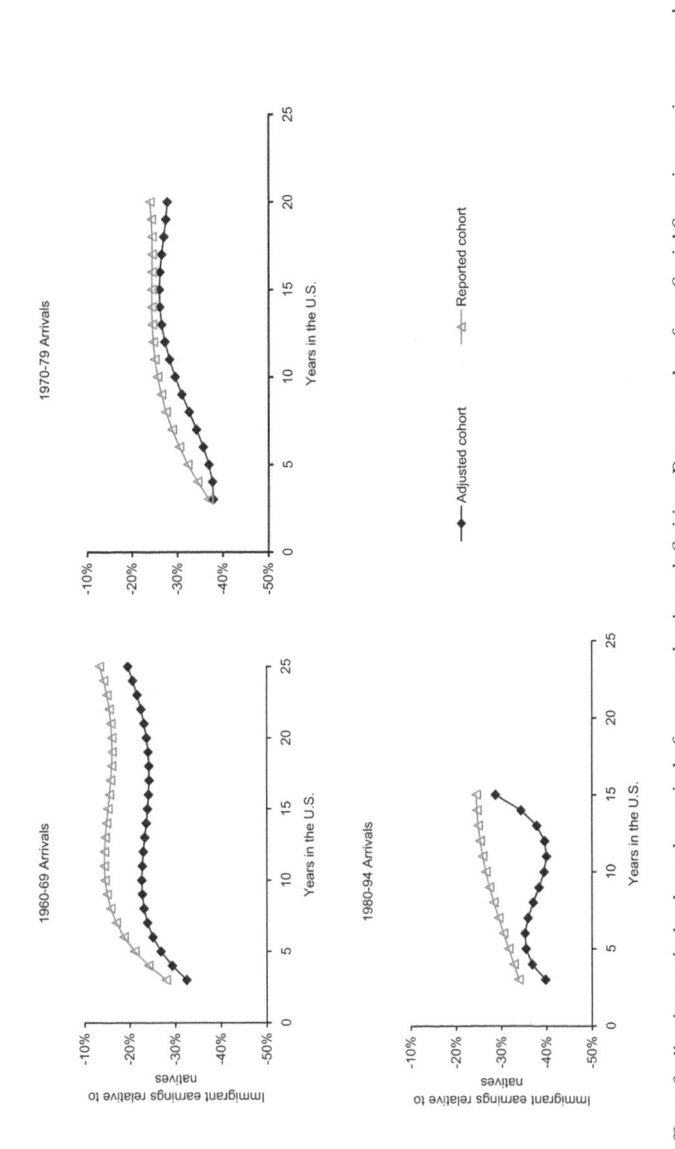

FIG. 4.—The effect of adjusting arrival cohorts by period of entry and cohort definition. Data are taken from Social Security earnings records matched to individuals in the 1990 and 1991 SIPPs and in the 1994 CPS. Each line represents the predicted median earnings of immigrants relative to native-born workers based on different cohort definitions. The models also include controls for total potential experience and calendar time. The levels of the curves pertain to an immigrant who arrives in the United States with five years of potential experience. See the text for additional details.

FIG. 5.—The effect of changes in cohort composition on estimated immigrant earnings. Data are taken from longitudinal earnings records matched to individuals in the 1990 and 1991 SIPPs and in the 1994 CPS. Each line represents the predicted median earnings of immigrants relative to native-born workers. The cohorts are defined by the earlier of an immigrant's reported date of entry and his first year of earnings. The models also include controls for total potential experience and calendar time. The levels of the curves pertain to an immigrant who arrives in the United States with five years of potential experience. See the text for additional details.

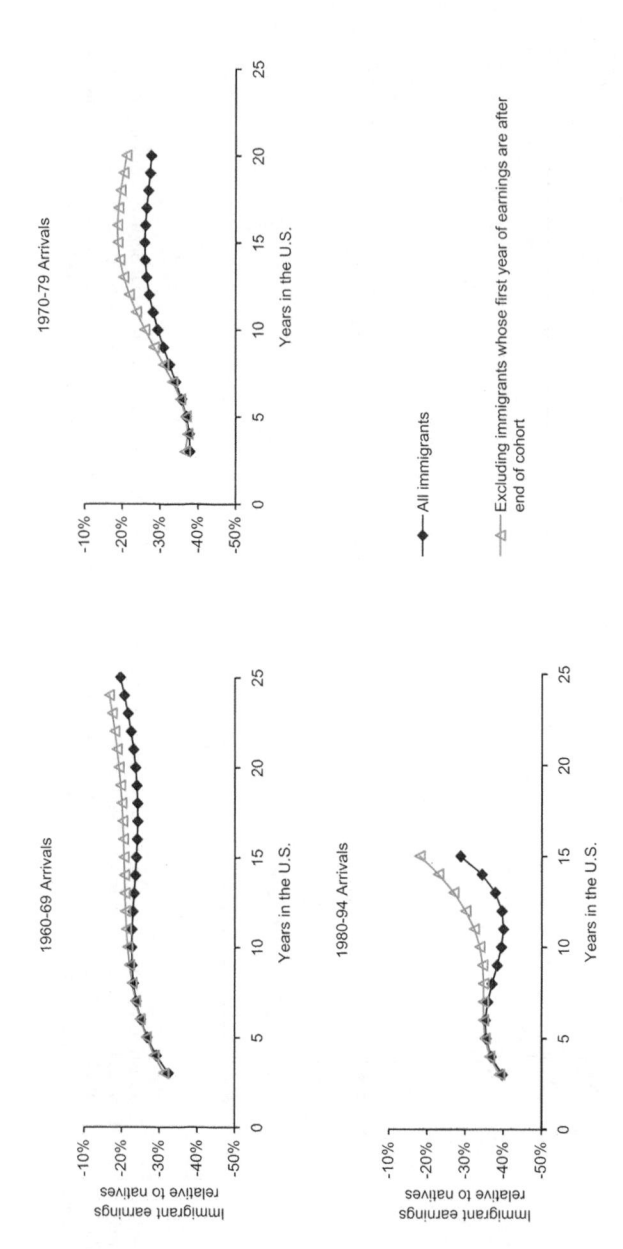

where the gap after 10 years decreases from 39 to 34 percent, and the downward trend in immigrants' relative earnings is eliminated. It is important to note that a similar composition bias may exist in repeated cross-sectional data if immigrants are more likely to be included in the data when they transition from an illegal to a legal immigrant, or if successive censuses are more likely to pick up low-wage or illegal immigrants over time.

Finally, figure 6 compares immigrant-native earnings gaps, by cohort, in the repeated cross-sectional data and in the longitudinal data. To avoid the compositional changes in immigrant cohorts documented in figure 5, I grouped immigrants by their first year of covered earnings (and their time in the United States is measured from their first year of covered earnings). These pictures indicate that the discrepancies in immigrant assimilation between the longitudinal and repeated cross-sectional data appear to be concentrated in the immigrant arrival cohorts that arrived in the 1970s and, to a lesser extent, between 1980 and 1994. For example, the immigrant-native earnings gap among the 1960–69 arrivals closes by 15 percentage points during the first 10 years in the United States according to the longitudinal data and by 12 percentage points according to the repeated cross-sectional data. Yet, the earnings gap among the 1970–79 arrivals closes by 33 percentage points according to the repeated cross-sectional data, but by only 20 percentage points according to the longitudinal data. The earnings gap among the 1980–94 arrivals closes by 29 percentage points according to the repeated cross-sectional data, but by only 22 percentage points according to the longitudinal data. The longitudinal data also point to small differences in the rate of earnings growth across cohorts: during their first 10 years in the United States, the immigrant-native earnings gap among the 1960–69 arrivals closed by 15 percentage points, which is slightly slower than the 20- and 22-percentage-point change among the 1970–79 and 1980–84 arrivals.

V. Conclusion

Using longitudinal earnings records from 1951 to 1997, this work has addressed several important issues in the study of immigrant earnings. Many immigrants to the United States do not remain in the country throughout their working lives. Some permanently leave the country, and others reenter at a later date. Both types of migration decisions may bias the measured earnings progress of immigrants in repeated cross sections of the decennial census, by far the most common source of data used to examine immigrants' performance in the American labor market. Whereas permanent out-migration by low-earning immigrants will lead to an overstatement of earnings growth across census cross

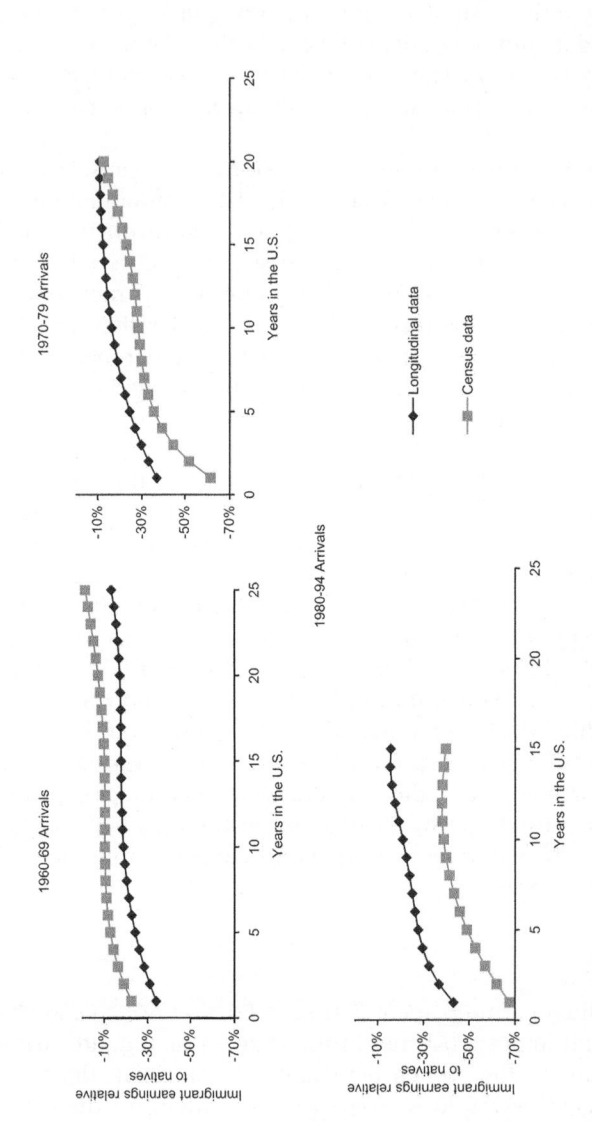

FIG. 6.—Immigrant-native earnings gaps in longitudinal and repeated cross-sectional data. Each line represents the predicted median earnings of immigrants relative to native-born workers. Samples are the same as those used in table 5. The cohorts in the longitudinal data are defined by the earlier of an immigrant's reported date of entry and his first year of earnings. The level of earnings pertains to immigrants who arrived in the United States with five years of potential experience.

sections, temporary out-migration by low-earning immigrants may lead to the appearance of a decline in the level of earnings of successive arrival cohorts if reentrants tend to report the date of their most recent arrival in the census questionnaire. Though the longitudinal data set is not ideal, it can correct some of the shortcomings of repeated cross sections of the census.

This study provided evidence for several new empirical results: First, actual earnings growth among immigrants who remained in the United States until the 1990s was considerably slower than that implied by estimates from repeated cross sections of the decennial census. Measured in longitudinal data, over their first 20 years in the United States, immigrant earnings grow by 10–15 percent relative to the earnings of native-born workers. Repeated cross sections of the census suggest that immigrant earnings grow twice as fast, by about 26 percent over the same time period. Selective out-migration by low-earning immigrants, therefore, gives the misleading impression that the economic status of immigrants to the United States improves substantially faster as they assimilate into the labor market.

This result has two important implications for interpreting assimilation across generations. Selective emigration by low-earning immigrants means that the gains in educational attainment between the first and second generations will also be overestimated in repeated cross-sectional data, since the second generation is born largely to the more successful subset of immigrants who remain in the United States. Like computing earnings assimilation, correctly computing changes in educational attainment from immigrant parents to their native-born children requires knowing which immigrants stayed in the United States and gave birth, and which left. Second, previous research indicates that the earnings of children of immigrants tend to be equal to, or perhaps above, those of third-generation and higher Americans (see, e.g., Borjas 1993; Card 2005). To the extent that wage growth among first-generation immigrants is slower than previously reported in other research, more of the assimilation, therefore, occurs between the first and second generations rather than during first-generation immigrants' own working life.

The second key result of this paper is that there is a great deal of disagreement between immigrants' self-reported date of arrival "to stay" in the United States and their first year of covered Social Security earnings, a discrepancy caused in part by out-migration and the subsequent reentry into the United States. Nearly one-third of the decline in the level of earnings of immigrants between the 1960s and 1980s can be accounted for by the misclassification of many low-wage immigrants as more recent arrivals, when in fact they had entered the United States considerably earlier. A corollary of this finding is that the standard model in the economics literature in which immigrants remain in the United

States throughout their working life may not be appropriate for analyzing contemporary migration. Better understanding of the immigrant experience will require better data on migration patterns.

References

Baker, Michael, and Dwayne Benjamin. 1997. "The Role of the Family in Immigrants' Labor-Market Activity: An Evaluation of Alternative Explanations." *A.E.R.* 87 (September): 705–27.

Bean, Frank D., Barry Edmonston, and Jeffrey S. Passel, eds. 1990. *Undocumented Migration to the United States: IRCA and the Experience of the 1980's*. Washington, DC: Urban Inst. Press.

Bean, Frank D., and Michael Fix. 1992. "The Significance of Recent Immigration Policy Reforms in the United States." In *Nations of Immigrants: Australia, the United States, and International Migration*, edited by Gary P. Freeman and James Jupp. Melbourne: Oxford Univ. Press.

Bilias, Yannis, Songnian Chen, and Zhiliang Ying. 2000. "Simple Resampling Methods for Censored Regression Quantiles." *J. Econometrics* 99 (December): 373–86.

Borjas, George J. 1985. "Assimilation, Changes in Cohort Quality, and the Earnings of Immigrants." *J. Labor Econ.* 3 (October): 463–89.

———. 1989. "Immigrant and Emigrant Earnings: A Longitudinal Study." *Econ. Inquiry* 27 (January): 21–37.

———. 1993. "The Intergenerational Mobility of Immigrants." *J. Labor Econ.* 11, no. 1, pt. 1 (January): 113–35.

———. 1994. "The Economics of Immigration." *J. Econ. Literature* 32 (December): 1667–1717.

———. 1995. "Assimilation and Changes in Cohort Quality Revisited: What Happened to Immigrant Earnings in the 1980s?" *J. Labor Econ.* 13 (April): 201–45.

———. 1999. "The Economic Analysis of Immigration." In *Handbook of Labor Economics*, vol. 3A, edited by Orley Ashenfelter and David Card. Amsterdam: Elsevier Sci.

Borjas, George J., and Bernt Bratsberg. 1996. "Who Leaves? The Outmigration of the Foreign-Born." *Rev. Econ. Statis.* 78 (February): 165–76.

Borjas, George J., and Rachel Friedberg. 2006. "The Immigrant Earnings Turnaround of the 1990s." Manuscript (July), Harvard Univ.

Borjas, George J., and Lawrence Katz. 2007. "The Evolution of the Mexican-Born Workforce in the United States." In *Mexican Immigration to the United States*, edited by George J. Borjas. Chicago: Univ. Chicago Press (for NBER).

Bound, John, and Alan B. Krueger. 1991. "The Extent of Measurement Error in Longitudinal Earnings Data: Do Two Wrongs Make a Right?" *J. Labor Econ.* 9 (January): 1–24.

Buchinsky, Moshe. 1994. "Changes in the U.S. Wage Structure 1963–1987: Application of Quantile Regression." *Econometrica* 62 (March): 405–58.

Card, David. 2005. "Is the New Immigration Really So Bad?" *Econ. J.* 115 (November): F300–F323.

Card, David, and Alan B. Krueger. 1993. "Trends in Relative Black-White Earnings Revisited." *A.E.R. Papers and Proc.* 83 (May): 85–91.

Carliner, Geoffrey. 1996. "The Wages and Language Skills of U.S. Immigrants." Working Paper no. 5763 (September), NBER, Cambridge, MA.

Chay, Kenneth Y. 1995. "Evaluating the Impact of the 1964 Civil Rights Act on the Economic Status of Black Men Using Censored Longitudinal Earnings Data." Manuscript (October), Princeton Univ.

Chay, Kenneth Y., and Bo E. Honoré. 1998. "Estimation of Semiparametric Censored Regression Models: An Application to Changes in Black-White Earnings Inequality during the 1960s." *J. Human Resources* 33 (Winter): 4–38.

Chiquiar, Daniel, and Gordon H. Hanson. 2005. "International Migration, Self-Selection, and the Distribution of Wages: Evidence from Mexico and the United States." *J.P.E.* 113 (April): 239–81.

Chiswick, Barry R. 1978. "The Effect of Americanization on the Earnings of Foreign-Born Men." *J.P.E.* 86 (October): 897–921.

———. 1980. *An Analysis of the Economic Progress and Impact of Immigrants.* National Technical Information Service, no. PB80-200454. Washington, DC: U.S. Dept. Labor.

———. 1986. "Human Capital and the Labor Market Adjustment of Immigrants: Testing Alternative Hypotheses." In *Research in Human Capital and Development*, vol. 4, *Migration, Human Capital and Development*, edited by Oded Stark. Greenwich, CT: JAI.

Deaton, Angus. 1997. *The Analysis of Household Surveys: A Microeconometric Approach to Development Policy.* Baltimore: Johns Hopkins Univ. Press (for World Bank).

Duleep, Harriet Orcutt, and Daniel J. Dowhan. 2002. "Insights from Longitudinal Data on the Earnings Growth of U.S. Foreign-Born Men." *Demography* 39 (August): 485–506.

Duleep, Harriet Orcutt, and Mark C. Regets. 1996. "The Elusive Concept of Immigrant Quality: Evidence from 1970–1990." Program for Research on Immigration Policy PRIP-UI-41 (April), Urban Inst., Washington, DC

———. 1997. "Immigrant Entry Earnings and Human Capital Growth: Evidence from the 1960–1980 Censuses." In *Research in Labor Economics*, vol. 16, edited by Soloman W. Polachek. Greenwich, CT: JAI.

Ellis, Mark, and Richard Wright. 1998. "When Immigrants Are Not Migrants: Counting Arrivals of the Foreign Born Using the U.S. Census." *Internat. Migration Rev.* 32 (Spring): 127–44.

Friedberg, Rachel M. 1993. "The Labor Market Assimilation of Immigrants in the United States: The Role of Age at Arrival." Manuscript (March), Brown Univ.

Funkhouser, Edward, and Stephen J. Trejo. 1995. "The Labor Market Skills of Recent Male Immigrants: Evidence from the Current Population Survey." *Indus. and Labor Relations Rev.* 48 (July): 792–811.

Hu, Wei-Yin. 1999. "Assimilation and the Earnings of Immigrants: New Evidence from Longitudinal Data." Manuscript (August), Univ. California, Los Angeles.

———. 2000. "Immigrant Earnings Assimilation: Estimates from Longitudinal Data." *A.E.R. Papers and Proc.* 90 (May): 368–72.

Ibarraran, Pablo, and Darren Lubotsky. 2007. "Mexican Immigration and Self-Selection: New Evidence from the 2000 Mexican Census." In *Mexican Immigration to the United States*, edited by George J. Borjas. Chicago: Univ. Chicago Press (for NBER).

Jasso, Guillermina, and Mark R. Rosenzweig. 1990. *The New Chosen People: Immigrants in the United States.* New York: Sage Found.

Jasso, Guillermina, Mark R. Rosenzweig, and James P. Smith. 1998. "The Changing Skills of New Immigrants to the United States: Recent Trends and Their Determinants." Working Paper no. 6764 (October), NBER, Cambridge, MA.

LaLonde, Robert J., and Robert H. Topel. 1992. "The Assimilation of Immigrants in the U.S. Labor Market." In *Immigration and the Work Force*, edited by George J. Borjas and Richard B. Freeman. Chicago: Univ. Chicago Press (for NBER).

———. 1997. "Economic Impact of International Migration and the Economic Performance of Migrants." In *Handbook of Population and Family Economics*, vol. 1B, edited by Mark R. Rosenzweig and Oded Stark. Amsterdam: Elsevier Sci.

Lindstrom, David P., and Douglas S. Massey. 1994. "Selective Emigration, Cohort Quality, and Models of Immigrant Assimilation." *Soc. Sci. Res.* 23 (December): 315–49.

Lubotsky, Darren. 2007. "The Effect of Changes in the U.S. Wage Structure on Recent Immigrants' Earnings." Working paper, Univ. Illinois, Urbana-Champaign.

Nevo, Aviv. 2003. "Using Weights to Adjust for Sample Selection When Auxiliary Information Is Available." *J. Bus. Econ. Statis.* 21 (January): 43–52.

Powell, James L. 1984. "Least Absolute Deviations Estimation for the Censored Regression Model." *J. Econometrics* 25 (July): 303–25.

Redstone, Ilana, and Douglas S. Massey. 2004. "Coming to Stay: An Analysis of the U.S. Census Question on Immigrants' Year of Arrival." *Demography* 41 (November): 721–38.

Schoeni, Robert F. 1997. "New Evidence on the Economic Progress of Foreign-Born Men in the 1970s and 1980s." *J. Human Resources* 32 (Fall): 683–740.

Schoeni, Robert F., Kevin F. McCarthy, and Georges Vernez. 1996. *The Mixed Economic Progress of Immigrants*. Santa Monica, CA: Center Res. Immigration Policy, Rand Corp.

Smith, James P., and Barry Edmonston, eds. 1997. *The New Americans: Economic, Demographic, and Fiscal Effects of Immigration*. Washington, DC: Nat. Acad. Press.

Social Security Administration. Office of the Chief Actuary. 1997. *History of the Provisions of Old-Age, Survivors, Disability, and Health Insurance, 1935–1996.* SSA Publication no. 11-11515 (October). Washington, DC: Soc. Security Admin.

———. Office Policy and Office of Research, Evaluation, and Statistics. 2006. *Annual Statistical Supplement to the Social Security Bulletin, 2005.* SSA Publication no. 13-11700 (February). Washington, DC: Soc. Security Admin.

Wealth Distributions of Migrant and Australian-born Households*

DENISE DOIRON and ROCHELLE GUTTMANN
School of Economics, University of New South Wales, Sydney, Australia

Wealth is an important measure of overall economic well-being and a crucial factor in migrants' ability to integrate into their new country. Using data from the 2002 HILDA survey, this study explores the disparity between the wealth distributions of native-born and foreign-born households in Australia. Using quantile regressions the results reveal that migrants have significantly less wealth than their Australian-born counterparts throughout the wealth distribution. This is despite the greater wealth-generating characteristics of the foreign-born. The wealth differentials are reduced but still negative for the migrant cohorts who have been in Australia for over 25 years.

I Introduction

The economic integration of immigrants is a key policy issue in Australia where a large proportion of the population are foreign-born. Over one-fifth of the Australian population was born overseas, with net overseas migration being the major contributor to population growth (ABS, 2007, 2008). A key measure of migrants' settlement success is their wealth position relative to the native-born. Although there has been considerable focus on immigrants' labour market outcomes, including gaps in earnings and probabilities of employment (e.g. Cobb-Clark, 2003; Wilkins, 2003; Thapa, 2004), wealth accumulation has received little attention in the Australian literature. The Household, Income and Labour Dynamics in Australia (HILDA) survey enables us to compare the wealth distributions of Australian-born versus foreign-born households.

Wealth is an important gauge of the success of immigrants' economic assimilation. Focusing on labour market earnings ignores other sources of income, such as savings, inheritance and returns from investment. Wealth is also a more permanent and stable measure of one's economic situation than income, as it allows the financing of both current and future consumption. Wealth facilitates economic success in broader ways. As Zhang (2003) noted, 'wealth affects access to the credit market, and allows family members to venture into business activities, pursue higher education, or spend more time looking for a better job'. Thus, wealth can enhance the speed of economic integration and earnings assimilation into an immigrant's new home.

The theoretical literature suggests a number of reasons why immigrants' wealth might differ from native-born families, but offers no clear guide on

---

* We would like to thank Garry Barrett, Denzil Fiebig, Paul Miller, the participants at the 3rd Annual National Honours Colloquium and two anonymous referees for their useful comments. Also, we are grateful to the Department of Family, Housing, Community Services and Indigenous Affairs (FaHCSIA) and the Melbourne Institute for Applied Economic and Social Research for providing the data used in this research, although the research does not necessarily reflect the views of FaHCSIA or the Melbourne Institute. Any remaining errors are ours.
JEL classifications: D31, J61, C39
Correspondence: Denise Doiron, School of Economics, University of New South Wales, Sydney, NSW 2052, Australia. Email: d.doiron@unsw.edu.au

the direction of the gap. Immigrants generally self-select to move to a new country and therefore are not a random sample drawn from the source country's population (Borjas, 1994). Furthermore, Australia's strict regulations as to the number and type of visas offered accentuate selectivity (Cobb-Clark, 2003). As such, migrants' motives and incentives to save, and thus accumulate wealth, are likely to differ from the general native-born population. Given the possibility of return migration and the prevailing assumption that expected earnings in the host country exceed expected earnings in the source country, Galor and Stark (1990) establish that migrants have an incentive to save more than natives do. Dustmann (1997) further illustrates that if labour market shocks between countries are correlated, then the sign and size of the savings of migrants relative to natives is ambiguous. A further reason why immigrant wealth might differ from a native-born's wealth is discrimination. The existence of labour market discrimination, particularly of migrants from non-English speaking backgrounds (Junankar et al., 2002; Thapa, 2004; Junankar & Mahuteau, 2005), and possible initial difficulties in asset market engagement would create nativity wealth differentials.

Nativity wealth differentials exist in many traditionally immigrant-receiving countries; although a country's institutional setting makes it difficult to compare results across countries. Like Australia, New Zealand's and Canada's immigration policy has an emphasis on skill, and both countries exhibit nativity wealth differentials. However, the direction of the gap is not uniform: in New Zealand a positive wealth gap is generally found for singles; in Canada migrants in the mid- to upper part of the distribution have greater wealth compared to native-born, whereas negative wealth gaps exist for the other parts of the distribution (Zhang, 2003; Gibson et al., 2007). The USA and Germany have very different immigrant selection policies than Australia. In these countries immigrants have less wealth than those that are native-born (Carroll et al., 1998; Hao, 2004; Cobb-Clark & Hildebrand, 2006; Bauer et al., 2007). Thus, the available international evidence shows a nativity wealth gap is likely to exist but there is no consensus on the direction of the gap. This paper is the first to conduct a comparative analysis of the wealth distributions between different migrant groups in Australia. Nonparametric tests show that for couples, migrants have less wealth throughout the distribution whereas for singles, the distributions are statistically indistinguishable. Parametric methods are used to decompose the nativity wealth gaps across the distribution into the contribution of characteristics (lifecycle and human capital factors) and returns to these characteristics. The decompositions reveal that migrants have more wealth-increasing characteristics compared to native households; the negative gap is due to differences in coefficients, especially a systematic shift in the constant. We also find that country-of-origin is irrelevant in explaining the wealth gap, whereas a migrant's length-of-time in Australia is an important factor throughout the distribution.[1]

II Data

(i) The Household, Income and Labour Dynamics in Australia (HILDA) Survey

The HILDA Survey is a national household panel that provides comprehensive data on a variety of labour market and earnings characteristics, including wealth. The first wave in 2001 comprised 7682 household interviews (13 969 personal interviews). In the second wave in 2002, interviews from 7245 households (13 041 individuals) were obtained, representing an 87 per cent household response rate. A supplementary wealth module, covering detailed questions on household assets and liabilities, was included in 2002. This was the first representative survey in over 30 years to directly measure household wealth and its components in Australia. This study is based on the 2002 cross-section data.

Wealth is defined as total assets less total liabilities. Most questions in the wealth module were asked at the household level, since many assets and debts are difficult to divide among individuals (e.g. housing). Assets comprise financial assets – bank deposits, life insurance, superannuation, trust funds, equity (e.g. shares, managed funds) and cash investments (e.g. bonds, debentures) – and non-financial assets, particularly housing, collectibles, businesses and vehicles. Debts include housing, business, credit card, HECS and other personal debt. Heady et al. (2005) find that the HILDA survey understates wealth at the top-tail of the distribution, as is typical of a representative household survey, but

---

[1] Since the submission of this paper, a few studies on nativity wealth gaps in Australia have emerged: Cobb-Clark and Hildebrand (2008) and Bauer et al. (2007). Although the overall results from these studies are consistent with ours, different aspects of wealth are also explored. Additional findings from these studies are included in the discussions below.

© 2009 The Economic Society of Australia

conclude that the survey adequately captures the wealth of households over most of the wealth distribution.[2]

The unit of analysis is the household. A reference person is chosen on the basis of the highest income, highest salary, labour force status, age and respondent number from each household, in this order. This person is most likely to be involved in household finance decisions and be attached to the labour market, and thus a valid representation of the household. In this study a migrant household is one where the reference person is a migrant.[3] This raises the issue of how to treat mixed households, where one partner is Australian-born and the other not. This is addressed in Section IV.

(ii) Sample Characteristics

The analysis sample consists of 7129 households.[4] Of these, 5385 (75.5 per cent) are Australian-born and 1744 (24.5 per cent) are migrant households, consistent with the proportion of migrants and natives in the Australian population. The sample is split into couple-headed (married or de facto) and single-headed households as they are likely to have distinct wealth accumulation behaviour (Schmidt & Sevak, 2006).[5]

Table 1 provides weighted means and percentiles of household net wealth, assets and debts and financial year gross income.[6] It is clear that the wealth distributions for both Australian-born and foreign-born households are highly skewed, particularly for singles, with mean net wealth being almost double the median. For example, the average net wealth among Australian-born single households is $249 570 compared to the median of $115 000. Assets and particularly debt are also highly skewed, whereas income is much less so. Foreign-born households have on average less wealth than native-born households; this originates from both greater debt and smaller levels of assets. It is noteworthy that the wealth gap between foreign- and Australian-born households is much wider than for income. This suggests that income differentials do not give a complete picture of migrant economic outcomes.

Figure 1(a,b) present weighted kernel density estimates of household wealth for native- and foreign-born households, for couples and singles, respectively.[7] The figures highlight the right-skewness of the distributions. For couples, there is a greater proportion of foreign-born households at the bottom of the wealth distribution. In contrast, there is little disparity in wealth distributions for single households except at the top of the wealth distribution. The Kolmogorov–Smirnov tests of the null hypothesis of equal densities confirm this, with P-values of 0.02 and 0.679 for couples and singles, respectively.

III Determinants of Wealth

(i) Model

One obstacle to modelling wealth is the non-normality of its distribution. The typical approach is to take the natural logarithm of wealth, and therefore either exclude negative and zero observations or set these to an arbitrarily small value, such as

---

[2] The survey asks about wealth held overseas; however, it is believed that this may be underreported. Since this is likely to be more severe for migrants as they are more likely to hold off-shore assets or remit savings to their home country, the migrant wealth differential could be overestimated.

[3] There is no single definition of a migrant household in the literature. For example, Shamsuddin and DeVoretz (1998) base it on the husband's migrant status, Carroll *et al.* (1998), Cobb-Clark and Hildebrand (2006) and Bauer *et al.* (2007) choose households where both partners have the same migrant status and omit mixed households, Zhang (2003) chooses the highest income earner's nativity and Hao (2004) defines a migrant household as one where at least one partner is a migrant.

[4] From the 7245 responding households, 116 observations are deleted due to missing country of birth, employment experience, employment status or years of partnership.

[5] The split partly controls for household size. In addition, the number of children is included as a control variable. As a final robustness check, household size was explicitly controlled for by adjusting household wealth by two equivalence scales – dividing by the number of people in the household and the square root of this. The conclusions were largely unchanged using either set of scales.

[6] Wealth data are based on actual responses. Imputed data, provided by the Melbourne Institute, are used where some response components were missing (Watson, 2004), comprising close to 40 per cent of cases. An indicator for the use of imputed wealth is added in the regressions. Wealth is top-coded at $3 000 000. To preserve means, wealth is replaced by the average in the top-coded group for all the cases which exceed the threshold. Around 1 per cent of observations are top-coded. Since most of the analysis below consists of quantile regressions at the percentile level, the top-coding is unlikely to affect results (Buchinsky, 1998).

[7] The illustrated distributions are censored at the 1st and 95th percentiles to provide a clearer visual representation of the densities, although the analysis covers the whole distribution. For more details on kernel density estimation, see Pagan and Ullah (1999).

© 2009 The Economic Society of Australia

TABLE 1
Descriptive Statistics on Wealth and Income by Migrant Status, 2002 Dollars

	Observations	Mean ($)	Percentile		
			Median ($)	10th ($)	90th ($)
Australian-born	5 385				
Couple households	3 000				
Net wealth		539 659	333 900	32 500	1 182 800
Assets		628 173	425 504	58 750	1 320 000
Debts		88 904	31 100	0	225 000
Income		76 409	65 426	21 466	133 044
Single households	2 385				
Net wealth		249 570	115 000	400	635 500
Assets		281 916	148 067	2 900	693 000
Debts		32 562	1 300	0	102 400
Income		40 125	30 589	10 690	82 400
Foreign-born	1 744				
Couple households	1 118				
Net wealth		488 352	299 000	18 000	1 026 100
Assets		587 660	382 700	25 400	1 270 038
Debts		99 225	23 000	0	275 000
Income		74 708	60 378	18 500	139 854
Single households	626				
Net wealth		224 897	102 200	299	507 450
Assets		266 364	130 600	3 000	640 600
Debts		39 312	800	0	144 000
Income		38 796	29 681	10 660	76 000

Notes: (a) An Australian- (foreign-) born household is one where the household reference person is a native (migrant). (b) Net wealth is defined as total financial and non-financial assets less total debt. (c) Statistics are weighted to represent population figures.

FIGURE 1
(a) Distribution of Household Wealth for Couples; (b) Distribution of Household Wealth for Singles

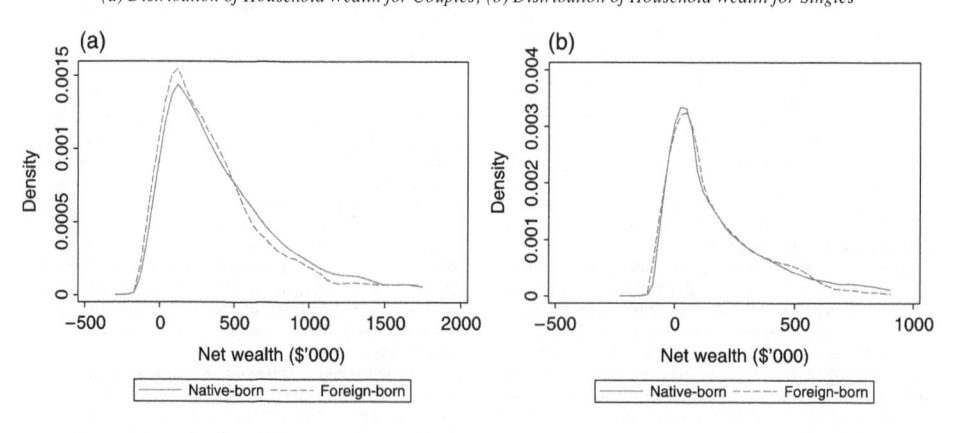

© 2009 The Economic Society of Australia

$1. The drawback to these transformations and exclusions is that they may affect subgroups differently and thus bias results. For example, excluding all families with net worth less than a certain level could result in a different selection of migrants and the native-born. Taking a logarithmic or inverse hyperbolic sine transformation diminishes the effects of very large values of wealth and exaggerates small values, so is not a robust procedure (Carroll et al., 2003). A behavioural model could be used to justify the choice of transformation; however, to date this is lacking in the literature and it is still unclear as to which approach is best. In this study no transformation of wealth is made.

To characterise the entire conditional wealth distribution, the simultaneous quantile regression estimator, introduced by Koenker and Bassett (1978), is employed. This estimator enables inference to be drawn where, for instance, a nativity wealth gap exists only at the bottom of the distribution.[8] To estimate the nativity wealth gap at the qth quantile the following is estimated:

$$W_i = X_i \beta^q + I_i \delta^q + \varepsilon_i^q \qquad (1)$$

assuming $Q^q(\varepsilon^q \mid I_i, X_i) = 0$, where W_i is the wealth level of the ith household, X_i is a vector of characteristics, β^q is the qth quantile-specific vector of coefficients, I_i is a dummy variable that equals one if the reference person in the ith household is a migrant and zero if Australian-born, ε_i is the error term and $Q^q(\cdot)$ denotes the qth conditional quantile. The coefficient δ^q is interpreted as the estimated conditional nativity wealth gap at the qth quantile controlling for other factors through the inclusion of X_i. A more general model would allow all coefficients (β^q) to vary by migrant status. We test for this below.

(ii) Variables

The dependent variable is household net wealth. Two main specifications of the determinants of wealth are estimated. First, a reduced model is used, drawing on factors that describe the lifecycle stage of the family and thus directly influence saving behaviour (Model 1). Age is modelled as a quadratic to reflect accumulation and dissipation of wealth over the lifecycle. Having children will alter saving motives – perhaps to save for children's education

or to leave a bequest. Since wealth is accumulated or run down over time, marital history is likely to be important. The length of current marriage (or partnership) is included for couples.[9] Finally, an indicator for whether wealth was imputed is included, so as to check for bias that could result from the imputation procedure. The variable definitions and sub-sample means are presented in Table 2.

A larger model (Model 2) is estimated with variables the human capital literature predicts are important explanators of labour income differentials, and thus wealth differentials. This includes educational attainment and labour market experience – specifically, current labour market status and years spent in and out of the labour market (as a quadratic). Gender, health and locality are also all likely to be important explanators of wealth differentials (Richardson et al., 2004; Wenzlow et al., 2004; Deere & Doss, 2006).[10]

Lifecycle theory suggests that households base saving decisions on permanent income. However, income may be endogenous as wealth generates income, rendering an instrument necessary. Finding an instrument is difficult as factors which explain permanent income are likely to explain wealth directly.[11] Finally, ethnicity may affect wealth through channels such as attitudes to risk and saving and discrimination. This is addressed in Section IV.

Time since arrival in Australia is likely to have a significant impact on wealth for migrants as it captures both the differential speed of accumulation in the host versus the home country as well as differences across cohorts of migrant. Additional models are estimated to capture these differences. Two specifications are used consistent with existing literature. First a linear effect of years since arrival is estimated. In the second specification, dummy variables are used to distinguish across cohorts of migrants based on major policy shifts.

---

[8] Another advantage, particularly under non-normality, is that no distributional assumptions are required so the method is robust to extreme observations in the dependent variable. Also, the estimator is consistent and asymptotically normal (Buchinsky, 1998).

[9] An indicator for being previously divorced or widowed was also included initially. This variable proved to be insignificant throughout the distribution and since its inclusion reduced sample sizes due to missing values, it was deleted from the analysis.

[10] Information on English proficiency is also available in HILDA and likely to be important in determining wealth. Since the language indicators have low variance for the native-born households, they are not useful for our purposes and are excluded from the analysis.

[11] HILDA provides information on food and rent expenditures that could proxy consumption and thus potentially act as instruments. However, this is left for future work.

© 2009 The Economic Society of Australia

TABLE 2
Variable Definitions and Sub-sample Means

Variable	Definition	Australian-born n = 5385	Foreign-born n = 1744
Dependent variable			
Wealth	Household wealth	412.20	395.87
	(in 2002 dollars; $'000)	(628.49)	(630.14)
Couple	1 if married or de facto	0.56	0.65
Model 1			
Migrant	1 if foreign-born	0.00	1.00
Age	Age of reference person in years	46.74	49.94
		(16.99)	(16.05)
Kids dummy	1 if has children	0.29	0.25
Kids	Number of children	1.82	1.79
	(dependent and non-dependent)	(1.61)	(1.48)
Couple years	Length of current marriage	11.19	13.81
	(or partnership)	(15.44)	(16.12)
Imputation dummy	1 if net wealth was imputed	0.44	0.49
Model 2			
Tertiary	1 if university or graduate diploma	0.19	0.26
Trade	1 if trade qualification	0.33	0.29
High school	1 if no higher education	0.48	0.45
Employ years	Years in employment	23.11	24.05
		(14.23)	(14.31)
Unemploy years	Years in unemployment	0.60	0.59
		(1.92)	(2.05)
Employ	1 if employed	0.68	0.63
Unmploy	1 if unemployed	0.03	0.04
Nilf	1 if not in the labour force	0.29	0.34
Gender	1 if female	0.41	0.40
Health	1 if has a long-term illness or disability	0.24	0.23
Region	1 if living in a remote area	0.15	0.06
Other			
Year Aus	Years in Australia	–	26.07
			(16.15)
Cohort 5	1 if 5 or less years living in Australia	–	0.10
Cohort 625	1 if 6–25 years living in Australia	–	0.40
Cohort 26	1 if >25 years living in Australia	–	0.50
Parent migrant	1 if second generation migrant	0.25	–

Notes: Standard deviations are in brackets for continuous variables. All variables are weighted to represent population figures.

Table 2 shows that on average migrants have more human capital investments in terms of education and experience. This is not surprising given the advantages given to skilled migrants in immigration policies (more details are provided below). They are also more likely to be married and less likely to live in a remote area and to be employed. This is in agreement with previous findings for Australia (Wilkins, 2003).

(iii) Nativity Wealth Gap

Table 3 presents the coefficient estimates for migrant status (δ) from the two models estimated at the 10th through 90th percentiles, along with the unconditional wealth gap. For example, the second coefficient in column 3 indicates that the 10th percentile of the wealth distribution for native-born persons is close to $34 000 greater than the 10th percentile for migrants. This is a systematic shift between the two groups controlling for the factors included in Model 1 and listed in Table 2.

Several findings are evident from Table 3. Consider couples. We see that Australian-born persons have significantly greater wealth than migrants; this gap generally increases as we move up the distribution;

© 2009 The Economic Society of Australia

TABLE 3
The Nativity Wealth Gap Quantile Regression Coefficient Estimates ($'000)

	Couples			Singles		
	Unconditional	Model 1	Model 2	Unconditional	Model 1	Model 2
Mean (OLS)	−33.52* (17.16)	−88.74*** (16.02)	−90.83*** (15.46)	−13.09 (15.04)	−32.38** (14.43)	−43.11*** (14.07)
10th	−12.42*** (4.27)	−33.68*** (5.98)	−34.01*** (5.96)	0.13 (0.43)	−1.80* (1.08)	−3.69* (1.95)
20th	−19.60** (8.83)	−39.80*** (7.10)	−52.05*** (9.09)	1.60 (2.04)	−4.82* (2.85)	−9.48*** (3.23)
30th	−14.57 (9.29)	−51.75*** (8.24)	−60.72*** (9.85)	−0.55 (4.42)	−9.10** (3.81)	−15.13*** (5.62)
40th	−25.65** (11.84)	−66.32*** (10.57)	−73.78*** (9.33)	−5.76 (8.30)	−16.35*** (5.52)	−19.91*** (6.46)
50th	−26.59* (14.47)	−80.69*** (12.14)	−68.16*** (12.35)	−5.50 (11.97)	−18.88*** (6.85)	−25.24*** (7.76)
60th	−48.10** (19.75)	−92.06*** (15.22)	−75.64*** (13.39)	−0.90 (14.83)	−29.11*** (8.50)	−27.15*** (9.56)
70th	−68.00*** (24.84)	−103.10*** (19.54)	−102.95*** (19.02)	−20.00 (18.43)	−36.66*** (12.19)	−24.41* (14.74)
80th	−56.32* (34.40)	−123.04*** (31.51)	−131.68*** (24.69)	−27.50 (25.53)	−42.19** (21.39)	−29.87 (19.41)
90th	−120.64 (89.01)	−120.73*** (46.51)	−154.27 (47.55)	−95.00** (39.83)	−73.97** (32.86)	−105.67*** (30.14)
F-test	0.99	2.40**	3.89***	1.50	1.84*	2.84***
N	4118	4118	4118	3011	3011	3011

Notes: (a) Standard errors in parenthesis; obtained using 200 bootstrap repetitions. (b) *** significant at 1% level, ** significant at 5% level, * significant at 10% level. (c) Variables used in Model 1 and Model 2 are described in Table 2 and additional estimation results are available upon request. (d) F-test statistic for the null hypothesis that the nativity wealth gaps are jointly equal for quantiles 10 through 90.

and controlling for factors generally causes the gap to increase. The results for singles are similar but the gap is smaller and is generally not significant when regressors other than migrant status are not included. The gap at the mean is also negative and mostly significant. Consistent with the skewness in the wealth distributions, especially for singles, the mean wealth gap falls at percentiles above 50.

These findings are consistent with the descriptive statistics presented above; there is a gap in the observed raw wealth distributions, at least for couples, despite the fact that migrants have more wealth generating characteristics. When controlling for observed characteristics the gap is substantial. For couples, the difference in wealth levels for Model 2 is around $70 000 in the middle of the distribution and varies between $34 000 at the 10th percentile to over $154 000 at the 90th percentile. For singles, the gap rises from $4000 at the 10th percentile to $25 000 at the median. It is then fairly constant reaching $30 000 at the 80th percentile and then rising sharply to over $100 000 at the 90th percentile.

Variables that enhance wealth include age, years of marriage, tertiary qualifications, employment and gender at the top of the distribution. Explanators that reduce wealth are children (at the lower half of the distribution), health and remoteness.[12] In the models reported so far, it has been assumed that the impact of variables on wealth is the same across the migrant and Australian-born groups. To confirm this, interactions for each variable were added to Model 2, but the vast majority were highly insignificant. Only the age interaction was significant at the top tail of the distribution. None of the main results were affected by this. Additional results confirming this are presented below.

[12] The full-model estimation results are available upon request.

© 2009 The Economic Society of Australia

Using the estimated variance–covariance matrix, the equality of nativity wealth gaps along the distribution can be tested. With an F-statistic of 2.40 and 3.89 for couples in Model 1 and Model 2, respectively, and 1.84 and 2.84 for singles, each with an associated P-value < 0.1, the equality of gaps throughout the whole distribution is rejected. A model such as the OLS regression in which the migrant coefficients are kept constant throughout the distribution is thus unable to fully capture the features of the migrant wealth gap.

(iv) Decomposition of the Nativity Wealth Gap

In order to quantify the contribution of characteristics on the observed wealth gap, we decompose the differences in wealth quantiles into components representing differences in coefficients and variables. The most popular method used in recent published studies is due to Machado and Mata (2005) (henceforth MM). We implement this approach with the following steps:

1 Estimation of the wealth quantiles using quantile regressions at a large number of randomly chosen points along the native- and the foreign-born distributions of wealth. Specifically, for couples 1100 points are randomly chosen from a $U[0, 1]$ and the quantiles for each sample of couples are fitted at each of these points. The number of points is limited by the size of the foreign-born sample, which numbers 1118 for couples. This yields two matrices of coefficients: γ^j for j = foreign or native, with 1100 rows and k columns, where k is the number of variables used in the regressions. Let X^j denote the matrix of k explanatory variables used in the quantile regressions for group j with j = foreign or native.
2 Derivation of the predicted distributions consistent with the model and the observed characteristics. This is done by simulation. Specifically, for couples 1100 draws with replacement are taken from each matrix X^j and predicted quantiles are computed as: $\gamma_i^j Z_i^j$ for $i = 1 \ldots 1100$, j = foreign or native, and where Z denotes the random draws transposed (i.e. Z_i^j is a $k \times 1$ vector).
3 Computation of a counterfactual wealth distribution by using one group's coefficients and the other group's characteristics. Specifically let $\gamma_i^n Z_i^f$ represent the counterfactual wealth value for migrant household i if it was given the native-born returns on its characteristics.
4 The migrant gap in the predicted qth wealth quantiles can then be decomposed as:

$$\hat{Q}_q^f - \hat{Q}_q^n = (\gamma_q^n Z_q^f - \gamma_q^n Z_q^n) + (\gamma_q^f Z_q^f - \gamma_q^n Z_q^f) \quad (2)$$

where $\gamma_q^j Z_q^j$ generates the qth quantile in the predicted wealth distribution for group j, that is, $\hat{Q}_q^j = \gamma_q^j Z_q^j$ for j = foreign or native and $\gamma_q^n Z_q^f$ generates the qth quantile in the counterfactual distribution. The first term in parenthesis on the right-hand side represents the contribution to the gap due to differences in the distribution of covariates and the second term is the impact from differences in the returns to the characteristics.[13]

Separate analyses are conducted for couples and singles. For singles, 600 points for each of the foreign- and native-born wealth distributions are fitted with quantile regressions and 600 draws are taken to simulate the predicted and counterfactual distributions. For more details on the approach including a comparison to other methods, see Machado and Mata (2005).

Table 4 presents the decomposition of the predicted nativity gap in wealth quantiles at various percentiles using the MM method and a slightly reduced version of Model 2.[14] All coefficients are allowed to vary between the foreign- and native-born groups. Total represents the predicted wealth gap, Covar is the contribution of differences in covariates (the first term in parentheses on the right-hand side of (2)) and Coeff is the component due to differences in coefficients (the last term in (2)). The Oaxaca–Blinder decomposition of the mean of the distribution is also provided.

The decomposition confirms that migrants have characteristics that are wealth enhancing relative to Australian-born persons. This is the case throughout the distribution but the differences in covariates become more important as we move up the distribution. For example, at the same coefficients, migrant couples would have $33 670 more wealth

---

[13] Since the empirical wealth distribution differs from the estimated distribution, the decomposition in Equation (2) is not exact. With a few exceptions, the predicted wealth differentials are smaller than the observed gaps. From the middle to the upper end of the distributions, specifically from the 50th to the 90th percentiles where the differentials are more substantial, 70–90 per cent of the observed gap is explained by the model. More details are available from the authors.

[14] In order to generate bootstrap standard errors, variables with small cells are excluded; specifically, current employment status and region are dropped (employment history is retained), tertiary and trade qualifications are grouped together and the effect of the number of children is linear with no jump at one. With these restrictions, quantile regressions could be estimated from all but a few bootstrap samples. The estimated wealth gaps are largely unchanged due to these restrictions.

© 2009 The Economic Society of Australia

TABLE 4
Decomposition of Nativity Gaps in Predicted Wealth Quantiles ($'000)

	Couples			Singles		
	Total	Covar	Coeff	Total	Covar	Coeff
Mean	−33.52	47.67	−81.19	−13.09	31.13	−44.22
	(17.38)	(8.41)	(16.82)	(16.16)	(6.68)	(15.69)
10th	−6.25	33.67	−39.92	3.33	10.48	−7.15
	(13.53)	(11.61)	(8.99)	(3.18)	(3.61)	(2.77)
30th	−18.59	33.37	−51.96	−0.22	22.14	−22.36
	(13.23)	(9.57)	(10.52)	(6.89)	(6.62)	(7.03)
50th	−20.45	55.73	−76.18	0.53	23.65	−23.12
	(17.39)	(13.63)	(14.21)	(14.37)	(10.10)	(12.04)
70th	−54.24	44.14	−98.38	−17.64	38.82	−56.46
	(24.73)	(18.43)	(21.40)	(24.59)	(14.50)	(20.49)
90th	−67.55	80.26	−147.81	−38.63	36.03	−74.66
	(58.78)	(33.14)	(51.31)	(40.79)	(24.80)	(35.65)

Notes: (a) Standard errors in parenthesis; obtained using 100 bootstrap repetitions for quantiles and 200 repetitions for the means. (b) Total refers to the predicted wealth gap at the indicated percentile, Covar represents the component of the predicted gap due to differences in covariates (weighted by the native-born coefficients) and Coeff represents the component of the wealth gap due to differences in coefficients (weighted by the foreign-born covariates). (c) Model 2 is used to represent wealth with the following restrictions: the unemployed, employed, region and presence of children indicators are excluded, and tert and trade qualifications are grouped together. This causes the quantile regressions to be estimable with all but a few bootstrap samples. The Machado and Mata method is used to generate predicted quantiles and decomposition terms. For couples, 1100 quantiles are fitted whereas for singles, 600 draws are taken. See the main text for more details.

than Australian-born persons at the 10th percentile and $80 260 greater wealth at the 90th percentile. The reason for the lower migrant wealth lies with differences in returns to characteristics.

An alternative decomposition to that presented in Equation (2) would use the foreign-born coefficients to evaluate differences in covariates and native-born characteristics to weigh differences in coefficients. We check the consistency of our results to this alternative approach. Also, since most coefficients are similar for native- and foreign-born regressors, an alternate procedure is implemented in which the coefficients (except for the constant) are constrained to be equal for migrant and native-born households in the quantile regressions. The results are discussed below.

For the purposes of this paper, there is some concern with the use of the MM method. Given the fairly small sample size of the migrant group, the simulated distributions may not characterise the underlying distributions well. In order to check the robustness of our results, we use an alternative approach due to Blaise Melly (2005) (henceforth BM). This method uses the whole sample to obtain the predicted and the counterfactual distributions and hence is more efficient than the MM method especially for small samples. This is shown in Melly (2006).

Briefly, in step 2 above, rather than associating each coefficient vector with one draw from the matrix of regressors, the predicted quantiles are computed at each sample point. The number of predicted quantiles is $m \times s$, where m is the number of estimates of the coefficient vector (1100 for couples and 600 for singles) and s is the sample size for the group. For example, in the case of couples, the predicted native-born distribution is characterised using 3300 000 (1100 × 3000) points and the migrant distribution with 1229 800 (1100 × 1118) points, where 3000 and 1118 are the sample sizes for the native- and foreign-born groups, respectively. The derivation of this method and the properties of the estimates are presented in Melly (2005, 2006).[15]

These additional results and robustness checks are presented in Table 5. One way to summarise

[15] See, Cai and Liu (2007) for an application of the Melly method to the decomposition of union wage effects. Also for a different approach to decompositions based on influence functions, see the work in progress by Firpo et al. (2007).

© 2009 The Economic Society of Australia

TABLE 5
Trends in Components of the Wealth Gap, OLS Regressions-various Models

	Couples			Singles		
	Constant	Slope	R^2	Constant	Slope	R^2
MM model:						
Covariates	26.31	0.54	0.52	7.29	0.37	0.66
Coefficients	−25.80	−1.22	0.87	6.26	−0.85	0.91
Alternate weighting:						
Covariates	16.07	0.58	0.57	8.99	0.16	0.33
Coefficients	−15.56	−1.27	0.93	4.56	−0.64	0.82
MM model with restricted coefficients:						
Covariates	16.14	0.51	0.71	0.86	0.44	0.70
Coefficients	−29.83	−1.04	0.96	−0.83	−0.52	0.83
Alternate weighting:						
Covariates	23.58	0.35	0.47	1.04	0.46	0.69
Coefficients	−37.27	−0.88	0.90	−1.01	−0.53	0.88
BM model:						
Covariates	26.32	0.44	0.91	2.22	0.42	0.92
Coefficients	−30.41	−1.10	0.93	5.19	−0.79	0.94
Alternate weighting:						
Covariates	15.27	0.51	0.69	3.26	0.31	0.76
Coefficients	−19.36	−1.17	0.93	4.15	−0.68	0.92

Notes: (a) The results are from OLS regressions fitted through the components of the decomposition at the percentiles of the distributions up to the 90th percentile. Each row and each block of columns corresponds to a separate OLS regression. (b) Alternate weighting uses the foreign-born coefficients to weigh the differences in characteristics; MM with restricted coefficients means that only the constant term is allowed to vary between migrants and non-migrants; BM is the Melly (2005) model (with unrestricted coefficients). Model 2 as described in Table 2 is used to estimate all quantile regressions.

the results of the decompositions is to look at the trends in the components over the distribution. This is done by fitting a straight line (an OLS regression) through the Covar and Coeff terms at the percentiles[16] of the distributions.[17] Each row and each block of columns in Table 5 corresponds to a separate OLS regression. A positive (negative) constant and slope indicate that the component is wealth increasing (decreasing) for migrants compared to non-migrants and that the difference grows (falls) as we move up the distribution, respectively. Different models are used to decompose the differentials in the wealth distributions. Alternate weighting refers to the use of the foreign-born coefficients to weigh the differences in characteristics; MM with restricted coefficients means that only the constant term is allowed to vary between migrants and non-migrants in the quantile regressions; BM refers to the Melly model with unrestricted coefficients. The full Model 2 specification is used to estimate the quantile regressions.

The results of the decompositions are surprisingly robust across the different approaches. In all cases, the covariates are found to be wealth increasing for migrants compared to non-migrants and this component increases as we move up the distribution. The differences in coefficients cause migrant wealth to be lower than that of non-migrants and this effect is also stronger as we move up the distribution. (For singles the contribution of differences in coefficients is positive in some models at the very bottom of the distribution, below the 10th percentile in all cases). Most of the differences in coefficients come from the shift in the constant term, that is, a systematic shift between migrants and non-migrants.

---

[16] The regressions fit up to the 90th percentiles only; there is quite a lot of variation in the top 10 percentiles and they affect the regression results and the fit substantially.

[17] Machado and Mata (2005) use a similar method to look at trends in individual coefficients.

© 2009 The Economic Society of Australia

TABLE 6
Decomposition of Cohort-specific Nativity Gaps in Predicted Wealth Quantiles ($'000)

	Couples			Singles		
	Total	Covar	Coeff	Total	Covar	Coeff
Younger cohort: ≤25 years in Australia						
10th	−55.98	−8.73	−47.25	−8.84	0.08	−8.92
30th	−82.33	12.84	−95.17	−31.55	−11.01	−20.54
50th	−75.04	48.11	−123.15	−69.37	−36.77	−32.60
70th	−78.88	76.61	−155.49	−53.52	2.87	−56.39
90th	−230.70	−56.26	−174.44	−26.22	53.74	−79.96
Older cohort: >25 years in Australia						
10th	24.61	45.77	−21.16	6.85	8.30	−1.45
30th	35.49	60.67	−25.18	10.71	24.09	−13.38
50th	64.12	109.81	−45.69	34.45	47.57	−13.12
70th	113.30	164.55	−51.25	117.77	124.88	−7.11
90th	80.44	210.15	−129.71	81.52	128.32	−46.80

Notes: (a) Please see notes to Table 4 for definitions of the columns. (b) Model 2 is used to predict wealth and the Machado and Mata method is used to generate predicted quantiles and decomposition terms. For couples, 500 quantiles are fitted whereas for singles, 250 draws are taken. See the main text for more details.

(v) Cohort Effects

The analysis so far does not distinguish between migrants who have recently arrived and those who have been in Australia a longer time. The addition of a variable measuring years since arrival in quantile regressions such as those reported in Table 3 shows that wealth increases with years in the host country; specifically, a positive and statistically significant coefficient on years since arrival, between $200 and $3500, is found for each quantile. The interpretation of this coefficient is ambiguous in a cross-section; it may reflect either greater assimilation or a decline in relative skills across successive migrant cohorts (Borjas, 1994, 1999). In Australia, policy changes were made to increase the proportion of skilled migrants. This has led some to interpret the positive coefficient as reflecting assimilation (Withers, 1987). Panel data are needed to verify this hypothesis.

Following Zhang's (2003) study of Canadian migrants' wealth, the wealth regressions are re-estimated, replacing the migrant status with three cohort dummies. We choose categories to correspond to a change in policy with a growing emphasis on skills: five or less years in Australia, 6–25 years in Australia (arriving between 1977 and 1996), and over 25 years in Australia. From 1977, immigration policy began to focus on the quality of migrants and strengthened considerably in 1997 (DIMA, 2001). Consequently, from a policy perspective, the performance of the separate cohorts will be of interest.

The unconditional wealth differentials across cohorts are consistent with the results from the models that include the years since arrival variable. For both couples and singles, the two most recent cohorts have negative wealth gaps compared to native-born households, whereas the earliest cohort has a positive wealth differential. Furthermore, the gap becomes larger for the most recent cohort relative to the middle cohort of migrants. These are statistically significant differences except for singles in the tails of the distribution. (Results are available upon request.)

Table 6 presents results on the decomposition of predicted nativity wealth differentials using the MM method. The youngest two cohorts have been grouped to increase sample sizes. These results show that the positive wealth gap for the group of migrants who have been in Australia more than 25 years is due to large and positive contributions of characteristics that overcompensate for the negative effects of coefficients. Furthermore, the negative effects of coefficients are smaller for the earliest cohort. As for the migrant group as a whole, a constant shift for migrants captures most of the effects from the shift in coefficients (not shown). The reduction in the unexplained component of the wealth gap does suggest assimilation of the

© 2009 The Economic Society of Australia

migrants over time. The greater positive effect of differences in characteristics could be due to innate differences across migrant groups or different behaviour of migrants once in Australia. Further research is needed to address these issues.

IV Extensions

(i) Second Generation Migrants

The above analysis confirms that, on average, migrants have less accumulated wealth than their Australian-born counterparts and this difference is greater once lifecycle and human capital determinants are accounted for. Is this the case for second-generation migrants, that is, native Australians born to a foreign-born parent? This section of society comprises 24.1 per cent of our sample of Australian-born households.

A dummy variable, equal to one if the reference person is a second-generation migrant and zero otherwise, is added to the full model (Model 2). For couples, the coefficients are small and insignificant throughout the distribution. For singles, results are similar except for a few significant and positive coefficients at the top end of the distribution. Consequently, the wealth gap that migrants experience may not be mirrored in their children's asset and labour market outcomes, (except for singles at the top of the wealth distribution). This result is consistent with Chiswick and Miller's (1985) Australian analysis where second-generation migrants were not discriminated against in the labour market.

(ii) Country of Birth

Grouping migrants together ignores possible heterogeneity of migrant outcomes arising from country of birth or ethnicity. Wealth accumulation may differ due to attitudes to risk and saving and labour market discrimination. The sensitivity of our results to country of birth is tested by replacing the migrant status dummy in Model 2 with seven country of birth dummies – New Zealand, other main English speaking (UK, USA and South Africa), Western Europe, Eastern Europe and former USSR, South East Asia, other Asia and other. For each region of origin, migrants are less wealthy than Australian-born households. Although the wealth gap is significant for couples, among single-headed households significance is chiefly found for other main English speaking, other Asia in the middle of the distribution and Eastern Europe at the top-tail.

Testing for equality of country of birth coefficients confirms that the nativity wealth differentials are statistically indistinguishable across country of birth, except for singles at the 20th and 30th quantile. Therefore, it is migrant status per se that influences wealth accumulation rather than individual countries of birth.[18]

(iii) Mixed Households

As discussed above, there is no single definition of a migrant household in the empirical literature. To check for robustness of our results to the definition, Model 2 is re-estimated excluding mixed households entirely. Mixed households comprise 21 per cent of coupled households in the sample. The qualitative results still hold with this reduced sample. Preliminary investigations using dummy variables to distinguish between types of mixed households (migrant reference person with Australian-born partner and vice versa) suggest that these households have significantly different wealth distributions and hence how one defines a migrant household may affect results. In particular, a household in which a migrant reference person is partnered with an Australian-born person is found to have an advantage in terms of its wealth levels. Although Cobb-Clark and Hildebrand (2008) also address the role of mixed households, further research using panel data is needed to clarify the role of partnering on the assimilation of migrants in the Australian context.

V Conclusion

This paper explores the existence and magnitude of a nativity wealth gap in Australia, using the 2002 HILDA survey. By exploring migrant outcomes from a wealth perspective, rather than that of labour market performance, a more comprehensive indication of migrants' settlement success is provided. Furthermore, the Australian distribution of wealth is highly unequal, and for policymakers it is important to uncover what generates this inequality. This study shows that migrant status has a significant role in explaining wealth differentials. Specifically migrant couples have significantly lower wealth distributions despite greater wealth-generating characteristics. For singles, the observed wealth distributions are statistically indistinguishable despite migrants having greater wealth-generating characteristics. The migrant wealth gaps increase as we move up the distributions.

---

[18] Although net wealth does not differ by country of birth, wealth portfolios may (Cobb-Clark & Hildebrand, 2008).

© 2009 The Economic Society of Australia

Immigration policy has increasingly focused on attracting skilled migrants. Although these policies have improved migrants' labour-market outcomes (Cobb-Clark, 2003), this study suggests that the improvements may not have flowed to wealth. The most recent migrant cohorts have the greatest (negative) gap in wealth compared to Australian-born households. This is due to both lower wealth-generating characteristics and stronger negative impacts from coefficients, especially the constant term. Policy may have a role in removing barriers to wealth accumulation for migrants, as well as improving labour market performance. However, without information on visa categories and without any control for possibly differential speeds of accumulation, only tentative policy implications can be drawn.

Migrants from different countries of origin all had less wealth than their Australian-born counterparts, but were indistinguishable to each other. Among Australian-born households, children of migrants experienced no difference in wealth levels, except singles at the top of the wealth distribution, who have less wealth than other native-born households.

A notable limitation to this study is the use of cross-section data, which prevents a separation of assimilation effects from cohort effects. Panel data would make possible this distinction, offering a richer picture of migrant performance in the host country. Furthermore, questions of whether, say, skilled migrants can close the nativity wealth gap faster than other migrants could be addressed. Fortunately, Wave 6 of the HILDA survey includes another wealth module, allowing a longitudinal study of wealth dynamics.

REFERENCES

Australian Bureau of Statistics (ABS) (2007), *2006 Census of Population and Housing*, Cat. no. 2068.0, Commonwealth of Australia, Canberra.

Australian Bureau of Statistics (ABS) (2008), *Migration, Australia, 2006–07*, Cat. no. 3412.0, Commonwealth of Australia, Canberra.

Bauer, T.K., Cobb-Clark, D.A., Hildebrand, V. and Sinning, M. (2007), 'A Comparative Analysis of the Nativity Wealth Gap', *IZA Discussion Paper*, No. 2772.

Borjas, G.J. (1994), 'The Economics of Immigration', *Journal of Economic Literature*, **32**, 1667–717.

Borjas, G.J. (1999), 'The Economic Analysis of Immigration', in Ashenfelter, O. and Card, D. (eds), *Handbook of Labor Economics*, Vol. 3C. Elsevier Science Press, Amsterdam, NY, 1697–760.

Buchinsky, M. (1998), 'Recent Advances in Quantile Regression Models: A Practical Guideline for Empirical Research', *Journal of Human Resources*, **33**, 88–126.

Cai, L. and Liu, Y.C. (2007), 'Union Wage Effects in Australia: Are There Variations in Distribution?' Melbourne Institute Working Paper Series Working Paper No. 17/07.

Carroll, C.D., Dynan, K.E. and Krane, S.D. (2003), 'Unemployment Risk and Precautionary Wealth: Evidence from Households' Balance Sheets', *Review of Economics and Statistics*, **85**, 586–604.

Carroll, C.D., Rhee, B.K. and Rhee, C. (1998), 'Does Cultural Origin Affect Saving Behaviour? Evidence from Immigrants'. *NBER Working Paper Series*, No. 6568.

Chiswick, B. and Miller, P. (1985), 'Immigrant Generation and Income in Australia', *Economic Record*, **61**, 540–53.

Cobb-Clark, D.A. (2003), 'Public-policy and the Labour Market Adjustment of New Immigrants to Australia', *Journal of Population Economics*, **16**, 655–81.

Cobb-Clark, D.A. and Hildebrand, V. (2006), 'The Wealth and Asset Holdings of US-born and Foreign-born Households: Evidence From SIPP Data', *Review of Income and Wealth*, **52**, 17–42.

Cobb-Clark, D.A. and Hildebrand, V. (2008), 'The Asset Portfolios of Native-born and Foreign-born Households', *IZA Discussion Paper*, No. 3304.

Deere, C. D. and Doss, C. (2006), 'The Gender Asset Gap: What do we Know and Why Does it Matter?', *Feminist Economics*, **12**, 1–50.

Department of Immigration and Multicultural Affairs (DIMA) (2001), 'Immigration-Federation to Century's End', October, AGPS, Canberra.

Dustmann, C. (1997), 'Return Migration, Uncertainty and Precautionary Savings', *Journal of Development Economics*, **52**, 295–316.

Firpo, S., Fortin, N. and Lemieux, T. (2007), 'Unconditional Quantile Regressions'. NBER Technical Working Paper 339.

Galor, O. and Stark, O. (1990), 'Migrants' Savings, the Probability of Return Migration and Migrants' Performance', *International Economic Review*, **31**, 463–7.

Gibson, J.K., Le, T. and Stillman, S. (2007), 'What Explains the Wealth Gap Between Immigrants and the New Zealand Born?', *Motu Working Paper*, No. 07-12.

Hao, L. (2004), 'Wealth of Immigrant and Native-born Americans', *International Migration Review*, **38**, 518–46.

Heady, B., Marks, K. and Wooden, M. (2005), 'The Structure and Distribution of Household Wealth in Australia', *The Australian Economic Review*, **38**, 159–75.

Junankar, P.N. and Mahuteau, S. (2005), 'Do Migrants get Good Jobs? New Migrant Settlement in Australia?', *Economic Record*, **81** (Special Issue), S34–S46.

Junankar, P.N., Paul, S. and Yasmeen, W. (2004), 'Are Asian Migrants Discriminated Against in the Labour Market? A Case Study of Australia', *IZA Discussion Paper* No. 1167.

Koenker, R.W. and Bassett, G. (1978), 'Regression Quantiles', *Econometrica*, **46**, 33–50.

Machado, J.A.F. and Mata, J. (2005), 'Counterfactual Decomposition of Changes in Wage Distributions using Quantile Regression', *Journal of Applied Econometrics*, **20**, 445–65.

© 2009 The Economic Society of Australia

Melly, B. (2005), 'Decomposition of Differences in Distribution using Quantile Regression', *Labour Economics*, **12**, 577–90.

Melly, B. (2006), 'Estimation of Counterfactual Distributions Using Quantile Regressions', University of St. Gallen Working Paper.

Pagan, A. and Ullah, A. (1999), *Nonparametric Econometrics*. Cambridge University Press, New York.

Richardson, S., Stack, S., Lester, L., Healy, J., Ilsley, D. and Horrocks, J. (2004), 'The Changing Labour Force Experience of New Migrants. Inter-wave Comparisons for Cohort 1 and 2 of the LSIA', AGPS, Canberra.

Schmidt, L. and Sevak, P. (2006), 'Gender, Marriage, and Asset Accumulation in the United Status', *Feminist Economics*, **12**, 139–66.

Shamsuddin, A.F.M. and DeVoretz, D.J. (1998), 'Wealth Accumulation of Canadian and Foreign-born Households in Canada', *Review of Income and Wealth*, **44**, 515–33.

Thapa, P.J. (2004), 'On the Risk of Unemployment: A Comparative Assessment of the Labour Market Success of Migrants in Australia', *Australian Journal of Labour Economics*, **7**, 199–229.

Watson, N. (2004), 'Income and Wealth Imputation for Waves 1 and 2', *Hilda Project Technical Paper Series*, 3/04.

Wenzlow, A.T., Mullahy, J., Robert, S.A. and Wolfe, B.L. (2004), 'An Empirical Investigation of the Relationship Between Wealth and Health: Using the Survey of Consumer Finances', *Institute for Research on Poverty Discussion Paper*, 1287–04.

Wilkins, R. (2003), 'Immigrant and Native-born Earnings Distributions in Australia: 1982–96', *Australian Journal of Labour Economics*, **6**, 83–115.

Withers, G. (1987), 'Immigration and Australian Economic Growth', in Miller, P. and Baker, L. (eds), *The Economics of Immigration*. AGPS, Canberra, 29–55.

Zhang, X. (2003), 'The Wealth Position of Immigrant Families in Canada', *Statistics Canada Working Paper*, No. 197.

© 2009 The Economic Society of Australia

[10]

Do Enclaves Matter in Immigrant Adjustment?

Barry R. Chiswick*
University of Illinois at Chicago and the Institute for the Study of Labor

Paul W. Miller
University of Western Australia

> This paper is concerned with the determinants and consequences of immigrant/linguistic concentrations (enclaves). The reasons for the formation of these concentrations are discussed. Hypotheses are developed regarding "ethnic goods" and the effect of concentrations on the immigrant's language skills, as well as the effects on immigrant earnings of destination language skills and the linguistic concentration. These hypotheses are tested using PUMS data from the 1990 U.S. Census on adult male immigrants from non-English speaking countries. Linguistic concentrations reduce the immigrant's own English language skills. Moreover, immigrant's earnings are lower the lower their English-language proficiency and the greater the linguistic/ethnic concentration in their origin language of the area in which they live. The adverse effects on earnings of poor destination language skills and of immigrant concentrations exist independently of each other. The hypotheses regarding ethnic goods are supported by the data.

INTRODUCTION

This paper is concerned with the issue of immigrant/ethnic concentrations, that is, the tendency of immigrants to concentrate geographically by ethnicity or country of origin within the host country.[1] In particular, it is concerned with the consequences of enclaves or concentrations for two characteristics of immigrant adjustment—destination language proficiency and labor market earnings. Other aspects of immigrant life influenced by concentrations, including political participation and influence, are beyond the scope of this paper.

There are two basic research questions of interest. One is the effect of immigrant concentrations on proficiency in destination language skills. The other is the direct effect of the immigrant's proficiency in the destination language and the effects of these immigrant concentrations on their labor market earnings. In particular, this study separates the direct effects and indirect effects via language proficiency of immigrant concentrations on earnings. The application is to the United States. The methodology developed, however, could be applied to any immigrant-receiving country for which there is appropriate census or survey data.

---

*Correspondence should be addressed to Barry R. Chiswick, Department of Economics, University of Illinois at Chicago, College of Business Administration, 601 S. Morgan Street (Room 2103 UH), Chicago, IL 60607-7121; Brchis@uic.edu.

City & Community 4:1 March 2005
© American Sociological Association, 1307 New York Avenue, NW, Washington, DC 20005-4701

CITY & COMMUNITY

The section "Immigrant Concentrations: Hypotheses" provides a brief introduction to the broader setting within which the issue of immigrant concentrations arises. Testable hypotheses are developed, with a particular emphasis on ethnic goods. "The Data" section discusses the data used in the empirical analysis. In the "Analysis of Language" section a model of dominant language acquisition is presented and estimated, with a particular focus on the effects of immigrant/linguistic concentrations on dominant language proficiency. "Analysis of the Earnings" section is the analysis of the earnings of immigrants with a particular focus on the effects of the immigrant's destination language skills and living in a linguistic concentration area on the respondent's labor market earnings. The paper closes with a summary and conclusion, with implications for public policy.

IMMIGRANT CONCENTRATIONS: HYPOTHESES

IMMIGRANT FLOWS

A characteristic of the late 20th century that is surely to continue into at least the early 21st century is an increase in the movement of people across international borders (Chiswick and Hatton, 2003). International migration has increased into the traditional immigrant-receiving countries, such as the United States, Canada, and Australia. Yet, international migration into traditional countries of emigration has also become commonplace. Italy, Ireland, Germany, and Japan, among others, are now experiencing large net in-migration, or where restricted by law, as in Japan, pressures for in-migration as evidenced by illegal flows.

These migration flows have, in part, been "East" to "West," that is, from the former Soviet Union and the Eastern block countries to the United States, Canada, Germany, and Israel. More pronounced, however, are the migration flows from the "South" to the "North," more precisely, from less developed countries to highly developed economies. Unprecedented immigration flows have been experienced from Latin America to North America, from Africa to Western Europe, and from Asia to North America, Western Europe, Australia, and Japan (Chiswick and Hatton, 2003).

An important characteristic of these international migration flows is that the immigrants are "different" from the natives. As was true of the immigration flows from Southern and Eastern Europe to North America at the turn of the 20th century, the immigrants to the developed countries at the turn of the 21st century "sound" and "look" different.

In spite of the world becoming a smaller place with the ease (falling cost) of the transmission of information and ideas, and the falling cost of transportation for people and goods, and hence the "Westernization" of much of the world, new immigrants are frequently distinctive. Although distinctive clothing, especially for men, is less common than in the past, immigrants as a group frequently differ from natives as a group in appearance, religion, customs, belief-systems, language, and other characteristics associated with ethnicity.

IMMIGRANT CONCENTRATIONS

The immigrant groups typically have a spatial distribution in their host countries that differ sharply from that of the native born. For obvious reasons, new immigrants typically

IMMIGRANT ADJUSTMENT

settle in areas based on three characteristics (Bartel, 1989).[2] The first is "ports" of entry, near seaports in the past, near airports in the current era. The second is where family and friends (co-ethnics) from earlier migrations have settled. Even if the location choice of the first settler from the ethnic group is purely random among a set of equally attractive locations in a destination country, once that first settler is established, future settlers are no longer indifferent among destination sites. The third is where the jobs are, that is, where the immigrants are most able to gain employment that makes best use of their skills, or lack thereof. With the passage of time "ports of entry" and "family and friends" become less central and economic factors relatively more central in deciding where to live in the host country, and immigrants tend to disperse to some extent.

Some interpret the "family and friends" or chain migration effect on immigrant formations of concentrations as "clannishness." Yet to say it is clannishness is to beg the question as "clannishness" per se has no content. An alternative interpretation, however, is that settling in areas with others from the same origin provides for economies in communication, information, consumption, and in the labor market.

Where new immigrants differ from the host population in terms of language skills, communication in all spheres of life are that much more difficult. These communication costs can be reduced if the host population were to learn the immigrant's language. Yet, it is not cost effective for a majority host population speaking the dominant language to learn the myriad of new languages that minority immigrants bring with them from various linguistic backgrounds.

These communication costs are reduced when immigrants learn the dominant language of the destination country. Yet, this learning can be costly and cannot be done instantaneously in the destination. Thus, to varying degrees, new immigrants from a different linguistic origin tend to lack complete proficiency in the dominant language of the host economy, unless dominant language proficiency is a requirement for entry. Moreover, as with the production of other forms of human capital and of market goods and services, beyond some point, costs per unit of improved proficiency increase with a faster speed of language acquisition. Thus, the optimal acquisition of dominant language proficiency among immigrants takes time and, for some, full proficiency may never be obtained in their lifetime.

Finally, these communication costs for the immigrants can be reduced by living and/or working in a linguistic concentration area (Bauer, Epstein, and Gang, 2002). Not all members of the group need dominant language proficiency, and the earlier arrivals and those more efficient in language acquisition are more likely to become proficient. They can serve as either direct or indirect translators for communication between the enclave and the host society. The demand for this specialized function increases with the size of the linguistic minority group and decreases as the members of the group learn the dominant language or as the native population learns the immigrant language.

Even aside from issues of language skills, immigrant/ethnic concentrations provide information networks that can be very valuable in social interaction, consumption, and employment activities. Natives of an area have acquired location-specific human capital, which includes information obtained directly and indirectly through established networks. Not being connected to host country information networks when they arrive, immigrants have an incentive to create or "import" information networks through living in geographic concentrations with other new and longer term immigrants from the same origin.

ETHNIC GOODS

Immigrants tend to differ from the native or host population in many dimensions related to ethnicity. They may differ in the foods they eat, the clothing they wear, the holidays they celebrate, the religion they practice, the media they read or hear (e.g., newspapers and radio), their social organizations, and the languages they speak, among other characteristics.[3] There is frequently a tension among immigrants between preserving the culture of the "old country" in the new setting and adopting the culture of the host country.

Let us call "ethnic goods" the consumption characteristics of an immigrant/ethnic group not shared with the host population, or with other immigrant groups, broadly defined to include market and nonmarket goods and services, including social interactions for themselves and their children with people of their same origin.[4] To the extent that "ethnic goods" are distinctive and are important in the market basket, immigrants from a particular origin have a different market basket than the native born and immigrants from other origins. The full cost of consumption of these ethnic goods varies with the price of purchased market goods and services and the value of time, but also with the importance and distinctiveness of the ethnic goods and the size of the group.[5]

There are certain fixed costs and economies of scale in the production and distribution of ethnic goods. Social interaction with others of the same origin (including finding an appropriate marriage partner) may involve little in the way of conventional market goods and services, but importantly involves the number of other individuals in the group. The cost would decrease (presumably at a decreasing rate) the larger the size of the group.[6] Up to a point, an ethnic religious institution (e.g., church, mosque, temple, or synagogue) or an ethnic school for the children of immigrants has a lower per capita cost for members for the same type of facility providing the same level of services to the congregants or students if it is in a larger rather than in a smaller ethnic community.[7] There are fixed costs for buildings and hiring religious officials, among other items, including the probability that enough individuals will show up on a given occasion for the religious service.

The cost of "importing" into the community ethnic-specific goods (e.g., saris, Chinese vegetables, kosher meats) also varies with the size of the market because of economies of scale. Indeed, as the size of the community increases, the manner of "importation" may change from a family making a trip to a larger nearby community, to collective/cooperative efforts to place periodic bulk orders, to the establishment of a single (monopoly) outlet, to many competitive outlets selling the product. The full price declines, the larger the size of the community.

The cost of living in an area then depends on the relative cost of ethnic goods, broadly defined, and the importance and distinctiveness of ethnic goods in the person's market basket. The cost of ethnic goods is lower, the larger is the size of the particular ethnic/immigrant community. The share of ethnic goods in the market basket is likely to be lower, the closer culturally the group is in the origin to the host society, the greater the extent of assimilation into the host society, the longer the immigrant's duration of residence in the destination, and among the native-born descendants of immigrants.

Ethnic goods have implications for living in an ethnic concentration area as well as for geographic differences in earnings. If ethnic goods, defined broadly, are an important part

IMMIGRANT ADJUSTMENT

of the market basket, the person faces a higher real cost of living where ethnic goods are more expensive (an area where fewer co-ethnics live) than where they are less expensive (a high ethnic concentration area). Then the ethnic immigrant would be indifferent between a similar job in a high-concentration area and a low-concentration area only if the latter provided a higher nominal wage that was just sufficient to compensate for the higher cost of living.[8]

Thus, ethnic goods can result in different geographic concentrations of various immigrant groups and differences in the pattern of regional wage differentials across immigrant groups and between immigrants and natives. The general observation would be lower nominal wages, the larger the size of the concentration, other variables being the same. Note that the "ethnic goods" hypothesis regarding the negative relation between the concentration measure and earnings is an equilibrium situation based on differences in the real (ethnic-specific) cost of living. It reflects compensating wage differentials.[9]

When a new immigrant group initially arrives in a destination it may be indifferent among alternative regions in the destination that are equally attractive in terms of job opportunities and ports of entry. The initial settlers would tend to be immigrants with a lower demand for ethnic goods. Subsequent immigrants from this ethnic group will not be indifferent among the alternative destinations as ethnic goods will be cheaper where their co-ethnics have already settled. With the ethnic community established, those with a higher demand for ethnic goods would find immigration much more attractive.

New ethnic concentrations away from the original center in the destination can be formed under any one of several scenarios. An individual with a very low demand for ethnic goods may settle elsewhere and gradually (and perhaps inadvertently) serve as a nucleus for others to follow. An individual with a high demand for ethnic goods may randomly receive a very high wage offer from the distribution of wage offers and settle in a new area. This person may serve as a nucleus and may even have an economic incentive to subsidize ethnic goods to encourage others to join him or her in the new location. Moreover, if a very "large" number of immigrants settle in the initial location and they are less than perfect substitutes in production for native workers, under the crowding hypothesis their wages decline relative to what they could earn in alternate locations with fewer (perhaps none) of their group. If the wage gap compensates for the higher cost of living because of ethnic goods, a second enclave can be established. Thus, the number of enclaves or areas of concentration will vary systematically with the size of the immigrant/ethnic group and the distinctiveness and intensity of the demand for ethnic goods.

IMMIGRANT "CROWDING"

An alternative to the "ethnic goods" hypothesis is a labor supply or "crowding" hypothesis. If there are a large number of immigrants with a given skill level, and if they are not good substitutes in production for others with the same skill level, their earnings would be depressed, as indicated in the previous paragraph. This is, however, a disequilibrium situation as immigrant workers with a given level of skill could receive higher real wages outside the enclave. The internal mobility of immigrant and native-born labor, and other factors of production, as well as goods and services, would bring about factor price equalization, eliminating the negative relation between concentration and earnings.

The "crowding hypothesis" is not likely to be compelling for the United States. The United States has highly fluid labor, capital, and product markets where inter-regional mobility is the norm rather than the exception. The largest single group of immigrants is from Mexico, and they tend to have low levels of skill, without a high degree of specialized skills.[10] As such, they are good substitutes in production for other low-skilled labor, whether native born or foreign born. Among the non-Mexican immigrants, the countries and languages of origin are numerous and skill levels are more highly varied. It is difficult to think of any groups in the U.S. that are sufficiently large and specialized with a low substitutability with native-born and other foreign-born workers. To the extent that a sudden exogenous infusion of immigrant labor with specialized skills impacts a local labor market, disequilibrium earnings differentials would emerge, but would be dissipated over time with internal mobility of factors of production (including immigrant labor) and tradable goods. The persistence over time of immigrant concentrations is not consistent with the implications of the crowding hypothesis effect on wages.

CONSEQUENCES OF CONCENTRATIONS

Limited destination language proficiency is likely to reduce the earnings potential of immigrants (Chiswick and Miller, 1992, 1995). It raises the cost or lowers the efficiency of job search and in many jobs may restrict access (e.g., if there is a need to pass a test that requires proficiency) or merely lower productivity. There may also be discrimination in the labor market by the native population (either as employers, co-workers, or consumers) against those who are less proficient in the dominant language or who speak it with an accent. Working within a linguistic enclave is a mechanism for sheltering oneself from, or mitigating the adverse labor market consequences of, limited destination language proficiency.

Living and working within a linguistic concentration area has feedback effects on destination language proficiency. The greater the extent to which an individual can avoid communicating in the destination language, the slower is likely to be the rate of acquisition of dominant language skills. Consider two individuals: one lives in a large linguistic concentration area where one can work, consume, socialize, and engage in other activities using the origin language and the other lives in a linguistically isolated area; communication can be done only in the dominant language. The latter may have a more difficult initial adjustment, but has a stronger incentive to acquire destination language skills and has greater exposure that facilitates learning the destination language.

Thus, what has emerged in many developed countries is the existence of distinct immigrant communities that differ in language, culture, and other characteristics from the host society. These immigrant/linguistic concentrations are expected to have an adverse effect on the immigrant's acquisition of dominant language skills. The immigrant's dominant language skills, as well as the size of the linguistic concentration area, will also affect the person's earnings, other things being the same. Greater proficiency would have a positive effect, and a larger concentration a negative effect on nominal earnings. These hypotheses are tested in the empirical analysis.

IMMIGRANT ADJUSTMENT

THE DATA

DEFINING THE POPULATION UNDER STUDY

The empirical analysis is performed using data from the 1990 Census of Population of the United States for adult male immigrants.[11] The U.S. Census provides a very large sample, a rich array of variables, and immigrants from diverse origins arriving at various periods of time. The analysis at this stage is limited to adult (nonaged) males as the analysis for females or aged males becomes more complex because of the need to model labor supply decisions, in addition to the language and earnings equations. Moreover, the formation of enclaves or concentrations is taken as exogenous for the individual in the empirical analysis, although there was a discussion in Section II as to why such concentrations are formed.

The data for the statistical analysis are from the 5 percent Public Use Microdata Sample from the 1990 Census. The sample is limited to males aged 25 to 64 years who were foreign born, but not from an English-speaking developed country. Thus, the native born, those born in a U.S. territory (e.g., Puerto Rico), born at sea, or born abroad of American parents are excluded, as are those born in the United Kingdom, Ireland, Canada, Australia, and New Zealand.

DEFINING THE VARIABLES

The English language proficiency variable comes from question number 15 in the census long form. Respondents were asked if there was a language other than English spoken at home (other than just a few words), and if so the identity of that language and how well they spoke English, where the response categories were Very Well, Well, Not Well, and Not at All. For the purpose of this analysis, the foreign born who spoke only English or who spoke another language but reported that they spoke English "very well" or "well" were considered fluent; those who spoke English "not well" and "not at all" were considered not fluent.

The other dependent variable is earnings, which is the sum of wage, salary, and self-employment income in 1989. Those with earnings of less than $100, including those with negative earnings, were assigned a value of $100. Those who worked 0 weeks in 1989 were deleted from the sample for the analysis of earnings.

The enclave variable is a minority language concentration measure (CON).[12] The 24 languages other than English most frequently spoken in the United States were identified. The speakers of these top 24 languages constitute around 94 percent of those reporting a foreign language spoken at home. For each of these 24 languages, for the 50 states and the District of Columbia, the percent of the states' population aged 18 to 64 years (whether native or foreign born) speaking that language, was computed. The concentration measure for each respondent is the percentage speaking the person's origin language in the state of current residence. For other languages, since the number of speakers is too low, the percentage was assumed to be zero. Those who reported speaking only English were assigned the mean value of the concentration ratio for foreign language speakers in their birthplace group.

Within states, the density of population is less in rural areas than in urban areas. A variable for residence in a rural area (RURAL) is included because of a smaller concentration

CITY & COMMUNITY

of origin language speakers in rural than in urban centers. The other explanatory variables are straightforward and are discussed in Appendix B and as the variables are introduced in the text.

THE STATISTICAL TECHNIQUES

The main statistical methodology that is employed is ordinary least squares (OLS) with standard errors corrected for heteroskedasticity, and where indicated below instrumental variables (IV) analysis.

ANALYSIS OF LANGUAGE

THE LANGUAGE MODEL

This section presents the development of the model for dominant language proficiency. While largely based on previous work, in particular Chiswick and Miller (1995, 1998), the model is expanded to include new variables (refugees, persons from former colonies of English-speaking countries, and persons who lived abroad 5 years earlier). Particular attention is given to the variable measuring the degree of minority language concentration (CON).

The language proficiency model adopts a human capital approach in which destination language proficiency (LANG) is a function of three fundamental determinants, namely, "exposure," "efficiency," and "economic incentives." Since the application is to the English language for immigrants in the United States in the 1990 Census, the discussion of these variables will be in this context. The principles apply to any destination language, country, and data set.

Exposure Variables

"Exposure" refers to exposure to the destination language either pre- or postimmigration. The Census identifies country of birth, but provides no other information on preimmigration experiences relevant for acquiring English language proficiency. A set of country-of-origin dichotomous variables is included in the analysis to control for country of origin fixed effects. Western Europe (other than the U.K. and Ireland) is the benchmark. Moreover, a dichotomous variable is created for whether the origin was a colony (COLONY) of an English-speaking country, that is, of either the United States or the United Kingdom. Recall that respondents born in current U.S. territories are excluded from the analysis.

Postimmigration exposure to English can be measured in time units and in intensity per unit of time. Time in the destination is measured as the number of years since migration and its square (YSM, YSMSQ). It is expressed as a quadratic variable to allow for the effect of an extra year in the United States to be larger in the early years than in subsequent years.

The duration variable refers to when the immigrant first came to the United States to stay. Exposure to English in the United States may have been interrupted by sojourns outside the country after the initial migration. For immigrants in the United States for more than 5 years the variable "lived abroad five years ago" (ABROAD5) is unity if this was the situation, otherwise it is zero. It is expected that, other variables being the same,

12

IMMIGRANT ADJUSTMENT

having lived outside the United States would be associated with lesser proficiency in English compared to otherwise similar immigrants who did not live elsewhere in 1985.

Intensity of exposure per unit of time in the United States can be measured by several variables. Of particular interest is the minority language concentration measure (CON), which is computed on a state level, as was discussed above. Within states the density of population is less in rural areas than in urban areas. A variable for residence in a rural area (RURAL) is included because of a smaller concentration of origin language speakers in rural than in urban areas within states.

For immigrants from Mexico the analysis also includes an index for Spanish language media, namely, a variable for the number of radio stations in Spanish normalized for the size of the state in square miles and population (RADIO) (Chiswick and Miller, 1998). Because of possible endogeneity in this variable, a predicted value (IV technique) rather than an observed value for radio is used.

A marital status variable (MARR is unity if married, spouse present) is also included here. It is not possible in the 1990 Census to distinguish between pre- and postmigration marriages, but it was possible to do in the 1980 Census (Chiswick and Miller, 1992).

Efficiency Variables

"Efficiency" refers to the ability to convert exposure into language skills. Greater efficiency means more language skills are acquired for the same level of exposure. The efficiency variables include age at migration (age with years since migration held constant), years of schooling, whether the respondent may have been a refugee, and a measure of the "distance" between the origin language and English.

Older immigrants (AGE) at arrival have greater difficulty learning a new language. Age is entered as a quadratic variable (age and its square) as it is expected that an extra year of age at migration would have a larger adverse effect among younger than among older immigrants.

Those with more schooling (EDUC) are assumed to be more able and to have more knowledge of the structure of languages, and hence are likely to be more efficient in learning new languages, including the destination language. It may also be that those with more schooling in the origin were exposed to English at higher grades prior to immigration, or that schooling in the United States enhanced proficiency.[13]

The refugee variable (REFUGEE) is included because refugees tend to be less favorably selected for a successful adjustment in the destination than are economic migrants. The migration decision of refugees is influenced to an important extent by factors other than the expectation of a successful economic adjustment. The refugee variable is based on country of birth and period of immigration.

Another efficiency variable is "linguistic distance" (DISTANCE), that is, a measure of how difficult it is for non-English speakers to learn English (see Chiswick and Miller, 1998). For example, Korean would be more "distant" from English than would be French. The more "distant" is the origin language from English, the lower the efficiency in learning English and hence the lower the expected proficiency in English.

Economic Variables

"Economic incentives" is the most difficult conceptual variable to model. In principle, one would like to add an explanatory variable that measures the expected increment in earnings for a unit increase in proficiency for each respondent. Given currently available data it is not possible to do this. It has been found that immigrants with higher levels of schooling have a greater economic return from becoming proficient (Chiswick and Miller, 2003). That is, that there is a complementarity between language skills and education in generating labor market earnings. This effect on incentives to invest in destination language skills would be captured by the education variable (EDUC).

The economic benefits in the labor market and in other activities from increased proficiency in English would be greater the longer the expected duration in the United States. Immigrants from countries with a high propensity for return migration would expect a shorter period in the U.S. data on emigration (EMIG) by country of origin are used for this purpose, but not for Mexico (Ahmed and Robinson, 1994). The methodology for developing the country-specific emigration rates in Ahmed and Robinson (1994) is not applicable to Mexico because of the 1986 amnesty and the very large proportion of illegal aliens among the foreign born from Mexico.

Immigrants from countries farther from the United States are more likely to be favorably self-selected as they have higher costs of migration (Chiswick, 1999). This implies a higher level of efficiency in learning English. They also have a lower return migration rate, again because of the higher migration costs. Those from origins at a greater distance from the United States are, therefore, expected to be more fluent (Chiswick and Miller, 1998). This is measured as the number of miles (XMILES) from the major city in the origin to New York, Miami, or Los Angeles, whichever is the shortest. It is entered as a quadratic variable.

While state-specific (fixed) effects are not held constant because the concentration ratio is based on state data, a control variable is entered for Southern states (SOUTH).

STATISTICAL ANALYSIS

The means and standard deviations of the language variable (LANG) and the explanatory variables, overall and separately for Mexican and non-Mexican immigrants, are reported in Table A1. The regression equations for English language proficiency are reported in Table 1 for all immigrants, non-Mexican immigrants, and Mexican immigrants.

The data are found to be consistent with the hypotheses developed above. In particular, English language proficiency is greater the higher the level of schooling, the longer the duration of residence (quadratic effect), the younger the age at immigration (negative effect of age), among those from a former British or American colony, and from countries more distant from the United States. It is less among refugees, among transients (i.e., immigrants who first came to the United States more than 5 years earlier—prior to 1985—but who were outside the United States in 1985), and where the expected duration in the United States (emigration rate variable) is shorter. The linguistic distance variable is not statistically significant when country of origin fixed effects are included in the analysis, as is the case in Table 1, but it is significant with the expected negative effect when the country dichotomous variables are excluded from the equation. This arises from the close relation between country of origin and language of origin.

The minority language concentration variable (CON) is highly statistically significant as is the rural variable (RURAL), which is a proxy for the concentration of foreign language speakers within areas in states. According to the regression for all immigrants, going from a minority language concentration of zero to the mean value of 7.8 percent lowers the

14

IMMIGRANT ADJUSTMENT

TABLE 1. Regression Estimates of Language Equation, Adult Foreign-Born Men by Origin, 1990

Variable	Total Sample[a]	Excludes Immigrants from Mexico[a]	Immigrants from Mexico Only[b]
Constant	0.409	0.478	0.440
	(26.28)	(26.76)	(10.64)
Age	−0.010	−0.011	−0.006
	(15.69)	(16.59)	(3.96)
Age squared/100	0.003	0.006	−0.003
	(4.96)	(7.55)	(1.33)
Years of education	0.029	0.030	0.028
	(141.10)	(119.57)	(64.67)
Years since migration (YSM)	0.021	0.018	0.027
	(100.30)	(83.11)	(48.35)
YSM squared/100	−0.025	−0.023	−0.027
	(56.69)	(50.82)	(22.23)
Married	0.033	0.020	0.053
	(19.29)	(11.02)	(12.06)
Rural	0.010	0.021	0.002
	(3.00)	(6.93)	(0.26)
South	0.013	0.010	0.028
	(7.16)	(5.41)	(5.75)
S. Europe	−0.028	−0.033	c
	(9.47)	(10.88)	
E. Europe	−0.047	−0.063	c
	(12.19)	(15.41)	
USSR	−0.030	−0.039	c
	(4.75)	(6.19)	
IndoChina	−0.090	−0.093	c
	(9.19)	(9.22)	
Philippines	0.024	0.014	c
	(3.43)	(1.78)	
China	−0.123	−0.128	c
	(17.17)	(16.15)	
S. Asia	−0.011	−0.020	c
	(1.38)	(2.26)	
Other Asia	−0.036	−0.044	c
	(3.27)	(3.91)	
Korea	−0.202	−0.207	c
	(21.62)	(18.04)	
Japan	−0.108	−0.116	c
	(10.74)	(9.84)	
Middle East	0.010	0.009	c
	(2.52)	(1.10)	
Sub-Saharan Africa	0.032	0.028	c
	(6.28)	(2.79)	
Mexico	−0.067	c	c
	(12.10)		
Cuba	0.044	0.040	c
	(5.17)	(3.97)	
C. and S. America (Spanish)	−0.019	−0.042	c
	(4.10)	(8.25)	
C. & S. America (non-Spanish)	0.219	0.208	c
	(32.97)	(30.76)	
Minority language concentration	−0.004	−0.003	−0.010
	(17.81)	(9.73)	(7.84)

(*continued overleaf*)

TABLE 1. (Continued.)

Variable	Total Sample[a]	Excludes Immigrants from Mexico[a]	Immigrants from Mexico Only[b]
Linguistic distance	−0.005	−0.006	c
	(0.36)	(0.44)	
Miles from origin/1,000	0.050	0.054	c
	(14.57)	(15.19)	
Square of miles from origin/1,000	−0.034	−0.038	c
	(9.16)	(10.19)	
Refugee	−0.123	−0.138	c
	(32.12)	(35.19)	
Colony	0.012	0.013	c
	(3.53)	(3.90)	
Resident overseas 5 years ago	−0.069	−0.046	−0.073
	(11.34)	(6.76)	(3.13)
Emigration rate	c	−0.010	c
		(2.37)	
Spanish radio	c	c	−21.98
			(4.11)
$\bar{R}^2$	0.3244	0.3176	d
Sample size	237,766	169,253	68,512

[a]Equation estimated using ordinary least squares; [b]equation estimated using instrumental variables (IV) estimator; [c]variable not applicable; [d]R^2 not defined for the IV Model. IV estimator used for Spanish Radio variable.
Note: *t*-statistics have been computed using White's (1980) heteroskedasticity-consistent covariance matrix estimator.
Source: 1990 Census of Population of the United States, Public Use Microdata Sample, 5 percent sample.

probability of being fluent in English by 3.1 percentage points, which is 4.2 percent of the mean proficiency of 0.73 or 73 percent. Rural residence (5.5 percent of the foreign born) raises proficiency by 1.0 percentage point overall and by 2 percentage points among non-Mexican immigrants.

Among Mexican immigrants three variables reflect the effect of the linguistic concentration of Spanish speakers. One is the direct minority language concentration measure, the second is the rural variable, while the third is the (predicted) Spanish language radio station variable. The minority concentration measure and the radio station variable, but not the rural variable, are highly statistically significant with the expected negative signs.

Thus, the analysis of English language proficiency among immigrants from non-English origins in the United States indicates that the data are consistent with the model based on exposure, efficiency, and economic variables. Moreover, it is found that linguistic concentrations or enclaves are associated with a lesser proficiency in English among all, Mexican and non-Mexican immigrants.

ANALYSIS OF EARNINGS

THE EARNINGS MODEL

The econometric analysis of earnings is based on the human capital earnings function, modified for immigrant adjustment (Chiswick, 1978). In this specification, the natural logarithm of annual earnings (LNEARN) is regressed on years of schooling (EDUC), years of potential labor market experience and its square (EXP, EXPSQ), duration in the United States and its square (YSM, YSMSQ), the natural logarithm of weeks worked (LNWW),

IMMIGRANT ADJUSTMENT

marital status (MARR), and place of residence (RURAL, SOUTH). Three dichotomous variables are added to the equation which take the value of unity for immigrants whose race is Black, are Veterans of the U.S. Armed Forces, and who are Citizens of the United States. Two other variables are also added to this equation, the respondent's proficiency in English (LANG), which is unity for those fluent in English, as defined above, and zero otherwise, and the minority language concentration measure (CON).

STATISTICAL ANALYSIS

The earnings equation is estimated separately for all immigrants, Mexican immigrants, and non-Mexican immigrants. The means and standard deviations of the variables are reported in Table A2, while Tables A3–A5 report the regression equations for each group. A basic earnings function in these tables is reported in column (*i*) without the language and concentration variables, column (*ii*) adds the English language proficiency variable (LANG), column (*iii*) adds the concentration variable (CON) to the basic equation, column (*iv*) adds both variables, while column (*v*) substitutes a predicted English language proficiency variable obtained through the IV technique. (The auxiliary equation is reported in Table A6.) A summary of the language and concentration variable results are presented in Table 2.

Ordinary Least Squares Analysis

As has been found elsewhere, the basic determinants of earnings among immigrants are also found to be important here (see Tables A3–A5). For immigrants from non-English speaking countries, earnings increase with years of schooling (by about 5 percent per year of schooling), duration in the United States (at a decreasing rate), preimmigration labor market experience (total experience when duration is held constant), and weeks worked (with an elasticity of annual earnings with respect to weeks worked close to unity), and are higher for married men (by about 20 percent) and citizens (9 percent). Earnings are lower for immigrants who are veterans of the U.S. Armed Forces (8 percent), and among those living in rural areas (4 percent) and in the south (11 percent).

Similar patterns are found when the analysis is done separately for non-Mexican and for Mexican origin immigrants (Tables A4 and A5).[14] Note that the effects of several variables

TABLE 2. Partial Effects on Earnings of the Language and Concentration Variables, Adult Foreign-Born Men from Non-English Speaking Countries, 1990

Variables	Total Sample OLS	Total Sample IV	Excludes Immigrants from Mexico OLS	Excludes Immigrants from Mexico IV	Immigrants from Mexico Only OLS	Immigrants from Mexico Only IV
Proficient in English	0.148	0.592	0.151	0.678	0.146	[a]
	(31.60)	(16.53)	(22.40)	(16.40)	(23.52)	
Minority language concentration	−0.0056	−0.0039	−0.0070	−0.0050	−0.0033	[a]
	(15.25)	(9.62)	(11.77)	(7.85)	(7.13)	

[a] IV equation is not computed for Mexico; *t*-ratios are in parenthesis.
Note: Full regression equations are reported in column (*iv*) and column (*v*) of Tables A3–A5. OLS refers to ordinary least squares. IV refers to instrumental variables technique using predicted value of respondent's proficiency in English.
Source: Tables A3–A5.

reflecting human capital are smaller for Mexican immigrants than for other immigrants. These include schooling, experience, and weeks worked, but not duration in the United States.

The OLS analysis in Tables A3–A5 indicates that earnings are about 15 percent higher for all immigrants, Mexican immigrants and non-Mexican immigrants who are proficient in English, compared to those lacking proficiency. The difference is statistically significant and the magnitude of the effect and level of significance do not vary with whether the concentration measure is included in the analysis.

Assuming a long working life, the real rate of return on the investment in language proficiency can be estimated (approximately) as $r = b/k$, where r is the real rate of return, b is the regression coefficient of the language proficiency variable, and k is the number of full-year equivalents of lost earnings (including out-of-pocket expenditures and foregone earnings), to go from not proficient ("not well," "not at all") to proficient (English only, "very well" or "well"). Then, if the coefficient of the language variable is $b = 0.15$ and if the full cost is the equivalent of a full year's potential earnings ($k = 1$), the rate of return is about 15 percent. If the cost were the equivalent of 2 years of full-time equivalent earnings ($k = 2.0$), the rate of return on the investment would be about 7.5 percent. If proficiency required the equivalent of only 6-months foregone earnings ($k = 0.5$), the estimated rate of return would be about 30 percent. The rate of return would be even higher if the positive effects of proficiency on weeks worked in the year were included in the calculation and if the consumption benefits from English language proficiency could be estimated. Thus, investments in English language skills appear to be profitable for immigrants from non-English speaking countries.

The concentration measure is also statistically significant in all three analyses. Earnings are lower where the concentration index is higher.[15] The coefficient and level of significance are also largely invariant with respect to the inclusion in the analysis of the respondent's fluency in English. Among all immigrants, going from a zero concentration area to the mean level (7.8 percent) lowers earnings by about 4.4 percent (i.e., 7.8 times 0.0056 from Table A3, column (iv)). For non-Mexican immigrants (mean concentration 3.9 percent) it lowers earnings by about 2.7 percent. Among Mexican immigrants, the mean of the concentration ratio is much higher (18.1 percent), but the coefficient of the concentration ratio is lower (−0.0033 compared to −0.0070 for other countries). For Mexican immigrants, the effect of going from a zero concentration to the mean concentration ratio is to lower earnings by about 6.0 percent. Thus, other variables the same, including the respondent's own proficiency in English, living in a linguistic/ethnic concentration area lowers the earnings of immigrants.[16] Moreover, the estimated magnitude of the effect is in a reasonable range.

The effect of the concentration ratio on earnings varies systematically with the level of education. If an education–concentration ratio interaction term is added to the regression in Table A3, column iv, it has a negative and highly significant effect.[17] That is, the adverse effect on earnings from living in a high-concentration area is greater the higher the level of schooling.[18] There is no effect for those with only 5 years of schooling, but the negative effect of living in a high-concentration area grows larger at higher levels of schooling. Alternatively, this can be expressed as the effect of education on earnings is smaller in the high-concentration (enclave) area than in an area where fewer other individuals speak the same origin language.

18

IMMIGRANT ADJUSTMENT

Instrumental Variables Analysis

There are several potential econometric problems with the OLS analysis using the respondent's reported level of English language proficiency. One problem is that language skills may be endogenous to, that is, determined by, earnings. Those who anticipate higher earnings if they were to become proficient will make greater investments to acquire proficiency (Chiswick and Miller, 1995).

A second problem is that there may be substantial measurement error in reported language skill. Purely random measurement error would bias the coefficient toward zero, but the measurement error need not be purely random (Kruger and Dunning, 1999). For example, those who are more successful in the labor market for unmeasured reasons may be more likely to overestimate their English language skills. A positive correlation in the measurement error terms could bias the coefficient upward.

A third problem is that there may be dimensions of ability that are not in the equation, but which enhance both English language proficiency and earnings. Those with greater innate ability among the foreign born may have superior English language skills and earn more, even though the higher earnings may be unrelated to their English proficiency. Yet there are no independent measures of ability in these data. This form of omitted variables bias would tend to overstate the true effect of language skills on earnings in an OLS equation.

Instrumental variables is a statistical technique that can, in principle, correct for these potential problems by using a predicted rather than the observed value of language proficiency. An auxiliary regression is computed (Table A6), which includes at least some variables that are not in the earnings function and which has a more complex functional form (various quadratic and interaction terms) to permit statistical identification. This auxiliary regression is used to obtain predicted values of the language variable, and it is these values, rather than the reported or observed values, that are used in the earnings equation. Because the statistical identification is so dependent on variables that vary across countries of origin, a reliable IV model cannot be estimated using these data for immigrants from only one country, Mexico.

The results for the IV earnings function are reported in column (v) in Tables A3 and A4 and are summarized in Table 2 for all and non-Mexican immigrants. The IV technique results in a very large coefficient for the language proficiency variable. It implies about 80 percent higher earnings for those proficient in English in the all immigrant analysis.[19] Yet, similar very large coefficients on destination language skills have been found elsewhere and for other countries using this technique.[20] Perhaps the unbiased effect of English language fluency on earnings among immigrants is somewhere between the OLS and the IV estimates. Yet, even the OLS estimate of about 15 percent implies a large pay-off from obtaining English language skills.

SUMMARY AND CONCLUSION

SUMMARY

This paper has been concerned with whether immigrant linguistic concentrations or enclaves affect immigrant adjustment in terms of destination language proficiency and earnings.

The reasons for the development of these concentrations are discussed. New immigrants tend to settle near ports of entry, where previous immigrants from their origin (friends and family) have settled and where their employment opportunities are best. The "friends and family" or chain migration effect is a consequence of economies in communication, information, consumption, and the labor market.

"Ethnic goods" are market and nonmarket goods and services consumed by members of an immigrant/ethnic group that are not consumed by others. Ethnic-specific goods are an important factor in location choice. Because of economies of scale in the production of ethnic goods, the full cost of ethnic goods is lower the larger the size of the immigrant/ethnic group. Then an immigrant would be indifferent between working in two alternative areas (equal real wages) only if the area with the high cost ethnic goods (lower concentration ratio) provided a higher nominal wage.

Several hypotheses emerge from the analysis. Linguistic concentrations are expected to have an adverse effect on the destination language proficiency of immigrants. Greater proficiency is expected to result in higher earnings and a larger ethnic/immigrant concentration is expected to have a negative effect on nominal earnings.

The modeling of the language equation is based on three fundamental variables, exposure (pre- and postimmigration) to the destination language, efficiency in destination language acquisition, and economic incentives for destination language acquisition. Variables are developed to measure the effects of these concepts. The concentration ratio and the rural variable measure, in part, postimmigration exposure to the destination language.

The earnings equation is based on the standard human capital earnings function augmented for immigrant adjustment. Two additional variables are the immigrant's proficiency in the destination language and the minority language concentration ratio.

The empirical testing is done using adult (nonaged) male immigrants in the United States from non-English speaking countries as reported in the 1990 Census 5 percent microdata sample. Immigrant language skills are found to vary positively with exposure to the destination language, efficiency in language acquisition, and economic incentives. In particular, English language proficiency is greater the higher the level of schooling, the longer the duration of residence, the younger the age at immigration, the further the origin from the United States, if the origin was a colony of the United States or the United Kingdom, if the immigrant was not a refugee, has a lower probability of return migration, and among immigrants who do not go back and forth between their origin countries and the United States. A smaller minority language concentration ratio and living in a rural area, and hence living among a lower density of origin language speakers, are both associated with greater proficiency in English. Among immigrants from Mexico, greater access to Spanish language radio stations are associated with poorer English language skills.

Annual earnings are found to increase with skill level (schooling, experience, duration in the United States), and weeks worked, and are higher among married men, those living in urban areas outside the south, those who are citizens, and those who are not black. Veteran status is associated with higher earnings among Mexican immigrants, but lower earnings among other immigrants. In the OLS analysis earnings are higher by about 15 percent for those proficient in English, compared to those lacking fluency, and are lower for those living in an area with a higher minority language concentration ratio. The earnings advantage from proficiency is even greater when the respondent's English language proficiency is estimated using the IV technique.

IMMIGRANT ADJUSTMENT

POLICY IMPLICATIONS

The answer to the question in the title is "yes." Enclaves matter for immigrant adjustment. Immigrant linguistic concentrations are associated with a lower level of proficiency in the destination language (English). Poorer English language skills result in lower nominal and real earnings. Even after controlling for one's own language skills, living within an immigrant/ethnic concentration area also results in lower nominal earnings, presumably because of the ethnic goods effect. Thus, linguistic concentrations have both an indirect effect (via destination language skills) and a direct effect on lowering the observed earnings of immigrants. The direct effect of concentration on earnings may be an equilibrium situation, where earnings differences are compensating differentials reflecting geographic differences in the cost of ethnic goods.

Immigrant/linguistic concentrations serve a useful role. They provide information networks and channels of communication in consumption and in the labor market for those without, or with only limited, destination-specific information and language proficiency, and they lower the cost of ethnic goods. On the other hand, they tend to retard the acquisition of, or investment in, destination-specific skills (e.g., language proficiency) and to lower nominal earnings. The assimilation or adjustment of immigrants is enhanced the smaller the extent of the immigrant/ethnic concentration.

It would be difficult to implement incentives for immigrants to settle outside of concentrated areas for their group. Focusing immigration on countries of origin "culturally similar" to the United States would be an unwarranted return to the pernicious national origins quota system in place from 1921 to 1965. A reduced emphasis on family ties in issuing immigration visas, and placing a greater emphasis on the applicant's own skills is likely to increase the diversity of origins and reduce the extent of immigrant–linguistic concentrations.

Yet, in the highly mobile United States these concentrations tend to be first generation, and at most also second-generation, phenomena. Reliance on self-correcting mechanisms is likely to be the most effective public policy, such as the acquisition of English language skills and the decline in the importance in the market basket of ethnic goods with a longer duration of residence.

Acknowledgments

Earlier versions of this paper were presented at the Conference on Magnet Societies, Loccum, Germany, June 2000, the Annual Meeting of the European Society for Population Economics, June 2000, Bonn, Germany, the Joint Center for Poverty Research, Northwestern University, February 2001, the Education and Employment Economics Group (UK) Annual Meeting, Leicester, July 2001, the Annual Meeting of the American Economic Association, Atlanta, January 2002, the Center for Economic Policy Research Conference on Discrimination and Unequal Outcomes, Le Mans, France, January 2002, the Gideon Fishelson Lecture at Tel Aviv University, January 2003, the Institute of Government and Public Affairs, University of Illinois at Chicago, October 2003, conference Trading Borders: Migration, Ethnicity and Incorporation in the Age of Globalism, New York, October 2003, and Department of Economics seminars at George Washington University (November 2001) and Hebrew University, Jerusalem (December 2001). Comments received from participants at these presentations are appreciated although all errors of omission and commission are solely those of the authors.

CITY & COMMUNITY

Chiswick acknowledges the research support of the Institute of Government and Public Affairs, University of Illinois, and Miller acknowledges the support of an Australian Research Council grant. This paper received the Milken Institute Award for Distinguished Research in Regional and Demographic Studies, 2001, and an earlier version with the same title was published in Hebrew in Revon L'Kalcalah (Vol. 50, No. 2, June 2003).

Notes

[1] Other work on the determinants of immigrant or ethnic concentrations include Bartel (1989), Brettell (2003), Cutler and Glaeser (1977), Lazear (1999), Bauer, Epstein, and Gang (2002), and Sierminska (2002). Lazear (1999, p. S99) describes concentrations as forming "in large part because doing so enhances trade" in market and non-market goods and services.

[2] Epstein (2003) distinguishes theoretically between "herd behavior" and "network externalities" in the choice of destination among those from the same origin. Herd behavior refers to following those from the same origin, even if they are few in number, under the belief that they have better information, while "network externalities" implies a larger group and a lower cost of settlement in a specific destination because of linguistic and information networks.

[3] Ross (2002) develops a model in which preferences for social interaction by the majority or a minority (whether negative as in prejudice or positive as in cultural affinity) result in social segregation of neighborhoods.

[4] For research on network externalities see Economides (1996) and Katz and Shapiro (1985).

[5] Distinctiveness is important as the ethnic goods of English immigrants to the United States would be much less distinctive than would those of, say, Chinese immigrants. To some extent the cost of ethnic goods can be reduced if the host society "adopts" the ethnic good, as, for example, often happens for certain foods, such as in Chinese restaurants. The "Americanized" version of the ethnic good may well differ from the version consumed in the origin or by members of the ethnic group in the destination.

[6] For a study of consumer network markets and group size, see Etziony and Weiss (2001).

[7] For a discussion of Chinese schools, see Zhou and Li (2003).

[8] Workers of a given level of skill can be thought of as randomly drawing wage offers from a given distribution of wage offers available in the high concentration and the low-concentration areas. If ethnic goods are an important part of their market basket, the ethnic immigrants will move to or stay in a low-concentration area only if their wage offer in this area exceeds by a sufficient margin the wage offer from the high-concentration area to compensate for the higher cost of living. Once settled in a specific area explicit and implicit location-specific investments in human capital, relevant for consumption and the labor market, tend to reduce subsequent migrations. Thus, those who leave a high concentration enclave for a low or zero concentration area will tend to be those who receive a high wage offer in the latter location and those for whom ethnic goods (including ties to the ethnic community) are least important.

[9] The "ethnic goods" concept and its implications for concentrations and wage differentials can be applied to other affinity groups, for example, the gay population.

[10] In the data under study for earnings, Mexican immigrants are 29 percent of the sample and have a mean schooling level of 7.9 years, in contrast to 13.3 years for the other immigrants.

[11] The definition of the population under study and the variables used in the analysis are described in more detail in Appendix B.

[12] Bertrand, Luttmer, and Mullainathan (2002) also use language as the basis for their "networks" (concentrations) in an analysis of welfare participation.

[13] The finding that a higher level of secular schooling is associated with greater proficiency in Hebrew among immigrants in Israel suggests that exposure to English in school prior to immigration is not the primary

22

IMMIGRANT ADJUSTMENT

mechanism for the positive effect of schooling on English language skills in the United States (Chiswick and Repetto, 2001).

[14] On the other hand, the effect of having been in the U.S. Armed Forces differs sharply between these two groups. Veteran status is associated with about 8 percent higher earnings for Mexican immigrants but 10 percent lower earnings for non-Mexican immigrants.

[15] Clark and Drinkwater (2002) find that unemployment rates for racial and ethnic minorities are higher among those living in ethnically concentrated areas of England and Wales.

[16] The labor supply or "crowding" hypothesis would imply a larger coefficient on the concentration measure for Mexican immigrants than for the much more heterogeneous group of immigrants from other countries. That the opposite is found suggests that the negative relation between concentration and earnings is not a consequence of ethnic crowding in the labor market.

[17] Partial effects of education and the concentration ratio on earnings:

	Table A3 Column *iv*	Table A3, Column (*iv*), Plus Interaction
Education	0.045	0.056
	(82.9)	(78.3)
Minority Language	−0.0056	0.0062
Concentration	(15.3)	(10.9)
Education-Concentration Interaction	—	−0.0012 (26.9)

[18] For a similar finding for Sweden, see Edin, Fredriksson, and Aslund (2002).

[19] The regression coefficient is $\ln(1 + X) = 0.59$, where X is the percentage increase in earnings. X is then 0.80 or 80 percent. $\ln(1 + X)$ is approximately equal to X when X is a small number. When $\ln(1 + X) = 0.15$, X is approximately 16 percent.

[20] See Chiswick and Miller (1995), and the references therein, for the United States, Canada, Australia, and Israel, and Dustmann and van Soest (2001) for Germany. The difference between the OLS and IV effects on earnings is much smaller in the United Kingdom (Dustmann and Fabbri, 2000).

References

Ahmed, B., and Robinson, J. G. 1994. *Estimates of Emigration of the Foreign-Born Population, 1980–1990*. Technical Working Paper No. 9. Washington, DC: U.S. Bureau of the Census.
Bartel, A. 1989. "Where Do the New Immigrants Live?" *Journal of Labor Economics* 7(4), 371–391.
Bauer, T., Epstein, G. S., and Gang, I. N. 2002. *Enclaves, Language and the Location Choice of Migrants*. Institute for the Study of Labor, Bonn, Xerox.
Bertrand, M., Luttmer, E. F. P., and Mullainathan, S. 2002. "Network Effects and Welfare Cultures," *Quarterly Journal of Economics* August, 1019–1055.
Brettell, C. 2003. "Meet Me at the Chat Corner: The Embeddedness of Immigrant Entrepreneurs," Department of Anthropology, Southern Methodist University, Dallas.
Broadcasting and Cable Yearbook, 1994. 1994. New Providence. NJ: R.R. Bowker Publishers.
Chiswick, B. R. 1978. "The Effect of Americanization on the Earnings of Foreign-Born Men," *Journal of Political Economy* 86(5), 897–922.
Chiswick, B. R. 1999. "Are Immigrants Favorably Self-Selected?" *American Economic Review*, 89(2), 181–185.
Chiswick, B. R., and Hatton, T. 2003. "International Migration and the Integration of Labor Markets," in M. D. Bordo, A. M. Taylor, and J. Williamson (eds.), *Globalization in Historical Perspective*, pp. 65–119. Cambridge: National Bureau of Economic Research.

Chiswick, B. R., and Miller, P. W. 1992. "Language in the Immigrant Labor Market" in B. R. Chiswick (ed.), *Immigration, Language and Ethnicity: Canada and the United States*, pp. 229–296. Washington: American Enterprise Institute.

Chiswick, B. R., and Miller, P. W. 1995. "The Endogeneity Between Language and Earnings: International Analyses," *Journal of Labor Economics* 13(2), 246–288.

Chiswick, B. R., and Miller, P. W. 1998. "English Language Fluency Among Immigrants in the United States," *Research in Labor Economics* 17, 151–200.

Chiswick, B. R., and Miller, P. W. 2003. "The Complementarity of Language and Other Human Capital: Immigrant Earnings in Canada," *Economics of Education Review* 22, 469–480.

Chiswick, B. R., and Repetto, G. 2001. "Immigrant Adjustment in Israel: Literacy and Fluency in Hebrew and Earnings," in S. Djajic (ed.), *International Migration: Trends, Policy and Economic Impact*, pp. 204–228. New York: Routledge.

Clark, K., and Drinkwater, S. 2002. "Enclaves, Neighbourhood Effects and Employment Outcomes: Ethnic Minorities in England and Wales," *Journal of Population Economics* 15, 5–29.

Cutler, D. M., and Glaeser, E. L. 1997. "Are Ghettos Good or Bad?" *Quarterly Journal of Economics* 112, 827–872.

Dustmann, C., and Fabbri, F. 2000. "Language Proficiency and Labor Market Performance in the UK," University College London, London, Xerox.

Dustmann, C., and van Soest, A. 2001. "Language Fluency and Earnings: Estimation with Misclassified Language Indicators," *Review of Economics and Statistics* 83(4), 663–674.

Economides, N. 1996. "The Economics of Networks," *International Journal of Industrial Organization* 14, 673–699.

Edin, P.-A., Fredriksson, P., and Aslund, O. 2002. "Ethnic Enclaves and the Economic Success of Immigrants—Evidence from a Natural Experiment," Department of Economics, Uppsala University, Sweden.

Epstein, G. S. 2003. "Informational Cascades and the Decision to Migrate," Department of Economics, Bar Ilan University.

Etziony, A., and Weiss, A. 2001. "Coordination and Critical Mass in a Network Market: An Experimental Evaluation," Department of Economics, Bar Ilan University, October, Xerox.

Fitzpatrick, G. L., and Modlin, M. J. 1986. *Direct-line Distances: United States Edition*. Metuchen, NJ: The Scarecrow Press, Inc.

Grimes, J. E., and Grimes, B. F. 1993. *Ethnologue: Languages of the World*, (13th ed.). Dallas: Summer Institute of Linguistics.

Hart-Gonzalez, L., and Lindermann, S. 1993. "Expected Achievement in Speaking Proficiency, 1993," School of Language Studies, Foreign Service Institute, U.S. Department of State, Mimeographed.

Katz, M., and Shapiro, C. 1985. "Network Externalities, Competition and Compatibility," *American Economic Review* 75, 424–440.

Kruger, J., and Dunning, D. 1999. "Unskilled and Unaware of it: How Difficulties in Recognizing One's Own Competence Lead to Inflated Self-Assessments," *Journal of Personality and Social Psychology* 77(6), 1121–1134.

Lazear, E. P. 1999. "Culture and Language," *Journal of Political Economy* 107(6, part 2), pp. S95–S126.

Ross, S. 2002. "Segregation and Racial Preferences: An Analysis of Choice Based on Satisfaction and Outcome Measures," Paper presented at the conference on Discrimination and Unequal Outcomes, Le Mans, France.

Sierminska, E. 2002. "Immigrants and State Clustering: Effect of Welfare Benefits," Department of Economics, Johns Hopkins University, October, Xerox.

White, H. 1980. "A Heteroskedastic Consistent Covariance Matrix Estimator and a Direct Test for Heteroskedasticity," *Econometrica* 48, 817–838.

Zhou, M., and Li, Y.-Y. 2003. "Ethnic Language Schools and the Development of Supplementary Education in an Immigrant Chinese Community in the U.S.," Department of Sociology, UCLA.

IMMIGRANT ADJUSTMENT

APPENDIX A

TABLE A1. Means and Standard Deviations of Variables, Sample Used for Language Model

Variable	Total Sample	Excludes Immigrants from Mexico	Immigrants from Mexico Only
English proficiency	0.730	0.808	0.524
	(0.44)	(0.39)	(0.50)
Age	37.79	40.92	36.83
	(10.63)	(10.75)	(9.69)
Years of education	11.63	13.09	7.80
	(4.99)	(4.27)	(4.69)
Years since migration	15.21	15.43	14.64
	(11.08)	(11.51)	(9.84)
Married	0.655	0.673	0.610
	(0.48)	(0.47)	(0.49)
Rural	0.055	0.042	0.089
	(0.23)	(0.20)	(0.28)
South	0.237	0.234	0.244
	(0.43)	(0.42)	(0.43)
S. Europe	0.078	0.107	[a]
	(0.27)	(0.31)	
E. Europe	0.036	0.049	[a]
	(0.19)	(0.22)	
USSR	0.016	0.022	[a]
	(0.12)	(0.15)	
IndoChina	0.048	0.066	[a]
	(0.21)	(0.25)	
Philippines	0.051	0.070	[a]
	(0.22)	(0.26)	
China	0.062	0.085	[a]
	(0.24)	(0.28)	
S. Asia	0.049	0.067	[a]
	(0.21)	(0.25)	
Other Asia	0.012	0.016	[a]
	(0.11)	(0.13)	
Korea	0.031	0.044	[a]
	(0.17)	(0.20)	
Japan	0.015	0.020	[a]
	(0.12)	(0.14)	
Middle East	0.060	0.083	[a]
	(0.24)	(0.28)	
Sub-Saharan Africa	0.024	0.034	[a]
	(0.15)	(0.18)	
Mexico	(0.276)	0.00	1.00
	(0.45)	(0.00)	(0.00)
Cuba	0.051	0.070	[a]
	(0.22)	(0.26)	
C. and S. America (Spanish)	0.125	0.173	[a]
	(0.33)	(0.38)	
C. and S. America (non-Spanish)	0.009	0.012	[a]
	(0.09)	(0.11)	
Minority language concentration	7.784	3.816	18.178
	(8.87)	(6.19)	(5.95)
Linguistic distance	0.515	0.542	[a]
	(0.15)	(0.17)	

(*continued overleaf*)

25

TABLE A1. (Continued.)

Variable	Total Sample	Excludes Immigrants from Mexico	Immigrants from Mexico Only
Miles from origin	3841.1	4756.6	a
	(2574.9)	(2475.4)	
Refugee	0.096	0.133	a
	(0.29)	(0.34)	
Colony	0.147	0.203	a
	(0.35)	(0.40)	
Resident overseas 5 years ago	0.019	0.017	0.025
	(0.14)	(0.13)	(0.16)
Emigration rate	a	2.049	a
		(0.76)	
Spanish radio	a	a	0.002
			(0.01)
Sample size	237,766	169,253	68,512

Note: Standard errors are in parentheses.
[a] Variable not applicable.
Source: 1990 Census of Population of the United States, Public Use Microdata Sample, 5 percent sample.

TABLE A2. Means and Standard Deviations of Variables, Sample Used for Earnings Model

Variable	Total Sample	Excludes Immigrants from Mexico	Immigrants from Mexico Only
Natural log of earnings	9.787	9.942	9.387
	(1.03)	(1.04)	(0.90)
English proficiency	0.747	0.830	0.535
	(0.43)	(0.38)	(0.50)
Labor market experience	22.76	22.41	23.63
	(11.46)	(11.53)	(11.25)
Years of education	11.79	13.30	7.90
	(4.92)	(4.11)	(4.68)
Years since migration	15.43	15.75	14.60
	(10.85)	(11.30)	(9.52)
Married	0.673	0.691	0.627
	(0.47)	(0.46)	(0.48)
Rural	0.057	0.044	0.091
	(0.23)	(0.20)	(0.29)
South	0.240	0.238	0.244
	(0.43)	(0.43)	(0.43)
Race (Black)	0.033	0.044	0.004
	(0.18)	(0.21)	(0.06)
Citizen	0.417	0.484	0.247
	(0.49)	(0.50)	(0.43)
Veteran	0.068	0.083	0.030
	(0.25)	(0.28)	(0.17)
Log weeks worked	3.752	3.774	3.693
	(0.47)	(0.46)	(0.51)
S. Europe	0.078	0.108	a
	(0.27)	(0.31)	
E. Europe	0.036	0.050	a
	(0.19)	(0.22)	
USSR	0.013	0.019	a
	(0.12)	(0.14)	
IndoChina	0.041	0.057	a
	(0.20)	(0.23)	

IMMIGRANT ADJUSTMENT

TABLE A2. (Continued.)

Variable	Total Sample	Excludes Immigrants from Mexico	Immigrants from Mexico Only
Philippines	0.053	0.073	a
	(0.22)	(0.26)	
China	0.061	0.085	a
	(0.24)	(0.28)	
S. Asia	0.051	0.071	a
	(0.22)	(0.26)	
Other Asia	0.011	0.016	a
	(0.11)	(0.12)	
Korea	0.031	0.043	a
	(0.17)	(0.20)	
Japan	0.015	0.021	a
	(0.12)	(0.14)	
Middle East	0.059	0.082	a
	(0.24)	(0.27)	
Sub-Saharan Africa	0.024	0.034	a
	(0.15)	(0.18)	
Mexico	0.279	0.00	1.00
	(0.45)	(0.00)	(0.00)
Cuba	0.051	0.069	a
	(0.22)	(0.25)	
C. and S. America (Spanish)	0.127	0.176	a
	(0.33)	(0.38)	
C. and S. America (non-Spanish)	0.009	0.012	a
	(0.09)	(0.11)	
Minority language concentration	7.834	3.850	18.129
	(8.88)	(6.21)	(6.00)
Sample size	212,381	150,680	61,700

Note: Standard errors are in parentheses.
[a]Variable not applicable.
Source: 1990 Census of Population of the United States, Public Use Microdata Sample, 5 percent sample.

TABLE A3. Regression Estimates of Earnings Equation, Adult Foreign-Born Men from Non-English Speaking Countries, 1990

Variable	OLS (i)	(ii)	(iii)	(iv)	IV (v)
Constant	5.063	5.006	5.074	5.017	4.845
	(173.18)	(171.67)	(173.47)	(171.96)	(150.58)
Years of education	0.049	0.045	0.048	0.045	0.035
	(91.10)	(83.48)	(90.24)	(82.85)	(35.19)
Experience	0.023	0.025	0.023	0.025	0.029
	(35.72)	(38.04)	(35.77)	(38.04)	(38.55)
Experience squared/100	−0.037	−0.038	−0.038	−0.038	−0.041
	(31.33)	(32.20)	(31.47)	(32.30)	(33.27)
Years since migration (YSM)	0.028	0.025	0.028	0.025	0.017
	(49.29)	(43.73)	(49.76)	(44.24)	(18.36)
YSM squared/100	−0.039	−0.035	−0.039	−0.036	−0.026
	(30.24)	(27.56)	(30.54)	(27.88)	(16.85)
Log of weeks worked	0.970	0.964	0.967	0.963	0.952
	(135.52)	(134.94)	(135.43)	(134.88)	(131.21)
Married	0.213	0.208	0.214	0.209	0.195
	(55.22)	(54.02)	(55.43)	(54.23)	(47.54)

(*continued overleaf*)

TABLE A3. (Continued.)

	OLS				IV
Variable	(i)	(ii)	(iii)	(iv)	(v)
Rural	−0.037	−0.038	−0.043	−0.044	−0.047
	(4.67)	(4.89)	(5.43)	(5.58)	(5.89)
South	−0.112	−0.113	−0.109	−0.110	−0.113
	(26.11)	(26.36)	(25.40)	(25.71)	(25.90)
Race (Black)	−0.182	−0.190	−0.187	−0.195	−0.218
	(12.36)	(12.95)	(12.68)	(13.22)	(14.48)
Veteran	−0.078	−0.080	−0.079	−0.081	−0.085
	(10.25)	(10.48)	(10.39)	(10.61)	(11.12)
Citizen	0.090	0.082	0.088	0.080	0.056
	(21.36)	(19.35)	(20.87)	(18.94)	(11.83)
S. Europe	−0.063	−0.060	−0.058	−0.056	−0.049
	(6.23)	(5.98)	(5.70)	(5.51)	(4.85)
E. Europe	−0.077	−0.073	−0.077	−0.074	−0.062
	(6.40)	(6.09)	(6.44)	(6.13)	(5.14)
USSR	−0.133	−0.125	−0.134	−0.127	−0.103
	(7.37)	(6.95)	(7.43)	(7.02)	(5.65)
IndoChina	−0.282	−0.270	−0.283	−0.271	−0.236
	(23.21)	(22.31)	(23.31)	(22.42)	(19.02)
Philippines	−0.224	−0.234	−0.217	−0.227	−0.259
	(21.11)	(22.07)	(20.39)	(21.39)	(23.42)
China	−0.274	−0.254	−0.270	−0.251	−0.193
	(24.10)	(22.41)	(23.73)	(22.11)	(15.84)
S. Asia	−0.021	−0.028	−0.023	−0.029	−0.049
	(1.83)	(2.41)	(2.00)	(2.55)	(4.13)
Other Asia	−0.201	−0.203	−0.202	−0.203	−0.208
	(10.45)	(10.54)	(10.49)	(10.57)	(10.70)
Korea	−0.233	−0.209	−0.233	−0.209	−0.137
	(14.95)	(13.41)	(14.94)	(13.43)	(8.25)
Japan	0.347	0.357	0.347	0.357	0.389
	(18.75)	(19.45)	(18.76)	(19.44)	(20.97)
Middle East	−0.098	−0.104	−0.099	−0.105	−0.122
	(8.26)	(8.77)	(8.36)	(8.85)	(10.18)
Sub-Saharan Africa	−0.064	−0.070	−0.062	−0.068	−0.087
	(3.38)	(3.71)	(3.29)	(3.62)	(4.54)
Mexico	−0.341	−0.313	−0.235	−0.218	−0.167
	(37.39)	(34.39)	(21.28)	(19.80)	(14.23)
Cuba	−0.242	−0.216	−0.172	−0.153	−0.095
	(21.54)	(19.22)	(14.35)	(12.77)	(7.44)
C. and S. America (Spanish)	−0.244	−0.227	−0.168	−0.158	−0.129
	(25.62)	(23.89)	(15.93)	(15.05)	(11.96)
C. and S. America (non-Spanish)	−0.081	−0.100	−0.073	−0.092	−0.150
	(3.61)	(4.45)	(3.27)	(4.12)	(6.47)
Proficient in English	a	0.151	a	0.148	0.592
		(32.26)		(31.60)	(16.53)
Minority language concentration	a	a	−0.0062	−0.0056	−0.0039
			(16.75)	(15.25)	(9.62)
$\bar{R}^2$	0.4157	0.4185	0.4164	0.4190	b
Sample size	212,381	212,381	212,381	212,381	212,381

[a]Variable not entered; [b]R^2 not defined for the IV Model, IV estimator used for Proficient in English variable. t-statistics have been computed using White's (1980) heteroskedasticity-consistent covariance matrix estimator.
Source: 1990 Census of Population of the United States, Public Use Microdata Sample, 5 percent sample.

IMMIGRANT ADJUSTMENT

TABLE A4. Regression Estimates of Earnings Equation, Adult Foreign-Born Men from Non-English Speaking Countries Other than Mexico, 1990

Variable	OLS (i)	OLS (ii)	OLS (iii)	OLS (iv)	IV (v)
Constant	4.824	4.757	4.839	4.773	4.542
	(132.90)	(131.27)	(133.15)	(131.52)	(111.69)
Years of education	0.058	0.055	0.058	0.054	0.041
	(85.04)	(77.84)	(83.96)	(76.98)	(33.96)
Experience	0.023	0.025	0.024	0.025	0.030
	(29.48)	(31.39)	(29.80)	(31.64)	(33.21)
Experience squared/100	−0.037	−0.038	−0.038	−0.039	−0.042
	(24.66)	(25.42)	(25.05)	(25.77)	(26.90)
Years since migration (YSM)	0.026	0.024	0.027	0.024	0.016
	(37.82)	(33.87)	(38.05)	(34.15)	(15.63)
YSM squared/100	−0.037	−0.034	−0.038	−0.035	−0.024
	(24.46)	(22.43)	(24.66)	(22.64)	(13.87)
Log of weeks worked	0.994	0.991	0.994	0.990	0.978
	(108.94)	(108.53)	(108.89)	(108.50)	(105.98)
Married	0.218	0.215	0.217	0.215	0.205
	(44.77)	(44.23)	(44.70)	(44.18)	(40.86)
Rural	−0.002	−0.005	−0.006	−0.009	−0.018
	(0.18)	(0.43)	(0.50)	(0.72)	(1.48)
South	−0.087	−0.088	−0.091	−0.091	−0.093
	(16.22)	(16.38)	(16.85)	(16.95)	(16.90)
Race (Black)	−0.189	−0.197	−0.196	−0.203	−0.228
	(12.25)	(12.77)	(12.65)	(13.13)	(14.40)
Veteran	−0.093	−0.095	−0.094	−0.095	−0.101
	(11.12)	(11.33)	(11.18)	(11.38)	(11.90)
Citizen	0.107	0.098	0.105	0.097	0.069
	(19.99)	(18.41)	(19.63)	(18.12)	(11.85)
S. Europe	−0.028	−0.025	−0.023	−0.020	−0.012
	(2.72)	(2.46)	(2.18)	(1.96)	(1.17)
E. Europe	−0.069	−0.063	−0.071	−0.065	−0.045
	(5.66)	(5.21)	(5.81)	(5.36)	(3.67)
USSR	−0.133	−0.123	−0.136	−0.125	−0.090
	(7.28)	(6.74)	(7.44)	(6.90)	(4.84)
IndoChina	−0.266	−0.251	−0.269	−0.253	−0.199
	(21.30)	(20.11)	(21.50)	(20.32)	(15.19)
Philippines	−0.225	−0.232	−0.217	−0.225	−0.253
	(20.62)	(21.33)	(19.91)	(20.66)	(22.53)
China	−0.274	−0.251	−0.270	−0.248	−0.169
	(23.67)	(21.67)	(23.33)	(21.39)	(12.94)
S. Asia	−0.041	−0.044	−0.043	−0.047	−0.058
	(3.45)	(3.75)	(3.69)	(3.96)	(4.85)
Other Asia	−0.207	−0.206	−0.209	−0.207	−0.203
	(10.68)	(10.63)	(10.77)	(10.71)	(10.36)
Korea	−0.237	−0.208	−0.238	−0.210	−0.112
	(14.94)	(13.17)	(15.01)	(13.26)	(6.40)
Japan	0.339	0.353	0.338	0.352	−0.402
	(18.12)	(18.99)	(18.07)	(18.93)	(21.06)
Middle East	−0.105	−0.108	−0.107	−0.110	−0.121
	(8.72)	(9.01)	(8.89)	(9.16)	(9.99)
Sub-Saharan Africa	−0.071	−0.074	−0.068	−0.071	−0.082
	(3.63)	(3.78)	(3.48)	(3.65)	(4.17)

(*continued overleaf*)

TABLE A4. (Continued.)

	OLS				IV
Variable	(i)	(ii)	(iii)	(iv)	(v)
Cuba	−0.230	−0.203	−0.141	−0.120	−0.051
	(19.99)	(17.56)	(10.42)	(8.93)	(3.48)
C. and S. America (Spanish)	−0.217	−0.197	−0.124	−0.112	−0.067
	(22.14)	(20.07)	(10.21)	(9.17)	(5.25)
C. and S. America (non-Spanish)	−0.060	−0.077	−0.052	−0.069	−0.129
	(2.62)	(3.36)	(2.25)	(3.00)	(5.44)
Proficient in English	a	0.154	a	0.151	0.678
		(22.82)		(22.40)	(16.40)
Minority language concentration	a	a	−0.0076	−0.0070	−0.0050
			(12.71)	(11.77)	(7.85)
$\bar{R}^2$	0.3770	0.3792	0.3776	0.3797	b
Sample size	150,680	150,680	150,680	150,680	150,680

[a]Variable not entered; [b]R^2 not defined for the IV Model. IV estimator for Proficient in English variable. *t*-statistics have been computed using White's (1980) heteroskedasticity-consistent covariance matrix estimator.
Source: 1990 Census of Population of the United States, Public Use Microdata Sample, 5 percent sample.

TABLE A5. Regression Estimates of Earnings Equation, Adult Foreign-Born Men from Mexico, 1990

	OLS			
Variable	(i)	(ii)	(iii)	(iv)
Constant	5.208	5.194	5.279	5.254
	(115.30)	(115.28)	(114.92)	(114.70)
Years of education	0.027	0.024	0.027	0.024
	(29.94)	(26.67)	(29.77)	(26.58)
Experience	0.015	0.016	0.015	0.016
	(12.23)	(13.35)	(12.11)	(13.23)
Experience squared/100	−0.026	−0.026	−0.025	−0.026
	(12.74)	(12.90)	(12.64)	(12.81)
Years since migration (YSM)	0.029	0.025	0.029	0.025
	(29.47)	(25.36)	(29.82)	(25.70)
YSM squared/100	−0.037	−0.033	−0.037	−0.033
	(15.40)	(13.69)	(15.57)	(13.85)
Log of weeks worked	0.918	0.913	0.918	0.913
	(82.30)	(81.83)	(82.25)	(81.79)
Married	0.207	0.199	0.208	0.200
	(33.54)	(32.43)	(33.78)	(32.65)
Rural	−0.098	−0.099	−0.105	−0.105
	(10.58)	(10.73)	(11.27)	(11.29)
South	−0.184	−0.184	−0.174	−0.175
	(26.73)	(26.81)	(24.85)	(25.16)
Race (Black)	−0.039	−0.055	−0.038	−0.054
	(0.82)	(1.16)	(0.80)	(1.14)
Veteran	0.087	0.078	0.085	0.076
	(4.73)	(4.24)	(4.63)	(4.17)
Citizen	0.042	0.028	0.040	0.026
	(6.17)	(4.04)	(5.86)	(3.82)
Proficient in English	a	0.149	a	0.146
		(23.98)		(23.52)
Minority language concentration	a	a	−0.0039	−0.0033
			(8.53)	(7.13)
$\bar{R}^2$	0.4080	0.4135	0.4086	0.4139
Sample size	61,700	61,700	61,700	61,700

[a]Variable not entered; *t*-statistics have been computed using White's (1980) heteroskedasticity-consistent covariance matrix estimator.
Source: 1990 Census of Population of the United States, Public Use Microdata Sample, 5 percent sample.

IMMIGRANT ADJUSTMENT

TABLE A6. Regression Estimates of Language Equation Used in IV Estimation, Adult Foreign-Born Men by Origin, 1990

Variable	Total Sample	Excludes Immigrants from Mexico
Constant	0.350	0.398
	(25.24)	(24.06)
Experience	−0.007	−0.007
	(23.10)	(21.09)
Experience squared/100	0.004	0.004
	(6.62)	(6.87)
Years of education	0.022	0.022
	(67.15)	(65.15)
Years since migration (YSM)	0.013	0.012
	(54.17)	(44.62)
YSM squared/100	−0.019	−0.016
	(41.42)	(33.24)
Married	0.028	0.016
	(15.33)	(8.35)
Rural	0.010	0.020
	(3.07)	(6.62)
South	0.005	0.004
	(2.53)	(2.15)
Citizen	0.064	0.055
	(33.65)	(27.59)
Race (Black)	0.068	0.065
	(12.22)	(11.61)
Veteran	0.019	0.012
	(8.46)	(5.17)
Natural logarithm of weeks worked	0.026	0.022
	(14.14)	(10.77)
S. Europe	−0.055	−0.056
	(18.47)	(18.16)
E. Europe	−0.072	−0.087
	(18.72)	(20.88)
USSR	−0.039	−0.053
	(6.22)	(8.22)
IndoChina	−0.156	−0.134
	(15.12)	(12.78)
Philippines	−0.065	−0.038
	(9.10)	(4.72)
China	−0.163	−0.144
	(21.67)	(17.56)
S. Asia	−0.102	−0.072
	(12.31)	(7.79)
Other Asia	−0.120	−0.100
	(10.44)	(8.15)
Korea	−0.242	−0.196
	(25.25)	(16.82)
Japan	−0.137	−0.101
	(13.30)	(8.42)
Middle East	−0.038	0.008
	(9.17)	(0.99)
Sub-Saharan Africa	−0.081	−0.024
	(10.71)	(2.04)
Mexico	−0.110	a
	(18.91)	

(*continued overleaf*)

TABLE A6. (Continued.)

Variable	Total Sample	Excludes Immigrants from Mexico
Cuba	−0.024	−0.008
	(2.66)	(0.73)
C. and S. America (Spanish)	−0.057	−0.053
	(11.40)	(9.84)
C. and S. America (non-Spanish)	0.106	0.133
	(13.69)	(15.99)
Minority language concentration (CON)	0.028	0.022
	(7.61)	(5.76)
Linguistic distance	−0.002	0.009
	(0.16)	(0.59)
Miles from origin/1,000	0.035	0.047
	(8.43)	(10.12)
Square of miles from origin/10 m.	−0.012	−0.023
	(2.85)	(5.08)
Refugee	−0.116	−0.113
	(28.94)	(27.36)
Colony	0.019	0.022
	(5.70)	(6.57)
Resident overseas 5 years ago	−0.066	−0.045
	(10.37)	(6.37)
Emigration rate	a	−0.033
		(7.61)
CON × years of education/1,000	−0.024	0.103
	(0.84)	(2.12)
CON × experience/1,000	−0.206	−0.270
	(17.89)	(15.59)
CON × YSM/1,000	0.527	0.666
	(50.63)	(37.23)
CON × linguistic distance	−0.078	−0.078
	(9.26)	(9.11)
CON × miles from origin/1 m	0.181	−0.349
	(1.40)	(2.41)
CON × emigration rate	a	0.003
		(8.00)
$\bar{R}^2$	0.3345	0.3164
Sample Size	212,381	150,680

[a]Variable note entered; t-statistics have been computed using White's (1980) heteroskedasticity-consistent covariance matrix estimator.
Source: 1990 Census of Population of the United States, Public Use Microdata Sample, 5 percent sample.

APPENDIX B

DEFINITIONS OF VARIABLES

The variables used in the statistical analyses are defined below. Mnemonic names are also listed where relevant. The means and standard deviations are reported in Appendix Tables A1 and A2 for the samples used in the analyses of language attainment and earnings, respectively.

Data Source: 1990 Census of Population, Public Use Microdata Sample, 5 percent sample of the foreign born, except where noted otherwise.

IMMIGRANT ADJUSTMENT

Definition of Population: The sample used in this study comprises foreign-born men aged 25 to 64, born in countries other than the English-speaking developed countries (UK, Ireland, Canada, Australia, New Zealand), territories of the United States, at sea, or born abroad of American parents. Those who worked 0 weeks in 1989 were deleted from the analysis of earnings, as they were not labor force participants.

DEPENDENT VARIABLES

English Language Fluency (LANG): LANG is set equal to 1 for individuals who speak only English at home, or if a language other than English is spoken in the home, who speak English either "very well" or "well." The variable is set to 0 where a language other than English is spoken in the home and the respondent speaks English either "not well" or "not at all."

Earnings (LNEARN): The natural logarithm of the sum of wage or salary income and self-employment income (either nonfarm or farm) received in 1989. Individuals with earnings less than $100, including those with negative earnings, were assigned a value of $100.

EXPLANATORY VARIABLES

Minority Language Concentration (CON): Each respondent is assigned a measure equal to the percentage of the population aged 18 to 64 in the state in which he lives, who reports the same non-English language as the respondent. In the construction of this variable, only the 24 largest language groups nationwide are considered. In descending order there are: Spanish; French; German; Italian; Chinese; Tagalog; Polish; Korean; Vietnamese; Japanese; Portuguese; Greek; Arabic; Hindi; Russian; Yiddish; Thai; Persian; French Creole; Armenian; Hebrew; Dutch; Hungarian; Mon-Khmer (Cambodian). These constitute 94 percent of all responses that a language other than English is used at home. Representation in the other language groups is so small numerically that the proportions are approximately zero, and this value is assigned. Those who reported speaking only English are assigned the mean value of the CON measure for other language speakers of their birthplace group.

Location: The two location variables record residence in a rural area (RURAL) or in the Southern States (SOUTH). The states included in the latter are: Alabama, Arkansas, Delaware, District of Columbia, Florida, Georgia, Kentucky, Louisiana, Maryland, Mississippi, Missouri, North Carolina, Oklahoma, South Carolina, Tennessee, Texas, Virginia, West Virginia.

Birthplace (BIRTH): A number of non-English speaking birthplace regions are considered in the analyses: Western Europe; Southern Europe; Eastern Europe; former Soviet Union; Indochina; South Asia (which comprises the regions of British influence, for example, India, Nepal, Pakistan); Other South-East Asia; Korea; Japan; Middle East and North Africa; SubSaharan Africa; Mexico; Cuba; Central and South America (Spanish influence); Central and South America (non-Spanish influence). The benchmark group (omitted category) in the regression analysis is Western Europe.

Colony (COLONY): Countries that are current or former colonies of English-speaking countries are coded one. All other countries are coded zero. Dependencies of the United

Kingdom, United States, Australia, New Zealand, and South Africa are coded as colonies under this definition.

Years Since Migration (YSM). The categorical Census information on year of immigration is converted to a continuous measure using the following values: 1987 to 1990 (1.75 years); 1985 to 1986 (4.25 years); 1982 to 1984 (6.75 years); 1980 to 1981 (9.25 years); 1975 to 1979 (12.75 years); 1970 to 1974 (17.75 years); 1965 to 1969 (22.75 years); 1960 to 1965 (27.75 years); 1950 to 1959 (35.25 years); before 1950 (49.75 years).

Lived Abroad 5 Years Ago (ABROAD5): This dichotomous variable is defined only for immigrants who have resided in the United States for more than 5 years. It is set equal to 1 if the individual lived abroad in 1985, otherwise it is set equal to 0 for immigrants in the United States 5 or fewer years and for longer duration immigrants living in the United States in 1985.

Radio (RADIO): The number of radio stations broadcasting entirely or nearly entirely in Spanish in the state were obtained from *Broadcasting and Cable Yearbook, 1994* (1994), R.R. Bowker, New Providence, NJ, pp. B566–B567. In 1994, there were 315 Spanish language radio stations broadcasting in 25 states. Chiswick and Miller (1998) present details. The number of Spanish-language radio stations in the state was normalized by the area of the state to give the number of radio stations per 1,000 square miles. Then this variable was normalized by the number of Spanish speakers in the state of residence to give the number of Spanish language radio stations per unit of area per 10,000 Spanish speakers. This variable provides an index of the intensity of the infrastructure supporting the Spanish language in the state of residence. There were too few radio stations broadcasting in languages other than Spanish to compute a meaningful index for other languages. Because of the possible endogeneity of this variable, an IV approach was used.

Marital Status (MARR): This is a binary variable that distinguishes individuals who are married, spouse present (equal to 1) from all other marital states.

Years of Education (EDUC): This variable records the total years of full-time education. It has been constructed from the Census data on educational attainment by assigning the following values to the Census categories: completed less than fifth grade (2.5 years); completed fifth through eighth grade (7 years); completed ninth grade (9); completed tenth grade (10); completed 11th grade (11); completed 12th grade or high school (12); attended or completed college (14); Bachelor's degree (16); Master's degree (17.5); Professional degree (18); Doctorate (20).

Refugee (REFUGEE): This variable is constructed to identify the major sources of post-WWII refugees to the United States. It is defined only for immigrants who migrated at age 25 and older. Individuals who migrated from Cambodia, Laos, or Vietnam in 1975 or later, Iran in 1980 or later, Cuba in 1960 or later, or the USSR and Baltic States are assigned a value of one for this variable. All other immigrants are assigned a value of zero.

Linguistic Distance (DISTANCE): This is a measure of the difficulty of learning a foreign language for English-speaking Americans. It is based on a set of language scores (LS) measuring achievements in speaking proficiency in foreign languages by English-speaking Americans at the U.S. Department of State, School of Language Studies, reported by Hart-Gonzalez and Lindermann (1993). It is described in detail in Chiswick and Miller (1998, Appendix B). For the same number of weeks of instruction, a lower score (LS) represents less language facility, and, it is assumed, greater linguistic distance between English and the specific foreign language. For example, French is scored at 2.5 (in a range from 1 to 3), while Japanese is scored at 1.0. The language groups reported in the Hart-Gonzalez

IMMIGRANT ADJUSTMENT

and Lindermann (1993) study are then matched to language codes in the 1990 Census using the Ethnologue Language Family Index published by Grimes and Grimes (1993). Adam Makkai, Professor of Linguistics, University of Illinois at Chicago, assisted in the matching of language codes, and in expanding the list of languages for which scores were assigned.

In the construction of this variable, foreign-born persons who speak only English at home and hence do not report speaking a non-English language are assigned the mean value of the linguistic score measure for individuals reporting a foreign language from their birthplace group.

The variable in the regression equations is linguistic distance, which is 1 divided by the linguistic score, DISTANCE = 1/LS.

Emigration Rate (EMIG): Yearly emigration rates of the foreign born by country of birth and sex are computed by dividing the yearly emigration levels between 1980 and 1990 from Ahmed and Robinson (1994) by the number of immigrants of the specific birthplace–gender group in 1980 from the 1980 U.S. Census. Thirty-three countries are separately identified in the data, together with seven residual regions.

Direct-Line Distances (MILES): The miles between the major city in the immigrant's country of origin and the nearest large port of entry in the United States (New York, Miami, Los Angeles) are constructed from data in Fitzpatrick and Modlin's (1986) *Direct Line Distances, United States Edition*.

Years of Experience (EXP): This is computed as age minus years of education minus 5 (that is, EXP = AGE − EDUC − 5). A quadratic specification is used.

Log of Weeks Worked (LNWW): The number of weeks worked in 1989 is used in natural logarithmic form.

Race: This is a dichotomous variable, set to 1 if the individual is Black, and set to 0 for all other racial groups (White, Asian, and Pacific Islander groups, American Indian, other groups).

Veteran Status (VETSTAT): This is a dichotomous variable, set to 1 where the respondent is a veteran of the U.S. armed forces. In all other cases it is set to 0.

Citizen (CITIZEN): This is a dichotomous variable, set to 1 for individuals who are naturalized citizens.

[11]

Ethnic Enclaves and Immigrant Labor Market Outcomes: Quasi-Experimental Evidence

Anna Piil Damm, *University of Aarhus*

I examine the effects of the ethnic enclave size on labor market outcomes of immigrants. I account for ability sorting into enclaves by exploiting a Danish spatial dispersal policy under which refugees were randomly dispersed across locations. First, I find strong evidence that refugees with unfavorable unobserved characteristics self-select into ethnic enclaves. Second, a relative standard deviation increase in the ethnic enclave size increases annual earnings by 18% on average, irrespective of skill level. Third, further findings are consistent with the explanation that ethnic networks disseminate job information, which increases the job-worker match quality and thereby the hourly wage rate.

I have benefited from helpful comments from Christian Dustmann, Joshua Angrist, Stephen Lich-Tyler, Yoram Weiss, Helena Skyt Nielsen, Peter Fredriksson, Michael Rosholm, and Anders Frederiksen; conference participants at the 2006 Center for Research and Analysis of Migration–Team for Advanced Research on Globalization, Education, and Technology Immigration Conference, 2004 European Society for Population Economics, and 2004 Econometric Society European meetings; workshop participants at the 2004 Center for Research in Integration, Education, Qualifications, and Marginalization workshop, and seminar participants at the Centre for Applied Microeconometrics, Copenhagen University, Aarhus School of Business, University of Aarhus, Research School of Social Sciences, and Australian National University. I would like to thank Bente Bondebjerg and Morten Iversen, Danish Refugee Council, for valuable information about the 1986–98 Danish spatial dispersal policy on refugees and the Institute of Local Government Studies and the Rockwool Research Unit for access to administrative register data from Statistics Denmark. The project was financed by grant 24-03-0288 from the Danish Research Agency. Contact the author at apd@asb.dk.

I. Introduction

Immigrants in advanced societies tend to live spatially concentrated in the larger cities; see, for instance, Bartel (1989) or Borjas (1998) for U.S. evidence. Residential segregation of immigrants is commonly believed to hamper integration of immigrants. This is a key reason why many Western European countries spatially disperse refugees and asylum seekers. Migration researchers agree that integration of immigrants into the labor market is of major importance for overall integration of immigrants into the society. It is therefore important to know how residence in ethnic enclaves affects labor market outcomes of immigrants.

Empirical evidence of the effect of ethnic enclave size on economic success of immigrants is scarce because of difficulties in identifying the effect of ethnic enclave size. Difficulties arise if individuals sort into cities and neighborhoods on the basis of unobserved personal characteristics that also affect their labor market outcomes. Recent research has made progress in addressing this issue. Cutler and Glaeser (1997) and Bertrand, Luttmer, and Mullainathan (2000) exploit the variation across a larger geographical area to avoid within-city sorting by ability. They find that blacks and immigrants, respectively, are hurt by residential segregation. This approach does not avoid the issue of sorting by ability across cities. The ideal approach would be to exploit evidence from an experiment in which ethnic minorities are randomly distributed across locations and persuaded to stay in the location of assignment for a considerable period of time.

The 1986–98 Danish spatial dispersal policy on refugees and asylum seekers is such an experiment and can be exploited to obtain quasi-experimental evidence on the return to living in an ethnic enclave. A similar identification strategy is used by Edin, Fredriksson, and Åslund (2003), who exploit a former Swedish spatial dispersal policy on refugees and asylum seekers to obtain quasi-experimental evidence on the effect of ethnic enclave size on annual earnings. Edin et al. measure the ethnic enclave size by the number of conationals living in individual i's current area of residence. They instrument the ethnic enclave size by the number of conationals living in individual i's area of assignment in the year of assignment, that is, by the initial local ethnic *stock*. When one takes account of sorting into ethnic enclaves, the earnings gain associated with a standard deviation increase in the local ethnic stock is 13%.

The implicit exogeneity assumption in Edin et al. (2003) is invalid if the stock of immigrants of a particular descent is driven by ethnic group–specific selection into areas, for example, areas providing better job opportunities for the group in question. In that case, assignment to an area with a relatively large local ethnic stock implies assignment to an area with relatively favorable ethnic group–specific earnings opportunities for earlier cohorts. Therefore, the finding of the positive instrumental variable estimate of the ethnic enclave size on annual earnings may not be evidence of a positive causal effect of ethnic enclave size on annual earnings. It may instead capture the tendency for earlier cohorts of conationals to settle in areas with favorable ethnic group–specific earnings opportunities.

My study handles this potential problem of ethnic group–specific selection into areas of earlier cohorts by using the *inflow* of *placed* conationals to individual i's location of assignment since the year of implementation of the dispersal policy until the (end of the) year of immigration of individual i as an instrument for the stock of conationals in individual i's current area of residence.

The paper provides new empirical results. First, I find strong negative ability sorting into ethnic enclaves. Second, when one takes account of sorting, 7 years after immigration a relative standard deviation increase in the local ethnic stock increases annual earnings by 18%, irrespective of skill level. Third, an increase in the ethnic enclave size decreases the employment probability of high-skilled refugees and reduces the probability of full-time work for high-skilled wage earners; the estimated effects are insignificant for low-skilled refugees. These findings suggest that living in an ethnic enclave increases annual earnings by increasing the hourly wage rate rather than by increasing annual hours worked. The findings are consistent with information spillover within the ethnic network that increases the job-worker match quality and thereby the hourly wage rate. Fourth, in line with such information spillover, I find weak evidence that the return to living in an ethnic enclave increases with the quality of the ethnic enclave. Finally, descriptive evidence on the ethnic concentration at the workplace of private-sector refugees renders probable that a considerable share of refugees have found their job through their ethnic network.

Section II briefly reviews existing theories. Section III provides background on the Danish spatial dispersal policy on refugees and asylum seekers. Section IV describes the administrative records on refugees used in the empirical analysis and discusses the instrument. Section V presents my results on the effect of ethnic enclave size on earnings. Section VI looks at the reason why living in an ethnic enclave increases earnings. Section VII offers conclusions.

II. Theories on the Return to Living in an Ethnic Enclave

Many researchers believe that ethnic enclaves create closer social networks between people of a common ethnicity living in geographical proximity to each other, henceforth referred to as ethnic networks. As noted by Bertrand et al. (2000), social networks affect individual behavior through two potentially important channels: information and norms.[1] The informational channel operates through contacts with valuable knowledge of various kinds. Contacts may have knowledge about job vacancies, for instance, in ethnic businesses or ethnic niches, or valuable information for establishment of own business such as knowledge about business and loan opportunities and knowledge about disciplined co-ethnic workers searching for a job (Portes 1998).[2] Alternatively, contacts may disseminate information about income alternatives to employment, such as welfare eligibility (Bertrand et al. 2000). With regard to the social norms channel, social norms may influence employment status directly (e.g., work ethics, self-employment traditions, attitudes toward receipt of social benefits, and division of labor between spouses) and indirectly (e.g., norms regarding early marriage that may affect the fertility rate and the level of educational attainment of women; see, e.g., Coleman et al. 1966; Wilson 1987; Case and Katz 1991; Borjas 1995; Glaeser, Sacerdote, and Scheinkman 1996; Bertrand et al. 2000). Residence in an ethnic enclave may therefore promote or hinder economic success of immigrants depending on the nature of the spillover of information and social norms in the ethnic community. According to another hypothesis, living in an ethnic enclave hampers economic assimilation of recent immigrants by decreasing the rate of acquisition of host country–specific human capital (e.g., language) due to reduced social interaction with natives, which reduces the incentive to acquire host country–specific human capital such as host country language skills (Chiswick 1991; Lazear 1999). Furthermore, Chiswick and Miller (2005) speculate that ethnic minorities will be willing to accept a job at a lower wage rate if the job is located in an ethnic enclave, because residence in an ethnic enclave reduces the cost of consumption of ethnic goods and services such as traditional food products from the source country, clubs for conationals, and places for practicing religion. In standard search models, a relatively low reservation wage implies a relatively high probability of accepting a job offer. In that case, the short-run effect of living in an ethnic enclave on individual annual earnings is ambiguous, because annual earnings are the product of hours of work throughout the year—which may increase—and hourly wages—which may decrease. Furthermore, the medium-run effect of living in an ethnic enclave may be unambiguously positive because hourly wages tend to increase with work experience.

The short description of the three theories mentioned above demon-

[1] For theoretical analyses, see Banerjee (1992) and Bikhchandani, Hirshleifer, and Welch (1992) for the informational channel and Akerlof (1980) for the norms channel.
[2] Studies of Chinatown in New York, Little Havana in Miami, and Koreatown in Los Angeles provide empirical evidence that ethnic networks constitute a crucial resource for ethnic businesses (Portes 1998, 13).

strates that theoretically the effect of residence in an ethnic enclave on labor market outcomes of immigrants is ambiguous in sign. Therefore, the effect of living in an ethnic enclave on labor market outcomes of immigrants must be determined by an empirical analysis, to which I now turn.

III. The Danish Spatial Dispersal Policy on Refugees

The mid-1980s saw a surge of refugee applications in Denmark that made it increasingly difficult for the Danish Refugee Council to satisfy the location preferences of most new refugees for accommodation in the larger cities. As a consequence, the Danish government urged the council to implement a spatial dispersal policy. The year 1986 marks the start of the first Danish spatial dispersal policy on refugees and asylum seekers who had their applications approved.[3] Henceforth, I refer to such recognized refugees and asylum seekers as "refugees." The policy was in force until 1999 under the charge of the council.

Spatial dispersal was a two-stage process. At the country level, the council tried to allocate an equal number of refugees to counties relative to the number of inhabitants.[4] Within counties, the council aimed at attaining an equal number of refugees relative to the number of inhabitants across municipalities (local authority districts) with suitable facilities for reception such as housing, educational institutions, employment opportunities, and conationals.[5] One implication of these dispersal criteria was that refugees were provided with permanent housing in cities and towns and to a lesser extent in the rural districts (Ministry of Internal Affairs 1996). Another implication was ethnic clustering: in order to facilitate local refugee reception and refugees' well-being, the council aimed at attainment of local ethnic clusters of 70–100 refugees of a particular descent over a 3-year period.

In practice, as soon as a refugee was granted asylum, the individual was offered assistance from the council in finding housing. Approximately 10 days later, the council assigned a refugee to one of 15 counties. When refugees were provided with temporary housing in the receiving county, local offices of the council assisted the assigned refugees in finding per-

---

[3] Until June 2002, Denmark gave asylum to convention refugees, i.e., persons who were defined as refugees according to the Geneva Convention of 1951, and to foreigners who were not defined as refugees according to the Geneva Convention, but who for similar reasons as stated in the convention or other weighty reasons should not be required to return to their home country (de facto refugees; Coleman and Wadensjö 1999, 249).

[4] At the regional level, Denmark was divided into two county-municipalities and 14 counties with 324,000 inhabitants per county on average in 1993.

[5] At the local level, Denmark was divided into 275 municipalities with 19,000 inhabitants per municipality on average.

manent housing in the county. The local offices were mobile within a county. They typically stayed in the same area for about 3 years.

The take-up rate for housing assistance was extremely high. In an interview, a former placement officer at the council[6] says that she does not recall that any refugees rejected the offer of housing search assistance from the council. I also compare the official figures on the number of residence permits granted to refugees[7] with the council's statistics on location assignment of refugees.[8] These suggest that over the period 1986–97, at least 90% of refugees were provided with permanent housing under the terms of the dispersal policy.

Once settled, refugees participated in Danish language courses during an introductory period of 18 months while receiving social assistance. Refugees were urged to stay in the assigned municipality during the entire introductory period. However, there were no relocation restrictions. Refugees could move away from the municipality of assignment at any time, insofar as they could find alternative housing elsewhere. Receipt of welfare was unconditional on residing in the assigned municipality.

The dispersal policy was very successful and led to an equal distribution of refugees across counties (Damm 2005). A figure from the council's annual report in 1987 (30–31) shows the distribution of refugees across municipalities. Only 2 years after the introduction of the dispersal policy, refugees lived in 243 out of the 275 municipalities. The number of refugees who were assigned to permanent housing between 1985 and 1987 across municipalities was 33 refugees per 10,000 inhabitants. The number of refugees per 10,000 inhabitants was twice as large as the country average in only 17 municipalities. The effect of the dispersal policy on the settlement pattern of refugees is clearly visible from table 1, which shows the geographical distribution of the overall population in Denmark, refugees, and nonrefugee immigrants across the capital area, towns, and rural areas in 1993. The geographical distribution of nonrefugee immigrants differs greatly from the distribution of the overall population: 71% of nonrefugee immigrants live in the capital area, where 26% of the overall population live. In contrast, the geographical distribution of refugees closely resembles the distribution of the overall population. Refugees are only slightly overrepresented in the capital area.

---

[6] Interview on March 7, 2008, with former placement officer Bente Bondebjerg, chief consultant, Danish Refugee Council. Note also that the council had a financial incentive to assist as many refugees as possible in finding housing because of economies of scale and receipt of a fixed governmental transfer per refugee assigned to a location.

[7] The 1992 and 1997 *Statistical Yearbook* and *Statistical News* (Statistics Denmark 2000).

[8] The 1986–94 annual reports of the Danish Refugee Council and the council's internal administrative statistics for 1995–98.

Table 1
Geographical Distribution in 1993 (%)

	Total Population	Refugees	Nonrefugee Immigrants
Capital and its suburbs	26	33	71
Towns	59	56	24
Rural areas	15	11	5

SOURCE.—Danish Refugee Council (1993).

Were refugees randomly distributed across locations under the spatial dispersal policy? Upon asylum, refugees filled in a questionnaire from the council with a few personal details: the individual's birth date, marital status, number of children, nationality, and addresses of potential family relations and friends in Denmark.[9] According to interviews with two former placement officers, the council used the information about nationality to spatially disperse refugees in ethnic clusters and considered wishes of refugees to be assigned to a location near close family members.[10] The information about household composition was used to determine whether to search for housing for a single individual or family in the municipality of assignment. Over time it became increasingly difficult for the council to find vacant rental housing in the larger and medium-sized towns, which led to later arrivals of refugees being more likely to be settled in smaller towns. Therefore, the council's allocation may have been influenced by nationality, family size, and year of immigration—characteristics on which I condition in the analysis.

As a result of the way in which the dispersal policy was implemented, municipalities had little opportunity to cream-skim refugees, that is, to ask for, say, well-educated refugees. Although the council did not know in advance which groups of asylum seekers would next be granted asylum, it had to provide refugees with temporary housing shortly after receipt of the residence permit. This procedure left little time for negotiation between the council and municipalities. Moreover, the council acted as a private agent searching for housing in the local housing market on behalf of refugees who had just received a residence permit. The local authorities were typically not informed about the settlement of a refugee until after a refugee had been provided with housing in the municipality.

---

[9] The question about the addresses of potential family relations replaced a question about location wishes that was asked at the beginning of the dispersal policy period. The question was replaced because the spatial dispersal criteria led to the inability of the council to comply with location wishes.

[10] Interview on June 8, 2001, with former placement officers Bente Bondebjerg and Morten Iversen.

IV. Data

A. Data and Sample Selection

The empirical analysis is based on administrative records for the immigrant population in Denmark for 1984–2000. Earnings data are obtained from the income tax registers, employment status from the labor force registers, demographic characteristics (country of origin, gender, age, family composition, municipality of residence, date of immigration) from the population registers, and Danish education from the integrated pupil registers; education attained prior to immigration comes from a survey-based register. The individual records are linked using a unique person identifier. Real annual labor market earnings, henceforth referred to as real annual earnings, are defined as the sum of wage earnings, profits from own company, and sickness benefits deflated by the consumer price index, which has 1980 as its base year. An individual is regarded as being employed if his main occupation is wage employment or self-employment. Throughout I use country of origin as a proxy for ethnicity.

Local characteristics are measured at the municipality level. There are 275 municipalities, and the median municipality has close to 10,000 inhabitants. I calculate the number of immigrants from a particular source country and use it to represent the size of the ethnic group in a municipality. I use population-counted data from Statistics Denmark to represent other characteristics of the municipalities, including the unemployment rate.

I identify the 11 largest refugee-sending countries in the period 1986–93 (ranked in descending order): Lebanon, Iran, Iraq, Somalia, Sri Lanka, Vietnam, Poland, Afghanistan, Ethiopia, Romania, and Chile.[11] I focus on the immigration cohorts during 1986–93 because labor market outcomes 7 years after immigration are not observed for later cohorts in the administrative records that are currently available. An immigrant is a refugee if he or she meets the following two criteria. First, the individual emigrated from one of the 11 largest refugee-sending countries in the period 1986–93. Second, at the time of immigration, that is, the year of receipt of a residence permit, the individual was not married to (1) an individual from a non-refugee-sending country or (2) an immigrant from a refugee-sending country who had immigrated at least 1 year earlier. The latter criterion is imposed to limit the refugee sample to refugees who were assigned to a location by the council after receipt of asylum. Only

---

[11] I identify the 11 largest refugee-sending countries using official statistics from Statistics Denmark on the total number of residence permits granted to refugees between 1986 and 1993 reported in the 1992 and 1997 *Statistical Yearbook* and *Statistical News*. Residence permits granted to refugees from the 11 refugee-sending countries constitute 94% of the total number of residence permits granted to refugees between 1986 and 1993.

individuals aged 18–59 at the time of immigration are included in the sample. The annual inflow of conationals assigned to a particular municipality is calculated from the resulting sample of 16,076 individuals. In the period 1986–93, refugees were assigned to 248 municipalities, or 90% of municipalities.

The refugee sample used in the earnings and employment analysis is obtained after imposing a final restriction, that is, annual observations from 1 year after immigration until 7 years after immigration. This results in a balanced panel of 13,927 individuals, of whom 41% have positive annual earnings 7 years after immigration.[12] The subsample of refugees with positive annual earnings 7 years after immigration is referred to as the earnings sample.

I identify the municipality of assignment by using the following algorithm based on information on the council's internal administrative statistics on temporary housing. The first municipality of residence observed in the registers is defined as a municipality of temporary housing if the person relocates to another municipality within the county within 1 year after receipt of the residence permit. The reason is that refugees may initially have lived in temporary housing in proximity to the municipality to which they were later assigned on average after 6–7 months and in general after 3 months. Otherwise, the first municipality is defined as the municipality of assignment. (Variable definitions and descriptive statistics are reported in tables A1–A3 in the appendix.)

B. Initial Assignment and Subsequent Mobility

Following Edin et al. (2003), I measure the ethnic enclave size by the local ethnic stock of individual i, which is defined as the number of conationals living in individual i's municipality of residence. Hence, implicitly *ethnicity* is measured by country of origin following Borjas (1992, 1995, 1998). Conationals are first- and second-generation immigrants from individual i's country of origin. The implicit definition of an ethnic enclave underlying the empirical analysis is the following. The individual lives in

[12] Fifty-one individuals who were observed in the registers 7 years after immigration but not annually up to that point are excluded from the sample. The number of permanent return migrants, i.e., individuals who emigrated prior to 7 years of residence in Denmark, amounts to 2,098 individuals. Results from linear regression of an indicator for having emigrated between year t and $t + 7$ on a range of initial individual and location characteristics show that singles, older individuals, women, and individuals without older children have the highest tendency to emigrate. The economically least successful refugees do not appear to be more likely to emigrate; the effect of real annual earnings in year $t + 1$ is negative but insignificant. The estimated effects of location characteristics suggest that individuals emigrate in response to assignment to an unattractive location, i.e., a location with a relatively high unemployment rate and a low inflow of assigned conationals.

Table 2
Summary Statistics for Refugees with Positive Earnings 7 Years after Immigration: Means and Standard Deviations (Parentheses)

	ln(Local Inflow of Assigned Conationals)		t-Test of Difference in Means
	Below Average	Above Average	
Education missing and < 10 years	.47	.47	1.00
	(.50)	(.50)	
High school	.39	.40	1.39
	(.49)	(.49)	
University	.13	.13	.56
	(.34)	(.33)	
Female	.24	.21	3.37
	(.43)	(.41)	
Age	26.43	26.10	2.98
	(6.36)	(6.19)	
Number of children	.71	.61	5.08
	(1.17)	(1.12)	
Married	.35	.31	5.20
	(.48)	(.46)	
Number of observations	2,631	3,016	

NOTE.—Variables refer to the values in year t, where t is the year of immigration. Mean (standard deviation) of ln(local inflow of assigned conationals) is 3.45 (1.41).

an ethnic enclave if he lives in a municipality in which the number of conationals exceeds a given threshold. As reported in appendix table A3, the mean local ethnic stock 7 years after immigration is 1,010; that is, on average, individuals in the sample have 1,009 compatriots in the municipality of residence 7 years after immigration.

The instrument I propose to use for the ethnic enclave size 7 years after immigration is the inflow of placed conationals (aged 18–59) to individual i's location of assignment since the year of implementation of the dispersal policy, that is, 1986, until the (end of the) year of immigration of individual i.

Did the spatial dispersal provide random variation in the instrumental variable? To find out, I first divide individuals in the earnings sample into two groups: individuals who were placed in a municipality with a below- or above-average number of assigned conationals since 1986 until the year of immigration of individual i. Table 2 compares the personal characteristics of the two groups in the year of immigration. The two groups are very similar in terms of demographic characteristics and educational attainment.

Second, for refugees in the earnings sample I regress the log of the number of assigned conationals since 1986 until the year of immigration of individual i linearly on education category dummies. None of the education category dummies are significant, and the explained variation is virtually zero. In a second regression, I extend the set of explanatory variables with a range of demographic characteristics. The only variables that enter significantly are age, year of immigration, source country, and the log of the number of conationals in Denmark. Henceforth, I refer to the number of conationals of individual i in Denmark as the ethnic stock in Denmark. Not surprisingly, there is a positive relationship between the log of ethnic stock in Denmark and the log of the number of assigned conationals. It suggests that refugees with a larger ethnic stock in Denmark were dispersed in larger ethnic clusters. Some ethnic groups were apparently less likely to be assigned to larger cities (e.g., Tamils) than the reference group (Iranian). Earlier cohorts of refugees are assigned to a municipality with a significantly lower number of assigned conationals since 1986 until the year of immigration; this captures the fact that earlier cohorts had a higher chance of being assigned to municipalities with no previous inflow of (assigned) conationals. I conclude that the inflow of placed conationals to individual i's location of assignment since 1986 until the year of immigration of individual i is random, conditional on year of immigration, source country, age, and ethnic stock in Denmark.

In the empirical analysis, I intend to exploit the within variation in the instrument, that is, the variation in the local inflow of placed conationals that remains after inclusion of municipality of assignment fixed effects that captures the local number of inhabitants. By consequence, I propose to exploit the within variation in the local inflow of placed conationals relative to the number of inhabitants. Within variation exists in this variable because municipalities tended to receive assigned refugees from source country k over a 3-year period. To assess the extent of within variation in the instrument, I calculate the number of assigned refugees from source country k from 1986 until year t per 10,000 inhabitants in the municipality for each source country. Summary statistics for the variable are reported for each source country in appendix table A4. For all source countries, there is less within than between variance, but for the majority of countries the ratio between within and between variance is at least 24%.

A related question is whether some individuals were more likely to realize their preferred location choice than others. I investigate this question by analyzing placed refugees' subsequent migration decision. The results from linear regression of the indicator for having moved out of the municipality of assignment on a range of individual, group, and location (demographic, labor market, and housing market) characteristics at the time of immigration are shown in table 3. The effects of demographic characteristics of the individual are quite standard: men, younger individuals, and singles have a significantly higher out-migration rate, probably because of lower costs of moving. By contrast, there are no significant differences in out-migration rates between educational groups. The latter result is reassuring: it suggests that all educational groups had the same

Table 3
OLS Estimates: Dependent Variable: Indicator for Having Moved Out of the Assigned Municipality between Years t and $t + 7$

	All (1)	Positive Earnings in $t + 7$ (2)	(3)
Individual and group characteristics in year $t + 7$:			
Education missing and < 10 years			Ref.
High school			.001
			(.014)
University ≤ 2 years			.007
			(.024)
University > 2 years			.049**
			(.025)
ln(real annual earnings)			−.013***
			(.004)
Individual and group characteristics in year t:			
Education missing and < 10 years	Ref.	Ref.	
High school	−.000	.003	
	(.009)	(.014)	
University ≤ 2 years	−.009	−.009	
	(.016)	(.027)	
University > 2 years	.007	.032	
	(.017)	(.027)	
Female	−.030***	−.056***	−.058***
	(.009)	(.016)	(.016)
Age	−.005***	−.006***	−.006***
	(.001)	(.001)	(.001)
Married	−.090***	−.100***	−.099***
	(.013)	(.024)	(.022)
Young child (0–2 years)	−.004	.016	.015
	(.012)	(.022)	(.022)
Old child (3–17 years)	−.036***	−.067***	−.066***
	(.012)	(.022)	(.022)
ln(ethnic stock in Denmark)	−.057**	.021	.015
	(.023)	(.039)	(.039)
Immigration year dummies	Yes	Yes	Yes
Country of origin dummies	Yes	Yes	Yes
Municipality of assignment characteristics in year t:			
Large	Ref.	Ref.	Ref.
Medium	.252***	.181***	.183***
	(.021)	(.035)	(.035)
Small	.340***	.267***	.270***
	(.031)	(.049)	(.049)
ln(immigrant stock)	−.003	.007	.007
	(.008)	(.007)	(.138)
ln(inflow of assigned conationals)	−.044***	−.066***	−.065***
	(.004)	(.007)	(.007)
Unemployment rate	.008***	−.004	−.004
	(.003)	(.004)	(.004)
% right-wing votes	.000	−.001	−.001
	(.001)	(.001)	(.001)

(continued overleaf)

Table 3 (*Continued*)

	All (1)	Positive Earnings in $t + 7$ (2)	(3)
Number of educational institutions	.003**	.002	.002
	(.001)	(.002)	(.002)
% social housing	−.007***	−.006***	−.006***
	(.001)	(.001)	(.001)
R^2	.181	.159	.160
Number of observations	13,927	5,647	5,647

NOTE.—The regressions use the linear probability model. The number of movers in the full sample is 7,266; the number of movers in the earnings sample is 2,953. Standard errors are in parentheses. Ref. = reference category.
* Significant at the 10% level.
** Significant at the 5% level.
*** Significant at the 1% level.

chance of realizing their preferred location choice. The characteristics of the municipality of assignment had a substantial influence on the migration decision. For the full sample, the explanatory power increases from 6.2% to 18.1% after inclusion of location characteristics. In particular, the migration probability decreases with the local inflow of assigned conationals. This result suggests that placed refugees derive high utility from living in the same location as conationals, which is consistent with the ethnic network hypothesis by Piore (1979) and Kobrin and Speare (1983) and the ethnic goods hypothesis by Chiswick and Miller (2005). Movers also seem to escape municipalities with a relatively small number of inhabitants, a high unemployment rate, and lack of social housing.

Further descriptive evidence reveals that after the relocation, movers are overrepresented in municipalities with a large local population and a large local ethnic stock and in municipalities in which immigrants constitute a large share of the local population.

Another important issue is whether the local inflow of assigned conationals by the end of the year of immigration of individual i should be expected to be a strong predictor of the ethnic stock in the location of residence 7 years after immigration. This depends on the extent of subsequent out-migration from the municipality of assignment. Since almost half of the sample (48%) stayed in the assigned municipality, I expect the instrument to have a strong predictive power in the first-stage regressions.

V. Model and Empirical Estimates of Effects of Living in an Ethnic Enclave

A. Model

I focus on real annual earnings 7 years after immigration, at which time individuals are recent immigrants but have had time to establish social networks in the host country and to acquire basic skills necessary for job search in the host country. I employ the following baseline specification:

$$y_{ijk(t+7)} = \alpha \ln e_{jk(t+7)} + \beta' X_{ikt} + \delta_j + \delta_k + \delta_t + \varepsilon_{ijk(t+7)}, \qquad (1)$$

where i indexes individuals, j municipalities of assignment, k countries of origin, and t years of immigration. The parameter of interest is α, which measures the average effect of the logarithmic value of the ethnic stock in municipality j at time $t + 7$ ($e_{jk(t+7)}$) on real annual earnings in year $t + 7$ of individual i living in municipality j from country of origin k ($y_{ijk(t+7)}$). The estimate of α is obtained by regressing y on e; fixed effects for j, k, and t; and a set of controls for observed personal and ethnic group characteristics in year t.[13]

The estimate of α based on equation (1) may still suffer from omitted variables bias. Individuals choose where to live in year $t + 7$, that is, the ethnic enclave size. Individuals with certain unobserved characteristics, for example, poor abilities or lack of ambition about socioeconomic assimilation in the host country, may therefore be overrepresented in large ethnic enclaves. I account for potential sorting into ethnic enclaves by using instrumental variables (IV) methods. The instrument I use for ethnic enclave size in year $t + 7$ is the *inflow* of placed conationals (aged 18–59) to individual i's location of assignment since the year of implementation of the dispersal policy until (the end of) year t. The identifying assumption is that the local inflow of assigned conationals is random, conditional on age, year of immigration, source country, and ethnic stock in Denmark. Evidence in support of this assumption was presented in Sections III and IV.[14]

The instrument has the advantage relative to the instrument used by Edin et al. (2003) of being robust to differential sorting of ethnic groups into locations; that is, ethnic groups relocate into different locations after initial assignment based on potential group-specific earnings returns to residence in a given local labor market. In case of differential sorting of ethnic groups into locations, the local ethnic stock in year t may not be the result of random assignment of refugees under the dispersal policy. If conationals who immigrated before the implementation of the dispersal policy settled primarily in areas with relatively favorable group-specific

---

[13] Administrative records are missing in year t for 14.7% of the individuals. For these individuals the vector of personal characteristics other than educational attainment refers to year $t + 1$. The only exception is educational attainment, which refers to year $t + 7$ because educational attainment is missing for "only" 27.4% in year $t + 7$ as opposed to 34% in year $t + 1$.

[14] The consistency of the earnings result rests on the assumption of no sample selection into the labor force in year $t + 7$. To test for and take account of potential sample selection, we need an instrument for labor force participation, i.e., one or more variables that affect the labor force participation decision but not annual earnings. Unfortunately, I have not been able to find such an instrument.

earnings opportunities or if earlier cohorts of assigned conationals have subsequently relocated to areas with relatively favorable group-specific earnings opportunities, a relatively large local ethnic stock in year t partly reflects presence of favorable ethnic group–specific earnings opportunities in the past. Therefore, if one estimates the effect of ethnic enclave size on annual earnings according to equation (1) using the local ethnic stock in year t as an instrument for the local ethnic stock in year $t + 7$ and finds a positive IV estimate of the ethnic enclave size on annual earnings, this may not be evidence of a positive causal effect of ethnic enclave size on annual earnings, but evidence that earlier cohorts of conationals have settled in areas with favorable ethnic group–specific earnings opportunities.[15]

B. Baseline Estimates

The first-stage equations in the IV (two-stage least squares [2SLS]) procedure amount to regressing the log of the local ethnic stock in year $t + 7$ on the instrument, the log of the local inflow of assigned conationals since 1986 until the end of year t, and on individual, group, and location characteristics in year t. The first-stage regression estimates are reported in table 4. The log of local inflow of assigned conationals enters the equations with a coefficient of .273–.308, depending on the skill group. The instrument has a strong predictive power. The null hypothesis of a zero effect of the identifying variable is rejected at a 1% significance level for all samples. The t-values range from 7.54 to 2.90. The partial R-squared values that show how much inclusion of the identifying variable improves the R-squared of the first-stage regression are just above 0.01.

Table 5 reports the estimation results of the earnings model given by equation (1). Columns 1, 3, and 5 report ordinary least squares (OLS) estimates of the model, and columns 2, 4, and 6 give the results of the IV procedure. According to the OLS estimate for the full earnings sample (col. 1), when we control for other observed characteristics of the individual and for three types of fixed effects, the log of the local ethnic stock in year $t + 7$ on average has a significantly negative effect on earnings. The t-test for weak exogeneity of the local ethnic stock in year $t + 7$ is rejected at a 1% significance level. The negative sign of the estimate of the predicted residual from the first-stage regression suggests that individuals with relatively unfavorable personal characteristics sort into ethnic

---

[15] In the case of differential sorting of ethnic groups into locations, the initial local ethnic stock would be a valid instrument for future ethnic group size only if interaction terms between municipality of assignment fixed effects and ethnic group fixed effects were included as controls in eq. (1). In the present study that would reduce the degrees of freedom by 2,673, i.e., 243 municipality of assignment indicator variables times 11 ethnic group indicator variables.

Table 4
OLS First-Stage Earnings Regression Estimates of 2SLS: Dependent Variable: ln(Local Ethnic Stock)

	Full Sample (1)	Low Education (12 Years or Less) (2)	High Education (More than 12 Years) (3)
ln(local inflow of assigned conationals)	.306***	.308***	.273***
	(.041)	(.042)	(.094)
Female	.051	.021	.217
	(.073)	(.076)	(.132)
Age	.004	−.002	−.026
	(.012)	(.023)	(.055)
Age squared	.022	−.010	.028
	(.021)	(.039)	(.083)
Married	−.023**	−.161	−.231
	(.088)	(.102)	(.225)
Married × female	.045	−.003	−.059
	(.122)	(.136)	(.288)
Young child (0–2 years)	.005	.020	−.033
	(.085)	(.100)	(.196)
Young child × female	−.014	.020	−.051
	(.095)	(.110)	(.270)
Old child (3–17 years)	.065	−.025	.232
	(.093)	(.106)	(.215)
Old child × female	−.193*	−.122	−.169
	(.109)	(.120)	(.286)
Education missing and < 10 years	Ref.	Ref.	
High school	.038	.044	
	(.038)	(.038)	
University ≤ 2 years	.033		Ref.
	(.076)		
University > 2 years	.007		−.169
	(.084)		(.286)
ln(ethnic stock in Denmark)	.456***	.452***	.498
	(.143)	(.150)	(.419)
Immigration year dummies	Yes	Yes	Yes
Country of origin dummies	Yes	Yes	Yes
Municipality of assignment dummies	Yes	Yes	Yes
R^2	.379	.397	.469
Number of individuals	5,647	4,745	902

NOTE.—Explanatory variables refer to the values in year t, where t is the year of immigration. Standard errors, reported in parentheses, are corrected for heteroskedasticity and clustering of the residuals by municipality of assignment and year of immigration.
* Significant at the 10% level.
** Significant at the 5% level.
*** Significant at the 1% level.

enclaves. As a result, the OLS estimate of the earnings effect of the local ethnic stock is downward biased. In contrast, the IV procedure should produce consistent estimates. The IV estimate of the local ethnic stock on earnings reported for the full earnings sample in column 2 is striking: it is positive and significant, indicating that residence in an ethnic enclave increases annual earnings of refugees.

To interpret the economic significance of the estimate, I calculate the effect of a standard deviation (1,176) increase in the local ethnic stock

Table 5
Baseline Estimates: Dependent Variable: ln(Earnings)

	Full Sample OLS (1)	Full Sample IV (2)	Low Education (12 Years or Less) OLS (3)	Low Education (12 Years or Less) IV (4)	High Education (More than 12 Years) OLS (5)	High Education (More than 12 Years) IV (6)
ln(local ethnic stock)	−.066*** (.015)	.216** (.112)	−.052*** (.017)	.224* (.118)	−.132*** (.037)	.213 (.332)
Female	−.297*** (.080)	−.311*** (.082)	−.345*** (.088)	−.350** (.090)	.099 (.220)	.026 (.262)
Age	.042* (.025)	.042* (.026)	.039 (.028)	.041 (.029)	.090 (.067)	.101 (.070)
Age squared	−.062 (.043)	−.058 (.045)	−.058 (.050)	−.058 (.051)	−.142 (.107)	−.156 (.110)
Married	−.000 (.095)	.049 (.100)	−.067 (.107)	−.034 (.112)	.369* (.218)	.438* (.248)
Married × female	.106 (.120)	.102 (.127)	.215 (.140)	.225 (.147)	−.461 (.300)	−.456 (.330)
Young child (0–2 years)	−.140* (.089)	−.141 (.091)	−.071 (.106)	−.070 (.108)	−.359* (.198)	−.351* (.215)
Young child × female	.216* (.120)	.214* (.122)	.152** (.136)	.138 (.114)	.368 (.103)	.390 (.324)
Old child (3–17 years)	.066 (.098)	.052 (.100)	.127 (.113)	.138 (.114)	−.081 (.192)	.158 (.224)
Old child × female	−.770 (.122)	−.032 (.129)	−.108 (.149)	−.083 (.152)	−.102 (.248)	−.041 (.287)
Education missing and < 10 years	Ref.	Ref.	Ref.	Ref.		
High school	.097** (.047)	.088* (.048)	.108** (.047)	.098** (.049)		
University ≤ 2 years	.106 (.078)	.101 (.086)			Ref.	Ref.
University > 2 years	.282*** (.081)	.286*** (.086)			.143 (.099)	.146 (.108)
ln(ethnic stock in Denmark)	−.363*** (.139)	−.539*** (.165)	−.416*** (.152)	−.588*** (.176)	−.123 (.372)	−.350 (.471)
Immigration year dummies	Yes	Yes	Yes	Yes	Yes	Yes
Country of origin dummies	Yes	Yes	Yes	Yes	Yes	Yes
Municipality of assignment dummies	Yes	Yes	Yes	Yes	Yes	Yes
R^2	.093	.025	.098	.035	.270	.182
Number of individuals	5,647		4,745		902	

NOTE.—Explanatory variables refer to the values in year t, where t is the year of immigration. The instrument for the log of the local ethnic stock in year $t+7$ is the log of the inflow of assigned conationals to individual i's municipality of assignment since 1986 until the end of year t. Standard errors, reported in parentheses, are corrected for heteroskedasticity and clustering of the residuals by municipality of assignment and year of immigration.
* Significant at the 10% level.
** Significant at the 5% level.
*** Significant at the 1% level.

relative to its mean of 1,010 conationals. Such a relative standard deviation increase corresponds to a 116% increase of the local ethnic stock and to a log increase of 0.77. As a result, a relative standard deviation increase in the local ethnic stock 7 years after immigration on average increases log earnings by (0.77 × 0.216 =) 0.17, corresponding to an 18% earnings increase.

The finding of negative self-selection into ethnic enclaves is supported by the descriptive evidence on out-migration from the municipality of assignment shown in column 3 in table 3. When we control for educational attainment in year $t + 7$ and demographic, group, and location characteristics in year t, individuals with lower annual earnings in year $t + 7$ are significantly more likely to have left the municipality of assignment during the first 7 years after immigration. A relative standard deviation decrease in real annual earnings is associated with a 1.3-percentage-point increase in the out-migration probability.

To explore differences in the return to living in an ethnic enclave across skill groups, I divide the sample into two subsamples, for low-educated and high-educated individuals. Low-educated individuals are individuals with at most an upper-secondary education, that is, less than 13 years of education. High-educated individuals are individuals with a tertiary education, that is, at least 13 years of education. The OLS and IV estimates for the subsample of low-educated refugees are given in columns 3 and 4, respectively. The corresponding estimates for high-educated refugees are reported in columns 5 and 6. On average, the local ethnic stock in year $t + 7$ has a significant negative effect on earnings for both subsamples. That is, according to the OLS estimates, current residence in an ethnic enclave decreases earnings of refugees, irrespective of educational level. Separate IV estimations for low- and high-skilled refugees yield estimates of virtually the same magnitude as for the overall sample. I therefore conclude that the earnings return to living in an ethnic enclave is positive and does not vary across educational groups.

The return to living in an ethnic enclave may also vary across genders. However, separate estimations of the model given by equation (1) for men and women show no significant difference in the return to living in an ethnic enclave.

Finally, the return to living in an ethnic enclave may vary across ethnic groups. I estimate the model given by equation (1) separately for refugees from each of the four regions of origin: Europe, Africa, the Middle East, and Asia. The IV estimate is positive for all regions except Africa.

As a specification check, I check whether the return to ethnic enclave size is nonlinear. I include the squared value of the local ethnic stock in year $t + 7$ in equation (1) and use the squared value of the local inflow of assigned conationals since 1986 until year t as an additional identifying variable in the first-stage regression of 2SLS. The IV estimate of the effect of the local ethnic stock in year $t + 7$ remains strongly significant and positive after inclusion of the squared value. The IV estimate of the effect of the squared value of the local ethnic stock in year $t + 7$ is negative and strongly significant. This suggests that the return to ethnic enclave size increases with ethnic size but at a decreasing rate.[16]

VI. Empirical Investigation of Possible Mechanisms

The empirical analysis presented in Section V shows that living in an ethnic enclave increases annual earnings of refugees 7 years after immigration. This result suggests that the potential negative effect of living in an ethnic enclave due to a reduced rate of acquisition of host country–specific human capital is more than outweighed by a positive effect. Part of the reason may be that the earnings return to host country language skills is relatively low within the ethnic enclave. A positive earnings return to living in an ethnic enclave can be explained by the ethnic goods consumption hypothesis or, alternatively, by spillover of information and/or norms within the ethnic network that promote earnings of enclave members. The goal of this section is to investigate the empirical importance of these two potential explanations for the finding of a positive net effect.

For the positive earnings return to be consistent with the ethnic goods consumption hypothesis, the negative enclave effect on the hourly (reservation) wage must be dominated by a positive enclave effect on annual hours worked. In addition, because of the decrease in the hourly reservation wage, we should expect to find a positive enclave effect on the employment probability.

The administrative registers enable me to estimate the effect of enclave size on the employment probability and on the probability of working full-time in year $t + 7$. The OLS and IV (2SLS) estimates of the effect of the log of the local ethnic stock on (i) the employment probability in year $t + 7$ and (ii) the probability of full-time work in year $t + 7$ (conditional on being a wage earner) are reported in tables 6 and 7, respectively.[17] I use the same set of controls as in equation (1) and the same

---

[16] The IV estimates of the coefficients (standard error) of the log of the local ethnic stock and its squared value are 1.707 (.556) and −.150 (.050), respectively. According to this specification, a relative standard deviation increase in ethnic enclave size (measured around the sample means of the distribution) increases annual earnings by 23%.

[17] I treat the models as linear probability models in order to facilitate interpretation of the estimates. Probit and Amemiya generalized least squares yield similar estimates.

Table 6
Marginal Effect of ln(Local Ethnic Stock) on Pr(Employed), Pr(Wage Earner), and Pr(Self-Employed) in Year $t + 7$

Sample	Dependent Variable: Pr(Employed) OLS (1)	IV (2)	Dependent Variable: Pr(Wage Earner) OLS (3)	IV (4)	Dependent Variable: Pr(Self-Employed) OLS (5)	IV (6)
Full	−.022*** (.003)	.025 (.023)	−.023*** (.003)	.018 (.023)	.001 (.002)	.008 (.011)
Low educated	−.021*** (.003)	.036 (.025)	−.021*** (.003)	.031 (.024)	.000 (.002)	.005 (.012)
High educated	−.027*** (.007)	−.027 (.057)	−.031*** (.008)	−.065 (.057)	.004 (.005)	.038 (.033)

NOTE.—The number of observations is 13,927, of which 5,639 are employed, 4,666 are wage earners, and 973 are self-employed workers in year $t + 7$. Controls are the same as in table 5. The instrument for the log of the local ethnic stock in year $t + 7$ is the log of the inflow of assigned conationals to individual i's municipality of assignment since 1986 until the end of year t. The regressions use the linear probability model. Standard errors, reported in parentheses, are corrected for heteroskedasticity and clustering of the residuals by municipality of assignment and year of immigration.
* Significant at the 10% level.
** Significant at the 5% level.
*** Significant at the 1% level.

Table 7
Marginal Effect of ln(Local Ethnic Stock) on Pr(Full-Time Work) in Year $t + 7$: Wage Earners Only

	Full Sample OLS (1)	IV (2)	Low Educated OLS (3)	IV (4)	High Educated OLS (5)	IV (6)
ln(local ethnic stock)	−.017 (.005)***	−.045 (.028)	−.017 (.006)***	−.030 (.031)	−.005 (.018)	−.206 (.120)*
R^2	.106	.098	.111	.110	.236	.048
Number of individuals	4,666		3,950		716	

NOTE.—Controls are the same as in table 5. The share of wage earners who work full-time, i.e., on average at least 27 hours per week during the year, is 23.47% for the full sample, 22.81% for low-educated wage earners, and 27.09% for high-educated wage earners. The instrument for the log of the local ethnic stock in year $t + 7$ is the log of the inflow of assigned conationals to individual i's municipality of assignment since 1986 until the end of year t. The regressions use the linear probability model. Standard errors, reported in parentheses, are corrected for heteroskedasticity and clustering of the residuals by municipality of assignment and year of immigration.
* Significant at the 10% level.
** Significant at the 5% level.
*** Significant at the 1% level.

instrument as in the earnings analysis in Section V.[18] By contrast, the administrative registers do not contain information on the hourly wage and annual hours worked.

According to the OLS estimates in column 1 of table 6, the ethnic enclave size has a negative and significant effect on the employment probability in year $t + 7$, irrespective of skill level. Comparison with the IV estimates in column 2 shows that the OLS estimate is downward biased for low-educated individuals because of negative self-selection into ethnic enclaves but consistent for high-educated individuals because of an absence of sorting. When we take account of sorting, the ethnic enclave size has a positive but insignificant effect on the employment probability of low-educated individuals. For high-educated individuals, one relative standard deviation increase in ethnic enclave size decreases the employment probability by (0.77 × 0.027 =) 0.021, that is, 2.1 percentage points.[19]

Wage earners are obliged to contribute to a supplementary pension scheme, ATP, as an increasing function of the annual hours worked.[20] On the basis of the annual ATP contribution, I can therefore construct an indicator for full-time work for wage earners. Full-time work is defined as working on average at least 27 hours per week during the year. It is seen from table 7 that OLS and IV both yield negative estimates of the effect of ethnic enclave size on the probability of full-time work in year $t + 7$, but the IV estimate is significant only for high-educated wage earners for whom a relative standard deviation increase in the local ethnic stock reduces the probability of working full-time by 16%.

The finding of zero (negative) effect of the ethnic enclave size on the probability of working full-time suggests that the ethnic enclave size has zero (negative) effect on the annual hours worked. The implication is that the ethnic enclave size increases annual earnings by increasing the hourly wage rate rather than by increasing annual hours worked. A positive effect of ethnic enclave size on the hourly wage is difficult to reconcile with

---

[18] Descriptive evidence suggests that the overall sample of refugees was initially randomly distributed across locations; in particular, there are no significant differences in educational attainment of refugees assigned to a municipality with below/above-average local inflow of assigned conationals. The instrument has a strong predictive power. The log of local inflow of assigned conationals enters the first-stage regressions with a coefficient of .274–.321, depending on the skill group. The null hypothesis of a zero effect of the identifying variable is rejected at a 1% significance level for all samples. The t-values range from 5.04 to 9.54.

[19] Further IV estimates shown in table 6 suggest that living in an ethnic enclave worsens the wage employment chances of high-educated individuals.

[20] Workers were given no ATP contribution if they worked 0–8 weekly hours, one-third of the full ATP contribution if 9–17 weekly hours, two-thirds of the full ATP contribution if 18–26 weekly hours, and the full ATP contribution (1,166.40 Danish kroner [DKK]) if 27 weekly hours or more.

the ethnic goods consumption hypothesis. So is the negative enclave effect on the employment probability for high-skilled refugees.

Can the results then be explained by spillover of information or norms within the ethnic network? In my view, they cannot be easily explained by norms spillover. In particular, for the high-skilled, one can rule out spillover of norms that endorse self-sufficiency, because it would increase the job search effort and thereby the employment probability, contradicting my findings. By contrast, the results are consistent with information spillover within the ethnic network that increases the job-worker match quality and thereby hourly wages.

If the results are due to such information spillover within the ethnic network, we should expect the following. First, enclave members should gain more from interaction with high-ability and employed workers than low-ability and unemployed workers (see, e.g., Montgomery 1991; Topa 2001; Calvo-Armengol and Jackson 2002); that is, the earnings return to living in an ethnic enclave should increase with enclave quality. Second, a considerable share of the refugees should have found their current job through their ethnic network.

I examine whether the earnings return to living in an ethnic enclave does in fact increase with enclave quality along the lines of Bertrand et al. (2000) and Edin et al. (2003). I include an interaction between enclave quality and the log of the local ethnic stock in year $t + 7$ in equation (1). The main effect of enclave quality is not identified separately from the country of origin fixed effects. I use four different measures of enclave quality in 1985, that is, the year prior to the implementation of the spatial dispersal policy: (i) mean annual earnings of the ethnic group; (ii) the share of self-employed in the ethnic group; (iii) the share of the ethnic group with upper-secondary or tertiary education, that is, at least 10 years of education; and (iv) the share of the ethnic group with tertiary education.

The IV estimates of the main effect of the log of the local ethnic stock in year $t + 7$ and the interaction between this variable and enclave quality are reported in table 8. The instrument for the log of the local ethnic stock in year $t + 7$ is the same as in the baseline earnings model, the log of the local inflow of assigned conationals. As an instrument for the interaction term I use the interaction between quality and the log of the local inflow of assigned conationals. The estimated main effect remains positive but decreases in magnitude and turns insignificant after inclusion of the interaction term. The estimated interaction effects are all positive but significant only when enclave quality is measured as mean annual earnings of the ethnic group or the share of the ethnic group with upper-secondary or tertiary education. The results provide weak

Table 8
The "Quality" of Enclaves (IV Estimates): Dependent Variable: ln(Earnings)

	Full Sample				Low Education (12 Years or Less)				High Education (More than 12 Years)			
	(1)	(2)	(3)	(4)	(5)	(6)	(7)	(8)	(9)	(10)	(11)	(12)
ln(local ethnic stock)	.07 (.15)	.13 (.15)	.06 (.17)	.11 (.15)	.06 (.16)	.18 (.16)	.05 (.19)	.14 (.16)	.26 (.45)	.10 (.42)	.26 (.48)	.08 (.43)
ln(local ethnic stock) × ethnic earnings (×10⁻⁴)	.07** (.03)				.08* (.04)				−.02 (.08)			
ln(local ethnic stock) × ethnic self-employment rate		2.67 (2.28)				1.49 (2.60)				3.62 (5.36)		
ln(local ethnic stock) × ethnic group share with at least 10 years of education			.55* (.33)				.61 (.40)				−.15 (.75)	
ln(local ethnic stock) × ethnic group share with at least 13 years of education				1.32 (.97)				1.10 (1.13)				1.21 (1.83)
R²	.026	.022	.033	.028	.032	.033	.042	.035	.176	.182	.175	.199
Number of individuals		5,647				4,745				902		

NOTE.—Controls are the same as in table 5. The instrument for the log of the local ethnic stock in year $t+7$ is the log of the inflow of assigned conationals to individual i's municipality of assignment since 1986 until the end of year t. The instrument for the interaction between quality and the log of the local ethnic stock in year $t+7$ is the interaction between quality and the log of the inflow of assigned conationals to individual i's municipality of assignment since 1986 until the end of year t. Standard errors, reported in parentheses, are corrected for heteroskedasticity and clustering of the residuals by municipality of assignment and year of immigration.
* Significant at the 10% level.
** Significant at the 5% level.
*** Significant at the 1% level.

Table 9
Distribution of the Number of Conationals at the Workplace in Year $t + 7$ (%)

	Number of Employed Individuals	\multicolumn{6}{c}{Number of Conationals at Workplace}
		0	1	2–4	5–9	10–29	30 or More
Low educated	989	43.78	18.81	19.92	7.99	5.56	3.94
High educated	196	54.59	16.33	18.88	3.57	3.06	3.57
All	1,185	45.57	18.40	19.75	7.26	5.15	3.88
With at least 10 years of education: low educated	989	73.31	9.91	10.41	2.12	4.15	.10
With at least 13 years of education: high educated	196	77.04	14.80	5.10	3.06	0	0

NOTE.—Private-sector workers in refugee sample, 1986 and 1987 cohorts excluded.

evidence that the return to living in an ethnic enclave increases with enclave quality.[21]

Finally, I would like to know the share of employed refugees who have obtained a job through their ethnic network. No precise information exists on the job search channels used to find a job for individuals in the refugee sample. However, the administrative registers enable me to calculate the share of private-sector refugee workers who have at least one co-ethnic colleague.[22] Refugees who have at least one co-ethnic colleague may potentially have obtained the job through their ethnic network. The first three rows of table 9 show the distribution of the number of conationals at the workplace in year $t + 7$ for private-sector refugee workers in the refugee sample:[23] 54% of private-sector refugee workers have at least one co-ethnic colleague at the workplace, 36% have at least two co-ethnic colleagues, and 16% have at least five co-ethnic colleagues.

[21] Evaluated at the sample means of the ethnic group share with upper-secondary or tertiary education, the overall effect of a relative standard deviation increase in the local ethnic stock on earnings is 17%.
[22] I link administrative records on the workplace in November, available for the full population of private-sector workers in Denmark in the period 1995–2000, with the population registers in the period 1995–2000. Next, I calculate the number of employees who are immigrants or descendants from source country k. Finally, I link this workplace information with the refugee sample and obtain the number of conationals at the workplace in year $t + 7$ as the number of immigrants and descendants from individual i's source country at individual i's workplace minus one.
[23] Workplace information is available for individuals in the refugee sample who got asylum in the period 1988–93 and who worked in the private sector in November 7 years after immigration: 3,319 individuals of the 1988–93 cohorts in the refugee sample were employed in year $t + 7$. Workplace information exists for 1,185 of these individuals.

If refugees primarily learn about relevant job vacancies from relatively high-skilled co-ethnic workers, the figures reported in the fourth and fifth rows of table 9 are more relevant than the figures in the first three. According to the last two rows, 7 years after immigration 27% of low-educated private-sector refugee workers had at least one co-ethnic colleague with upper-secondary or tertiary education and 23% of high-educated private-sector refugee workers had at least one high-educated co-ethnic colleague. These figures render probable that a considerable share of refugees have found their job through their ethnic network. In a Danish immigrant survey conducted in 1999 among 3,616 immigrants from the eight largest source countries, including six refugee-sending countries, 23% of employed immigrants had found their current job through the informal network (friends, relatives, and acquaintances; Schultz-Nielsen 2000).

Overall, the results presented in this section are consistent with the view that the ethnic network passes on information about job vacancies, which increases the job-worker match quality and thereby the hourly wage rate.

VII. Conclusion

Estimates based on the 1986–98 Danish spatial dispersal policy on refugees indicate that 7 years after immigration, refugees who lived in an ethnic enclave earned substantially more than non–enclave members. A relative standard deviation increase in the local ethnic stock on average increases annual earnings by 18%, irrespective of skill level. Edin et al. (2003) report an estimate of the enclave effect on annual earnings for low-skilled refugees similar to the estimate in this study, but they find a negative and insignificant effect for high-skilled refugees.

This finding of a positive earnings return to ethnic enclave size suggests that the potential negative effect of living in an ethnic enclave on the rate of acquisition of host country–specific human capital is more than outweighed by a positive effect.

Investigation of theoretical explanations for the positive net effect of ethnic enclave size on annual earnings of refugees reveals the following. First, one relative standard deviation increase in the ethnic enclave size decreases the employment probability of high-skilled individuals by 2.1 percentage points and decreases the probability of working full-time by 16% for high-skilled wage earners. The ethnic enclave size affects neither the employment probability of low-skilled individuals nor the probability of working full-time of low-skilled wage earners. These skill group differences in the return to living in an ethnic enclave may help explain the finding by LaLonde and Topel (1997) and Borjas (1998) that low-skilled immigrants have a higher tendency to live in ethnic enclaves than high-skilled immigrants. The absence of a positive effect on working hours suggests that the ethnic enclave size increases annual earnings of wage earners by increasing the hourly wage rate rather than by increasing annual hours worked. A positive effect of enclave size on the hourly wage rate and the negative enclave effect on the employment probability for the high-skill group are difficult to reconcile with the ethnic goods consumption hypothesis but are consistent with spillover of information within the ethnic network, which increases the job-worker match quality and thereby the wage rate. Also in line with favorable information spillover within the ethnic network, I find weak evidence that the return to living in an ethnic enclave increases with the quality of the ethnic enclave, in particular with mean annual earnings in the ethnic enclave and the share of enclave members who have upper-secondary or tertiary education. Finally, descriptive evidence on the distribution of the number of co-ethnic workers at the workplace for private-sector refugee workers renders probable that a substantial share of private-sector refugee workers have found their current job through their ethnic network.

Overall, the findings of the study are consistent with the hypothesis that the ethnic network passes on valuable information that increases annual earnings by increasing the job-worker match quality and thereby the hourly wage rate, irrespective of skill level.

Appendix

Table A1
Variable Definitions and Primary Data Sources

Variable	Definition	Primary Data Source
Individual characteristics:		
Employment status	Dummy for having one of the following types of main occupation during the year: (1) wage earner or (2) self-employed	Register-based labor force statistics, Statistics Denmark (DST)
Annual earnings	Sum of income from work and income from business in 1980 prices; all transfers unrelated to the employment position are excluded	Income tax registers, DST
Female	Dummy for sex	Population register, DST
Age	Age	Population register, DST
Married	Dummy for being married	Population register, DST
Young child	Dummy for presence of children between 0 and 2 years of age in the household	Population register, DST
Old child	Dummy for presence of children between 3 and 17 years of age in the household	Population register, DST
Country of origin	Dummy for immigrant source country	Population register, DST
Immigration year	Dummy for first year of receipt of residence permit	Population register, DST
Basic schooling	Dummy for 0–9 years of education constructed from an education code of highest degree attained	Survey-based register on immigrants' education level attained prior to immigration and integrated pupil register, DST
High school	Dummy for 10–12 years of education constructed from an education code of highest degree attained	Survey-based register on immigrants' education level attained prior to immigration and integrated pupil register, DST
University	Dummy for 13 or more years of education constructed from an education code of highest degree attained	Survey-based register on immigrants' education level attained prior to immigration and integrated pupil register, DST
Unknown education	Dummy for lack of information on highest degree attained	Survey-based register on immigrants' education level attained prior to immigration and integrated pupil register, DST

Table A1 (*Continued*)

Variable	Definition	Primary Data Source
Group characteristics:		
Ethnic stock in Denmark	Number of immigrants and descendants from source country k in Denmark	Population register, DST; author's calculations based on the 100% sample of immigrants
Local ethnic stock	Number of immigrants and descendants of immigrants from source country k residing in municipality j	Population register, DST; author's calculations based on the 100% sample of immigrants
Local inflow of assigned conationals	Sum of the number of immigrants from source country k assigned to municipality j by the authorities since 1986 until (the end of) year t, where t refers to the year of immigration of individual i	Population register, DST; author's calculations based on the 100% sample of immigrants
Ethnic earnings	Mean real annual earnings in 1985 (including zeros and in 1980 prices) of immigrants and descendants aged 18–59 from source country k	Income tax registers linked with population statistics, DST; author's calculations
Ethnic self-employment rate	Share of immigrants and descendants aged 18–59 from source country k with main occupation as self-employed in 1985	Register-based labor force statistics linked with population statistics, DST; author's calculations
Ethnic group share with at least 10 years of education	Share of immigrants and descendants aged 18–59 from source country k with at least 10 (imputed) years of education in 1985	Information on immigrants' educational attainment from surveys and the integrated pupil register linked with population statistics, DST; author's calculations
Ethnic group share with at least 13 years of education	Share of immigrants and descendants aged 18–59 from source country k with at least 13 (imputed) years of education in 1985	Information on immigrants' educational attainment from surveys and the integrated pupil register linked with population statistics, DST; author's calculations
Municipality characteristics:		
Number of inhabitants	Number of inhabitants in municipality j	Population statistics (population-counted data), DST
Immigrant stock	Number of immigrants and descendants of immigrants residing in municipality j	Population register, DST; author's calculations based on the 100% sample of immigrants
Unemployment rate	Unemployment rate in a radius of 60 DKK (approximately US$10) of transport around the largest post office in municipality j	Unemployment register (population-counted data), DST, and statistics on the cost of transport, the Ministry of Transport; constructed by local government studies

(*continued overleaf*)

% right-wing votes	Sum of votes for the Liberal Party and the Conservative People's Party in percentage of the sum of votes for the Liberal Party, the Conservative People's Party, the Social Democratic Party, and the Socialist People's Party at the latest municipal election; the two former parties are traditional right-wing parties whereas the latter two are traditional left-wing parties	Election statistics, DST
Number of educational institutions	Number of institutions for vocational and higher education in municipality j	Integrated pupil register (population-counted data), DST
% social housing	Number of social housing dwellings for all-year residence in percentage of the total number of dwellings for all-year residence in municipality j	Buildings and housing statistics (population-counted data), DST

Table A2
Summary Statistics: Means and Standard Deviations (Parentheses)

	All	Positive Earnings in $t+7$	Stayers	Movers	Permanent Return-Migrants
Individual characteristics:					
Female	.34 (.47)	.23 (.42)	.39 (.49)	.29 (.46)	.39 (.49)
Age	27.86 (7.60)	26.25 (6.27)	28.87 (8.08)	26.94 (7.00)	32.39 (13.08)
Married	.44 (.50)	.33 (.47)	.51 (.50)	.37 (.48)	.40 (.49)
Young child (0–2 years)	.24 (.43)	.15 (.35)	.24 (.43)	.19 (.39)	.13 (.33)
Old child (3–17 years)	.34 (.47)	.21 (.41)	.36 (.48)	.25 (.43)	.23 (.42)
Poland	.03 (.17)	.04 (.20)	.03 (.18)	.03 (.16)	.05 (.22)
Romania	.02 (.12)	.03 (.16)	.02 (.14)	.01 (.11)	.01 (.10)
Ethiopia	.01 (.10)	.01 (.11)	.01 (.11)	.01 (.10)	.03 (.17)
Somalia	.06 (.24)	.06 (.23)	.06 (.23)	.07 (.25)	.06 (.23)
Chile	.002 (.04)	.002 (.05)	.002 (.04)	.002 (.04)	.003 (.06)
Afghanistan	.02 (.14)	.02 (.14)	.02 (.14)	.02 (.14)	.01 (.11)
Iraq	.16 (.37)	.14 (.35)	.15 (.35)	.17 (.38)	.12 (.32)
Iran	.20 (.40)	.22 (.41)	.18 (.39)	.22 (.42)	.24 (.43)
Lebanon	.28 (.45)	.16 (.37)	.26 (.44)	.29 (.46)	.21 (.41)
Vietnam	.10 (.29)	.11 (.31)	.14 (.34)	.06 (.24)	.11 (.32)
Sri Lanka	.13 (.33)	.22 (.41)	.14 (.35)	.12 (.32)	.15 (.36)
Immigration year 1986	.26 (.44)	.33 (.47)	.24 (.43)	.29 (.45)	.28 (.45)
Immigration year 1987	.13 (.34)	.13 (.33)	.13 (.34)	.14 (.35)	.14 (.35)
Immigration year 1988	.10 (.30)	.10 (.29)	.10 (.29)	.11 (.31)	.13 (.33)
Immigration year 1989	.12 (.32)	.10 (.30)	.12 (.32)	.12 (.33)	.11 (.32)
Immigration year 1990	.09 (.28)	.07 (.26)	.19 (.29)	.08 (.27)	.08 (.27)
Immigration year 1991	.10 (.30)	.09 (.28)	.10 (.30)	.09 (.29)	.09 (.29)
Immigration year 1992	.11 (.32)	.11 (.31)	.13 (.34)	.07 (.26)	.09 (.29)
Immigration year 1993	.09 (.28)	.09 (.28)	.10 (.30)	.07 (.26)	.08 (.28)
Basic schooling	.14 (.34)	.10 (.30)	.15 (.36)	.13 (.34)	.01 (.10)
High school	.39 (.49)	.40 (.49)	.39 (.49)	.39 (.49)	.04 (.49)
University	.13 (.34)	.13 (.34)	.13 (.34)	.13 (.34)	.01 (.11)
Unknown education	.34 (.48)	.37 (.48)	.33 (.47)	.36 (.48)	.94 (.23)
Group characteristics:					
ln(ethnic stock in Denmark)	8.02 (.72)	7.99 (.72)	8.05 (.71)	7.99 (.72)	8.05 (.73)
ln(local ethnic stock)	4.81 (1.54)	4.71 (1.53)	5.32 (1.41)	4.34 (1.50)	4.77 (1.53)
ln(local inflow of assigned conationals)	3.45 (1.41)	3.35 (1.41)	3.84 (1.35)	3.09 (.137)	3.32 (1.46)
Municipality characteristics:					
Number of inhabitants	111,669 (136,851)	105,171 (134,241)	139,415 (138,574)	86,234 (130,168)	113,358 (141,279)
Large ($\geq$ 100,000 inhabitants)	.32 (.47)	.29 (.45)	.44 (.50)	.20 (.40)	.30 (.46)
Medium (10,000–99,999 inhabitants)	.59 (.49)	.61 (.49)	.52 (.50)	.66 (.47)	.61 (.49)
Small (< 10,000 inhabitants)	.09 (.29)	.10 (.30)	.04 (.19)	.15 (.35)	.09 (.28)
Immigrant stock	8,759 (15,784)	8,141 (15,522)	10,759 (16,322)	6,925 (15,044)	9,093 (16,483)
Unemployment rate	10.21 (2.40)	10.07 (2.45)	10.48 (2.34)	9.96 (2.43)	10.01 (2.43)
% right-wing votes	40.21 (12.16)	40.78 (12.36)	37.93 (10.39)	42.31 (13.25)	40.45 (12.89)
Number of educational institutions	9.14 (10.03)	8.64 (9.83)	11.55 (10.10)	6.92 (9.44)	9.22 (10.20)

(*continued overleaf*)

Table A2 (Continued)

	All	Positive Earnings in $t+7$	Stayers	Movers	Permanent Return-Migrants
% social housing	20.35 (9.96)	19.79 (9.85)	22.53 (8.84)	18.35 (10.49)	20.51 (10.27)
Number of observations	13,927	5,647	6,661	7,266	2,098

NOTE.—Variables refer to the values in year t, where t is the year of immigration. "Stayers" are those who stayed on in the assigned municipality between t and $t+7$. "Movers" are those who moved between these two time points.

Table A3
Summary Statistics for Dependent Variables and Key Explanatory Variables: Means and Standard Deviations (Parentheses)

	All	Positive Earnings in $t+7$
Mean real annual earnings	20,276	50,774
	(36,863)	(41,848)
Employment rate	.40	.81
	(.49)	(.40)
Wage employment rate	.33	.70
	(.47)	(.46)
Self-employment rate	.07	.10
	(.25)	(.30)
Mean local ethnic stock	1,010	825
	(1,177)	(182)
Mean real annual earnings in 1985[a]	22,753	21,932
	(12,548)	(13,110)
Self-employment rate in 1985[a]	.04	.03
	(.02)	(.02)
Share with at least 10 years of education in 1985[a]	.26	.26
	(.12)	(.13)
Share with at least 13 years of education in 1985[a]	.08	.08
	(.04)	(.05)
Number of observations	13,927	5,647

NOTE.—Unless otherwise stated, variables refer to the values in year $t+7$, where t is the year of immigration. Real annual earnings (in 1980 prices) are reported in DKK. In the period 1994–2000, mean real annual earnings conditional on having positive earnings of the overall Danish population aged 18–59 was 124,533 DKK for men and 84,118 DKK for women. In the same period the average employment rate of the overall Danish population aged 18–59 was 85% for men and 77% for women.

[a] Data source: Longitudinal administrative registers from Statistics Denmark on the immigrant population in Denmark, 1985.

Table A4
Summary Statistics of the Local Inflow of Assigned Refugees of Descent k from 1986 until the End of Year t per 10,000 Inhabitants: Means, Standard Deviations, and Variance Decomposition

Source Country k	Mean	Standard Deviation	Number of Municipalities of Assignment	Mean Number of Years	Within Variance Relative to Between Variance
Poland (1986–89)	1.87	1.99	100	1.58	26%
Romania (1986–91)	2.06	2.56	36	1.69	3%
Ethiopia (1986–90)	1.08	.78	27	2	40%
Somalia (1989–93)	2.88	3.64	68	2.04	55%
Chile (1986–88)	.55	.65	10	1.50	5%
Afghanistan (1986–93)	1.40	1.46	44	2.07	78%
Iraq (1986–93)	4.68	4.85	135	3.01	71%
Iran (1986–93)	7.81	7.14	144	3.41	40%
Lebanon (1986–93)	10.19	11.40	183	3.56	10%
Sri Lanka (1986–93)	10.80	10.73	145	2.45	9%
Vietnam (1986–93)	6.84	9.93	66	3.32	24%

NOTE.—Year t refers to the years 1986–93. The years in parentheses refer to the period (within the observation period) during which source country k was a refugee-sending country.

References

Akerlof, George A. 1980. A theory of social custom, of which unemployment may be one consequence. *Quarterly Journal of Economics* 94, no. 4:749–75.

Banerjee, Abhijit. 1992. A simple model of herd behavior. *Quarterly Journal of Economics* 107:797–818.

Bartel, Ann P. 1989. Where do the new U.S. immigrants live? *Journal of Labor Economics* 7, no. 4:371–91.

Bertrand, Marianne, Erzo F. P. Luttmer, and Sendhil Mullainathan. 2000. Network effects and welfare cultures. *Quarterly Journal of Economics* 115:1019–55.

Bikhchandani, Sushil, David Hirshleifer, and Ivo Welch. 1992. A theory of fads, fashion, custom, and cultural change in informational cascades. *Journal of Political Economy* 100:992–1026.

Borjas, George J. 1992. Ethnic capital and intergenerational mobility. *Quarterly Journal of Economics* 107, no. 1:123–50.

———. 1995. Ethnicity, neighborhoods, and human-capital externalities. *American Economic Review* 85, no. 3:365–90.

———. 1998. To ghetto or not to ghetto: Ethnicity and residential segregation. *Journal of Urban Economics* 44:228–53.

Calvo-Armengol, Antoni, and Matthew O. Jackson. 2002. Social norms and recruiting patterns in dynamics of employment and wages. Working Paper no. 1213, California Institute of Technology.

Case, Anne C., and Lawrence F. Katz. 1991. The company you keep: The effects of family and neighborhood on disadvantaged youths. Working Paper no. 3705, National Bureau of Economic Research, Cambridge, MA.

Chiswick, Barry R. 1991. Speaking, reading, and earnings among low-skilled immigrants. *Journal of Labor Economics* 9, no. 2:149–70.

Chiswick, Barry R., and Paul W. Miller. 2005. Do enclaves matter in immigrant adjustment? *City and Community* 4, no. 1:5–35.

Coleman, David, and Eskil Wadensjö. 1999. *Indvandringen til Danmark: Internationale og nationale perspektiver.* Viborg: Spektrum.

Coleman, J. S., E. Campbell, J. Hobson, J. McPartland, A. Mood, F. Weinfeld, and R. York. 1966. *Equality of educational opportunity.* Washington, DC: U.S. Government Printing Office.

Cutler, David, and Edward Glaeser. 1997. Are ghettos good or bad? *Quarterly Journal of Economics* 112, no. 3:827–72.

Damm, Anna P. 2005. The Danish dispersal policy on refugee immigrants 1986–1998: A natural experiment? Working Paper no. 05-03, Department of Economics, Aarhus School of Business, University of Aarhus.

Danish Refugee Council (Dansk Flygtningehjælp). 1993. Om geografisk spredning af asylansøgere, flygtninge og indvandrere. Internal report by Bente Bondebjerg and Morten Iversen. Danish Refugee Council, Copenhagen.

Edin, Per-Anders, Peter Fredriksson, and Oluf Åslund. 2003. Ethnic enclaves and the economic success of immigrants—evidence from a natural experiment. *Quarterly Journal of Economics* 118:329–57.

Glaeser, Edward L., Bruce Sacerdote, and José A. Scheinkman. 1996. Crime and social interactions. *Quarterly Journal of Economics* 111: 507–48.

Kobrin, Francis E., and Alden Speare. 1983. Outmigration and ethnic communities. *International Migration Review* 17:425–44.

LaLonde, Robert, and Robert Topel. 1997. Economic impact of international migration and the economic performance of migrants. In *Handbook of population economics*, ed. Mark Rosenzweig and Oded Stark. Amsterdam: North-Holland.

Lazear, Edward P. 1999. Culture and language. *Journal of Political Economy* 107, no. 6, pt. 2 (December): S95–S126.

Ministry of Internal Affairs (Indenrigsministeriet). 1996. *Udlændinge '96: En talmæssig belysning af udlændinge i Danmark.* Copenhagen: Indenrigsministeriet.

Montgomery, James D. 1991. Social networks and labor market outcomes: Towards an economic analysis. *American Economic Review* 81, no. 5: 1408–18.

Piore, Michael J. 1979. *Birds of passage: Migrant labor and industrial societies.* Cambridge: Cambridge University Press.

Portes, Alejandro. 1998. Social capital: Its origins and applications in modern sociology. *Annual Review of Sociology* 24:1–24.
Schultz-Nielsen, Marie L. 2000. Hvilke individuelle faktorer har betydning for integrationen på arbejdsmarkedet? In *Integration i Danmark omkring årtusindskiftet*, ed. Gunnar V. Mogensen and Poul C. Matthiessen. Aarhus: Aarhus Universitetsforlag, Rockwool Fondens Forskningsenhed.
Statistics Denmark. Various years. *Statistisk årbog* [Statistical yearbook]. Copenhagen: Statistics Denmark.
———. 2000. *Statistiske efterretninger 2000(1) om befolkning og valg* [Statistical news 2000(1) on population and elections]. Copenhagen: Statistics Denmark.
Topa, Georgio. 2001. Social interactions, local spillovers and unemployment. *Review of Economic Studies* 68, no. 2:261–95.
Wilson, William J. 1987. *The truly disadvantaged: The inner city, the underclass, and public policy.* Chicago: University of Chicago Press.

[12]

PRODUCTIVITY OF HIGHLY SKILLED IMMIGRANTS: ECONOMISTS IN THE POSTWAR PERIOD

JOHN M. MCDOWELL and LARRY D. SINGELL, JR*

Prior work finds declining immigrant quality in the postwar period that is linked to source-country and skill-composition changes associated with the 1965 Immigration Act. This paper uses a unique panel of foreign- and native-born American Economic Association members to show that the highly skilled experienced a similar shift away from European migrants toward those from Asia. However, the findings do not indicate that this change in source-country composition has been accompanied by a decline in quality; rather, the most recent cohorts of foreign-born economists appear to be more productive than their native counterparts. (JEL J61)

I. INTRODUCTION

This article is the first systematic analysis of the attributes and abilities of foreign-born U.S. economists since a descriptive study of the brain drain by Grubel and Scott [1967]. It also provides some of the first formal evidence for the largely theoretical proposition in earlier work by Bhagwati and Rodriquez [1975] that the United States draws the best skilled workers from abroad. However, recent immigration literature has not focused on the brain drain but has generated considerable debate concerning whether the 1965 Immigration and Nationality Act has reduced the skill quality of U.S. immigrants. In particular, descriptive evidence in Borjas [1987] and Greenwood [1983], respectively, indicates that the 1965 law shifted the composition of U.S. immigrants toward non-European nations and increased the number of low-skilled migrants to the United States. Our article extends this work by examining whether there has been a post-1965 change in the source-country mix of Ph.D. economists and whether such changes impact the productivity of the foreign born in comparison to their native counterparts.

Most empirical studies of immigrant productivity have focused on earnings. Early cross-sectional studies of immigrant earnings, including Chiswick [1978a], concluded that the age–earnings profile of immigrants is steeper than that of comparable native-born workers and, though initially lower, crosses the native profile 10 to 15 years after immigration. These results are consistent with the widely held belief that the immigration process self-selects the highly motivated and industrious from their respective source countries. Thus immigrants, although they initially enter the United States with relatively low levels of human capital, eventually become more productive than their native counterparts.

More recent work by Borjas [1985, 1987] has contested these conclusions, arguing that it is not possible to separately identify assimilation and cohort effects using a single cross-sectional data set. In particular, the positive correlation between earnings and years since migration in cross-sectional data may be due to immigrant assimilation or a cohort effect that arises from the declining skill quality of more recent immigrant groups. Borjas combines multiple cross-sectional data sets to separately identify assimilation and cohort effects and finds evidence indicating that earlier cohorts of immigrants do relatively better than both natives and more recent immigrant cohorts, suggesting a decline in immigrant quality. Although

---

*We would like to thank George Borjas, Daniel Hamermesh, and Michael Greenwood for their insights and suggestions. We are responsible for any remaining mistakes.

McDowell: Professor, Department of Economics, Arizona State University, Tempe, Ariz. 85287-3806. Phone 1-480-965-7109, Fax 1-480-965-0748, E-mail john.mcdowell@asu.edu.

Singell: Associate Professor, Department of Economics, University of Oregon, Eugene, Or. 97403-1285. Phone 1-541-346-4672, Fax 1-541-346-1243, E-mail lsingell@oregon.uoregon.edu.

Chiswick [1986] challenges the contention of declining immigrant quality and Funkhouser and Trejo [1995] find evidence that immigrant quality may have increased during the 1980s, Borjas [1995] contends that the empirical evidence consistently shows that immigrant quality has declined for most of the postwar period.

However, the decline in immigrant quality has not necessarily been found within specific groups of immigrants. In particular, Greenwood and McDowell [1986] find that the change in skill quality is related to the shift in the source-country composition of immigrants away from European nations toward those from Asia and Latin American after the 1965 Immigration Act. Thus, explanations for the relatively poor performance of recent immigrants, including those in LaLonde and Topel [1991, 1992] and Borjas [1992], focus on the post-1965 changes in the incentives to migrate to the United States that have increased the number of low-skilled, non- European immigrants.

This article takes an alternative approach by focusing on a group of highly skilled workers (i.e., Ph.D. economists). In particular, we use publication and personal data for a panel of native- and foreign-born economists who are members of the American Economics Association (AEA). Our analysis finds a source-country composition shift for the economics profession over the last 60 years that is similar to the broader population of immigrants. We use a tobit model of research productivity to examine whether, consistent with prior analysis in Borjas [1995], the shift in the national origin mix away from traditional European source countries has generated a less "successful" immigrant flow.

In the article, traditional cross-sectional specifications that focus on assimilation effects are compared with longitudinal specifications that distinguish between assimilation and cohort effects. In addition, our unique data permit us to extend prior work by using both detailed personal/regional controls and panel techniques to examine whether observed assimilation and cohort effects can be attributed to changes in either observed and/or unobserved heterogeneity, respectively. This permits us to examine more clearly whether there are changes in the relative productivity of foreign-born economists over time. Our results provide evidence of systematic productivity differences between highly skilled foreign- and native-born workers that varies over time in response to both immigration policy and market conditions.

II. THE PANEL

The analysis uses a panel of foreign- and native-born American Economic Association (AEA) members who entered the economics profession over a period prior to World War II and ending in the mid-1980s. These unique data, though contained in readily available sources, have not previously been organized in a way that could be empirically exploited. Thus, it is useful to examine briefly how the panel is constructed to study changes in the characteristics of foreign-born AEA members, both in absolute terms and in relative comparison to the native born, over a time period that encompasses the passage of the 1965 Immigration Act.

Construction of the Panel

The primary sources for the panel is the biographical listings in the 1964 and 1974 AEA directories and the 1985 computer tape, which are used to identify the native- or foreign-born status of AEA members.[1] We select all foreign-born AEA members aged 65 or less if the individual received a Ph.D. (or equivalent degree) from: (1) a U.S. institution, or (2) a foreign institution, but works for an employer located in the United States.[2] The native-born control group must also be aged 65 or less and meet criterion (1) or (2). The native sample group is initially selected at a 50% rate of the foreign-born population within each of the respective 1964, 1974,

1. The biographical listings in the published AEA directories provide data on the year and place of birth in the 1964, 1969, and 1974 editions. After 1974, only the year of birth is available in the published AEA directories. For surveys after 1974, the computer tapes containing the responses to the AEA Survey of Members can be used to retrieve information on birthplace. Diamond and Haurin [1994] were the first to use the computer tapes for research purposes.

2. An AEA member is included if he or she is age 65 or less. For example, an economist who is 45 in 1964, 55 in 1974, and 66 in 1985 would be included in the panel for 1964 and 1974 but not 1985. Not all AEA members respond to the portion of the survey that relates to nativity. The percentages of respondents providing data on birthplace are 73.1% (1964), 68.1% (1974), and 71.1% (1985).

and 1985 cross-sections. For all individuals, demographic and career-related data are collected from the biographical listings in various AEA directories.[3] These data include date and place of birth, gender, degree years and source institutions, principal employment and (if foreign born) the year of entry into U.S. employment, and the individual's major fields of interest.[4]

The panel is constructed in several steps. First, the foreign-born panel is obtained by simply cross-checking and linking the names of individuals who match in each of the cross-sections. This yields a panel that traces the careers of 65% of foreign-born economists in more than one cross-section. Next, the initial native-born control group is supplemented by adding observations for the originally sampled native-born economists in each of the other cross-sections in which they are also found. For example, the name of a native-born economist in the initial 1974 random sample is cross-checked and observations added in other cross-sections if this individual also is observed in the 1964 or 1985 AEA directories. Because the overlap of the initial random cross-sectional samples of native-born economists for 1964, 1974, and 1985 is relatively small, the number of native-born economists in the final panel data actually exceeds that of the foreign born even though the native born are originally selected at a 50% rate of the foreign born in each cross-section. Nonetheless, following all cross-sectional observations of the control group over time is consistent with the construction of the foreign-born panel and ensures a sizable panel that includes approximately 65% of the native-born economists originally sampled.

The final step in constructing the panel involves adding data relating to a 1989 cross-section. The 1989 cross-section is constructed by taking all foreign- and native-born individuals in their respective 1985 cross-section and including individuals in the 1989 data if they otherwise met the criteria for sample inclusion. Thus, no attempt is made to add "new" names in the 1989 cross-section.[5] By adding the 1989 cross-section, the panel data include individuals who received their Ph.D. after 1974 and include the most recent year for which all the data necessary for the analysis of research output are available.

The personal data are supplemented with information pertaining to publication activity that is collected from various issues of the AEA *Index of Economic Articles*. Publications are recorded over a 2-year period and then aggregated to provide a measure of research output. More specifically, an individual's publications are represented by articles that are published in the year of the cross-sectional observation plus articles published in the year immediately following (i.e., 1964–65, 1974–75, 1985–86, or 1989–90).[6] The publication data also include information on the number of coauthors and journal placement. This latter information is used to provide alternative weighted measures of publication activity.[7]

---

3. To a much lesser extent, other data sources also are used (e.g., *American Men and Women of Sciences: Social and Behavioral Science*).

4. The 1985 computer tape only provides information on whether the individual is native or foreign born. For foreign-born individuals, several steps were taken to identify the precise country of birth (or origin). First, if the individual is also found in the 1964, 1969, or 1974 published AEA directories, the country of birth is determined from these sources. For the remaining individuals who had degrees from foreign institutions (e.g., a U.S. Ph.D. but a B.A. from a foreign institution), the location of the foreign degree–granting institution is used as the country of origin. Finally, for the foreign born who had degrees only from U.S. institutions, a phone survey was conducted in which the individual was asked the place of birth. This survey resulted in country-of-birth data on 132 of 154 individuals surveyed. The 22 individuals for which precise country of birth could not be determined were dropped from the sample.

5. To keep a similar time span between cross-sections, a 1989 observation is included only if the individual is found in the 1993 AEA directory.

6. Only articles published in journals are enumerated in the publication counts. Thus, published books and articles published in books of collected works are not included.

7. Following Sauer's [1988] findings for the rewards to coauthorship, weighted measures use the simple $1/n$ rule. For "quality" of journal placement, the weighted measures use as weights the journal's "impact factor" as reported in the *SSCI Journal Citation Reports*. Native- and foreign-born individuals in the sample published articles in 412 publication outlets (as recorded in the *Index of Economic Articles*). A quality index or impact factor is available for 224 of these 412 publication outlets. For the remaining 188 outlets, a weight of zero is used. Of the 188 outlets assigned a weight of zero, 106 outlets are not contained in the *World List of Social Science Periodicals* [UNESCO 1991], which lists 4,459 periodicals that meet their criteria of being a "scientific periodical." Only 11 of the remaining 82 journals, which are noted as a "scientific periodical" in the *World List* but are assigned a zero weight, are published in the United States.

The use of panel data follows the precedent established in Huang [1987] and Borjas [1985] that has shifted the focus from a single cross-section of data to longitudinal data constructed by aggregating cross-sectional random samples of different sets of individual in several time periods. However, our panel offers a number of advantages over prior analyses. First, while recent analyses have used longitudinal data, most do not follow the same individuals over time, as permitted by our AEA data.[8] Without a panel, longitudinal studies are not able to separate aggregate changes in cohort ability (e.g., less able persons migrate to the United States) from changes in the unobserved quality of time varying immigrant attributes (e.g., a decline in the quality of a foreign versus a U.S. education). This is particularly a problem because the source country for the time-varying attributes, such as education, is generally unknown. Second, prior studies use earnings that are only an indirect measure of productivity. However, our publication measure is a direct qualitative measure of output. Finally, the homogeneity of economists, although limiting generalizations to broader populations, permits us to examine cohort effects for workers who have similar training and opportunities.

Descriptive Statistics

Descriptive statistics for foreign- and native-born AEA members who enter the profession before and after 1965 are included in Table I. The data include 2,958 person-year observations of 1,180 foreign-born economists and 3,385 person-year observations of 1,354 native-born economists. Thus, on average, both native- and foreign-born economists contribute roughly 2.5 panel years to the data. Overall, the descriptive statistics suggest that foreign-born economists are older with more experience, and they are more likely to be male and placed in academia than their native-born counterparts. Foreign-born economists also are less likely to attend a top-35 Ph.D. institution, but this may simply reflect that their degrees are more frequently conferred by institutions outside the United States.

Table I suggests a number of differences in the profession before versus after 1965. The most notable change is the source-region mix of the foreign born. In particular, among those who entered the economics profession prior to 1965, over 70% of foreign-born economists migrated from Europe or Canada, whereas these regions contributed only 40% of foreign-born economists entering after 1965. At the same time, foreign-born economists from Asia nearly doubled, from 20% to 37%, between the two periods. The most distinct difference between the post-1965 source-region mix of economists and that of the general population of U.S. immigrants is the relatively small representation of economists from Latin America after 1965.[9] Our empirical analysis examines if there are changes in relative productivity over time after controlling for observed and unobserved heterogeneity of native- and foreign-born economists.

III. THE EMPIRICAL MODEL

The empirical model encompasses the traditional cross-sectional approach, subsequent modifications by longitudinal studies, and more recent attempts to explain observed cohort effects by including more detailed controls for worker and country attributes. In addition, we extend prior analyses by the introduction of panel techniques to control for unobserved worker heterogeneity. A general tobit model is developed to show how the specifications are related.

Tobit Model of Research Productivity

Economists, whether foreign or native born, are viewed as allocating time and resources to maximize utility over their career. The utility of professional economists is likely to depend on research output both because it enters as an argument in their utility function and because the institutions for which they work compensate them to various degrees for research activities. Thus, util-

---

8. Typically, these analyses track the progress of a particular cohort over successive cross-sectional data bases. Analyses using actual longitudinal data are provided in Chiswick [1978b], Jasso and Rosenzweig [1986, 1988], and Borjas [1989].

9. McDowell and Singell [1998] provide a more detailed, descriptive analysis of these data.

TABLE I
Descriptive Statistics

	All Years		Pre-1965		Post-1965	
	Foreign Born	Native Born	Foreign Born	Native Born	Foreign Born	Native Born
Attributes						
Age	46.570	44.310	50.480	48.680	43.510	41.120
Experience	15.010	13.750	19.320	17.780	11.640	10.800
Female	0.033	0.073	0.037	0.050	0.031	0.090
B.A. in the U.S.	0.349	0.999	0.400	1.000	0.308	0.999
Foreign Ph.D.	0.084	0.007	0.131	0.011	0.047	0.005
Ph.D. in Top 35[a]	0.660	0.739	0.710	0.804	0.624	0.692
Occupation academic	0.749	0.724	0.783	0.775	0.722	0.686
Occupation government	0.054	0.092	0.056	0.073	0.053	0.106
Occupation business	0.086	0.105	0.072	0.087	0.096	0.118
Occupation other	0.112	0.080	0.089	0.065	0.129	0.090
Source Region						
Africa	0.030	0.000	0.012	0.000	0.044	0.000
Asia	0.296	0.000	0.201	0.000	0.370	0.000
Canada	0.096	0.000	0.103	0.000	0.090	0.000
Carribean	0.025	0.000	0.009	0.000	0.037	0.000
Eastern Europe	0.101	0.000	0.186	0.000	0.035	0.000
Mexico/Central America	0.012	0.000	0.007	0.000	0.016	0.000
Middle East	0.062	0.000	0.039	0.000	0.079	0.000
Northwest Europe	0.254	0.000	0.317	0.000	0.204	0.000
Oceania	0.019	0.000	0.012	0.000	0.025	0.000
Southeast Europe	0.080	0.000	0.103	0.000	0.062	0.000
South America	0.023	0.000	0.009	0.000	0.033	0.000
Productivity Measures						
Published pages	11.513	9.518	8.647	6.535	13.753	11.700
Published pages: weight by coauthors and quality	8.424	6.899	7.053	5.130	9.497	8.192
Articles	0.540	0.670	0.480	0.540	0.620	0.820
Articles: weight by coauthors and quality	0.417	0.427	0.388	0.416	0.439	0.435
Number of Observations	2958	3385	1298	1430	1660	1955

[a] Quality of academic institution is determined from data provided in Graves et al. [1982].

ity maximization is postulated to generate an optimal amount research for an economist i at time interval t, Q_{it}^* that can be expressed as a linear function:

(1) $\quad Q_{it}^* = \alpha X_{it} + \beta Y_{it} + \gamma Z_{it} + \varepsilon_{it}$

where X_{it} is the vector of variables included in traditional cross-sectional studies; Y_{it} is a vector of cohort effects found in longitudinal studies; Z_{it} is a vector observable ability measures that include regional dummies and personal characteristics; α, β, and γ are parameter vectors; and ε_{it} is the error term.

Like many optimization problems, the optimal amount of research consumed (produced) is not restricted to be greater than zero (e.g., the labor-leisure model). Nonetheless, observed research output, Q_{it}, must be nonnegative. Using equation (1), Q_{it} can be described by a semidiscrete function:

(2.1) $\quad Q_{it} = 0 \sim if\ \varepsilon_{it} \leq (\alpha X_{it} + \beta Y_{it} + \gamma Z_{it})$

(2.2) $\quad Q_{it} = Q_{it}^* \sim if\ \varepsilon_{it} > (\alpha X_{it} + \beta Y_{it} + \gamma Z_{it})$.

Expressions (2.1) and (2.2) form the basis for several specifications of a tobit model of the research output, which differ from one another based on the assumptions regarding the parameters and/or the error term.

The Empirical Specification

As a point of departure we use the number of published pages to measure Q_{it} because it has relatively more variation than its alternatives. Nonetheless, the other publication measures are also used and show that the results are robust to the choice of dependent variable. Our base specification follows the early cross-sectional work that assume β and γ equal zero and includes measures of human capital (i.e., age and experience) and, for immigrants, the differential return to post-Ph.D. U.S. experience. For all economists, research output is expected to increase with post-Ph.D. experience, whereas its square and cubic are included to account for possible nonlinearities in research output documented in Oster and Hamermesh [1998] and McDowell [1982]. The individual's age and its square are also included to account for the depreciation of human capital that occurs, if nothing else, because technical skills eventually become dated. The number of years since entry, as measured by years since first post-Ph.D. U.S. employment, and its square are used to proxy for the assimilation effect. The inclusion of the years-since-entry variable roughly follows the methodology found in Borjas [1990] and Chiswick [1978a]. Unfortunately, the AEA directories include information on an economist's first U.S. appointment, but not when they actually first entered the United States. Thus, the years-since-entry variable measures the immigrant-specific return to post-Ph.D. U.S. experience.

Contrary to early cross-sectional work, our data include multiple time periods and male and female workers. Thus, X_{it} includes two additional variables. First, to account for possible gender differences in research output documented in Hansen et al. [1978], the model includes a binary variable that equals one for female economists. Second, following longitudinal studies that use multiple cross-sections, a dummy variable is included for the 1974, 1985, and 1989 cross-sections to test for possible period effects relative to the 1964 sample.

To make use of the longitudinal aspects of our data, several specifications supplement X_{it} with Y_{it} that includes 10 entry cohort dummies for the 5-year intervals, starting with the first observed cohort in 1936–40 and ending with the last observed cohort in 1981–85. The 5-year interval ensures at least 30 observations in each interval and has the added advantage of being directly comparable to the time intervals used in prior longitudinal studies. These entry cohort variables permit us to observe whether the quality of foreign-born economists has changed over time.

Prior work suggests that the observed cohort effects for a random sample of immigrants can be attributed to changes in the source country mix of the foreign born and their associated differences in observed attributes. This hypothesis is tested by introducing the vector Z_{it} that includes two groups of variables that broadly proxy for immigrant quality. First, a set of 10 binary variables for region of origin are used and include (in alphabetical order) Africa, Asia, the Caribbean, Eastern Europe, Mexico and Central America, the Middle East, Northwest Europe, Oceania (i.e., Australia, New Zealand, and the Pacific Islands), South America, and Southwest Europe. Canada is used as the excluded region because it includes a large number of immigrants across all time periods and because of its cultural similarity and spacial proximity to the United States. Although the actual country of origin is known for each of the foreign-born economists, the relatively broad regions ensure a reasonable number of observations in each category and conserve degrees of freedom.

Second, research output may differ over time and by country because of changes in: (1) the occupational distribution toward jobs that are less research oriented (i.e., from academia to government), (2) the quality of education with relatively fewer graduates from top Ph.D. programs, or (3) the choice of field toward those that produce less research or those that have experienced less growth in research opportunities. Thus Z_{it} also includes 3 measures for occupation type, 4 schooling measures, and 15 field-of-specialization variables that are used to examine whether these observed differences can account for possible cohort or regional differences among immigrants.[10]

The model in its most general form permits the productivity of the foreign born to vary over time via experience (including a differential return to U.S. experience), period,

---

10. Academics are distinguished from other occupations by three binary variables that are equal to one if the individual is employed in business, government, or

and cohort effects. However, because there are only two sources of variation in the model (i.e., time and individual), all of these effects cannot be separately identified for the foreign born. Following the identification strategy in Borjas [1985], the native- and foreign-born samples are combined and the model is estimated with the restriction that the human-capital measures (except for years since entry), the personal attributes (except for the entry-cohort variables), and period effects are the same for native-born and foreign-born economists. The period effects capture overall changes in the tendency to publish in the profession over time, which may reasonably be assumed to be the same for native-born and foreign-born economists.[11]

The Error Term

The error term, ε_{it}, is likely to arise naturally in this problem and is modeled as having two possible sources. First, while the production of research requires generally a continuous effort on the part of the researcher, observed publications are inherently discrete. Thus, publication measures for a given time interval may overstate the true output in the period (if the author had a backlog of articles accepted), or understate the true output (if the author had a rash of rejections). Moreover, any criterion used to compare research output across individuals is imperfect and is likely, for example, to exclude some relevant research outlets and give an inappropriate weight to some others that are included. In this case, observed output is measured with error that varies by individual and time, which we denote as u_{it}, where $u_{it} \sim N(0, \sigma_u^2)$.

Second, there may be idiosyncratic publishing tendencies of a given individual that are not fully captured by even a detailed list of explanatory variables. This unobserved publishing tendency is likely to be correlated over time; for simplicity, we specify the error process as AR(1), $\rho \varepsilon_{it}$. It is assumed that $\rho \varepsilon_{it}$ and u_{it} are independent, which essentially requires that the individual's unmeasured ability is uncorrelated with the measurement error in the dependent variable beyond that attributable to the first-order correlation.[12]

Thus, in the most general form, the error term can be expressed as:

$$\varepsilon_{it} = \rho \varepsilon_{it-1} + u_{it}. \quad (3)$$

Our empirical analysis uses two different assumptions regarding the error. First, we estimate a standard tobit model that assumes that the only source of the randomness is the stochastic nature of the publication process, u_{it}. Second, we estimate an autoregressive tobit model using the error specification in equation (3), which is estimated using the hermite integral approximation of the type described by Butler and Moffit [1982].[13] Comparisons of the two models provide some

---

other nonacademic institutions. Two schooling measures are constructed from departmental publication rankings in Graves et al. [1982]. First, a binary variable that equals one if the individual received a Ph.D. from a top 35 program is used to broadly distinguish research- versus nonresearch-oriented departments. Second, this variable is interacted with the log of the Graves ranking to distinguish among research-oriented institutions. Because foreign institutions are not included in the Graves ranking, a binary variable that is equal to one for those individuals who obtain a Ph.D. from an institution located outside the United States is also included. Immigrants who received their B.A. in the United States are also distinguished from those who did not, because migration decisions that occur at a younger age (particularly if the migrant is a child) are likely to differ from those that occur for employment reasons. Finally, a set of 15 dummy variables is included to control for the primary area of research interest, where the category "general" (as defined by *Journal of Economic Literature* prior to 1991) is excluded.

11. The period-effect restriction is the minimum identification requirement. The human-capital and personal-attribute coefficients are also restricted to be the same for native- and foreign-born economists because less restrictive empirical specifications find no statistical differences by origin of birth. Thus, we follow prior work and focus on cohort and year-since-entry effects.

12. As an alternative to the proposed model, the random-effects tobit model specifies an individual-specific random component, α_i, that measures unobserved heterogeneity instead of $\rho \varepsilon_{it}$. Hsiao [1986] proposes including a lag of research output and conducting a t-test on its coefficient to confirm the possible presence of an individual effect. This test is conducted for several specifications and supports the presence of an individual effect, which could arise from several sources, including serial correlation or unobserved heterogeneity. We select the AR(1) model because its likelihood function is significantly more stable in convergence; replication of our AR(1) specifications using a random-effects tobit model yield the same qualitative conclusions when the random-effects model converges.

13. A first-order, autoregressive structure can arise if there is serial correlation or state dependence. The difference between the two hypothesis is that the former implies research output depend on the entire history of the errors, whereas the latter output depends only on a one-period lag of output. We conduct a test for state

insights into the importance of unobserved heterogeneity in determining the assimilation and cohort effects.

IV. EMPIRICAL RESULTS

To make our analysis directly comparable to prior immigration studies, we restrict our analysis to Ph.D. economists working in the United States. The analysis first compares and contrasts the results of the cross-sectional and longitudinal models to examine whether assimilation and cohort effects that are found for broader populations of immigrants are also present for foreign-born economists. Subsequent analysis examines whether observed individual heterogeneity can explain the possible differential return to U.S. experience and cohort effects. Each of the specifications is estimated using both a standard and an autoregressive tobit model to examine the role of unobserved heterogeneity in assimilation and cohort quality.

Cross-Sectional and Longitudinal Estimates

The results applying cross-sectional and longitudinal specifications to the number of published pages using both the standard and autoregressive tobit models are presented in Table II. Each of specifications presented are replicated and are robust to the use of alternative publication measures.[14] Moreover, the coefficients on the human capital, gender, and period variables are also qualitatively equivalent across the models. In particular, research output appears to increase with

---

dependence proposed by Chamberlain [1982] that uses a likelihood-ratio test to compare a specification with and without the lagged values of the time varying explanatory variables. The chi-squared statistic of 14.1 rejects the null of state dependence at the 5% level. Thus, the AR(1) model is used in the estimations.

14. As a point of comparison, columns 1 and 2 of Appendix Table A1 include the base longitudinal specification using the number of articles weighted by coauthors and the quality index, which is the publication measure that is most distinct from published pages. The results are qualitatively equivalent but yield less significant cohort effects than those presented subsequently. The descriptive statistics provided by McDowell and Singell [1998] indicate that foreign-born economists are more likely to coauthor than native-born economists, particularly those in early cohorts, which may account for the smaller observed cohort effect when using a coauthor adjusted publication measure.

experience, and publication skills depreciate with age.[15] Overall, the period effects suggest that research production has increased over time, which likely reflects both the increase in the number of research outlets and the expansion of institutions that require research for promotion.[16] In addition, female AEA members appear to produce significantly less than their male counterparts. Given the robustness of the findings for the non-immigrant-specific results, the remaining discussion focuses on the predicted differences between foreign- and native-born economists.

The first two columns of Table II replicate the traditional cross-sectional model of immigrant productivity and confirm prior findings that productivity increases at a decreasing rate with years since entry. Finding an assimilation effect from the first year of U.S. employment is not necessarily expected because 35% of foreign-born economists obtain their B.A. in the United States, and roughly 90% have a U.S. Ph.D. Thus the assimilation process is likely to have already begun before our defined point of U.S. labor-force entry. Moreover, the educational backgrounds of the foreign born who ultimately select a U.S. professional career are likely to have begun the assimilation process well before they actually migrate. Therefore, it is not surprising that the inclusion of controls for possible cohort effects (columns 3 and 4) and the use of panel techniques (columns 7 and 8) eliminate the significant differential return to U.S. experience for the foreign-born economists by controlling for observed and unobserved heterogeneity. To the extent that foreign-born economists are not expected to benefit from assimilation in these data, the finding of a significant assimilation effect in the cross-sectional specification suggests that the failure to control for changes in immigrant quality can yield predicted increases in productivity with years since entry when none is, in fact, present.

The cohort effects presented in Table II suggest a U-shaped productivity differential

---

15. The negative coefficient on age could also reflect unobserved differences in ability or motivation between those who finish their Ph.D. at older and younger ages.
16. Although the number of published pages have increased over time, the number of articles weighted by quality and coauthors has not increased (Appendix Table A1).

TABLE II
Cross-Sectional and Longitudinal Specifications[a]

	Standard Tobit				Auto-regressive Tobit			
	Cross-Sectional		Longitudinal		Cross-Sectional		Longitudinal	
	Coeff.	SE	Coeff.	SE	Coeff.	SE	Coeff.	SE
Constant	172.08*	23.30	166.77*	23.23	135.26*	20.99	135.84*	20.98
Experience	527.39*	78.23	531.56*	80.84	493.25*	66.46	531.63*	67.36
(Experience)^2	−1,673.40*	451.22	−1,428.30*	458.24	−1,615.84*	371.10	−1,595.09*	375.86
(Experience)^3	2,733.00*	791.12	1,954.80*	808.91	2,781.32*	650.22	2,419.41*	662.90
Age	−760.41*	112.41	−749.50*	112.83	−591.37*	99.03	−612.49*	99.55
(Age)^2	441.35*	121.33	438.22*	121.83	264.55*	105.54	296.22*	106.64
Female	−9.69*	3.43	−8.45*	3.41	−8.73*	4.16	−7.14**	4.13
Year 1974	0.86	2.59	0.98	2.72	4.16**	2.21	2.80	2.45
Year 1985	8.88*	2.57	6.14*	3.10	10.83*	2.69	7.19*	3.35
Year 1989	14.26*	2.71	10.41*	3.42	14.38*	2.99	10.04*	3.82
Years since entry	85.61*	27.23	20.59	56.17	67.13*	29.25	−25.96	37.67
(Years since entry)^2	−218.82**	113.32	−21.08	169.45	−152.06	112.04	115.72	131.88
Entry 1936–40			31.01*	11.88			20.90**	11.58
Entry 1941–45			−5.83	11.78			−2.42	8.12
Entry 1946–50			0.57	8.35			2.83	7.32
Entry 1951–55			1.05	6.47			−0.65	5.64
Entry 1956–60			3.33	5.51			6.88**	4.19
Entry 1961–65			3.32	5.28			7.99*	4.06
Entry 1966–70			4.21	5.01			6.67*	3.36
Entry 1971–75			−2.26	4.58			2.77	3.47
Entry 1976–80			15.03*	5.03			16.11*	4.37
Entry 1981–85			27.47*	4.70			28.30*	4.78
Sigma	48.19*	0.82	47.75*	0.81	48.00*	0.49	47.54*	0.51
Rho	—	—	0.60*	0.01	—	—	0.60*	0.01
Log likelihood	−13,483.33		−13,450.24		−13,040.53		−13,017.69	

[a]Convergence of the autoregressive tobit model required the units of the explanatory variables to be similar; it follows that years since entry, age, and experience are divided by 100, while the quadratic and cubic terms are divided by 1,000 and 10,000, respectively.

*(**) Significant at the 5 (10)% level.

between native- and foreign-born economists from 1936 to 1985. This finding is similar to that found in Funkhouser and Trejo [1995], which includes a broader population of immigrants. In particular, the standard tobit model in columns 3 and 4 suggest that foreign-born economists entering the U.S. economics profession before 1941 and after 1975 produce significantly more research than their native-born counterparts, while those entering in the intervening years do not differ significantly from native-born economists. The greater research productivity of the foreign born prior to 1941 likely reflects the influx of highly skilled economists that migrated as a result of World War II. The post-1975 productivity differential may reflect both the 1972 immigration law changes that affected the ability of the foreign born to remain in the United States after their Ph.D. and the recession in academia beginning in the 1970s as documented in Cartter [1976], Breneman [1975], and Brook and Marshall [1974]. Jointly, these changes might make economics departments relatively more selective in their hiring of foreign-born economists.[17]

The results for the autoregressive tobit model presented in columns 7 and 8 of

17. Native-born economists have been significantly more likely to work in nonacademic positions than their foreign-born counterparts, particularly in recent years. However, two longitudinal specifications using only academics presented in columns 3 and 4 of Appendix Table A1 yield the same qualitative conclusions as those that use all AEA members. Thus, the cohort effects do not appear to be related to different occupational choices by native- and foreign-born economists.

Table II also suggest a U-shaped pattern for the cohort effects, but these results also indicate that the foreign-born are relatively more productive than the native born between 1956 and 1970. The findings concerning these latter immigrant cohorts may reflect other changes in immigration law that made it easier to migrate from Eastern Europe in the mid-1950s and Asia in the early 1960s.[18] These results suggest that the highly skilled from these countries may have had pent-up demand to migrate to the United States, which lead to a large, temporary influx of relatively able economists from these regions. Overall, these panel results strengthen the contention that immigrant quality changes over time in response to changes in immigration law. Nonetheless, while the cohort effects for the highly skilled roughly correspond to those of the broader population of immigrants, the results do not suggest a pronounced change in the quality of the foreign born corresponding to the 1965 Immigration Act.

Country Effects

The results presented in Table III introduce source-region controls and observed quality controls to the longitudinal specification. The results from the standard tobit model indicate that foreign-born economists from Eastern European nations produce significantly more research than native and Canadian-born economists. The autoregressive panel model that includes country controls indicates that the foreign-born from Asia, Africa, and the Caribbean publish significantly less than Canadian economists working in the United States. However, once the observed quality controls are applied, only foreign-born economists from Africa appear to be significantly different. This suggests that the source-region controls measure observed attributes of the foreign born that originate from the region. On the other hand, unlike LaLonde and Topel [1992] who

---

18. For instance, during the 1950s, Congress passed several acts that facilitated the flow of refugees (e.g., Eastern Europeans) to the United States. In addition, the Act of September 26, 1961, eliminated the ceiling of 2,000 on the aggregate quota of the Asia-Pacific triangle, thus partially lowering restrictions that had been particularly binding on potential immigrants from Asian nations.

suggest that much of the change in cohort quality can be attributed changes in source country, the magnitude and significance of the cohort effects do not change qualitatively when the binary variables for source region are used in the model. Moreover, most of the cohort effects do not change qualitatively when a detailed list of field, occupation, and quality of Ph.D. institution are introduced. Thus, the cohort effects appears to be relatively more robust for Ph.D. economists than for the broader population of immigrants.

V. CONCLUSION

This article uses a unique, unbalanced panel of native- and foreign-born members of the AEA in 1964, 1974, 1985, and 1989 to analyze how the research productivity of foreign-born economists has changed before and after the Immigration and Nationality Act of 1965 and with respect to their native-born counterparts. Our study provides some of the first formal evidence that the post-1965 shift in source-country mix of the broader population of U.S. immigrants away from Europe toward Asia also has occurred among the highly skilled. The analysis compares and contrasts cross-sectional, longitudinal, and panel specifications to examine the role of observed and unobserved heterogeneity in immigrant assimilation and cohort differences in productivity over time.

The empirical analysis first estimates a traditional cross-sectional specification and finds an immigrant-specific return to experience, which suggests that foreign-born economists assimilate over time. Our analysis uses a longitudinal specification to control for cohort effects, which eliminates the observed differential return to U.S. experience. Given that the assimilation process for foreign-born economists likely begins well before their first post-Ph.D. U.S. employment, this result is not surprising.

Consistent with the findings for broader populations of immigrants, the longitudinal specifications suggest a U-shaped pattern for the cohort effects. In particular, foreign-born economists are found to produce more research than their native-born counterparts prior to World War II, when the tyranny in Europe induced the highly

TABLE III
Longitudinal Specification with Country Effects and Observed Quality Controls[a]

	Standard Tobit				Autoregressive Tobit			
	Country Effects		Quality Controls[b]		Country Effects		Quality Controls[b]	
	Coeff.	SE	Coeff.	SE	Coeff.	SE	Coeff.	SE
Years since entry	16.86	56.08	23.56	53.25	−7.92	40.19	−21.32	39.67
(Years since entry)^2	−2.17	169.14	−17.42	160.95	80.87	134.83	106.09	132.97
Entry 1936–40	31.25*	12.21	21.23**	11.62	23.45*	11.53	24.18*	12.42
Entry 1941–45	−7.15	12.17	−6.78	11.48	−1.19	8.18	2.33	8.15
Entry 1946–50	−1.65	8.84	−3.03	8.40	2.95	7.34	5.65	7.33
Entry 1951–55	−0.86	7.16	−2.16	6.82	−0.12	5.92	2.10	5.98
Entry 1956–60	1.00	6.45	−2.61	6.15	7.64**	4.59	7.38	4.63
Entry 1961–65	4.00	6.21	−2.16	5.90	11.00*	4.50	8.15**	4.42
Entry 1966–70	6.53	5.92	1.42	5.62	10.88*	4.00	9.46*	3.88
Entry 1971–75	−0.17	5.60	−4.17	5.34	6.73**	4.02	5.18	3.99
Entry 1976–80	16.67*	6.08	8.58	5.78	19.94*	4.98	15.56*	4.92
Entry 1981–85	28.95*	5.61	20.00*	5.32	31.89*	5.53	26.03*	5.17
Africa	−10.83	7.33	−9.66	6.99	−16.82**	8.91	−15.87**	8.42
Asia	−4.65	3.95	−1.76	3.80	−8.88*	4.37	−5.79	4.26
Carribean	−15.54*	7.95	−0.54	7.64	−21.78*	10.18	−8.76	9.17
Eastern Europe	11.42*	4.86	15.10*	4.77	4.35	5.14	7.41	4.99
Mexico/Cent. Amer.	−3.98	10.47	11.79	10.01	−6.97	12.61	6.07	12.22
Middle East	1.32	5.48	0.12	5.23	−4.34	6.24	−6.40	5.89
Northwest Europe	−1.12	3.94	5.21	3.85	−5.84	4.28	−1.01	4.16
Oceania	6.79	8.04	3.98	7.59	6.73	9.26	2.56	0.32
Southeast Europe	3.09	5.01	9.83*	4.88	−2.64	5.49	3.51	5.34
South America	2.43	7.77	10.61	7.54	−5.71	8.34	1.79	8.19
BA in the U.S.			−7.43*	2.35			−6.46*	2.83
Foreign Ph.D.			11.66*	4.01			9.05**	5.22
Ph.D. in Top 35			32.71*	2.47			32.16*	3.00
log(Ph.D. Top 35)			−7.47*	0.84			−7.26*	1.05
Government[c]			−29.46*	3.15			−24.90*	3.41
Business[c]			−44.15*	3.22			−37.93*	3.20
Other occupation[c]			−19.84*	2.52			−17.32*	2.44
Loglikelihood	−13,439.69		−13,123.74		−13,009.56		−12,817.83	

[a] All specifications also include human capital (i.e., age and experience), gender, and period effects; these regressors are omitted for simplicity and because their estimated coefficients do not differ qualitatively from those presented in Table II.
[b] The specifications with observed quality controls also include 15 field dummies.
[c] Employed at an academic institution is the excluded occupation.
*(**) Significant at the 5 (10)% level.

skilled to migrate to the United States, and after 1975, when stricter visa requirements and a poor job market for academics may have made economics departments relatively selective. These cohort effects are robust to the inclusion of a detailed list of qualitative and regional variables. Moreover, with the inclusion of panel controls for unobserved heterogeneity, there is evidence to suggest that the relaxation of immigration restrictions on migrants from Eastern Europe in the 1950s and Asia in the 1960s also led to an influx of relatively productive economists. The foreign-born economists who entered the United States in the years immediately following World War II were less productive than those who entered right before the war. However, the 1965 Immigration Act and its resulting change in the source-country compositional mix do not appear to have resulted in any decline in quality. Thus, overall, our findings suggest that foreign-born economists are at least as productive as their native-born counterparts and that the theoretically postulated brain drain of relatively able foreign-born economists to the United States did occur at several times during the postwar period.

APPENDIX TABLE A1
Different Publication Measures and Academics Only

	Articles Weighted by Coauthor and Quality		Academics Only[a]	
	Standard Tobit	Autoreg. Tobit	Standard Tobit	Autoreg. Tobit
Constant	9.756*	8.123*	161.82*	134.645*
	(1.25)	(1.11)	(26.03)	(23.03)
Experience	25.230*	25.851*	657.10*	628.112*
	(4.30)	(3.66)	(90.64)	(74.11)
(Experience)^2	−44.382**	−57.854*	−1,916.2*	−1,903.205*
	(24.47)	(20.76)	(511.73)	(420.43)
(Experience)^3	51.494	82.332*	2,712.7*	2,894.603*
	(43.26)	(36.92)	(899.21)	(736.76)
Age	−41.963*	−35.018*	−697.89*	−569.452*
	(6.10)	(5.38)	(126.63)	(108.95)
(Age)^2	24.48*	17.254*	322.92*	189.918**
	(6.62)	(5.86)	(137.06)	(116.39)
Female	−0.490*	−0.391**	−9.32*	−9.147*
	(0.18)	(0.24)	(3.86)	(4.62)
Year 1974	−0.168	−0.048	2.267	3.328
	(0.14)	(0.11)	(2.96)	(2.69)
Year 1985	−0.356	−0.259**	11.48*	11.399*
	(2.16)	(0.15)	(3.41)	(3.65)
Year 1989	−0.296**	−0.271	16.16*	14.901*
	(0.18)	(0.18)	(3.78)	(4.14)
Years Since Entry	2.522	−1.746	1.120	−41.21
	(2.99)	(2.25)	(62.68)	(42.19)
(Years Since Entry)^2	−8.006	4.079	33.15	171.17
	(9.07)	(7.75)	(188.01)	(144.26)
Entry 1936–40	1.173**	0.759	44.108*	27.59*
	(0.62)	(0.55)	(12.85)	(12.61)
Entry 1941–45	0.782	−0.365	4.364	5.993
	(0.63)	(0.42)	(13.93)	(8.49)
Entry 1946–50	0.269	0.073	5.97	5.027
	(0.44)	(0.34)	(9.06)	(7.80)
Entry 1951–55	−0.075	0.111	6.738	3.248
	(0.34)	(0.27)	(7.09)	(6.15)
Entry 1956–60	−0.068	0.340	6.195	8.768**
	(0.29)	(0.21)	(6.02)	(4.58)
Entry 1961–65	−0.058	0.358**	2.697	6.11
	(0.27)	(0.21)	(5.78)	(4.27)
Entry 1966–70	−0.004	0.265	3.825	7.623*
	(0.26)	(0.20)	(5.53)	(3.49)
Entry 1971–75	−0.215	0.135	2.181	4.784
	(0.24)	(0.19)	(5.17)	(3.90)
Entry 1976–80	0.667*	0.858*	16.204*	17.921*
	(0.26)	(0.27)	(5.60)	(4.95)
Entry 1981–85	1.200*	1.34*	24.77*	27.788*
	(0.24)	(0.28)	(5.16)	(4.76)
Log likelihood	−6,340.32	−5,968.10	−11,121.23	−10,805.85

[a] Dependent variable is the number of published pages.
*(**) Significant at the 5 (10)% level. Standard errors are in parentheses.

REFERENCES

Bhagwati, Jagdish, and Carlos Rodriquez. "Welfare-Theoretical Analysis of the Brain Drain." *Journal of Development Economics*, September 1975, 193–221.

Borjas, George J. "Assimilation, Changes in Cohort Quality, and the Earnings of Immigrants." *Journal of Labor Economics*, October 1985, 463–89.

———. "Self-Selection and the Earnings of Immigrants." *American Economic Review*, September 1987, 531–53.

———. "Immigrant and Emigrant Earnings: A Longitudinal Study." *Economic Inquiry*, January 1989, 21–37.

———. *Friends or Strangers: The Impact of Immigration of the U.S. Economy*. New York: Basic Books, 1990.

———. "National Origin and the Skills of Immigrants in the Postwar Period," in *Immigration and the Work Force: Economic Consequences for the United States and Source Areas*, edited by George J. Borjas and Richard B. Freeman. Chicago: University of Chicago Press, 1992, 17–47.

———. "Assimilation and Changes in Cohort Quality Revisited: What Happened to Immigrant Earnings in the 1980s?" *Journal of Labor Economics*, April 1995, 201–45.

Breneman, David W. *Graduated School Adjustments to the "New Depression" in Higher Education*. National Board on Graduate Education, Technical Report Number Three, February 1975.

Brook, Kathleen, and J. Ray Marshall. "The Labor Market for Economists." *American Economic Review*, May 1974, 488–511.

Butler, J. S., and Robert Moffit. "A Computationally Efficient Quadrature Procedure for the One-Factor Mutinomial Probit Model." *Econometrica*, May 1982, 761–65.

Cartter, Allan M. *Ph.D.'s and the Academic Labor Market*. New York: McGraw-Hill, 1976.

Chamberlain, Gary. "Multivariate Regression Models for Panel Data." *Journal of Econometrics*, January 1982, 5–46.

Chiswick, Barry R. "The Effect of Americanization of the Earnings of Foreign-Born Men." *Journal of Political Economy*, October 1978a, 897–921.

———. "A Longitudinal Analysis of the Occupational Mobility of Immigrants," in Industrial Relations Research Association, *Proceedings of the Thirteenth Annual Winter Meetings*, December 1977. New York. Madison, Wis.: IRRA, 1978b, 20–27.

———. "Is the New Immigration Less Skilled Than the Old?" *Journal of Labor Economics*, April 1986, 168–92.

Diamond, Arthur M., Jr., and Donald R. Haurin. "Determinants among Ph.D. Economists of Membership in a Professional Association." *Education Economics*, 2(1), 1994, 13–28.

Funkhouser, Edward, and Stephen J. Trejo. "The Labor Market Skills of Recent Male Immigrants: Evidence from the Current Population Survey." *Industrial and Labor Relations Review*, July 1995, 792–811.

Graves, Philip E., James R. Marchand, and Randall Thompson. "Economics Department Rankings: Research Incentives, Constraints, and Efficiency." *American Economic Review*, December 1982, 1131–41.

Greenwood, Michael J. "The Economics of Mass Migration from Poor to Rich Countries: Leading Issues of Fact and Theory." *American Economic Review*, May 1983, 173–77.

Greenwood, Michael J., and John M. McDowell. "The Factor Market Consequences of U.S. Immigration." *Journal of Economic Literature*, December 1986, 1738–72.

Grubel, Herbert G., and Anthony Scott. "The Characteristics of Foreigners in the U.S. Economics Profession." *American Economic Review*, March 1967, 131–45.

Hansen, W. Lee, Burton A. Weisbrod, and Robert P. Strauss. "Modeling the Earnings and Research Productivity of Academic Economists." *Journal of Political Economy*, August 1978, 729–41.

Hsiao, Cheng. *Analysis of Panel Data*. Cambridge: Cambridge University Press, 1986.

Huang, Wei-Chiao. "A Pooled Cross-Section and Time-Series Study of Professional Indirect Immigration to the United States." *Southern Economic Journal*, July 1987, 95–109.

Jasso, Guillermina, and Mark R. Rosenzweig. "What's in a Name? Country-of-Origin Influences on the Earnings of Immigrants in the United States," in *Human Capital and Development*, vol. 5, edited by Oded Stark and Ismail Sirageld. Stamford, Conn.: JAI Press, 1986, 75–106.

———. "How Well Do U.S. Immigrants Do? Vintage Effects, Emigration Selectivity, and Occupational Mobility," in *Research in Population Economics*, edited by T. Paul Schultz. Stamford, Conn.: JAI Press, 1988, 229–253.

LaLonde, Robert J., and Robert H. Topel. "Immigration in the American Labor Market: Quality, Assimilation, and Distributional Effects." *American Economic Review*, May 1991, 297–302.

———. "Assimilation of Immigrants in the U.S. Labor Market," in *Immigration and the Work Force: Economic Consequences for the United States and Source Areas*, edited by George J. Borjas and Richard B. Freeman. Chicago: University of Chicago Press, 1992, 67–92.

McDowell, John M. "Obsolescence of Knowledge and Career Publication Profiles: Some Evidence of Differences among Fields in Costs of Interrupted Careers." *American Economic Review*, September 1982, 752–68.

McDowell, John M., and Larry D. Singell, Jr. "The Foreign Born in the U.S. Economics Profession: Attributes, Composition, and Relative Productivity." Working paper, University of Oregon, 1998.

Oster, Sharon M., and Daniel S. Hamermesh. "Aging and Productivity among Economists: What and Why?" *The Review of Economics and Statistics*, February 1998, 154–56.

Sauer, Raymond D. "Estimates of the Returns to Quality and Coauthorship in Economic Academia." *Journal of Political Economy*, August 1988, 855–66.

UNESCO. *World List of Social Science Periodicals*, 8th. ed. Paris: United Nations Educational, Scientific and Cultural Organization, 1991.

Labor market assimilation and the self-employment decision of immigrant entrepreneurs

Magnus Lofstrom

University of California, Irvine, School of Social Sciences, 3151 Social Science Plaza, Irvine CA 92697-5100, USA
(Fax: +949-824-4717; e-mail: mlofstro@uci.edu)

Received: 10 November 1999/Accepted: 3 August 2000

Abstract. This paper uses data from the 1980 and 1990 U.S. Censuses to study labor market assimilation of self-employed immigrants. Separate earnings functions for the self-employed and wage/salary workers are estimated. To control for endogenous sorting into the sectors, models of the self-employment decision are estimated. Self-employed immigrants are found to do substantially better in the labor market than wage/salary immigrants. Earnings of self-employed immigrants are predicted to converge with natives' wage/salary earnings at about age 30 and natives' self-employed earnings at about age 40. Including the self-employed in the sample reduces the immigrant-native earnings gap by, on average, 14%.

JEL classification: J15, J23, J61

Key words: Immigration, assimilation, self-employment

1. Introduction

One of the "stylized facts" in the economics of immigration is that immigrants arriving in the U.S. in the last decades are not performing as well in the labor

---

I am very thankful to Julian Betts for numerous insightful comments on several revisions of this paper. I am also grateful to Jörgen Hansen, Shoshana Neuman, Steve Raphael, James Rauch, Mark Regets, David Riker, Akos Rona-Tas, two anonymous referees and participants at the European Summer Symposium in Labor Economics in Ammersee, 1999, the conference on Marginal Labor Markets in Metropolitan Areas in Dublin, 1999 and seminar participants at IZA, UC San Diego, and UC Irvine for helpful comments. *Responsible editor:* Alan Barrett.

market as their counterparts who arrived in the 1940's and 1950's and are not likely to reach earnings parity with natives (e.g., Borjas 1985, 1995). Notably, self-employed immigrants have continuously been excluded from these studies. This paper takes a closer look at the performance and assimilation in the labor market of self-employed immigrants. The paper explores two aspects of self-employment among immigrants. The first is the self-employment decision. More specifically, what are the main factors that cause the self-employment rates to differ between immigrants and natives, and what are the roles of these factors? The other aspect explored in the paper is the relative labor market performance of self-employed immigrants, compared to wage/salary immigrants and natives. I ask whether self-employed immigrants assimilate into the labor market, in terms of earnings, at the same rate as wage/salary workers. Also, at what point, if at all, do immigrants' earnings reach parity with self-employed native born Americans? The consequence of excluding the self-employed on the immigrant-native wage gap is also analyzed.

The lack of attention to the self-employed sector could easily be justified if either it was represented by a relatively small proportion of the labor force or if self-employed individuals possess very similar socioeconomic characteristics to wage and salary workers (i.e. they are simply a random sub-sample of the labor force). Neither of these statements is in fact true. Using the 1980 and 1990 Census of Population, I find that 10.39% of native born American males in the labor force were self-employed in 1980 and this increased to 11.21% in 1990. The proportions for immigrant men in 1980 and 1990 were 11.63% and 12.20% respectively, but vary greatly over ethnic groups and arrival cohorts (see Table 1). This is certainly not a small number of workers given that the total male labor force consists of over 70 million individuals[1].

As will be shown, self-employed immigrant workers are also, on average, older by about 5 to 6 years, display higher levels of English language fluency and are generally more educated than wage/salary immigrants. For example, in 1990 self-employed immigrants had on average 1.5 years more schooling than immigrants in the wage/salary sector. Self-employed workers also have higher total annual earnings than wage/salary workers do[2]. However, earnings from self-employment may not only reflect returns to human capital, but also returns to physical capital. A better comparison between wage/salary workers and self-employed individuals may be income including total earnings and investment income. This too is higher for self-employed persons. The fact that self-employed individuals are both more educated and older is likely to explain some of these differences.

Overall, both immigrants and natives who chose self-employment increased their earnings advantage over wage/salary workers in the last decade. In 1980 the self-employment to wage/salary earnings ratio was 1.42 for natives and 1.57 for all immigrants. By 1990 it increased slightly to 1.43 for natives and to 1.62 for immigrants.

Self-employment is also commonly believed to be an important tool in immigrants' cultural and economical assimilation process. As such, it may be an important stepping stone towards upward social and economic mobility (Cummings 1980).

In this paper I estimate separate earnings functions for the self-employed and wage/salary workers. To control for endogenous sorting into the sectors, models of the self-employment decision are estimated. Variables for immigrant population proportion and the ratio of average self-employment earn-

Table 1. Self-employment rates by national origin group and arrival cohort

Group:	National origin Group:				Arrival cohort:		
	Sample size		Self-employment rates		Group:	Self-employment rates	
	1980	1990	1980	1990		1980	1990
Natives	472,046	489,821	0.104	0.112			
All immigrants	151,010	229,902	0.116	0.122			
National origin group:					Cohort:		
Mexico	31,360	66,972	0.041	0.057	1985–89 Arrivals		0.061
Central/South America	11,554	26,184	0.083	0.091	1980–84 Arrivals		0.100
South East Asia	9,070	20,181	0.065	0.079	1975–79 Arrivals	0.060	0.127
North East Asia	10,215	19,069	0.172	0.205	1970–74 Arrivals	0.094	0.145
India, Pakistan, etc	4,518	9,190	0.114	0.140	1965–69 Arrivals	0.115	0.150
Middle East/Egypt	4,402	9,950	0.225	0.245	1960–64 Arrivals	0.133	0.171
Europe, CAN, AUS, NZ	61,663	52,897	0.154	0.176	1950–59 Arrivals	0.149	0.180
Africa	1,756	3,838	0.126	0.131	Pre–1950 Arrivals	0.182	0.193
Caribbean	7,780	11,342	0.052	0.080			
Cuba	8,692	10,279	0.152	0.177			

ings to average wage/salary earnings ratios, by national origin group and SMSA, are used as instruments to identify the inverse Mills correction terms. The estimated earnings functions are used to generate sector specific measures of labor market assimilation. I find that wage/salary immigrants do not reach earnings parity with natives. However, earnings of self-employed immigrants appear to converge with and surpass earnings of both wage/salary and self-employed natives. Using the consistent estimators from the earnings equations, I develop a new economy wide measure of assimilation that accounts for the distribution across sectors. This shows that the immigrant-native earnings gap is overstated when the self-employed are excluded from the study.

The paper is organized in the following way. Section 2 describes the data used and how national origin groups were created. Section 3 outlines and compares traits of immigrants and natives in the two sectors. Implications of these characteristics on self-employment rates and earnings are discussed. In Sect. 4, the self-employment decision model is described and Sect. 5 shows the empirical results. Earnings equations are presented in Sect. 6. Age-earnings profiles are derived and discussed in this section, as is the implication of excluding the self-employed. Finally, Sect. 7 summarizes the results of the study.

2. Data and national origin group definition

The data used in this paper are drawn from the 1980 5% a Sample and the 1990 5% Sample of the U.S. Census of Population. The study includes males between the ages of 18 and 64 who are not residing in group quarters, who are not in military service or enrolled in school, and who reported working in the year prior to the census[3]. Given the extremely large data set this leaves us with, I extracted a 20% randomly selected sub-sample of native born Americans from the 5% Sample, but kept all immigrants.

It is interesting to note that the selection process that determines who migrates or not, and hence the labor market performance of immigrants, is believed to be determined by the relative conditions in host and source country (see for example, Borjas 1987). However, the majority of studies on immigrant performance have been done based on *ethnic* groups, and not on *country of origin*. In this paper I try to create 10 relatively homogenous groups based on countries' geographic location and cultural and economic conditions, while maintaining a large enough sample size for each group.

It should be noted that any attempt to create homogenous groups will be scarred by compromises. As noted above, there *are* substantial differences in characteristics such as self-employment rates and educational attainment between immigrant groups. If the group is defined too widely, the impact of variations in these variables may not be accurately estimated. If the group is too narrowly defined, by country for example, the sample size will be small for some of the countries. This is particularly true when studying self-employed immigrants, a group that represents approximately one percent of the male labor force[4]. However, if different ethnic groups face different labor market constraints, such as discrimination, creating groups based on national origin may not be the best way to compose groups. Table A1 in the Appendix describes the countries represented in each national group used in this paper[5].

3. Characteristics – The self-employed v. wage/salary workers

In this section I outline traits of immigrants and natives in the two sectors. This descriptive portrait suggests that immigrants are highly heterogeneous, that the way they self-select into the self-employment and wage/salary sectors is not random, and that the nature of this self-selection may have changed somewhat during the 1980's.

Self-employment rates vary greatly over both national origin groups and arrival cohort. These are presented in Table 1. It is shown in this table that the Mexican national origin group displays the lowest self-employment rates both in 1980 and 1990 of any group. The group with the highest self-employment rate in both census years is the Middle Eastern national origin group. Table 1 also shows that immigrant self-employment probabilities increase with time spent in the U.S. The most recent arrival cohorts in both census years display the lowest self-employment rates while the most senior cohort exhibits the highest rate. The rate also increases for each cohort between 1980 and 1990. Some of these increases are likely due to the fact that the average age of a cohort increases over time.

As stated above, self-employed individuals have higher earnings than wage/salary workers. Table 2 presents mean earnings and a measure of earnings dispersion, the ratio of the 90th earnings percentile to the 10th earnings percentile, by arrival cohort; Table 3 shows these statistics by national origin groups. Earnings are shown in 1989 dollars and are adjusted for inflation by the annual Consumer Price Index. From the average earnings shown in Tables 2 and 3, earnings differentials between groups were calculated. Self-employed immigrants earned on average 4.6% more than self-employed natives did in 1980. This advantage had disappeared by 1990 when self-employed natives earned approximately 1.5% more than immigrants. Wage/salary immigrants displayed an earnings disadvantage of 6% and 15.3% respectively in 1980 and 1990. The tables also show that annual earnings vary greatly across national origin groups and increases with time spent in the U.S.

It is quite likely that differences in human capital explain some of the earnings disparity over national origin groups and arrival cohorts. The differences in educational attainment and English ability are seen in Tables 4, 5 and 6. These tables show the average years of schooling[6], high school drop out rates, college graduation rates and the percentage of immigrants in the group who report that they do not speak English well or not at all.

Self-employed immigrants display lower high school drop out rates and higher college graduation rates than immigrant wage/salary employees. This is shown in Table 4. The educational attainment gap between self-employed and wage/salary immigrants increased in the 1980's while during the same period the gap between self-employed and wage/salary natives decreased. If immigrants' education is valued less by U.S. employer than natives' education, as is found in Betts and Lofstrom (2000), it is plausible that relatively highly educated immigrants are more likely to choose self-employment compared to relatively highly educated natives. This is possibly one of the reasons why the educational gap between the self-employed and wage/salary employees is greater for immigrants than for natives.

The decline in earnings of recently arrived immigrants, relative to natives, is possibly due to a decline in educational attainment. Table 5 displays the human capital variables described above by arrival cohorts. The most recent

Table 2. Annual earnings, mean and ratio 90th/10th percentile, by arrival cohort

Group	1980 Self-employed Mean	1980 Self-employed P90/10	1980 Wage/salary Mean	1980 Wage/salary P90/10	1990 Self-employed Mean	1990 Self-employed P90/10	1990 Wage/salary Mean	1990 Wage/salary P90/10
Natives	40,388	11.12	28,459	5.75	41,993	14.29	29,378	6.78
All immigrants	42,246	11.53	26,841	6.42	41,364	14.09	25,479	8.33
Ratio: natives ÷ immigrants	0.956	0.965	1.060	0.895	1.015	1.014	1.153	0.813
Cohort:								
1985–89 Arrivals					25,462	13.75	18,253	9.34
1980–84 Arrivals					31,464	11.00	20,604	6.67
1975–79 Arrivals	32,295	13.72	19,800	8.66	40,582	12.50	24,782	6.70
1970–74 Arrivals	38,534	10.79	22,954	5.21	45,492	15.44	27,303	6.94
1965–69 Arrivals	42,589	11.23	27,018	5.60	47,272	13.72	31,245	6.29
1960–64 Arrivals	44,845	9.99	29,357	5.45	48,700	13.72	35,229	6.44
1950–59 Arrivals	43,900	9.99	32,374	4.56	48,003	12.15	37,728	5.91
Pre–1950 arrivals	46,516	11.16	35,391	5.14	55,467	16.17	40,301	7.65

Note: Earnings are shown in 1989 dollars and are adjusted for inflation by the annual Consumer Price Index

Table 3. Annual earnings, mean and ratio 90th/10th percentile, by national origin group

Group	1980 Self-employed Mean	P90/10	Wage/salary Mean	P90/10	1990 Self-employed Mean	P90/10	Wage/salary Mean	P90/10
Natives	40,388	11.12	28,459	5.75	41,993	14.29	29,378	6.78
All immigrants	42,246	11.53	26,841	6.42	41,364	14.09	25,479	8.33
Ratio: natives ÷ immigrants	0.956	0.965	1.060	0.895	1.015	1.014	1.153	0.813
National origin group:								
Mexico	27,708	8.70	17,702	5.93	21,957	9.93	14,807	6.09
Central/South America	40,880	11.99	23,253	6.24	34,076	13.00	20,653	6.50
South East Asia	65,046	15.70	23,919	6.00	45,022	20.59	24,478	6.26
North East Asia	39,582	11.35	29,714	7.38	42,441	10.75	33,561	9.07
India, Pakistan, etc	65,000	11.23	35,788	5.98	69,864	19.48	36,813	7.78
Middle East/Egypt	46,753	13.26	30,016	6.72	48,299	12.35	34,830	7.30
Europe, CAN, AUS, NZ	42,628	9.16	33,152	5.42	46,487	11.67	37,733	6.18
Africa	47,517	13.20	29,259	7.10	43,328	15.44	29,823	7.35
Caribbean	33,882	11.22	19,949	5.90	27,348	9.67	21,324	6.67
Cuba	37,395	10.19	24,750	5.00	35,912	11.43	25,806	6.71

Note: Earnings are shown in 1989 dollars and are adjusted for inflation by the annual Consumer Price Index

Table 4. Educational attainment and English proficiency – immigrants and natives

Group	Self-employed				Wage/salary			
	Years of schooling	High school drop out	College graduate	Limited English	Years of schooling	High school drop out	College graduate	Limited English
		1980				1980		
Natives	13.30	0.204	0.291	N/A	12.55	0.235	0.196	N/A
All immigrants	12.82	0.294	0.306	0.112	11.55	0.394	0.225	0.226
Ratio: natives ÷ immigrants	1.04	0.69	0.95	N/A	1.09	0.60	0.87	N/A
		1990				1990		
Natives	13.65	0.141	0.319	N/A	13.00	0.162	0.236	N/A
All immigrants	12.64	0.289	0.323	0.167	11.14	0.415	0.23.3	0.267
Ratio: natives ÷ immigrants	1.08	0.49	0.99	N/A	1.17	0.39	1.02	N/A

Table 5. Educational attainment and English proficiency by arrival cohort

Group	Self-Employed				Wage/salary			
	Years of schooling	High school drop out	College graduate	Limited English	Years of schooling	High school drop out	College graduate	Limited English
Cohort:		1980				1980		
1975–79 Arrivals	13.22	0.243	0.370	0.254	11.13	0.446	0.235	0.419
1970–74 Arrivals	13.01	0.292	0.360	0.187	10.91	0.471	0.211	0.310
1965–69 Arrivals	12.87	0.317	0.331	0.151	11.49	0.414	0.225	0.224
1960–64 Arrivals	12.84	0.290	0.293	0.103	11.97	0.338	0.221	0.139
1950–59 Arrivals	12.51	0.302	0.258	0.052	12.14	0.309	0.229	0.077
Pre–1950 Arrivals	12.78	0.298	0.278	0.020	12.14	0.334	0.227	0.046
		1990				1990		
1985–89 Arrivals	12.03	0.319	0.293	0.365	10.71	0.467	0.221	0.459
1980–84 Arrivals	12.24	0.304	0.288	0.276	10.65	0.466	0.202	0.331
1975–79 Arrivals	12.89	0.256	0.366	0.162	10.85	0.441	0.233	0.241
1970–74 Arrivals	12.58	0.318	0.337	0.155	10.90	0.440	0.225	0.210
1965–69 Arrivals	12.64	0.314	0.310	0.121	11.78	0.350	0.253	0.147
1960–64 Arrivals	12.90	0.266	0.320	0.074	12.36	0.284	0.279	0.100
1950–59 Arrivals	12.99	0.269	0.317	0.038	12.44	0.267	0.273	0.059
Pre–1950 arrivals	13.54	0.218	0.387	0.033	12.68	0.256	0.318	0.045

Table 6. Educational attainment and English proficiency by national origin group

National origin group:	Self-employed				Wage/Salary			
	Years of schooling	High school drop out	College graduate	Limited English	Years of schooling	High school drop out	College graduate	Limited English
		1980				1980		
Mexico	9.20	0.621	0.101	0.339	7.73	0.761	0.028	0.521
Central/South America	13.56	0.217	0.317	0.128	11.85	0.346	0.171	0.252
South East Asia	16.84	0.066	0.722	0.059	13.59	0.184	0.371	0.113
North East Asia	14.43	0.151	0.514	0.233	14.41	0.163	0.511	0.244
India, Pakistan, etc	17.39	0.052	0.780	0.012	17.08	0.061	0.779	0.026
Middle East/Egypt	13.61	0.232	0.360	0.056	13.86	0.213	0.421	0.085
Europe, CAN, AUS, NZ	12.44	0.311	0.247	0.046	12.28	0.311	0.237	0.091
Africa	14.55	0.149	0.434	0.014	14.57	0.134	0.463	0.035
Caribbean	12.23	0.335	0.199	0.112	11.18	0.401	0.119	0.153
Cuba	12.08	0.361	0.246	0.312	11.59	0.375	0.186	0.326
		1990				1990		
Mexico	8.11	0.710	0.064	0.385	7.45	0.770	0.026	0.497
Central/South America	12.35	0.311	0.261	0.231	10.75	0.438	0.138	0.325
South East Asia	14.03	0.181	0.446	0.143	12.91	0.204	0.327	0.143
North East Asia	13.96	0.144	0.461	0.288	13.90	0.169	0.497	0.281
India, Pakistan, etc	16.63	0.055	0.751	0.018	15.55	0.092	0.691	0.048
Middle East/Egypt	14.12	0.152	0.464	0.046	14.47	0.129	0.527	0.050
Europe, CAN, AUS, NZ	12.85	0.254	0.288	0.050	12.95	0.230	0.316	0.081
Africa	14.65	0.105	0.512	0.015	14.68	0.099	0.544	0.035
Caribbean	11.87	0.350	0.180	0.152	11.23	0.402	0.126	0.173
Cuba	11.82	0.396	0.217	0.336	11.60	0.384	0.181	0.283

cohort of immigrants who chose self-employment appear to have higher high school drop out rates and a lower percentage of college graduates in 1990 compared to 1980. Table 5 also shows that in 1990 recent wage/salary immigrants displayed lower educational attainment levels than did recent wage/salary immigrants in 1980. The decline relative to natives is quite notable since during the 1980's, educational attainment levels increased quite considerably for both self-employed and wage/salary natives.

The apparent relative decline in schooling levels of immigrants does not hold for all immigrant groups. In fact, there is quite a difference in changes of educational attainment in the 1980's over national origin groups. These statistics are presented in Table 6. In general, the groups who displayed an improvement of relative earnings over the decade also exhibited increases in educational attainment levels.

Educational attainment of immigrants overall appears to have declined relative to natives in the 1980's. The decline seems to be slightly greater among wage/salary immigrants than among self-employed immigrants. Furthermore, the educational attainment gap is generally smaller for self-employed immigrants than it is for wage/salary immigrants and in fact, the percentage of college graduates is greater for immigrant entrepreneurs than for self-employed natives.

The level of English ability of immigrants, measured here as limited English proficiency, appears to have changed in the last decade, as shown in Tables 4 through 6[7]. Overall, there appears to be a shift in the distribution of English proficiency levels of immigrants from higher ability to lower ability. Self-employed immigrants report speaking limited English to a lesser extent than wage/salary immigrants. This is true for all arrival cohorts and national origin groups except for North East Asians and Cubans in 1990.

The increase in the numbers of immigrants coming to the U.S. in the last decade may have made it easier to "get by" with limited English ability. The increase makes it more likely or easier for immigrants to settle in areas with higher proportion of co-nationals, or in so called enclaves. The role of enclaves will be analyzed in the self-employment decision models below.

4. The self-employment decision

Individuals choose whether to participate in the wage/salary sector of the labor market or to become self-employed. The decision will depend on several factors that determine expected utility in each sector. In this paper I assume that the utility function is a function of expected earnings, y_i^{s-e} for self-employment work and $y_i^{w/s}$ for work in the wage/salary sector, and that the function also indicates preferences for the characteristics of work in the two sectors, denoted z_i. Furthermore, earnings in each sector will depend on a vector of observable characteristics, X_i and unobserved characteristics ε_i. Note that the characteristics z_i are assumed to affect utility but not earnings in each sector. Assuming that individuals maximize expected utility, a person will chose self-employment if the expected utility from self-employment, denoted $E(u_i^{s-e})$, is greater than the expected utility in the wage/salary sector, represented here by $E(u_i^{w/s})$. Expected utility in the two sectors can be defined as:

$$E(u_i^{w/s}) = z_i^{w/s}\lambda^{w/s} + y_i^{w/s} = z_i^{w/s}\lambda^{w/s} + X_i\beta^{w/s} + \varepsilon_i^{w/s} \tag{1}$$

$$E(u_i^{s-e}) = z_i^{s-e}\lambda^{s-e} + y_i^{s-e} = z_i^{s-e}\lambda^{s-e} + X_i\beta^{s-e} + \varepsilon_i^{s-e} \tag{2}$$

where $\varepsilon^{w/s}$ and ε^{s-e} are jointly normally distributed with mean zero and variances $\sigma_{w/s}^2$ and σ_{s-e}^2. An individual chooses self-employment if:

$$I_i^* = E(u_i^{s-e}) - E(u_i^{w/s}) > 0 \tag{3}$$

Clearly the index function I_i^* is unobservable. However, from Eqs. (1), (2) and (3) I_i^* can be defined as:

$$\begin{aligned} I_i^* &= E(u_i^{s-e}) - E(u_i^{w/s}) \\ &= X_i\beta^{s-e} - X_i\beta^{w/s} + z_i^{s-e}\lambda^{s-e} - z_i^{w/s}\lambda^{w/s} + \varepsilon_i^{s-e} - \varepsilon_i^{w/s} \\ &= W_i\pi + e_i \end{aligned} \tag{4}$$

If we set $I = 1$ if $I_i^* > 0$, if self-employment is chosen, and $I = 0$ if $I_i^* \leq 0$, if the wage/salary sector is selected, then Eq. (4) can be seen as a probit model of sectoral choice of self-employment.

Estimating the self-employment decision in Eq. (4) has two main benefits. The first is that it will give us insight to the role of the different characteristics in choosing a sector. The question that can be answered through this process is: What are the reasons for the differences in self-employment rates between immigrants and natives and what are the roles of the factors? The second advantage is that from the probit estimates, when the instruments z_i are included in the model, the inverse Mills ratio can be calculated. This will help to correct for self-selection problems in the earnings functions through use of the Heckman two-step procedure.

5. Empirical model and findings: The self-employment decision

The sectoral choice an individual makes will depend on several factors. As explained above, an individual is assumed to compare the expected utility from work in the self-employment sector to the expected utility from employment in the wage/salary sector. If this difference is positive, the individual chooses to be self-employed. The model to be estimated by probit is:

$$I_i^* = W_i\pi + e, \quad \text{where } e \sim N(0, 1)$$

The probability an individual chooses self-employment is:

$$\text{Prob}[I_i = 1] = \Phi(W\pi),$$

where $\Phi(\cdot)$ is the standard normal cumulative density function. The probability a person chooses the wage/salary sector is then simply:

$$\text{Prob}[I_i = 0] = 1 - \Phi(W\pi)$$

The choice over self-employment will likely depend on socio-economic characteristics such as age, education, marital status and geographic location. If there are differences in the impact any of these variables have on earnings, we would expect these variables to affect the self-employment decision. For immigrants, it is likely that the number of years in the U.S. will also have an effect on this decision. Furthermore, both age and education may impact earnings and self-employment probabilities differently for immigrants compared to natives. This too needs to be incorporated in the model. All these individual characteristics and a period effect for 1980 are included in the matrix W. The probit estimation results for the above described model are presented in Table 7 as model 1. As expected, age and education are positively related to the probability of self-employment, as is years since migration for immigrants. It also appears that after controlling for years since migration, there is very little difference in self-employment probabilities between arrival cohorts. Also, immigrants are more likely to choose self-employment than natives even after the above described characteristics are controlled for.

Light (1984) argues that differences in traditions of commerce among immigrants from different countries help explain differences in self-employment rates among immigrants in the U.S. This may be one of the reasons for variations in self-employment rates over countries of origin that is not captured by the observable traits in the model. Also, if immigrants experience discrimination in the labor market and if discrimination varies over source countries, this also needs to be controlled for in the model. To attempt to incorporate these country specific unobservables, Model 2 in Table 7 adds dummy variables for the national origin groups. The African national origin group is the reference group. Adding these variables has a considerable impact on the arrival cohort and immigrant coefficients. Model 1 predicts that an immigrant who arrived between 1965 and 1969 is approximately 0.7% less likely, but statistically insignificantly so, to be self-employed than an immigrant who arrived in the most recent cohort in 1990. The same individual, statistically defined, is according to Model 2 around 3% significantly less likely to choose self-employment than a co-national who arrived between 1985 and 1989. By simply including a dummy variable for immigrants and not controlling for country of origin, differences in self-employment probabilities are greatly understated.

The impact of number years of education on the self-employment decision is also inaccurately estimated if no country of origin variables are included. Using the immigrant characteristics above, Model 1 predicts a positive marginal effect of slightly more than 7% on the probability of self-employment for an additional year of schooling. However, the estimates in Model 2 suggest that the marginal increase is only about 2.5%. The substantial change in probabilities from adding national origin variables may be related to both differences in levels and quality of education across countries. Nonetheless, it is quite clear that it is important to control for country of origin in the sectoral choice models of self-employment. The role of education in the self-employment decision is also very different for immigrants compared to natives. The marginal impact of education for a native with same characteristics as the immigrant described above is close to 7%. Education appears to play a greater role in choosing sector for natives than it does for immigrants.

Table 7. Probit models for self-employment for males aged 18–64, based on 1980 and 1990 public use samples of the U.S. census

Variable	Model 1	Model 2	Model 3	Model 4
Constant	−4.9720	−4.9700	−4.9703	−4.9869
	(0.0603)	(0.0603)	(0.0612)	(0.0612)
Immigrant	1.1556	1.7160	1.7072	1.6247
	(0.2242)	(0.2322)	(0.2322)	(0.2363)
Mexico		−0.3721	−0.4392	−0.4526
		(0.0424)	(0.0441)	(0.0451)
South and Central America		−0.1544	−0.1558	−0.1678
		(0.0428)	(0.0428)	(0.0438)
South East Asia		−0.3550	−0.3621	−0.3716
		(0.0443)	(0.0443)	(0.0453)
North East Asia		0.2305	0.2280	0.2239
		(0.0422)	(0.0422)	(0.0431)
India/Pakistan		−0.0571	−0.0599	−0.0676
		(0.0467)	(0.0467)	(0.0476)
Middle East		0.3985	0.3979	0.3925
		(0.0445)	(0.0445)	(0.0454)
Europe/Canada/Australia/New Zealand		0.0967	0.0927	0.0920
		(0.0405)	(0.0405)	(0.0413)
Caribbean		−0.3065	−0.3115	−0.3197
		(0.0465)	(0.0466)	(0.0475)
Cuba		0.1202	0.0144	0.0122
		(0.0451)	(0.0489)	(0.0498)
Period Effect 1980	−0.0751	−0.0754	−0.0751	−0.0596
	(0.0135)	(0.0136)	(0.0136)	(0.0137)
Age	0.2075	0.2075	0.2075	0.2059
	(0.0048)	(0.0048)	(0.0048)	(0.0048)
Age2	−0.0042	−0.0042	−0.0042	−0.0042
	(0.0001)	(0.0001)	(0.0001)	(0.0001)
Age3/1000	0.2898	0.2898	0.2898	0.2870
	(0.0098)	(0.0098)	(0.0098)	(0.0099)
Years of Schooling	0.0390	0.0390	0.0390	0.0388
	(0.0007)	(0.0007)	(0.0007)	(0.0008)
Years of Schooling* Immigrant	−0.0139	−0.0300	−0.0295	−0.0295
	(0.0016)	(0.0017)	(0.0017)	(0.0018)
Age* immigrant	−0.1002	−0.1199	−0.1196	−0.1143
	(0.0177)	(0.0180)	(0.0180)	(0.0183)
Age2* immigrant	0.0028	0.0032	0.0031	0.0030
	(0.0004)	(0.0005)	(0.0005)	(0.0005)
Age3/1000* immigrant	−0.2406	−0.2677	−0.2670	−0.2570
	(0.0361)	(0.0366)	(0.0366)	(0.0371)
Speaks little or no English	−0.1262	−0.0881	−0.0936	−0.0961
	(0.0154)	(0.0162)	(0.0163)	(0.0166)
Years since migration	0.0352	0.0463	0.0450	0.0450
	(0.0048)	(0.0049)	(0.0050)	(0.0050)
Years since migration2	−0.0011	−0.0012	−0.0012	−0.0012
	(0.0002)	(0.0002)	(0.0002)	(0.0002)
Years since migration3/1000	0.1075	0.1091	0.1112	0.1104
	(0.0300)	(0.0303)	(0.0303)	(0.0307)
Arrival cohort pre–1950	0.0588	−0.4240	−0.3593	−0.3661
	(0.1510)	(0.1541)	(0.1548)	(0.1559)
Arrival cohort 1950–59	−0.0070	−0.3631	−0.3157	−0.3227
	(0.1032)	(0.1056)	(0.1061)	(0.1069)

Table 7 (continued)

Variable	Model 1	Model 2	Model 3	Model 4
Arrival cohort 1960–64	−0.0135	−0.2744	−0.2382	−0.2438
	(0.0805)	(0.0824)	(0.0827)	(0.0834)
Arrival cohort 1965–69	−0.0335	−0.2237	−0.1967	−0.2002
	(0.0656)	(0.0671)	(0.0674)	(0.0680)
Arrival cohort 1970–74	0.0193	−0.0990	−0.0789	−0.0819
	(0.0515)	(0.0526)	(0.0528)	(0.0534)
Arrival cohort 1975–79	0.0149	−0.0579	−0.0444	−0.0482
	(0.0379)	(0.0387)	(0.0389)	(0.0393)
Arrival cohort 1980–84	0.0458	0.0086	0.0153	0.0132
	(0.0304)	(0.0311)	(0.0311)	(0.0318)
Proportion of immigrants from same			0.6650	0.6655
country in SMSA			(0.1167)	(0.1188)
Ratio of S-E earnings to W/S earnings				0.0182
by SMSA and ethnicity of natives				(0.0089)
Ratio of S-E earnings to W/S earnings				0.0483
by SMSA and national origin group				(0.0105)
Sample size	1342779	1342779	1342779	1342779
Log likelihood	−454043	−453178	−453161	−441567

Note: Standard errors are presented in parentheses. all models include interactions between education and period effect, education interacted with period effect and immigrant status, in addition to dummies for regions, SMSA residency, disability and for being married.

One of the reasons for estimating the probits of the self-employment decision is to calculate the inverse Mills ratio. The objective in doing so is to reduce the possible selection bias that may arise in the estimated wage models. The goal is to include in the probit model variables that will influence the self-employment decision, but that will not affect earnings, i.e. some characteristics z_i from the self-employment decision model above. It is highly desirable, but not necessary, for the probit model to include instruments that help to predict self-employment but which do not belong directly in the earnings function. I now discuss these additional instruments.

The first instrument added to Model 2 is a variable to test whether immigrants living in areas where relatively many co-nationals reside, so called enclaves, may be the reason we observe higher self-employment rates for some immigrant groups. The sociology literature commonly speaks of ethnic resources as a determinant in an individual's choice of whether or not to choose self-employment (see for example, Light 1984 and Aldrich and Waldinger 1990). Examples of ethnic resources are skills or knowledge to provide services or goods to other co-ethnics or co-nationals, availability of low wage labor, social support networks that assist an individual in obtaining necessary start-up capital or in transferring managerial skills. Aldrich and Waldinger (1990) describe "opportunity structures" as market conditions that may favor goods or services oriented towards co-ethnics or co-nationals. Immigrants who are living in areas with relatively high proportions of co-nationals may have a comparative advantage in providing certain goods or services, food or restaurant services for example, to their co-nationals compared to natives or other immigrants. The result, according to this theory, is higher self-employment rates among immigrants living in enclaves.

Hence, Model 3 extends Model 2 by adding a variable for the proportion of immigrants in the census year of the total population by SMSA and country of origin. This is calculated by adding up the number of male immigrants in the sample from a particular country in the SMSA and then dividing this by the total male population in the sample in the SMSA. For immigrants living in a non-SMSA area, the proportion is calculated based on the state's non-SMSA immigrant population. Given the definition above, it follows that the value of this variable is zero for all natives. The coefficient of this variable is positive and highly significant. This indicates that immigrants living in an area where a greater proportion of co-nationals are living, increases the probability of self-employment. For example, for a Mexican immigrant living in a SMSA where 10% of the population also comes from Mexico, the mean value for Mexican immigrants, an increase in the proportion of Mexicans by 1% in the area increases the probability of self-employment by 0.1%. The proportion of co-nationals in the area appears to greatly influence the self-employment decision of Cuban immigrants. Model 2 predicts that Cubans are approximately 3.5% more likely to be self-employed compared to a statistically similar African immigrant. When the immigrant proportion ratio is added, Cubans are found to be no more likely to be self-employed than African immigrants. That is, the difference in self-employment rates between Cuban and African immigrants possessing similar individual characteristics can be explained completely by the proportion of co-nationals living in the area.

The last model presented in Table 7, Model 4, adds to the previous model two instruments measuring the ratio of self-employment earnings to wage/salary earnings. The first variable is calculated by dividing the average native self-employment earnings in the SMSA in a given census year by the average native wage/salary earnings in the same SMSA and by natives' ethnicity[8]. The second variable measures the same ratio, but for immigrants by SMSA and national origin group. The latter variable is set to zero for all natives and the former is set to zero for all immigrants. It is expected that higher self-employment earnings to wage/salary earnings ratios are associated with higher self-employment rates, given a set of individual characteristics, since it essentially measures the relative success of the self-employed in the area[9]. The signs of both of the estimated coefficients are positive, as expected, and significant. However, the impact of a change in the earnings ratio on the probability of self-employment appears to be stronger for immigrants than natives. An increase in the earnings ratio by 0.1 increases the probability of self-employment for natives by 0.17%. The effect of the same change in the ratio on a Mexican immigrant who arrived between 1975 and 1979 is an increase in the probability of self-employment by 0.46%[10]. The effect is close to 3 times stronger for immigrants as compared to natives. The overall entrepreneurial success of an immigrant's co-nationals in the area seems to be quite important in the self-employment decision process. Natives are less influenced by the relative rewards between self-employment and wage/salary work in the area than immigrants.

The models described above show that it is important to include controls for country of origin when analyzing the self-employment decision. They also show differences in the role of education and earnings ratios in the self-employment choice process between immigrants and natives. The specification in Model 4 is used for the two-step Heckman selection correction models estimated and described below.

6. Empirical model and findings: Labor market assimilation

Immigrants' earnings in the wage/salary sector have been found not to converge with natives' earnings (Borjas 1985, 1995) over the work life. Earnings of immigrants start out at a lower point and rise more rapidly over time than natives' earnings. However, parity is not reached. This section will look at whether this also holds for self-employed immigrants when compared to self-employed natives. Comparisons of immigrant labor market performance between the two sectors will also be made. The main goal of this section is to establish whether self-employed immigrants do better or worse in the labor market than wage/salary immigrants, both relative to each other and relative to natives in their own sector.

The earnings models estimated in this paper use as the dependent variable log of weekly earnings[11]. To try to take into account the possibility that self-employed workers earn a return on physical capital, I also estimate models using as the dependent variable the log of weekly income, which includes any earnings from wage/salary work and/or self-employment earnings and in addition any interest, rental or dividend income. If an individual is deciding between a wage/salary job or self-employment, he/she can keep his/her assets in, for example, savings accounts, the stock market, bonds, or real estate and work in the wage/salary sector. Alternatively he/she can use a proportion, or all, of his/her assets to start a business. In the former, returns to physical capital will be observed in terms of interest, rental or dividend income. If self-employment is chosen, returns may show up both in increased earnings and interest, rental or dividend income. Therefore, as an alternative outcome measure, I use log income, where income is sum of total earnings and interest, rental or dividend income. With this measure, both groups are put on "par", and this measure of income can be compared reasonably between the two sectors. It appears that the results are not very sensitive to whether earnings or income is used[12]. In light of this, I use the log of weekly earnings as the dependent variable in all wage regressions presented and discussed in this paper. Furthermore, all earnings are deflated to 1989 dollars using the CPI.

One convenient way of analyzing labor market assimilation is to estimate earnings equations and use the estimated coefficients to trace out age-earnings profiles or alternatively use the predicted earnings to derive the profiles. The wage models are estimated separately for the self-employed and the wage/salary workers. The regressions are specified as:

$$\log y_i^{s-e} = \mathbf{X}_i \beta^{s-e} + \mathbf{A}_i \delta^{s-e} + \mathbf{YSM}_i \gamma^{s-e} + \varepsilon_i^{s-e}, \quad \text{for the self-employed}$$

$$\log y_i^{w/s} = \mathbf{X}_i \beta^{w/s} + \mathbf{A}_i \delta^{w/s} + \mathbf{YSM}_i \gamma^{w/s} + \varepsilon_i^{w/s}, \quad \text{for wage/salary workers}$$

where $\mathbf{X}$ is a vector of socio-economic and geographic characteristics, including dummy variables for immigrant status, national origin group and arrival cohort, $\mathbf{A}$ is a vector of age variables, i.e. age, age^2 and age^3, and $\mathbf{YSM}$ is a vector of years since migration variables, i.e. YSM, YSM^2 and YSM^3. The vector $\mathbf{A}$ also includes the age variables interacted with an immigrant dummy variable. The years since migration variable is equal to zero for all natives.

The models described above were estimated both by ordinary least squares with no correction and also by heteroskedastic robust ordinary least squares using the inverse Mills ratio to correct for selection bias. The estimated coefficients from the earnings models are presented in Table 8 where Model 1 is

Table 8. OLS weekly wage models for males aged 18–64, based on 1980 and 1990 public use samples of the U.S. census

Variable	Self-employed		Wage/salary	
	Model 1	Model 2	Model 1	Model 2
Constant	3.0797	−0.7753	2.7430	3.0173
	(0.0968)	(1.0676)	(0.0168)	(0.0224)
Immigrant	0.9177	1.9554	1.1660	0.7977
	(0.3617)	(0.4612)	(0.0652)	(0.0682)
Mexico	−0.1325	−0.3713	−0.0697	−0.0082
	(0.0602)	(0.0893)	(0.0154)	(0.0158)
South and Central America	−0.0965	−0.1962	−0.0562	−0.0252
	(0.0606)	(0.0665)	(0.0157)	(0.0158)
South East Asia	−0.0265	−0.2554	−0.0799	−0.0134
	(0.0637)	(0.0897)	(0.0159)	(0.0163)
North East Asia	−0.0938	0.0455	0.0387	−0.0160
	(0.0584)	(0.0699)	(0.0161)	(0.0164)
India/Pakistan	0.1448	0.1070	0.0870	0.0979
	(0.0652)	(0.0660)	(0.0174)	(0.0175)
Middle East	0.0616	0.3027	0.0924	−0.0112
	(0.0602)	(0.0897)	(0.0177)	(0.0185)
Europe/Canada/Australia/New Zealand	0.0549	0.1124	0.1633	0.1406
	(0.0564)	(0.0586)	(0.0152)	(0.0152)
Caribbean	−0.1593	−0.3583	−0.1043	−0.0483
	(0.0677)	(0.0871)	(0.0165)	(0.0168)
Cuba	−0.0963	−0.0168	−0.0229	−0.0490
	(0.0624)	(0.0661)	(0.0171)	(0.0172)
Period effect 1980	0.3884	0.3502	0.4061	0.4160
	(0.0182)	(0.0210)	(0.0048)	(0.0049)
Age	0.0676	0.2075	0.1136	0.0968
	(0.0075)	(0.0393)	(0.0014)	(0.0017)
Age2	−0.0007	−0.0035	−0.0017	−0.0015
	(0.0002)	(0.0008)	(0.00004)	(0.00004)
Age3/1000	−0.0072	0.1894	0.0758	0.0606
	(0.0147)	(0.0562)	(0.0031)	(0.0032)
Years of schooling	0.0983	0.1229	0.0796	0.0714
	(0.0010)	(0.0068)	(0.0003)	(0.0005)
Years of schooling* immigrant	−0.0363	−0.0553	−0.0350	−0.0290
	(0.0023)	(0.0057)	(0.0006)	(0.0007)
Age* immigrant	−0.0422	−0.1138	−0.0589	−0.0338
	(0.0275)	(0.0338)	(0.0053)	(0.0054)
Age2* immigrant	0.0009	0.0028	0.0011	0.0005
	(0.0007)	(0.0009)	(0.0001)	(0.0001)
Age3/1000* immigrant	−0.0625	−0.2226	−0.0757	−0.0187
	(0.0537)	(0.0695)	(0.0116)	(0.0120)
Speaks little or no English	−0.1484	−0.2064	−0.1488	−0.1374
	(0.0237)	(0.0286)	(0.0052)	(0.0052)
Years since migration	0.0428	0.0718	0.0289	0.0222
	(0.0072)	(0.0108)	(0.0016)	(0.0016)
Years since migration2	0.00002	−0.0008	0.0003	0.0004
	(0.0003)	(0.0004)	(0.0001)	(0.0001)
Years since migration3/1000	0.0076	0.0775	−0.0367	−0.0481
	(0.0410)	(0.0453)	(0.0115)	(0.0115)
Arrival cohort pre–1950	−1.6573	−1.9049	−1.3338	−1.2617
	(0.2173)	(0.2278)	(0.0515)	(0.0517)
Arrival cohort 1950–59	−1.0811	−1.2954	−0.8453	−0.7818
	(0.1504)	(0.1616)	(0.0345)	(0.0346)

Table 8 (continued)

Variable	Self-employed		Wage/salary	
	Model 1	Model 2	Model 1	Model 2
Arrival cohort 1960–64	−0.7429	−0.9044	−0.5768	−0.5308
	(0.1184)	(0.1265)	(0.0265)	(0.0266)
Arrival cohort 1965–69	−0.5662	−0.6973	−0.4374	−0.3996
	(0.0973)	(0.1038)	(0.0212)	(0.0213)
Arrival cohort 1970–74	−0.3888	−0.4442	−0.3103	−0.2956
	(0.0770)	(0.0785)	(0.0164)	(0.0164)
Arrival cohort 1975–79	−0.2657	−0.2977	−0.1912	−0.1836
	(0.0575)	(0.0582)	(0.0117)	(0.0117)
Arrival cohort 1980–84	−0.1637	−0.1538	−0.1107	−0.1117
	(0.0465)	(0.0466)	(0.0096)	(0.0096)
Correction term		−0.7830		0.6799
		(0.2160)		(0.0368)
Sample size	152243	152243	1190536	1190536
R-square	0.1841	0.1843	0.3088	0.3090

Note: Standard errors are presented in parentheses. Model 2 standard errors are White corrected standard errors since the Heckman two-step procedure introduces heteroskedasticity of the disturbance term. All models include interactions between education and period effect, education interacted with period effect and immigrant status, in addition to dummies for regions, SMSA residency, disability and for being married.

the equation without correction and Model 2 includes the correction term calculated based on estimation of Model 4 in Table 7.

The sign of the coefficient on the inverse Mills ratio variable tells us whether there is an overall positive or negative selection into each sector. Not surprisingly, the correction term indicates that there is positive selection into both wage/salary work and self-employment. That is, individuals who choose self-employment are better suited for self-employment, at least in terms of earnings, than are the persons who choose to work in the wage/salary sector and vice versa. Fairlie and Meyer (1994) also find indication of positive selection into both sectors. However, the coefficient on the correction term for the self-employed is not found to be statistically significant in their study.

Comparing the estimated coefficients from the models with and without correction for selectivity gives further insight to the selection process. The coefficient for limited English proficiency is of similar magnitude in both sectors in the models without correction. When correction is controlled for, the estimated coefficient does not change much for wage/salary workers but becomes substantially greater in absolute terms for the self-employed. The higher penalty for limited English ability in the self-employment sector may be one of the reasons for the observed lower proportion of individuals with this proficiency level of English among the self-employed.

Returns to education appear to be greater for self-employed immigrants and natives, as compared to wage/salary employees, both in models with and without a correction term. Also, the effect of controlling for self-selection is much greater on the schooling coefficient for the self-employed. As was found in Betts and Lofstrom (2000), returns to education for immigrants are lower than for natives. The returns from an additional year of schooling are greater

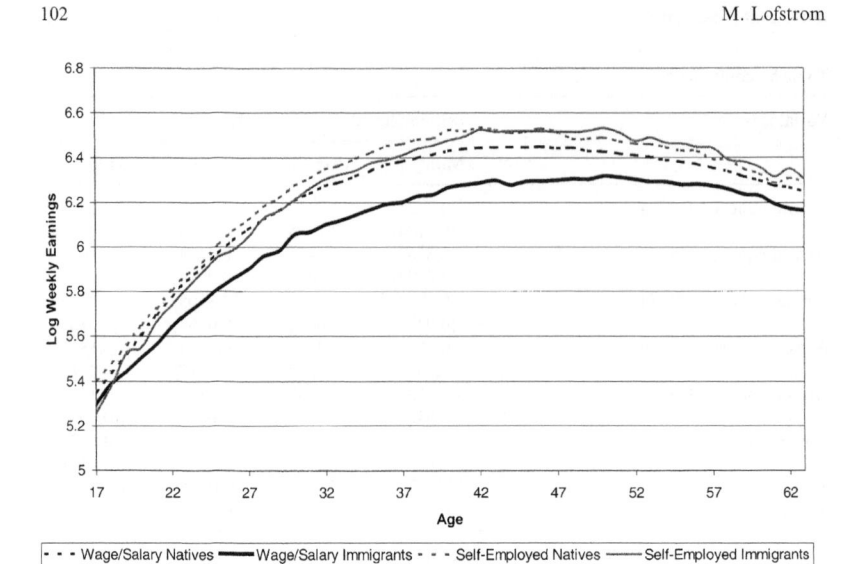

Fig. 1. Predicted age-earnings profiles, no control for self selection

for self-employed immigrants compared to wage/salary immigrants. However, when selection is controlled for it appears that immigrant education is discounted to a greater extent for the self-employed.

The self-employment decision models indicate that age affects self-employment probabilities differently between immigrants and natives. One possible reason for this is that age also impacts earnings differently for immigrants and natives. Model 1 in Table 8 suggest that this is the case and that there are also differences in returns to experience, or age, between the two sectors. For immigrants it also appears that years since migration impacts earnings differently between the self-employed and wage/salary workers. Since the models allow for non-linearities in both age and years since migration, it is difficult to analyze labor market assimilation by a simple comparison of the estimated coefficients. Instead, as stated above, a convenient way to analyze this is to look at age-earnings profiles. Figure 1 shows the predicted age-earnings profiles derived from Model 1. It traces out the average predicted log weekly earnings over age. In other words, the estimated coefficients from Model 1 are used to calculate the predicted earnings for *each* individual by age for the four groups, self-employed immigrants and natives and, wage/salary immigrants and natives.

The age-earnings profiles suggest that both wage/salary and self-employed immigrants start out at lower earnings than natives. They also indicate that wage/salary immigrants never reach earnings parity with natives. The supports the findings by Borjas (1995). A very interesting finding here is that self-employed immigrants' earnings appear to catch up with wage/salary natives' earnings at around age 30 and overtake, but stay close to, self-employed natives' earnings at around age 40. The greater labor market assimilation rate of self-employed immigrants, as compared to wage/salary immigrants, allows these immigrants to overcome their initial earnings disadvantage compared to

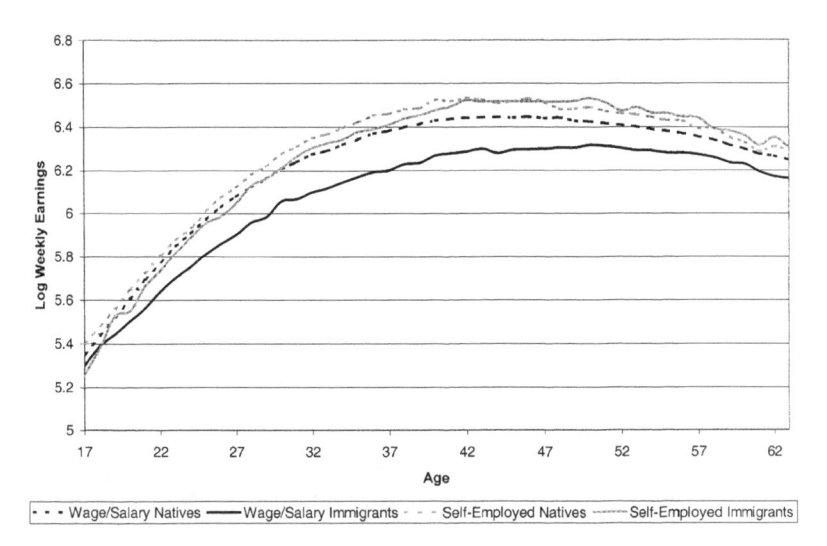

Fig. 2. Predicted age-earnings profiles with self selection correction

wage/salary immigrants and natives and self-employed natives. As can be seen in Fig. 2, this also holds true when correction for self-selection is incorporated into the model. Figure 2 shows the predicted age-earnings profile obtained from Model 2 in Table 8.

The results shown in Fig. 2 do not answer the question if self-employed immigrants do *statistically* significantly better in the labor market than do, say, self-employed natives? One way of answering this question is to look at whether expected lifetime earnings of the different groups are significantly different. From the estimated results in Models 2 in Table 8, the expected lifetime earnings for the four groups were calculated under the assumption of equal hours worked per week. The expected lifetime earnings of self-employed immigrants are about 1.5% less than the predicted earnings over the work life of self-employed natives, but within 2 standard errors of each other. In other words, there appears to be no significant difference in predicted lifetime earnings between self-employed immigrants and natives. In contrast, wage/salary immigrants are predicted to earn close to 15% less over their work life, compared to wage/salary natives. The difference is measured relatively precisely and is statistically significant.

A methodological concern in regards to the method used in this paper to analyze labor market assimilation of immigrants has been raised by Duleep and Regets (e.g., 1999). The concern is that wage convergence of immigrants may be underestimated if there is negative correlation between immigrant wage growth and time of entry human capital. According to Duleep and Regets, the observed decline in immigrant entry earnings is less of a concern since these individuals are likely to experience greater earnings growth than earlier relatively more skilled cohorts. One implication of their work is that the slope of age earnings profiles may differ across arrival cohorts. A solution that addresses this concern is to interact the variables for years since migration

Table 9. Change in median weekly earnings 1979–1989, by arrival cohort

Sample:	Wage/salary only	Wage/salary and self-employed*
Natives	−0.056	−0.056
Immigrant cohort:		
1975–79 Arrivals	0.275	0.298
1970–74 Arrivals	0.170	0.177
1965–69 Arrivals	0.154	0.175
1960–64 Arrivals	0.151	0.146
1950–59 Arrivals	0.112	0.121
Pre-1950 arrivals	0.024	0.030

* Sample includes self-employed individuals who reported negative earnings.

with the indicator variables for arrival cohorts. This method, however, does not allow for identification of cohort effects in levels of earnings.

Duleep and Regets (1999) find evidence of an inverse relationship between immigrant entry earnings and immigrant earnings growth. It should be pointed out that the finding of this relationship is based on holding educational attainment upon arrival constant. Borjas (2000) results corroborate the finding of Duleep and Regets, but he finds no evidence of earnings convergence if entry schooling level is not held constant. One implication of these results is that less skilled immigrant groups, like Mexican immigrants, are unlikely to reach the earnings levels of relatively more skilled groups, like North East Asian immigrants. However, a Mexican immigrant with a high school diploma is likely to reach earnings parity with a statistically similar high school graduate from North East Asian, even if he has lower initial earnings than the North East Asian migrant.

The discussion above points out that studies of labor market assimilation of immigrants is sensitive to whether immigrant entry skill levels are held constant or not. The results presented above are based on estimates in which I control for educational attainment and English proficiency of immigrants. To ensure that these results are not driven by the critique brought up by Duleep and Regets, or the exclusion in the sample of the self-employed who report negative earnings, I derived median weekly earnings for the cohorts included in both census years and calculated the unadjusted earnings growth rate for each cohort between the ages of 18 and 54 in 1980 and between the ages of 28 and 64 in 1990. These calculations were made based on two samples, one including only wage/salary workers and one including both wage/salary workers and the self-employed. The results are shown in Table 9. It appears that the regression results are driven neither by the potential bias in earnings assimilation stemming from a negative correlation between earnings growth and initial earnings, nor the exclusion of negative earners. For most arrival cohort, the increase in median weekly earnings increases somewhat when the self-employed, including negative earners, are included in the sample.

The finding that self-employed immigrants do better in the U.S. labor market and display greater earnings growth than wage/salary immigrants suggests that the wage gap between natives and immigrants is measured somewhat inaccurately unless self-employed immigrants are included in the sample. The

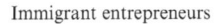

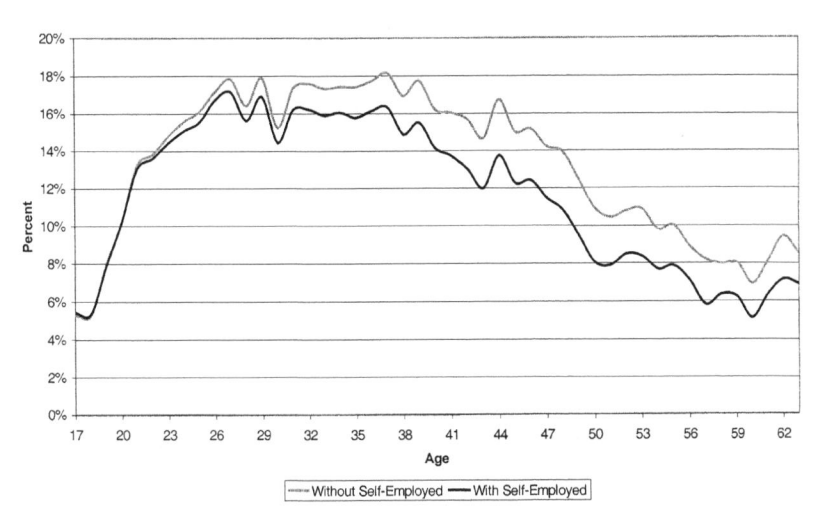

Fig. 3. Predicted log weekly earnings gap, immigrants-natives

important question is then: how does this gap change when the self-employed are included? This can be answered by calculating "weighted" age-earnings profiles separately for immigrants and natives in the following way:

$$\bar{y}_j^k = \frac{n_j^{w/s}}{n_j} \hat{y}_j^{w/s} + \frac{n_j^{s-e}}{n_j} \hat{y}_j^{s-e}$$

where n is the number of individuals in age group j, j varies between 17 and 63, and where k indicates the group, i.e. immigrants or natives. I suppress the superscript on the right hand side variables to simplify the notation. By subtracting $\bar{y}_j^{immigrants}$ from $\bar{y}_j^{natives}$ the wage gap when the self-employed are included can be calculated for each age group. Figure 3 shows the log wage gap calculated in this way, based on Model 2 in Table 8, and also the log wage gap when the self-employed are excluded.

The immigrant native earnings gap changes very little for individuals under the age of 30 when the self-employed are included. However, the gap becomes more exaggerated with age and is most overstated for individuals in their fifties. Excluding the self-employed when studying labor market assimilation overstates the gap between natives and immigrants by up to 30% of the earnings gap. This is mainly driven by two components. The first is that the most successful self-employed immigrants, relative to natives, are 40 years old or older. The second reason can be seen in Fig. 4. The greatest difference in self-employment rates between natives and immigrants is for individuals in their forties and fifties. The observed overall higher self-employment rate among immigrants is caused by the higher self-employment rates of this age group. It is not surprising that the most successful self-employed immigrants, relative to natives, also have the highest relative self-employment rates. This is in fact what the theoretical model described above predicts.

Using the predicted earnings and the method described above, I also cal-

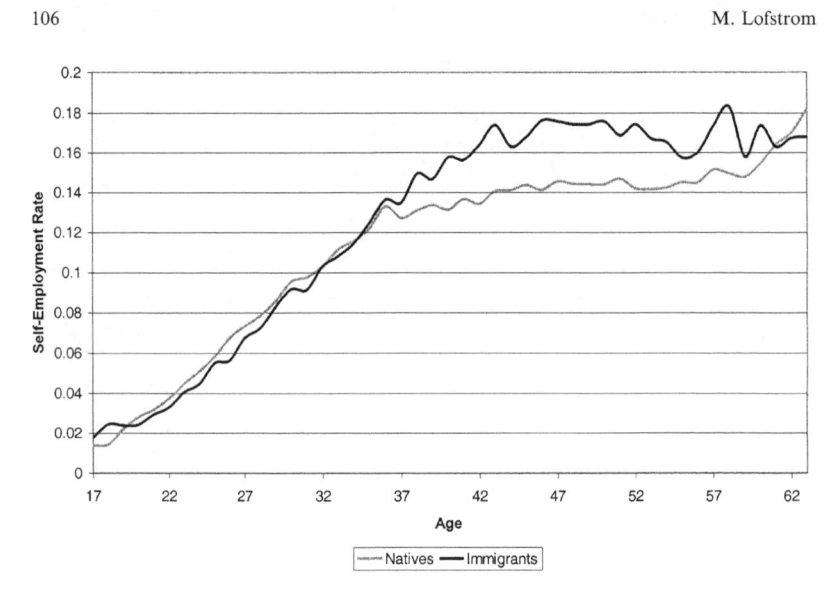

Fig. 4. Self-employment rates by age

culate the overall average immigrant-native earnings gap both when the self-employed are excluded and included in the sample. Without the self-employed, the predicted immigrant-native wage gap is about 12.7% (using the observed differences, the gap is 15.3%). When the self-employed are included, the predicted earnings gap decreases to around 10.8% (or 13.2% if no controls are included). The predicted gap is overstated on average by slightly more than 14% when the self-employed are not accounted for in the sample.

The estimated earnings models for wage/salary workers and the self-employed that include a correction term, Model 2 in Table 8, can also be used to predict earnings of the self-employed had they chosen the wage/salary sector. This gives us further insight into the effects of self-selection. Figure 5 displays the predicted age-earnings profile for wage/salary workers and the predicted age-earnings profiles for the self-employed had they chosen wage/salary work. These are calculated by applying the estimated coefficients for wage/salary workers and individuals' inverse Mills ratio to the self-employed as well as wage/salary employees. The predicted wage/salary earnings indicate that self-employed immigrants would barely reach earnings parity with wage/salary natives if they had selected the wage/salary sector. Furthermore, convergence is now delayed until approximately age 55. The predicted wage/salary earnings of self-employed immigrants is estimated to never reach the predicted wage/salary earnings of self-employed natives. Self-employed immigrants are predicted to do worse in the wage/salary sector compared to self-employed natives. Self-employed immigrants appear to be relatively more positively selected into self-employment than natives.

Is it possible that cohort effects may be the reason labor market assimilation appears to be more rapid for self-employed immigrants? It has been suggested that the drop in relative labor market performance of immigrants in the last decades is due to changes in U.S. immigration policy (see for example

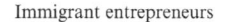

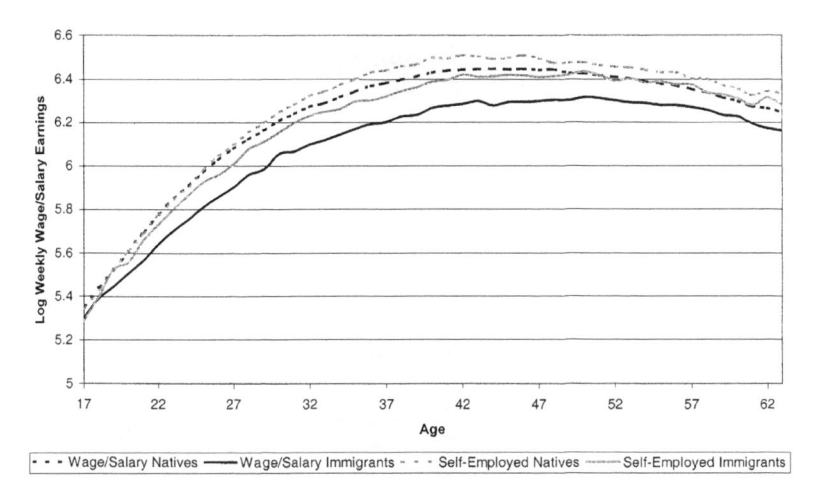

Fig. 5. Predicted age-wage/salary earnings profiles with self selection correction

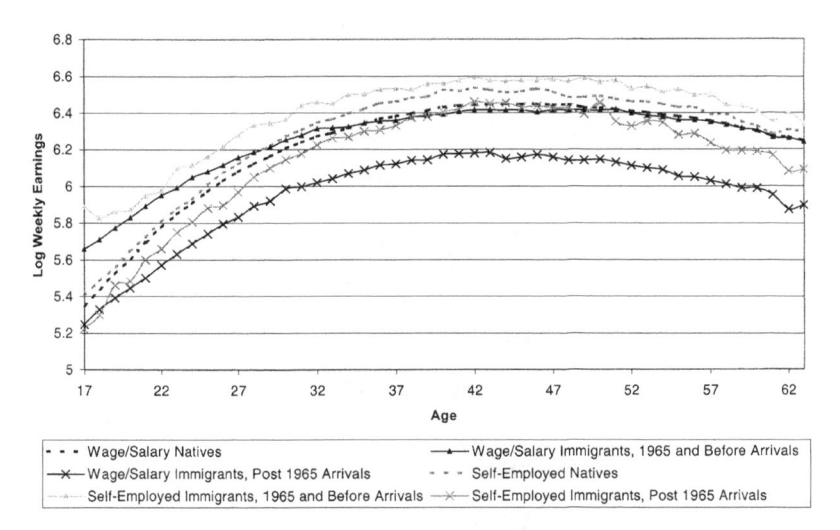

Fig. 6. Predicted age-earnings profiles by post 1965 arrival cohorts and 1965 and before arrival cohorts

Borjas 1994). The 1965 Amendments to the Immigration and Nationality Act repealed the national origin restrictions and made family re-unification the main criteria in deciding who is allowed to immigrate to the U.S. The effect of the policy change is believed to have led to changes in the national origin composition of immigrants toward immigrants of lower skill levels.

To ensure that cohort effects are not the cause of the observed relative attainment of self-employed immigrants, separate age-earnings profiles were derived for post 1965 arrival cohorts and 1965 and before arrival cohorts. Figure 6 shows these age-earnings profiles. It can be seen that the more recent

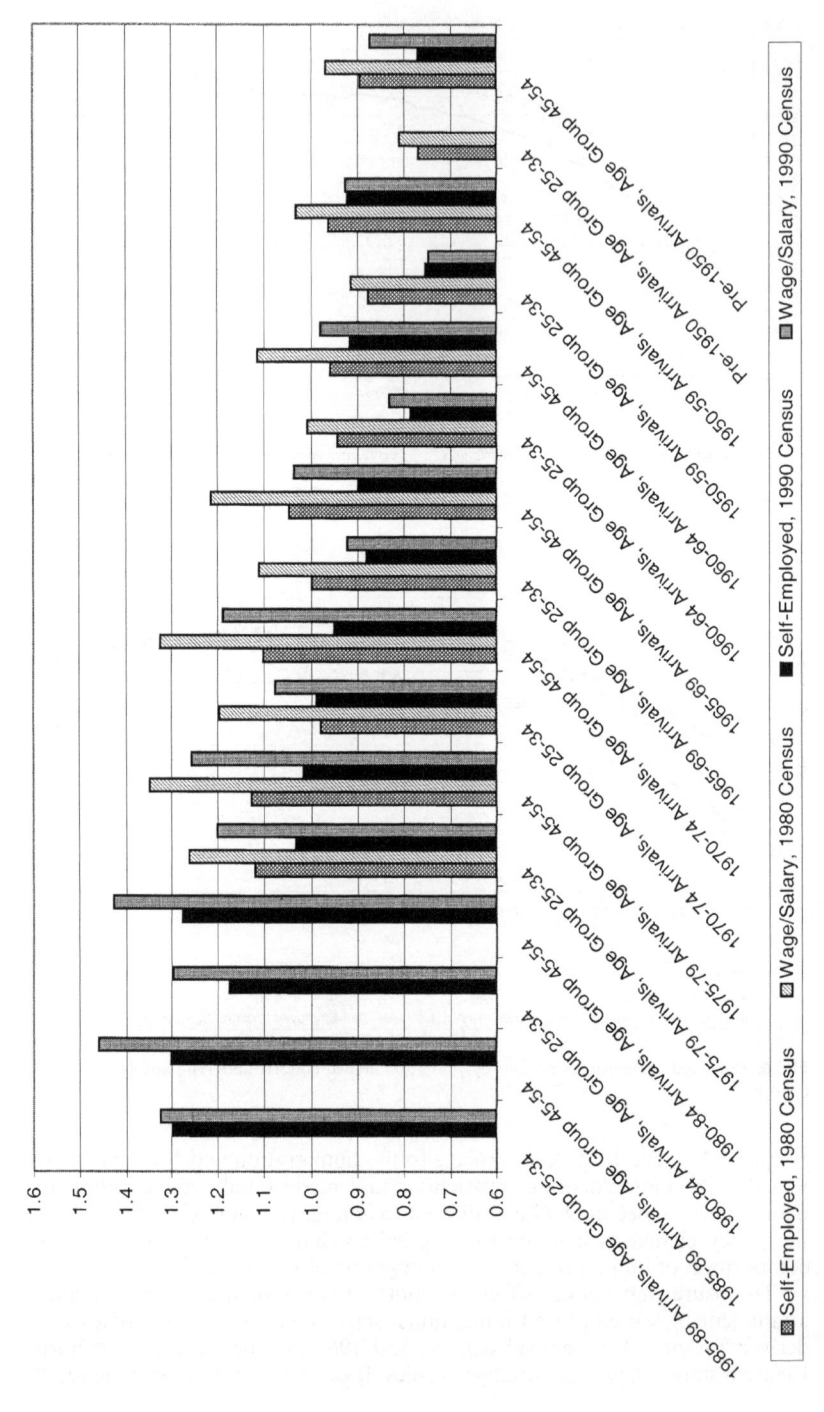

Fig. 7. Predicted relative weekly earnings, natives/immigrants, by arrival cohorts and age groups

arrival cohorts do not perform as well in the labor market as the earlier cohorts[13]. However, recent self-employed immigrants still do substantially better in the labor market than wage/salary immigrants. Their assimilation rate is greater and they also appear to be close to reaching earnings parity with self-employed natives. Self-employed immigrants who arrived in the earlier cohorts are also better performers in the labor market than wage/salary immigrants who arrived prior to 1965. The difference in earnings between post 1965 arrival cohorts and earlier cohorts appear to be smaller for self-employed immigrants.

Self-employed immigrants also appear to do better in the labor market than wage/salary immigrants when compared to natives of the same age. Figure 7 shows the predicted average weekly earnings for immigrants of two age groups, 25–34 and 45–54 year olds, relative to natives' average predicted earnings of the same age group. Although not presented here, the general findings for these age groups also hold for other age groups. For virtually all age groups and cohorts, self-employed immigrants perform better in the labor market, relative to natives of the same age, than immigrants in the wage/salary sector. For example, self-employed natives aged 25–34 in 1990 are predicted to earn 18% more than self-employed immigrants in this age group who arrived in the U.S. between 1980 and 1984 (i.e. a ratio of approximately 1.18). Wage/salary natives of the same age are predicted to earn 30% more than wage/salary immigrants in this age group and who arrived in the 1980–1984 period. The finding that self-employed immigrants display higher relative earnings than immigrant employees appear to hold for both the earlier and the more recent arrival cohorts. It seems unlikely that any cohort effects that are not absorbed by the estimated models are the driving forces behind the observed relative success of self-employed immigrants.

7. Conclusion and summary

Using data from the 1980 and 1990 U.S. Censuses, this paper shows that there are substantial differences between wage/salary immigrants and self-employed immigrants in terms of earnings and characteristics such as educational attainment. Self-employed immigrants have higher earnings, are more educated and display lower rates of limited English proficiency levels than wage/salary immigrants. Immigrants are more likely to be self-employed than natives but self-employment rates vary greatly across national origin groups and arrival cohorts.

Earnings of both self-employed and wage/salary immigrants declined relative to natives in the 1980's. The relative decline appears to be slightly stronger among the immigrants who chose wage/salary work.

Models of the self-employment decision are also estimated. Controlling for national origin groups affects the estimated impact of years of education on self-employment probabilities. Evidence of different roles of years of schooling in the self-employment decision between natives and immigrants is also found. Education has a greater influence on natives' self-employment probabilities compared to immigrants'.

The paper also finds evidence that the proportion of co-nationals living in the same SMSA has a positive impact on self-employment probabilities for immigrants. This variable alone appears to explain differences in self-employment rates between Cuban immigrants and African immigrants. This supports Borjas' (1986) finding of enclave effects in explaining some of the differences in self-employment rates between natives and immigrants.

The ratio of average self-employment earnings to wage/salary earnings in an individual's SMSA affects self-employment rates of natives substantially less than it does for immigrants.

The estimated earnings models suggest that wage/salary immigrants will not reach earnings parity with wage/salary natives. Earnings of self-employed immigrants are predicted to converge with native wage/salary earnings at around age 30 and native self-employed earnings at around age 40. The higher earnings of the self-employed suggest that the immigrant native earnings gap is overstated if the self-employed are not included in the sample. Calculations indicate the gap may be overstated by up to 30% for some age groups, but on average, the gap is overstated by roughly 14%.

Estimated models with correction for self-selectivity indicate that self-employed immigrants would not reach earnings parity with self-employed natives had they chosen to work in the wage/salary sector. The greater relative difference for immigrants between expected earnings in the wage/salary sector and self-employment earnings, compared to the difference for natives, is quite plausibly one important reason why immigrants display overall higher self-employment rates.

Appendix

Table A1. Definition of national origin groups

Mexico:
Mexico

South and Central America:
Argentina, Bolivia, Brazil, Chile, Colombia, Ecuador, Falkland Islands, French Guyana, Guyana, Paraguay, Peru, Suriname, Uruguay, Venezuela, Belize, Costa Rica, El Salvador, Guatemala, Honduras, Nicaragua, Panama.

South East Asia:
Bangladesh, Brunei, Burma, Cambodia, Indonesia, Laos, Macau, Malaysia, Philippines, Thailand, Vietnam.

North East Asia:
China, Hong Kong, Japan, North Korea, Singapore, South Korea, Taiwan.

India/Pakistan:
Bangladesh, Bhutan, India, Nepal, Pakistan, Sri Lanka.

Middle East/Egypt:
Bahrain, Cyprus, Iran, Iraq, Israel, Jordan, Kuwait, Lebanon, Oman, Qatar, Saudi Arabia, Syria, Turkey, United Arab Emirates, Yemen, Egypt.

Europe, Canada, Australia, New Zealand:
Albania, Andorra, Austria, Belgium, Bulgaria, Czechoslovakia, Denmark, Faeroe Islands, Finland, France, Germany, Gibraltar, Greece, Hungary, Iceland, Ireland, Italy, Liechtenstein, Luxembourg, Malta, Monaco, Netherlands, Norway, Poland, Portugal, Romania, San Marino, Spain, Sweden, Switzerland, United Kingdom, Vatican, Yugoslavia, Soviet Union, Canada, Australia, New Zealand.

Caribbean:
Anguilla, Antigua and Barbuda, Aruba, Bahamas, Barbados, British Virgin Islands, Cayman Islands, Dominica, Dominican Republic, Grenada, Guadeloupe, Haiti, Jamaica, Martinique, Montserrat, Netherlands Antilles, St. Barthelemy, St. Kitts-Nevis, St. Lucia, St. Vincent and the Grenadines, Trinidad and Tobago, Turks and Caicos Islands.

Cuba:
Cuba

Africa:
Algeria, Angola, Benin, Botswana, British Indian Ocean Territory, Burkina Faso, Burundi, Cameroon, Cape Verde, Central African Republic, Chad, Comoros, Congo, Djibouti, Equatorial Guinea, Ethiopia, Gabon, Gambia, Ghana, Glorioso Islands, Guinea, Guinea-Bissau, Ivory Coast, Juan de Nova Island, Kenya, Lesotho, Liberia, Libya, Madagascar, Malawi, Mali, Mauritania, Mayotte, Morocco, Mozambique, Namibia, Niger, Nigeria, Reunion, Rwanda, Sao Tome and Principe, Senegal, Mauritius, Seychelles, Sierra Leone, Somalia, South Africa, St. Helena, Sudan, Swaziland, Tanzania, Togo, Tromelin Island, Tunisia, Uganda, Western Sahara, Zaire, Zambia, Zimbabwe.

Table A2. Ethnic composition of national origin groups, percent of group population

Group	1980					1990				
	White	Black	Asian	Hispanic	Other	White	Black	Asian	Hispanic	Other
Natives	86.3	8.9	0.6	3.6	0.6	86.7	7.9	0.7	4	0.7
All immigrants	44.5	5	15.3	34.6	0.6	28.3	5.6	21.2	44.7	0.2
National origin group:										
Mexico	0.8	0.2	0.1	98.6	0.3	0.4	0.3	0.2	98.8	0.3
Central/South America	9.2	9.2	2	78.7	0.9	5.1	6.6	2.1	85.8	0.4
South East Asia	5.4	0.2	92.4	0.6	1.4	1.9	0.1	97.8	0.2	0
North East Asia	4.2	0.2	95.1	0.2	0.3	2	0.1	97.7	0.1	0.1
India, Pakistan, etc	5.9	0.3	92.3	0.1	1.4	3.9	0.2	95.1	0.2	0.6
Middle East/Egypt	95.2	0.2	1	1.1	2.5	97.6	0.2	1.5	0.6	0.1
Europe, CAN, AUS, NZ	96.6	0.4	0.3	2.4	0.3	96.3	0.6	0.4	2.7	0
Africa	48.5	36.7	9.5	2.3	3	32.8	55.9	10.1	1.2	0
Caribbean	4	68.9	2.4	23.6	1.1	2.6	72.4	2.2	22.5	0.3
Cuba	0.9	1.7	0.2	97.1	0.1	0.8	2.4	0.3	96.5	0

Endnotes

[1] Using the Current Population Survey, Bregger (1996) estimated that 6.7 million men were self-employed in 1994.

[2] Total earnings in this paper is defined as the sum of annual earnings from wage/salary work and self-employment earnings. The reason for this is that an individual may report earnings from both sectors. A person is defined to be self-employed if he reports to be self-employed in own incorporated or not incorporated business, professional practice or farm and if he has no farm self-employment income, i.e. self-employed farmers are excluded from the study. All other working individuals are defined as wage/salary workers.

[3] Individuals who reported a weekly wage over $20,000, in 1989 dollars, are excluded from the study. Also, individuals who reported a weekly wage of less than $50 are ignored. Since the 1990 Census is not a random sampling of the population, sample weights are used for all calculations and estimations.

[4] The U.S. Immigration and Naturalization Service estimates that in 1990, 7.9% of the total U.S. population was foreign born. Given a self-employment rate of 12.2% for male immigrants, the proportion of self-employed immigrants of the total male population would be 0.96%, assuming men and women comprise an equal share of foreign born.

[5] The goal of creating national origin groups is to obtain groups that are relatively homogenous within the group to reduce the observed heterogeneity among immigrants overall. The national origin groups used in this paper seem to be relatively homogenous in terms of the ethnic composition and educational attainment and appear to be reasonably defined groups. An earlier version of this paper contains more details about the national origin groups, see IZA Discussion Paper No. 54, August 1999.

[6] The coding of educational attainment changed in the 1990 Census. The data from 1990 is recoded in the following fashion. No school completed, nursery school and kindergarten are coded as 0 years of education; first through fourth grade are recoded as 2.5 years; fifth through eighth grade as 6.5 years; ninth grade as 9 years; tenth grade as 10 years; eleventh or twelfth grade without a high school diploma as 11 years; high school graduate as 12 years; some college, no degree as 13 years; associate degree as 14 years; bachelor's degree as 16 years; master degree as 17 years and professional and doctorate degree as 20 years.

[7] This variable is set equal to one if the respondent indicated that they did not speak English well or if they did not speak English at all.

[8] The ethnic groups used are the mutually exlusive ones shown in Table A2, i.e. white, black, Asian, Hispanic and all other.

[9] One concern with incorporating these variables into the self-employment decision models is that they may be determined endogenously and consequently lead to inconsistent estimators. However, given that the ratios are relative group characteristics by SMSA and not individual characteristics, this seems somewhat unlikely. The earnings ratio is not clearly endogenous, but may simply reflect entrepreneurial conditions or opportunities in an area.

[10] The interquartile range for the earnings ratios are approximately 0.4 for immigrants and 0.15 for natives. This implies that the model predicts roughly 1.8% of the variation in immigrant self-employment rates over SMSAs and 0.25% of the variation in native self-employment rates.

[11] Weekly earnings are calculated by adding up a person's earnings from wage/salary work and self-employment. This is divided by the number of weeks worked to obtain weekly earnings. Note that an individual may report earnings from both wage/salary work and self-employment. In these cases, both sources are included in the sum of earnings. In 1980 earnings were top coded at $75,000 while in 1990 the top code was $140,000. The real difference between the top code is approximately 10%. The reported top coded earnings in 1980 are adjusted by multiplying them by 1.1.

[12] Models using log hourly earnings were also estimated. The general results reported in this paper also hold for this outcome measure. Overall, the earnings advantage the self-employed hold over wage/salary workers is somewhat reduced when reported hours worked are corrected for.

[13] One possible reason for the higher earnings of the earlier arrival cohorts is that they consist of a greater proportion of immigrants who migrated at a relatively young age. Borjas (1995) finds that the assimilation process of immigrants who arrive in the U.S. at a young age have age-earnings profiles that are similar to the age-earnings profiles of natives.

References

Aldrich HE, Waldinger R (1990) Ethnicity and Entrepreneurship. *Annual Review of Sociology* 16:111–35

Betts JR, Lofstrom M (2000) The Educational Attainment of Immigrants: Trends and Implications. In: Borjas GJ (ed) *Issues in the Economics of Immigration*. University of Chicago Press

Borjas GJ (1985) Assimilation Changes in Cohort Quality and the Earnings of Immigrants. *Journal of Labor Economics* 4:463–89

Borjas GJ (1986) The Self-Employment Experience of Immigrants. *Journal of Human Resources* 21:485–506

Borjas GJ (1987) Self-Selection and the earnings of Immigrants. *The American Economic Review* 4:531–53

Borjas GJ (1994) The Economics of Immigration. *Journal of Economic Literature* 32:1667–717

Borjas GJ (1995) Assimilation Changes in Cohort Quality Revisited: What Happened to Immigrant Earnings in the 1980's? *Journal of Labor Economics* 2:201–45

Borjas GJ (2000) The Economic Progress of Immigrants. In: Borjas GJ (ed) *Issues in the Economics of Immigration*. University of Chicago Press

Bregger JE (1996) Measuring Self-employment in the United States. *Monthly Labor Review*: 3–9

Carliner G (1980) Wages, Earnings and Hours of First, Second, and Third Generation American Males. *Economic Inquiry* 1:87–102

Chiswick BR (1978) The Effect of Americanization on the Earnings of Foreign-born Men. *Journal of Political Economy* 5:897–921

Cummings S (1980) *Self-Help in Urban America: Patterns of Minority Business Enterprise*. Kenikart Press, New York

Duleep HO, Regets MC (1999) Immigrants and Human-Capital Investments. *American Economic Review* 82:186–191

Fairlie RW, Meyer BD (1996) Ethnic and Racial Self-Employment Differences and Possible Explanations. *Journal of Human Resources* 31:757–93

Light I (1984) Immigrant and Ethnic Enterprise in North America. *Ethnic and Racial Studies* 7:195–216

Yuengert AM (1995) Testing Hypotheses of Immigrant Self-Employment. *Journal of Human Resources* 30:194–204

[14]

The Role of the Family in Immigrants' Labor-Market Activity: An Evaluation of Alternative Explanations: Comment

By FRANCINE D. BLAU, LAWRENCE M. KAHN, JOAN Y. MORIARTY, AND ANDRE PORTELA SOUZA*

Most research on the labor-market outcomes of immigrants has studied the behavior of individuals, focusing primarily on the wage assimilation process, or the excess returns to experience which immigrants obtain in their destination country's labor market (e.g., Barry R. Chiswick, 1978; George J. Borjas, 1985). Recently, however, attention has been directed to analyzing immigrant labor-market outcomes in a family context, an approach which combines information about an individual's own labor-market opportunities and the family context in which labor-market decisions take place. In a previously published paper in this *Review*, Michael Baker and Dwayne Benjamin (1997) evaluate alternative explanations for the observed labor-supply patterns of Canadian immigrants in the 1986–1991 period. Specifically, when immigrant husbands arrive in Canada, they typically work less than comparable natives; however, immigrant wives work more than natives, other things equal. With assimilation, the labor supply of immigrant husbands eventually catches up to that of natives, while immigrant wives' labor supply falls relative to comparable natives and is ultimately overtaken by that of natives.

The authors take these patterns to be most consistent with a family investment model. In this scenario, upon arrival, husbands invest in their human capital, while wives work to provide the family with liquidity during this investment period. With increased time in Canada, husbands' labor supply increases rapidly due to their growing skills in the Canadian labor market, while wives' labor supply falls off in part because they originally took "dead-end" jobs upon arrival in order to finance their husbands' investments in human capital. Interestingly, while most of the findings reported by Baker and Benjamin are consistent with the family investment model, their estimated wage equations are not, although they do not comment on this in discussing the appropriateness of the family investment model. Specifically, they find *similar* rates of wage assimilation for husbands and wives. This finding suggests roughly equal propensities to invest in one's own human capital for both groups. This is contrary to the family investment hypothesis and does not match their story of dead-end jobs for wives and large human-capital investments of their husbands.

An alternative possible explanation for the patterns observed by Baker and Benjamin involves a simple price model in which the observed labor-supply patterns reflect labor-supply responses to each spouse's wages. For example, the initially high but eventually falling level of wives' labor supply (relative to comparable natives) could be a response to their husbands' initially low, but rising, wages. While this reasoning, like the family investment model, is broadly consistent with the data, the authors conclude that the simple price model cannot be the entire explanation since, in order to explain the full labor-supply patterns of immigrants, it would require unrealistically high labor-supply elasticities, and, further, that the assimilation patterns noted above remain even when wages of husband and wife are controlled

---

* Blau: School of Industrial and Labor Relations, Cornell University, 265 Ives Hall, Ithaca, NY 14853, and NBER and CESifo; Kahn: School of Industrial and Labor Relations, Cornell University, 264 Ives Hall, Ithaca, NY 14853, and CESifo; Moriarty: School of Industrial and Labor Relations, Cornell University, ILR Graduate Student Mailboxes, Ives Hall, Ithaca, NY 14853; Souza: Faculdade de Economia, Administracao e Contabilidade, University of Sao Paulo, Avenida Professor Luciano Gualberto, 908, Cidade Universitaria, Predio FEA 1, Sao Paulo, SP 05508, Brazil.

The authors thank three anonymous referees for helpful comments and suggestions. Portions of this paper were written while Blau and Kahn were Visiting Scholars at the Russell Sage Foundation, to which they are grateful for research support.

for. The authors then go on to present a variety of evidence that is consistent with wives in immigrant families in Canada financing their husbands' human-capital investments early in their stay in Canada.

In this paper, we use microdata from the U.S. Census of Population for 1980 and 1990 to examine whether these patterns characterize the experience of immigrants in the United States. While Baker and Benjamin cite studies by David A. MacPherson and James B. Stewart (1989) and Harriet Orcutt Duleep and Seth Sanders (1993) for the United States that obtain results which they characterize as consistent with their Canadian findings, these studies are based on a single cross-section of data. As Borjas (1985) showed, if the unmeasured characteristics of cohorts of immigrants are changing over time, as appears to be the case in the United States, such studies may produce biased estimates of immigrant assimilation effects. This problem may be mitigated by employing more than one nationally representative cross section as we do here and as Baker and Benjamin did in their analysis of Canada.[1]

In contrast to the patterns which Baker and Benjamin found for Canada, we find that, among immigrants to the United States, both husbands and wives work less than comparable natives upon arrival. Further, both immigrant husbands and wives have positive assimilation profiles in labor supply and eventually overtake the labor supply of comparable natives. Both the male and female immigrant hours shortfalls upon arrival and the positive assimilation profiles for men and women have similar magnitudes. It thus appears that in the United States the labor-supply patterns of immigrant husbands and wives similarly reflect assimilation into the new country's market. Our results suggest that investment is indeed important, but that, in sharp contrast to the family investment model, both spouses seem to invest primarily in their own human capital rather than their spouse's. In this respect our findings are consistent with a long line of research on the growth in married women's labor supply in the United States which suggests that married women's labor-supply decisions are more responsive to their own labor-market opportunities than to their husband's income (e.g., Jacob Mincer 1962; Claudia Goldin 1990; Chinhui Juhn and Kevin M. Murphy 1997). Finally, our paper has significance for the economics of gender. In the Baker and Benjamin model, married women are clearly "secondary earners" in the immigrant family. Our results for the United States suggest more similar economic behavior of men and women within the immigrant family in that they are both investing in their own human capital.

Our results imply that the extent to which the family investment model is the dominant pattern may vary depending on such factors as the composition of the immigrant group and conditions in the receiving country. While Baker and Benjamin have obtained some evidence suggesting that the model may hold in Canada, we have found that the model does not explain immigrant behavior in the United States. Similar studies of other countries need to be done in order to determine whether Canada or the United States is an exceptional case. However, our results do imply that the family investment model is inadequate for at least one major immigrant-receiving country, the United States.

I. The Labor-Supply and Wage Assimilation Patterns of Married Immigrants in the United States

A. Basic Results

We examine the labor-market assimilation patterns of married U.S. immigrants using a pooled sample of married couples from the 5% Public Use Samples of the 1980 and 1990 Censuses. These include native couples, immigrant couples, and "mixed couples" (i.e., those with one immigrant and one native spouse). The Census is particularly suitable for analyzing immigrant outcomes because of its large sample size (while immigration has been increasing rapidly, immigrants remained a relatively small proportion of population in 1980 and 1990) and its information on race and ethnicity, as well as on the source countries of immigrants. In order

---

[1] There may, however, be biases in this "synthetic cohort" approach as well. The chief concern is an alteration in the unmeasured composition of the group over the intervening period due say to the return migration of immigrants, or in our case movements into and out of the currently married category. We return to this point below.

to focus on differences between outcomes in the United States and Canada, we follow the specifications and sample restrictions in Baker and Benjamin's Canadian study as closely as possible.[2] The entire 5% sample is used for couples including immigrants, nonwhites, and Hispanics, but a random sample was employed for couples where both spouses were native whites.[3] In all the analyses reported below, observations are weighted to represent the U.S. population. Our weighting also takes into account Census sampling weights which are available for 1990 but not provided by the Census for 1980. Results were very similar when we ran unweighted regressions.

To analyze labor supply, we estimate the following equation on the pooled sample of married immigrants and married natives separately for wives and husbands:

(1) $H_{it} = \mathbf{B}'\mathbf{X}_{it} + \gamma_{Wc} + \gamma_{Hc}$

$+ a_1 YSMW_{it} + a_2 (YSMW_{it})^2$

$+ b_1 YSMH_{it} + b_2 (YSMH_{it})^2$

$+ k_t + u_{it},$

where for individual i in year t ($t = 1980$ or 1990), H_{it} is annual hours worked in the previous year (usual weekly hours × weeks worked, including those who did not work outside the home), γ_{Wc} and γ_{Hc} are immigrant cohort-of-arrival effects referring to cohort c for wives and husbands, respectively, YSMW and YSMH are years since migration for immigrant wives and immigrant husbands, respectively, but

equal 0 for natives, k is a common year effect, $\mathbf{X}$ is a vector of control variables to be discussed shortly, and u is an error term.

In equation (1), immigrants and natives are pooled. We define the cohort of arrival dummy variables (whose coefficients are the γs) to include each possible arrival cohort as coded in the Census: 1985–1989, 1980–1984, 1975–1979, 1970–1974, 1965–1969, 1960–1964, 1950–1959, and pre-1950. Since the sum of the wife (husband) cohort dummies in the wife (husband) labor-supply equation would be identical to an immigrant dummy variable, such an indicator is not separately included in (1). The equation allows each spouse's arrival cohort (if either spouse is an immigrant) to affect the labor-supply behavior of both spouses. In addition, the years since migration (YSMW and YSMH) variables allow us to estimate assimilation profiles with respect to the individual's own time in the United States as well as his or her spouse's time, if either spouse is an immigrant.[4] The pooled sample across two Census years and the assumption of a common time effect for immigrants and natives together allow us to separately identify immigrant cohort and assimilation effects (Borjas, 1985).[5]

The combination of the cohort dummies and the assimilation effects allows us to completely characterize immigrant labor supply over time starting with arrival in the United States of any arrival cohort relative to that of natives, controlling for the $\mathbf{X}$ variables and the time effect. The $\mathbf{X}$ variables include quadratics in age for both the husband and wife, years of schooling for both husband and wife, English language ability indicators (speaking English "well," "not well" or "not at all," with native English speakers as the omitted category) for both husband and wife, number of children, a dummy variable for the presence of children less than six years old,

---

[2] Following Baker and Benjamin, we restrict the sample to those couples in which both members are aged 16–64 and exclude the self-employed and individuals with positive wage and salary income but implausible values of wages (in our case, less than $1 or greater than $250 in 1989 dollars using the Personal Consumption Expenditures deflator). Also, as is standard in research examining immigrant outcomes in the United States or using U.S. Census data to study wages, we exclude natives born abroad, at sea, or in U.S. territories, individuals who are in the military, and those with allocated wage and salary income. Note that this is a sample of married couples. Thus, if one member of the couple did not meet the sample inclusion restrictions, both were excluded.

[3] This sample corresponded to 2/1000 of the U.S. population.

[4] Following Borjas (1995), we calculated the years since migration variables by evaluating the categorical period of immigration variables at the midpoints of the indicated intervals and used 40 years in 1980 and 50 years in 1990 for the open-ended category (before 1950).

[5] Of course, the common time effect may not hold to the extent that immigrants have different skill levels from natives. In our context, this factor could produce problems comparing the United States and Canada to the extent that immigrants' relative skill levels differ in the two countries. This point is pursued further below.

three race/ethnicity dummy variables for husband and wife (black, other nonwhite, and Hispanic, with white non-Hispanic the omitted category), a metropolitan area dummy variable, and regional dummy variables to account for the nine Census regions. Other than the control for race/ethnicity, the specification is very similar to that of Baker and Benjamin, and omitting these variables from our equations did not affect the basic results.[6]

Log-wage equations had a similar form to (1) except that, following Baker and Benjamin, no spouse cohort or assimilation variables were included. These were omitted by the authors in order to focus on individuals' own determinants of wage growth, while the labor-supply equations emphasize family considerations.[7] Wages were defined as the previous year's wage and salary income divided by (weeks worked × usual weekly work hours) and were expressed in 1989 dollars.

Table 1A contains basic regression results for work hours and wages from reduced form models. Overall, in contrast to Baker and Benjamin's Canadian results, we obtain similar wage and labor-supply assimilation patterns for immigrant husbands and wives in the United States. Consider first the results for the labor-supply equation for wives. We find that the coefficients on the years since migration (YSM) and cohort variables are similarly signed to the results obtained for Canada by Baker and Benjamin; however, there are some crucial differences in their magnitudes. As in the case of Canada, the annual hours of immigrant women increase with wife's own time in the United States (through 30.3 years)[8] and decrease with her husband's. However, while the coefficient on wife's own YSM is similar in magnitude to the coefficient estimated for Canada, the effect for her husband's YSM is small and insignificant. Similarly, while the impact of a woman's own cohort variables are all negative and of her husband's positive (with one exception), estimated husband's cohort effects are considerably smaller in magnitude in the United States than in Canada. Signs are also similar for the YSM and cohort variables of immigrant husbands in the United States and Canada. Both own and wives' cohort effects are negative; and immigrant husbands are found to increase their hours worked with both their own YSM (through 33.0 years) and their wives' YSM (through 30.4 years).[9] As in the case of Canada, own effects are larger than cross effects, although cross effects are found to be a bit larger in the United States than in Canada.

The net effects of the estimated YSM and cohort effects on the hours assimilation profiles of immigrant wives and husbands are illustrated in Table 1B for immigrant couples where both the wife and the husband arrived between 1975 and 1979. Results are qualitatively similar for other cohorts. Relative to natives with similar characteristics, we find that immigrant wives supply 212.7 fewer hours upon arrival (i.e. −264.592 + 51.897); and immigrant husbands 389.7 fewer hours. The assimilation effects for men and women both imply rising annual hours worked relative to comparable natives with time in the United States, with immigrant wives overtaking native-born wives after 10–15 years, and immigrant husbands surpassing native-born husbands after about 15 years. The hours assimilation profile is concave for both groups.

The U.S.–Canada comparison is clarified in Figure 1 which shows the hours assimilation profiles summarized in Table 1B for the United States and analogous results for Canada derived from Baker and Benjamin. We focus on hypothetical immigrant married couples that migrated at roughly the same time, where the base immigration entry cohort is assumed to be 1975–1979 for the United States and 1976–1980 for Canada. The figure shows that our results for immigrant husbands are similar to those obtained for Canada by Baker and Benjamin; however, our results differ sharply for

---

[6] Baker and Benjamin were unable to include controls for race and ethnicity in their analysis because this information was not available in their data, the 1986 and 1991 Canadian Survey of Consumer Finances.

[7] While we recognize that the family investment model implies that spouse's time in the United States affects one's own human capital, we use Baker and Benjamin's specification for comparability. Note that, following Baker and Benjamin, we include spouse's time in the U.S. and cohort variables when we examine results for immigrant and mixed families separately below. Inclusion of these variables does not alter our findings.

[8] Mean YSM of immigrant wives is 16.344.

[9] Mean YSM of immigrant husbands is 16.902.

TABLE 1A—ASSIMILATION PROFILES OF HOURS AND WAGES

	Hours				Log wages			
	Wives		Husbands		Wives		Husbands	
Independent variable	Coefficient	Standard error	Coefficient	Standard error	Coefficient	Standard error	Coefficient	Standard error
YSM, wife (×100 for log wage)	25.207	2.170	9.473	1.845	1.1410	0.1300		
YSM², wife (×100 for log wage)	−0.416	0.036	−0.156	0.031	−0.0154	0.0024		
YSM, husband (×100 for log wage)	−2.054	2.233	24.323	1.898			0.9950	0.1040
YSM², husband (×100 for log wage)	−0.043	0.036	−0.368	0.031			−0.0088	0.0019
IM8589, wife	−609.353	16.314	−80.765	13.839	−0.2731	0.0113		
IM8084, wife	−251.208	19.873	−95.234	16.879	−0.1630	0.0133		
IM7579, wife	−264.592	19.893	−122.841	16.939	−0.1153	0.0125		
IM7074, wife	−180.993	25.203	−78.472	21.457	−0.0788	0.0151		
IM6569, wife	−244.220	30.786	−94.549	26.197	−0.0946	0.0182		
IM6064, wife	−317.414	34.934	−98.459	29.722	−0.1353	0.0208		
IM5059, wife	−340.645	38.254	−108.739	32.548	−0.1612	0.0227		
IM50p, wife	−291.181	43.982	−97.112	37.423	−0.1604	0.0280		
IM8589, husband	−29.006	17.597	−422.652	14.904			−0.2120	0.0090
IM8084, husband	38.110	20.186	−217.384	17.117			−0.1792	0.0106
IM7579, husband	51.897	20.730	−266.833	17.647			−0.1513	0.0099
IM7074, husband	96.004	26.129	−214.143	22.238			−0.1058	0.0122
IM6569, husband	119.961	32.070	−277.808	27.281			−0.1111	0.0148
IM6064, husband	78.190	36.606	−307.492	31.133			−0.1238	0.0170
IM5059, husband	118.211	40.228	−317.708	34.208			−0.1676	0.0184
IM50p, husband	186.885	45.971	−312.185	39.088			−0.2257	0.0223
R^2	0.153		0.126		0.176		0.229	
Sample size	650,266		650,258		435,356		594,440	

Note: Additional controls for all equations include quadratics in age for both husband and wife, years of schooling of both husband and wife, English skill indicators for both husband and wife, number of children, a dummy variable for presence of children under 6 years old, race and ethnicity dummies for both husband and wife (black, other nonwhite, Hispanic), a metropolitan area dummy variable, regional dummy variables, and a year dummy.

TABLE 1B—IMMIGRANT-NATIVE DIFFERENCES IN HOURS FOR HUSBANDS AND WIVES IN THE 1975/1979 COHORT

Group	Net YSM	Net YSM²	Immigrant-native difference evaluated at YSM =						
			0	5	10	15	20	25	30
Wives	23.154	−0.459	−212.696	−108.394	−27.025	31.411	66.914	79.484	69.121
	(1.831)	(0.035)	(16.645)	(11.928)	(11.626)	(14.037)	(16.972)	(19.673)	(22.172)
Husbands	33.796	−0.524	−389.674	−233.793	−104.110	−0.625	76.664	127.754	152.647
	(1.558)	(0.030)	(14.175)	(10.150)	(9.875)	(11.918)	(14.411)	(16.709)	(18.838)

Note: Based on regression results reported in Table 1A evaluated assuming husbands and wives are in the same arrival cohort; i.e., the coefficients on own and spouse's YSM, YSM², and IM7579 are summed.

immigrant wives. Their results imply that, in Canada, immigrant wives work more than comparable natives upon arrival but that hours converge smoothly until reaching parity after 30 years. In contrast, as noted, immigrant wives in the United States initially have lower hours but eventually surpass hours of comparable natives. Note also the qualitatively similar profiles for

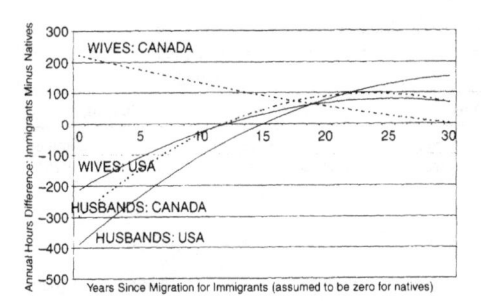

FIGURE 1. HOURS PROFILES FOR IMMIGRANT FAMILIES RELATIVE TO NATIVE FAMILIES

immigrant husbands and wives in the United States.

To assess the magnitudes of the assimilation and cohort entry effects for immigrant husbands and wives in the United States, recall that the dependent variable is annual hours worked.[10] In our pooled sample, the weighted means for annual hours (including those not employed) averaged 1,038.3 for wives and 1,961.0 for husbands.[11] If we convert the parameter values into elasticities evaluated at these means using the results in Table 1B for the 1975–1979 cohort, we find that the labor-supply behavior of immigrant husbands and wives relative to comparable natives is very similar, both at arrival and over time in the United States. At arrival, wives work 20.5 percent less than the average, all else equal, while husbands work 19.9 percent less. Over the next 25 years, immigrant wives increase their labor supply relative to comparable natives by 28.1 percent of the sample average, while immigrant husbands raise theirs by 26.4 percent.

The results in Table 1A indicate that, in the United States, wage assimilation profiles are also similar for immigrant husbands and wives.

---

[10] We use hours instead of log hours because we retain those with zero hours (i.e., the nonemployed) in the analysis.

[11] Annual work hours were 7–12 percent higher among natives than immigrants. For example, annual work hours averaged 934.4 hours for wives and 1,844.8 hours for husbands among immigrants; and 1,048.1 for wives and 1,971.14 for husbands among natives. Because the means for immigrants and natives are fairly close, we would obtain similar qualitative conclusions about elasticities using immigrant, native or pooled means.

Evaluating these results for the 1975/1979 cohort in Table 1C shows that both groups start 12–15 percent below comparable natives. But, after 25 years, immigrant wives have moved up 18.9 percent, while immigrant husbands' wages have increased 19.4 percent relative to comparable natives. Like the hours profiles (at least considered as elasticities), the log-wage profiles for husbands and wives display similar concavity. Interestingly, Figure 2 shows that our wage results are similar to those of Baker and Benjamin in that they also find similar wage assimilation profiles for immigrant husbands and wives. This suggests that some investment activity by both husbands and wives in their own human capital occurs in both countries. Moreover, the similarity of the wage assimilation profiles for husbands and wives in Canada (and our own findings for the United States) does not suggest that women are taking dead-end jobs to finance their husbands' human-capital investments. And, although wages increase considerably more rapidly with time in the receiving country for immigrant husbands in Canada than in the United States, the same is true for immigrant wives.[12] This suggests that the steeper slope of immigrant husbands' wage profiles in Canada compared to the United States is not necessarily due to the financing of their human capital investments by their wives.[13]

---

[12] Evaluated at the mean YSM in the United States of 16.623, the return to an additional year in the receiving country is 0.0063 for wives and 0.0070 for husbands in the United States, and 0.0140 for wives and 0.0124 for husbands in Canada.

[13] It is possible that the assumption of a common time effect for immigrants and natives has a larger negative effect on immigrants' wage assimilation profiles in the United States than in Canada. Specifically, according to Borjas (1993), immigrants are less skilled relative to natives in the United States than in Canada. Further, it appears that the fortunes of the less-skilled generally declined by more in the United States than in Canada in the 1980's (Richard B. Freeman and Karen Needels, 1993). Then if, as is necessary to account for immigrant cohort effects, we assume a common time effect, this may cause us to understate true immigrant assimilation profiles by more in the United States than in Canada. That is, the more negative immigrant time effect in the United States becomes a less steeply sloped assimilation profile in a model that forces a common time effect (this is similar to the argument made by Robert J. LaLonde and Robert H. Topel (1992) in assessing male immigrant wage assimilation in the United States in the

TABLE 1C—IMMIGRANT-NATIVE DIFFERENCES IN WAGES FOR HUSBANDS AND WIVES IN THE 1975/1979 COHORT

			\multicolumn{7}{c}{Immigrant-native difference evaluated at YSM =}
Group	YSM	YSM^2	0	5	10	15	20	25	30
Wives	1.141	−0.015	−11.527	−6.206	−1.652	2.134	5.152	7.403	8.886
	(0.130)	(0.002)	(1.245)	(0.871)	(0.795)	(0.938)	(1.138)	(1.328)	(1.500)
Husbands	0.995	−0.009	−15.132	−10.377	−6.062	−2.186	1.250	4.246	6.803
	(0.104)	(0.002)	(0.987)	(0.691)	(0.640)	(0.764)	(0.932)	(1.089)	(1.232)

Note: Based on regression results reported in Table 1A; wage effects and standard errors have been multiplied by 100.

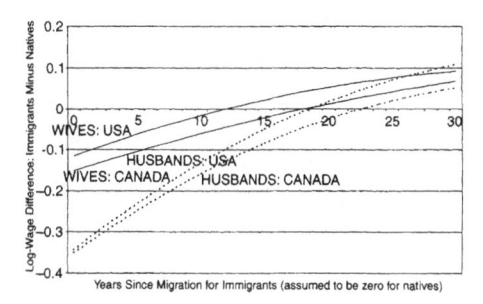

FIGURE 2. LOG-WAGE PROFILES FOR IMMIGRANT FAMILIES RELATIVE TO NATIVE FAMILIES

In Table 2, we present structural labor-supply equations where we include own and spouse's wages or estimated wage offers, as well as the couple's asset income, to see whether responses to these variables can account for the assimilation patterns which we observe in Tables 1A and B. Following Baker and Benjamin and Juhn and Murphy (1997), we impute wage offers to those without jobs by predicting log wages from a regression on a sample of those who worked less than 20 weeks in the previous year (estimated separately by gender).[14] Table 2 shows ordinary least-squares (OLS) and two-stage least-squares (2SLS) results, where in the latter, following Baker and Benjamin, own and spouse's wage offers are instrumented using the gender-specific decile in which one's wage offer (actual or predicted in the case of nonworkers) falls. This instrumental variable procedure can potentially correct for measurement error in the wage variables, since error is likely to be much less frequent in measuring wage decile than actual wages.[15]

The key findings in Table 2 are that, even controlling for wages, there are comparable positive hours assimilation profiles for immigrant husbands and wives. And, among immigrant couples in the same cohort, both husbands and wives are estimated to start out below comparable natives in work hours, controlling for wages, family asset income, period and the control variables. In contrast, using a similar specification, Baker and Benjamin continue to find that, among families that immigrated together, wives start out working more than comparable natives, but have negative assimilation profiles.

1980's). While a similar point may apply to the hours analyses as well, these relative biases cannot explain the divergent profiles for Canadian and U.S. immigrant wives shown in Figure 1. If anything, true U.S. immigrant women's employment assimilation profiles are even more positively sloped relative to those in Canada than Figure 1 indicates.

[14] This regression included the respondent's age, age squared, own and spouse's education, a metropolitan area indicator, regional dummies, a year effect, race/ethnicity, and own cohort dummies for immigrants. This specification is similar to Baker and Benjamin's, except for our inclusion of cohort dummies for immigrants (made possible by our larger sample size) and the addition of race. Due to an insufficient number of immigrants in the sample of individuals working less than 20 weeks, Baker and Benjamin obtain cohort effects from wage regressions using the sample of all working individuals. As noted above, Baker and Benjamin omit race/ethnicity from their analyses because it was not available in their data; recall that omitting race/ethnicity did not affect our results.

[15] While it is true that measurement error in wage deciles is less frequent than in actual levels, the consequences of making an error in denoting one's decile are likely to be greater than the consequences of a small measurement error in actual wage levels. For example, wrongly classifying a 9th decile worker as an 8th decile earner implies an error as large in log points as the difference between log wages in the 9th vs. the 8th deciles. Thus, the wage decile instrument may not adequately correct for measurement error in actual wages. Note that whatever the merit of this instrument, the OLS and 2SLS results in Table 2 are very similar.

TABLE 2—LABOR-SUPPLY EQUATIONS INCLUDING WAGE AND INCOME VARIABLES

	Wife's annual hours				Husband's annual hours			
	OLS		2SLS		OLS		2SLS	
Independent variable	Coefficient	Standard error	Coefficient	Standard error	Coefficient	Standard error	Coefficient	Standard error
Log (wife wage)	228.207	2.364	325.547	3.787	−13.944	2.025	−67.321	3.239
Log (husband wage)	−231.135	2.116	−360.818	3.690	−201.031	1.812	−135.717	3.150
Asset income	−0.008	0.000	−0.007	0.000	−0.002	0.000	−0.002	0.000
YSM, wife	24.767	2.135	24.628	2.143	10.051	1.827	10.144	1.830
YSM^2, wife	−0.401	0.035	−0.395	0.036	−0.158	0.030	−0.161	0.030
YSM, husband	−0.814	2.197	−0.141	2.206	25.922	1.879	25.601	1.882
YSM^2, husband	−0.048	0.036	−0.052	0.036	−0.383	0.031	−0.381	0.031
IM8589, wife	−568.967	16.059	−551.172	16.132	−88.542	13.708	−98.436	13.738
IM8084, wife	−243.437	19.554	−240.986	19.630	−104.014	16.713	−105.643	16.737
IM7579, wife	−263.405	19.573	−263.544	19.649	−131.590	16.772	−131.742	16.796
IM7074, wife	−191.417	24.798	−196.777	24.893	−85.858	21.245	−83.150	21.275
IM6569, wife	−251.773	30.290	−255.780	30.406	−101.737	25.938	−99.753	25.975
IM6064, wife	−322.160	34.372	−325.109	34.503	−107.715	29.429	−106.421	29.470
IM5059, wife	−345.041	37.639	−348.663	37.783	−122.279	32.227	−120.713	32.273
IM50p, wife	−299.962	43.274	−307.058	43.440	−115.040	37.053	−111.609	37.106
IM8589, husband	−71.885	17.319	−94.265	17.394	−463.298	14.761	−451.964	14.790
IM8084, husband	6.870	19.863	−9.996	19.943	−246.665	16.950	−238.305	16.977
IM7579, husband	20.996	20.398	4.190	20.480	−293.742	17.474	−285.333	17.502
IM7074, husband	75.490	25.708	64.338	25.808	−230.325	22.019	−224.730	22.050
IM6569, husband	98.866	31.555	88.010	31.676	−295.146	27.012	−289.689	27.051
IM6064, husband	56.450	36.018	45.576	36.156	−325.790	30.826	−320.325	30.870
IM5059, husband	88.738	39.581	73.365	39.734	−343.048	33.870	−335.410	33.919
IM50p, husband	149.303	45.232	128.256	45.408	−344.859	38.703	−334.385	38.759
R^2	0.180		0.175		0.143		0.131	
Sample size	650,266		650,266		650,258		650,258	

Notes: Additional controls for all equations include quadratics in age for both husband and wife, years of schooling of both husband and wife, English skill indicators for both husband and wife, number of children, a dummy variable for presence of children under 6 years old, race and ethnicity dummies for both husband and wife (black, other nonwhite, Hispanic), a metropolitan area dummy variable, regional dummy variables, and a year dummy. Two-stage least-squares (2SLS) estimates use the decile of husband's and wife's wage as instruments for the husband's and wife's log wages.

They take their results to imply that simple labor-supply models cannot account for their data. Our results similarly suggest that a simple labor-supply model cannot account for our findings, but in the case of the United States it appears that the primary pattern is for both immigrant wives and husbands to invest in their own human capital. We note however that one interpretation of our results, as well as those of Baker and Benjamin, is that time in the United States provides additional information about labor-market opportunities, even controlling for wages.[16]

[16] Note that, in addition to the YSM variables, a number of the control variables, including husband's and wife's education and presence of children, may capture some of the

A final point meriting comment in results presented in Tables 1A and 2 is the estimated effects of wages on labor supply. For the wives' results in Table 2, the coefficient on wife's own log wage (W_W) is smaller in absolute value than the coefficient on husband's log wage (W_H) in both the OLS and 2SLS regressions. This is counter to expectations based on the labor-supply literature cited above in which wives were found to be more responsive to their own wage opportunities than to their husband's income. However, when we estimated more conventional models we found the expected results. For example, when the models in Table 2 were reestimated continuing to include the YSM and immigrant cohort variables but omitting own and husband's education and presence of children, the estimated coefficients and standard errors were 338.969 (2.303) for W_W and −236.5 (2.149) for W_H in the OLS specification and 504.777 (3.402) for W_W and −334.854 (3.563) for W_H in the 2SLS specification.

TABLE 3—IMMIGRANT WIVES' ASSIMILATION AND COHORT PROFILES BY FAMILY TYPE

A. Assimilation Profiles:

	Annual hours				Log wages			
	Immigrant family		Mixed family		Immigrant family		Mixed family	
	Coefficient	Standard error	Coefficient	Standard error	Coefficient	Standard error	Coefficient	Standard error
YSM, wife	61.072	5.830	6.396	1.884	0.02309	0.00485	0.00011	0.00154
YSM², wife	−0.791	0.068	−0.120	0.041	−0.00031	0.00006	0.00002	0.00003
YSM, husband	−34.613	5.832	2.584	2.079	−0.00882	0.00484	0.00265	0.00163
YSM², husband	0.194	0.066	−0.048	0.046	0.00005	0.00005	−0.00002	0.00004
YSM, net	26.459	1.911			0.01427	0.00159		
YSM², net	−0.597	0.043			−0.00026	0.00004		

B. Cohort Profiles:

	Annual hours						Log wages					
	Both immigrants in same cohort		Immigrant wife and native husband		Native wife and immigrant husband		Both immigrants in same cohort		Immigrant wife and native husband		Native wife and immigrant husband	
	Coefficient	Standard error	Coefficient	Standard error	Coefficient	Standard error	Coefficient	Standard error	Coefficient	Standard error	Coefficient	Standard error
IM8589	−631.996	15.506	−476.796	29.030	−117.705	33.256	−0.29394	0.01404	−0.17346	0.02302	−0.03013	0.00023
IM8084	−208.937	19.884	−179.724	31.413	−54.065	32.103	−0.17543	0.01618	−0.08049	0.02431	−0.00896	0.00023
IM7579	−202.970	16.689	−174.166	23.647	−86.942	25.818	−0.10534	0.01446	−0.06152	0.01916	−0.03327	0.00019
IM7074	−60.489	21.068	−89.243	24.957	−62.705	28.266	−0.06077	0.01723	−0.00377	0.02012	0.01858	0.00022
IM6569	−98.964	24.765	−87.253	26.908	−32.700	31.273	−0.07502	0.02021	0.01029	0.02164	0.02000	0.00024
IM6064	−203.834	28.487	−101.328	27.140	−61.307	31.413	−0.10624	0.02332	−0.00592	0.02201	0.02006	0.00024
IM5059	−149.228	27.817	−89.780	21.518	−51.171	23.510	−0.07048	0.02347	−0.03333	0.01785	−0.01833	0.00019

Notes: To obtain net YSM effects the coefficients on own and spouse's YSM and YSM² are summed giving the effect for an immigrant whose spouse is in the same cohort. Additional controls for all equations include quadratics in age for both husband and wife, years of schooling of both husband and wife, English skill indicators for both husband and wife, number of children, a dummy variable for presence of children under 6 years old, race and ethnicity dummies for both husband and wife (black, other nonwhite, Hispanic), a metropolitan area dummy variable, regional dummy variables, and a year dummy.

positive effect of wife's YSM on husband's labor supply in all the models estimated. As noted above, Baker and Benjamin obtain the same result but in their case there is a ready interpretation for this finding. Wives are found to scale back their labor supply with time in Canada and hence it makes sense that husband's labor supply is increasing in wife's YSM. How can we explain our result in the face of rising wife's labor supply and wages with own YSM? It is possible that this positive coefficient is the result of greater information that the wife brings to her partner with additional time in the United States, thus furthering his assimilation process. However, if that is the case, we would expect to find a similar positive effect of husband's YSM on wife's labor supply. The fact that we find no evidence of this might be taken as indirect evidence in support of the family investment model. That is, it may be that the positive information effect of husband's YSM on wife's hours is offset by the wife's reduction in her labor supply as her husband accumulates human capital and no longer needs her contribution to family liquidity. However, if wives undertake such a role to some extent in the United States, our evidence strongly suggests that the dominant pattern for immigrant husbands and wives is a simple process of human-capital accumulation: both husbands and wives start with low wages and low hours but both have positive assimilation profiles, and the magnitudes of these effects are similar for husbands and wives.

Further evidence on the family investment model is provided in Tables 3 and 4 which show results for labor supply and wages separately for wives and husbands in immigrant families (i.e., where both spouses are immigrants) and mixed families (i.e., where only one spouse is an immigrant).[17] This analysis follows that of Baker and Benjamin, who reasoned that

---
[17] These results are estimated in regression equations specified as in (1), which include separate assimilation and cohort variables for immigrant husbands and wives in immigrant and mixed families.

TABLE 4—IMMIGRANT HUSBANDS' ASSIMILATION AND COHORT PROFILES BY FAMILY TYPE

A. Assimilation Profiles:

	Annual hours				Log wages			
	Immigrant family		Mixed family		Immigrant family		Mixed family	
	Coefficient	Standard error	Coefficient	Standard error	Coefficient	Standard error	Coefficient	Standard error
YSM, wife	−12.238	4.942	5.326	1.605	−0.00476	0.00368	−0.00083	0.00120
YSM^2, wife	−0.020	0.058	−0.103	0.035	0.00004	0.00004	0.00004	0.00003
YSM, husband	41.519	4.944	7.359	1.769	0.01164	0.00369	−0.00047	0.00132
YSM^2, husband	−0.539	0.056	−0.133	0.039	−0.00012	0.00004	0.00004	0.00003
YSM, net	29.282	1.627			0.00688	0.00123		
YSM^2, net	−0.560	0.037			−0.00008	0.00003		

B. Cohort Profiles:

	Annual hours						Log wages					
	Both immigrants in same cohort		Immigrant wife and native husband		Native wife and immigrant husband		Both immigrants in same cohort		Immigrant wife and native husband		Native wife and immigrant husband	
	Coefficient	Standard error	Coefficient	Standard error	Coefficient	Standard error	Coefficient	Standard error	Coefficient	Standard error	Coefficient	Standard error
IM8589	−483.752	13.143	−91.295	24.708	−374.356	28.066	−0.19449	0.01018	−0.05483	0.01805	−0.21324	0.02103
IM8084	−265.364	16.889	−67.113	26.768	−107.121	27.093	−0.16135	0.01266	−0.02105	0.01957	−0.08417	0.01983
IM7579	−341.801	14.216	−109.895	20.133	−144.199	21.952	−0.12541	0.01084	−0.01459	0.01484	−0.07709	0.01620
IM7074	−210.013	17.941	−65.830	21.258	−90.018	24.034	−0.06260	0.01337	0.00872	0.01569	−0.00611	0.01767
IM6569	−264.470	21.087	−70.221	22.935	−83.325	26.584	−0.05035	0.01575	0.01654	0.01703	0.03028	0.01958
IM6064	−262.723	24.261	−54.264	23.133	−86.779	26.681	−0.04781	0.01812	0.01347	0.01724	0.03717	0.01970
IM5059	−204.817	23.692	−58.494	18.333	−72.431	20.001	−0.04857	0.01788	−0.00715	0.01386	0.00926	0.01495

Notes: To obtain net YSM effects the coefficients on own and spouse's YSM and YSM^2 are summed giving the effect for an immigrant whose spouse is in the same cohort. Additional controls for all equations include quadratics in age for both husband and wife, years of schooling of both husband and wife, English skill indicators for both husband and wife, number of children, a dummy variable for presence of children under 6 years old, race and ethnicity dummies for both husband and wife (black, other nonwhite, Hispanic), a metropolitan area dummy variable, regional dummy variables, and a year dummy.

a mixed family would be less liquidity constrained than an immigrant family. They found that immigrant wives in mixed families behaved much less according to the family investment model than those in immigrant families. Specifically, immigrant wives in mixed families worked less than comparable natives upon arrival in Canada but had a positive assimilation profile, while immigrant wives in immigrant families generally worked more than comparable natives upon arrival, but had negative assimilation profiles.

In contrast to Baker and Benjamin, the results for the United States shown in Table 3 indicate that immigrant wives in *both* types of family work significantly less than comparable natives upon arrival and *both* have significantly positively sloped hours assimilation profiles. The hours shortfall at arrival relative to natives is generally smaller in mixed than in immigrant families, and the hours assimilation profile is more steeply sloped for wives in immigrant than in mixed families. These two contrasts could reflect a lower initial level of human capital and labor-market knowledge among immigrant wives in immigrant than in mixed families. This interpretation is bolstered by the wage results in Table 3. Specifically, while immigrant wives in both types of families start below comparable natives, the effects are much smaller in absolute value in mixed families, and the wage assimilation profile is much flatter in mixed families as well. These findings in Table 3 are not consistent with the idea that immigrant wives in immigrant families behave more according to the family investment model than those in mixed families. One result from Table 3 is consistent with the family investment hypothesis, however. Husbands' YSM is significantly related to wives' annual hours in immigrant but not in mixed families. Specifically, all else equal, wives in immigrant families work less as their husbands' years since migration increase (with the negative effect diminishing over time). But,

TABLE 5—POOLED RESULTS ALLOWING DIFFERENTIAL EFFECTS ACROSS FAMILY TYPES

A. Assimilation Profiles:

| | Husband's school attendance[a] |||| Presence of young children ||||
| | Immigrant family || Mixed family || Immigrant family || Mixed family ||
	Coefficient	Standard error	Coefficient	Standard error	Coefficient	Standard error	Coefficient	Standard error
YSM, wife	−0.0614	0.1470	−0.0085	0.0478	−0.1160	0.2630	−0.0268	0.0852
YSM^2, wife	0.0019	0.0017	−0.0001	0.0011	0.0035	0.0031	0.0013	0.0019
YSM, husband	−0.0479	0.1470	−0.1350	0.0527	−0.0155	0.2630	0.4000	0.0940
YSM^2, husband	0.0009	0.0017	0.0035	0.0012	−0.0026	0.0030	−0.0081	0.0021
YSM, net	−0.1093	0.0484			−0.1315	0.0866		
YSM^2, net	0.0028	0.0011			0.0009	0.0020		

B. Cohort Profiles:

| | Husband's school attendance[a] |||| Presence of young children ||||
| | Both immigrants in same cohort || Native wife and immigrant husband || Both immigrants in same cohort || Immigrant wife and native husband ||
	Coefficient	Standard error	Coefficient	Standard error	Coefficient	Standard error	Coefficient	Standard error
IM8589	0.1080	0.0039	0.0930	0.0084	−0.0086	0.0069	−0.0618	0.0131
IM8084	0.0678	0.0050	0.0740	0.0081	0.1150	0.0090	0.1038	0.0142
IM7579	0.0610	0.0042	0.0602	0.0065	0.0808	0.0075	0.0082	0.0107
IM7074	0.0215	0.0053	0.0365	0.0072	0.1003	0.0095	0.0326	0.0113
IM6569	0.0173	0.0063	0.0204	0.0079	0.0370	0.0112	−0.0075	0.0122
IM6064	0.0154	0.0072	0.0220	0.0079	−0.0019	0.0129	−0.0197	0.0123
IM5059	0.0133	0.0071	0.0192	0.0060	0.0237	0.0126	−0.0186	0.0097

Notes: To obtain net YSM effects the coefficients on own and spouse's YSM and YSM^2 are summed giving the effect for an immigrant whose spouse is in the same cohort. Additional controls for husband's school attendance include quadratics in age for both husband and wife, years of schooling of both husband and wife, English skill indicators for both husband and wife, number of children, a dummy variable for presence of children under 6 years old, race and ethnicity dummies for both husband and wife (black, other nonwhite, Hispanic), a metropolitan area dummy variable, regional dummy variables, and a year dummy. Controls are the same for the presence of young children regression except that number of children and the dummy variable for presence of children under 6 years old are excluded.

[a] Coefficients and standard errors multiplied by 100 in the husband's school attendance regressions.

this effect is strongly outweighed by wives' own positive hours assimilation profiles. Baker and Benjamin also find positive effects of wives' own YSM and negative effects of their husbands' YSM for the annual hours of immigrant wives. However, in Canada, the husbands' time effect dominates, while in the United States, the wives' own time effect dominates. This yields *overall* assimilation profiles (i.e., net YSM effects) that support the family investment model for Canada but not for the United States.

Table 4 shows that the same patterns characterize immigrant husbands as immigrant wives in mixed versus immigrant families. For both husbands and wives, being married to a native is generally associated with a higher initial level of hours and wages and less steeply sloped assimilation profiles than being married to an immigrant. Indeed, perhaps surprisingly, we show no evidence of wage assimilation for immigrant husbands in mixed families—we return to this point below.

Table 5 shows results for some direct measures of husband's human-capital investment and wife's role in financing this investment. First, the table shows that, upon arrival, immigrant husbands in immigrant families are more likely to be in school than comparable natives, but over time, this difference decays. This matches Baker and Benjamin's findings for Canada and suggests front-loading of immigrant husband's human-capital investment upon arrival in the United States. While this is consistent with the family investment model, such front-loading would of course also be predicted by human-capital models applied to individual investment behavior (Gary S. Becker, 1975). The latter seems a better explanation of our results in that, in contrast to Baker and Benjamin, we find similar results for immigrant husbands in mixed families, while for Canada, they found that husbands in mixed families were usually less likely to attend school than natives and had positive school attendance assimilation profiles. Moreover, again in contrast to the results for Canada, we find no evidence that wives' assimilation drives the excess enrollment decrease of men in immigrant families.[18]

Evidence on childbirth patterns can also shed light on the role of wives in financing their husbands' school attendance. If immigrant wives in immigrant families are more likely to be performing this role than those in mixed families, then we expect the latter to front-load their childbearing to a greater degree than the former and indeed Baker and Benjamin found evidence that this was the case in Canada. However, the results in Table 5 are not consistent with this scenario. Specifically, relative to natives, the presence of young children (a proxy for recent childbearing) appears to be more front-loaded for immigrant than for mixed families. While husbands are clearly investing in human capital relatively intensively upon arrival, there is little evidence that wives in immigrant families are financing this activity by postponing childbearing.[19]

B. *Alternative Specifications: Age at Immigration and Region-of-Origin Effects*

Up to now we have attempted to replicate as closely as possible Baker and Benjamin's specifications and have found that, in contrast to their results for Canada, immigrant wives in the United States appear to follow similar human capital accumulation patterns relative to natives as their husbands. In this subsection, we determine whether these results hold up to alternative specifications. We first consider issues relating to the age at which individuals migrated to the United States, and second, whether our results could be explained by region-of-origin effects, which were not included in (1).

Regarding the impact of age at migration, in our full sample of immigrants, some will have arrived in the United States as children and will have attained age 16, and therefore eligibility for our sample, some time between 1980 and 1990. While equation (1) relies on within-cohort changes to estimate assimilation effects, we do not observe a true within-cohort change in labor supply for those who recently arrived as children because they are not in the 1980 sample. More generally, results including those migrating to the United States as children may be misleading to some extent since they are more like Americans when they reach adulthood than those migrating as adults. To address these issues, following Rachel M. Friedberg (1993) and Borjas (1995), we have reestimated all of our models on a sample of immigrants who migrated to the United States at age 18 or older.[20]

Representative results for the adult immigrant sample are shown in Tables 6 and 7, and are similar in most respects to the corresponding Tables 3 and 4 for the sample including all immigrants. Specifically, immigrant wives and immigrant husbands who came to the United States when they were at least 18 both work less than comparable natives upon arrival, regardless of whether they are in an immigrant family

---

[18] The individual husband and wife YSM (and YSM²) effects are roughly similar in magnitude though none are significant. The net YSM (and YSM²) effects are however significant and consistent with a reduction in school attendance with years in the United States (through 19.5 years).

[19] In an examination of immigrant-native differences in total fertility (i.e., children ever born), Blau (1992) found evidence for the 1970–1980 period, that women's fertility tended to be disrupted by immigration. That is, upon arrival, immigrant women had fewer children than otherwise similar natives but that children increased relative to similar natives with time in the United States. The results in Table 5 suggest the possibility that this pattern may no longer hold although it is possible that the positive coefficient on most of the cohort variables for presence of young children reflects an attempt by immigrants whose fertility has been disrupted to attain their desired family size.

[20] To implement this sample selection, we evaluated the categorical period of immigration variables as in our computation of the YSM variables.

TABLE 6—IMMIGRANT WIVES' ASSIMILATION AND COHORT PROFILES BY FAMILY TYPE, ADULT IMMIGRANTS

A. Assimilation Profiles:

	Annual hours				Log wages			
	Immigrant family		Mixed family		Immigrant family		Mixed family	
	Coefficient	Standard error	Coefficient	Standard error	Coefficient	Standard error	Coefficient	Standard error
YSM, wife	86.751	8.760	26.730	5.025	0.0304	0.0073	0.0083	0.0044
YSM², wife	−1.436	0.160	−0.593	0.127	−0.0004	0.0001	−0.0002	0.0001
YSM, husband	−37.964	8.904	7.354	5.663	−0.0096	0.0074	0.0058	0.0043
YSM², husband	0.105	0.149	−0.126	0.142	−0.00004	0.0001	−0.0001	0.0001
YSM, net	48.787	3.421			0.0208	0.0029		
YSM², net	−1.330	0.102			−0.0004	0.0001		

B. Cohort Profiles:

	Annual hours						Log wages					
	Both immigrants in same cohort		Immigrant wife and native husband		Native wife and immigrant husband		Both immigrants in same cohort		Immigrant wife and native husband		Native wife and immigrant husband	
	Coefficient	Standard error	Coefficient	Standard error	Coefficient	Standard error	Coefficient	Standard error	Coefficient	Standard error	Coefficient	Standard error
IM8589	−689.347	18.836	−531.465	33.934	−127.477	39.334	−0.3129	0.0171	−0.1972	0.0273	−0.0317	0.0278
IM8084	−316.862	28.406	−305.311	46.088	−62.981	49.881	−0.2228	0.0234	−0.1367	0.0379	−0.0129	0.0367
IM7579	−298.483	22.864	−318.469	37.433	−115.751	41.869	−0.1492	0.0202	−0.1256	0.0328	−0.0486	0.0314
IM7074	−164.630	30.180	−265.245	46.174	−99.326	52.657	−0.1218	0.0247	−0.1032	0.0400	−0.0099	0.0402
IM6569	−227.597	35.106	−314.079	53.029	−115.789	62.431	−0.1427	0.0285	−0.0961	0.0455	−0.0208	0.0478
IM6064	−292.667	39.459	−350.232	53.897	−108.325	64.809	−0.1839	0.0320	−0.1342	0.0462	−0.0162	0.0497
IM5059	−253.824	42.097	−348.395	53.394	−92.855	60.710	−0.1482	0.0352	−0.1713	0.0471	−0.0409	0.0480

Notes: To obtain net YSM effects the coefficients on own and spouse's YSM and YSM² are summed giving the effect for an immigrant whose spouse is in the same cohort. Additional controls for all equations include quadratics in age for both husband and wife, years of schooling of both husband and wife, English skill indicators for both husband and wife, number of children, a dummy variable for presence of children under 6 years old, race and ethnicity dummies for both husband and wife (black, other nonwhite, Hispanic), a metropolitan area dummy variable, regional dummy variables, and a year dummy. Immigrants who came to the United States as children and their spouses are excluded.

or a mixed family. The effects are stronger for immigrant families than mixed families among men, while the relative magnitudes of cohort of arrival effects for women between immigrant and mixed families are ambiguous.[21] Moreover, immigrant husbands and wives in both types of families have positively sloped hours assimilation profiles, with stronger effects for immigrant families than mixed families.

Regarding wages, Table 6 shows that immigrant wives who came to the United States as adults have significantly positively sloped assimilation profiles regardless of family type, with a steeper slope for those in immigrant than in mixed families. Moreover, immigrant wives in immigrant families usually start with lower wages relative to comparable natives than those in mixed families. These findings are very similar to those in Table 3, although we now find stronger evidence of positive wage assimilation in mixed families. Immigrant husbands who came to the United States as adults now have wage patterns that are similar across the immigrant and mixed families (Table 7). Specifically, they start with low wages and have positively sloped assimilation profiles, and these effects are of similar magnitude across the two family types. It is possible that restricting the sample to adults has led to improved estimates of the wage profile for husbands and wives in mixed families because the latter may be more likely to include child immigrants. But, overall, our conclusion that wives appear to be investing in a similar manner to husbands (all relative to natives) is valid even restricting the immigrant sample to those who migrated as adults.

One possible reason for the differences we have obtained in the behavior of immigrant families in the United States compared to Baker

---

[21] For some cohorts, the cohort dummies are more negative for wives in immigrant families, while, for other cohorts, the effects are more negative for wives in mixed families.

TABLE 7—IMMIGRANT HUSBANDS' ASSIMILATION AND COHORT PROFILES BY FAMILY TYPE, ADULT IMMIGRANTS

A. Assimilation Profiles:

| | Annual hours |||| | Log wages ||||
| | Immigrant family || Mixed family || Immigrant family || Mixed family ||
	Coefficient	Standard error	Coefficient	Standard error	Coefficient	Standard error	Coefficient	Standard error
YSM, wife	−16.714	7.420	19.710	4.256	−0.0047	0.0055	0.0068	0.0033
YSM^2, wife	−0.209	0.137	−0.464	0.107	0.0002	0.0001	−0.0002	0.0001
YSM, husband	70.889	7.541	33.291	4.813	0.0150	0.0056	0.0098	0.0038
YSM^2, husband	−1.057	0.127	−0.773	0.121	−0.0003	0.0001	−0.0002	0.0001
YSM, net	54.176	2.903			0.0103	0.0023		
YSM^2, net	−1.267	0.086			−0.0001	0.000001		

B. Cohort Profiles:

| | Annual hours |||||| | Log wages ||||||
| | Both immigrants in same cohort || Immigrant wife and native husband || Native wife and immigrant husband || Both immigrants in same cohort || Immigrant wife and native husband || Native wife and immigrant husband ||
	Coefficient	Standard error	Coefficient	Standard error	Coefficient	Standard error	Coefficient	Standard error	Coefficient	Standard error	Coefficient	Standard error
IM8589	−554.264	15.961	−121.565	28.847	−450.709	33.181	−0.2042	0.0125	−0.0725	0.0213	−0.2423	0.0251
IM8084	−430.509	24.110	−150.934	39.156	−281.037	42.163	−0.2159	0.0184	−0.0714	0.0294	−0.1538	0.0319
IM7579	−469.900	19.444	−196.844	31.790	−327.287	35.640	−0.1734	0.0151	−0.0686	0.0242	−0.1524	0.0273
IM7074	−366.149	25.650	−177.271	39.183	−312.392	44.791	−0.1219	0.0194	−0.0634	0.0299	−0.1053	0.0342
IM6569	−425.442	29.838	−207.426	45.001	−338.467	53.061	−0.1079	0.0225	−0.0702	0.0344	−0.0679	0.0405
IM6064	−397.055	33.565	−184.813	45.751	−274.212	55.054	−0.1144	0.0253	−0.0850	0.0351	−0.0582	0.0420
IM5059	−367.675	35.806	−175.768	45.279	−252.403	51.632	−0.1258	0.0271	−0.1059	0.0351	−0.0840	0.0403

Notes: To obtain net YSM effects the coefficients on own and spouse's YSM and YSM^2 are summed giving the effect for an immigrant whose spouse is in the same cohort. Additional controls for all equations include quadratics in age for both husband and wife, years of schooling of both husband and wife, English skill indicators for both husband and wife, number of children, a dummy variable for presence of children under 6 years old, race and ethnicity dummies for both husband and wife (black, other nonwhite, Hispanic), a metropolitan area dummy variable, regional dummy variables, and a year dummy. Immigrants who came to the United States as children and their spouses are excluded.

and Benjamin's findings for Canada is that the U.S. and Canadian immigrants tend to come from different source countries and there may be behavioral differences associated with country of origin.[22] For example, it is possible that female immigrants to the United States come from areas where women are more prone to invest in their own human capital than female immigrants to Canada. To investigate this possibility, we estimated the labor-supply model in equation (1) and the associated wage equation separately for immigrants from each major world region. The regions were: Europe, North America, South America, Central America, the Caribbean, Africa, Asia, and Oceania, where region was defined by the focal individual (i.e., wife or husband).

Our region-by-region series of regressions of immigrants versus natives showed results very similar to those in Tables 1A–1C. First, husbands and wives who migrated at the same time had positively sloped, concave hours assimilation profiles for both husbands and wives within a region. Second, both husbands and wives within a region usually showed positive wage assimilation profiles.[23] Finally, in almost every case, both husbands and wives started below comparable natives upon arrival in the United States with respect to hours and wages.[24] Since

---

[22] For example, European immigrants are a larger share of the total in Canada than in the United States. For further evidence on U.S.-Canadian differences in source countries, see Borjas (1993). Since Baker and Benjamin's data did not include information on source country, they were unable to examine region-of-origin effects.

[23] Exceptions were negatively sloped profiles for husbands and wives from Central America and husbands from Oceania.

[24] There were three exceptions: Central America where, for some cohorts, husbands and wives worked more or earned more on arrival than comparable natives, and for other cohorts, they earned or worked less; wives from the Caribbean who had some positive and some negative hours

our basic findings characterize almost all cohorts for every region, even if immigrants to the United States came from the same regions in the same proportions as those in Canada, we would have obtained results similar to the ones presented here in Tables 1A–1C.[25]

C. *Qualifications and Possible Explanations*

The results we have presented suggest that for the United States, immigrant husbands and wives appear to invest similarly in their own human capital with time in the United States. Our results are not consistent with the family investment model, and contrast strongly with Baker and Benjamin's evidence in support of that model for Canada. However, there are some potential problems with the data and the empirical analysis that potentially apply to both studies which deserve serious consideration.

First, with the exception of recent arrivals, in neither the Canadian nor the U.S. data are we able to observe marital status at the time of arrival in the receiving country. Hypothetical assimilation profiles for married couples are constructed on the assumption that all currently observed married couples were married to each other for their entire stay in the United States or in Canada. To the extent that this assumption does not hold, the inferences made about assimilation profiles may be incorrect. Essentially, the problem is that the composition of the married populations may shift over time.[26] However, it should be pointed out that for those in the most recent cohort, we do observe marital status close to the time of entry in the receiving country.[27] Thus, our basic finding that U.S. immigrant men and women start out with work hours below that of comparable natives, and by similar percentages, is likely to be accurate, as are Baker and Benjamin's findings that Canadian immigrant wives start out with hours greater than comparable native wives and that immigrant husbands begin with hours below those of comparable native husbands. Moreover, a related study by Edward Funkhouser (2000) found that both male and female immigrants to the United States initially have lower employment rates than natives, but that employment rates tend to converge after six–ten years in the country. While he did not look explicitly at the family context (i.e., did not focus on married women or examine the impact of spouse's characteristics), Funkhouser's findings provide us with some confidence that the assimilation pattern which we observe for married immigrant women is not due to selection into the currently married category.[28]

Second, as we have seen, Baker and Benjamin estimated structural labor-supply models to assess the simple labor-supply hypothesis as an alternative to the family investment model in explaining the hours assimilation profiles they estimated. One can, however, question the estimation strategy for these labor-supply models. In particular, the authors do not take account of the endogeneity of husband's and wife's wages which is implied by the human-capital investment and family investment models,[29] and they also treat asset income (which is clearly affected by wages) as exogenous. Thus, the true magnitudes of the wage elasticities and the assimilation profiles controlling for wages may be

---

arrival effects for different cohorts; and both husbands and wives from North America who had some positive and some negative wage arrival effects for different cohorts.

[25] We also reestimated the labor-supply and wage equations including a full set of husband and wife country-of-origin dummy variables. There were 87 country dummies, resulting in a total of 174 additional variables included in the labor-supply equations and 87 in the wage equations. The results for the cohort and assimilation variables were very similar to those in Table 1A.

[26] Some well-known longitudinal data sets such as the National Longitudinal Surveys or the Michigan Panel Study of Income Dynamics allow one to observe marital status over time. However, concerns about sample size and the representativeness of the immigrant subsamples in these data files reduce their usefulness for our purposes compared to the Census.

[27] There may be some individuals who move into or out of the married category during this brief time interval, but this is likely to be a fairly small group.

[28] A further possible explanation for upward-sloping immigrant employment assimilation profiles is that some immigrants who arrive in the United States under visas that limit their right to work are eventually able to change their status to permanent resident with rights to work. However, Funkhouser (2000) analyzed Immigration and Naturalization Service data on the incidence of such changes in visa status and concluded that they were too infrequent relative to the stock of immigrants to noticeably influence the measured employment assimilation rate for men or women.

[29] Recall that wages are instrumented by wage decile to account for measurement error, a procedure that does not take into account these sources of endogeneity.

different from those estimated by Baker and Benjamin for Canada and those that we estimated for the United States. However, Baker and Benjamin make the reasonable argument that in order for the labor-supply model to explain their reduced form assimilation patterns, the required elasticities would be implausibly high in absolute value. Thus, the likelihood that an appropriate treatment of these endogeneities (with suitable instruments) would lead to labor-supply elasticities that could completely explain the Canadian hours assimilation patterns is small.

In our case, we find in reduced form analyses for immigrants to the United States that husbands and wives have similar hours and similar wage assimilation profiles (Tables 1A–1C). For labor-supply responses to completely explain the reduced form results in Tables 1A–1C, the following labor-supply elasticities (evaluated at the sample mean hours and time in the United States) are required: own wage elasticities of 0.878 for husbands and 1.703 for wives; cross-wage elasticities of 0.332 for husbands, and -0.525 for wives.[30] The required own wage elasticities are larger than those reported in Richard Blundell and Thomas MaCurdy's (1999) review of labor-supply studies. These ranged from -0.25 to 0.25 for men with most studies showing an elasticity of less than 0.1 in absolute value and 0.05 to 2.03 for married women, with 16 of the 17 studies cited having an elasticity of 1.18 or below. Regarding the cross-elasticities, the positive required value for men (.332) is counter to the vast majority of studies showing negative income effects for men (Blundell and MaCurdy, 1999). For women, the required cross-elasticity of -0.525 is larger in absolute value than the income effect in every study cited by Blundell and MaCurdy, the vast majority of which ranged from -0.1 to -0.3.[31] Thus, as was the case for Canada, the pure labor-supply model implies parameter values that are implausible and thus is unlikely to be the full explanation for the hours profiles of U.S. immigrants.

We also note that for the family investment model to have any explanatory power in Canada, it is necessary for the labor-supply model to explain less than the full pattern of immigrant wives' labor supply there—i.e., the negative hours assimilation profile. And Baker and Benjamin do indeed conclude that this is the case. In the United States, the labor-supply model also explains less than the full pattern of immigrant wives' labor-supply assimilation. However, in this case, the hours assimilation profile is positively sloped. The fact that wives' hours assimilation profiles are more steeply sloped than may be explained by the response to own and spouse wages is counter to the family investment model. Only if conventional labor-supply parameters predicted a steeper than observed hours assimilation profile for immigrant women in the United States could we say that the assimilation profile of immigrant wives in the United States is what would be expected based on the family investment model. And of course we find exactly the opposite.

If simple labor-supply models are not the entire explanation for Baker and Benjamin's Canadian hours assimilation and wage profiles and those we have found for the United States, what can explain the differences between immigrant labor-supply patterns in the two countries? First, we note that although U.S. immigrants are less skilled relative to natives than those in Canada (Borjas 1993; Heather Antecol et al., 2001, 2003; Lawrence M. Kahn, 2002), this difference is unlikely to explain our results. Specifically, Borjas (1993) finds that the relative skills of immigrants coming from the same country are similar in Canada and the United States, implying that the overall difference in skills of immigrants in the two countries is entirely due to country of origin. Since we

---

[30] These elasticities are computed as $(\partial\ln(\text{Hours})/\partial\ln(\text{YSM}))/(\partial\ln(\text{Wages})/\partial\ln(\text{YSM}))$. Ideally, to the extent that the assimilation wage profile is anticipated by immigrants, these should be interpreted as intertemporal labor-supply elasticities, with the marginal utility of wealth fixed. However, as discussed by Baker and Benjamin and Blundell and MaCurdy (1999), it is not clear whether cross-sectional labor-supply equations can identify such elasticities, and one should therefore interpret this discussion cautiously.

[31] The required cross-wage elasticity of -0.525 for women is the same as the required income elasticity if all of the family's income is earned by the husband. If the wife is working or if there is nonlabor income, then a cross-wage elasticity of -0.525 implies an income elasticity even larger in absolute value, since a given percentage change in the husband's wage entails a smaller percentage change in family income, which is the denominator of the income elasticity.

find similar results for each region of origin, different immigrant skill levels are not likely to explain the differences between our results and those of Baker and Benjamin.[32]

Second, Baker and Benjamin used a 1986–1991 window to identify their immigrant assimilation profiles and cohort effects, while we used a 1980–1990 window. On the one hand, a shorter window means that there are fewer unmeasured effects that may change over time than a longer window. On the other hand, the closer the end points of one's interval (i.e., the shorter the period), the more like a single cross-section one's data becomes, limiting one's ability to separately identify cohort and assimilation effects. In any case, this difference in the data may help to explain our results. Note that we have used the Census rather than other microdata bases such as the Current Population Survey because the Census has far more observations on immigrants.

Third, Canada has greater union coverage and much more generous social insurance programs than the United States (David Card and Freeman, 1993). While it is not obvious how these differences could explain why the family investment model appears to work better in Canada than in the United States, there could be a connection between such institutional features of the economy and immigrant behavior.

Finally, we note that in tabulations based on the 1994–1996 International Adult Literacy Survey (IALS) microdata, we find that ever-married immigrant women were more likely to be currently widowed or divorced both absolutely and relative to natives in the United States than in Canada.[33] Specifically, among 16–65-year-old ever-married native women, the percentage currently married was 79.1 percent in the United States and 81.6 percent in Canada; however, among ever-married immigrant women, 72.4 percent were currently married in the United States, compared to 83.0 percent in Canada. These differences were not explained by differences in the composition of immigrants by age, schooling, or adult literacy between Canada and the United States (Blau et al., 2000). Thus, immigrant women's marriages in the United States are overall more fragile than those in Canada. It is possible that the greater anticipated likelihood of being on one's own in the United States leads women to invest in their own human capital to a greater degree than immigrant women in Canada.[34] Of course, immigrant wives and husbands investing in their own human capital to a similar extent in the United States and following a family investment model in Canada could be the cause of, rather than a response to, the observed differences in marital stability.

II. Conclusions

This paper has examined the wage and labor-supply assimilation patterns of immigrant husbands and wives in the United States in 1980 and 1990. We find that, upon arrival in the United States, both immigrant husbands and wives earn and work less than comparable natives, with comparable shortfalls for men and women. However, with time in the United States, the wage rates and work hours of both immigrant husbands and wives increase to a similar extent and eventually overtake those of comparable natives. It thus appears that husbands and wives are investing equally in their human capital.

These patterns for women contrast sharply with those of Baker and Benjamin for Canada over the 1986–1991 period. They found that,

---

[32] It is possible, however, that U.S.-Canadian differences in immigrant relative skill levels by *gender* play a role in explaining why our results differ from those of Baker and Benjamin. Unfortunately the evidence on gender differences in immigrant relative skill levels is mixed. Looking at the stock of immigrants in 1994 and comparing them to all natives, Kahn (2002) reports that Canadian immigrant women are better qualified relative to immigrant men (in comparison to natives) than immigrant women in the United States with respect to both cognitive skills (as measured by an adult literacy test) and schooling levels. In contrast, for a sample of recent immigrants (arriving after 1980/1 as of 1990/1) compared to white natives (only), results presented in Antecol et al. (2001, 2003) give the opposite pattern, indicating that U.S. immigrant women were relatively better qualified. Further examination of the role of immigrant skills in affecting family labor supply and human-capital investment decisions would be a fruitful area for future research.

[33] The IALS is the result of an international cooperative effort; for a description, see OECD (1998).

[34] For evidence of the impact of divorce rates on married women's labor-force supply, see William R. Johnson and Jonathan Skinner (1986).

upon arrival in Canada, immigrant wives worked more than natives but that this advantage declined with time in the country. Immigrant husbands, however, had the same pattern we found for the United States: they started below natives in their labor supply but eventually caught up. These results were interpreted as consistent with a family investment model in which immigrant wives initially work to finance their husbands' human-capital investments but then reduce their labor-force commitment (relative to comparable natives) when this investment is completed.

It is certainly possible that the labor-supply assimilation profiles of immigrant wives in families that migrate together are affected by the opposing forces of own human-capital investment (implying positively sloped profiles) and family investments supporting their husbands' careers (implying negatively sloped profiles)—indeed this possibility is consistent with our regression results and those of Baker and Benjamin for immigrant families (i.e., where both spouses are immigrants). Viewed in this context, the contrast between our results for the United States and those of Baker and Benjamin for Canada is that we find that for the United States the own human-capital effect strongly dominates whereas they find the opposite for Canada. The broader significance of our findings is that the extent to which the family investment model prevails for immigrants is likely to vary with the composition of the immigrant group and the economic and legal circumstances in the receiving country. We have found that for at least one major country, the United States, this model is inadequate to explain immigrant assimilation patterns.

REFERENCES

Antecol, Heather; Cobb-Clark, Deborah A. and Trejo, Stephen J. "The Skills of Female Immigrants to Australia, Canada, and the United States." Claremont Colleges Working Paper 2001-12, April 2001.
_____. "Immigration Policy and the Skills of Immigrants to Australia, Canada, and the United States." *Journal of Human Resources*, Winter 2003, *38*(1), pp. 192–218.
Baker, Michael and Benjamin, Dwayne. "The Role of the Family in Immigrants' Labor-Market Activity: An Evaluation of Alternative Explanations." *American Economic Review*, September 1997, *87*(4), pp. 705–27.
Becker, Gary S. *Human capital*. New York: Columbia University Press, 1975.
Blau, Francine D. "The Fertility of Immigrant Women: Evidence from High-Fertility Source Countries," in George J. Borjas and Richard B. Freeman, eds., *Immigration and the work force: Economic consequences for the United States and source areas*. Chicago: University of Chicago Press, 1992, pp. 93–133.
Blau, Francine D.; Kahn, Lawrence M.; Moriarty, Joan and Souza, Andre. "The Role of the Family in Immigrants' Labor-Market Activity: Evidence from the United States." Working paper, Cornell University, September 2000.
Blundell, Richard and MaCurdy, Thomas. "Labor Supply: A Review of Alternative Approaches," in Orley Ashenfelter and David Card, eds., *Handbook of labor economics, volume 3A*. Amsterdam: Elsevier, 1999, pp. 1559–695.
Borjas, George J. "Assimilation, Changes in Cohort Quality, and the Earnings of Immigrants." *Journal of Labor Economics*, October 1985, *3*(4), pp. 463–89.
_____. "Immigration Policy, National Origin, and Immigrant Skills: A Comparison of Canada and the United States," in David Card and Richard B. Freeman, eds., *Small differences that matter: Labor markets and income maintenance in Canada and the United States*. Chicago: University of Chicago Press, 1993, pp. 21–43.
_____. "Assimilation and Changes in Cohort Quality Revisited: What Happened to Immigrant Earnings in the 1980s?" *Journal of Labor Economics*, April 1995, *13*(4), pp. 201–45.
Card, David and Freeman, Richard B. *Small differences that matter: Labor markets and income maintenance in Canada and the United States*. Chicago: University of Chicago Press, 1993.
Chiswick, Barry R. "The Effect of Americanization on the Earnings of Foreign-born Men." *Journal of Political Economy*, October 1978, *86*(5), pp. 897–921.
Duleep, Harriet Orcutt and Sanders, Seth. "The

Decision to Work by Married Immigrant Women." *Industrial and Labor Relations Review*, July 1993, *46*(4), pp. 677–90.

Freeman, Richard B. and Needels, Karen. "Skill Differentials in Canada in an Era of Rising Labor Market Inequality," in David Card and Richard B. Freeman, eds., *Small differences that matter: Labor markets and income maintenance in Canada and the United States.* Chicago: University of Chicago Press, 1993, pp. 45–67.

Friedberg, Rachel M. "Immigration and the Labor Market." Ph.D. dissertation, MIT, 1993.

Funkhouser, Edward. "Convergence in Employment Rates of Immigrants," in George J. Borjas, ed., *Issues in the economics of immigration.* Chicago: University of Chicago Press, 2000, pp. 143–84.

Goldin, Claudia. *Understanding the gender gap: An economic history of American women.* Oxford: Oxford University Press, 1990.

Johnson, William R. and Skinner, Jonathan. "Labor Supply and Marital Separation." *American Economic Review*, June 1986, *76*(3), pp. 455–69.

Juhn, Chinhui and Murphy, Kevin M. "Wage Inequality and Family Labor Supply." *Journal of Labor Economics*, January 1997, *15*(1), pp. 72–97.

Kahn, Lawrence M. "Immigration and Labor Market Skills: International Evidence." Working paper, Cornell University, January 2002.

LaLonde, Robert J. and Topel, Robert H. "The Assimilation of Immigrants in the U.S. Labor Market," in George J. Borjas and Richard B. Freeman, eds., *Immigration and the work force: Economic consequences for the United States and source areas.* Chicago: University of Chicago Press, 1992, pp. 67–92.

MacPherson, David A. and Stewart, James B. "The Labor Force Participation and Earnings Profiles of Married Immigrant Females." *Quarterly Review of Economics and Business*, Autumn 1989, *29*(3), pp. 57–72.

Mincer, Jacob. "Labor Force Participation of Married Women," in H. Gregg Lewis, ed., *Aspects of labor economics.* Princeton, NJ: Princeton University Press, 1962, pp. 63–105.

Organization for Economic Cooperation and Development (OECD). *Human capital investment: An international comparison.* Paris: OECD, 1998.

[15]

Assimilation via Prices or Quantities?
Sources of Immigrant Earnings Growth in Australia, Canada, and the United States

Heather Antecol
Peter Kuhn
Stephen J. Trejo

ABSTRACT

Using 1980/81 and 1990/91 census data from Australia, Canada, and the United States, we estimate the effects of time in the destination country on male immigrants' wages, employment, and earnings. We find that total earnings assimilation is greatest in the United States and least in Australia. Employment assimilation explains all of the earnings progress experienced by Australian immigrants, whereas wage assimilation plays the dominant role in the United States, and Canada falls in between. We argue that relatively inflexible wages and generous unemployment insurance in countries like Australia may cause assimilation to occur along the quantity rather than the price dimension.

I. Introduction

Economists have been studying the economic assimilation of immigrants for over a quarter century (Chiswick 1978). Despite the widespread interest in this question, however, the vast majority of studies have focused their attention on a single country, usually the United States.[1] Further, almost all studies restrict attention

---

Heather Antecol is an associate professor of economics at Claremont McKenna College and Simon Fraser University. Peter Kuhn is a professor of economics at the University of California, Santa Barbara. Stephen J. Trejo is an associate professor of economics at the University of Texas, Austin. The authors thank the University of California's Pacific Rim Research Grant program for support. Some data in this paper are only available through the Australian Bureau of Statistics. Researchers who wish to obtain these or other data may contact the authors beginning March 2007 through February 2010 from Heather Antecol, Department of Economics, Simon Fraser University, Burnaby, BC V5A 1S6, Canada<hantecol@sfu.ca>
[Submitted April 2005; accepted February 2006]
ISSN 022-166X E-ISSN 1548-8004 © 2006 by the Board of Regents of the University of Wisconsin System

1. A notable exception is Borjas (1988), who uses earlier data on the same countries as we do. Unfortunately, because he only had access to a single cross-section of data for Australia, he could not separately identify assimilation and cohort effects in that country. Miller and Neo (2001) compare the United States and Australia using a single cross-section in each country.

to a single dimension of immigrant assimilation, typically the wages or earnings of those immigrants who are employed. Thus, relatively little is currently known about international differences in the amount of immigrant assimilation, or in the *form* (wages versus employment) this assimilation takes. In this paper, we characterize both the amount and form of total earnings assimilation in three countries—Australia, Canada, and the United States—using (as far as possible) identical samples and procedures for the same period of time. We find large differences.

Specifically, we find that new immigrants face by far the largest wage disadvantage in the United States, but also experience by far the greatest rate of wage growth after arrival. Estimated wage assimilation is smaller in Canada and is actually *negative* in Australia, as some immigrant cohorts to that country earn a positive wage premium upon arrival, and then assimilate downward toward the Australian norm. On the employment dimension, we detect assimilation in all three countries, but do not find large differences among countries. Overall, the amount of total earnings assimilation is highest in the United States, and the share of total earnings assimilation attributable to wage growth is highest in that country as well, with Australia at the other extreme and Canada in between.

What might cause these dramatic international differences in the amount and form of immigrant assimilation? After ruling out some obvious possible explanations—for example, differences in observable immigrant characteristics and the greater predominance of Latin American immigrants in the United States—we note that the differences we document are strikingly similar to what one would predict from a simple model that emphasizes the effects on assimilation of two institutional features of the host country: the degree of wage inequality and the generosity of income floors for the unemployed. In particular, the observed patterns are consistent with a scenario in which Australia's (and to a lesser extent Canada's) more compressed wage distribution and generous income support (1) force assimilation to occur along the quantity rather than the price dimension, and (2) reduce the potential for immigrant wage growth after arrival.[2]

II. Data

We analyze individual-level data from the 1981 and 1991 Australian and Canadian censuses and the 1980 and 1990 U.S. census. For each country, these censuses provide comparable cross-section data at two points in time on demographic characteristics and labor force behavior, as well as the requisite information on country of birth and year of arrival for foreign-born individuals (henceforth referred to as immigrants). Having at least two cross-sections of data for each country is advantageous for estimating immigrant assimilation effects, as we explain in the next section,

---

2. To our knowledge, only two other papers have considered the interaction of national labor market institutions and immigration. Angrist and Kugler (2003) analyze how the impact of immigrants *on natives* varies with labor market flexibility. Kahn (2004) reports evidence consistent with the hypothesis that greater wage flexibility in the U.S. labor market makes it easier for male immigrants to find jobs, especially when the immigrants have low skills.

and the large samples of individuals available in census data produce relatively precise estimates. The Australian data constitute 1 percent samples of the population, the Canadian data are 3 percent samples, and the U.S. data are 5 percent samples.[3]

The similarities between our three countries that make them, collectively, a good "laboratory" in which to study the determinants of immigrant assimilation are well known; they include a high level of economic development; a common Anglo-Saxon cultural heritage, language, and legal system; a definition of citizenship that is based on country of birth or "naturalization" rather than ethnicity; the feature of being recently colonized by Europeans with only small aboriginal populations remaining in the country; relatively low population densities; a long tradition of immigration; and large immigrant population shares by international standards. As we argue below, these many basic similarities increase the likelihood that the large differences in immigrant assimilation patterns identified here are related to current institutional differences between the countries.

We restrict our analysis to men between the ages of 25 and 59 who are not institutional residents. We exclude women in order to minimize biases arising from selective labor force participation, and we choose this age range so as to focus on men who have completed their formal schooling and who have a strong attachment to the labor market. By comparing outcomes for immigrants with those for natives who reside in the same destination country, natives can serve as a control for cross-country differences in social or economic conditions or in how the census data were collected. To increase comparability of the native samples across countries and improve their usefulness as a control group, we exclude nonwhites from the native (but not the immigrant) samples. In addition, residents of the Atlantic Provinces and the Territories are excluded from the Canadian samples, because for these individuals the information about country of birth and year of immigration is not reported in sufficient detail. In the U.S. samples, we exclude individuals born in Puerto Rico and other outlying areas of the United States because the 1980 U.S. census does not provide information on year of arrival for such individuals. Finally, because the inclusion of immigrants who arrived as children can bias estimates of assimilation effects, we exclude all foreign-born individuals whose age and arrival cohort imply any possibility that they entered the destination country prior to age 16.

III. Empirical Framework

As noted, a key goal of this paper is to compare the relative importance of employment versus wage adjustments in accounting for the labor market assimilation of immigrants to Australia, Canada, and the United States. To do so, we start with the identity $E = pw$, where E denotes the expected earnings of an immigrant, p is the probability that the immigrant is employed, and w is the wage paid to the immigrant when he is employed. It is perhaps most natural to think of p as the frac-

---

3. The U.S. samples are much larger than the samples from the other two countries. To lighten the computational burden, we employ 0.1 percent (or one in a 1,000) samples of U.S. natives, but we use the full 5 percent samples of U.S. immigrants, and we use the full samples of natives and immigrants available in the Australian and Canadian data.

tion employed in a cohort of immigrants, w as the mean earnings of the employed members of the cohort, and E as the mean earnings of all members of the cohort (including those who are not employed and therefore have zero earnings). In our data, E, p, and w are all measured on a *weekly* basis; that is, w represents weekly earnings of persons who are employed in the census reference week, p represents the probability of being employed during the reference week, and E is the average total weekly earnings of a representative member of an immigrant arrival cohort including both its employed and nonemployed members.

Consider how the cohort's earnings potential evolves over time as its members adapt to the destination country's labor market. To a first-order approximation, the above identity implies that

(1) $\%\Delta E = \%\Delta p + \%\Delta w$.

In percentage terms, the growth in expected earnings arising from immigrant assimilation is equal to the sum of assimilation's impacts on employment rates and wages. To implement Equation 1 empirically, we define assimilation as the independent effect of duration of destination-country residence on immigrant outcomes. In other words, for each of our three host countries, we shall ask how immigrant wage and employment outcomes change with greater exposure to that country.

To distinguish assimilation effects from cohort effects, we adopt the regression framework developed by Borjas (1985, 1995). Specifically, let y_j^g represent the outcome for individual j, where the superscript g takes on the values I for immigrants and N for natives. Pooling data from the 1981 and 1991 censuses,[4] immigrant outcomes are determined by the equation

(2) $y_j^I = C_j \lambda^I + A_j \delta^I + \pi T_j + (1 - T_j) X_j \beta_{81}^I + T_j X_j \beta_{91}^I + \varepsilon_j^I$,

where the vector C is a set of mutually exclusive dummy variables identifying immigrant arrival cohorts, the vector A is a set of mutually exclusive dummy variables indicating how long an immigrant has lived in the destination country, T is a dummy variable marking observations from the 1991 census, the vector X contains other determinants of outcomes, ε is a random error term, and the remaining parameters are the objects of estimation. This specification gives each immigrant arrival cohort its own intercept, and differences in these intercepts represent permanent outcome differentials between cohorts. The coefficients of the duration of destination-country residence dummies measure the effects of immigrant assimilation on the outcome variable. In addition, the coefficients of the variables in X are allowed to vary across census years, with the Subscripts 81 and 91 indicating the survey year of a particular parameter vector.

The corresponding equation for natives is

(3) $y_j^N = \alpha^N + \pi T_j + (1 - T_j) X_j \beta_{81}^N + T_j X_j \beta_{91}^N + \varepsilon_j^N$,

where α^N is the intercept for natives, and the arrival cohort and duration of destination-country residence variables are excluded from this equation because they are not relevant for natives.

---

4. These are the years relevant for the Australian and Canadian census data. For the U.S. census data, the corresponding years are 1980 and 1990.

An analysis of immigrant outcomes must confront the classic problem of distinguishing cohort, age, and period effects. The main identifying restriction imposed in Equations 2 and 3 is that the period effect π is the same for immigrants and natives, as indicated by the absence of a superscript on this parameter. In essence, the period effect is estimated from natives, and this information is used to identify cohort and assimilation effects for immigrants. A key assumption of this approach is that compositional changes in the subsample of an immigrant cohort observed—such as those caused by emigration, mortality, and labor force entry and exit—do not bias measured outcome changes. To estimate the parameters of Equations 2 and 3, we pool observations on immigrants and natives from both years of census data into a single regression, and then impose the restrictions implicit in these equations by introducing the appropriate interaction terms between nativity, the 1990/91 census dummy, and the other explanatory variables.

Equation 2 also imposes the restriction that the rate of immigrant assimilation does not vary across arrival cohorts. This restriction conveniently synthesizes the experiences of various arrival cohorts over the 1980s into a single assimilation profile for each outcome and country, but we obtain similar results from less restrictive specifications that allow for cohort-specific assimilation profiles. For U.S. immigrants, Duleep and Regets (1999) and Borjas (2000) present evidence on how assimilation patterns differ by arrival cohort.

IV. Estimation Results

In this section, we use the empirical approach just described to estimate the impact of assimilation on the employment and wage opportunities of immigrants to Australia, Canada, and the United States. Interpreting these estimates in the context of Equation 1, we then compare the relative importance of employment versus wage adjustments in accounting for immigrant labor market assimilation in these three countries.

A. Employment Assimilation

Table 1 presents selected coefficients from estimating Equations 2 and 3 for employment. The dependent variable is a dummy identifying whether the individual was employed during the census survey week. The coefficients were estimated by least squares, and robust standard errors are shown in parentheses. In addition to the variables listed in Table 1, all regressions include controls for age and geographic location.[5] Two specifications are reported for each destination country. The first

---

5. The age variables are dummies identifying five-year age groups from 30–34 through 55–59, with 25–29 year-olds as the omitted reference group. The geographic variables indicate region of residence within each destination country (with eight regions defined for Australia, six regions for Canada, and nine regions for the United States) and whether the individual lives in a metropolitan area. The coefficients of the geographic controls are restricted to be the same for immigrants and natives, but these coefficients can differ across survey years. The coefficients of the age and education variables are allowed to vary both by nativity and survey year.

Table 1
Employment Regressions: Assimilation, Cohort and Period Effects

	Australia		Canada		United States	
Regressor	(1)	(2)	(1)	(2)	(1)	(2)
Time in destination country						
6–10 years	0.101	0.099	0.039	0.031	0.099	0.100
	(0.029)	(0.029)	(0.016)	(0.016)	(0.006)	(0.006)
11–15 years	0.112	0.120	0.060	0.055	0.113	0.110
	(0.023)	(0.025)	(0.012)	(0.013)	(0.005)	(0.005)
16–20 years	0.121	0.130	0.083	0.070	0.115	0.113
	(0.027)	(0.029)	(0.017)	(0.019)	(0.007)	(0.008)
More than 20 years	0.126	0.140	0.096	0.086	0.130	0.122
	(0.031)	(0.033)	(0.019)	(0.021)	(0.009)	(0.010)
Immigrant arrival cohort						
Pre-1961			−0.069	−0.023	−0.160	−0.118
			(0.021)	(0.027)	(0.010)	(0.013)
1961–65			−0.060	−0.014	−0.141	−0.103
			(0.019)	(0.024)	(0.009)	(0.011)
1966–70			−0.044	−0.011	−0.147	−0.107
			(0.016)	(0.021)	(0.007)	(0.010)
Pre-1971	−0.150	−0.168				
	(0.029)	(0.038)				
1971–75	−0.147	−0.161	−0.054	−0.017	−0.141	−0.101
	(0.030)	(0.036)	(0.017)	(0.020)	(0.007)	(0.009)
1976–80	−0.145	−0.164	−0.054	−0.026	−0.140	−0.103
	(0.018)	(0.026)	(0.009)	(0.012)	(0.004)	(0.006)
1981–85	−0.167	−0.172	−0.065	−0.037	−0.146	−0.113
	(0.033)	(0.035)	(0.018)	(0.019)	(0.007)	(0.008)
1986–91	−0.125	−0.140	−0.130	−0.110	−0.124	−0.094
	(0.017)	(0.018)	(0.008)	(0.009)	(0.004)	(0.004)
1990/91 census dummy	−0.086	−0.188	−0.053	−0.128	0.008	−0.017
	(0.010)	(0.019)	(0.004)	(0.007)	(0.006)	(0.007)
R^2	0.033	0.045	0.033	0.059	0.024	0.034
Controls for education	No	Yes	No	Yes	No	Yes

Note: The dependent variable is a dummy identifying whether the individual was employed during the census survey week. The coefficients were estimated by least squares, and robust standard errors are shown in parentheses. Data are from the 1981 and 1991 Australian and Canadian censuses and the 1980 and 1990 U.S. censuses. The samples include men ages 25–59, with nonwhites excluded from the native but not the foreign-born samples. The sample sizes for these regressions are 52,664 for Australia, 259,777 for Canada, and 432,179 for the United States. In addition to the variables listed above, all regressions include indicators for age and geographic location. The coefficients of the geographic controls are restricted to be the same for immigrants and natives, but these coefficients can differ across census years. The coefficients of the age and education variables are allowed to vary both by nativity and census year. The reference group for the "time in destination country" dummies is 0–5 years. The intervals listed above for the immigrant arrival cohorts are those defined in the Australian and Canadian data; the slightly different immigrant cohorts defined in the U.S. data are as follows: pre-1960, 1960–64, 1965–69, 1970–74, 1975–79, 1980–84, and 1985–90. The immigrant cohort coefficients reported in this table have been normalized to represent immigrant-native employment differentials for men who are aged 25–29 (in both specifications) and who have 12 years of education in 1990/91 (in Specification 2).

specification, in each Column 1, includes the independent variables mentioned so far, whereas the second specification, in each Column 2, also controls for years of schooling. Immigrants, even those who migrate as adults, frequently acquire additional education after arriving in the destination country (Chiswick and Miller 1992; Betts and Lofstrom 2000). For this reason, we focus our discussion on results from the specification that does not control for education, because this specification allows for a broader notion of labor market assimilation that includes the effects of post-migration investments in schooling. In general, however, the two specifications yield similar results.

Table 1 reports the immigrant cohort and assimilation effects, as well as the period effects, from the employment regressions.[6] The estimated period effects, which are the coefficients on the 1990/91 census dummy, indicate that employment opportunities deteriorated between 1981 and 1991 in Australia and Canada and did not change much in the United States over the same decade. The immigrant arrival cohort coefficients reported in Table 1 have been normalized to represent immigrant-native employment differentials for men who are aged 25–29 (in both specifications) and who have 12 years of education in 1990/91 (in Specification 2). In addition, these differentials pertain to immigrants from the relevant arrival cohort when they have lived in the destination country for five years or less. For example, the estimated coefficient for 1976–80 Australian immigrants in Column 1 indicates that, in their first five years after arriving, this cohort had an employment rate 14.5 percentage points below that of otherwise similar natives.

That the cohort coefficients are uniformly negative implies that, in all three countries, immigrants from every arrival period initially experienced lower employment than natives, but these employment deficits for new immigrants are much larger in Australia and the United States than in Canada. Within each country, the coefficients tend to be similar in magnitude for the various arrival cohorts. This finding suggests that, after controlling for years spent in the destination country, employment rates do not differ much across cohorts. The one important exception is the 1986–91 cohort of Canadian immigrants, whose employment rate is estimated to be permanently below that of other Canadian arrival cohorts by at least six percentage points.

We now turn to the assimilation effects that are the focus of our analysis. In Table 1, the coefficients of the "time in destination country" dummy variables indicate how employment rates change as an immigrant cohort becomes more familiar with its new surroundings. Australian and American immigrants display virtually identical patterns in which the bulk of employment assimilation takes place within the first decade after arrival.[7] In both Australia and the United States, employment rates shoot up by 10 per-

---

6. The intervals listed for immigrant arrival cohorts are those defined in the Australian and Canadian data; the slightly different immigrant cohorts defined in the U.S. data are as follows: pre-1960, 1960–64, 1965–69, 1970–74, 1975–79, 1980–84, and 1985–90. The 1991 Australian census does not distinguish 1960s arrivals from earlier immigrants, and therefore "pre-1971" is the most precise arrival cohort that can be defined consistently across censuses for Australian immigrants. For Canada and the United States, however, immigrants arriving during these years are disaggregated into "1966–70," "1961–65," and "pre-1961" cohorts.

7. For the United States, several earlier studies find this same pattern of immigrant employment adjustment. See, for example, Chiswick, Cohen, and Zach (1997) and Funkhouser (2000). For Australia, McDonald and Worswick (1999b) report a similar finding for *unemployment*: the unemployment rates of immigrant men decline sharply, both in absolute terms and relative to native unemployment rates, during the first decade after arrival.

centage points as immigrants pass from 0–5 to 6–10 years in the destination country, but thereafter employment increases only modestly (2–4 percentage points) with further exposure to the host labor market.

Employment assimilation for Canadian immigrants, by contrast, is a much more continuous process that takes longer to play out. For example, according to the estimates that do not control for education (Specification 1), immigrant employment rates rise (relative to their level during the initial five years of Canadian residence) by four percentage points after 6–10 years, six percentage points after 11–15 years, eight percentage points after 16–20 years, and 10 percentage points after more than 20 years in Canada. Despite the fact that employment assimilation beyond the first decade of residence is strongest for Canadian immigrants, the much greater initial adjustments of Australian and American immigrants result in total employment growth, even after more than 20 years of assimilation, that is larger in Australia and the United States (12–14 percentage points) than in Canada (9–10 percentage points).

Finally, recall the negative cohort coefficients discussed earlier. These coefficients indicate that, upon arrival, all immigrant cohorts had employment rates lower than those of comparable natives. Employment growth from assimilation, however, eventually erases all or most of this initial employment deficit for every immigrant arrival cohort. Consider, for example, the 1971–75 cohort of U.S. immigrants. According to the Specification 1 estimates that do not control for education, during its first five years in the United States this cohort had an employment rate 14 percentage points below that of natives. After just 6–10 years of U.S. residence, however, assimilation narrows the employment gap of this cohort by 10 percentage points, and after 20 years in the United States the cohort's employment rate closes to within a percentage point of the rate for comparable natives. Immigrants from other arrival cohorts and in other host countries display the same basic pattern. With sufficient time for adjustment, male immigrants in these three countries attain employment rates similar to those of natives.

B. Wage Assimilation

Table 2 presents analogous estimates for the natural logarithm of wages, our other outcome variable. These log wage regressions are identical in structure to the employment regressions in Table 1, except that now the sample is restricted to employed men, and controls have been added for hours worked during the census survey week. These controls for weekly hours of work are included so that our estimates using the available information on *weekly* income (for Australia) or earnings (for Canada and the United States) more closely approximate the effects on *hourly* wages (that is, the "price" of labor) that we seek. The coefficients of the weekly hours indicators are allowed to vary across census years but not by nativity. Because the dependent variables in Table 2 represent nominal wages, the estimated period effects (that is, the coefficients on the 1990/91 census dummy) reflect whatever inflation occurred during the 1980s, as well as the effects on real wages of any changes in national economic conditions that took place over the decade.

In Table 2, the estimated coefficients of the arrival cohort dummies reveal the extent of permanent wage differences between immigrant cohorts. Such wage differences are relatively modest in Australia and somewhat larger in Canada and the United

Table 2
Wage Regressions: Assimilation, Cohort and Period Effects

	Australia		Canada		United States	
Regressor	(1)	(2)	(1)	(2)	(1)	(2)
Time in destination country						
6–10 years	0.032	0.009	0.046	0.052	0.052	0.070
	(0.047)	(0.046)	(0.043)	(0.042)	(0.017)	(0.015)
11–15 years	−0.063	−0.086	0.111	0.139	0.144	0.183
	(0.037)	(0.039)	(0.028)	(0.031)	(0.011)	(0.012)
16–20 years	−0.061	−0.087	0.094	0.115	0.158	0.203
	(0.044)	(0.046)	(0.045)	(0.047)	(0.018)	(0.018)
More than 20 years	−0.090	−0.120	0.123	0.160	0.236	0.271
	(0.049)	(0.053)	(0.046)	(0.051)	(0.020)	(0.022)
Immigrant arrival cohort						
Pre-1961			−0.083	−0.019	−0.102	−0.056
			(0.052)	(0.064)	(0.023)	(0.028)
1961–65			−0.109	−0.042	−0.135	−0.082
			(0.047)	(0.057)	(0.020)	(0.024)
1966–70			−0.102	−0.087	−0.224	−0.146
			(0.038)	(0.049)	(0.017)	(0.022)
Pre-1971	−0.009	0.065				
	(0.046)	(0.060)				
1971–75	−0.058	0.004	−0.174	−0.139	−0.253	−0.142
	(0.048)	(0.057)	(0.045)	(0.049)	(0.018)	(0.020)
1976–80	−0.040	−0.009	−0.222	−0.196	−0.300	−0.206
	(0.025)	(0.038)	(0.021)	(0.029)	(0.009)	(0.013)
1981–85	−0.137	−0.100	−0.239	−0.206	−0.338	−0.230
	(0.053)	(0.053)	(0.048)	(0.048)	(0.018)	(0.017)
1986–91	−0.077	−0.098	−0.393	−0.354	−0.373	−0.271
	(0.023)	(0.024)	(0.021)	(0.021)	(0.008)	(0.009)
1990/91 census dummy	0.705	0.560	0.510	0.337	0.435	0.354
	(0.016)	(0.031)	(0.009)	(0.018)	(0.013)	(0.016)
R^2	0.334	0.369	0.148	0.189	0.184	0.288
Controls for education	No	Yes	No	Yes	No	Yes

Note: The dependent variable is the natural logarithm of weekly personal income (for Australia) or weekly earnings (for Canada and the United States). The coefficients were estimated by least squares, and robust standard errors are shown in parentheses. Data are from the 1981 and 1991 Australian and Canadian censuses and the 1980 and 1990 U.S. censuses. The samples include employed men ages 25–59, with nonwhites excluded from the native but not the foreign-born samples. The sample sizes for these regressions are 43,590 for Australia, 217,773 for Canada, and 359,999 for the United States. In addition to the variables listed above, all regressions include indicators for age, geographic location, and hours worked during the census survey week. The coefficients of the controls for geographic location and weekly hours of work are restricted to be the same for immigrants and natives, but these coefficients can differ across census years. The coefficients of the age and education variables are allowed to vary both by nativity and census year. The reference group for the "time in destination country" dummies is 0–5 years. The intervals listed above for the immigrant arrival cohorts are those defined in the Australian and Canadian data; the slightly different immigrant cohorts defined in the U.S. data are as follows: pre-1960, 1960–64, 1965–69, 1970–74, 1975–79, 1980–84, and 1985–90. The immigrant cohort coefficients reported in this table have been normalized to represent immigrant-native wage differentials for men who are aged 25–29 (in both specifications) and who have 12 years of education in 1990/91 (in Specification 2).

States. Wage profiles tend to be lower for more recent arrival cohorts, especially in Canada and the United States. For example, in the Specification 1 regression that does not control for education, Canadian immigrants arriving in 1986–91 have a permanent wage disadvantage of about 30 percent relative to their predecessors who arrived before 1970. The corresponding wage deficit is smaller but still sizeable for the most recent cohort of U.S. immigrants. The pattern in Table 2 of a steady decline in wages for successive cohorts of male immigrants to Canada and the United States confirms the findings of previous studies (for example, Baker and Benjamin 1994 and Bloom, Grenier, and Gunderson 1995 for Canada; Borjas 1985, 1995 and Funkhouser and Trejo 1998 for the United States).

The estimated coefficients of the "time in destination country" dummy variables measure wage growth due to immigrant assimilation. Consistent with earlier research by Borjas (1988) and McDonald and Worswick (1999a), we find no evidence of positive wage assimilation for Australian immigrants. Although both Canadian and U.S. immigrants enjoy significant wage boosts arising from increased exposure to the destination country's labor market, the magnitude and duration of such wage assimilation is greater in the United States. For example, without controlling for education, the estimates imply that wages grow by 11 percent as an immigrant cohort in Canada extends its time in the country from 0–5 to 11–15 years, but additional exposure to Canada beyond this point produces little wage improvement. For U.S. immigrants, the corresponding wage growth is 14 percent after 11–15 years in the country and 24 percent after 20-plus years of residence. Estimates of immigrant wage assimilation and the pattern of differences across destination countries are similar in Specification 2, which controls for education.

C. Total Earnings Assimilation and its Components

Given the estimates, from Tables 1 and 2, of how immigrant employment and wage opportunities evolve with greater exposure to the host country, we can now implement Equation 1. As discussed earlier, Equation 1 decomposes the labor market assimilation of immigrants into employment and wage components, where each component is simply the percentage impact of assimilation on the relevant outcome. The log specification of the dependent variable in the wage regressions implies that the assimilation coefficients from these regressions already approximate percentage effects, but the corresponding coefficients in the employment regressions do not. We transform the estimated employment effects of assimilation into percentage terms by comparing these effects with the employment rates of the most recent arrival cohort in the 1990/91 data.

For each destination country, Table 3 reports the resulting estimates of the components of Equation 1, with standard errors in parentheses. The top panel of Table 3 presents estimates based on the regressions that do not control for education, whereas the bottom panel shows results from the alternative specification that conditions on education. As prescribed by Equation 1, "total" immigrant earnings growth due to assimilation is computed as the sum of the estimates of earnings growth from employment assimilation and from wage assimilation. These calculations are reported for the assimilation-induced growth that occurs for an immigrant cohort between its first five years in the destination country and each of the durations of residence ranging from "6–10 years" to "more than 20 years." Finally, in order to highlight differ-

Table 3
Components of Immigrant Earnings Growth from Assimilation

<table>
<tr><th rowspan="4"></th><th colspan="3">Australia</th><th colspan="4">Canada</th><th colspan="4">United States</th></tr>
<tr><th colspan="2">Percentage Earnings Growth from Assimilation in</th><th rowspan="3">Percent of Total Due to Employment</th><th colspan="3">Percentage Earnings Growth from Assimilation in</th><th rowspan="3">Percent of Total Due to Employment</th><th colspan="3">Percentage Earnings Growth from Assimilation in</th><th rowspan="3">Percent of Total Due to Employment</th></tr>
<tr><th rowspan="2">Employment</th><th rowspan="2">Wage Total</th><th rowspan="2">Employment</th><th rowspan="2">Wage</th><th rowspan="2">Total</th><th rowspan="2">Employment</th><th rowspan="2">Wage</th><th rowspan="2">Total</th></tr>
<tr></tr>
<tr><td colspan="12">A. Without education controls
Time in destination country</td></tr>
<tr><td>6–10 years</td><td>13.5
(3.9)</td><td>3.2 16.7
(4.7) (6.1)</td><td>80.9
(23.2)</td><td>5.3
(2.2)</td><td>4.6
(4.3)</td><td>9.9
(4.8)</td><td>53.7
(25.4)</td><td>12.5
(0.8)</td><td>5.2
(1.7)</td><td>17.7
(1.9)</td><td>70.7
(6.9)</td></tr>
<tr><td>11–15 years</td><td>15.0
(3.1)</td><td>-6.3 8.7
(3.7) (4.8)</td><td>> 100</td><td>8.2
(1.6)</td><td>11.1
(2.8)</td><td>19.3
(3.2)</td><td>42.5
(7.9)</td><td>14.3
(0.6)</td><td>14.4
(1.1)</td><td>28.7
(1.3)</td><td>49.9
(2.2)</td></tr>
<tr><td>16–20 Years</td><td>16.2
(3.6)</td><td>-6.1 10.1
(4.4) (5.7)</td><td>> 100</td><td>11.3
(2.3)</td><td>9.4
(4.5)</td><td>20.7
(5.1)</td><td>54.7
(12.9)</td><td>14.6
(0.9)</td><td>15.8
(1.8)</td><td>30.4
(2.0)</td><td>48.0
(3.2)</td></tr>
<tr><td>More than 20 years</td><td>16.9
(4.1)</td><td>-9.0 7.9
(4.9) (6.4)</td><td>> 100</td><td>13.1
(2.6)</td><td>12.3
(4.6)</td><td>25.4
(5.3)</td><td>51.6
(10.6)</td><td>16.5
(1.1)</td><td>23.6
(2.0)</td><td>40.1
(2.3)</td><td>41.1
(2.6)</td></tr>
</table>

Table 3 (*continued*)

	Australia			Canada				United States			
	Percentage Earnings Growth from Assimilation in Employment	Wage	Total	Percent of Total Due to Employment	Percentage Earnings Growth from Assimilation in Employment	Wage	Total	Percent of Total Due to Employment	Percentage Earnings Growth from Assimilation in Employment	Wage	Total	Percent of Total Due to Employment

B. With education controls

Time in destination country

	Australia				Canada				United States			
6–10 years	13.3 (3.9)	0.9 (4.6)	14.2 (6.0)	93.6 (30.5)	4.2 (2.2)	5.2 (4.2)	9.4 (4.7)	44.9 (23.7)	12.7 (0.8)	7.0 (1.5)	19.7 (1.7)	64.4 (5.1)
11–15 years	16.1 (3.3)	−8.6 (3.9)	7.5 (5.1)	>100	7.5 (1.8)	13.9 (3.1)	21.4 (3.6)	35.1 (7.4)	13.9 (0.6)	18.3 (1.2)	32.2 (1.4)	43.2 (2.0)
16–20 years	17.4 (3.9)	−8.7 (4.6)	8.7 (6.0)	>100	9.6 (2.6)	11.5 (4.7)	21.1 (5.4)	45.4 (12.2)	14.3 (1.0)	20.3 (1.8)	34.6 (2.1)	41.4 (2.8)
More than 20 years	18.7 (4.4)	−12.0 (5.3)	6.7 (6.9)	>100	11.7 (2.9)	16.0 (5.1)	27.7 (5.9)	42.3 (9.8)	15.5 (1.3)	27.1 (2.2)	42.6 (2.5)	36.3 (2.7)

Note: These calculations are based on the employment and wage regressions reported in Tables 1 and 2, with standard errors shown in parentheses. The results in Panel A, which do not control for education, derive from regression Specification 1, and the results in Panel B, which do control for education, derive from regression Specification 2. The estimated effects of assimilation on immigrant employment probabilities are converted into percentage terms using the employment rates (reported in Table 1) of the most recent immigrant arrival cohort in the 1990/91 data. Because the dependent variables of the wage regressions are in natural logarithms, the estimated coefficients of the "time in destination country" dummies represent the percentage effects of assimilation on immigrant wage growth. Total immigrant earnings growth due to assimilation is the sum of the earnings growth from employment assimilation and the earnings growth from wage assimilation.

ences across countries in the nature of immigrant labor market adjustment, Table 3 also shows the percentage of total earnings growth from assimilation that arises from employment assimilation rather than from wage assimilation.

Initially consider the estimates in the top panel of Table 3, which do not control for education. Employment assimilation is an important contributor to immigrant earnings growth in all three countries, but the timing of this contribution varies. In Australia and the United States, the vast majority of immigrant employment assimilation occurs during the first decade after arrival, whereas employment rates for Canadian immigrants rise more continuously with duration of residence. In addition, the ultimate impact of employment assimilation is somewhat less in Canada than in the other two countries. After more than two decades in the destination country, employment assimilation increases immigrant earnings by about 17 percent in Australia and the United States and by 13 percent in Canada. Earnings growth from wage assimilation, on the other hand, is largest in the United States, sizeable in Canada, and zero or negative in Australia. Summing together the effects of employment and wage assimilation, earnings grow with duration of residence the most for U.S. immigrants and the least for Australian immigrants. After more than 20 years in the destination country, for example, total earnings growth from immigrant assimilation is 40 percent in the United States, 25 percent in Canada, and 8 percent in Australia.

Finally, Table 3 quantifies the *relative* contributions of wage and employment assimilation to total immigrant earnings assimilation in these three countries using the simple decomposition in Equation 1. The top panel of Table 3 shows that, at almost any duration of residence, the earnings growth of Canadian immigrants derives in roughly equal parts from employment assimilation and from wage assimilation. For Canadian immigrants, employment and wages rise at about the same rate with greater exposure to their adopted country. For U.S. immigrants, however, wage assimilation proceeds continuously but employment gains are concentrated in the first decade after arrival. As a result, for the United States, the share of immigrant earnings growth attributable to employment assimilation falls from 71 percent after 6–10 years of residence to 41 percent after more than 20 years of residence. For the first 15 years after arrival, employment adjustments account for a larger share of immigrant earnings growth in the United States than in Canada, but the opposite pattern emerges at longer durations of residence.

The bottom panel of Table 3 reports analogous estimates that control for education. Overall, the patterns are very similar to the top panel. For Canada and the United States, controlling for education generates somewhat lower estimates of employment assimilation and the share of total earnings growth arising from employment assimilation, but the comparisons across countries remain as described above. We note, however, that only for the United States is the share of earnings growth due to employment assimilation estimated with much precision, so although cross-country differences in our estimates of this share are suggestive, they are not statistically significant.

V. Possible Explanations

One obvious factor that might explain the dramatic differences in immigrant assimilation documented above is the marked difference in the source country composition of immigrant flows to Australia, Canada and the United States (Reitz 1998; Antecol, Cobb-Clark, and Trejo 2003). In particular, Borjas (1993) and Antecol, Cobb-Clark, and Trejo (2003) show that the skill deficit for U.S. immigrants relative to Australian and Canadian immigrants arises primarily because the United States receives a much larger share of immigrants from Latin America than do the other two countries. Consequently, an important concern is whether broad differences in region of origin drive the cross-country patterns of immigrant assimilation that we observe.

To investigate this issue, we replicated our analyses for two subsamples of the immigrant population that are fairly homogeneous in national origins yet still provide sufficiently large sample sizes for each country: only men born in Europe and only men born in Asia. The patterns for European and Asian immigrants considered separately are similar to those for all source countries combined. (We do not report these results here, but they are available upon request.) Thus, it does not appear that broad differences in region of origin, and in particular the large role of Latin American immigrants in the United States, explain our results.

Could host-country differences in immigration policy (including perhaps their effects on the more detailed national origin mix of immigrants) explain why immigrant assimilation patterns are so different across these three countries? On the surface, this might be an appealing explanation of at least the differences in wage assimilation: could it be that, because of Australian immigration policy, Australian immigrants are so well "matched" to the Australian labor market that they earn as much as (or more than) Australian natives on arrival, making further progress relative to natives impossible? Because a larger fraction of Australian (and Canadian) immigrants are selected on the basis of labor market qualifications, this is a potentially appealing hypothesis. However, as Borjas (1993) and Antecol, Cobb-Clark and Trejo (2003) have shown, once the large share of U.S. immigrants from Latin America is controlled for, the Australian and Canadian points systems have little demonstrable impact on the qualifications of immigrants. Since our main results continue to hold very strongly for subsets of immigrants from Europe or Asia, these "points systems" are thus unlikely to account for all the international differences in assimilation patterns documented here. Further, a more labor-market-oriented immigration policy should *raise* immigrants' relative employment rates on arrival, and this is clearly not the case in Australia or Canada relative to the United States.[8]

Another possible explanation of differences in immigrant assimilation patterns is international differences in host-country labor market institutions *other* than immigration policy. Such differences, including unionization and income support policies, have recently been linked to international differences in wage inequality (DiNardo,

---

8. Another possible source of bias in our results stems from the fact that universities in Australia, Canada, and the United States host a sizeable number of foreign undergraduate and graduate students who typically return to their home countries after completing their studies. Return migration by these foreign students could cause immigrant employment rates to rise sharply after an arrival cohort has spent 5–10 years in the destination country. More generally, the presence of temporary immigrants such as foreign students in our samples can bias estimates of assimilation profiles, and the nature of this bias might vary across destination countries. To explore this issue, we redid our analyses after dropping from the samples anyone currently enrolled in school. Very little change was observed.

Fortin, and Lemieux 1996; Blau and Kahn 1996), in the manner in which economies respond to adverse shocks to the demand for unskilled labor (Card, Kramarz, and Lemieux 1999; McDonald and Worswick 2000), in the size of the gender wage gap (Blau and Kahn 2000), in the magnitude of wage losses experienced by displaced workers (Kuhn 2002), in youth unemployment (Abowd et al. 2000), in work hours (Bell and Freeman 2001), in technical progress (Moene and Wallerstein 1997), and in the amount of labor reallocation across industries (Bertola and Rogerson 1997).

Given this extensive literature, it seems natural to ask whether a nation's labor market institutions also might shape the way in which new immigrants integrate into its economy. For example, any national policy or institution that effectively imposes a binding wage floor, or any policy that provides income support for unemployed immigrants, might "force" immigrant assimilation to occur along the employment rather than the wage dimension (for example, Harris and Todaro 1970). Any institution that *compresses* a country's wage distribution would operate in two distinct ways. The first of these is purely mechanical: Suppose that, over the course of his first ten years in the country, an immigrant to *any* country advances five percentiles in the native wage distribution. Simply because the rungs of the wage "ladder" are farther apart in high-inequality countries, immigrants to those countries will experience greater wage growth (relative to natives) than immigrants to other countries.[9] The second effect is behavioral: suppose that the investment required to rise one rung on the wage ladder (for example, learning English) is equally costly in these three countries. Then immigrants to compressed-wage countries will be less inclined to make such investments.

Do the actual institutional differences across the three countries studied in this paper accord with the differences required by the above discussion? Concerning the wage-setting process, Table 4 shows the well-known difference in union density between the United States and Canada, as well as the well-known decline in U.S. union density between 1980 and 1990. While union density in both countries is low by OECD standards, by the end of our sample period union density in Canada was more than double that in the United States (36 versus 16 percent). In both countries, coverage is only marginally greater than density, and wage bargaining is extremely decentralized. (Among 19 OECD countries, only one country ranks lower than Canada and the United States in terms of bargaining centralization.) Australia's union membership rates are higher than those of both Canada and the United States, but the most dramatic difference is in union coverage: In both our sample years, 80 percent or more of Australian workers' wages were determined by collective bargaining agreements. Further, this wage-setting process is highly centralized and coordinated. In 1990, Australia was ranked first (tied with Austria, Belgium, Finland, Norway, Portugal, and Sweden) among 19 countries in bargaining centralization by the OECD.[10]

---

9. For the United States, this "mechanical" effect of wage structure on the immigrant-native wage gap has been explored by Butcher and DiNardo (2002) and Lubotsky (2001).
10. During our sample period, the dominant institution in Australian wage-setting was the "award" system, a system whereby unions, employers, and government representatives met at the national level to negotiate wage rates specific to hundreds of occupations. Although firms were free to pay above-award wages, this was rare in practice. Thus, for all intents and purposes, Australian wages during our sample period were centrally administered at the occupation level. Statutory minimum wages were set at similar (low) fractions of the average wage in Canada and the United States, and they did not exist in Australia because they were superseded by the award system.

Table 4
Institutional Differences Among Australia, Canada, and the United States

	Australia 1980	Australia 1990	Canada 1980	Canada 1990	United States 1980	United States 1990
A. Indicators of union power						
1. Density (percent)	48	41	36	36	22	16
2. Coverage (percent)	88	80	37	38	26	18
3. Centralization (ranking)	3	1	17	17	17	17
4. Coordination 1980 (ranking)	7	5	18	17	18	17
B. Indicators of wage dispersion						
1. 90/10 wage ratio, men	2.67	3.93	3.73	4.21	4.04	4.80
2. 90/50 wage ratio, men	1.78	2.00	1.78	1.82	1.89	2.08
3. 50/10 wage ratio, men	1.50	1.96	2.10	2.31	2.13	2.31
4. Standard deviation of log wages	0.499	0.596	0.684	0.797	0.775	0.797
C. Indicators of income support						
1. UI Benefit Replacement Rate Index (percent)	24	26	25	28	13	13

Notes: Rankings of bargaining centralization and coordination are among 19 OECD countries; 1 is highest, ties allowed.
Australian wage data refer to weekly income of employees.
Canadian and U.S. wage data refer to weekly earnings of employees.
UI replacement rate index is an average of replacement rates for two earnings levels, three family situations, and three durations of unemployment, computed by OECD.
Sources: Union data from OECD, *Employment Outlook*, July 1997, Table 2.3.
Wage data from the 1981 and 1991 Australian and Canadian censuses and the 1980 and 1990 U.S. census. Sample is restricted to employed, white native-born men aged 25–59.
UI replacement rate index is from OECD *Employment Outlook*, July 1996, Chart 2.2 (numerical rates estimated from graph).

The consequences of these different wage-setting institutions for wage dispersion can be seen in Panel B of Table 4. As Blau and Kahn (1996) have argued, high levels of union coverage tend to be associated with low levels of wage dispersion, and this is certainly borne out in our data. By all measures—the 90/10 ratio (ratio of the ninetieth to the tenth percentiles of the weekly earnings distribution), 90/50 ratio, 50/10 ratio, or the standard deviation of log wages—Australia had the most compressed wage distribution in both years of our data, and the United States the most dispersed. Canada stands between these two extremes on most measures, though it is tied with the United States on two of these measures in 1990, perhaps reflecting a more severe recession at that time. All three countries exhibit increasing wage inequality between 1980 and 1990.

Concerning the income support available to unemployed workers, an aggregate, comparable index of benefit generosity computed by the OECD in Table 4 shows similar overall replacement rates in Canada and Australia, and a much lower rate in the United States. While this probably summarizes overall generosity reasonably well, there are a number of reasons to suspect that these figures understate the differences among the three countries, especially as it affects immigrants. One such difference is the takeup rate of unemployment insurance (UI) benefits: In 1990, the ratio of UI beneficiaries to the total number of unemployed was 34 percent in the United States, 82 percent in Australia, and 87 percent in Canada.[11] Thus, it is much less likely that an unemployed worker in the United States will actually receive UI benefits than in Australia or Canada. Second, the Australian income support system has three features that make it especially generous for immigrants: Unlike the United States and Canadian systems, eligibility does not require prior employment, recent immigrants are not explicitly disqualified from receiving benefits, and benefits do not depend on previous wages. Furthermore, in Australia these benefits are payable for an indefinite period, in contrast to maximum entitlement periods of a year in Canada and 26 weeks in the United States. Overall, it thus appears that Australia's income support system is the most generous to immigrants, and both Canada and Australia are clearly more generous than the United States.

In sum, the institutional differences summarized above are consistent with the patterns of immigrant assimilation documented in this paper. The broad institutional features of these labor markets lead us to expect wages to be the primary mode of assimilation in the United States, employment in Australia, with Canada in between. Empirically we find that employment gains explain *all* of the labor market progress experienced by Australian immigrants, that the magnitude of wage assimilation is greatest in the United States, and that (for sufficiently long periods of adjustment) the share of immigrant earnings growth due to wage assimilation rather than employment assimilation is also largest in the United States.

---

11. OECD, 1994, Table 8.4, plus CANSIM Series v384773 [the OECD's table includes UI *and* welfare cases for Canada; thus we retrieved our own beneficiary counts from Statistics Canada's CANSIM database]. Australian figures refer to 1991. For Canada, our figures include regular UI beneficiaries only (thus they exclude UI benefits for job training, maternity, sickness, etc.). As noted, Australia has only a means-tested program—these figures refer to it. U.S. figures, like those for Canada, include UI claimants only (thus excluding welfare). In all cases the count of beneficiaries refers to an annual average stock (not to the total number of persons receiving benefit at any time during the year).

A final concern with the "institutional" hypothesis described above is the notion that institutional differences among these three countries cause systematically different types of immigrants to be *attracted* to each country. For example, individuals with high learning capacities should be disproportionately attracted to the U.S. market, where investments in additional human capital are more likely to be rewarded. We do not dispute this possibility; in fact we think it is quite likely. Instead we simply note, first, that any self-selection of this nature that is *induced* by international institutional differences would simply reinforce the international differences in assimilation patterns that we observe. Second, self-selection on "ambition" or "learning ability" that is induced by international institutional differences can be seen as a logical extension of Borjas' (1987) argument that international differences in wage inequality should affect the average ability *level* of immigrants. Indeed, it is exactly what we should expect if host country labor market institutions really matter.

VI. Conclusion

In this paper we generate estimates of employment and wage assimilation among immigrants to Australia, Canada, and the United States using census data spanning the decade of the 1980s. We find that total earnings assimilation is greatest in the United States and least in Australia. Further, employment assimilation explains *all* of the earnings progress experienced by Australian immigrants, whereas wage assimilation plays the dominant role in the United States, and Canada falls in between.

We argue that these patterns are suggestive of an effect of host-country labor market institutions on the immigrant assimilation process, with relatively inflexible wages and generous unemployment insurance in countries like Australia causing assimilation to occur along the quantity rather than the price dimension. Also, Australia's relatively compressed wage distribution reduces the scope for immigrant wage growth and might reduce incentives to make post-arrival investments in human capital.

Of course, it is certainly possible that the dramatic international differences in immigrant assimilation documented here derive from idiosyncrasies of these countries other than the labor market institutions that we emphasize. After all, with only three countries, we have very few degrees of freedom for discriminating among alternative hypotheses. Nonetheless, our results strongly suggest that greater attention to the role of national labor market institutions—in particular those that influence the dispersion of wages and the incomes of the unemployed—may help to advance our understanding of why the immigrant assimilation process appears to operate so differently across destination countries.

References

Abowd, John M., Francis Kramarz, Thomas Lemieux, and David N. Margolis. 2000. "Minimum Wages and Youth Employment in France and the United States." In *Youth Employment and Joblessness in Advanced Countries*, ed. David Blanchflower and Richard B. Freeman, 427–72. Chicago: University of Chicago Press.

Angrist, Joshua D., and Adriana D. Kugler. 2003. "Protective or Counter-Productive? Labour Market Institutions and the Effect of Immigration on EU Natives." *Economic Journal* 113(488): F302–F331.

Antecol, Heather, Deborah A. Cobb-Clark, and Stephen J. Trejo. 2003. "Immigration Policy and the Skills of Immigrants to Australia, Canada, and the United States." *Journal of Human Resources* 38(1):192–218.

Baker, Michael, and Dwayne Benjamin. 1994. "The Performance of Immigrants in the Canadian Labor Market." *Journal of Labor Economics* 12(3):369–405.

Bell, Linda A., and Richard B. Freeman. 2001. "The Incentive for Working Hard: Explaining Hours Worked Differences between the U.S. and Germany." *Labour Economics* 8(2):181–202.

Bertola, Giuseppe, and Richard Rogerson. 1997. "Institutions and Labor Reallocation." *European Economic Review* 41(6): 937–57.

Betts, Julian R., and Mangus Lofstrom. 2000. "The Educational Attainment of Immigrants: Trends and Implications." In *Issues in the Economics of Immigration*, ed. George J. Borjas, 51–116. Chicago: University of Chicago Press.

Blau, Francine D., and Lawrence M. Kahn. 1996. "International Differences in Male Wage Inequality: Institutions versus Market Forces." *Journal of Political Economy* 104(4): 791–836.

Blau, Francine D., and Lawrence M. Kahn. 2000. "Gender Differences in Pay." *Journal of Economic Perspectives* 14(4):75–99.

Bloom, David E., Gilles Grenier, and Morley Gunderson. 1995. "The Changing Labour Market Position of Canadian Immigrants." *Canadian Journal of Economics* 28(4b): 987–1005.

Borjas, George J. 1985. "Assimilation, Changes in Cohort Quality, and the Earnings of Immigrants." *Journal of Labor Economics* 3(4):463–89.

———. 1987. "Self-Selection and the Earnings of Immigrants." *American Economic Review* 77(4):531–53.

———. 1988. *International Differences in the Labor Market Performance of Immigrants*. Kalamazoo, Mich.: W. E. Upjohn Institute for Employment Research.

———. 1993. "Immigration Policy, National Origin, and Immigrant Skills: A Comparison of Canada and the United States." In *Small Differences That Matter: Labor Markets and Income Maintenance in Canada and the United States*, ed. David Card and Richard B. Freeman, 21–43. Chicago: University of Chicago Press.

———. 1995. "Assimilation and Changes in Cohort Quality Revisited: What Happened to Immigrant Earnings in the 1980s?" *Journal of Labor Economics* 13(2):201–45.

———. 2000. "The Economic Progress of Immigrants." In *Issues in the Economics of Immigration*, ed. George J. Borjas, 15–50. Chicago: University of Chicago Press.

Butcher, Kristin F., and John DiNardo. 2002. "The Immigrant and Native-Born Wage Distributions: Evidence from United States Censuses." *Industrial and Labor Relations Review* 56(1):97–121.

Card, David, Francis Kramarz, and Thomas Lemieux. 1999. "Changes in the Relative Structure of Wages and Employment: A Comparison of the United States, Canada, and France." *Canadian Journal of Economics* 32(4):843–77.

Chiswick, Barry R. 1978. "The Effect of Americanization on the Earnings of Foreign-Born Men." *Journal of Political Economy* 86(5):897–921.

Chiswick, Barry R., Yinon Cohen, and Tzippi Zach. 1997. "The Labor Market Status of Immigrants: Effects of the Unemployment Rate at Arrival and Duration of Residence." *Industrial and Labor Relations Review* 50(2):289–303.

Chiswick, Barry R., and Paul W. Miller. 1992. *Post-Immigration Qualifications in Australia: Determinants and Consequences*. Canberra: Australian Government Publishing Service.

DiNardo, John, Nicole M. Fortin, and Thomas Lemieux. 1996. "Labor Market Institutions and the Distribution of Wages, 1973–1992: A Semiparametric Approach." *Econometrica* 64(5):1001–44.

Duleep, Harriet Orcutt, and Mark C. Regets. 1999. "Immigrants and Human-Capital Investment." *American Economic Review* 89(2):186–91.

Funkhouser, Edward. 2000. "Convergence in Employment Rates of Immigrants." In *Issues in the Economics of Immigration,* George J. Borjas, 143–84. Chicago: University of Chicago Press.

Funkhouser, Edward, and Stephen J. Trejo. 1998. "Labor Market Outcomes of Female Immigrants in the United States." In *The Immigration Debate: Studies on the Economic, Demographic, and Fiscal Effects of Immigration,* ed. James P. Smith and Barry Edmonston, 239–88. Washington, D.C.: National Academy Press.

Harris, John R., and Michael P. Todaro. 1970. "Migration, Unemployment & Development: A Two-Sector Analysis." *American Economic Review* 60(1):126–42.

Kahn, Lawrence M. 2004. "Immigration, Skills and the Labor Market: International Evidence." *Journal of Population Economics* 17(3):501–34.

Kuhn, Peter. 2002. "Summary and Synthesis." In *Losing Work, Moving On: International Perspectives on Worker Displacement,* ed. Peter Kuhn, 1–104. Kalamazoo, Michigan: W.E. Upjohn Institute for Employment Research.

Lubotsky, Darren. 2001. "The Effect of Changes in the U.S. Wage Structure on Recent Immigrants' Earnings." Working paper no. 458, Industrial Relations Section, Princeton University.

McDonald, James T., and Christopher Worswick. 1999a. "The Earnings of Immigrant Men in Australia: Assimilation, Cohort Effects, and Macroeconomic Conditions." *Economic Record* 75(228):49–62.

———. 1999b. "Immigrant Assimilation in a Regulated Labour Market: Unemployment of Immigrant Men in Australia." Hobart: University of Tasmania. Unpublished.

———. 2000. "Earnings and Employment Probabilities of Men by Education and Birth Cohort, 1982–96: Evidence for the United States, Canada and Australia." Hobart: University of Tasmania. Unpublished.

Miller, Paul, and Leanne Neo. 2001. "Labor Market Flexibility and Immigrant Adjustment." Unpublished paper. Perth: University of Western Australia.

Moene, K. O., and M. Wallerstein. 1997. "Pay Inequality." *Journal of Labor Economics* 15(3.1): 403–30.

OECD. 1994. *The OECD Jobs Study: Evidence and Explanations, Part II, The Adjustment Potential of the Labour Market.* Paris: OECD.

Reitz, Jeffrey G. 1998. *Warmth of the Welcome: The Social Causes of Economic Success for Immigrants in Different Nations and Cities.* Boulder, Colo.: Westview Press.

Part III
Demographic Adjustment of Immigrants

Part III
Demographic Adjustment of Immigrants

[16]

UNHEALTHY ASSIMILATION: WHY DO IMMIGRANTS CONVERGE TO AMERICAN HEALTH STATUS LEVELS?*

HEATHER ANTECOL AND KELLY BEDARD

It is well documented that immigrants are in better health upon arrival in the United States than their American counterparts but that this health advantage erodes over time. We study the potential determinants of this "healthy immigrant effect," with a particular focus on the tendency of immigrants to converge to unhealthy American BMI levels. Using data from the National Health Interview Survey, we find that average female and male immigrants enter the United States with BMIs that are approximately two and five percentage points lower than native-born women and men, respectively. Consistent with the declining health status of immigrants the longer they remain in the United States, we also find that female immigrants almost completely converge to American BMIs within 10 years of arrival, and men close a third of the gap within 15 years.

According to the U.S. census, the foreign-born population reached an all-time high of 32 million persons in 2000, an increase of 12 million people since 1990. Thus, immigrants constituted 10% of the U.S. population in 2000, compared with only 8% in 1990. The large and increasing presence of immigrants highlights the importance of monitoring immigrant health because the health of immigrants (and of their descendants) has a larger impact on the overall health outcomes of the American population as the immigrant population grows. Further, larger immigrant populations may increase pressure on the U.S. health care system; empirical evidence shows that immigrants place a burden on Medicaid (Borjas and Hilton 1996).[1]

Researchers from a wide array of disciplines have studied health differences between immigrants and native-born Americans. A key stylized fact that is generally supported in the literature is that upon arrival in the United States, immigrants are healthier than their native counterparts but that over time, this health advantage dissipates (House et al. 1990; Stephen et al. 1994). A similar pattern has also been documented in other major immigrant-receiving countries. For Canadian evidence, see Chen, Ng, and Wilkins (1996), Deri (2003), McDonald (2003), and Perez (2002); for Australian evidence, see Donovan et al. (1992). This phenomenon is often called the "healthy immigrant effect," henceforth referred to as the HIE.

The existence of the HIE has spawned a growing literature that seeks to explain this effect. The usual hypothesized contributing/mitigating factors include selective immigration, health care access, income assimilation, and acculturation. We discuss each of these in turn.

SELECTIVE IMMIGRATION

Several countervailing selection effects are at work with regard to the HIE. First, immigrants are positively selected and are hence in better health either by choice or due to the U.S. immigration screening process (Jasso et al. 2004; McDonald 2004; Marmot, Adelstein, and Bulusu 1984). Second, unhealthy immigrants may be more likely to return to their home

---

*Heather Antecol, Department of Economics, Claremont McKenna College, Claremont, CA 91711; E-mail: heather.antecol@claremontmckenna.edu. Kelly Bedard, Department of Economics, University of California, Santa Barbara, CA 93106; E-mail: Kelly@econ.ucsb.edu.

1. Borjas and Trejo (1991) similarly found that recent immigrant cohorts are more welfare dependent than earlier cohorts and that immigrant households are more likely to receive welfare the longer they reside in the United States. They also showed that the changing national origin mix explains the increased take-up in welfare among recent immigrant cohorts.

countries (Palloni and Arias 2003). Or third, more economically successful immigrants may be more likely to remain in the United States, and the extent to which higher-income individuals are healthier biases the immigrant sample toward being healthier. Finally, less-healthy immigrants may be more likely to die prematurely, making it important for researchers to consider the age range of the sample carefully. While positive selection into the Unites States upwardly biases the estimated health premium for immigrants upon entry (i.e., the cohort effects, according to Jasso et al. 2004; Marmot et al. 1984; McDonald 2004), the remaining selection mechanisms downwardly bias the estimates of immigrant health convergence toward lower U.S. health levels. As such, all the assimilation estimates reported in this article should be interpreted as lower bounds.

HEALTH CARE ACCESS

Improved access to health care for immigrants with time in residence might reduce reported health status by increasing the diagnosis of preexisting conditions (Jasso et al. 2004; McDonald and Kennedy 2004). On the other hand, it has also been suggested that increased access to health care may improve reported health status by reducing immigrant-native gaps in preventative health care screening, diagnosis, and treatment of health care problems (Laroche 2000; Leclere, Jensen, and Biddlecom 1994; McDonald and Kennedy 2004). As such, predicting the direction of the change in immigrant self-reported health status over time that results from changes in health care access is difficult.

However, we do know that immigrant health status is initially higher than that of natives and then falls toward American levels. Two things are therefore necessary for health care access to play a role in immigrant assimilation toward American health levels. First, immigrants' access to health care must change with the length of time that cohorts remain in the United States. Second, health care access must either fall the longer immigrants remain in the country, which seems incredibly unlikely, or must lead to the detection of previously unknown health problems that cause immigrants to report worse health.

INCOME ASSIMILATION

It is well known that most immigrant groups enter the United States with lower incomes and employment rates and subsequently converge toward native levels the longer they remain in the country (see, e.g., Antecol, Kuhn, and Trejo forthcoming; Borjas 1985, 1995; Chiswick 1986; Duleep and Regets 1994, 1999, 2002; Funkhouser and Trejo 1995; Hu 2000; LaLonde and Topel 1992; Schoeni 1997, 1998). Given immigrant income assimilation and the general finding that health is positively related to income (Sorlie et al. 1993), immigrants should become healthier the longer they remain in the country (Jasso et al. 2004). This is exactly the opposite of the HIE: immigrants arrive healthier and then become less healthy, not the reverse.

ACCULTURATION

Exposure to the U.S. environment causes immigrants to adopt native-born behaviors (such as diet and exercise) that have important health implications (Kasl and Berkman 1983; Marmot and Syme 1976; McDonald 2004; Stephen et al. 1994).[2] One of the most important but largely overlooked types of acculturation is the role that BMI (body mass index) assimilation plays in explaining the HIE. While the growing rate of obesity is well documented for the American population (Chou, Grossman, and Saffer 2002; Costa and Steckel 1995; Cutler, Glaeser, and Shapiro 2003; Himes 2000; Lakdawalla and Philipson 2002; Philipson

---

2. Alternatively, the act of migration may lead to worse health due to either the stress associated with the immigration process (Kasl and Berkman 1983) or exposure to discrimination in the host country (Vega and Amaro 1994).

2001; Philipson and Posner 1999), it has been essentially overlooked for the foreign-born population.[3]

The rising rate of obesity is of great concern to policymakers because of its associated health risks and hence costs. To put it in context, only tobacco use leads to higher rates of premature death than obesity (Chou et al. 2002). In particular, obesity increases the risk of heart disease, stroke, some types of cancer, and diabetes, and hence the financial burden due to greater health care consumption and/or productivity loss (Sturm 2002; Wolf and Colditz 1998).[4] Of course, these elevated costs are not borne entirely by the obese themselves; half of all health care is paid for by federal, state, and local governments (Chou et al. 2002).

THE HEALTHY IMMIGRANT EFFECT AND BMI CONVERGENCE

The objective of this paper is twofold. We first document the HIE by using the National Health Interview Surveys (NHIS). However, unlike in much of the previous literature, we control for differences in cohort quality.[5] Second, we examine a complementary explanation of the HIE: the BMI (kgs/meters^2) assimilation aspect of acculturation, which has received limited attention in the literature. The absence of research in this area is, in part, due to data limitations—few data sources provide information on weight and height as well as immigrant status. Fortunately, the 1989–1996 NHIS includes detailed information on immigration (e.g., year of arrival) and demographics (age, education, and so on) as well as weight and height.

We find support for the HIE in the NHIS by using three measures of health (self-reported health status, health conditions, and activity limitations). Immigrants enter healthier but then converge toward health levels of natives. Consistent with this finding, we find that immigrant women enter the country with BMIs that are approximately 2 percentage points lower than those of native-born women but that almost entirely converge to American BMIs within the first decade of residence in the United States. In contrast, immigrant men enter with BMIs that are approximately 5 percentage points lower than those of native-born men and close only one-third of the gap even after 15 years of U.S. residence. While convergence in average BMI is interesting, it masks an even greater difference in the percentage of natives and immigrants who are overweight (BMI $\geq$ 25) and obese (BMI $\geq$ 30). For example, immigrant women are about 10 percentage points less likely to be overweight than natives at entry, and they close 90% of the gap within 10 years of U.S. residence. Immigrant men are about 16 percentage points less likely to be overweight than native men, and they close half the gap after 15 or more years of U.S. residence.

Later in the article, we discuss the results further and offer conclusions. We begin, however, with a description of the data and then a presentation of the estimation strategy.

DATA

All data are drawn from the National Health Interview Surveys (NHIS) from 1989 to 1996. The NHIS is an annual cross-sectional survey intended to obtain information about the distribution of illness and the health services that people receive. Approximately 120,000 individuals in 45,000 households are surveyed each year. Information regarding basic socioeconomic characteristics as well as summary health measures, such as self-reported health status and activity limitations, are collected for all individuals, and

---

3. One exception is McDonald (2004), who examined the role obesity plays in explaining the HIE in Canada. And a growing literature documents obesity rates among foreign-born adolescents (see, e.g., Gordon-Larsen et al. 2003; Popkin and Udry 1998).

4. A related literature has also found that a wage penalty is associated with obesity (Averett and Korenman 1996; Cawley 2000; Hamermesh and Biddle 1994; Pagan and Davila 1997; Register and Williams 1990).

5. This technique is commonly used in the labor economics literature to examine wage and employment assimilation (see Borjas 1985 for the classic study).

measures of weight and height are collected for individuals aged 18 and older. Our analysis is restricted to 1989–1996 because years of U.S. residence are reported only in these years. To ensure a representative sample, we also restrict the sample to men and women aged 20–64 because overweight individuals may be less healthy and hence have higher premature mortality rates.

All of the analysis is carried out on four groups by nativity: all racial/ethnic origin groups, Hispanics, non-Hispanic whites, and non-Hispanic blacks—henceforth referred to as all origins, Hispanics, whites, and blacks. Immigrant groups are further broken down by year since arrival to the United States (0–4, 5–9, 10–14, and 15+). The sample includes 429,482 natives—comprising 20,510 Hispanics, 342,899 whites, and 60,179 blacks—and 61,234 immigrants—comprising 26,496 Hispanics, 17,793 whites, and 4,439 blacks.[6] Not surprisingly, given the open-ended nature of the 15+ years since arrival category, it is by far the largest group of immigrants, with 29,099 immigrants, while 0–4 years since arrival includes 11,047 immigrants, 5–9 years since arrival includes 11,033 immigrants, and 10–14 years since arrival includes 10,145 immigrants. However, due to a small amount of nonreporting for some health measures, the exact sample sizes vary slightly across outcomes.

Tables 1 and 2 report summary statistics by race/ethnic origin (henceforth referred to as race) for the variables used throughout the analysis for women and men, respectively.[7] For both natives and immigrants, we have measures for age and years of education, and indicators for currently married, currently employed, urban residence, and region of residence.[8] For all immigrants, Tables 1 and 2 also report immigrant arrival cohorts (1980 or before, 1981–1985, 1986–1990, and 1991–1996)[9] and the years since arrival (0–4, 5–9, 10–14, and 15+).

Throughout the analysis, we use three self-reported health indicators: poor health, the presence of at least one health condition, and the existence of at least one activity limitation. Poor health is defined as 1 if the individual's reported health status is fair or poor and 0 if his or her reported health status is excellent, very good, or good. An individual is defined as having at least one health condition if he or she reported one or more health conditions. Finally, the activity limitation indicator is set equal to 1 if the respondent is unable to perform a major activity (i.e., work), is limited in the kind or amount of the major activity, or is limited in any activity. For the sample as a whole, approximately 11% and 12% of native and immigrant women, respectively, report poor health; approximately 9% of both native and immigrant men report poor health. Of native and immigrant women, 46% and 34% report at least one health condition, and 15% and 11% report an activity limitation, respectively. Figures for native and immigrant men are slightly lower: 40% of native and 26% of immigrant men report at least one health condition, and 14% and 9% report an activity limitation, respectively. While the magnitudes vary by race, the overall patterns generally hold.[10]

---

6. The sample size for the all origins category is larger than the sum of the Hispanic, white, and black samples because it also includes all "other" racial/ethnic origins (e.g., Asians, Indians). However, this category is not analyzed separately because of small sample sizes.

7. All variables are defined in Appendix Table A.

8. To conserve space, the regional indicators are not reported in Tables 1 and 2 but are included in all models.

9. The NHIS reports years since U.S. arrival rather than immigrant arrival cohorts. As such, we assign individuals to five-year cohorts to maximize the number of immigrants placed in the correct arrival cohort. Immigrants reporting 15+ years of U.S. residence in all NHIS years and those reporting 10–14 years in 1989–1992 are designated as arriving in 1980 or earlier. Immigrants reporting 10–14 years in 1993–1996 and 5–9 years in 1989–1992 are designated as arriving in 1981–1985. Immigrants reporting 5–9 years in 1993–1996 and 0–4 years in 1989–1992 are designated as arriving in 1986–1990. Finally, immigrants reporting 0–4 years in 1993–1996 are designated as arriving in 1991–1996.

10. The main exception is reports of poor health for black women and men, where natives are 10 percentage points more likely to report poor health than their immigrant counterparts.

Table 1. Summary Statistics for Women, by Nativity and Race/Ethnic Origin

Variable	All Origins Native	All Origins Immigrant	Hispanic Native	Hispanic Immigrant	White Native	White Immigrant	Black Native	Black Immigrant
Poor Health	0.105 (0.306)	0.122 (0.327)	0.145 (0.352)	0.163 (0.369)	0.088 (0.284)	0.100 (0.300)	0.191 (0.393)	0.099 (0.298)
Health Conditions	0.460 (0.498)	0.340 (0.474)	0.410 (0.492)	0.341 (0.474)	0.465 (0.499)	0.392 (0.488)	0.445 (0.497)	0.310 (0.462)
Activity Limitations	0.149 (0.356)	0.108 (0.311)	0.132 (0.339)	0.121 (0.327)	0.145 (0.352)	0.124 (0.330)	0.175 (0.380)	0.084 (0.277)
Poverty	0.103 (0.304)	0.187 (0.390)	0.206 (0.404)	0.322 (0.467)	0.071 (0.257)	0.091 (0.287)	0.277 (0.447)	0.165 (0.371)
BMI	25.459 (5.808)	25.259 (4.842)	26.739 (6.222)	26.817 (4.876)	24.980 (5.497)	25.015 (4.494)	28.018 (6.646)	26.689 (5.204)
Overweight (BMI 25+)	0.435 (0.496)	0.438 (0.496)	0.529 (0.499)	0.593 (0.491)	0.400 (0.490)	0.393 (0.488)	0.630 (0.483)	0.594 (0.491)
Obese (BMI 30+)	0.186 (0.389)	0.145 (0.352)	0.261 (0.439)	0.225 (0.417)	0.161 (0.367)	0.112 (0.315)	0.324 (0.468)	0.221 (0.415)
Immigrated in 1980 or Before		0.562 (0.496)		0.564 (0.496)		0.670 (0.470)		0.509 (0.500)
Immigrated in 1981–1985		0.158 (0.365)		0.162 (0.368)		0.110 (0.313)		0.205 (0.404)
Immigrated in 1986–1990		0.182 (0.386)		0.183 (0.387)		0.139 (0.346)		0.207 (0.405)
Immigrated in 1991–1996		0.098 (0.298)		0.091 (0.287)		0.080 (0.272)		0.080 (0.271)
0–4 Years Since Arrival		0.187 (0.390)		0.173 (0.379)		0.150 (0.357)		0.173 (0.378)
5–9 Years Since Arrival		0.170 (0.375)		0.178 (0.383)		0.125 (0.331)		0.215 (0.411)
10–14 Years Since Arrival		0.154 (0.361)		0.165 (0.372)		0.104 (0.306)		0.192 (0.394)
15 or More Years Since Arrival		0.489 (0.500)		0.483 (0.500)		0.621 (0.485)		0.420 (0.494)
Age	39.423 (12.132)	38.747 (11.817)	35.138 (11.510)	37.203 (11.517)	39.876 (12.129)	41.383 (12.130)	38.064 (11.972)	36.912 (10.950)
Married	0.661 (0.473)	0.679 (0.467)	0.590 (0.492)	0.663 (0.473)	0.709 (0.454)	0.729 (0.444)	0.391 (0.488)	0.461 (0.499)
Years of Education	13.064 (2.467)	11.743 (4.140)	11.932 (2.850)	9.581 (4.247)	13.220 (2.407)	12.879 (3.365)	12.452 (2.480)	12.485 (3.159)
Working/Employed	0.675 (0.469)	0.567 (0.496)	0.617 (0.486)	0.473 (0.499)	0.686 (0.464)	0.600 (0.490)	0.628 (0.483)	0.701 (0.458)
Urban	0.776 (0.417)	0.941 (0.236)	0.904 (0.295)	0.950 (0.218)	0.758 (0.428)	0.912 (0.283)	0.854 (0.353)	0.988 (0.110)
Sample Size	226,611	32,107	11,034	13,548	176,853	9,388	35,642	2,446

Notes: NHIS data from 1989–1996 for individuals aged 20–64. All statistics use NHIS annual weights. The sample size is based on activity limitation reports, since activity limitation has the highest reporting rate. Standard deviations are in parentheses.

Table 2. Summary Statistics for Men, by Nativity and Race/Ethnic Origin

	All Origins		Hispanic		White		Black	
Variable	Native	Immigrant	Native	Immigrant	Native	Immigrant	Native	Immigrant
Poor Health	0.089	0.085	0.106	0.110	0.080	0.076	0.149	0.044
	(0.285)	(0.280)	(0.307)	(0.313)	(0.271)	(0.264)	(0.356)	(0.205)
Health Conditions	0.395	0.262	0.339	0.246	0.403	0.315	0.358	0.222
	(0.489)	(0.440)	(0.473)	(0.430)	(0.490)	(0.464)	(0.480)	(0.415)
Activity Limitations	0.144	0.090	0.126	0.096	0.140	0.104	0.174	0.062
	(0.351)	(0.286)	(0.332)	(0.295)	(0.347)	(0.305)	(0.379)	(0.242)
Poverty	0.070	0.161	0.133	0.268	0.054	0.080	0.167	0.124
	(0.255)	(0.367)	(0.339)	(0.443)	(0.226)	(0.271)	(0.373)	(0.330)
BMI	26.504	25.367	27.233	26.024	26.475	25.878	26.540	25.055
	(4.490)	(3.826)	(4.803)	(4.091)	(4.390)	(3.804)	(5.008)	(3.163)
Overweight (BMI 25+)	0.589	0.485	0.661	0.565	0.590	0.540	0.570	0.492
	(0.492)	(0.500)	(0.473)	(0.496)	(0.492)	(0.498)	(0.495)	(0.500)
Obese (BMI 30+)	0.177	0.097	0.241	0.129	0.171	0.116	0.199	0.059
	(0.382)	(0.297)	(0.428)	(0.336)	(0.377)	(0.320)	(0.399)	(0.236)
Immigrated in 1980 or Before		0.534		0.531		0.626		0.492
		(0.499)		(0.499)		(0.484)		(0.500)
Immigrated in 1981–1985		0.179		0.184		0.129		0.232
		(0.384)		(0.388)		(0.335)		(0.422)
Immigrated in 1986–1990		0.193		0.201		0.158		0.202
		(0.394)		(0.401)		(0.365)		(0.402)
Immigrated in 1991–1996		0.094		0.084		0.087		0.074
		(0.292)		(0.277)		(0.282)		(0.262)
0–4 Years Since Arrival		0.185		0.173		0.163		0.162
		(0.388)		(0.378)		(0.369)		(0.368)
5–9 Years Since Arrival		0.189		0.201		0.146		0.228
		(0.391)		(0.401)		(0.353)		(0.420)
10–14 Years Since Arrival		0.172		0.182		0.126		0.220
		(0.378)		(0.386)		(0.332)		(0.414)
15 or More Years Since Arrival		0.454		0.444		0.565		0.391
		(0.498)		(0.497)		(0.496)		(0.488)
Age	39.306	37.692	34.922	36.157	39.723	39.988	37.942	36.508
	(12.005)	(11.493)	(11.459)	(11.243)	(11.967)	(11.789)	(12.020)	(10.177)
Married	0.688	0.687	0.611	0.697	0.713	0.711	0.540	0.601
	(0.463)	(0.464)	(0.488)	(0.459)	(0.452)	(0.453)	(0.498)	(0.490)
Years of Education	13.196	12.109	12.214	9.473	13.372	13.565	12.243	13.117
	(2.694)	(4.285)	(2.825)	(4.272)	(2.647)	(3.447)	(2.701)	(3.140)
Working/Employed	0.837	0.822	0.809	0.831	0.854	0.838	0.733	0.798
	(0.369)	(0.383)	(0.393)	(0.375)	(0.353)	(0.368)	(0.442)	(0.401)
Urban	0.771	0.943	0.898	0.936	0.756	0.932	0.850	0.985
	(0.420)	(0.232)	(0.302)	(0.245)	(0.429)	(0.251)	(0.357)	(0.120)
Sample Size	202,871	29,217	9,476	12,948	166,046	8,405	24,537	1,993

Notes: NHIS data from 1989–1996 for individuals aged 20–64. All statistics use NHIS annual weights. The sample size is based on activity limitation reports, since activity limitation has the highest reporting rate. Standard deviations are in parentheses.

While reported height and weight can be used to construct the BMI (kgs/meters^2), which adjusts weight for height differences, self-reported height and weight are subject to reporting errors that may bias coefficient estimates. Unfortunately, the NHIS does not include measured height and weight. As such, we are forced to use self-reported measures. For our purposes, we are particularly concerned that different racial and/or immigrant groups may differentially misreport. For example, in a similarly aged sample in the Third National Health and Nutrition Examination Survey (NHANES III) conducted in 1988–1994, the average immigrant woman underreported her weight by 1.3%, while the average native woman underreported her weight by 2.4%. On the other hand, the average native and immigrant man both underreported their actual weight by 0.8%.

Following Cawley (2000), we address this misreporting problem by using the strategy described in Lee and Sepanski (1995) and Bound, Brown, and Mathiowetz (2001). More specifically, we correct self-reported weight and height, using data from NHANES III, which is a nationally representative sample containing information on immigrant status as well as self-reported weight and height and professionally measured weight and height. As such, we regress measured true weight and height on reported weight and height and reported weight and height squared separately for men and women by race/immigrant group (white, black, Hispanic, and other immigrants and natives—16 groups in total).[11] The estimates used for the adjustment of weight and height are available upon request. We then use the coefficient estimates to predict measured weight and height in the NHIS data.[12] All summary BMI statistics and estimates reported in this article are based on predicted weight and height. Nevertheless, all results are similar if reported weight and height are used instead (this is discussed in detail in the section on immigrant BMI patterns).

Rows 5–7 in Tables 1 and 2 report the average BMI, the percentage defined as overweight (BMI $\geq$ 25) and the percentage defined as obese (BMI $\geq$ 30) for women and men, respectively.[13] While average BMI is virtually identical for natives and immigrants, irrespective of gender and race,[14] the same is not always true for the percent overweight and the percent obese. Specifically, immigrant women are equally as likely as native women to be overweight (44%) but are less likely to be obese (15%) than their native counterparts (19%). In contrast, 59% of native men are overweight and 18% are obese, compared with only 49% and 10% of immigrant men. These averages, however, hide interesting differences by race, particularly for women. For example, while Hispanic immigrant women are 6 percentage points more likely to be overweight than their native-born counterparts and black immigrant women are 4 percentage points less likely to be overweight than their native-born counterparts, white native and immigrant women are indistinguishable.

EMPIRICAL FRAMEWORK

As previously stated, our goal is to document the HIE and to examine the BMI assimilation pattern of immigrants to the United States. For all outcome measures, we examine immigrant assimilation by using the regression framework developed by Borjas (1985, 1995). To begin, we focus on the assimilation of immigrants to natives for all origin groups combined, using eight NHIS cross sections from 1989 to 1996. The availability of repeated cross sections is crucial because it allows us to track health outcomes for immigrant arrival cohorts over time.[15]

---

11. All models are appropriately weighted.
12. See Cawley (2000: appendix A) for a more detailed discussion of these issues. This, of course, assumes that the relationship between reported and measured height is the same in the NHANES III and NHIS.
13. We exclude 52 respondents who reported extreme heights (under 48 inches or over 84 inches) from the weight analysis. However, all results are similar if these individuals are included.
14. The one exception is that black native women have a higher average BMI (28) than black immigrant women (26.7).
15. However, not every arrival cohort is observed in every category of years since migration.

In particular, we estimate equations of the following form:

$$Y_i = X_i\beta + A_i\delta + C_i\gamma + T_i\pi + \varepsilon_i, \qquad (1)$$

where i denotes individuals, y represents the outcome measure of interest, X is a vector of control variables, A is vector of dummy variables indicating how long an immigrant has lived in the United States (set equal to 0 for natives), C is a vector of dummy variables identifying immigrant arrival cohorts, T is a vector of dummy variables indicating the survey year, and ε is a random error term. This specification gives each immigrant arrival cohort its own intercept, and differences in these intercepts represent permanent outcome differences between cohorts. The coefficients for the duration of U.S. residence dummy variables (A) measure the effects of immigrant assimilation with respect to the outcome measure in question.[16]

In order to identify the cohort and assimilation effects, we restrict the period effect, π, to be the same for both immigrants and natives. In essence, this means that the period effects are estimated from natives, and this information is used to identify cohort and assimilation effects for immigrants. Although not necessary for identification, Eq. (1) also restricts the effects of the variables in the control vector (X) to be the same for immigrants and natives and across survey years. We also estimated less-constrained models that did not impose these latter restrictions and obtained very similar results.

We then estimate Eq. (1) separately by race. Specifically, we focus on the assimilation of Hispanic immigrants to Hispanic natives, white immigrants to white natives, and black immigrants to black natives. By estimating the model within race, as opposed to using white natives as the base group (which is the usual approach in the literature on labor market assimilation), we avoid confounding possible racial differences with assimilation.

THE HEALTHY IMMIGRANT EFFECT

Do immigrants arrive in the United States healthier than their native counterparts? And do immigrants converge to American health levels? To answer these questions, we estimate Eq. (1) for three indicator variables for health: poor health (1 if self-reported health is either fair or poor), health conditions (1 if one or more health conditions are reported), and activity limitations (1 if activity or work is limited).

Tables 3 and 4 present the immigrant cohort and assimilation effects for our three health measures by race for women and men, respectively. All health equations are estimated as probit models. To more easily describe the quantitative importance of the explanatory variables in the probit specifications, Tables 3 and 4 and all remaining tables report the marginal effects for continuous variables and average treatment effects for the discrete variables, in both cases evaluated at means, as well as standard errors calculated using the "delta" method. In addition to the variables listed in Tables 3 and 4, all regressions include controls for age, age squared, years of education, and indicator variables for married, employed, residence in an urban area, region of residence, and survey year.[17]

Overall, the period effects indicate that Americans are getting less healthy over time irrespective of gender and the health measure analyzed. Between 1989 and 1996, holding all else constant, the average female probability of being in poor health increased by 1.3 percentage points, and the average male probability of being in poor health increased by 0.8 percentage points. While the same pattern holds for whites, the period effects are less pronounced for Hispanics and blacks. In order to avoid overly cluttered tables, and because

---

16. Given these variables, the specification defined in Eq. (1) assumes that the assimilation pattern is constant across arrival cohorts.
17. The coefficient estimates and marginal effects for these variables are available upon request.

Table 3. Immigrant Cohort and Assimilation Effects of Health Status for Women, by Race/Ethnic Origin

Variable	All Origins Poor Health	All Origins Health Conditions	All Origins Activity Limitations	Hispanic Poor Health	Hispanic Health Conditions	Hispanic Activity Limitations	White Poor Health	White Health Conditions	White Activity Limitations	Black Poor Health	Black Health Conditions	Black Activity Limitations
Cohort Effects												
Immigrated in 1980 or before	-0.042† (0.009)	-0.212† (0.021)	-0.102† (0.019)	-0.099† (0.024)	-0.214† (0.037)	-0.102† (0.019)	-0.014 (0.022)	-0.174† (0.046)	-0.072† (0.020)	-0.071 (0.053)	-0.090 (0.082)	-0.079 (0.034)
Immigrated in 1981–1985	-0.038† (0.007)	-0.199† (0.016)	-0.074† (0.010)	-0.079† (0.014)	-0.177† (0.025)	-0.074† (0.010)	-0.026 (0.013)	-0.176† (0.034)	-0.064† (0.017)	-0.058 (0.046)	-0.097 (0.064)	-0.093† (0.018)
Immigrated in 1986–1990	-0.031† (0.004)	-0.202† (0.009)	-0.070† (0.006)	-0.067† (0.009)	-0.160† (0.015)	-0.070† (0.006)	-0.003 (0.010)	-0.168† (0.018)	-0.063† (0.009)	-0.059 (0.030)	-0.163† (0.038)	-0.089† (0.013)
Immigrated in 1991–1995	-0.021† (0.005)	-0.191† (0.010)	-0.059† (0.007)	-0.039† (0.010)	-0.121† (0.016)	-0.059† (0.007)	-0.002 (0.010)	-0.162† (0.020)	-0.068† (0.008)	-0.102† (0.017)	-0.148† (0.040)	-0.092† (0.012)
Assimilation Effects												
5–9 years since arrival	0.027† (0.011)	0.039† (0.016)	0.035† (0.019)	0.032† (0.019)	0.059† (0.025)	0.035† (0.019)	0.023 (0.020)	0.042 (0.032)	0.021 (0.027)	0.008 (0.055)	0.048 (0.059)	0.084 (0.063)
10–14 years since arrival	0.034† (0.016)	0.052† (0.023)	0.054† (0.031)	0.059† (0.032)	0.081† (0.038)	0.054† (0.031)	0.031 (0.031)	0.068 (0.048)	0.050 (0.043)	0.015 (0.076)	0.024 (0.079)	0.063 (0.081)
15 or more years since arrival	0.053† (0.020)	0.140† (0.026)	0.101† (0.036)	0.096† (0.036)	0.167† (0.044)	0.101† (0.036)	0.010 (0.029)	0.125† (0.053)	0.075† (0.052)	0.035 (0.093)	0.000 (0.089)	0.070 (0.096)
Sample Size	257,714	258,718	24,582	24,430	24,582	24,582	185,626	186,241	186,241	37,897	38,088	38,088

Notes: All models also include age, age squared, years of education, and indicators for married, employed, urban, region, and survey year. NHIS annual weights are used. Marginal effects are reported for all probit models. Standard errors are in parentheses. The sample size varies due to nonreporting of the dependent variable.
†Statistically significant at the 10% level.

Table 4. Immigrant Cohort and Assimilation Effects of Health Status for Men, by Race/Ethnic Origin

Variable	All Origins Poor Health	All Origins Health Conditions	All Origins Activity Limitations	Hispanic Poor Health	Hispanic Health Conditions	Hispanic Activity Limitations	White Poor Health	White Health Conditions	White Activity Limitations	Black Poor Health	Black Health Conditions	Black Activity Limitations
Cohort Effects												
Immigrated in 1980 or before	-0.025† (0.009)	-0.208† (0.019)	-0.082† (0.009)	-0.053† (0.020)	-0.142† (0.035)	-0.075† (0.018)	-0.018 (0.017)	-0.140† (0.046)	-0.051 (0.026)	-0.061 (0.035)	-0.124 (0.076)	-0.103† (0.022)
Immigrated in 1981–1985	-0.026† (0.006)	-0.190† (0.015)	-0.077† (0.006)	-0.043† (0.012)	-0.115† (0.024)	-0.058† (0.010)	-0.025† (0.011)	-0.154† (0.034)	-0.051† (0.020)	-0.054 (0.029)	-0.143† (0.057)	-0.092† (0.023)
Immigrated in 1986–1990	-0.021† (0.004)	-0.200† (0.008)	-0.077† (0.004)	-0.045† (0.007)	-0.129† (0.014)	-0.052† (0.007)	-0.019† (0.007)	-0.171† (0.019)	-0.065† (0.009)	-0.049† (0.018)	-0.138† (0.038)	-0.089† (0.018)
Immigrated in 1991–1995	-0.017† (0.005)	-0.197† (0.009)	-0.078† (0.003)	-0.035† (0.009)	-0.113† (0.015)	-0.036† (0.008)	0.000 (0.011)	-0.181† (0.020)	-0.079† (0.007)	-0.067† (0.018)	-0.165† (0.043)	-0.103† (0.009)
Assimilation Effects												
5–9 years since arrival	0.026† (0.011)	0.053† (0.018)	0.027† (0.015)	0.039† (0.018)	0.022 (0.024)	0.031† (0.019)	0.041† (0.024)	0.033 (0.035)	0.000 (0.026)	-0.019 (0.037)	0.065 (0.067)	0.052 (0.083)
10–14 years since arrival	0.030† (0.015)	0.066† (0.025)	0.047† (0.023)	0.045† (0.027)	0.031 (0.036)	0.057† (0.031)	0.057† (0.039)	0.047 (0.050)	0.017 (0.040)	-0.009 (0.057)	0.080 (0.090)	0.123 (0.130)
15 or more years since arrival	0.025† (0.016)	0.146† (0.028)	0.091† (0.030)	0.047† (0.029)	0.082† (0.044)	0.075† (0.034)	0.022 (0.033)	0.099† (0.056)	0.048 (0.051)	0.015 (0.077)	0.058 (0.101)	0.173 (0.160)
Sample Size	231,262	232,088	232,088	22,313	22,424	22,424	173,932	174,451	174,451	26,360	26,530	26,530

Notes: All models also include age, age squared, years of education, and indicators for married, employed, urban, region, and survey year. NHIS annual weights are used. Marginal effects are reported for all probit models. Standard errors are in parentheses. Sample size varies due to nonreporting of the dependent variable.

†Statistically significant at the 10% level.

the results mirror those in the established literature, we do not report these marginal effects in Tables 3 and 4.

The immigrant arrival cohort marginal effects reported in Tables 3 and 4 represent immigrant-native health differences evaluated at 0–4 years of U.S. residence. For example, the estimated marginal effect for 1986–1990 Hispanic female immigrants in the health conditions specification indicates that in their first four years after arriving, this cohort was 7 percentage points less likely to be in poor health relative to otherwise similar Hispanic natives.

That the cohort marginal effects are uniformly negative (although sometimes imprecisely estimated) irrespective of race implies that immigrants who have recently arrived in the United States (those with 0–4 years of residency) are less likely to report poor health, health conditions, and activity limitations than natives. Furthermore, the fact that the marginal effects tend to be similar in magnitude for all of the various recent arrival cohorts suggests that, after controls for years of U.S. residence, health is similar across cohorts.

We now turn to the assimilation effects. In Tables 3 and 4, the marginal effects for the duration of U.S. residence indicate how health changes the longer an immigrant cohort remains in the United States. The overall assimilation patterns are similar for male and female immigrants; thus, we focus on the female assimilation patterns here. While the bulk of assimilation for the probability of being in poor health takes place within the first decade after arrival, immigrant assimilation in terms of health conditions and activity limitations occurs more slowly. For example, the probability of being in poor health increases by 2.7 percentage points as female immigrants pass from 0–4 to 5–9 years in the United States but thereafter increases only a modest 2.6 percentage points. In contrast, the percentage of female immigrants with health conditions, relative to their level during the initial four years of U.S. residence, rises by 3.9 percentage points after 5–9 years, by 5.2 percentage points after 10–14 years, and by 14 percentage points after more than 15 years.

The overall patterns hide some interesting racial differences. First, the overall assimilation patterns hold for Hispanic immigrants, irrespective of gender. Second, the point estimates for black immigrants reveal that neither men nor women assimilate to their black native-born counterparts. Third, the point estimates for white immigrants suggest some convergence toward their white native-born counterparts, though these estimates are often imprecise. In particular, the point estimates are more precise for health conditions and activity limitations for white female immigrants, while for white male immigrants, the point estimates are more precise for poor health and health conditions.

Finally, recall the negative cohort marginal effects discussed earlier. These marginal effects indicate that for all races, all immigrant cohorts are less likely than natives to be in poor health, by all measures, at the time of arrival (defined as having arrived in the United States during the five years before the survey). However, assimilation toward U.S. levels eventually erases all or most of the initial health advantage for all immigrants, for Hispanic immigrants, and depending on the health measure for white immigrants, but not for black immigrants. As an illustration, consider the 1981–1985 arrival cohort for Hispanics. During their first five years in the United States, this cohort had an incidence of being limited in activities that was 7.4 and 5.8 percentage points below that of Hispanic natives for women and men, respectively. But after 10–14 years of U.S. residence, assimilation reduces the gap by 5.4 percentage points for women and 5.7 percentage points for men. After 15 years of U.S. residence, Hispanic female and male immigrants are actually 2.7 and 1.7 percentage points more likely than Hispanic natives to be classified as limited in activities. To summarize, these results are generally consistent with an immigrant health assimilation process, as opposed to permanent health differences across immigrant cohorts.

Overall, these results confirm the existence of the HIE found in previous research. In particular, we find that recent immigrants (those with 0–4 years of U.S. residency) are healthier than natives irrespective of race and gender, though this health advantage declines (and/or is erased) with time in the United States for all immigrants, for Hispanic immigrants, and (depending on the health measure) for white immigrants, but not for black immigrants.

IMMIGRANT BMI PATTERNS

As previously stated, a growing literature has documented the ever-increasing American waistline and the rapidly growing incidence of obesity. The rising rate of obesity is of great concern to policymakers because of the associated health risks (e.g., heart disease, stroke, some types of cancer, and diabetes) and hence costs. These facts suggest a possible explanation for why immigrants become less healthy the longer they reside in the United States: immigrant BMIs may be approaching the unhealthy BMIs of their American counterparts.[18] We focus on three BMI measures: the natural logarithm of BMI[19] (we use logs for interpretative ease), an indicator variable for overweight (1 if BMI ≥ 25), and an indicator variable for obese (1 if BMI ≥ 30).

BMI by Nativity

Do immigrants converge to the unhealthy BMIs of U.S. natives? We begin to answer this question by simply graphing the average BMI for all origins, Hispanic, white, and black women (Figure 1a) and men (Figure 1b) from 1989–1996. For easy visual analysis of immigrant assimilation patterns, each graph includes a line for natives, immigrants with 0–4 years of U.S. residence, and immigrants with 15 or more years of U.S. residence.

Consistent with findings reported by Lakdawalla and Philipson (2002) and Cutler et al. (2003), men's and women's average BMIs rose between 1989 and 1996 for all racial groups, although the average BMI level did differ across racial groups. To put this in perspective, in 1989, the average native white woman had a BMI of 24.5. Over the next seven years, this rose by 4% to 25.4. While the BMIs for the average native black and Hispanic woman in 1989 were 27.3 and 26.2, respectively, the growth rates were about the same as for native white women. The average upward trend for men was slightly slower, with a growth rate of approximately 3% for all racial groups. The major difference between men and women is that the racial spread is much smaller for men.

Although the upward native trends are important for comparison, the immigrant patterns are of greater importance for our purposes. Two patterns are noteworthy. First, just as for natives, there is an upward trend for immigrants over time, holding years since arrival constant. Second, the longer immigrants reside in the United States, the higher their BMIs become. The BMI for the average female immigrant rises by approximately 6% between 0–4 years of U.S. residence and 15 or more years of U.S. residence. However, the average for the all-origin group masks important race-specific assimilation patterns. For example, Hispanic immigrant women who have lived in the United States for 0–4 years have lower

---

18. Ideally, we would like to examine other determinants of the HIE, such as access to health care and poverty. Unfortunately, the only measure of access to health care that is reported in the NHIS is a binary indicator for whether the respondent visited a doctor in previous months. This is a questionable measure of health care access because it confounds access and utilization. As a result, we cannot empirically investigate this potential HIE channel. Turning to poverty, the NHIS includes only a categorical measure of nominal family income (with a low top code and a high nonreporting rate) and an indicator variable for households falling below the poverty line. Given the high nonreporting for family income and the difficulty associated with converting nominal categories into real values over time, we can analyze the probability of being in poverty but not family income. We estimate immigrant entry and assimilation effects by using the estimation strategy described in the section on the empirical framework and Eq. (1). The results are available upon request. Consistent with previous studies, we find that overall, all immigrant arrival cohorts are more likely to be in poverty than their native counterparts and that there is a small amount of convergence toward lower rates of poverty among natives with increasing years of U.S. residency. While similar cohort effects are generally found by race (the one exception is black women), there are no assimilation effects by race. As such, the poverty and health assimilation processes move in opposite directions, which is incompatible with the HIE.

19. All results are similar using BMI levels.

Figure 1. BMI by Race/Ethnic Origin and Nativity

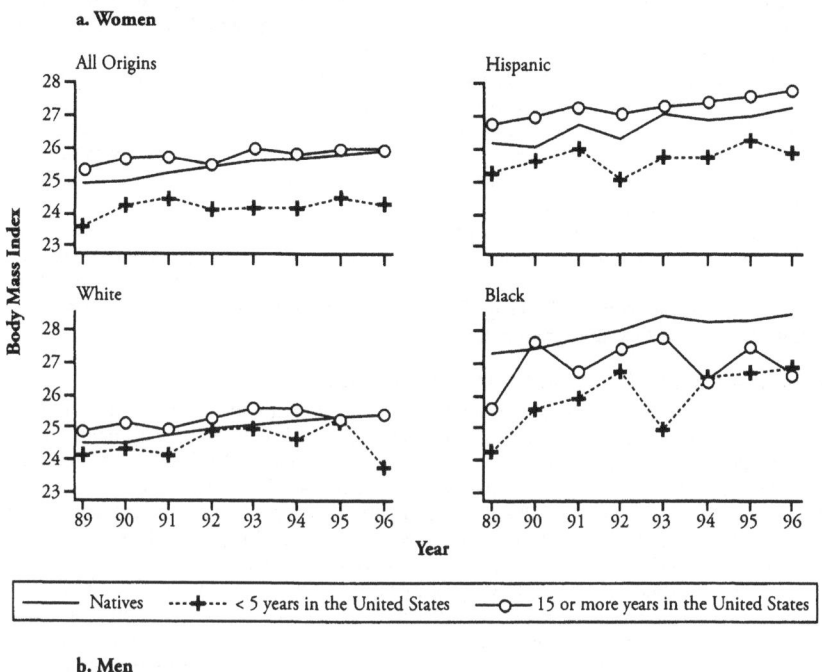

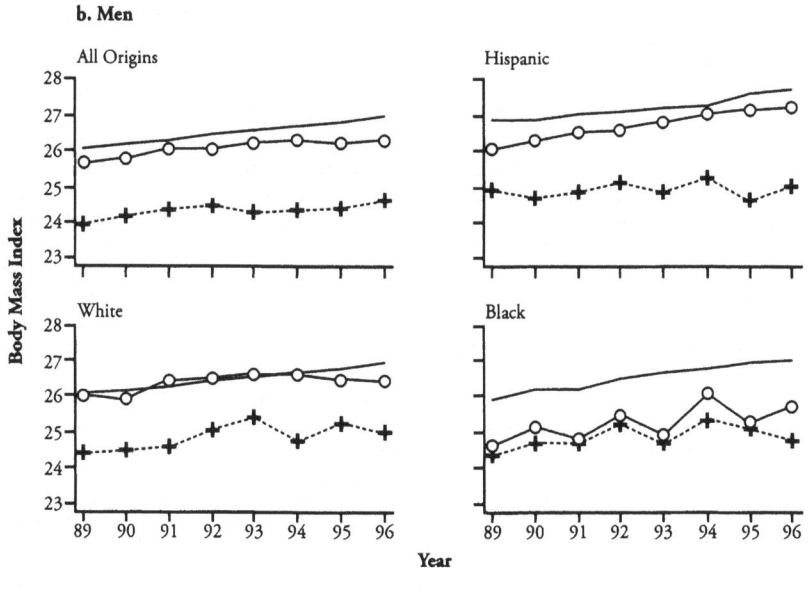

a. Women

Legend: —— Natives ···+··· < 5 years in the United States —○— 15 or more years in the United States

b. Men

BMIs than native Hispanics, while Hispanic immigrant women who have lived the United States for 15 or more years have higher BMIs than native Hispanics. In contrast, both newly arrived black immigrants and those who have resided in the United States for more than 15 years have lower BMIs than native blacks, although the group with longer U.S. residence has a higher average BMI than the recently arrived group.

There are two important differences between the female and male patterns. First, for most racial groups, the average BMI difference between natives and recent immigrants is substantially larger for men than for women. Second, with the exception of white immigrants, male immigrants' BMIs do not converge to the comparable native level even for the group with 15 or more years of U.S. residency. This pattern contrasts with the overshooting that we see for female immigrants.

Figures 2 and 3 replicate Figure 1 for the percentage of people classified as overweight and obese, respectively. In both cases, the patterns are very similar. The one noticeable difference is that there appears to be somewhat less immigrant convergence in obesity relative to the BMI and the overweight designation. The remainder of the article provides a more formal analysis of this immigrant convergence.

Immigrant Assimilation and Cohort Differences

Following the standard Borjas (1985, 1995) approach, we begin by presenting the immigrant cohort and assimilation effects for Eq. (1) for our three BMI measures for all immigrants in the first three columns of Tables 5 (for women) and 6 (for men). We then present the results for Hispanics, whites, and blacks separately in columns 4–12. Furthermore, for each of the four racial group specifications, the native comparison group is the equivalent racial group: all origins (i.e., all American-born individuals), Hispanics, whites, and blacks.

The period effects indicate that U.S. BMIs are rising. Between 1989 and 1996, holding all else constant, the average BMI, probability of being overweight, and probability of being obese increased, respectively, by 3.8, 8.4, and 6.0 percentage points for women and 3.0, 8.0, and 6.0 percentage points for men (these results are available upon request).[20] Moreover, this pattern holds irrespective of race, in sharp contrast to the results for our three health measures presented in Tables 3 and 4, where the period effects were largely driven by whites.

We begin by focusing on the all-origins group. As with the health outcomes, the uniformly negative cohort marginal effects imply that both male and female immigrants with 0–4 years of U.S. residency from every arrival cohort have lower BMIs, a lower proportion of overweight individuals, and a lower proportion of obese individuals than natives do. Furthermore, we find no evidence of differences across cohorts (i.e., the magnitude of the marginal effects are similar across recent arrival cohorts). However, unlike the health outcomes, there are some important differences across racial groups with respect to cohort effects. While Hispanic and black immigrants closely resemble the all origins patterns, irrespective of gender, the pattern for white immigrants is very different. In particular, with the exception of obesity rates, white female immigrants are indistinguishable from their white native counterparts, while white male immigrants from every arrival period initially have lower BMIs, probabilities of being overweight, and probabilities of being obese than their native counterparts. In particular, white male immigrants have BMIs that are 3%–4% lower and overweight and obesity rates that are 11–14 and 7–11 percentage points lower, depending on the arrival cohort, than their white native counterparts.

Turning to the overall assimilation effects (columns 1 to 3 of Tables 5 and 6), the bulk of assimilation (regardless of the outcome measure) takes place within the first decade after arrival for female immigrants. The probability of being overweight or obese increases

---

20. The parameter estimates for age, age squared, years of education, and indicator variables for married, employed, residence in an urban area, region of residence, and survey year are available upon request.

Unhealthy Assimilation of Immigrants

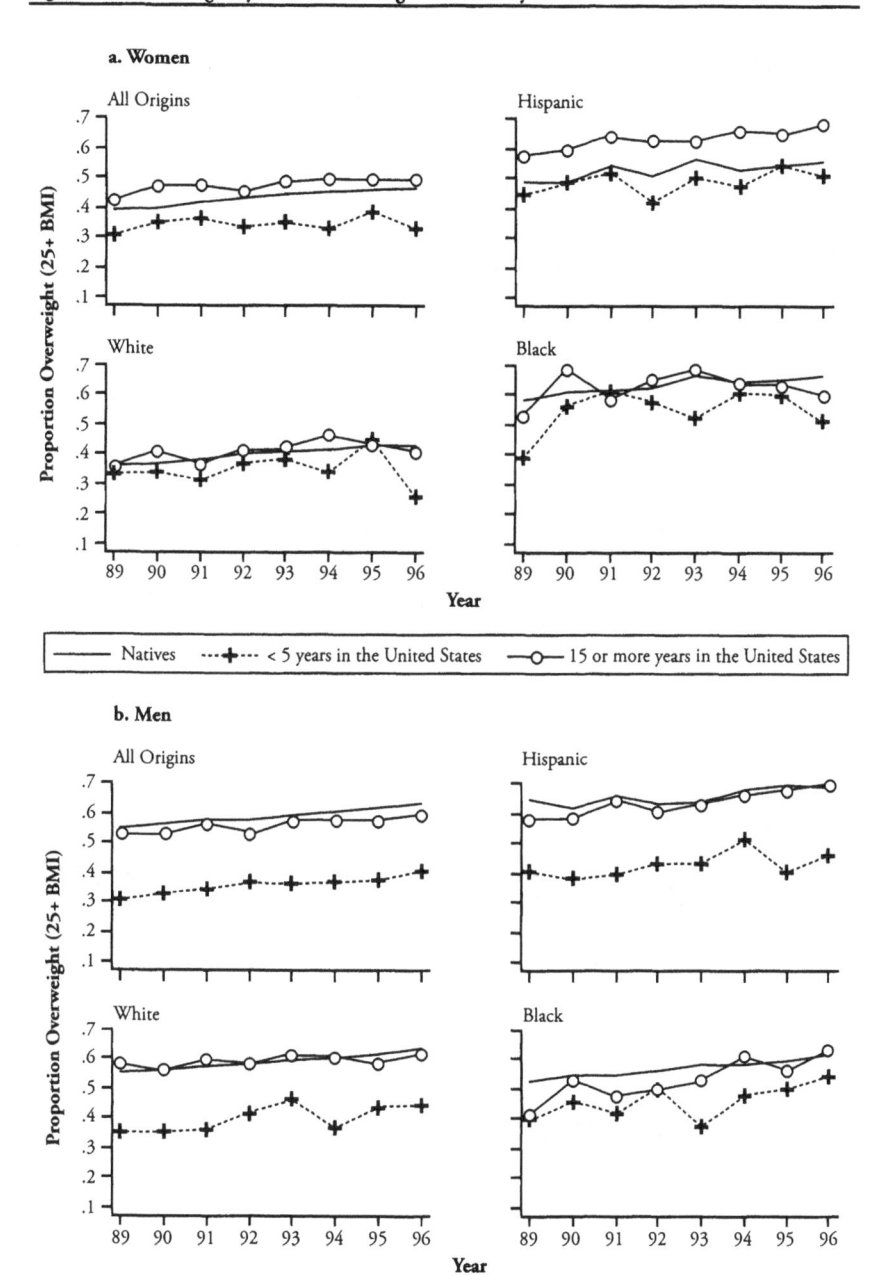

Figure 2. Overweight by Race/Ethnic Origin and Nativity

a. Women

——— Natives   ···+··· < 5 years in the United States   —○— 15 or more years in the United States

b. Men

Figure 3. Obesity by Race/Ethnic Origin and Nativity

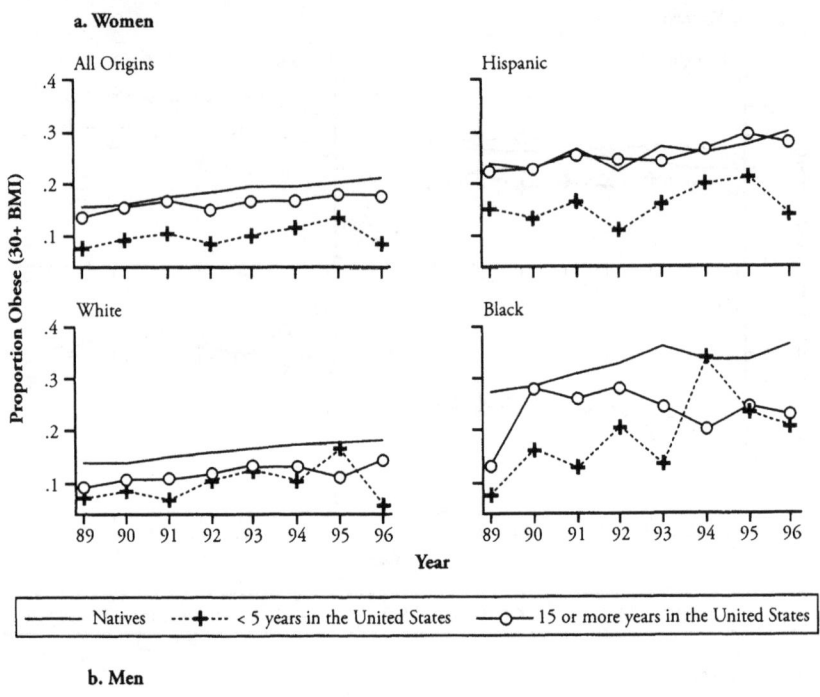

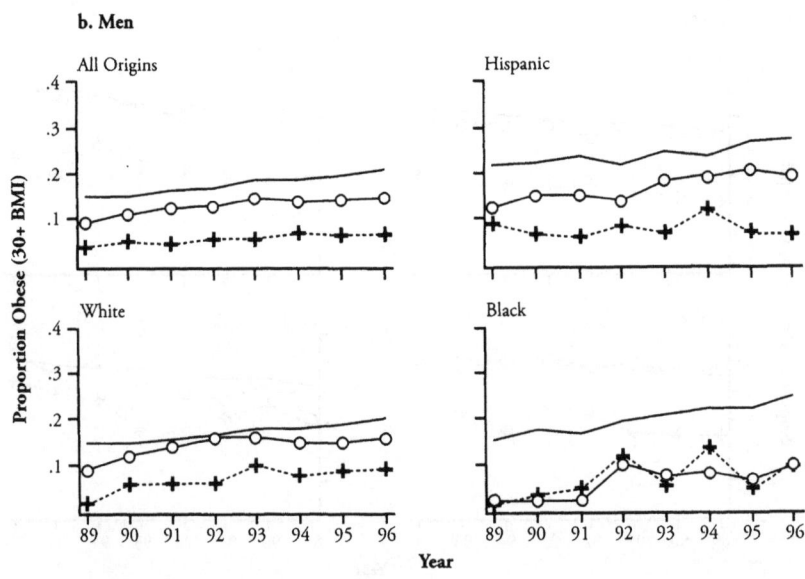

a. Women

——— Natives   ---+--- < 5 years in the United States   —○— 15 or more years in the United States

b. Men

Table 5. Immigrant Cohort and Assimilation Effects of BMI for Women, by Race/Ethnic Origin

Variable	All Origins Log BMI	All Origins Overweight	All Origins Obese	Hispanic Log BMI	Hispanic Overweight	Hispanic Obese	White Log BMI	White Overweight	White Obese	Black Log BMI	Black Overweight	Black Obese
Cohort Effects												
Immigrated in 1980 or before	-0.025† (0.008)	-0.099† (0.024)	-0.095† (0.013)	-0.037† (0.014)	-0.113† (0.044)	-0.176† (0.030)	0.013 (0.015)	-0.048 (0.050)	-0.053 (0.031)	0.010 (0.028)	0.016 (0.076)	-0.053 (0.075)
Immigrated in 1981–1985	-0.034† (0.006)	-0.095† (0.018)	-0.099† (0.009)	-0.045† (0.010)	-0.120† (0.032)	-0.153† (0.017)	0.000 (0.012)	-0.043 (0.037)	-0.072† (0.019)	-0.025 (0.020)	0.003 (0.059)	-0.114† (0.049)
Immigrated in 1986–1990	-0.025† (0.003)	-0.058† (0.011)	-0.085† (0.006)	-0.034† (0.006)	-0.069† (0.019)	-0.128† (0.012)	0.013† (0.006)	0.001 (0.021)	-0.058† (0.012)	-0.039† (0.010)	-0.022 (0.036)	-0.137† (0.027)
Immigrated in 1991–1995	-0.041† (0.004)	-0.092† (0.011)	-0.087† (0.006)	-0.044† (0.006)	-0.080† (0.019)	-0.115† (0.011)	0.007 (0.007)	-0.017 (0.021)	-0.042† (0.013)	-0.057† (0.016)	-0.055 (0.044)	-0.106† (0.036)
Assimilation Effects												
5–9 years since arrival	0.017† (0.005)	0.066† (0.016)	0.043† (0.014)	0.019† (0.008)	0.081† (0.023)	0.064† (0.024)	-0.001 (0.009)	0.012 (0.031)	0.017 (0.027)	0.009 (0.017)	-0.005 (0.049)	0.051 (0.054)
10–14 years since arrival	0.016† (0.007)	0.085† (0.023)	0.060† (0.022)	0.024† (0.012)	0.111† (0.035)	0.114† (0.039)	-0.002 (0.014)	0.040 (0.047)	0.002 (0.038)	-0.020 (0.025)	-0.038 (0.071)	0.008 (0.075)
15 or more years since arrival	0.022† (0.008)	0.097† (0.026)	0.072† (0.025)	0.029† (0.015)	0.124† (0.042)	0.138† (0.043)	-0.011 (0.015)	0.022 (0.053)	-0.001 (0.042)	-0.041 (0.029)	-0.038 (0.081)	-0.034 (0.079)
Sample Size	251,366	251,366	251,366	23,822	23,822	23,822	180,968	180,968	180,968	37,007	37,007	37,007

Notes: All models also include age, age squared, years of education, and indicators for married, employed, urban, region, and survey year. NHIS annual weights are used. Marginal effects are reported for all probit models. Standard errors are in parentheses.
† Statistically significant at the 10% level.

Table 6. Immigrant Cohort and Assimilation Effects of BMI for Men, by Race/Ethnic Origin

Variable	All Origins Log BMI	All Origins Overweight	All Origins Obese	Hispanic Log BMI	Hispanic Overweight	Hispanic Obese	White Log BMI	White Overweight	White Obese	Black Log BMI	Black Overweight	Black Obese
Cohort Effects												
Immigrated in 1980 or before	-0.040† (0.007)	-0.146† (0.025)	-0.089† (0.014)	-0.042† (0.013)	-0.165† (0.043)	-0.111† (0.029)	-0.029† (0.013)	-0.136† (0.051)	-0.105† (0.024)	-0.012 (0.021)	-0.076 (0.088)	-0.048 (0.074)
Immigrated in 1981–1985	-0.051† (0.005)	-0.158† (0.019)	-0.098† (0.010)	-0.052† (0.009)	-0.178† (0.032)	-0.111† (0.016)	-0.032† (0.009)	-0.108† (0.039)	-0.096† (0.020)	-0.021 (0.017)	-0.053 (0.068)	-0.090 (0.045)
Immigrated in 1986–1990	-0.055† (0.003)	-0.170† (0.011)	-0.104† (0.005)	-0.062† (0.005)	-0.200† (0.019)	-0.122† (0.009)	-0.038† (0.005)	-0.143† (0.021)	-0.098† (0.011)	-0.038† (0.011)	-0.070 (0.044)	-0.117† (0.020)
Immigrated in 1991–1995	-0.065† (0.003)	-0.172† (0.012)	-0.103† (0.006)	-0.082† (0.006)	-0.207† (0.020)	-0.127† (0.007)	-0.038† (0.006)	-0.127† (0.023)	-0.072† (0.014)	-0.050† (0.014)	-0.085† (0.050)	-0.103† (0.026)
Assimilation Effects												
5–9 years since arrival	-0.003 (0.004)	0.023 (0.015)	-0.006 (0.014)	-0.011† (0.007)	0.011 (0.024)	-0.021 (0.020)	0.002 (0.007)	0.058† (0.029)	0.032 (0.033)	-0.036† (0.014)	-0.103† (0.058)	-0.070 (0.043)
10–14 years since arrival	0.001 (0.006)	0.038† (0.022)	0.003 (0.021)	-0.008 (0.011)	0.044 (0.035)	-0.008 (0.031)	0.002 (0.012)	0.064 (0.043)	0.056 (0.051)	-0.032† (0.019)	-0.013 (0.079)	-0.084 (0.054)
15 or more years since arrival	0.018† (0.007)	0.085† (0.024)	0.053† (0.027)	0.006 (0.013)	0.072† (0.042)	0.027 (0.038)	0.021 (0.013)	0.107† (0.046)	0.130† (0.065)	-0.040† (0.022)	-0.006 (0.089)	-0.105 (0.052)
Sample Size	228,768	228,768	228,768	21,781	21,781	21,781	172,548	172,548	172,548	25,931	25,931	25,931

Notes: All models also include age, age squared, years of education, and indicators for married, employed, urban, region, and survey year. NHIS annual weights are used. Marginal effects are reported for all probit models. Standard errors are in parentheses.

†Statistically significant at the 10% level.

by 6.6 and 4.3 percentage points, respectively, as female immigrants pass from 0–4 to 5–9 years in the United States, but thereafter increases only by 3.1 percentage points for overweight and 2.9 percentage points for obesity. In contrast, male immigrants assimilate more slowly. The percentage of male immigrants designated overweight, relative to their level during the initial four years of U.S. residence, rises by 2.3 percentage points after 5–9 years, by 3.8 percentage points after 10–14 years, and by 8.5 percentage points after more than 15 years; obesity rates for this group stay virtually stagnant until after 15 years of U.S. residence, when they rise by 5.3 percentage points (although some of these effects are imprecisely estimated).

The overall assimilation patterns, however, mask some important differences by race. First, for female immigrants, only Hispanic immigrants converge to their native counterparts irrespective of the BMI measure considered. In other words, the results for the all-origins specification for female immigrants appear to be largely driven by Hispanic immigrants. Second, Hispanic male immigrants also converge to their native counterparts, but only in terms of overweight rates. Moreover, unlike for female immigrants, evidence shows that white male immigrants do assimilate in terms of overweight and obesity rates. After more than 15 years in the United States, white male immigrants narrow the immigrant-native overweight gap by 11 percentage points and more than eliminate the obesity gap. Finally, black immigrants do not assimilate in terms of BMI irrespective of gender. Caution, however, should be used in interpreting these results because of the small number of black immigrants.

Finally, BMI assimilation eventually erases the entire initial BMI advantage for all female immigrant arrival cohorts for the all origins and Hispanic samples and a substantial fraction of the initial BMI advantage for immigrant men for the all origins sample, and depending on the BMI measure for the Hispanic and white samples. For example, during their first four years in the United States, the 1981–1985 Hispanic cohort had an incidence of being overweight that was 12.0 (for women) and 17.8 (for men) percentage points below that of Hispanic natives. But after 15 years of U.S. residence, assimilation had more than completely eliminated the female gap and reduced the male gap by 7.2 percentage points. These results are consistent with an immigrant adjustment process as opposed to permanent cohort differences.

Overall, the general patterns found in terms of BMI (irrespective of the measure) mirror the patterns found for general health measures. Recent immigrants have lower BMIs and are healthier than natives but become heavier and less healthy with time in residence. This suggests that BMI, which is largely determined by diet and exercise,[21] is an important contributing factor for explaining the HIE.

Moreover, the overall results hide some important racial differences, particularly for Hispanic women. The high and increasing female Hispanic immigrant BMIs are particularly interesting when considered in conjunction with the health and poverty assimilation patterns, which are inconsistent with the Hispanic paradox, the finding of lower mortality rates among Hispanic immigrants despite their relatively low socioeconomic status (see Palloni and Arias 2003 and the references therein). Consistent with the paradox, Hispanic immigrant women are 2–11 percentage points (depending on their arrival cohort) more likely to be in poverty than their native-born counterparts upon arrival and do not converge

---

21. Unfortunately, separating the contributions of diet and exercise from each other is difficult because of data limitations. Two NHIS supplements (in 1990 and 1991) include information on exercise. However, given the essentially cross-sectional nature of these data, it is impossible to separately identify cohort and assimilation effects. However, simple comparisons of immigrant (combining cohort and assimilation factors) and native probabilities show that immigrant women are somewhat less likely to exercise regularly than native women, but no male differences are found. Although this evidence is somewhat difficult to interpret because of the inability to separate the cohort and assimilation effects, it does suggest that both diet and exercise play a role for women, while male BMI assimilation is likely largely driven by dietary changes with time in U.S. residence.

to native levels with time of residence (see footnote 18). Inconsistent with the paradox, however, Hispanic women have lower probabilities of poor health at entry into the United States but assimilate to, or beyond, natives' levels of poor health within 10 to 15 years after arrival. However, the declining relative health of Hispanic immigrant women does match closely with their rising BMIs and is consistent with the higher rates of diabetes among Hispanic women (see Jasso et al. 2004). Unlike female Hispanic immigrants, male Hispanic immigrants' lack of BMI assimilation seems at odds with their relatively high rates of death due to diabetes (Arias et al. 2003).

Checks of Robustness

One potential limitation of the preceding analysis is the use of predicted BMI measures based on the NHANES (see the section on data for a detailed discussion). To ensure that the predicted measures are not driving our cohort and assimilation effects, we reestimate Eq. (1) by using our unadjusted BMI measures (i.e., BMI based on self-reported weight and height from the NHIS). We find very similar results with the unadjusted measures (these results are available on request); thus, the patterns found are not an artifact of the BMI measure used.

Another concern is that some immigrants in our sample arrived in the United States as children. This may lead to cohort effects that are biased downward, or assimilation effects that are biased upward, because immigrants who came as children will more likely have health outcomes that more closely align with natives. In an attempt to control for this possibility, we reestimate Eq. (1), excluding immigrants who arrived before age 15. To determine the age of the immigrant at arrival, we used their current age and years since migration. For example, individuals who are 24 and have been in the United States for 12 years (the midpoint of the category 10–14 years since migration), were age 12 at arrival and are therefore excluded from the analysis. Because years since migration is open-ended at the top (i.e., 15 *or more* years since migration), we estimate two specifications: specification 1 top-codes the migration group with 15 or more years in the United States at 29 years, and specification 2 deletes the migration group with 15 or more years in the United States. The latter is a more conservative measure because we are able to exactly identify all individuals' ages at arrival.[22] The results are very similar to those presented in Tables 5 and 6, in which all immigrants are included. Thus, they are not reported here but are available upon request.

One may also be concerned that our female estimates partly reflect differential fertility rates across immigrant and native groups. Unfortunately, the person file in the NHIS does not report pregnancy status. Given this data limitation, we are unable to exclude pregnant women from the sample. To check the robustness of our results, we can, however, exclude women of childbearing age. While the estimated cohort and assimilation effects for women aged 35 and older are very similar to those reported in Table 5, some of the point estimates are statistically imprecise due to the substantial reduction in sample size associated with excluding all women under age 35 (these results are available on request).

A final concern is that we are not picking up assimilation but merely the trends in BMI in the country of origin. For example, Popkin and Gordon-Larsen (2004) showed that overweight trends in Mexico have grown several times faster than in the United States over the past few decades. Although we do not have direct evidence on trends in obesity in the immigrant's country of origin, we can proxy these trends by using the NHIS. Specifically, we examine the change in BMI for young, recent immigrants (those with 0–4 years of U.S. residency, who likely closely reflect the trends in their countries of origin) and compare them with the trends of young natives by gender, age, and race. We consider two age

---

22. We focus on the overall and Hispanic samples in this table because the white and black results are noisy even without these further exclusions. However, all results are similar for these samples and are available on request.

groups, 20–29 and 30–39. If the trends are similar, then it does not appear that the trends of the home country are biasing our results. Overall, immigrants have lower BMIs than their native counterparts in 1989, and both immigrants and natives see an increase in BMI from 1989 to 1996, but the rate of the increase is roughly similar for the two groups irrespective of gender or age group considered. In general, similar patterns are found by race, although the rate of increase at times is higher for natives depending on the racial group considered. Thus, it seems unlikely that trends, rather than assimilation, are driving our results (these results are available upon request).

CONCLUSION

It is well documented that immigrants are in better health upon arrival in the United States than their American counterparts but that this health advantage erodes over time. This phenomenon is known as the healthy immigrant effect, or HIE. We find support for the HIE in the NHIS by using three measures of health (self-reported health status, health conditions, and activity limitations). We also find substantial evidence that the BMI assimilation patterns of immigrants closely mirror self-reported health assimilation. Overall, immigrants arrive in the United States with lower BMIs than natives but then converge toward natives. However, this overall pattern is somewhat misleading. For example, while white female immigrants are indistinguishable from their native counterparts upon arrival, Hispanic female immigrants enter the United States with lower BMIs than native Hispanics and then converge toward native levels. On the other hand, male immigrants of all races/ethnic origins generally enter the United States lighter than natives and never fully assimilate.

Understanding the intricacies of the immigrant weight assimilation path may give us some insight into the causes of elevated U.S. weight levels. The fact that most immigrant groups arrive with lower BMIs than U.S. natives and then converge toward native levels suggests that the new cultural or environmental factors that immigrants are exposed to alter their behaviors. Unfortunately, their newly acquired eating habits and weight gain increase the probability of health problems and premature death, as well as raise health care costs.

Appendix Table A. Variable Definitions

Variable Name	Definition
Poor Health	= 1 if self-reported health status = 4 (fair) or 5 (poor)
Health Conditions	= 1 if 1 or more health conditions are reported
Activity Limitations	= 1 if activity or work is limited
Poverty	= 1 if below the NHIS poverty index
BMI	kilograms/meters^2
Overweight	= 1 if BMI 25+
Obese	= 1 if BMI 30+
Immigrated in 1980 or Before	Immigrated to the United States in or before 1980 (see the text for more detail)
Immigrated in 1981–1985	Immigrated to the United States between 1981 and 1985 (see the text for more detail)
Immigrated in 1986–1990	Immigrated to the United States between 1986 and 1990 (see the text for more detail)
Immigrated in 1991–1996	Immigrated to the United States between 1991 and 1996 (see the text for more detail)

(Appendix Table A, continued)

Variable Name	Definition
0–4 Years Since Arrival	Arrived in the United States 0–4 years ago
5–9 Years Since Arrival	Arrived in the United States 5–9 years ago
10–14 Years Since Arrival	Arrived in the United States 10–14 years ago
15 or More Years Since Arrival	Arrived in the United States 15 or more years ago
Age	Continuous measure from 20 to 64
Married	= 1 if married
Years of Education	Continuous measure from 0 to 18
Working/Employed	= 1 if worked in the past two weeks
Urban	= 1 if resides in a metropolitan statistical area

REFERENCES

Antecol, H., P. Kuhn, and S. Trejo. Forthcoming. "Assimilation via Prices or Quantities? Labor Market Institutions and Immigrant Earnings Growth in Australia, Canada, and the United States." *Journal of Human Resources*.

Arias, E., R.N. Anderson, H.-C. Kung, S.L. Murphy, and K.D. Kochanek. 2003. "Deaths: Final Data for 2001." *National Vital Statistics Reports*, Vol. 52, No. 3. Hyattsville, MD: National Center for Health Statistics. Available online at http://www.cdc.gov/nchs/data/nvsr/nvsr52/nvsr52_03.pdf

Averett, S. and S. Korenman. 1996. "The Economic Reality of the Beauty Myth." *Journal of Human Resources* 31:304–30.

Borjas, G.J. 1985. "Assimilation, Changes in Cohort Quality, and the Earnings of Immigrants." *Journal of Labor Economics* 3:463–89.

———. 1995. "Assimilation and Changes in Cohort Quality Revisited: What Happened to Immigrant Earnings in the 1980s?" *Journal of Labor Economics* 13:201–45.

Borjas, G.J. and L. Hilton. 1996. "Immigration and the Welfare State: Immigrant Participation in Means-Tested Entitlement Programs." *The Quarterly Journal of Economics* 111:575–604.

Borjas, G.J. and S. Trejo. 1991. "Immigration Participation in the Welfare System." *Industrial and Labor Relations Review* 44:195–211.

Bound, J., C. Brown, and N. Mathiowetz. 2001. "Measurement Error in Survey Data." Pp. 3705–843 in *Handbook of Econometrics*, Vol. 5, edited by J.J. Heckman and E.E. Leamer. New York: Springer-Verlag.

Cawley, J. 2000. "Body Weight and Women's Labor Market Outcomes." NBER Working Paper No. 7841. National Bureau of Economic Research, Cambridge, MA.

Chen, J., E. Ng, and R. Wilkins. 1996. "The Health of Canada's Immigrants in 1994–95." *Health Reports* 7(4):33–45.

Chiswick, B.R. 1986. "Is the New Immigration Less Skilled than the Old?" *Journal of Labor Economics* 4:168–92.

Chou, S.Y., M. Grossman, and H. Saffer. 2002. "An Economic Analysis of Adult Obesity: Results From the Behavioral Risk Factor Surveillance System." NBER Working Paper No. 9247. National Bureau of Economic Research, Cambridge, MA.

Costa, D.L. and R.H. Steckel. 1995. "Long-Term Trends in Health, Welfare, and Economic Growth in the United States." NBER Historical Working Paper No. 76. National Bureau of Economic Research, Cambridge, MA.

Cutler, D.M., E.L. Glaeser, and J.M. Shapiro. 2003. "Why Have Americans Become More Obese?" *Journal of Economic Perspectives* 17(3):93–118.

Deri, C. 2003. "Understanding the 'Healthy Immigrant Effect' in Canada." Working paper 0502E. Department of Economics, University of Ottawa, Ontario, Canada. Available online at http://www.socialsciences.uottawa.ca/eco/pdf/cahiers/0502E.pdf

Donovan, J., E. d'Espaignet, C. Metron, and M. van Ommeren. 1992. "Immigrants in Australia: A Health Profile." Australian Institute of Health and Welfare Ethnic Health Series, No 1. Canberra: AGPS.

Duleep, H.O. and M.C. Regets. 1994. "The Elusive Concept of Immigrant Quality." Working Paper No. PRIP-UI-28. Urban Institute, Washington, DC.

———. 1999. "Immigrants and Human Capital Investment?" *American Economic Review* 89: 186–91.

———. 2002. "The Elusive Concept of Immigrant Quality: Evidence From 1970–1990." IZA Discussion Paper, No. 631. Institute for the Study of Labor, Bonn, Germany.

Funkhouser, E. and S.J. Trejo. 1995. "The Labor Market Skills of Recent Male Immigrants: Evidence From the Current Population Survey." *Industrial and Labor Relations Review* 48:792–811.

Gordon-Larsen, P., K.M. Harris, D.S. Ward, and B.M. Popkin. 2003. "Acculturation and Overweight-Related Behaviors Among Hispanic Immigrants to the US: The National Longitudinal Study of Adolescent Health." *Social Science and Medicine* 57:2023–34.

Hamermesh, D.S. and J.E. Biddle. 1994. "Beauty and the Labor Market." *American Economic Review* 84:1174–94.

Himes, C. 2000. "Obesity, Disease, and Functional Limitation in Later Life." *Demography* 37: 73–82.

House, J.S., R.C. Kessler, A.R. Herzog, R.P. Mero, A.M. Kinney, and M.J. Breslow. 1990. "Age, Socioeconomic Status and Health." *The Milbank Quarterly* 68:383–411.

Hu, W.Y. 2000. "Immigrant Earning Assimilation: Estimates From Longitudinal Data." *American Economic Review* 90:368–72.

Jasso, G., D.S. Massey, M.R. Rosenzweig, and J.P. Smith. 2004. "Immigrant Health—Selectivity and Acculturation." Unpublished Manuscript. RAND. Available online at http://econwpa.wustl.edu/eps/lab/papers/0412/0412002.pdf

Kasl, S.V. and L. Berkman. 1983. "Health Consequences of The Experiences of Migration." *Annual Review of Public Health* 4:69–90.

Lakdawalla, D. and T. Philipson. 2002. "The Growth of Obesity and Technological Change: A Theoretical and Empirical Examination." NBER Working Paper No. 8946. National Bureau of Economic Research, Cambridge, MA.

LaLonde, R.J. and R.H. Topel. 1992. "The Assimilation of Immigrants in the U.S. Labor Market." Pp. 67–92 in *Immigration and the Work Force: Economic Consequences for the United States and Source Areas*, edited by G.J. Borjas and R.B. Freeman. Chicago: University of Chicago Press.

Laroche, M. 2000. "Health Status and Health Services Utilization of Canada's Immigrant and Non-Immigrant Populations." *Canadian Public Policy* 26(2):51–75.

Leclere, F.B., L. Jensen, and A.E. Biddlecom. 1994. "Health Care Utilization, Family Context, and Adaptation Among Immigrants to the United States." *Journal of Health and Social Behavior* 35:370–84.

Lee, L.F. and J.H. Sepanski. 1995. "Estimation of Linear and Nonlinear Errors in Variables Models Using Validation Data." *Journal of the American Statistical Association* 90(429):130–40.

Marmot, M.G., A.M. Adelstein, and L. Bulusu. 1984. "Lessons From the Study of Immigrant Mortality." *Lancet* 30:1455–57.

Marmot, M.G. and S.L. Syme. 1976. "Acculturation and Coronary Heart Disease in Japanese-Americans." *American Journal of Epidemiology* 104:225–47.

McDonald, J.T. 2003. "The Health of Immigrants to Canada." Unpublished manuscript. Department of Economics, University of New Brunswick, Fredericton.

———. 2004. "BMI and the Incidence of Being Overweight and Obese Among Canadian Immigrants: Is Acculturation Associated with Unhealthy Weight Gain?" Unpublished manuscript. Department of Economics, University of New Brunswick, Fredericton.

McDonald, J.T. and S. Kennedy. 2004. "Insights Into the 'Healthy Immigrant Effect': Health Status and Health Service Use of Immigrants to Canada." *Social Science and Medicine* 59:1613–27.

Pagan, J.A. and A. Davila. 1997. "Obesity, Occupational Attainment, and Earnings." *Social Science Quarterly* 78:756–70.

Palloni, A. and E. Arias. 2003. "A Re-Examination of the Hispanic Mortality Paradox." CDE Working Paper No. 2003-01. Center for Demography and Ecology, University of Wisconsin–Madison.

Perez, C.E. 2002. "Health Status and Health Behaviour Among Immigrants." *Health Reports* 13(Suppl.):1–12.

Philipson, T. 2001. "The World-Wide Growth in Obesity: An Economic Research Agenda." *Health Economics* 10(1):1–7.

Philipson, T. and R.A. Posner. 1999. "The Long-Run Growth in Obesity as a Function of Technological Change." NBER Working Paper No. 7423. National Bureau of Economic Research, Cambridge, MA.

Popkin, B.M. and P. Gordon-Larsen. 2004. "The Nutrition Transition: Worldwide Obesity Dynamics and the Determinant." *International Journal of Obesity* 28:S2–S9.

Popkin, B.M. and J.R. Udry. 1998. "Adolescent Obesity Increases Significantly in Second and Third Generation U.S. Immigrants: The National Longitudinal Study of Adolescent Health." *Journal of Nutrition* 128:701–706.

Register, C.A. and D.R. Williams. 1990. "Wage Effects of Obesity Among Young Workers." *Social Science Quarterly* 71:130–41.

Schoeni, R.F. 1997. "New Evidence on the Economic Progress of Foreign-Born Men in the 1970s and 1980s." *Journal of Human Resources* 32:683–740.

———. 1998. "Labor Market Assimilation of Immigrant Women." *Industrial and Labor Relations Review* 51:483–504.

Sorlie, P.D., E. Backlund, N.J. Johnson, and E. Rogot. 1993. "Mortality by Hispanic Status in the United States." *Journal of American Medical Association* 270(20):2464–68.

Stephen, E.H., K. Foote, G.E. Hendershot, C.A. Schoenborn. 1994. "Health of the Foreign-Born Population." *Advance Data From Vital and Health Statistics* 241:1–10.

Sturm, R. 2002. "The Effects of Obesity, Smoking and Drinking on Medical Problems and Costs." *Health Affairs* 21:245–53.

Vega, W. and H. Amaro. 1994. "Latino Outlook: Good Health, Uncertain Prognosis." *Annual Review of Public Health* 15:39–67.

Wolf, A. and G. Colditz. 1998. "Current Estimates of the Economic Cost of Obesity in the United States." *Obesity Research* 6:97–106.

[17]

Health of Immigrants in European Countries

Aïda Solé-Auró
University of Barcelona

Eileen M. Crimmins
University of Southern California

> The health of older immigrants can have important consequences for needed social support and demands placed on health systems. This paper examines health differences between immigrants and the native-born populations aged 50 years and older in 11 European countries. We examine differences in functional ability, disability, disease presence, and behavioral risk factors for immigrants and nonimmigrants using data from the Survey of Health, Aging and Retirement in Europe (SHARE) database. Among the 11 European countries, migrants generally have worse health than the native population. In these countries, there is a little evidence of the "healthy migrant" at ages 50 years and over. In general, it appears that growing numbers of immigrants may portend more health problems in the population in subsequent years.

INTRODUCTION

In recent decades, with the development and expansion of the European Union, emigrating within Europe is not as difficult as in the past and international borders are no longer restrictive to many individuals. This has resulted in a dramatic increase in immigration rates for many countries in Europe (Österle, 2007). It is of importance to social planning to understand whether immigrants differ from the native-born population in ways that will affect the demand for social support and health care. This is particularly true for older immigrants who are approaching the age of retirement and the age when healthcare costs may increase. Our aim is to examine the health of immigrants relative to the native-born populations in the population aged 50 years and older in 11 European countries. Ten of these countries are members of the European Union.

While immigration from within the European Union accounts for some of the immigration to these 11 European countries, movement of people into

---

[1] Support was provided by federal grants from the Spanish Ministry of Education and Science, FEDER grant SEJ2007-63298, and the U.S. National Institutes of Health, grant P30 AG17265.

© 2008 by the Center for Migration Studies of New York. All rights reserved.
DOI: 10.1111/j.1747-7379.2008.00150.x

the Union from poorer countries characterizes a significant portion of European migration over recent decades (Massey *et al.*, 1993). People nearing retirement age generally migrated decades ago as migration is most likely to occur in the early working ages, often motivated by the economic possibilities at the destination (Karras and Chiswick, 1999; Barrell, Guillemineau, and Liadze, 2006). In general, immigrants have lower socioeconomic status than the populations into which they move (Ringbäck *et al.*, 1999). The relative health of immigrants is less clear a priori. Some evidence from both the United States and Europe suggests that immigrants may be healthier than might be expected given their social status (Razum and Twardella, 2002; Jasso *et al.*, 2004); on the other hand, other research in Europe has found mixed patterns of immigrant health depending on country of origin (Gadd *et al.*, 2006; Sundquist and Li, 2006).

BACKGROUND

Between 1950 and 1982, the number of foreign residents increased from 3.1 to 11.2 million in the traditional receiving countries (Belgium, France, Germany, Luxembourg, the Netherlands, Sweden, and Switzerland), which accounted for 70–80 percent of all European immigrants over the three decades (Maillat, 1987). In the early part of this period large numbers of immigrants were still being resettled after World War II. There was also significant immigration from once colonized countries in Asia, Africa, and the Middle East to the original colonial power (Fassmann and Munz, 1992; Zimmermann, 1994). By the 1960s, there was extensive migration from Southern to Northern Europe. Spain and Portugal were the most important European emigration countries, followed by Greece and Yugoslavia; Sweden, France, the United Kingdom, and Switzerland were the main poles of attraction. In the 1980s, the Southern Europe countries themselves became places of immigration. Africa generated new surges of immigration to Greece, Italy, Spain, and Portugal as well as to traditional receiving countries (Salt, 1989). Most of the people whom we study here, now 50 and over, would have migrated to the countries where they are now living in their prime working years or before 1980. Since that time, migration from Eastern Europe has been a significant source or immigrants for many countries in the European Union.

Many recent studies in the United States have noted that immigrants from Mexico have better health than nonimmigrants or better than expected health given their social status (Cho *et al.*, 2004; Palloni and Arias, 2004; Crimmins *et al.*, 2007). The relatively good health of the Hispanic immigrant population is known as the "Hispanic paradox." The paradox is that a socioeconomically deprived population has health as good as that of the mainstream population. European researchers have also noted an "immigrant paradox" which describes the better than expected health of some immigrant populations (Ronellenfitsch and Razum, 2004).

In Europe the observed health differences between native-born and immigrants vary by country of study and origin of migrants and also gender. In Sweden male immigrant groups appear to have worse mortality and heart disease than Swedes but better than the populations they came from (Gadd et al., 2003; Sundquist and Li, 2006). This work also finds that the relative health of immigrant populations, however, may depend on area of origin. Marmot, Adelstein, and Bulusu (1984) reports that in England and Wales, migrants from Europe have better health than the native-born, but female migrants from the Caribbean and Africa had higher mortality than natives. In France, male immigrants from Morocco have lower mortality than native-born men but women from Morocco have higher mortality than French women (Khlat and Courbage, 1996).

Jasso et al. (2004) have emphasized the effects of both selectivity and acculturation on immigrant health. Initially, immigrants may be selected for good health from the population they are leaving; but as time since migration increases, their health may become more like the population in the country where they live (Williams, 1993). So the health of immigrants relative to the native population may depend on the age at migration and the age when health is examined. For instance, immigrants from Eastern Europe to Germany had better health than native West Germans initially; however, five years after immigration the health differences disappeared (Stronks, 2003) and at the same time the socioeconomic disadvantage of immigrants compared to native Germans had diminished. This reduction in differences may occur because some health conditions appear later in life and would not be related to the propensity to migrate or because over time the immigrants become more like the population at their destinations in socioeconomic status and health-related behaviors (Stronks, 2003; Lopez-Gonzalez, Aravena, and Hummer, 2005).

There are many reasons why there may not be a consistent pattern of health differences between immigrants and native-born populations across time and place. First, migration occurs for a variety of reasons and immigrant characteristics may differ with those reasons and according to the obstacles to be overcome in migrating. It is also true that differentials between immigrants and the native populations may differ across dimensions of health (Jasso et al., 2004; Hayward, Warner, and Crimmins, 2007). For instance, there may be differentials in disability but not mortality because immigrants who are ill may return to their native countries for treatment or to die (Palloni and Arias, 2004). It is also possible that differences in use of healthcare resulting from lack of access or language barriers could result in differences in the progression of health problems as well as reporting of health problems. For example, if immigrants do not use the medical system in the same way as the native population, they may not know they have diseases. In addition, if immigrants are less likely to be treated for some conditions, they could die more quickly and paradoxically have a lower prevalence of a condition than the surviving population. It is also possible that data quality may differ between immigrants and the native population (Smith and Bradshaw, 2006).

There are many ways that immigrants are likely to differ from native populations that may be related to health differentials that are important in understanding observed differentials. Immigrants tend to have lower socioeconomic status than the populations into which they move because they are moving for improved job opportunities. Worse health could be due to the psychological stress of living in a new environment or stress resulting from discrimination in the new living situation (Silveira *et al.*, 2002). The foreign-born are also less likely to have adequate health care coverage or familiarity with and established connections to health care systems (Carrasquillo, Carrasquillo, and Shea, 2000; Tovar *et al.*, 2007). Health behaviors may also affect population health differences. Immigrants can have healthier or less healthy life styles than native-born members of the population (Carrasco-Garrido *et al.*, 2007).

Our study affords a new examination of disparities in health and health behavior between immigrants and the native-born population in 11 different European countries. We are interested in whether there are systematic health differences between these groups and whether differences are a reflection of socioeconomic differences.

DATA AND METHODS

Data

We use data from the Survey of Health, Aging and Retirement (SHARE), which provides information on health, socioeconomic status, and social and family networks of individuals aged 50 and over in participating countries. The first wave of this survey was collected in 2004/2005 in 11 European countries; additional waves are being planned and additional countries are now being added. While this is a multicountry project, countries conducted their own national surveys using a common questionnaire translated into the appropriate

TABLE 1
SAMPLE CHARACTERISTICS BY COUNTRY, GENDER, AND IMMIGRANT STATUS, 2004

Country	Total (N)	Immigrants	% of immigrants Total	% of immigrants Males	% of immigrants Females	% of Immigrants with Citizenship	Mean Year of Immigration
Austria	1,849	173	9.4	41.0	59.0	73.5	1963
Belgium	3,649	253	6.9	46.6	53.4	50.0	1960
Denmark	1,615	59	3.7	47.5	52.5	66.7	1963
France	3,038	454	15.1	46.3	53.7	65.1	1964
Germany	2,941	550	18.7	47.6	52.4	87.3	1961
Greece	2,669	64	2.4	39.0	61.0	90.3	1953
Italy	2,508	37	1.5	27.0	73.0	100.0	1962
Netherlands	2,865	173	6.0	46.8	53.2	82.5	1967
Spain	2,353	52	2.2	32.7	67.3	50.0	1980
Sweden	2,997	250	8.4	41.2	58.8	67.6	1965
Switzerland	960	155	16.2	45.8	54.2	52.9	1964
Total	27,444	2,220					

Source: SHARE database, 2004 (Individuals aged 50 and over).

languages; The Mannheim Research Institute for the Economics of Aging in Germany coordinates this collaborative effort. Our study includes information from the 11 countries, which provide a balanced representation of the various regions in Europe, ranging from Scandinavia through Central Europe to the Mediterranean. The names of the individual countries are shown in Table 1. In comparing countries we need to be mindful of some differences in the quality of the surveys. Household response rates vary markedly across the countries from a low of 39% in Switzerland to a high of 81% in France; and individual response rates range from 74% in Spain to a high of 93% in France (SHARE, 2007).

Measuring Immigration Status, Health, and Other Variables in SHARE

Each survey respondent indicates whether he/she was born in the country of residence where the survey is taking place. This response is used to divide the residents of each country into the native-born and the foreign-born or immigrants. Individuals born outside the country where they are interviewed are asked what year they came to the country. While people indicate where they were born, these data are not yet available for analysis.

The SHARE datasets contain comparable indicators of disease, disability, and functioning, as well as health behaviors. We use three indicators of problems with functioning and disability: self-reported difficulty performing at least one of 10 tasks related to mobility, strength, and endurance (Nagi, 1976), difficulty doing at least one of six activities of daily living (ADLs) indicating ability to care for oneself, and difficulty with at least one of seven instrumental activities of daily living (IADLs) needed for independent living. The ten indicators of functioning ability include walking one block, climbing several flights of stairs, climbing one flight of stairs, sitting for about 2 hours, getting up from a chair, lifting or carrying weights over 10 pounds, stooping, kneeling or crouching, picking up a dime from a table, reaching or extending arms, and pulling or pushing large objects. ADL functions include walking across a room, getting in and out of bed, bathing or showering, eating (such as cutting up food), dressing (including putting on shoes and socks), and using the toilet (including getting up or down). IADL abilities include using a map to figure out how to get around in a strange place, preparing a hot meal, shopping for groceries, making telephone calls, taking medications, doing work around the house or garden, and managing money, such as paying bills and keeping track of expenses.

In addition information on the presence of seven chronic diseases is reported in response to the question "Has a doctor ever told you that you had any of the following conditions?" Chronic medical measures include high blood pressure, diabetes, cancer, lung disease, heart disease, stroke, and arthritis. We use a variable indicating the presence of two or more of these chronic diseases in our analysis. Self-perceived health is assessed using the question "Would you say your health is excellent, very good, good, fair or poor?" We group self-perceived health into two categories: good or very good health and less than good health. Each of the health indicators is coded as a dichotomous variable.

We also examine indicators of weight and smoking behavior. Information on height and weight is converted into body mass index (BMI), which is categorized as overweight (BMI ≥ 25) or not overweight. Smoking is coded as being a current smoker or not.

In order to examine how the socioeconomic status (SES) of immigrants is related to their relative health status, we control for education in our analysis. Education is the most appropriate indicator of SES when one is examining people across a wide range of ages and across multiple countries. Since education systems vary across the countries, SHARE provides an equivalence scale based on the International Standard Classification of Education (ISCED) designed for UNESCO in the early 1970s (UNESCO, 1997). Education is categorized into seven categories: pre-primary education, primary education (first stage of basic education), lower secondary education (second stage of basic education), upper secondary education, post-secondary non tertiary education, first stage of tertiary education (not leading directly to an advanced research qualification), and second stage of tertiary education (leading to an advanced research qualification). To make this a continuous variable we code each category at its midpoint to indicate years of education.

We also examine differences in labor force status of immigrants and nonimmigrants using responses to the question "How would you describe your current situation?": retired, employed or self-employed (including working for a family business), unemployed, permanently sick or disabled, or homemaker. We group respondents into two categories: employed or not employed. Moreover, we examine differences in healthcare usage among immigrants and the native-born population that might be relevant to their reports of diseases. Healthcare usage is reported using the following question: "During the last 12 months, about how many times in total have you seen or talked to a medical doctor about your health?" We group healthcare usage into one or more visits versus no visits.

The Sample

Table 1 shows the size and composition of the SHARE sample in each country. The data used for this analysis include information from 27,444 individuals living in 11 European countries who have provided responses for all variables used in the analysis. The sample is composed of 12,552 males (996 immigrants) and 14,892 females (1,224 immigrants). There are 758 individuals eliminated from the sample because of missing data on variables used in the analysis, leaving an analytic sample of 26,686 individuals. Those who are excluded from our analysis are significantly more likely to be female (70.7%) than included individuals (53.8%). The average age of those nonincluded is older (69) than that of the nonmissing (65). Among the 2,220 immigrants, 3.1% have missing information. If we compare missing and nonmissing immigrants in terms of age, those who are excluded from our sample are significantly older (average 68) than included individuals (average 64). Also, the missing immigrants are significantly more likely to be female than the nonmissing immigrants.

The percentage of immigrants in the population age 50 and over in each country ranges from 18.7 percent in Germany to 1.5 percent in Italy (Table 1). The percentage of immigrants is highest in Northern European countries – Germany, France, and Switzerland; and lowest in Southern European countries – Italy, Spain, and Greece. In all countries, the number of immigrant females exceeds that of immigrant males; the countries with the highest proportion of female immigrants are Italy, Greece, and Spain. Since this is an older group, the preponderance of women may reflect mortality differences more than past differences in immigration. Immigrants are most likely to be citizens in Italy, Greece, and Germany and least likely in Belgium, Spain, and Switzerland.

While the sample ranges in age from 50 to 104, the average age of the entire sample is 65 years old. However, immigrants are a year younger on average (64). Immigrants from Austria, Belgium, Germany, and Greece have a higher mean age than nonimmigrants in their countries (data not shown). The nonimmigrant individuals in the seven remaining countries are older on average than the immigrants. The difference in mean age between immigrants and native-born populations ranges from 5.5 years to less than one year. We also indicate the mean year of migration for immigrants in each country in Table 1. As expected, in most countries the average time of immigration for those who are now in their mid-60s in age was about forty years before the survey in the mid-1960s when they were about 20. There are two notable exceptions to this. In Spain immigrants are much more recent, with an average year of migration of 1980. On the other hand, immigrants in Greece have been there since 1953 on average, 50 years before the survey.

In terms of education, immigrants living in Belgium, France, Germany, Netherlands, and Switzerland have significantly less education than the native-born residents (data not shown). On the other hand, the greatest difference is in the other direction in Spain where immigrants have almost 4.5 years more education than nonimmigrants. This indicates the tremendous differences in the characteristics of the immigrant population relative to the native-born population across these countries.

Immigrants living in Spain, Denmark, France, Italy, Netherlands, and Sweden are more likely to be in the labor force than nonimmigrants, perhaps due to the fact that immigrants in these countries are younger than nonimmigrants. For example, older immigrants to Spain are twice as likely to be working as nonimmigrants. On the other hand, immigrants to Germany are less likely to work than nonimmigrants.

Methods

We used logistic regressions to examine the effect of being an immigrant on each of the indicators of health and health behavior. Each country is examined separately. We estimate two models: the first shows the odds ratios indicating the relative likelihood that immigrants are in each poor health category with age and sex controlled. These controls adjust for compositional differences that might affect health independent of immigrant status. Then we add education as a control to see how the odds ratios indicating the link between immigrant status and health are changed with this added control, which adjusts for socioeconomic differences between immigrants and nonimmigrants.

TABLE 2
PERCENT IN TOTAL SAMPLE WITH HEALTH PROBLEMS, LOW SELF-PERCEIVED HEALTH, AND RISK FACTORS

Country	Functioning Difficulties	ADL Difficulties	IADL Difficulties	Chronic Diseases	Low Self-Perceived Health	Current Smokers	Overweight
Austria	52.5	9.2	17.4	33.4	39.2	17.9	61.4
Belgium	48.3	12.0	18.1	46.7	31.9	17.3	59.8
Denmark	42.3	10.3	17.3	43.4	31.3	31.2	51.8
France	48.5	11.8	16.5	42.4	38.2	14.3	54.6
Germany	53.8	9.5	14.1	40.3	45.5	18.6	61.1
Greece	54.4	9.0	18.7	39.9	37.5	25.3	67.3
Italy	52.3	10.7	14.7	45.4	51.8	18.2	61.7
Netherlands	42.0	8.4	16.1	34.9	32.1	24.4	56.8
Spain	57.4	13.5	25.6	51.1	51.5	15.1	68.9
Sweden	45.3	9.7	16.1	42.1	36.6	17.1	53.9
Switzerland	38.7	6.9	8.6	28.2	20.1	19.6	50.3

Data: SHARE database, 2004 (Individuals aged 50 and over).
Functioning: difficulties performing at least one out of ten tasks; ADL: difficulty performing at least one activity of daily living; IADL: difficulty performing at least one instrumental activity of daily living; Chronic diseases: two or more chronic diseases; Low self-perceived health: less than good health; Smoking: current smokers; and Overweight: BMI ≥ 25.

RESULTS

Descriptive Analysis

First, we examine the variability across countries in the percent of the population reporting each of the health problems (Table 2). The prevalence of functioning problems ranges from just over a third to over half the population (38.7–57.4 percent). The prevalence of ADL limitations ranges from 6.9 to 13.5 percent; IADL disability ranges between 8.6 and 25.6 percent. The percent with at least two chronic diseases varies from a low of 28.2 to a high of 51.1 percent. Spain has the highest prevalence of health problems according to many of these indicators, while Switzerland in many cases has the lowest percentage of its population suffering from these health problems. Overall self-reported health aligns somewhat with these indicators of functioning problems, disability, and disease. The Swiss rate their health the highest with only 20.1% saying health is less than good. On the other hand, people in Spain and Italy are most likely to rate their health as less than good. Health behaviors also vary across these countries. Denmark, Greece, and Spain have the highest levels of current smoking. Overweight is highest in Greece, Spain, Austria, and Germany (Michaud, Soest, and Andreyeva, 2007).

Table 3 addresses whether there is a difference between immigrants and the native-born in each country in the likelihood of having each type of health problem, risky behavior, and low self-perceived health. Odds ratios from logistic regressions within each country are presented. As indicated above, model 1 is

TABLE 3
ODDS RATIOS INDICATING RELATIVE LIKELIHOOD THAT IMMIGRANTS HAVE HEALTH PROBLEMS AND RISKY HEALTH BEHAVIORS, WITH CONTROLS FOR AGE AND SEX AND ADDING CONTROLS FOR EDUCATION, 2004

Country	Functioning Difficulty M1	M2	ADL Difficulty M1	M2	IADL Difficulty M1	M2	Two Chronic Diseases M1	M2	Low Self-Perceived Health M1	M2	Current Smoker M1	M2	Overweight M1	M2
Austria	0.78	0.80	0.78	0.79	1.04	1.02	0.66*	0.66*	0.84	0.88	1.71*	1.73*	0.89	0.90
Belgium	1.04	1.03	1.04	0.94	1.12	1.03	1.00	0.93	1.12	1.00	1.29	1.31	1.14	1.12
Denmark	1.95*	2.20*	1.32	1.58	1.88	2.30*	1.32	1.38	1.44	1.74	1.08	1.13	0.84	0.90
France	1.23	1.15	0.99	0.91	1.49*	1.39*	0.89	0.85	2.06*	1.88*	1.18	1.31	0.99	0.91
Germany	1.20	1.18	1.22	1.14	1.08	1.02	1.26*	1.23*	1.47*	1.41*	0.95	0.91	1.41*	1.39*
Greece	1.12	1.13	1.72	1.78	0.86	0.96	0.93	0.98	1.48	1.77	0.94	0.96	1.24	1.34
Italy	1.10	1.25	0.50	0.57	0.63	0.80	1.31	1.45	0.55	0.69	1.58	1.55	0.37*	0.43*
Netherlands	1.43*	1.43*	1.42	1.42	1.12	1.12	0.91	0.91	2.43*	2.44*	1.15	1.11	0.95	0.92
Spain	0.83	1.19	0.80	1.17	0.58	1.06	1.60	2.01*	0.53*	0.76	1.10	1.01	0.37*	0.50*
Sweden	1.32*	1.44*	1.25	1.47	1.19	1.22	1.28	1.43*	2.04*	2.29*	0.94	1.03	1.45*	1.61*
Switzerland	1.48*	1.58*	2.12*	2.48*	1.91*	1.84*	1.52*	1.52*	2.19*	2.24*	1.06	1.13	0.98	0.95

Data: SHARE database (Individuals aged 50 and over).
Model 1: controlled for age and sex.
Model 2: controlled for age, sex, and education.
Functioning: difficulties performing at least one out of ten tasks; ADL: difficulty performing at least one activity of daily living; IADL: difficulty performing at least one instrumental activity of daily living; Chronic diseases: two or more chronic diseases; Low self-perceived health: less than good health; Smoking: current smokers; and Overweight: BMI ≥ 25.
*p < 0.05.

run with controls for age and sex. The interpretation of the results for Switzerland is that immigrants are 2.1 times as likely as nonimmigrants to have ADL problems, assuming that the age and sex structure of the migrant and nonmigrant populations are the same.

There is no indication that immigrants have fewer functioning problems or less disability than the native populations. All significant differences between immigrants and nonimmigrants indicate worse functioning and disability for immigrants. Swiss, Swedish, Danish, and Dutch immigrants are more likely to have functioning difficulties than the native population in each of these countries. The relative likelihood is highest in Denmark where the immigrants are almost twice as likely to have functioning problems. As indicated above, Swiss immigrants are twice as likely as the native-born population to have ADL difficulties. In no other country is there a significant difference between immigrants and the native-born in ADL problems.

In two countries, Switzerland and France, immigrants are 1.5 to 2 times as likely to have IADL difficulties as nonimmigrants. Because of the nature of IADL activities, these differences may relate to social and cultural integration as well as underlying functioning problems.

Immigrants in Switzerland are 1.5 times more likely to have at least two chronic diseases than nonimmigrants. In contrast, Austrian immigrants are one-third less likely to have chronic diseases than nonimmigrants. This is one of the few indicators of better health among an immigrant population than a native-born population. Chronic diseases are reported in response to a question whether a "doctor ever told you" about a disease. If immigrants were less likely to go to doctors, they would be less likely to know of a disease. However, when we examine the use of healthcare by immigrants and nonimmigrants we find that it is very similar in most of the countries and it is unlikely to be a source of differential reporting (Table 4). Only in Austria is there a substantial difference in the reports of seeing a doctor in the last year; in Austria, immigrants are about 6 percent less likely to report a doctor visit. This may be related to the finding that Austrian immigrants are less likely to report having diseases.

Self-perceived health can be viewed as the individual's self-assessment of the importance of problems with functioning, disability, and disease. In five countries, immigrants are more likely to have worse self-perceived health than nonimmigrants (Table 3). These are the countries where immigrants have had more functioning problems, disability, or disease (Switzerland, Netherlands, Germany, Sweden, and France). Only in Spain do immigrants perceive their health to be better than the native-born population.

TABLE 4
PERCENT SEEING DOCTOR IN LAST 12 MONTHS

Country	Immigrants	Native-Born (NB)	Difference (Immigrants − NB)
Austria	80.4	86.3	−5.9
Belgium	93.1	92.7	0.4
Denmark	87.5	81.3	6.2
France	94.1	93.5	0.6
Germany	92.5	92.1	0.4
Greece	77.4	78.7	−1.3
Italy	81.8	83.9	−2.1
Netherlands	85.1	81.3	3.8
Spain	87.7	88.9	−1.2
Sweden	77.1	77.3	−0.2
Switzerland	85.7	84.0	1.7

Data: SHARE database (Individuals aged 50 and over).
*Significantly differed from native-born at the 0.05 level.

We also examine differences between immigrants and nonimmigrants in smoking and being overweight to see how immigrants differ from the native-born populations in health habits (Table 3). Immigrants in Austria exhibit a 71 percent higher likelihood of being current smokers compared to nonimmigrants. In all other countries, smoking behavior does not differ significantly between immigrants and the native-born population. Immigrants are more likely to be overweight than nonimmigrants in Germany and Sweden and less likely to be overweight in Spain and Italy.

In the second model under each health outcome, we examine the differences between immigrants and nonimmigrants adding a control for education in order to see if the worse health of immigrants is due to their lower levels of education or SES. When we include the education variable, the results do not change much; a couple of coefficients become significant and a couple become nonsignificant. Functioning problems are still lower for immigrants than nonimmigrants in four countries. In terms of IADL, the effect of controlling for education is to raise the difference in IADL difficulties to significance for persons in Denmark. On the other hand, the difference becomes nonsignificant in France. Controls for education also result in significantly higher levels of chronic diseases among immigrants in Sweden and Spain. Education control also reduces the difference between migrants and nonmigrants in Spanish self-perceived health to nonsignificance. In general, the differences are relatively stable with controls for education meaning that differences in socioeconomic status between immigrants and nonimmigrants do not appear to be the cause of health differences.

DISCUSSION

The debate about the effect of immigrant populations on demands for health and social services has gone on for many years. While we cannot examine the differences between immigrants and the native populations at the time of immigration, we do examine health differences at the ages when health tends to deteriorate and place more demands on the healthcare system. Where there are differences in health between migrants and nonmigrants in these 11 European countries, migrants generally have worse health. In these countries there is little evidence of the "healthy migrant" at ages 50 and over.

Immigrants appear relatively worse off than native-born individuals in terms of self-perceived health and functioning in France, Germany, Netherlands, Sweden, and Switzerland. These countries tend to be the countries with the best overall levels of the health indicators for the entire population, that is, the countries with good functioning and low levels of ADL and IADL problems. For example, Switzerland has the lowest percent with ADL and IADL problems (6.9 and 8.6, respectively) and the highest likelihood of immigrants relative to the native-born population having ADL and IADL difficulties (almost twice as high in both cases). In reverse, Spain has the highest level of ill health according to many of the indicators studied, but immigrants to Spain have lower levels of some health problems than the native-born. For instance, Spain and Italy have immigrants who are less likely than native-born to be overweight. These findings point to the fact that both the health of the native-born population and the health of the immigrants contribute to the observed health differences.

We also addressed the question of whether there were significant differences by country in the health of immigrants. We limited our analysis to immigrants to see if there were countries where immigrants appeared to be healthier or less healthy than immigrants in other countries (data not shown). We do not find evidence of differences. For instance, immigrants to Switzerland do not appear to have worse health than immigrants to other countries.

Controls for education in our analysis do not affect our results indicating that the worse health of immigrants in these countries is not due to their lower levels of education or SES. In addition, differences between native-born and immigrants in healthcare use do not appear to be common in these countries. On the other hand, we do not know many ways in which immigrants and native-born might differ. For instance, we do not know how the jobs that people worked over their lives differed. It is possible that immigrants were more likely to perform manual labor than the native-born resulting in the higher levels of functioning loss and disability observed in some countries.

There are some limitations to our results. We must note that migrants observed at one point in time represent those who remain. People may have died at different rates and the group of immigrants remaining may be more or less selected than the native-born population. Some immigrants may have returned to their origins after becoming ill, another selection process relating to observed differences. In addition, there are differences in the response rates to the surveys across countries, which could affect our results. We should note again that the lowest response levels were in Switzerland. Differential response by people with and without health problems among immigrants and non-immigrants may affect observed differences.

As indicated above, we do not have information on the area of origin of migrants and how that differs across countries. The migration streams during which these European migrants moved differed across the 11 countries. For instance, the Southern European countries of Spain, Greece, and Italy were sending immigrants to the Northern countries in the 1960s. In the 1980s the characteristics of migrants to European countries changed and many migrants were motivated to move by political conflicts, civil wars, and economic crises in the Middle East, South America, and Africa. Migrants to Spain studied here are especially likely to be from these new streams (Massey, 1990). Future research should examine the link between health of migrants and the place of origin.

The results of this study should be useful in expanding our understanding of current health issues facing Europe, and provide baseline information from which policy-makers can predict the impact of growing immigration on the health and social security needs of a growing and aging immigrant population. In general, growing numbers of immigrants may be linked to more health problems in the population in subsequent years.

REFERENCES

Barrell, R., C. Guillemineau, and I. Liadze
2006 "Migration in Europe." *National Institute Economic Review* 198:36–39.

Carrasco-Garrido, P., A. Gil, V. Hernández, and R. Jiménez-García
2007 "Health Profiles, Lifestyles and Use of Health Resources by the Immigrant Population Resident in Spain." *European Journal of Public Health* 17:503–507.

Carrasquillo, O., A. I. Carrasquillo, and S. Shea
2000 "Health Insurance Coverage of Immigrants Living in the United Statues: Differences by Citizenship Status and Country of Origin." *American Journal of Public Health* 90(6):917–923.

Cho, Y., W. P. Frisbie, R. A. Hummer, and R. G. Rogers
2004 "Nativity, Duration of Residence and the Health of Hispanic Adults in the United States." *The International Migration Review New York* 38(1):184.

Crimmins, E. M. et al.
2007 "Hispanic Paradox in Biological Risk Profiles." *American Journal of Public Health, Washington* 97(7):1305–1310.

Fassmann, H., and R. Munz
1992 "Patterns and Trends of International Migration in Western Europe." *Population and Development Review* 18(3):457–480.

Gadd, M., S. E. Johansoon, J. Sundquist, and P. Wändell
2006 "Are There Differences in All-cause and Coronary Heart Disease Mortality between Immigrants in Sweden and in Their Country of Birth? A Follow-up Study of Total Populations." *BMC Public Health* 6:102.

——— 2003 "Morbidity in Cardiovascular Disease in Immigrants in Sweden" *Journal of Internal Medicine* 254:236–243.

Hayward, M. D., D. F. Warner, and E. M. Crimmins
2007 "Does Longer Life Mean Better Health? Not for Native-Born Mexican Americans in the Health and Retirement Survey." *Springer* 7:85–95.

Jasso, G., S. D. Massey, M. R. Rosenzweig, and J. P. Smith
2004 "Immigrant Health: Selectivity and Acculturation." In *Critical Perspectives on Racial and Ethnic Differences in Health in Late Life*. Ed. Norman B. Anderson. Washington, DC: National Academies Press. Pp. 227–266.

Karras, J., and C. U. Chiswick
1999 "Macroeconomic Determinants of Migration: The Case of Germany 1964–1988." *International Migration Review* 37(4):657–677.

Khlat, M., and Y. Courbage
1996 "Mortality and Causes of Death of Moroccans in France, 1979–91." *Population* 8:59–94.

Lopez-Gonzalez, L., V. C. Aravena, and R. A. Hummer
2005 "Immigrant Acculturation, Gender and Health Behavior: A Research Note." *Social Forces* 84(1):581–593.

Maillat, D.
1987 "Long-Term Aspects of International Migration Flows: The Experience of European Receiving Countries." *The Future of Migration*. Paris: Organization for Economic Co-operation and Development (OECD). Pp. 38–63.

Marmot, M. G., A. M. Adelstein, and L. Bulusu
1984 "Immigrant Mortality in England and Wales 1970–78. Causes of Death by Country of Birth." *Studies on Medical and Population Subjects* 47:145.

Massey, D. S.
1990 "The Social and Economic Origins of Immigration." *Annals of the American Academy of Political and Social Science* 510:60–72.

——— et al.
1993 "Theories of International Migration: A Review and Appraisal." *Population and Development Review* 19(3):431–466.

Michaud, P. C., A. Soest, and T. Andreyeva
2007 *Cross-Country Variation in Obesity Patterns among Older Americans and Europeans*. Santa Monica, CA: RAND Corporation. Working paper.

Nagi, S. Z.
1976 "An Epidemiology of Disability among Adults in the United States." *Milbank Memorial Fund* 54:439–467.

Österle, A.
2007 "Health Care across Borders: Austria and Its New EU Neighbours." *Journal of European Social Policy* 17(2):112–124.

Palloni, A., and E. Arias
2004 "Paradox Lost: Explaining the Hispanic Adult Mortality Advantage." *Demography* 41:385–415.

Razum, O., and D. Twardella
2002 "Towards an Explanation for a Paradoxically Low Mortality among the Recent Immigrants." *Tropical Medicine and International Health* 7(1):4–10.

Ringbäck, G., A. Gullberg, A. Hjern, and M. Rosén
1999 "Mortality Statistics in Immigrant Research: Method for Adjusting Underestimation of Mortality." *International Journal of Epidemiology* 28:756–763.

Ronellenfitsch, U., and O. Razum
2004 "Deteriorating Health Satisfaction among Immigrants from Eastern Europe to Germany." *International Journal for Equity in Health* (13 June):3–4. <http://www.equityhealthj.com/content/3/1/4>.

Salt, J.
1989 "A Comparative Overview of International Trends and Types, 1950–80." *International Migration Review* 23(3):431–456.

SHARE (Survey of Health, Aging and Retirement in Europe)
2007 December <http://www.share-project.org/>.

Silveira, E., I. Skoog, V. Sundh, and B. Steen
2002 "Health and Well-Being among 70-Year-Old Migrants Living in Sweden – Results from the H 70 Gerontological and Geriatric Population Studies in Göteborg." *Social Psychiatry and Psychiatric Epidemiology* 37:13–22.

Smith, D. P., and B. S. Bradshaw
2006 "Rethinking the Hispanic Paradox: Death Rates and Life Expectancy for US Non-Hispanic White and Hispanic Populations." *American Journal of Public Health* 96(9):1686–1692.

Stronks, K.
2003 "Public Health Research among Immigrant Populations: Still a Long Way to Go." *European Journal of Epidemiology* 18(9):841–842.

Sundquist, K., and X. Li
2006 "Coronary Heart Disease Risks in First- and Second-Generation Immigrants in Sweden: A Follow-Up Study." *Journal of Internal Medicine* 259:418–427.

Tovar, J. J. et al.
2007 "Hispanic Established Populations for the Epidemiologic Studies of the Elderly: Selected Longitudinal Findings." *Aging Health* 3(3):325.

UNESCO Institute for Statistics
1997 *International Standard Classification of Education.* <http://www.uis.unesco.org/TEMPLATE/pdf/isced/ISCED_A.pdf>.

Williams, R.
1993 "Health and Length of Residence among South Asians in Glasgow: A Study Controlling for Age." *Journal of Public Health Medicine* 15:52–60.

Zimmermann, K. F.
1995 "European Migration: Push and Pull." *The World Bank Research Observer* 310:313–342.

Ethnic intermarriage among immigrants: human capital and assortative mating

Barry R. Chiswick · Christina Houseworth

Received: 17 March 2009 / Accepted: 25 June 2010 / Published online: 25 July 2010
© Springer Science+Business Media, LLC 2010

Abstract This paper analyzes the determinants of interethnic marriages by immigrants in the United States. The dependent variable is intermarriage across ethnic groups (on the basis of ancestry and country of birth) and the inclusion of the explanatory variables is justified by a simple rational choice economic model. A binomial logistic regression is estimated using data from the 1980 US Census, the last Census where post-migration marriages can be identified. Results show that the probability of intermarriage increases the longer a migrant resides in the U.S. and the younger the age at arrival. Both relationships can be attributable to the accumulation of US-specific human capital and an erosion of ethnic-specific human capital. Inter-ethnic marriages are more likely between individuals with similar education levels, providing evidence of positive assortative mating by education for immigrants. The construction of the "availability ratio" for potential spouses from one's own group and group size where one lives using data from several Censuses provides a the measure of the marriage market. Intermarriage is lower the greater the availability ratio and the larger the size of one's own group. Linguistic distance of the immigrant's mother tongue from English indirectly measures the effect of English language proficiency at arrival and is found to be a significant negative predictor of intermarriage. Those who report multiple ancestries and who were previously married are more likely to intermarry.

B. R. Chiswick (✉) · C. Houseworth
University of Illinois at Chicago, Chicago, IL, USA
e-mail: brchis@uic.edu

B. R. Chiswick
IZA, Bonn, Germany

C. Houseworth
Litigation Analytics, New York, NY, USA

JEL Classification J12 · J15 · J61 · F22

Keywords Immigrants · Marriage · Ethnicity/Ancestry · Country of Birth

1 Introduction

This paper examines the determinants of ethnic intermarriage (or exogamous marriage) among immigrants to the US, where interethnic marriage is defined as the marital union between two individuals of different ethnic backgrounds/ancestries. Immigrant ethnicity is measured using responses to the two questions on ancestry and country of birth in the US Census of Population. Ethnic intermarriage rates vary considerably among married adult immigrants in the US. Using the 1980 Census, the primary data for this study, if ethnicity is defined by ancestry the range is from 89% among Icelanders to 11% for Asian Indians, and if defined by country of birth it is from 90 percent for those born in Luxembourg to 15 percent for those born in Haiti.[1] Intermarriage rates for immigrants for the full set of 85 ancestries and 79 countries of birth are reported in an Appendix (available upon request). The purpose of this paper is to analyze the individual and environmental characteristics that are responsible for influencing the probability of intermarriage. A study of the determinants of intermarriage is important for understanding the underlying factors that may influence immigrant adjustment and the adjustments of their children.

Since the passage of the 1965 Amendments to the Immigration and Nationality Act, there has been a steady increase in the flow of immigrants to the United States. According to the Department of Homeland Security, there were 300,000 legal permanent residents admitted to the US in 1970, about 700,000 admitted in 1990, and 1.12 million in 2005.[2] Some have argued that immigration flows will alter the character and culture of the country in undesirable ways (Buchanan 2006). The

---

[1] Immigrant Ethnic Intermarriage Rates, Age 18–64, By Selected Ancestry and Country of Birth, 1980 Census

Intermarriage defined by			
Ancestry	Percent	Country of birth	Percent
Icelander	89	Luxembourg	90
Thai	57	Germany	76
Ukrainian	51	Canada	72
Jamaican	31	Honduras	51
Puerto Rican	30	Cuba	22
Italian	24	Portugal	19
Asian Indian	11	Haiti	15

Source 1980 Census of Population, Public Use Microdata Sample, Five Percent Sample

[2] While reportedly 1.7 million legal permanent resident visas were issued in 1990, this includes about 1.0 million illegal aliens who received permanent resident alien status under one of the two provisions of the

validity of this concern depends on the dimensions of assimilation of interest and how fast immigrant groups assimilate to the US culture and economy. One dimension of assimilation is an individual's economic status, such as education, earnings, or occupation. Another dimension of assimilation is the extent of intermarriage by the foreign born, where marriages among individuals of different ethnic or ancestry groups are commonly referred to as ethnic intermarriages.

Assimilation is the process by which the foreign born acquire human capital specific to the host country.[3] This perspective dates back to B. Chiswick (1978) who demonstrated that economic assimilation is a process occurring after immigration, with immigrants reaching parity in earnings with the native born at about 12–15 years after entering the country, controlling for age and education, among other variables. Country-specific human capital consists of investments in language and culture, as well as knowledge about local job markets and specific occupations. For a variety of reasons, the extent of intermarriage by an immigrant group in the US may be considered one signal of the level of assimilation, that is, the level of US-specific human capital accumulation.

Marriage is facilitated if there is effective verbal communication between spouses. Migrants from different linguistic groups that marry will need to learn a common language to communicate effectively, and the host country language is likely the most cost effective language to learn. Considering that most immigrants from non-English speaking countries make large investments in English language skills after arrival in the US, learning a third language (i.e., the mother tongue of an immigrant spouse) may not be an efficient allocation of time and other resources. Migrants from the same linguistic group are likely to speak their native language at home, and this reduces the need to learn and speak the language of the host country. There is more incentive for intermarried individuals to acquire English language skills and, therefore, intermarried immigrants are likely to have higher levels of English language ability than their endogamously (same ethnic background) married counterparts. Greater English language ability corresponds to a higher level of assimilation.

Intermarriage propensities and observed or current English language skills are likely to be endogenously determined. An individual is more likely to marry someone who is not from the same ancestry group or country of origin the better their English language proficiency. On the other hand, a measure of the "linguistic distance" of their mother tongue from English would be exogenous to the intermarriage decision. Such a measure is used here.

Moreover, there is literature showing empirically that intermarriage is an indicator of assimilation. Intermarried immigrants in Australia, France, and the US earn significantly higher incomes than their endogamously married counterparts, even after controlling for human capital endowments unrelated to marriage (Meng

---

Footnote 2 continued
1986 Immigration Reform and Control Act. Therefore, about 700,000 of the 1990 immigrants are comparable to the 300,000 immigrants admitted in 1970.

[3] The acquisition of US-specific human capital need not necessarily imply an eroding of the individual's ethnic-specific human capital.

and Gregory 2005; Meng and Meurs 2006; Kantarevic 2004). There is also evidence, however, that the direction of causality runs in the opposite direction, and that higher earnings are a consequence of intermarriage rather than an indicator or predictor of intermarriage (Meng and Gregory 2005; Meng and Meurs 2006). Holding all else fixed, favorable labor market outcomes are often an indication of assimilation as high earnings in the US are associated with a good knowledge of local labor markets and substantial English proficiency. Because intermarried immigrants earn higher incomes than their endogamously married counterparts, intermarried couples appear to be more assimilated. Furthermore, intermarriage is an index of social assimilation and acceptance of the immigrant group by other ethnic groups. Those groups whose members are bound to the ethnic community, or whose members are shunned by other groups, are less likely to intermarry. Because of the absence of good identifying instruments, it is not possible to analyze the endogenous relationship between marriage and labor market outcomes.

In this study intermarriage for a person of mixed background is defined as a marriage to a person of an ethnicity other than *either* of the respondent's ethnicities. Furthermore, a marriage between a native born and an immigrant of a similar ancestry is not considered an inter-ethnic marriage.[4] Consider a German immigrant married to a native born of German decent. This marriage will be considered endogamous if the native born marks German as their first choice for the ancestry question on the Census. This may bias the intermarriage rate downward, if the native born is from much earlier generations of immigrants, and therefore more American than German per se. However, the alternative to this would be to consider the above couple intermarried, which would then bias the intermarriage rate upward if the native born are from relatively recent immigrant arrivals.

Among other results of this study, support is found for positive assortative mating by education level for men and women. Several variables are used to construct ethnic marriage market conditions, where an availability ratio and ethnic group size are found to have significant effects on the probability of intermarriage. This paper explores the relationship between ethnic-specific human capital and US-specific human capital. Findings indicate that the probability of intermarriage increases with educational attainment and as the age of migration falls, as well as with duration of residence in the U.S. The greater the "linguistic distance" of the immigrant's mother tongue from English the lower is the inter-marriage rate, except for immigrant Korean and Japanese women who married veterans of the US Armed Forces, referred to as "war brides" even if these are peacetime marriages.

The paper is organized as follows. Section 2 provides a review of the literature on the determinants of ethnic intermarriage for immigrants. In Sect. 3, a simple economic model of intermarriage is presented. A description of the data set is in Sect. 4, followed by the empirical results in Sect. 5, and a conclusion in Sect. 6.

---

[4] There is no way to distinguish between the native-born who are second generation from those who are third or higher order generations in the 1980 Census or later Censuses.

2 Literature review: determinants of ethnic intermarriage

There is a large literature on the economics of marriage in which, among other things, the potential gains from marriage are discussed. The underlying assumption of the model employed in this paper is that benefits accrue to those who marry within their ethnicity. As discussed in Becker's "A Theory of Marriage", positive assortative mating implies that there are benefits from marriage that are most efficiently utilized when individuals match up with people of similar traits (Becker 1974). Such characteristics may be education, intelligence, health, language, ethnicity, and religion. There are numerous benefits to marrying within one's group, derived from the activities performed jointly in marriage, such as rearing children, joint decision making regarding the distribution of time and money, the observance of customs and rituals, and many others.

In a recent study of ethnic intermarriage in the United Kingdom, Belot and Fidrmuc (2009) focus on a marriage model where there is a preference for the husband being taller than the wife. With ethnic group differences in the mean and distribution of height, this generates differences in inter-marriage patterns by gender which are found to be consistent with the data. The US Census does not include data on height or other physical characteristics.

The determinants of intermarriage can be categorized in one of three groups: preferences, opportunity for contact, and factors that influence both. "Preferences" describe the degree of importance that an individual attaches to marrying someone within their ethnic group. "Opportunity for contact" refers to availability and accessibility to potential spouses in the individual's ethnic group. Education and military status are discussed separately, as they may affect both an individual's marriage market and their individual preferences.

Preferences for a partner of a similar ethnic background can be altered by a variety of factors, such as language, levels of human capital, modernization, and a host of other characteristics.[5] Researchers have used language and education as proxies for levels of ethnic human capital. Continuing facility with one's native language has been found to be negatively related to intermarriage in Anderson and Saenz (1994). Kalmijn (1998) uses the term modernization, which correlates to high levels of US-specific human capital, and hypothesizes that the US-born children of immigrants are more likely to intermarry than their immigrant parents. Alba and Golden (1986) look at rates of ethnic intermarriage among the native born in the US. They find a positive relationship between immigrant cohort and intermarriage, that is, intermarriage rates increase with generation in the US. Alba and Golden (1986) also find that individuals with mixed ancestry are more likely to intermarry than the children of endogamously married parents. In addition, Gilbertson et al. (1996) finds that among second-generation Hispanics living in New York, those with a mixed ancestry are more likely to intermarry than those with a single Hispanic ancestry living in New York.

---

[5] Ethnic-specific human capital refers to capital that is productive in terms of ethnicity (e.g., knowing how to celebrate ethnic holidays). US-specific human capital refers to human capital that is productive in the US, but is general across ethnic groups in the US (e.g., English language).

Opportunity for contact is indicated by the size of the ethnic group, the size of the population as a whole, and the number of the opposite sex in relation to the number of individuals of the same sex. The ratio of available men to women in a given region has commonly been used to explain various behaviors in Schoen (1983), Lichter et al. (1991), Fossett and Kiecolt (1991), Fitzgerald (1991), Brien (1997), and Goldman et al. (1984). Lichter et al. (1992) find a negative relationship between availability ratios and age at first marriage. They find that individuals marrying at later ages typically faced a lower availability ratio than those who married early in life. Several studies include only employed males as relevant for the marriage market (Wilson 1987; Lichter et al. 1992; Wood 1995; Fitzgerald 1991; Brien 1997; Fossett and Kiecolt 1991; Lichter et al. 1991; South and Lloyd 1992).

The probability of finding a "good match" increases not only as the ratio of opposite to same gender grows, but also the larger the absolute size of the population. Alba and Golden (1986) look at ethnic intermarriage among European origin groups in the US. They find a significant and negative relationship between group size and intermarriage. Other studies come to the same conclusion (e.g., Gilbertson et al. 1996).

General education may affect the probability of intermarriage through three venues. Education may alter an individual's preferences for marrying outside their ethnicity. As discussed in Cohen (1977), those who have higher levels of secular education may have spent more time among people of diverse backgrounds which may decrease aversion to (or increase understanding of) members of other groups. The effect that education may have on preferences for marrying outside one's ethnicity is referred to by Furtado (2006) as the "cultural adaptability effect". On the other hand, ethnic or religious education may have the opposite effects and discourage intermarriage (see, Grossbard-Shechtman 1993; Reinharz and DellaPergola 2009).

Education is also examined as a determinant of intermarriage in other papers, with most of the findings supporting the hypothesis that the highly educated are more likely to intermarry (Lieberson and Waters 1988; Schoen and Wooldredge 1989; Sandefur and McKinnell 1986; Meng and Gregory 2005; Lichter and Qian 2001). Celikaksoy et al. (2006) find support for positive assortative mating in Denmark, even after accounting for other potential tradeoffs. However, Furtado (2006) finds no support for the cultural adaptability effect of education after controlling for the other avenues through which education may affect the probability of intermarriage.

Highly educated individuals may also be less attached to their family or community of origin as they left their family and ethnic environment to obtain higher education (Kalmijn 1998). Furtado (2006) refers to this effect as the "enclave effect". She assumes that individuals remain in the area where they received the education that removed them from the enclave and concludes that the enclave effect is well measured by the proportion of the individual's ethnic group in the geographical area.

If there is assortative mating by education, education also affects the size of the relevant marriage market. Furtado (2006) examines the effect of education on the probability of intermarriage by controlling for the average level of education within the group for 2nd generation immigrants using 1970 Census data. She finds that the effect is strongest for immigrants from countries whose mean education values are very different from the rest of the population. Individuals with educational levels much higher or much lower than their ethnic group's average have a significantly higher probability of intermarriage. Similar results are found in Lehrer (1998) in connection with religious intermarriage.

The literature cited above suggests that several individual and environmental characteristics are important in determining the probability of intermarriage. This paper draws on some of the techniques used in the literature, such as the availability ratio. However, a more accurate measure of the availability ratio is created by using several Censuses to construct this variable. In addition to expanding on previous methods, this paper addresses some issues that were not previously studied. For instance, using current English language skill as a determinant of intermarriage creates econometric problems as it is likely to be endogenous to the probability of intermarriage. An alternative exogenous measure of language, linguistic distance, is used here.

3 Theory and hypotheses

In general, economic theories of marriage assume that individuals make marriage decisions by comparing costs and benefits. C. Chiswick and Lehrer (1991) and Lehrer (1998) model intermarriage using a marginal cost/marginal benefit model. The process of dating and finding an acceptable spouse is similar to a job search. The marginal cost of continuing to search is the delay in marriage and family formation, and the foregone benefits of marrying the current partner. The marginal benefit of continuing to search for a marriage partner arises from the probability of finding a more suitable partner, in particular, a partner who is personally, financially and ethnically more compatible.

Because the data to be studied are on marriages that have already taken place, an ex post analysis will be used, while the discussion and interpretation will continue to relate the variables of the model to a search process.[6]

3.1 Individual characteristics

The 1980 Census data, the last US Census to ask age at first marriage, show that the median age at first marriage among immigrants was 22 years for females and 25 years for males. Preferences for intermarriage may change over time; 30 year olds may have different preferences than those they had when they were 22. In addition, an individual's ethnic marriage market becomes smaller as they age, as other potential mates in their ethnic group marry or otherwise leave the marriage market. Thus, as age while still unmarried increases for immigrants, the marginal cost of search for ethnic compatibility will increase and the probability of intermarriage increases. Recent findings by Lehrer (2008), for example, show that women who marry at an older age are more likely to make tradeoffs in regards to several characteristics.

---

[6] It should be noted that the theory predicts changes in the probability of intermarriage, a continuous variable, while the data measures intermarriage as a dichotomous variable. However, there is no qualitative effect of this distinction on the conclusions.

Most men and women are likely to have increased utility from a marriage that results in childbirth. This particular benefit from marriage has lower odds of occurring as women age; therefore, unmarried women closer to the age at which the probability of pregnancy starts to decline may be more likely to intermarry.

Time spent in the US and the age at which an individual migrated to the US both affect levels of human capital. Age at migration is used as a proxy for the speed at which an individual may acquire US-specific human capital. Those who migrate at younger ages are likely to acquire US-specific human capital at a faster rate than those who migrate at older ages. Language, customs and traditions can be more easily acquired the younger the age at migration. For example, children who learn a foreign language after the age of 6 are more likely to develop an accent in that language (Asher 1969). B. Chiswick and Miller (2008) show that there is a lower level of English language proficiency with a greater age at migration, other variables the same.

C. Chiswick (2009) provides a theoretical model that evaluates the association between ethnic and US-specific human capital and the corresponding impact on intermarriage. The rate of acquisition ultimately affects the stock of US-specific human capital which may alter preferences for intermarriage, depending on the relationship between ethnic and US-specific human capital. US-specific and ethnic human capital may be complementary in the learning process (C. Chiswick 2009). If the acquisition of US-specific human capital also increases the level of ethnic human capital, then ethnic and US-specific human capital have positive externalities. For example, a Japanese child will learn English in school and may speak Japanese with his parents at home. If learning English also improves his Japanese, then the two types of human capital (US-specific and ethnic) are acquired in a complementary learning process.

Assortative models of marriage indicate that high levels of ethnic-specific human capital will decrease the probability of intermarriage. High levels of ethnic-specific human capital imply some preference for ethnic goods, and marriage to a partner with similar levels of ethnic-specific human capital will insure that the acquisition of these goods and transmitting them to one's children is less costly. If there are positive externalities there should be little difference between the probability of intermarriage between the two types of human capital among individuals who migrated as children and those who migrated as adults.

Conversely, if ethnic and US-specific human capital are competitive in the development of knowledge, in the sense that more of one detracts from the acquisition of more of the other, they would compete for the individual's resources (including time). This indicates that high levels of US-specific human capital will be accompanied by low levels of ethnic human capital, and vice versa. A child fully engaged in American customs and traditions would be less inclined to participate in ethnic-specific customs and traditions. Consequently, individuals who migrate as children are less likely to have high levels of ethnic human capital. Thus, they have a lower marginal benefit of ethnic compatibility, raising the probability of intermarriage.

The amount of time an individual has been living in the US and the speed at which human capital is acquired provide a second link between age and ethnic human capital. Duration is important since human capital increases as time spent in the host country rises. The rate at which ethnic human capital is attained depends on the relationship between ethnic and US-specific human capital. Similar to that explained above, C. Chiswick's (2009) model of ethnic human capital and assimilation is used to discuss the possible effects of ethnic human capital on the probability of intermarriage.

If ethnic and US-specific human capital are competitive in the development of knowledge, high levels of US-specific human capital will generally be accompanied by low levels of ethnic human capital, and vice versa. Consider an individual enrolled in a time intensive course of study in the host country. Most likely he or she will have less time to engage in ethnic related activities, and therefore have lower levels of ethnic human capital than his/her un-enrolled counterparts. This competitive relationship implies that individuals residing in the US for longer periods of time are more likely to be intermarried because of the acquisition of general (US-specific) human capital and the depreciation of ethnic human capital.

Other individual characteristics affecting the probability of intermarriage include previous marriages, the ethnic mix of the respondent's parents, gender, and race. To the extent that potential partners view a previous divorce as a signal of undesirable characteristics, individuals with this trait will generate fewer marriage offers, and, therefore, have higher marginal cost of search. In addition, ties to the parental home are weaker if an individual has been married, and, therefore, the individual may have a lower marginal benefit of ethnic compatibility, increasing the probability of intermarriage.

Parents may affect choice of spouse, even if their wishes are not verbalized or even indirectly implied. Using information on ancestry, a proxy for intermarried parentage can be constructed. If the respondent lists multiple ancestries, it is assumed they come from an intermarried background. An individual from single ethnic parentage may have preferences for a potential partner of the same ethnicity, while this preference is less likely to be present among those with an intermarried background (lower marginal benefit from search). In addition, potential marriage partners from a particular ethnic group may view a person of mixed parentage, partly from that group and partly from another, as being less ethnically compatible. If mixed parentage is used as a signal of lower ethnic compatibility, then the marginal cost of search for a potential partner of either ethnic group will increase. Thus, children from intermarried parents will have a lower marginal benefit and higher marginal cost of search for a partner of the same ethnicity, and therefore a higher probability of intermarriage (i.e., marriage to a person whose ethnicity differs from that of either parent) than those from the same ethnic parentage.

The gender of the respondent is included to examine gender differences in the probability of intermarriage. Immigrant women who marry in the US may be more tied to the family home, and therefore have a higher marginal benefit of ethnic compatibility, than immigrant males. Immigrant groups may differ in their attitudes towards, and ability to limit, males and females socializing and marrying outside their ethnic group.

3.2 Marriage market characteristics

Marriage market variables give an estimate of the respondent's pool of potential mates at the time of consideration of marriage. Four aspects with regard to the marriage market are considered: availability of potential partners of the same ethnicity and relevant age group, group size, modal education of the individual's ethnic group and gender, and a measure of linguistic distance between English and the person's mother tongue.

Following Goldman et al. (1984), and with some minor alterations, the marriage market availability ratio is specified by ethnicity and by geographic region, giving the following "availability ratio" for females ($^F AR_{ijk}$):

$$^F AR_{ijk} = \frac{\sum_{i}^{i+10} M_{ijk}}{\sum_{i-2}^{i+8} F_{ijk}}$$

M_{ijk} is the number of men of age i in region j from ethnic group k. F_{ijk} is the number of women in the age group "competing" for the men in the numerator, in region, j, and of race/ethnicity, k.[7] Marriages tend to occur where the male partner is on average 2 years older than the female and following Goldman et al. (1984) the availability ratio is constructed to reflect this fact. For example, the appropriate sex ratio for a white female age 20 is the number of white men aged 20–30 divided by the number of white females aged 18–28. The relevant cohort group will span a total of 11 years. Fossett and Kiecolt (1991) provide support for using broad age groups, finding that constricting age groups can overly restrict comparisons by age and ignore possible competition in close cohorts.[8] In the absence of information on where in the US they lived at the time they married, the individual's current location is assumed to be the same as when he or she was in the marriage market.

Using several Censuses to construct availability ratios provides a more accurate portrayal of actual marriage markets according to specifications discussed in Sect. 4. As an individual's availability ratio increases, the marginal cost of ethnic compatibility decreases, and the probability of intermarriage decreases.

The availability ratio measures possible differences in the marriage market for men and women by taking into account competition by members of the same sex. Another important characteristic of the relative ethnic marriage market is the absolute size of the ethnic group. Group size measures the number of the opposite sex in a specific ethnicity by geographic region and age group. While the availability ratio may be close to one, indicating a relatively "balanced" marriage

---

[7] For men the ratio is $^M AR_{ijk} = \frac{\sum_{i-2}^{i+8} F_{ijk}}{\sum_{i}^{i+10} M_{ijk}}$

[8] Fossett and Kiecolt (1991) point out that there is a structure of preference within the broad age ranges and suggest using weights. While this appears to be useful, Goldman et al. (1984) have found weighted and un-weighted sex ratios to be statistically similar. In addition, assigning weights to particular age groups would be rather arbitrary, as personal preferences vary.

market, the actual number of the opposite sex in one's group would still be relevant as the probability of finding a "good match" within one's ethnic group increases with the size of the group. Thus, as an individual's group size increases, the marginal cost of search for a partner of the same ethnicity decreases and the probability of intermarriage decreases.

The size of the total population in the relevant age group for the time at which the individual was most likely in the marriage market is included to measure the size of the non-ethnic-specific marriage market. Intermarriage is more likely for those living in an area with a larger total population, controlling for the size of their group and the availability ratio.

Experience in the US Armed Forces may affect the relevant marriage market. Since 1973, the United States had had an all-volunteer military force. Prior to 1973 men between the ages of 18 and 25 were required to register for the draft, and in times of need would be selected for service. Therefore, the individuals in this sample aged 18 after 1973 are all voluntarily providing service and those prior to 1973 may or may not be. Those in the US military may be more likely to marry outside their ethnicity than non-veterans because of separation from one's parents and ethnic community. Those in the military are exposed to a broader range of ethnic groups than they would in civilian life and members of other ethnic groups in the local community in postings in the US and overseas. The pertinent ethnic marriage market may be virtually non- existent for those overseas, which increases the marginal cost of search for ethnic compatibility. In addition, men based overseas are exposed to a different culture and may have a higher marginal benefit for intermarriage than non-veterans and, consequently, a lower marginal benefit of ethnic compatibility. Both the increase in marginal cost and the decrease in marginal benefit will decrease the level of ethnic compatibility and, therefore, will increase the probability of intermarriage. The probability of intermarriage may vary by period of time of military service.

3.3 Human capital

Linguistic distance refers to the extent that languages differ from one another. The US Department of State, School of Language Studies teaches English-speaking Americans foreign languages and then assesses the proficiency in these languages. A paper by Hart-Gonzalez and Lindermann (1993) reports these scores for 43 languages. B. Chiswick and Miller (1998, 2005) convert these scores into a measure of linguistic distance from English for nearly all of the languages (except American Indian languages) coded in the US Census PUMS file. A lower score corresponds to a greater distance between the foreign language and English. They find that lower levels of linguistic distance are associated with higher levels of English fluency. Linguistic distance can be used to predict the probability of intermarriage, as those with the potential for greater English ability are likely to have lower costs and greater benefits from intermarriage. A greater distance between the individual's foreign language and English will result in a lower probability of intermarriage.

As mentioned in the literature review above, education has many effects on the probability of intermarriage. First, education may affect an individual's preferences for ethnic compatibility. Individuals with high levels of secular education may have a lower marginal benefit of search for a partner of the same ethnicity and, hence, are more likely to be intermarried than those with lower educational levels. Second, education may alter an individual's marriage market because he or she may be more likely to move out of the ethnic enclave and family influences when attending college. This effect can not be measured directly, as the data do not provide a direct measure for individuals who are likely to move out of an ethnic enclave, but schooling level serves as a proxy.

Another avenue through which education may alter the probability of intermarriage depends on preferences for education levels of a spouse and changes in the relevant marriage market. Specifically, education levels may be used, in addition to ethnicity, as a trait by which people try to match themselves. Education can be used to signal possible compatibility. Positive assortative mating implies that individuals with high levels of education, in ethnic groups with relatively low levels of education, are more likely to be intermarried because of a thinner marriage market for their ethnic group within their educational level. Similarly, individuals with low levels of education, in groups with relatively high levels of education, are more likely to be intermarried.

Although most studies use average levels of education, this study uses modal education levels. Modal values may provide a better measure of central tendency to make comparisons across ethnic groups. For example, the majority of immigrants in the sample have education levels above the 6th grade, while only a small percentage have more than a bachelor's degree. Therefore, for small ethnic groups, a few individuals with high levels of education can skew the average to overestimate the "typical" education level of the ethnic group. The modal education levels by ethnic/racial groups will be taken from the relevant Census and will be determined by the same age groupings as used in construction of group size. It is understood that some individuals may pursue higher levels of education *after* marriage. However, this issue is not addressed as there is no information on the year the education was completed.

4 Data and estimating equation

The US 1980 Census of Population and Housing, Public Use Microdata Sample (B-Sample) 1% Sample (PUMS) is used to address the determinants of ethnic intermarriage among immigrants. The 1980 Census is specifically used because it includes "age at first marriage", a question that has not been included in more recent Censuses. The questions, "age at first marriage" and "migration year" ("When did this person come to the United States to stay?") are used to determine whether the individual's first marriage took place after immigration, permitting examination of an immigrant's decision to marry outside of his/her ethnicity in the US. Many of the characteristics of the US marriage market are not relevant for immigrants married prior to migration, therefore, the sample is restricted to individuals married after migration. It is important to note that the Census data only give information on spouses that exist at the time of the Census. Thus only those currently married and living with their spouse can be studied. While the respondent is an immigrant, the spouse may be either native-born or foreign-born.

Springer

Appendix to this paper reports the definition of each of the variables used in the analysis, and their code names. The dependent variable, intermarried, is dichotomous and equal to one if the respondent is currently married to an individual of a different "ethnicity" which is used as a measure of intermarriage. Two proxies are used for ethnicity: ancestry and country of birth. Under the ancestry definition, immigrants are considered to be intermarried if their spouse is of a different ancestry, without regard for country of birth. When multiple ancestries are reported in response to the Census question, the first response is taken as the person's ethnicity.[9] Under the country of birth definition, immigrants are considered to be intermarried if their spouse was born in a different country, including the United States.

To test the hypotheses developed above for immigrants, the following equation is run with both sexes, and also separately by gender for both definitions of ethnicity.

$$\ln[P(INTRMAR = 1)/P(INTRMAR = 0)] = b_0 + b_1 SEX + b_2 GRADE$$
$$+ b_3 GRADE2 + b_4 DEVMODE + b_5 TIMESMAR + b_7 AR + b_8 GRPSIZE$$
$$+ b_9 VETERAN^m + b_{10} SPSVET^f + b_{11} YSM + b_{12} AGM14\_17 + b_{13} AGM18\_23$$
$$+ b_{14} AGM24\_28 + b_{15} AGM29\_35 + b_{16} AGM36\_ + b_{17} MULTANC$$
$$+ b_{18} AGMAR31\_45 + b_{19} AGMAR64\_ + b_{20} RACE + b_{21} LINGDIS$$
$$+ b_{22} ENGONLY + b_{22} POP$$

SEX is a dichotomous variable equal to 0 if the respondent is male and 1 if female. TIMESMAR is a dichotomous variable equal to 0 if married once and equal to 1 if married more than once. To test the effect that later marriages may have on the probability of intermarriage two dichotomous variables are included, AGMAR31_45 and AGMAR46_64 are constructed and equal to one if the respondent was married in the age ranges listed. AGMAR18_30 is the benchmark group.

For the period under study, the decades prior to 1980, the military was composed primarily of males. Thus, the veteran variable (VETERAN) is defined only for males, while the variable for the spouse of a veteran (SPSVET) is defined only for females. Separate veteran variables are defined for specific time periods.[10]

---

[9] Appendix includes a list of these ethnicities and their components and a lit of countries of birth which are used as the second proxy for ethnicity. Tables in these Appendices show intermarriage rates among immigrants where ethnicity is defined by ancestry and country of birth. Only eight percent of the sample reports a multiple ancestry for the 1980 Census data.

[10] The analysis for Veterans is reported in the gender specific equations in Chiswick and Houseworth (2008, Tables B1 and B3). The veteran variable is defined as follows: VET75 is equal to 1 if the respondent served in the US military in May 1975 or later and equal to 0 otherwise. VETVIET is equal to 1 if the respondent served in the military during the Vietnam War (August 1964–April 1975) and equal to 0 otherwise. VET55_64 is equal to 1 if the respondent served in the military between February 1955 and July 1964 and equal to 0 otherwise. VETKOR is equal to 1 if the respondent served in the military during the Korean Conflict (June 1950–January 1955) and equal to 0 otherwise. VETWWII is equal to 1 if the respondent served in the military during WWII (September 1940–July 1947) and equal to 0 otherwise. VETOTHER is equal to one if the respondent served in the military at any other time. SPSVET is a dichotomous variable equal to one if the immigrant female's husband served in the US military, referred to as "war brides", even if the sources was not in a period of war.

The availability ratio, AR, is as specified in Sect. 3 and is taken from the relevant marriage market, based on SMSAs and states. The relevant marriage market for an individual is more accurately estimated at the time during which they were most likely to have been "in the market". Because the Census survey data are collected every 10 years, a good estimate for a female aged 30 in 1980 is information on the population she potentially encountered at age 20: characteristics for men aged 20–30 from the 1970 Census. Given the limitations in the Census data, it is assumed the individual lived in the same location in 1980 and the year they were in the marriage market.[11]

Thus, marriage market variables are extracted in the following manner: Group 1- Marriage market variables for 18–27 year olds are estimated with the 1980 Census. Group 2- Marriage market variables for 28–45 year olds are estimated with the 1970 Census. Group 3- Marriage market variables for 46–64 year olds are estimated with the 1960 Census.

Group size, GRPSIZE, is a variable equal to the number of individuals of the opposite sex (in thousands) estimated for the respondent's ethnic group and region. Group size is estimated separately for ethnicity defined by ancestry and country of birth. GRPSIZE for Group 1 (using the 1980 Census) is estimated from the number of individuals aged 18–35 by geographic region and ethnicity. GRPSIZE for Group 2 (using the 1970 Census) is estimated from the number of individuals aged 18–35 by geographic region and ethnicity. GRPSIZE for Group 3 (using the 1960 Census) is estimated from the number of individuals aged 28–45 by geographic region and ethnicity. Population (POP) is measured by region and uses the same age ranges as GRPSIZE, but includes the total population, regardless of ethnicity.

Location is defined by SMSA for data from the 1980 and 1970 Censuses and state for the 1960 Census. The 1960 Census does not provide information on SMSA. An SMSA is defined as an area of 100,000 or more. Many large cities, groups of cities and counties are defined within large SMSA's.

GRADE represents years of education. GRADE2 (GRADE squared) is included to measure the non-linear effects of education. To test the theory of positive assortative mating, two variables equal to the deviation of the individual's education from the modal education level (DEVMODE) of the group are included: HIGHL, the deviation from the mode if the respondent has an education level higher than the mode of the ethnic group, and LOWHI, the deviation from the mode if the respondent has an education level lower than the mode of the ethnic group. Education modes for the ethnic group are estimated by ethnic group, geographic region and age group. In addition, education modes are estimated separately by ethnicity defined by ancestry and country of birth.

To test the effect of age at immigration, immigrants are divided into 5 age groups, each represented by a dichotomous variable. The variables are labeled AMXXX, where XXX refers to the age group. The 1980 Census gives information on immigration year in intervals. By using a midpoint of the migration intervals and

---

[11] The Census permits the identification of state or country of birth, state of residence 5 years ago if it was in the US, and current place of residence.

the individual's exact age, a variable representing the age at immigration is constructed.[12]

LINGDISXXX represents eight dichotomous variables for each level of linguistic distance, where XXX stands for the value of linguistic distance. The benchmark is individuals from English-speaking developed countries.

The effect of duration of residence in the US is estimated using years since migration, YSM. MULTANC is a dichotomous variable equal to 1 if the respondent lists multiple ancestries, thereby implying parental intermarriage, and is 0 if only one ancestry is listed. Dichotomous variables indicating race are non-Hispanic WHITE (the benchmark group), BLACK (non-Hispanic), AMINDIAN (American Indian), ASIAN, HISPANIC, ASINDIAN (South Asian) and OTHER.

5 Empirical results

5.1 Pooled across gender

Results of the logistic regression using the 1980 Census are shown in Table 1 (Columns 1 and 2) for the pooled sample of immigrant women and men, estimated separately for ethnicity defined by ancestry and country of birth, respectively. The signs of the coefficients are similar regardless of the definition of ethnicity, although they are stronger when ethnicity is defined by country of birth. In addition, the overall explanatory power of the equation is more robust when ethnicity is defined by country of birth. This pattern is generally shown throughout.

In the United States, ethnic and US-specific human capital do compete for space within an individual and are not overall complements in the learning process. The coefficients on the age at migration variables are significant and negative for AM14_17, AM18_23 and AM24_28, indicating that these groups are less likely to intermarry than those that migrated before the age of 13, regardless of which of the two definitions of ethnicity is used. Further support that ethnic and US-specific human capital are not overall complements in the learning process can be seen through the variable years since migration. Each year spent in the US, measured by YSM, increases the probability of intermarriage by .1% when intermarriage is defined by ancestry and .8% when intermarriage is defined by country of birth. An individual who has been living in the US for 30 years is 16% more likely to marry someone from a different country than an individual who has been living in the US for 10 years, all else equal.

Immigrant women (whose first marriage is after migration) are significantly less likely to be intermarried than immigrant men for both definitions of ethnicity. The odds of intermarriage decrease by 20% if the respondent is female when ethnicity is defined by ancestry and by 32% when ethnicity is defined by country of birth.

---

[12] Individuals that migrated as children are the benchmark group and range in age from 0 to 13 (AGM0_13). Teenagers are classified as having immigrated between the ages of 14 and 17 (AGM14_17) and young adults as between the ages of 18–23 (AGM18_23). Adults are divided into three groups: those who migrated between the ages of 24 and 28 (AGM24_28), the ages of 29 and 35 (AGM29_35), and those who migrated at age 36 or after (older immigrants) (AGM36).

Table 1 Logistic regressions estimates of intermarriage for immigrants with ethnicity defined by ancestry (Column 1) and country of birth (Column 2), US, 1980 Census
Dependent variable: Intermarriage pooled

Variable	Column 1-ancestry					Column 2-country of birth				
	Coeff	z-score	dy/dx[a]	Odds ratio		Coeff	z-score	dy/dx	Odds ratio	X[d]
OTHER	0.02	0.19	0.005	**1.02**		0.15	1.45	0.029	**1.16**	0.02
BLACK	−0.45	−7.03	−0.111	**0.64**		−0.78	−10.98	−0.176	**0.46**	0.05
AMINDIAN	−0.03	−0.09	−0.006	**0.97**		0.17	0.50	0.032	**1.18**	0.002
ASIAN	−0.42	−10.37	−0.105	**0.66**		−0.75	−17.07	−0.167	**0.47**	0.13
ASINDIAN	−1.01	−10.82	−0.235	**0.36**		−0.91	−9.65	−0.209	**0.4**	0.02
HISPANIC	−0.18	−3.90	−0.045	**0.84**		−0.06	−1.26	−0.012	**0.94**	0.10
AGMAR31_45	0.18	4.20	0.045	**1.20**		−0.36	−7.74	−0.076	**0.69**	0.13
AGMAR46_64	0.30	2.08	0.075	**1.36**		−0.53	−3.38	−0.117	**0.59**	0.008
TIMESMAR	0.81	17.83	0.195	**2.25**		1.16	17.91	0.182	**3.19**	0.10
HIGHL	0.01	1.77	**0.002**	1.01		0.01	2.43	**0.002**	1.01	3.62
LOWHI	0.04	5.06	**0.009**	1.04		0.003	0.40	**0.001**	1.00	1.51
GRADE	0.13	10.56	**0.032**	1.14		0.04	3.35	**0.007**	1.04	11.73
GRADE2	−5.00E − 04	−4.79	**−0.001**	1.00		−8.00E − 05	−0.18	**−2.00E − 05**	1.00	158.41
GRPSIZE[b]	−0.13	−16.87	**−0.032**	0.88		−0.05	−6.89	**−0.010**	0.95	0.81
AR	−0.43	−8.98	**−0.108**	0.65		−0.31	−5.73	**−0.063**	0.73	0.78
POP	0.002	8.06	**0.001**	1.00		0.0005	1.72	**0.0001**	1.00	49.26
AM14_17[c]	−0.35	−7.26	−0.087	**0.70**		−0.55	−10.48	−0.120	**0.58**	0.12
AM18_23	−0.33	−7.99	−0.081	**0.72**		−0.43	−9.43	−0.089	**0.65**	0.30
AM24_28	−0.36	−8.14	−0.09	**0.7**		−0.24	−4.84	−0.050	**0.79**	0.23
AM29_35	−0.30	−5.70	−0.075	**0.74**		0.23	3.63	0.044	**1.25**	0.13
AM36_	−0.28	−3.18	−0.07	**0.75**		0.76	7.34	0.127	**2.13**	0.04
YSM	0.0007	1.65	**0.001**	1.00		0.04	21.34	**0.008**	1.04	16.88

Table 1 continued

Variable	Column 1-ancestry				Column 2-country of birth			
	Coeff	z-score	dy/dx[a]	Odds ratio	Coeff	z-score	dy/dx	Odds ratio	X[d]
MULTANC	0.39	7.79	0.097	**1.48**	0.80	11.45	0.134	**2.21**	0.08
SPSVET	1.12	29.75	0.266	**3.06**	1.97	38.03	0.293	**7.16**	0.21
SEX	−0.22	−7.37	−0.055	**0.80**	−0.38	−12.22	−0.076	**0.68**	0.53
Constant	−0.87	−7.56			−0.02	−0.2			−0.64, 0.19
	Sample size = 29,137				Sample size = 29,137			
	Pseudo R2 = .1008				Pseudo R2 = .1728			

Variable names are defined in Appendix. Odds ratios and marginal effects are bolded to indicate significance for dichotomous variables and continuous variables, respectively. Z-scores for a 5 percent significance test and a 1 percent significance test are 1.65 and 2.33, respectively

[a] dy/dx = Pr(INTRMR)(predict)—marginal effects are the partial derivative with respect to X (mean) of the probability of intermarriage, except for dichotomous variables. The marginal effect for a dichotomous variable is the discrete change from 0 to 1. An alternative measure of the effect of a dichotomous variable is the corresponding odds ratio

[b] GRPSIZE and POP are in thousands

[c] The benchmark group for age at migration (AMXXX) variables are individuals that migrated prior to age 14

Source 1960–1980 Censuses of Population, Public Use Microdata Samples

[d] Mean values are identical or within a very small range for all variables except for the constant, where the mean is equal to 0.19 for column one and −0.64 for column two

A possible explanation of the gender difference is that immigrant women are more tied to the family home. The rules of dating or socializing with members of the opposite sex may be stricter for females and they may have less opportunity to interact with individuals outside of their ethnicity. Alternatively, immigrant females may have stronger preferences for endogamy than immigrant males as they have the larger role in the raising of children.

Individuals who have been married more than once (TIMESMAR) have a higher probability of interethnic marriage. Previous marriages may be seen as a signal of other unmeasured undesirable characteristics, or that a previous marriage has weakened ties to family and ethnic community. The Census contains information on age at *first* marriage, but if an individual has been married more than once, the relevant variable for this estimation is age at *current* marriage, which is not available. Those who have been married more than once are likely to be in a marriage that took place at an "older" age than age at first marriage. Therefore, they faced a smaller ethnic marriage market when searching for their current spouse and have a higher probability of intermarriage. An individual who has been married more than once has a 125% increase in the odds of being intermarried compared to individuals in their first marriage when ancestry is used to define ethnicity. The effect is stronger (219%) when country of birth is used to define ethnicity.

The availability ratio, group size, and total population variables capture the best estimate of an individual's ethnic marriage market. The availability ratio shows that an increase in the number of members of the opposite sex in an individual's ethnic group relative to the number of members of the respondent's own sex decreases the probability of intermarriage.

The coefficient on group size implies a decrease in the likelihood of intermarriage as the size of the ethnic group increases when ethnicity is defined by ancestry. As the absolute size of the pool of potential partners increases, the probability of finding a suitable mate within one's group increases, and hence, immigrants are less likely to marry outside of their ancestry. The effect of group size is slightly smaller when ethnicity is defined by country of birth. Ethnic enclaves develop as a way to efficiently engage in ethnic related behavior, such as food preparation, celebration of holidays, and dress. They are likely to include individuals from different countries that share similar ancestries (e.g., Hispanics). Therefore, if the ethnic group spans several countries of origin, individuals who reside in ethnic enclaves have a larger ethnic marriage market by ancestry and are more likely to marry within their ancestry than to someone from their country of birth.

A person with intermarried parents (i.e., of mixed ancestry) is 48% more likely to be intermarried when intermarriage is defined by ancestry and 121% more likely when intermarriage is defined by country of birth. Individuals with intermarried parents are less likely to marry a person of *either* ethnicity of their parents' than are those with a single ancestry (endogamously married parents). Immigrants with parents who are from different countries are three times more likely to be intermarried than those with parents of different ancestries.

GRADE is positively related to intermarriage. GRADE2 has a negative coefficient, indicating that as educational levels increase the probability of

Table 2 Marginal effect of years of schooling completed on the probability of intermarriage among immigrants defined by ancestry, US, 1980 census

Years of schooling	Marginal effect (dy/dx)	z-score
3	0.021	65.60
4	0.020	38.07
5	0.024	26.83
6	0.026	20.97
7	0.027	17.47
8	0.029	15.19
9	0.030	13.65
10	0.030	12.59
11	0.032	11.87
12	0.032	11.41
13	0.033	11.17
14	0.033	11.11
15	0.033	11.26
16	0.032	11.61
17	0.031	12.20
18	0.030	13.08
19	0.029	14.37
20	0.027	16.24

Pooled male and female samples. The marginal effect of years of schooling is calculated at each specified year of schooling, controlling for all other variables based on regression in Table 1

Source 1980 Census of Population, Public Use Microdata Samples, 1 Percent Sample

intermarriage increases, but at a decreasing rate. The partial effect of GRADE is never negative, indicating that increases in education will always increase the probability of intermarriage. Education may alter preferences for ethnic compatibility or move individuals out of ethnic enclaves. Table 2 below shows the marginal effects of each year of education on the probability of intermarriage for immigrants.

From Table 1, Column 1, we see that as education increases by year, the probability of intermarriage increases by 3.2 percentage points. If the availability ratio increases by 1 unit from the mean, the probability of intermarriage decreases by 10.8 percentage points. The availability ratio is expressed as a percentage (percentage of opposite sex in relation to same sex of same ethnic origin). Therefore, as the availability ratio increases by 1 percentage point from the mean the probability of intermarriage decreases by 10.8 percentage points. Thus, a 3 year increase in schooling has the same effect on intermarriage as a one percentage point decline in the availability ratio.

When ethnicity is defined by ancestry, the variables HIGHL and LOWHI are both significant and positive. Individuals who have education levels at least 1 year above or at least 1 year below the mode of their group are more likely to intermarry, indicative of positive assortative theories of marriage. In this case, individuals trade off ethnicity for more compatible levels of education in their spouse. Individuals with high levels of education in groups with lower modal levels of education (HIGHL) have a harder time finding someone within their education level to marry. When ethnicity is defined by country of birth, only HIGHL is significant.

Race is included to examine whether patterns of intermarriage by immigrants vary by race. "Races" include white, black, American Indian, Asian Indian, Asian, Hispanic and Other. It is recognized that Hispanic is not a separate racial group. However, individuals within this group are likely to have broadly similar geographic and cultural origins and to speak Spanish. Black, Asian, Asian Indian and Hispanic immigrants are less likely to intermarry than whites (Table 1, Columns 1 and 2). One possible explanation is that the majority of the US population is white and there is a tendency for racial groups in the US to be largely endogamous in terms of marriage, perhaps because of racial discrimination by whites. Therefore, it is more likely for a white immigrant to marry a white native born or immigrant of a different ancestry or country of origin than immigrants of other racial groups.

The first major difference between the results for the alternate definitions of ethnicity relates to those who migrated to the US as adults. When ethnicity is defined by country of birth, immigrants who arrived at age 29 or older (AM29_35 and AM36_) have coefficients that are positive and statistically significant compared to the benchmark age at migration 13 or younger. When ethnicity is defined by ancestry the coefficients are statistically significant and negative. Individuals who migrate at older ages are more likely to marry outside their country of origin than individuals who migrate as children, but are less likely to marry outside of their ancestry group. That is, those who migrate at an older age are more likely to marry individuals with a similar ancestry but from a different country of birth.

Those who migrated past the age of 28, who married within their ancestry group and to individuals from other countries, are mainly: English, Scottish, French, German, Greek, Irish, Italian, Polish, Spanish, Mexican, Chinese, Filipino, Japanese and Korean. For European ancestries, the majority of the individuals were either born in the country associated with that ancestry, or in Canada. For example, persons of German ancestry born in Canada who migrated to the US at later ages are more likely to marry non-Canadians, but are more likely than Germans that migrated to the US as children to marry persons of German ancestry. Perhaps those of German ancestry born in Canada over age 28 have a greater attachment to their ancestry than Germans who migrated to the US before the age of thirteen.

Individuals who list Spanish ancestry were most likely born in Mexico, Cuba or Spain. To be clear, there are individuals who listed Spanish as their ancestry group, and others who listed Mexican, but both could be from Mexico. Individuals that migrated from Cuba at later ages are less likely to marry Cubans than those that migrated as children, but are more likely to marry individuals born in Mexico or Spain. Those that marry at older ages may lower their "reservation price", in this case choose to accept a spouse not born in Cuba. At the same time, because they migrate at later ages they have less destination specific human capital, which is valued in the marriage market for the native born and foreign born that migrated at young ages. They are less picky, but also are more constrained by low levels of destination specific human capital, namely English language skills. Therefore, they accept marriage offers outside of their country of birth, but must find a spouse who speaks Spanish.

The two definitions of ethnicity also produce differing coefficients on the age at first marriage variables. For ethnicity defined by birthplace, individuals who marry between the ages of 31 and 45 have a 1% *decrease* in the odds of intermarriage compared to those who married before the age of 31. When ethnicity is defined by ancestry, individuals that marry between the ages of 31 and 45 have a 1% *increase* in the odds of being intermarried. Thus, those who have their first marriage at an older age are more likely to involve mates from the same country of origin (same language) but different ancestry groups.

Odds ratios for the linguistic distance variables are presented in Table 3 for the pooled sample of immigrant women and men, separately estimated by gender and for ethnicity defined by ancestry and country of birth. LING1 represents languages furthest away from English, mainly made up of Korean and Japanese, LING3 are those closest to English, such as Swedish. The benchmark is those who come from English-speaking countries. The patterns are consistent for both definitions of ethnicity, with the exception of LING1 for ancestry for women. For instance, Table 3 shows that for ancestry for males and females pooled those who speak languages relatively far linguistically from English, LING175, are 60% less likely to be intermarried than those who come from English speaking countries, whereas those that speak languages closer to English, LANG275, are only 32% less likely to be intermarried. Interestingly, women who speak languages the furthest from English, like Korean and Japanese, are *more* likely to be intermarried (based on ancestry) than those who come from English-speaking countries. This suggests that this represents a "war brides" effect, that is, Korean and Japanese women who married members of the US Armed Forces stationed in these countries. Thus, a greater degree of distance of the origin language from English is associated with lower rates of intermarriage (defined either by ancestry or country of origin), except for Korean and Japanese "war brides".

Table 3 Logistic regression effect of linguistic distance on intermarriage for immigrants, 1980 (*Source* 1980 US Census Data, Dependent variable: Intermarriage)

Variable	Ancestry			Country of birth		
	All	Male	Female	All	Male	Female
LING1	1.42*	0.76	1.59*	0.65*	0.42*	0.72*
LING15	0.66*	0.80	0.51*	0.34*	0.48*	0.24*
LING175	0.40*	0.57*	0.25*	0.27*	0.42*	0.18*
LING2	0.88*	0.90	0.80*	0.38*	0.47*	0.29*
LING225	0.68*	0.64*	0.72*	0.36*	0.41*	0.34*
LING25	0.61*	0.55*	0.66*	0.35*	0.44*	0.28*
LING275	0.68*	0.78	0.62*	0.43*	0.61*	0.31*
LING3	0.89	0.70	1.16	0.75	0.80	0.78

Note Pooled Sample Size = 27,116. Variables are defined in Appendix. Odds ratios reported in table, controlling for the other explanatory variables in Table 1. * designates statistically significant at 5 percent level. Benchmark: Immigrated from English-speaking developed countries. LING1, languages furthest from English (e.g., Korean and Japanese), LING3, languages closest to English (e.g. Swedish)

Sources 1960–1980 Censuses of Population, Public Use Microdata Samples

Chiswick and Miller (2005)

5.2 Separate analyses by gender

Separate analyses are conducted by gender for the two definitions of ethnicity, where the regression results are reported in B. Chiswick and Houseworth 2008, Appendix.

GRADE and GRADE2 follow the same pattern as the pooled sample. As education levels increase, the probability of intermarriage increases, but at a decreasing rate. The coefficient on LOWHI (a person with a low education from a highly educated group) is significant, positive and of a similar magnitude for both men and women when ethnicity is defined by ancestry. This coefficient indicates that individuals with education levels below the modal education level of the group are more likely to intermarry. This result supports positive assortative mating models. Individuals with low education levels from a high education group will find a smaller pool of potential mates, as most of the individuals in their ethnic group will have been sorted with other highly educated individuals. When ethnicity is defined by country of birth, however, deviations from the mode are not statistically significant.

Immigrant men who served in the U.S. armed forces are more likely to be intermarried than those who are not veterans, especially if this service was during WWII, when so many were stationed overseas, or was in the most recent period, 1975–1980. Immigrant women with a spouse currently in or a veteran of the US armed forces (SPSVET) are almost 200% more likely to be intermarried when intermarriage is defined by ancestry and 588% when defined by country of birth. These variables account for the effect that "war brides" have on the probability of intermarriage, which is a stunningly large effect.[13] Women have lower intermarriage rates than men, except for "war brides". The age at migration variables for both men and women are significant and negative for almost all of the age groups. This relationship indicates that migrating before the age of 13 increases the probability of intermarriage, as individuals that migrated before age 13 are the benchmark group. When ethnicity is defined by the ancestry question, migrating past the age of 36 does not have a significant effect on the probability of intermarriage compared to the youngest age at migration group. When ethnicity is defined by country of birth, women who migrated past the age of 29 are more likely to be intermarried than those who migrated as children. As discussed above, this effect may be related to the types of individuals who migrate at later ages, those who marry within their ancestry group and to individuals from other countries. A large majority of those who marry within their ancestry group and outside their country of origin are from Canada.

Another interesting result is that race matters for both males and females, regardless of the definition of ethnicity. Immigrant blacks, Asians, Asian Indians, and Hispanics are all less likely to intermarry than immigrant whites, except for the "war brides" effect for immigrant women.

---

[13] Note in Table 3 the very high intermarriage rate among women, but not among men from language groups the most distant from English, in particular, Korean and Japanese.

6 Summary and conclusions

A number of results were obtained by examining the determinants of intermarriage for first generation immigrants using the 1980 US Census of Population and Housing, the last Census that included the question on age at first marriage. Ethnicity is defined by both ancestry and country of birth.

This paper contributes to the literature in this area of study in several ways. First, several data sets (1960–1980 Censuses) are used to construct marriage market variables, specifically group size, population size and the availability ratio. This method provides a more appropriate picture of marriage market characteristics. In addition, three variables are included to test for the relationship between education and intermarriage. By including both education level and deviations from the modal education level of the ethnic group, two possible venues are examined. There is evidence of both positive assortative mating and also an independent positive effect by education level. Finally, this paper provides an exogenous proxy for English language skill among immigrants. Because current English fluency is endogenously related to intermarriage, linguistic distance, serving as a proxy, can measure the effect indirectly.

Ethnic intermarriage rates among immigrants in the US are greater among whites than other racial groups, are greater for men than for women (except for "war brides"), but decrease with the age at migration. The intermarriage rates increase with duration of residence in the US, educational attainment, the disparity between one's own educational attainment and that of one's ethnic group, having had a previous marriage, and if one's parents were intermarried. Intermarriage rates are higher for men who were veterans, and higher for women who are married to veterans. Intermarriage rates are lower the greater the distance between the immigrant's mother tongue and English. A noticeable "war brides" effect is found in the analysis in contrast to the generally lower intermarriage rate for women. Intermarriage rates are also greater the smaller the potential availability of a spouse of the same ethnicity, and the smaller the size of one's ethnic group, although the absolute population size where one lives has little effect.

The lack of direct information on specific country of residence when education was completed, as well as information on the timing of the current marriage, hinders research on the determinants of intermarriage. In addition, the 1980 Census was the last time age at first marriage was asked in the decennial Census. This information is imperative for examining the marital decisions of more recent immigrants in the United States.

Acknowledgments We would like to thank those who made helpful comments at the IZA Third Migrant Ethnicity 2007 Meeting, the Society of Labor Economists Meetings (2008) and at the Stockholm University Linnaeus Center for Integration Studies (2009). We also appreciate the very helpful comments of the REHO editor and referees.

Appendix

See Appendix Tables 4 and 5.

Table 4 Data sources and definitions of the variables

Data sources		Description
Primary		1980 Census of Populations, Public Use Microdata Sample, 1 Percent Sample
Secondary		1970 and 1960 Census of Populations, Public Use Microdata Sample, 1 Percent Samples

Dependent variables		Description
Intermarried–based on ancestry		The dependent variable is dichotomous and equal to one if the respondent is currently married to an individual of a different ethnicity based on the first entry listed for the question regarding an individual's ancestry
Intermarried–based on country of birth		The dependent variable is dichotomous and equal to one if the respondent is currently married to an individual of a different ethnicity based on their place of birth

Explanatory variables	Code	Description
Race	BLACK, AMINDIAN, ASIAN, ASINDIAN, HISPANIC, WHITE, OTHER	Dichotomous variables equal to unity if the respondents race or Hispanic Ancestry is Black, American Indian, Asian, Asian Indian, Hispanic (regardless of race), White or other, where white is the benchmark group
Marital history	TIMESMAR	Equal to 0 if married once and equal to 1 if more than once
Age at marriage	AGEMAR	Equal to the age of first marriage
	AGEMAR18_30	Equal to 1 if the respondent married between the ages of 18 and 30
	AGEMR31_45	Equal to 1 if the respondent married between the ages of 31 and 45
	AGEMR_64	Equal to 1 if the respondent married between the ages of 46 and 64
Availability ratio	AR	Where i is age in year marriage market variables are taken from (1980,1970 or 1960), j is geographic region and k is ethnicity of respondent

Table 4 continued

Explanatory variables	Code	Description
AR used for females Parallel construction for the AR used for males		$FAR_{ijk} = \dfrac{\sum_{t=2}^{t+10} M_{tjk}}{\sum_{t=2}^{t+8} F_{tjk}}$

Variables	Code	Description
Size of group	GRPSIZE	Equal to the number (in thousands) of the opposite sex in the ethnic/racial group of the respondent by region and taken from the Census that represents the individual's marriage market, specified in Sect. 4
Population	POP	Total Population in SMSA or State
Spouse's veteran status	SPSVET	Equal to 1 for women if husband served in the US military and 0 if spouse did not and for males
Years of schooling completed	GRADE	Equal to the highest grade attended
Grade squared	GRADE2	Equal to grade squared
Deviations from the educational mode-high	HIGHL	Equal to the deviation from the modal educational level of the group if the respondent has a higher education level than the group, equal to 0 otherwise
Deviations from the educational mode-low	LOWHI	Equal to the deviation from the modal educational level of the group if the respondent has a lower educational level than the group, equal to 0 otherwise
Linguistic distance	LINGXX	Linguistic Distance (Table 3) ranges from LING1 (languages most distant from English) to LING3 (closest to English)
Multiple ancestry	MULTANC	Equal to 1 if the respondent has more than one ancestry listed, 0 otherwise
Years since migration	YSM	Equal to AGE–AGEIMM
Age at immigration variables	AM0_13 AM14_17 AM18_23 AM24_28 AM29_35 AM36_	Equal to AGEIMM for ages indicated by the name of the code; otherwise 0. The benchmark group for this category is 0_13

Table 5 List of Ancestries and Countries of birth

Group	Including
(A) *Ancestries*	
Austrian	
Belgian	
Icelander	
Danish	Danish, Faeroe Islander, Greenlander
Dutch	Dutch, Dutch-French-Irish, Dutch-German-Irish, Dutch-Irish-Scotch, Dutch and English Speaking Belgian
English	English, English-French-German, English-French-Irish, English-German-Irish, English-German-Swedish, English-Irish-Scotch, English-Scotch-Welsh, Manx
Welsh	
Scottish	
Finnish	
French	French, French-German-Irish, Alsatian
German	German, German-Irish-Italian, German-Irish-Scotch, German-Irish-Swedish
Greek	
Irish	
Italian	
Luxemburger	
Norwegian	
Portuguese	
Swedish	
Swiss	
Scandinavian	
Other European	European, Northern European, Slovak, Andorran, Armenian, Central European, Croatian, Eastern European, Georgian, Gibraltan, Lapp, Liechtensteiner, Maltese, Monegasque, Ruthenian, Serbian, Slav, Slovene, Southern European, Western European
Albanian	
Bulgarian	
Czechoslovakian	
Estonian	
Hungarian	
Latvian	
Lithuanian	
Polish	
Rumanian	
Yugoslavian	
Russian	
Ukrainian	
Byelorussian	
Spanish	Spanish, Spaniard, Basque

Table 5 continued

Group	Including
Mexican	
Puerto Rican	
Cuban	
Dominican	
Argentinean	
Bolivian	
Chilean	
Colombian	Columbian, Providencia, San Andres
Costa Rican	
Guatemalan	
Honduran	
Paraguayan	
Peruvian	
Uruguayan	
Ecuadorian	
Venezuelan	
South and Central American	Central and South American, Nicaraguan, Panamanian, Salvadoran, Surinam
Haitian	Haitian, French West Indies
Jamaican	
Trinidadian/Tobagonian	
U.S. Virgin Islander	
English Speaking West Indies	British West Indian, Anguilla Islander, British Virgin Islander, Cayman Islander, Turks and Caicos Islander Caribbean, Bahamian, Barbadian, Dominica Islander, Dutch West Indies, St. Christopher Islander, St. Lucia Islander, Bermudan, Guyanese
Belizean	
Brazilian	
Iranian	
Israeli	
Jordanian	Jordanian, Trans Jordan
Lebanese	
Syrian	
Turkish	
Muscat	
North African, Arabian Middle Eastern	Middle Eastern, Gazan, Afghan, Arabian, Bahraini, Bedouin, Iraqi, Kurd, Kuria Muria Islander, Kuwaiti, Muscat, Omani, Palestinian, People's Democratic Republic of Yemen, Qatar, Saudi Arabian, Trucial Oman, West Bank, Assyrian, Egyptian, Berber, Tunisian, Algerian, Moroccan, Alhucemas, Libyan, Yemeni, Aden, Comoros Islander, Rio de Oro, Moor
South African-White	Race White: South African, Lesotho, Rhodesian, Swaziland, Botswana
South African-Black	Race Black: South African, Lesotho, Rhodesian, Swaziland, Botswana

(*continued overleaf*)

Table 5 continued

Group	Including
Sub-Saharan African	Angolan, Congolese, Djibouti, Ethiopian, Madagascan, , Mozambican, Namibian, Rio de Oro, Somalian, Sudanese, Zairian, Zambian, Burundian, Cameroonian, Central African Republic, Equatorial Guinea, Gabonese, Kenyan, Rwandan, Tanzanian, Ugandan, Benin, Cape Verdean, Chadian, Gambian, Ghanaian, Guinea-Bissau, Guinean, Ivory Coast, Liberian, Malian, Mauritanian, Niger, Nigerian, Senegalese, Sierra Leonean, Togo, Kenyan, Upper Voltan, Afro-American, Eastern Africa, Western Africa, Central African and Other African
Asian Indian	
Pakistani	
Chinese	Taiwanese, Singaporean
Filipino	
Japanese	Japanese, Okinawan
Korean	
Other Asian: Malaysian & Indonesian	Asia, Malaysian, Indonesian
Vietnamese	
South East Asian	Burmese, Cambodian, Indo-Chinese, Laotian
(B) *Countries of birth*	
England	England, Channel Islands
Scotland	
Wales	
Ireland	Ireland, Northern Ireland
Norway	
Sweden	
Denmark	Denmark, Faeroe Islands, Greenland
Netherlands (Dutch)	
Belgium	
Switzerland	
France	
Germany	East and West Germany
Poland	
Czechoslovakia	
Austria	
Hungary	
Yugoslavia	
Latvia	
Estonia	
Lithuania	
Finland	
Romania	
Bulgaria	
Greece	

Table 5 continued

Group	Including
Italy	
Spain	
Portugal	
Iceland	
Luxembourg	
Albania	
Turkey	
Syria	
Lebanon	
Israel	
Pakistan	
India	
China	China, Hong Kong, Macau, Singapore, Taiwan
Japan	
Korea (n.e.c.)	
Philippines	
Byelorussia	
Ukrainia	
Jordan	
Iran	
Canada	
Mexico	
Guatemala	
Belize	
Honduras	
El Salvador	
Costa Rica	
Cuba	
Jamaica	
Dominican Republic	
Haiti	
Trinidad & Tobago	
Venezuela	
Ecuador	
Peru	
Bolivia	
Brazil	
Paraguay	
Uruguay	
Chile	
Argentina	

(*continued overleaf*)

Table 5 continued

Group	Including
Other Central and South America	Central and South America, Nicaragua, Panama, Surinam
Colombia	
Vietnam	
New Zealand	
North African/Arabian/ Middle Eastern	North Africa, Cyprus, Afganistan, Algeria, Egypt, Iraq, Kuwait, Libya, Morocco, Qatar, Saudi Arabia, Tadzhik, Tunisia, Yemen
Korea	South and North Korea
English Speaking West Indies	Antigua- Barbuda, Bermuda, British Virgin Islands, British West Indies, Caribbean, Cayman Islands, Dominica, Guyana, Aruba, Curacao, Bahamas, Barbados, Grenada, St. Lucia
Sub-Saharan Africa	Angola, Africa, Benin, Burundi, Cameroon, Cape Verde, Chad, Eastern Africa, Ethiopia, Gambia, Ghana, Guinea, Guinea-Bissau, Ivory Coast, Kenya, Liberia, Madagascar, Mauritlus, Mozambique, Nambia, Niger, Nigeria, Senegal, Sierra Leone, Somalia, Sudan, Tanzania, Togo, Uganda, Western Africa, Zaire, Botswana
South African Black	South Africa, Zimbabwe
South African White	South Africa, Zimbabwe
Pacific Islander	Fiji, Micronesia, Papua New Guinea, Tonga, Western Samoa
Other Asian	Burma, Indonesia, Cambodia, Laos, Malaysia, SE Asia
Thai	

Source 1980 Census of Population, Public Use Microdata Sample, 1 Percent Sample

References

Alba, R. D., & Golden, R. M. (1986). Patterns of ethnic intermarriage in the United States. *Social Forces, 65*, 202–223.

Anderson, R. N., & Saenz, R. (1994). Structural determinants of Mexican American intermarriage, 1975–1980. *Social Science Quarterly, 75*, 414–430.

Asher, J. J. (1969). The optimal age to learn a foreign language. *The Modern Language Journal, 53*, 334–341.

Becker, G. S. (1974). *A theory of marriage. Economics of the family* (pp. 299–344). Chicago/London: University of Chicago Press.

Belot, M., & Fidrmuc, J. (2009). *Anthropometry of love: Height and gender asymmetries in interethnic marriages*. Nuffield College, Oxford University: Center for Experimental Social Sciences.

Brien, M. J. (1997). Racial differences in marriage and the role of marriage markets. *Journal of Human Resources, 32*(4), 741–778.

Buchanan, P. J. (2006). *State of emergency: The third world invasion and conquest of America*. New York: Thomas Dunne Books/St. Martin's Press.

Celikaksoy, A., Helena, N., & Verner, M. (2006). Marriage migration: Just another case of positive assortative matching? *Review of Economics of the Household, 4*, 253–275.

Chiswick, B. R. (1978). The effect of americanization on earnings of foreign born men. *The Journal of Political Economy, 86*, 897–921.

Chiswick, C. U. (2009). The economic determinants of ethnic assimilation. *Journal of Population Economics, 22*(4), 859–880.

Chiswick, B. R. & Houseworth, C. (2008). Ethnic Intermarriage among Immigrants: Human Capital and Assortative Mating. IZA–Institute for the Study of Labor, Bonn, Discussion Paper No. 3740, September 2008.

Chiswick, B. R., & Miller, P. W. (1998). English language fluency among immigrants to the United States. *Research in Labor Economics, 17*, 151–200.

Chiswick, B. R., & Miller, P. W. (2005). Linguistic distance: A quantitative measure of the distance between English and other languages. *Journal of Multilingual and Multicultural Development, 26*, 1–11.

Chiswick, B. R., & Miller, P. W. (2008). A test of the critical period hypothesis for language learning. *Journal of Multilingual and Multicultural Development, 29*(1), 16–29.

Chiswick, C. U., & Lehrer, E. L. (1991). Religious intermarriage: An economic perspective. *Contemporary Jewry, 12*, 21–34.

Cohen, S. M. (1977). Socioeconomic determinants of intraethnic marriage and friendship. *Social Forces, 55*(4), 997–1010.

Fitzgerald, J. (1991). Welfare durations and the marriage market: Evidence from the survey of income and program participation. *The Journal of Human Resources, 26*, 545–561.

Fossett, M. A., & Kiecolt, K. J. (1991). A methodological review of the sex ratio: Alternatives for comparative research. *Journal of Marriage and the Family, 53*, 941–957.

Furtado, D. (2006). Human capital and interethnic marriage decisions. IZA–Institute for the Study of Labor, Discussion Paper Series No. 1989, Bonn, February 2006.

Gilbertson, G. A., Fitzpatrick, J. P., & Yang, L. (1996). Hispanic intermarriage in New York City: New evidence from 1991. *International Migration Review, 30*, 445–459.

Goldman, N., Westoff, C. F., & Hammerslough, C. (1984). Demography of the marriage market in the United States. *Population Index, 50*, 5–25.

Gordon, M. (1964) Assimilation and American life: The role of race, religion and national origins. Oxford University Press, Inc.

Grossbard-Shechtman, S. (1993). *On the economics of marriage: A theory of marriage, Labor, and Divorce*. Boulder: Westview Press.

Hart-Gonzalez, L., & Lindermann, S. (1993). *"Expected achievement in speaking proficiency, 1993" School of Language Studies, Foreign Service Institute, US*. Mimeographed: Department of State.

Kalmijn, M. (1998). Intermarriage and homogamy: Causes, patterns, trends. *Annual Review of Sociology, 24*, 395–421.

Kantarevic, J. (2004) Interethnic marriages and economic assimilation of immigrants. IZA–Institute for the Study of Labor, Discussion Paper Series No. 1142, Bonn, May 2004.

Lehrer, E. L. (1998). Religious intermarriage in the United States: Determinants and trends. *Social Science Research, 27*, 245–263.

Lehrer, E. L. (2008). Age at marriage and marital instability: Revisiting the becker-landes-michael hypothesis. *Journal of Population Economics, 21*(2), 463–484.

Lichter, D. T., LeClere, F. B., & McLaughlin, D. K. (1991). Local marriage markets and the marital behavior of black and white women. *The American Journal of Sociology, 96*, 843–867.

Lichter, D. T., Mclaughlin, D. K., Kephart, G., & Landry, D. J. (1992). Race and the retreat from marriage: A shortage of marriageable men? *American Sociological Review, 57*, 781–799.

Lichter, D. T., & Qian, Z. (2001). Measuring marital assimilation: Intermarriage among natives and immigrants. *Social Science Research, 30*, 289–312.

Lieberson, S., & Waters, M. C. (1988). *From many strands: Ethnic and racial groups in contemporary America*. New York: Russell Sage Foundation.

Meng, X., & Gregory, R. R. (2005). Intermarriage and the economic assimilation of immigrants. *Journal of Labor Economics, 23*, 135–175.

Meng, X., Meurs, D. (2006). Intermarriage, language, and economic assimilation process: A case study of France. IZA–Institute for the Study of Labor, Discussion Paper Series No. 2461, Bonn, November 2006.

Reinharz, S., & DellaPergola, S. (Eds.). (2009). Jewish intermarriage around the world. New Brunswick, NJ: Transaction Publishers.

Sandefur, G. D., & McKinnell, T. (1986). American Indian intermarriage. *Social Science Research, 347*, 347–348.

Schoen, R. (1983). Measuring the tightness of a marriage squeeze. *Demography, 20*, 61–78.

Schoen, R., & Thomas, B. (1989). Intergroup marriage in Hawaii, 1969–1971 and 1979–1981. *Sociological Perspectives, 32*, 365–382.

Schoen, R., & Wooldredge, J. (1989). Marriage choices in North Carolina and Virginia, 1969–1971 and 1979–1981. *Journal of Marriage and the Family, 51*, 465–481.

South, S. J., & Lloyd, K. M. (1992). Marriage markets and nonmarital fertility in the United States. *Demography, 29*, 247–264.

Statistical Abstract: 2007 Edition, U.S. Census Bureau, http://www.census.gov/compendia/statab/2007edition.html.

Wilson, W. J. (1987). *The truly disadvantaged*. Chicago: University of Chicago Press.

Wood, R. G. (1995). Marriage rates and marriageable men: A test of the wilson hypothesis. *Journal of Human Resources, 30*, 163–193.

[19]

Intermarriage and the Economic Assimilation of Immigrants

Xin Meng, *Australian National University*

Robert G. Gregory, *Australian National University*

This article investigates the assimilation role of intermarriage between immigrants and natives. Intermarried immigrants earn significantly higher incomes than endogamously married immigrants, even after we take account of human capital endowments and endogeneity of intermarriage. The premium does not appear to be a reward for unobservable individual characteristics. Natives who intermarry do not receive this premium, nor do immigrants who intermarry into another ethnic group. The premium is mainly attributable to a faster speed of assimilation rather than any difference in labor-market quality between intermarried and nonintermarried immigrants at the point of arrival.

I. Introduction

In most Western countries immigrants earn less, on average, than the native born, with this earnings gap falling as time spent in the host country increases. The rate at which the gap narrows is usually interpreted as a measure of economic assimilation. The sources of economic assimilation

We would like to thank Josh Angrist, Michael Baker, Jeff Borland, Trevor Breusch, Deborah Cobb-Clark, Tom Crossley, Tue Gorgens, Robert Haveman, and Paul Miller for their useful comments; seminar participants at the Research School of Social Sciences, Australian National University, the University of Adelaide, the University of Melbourne, and Monash University; and participants at the Society of Labor Economists Annual Conference, Austin, Texas, 2001. Contact the corresponding author, Xin Meng, at xin.meng@anu.edu.au

[*Journal of Labor Economics*, 2005, vol. 23, no. 1]
© 2005 by The University of Chicago. All rights reserved.
0734-306X/2005/2301-0006$10.00

are generally understood to be accumulation of the knowledge of the customs, language, and opportunities for finding good jobs in the host country (Chiswick 1978).

Considerable research effort, especially in the United States, Canada, and Australia, has been directed toward measuring the economic assimilation of immigrants (see Chiswick 1978; Borjas 1985, 1995a, 1999; Beggs and Chapman 1988; LaLonde and Topel 1992, 1997; Baker and Benjamin 1994; McDonald and Worswick 1999). Few studies, however, have attempted to investigate the process by which assimilation takes place, although some attention has been directed toward the effect of English proficiency on immigrant earnings, suggesting that linguistic adjustment is important (see, e.g., Chiswick and Miller 1992, 1994, 1995; Lazear 1999).

Recently, the effect of family structure on immigrant assimilation has begun to attract attention (Baker and Benjamin 1997; Eckstein and Weiss, forthcoming). This article adds to this literature from a new perspective. It studies intermarriage as a way through which immigrants acquire host country customs, language skills, and knowledge of the local labor market and obtain contacts and connections, which, in turn, improve their job prospects and increase the rate of economic assimilation.

Three important questions are posed in this article: (1) Who intermarries? (2) Is there an earnings premium associated with intermarriage? (3) And, if so, does the premium indicate a return to economic assimilation?

To address these questions, the article proceeds in the following ways. First, a model is outlined to analyze the determinants of intermarriage. Second, various techniques are used to estimate the causal effect of intermarriage on earnings. Finally, alternative hypotheses are examined to ascertain whether the observed intermarriage premium reflects a return to economic assimilation.

The article is organized as follows. Section II discusses the model specification and the data. Section III investigates the determinants of intermarriage, Section IV estimates the intermarriage premium, Section V explores the sources of the intermarriage premium, and conclusions are given in Section VI.

II. Model Specification and Data

Model Specification

According to the traditional assimilation literature, the earnings of immigrants are functions of their human capital characteristics and economic assimilation, where the latter is usually captured by time spent in the host country since migration and host country–speaking ability (Chiswick 1978; Borjas 1985, 1995a, 1999; and Chiswick and Miller 1992, 1994, 1995). Immigrants who have been in the host country longer have more time to find good jobs and to learn employment skills that fit the new environment. Good host country–speaking ability increases the range of available jobs and the speed of learning the local culture and labor-market skills.

Recent studies have suggested that the assimilation process may be affected by family structure. Eckstein and Weiss (forthcoming) conjecture that married couples can assist each other on arrival to a new country and, hence, may be able to catch up faster than single immigrants. They call this a "coordination effect," which leads to a higher marriage premium for immigrants relative to natives.

Baker and Benjamin (1997) focus on immigrant women and find that those from an intermarried family do better in the labor market than their counterparts from a nonintermarried family. They interpret this phenomenon as an outcome of an investment strategy that differs by family type. Immigrant women from an endogamous marriage often have to accept the first job they can find on arrival to finance their husbands' investment in the local labor market. They implicitly borrow against their future income by choosing jobs that do not offer steep experience-earnings profiles. Immigrant women from an exogamous marriage can afford to search and wait for jobs that promise a better future.

We are also interested in the effect of family structure on assimilation, but our emphasis differs from these two studies. Compared with Baker and Benjamin (1997), we propose that intermarriage should affect the economic assimilation of both male and female immigrants. This is because intermarried immigrant men and women can more quickly learn and understand the host country's customs, language skills, and knowledge of the local labor market from their native spouse. They obtain contacts and connections that improve their job prospects and increase the rate of economic assimilation. Compared with Eckstein and Weiss (forthcoming), our attention is mainly directed toward the difference in marriage premia between exogamous and endogamous marriages rather than to the difference in marriage premia for immigrants and natives.

Following the traditional economic assimilation literature and incorporating these recent developments and our own focus on intermarriage, the baseline earnings equation for immigrants may be specified as follows:

$$\ln W_{it} = X'_{it}\beta_{10} + ASM'_{it}\beta_{11} + \mu_1 M_{1it} + \mu_2 M_{2it} + \varepsilon_{it}, \quad (1)$$

where $\ln W_{it}$ refers to the log earnings of an immigrant i observed in census year t; X_{it} is a vector of human capital and demographic variables, including age and its squared term, years of schooling, religious belief, and birthplace.[1] The vector ASM_{it} is a vector of variables indicating economic

---

[1] The existence of religious beliefs is not usually included in an earnings equation. However, there is a literature suggesting a correlation between religious beliefs and earnings (Tomes 1985; Steen 1996).

assimilation, including years since migration and English language skill. The variable M_1 is the indicator for endogamous marriage, and M_2 is the indicator for exogamous marriage, while being single is used as the default group.

If the choice among being single, endogamous marriages, and exogamous marriages is regarded as exogenous, then equation (1) can be fitted directly to the data, and we can begin to explore the extent to which marriage premia are different for endogamously and exogamously married immigrants. However, if the decision to marry and the choice between endogamous and exogamous marriage depends, in part, on the potential earnings within each family type, marriage choices will be endogenous. It is commonly known that there is a positive and sizable marriage premium for male workers and a negative premium for female workers in many market economies (Nakosteen and Zimmer 1987; Korenman and Neumark 1991). But the literature does not provide conclusive results as to whether it is the marriage that increases individual productivity or whether more productive people are more likely to marry. If the latter is important, endogeneity of marriage should be taken into account in the estimation of a normal earnings equation. This should also apply to the choice between endogamous and exogamous marriages. Equation (1) would then need to be embedded in a system of equations derived from a theory of marriage and intermarriage.

To develop this system of equations, we can draw on the theoretical and empirical marriage literature derived from Becker (1973, 1974). However, there is no well-defined economic literature discussing the choice between an endogamous or exogamous marriage, although many of the considerations discussed by Becker would be relevant. Given our empirical focus, the full development of a formal model is outside the scope of this article, but the following is a sketch of an empirical model of endogamous and exogamous marriages based on economic principles.

Becker's (1973, 1974) marriage theory suggests that an individual's earnings potential should be highly correlated with the probability of being married. Thus, commonly used variables in the empirical marriage literature include the usual core of human capital variables, such as age and education, which proxy the potential earnings of individuals (Freiden 1974; Nakosteen and Zimmer 1987; Blau, Kahn, and Waldfogel 2000). Similar variables may well affect the probability of intermarriage.

The incidence of endogamous and exogamous marriages will also be affected by noneconomic factors such as religious beliefs. This variable, however, may affect different types of marriages in different directions. Individuals who are more religious may be more likely to marry into their own group, whereas intermarriage is more likely to require that an individual be willing to accept a different cultural system, beliefs, and lifestyle within a marriage. This willingness may be negatively correlated with strong religious beliefs. In addition, young and highly educated people may be more tolerant of other cultures and lifestyles and be more likely to intermarry.

Communication skills that are directly related to one of the most important components of utility from marriage—love and companionship—may also be correlated with endogamous and exogamous marriages. Thus, facility in the native language may be a particularly important determinant of marriage type.

The probability that an immigrant will intermarry may also be affected by their length of residency in the host country. Immigrants who have been in the host country for a longer period may have a better understanding of the culture of the host country than more recent arrivals and may, therefore, relate better to potential spouses from the set of available natives.

In addition, the economics and sociology literature suggest that individuals bond more easily within their own age, ethnic, and religious groups. It is to be expected, therefore, that the probability of meeting a potential partner from their own ethnic or religious background may be positively related to an immigrant's endogamous marriage probability and negatively related to the incidence of exogamous marriages (Glazer and Moynihan 1963; Borjas 1995b; Jones 1997; Bisin and Verdier 2000). For example, a Turkish Muslim woman in Australia may prefer to marry a Turkish Muslim man. However, if the number of Muslim male immigrants from Turkey is limited, her range of choice will be limited. Thus, other things being equal, she will have a lower probability of marrying within her own ethnic-religious group and a higher probability of marrying outside the group. Assuming that she treats other ethnic-religious groups equally, her most likely partner will be from the "native" pool. To approximate this effect on the probability of an immigrant woman (or man) forming an endogamous or exogamous marriage, we define the probability of a women (or man) marrying within her (his) own ethnic-religion-age group, $P_{it}^{f}(MI)$—or $P_{it}^{m}(MI)$—as the number of men (women) from her (his) own age-ethnic-religion group observed in census year t (n_t^m or n_t^f) divided by the total stock of all men (women) of marriageable age observed in census year t (N_t^m, or N_t^f). We refer to this ratio as the "probability of marry within," and for women (or men) it can be formally specified as:

$$P_{it}^{f}(MI) = \frac{n_t^m}{N_t^m} \left[\text{or } P_{it}^{m}(MI) = \frac{n_t^f}{N_t^f} \right].$$

There is another constraint that may affect the probability of an endogamous or an exogamous marriage. The probability may also depend on competition among fellow immigrants for partners of the same age, religious, and ethnic group (Freiden 1974; Angrist 2002). Thus, the sex ratio within each age-ethnic-religious cell may matter. If the sex ratio indicates a predominance of males then, ceteris paribus, there may be more exogamous marriages from immigrant men and less from immigrant women and vice versa for endogamous marriages. In addition, given age-ethnic-religious preference, a very unbalanced sex ratio should reduce the overall marriage rate. The sex ratio for female immigrants is defined as:

$$\text{SRATIO}_{it}^{f} = \frac{n_t^m}{n_t^f},$$

where n_t^m and n_t^f are the number of males and females, respectively, in the age-ethnic-religion group to which individual i of census year t belongs. The corresponding ratio for male immigrants is the inverse of that for female immigrants.

The above discussion suggests that endogamous-exogamous marriage equations for an immigrant i in census year t may be written as:

$$M_{1it} = X'_{it}\pi_{10} + ASM'_{it}\pi_{11} + Z'_{it}\pi_{12} + u_{1it}, \tag{2}$$

$$M_{2it} = X'_{it}\pi_{20} + ASM'_{it}\pi_{21} + Z'_{it}\pi_{22} + u_{2it}, \tag{3}$$

where M_{1t}, M_{2t}, X_{it}, and ASM_{it} are defined the same way as in equation (1); Z_i is a vector of additional exogenous variables that affect the marriage decision but do not directly affect earnings in equation (1) except through their impact on marital status. They include $P_{it}(MI)$, the probability of meeting a potential partner within the immigrant's own age-ethnic-religious group, and SRATIO$_{it}$, the sex ratio of the immigrant's own age-ethnic-religious group.

Equations (2) and (3) can be estimated by ordinary least squares (OLS), or by a single equation multinomial logit model, where M_1 and M_2, as different marriage status variables, are compared with the singles.[2] The earnings equation (1) will first be estimated as a single equation by OLS treating marriage status as exogenous. Equations (1)–(3) will then be estimated as two-stage models treating marital status as endogenous. Following Wooldridge (2002), when estimating a two-stage model, the predicted values of endogamous and exogamous marriages are obtained from the first-stage estimation (either OLS or multinomial logit) and plugged into the earnings equation. The vector Z_i is used as instruments and is excluded from the second-stage earnings estimation.

[2] In the case of the multinomial logit model, the functional form is specified as Prob$(y_i = M_j) = e^{x_i\beta_j}/\sum_{k=1}^{J} e^{x_i\beta_k}$, where M_j indicates marital status, which takes three values: M_0, M_1, and M_2. In addition, M_0 refers to singles, M_1 is endogamous marriage, and M_2 is exogamous marriage.

The Data

The data are taken from the 1% samples of the 1981, 1986, 1991, and 1996 Australian Census of Population and Housing. The four samples are stacked to increase the sample size sufficiently to allow separate estimations for males and females. In addition, stacking the four samples allows for the control of both "years since migration" and "cohort" effects when there is a need to control for both quality of the cohort and assimilation effects in Section V.

"Marriage" includes both formal and de facto marriages. "Intermarriage" is defined as the union of an immigrant from non-English-speaking background countries (NESB) with a "native," who is defined as Australian born or an immigrant from an English-speaking background country (ESB), such as New Zealand, the United Kingdom, the United States, and Canada.[3] We define "native" this way because most English-speaking countries have a similar culture and other formal and informal labor market structures. In addition, we show in table 1 below that endogamous and exogamous marriage premia are very similar for Australian born people and immigrants from ESB countries.

We should limit the immigrant sample to those who have the chance to intermarry in Australia. In principle, this includes all NESB immigrants because they always have the option of divorce. In practice, however, the probability of intermarriage will be lower if an immigrant is already married on arrival. Information on the date of marriage is available only from the 1981 census. To examine whether fitting the earnings equation to all NESB immigrants produces different results from fitting the equation to NESB immigrants who married after arrival in Australia, we also report our results for those who married after arrival in Australia for the 1981 data, and for those who entered Australia at age 19 years or below for all four censuses, under the assumption that those arriving at a younger age are less likely to have been married before migration.

The Australian census collects annual income rather than earnings. As the main interest here is the earnings premium of intermarriage, the samples are constrained to wage and salary earners who worked full-time (35 hours and more) in the census years. For this group the income measure may be a close approximation to earnings.[4] In the empirical section, we

---

[3] Ireland and Scotland are included in the United Kingdom. The 1996 census does not distinguish between North and South Americans, and this category is excluded from the 1996 data.

[4] We compared the weekly income (annual income divided by 52) for full-time wage and salary earners from the four census data sets with the weekly earnings of full-time wage and salary earners data obtained from the Survey of Employers conducted by the Australian Bureau of Statistics (Catalogue 6302.0 Average Weekly Earnings of Australia, Australian Bureau of Statistics, various years) and found that they are very close for both men and women. The average weekly

Table 1
Average Annual Nominal Income for the Sample of Immigrants and Natives

	Mean Income					Marriage Premia		
	Average (C1)	Single (C2)	Endogamous Marriage (C3)	Exogamous Marriage (C4)	Marry to ESBs (C5)	Endogamous Marriage [(C3/C2) − 1] × 100	Exogamous Marriage [(C4/C3) − 1] × 100	Marry to ESBs [(C5/C3) − 1] × 100
NESBs:								
Males:								
1981	13,587	12,640	13,101	15,243	15,803	3.7	16.4	20.6
1986	21,371	20,144	20,396	24,196	25,239	1.3	18.6	23.7
1991	29,469	24,929	28,909	33,531	35,659	16.0	16.0	23.3
1996	37,313	33,867	36,612	40,643	41,768	8.1	11.0	14.1
4-year average						7.2	15.5	20.4
Females:								
1981	10,093	10,952	9,506	12,067	10,887	−13.2	26.9	14.5
1986	16,243	18,032	15,026	18,190	18,850	−16.7	21.1	25.4
1991	23,376	22,904	22,240	27,147	27,833	−2.9	22.1	25.1
1996	29,970	31,001	27,673	34,029	34,417	−10.7	23.0	24.4
4-year average						−10.9	23.3	22.4
ESB:								
Males:								
1981	15,214	13,689	15,707	15,639	16,634	14.7	−.4	5.9
1986	24,225	21,224	24,773	25,432	25,502	16.7	2.7	2.9
1991	32,864	26,590	34,981	34,492	37,045	31.6	−1.4	5.9
1996	42,394	37,147	44,611	42,993	47,548	20.1	−3.6	6.6
4-year average						20.8	−.7	5.3

	ESB			NESB			Difference	
Females:								
1981	11,199	11,254	10,845	11,503	12,284	−3.6	6.1	13.3
1986	18,107	18,621	17,564	18,288	17,604	−5.7	4.1	.2
1991	25,650	24,418	25,637	27,090	25,867	5.0	5.7	.9
1996	32,936	33,487	32,761	32,557	32,578	−2.2	−.6	−.6
4-year average						−1.6	3.8	3.5
Australian born:								
Males:								
1981	14,630	12,282	15,467	15,918	15,844	25.9	2.9	2.4
1986	22,842	19,205	24,092	24,639	25,913	25.4	2.3	7.6
1991	30,873	24,480	33,336	35,250	34,853	36.2	5.7	4.6
1996	38,646	32,626	40,645	42,660	46,345	24.6	5.0	14.0
4-year average						28.0	4.0	7.1
Females:								
1981	11,173	10,959	11,318	11,696	11,459	3.3	3.3	1.2
1986	17,713	17,540	17,763	18,096	18,448	1.3	1.9	3.9
1991	24,401	23,069	25,100	26,514	26,631	8.8	5.6	6.1
1996	30,788	30,671	30,445	33,401	32,626	−.7	9.7	7.2
4-year average						3.2	5.1	4.6

NOTE.—ESB = English-speaking background countries; NESB = non-English-speaking background countries.
SOURCES.—1% samples of the 1981, 1986, 1991, and 1996 Australian Census of Population and Housing.

use the terms "earnings" and "income" interchangeably. The measurement of some other variables differs from census to census, and this is noted along with a full data description in the data appendix.

Intermarriage rates in Australia are high. For the total sample of married NESB immigrants, 26%, 27%, 29%, and 32% are intermarried at each of the 4 census years, respectively. Among individuals arriving in Australia at 19 years of age or below, the intermarriage rate is much higher at 48%, 46%, 48%, and 47% at each census date, respectively.[5] These intermarriage rates indicate the high rate of social assimilation of NESB immigrants in Australia and are a reflection of an immigration policy that has always placed considerable emphasis on social and economic assimilation.

The nominal annual incomes for native Australian born, ESB, and NESB immigrant full-time wage and salary earners is given in table 1. The samples are divided into single, endogamously and exogamously married, and males and females. The data are quite revealing.[6]

First, the raw income gap is quite small between single and endogamously married male NESB immigrants, an average of 7.2% for the 4 census years. In comparison, the average income gap for Australian born males is 28.0%, while for ESB males it is 20.8%. The endogamous marriage premium for NESB immigrant women is negative, averaging −10.9% for the 4 census years, while for Australian women it averages 3.2%, and for ESB women −1.6%.

Second, the exogamous marriage premia for NESB men and women are both positive and significant. Female and male NESB immigrants who marry the Australian born earned, at an average, 23.3% and 15.5% more than their endogamously married counterparts over the 4 census years, respectively. Similarly sized intermarriage premia are observed if they marry ESBs (22.4% and 20.4%, respectively). These differences are statistically significant. However, the Australian born who intermarry with an NESB immigrant gain a small positive premium, which averages 4.6% for women and 7.1% for men. Similar small positive premia are observed for ESB immigrants who intermarry with NESB immigrants, averaging 3.5 for women and 5.3 for men. Equally small premia are observed if the Australian born and ESBs are intermarried to each other; t-statistics for the differences between the mean incomes of Australian born and ESBs

---

income from census data is around 3.5% less than average weekly earnings from the employer data.

[5] The 1981 data show that among those who married after they arrived in Australia 37% are intermarried.

[6] Note that the premia for endogamous marriage are particularly high for 1991 data for all groups presented in table 1. To our knowledge, no study has compared the results of marriage premia across census years, and the reason for this volatility is not clear to us at this stage.

show that there is no statistically significant difference between these two groups for all 4 years of samples.

Thus, the main conclusions drawn from table 1 are the following. The NESB immigrants earn a significantly high premium if they marry the Australian born or ESB immigrants, whereas ESBs and the Australian born do not enjoy such a high premium if they marry NESB immigrants. The pattern of endogamous and exogamous marriage premia presented in table 1, therefore, should warrant our analytical strategy of combining the Australian born and ESBs into a single native group for simplicity.

The size of the intermarriage premium for NESB immigrants is surprising. It is much larger, for example, than the income gap between the average NESB immigrant and native full-time wage and salary earner, which was 9% and 11% for men and women, respectively, in the 1981 census. These gaps can be compared with the premia of 16% and 26% if NESB immigrants are intermarried to the Australian born and 21% and 15% if they are intermarried to ESBs. Of course, the intermarriage premia of table 1 make no allowance for any human capital differences between those who intermarry and those who do not, and there are some indications that these differences may contribute to the earnings gaps. The summary statistics presented in the data appendix suggest that relative to NESB immigrants who are in an endogamous marriage, intermarried immigrants are younger, are more educated, have been in Australia for a longer time, are less likely to be religious, and are more likely to speak English fluently. It is important to account for these differences. But first we turn to a fuller discussion of the determinants of endogamous and exogamous marriage.

III. Determinants of Intermarriage

To estimate the contribution of different factors to the probability of endogamous and exogamous marriages, equations (2) and (3) are estimated by OLS and as a single multinomial logit model for male and female samples separately. In the OLS estimation, the dependent variables are endogamous and exogamous marriages (M_1 and M_2), respectively. In the multinomial logit estimation, the dependent variable takes three values: singles ($M = 0$), endogamously married ($M = 1$), and exogamously married ($M = 2$). In this case, endogamous and exogamous marriages of NESB immigrants are compared with single NESB immigrants. The results of the multinomial logit estimation are reported in the left panel of table 2, while the results from the OLS estimation are reported in the right panel. In the multinomial logit case, the listed marginal effects (ME) are evaluated at the sample mean.[7] The results for both estimations are

[7] The model is also estimated for a sample of immigrants who arrived in Australia at 19 years of age and below, and the results, which are available on request from the authors, are consistent with those reported in table 2 for the full sample.

Table 2
Selected Results of the Determinants of Endogamous and Exogamous Marriage among NESB Immigrants

| | Multinomial Logit Model ||||| OLS ||||
| | Males || Females || Males || Females ||
	Endogamous Married	Exogamous Married	Endogamous Married	Exogamous Married	Endogamous Married	Exogamous Married	Endogamous Married	Exogamous Married
Constant	−.913** (.111)	−.201* (.078)	−.332** (.114)	−.207** (.059)	−.503** (.086)	−.064 (.080)	−.057 (.087)	.111 (.075)
Sex ratio	.053** (.011)	−.025** (.007)	.057** (.011)	−.022** (.008)	.043** (.009)	−.019** (.006)	.048** (.008)	−.025** (.008)
Probability of marry within	.026+ (.016)	−.022+ (.014)	.045** (.018)	−.040** (.014)	.024+ (.013)	−.031** (.012)	.028** (.011)	−.030** (.009)
Age	.060** (.005)	−.007* (.003)	.041** (.004)	−.001 (.003)	.051** (.004)	.009** (.003)	.036** (.004)	.003 (.003)
Age²/1,000	−.500** (.054)	−.031 (.038)	−.396** (.054)	−.038 (.038)	−.419** (.041)	−.197** (.039)	−.354** (.046)	−.085* (.043)
Years of schooling	−.007* (.004)	.005* (.003)	−.010+ (.006)	−.006 (.004)	−.004+ (.003)	.004* (.002)	−.004 (.004)	−.006* (.003)
English proficiency	−.278** (.036)	.306** (.028)	−.280** (.033)	.255** (.035)	−.208** (.026)	.245** (.017)	−.187** (.027)	.164** (.022)

Years since migration	-.015**	.012**	-.011**	.006**	-.013**	.012**	-.010**	.007**
	(.001)	(.001)	(.001)	(.001)	(.001)	(.001)	(.001)	(.001)
Dummy for no religion	-.076**	.026*	-.138**	.041*	-.067**	.020	-.122**	.041+
	(.016)	(.013)	(.027)	(.02)	(.014)	(.013)	(.024)	(.025)
Born in southern Europe	.255**	-.073**	.280**	-.067**	.218**	-.070**	.249**	-.077**
	(.020)	(.016)	(.027)	(.016)	(.018)	(.017)	(.024)	(.020)
Born in Asia	.237**	-.135**	.143**	-.044**	.201**	-.120**	.138**	-.050**
	(.029)	(.021)	(.023)	(.014)	(.024)	(.021)	(.022)	(.019)
Born in other NESB countries	.120**	-.023*	.089**	-.006	.115**	-.031+	.081**	.003
	(.019)	(.015)	(.024)	(.013)	(.017)	(.019)	(.023)	(.020)
No. of observations	12,743		5,901		12,743		5,901	
χ^2	7,913.5		8,797.33					
Pseudo R^2 or adjusted R^2	.21		.16		.26		.22	
F-test for inclusion of instruments	54.78		63.98		26.05		24.29		10.24
	(.00)		(.00)		(.00)		(.00)		(.00)

NOTE.—NESB = non-English-speaking background countries. Standard errors are displayed in parentheses below the coefficients. The standard errors are derived from a consistent variance-covariance matrix using Huber-White sandwich estimators. They are also corrected for age-ethnic-religion clustering. Other variables included in the estimation are 3-year dummy variables and interaction terms between the year dummy variables and years of schooling and English proficiency. The full results for the multinomial logit estimations are reported in table B1. The results reported for the multinomial estimations are marginal effects rather than coefficients. The F-tests reported are the test for the strength of sex ratio and probability of marry within. The values in parentheses below the F-tests are significance levels (p-value).
+ Significant at 10% level.
* Significant at 5% level.
** Significant at 1% level.

consistent, and, hence, the discussion below will focus mainly on the multinomial logit results.

Most variables have the expected sign and are statistically significant. An increase in age increases the incidence of endogamous marriage, relative to being single, and reduces the rate of intermarriage. An increase in education reduces the probability of an endogamous marriage for men, relative to being single, and increases the probability of being intermarried. The education relationships with both endogamous and exogamous marriages for women, however, are negative, and the relationship is insignificant for the exogamous marriage.

English proficiency among NESB immigrants has a strong and positive correlation with intermarriage but a negative correlation with endogamous marriage, relative to being single. It is likely, however, that English proficiency is endogenous, and the causality between intermarriage and English proficiency may run both ways—greater English proficiency increases the probability of intermarriage, while intermarriage increases English proficiency (Chiswick and Miller 1995; Lazear 1999). Longitudinal data would enable us to relate the change in English proficiency to a change in marital status, but such data are not available. Nevertheless, in the 1981 census a measure of marriage duration is available. These data reveal a statistically significant and positive relationship between duration of marriage and English proficiency for intermarried NESB immigrants, whereas this relationship does not exist for NESB immigrants in endogamous marriages. This suggests that there is a causality running from the nature of the marriage to the acquisition of English fluency. We discuss this issue later in the article.

The dummy variable for no religious belief has a statistically significant positive effect on intermarriage, suggesting that more adaptive individuals are more likely to intermarry. Its effect on endogamous marriage is negative, confirming a common belief that religious people are more likely to have an endogamous marriage.

It is also apparent that the longer immigrants have been in Australia, the more likely it is that they will marry a native, and the less likely they will be in an endogamous marriage in comparison with those who are single. These are very strong effects that apply both to male and female samples.

Relative to being single, those who were born in northern Europe, which is the omitted category, are more likely to be intermarried and less likely to be in an endogamous marriage than immigrants who were born in any other NESB country. We also included individual year dummy variables and their interaction terms with schooling and English proficiency, but they do not exhibit consistent patterns and have not been reported in table 2.[8]

---

[8] See app. B for the complete results.

An estimation using combined male and female samples also reveals that NESB immigrant men are significantly less likely to be in an endogamous marriage than women, while they are more likely to intermarry than immigrant women, which is consistent with Gray's (1987) finding.[9]

We now turn to the variables that will identify the endogamous and exogamous marriage effects in the earnings equation. As expected, an increase in the probability of an NESB immigrant meeting a potential partner within the same age-ethnic-religious group has a positive and significant effect on the incidence of endogamous marriages and a negative and significant impact on the incidence of intermarriage relative to singles. In addition, an increase in competition for a potential partner within the age-ethnic-religious group reduces the probability of endogamous marriage and increases the probability of exogamous marriage. The result for the relationship between endogamous marriage and the sex ratio is consistent with that found using the U.S. aggregated data (see Freiden 1974; Blau et al. 2000). Both variables are significant at below the 1% level.

The findings in this section indicate that, in general, immigrants who are younger, are educated, have good English skills, have been in the country for a longer period, and are without religious beliefs are more likely to intermarry. Male immigrants are also more likely to intermarry than female immigrants. In addition, immigrants who are less likely to meet partners or face higher competition for potential partners within their own age-ethnic-religious group are more likely to intermarry.

IV. Intermarriage and Earnings

The data from table 1 indicate that intermarriage by an NESB immigrant with a native (Australian born or ESB immigrant) is associated with a substantial and positive income premium. Is intermarriage still associated with a premium once we take account of the difference in economic and demographic characteristics between those who are intermarried and those who are not? Table 3 presents the estimated endogamous and exogamous marriage premia from an OLS estimation of equation (1) when both endogamous and exogamous marriages are treated as exogenous.[10]

Two dummy variables indicating whether an individual is endogamously or exogamously married are included. Thus, to observe the dif-

---

[9] The full results from the combined sample estimation are available on request from the authors.

[10] The variable "hours worked" may be important in this estimation. However, the variable is categorized differently across the four censuses. In particular, the 1981 census only has one category for full-time workers (35 hours and more). To test the sensitivity of this exclusion, an hours worked variable was included in the estimation for the other 3 years. The results show that including hours worked reduces the intermarriage premium slightly, but the conclusions remain unchanged.

Table 3
Selected Results from OLS Estimation of the Earnings Equation (1), 1981–96

	NESB Immigrants		Immigrant Arrived at 19 or Below		Immigrants Married after Arrival in Australia 1981 Data		Northern European Immigrants		Southern European Immigrants		Asian Immigrants		Other NESB Immigrants		Natives	
	Males	Females	Males	Females	Males	Females	Males	Females	Males	Females	Males	Females	Males	Females	Males	Females
Constant	8.104** (.054)	8.093** (.073)	7.804** (.078)	7.946** (.128)	8.262** (.097)	7.976** (.161)	8.138** (.128)	7.809** (.177)	8.572** (.079)	8.721** (.139)	7.888** (.113)	7.980** (.125)	7.747** (.161)	7.896** (.161)	7.432** (.037)	7.303** (.065)
Dummy for endogamous marriage (M_1)	.099** (.012)	−.052** (.013)	.086** (.020)	−.067** (.022)	.085** (.022)	−.070** (.028)	.099** (.023)	−.064** (.031)	.048** (.023)	−.086** (.029)	.106** (.021)	−.044** (.021)	.146** (.033)	−.018 (.030)	.138** (.004)	.009** (.004)
Dummy for exogamous marriage (M_2)	.147** (.012)	.046** (.016)	.141** (.019)	.038+ (.021)	.123** (.023)	.031 (.037)	.135** (.022)	.032 (.031)	.122** (.024)	.061+ (.038)	.138** (.027)	.000 (.028)	.180** (.036)	.106** (.035)	.160** (.008)	.011 (.011)
Age	.037** (.002)	.032** (.003)	.055** (.004)	.040** (.007)	.035** (.005)	.044** (.008)	.037** (.006)	.034** (.008)	.021** (.004)	.008 (.006)	.041** (.006)	.043** (.006)	.048** (.008)	.041** (.008)	.062** (.001)	.056** (.001)
Age²/1,000	−.413** (.029)	−.362** (.044)	−.651** (.052)	−.468** (.097)	−.429** (.061)	−.539** (.116)	−.413** (.062)	−.386** (.104)	−.255** (.042)	−.088 (.074)	−.462** (.068)	−.511** (.082)	−.537** (.097)	−.461** (.111)	−.681** (.012)	−.646** (.019)
Years of schooling	.035** (.002)	.032** (.003)	.034** (.0030)	.030** (.006)	.033** (.002)	.029** (.005)	.040** (.005)	.058** (.008)	.024** (.002)	.014** (.005)	.044** (.005)	.027** (.005)	.042** (.006)	.044** (.007)	.055** (.001)	.073** (.002)
English proficiency	.099** (.013)	.111** (.022)	.093** (.018)	.178** (.044)	.071** (.018)	.145** (.039)	.067** (.026)	.068 (.058)	.063** (.019)	.048 (.036)	.101** (.032)	.179** (.051)	.173** (.035)	.077+ (.044)	.095** (.030)	.059 (.054)
Years since migration	.003** (.000)	.002** (.001)	.004** (.001)	.001 (.001)	.004** (.001)	.000 (.003)	.001 (.001)	.003** (.001)	.003** (.001)	.002+ (.001)	.007** (.001)	.003** (.001)	.002+ (.001)	.001 (.001)	.000 (.000)	.000 (.001)

Dummy for no religion	.015	.056**	.042**	.055**	.013	.058	.020	.050	.007	.008	−.008	.066**	.067*	.072*	.019**	.040**
	(.012)	(.016)	(.017)	(.024)	(.023)	(.040)	(.020)	(.032)	(.032)	(.058)	(.018)	(.023)	(.034)	(.037)	(.004)	(.005)
Born in southern Europe	−.068**	−.054**	−.065**	−.050**	−.086**	−.101*										
	(.010)	(.016)	(.013)	(.023)	(.019)	(.040)										
Born in Asia	.001	.051**	.016	.082**	.008	.018										
	(.011)	(.016)	(.016)	(.024)	(.023)	(.050)										
Born in other NESB countries	.021	.054**	.014	.035	.052+	.039										
	(.013)	(.017)	(.019)	(.025)	(.028)	(.042)										
Born in New Zealand															.022+	.011
															(.013)	(.016)
Born in other ESB countries															.010+	.009
															(.005)	(.008)
Difference between M_2 and M_1	.048	.098	.055	.105	.038	.101	.04	.10	.07	.15	.03	.04	.03	.12	.022	.002
Wald F-test for $M_2 = M_1$	25.7	45.2	21.5	29.1	4.7	7.0	3.63	8.36	26.51	20.31	2.04	2.90	1.78	17.84	8.0	.0
	(.00)	(.00)	(.00)	(.00)	(.03)	(.01)	(.06)	(.00)	(.00)	(.00)	(.15)	(.09)	(.18)	(.00)	(.00)	(.90)
No. of observations	12,743	5,901	5,917	2,730	2,603	935	2,930	1,146	4,866	1,853	2,962	1,845	1,864	975	75,846	36,438
Adjusted R^2	.54	.59	.57	.61	.20	.21	.50	.54	.56	.60	.54	.56	.49	.60	.53	.53

NOTE.—OLS = ordinary least squares; NESB = non-English-speaking background countries; ESB = English-speaking background countries. Standard errors are displayed in parentheses below the coefficients. The standard errors are derived from consistent variance-covariance matrix using Huber-White sandwich estimators. Other variables included in the estimation are the 3-year dummy variables and interaction terms between the year dummy variables and years of schooling and English proficiency. The full results for the first, second, and the last sets of columns are reported in table C1 of app. C. A Wald F-test is used to test the difference in coefficients specified. The values in parentheses below the F-tests are significance levels (p-value).

+ Significant at 10% level.
* Significant at 5% level.
** Significant at 1% level.

ference in marriage premium between endogamous and exogamous marriages, table 3 also presents the difference between the two coefficients and the Wald F-tests indicating whether the differences are statistically significant.

There are eight column sets in table 3, and each set presents results for male and female samples separately. The first set reports results for NESB immigrants in total. The second and third column sets present results for two subsets of NESB immigrants—those who arrived before 19 years of age (available for each census year) and those who married after arrival (available from the 1981 census). These results enable us to judge whether including those who were married before immigration makes a significant difference to the results. The results are very similar across the first three sets of columns, and little seems to be lost from working with NESB immigrants in total.

The fourth to the seventh column sets present results for different ethnic groups. The results seem similar across the ethnic groups, which supports the decision to focus the discussion and analysis on NESB immigrants in total. Finally, the last column on the right presents the earnings equation for natives.[11] A comparison of the last and first column sets enables us to assess whether natives have the same marriage and intermarriage premia as NESB immigrants.

The estimated coefficients for the human capital variables—age, years of schooling, and English proficiency—have the expected signs and are statistically significant for both immigrants and natives. The rate of return to years of schooling is positive and significant for NESB immigrants. In 1981, an extra year of schooling brings an income increase of 3.5% and 3.2% for immigrant men and women, respectively. For the native born, the rate of return to an extra year of schooling is 5.5% and 7.3% for men and women, respectively. The complete specification of these earnings equations, reported in appendix C, allows the rate of return to vary by census year, and the results indicate that the rate of return to education has increased over time for immigrant men and women, almost doubling over the 4 census years, but has increased only marginally for the native born.

Male NESB immigrants have a steeper age-earnings profile than their female counterparts, while NESB immigrants who arrived at an early age have a steeper profile than immigrants on average. These differences among NESB immigrants, however, are smaller than the differences between immigrants and natives who have much steeper age-earnings profiles.

Consistent with other studies of immigrant earnings, English profi-

---

[11] As noted earlier, "native" in this study refers to the combination of Australian born with ESBs. Earnings eq. (1) is also estimated for the ESB sample only, and the results indicate a pattern that is largely consistent with that for the sample of Australian born only. These results are reported in app. C, table C2.

ciency has a strong and positive effect on immigrant earnings. For the sample of individuals who arrived at 19 years of age or less, however, the effect is not evident in 1986 and 1991 (see full results in table C1).

Years since migration has a positive and significant effect on the earnings of NESB male immigrants but an insignificant effect on the earnings of female NESB immigrants. These results are consistent with those found in Chiswick and Miller (1995), though their sample only included male immigrants.

The dummy variable indicating if an individual has religious beliefs or not has a positive effect on earnings for almost all groups, and the effect is larger for women than for men. But when estimating the equation for different ethnic groups, most of them become statistically insignificant, in particular, for eastern and southern Europeans. This may result from the lack of variation in religious belief among the ethnic groups.

The estimated effects of birthplace for NESB immigrants are relative to those born in northern Europe. The total sample estimations indicate that southern European males and females earn relatively less. Asians and other immigrant women earn more than northern European women. For the native sample, the category of Australian born is omitted and positive, and marginally significant results are observed for the male sample but not for the female sample.

Turning to the most important results of this study, the effects of endogamous and exogamous marriages are both positive and statistically significant for total male NESB immigrants. The endogamous marriage premium is 9.9% for male immigrants relative to singles, while for those who are intermarried, a 14.7% premium is observed, indicating a 4.8% intermarriage premium when compared with those who are endogamously married. Endogamously married NESB women, however, earned 5.2% less than single women, while intermarried women earned 4.6% more than single women. Thus, intermarried women on average earn 9.8% more than their endogamously married counterparts. The Wald F-tests indicate that the differences between the exogamous and endogamous marriage premia for both men and women are statistically significant. Results from the next two columns show that the size of the exogamous marriage premia does not change if we restrict our sample to those who arrived at age 19 and below (more likely to be married after migration) or, in the case of 1981 data, married after migration to Australia. Going further across the columns, we find that apart from Asian males and males from other NESB countries, the size and significance level of the exogamous marriage premia are consistent for immigrants from different ethnic groups.

A comparison of premia for endogamous and exogamous marriage for NESB immigrants and natives will provide a "difference in differences" estimate of the extent to which the two types of marriage facilitate the immigrant assimilation process. The endogamous marriage premium is much higher for natives. Married native men earn 13.8% more than single native men, ceteris paribus, which is 4 percentage points higher than for immigrants. Native women have a 0.9% positive and statistically significant endogamous marriage premium, while this premium is −5.2% for immigrant women. These results are different from those found in the Eckstein and Weiss's (forthcoming) study of immigrants to Israel, where they show a much larger marriage premium for immigrants than for native Israelis, suggesting that married immigrant couples are better off relative to their single counterparts in the assimilation process.

With regard to intermarriage, however, the premium seems to be much higher for immigrants than for natives. Ceteris paribus, an intermarried immigrant man earns 4.8% more than his endogamously married counterpart, while this premium for natives is only around 2.2%.[12] The intermarriage premium for native women is 0.2%, while for immigrant women it is 9.8%. The larger intermarriage premia for NESB immigrants than for natives suggest that the intermarriage premium may well capture a reward to intermarriage over and above to the special characteristics of people who intermarry. This issue will be discussed more in Section V.

The above analysis treats both endogamous and exogamous marriages as exogenous. Given the possible endogeneity of marriage, the estimated premia may be biased and inconsistent. At least two instruments are required to endogenize the marriage decision. Finding good instruments is difficult. We choose "probability of marry within" and the "sex ratio" as instruments in this study. There are a number of aspects related to the validity of these instruments that should be discussed.

First, the instruments should only affect earnings (the outcome) through their effect on marital status (endogenous variables). As mentioned before, our two instruments are constructed from the number of male and female individuals in each age-ethnic-religious sample cell. Although individuals' age, ethnicity, and religion all affect their earnings, as shown in table 3, our constructed variables should not present a problem. In the case of the variable probability to marry within, it is difficult to imagine that an individual's productivity, as reflected in earnings, will depend on the number of individuals of the opposite sex in the same age-ethnic-religious group as a ratio of the total stock of the opposite sex of marriageable age. Similar considerations apply to the sex ratio. Thus, our constructed variables are unlikely to make a direct contribution to income except through their effects on endogamous and exogamous marriages.

Second, the instruments should not be affected by earnings. In other

---

[12] The statistically significant intermarriage premium for native men is mainly because of the 1996 census data. Excluding 1996 data results in an insignificant intermarriage premium for native men.

words, they should be exogenous. In our case, the allocation of individuals across age-ethnic-religious cells, the number of individuals of the opposite sex within each cell, and the size of these cells should be exogenous.

Third, the instruments should directly affect marriage decisions. The results presented in table 2 show that both instruments are significant determinants of endogamous and exogamous marriage decisions.

Fourth, the relationship between the instruments and the marriage decisions must not be weak. Weak instruments are unlikely to be effective and may generate significant bias. There is no exact measure of sufficient instrument strength, but the F-statistics presented in table 2 indicate that the combined strength of the two instruments satisfies the indicative measure for strong instruments presented in Stock and Yogo (2001).

Our instruments, therefore, seem to satisfy these general conditions. Nevertheless, the two endogenous variables in our study are highly correlated, and finding instruments that can identify both endogamous and exogamous marriages may be difficult. We, therefore, begin with using the two instruments mentioned above and then explore other identification strategies if our instruments prove to be not satisfactory.

The identification issue is explored in table 4, which lists the endogamous and exogamous marriage coefficients, their standard errors, and the difference in the two coefficients and their F-test with the statistical significance in brackets. We adopt both a two-stage least squares (2SLS) estimation and a nonlinear two-stage (NL2S) procedure using multinomial logit as the first-stage estimation. The results are presented in the top and bottom panels, respectively.

The first row of table 4 in both panels presents the results from our initial instrument choice. In the top panel (2SLS), the magnitude and sign of the marital status coefficients are consistent with earlier results, but the differences in coefficients are not statistically significant. In the bottom panel (NL2S), the results are statistically significant for both genders but very large for women and with the wrong sign for men (the only wrong sign in coefficient difference in table 4). Further examination of the relationships between our two initial instruments and marital status suggests that a high degree of multicollinearity between our predicted value of endogamous and exogamous marriages might be causing the problem. Indeed, while the original correlation coefficients between M_1 and M_2 are 0.69 and 0.57 for male and female samples, respectively, the correlation coefficient between the predicted values increase to as high as 0.88 and 0.92 for the first-stage OLS estimation and to 0.87 and 0.91 for the first-stage multinomial logit estimation.[13]

---

[13] This is probably related to the fact that our instruments are not very strong in identifying being single, which makes the remaining two choices strongly correlated. For linear first-stage estimation, the F-statistics from the equation ex-

Table 4
Endogamous and Exogamous Marriage Premia Estimated from Two-Stage Estimation of the Earnings Equation (1), 1981–96

Instruments Used	Males Endogamous Marriage (M1)	Males Exogamous Marriage (M2)	Males Difference (M2 − M1)	Males F-Test for (M2 − M1)	Females Endogamous Marriage (M1)	Females Exogamous Marriage (M2)	Females Difference (M2 − M1)	Females F-Test for (M2 − M1)
2SLS:								
Probability of marry within and sex ratio	.24 (.27)	.27 (.37)	.03	.04 (.85)	−.47 (.48)	−.33 (.72)	.14	.21 (.64)
Probability of marry within and sex ratio plus nonlinear cohorts effects	.12 (.22)	.32 (.24)	.20	8.74** (.00)	−.15 (.39)	.31 (.60)	.46	3.65+ (.06)
Sex ratio plus nonlinear cohorts effects	.17 (.24)	.38 (.27)	.21	8.84** (.00)	.36 (.55)	1.18 (.89)	.81	5.14* (.02)
Probability of marry within plus nonlinear cohorts effects	−.63 (.48)	−.41 (.49)	.21	9.74** (.00)	−.19 (.52)	.27 (.72)	.46	3.40+ (.07)
Mlogit two-stage:								
Probability of marry within and sex ratio	.48** (.09)	.36** (.08)	−.12	3.85* (.05)	−.21 (.18)	.40* (.20)	.61	27.46** (.00)
Probability of marry within and sex ratio plus nonlinear cohorts effects	.42** (.09)	.49** (.09)	.08	2.73+ (.10)	−.20 (.18)	.40+ (.23)	.60	36.60** (.00)
Sex ratio plus nonlinear cohorts effects	.42** (.09)	.50** (.09)	.08	2.71+ (.10)	−.18 (.18)	.45* (.24)	.63	25.51** (.00)
Probability of marry within plus nonlinear cohorts effects	.46** (.10)	.52** (.09)	.07	1.63 (.20)	−.22 (.20)	.45* (.24)	.67	29.15** (.00)

NOTE.—2SLS = two-stage least squares; standard errors are displayed in parentheses below the coefficients. Other variables included in the estimation are all the variables included in table 3 plus 3-year dummy variables and interaction terms between the year dummy variables and years of schooling and English proficiency. The full results are available on request from the authors. The standard errors are derived from a consistent variance-covariance matrix using Huber-White sandwich estimators for both stage estimations. They are also corrected for age-ethnic-religion clustering in the first-stage estimation. Wald F-tests are used to test difference in coefficients specified. The values in parentheses below the F-tests are significance levels (p-value).
+ Significant at 10% level.
** Significant at 5% level.
*** Significant at 1% level.

To gain additional identification, we experimented with changing one of the other exogenous variables between the first- and second-stage equations. It is possible that the functional form of the relationship between "year since arrival" and earnings is different from its relationship to marital status. Thus, we included a group of dummy variables indicating the cohort of arrival in the first-stage estimation and a continuous years since migration variable in the second stage. This seems to have worked well. Adding this change produces significant coefficients with the right sign in terms of the additional return to exogamous marriage (second row in both panels of table 4).[14] It is also apparent that including this additional identification works equally well with one or both of our original instruments (rows 3 and 4 in both panels of table 4).

A more complete set of results from the specification of the second row of table 4 are presented in table 5.[15] Except for the two endogenized marriage dummy variables and the variable "English proficiency," the magnitudes of the results are largely consistent with those presented in table 3 (the OLS estimation). The discussion below, therefore, focuses mainly on the effect of the two marriage dummy variables and English proficiency.

With regard to the marriage variables, both sets of results support our general findings and are qualitatively consistent with the gross data and OLS estimates of a positive and statistically significant intermarriage pre-

---

plaining whether an individual is single or not are 4.2 and 8.6 from men and women, respectively. The weak instrument in the male sample is sex ratio with t-ratio of 0.01, while the weak instrument in the female sample is probability of marry within with t-ratio of 1.2.

[14] The estimated intermarriage premia do not change significantly if the continuous years since migration variable is included in the first stage and the group of cohort dummy variables are included in the second stage. In the case of the male sample, these changes increase the intermarriage premium from 7.9 to 10.6, while for the female sample these changes reduce the premium from 60.1 to 41.4 in the nonlinear two-stage procedure.

[15] It would be interesting to compare 2SLS and nonlinear two-stage procedure estimates between NESBs and natives as presented in table 3 for OLS results. In the case of the native sample, however, good instruments are very hard to find. The two instruments used in the NESB equation are based on variations across country of birth, religion, and age groups. For the native sample there is only a very limited number of country of birth groups (Australia, New Zealand, the United States, the United Kingdom, and Canada), and hence it is impossible to construct instruments that have sufficient variation. The coefficient of variations for sex ratio for native male and females, e.g., are 0.24 and 0.26, respectively, while for NESB male and females they are 0.67 and 0.65, respectively. Similarly, for probability of marry within the group the coefficient of variations for native males and females are 0.75 and 0.70, while for NESB male and females they are 1.32 and 1.40, respectively. Because of the lack of reliable instruments, no sensible results can be obtained from the 2SLS or nonlinear two-stage procedure estimation for the native sample.

Table 5
Selected Results from Two-Stage Estimation of the Earnings Equation (1), 1981–96

	2SLS Males	2SLS Females	MLogit Two-Stage Males	MLogit Two-Stage Females
Constant	8.115** (.135)	8.050** (.076)	8.288** (.073)	8.026** (.073)
Dummy for endogamous marriage (M_1)	.120 (.224)	−.151 (.388)	.415** (.091)	−.199 (.171)
Dummy for exogamous marriage (M_2)	.319 (.247)	.312 (.598)	.494** (.088)	.402[+] (.226)
Age	.034** (.013)	.035* (.016)	.018** (.006)	.037** (.007)
Age²/1,000	−.372** (.143)	−.382* (.194)	−.213** (.059)	−.395** (.086)
Years of schooling	.035** (.002)	.033** (.004)	.034** (.002)	.034** (.003)
English proficiency	.054* (.025)	.036 (.042)	.080** (.019)	.010 (.030)
Years since migration	.003** (.001)	.001[+] (.001)	.003** (.001)	.001 (.001)
Dummy for religion	.014 (.016)	.039 (.028)	.031** (.013)	.032 (.020)
Born in southern Europe	−.058[+] (.032)	−.002 (.052)	−.110** (.018)	.020 (.032)
Born in Asia	.027 (.023)	.092** (.029)	−.021 (.017)	.106** (.023)
Born in other NESB country	.033 (.023)	.073* (.035)	−.004 (.017)	.079** (.023)
Difference between M_2 and M_1	.199	.464	.079	.601
Wald F-test for $M_2 = M_1$	8.74 (.00)	3.65 (.06)	2.73 (.10)	26.78 (.00)
No. of observations	12,743	5,901	12,743	5,901
Adjusted R^2	.53	.59	.53	.59

NOTE.—2SLS = two-stage least squares; NESB = non-English-speaking background countries; standard errors are displayed in parentheses below the coefficients. The standard errors are derived from a consistent variance-covariance matrix using Huber-White sandwich estimators for both stage estimations. They are also corrected for age-ethnic-religion clustering in the first-stage estimation. Other variables included in the estimation are the 3-year dummy variables and interaction terms between the year dummy variables and years of schooling and English proficiency. The full results are available on request from the authors. Wald F-tests are used to test difference in coefficients specified. The values in parentheses below the F-tests are significance levels (p-value).
[+] Significant at 10% level.
* Significant at 5% level.
** Significant at 1% level.

mium. For 2SLS the estimated endogamous and exogamous marriage premia for males are 12.0% and 31.9%, and for females, −15.1%, and 31.2%, respectively. These indicate that the intermarriage premia for males and females are 19.9% and 46.3%, respectively. The nonlinear two-stage procedure produces endogamous and exogamous marriage premia for males of 41.5% and 49.4%, and for females of −19.9%, and 40.2%, respectively. The differences between endogamous and exogamous premia produce

7.9% and 60.1% intermarriage premia for the male and female samples, respectively.

The intermarriage premia for males seem plausible. The fact that the estimates from both 2SLS and NL2S procedures (19.9% and 7.9%) are higher than the OLS estimate (4.8%) suggests that selection into the intermarriage group contributes negatively to income. This indicates that there may be unobservable characteristics, which both increase the probability of intermarriage and depress earnings.

For females, however, the estimated intermarriage premia from both the 2SLS and the NL2S procedures, although of correct sign, seem too high. There may be a number of reasons for this. First, our sample only includes full-time workers. This may cause a selection bias, which should be more severe for women than for men because of the low levels of full-time employment of women in Australia. For example, the four censuses reveal that for the NESB immigrant population of working age, the full-time employment-population ratios for men in 1981, 1986, 1991, and 1996 are 73%, 60%, 56%, and 56%, respectively, while for women the ratios are 30%, 28%, 26%, 28%, respectively. Unfortunately the direction and the size of the potential selection bias on the estimated intermarriage premium is theoretically unclear.[16] Second, the low level of full-time employment ratio means that the sample size for women is relatively small, less than half of the male sample, and smaller samples require stronger instruments to produce good estimates.

The English proficiency variable should also be discussed a little further. A comparison of the OLS results of table 3 and the results presented in table 5 suggests that the relationships among earnings, intermarriage, and English proficiency may be complicated. In the OLS estimates of the earnings equation, where intermarriage is treated as exogenous, there is a statistically significant and positive coefficient of 10% on English proficiency in the male equation and 11% in the female equation (see table 3). When intermarriage is treated as endogenous in the two-stage estimations, there is a strong positive association between English proficiency and intermarriage at the first stage of estimation, and it may be partly through this effect that income increases. When English proficiency is added to the earnings equation to make an independent contribution, in addition to its effect through intermarriage, the coefficient is halved for men in the 2SLS estimation and not statistically significant for women in both estimations. The change in coefficients attached to English proficiency between estimation techniques is not trivial and matters in terms of the economic interpretation of the data.

The fact that English proficiency is exerting a large effect on income

---

[16] To move forward on these issues requires a more complicated model, which is beyond the scope of this article and requires a better database than is available.

through the intermarriage equation may result from multicollinearity between predicted intermarriage from the first-stage estimation and the dummy variable for speaking English fluently that is included in the earnings equation. If this is the case, our estimate of the effect of either variable may not be precise.

We responded to this possibility in a number of ways. First, we tried an alternative measure of English proficiency. The census includes the categories "speak English fluently" and "speak English very well." The results do not vary systematically when English proficiency is measured either as speak English fluently or as a combination of both.

Second, to avoid the multicollinearity problem, the earnings equation is estimated for a subsample of NESB immigrants who speak English fluently or very well. The results from the OLS, 2SLS, and NL2S estimations for this subgroup of individuals are reported in table 6. The results indicate that there is a substantial intermarriage premium for the sample of NESB immigrants who speak English perfectly and very well. The premia are similar to those estimated for the whole sample in all three estimations. These results suggest that the estimated intermarriage premia from tables 3–5 do not capture an English-speaking effect but measure the size of the reward for intermarriage.

The above analysis seems to indicate that the positive impact of intermarriage on income is quite robust, although the size of the effect is not precisely determined. The reason for such a premium, however, is not clear. This issue is now tackled from several different perspectives.

V. The Intermarriage Premium: A Reward for Economic Assimilation?

One reason why intermarriage might contribute to immigrant earnings may be that it provides a channel for immigrants to integrate better into the host society by a faster rate of acquisition of the customs, language, and opportunities relevant to finding a good job. Thus, the intermarriage premium is a reward for economic assimilation. Alternatively, there may be several other interpretations.

A Return to Unobservable Characteristics?

It is possible that immigrants who intermarry possess some unobservable personal characteristics, such as a willingness to accept cultural differences, which lead independently both to higher earnings and to intermarriage. If this is the case, the intermarriage premium may be a return to these unobservable characteristics and may have nothing to do with the contribution of the marriage to economic assimilation. Even though this issue might have been dealt with by our methods to endogenize intermarriage, it is worthwhile pursuing further.

Table 6
Selected Results of the Earnings Equation (1) for Immigrants Who Speak English Fluently or Very Well, 1981–96

	OLS Males	OLS Females	2SLS Males	2SLS Females	MLogit Two-Stage Males	MLogit Two-Stage Females
Constant	7.963** (.072)	7.699** (.094)	8.108** (.215)	7.587** (.104)	8.236** (.102)	7.595** (.099)
Dummy for endogamous marriage (M_1)	.106** (.015)	−.042** (.016)	.382 (.372)	.312 (.360)	.609** (.140)	.164 (.239)
Dummy for exogamous marriage (M_2)	.153** (.014)	.049** (.017)	.636 (.407)	.850 (.531)	.787** (.140)	.652* (.332)
Age	.042** (.003)	.043** (.004)	.022 (.023)	.026 (.017)	.010 (.009)	.033** (.011)
Age²/1,000	−.467** (.038)	−.501** (.055)	−.284 (.201)	−.232 (.244)	−.114 (.092)	−.362** (.130)
Years of schooling	.046** (.003)	.057** (.004)	.043** (.004)	.062** (.006)	.042** (.003)	.060** (.005)
Years since migration	.003** (.001)	.004** (.001)	.002** (.001)	.003** (.001)	.003** (.001)	.003** (.001)
Dummy for religion	.028* (.014)	.070** (.018)	.038+ (.023)	.078** (.026)	.052** (.016)	.068** (.022)
Born in southern Europe	−.072** (.012)	−.052** (.019)	−.084* (.046)	−.063 (.054)	−.120** (.023)	−.044 (.043)
Born in Asia	.006 (.014)	.064** (.018)	.024 (.032)	.069* (.033)	−.011 (.022)	.079** (.029)
Born in other NESB country	.030* (.015)	.069** (.019)	.029 (.029)	.043 (.040)	.006 (.019)	.056+ (.031)
Difference between M_2 and M_1	.047	.091	.254	.538	.178	.488
Wald F-test for $M_2 = M_1$	20.24 (.00)	35.19 (.00)	14.09 (.00)	7.01 (.00)	10.30 (.00)	12.03 (.00)
No. of observations	8,587	4,015	8,587	4,015	8,587	4,015
Adjusted R^2	.49	.55	.48	.55	.48	.55

NOTE.—OLS = ordinary least squares; 2SLS = two-stage least squares; NESB = non-English-speaking background countries; standard errors are displayed in parentheses below the coefficients. The standard errors are derived from a consistent variance-covariance matrix using Huber-White sandwich estimators. For 2SLS and two-stage estimations, the first-stage estimations are also corrected for age-ethnicity-religion clusters. Other variables included in the estimation are the 3-year dummy variables and interaction terms between the year dummy variables and years of schooling and English proficiency. The full results are available on request from the authors. Wald F-tests are used to test the difference between coefficients specified. The values in parentheses below the F-tests are significance levels (p-values).

+ Significant at 10% level.
* Significant at 5% level.
** Significant at 1% level.

If there are unobservable characteristics associated with intermarriage that also lead to higher earnings, these characteristics should be possessed by all intermarried people no matter to whom they intermarry. If this is the case, natives who marry immigrants or immigrants who marry immigrants from other ethnic groups should also have higher earnings relative to their nonintermarried counterparts.

The results from table 3 indicated that among married native women, those who are intermarried do not earn more than their nonintermarried counterparts, while among married native men there is a small intermarriage premium of 2.2%, but it is less than half the magnitude of that of their immigrant counterparts. Thus, in terms of labor-market earnings there does not seem to be anything very special or significant about natives who intermarry.

We also estimated the earnings regression for the sample of all NESB immigrants, which includes three dummy variables: endogamously married, intermarried to natives, and intermarried to immigrants from other ethnic groups. The coefficient for the third dummy variable is statistically insignificant. It seems unlikely, therefore, that the premium extends to intermarriage to other ethnic groups.[17]

Although these tests cannot definitely rule out a role for unobservable characteristics, they suggest indirectly that the intermarriage premium for NESB immigrants who marry natives may well be a reward for the improved ability, delivered by intermarriage, to integrate into the host country labor market. We now take a closer look at this issue.

A Return to Better Initial Labor-Market Quality?

It is possible that immigrants who choose to intermarry after arrival in the host country might have possessed higher quality labor-market attributes at the time of arrival, and these attributes led to intermarriage and generated higher earnings? Under these circumstances the observed premium to intermarriage may not be a return to economic assimilation facilitated by intermarriage. Alternatively, at the time of arrival, immigrants who subsequently intermarry might have had the same labor-market quality and on average earned the same as the nonintermarried group, but because of intermarriage they experience a faster rate of earnings growth and, hence, an earnings premium. If the intermarriage premium is the reward to better labor-market quality possessed at the time of arrival, an earnings difference should be observed between the two immigrant groups at the time of arrival. Otherwise, if intermarriage leads to a faster earnings growth, the change in earnings after migration should differ between the two groups.

To unpack these two different effects, we borrow from Borjas (1985) to disentangle the intermarriage premia (the difference between μ_1 and μ_2

---

[17] The results are not reported here but are available on request from the authors.

from eq. [1]) into an effect of years since migration (the assimilation effect) and cohort fixed effects (cohort quality effect at the time of arrival). The estimation allows the two effects to vary across three subgroups: single immigrants, immigrants who are in an endogamous marriage, and immigrants who intermarry. The estimated earnings equation is specified as follows:

$$\ln W_{it} = \beta G_{it} + \gamma_{M_0} \text{YSM}_{it} + \gamma_{M_1} M_{1it} \text{YSM}_{it}$$
$$+ \gamma_{M_2} M_{2it} \text{YSM}_{it} + \lambda_{M_0} \text{COH}_{it} \qquad (4)$$
$$+ \gamma_{M_1} M_{1it} \text{COH}_{it} + \lambda_{M_2} M_{2it} \text{COH}_{it} + \varphi \text{YEAR}_{it} + \nu_{it},$$

where the subscripts M_0, M_1, and M_2 refer to single, endogamous marriages, and exogamous marriages, respectively. The vector G_{it} is a vector of variables, including age and its squared term, years of schooling, English proficiency, and a dummy for no religious beliefs. The variable YSM_{it} represents years since migration, and COH_{it} is a vector of dummy variables indicating different immigration arrival cohorts, which are categorized into four groups: arrived before 1981, between 1981 and 1985, between 1986 and 1990, and between 1991 and 1996, where before 1981 is used as the omitted category. The vector YEAR_{it} is a vector of year effects. The variables $M_{1it}\text{YSM}_{it}$ and $M_{1it}\text{COH}_{it}$ refer to the interaction between the endogamous marriage dummy variable and YSM_{it} and COH_{it}, and $M_{2it}\text{YSM}_{it}$ and $M_{2it}\text{COH}_{it}$ refer to the interaction between the exogamous marriage dummy variable and YSM_{it} and COH_{it}.[18]

The parameter γ_{M_0} measures the assimilation effect for single immigrants, while γ_{M_1} and γ_{M_2} measure the additional assimilation effect for endogamously and exogamously married immigrants. The difference between γ_{M_1} and γ_{M_2} measures whether intermarriage leads to a faster assimilation process.[19] Similarly, the coefficient vector λ_{M_0} measures the cohort

---

[18] The nonlinear terms for years since migration (squared and cubic) were added to the regression, and none of them are statistically significant and, hence, were subsequently dropped. We also interacted endogamous and exogamous marriage dummies with age and its squared term. These variables are statistically insignificant in all estimations and are not included in the final regression.

[19] There is a debate in the literature over the definition of assimilation. Borjas (1985, 1995a) defines assimilation as the process whereby the earnings of immigrants approach that of natives, whereas LaLonde and Topel (1992) define assimilation as the process whereby the earnings of recent immigrants approach that of earlier immigrants. Given that this study compares the difference in the assimilation process across two groups, between immigrants of endogamous and exogamous marriage, the difference in the definition of assimilation is unlikely to affect the results of the econometric model as specified in eq. (4). In addition, it is possible that conditions in the host country at the point of arrival affect the rate of assimilation. Thus, if immigrants arrive in a period of high unemployment, this may have a permanent effect on their ability to find good jobs (see LaLonde

quality effects at the time of arrival for single, while λ_{M_1} and λ_{M_2} measure the additional cohort quality effects for endogamously and exogamously married immigrants. The differences between λ_{M_1} and λ_{M_2} indicate whether the initial labor-market quality of the intermarried immigrants is higher than those who are endogamously married; ϕ is a vector of coefficients for year dummy variables to adjust for the different earnings level at each census date and any period effects. We assume that such effects are common to intermarried and nonintermarried immigrants. Selected results together with Wald F-tests for significance of the difference between the coefficients for endogamous and exogamous marriages are reported in table 7.

With regard to cohort quality effects, the Wald F-tests indicate that exogamously married immigrant men arriving between 1986 and 1990 appear to be better qualified than their endogamously married counterparts, while exogamously married immigrant women who arrived between 1981 and 1985 and between 1991 and 1996 seem to be marginally better qualified than their endogamously married counterparts.[20]

These effects of better initial labor-market quality for exogamously married individuals relative to their endogamously married counterparts, however, are far from exhausting the intermarriage premia. After controlling for the effect of cohort quality on arrival (cohort effects), the additional years since migration effect for endogamously married immigrant men is significant. Relative to the single group, they gain 0.3% extra earnings for every additional year that they spend in Australia. For the group of male immigrants who intermarry, the relative gain is a 0.5% increase. The difference between premia for endogamous and exogamous marriage is 0.2%, and the Wald F-test indicates that this difference is statistically significant at less than the 1% level.

The story for women is slightly different. They incur a 0.1 (0.002 − 0.003)% income loss per annum if they are endogamously married. Immigrant women who are exogamously married, however, gain a 0.3 (0.002 + 0.001)% income increase for each additional year they spend in Australia, which suggests a 0.4% extra income gain each year relative to their endogamously married counterparts. This difference is statistically significant.

Controlling for initial labor-market quality, the income gains obtained

---

and Topel 1997). However, as this study compares two immigrant groups, it is assumed that if there is a period effect, it affects both groups equally, and there is no need to address this issue.

[20] In this study we do not discuss cohort effects in general. This is because McDonald and Worswick (1999) indicated that the cohort effects for Australian immigrants are very sensitive to the choice of survey years. As we are comparing relative cohort effects within each census year, our study should avoid this sensitivity issue.

Table 7
Selected Results from Earnings Equation (4)

	Males	Females
Years since migration	−.001 (.001)	.002* (.001)
Years since migration × endogamous married (γ_{M_1})	.003** (.001)	−.003** (.001)
Years since migration × exogamous married (γ_{M_2})	.005** (.001)	.001+ (.001)
Cohort arrives 1981–85	−.139** (.036)	.018 (.031)
Cohort arrives 1986–90	−.188** (.036)	−.083* (.040)
Cohort arrives 1991–96	−.14 2* (.060)	−.159+ (.086)
Cohort arrives 1981–85 × endogamous married ($\lambda_{M_1} 1$)	.142** (.039)	−.034 (.034)
Cohort arrives 1986–90 × endogamous married ($\lambda_{M_1} 2$)	.141** (.037)	.002 (.040)
Cohort arrives 1991–96 × endogamous married ($\lambda_{M_1} 3$)	.065 (.067)	−.053 (.091)
Cohort arrives 1981–85 × exogamous married ($\lambda_{M_2} 1$)	.141** (.049)	.063 (.050)
Cohort arrives 1986–90 × exogamous married ($\lambda_{M_2} 2$)	.274** (.055)	.023 (.052)
Cohort arrives 1991–96 × exogamous married ($\lambda_{M_2} 3$)	.185** (.088)	.098 (.114)
No. of observations	12,743	5,901
Adjusted R^2	.54	.60
Difference between γ_{M_2} and γ_{M_1}	.002	.004
Wald F-test for $\gamma_{M_2} = \gamma_{M_1}$	20.38 (.00)	35.76 (.00)
Wald F-test for $\lambda_{M_1} 1 = \lambda_{M_2} 1$	.00 (.98)	4.8 (.04)
Wald F-test for $\lambda_{M_1} 2 = \lambda_{M_2} 2$	8.41 (.00)	.24 (.63)
Wald F-test for $\lambda_{M_1} 3 = \lambda_{M_2} 3$	2.60 (.12)	3.04 (.08)

NOTE.—Standard errors are displayed in parentheses below the coefficients. The standard errors are derived from a consistent variance-covariance matrix using Huber-White sandwich estimators. Other variables included in the estimation are the 3-year dummy variables and interaction terms between the year dummy variables and years of schooling and English proficiency. The full results are presented in table D1. Wald F-tests are used to test the difference between coefficients specified. The values in parentheses below the F-tests are significance levels (p-values).
+ Significant at 10% level.
* Significant at 5% level.
** Significant at 1% level.

by immigrants who intermarry natives indicate that in the first 2 decades after arrival the earnings gap between them and their endogamously married counterparts grows from 0.2 to 4.0 and from 0.4 to 8.0 percentage points for the sample of male and female immigrants, respectively. These results further strengthen the conclusion that intermarriage to a native adds to income by improving the assimilation process.

A Return to Investment in Local Human Capital?

The family investment model of economic assimilation (Duleep and Sanders 1993; Baker and Benjamin 1997; Worswick 1999) suggests that one spouse, usually the female, in an endogamous marriage may take a dead-end job to finance the human capital investment of the other spouse in response to family credit constraints that particularly impinge on immigrants. Immigrants in intermarried families have no such need as their partner can either access credit or is already established in the local labor market. The immigrant partner in an intermarried family, therefore, can afford to wait for a good job or invest in local human capital first and then take a good job. This literature suggests that there may be an intermarriage premium for intermarried females, which arises from the "freedom" to invest in their own local human capital.

Two implications emerge from this model. First, on average, immigrant women in endogamous marriages will earn less than immigrant women who are married to a native. Second, because of the nature of dead-end jobs they take, immigrant women in endogamous marriages may have a much flatter assimilation profile than their counterparts in exogamous marriages. Thus, the earnings gap, as well as the difference in the assimilation process between intermarried and nonintermarried female immigrants observed in this study, may be an effect of this difference in family investment behavior.

However, the family investment model does not usually focus on a significant earnings gap between intermarried and nonintermarried immigrant men, nor does it predict a steeper years since migration-earnings profile for intermarried men. Immigrant men in either type of family should have a similar chance to invest in local human capital. The estimated results presented in tables 3, 4, 5, and 7 show that intermarried male immigrants receive an intermarriage premium and have a steeper postmigration experience-earnings profile, though to a lesser degree than intermarried women. These results indicate that perhaps the family investment hypothesis is at work to some extent, but a significant proportion of the intermarriage premium should not be attributed to this effect but to economic assimilation.

VI. Conclusions

Intermarriage should be an important input into the economic and social assimilation of immigrants in the host country. It is a little surprising, therefore, that intermarriage has not attracted more attention. To understand fully the relationships between intermarriage and economic assimilation, access to longitudinal data is ideal. In its absence, the analysis of the Australian census data suggests the following.

First, for immigrants from NESB countries, there is a high intermarriage rate of around 30% in Australia. In general, immigrants who are young, are educated, have good English skills, have spent a longer period in the host country, and have no religious beliefs are more likely to intermarry. In addition, male rather than female immigrants are more likely to intermarry. Immigrants who are less likely to find partners or face greater competition for potential partners within their own ethnic-religious group are more likely to intermarry.

Second, intermarried NESB immigrant full-time wage and salary earners earn significantly higher earnings than their endogamously married counterparts. The raw premium is around 17% for men and 22% for women. After account is taken of individual characteristics, this premium for men and women is estimated as 5% and 10%, respectively, when marriage types are treated as exogenous variables. Much larger effects are observed when marriage types are treated as endogenous variables. This pattern of results is very robust even within the group of NESB immigrants who speak English fluently.

Third, to strengthen the argument that the intermarriage premium is a reward for economic assimilation, we explored three alternative hypotheses and reached the following conclusions. (1) The observed intermarriage premium, after accounting for human capital differences among individuals, does not seem to be a reward to unobservable characteristics specifically associated with intermarried individuals. (2) Even though intermarried immigrants appear to be marginally better qualified than their endogamously married counterparts when they first arrive in the host country, this effect does not eliminate the estimated intermarriage premium. Even after controlling for the initial labor-market quality, the intermarriage premium increases with the passage of time in the host country, lending support to the suggestion that the intermarriage premium is a return to economic assimilation. (3) Although the family investment model suggests higher earnings and a steeper postmigration experience-earnings profile for intermarried immigrant women than for their endogamously married counterparts, our findings indicate that male immigrants also receive an intermarriage premium and have a steeper postmigration earnings profile. These findings suggest that the main force generating the premium and the steeper age-earnings profile for both genders is a reward for economic assimilation.

Where to now? This article has just begun the process of looking at the role of intermarriage, and it seems that there may be a significant research agenda ahead. Does the intermarriage premium extend to all ethnic groups who marry natives? What is the lifetime value of the premium? Does intermarriage affect other labor-market outcomes such as labor force participation, employment, and unemployment? Does a premium exist in other countries? Much remains to be done.

Appendix A

Data Appendix

Table A1
Category Variations of Some Variables in the Four Surveys

Variable Description	1981	1986	1991	1996
Age	In single years	28 categories	38 categories	38 categories
Birthplace of individual	101 categories	16 categories	36 categories	21 categories
Use of English language	5 categories	5 categories	4 categories	5 categories
Individual income	13 categories	8 categories	14 categories	14 categories
Period of residence/year of arrival	In single years	5 categories	7 categories	6 categories
Religious denomination	27 categories	12 categories	17 categories	14 categories

Variable description:

Income: Annual income is derived from the categorical variable "individual income" by taking the midpoint of each category.

Age: Age in 1981 is taken directly from the census. Age is recorded in single years if it is below 15 for the 1986 census or below 25 for the 1991 and 1996 censuses. Beyond these, it is recorded in 5-year categories. The midpoint is taken for these categories.

Period of residence/year of arrival: the 1981 and 1986 censuses report period of residence, while the 1991 and 1996 censuses report year of arrival in Australia. The variables "years since arrival" (YSAR) and year at arrival (COH) for the 1986–96 cemsuses are derived according to the following tabulation.

	1986			1991			1996	
Original	YSAR	COH	Original	YSAR	COH	Original	YSAR	COH
20+	30	Bf. 81	Bf. 71	30	Bf. 81	Bf. 81	25	Bf. 81
15–19	17	Bf. 81	71–75	18	Bf. 81	81–85	13	81–85
10–14	12	Bf. 81	76–80	13	Bf. 81	86–90	8	86–90
5–9	7	Bf. 81	81–85	8	81–85	91–92	5	91–96
0–4	2	82–86	86–87	5	86–91	93–94	3	91–96
			88–89	3	86–91	95–96	1	91–96
			90–91	1	86–91			

NOTE.—Bf. refers to before 1971 or before 1981.

English proficiency: there are five categories for the 1981, 1986, and 1996 censuses: (1) perfect, (2) very well, (3) well, (4) not well, and (5) not at all. For the 1991 census, categories 2 and 3 are grouped together. The dummy variable for English language is derived from this variable. The categories perfect and very well equal 1; otherwise equals zero.

Table A2
Summary Statistics

	Males								Females							
	Total		Single		Endogamous Marriage		Exogamous Marriage		Total		Single		Endogamous Marriage		Exogamous Marriage	
	Mean	SD	Mean	SD	Mean	SD	Mean	SD	Mean	SD	Mean	SD	Mean	SD	Mean	SD
NESB immigrants:																
Log (annual income)	9.96	.57	9.88	.60	9.92	.56	10.09	.56	9.76	.59	9.85	.57	9.66	.58	9.96	.57
Prob of marry within	.05	.07	.03	.05	.06	.08	.04	.06	.05	.07	.03	.05	.07	.08	.03	.00
Sex ratio	.88	.59	.87	.63	.90	.56	.85	.63	.94	.61	.87	.67	1.00	.58	.84	.62
Years of schooling	11.84	3.08	12.24	2.65	11.49	3.41	12.37	2.33	11.65	3.12	12.42	2.72	11.12	3.31	12.49	2.47
Age	41.85	10.68	37.15	12.07	43.98	10.03	40.01	9.86	38.63	10.05	36.62	11.09	39.89	9.54	36.89	9.70
Years since migration	20.25	10.66	18.63	11.16	18.68	10.73	24.78	8.69	18.26	10.83	18.81	11.15	17.03	10.59	21.65	10.44
Married to other ethnic groups	.04				.08				.04				.07			
Speak English fluently	.67		.72		.54		.94		.68		.80		.55		.96	
Dummy for no religion	.13		.20		.10		.14		.12		.18		.10		.15	
Arrive before 1981	.82		.77		.79		.93		.77		.76		.75		.82	
Arrive during 1981–85	.08		.11		.09		.04		.10		.10		.10		.08	
Arrive during 1986–90	.08		.10		.09		.02		.10		.09		.11		.08	
Arrive during 1991–96	.02		.02		.03		.01		.03		.04		.03		.02	
Born in northern Europe	.23		.29		.15		.37		.19		.25		.14		.31	
Born in southern Europe	.38		.21		.45		.33		.31		.16		.41		.19	
Born in Asia	.23		.28		.26		.14		.31		.33		.32		.28	
Born in other NESBs	.15		.17		.13		.17		.17		.18		.14		.22	
No. of observation	12,743		2,056		7,396		3,291		5,901		1,299		3,534		1,068	
Natives:																
Log (annual income)	10.05	.58	9.87	.59	10.11	.56	10.21	.57	9.85	.58	9.81	.58	9.88	.57	9.88	.58
Probability of marry within	1.13	.85	1.25	.90	1.10	.83	.94	.82	1.21	.85	1.24	.85	1.19	.85	1.11	.86
Sex ratio	1.04	.25	1.06	.26	1.04	.24	1.00	.28	.96	.25	.94	.25	.96	.25	.96	.25
Years of schooling	12.13	2.20	12.13	1.91	12.11	2.28	12.63	2.45	12.09	2.15	12.32	2.01	11.92	2.23	12.12	2.29
Age	37.60	11.37	31.64	11.38	39.87	10.56	39.60	9.74	34.63	11.26	31.96	11.63	36.50	10.63	36.44	10.12
Dummy for no religion	.18		.23		.15		.19		.16		.18		.14		.13	
Born in New Zealand	.02		.03		.02		.02		.03		.03		.02		.03	
Born in other ESBs	.13		.10		.13		.21		.11		.09		.13		.13	
No. of observations	75,846		20,826		52,531		2,489		36,438		15,037		19,968		1,433	

NOTE.—NESB = non-English-speaking background countries; ESB = English-speaking background countries.

Appendix B

Table B1
Full Results from Multinomial Logit Marital Status Equation

	Males		Females	
	Endogamous Married	Exogamous Married	Endogamous Married	Exogamous Married
Constant	−.913** (.111)	−.201** (.078)	−.332** (.114)	−.207** (.059)
Sex ratio	.053** (.010)	−.025** (.007)	.057** (.011)	−.022** (.008)
Probability of marry within	.026** (.017)	−.022 (.014)	.045** (.018)	−.040** (.014)
Age	.060** (.005)	−.007** (.003)	.041** (.004)	−.001 (.003)
Age^2/1,000	−.500** (.054)	−.031 (.038)	−.396** (.054)	−.038 (.038)
Years of schooling	−.007+ (.004)	.005 (.003)	−.010 (.006)	−.006 (.004)
Years of schooling × 1986	−.001 (.005)	.004 (.004)	−.005 (.008)	.014** (.004)
Years of schooling × 1991	−.003 (.006)	.004 (.004)	−.001 (.009)	.011** (.006)
Years of schooling × 1996	.023** (.005)	−.018** (.003)	.009 (.009)	.006 (.005)
English proficiency	−.278** (.036)	.306** (.028)	−.280** (.033)	.255** (.035)
English proficiency × 1986	−.004 (.042)	.026 (.030)	.011 (.052)	−.036 (.047)
English proficiency × 1991	−.166* (.094)	.222* (.112)	.132* (.068)	−.053 (.075)
English proficiency × 1996	−.027 (.037)	−.020 (.038)	−.072 (.061)	.006 (.050)
Years since migration	−.015** (.001)	.012** (.001)	−.011** (.001)	.006** (.001)
Dummy for no religion	−.076** (.016)	.026* (.013)	−.138** (.027)	.041* (.020)
Born in southern Europe	.255** (.020)	−.073** (.016)	.280** (.027)	−.067** (.016)
Born in Asia	.237** (.029)	−.135** (.021)	.143** (.023)	−.044** (.014)
Born in other NESB countries	.120** (.019)	−.023 (.015)	.089** (.024)	−.006 (.013)
Year dummy 1986	.011 (.062)	−.092 (.051)	.018 (.089)	−.131** (.064)
Year dummy 1991	.216+ (.114)	−.322** (.134)	−.109 (.106)	−.070 (.092)
Year dummy 1996	−.303** (.060)	.209** (.047)	−.130 (.094)	−.055 (.047)
No. of observations	12,743		5,901	
Pseudo R^2	.21		.16	

NOTE.—NESB = non-English-speaking background countries. The standard errors are derived from a consistent variance-covariance matrix using Huber-White sandwich estimators.
+ Significant at 10% level.
* Significant at 5% level.
** Significant at 1% level.

Appendix C

Table C1
Full Results from the OLS Estimation of the Earnings Equation (1), 1981–96

	Immigrant Total Sample		Immigrant Arrived at 19 or Younger		Natives (Australian and ESB Immigrants)	
	Males	Females	Males	Females	Males	Females
Constant	8.104** (.054)	8.093** (.073)	7.804** (.078)	7.946** (.128)	7.432** (.037)	7.303** (.065)
Dummy for endogamous marriage	.099** (.012)	−.052** (.013)	.086** (.020)	−.067** (.022)	.138** (.004)	.009** (.004)
Dummy for exogamous marriage	.147** (.012)	.046** (.016)	.141** (.019)	.038 (.021)	.160** (.008)	.011 (.011)
Age	.037** (.002)	.032** (.003)	.055** (.004)	.040** (.007)	.062** (.001)	.056** (.001)
Age²/1,000	−.413** (.029)	−.362** (.044)	−.651** (.052)	−.468** (.097)	−.681** (.012)	−.646** (.019)
Years of schooling	.035** (.002)	.032** (.003)	.034** (.003)	.030** (.006)	.055** (.001)	.073** (.002)
Years of schooling × 1986	.007** (.003)	.006 (.005)	.020** (.005)	.019** (.009)	.023** (.002)	.014** (.003)
Years of schooling × 1991	.017** (.004)	.020** (.006)	.035** (.006)	.045** (.009)	.023** (.002)	−.003 (.003)
Years of schooling × 1996	.022** (.004)	.026** (.006)	.040** (.007)	.025** (.009)	.035** (.002)	.013** (.003)
English proficiency	.099** (.013)	.111** (.022)	.093** (.018)	.178** (.044)	.095** (.030)	.059 (.054)
English proficiency × 1986	.007 (.018)	−.022 (.029)	−.065** (.028)	−.109* (.054)	.064 (.057)	.106 (.079)
English proficiency × 1991	.025 (.025)	.040 (.039)	−.050 (.060)	−.118⁺ (.060)	−.018 (.079)	.000 (.095)
English proficiency × 1996	.034 (.021)	.031 (.031)	−.021 (.034)	−.048 (.054)	−.032 (.063)	.019 (.073)
Years since migration	.003** (.000)	.002* (.001)	.004** (.001)	.001 (.001)	.000 (.000)	.000 (.001)
Dummy for no religion	.015 (.012)	.056** (.016)	.042** (.017)	.055** (.024)	.019** (.004)	.040** (.005)
Born in southern Europe	−.068** (.010)	−.054** (.016)	−.065** (.013)	−.050** (.023)		
Born in Asia	.001 (.011)	.051** (.016)	.016 (.016)	.082** (.024)		
Born in other NESB countries	.021 (.013)	.054** (.017)	.014 (.019)	.035 (.025)		
Born in New Zealand					.022 (.013)	.011 (.016)
Born in other ESB countries					.010 (.005)	.009 (.008)
Year dummy 1986	.323** (.038)	.351** (.0480)	.204** (.053)	.259** (.086)	.064 (.060)	.124⁺ (.086)
Year dummy 1991	.446** (.046)	.413** (.067)	.302** (.084)	.277** (.091)	.406** (.081)	.710** (.100)

(*continued overleaf*)

Table C1 (Continued)

	Immigrant Total Sample		Immigrant Arrived at 19 or Younger		Natives (Australian and ESB Immigrants)	
	Males	Females	Males	Females	Males	Females
Year dummy 1996	.536** (.053)	.532** (.063)	.324** (.088)	.618** (.091)	.431** (.067)	.666** (.079)
No. of observations	12,743	5,901	5,917	2,730	75,846	36,438
Adjusted R^2	.54	.59	.57	.61	.53	.53

NOTE.—NESB = non-English-speaking background countries; ESB = English-speaking background countries. The standard errors are derived from a consistent variance-covariance matrix using Huber-White sandwich estimators.
+ Significant at 10% level.
* Significant at 5% level.
** Significant at 1% level.

Table C2
Selected Results from the OLS Estimation of the Earnings Equation (1) for ESB and Australian Born Separately, 1981–96

	ESB Immigrants		Australian Born	
	Males	Females	Males	Females
Constant	7.804** (.113)	7.677** (.135)	7.215** (.041)	7.133** (.308)
Dummy for endogamous marriage (M_1)	.130** (.010)	.013 (.012)	.138** (.004)	.009+ (.005)
Dummy for exogamous marriage (M_2)	.133** (.018)	.001 (.031)	.168** (.009)	.013 (.012)
Age	.053** (.003)	.042** (.004)	.063** (.001)	.057** (.001)
Age^2/1,000	−.596** (.000)	−.501** (.046)	−.688** (.013)	−.665** (.020)
Years of schooling	.053** (.002)	.070** (.005)	.055** (.001)	.073** (.002)
English proficiency	−.060 (.099)	−.026 (.089)	.107** (.032)	.063 (.060)
Years since migration	−.000 (.000)	.000 (.001)		
Dummy for no religion	.014 (.009)	.057** (.013)	.019** (.004)	.036** (.006)
Born in other ESB countries	.014 (.013)	−.016 (.015)		
Difference between M_2 and M_1	.002	−.011	.029	.004
F-test for $M_2 = M_1$	4.46 (.04)	.14 (.70)	11.08 (.00)	.14 (.71)
No. of observations	11,173	5,131	64,673	31,307
Adjusted R^2	.53	.54	.53	.53

NOTE.—English-speaking background countries. The standard errors are derived from a consistent variance-covariance matrix using Huber-White sandwich estimators.
+ Significant at 10% level.
** Significant at 1% level.

Immigrant Intermarriage

Appendix D

Table D1
Full Results from Earnings Equation (4)

	Males Coefficient	SE	Females Coefficient	SE
Constant	8.188**	.055	8.094**	.074
Age	.038**	.002	.032**	.003
Age^2/1,000	−.428**	.029	−.359**	.044
Years of schooling	.035**	.002	.031**	.003
Years of schooling × 1986	.007**	.003	.004	.005
Years of schooling × 1991	.018**	.004	.021**	.006
Years of schooling × 1996	.025**	.004	.030**	.006
English proficiency	.109**	.013	.128**	.022
English proficiency × 1986	.002	.018	−.026	.030
English proficiency × 1991	.005	.025	.021	.039
English proficiency × 1996	.013	.022	−.006	.032
Years since migration	−.001	.001	.002	.001
Years since migration × endogamous married (γM_1)	.003**	.001	−.003**	.001
Years since migration × exogamous married (γM_2)	.005**	.001	.001	.001
Cohort arrives 1981–85	−.139**	.036	.018	.031
Cohort arrives 1986–90	−.188**	.036	−.083*	.040
Cohort arrives 1991–96	−.142**	.060	−.159+	.086
Cohort arrives 1981–85 × endogamous married (λM_1 1)	.142**	.039	−.034	.034
Cohort arrives 1986–90 × endogamous married (λM_1 2)	.141**	.037	.002	.040
Cohort arrives 1991–96 × (λM (λM_1 3)	.065	.067	−.053	.091
Cohort arrives 1981–85 × exogamous married (λM_2 1)	.141**	.049	.063	.050
Cohort arrives 1986–90 × exogamous married (λM_2 2)	.274**	.055	.023	.052
Cohort arrives 1991–96 × exogamous married (λM_2 3)	.185*	.088	.098	.114
Dummy for religion	.016	.012	.056**	.016
Born in southern Europe	−.067**	.010	−.050**	.016
Born in Asia	−.001	.011	.048**	.016
Born in other NESB countries	.020	.013	.049**	.017
Year dummy 1986	.328**	.039	.382**	.048
Year dummy 1991	.456**	.047	.435**	.066
Year dummy 1996	.537**	.054	.560**	.064
No. of observations	12,743		5,901	
Adjusted R^2	.54		.60	

NOTE.—NESB = non-English-speaking background countries. The standard errors are derived from a consistent variance-covariance matrix using Huber-White sandwich estimators.
+ Significant at 10% level.
* Significant at 5% level.
** Significant at 1% level.

References

Angrist, Josh. 2002. How do sex ratios affect marriage and labor markets? Evidence from America's second generation. *Quarterly Journal of Economics* 117, no. 3:997–1038.

Baker, Michael, and Dwayne Benjamin. 1994. The performance of immigrants in the Canadian labor market. *Journal of Labor Economics* 12, no. 3:369–405.

———. 1997. The role of the family in immigrants' labor-market activity: An evaluation of alternative explanations. *American Economic Review* 87, no. 4:705–27.

Becker, Gary S. 1973. A theory of marriage: Part I. *Journal of Political Economy* 81, no. 4:813–46.

———. 1974. A theory of marriage: Part II. *Journal of Political Economy* 82, no. 2, suppl.: S11–S26.

Beggs, John J., and Bruce J. Chapman. 1988. Immigrant wage adjustment in Australia: Cross section and time series estimates. *Economic Record* 64, no. 186:161–67.

Bisin, Alberto, and Thierry Verdier. 2000. "Beyond the melting pot": Cultural transmission, marriage, and the evolution of ethnic and religious traits. *Quarterly Journal of Economics* 115, no. 3:955–88.

Blau, Francine D., Lawrence M. Kahn, and Jane Waldfogel. 2000. Understanding young women's marriage decisions: The role of labor and marriage market conditions. *Industrial and Labor Relations Review* 53, no. 4:624–47.

Borjas, George J. 1985. Assimilation, changes in cohort quality, and the earnings of immigrants. *Journal of Labor Economics* 3, no. 4:463–89.

———. 1995a. Assimilation and changes in cohort quality revisited: What happened to immigrant earnings in the 1980s? *Journal of Labor Economics* 13, no. 2:201–45.

———. 1995b. Ethnicity, neighborhoods, and human capital externality. *American Economic Review* 85, no. 3:365–90.

———. 1999. Economic analysis of immigration. In *Handbook of labor economics*, vol. 3A, ed. Orley Ashenfelter and David Card, 1697–1760. Amsterdam: Elsevier Science/North-Holland.

Chiswick, Barry R. 1978. The effect of Americanization on the earnings of foreign-born men. *Journal of Political Economy* 86, no. 5:897–921.

Chiswick, Barry R., and Paul W. Miller. 1992. Language in the labor market: The immigrant experience in Canada and the United States. In *Immigration, language and ethnic issues: Canada and the United States*, ed. Barry R. Chiswick, 229–96. Washington, DC: American Enterprise Institute.

———. 1994. Language choice among immigrants in a multilingual destination. *Journal of Population Economics* 7, no. 2:119–31.

———. 1995. The endogeneity between language and earnings: International analyses. *Journal of Labor Economics* 13, no. 2:246–88.

Duleep, Harriet O., and Seth Sanders. 1993. The decision to work by married immigrant women. *Industrial and Labor Relations Review* 46, no. 4:677–90.

Eckstein, Zvi, and Yoram Weiss. Forthcoming. The integration of immigrants from the former Soviet Union in the Israeli labor market. In *A special volume in memory of Michael Bruno*, ed. A. Ben-Basat. Cambridge, MA: MIT Press.

Freiden, Alan. 1974. The United States marriage market. *Journal of Political Economy* 82, no. 2, suppl.: S34–S53.

Glazer, Nathan, and Daniel P. Moynihan. 1963. *Beyond the melting pot*. Cambridge, MA: MIT Press.

Gray, Alan. 1987. Intermarriage: Opportunity and preference. *Population Studies* 41, no. 3:365–79.

———. 1997. Individual and group effects on ethnic intermarriage: A multilevel analysis. *Australian Journal of Social Research* 3, no. 1:17–35.

Korenman, Sanders, and David Neumark. 1991. Does marriage really make men more productive? *Journal of Human Resources* 26, no. 2: 282–307.

LaLonde, Robert J., and Robert H. Topel. 1992. The assimilation of immigrants in the U.S. labor market. In *Immigration and the work force: Economic consequences for the United States and source areas*, ed. George J. Borjas and Richard B. Freeman, 67–92. Chicago: University of Chicago Press.

———. 1997. Economic impact of international migration and the economic performance of migrants. In *Handbook of population and family economics*, vol. 1B, ed. Mark R. Rosenzweig and Oded Stark, 799–850. Amsterdam: Elsevier Science/North-Holland.

Lazear, Edward P. 1999. Culture and language. *Journal of Political Economy* 107, no. 6, pt. 3, suppl.: S95–S126.

McDonald, Ted, and Christopher Worswick. 1999. The earnings of immigrant men in Australia: Assimilation, cohort and macroeconomic conditions. *Economic Record* 75, no. 228:49–62.

Nakosteen, Robert A., and Michael A. Zimmer. 1987. Marital status and earnings of young men: A model of endogenous selection. *Journal of Human Resources* 22, no. 2:248–68.

Steen, Todd P. 1996. Religion and earnings: Evidence from the NLS youth cohort. *International Journal of Social Economics* 23, no. 1:47–58.

Stock, James H., and Motohiro Yogo. 2002. Testing for weak instruments in linear IV regression. NBER Technical Working Paper no. 284, National Bureau of Economic Research, Cambridge, MA.

Tomes, Nigel. 1985. Religion and the earnings function. *American Economic Review* 75, no. 2:245–50.

Wooldridge, Jeffrey M. 2002. *Econometric analysis of cross section and panel data*. Cambridge, MA: MIT Press.

Worswick, Christopher. 1999. Credit constraints and the labour supply of immigrant families in Canada. *Canadian Journal of Economics* 32, no. 1:152–70.

[20]
Assortative Mating among Married New Legal Immigrants to the United States: Evidence from the New Immigrant Survey Pilot[1]

Guillermina Jasso
New York University

Douglas S. Massey
University of Pennsylvania

Mark R. Rosenzweig
University of Pennsylvania

James P. Smith
Rand Corporation

>This article provides a brief summary of the Pilot for the New Immigrant Survey (NIS) and presents new information, never before available, on one important aspect of immigrant behavior – assortative mating. Our intent is to provide a flavor for the kinds of questions that can be studied with this new data base and with the larger-sample full New Immigrant Survey by presenting new information on married couples who are part of immigration flows and whose characteristics are importantly shaped by immigration law. We distinguish between two types of couples, those in which one spouse is a U.S. citizen sponsor and those in which both spouses are immigrants. Our findings include the following: First, among married couples formed by a U.S. citizen sponsoring the immigration of a spouse, husbands and wives have similar levels of schooling, with the U.S. citizen slightly better educated than the immigrant spouse; however, U.S. citizen husbands and their immigrant wives have substantially higher schooling than U.S. citizen wives and their immigrant husbands (on average, two years higher). Second, unlike immigrants from other countries, Mexico-born spouses of U.S. citizens differ markedly in schooling depending on whether they are recently married, suggesting the continuing after-effects of the Immigration Reform and Control Act of 1986. Third, husband-wife schooling levels are less similar among

[1]This research was supported by the National Institutes of Health under grant HD33843, with partial support from the Immigration and Naturalization Service and the National Science Foundation.

© 2000 by the Center for Migration Studies of New York. All rights reserved.
0197-9183/00/3402.0130

married couples in which both spouses are immigrants than among couples involving a U.S. citizen sponsor and an immigrant spouse, except when the wife is the principal in an employment category. These findings suggest that immigration laws importantly shape the characteristics of families and thus the next generation – the children of immigrants and immigrant children.

Research on U.S. immigration during the past two decades can be characterized by three features: 1) a rapidly increasing sophistication in the theoretical frameworks and models developed to understand migration processes; 2) a growing catalog of deficiencies in the data available for empirically estimating and testing the theoretical models; and 3) a progressively sharper vision for collection of new data that would permit accurate and deeper understanding of migration phenomena. Notwithstanding the critical importance of immigration in the United States, the available data do not even provide such rudimentary information as the schooling of new legal immigrants or the proportion of legal immigrants who emigrate from the United States. Thus, it is not surprising that the reports issued by major study groups during the period argue for new data collection.[2]

The evolving vision for the requisite new data collection emphasizes four points. First, the data should be based on probability samples, drawn periodically from cohorts of new legal permanent resident aliens, of sufficient size to accommodate the diversity of immigrant origins. Second, information should be obtained both from the sampled individual and from or about all other persons in the household and the (extended) family, including persons living abroad and new members added over time. Third, the design should be longitudinal, with interviews at regular intervals over the lifecourse. Fourth, the information collected should cover pre-migration experience and include complete schooling, work, migration, sponsorship, linguistic, health, marital, and reproductive histories.

This longitudinal, multi-cohort design, which came to be called the New Immigrant Survey (NIS), would make it possible to address basic scientific

---

[2]For example, panels and committees which have urged new data collection include the U.S. House of Representatives Select Committee on Population (1978); the U.S. Select Commission on Immigration and Refugee Policy (1981); the National Academy of Sciences' Panel on Immigration Statistics (Levine, Hill, and Warren, 1985); the International Union for the Scientific Study of Population's (IUSSP) Committee on International Migration and Committee on Data Collection (Golini, 1987; Kritz, 1987; Zlotnik, 1987); the National Academy of Sciences' Panel on Demographic and Economic Impacts of Immigration (Smith and Edmonston, 1997); and the Binational Study on Migration between Mexico and the United States (Loaeza Tovar and Martin, 1997).

issues in the study of immigration. Multi-cohort, longitudinal data would substantially advance understanding of the factors associated with the decision to migrate, the process of assimilation among both immigrants and their children, and the impacts of immigration on the U.S. society and economy. Among other things, the new data would make it possible to assess changes over time in the characteristics at entry of successive cohorts of immigrants and to address fundamental questions about identity formation, language acquisition, gains and losses from immigration, development of human resources, and health.

From the earliest discussions of the NIS, it was recognized that a pilot would be essential. There were too many unknowns for comfort: how to construct a sampling frame of new legal immigrants; how to locate the sampled individuals; what languages would be required for the interviews; whether the new immigrants would be willing to be interviewed; whether the new immigrants would agree to be contacted over time. Moreover, a central aspect of the NIS design features would be their cost-effectiveness, and therefore a variety of procedures for locating and tracking sample members would have to be tried.

While twenty years ago it might not even have been possible to construct a sampling frame in a timely manner, technical improvements in the data systems of the U.S. Immigration and Naturalization Service enabled formulation of the threefold "who-when-where" key of the NIS sampling design: 1) draw the sample from batches of electronic administrative records of new permanent resident aliens; 2) contact them as soon as possible after their admission to permanent residence; 3) contact them at the address to which they have requested that their "green card" be mailed. There is no question that this address is the best possible address, as new immigrants typically are anxious to receive the green card – the paper evidence of their new status. Because immigrants may be mobile, however, rapid contact is crucial.

During the last twenty years there have also been major advances in the technical procedures of longitudinal data collection, and the design of the New Immigrant Survey Pilot (NIS-P) exploits the new knowledge gained from experience with the National Longitudinal Surveys of Labor Market Experience, the Panel Study of Income Dynamics, and other longitudinal studies. As well, many advances have been made in questionnaire construction, for example, in the measurement of labor force participation, wealth and assets, transfers, health, religiosity, and use of public assistance programs. By using question modules that have been honed by experts across many topical domains, the NIS and the NIS-P ensure not only state-of-the-art features but also, and importantly, comparability with the subject populations of other studies, especially with the native-born population of the United States.

The objective of the NIS-P was twofold: 1) to assess the cost-effectiveness of alternative methods for locating and tracking sampled immigrants; and 2) to obtain information about new legal immigrants that would both be immediately useful and also aid in the design of the full New Immigrant Survey. This article first provides a brief summary of the NIS-P design and next presents information, never before available, obtained from the NIS-P on one important aspect of immigrant behavior, assortative mating. The intent is to provide a flavor for the kinds of questions that can be studied with this new data base and with the larger-sample full New Immigrant Survey by presenting new information on married couples who are part of immigration flows and whose characteristics are importantly shaped by immigration law. We distinguish between two types of couples, those in which one spouse is a U.S. citizen sponsor and those in which both spouses are immigrants. INS administrative data provide no information on couples, only on individual immigrants, and census data, which do provide information on couples, do not distinguish the foreign-born by visa status or, accurately, by date of immigration. These play important roles. It is important to study assortative mating among immigrants because who is married to whom affects the environment in which the children of immigrants are born and raised. And these children are an important component of the long-term impact of immigration.

THE NEW IMMIGRANT SURVEY PILOT
NIS-P Sampling

The sampling frame for the NIS Pilot consists of all persons who were admitted to legal permanent residence during the months of July and August of 1996.[3] This is a sampling frame whose sampling units are specific named individuals. The total number of immigrants admitted during this period was 148,987. Because children are quite numerous among immigrants and because employment-based immigrants, in whom there is great interest, are a relatively small category, we drew a stratified random sample, undersampling children and oversampling the employment-based. The strata were defined

---
[3]Analysis of INS data indicates that there is little seasonality in admission to permanent residence; thus, immigrants admitted in July and August appear to be representative of a full year's cohort of immigrants. For further details, *see* Jasso, Massey, Rosenzweig and Smith, 2000.

as follows: 1) all children (defined as being under age 18 at admission to permanent residence) went into one stratum, with a probability of selection equal to .003715; 2) all adults (defined as age 18 or over) with employment-category visas (including the spouses and children aged 18+ of employment-based principal immigrants) went into the second stratum and were assigned the highest probability of selection (.047201); and 3) all other immigrants went into the third and last stratum, assigned a probability of selection of .013486. Accordingly, employment-based adult immigrants were 3.5 times as likely to be drawn as other adult immigrants.

The initial sample thus drawn numbered 2,001 persons. Of these, 20 declared as their place of intended residence a locale outside the 50 states (such as Puerto Rico, Guam, or the Virgin Islands); of these twenty, three adults were retained in the sample in order to test methods for contacting individuals outside the 50 states (two persons from Puerto Rico and one from the Virgin Islands), leaving an effective sample of 1,984 persons. Of these, 1,839 were adult immigrants (including the three resident in Puerto Rico and the Virgin Islands).

Our strategy was to conduct interviews with sample members from the second and third strata (these are age 18 and older) and with the parents or caregivers of the sample members in the first stratum. This study focuses on the second and third strata, examining data on adult sampled immigrants.

NIS-P Survey Cycle and Periodicity Experiment

The NIS Pilot consists of a baseline survey, a three-month follow-up of half (randomly chosen) of the baseline-interviewed sample, a six-month follow-up of all the baseline-interviewed sample, and a one-year follow-up, also of the baseline-interviewed sample. The purpose of the three-month interview is to assess the effects of interview number and frequency on sample attrition and recall bias.

Locating Sampled Immigrants

For budgetary reasons, the NIS-P was designed as a telephone survey, unlike the full NIS whose design calls for in-person interviews at the first and some of the subsequent interviews. Thus, the first step was to obtain telephone numbers for the sampled immigrants, using the addresses to which they had requested that the green card be mailed. The large array of methods for obtaining telephone numbers, described in detail in Jasso, Massey, Rosenzweig, and Smith (*Demography*, Vol. 37:127–138), produced telephone numbers for slightly over half of the sampled immigrants aged 18 and over (53.3% – 980 out of 1,839). To find the telephone number for the remainder (46.7%), it was necessary to change strategy midstream and undertake intensive fieldwork – an option which for budgetary reasons had been initially rejected. A staff of field trackers was sent out to locate respondents and obtain telephone numbers in areas where sampled immigrants were concentrated: the Los Angeles area, Northern California, and parts of the following states – New York, New Jersey, Connecticut, Florida, Texas, Washington, Michigan, Virginia, Maryland, Massachusetts – as well as Washington, DC.

Interview Language

Interviews were conducted in eighteen languages. The interview instruments were translated into six languages – Spanish, Chinese, Russian, Polish, Korean and Vietnamese. In addition, bilingual interviewers fluent in eleven other languages were hired to interview respondents in those languages.

Response Rates

Baseline interviews were conducted with 62% of the new-immigrant sample. This figure reflects the experiments with alternative procedures for locating the immigrants (and their telephone numbers). In the 69 percent of the cases where a correct telephone number was obtained, the response rate was 89 percent. We estimate that if fieldwork had been carried out on the full sample and in a timely manner, the overall response rate would have been 75 percent. The lesson for the full survey is clear: the first interview should be face-to-face and carried out soon after admission to legal permanent residence.

Much higher completion rates were obtained for the six- and twelve-month follow-ups, as would be expected given that contact attempts began with a correct telephone number. For the six-month round, the completion rate was 92 percent, and for the twelve-month round it was 95 percent.

Information from Administrative Record

A useful feature of the NIS design is that, because the sampling frame consists of the administrative records of all persons admitted to legal permanent residence in a particular time interval, there is some information on all sampled individuals, whether or not they are interviewed. This information – the INS New-Immigrant Record – can thus be used to assess sample selectivity. Importantly, linked data from both the INS record and the NIS interviews provide a powerful data base.

The INS immigrant record provides information on age, sex, marital status, as well as on several migration-relevant variables. These include country of origin, detailed information on the immigrant visa class of admission, the month and year of admission to legal permanent residence and, for the subset of immigrants who are adjusting from a nonimmigrant status, year of admission to that nonimmigrant status.[4]

We use the information on class of admission to construct indicator variables for major visa classes, including spouse of U.S. citizen, parent of (adult) U.S. citizen, employment-based, sibling of U.S. citizen, refugee/asylee, and diversity immigrants and to distinguish, where applicable, between the principal immigrant and his or her accompanying family members.

It is also possible from information on the immigrant record to construct a measure of immediately prior residence in illegal status. First, the immigrant visa type includes some categories designated for illegals who qualify for permanent residence; examples include suspension-of-deportation cases and registry-provision legalization.[5] Second, the nonimmigrant class codes include a category for persons who entered without inspection and are adjusting to legal permanent residence without first leaving the country, under the section 245(i) provisions of the Immigration and Nationality Act in effect in 1996. Accordingly, we construct a measure that classifies as having prior illegal experience those sampled immigrants whose immigrant visas signal prior illegal experience plus those whose nonimmigrant visas indicate prior illegal experience.[6]

The variables just listed, because they are available for all sampled immigrants whether or not they are interviewed, can be used to assess selectivity in response rates. Indeed, an analysis comparing the INS-record characteristics of the interviewed and non-interviewed sampled immigrants indicates little appreciable difference between the two groups (Jasso, et al., 2000). Moreover, combining the data collected in the NIS interviews with the INS-record characteristics provides a powerful set of information. For example, a richer understanding of prior illegal experience can be obtained by combining the immigrant-visa

[4]However, in the INS new-immigrant record long residence with a succession of nonimmigrant visas is ignored except for the final nonimmigrant status.
[5]The registry provisions of U.S. law grant permanent residence to individuals who have resided illegally in the United States for many years. Currently, as fixed by the Immigration Reform and Control Act of 1986, the requisite period of residence must have begun on or before January 1, 1972. Prior to this legislation, the registry cutoff date was June 30, 1948.
[6]This measure, constructed from the immigrant and nonimmigrant visa information in the INS new-immigrant record is largely a measure of prior "entry without inspection" experience and thus understates the true immediately prior illegal experience; as well, it understates the total prior illegal experience.

and nonimmigrant-visa information described above with respondent-provided information on entry without inspection, visa overstays, and unauthorized employment.

U.S. IMMIGRATION LAW, THE FAMILY, AND EDUCATIONAL ACHIEVEMENT

As is well known, U.S. law grants U.S. citizens the right to marry almost anyone they choose and to reside in the United States with the chosen mate (*see* Jasso and Rosenzweig, 1990). The United States also promotes the immigration of highly-educated persons, via the employment-based preference categories. Against this backdrop, there is a vigorous interplay of behavioral processes: a job market and a marriage market; the "smoke-gets-in-your-eyes" phenomenon, where the smoke is U.S. citizenship, and U.S. citizens may appear more attractive as potential mates than they actually are; employers optimizing for the short term and marital spouses for the long term.

Family phenomena and employment phenomena, always deeply intertwined, are even more deeply intertwined in foreign-born or mixed-nativity populations. But analyzing the operation of the mechanisms in this passionate immigration dance has been severely hampered by data deficiencies. In particular, the data base with information on immigration-law and immigration-status variables (INS data) does not contain information on spouses or on schooling; and the data bases rich in information about spouses and schooling (*e.g.*, Census and CPS) do not contain information about immigration status. NIS data will enable precise analysis of all the mechanisms in a long-term longitudinal context, and NIS-P data enable a first approximation.

A critical question in immigration research focuses on the childrearing environments provided by mixed-nativity families and immigrant families. The NIS-P enables, for the first time, a look at assortative mating in schooling, which shapes the children's home environment, among a probability sample of immigrants from a well-defined population. Seventy percent of immigrants aged 18 and over in the NIS-P were married. We examine assortative mating for two kinds of couples that are part of U.S. immigration flows – couples in which an immigrant spouse is sponsored by a U.S. citizen and couples in which both spouses are immigrants, having married prior to immigration.

Couples Formed by U.S. Citizen Sponsors and Spouse-Immigrants

Almost 41 percent of married immigrants aged 18 and over were sponsored by a U.S. citizen. The NIS-P indicates that, among married FY 1996 immigrants aged 25 and over who were sponsored by U.S. citizens, immigrant wives are substantially better educated than immigrant husbands – average schooling of immigrant brides is 14.5 years while among immigrant husbands it is 12.4 years, a difference of more than two years. This could reflect operation of two distinct mechanisms: 1) U.S. citizen men and women have similar education but have different tastes in marital partners; or 2) U.S. citizen men and women differ in education and they marry people like themselves. The twelve-month round of the NIS-P obtained information on the schooling of the spouse of the sampled immigrant, and we utilize this information to examine schooling and assortative mating among couples formed by the marriage of a U.S. citizen and the spouse sponsored for immigration.

Table 1 presents, in panel A, the average years of schooling among four groups of persons aged 25 and over: U.S. citizen brides who sponsor husbands, U.S. citizen grooms who sponsor wives, immigrant brides, and immigrant grooms. Married couples appear on the diagonals; for example, U.S. citizen brides are married to immigrant grooms, and U.S. citizen grooms are married to immigrant brides. The estimates reveal three things: 1) U.S. citizen men who sponsor immigrant spouses are substantially better educated than U.S. citizen women who sponsor immigrant spouses – averaging 15.1 years of schooling versus 12.7; 2) the immigrant spouses that these U.S. citizens sponsor are remarkably like themselves – U.S. citizen men marry women with almost as high schooling as their own (14.8 years versus 15.1), and U.S. citizen women similarly marry men with almost as high schooling as their own (12.4 years versus 12.7); 3) however slight the spousal differential, U.S. citizens nonetheless display the American penchant for education, being more educated than their immigrant spouses, on average, among both sexes.

To summarize the husband-wife schooling differential, we present in Table 1, panel B, the ln(difference) of their schooling levels, constructed as the natural logarithm of the ratio of wife's schooling to husband's schooling.

TABLE 1
ASSORTATIVE MATING AMONG U.S. CITIZENS AND THE IMMIGRANT SPOUSES THEY SPONSOR:
NIS-P 1996 IMMIGRANTS AND SPOUSES AGED 25 AND OVER

	Brides	Grooms
A. Average Years of Schooling		
U.S. Citizen Sponsor	12.73	15.13
Immigrant Spouse	14.78	12.38
B. Measures of Assortative Mating, by Immigrant Spouse		
Average of ln(difference) in schooling	-0.0551	0.0526
Correlation between spouses' schooling	0.270	0.377
Sample size	78	52

Notes: In panel A, married couples appear in the diagonals. The ln(difference) in panel B is the natural logarithm of the ratio of wife's to husband's schooling.

This measure has the interpretation that zero represents equal schooling, negative numbers represent the case where the wife has less schooling than the husband, and positive numbers represent the case where the wife has more schooling than the husband. This measure is reported for two subsets of couples – those in which the bride is the immigrant spouse and those in which the husband is the immigrant spouse. As expected from the average schooling in panel A, the ln(difference) is negative among couples in which U.S. citizen men marry immigrant brides – the immigrant brides have lower schooling than their U.S. citizen husbands – and it is positive among couples in which U.S. citizen women marry immigrant grooms – the U.S. citizen women have higher schooling than their immigrant husbands. Nativity is more important than gender; U.S. citizens, of whatever sex, have more schooling than their immigrant spouses.

Table 1 also reports the correlation between wife's and husband's schooling, again separately for the two subsets of couples. The correlation is higher among the group composed of immigrant husbands and citizen wives (r=0.38 versus 0.27), indicating differences in departures from linearity between the two groups. Sharper scrutiny would, with larger sample size and a longitudinal design (as called for in the full NIS), enable more precise characterization of the distribution of husband-wife differences in schooling.

It is possible that assortative mating patterns differ between couples in which the U.S. citizen sponsor is native born and couples in which the U.S. citizen sponsor is a former immigrant who naturalized. It is risky to undertake such an analysis with NIS-P data because of the modest sample size, but we did examine the subsets (aged 25 and over) in which the U.S. citizen sponsor is native born; these subsets contain 43 couples involving U.S. citizen men and 30 couples involving U.S. citizen women. Results, not shown, indicate that the direction of all effects is the same as in Table 1 (which is not surprising given that such couples are in the majority). However, the results suggest an intensifying of the mechanisms. For example, while in the entire group the average schooling of U.S. citizen husbands and their immigrant wives is 15.1 and 14.8 years, respectively, here the average schooling of native-born U.S. citizen husbands and their immigrant wives is 15.5 and 14.9 years, respectively; this sharpening is reflected in the ln(difference), which drops to -0.063 from -0.0551. Still, the difference in average schooling reaches only six-tenths of a year in both groups.

To fully understand the schooling distribution among the immigrant spouses of U.S. citizens, it is necessary also to pay attention to both the immigrant's country of origin and changes in U.S. immigration law because the Immigration Reform and Control Act (IRCA) of 1986 and the Immigration Fraud Amendments of 1986 played important roles in determining the schooling distribution of these immigration couples.

Table 2 reports the average years of schooling, measured in the NIS-P baseline survey, of persons who gained admission to permanent residence as the spouses of U.S. citizens and who were age 25 and over at admission, separately for Mexico and all other countries. Additionally, figures are presented separately for immigrants who received conditional visas – i.e., had been married less than two years at admission to permanent residence – and immigrants who received an unconditional visa (under the provisions of the Immigration Marriage Fraud Amendments of 1986). As shown, for both country groups and for both marital durations, wives of U.S. citizens are substantially better schooled than husbands of U.S. citizens. However, these differentials are larger among immigrants born in Mexico – 3.3 years of schooling for newlyweds and 4.8 years for the longer-married group – than among immigrants born elsewhere, where the differentials range between 1.8 and 2.1.

TABLE 2
AVERAGE YEARS OF SCHOOLING AMONG SPOUSES OF U.S. CITIZENS AGED 25 AND OVER, BY SEX, NATIVITY, AND MARITAL DURATION: NIS-P 1996 IMMIGRANTS AT BASELINE

	Immigrants			
	Born in Mexico		Born Elsewhere	
Marital Duration	Men	Women	Men	Women
Less than 2 years	13.9	17.2	12.7	14.5
More than 2 years	8.6	13.4	12.6	14.7
N	16	12	72	91

Table 2 also shows that while among spouses born outside Mexico there is little difference in average schooling across the two marital-duration groups – one tenth and one fifth of a year of schooling difference between newly-married and longer-married husbands and wives, respectively – there is a large difference in average schooling across the Mexico-born in the two marital-duration groups. Recently-married Mexico-born spouses are substantially better schooled than those who have been married longer. Among Mexico-born wives of U.S. citizens, those in recent marriages have an average schooling that is 3.8 years higher than that of immigrants in older marriages; among Mexico-born husbands of U.S. citizens, that differential is 5.3 years. This dramatic difference suggests that there may be a mechanism at work beyond ordinary increasing aspirations and ordinary birth cohort effects; just such a mechanism could be due to the unfolding of the IRCA amnesty. At the time of the amnesty, fewer aliens were legalized than had been anticipated based on demographic estimates; anecdotal evidence suggests that the deficit was due to couples hedging their bets and conserving their financial resources. It is believed that to guard against rejection of the legalization application, and consequent deportation of the entire family, and also because of the hardship imposed by the legalization fees, some married couples opted to have only one spouse apply for legalization. IRCA-legalized aliens started becoming eligible to naturalize in FY 1994, and thus the FY 1996 immigrant cohort would include immigrant spouses sponsored by naturalized U.S. citizens who had been legalized under IRCA.[7] Of course, these spouses would have been married longer than two years and thus eligible for unconditional visas.

The full NIS will obtain complete migration histories about spouses of sampled immigrants, and thus it will be possible to have direct and certain information about the sponsors of immigrant spouses. For now, it is highly likely that the U.S. citizen sponsors of Mexico-born spouses in longer-duration marriages were IRCA-legalized aliens. This is consistent with other evidence in the NIS-P that immigrants with prior illegal experience have less schooling – 10.5 years – than immigrants with no prior illegal experience – 13 years (Jasso, *et al.*, 2000) – and is consistent with the positive assortative mating among immigrant spouses and their U.S. citizen sponsors.

Immigrant Couples

Under U.S. immigration law, many classes of immigrant visas provide visa entitlement to the spouse and minor children of the qualifying individual; the latter is known as the "principal," and the spouse and minor children as "accompanying family members" (even though they need not travel together). For example, a professor who qualifies for an employment-based visa can also obtain visas for his or her spouse and minor children. Such family groups constitute the quintessential "immigrant families" so popular in the mass media, although they are less than 60 percent of all married couples involving an immigrant. As with the citizen-immigrant couples discussed in the preceding section, the childrearing environment they provide may be shaped by differences in schooling across the parents.

It has never been possible to study such families using INS data because the data do not include a family identifier. Thus, for example, while INS data

---

[7]Admission to permanent residence under IRCA provisions started in FY 1989, when 478,814 persons adjusted status. The peak year was FY 1991, when 1,123,162 IRCA-legalized aliens became permanent residents.

may characterize a given immigrant as a principal within a detailed visa classification and another immigrant as a spouse within the same detailed visa classification, it is not possible to ascertain that the two form a marital unit. The NIS-P, besides measuring the sampled immigrant's schooling, also measured the schooling of the immigrant's spouse.

In this section we focus on eight subsets of immigrant couples, defined by their visa category – employment-based, sibling-based, refugee/asylee, and diversity immigrants – and distinguishing between couples in which the wife is the principal immigrant and couples in which the husband is the principal immigrant. Because the NIS design calls for obtaining information on family members, the sample size available for this analysis is larger than it would be if the subsets were based only on the sampled immigrants (although sample sizes remain modest, and in some subsets quite small, except in the employment-based categories which were oversampled, as discussed above). To illustrate, we describe how the two employment-based subsets are constituted. The subset in which the wife is the immigrant principal includes all couples in which the sampled immigrant is either a female employment-based principal with a foreign-born spouse or a male employment-based accompanying spouse; and the subset in which the husband is the immigrant principal includes all couples in which the sampled immigrant is either a male employment-based principal with a foreign-born spouse or a female employment-based accompanying spouse. Couples are included only if both spouses are aged 25 or over.

This method of constructing the subsets produces an asymmetry whose effects are probably mild and which will disappear in the full NIS in which complete migration and marital histories will be obtained about all family members. The asymmetry is this: while it is certain that accompanying spouses are married to someone in the same visa classification (*e.g.*, a female accompanying spouse in an employment visa category is with 100% certainty married to a male principal in the same employment visa category), a married principal may have a spouse who is not an accompanying spouse (*e.g.*, a principal in the employment visa category may be married to a sibling principal – the marriage could have taken place after immigration or it might have taken place before, the employment principal having been in the spouse-of-permanent-resident-alien backlogs before finding an employer to sponsor him or her).

Table 3 reports the average schooling of the husbands and wives in the eight subsets. As in Table 1, couples are represented on the diagonals. For example, in panel A, couples in which the wife is the principal and the husband is the accompanying spouse appear in the top-left and bottom-right cells, and couples in which the husband is the principal and the wife is the accompanying spouse appear in the top-right and bottom-left cells. As discussed above, the accompanying-spouse groups include the spouses of principals. The estimates indicate two things: 1) among employment-based and sibling-based immigrants, men are more highly schooled than their wives, on average, regardless of which one is the principal immigrant; but the differential is substantially attenuated when the wife is the principal in an employment category (average schooling of 15.2 years for the wife-principal versus 15.3 years for the accompanying husband); and 2) in the refugee/asylee and diversity categories, the principal is more highly schooled than the spouse, regardless of sex; this may reflect both legal procedures and behavioral processes associated with qualifying for immigrant visas in these categories. For example, an asylee couple may put forward as principal the more highly schooled in hopes of a more favorable disposition; and diversity visas have an educational requirement for principals but not for accompanying spouses.

TABLE 3
AVERAGE YEARS OF SCHOOLING AMONG MARRIED NIS-P 1996 IMMIGRANTS AGED 25+,
BY VISA CATEGORY AND WHETHER WIFE OR HUSBAND IS PRINCIPAL IMMIGRANT

	Wives	Husbands
A. Employment-Based Immigrants		
Principal	15.18	17.16
Accompanying spouse	15.34	15.29
B. Sibling Immigrants		
Principal	10.62	14.00
Accompanying spouse	10.58	13.00
C. Refugee/asylee Immigrants		
Principal	16.00	13.66
Accompanying spouse	12.10	15.56
D. Diversity Immigrants		
Principal	15.20	15.43
Accompanying spouse	13.29	13.80

Notes: Married couples appear in the diagonals. Sample sizes for the eight subsets of married couples are: employment-based/wife-principal, 51; employment-based/husband-principal, 161; sibling-based/wife-principal, 13; sibling-based/husband-principal, 12; refugee-based/wife-principal, 9; refugee-based/husband-principal, 29; diversity-based/wife-principal, 5; diversity-based/husband-principal, 14.

Table 4 reports the average ln(difference) and the correlation between husband's and wife's schooling. As expected from Table 3, the ln(difference) is negative for all four subsets in the employment and sibling categories – wives have lower schooling than their husbands – but in the refugee/asylee and diversity categories it is negative only if the husband is the principal immigrant.

TABLE 4
ASSORTATIVE MATING AMONG NIS-P 1996 IMMIGRANTS AGED 25 AND OVER,
BY VISA CATEGORY AND WHETHER WIFE OR HUSBAND IS PRINCIPAL IMMIGRANT

Visa Category	ln(difference) between Spouses' Schooling Immigrant Principal		Correlation between Spouses' Schooling Immigrant Principal	
	Wives	Husbands	Wives	Husbands
Employment	-0.0392	-0.108	0.339	0.437
Sibling	-0.176	-0.310	0.480	0.717
Refugee/asylee	0.0249	-0.166	0.581	0.456
Diversity	0.110	-0.140	0.875	0.0411

Note: The ln(difference) is the natural logarithm of the ratio of wife's to husband's schooling.

It is illuminating to examine the magnitudes of the schooling differentials, as indicated by both the average schooling levels in Table 3 and the average ln(difference) in Table 4. In the two subsets in which the wife is better schooled than the husband – *i.e.*, when the wife is the principal in a refugee/asylee or diversity category – the schooling differential is modest (0.44 and 1.4 years in the refugee/asylee and diversity categories, respectively). In the other six subsets in which the wife is less schooled than the husband, the differential exceeds 1.5 years of schooling in all subsets except the one in which the wife is an employment-based principal, where it is only 0.11 years. In general, if the wife is a principal, either it is the case that she is more highly schooled or, if less schooled than her husband, the differential is less than the differential in the same category for the opposite situation. The differentials are larger in the sibling category than in all other categories.

These results hint at a number of mechanisms, including the long wait for visas in the sibling category. That is, immigrants admitted in FY 1996 as sibling immigrants had been approved for their visas more than ten years earlier – in the case of immigrants from the Philippines, almost twenty years earlier. As in Bleak House, the world changed while they waited for visas; immigrant applicant couples of more recent vintages appear to have greater schooling similarity. Note also that of all the couples in Table 4, only the wife-principal couples in the employment, refugee/asylee, and diversity categories resemble in this respect the citizen-spouse couples of the preceding section. Finally, note that in the employment sphere, if the objective is to maximize human resources and get a "two-fer," then the technique of choice is to sponsor married women.

However, we note again the critical importance of monitoring changes in schooling over time. The U.S. climate of rewarding investment in human resources and of wide educational opportunities unleashes aspirations and uncovers talents. It is possible that a decade later, the estimates of Tables 2 and 4 would look substantially different.

CONCLUSION

This article provided a brief summary of the Pilot for the New Immigrant Survey (NIS) and presented new information, never before available, on immigrant assortative mating by schooling. Over 70 percent of adult immigrants are married at immigration, yet there has been little information about the couples in these immigration flows.

Our findings on couples include the following. First, among married couples formed by a U.S. citizen sponsoring the immigration of a spouse, husbands and wives have similar levels of schooling, with the U.S. citizen slightly better educated than the immigrant spouse. However, U.S. citizen husbands and their immigrant wives have substantially higher schooling than U.S. citizen wives and their immigrant husbands (on average, two years higher). Second, unlike immigrants from other countries, Mexico-born spouses of U.S. citizens differ markedly in schooling depending on whether they are recently married, suggesting the continuing after-effects of the Immigration Reform and Control Act of 1986. Third, husband-wife schooling levels are less similar among married couples in which both spouses are immigrants than among couples involving a U.S. citizen sponsor and an immigrant spouse, except when the wife is the principal in an employment category. These findings suggest that immigration laws importantly shape the characteristics of families, and thus the next generation – the children of immigrants and immigrant children.

REFERENCES

Golini, A.
1987 "Population Movements: Typology and Data Collection, Trends, Policies." Paper presented at the European Population Conference. Finland.

Jasso, G. and M. R. Rosenzweig
1990 *The New Chosen People: Immigrants in the United States.* A volume in "The Population of the United States in the 1980s: A Census Monograph Series." New York: Russell Sage.

Jasso, G., *et al.*
2000 "The New Immigrant Survey Pilot (NIS-P): Overview and New Findings about U.S. Legal Immigrants at Admission," *Demography,* Vol. 37(1):127–138.

Kritz, M. M.
1987 "International Migration Policies: Conceptual Problems," *International Migration Review,* 21:947–964.

Levine, D. B., K. Hill and R. Warren, eds.
1985 *Immigration Statistics: A Story of Neglect.* Washington, DC: National Academy Press.

Loaeza Tovar, E. and S. Martin, eds.
1997 *Binational Study on Migration between Mexico and the United States*. Washington, DC, and Mexico City: U.S. Commission on Immigration Reform and Mexico's Secretaría de Relaciones Exteriores.

Smith, J. P. and B. Edmonston, eds.
1997 *The New Americans: Economic, Demographic, and Fiscal Effects on Immigration*. Report of the National Research Council. Washington, DC: National Academy Press.

U.S. Department of State
Various Issues. *Visa Bulletin*.

U.S. House of Representatives Select Committee on Population
1978 *Legal and Illegal Immigration to the United States*. Washington, DC: U.S. Government Printing Office.

U.S. Select Commission on Immigration and Refugee Policy
1981 *U.S. Immigration Policy and the National Interest: Final Report and Recommendations of the Select Commission on Immigration and Refugee Policy to the Congress and President of the United States*. Washington, DC: U.S. Government Printing Office.

Zlotnik, H.
1987 "The Concept of International Migration as Reflected in Data Collection Systems," *International Migration Review*, 21(4):925–946.

… Fertility assimilation of immigrants: Evidence from
count data models

Jochen Mayer[1,2], Regina T. Riphahn[1,2,3]

[1] University of Munich, Ludwigstr. 28RG, 80539 Munich, Germany
(Fax: +49-89-336392; e-mail: Regina.Riphahn@selapo.vwl.uni-muenchen.de)
[2] IZA, Bonn, Germany
[3] CEPR, London

Received: 7 January 1999/Accepted: 10 August 1999

Abstract. This study applies count data estimation techniques to investigate the fertility adjustment of immigrants in the destination country. Data on completed fertility are taken from the 1996 wave of the German Socioeconomic Panel (GSOEP). While the economic literature stresses the role of prices and incomes as determinants of fertility, the demographic literature discusses whether assimilation or disruption effects dominate immigrants' fertility after migration. We find evidence in favor of the assimilation model according to which immigrant fertility converges to native levels over time. In addition, we confirm the negative impact of female human capital on fertility outcomes.

JEL classification: C25, J13, J61

Key words: Immigrant fertility, assimilation, disruption

1. Introduction

Immigrants' assimilation to destination country standards is discussed in a wide and growing literature. Past assimilation research has focused on labor market aspects such as earnings, unemployment,[1] or transfer program participation.[2] With continuously accelerating flows of international migration (cf. Segal 1993) issues of *demographic* assimilation, increasingly gain in importance as well.

All correspondence to Regina T. Riphahn. We wish to thank Julia Dannenberg for very able research assistance, and three anonymous referees, Ralph Rotte, seminar participants at IZA-Bonn and the University of Munich for helpful comments. *Responsible editor:* Rainer Winkelmann.

This paper contributes to the literature on immigrant fertility assimilation, applying a count data estimation framework. Since the early contribution of Ben-Porath (1973) the literature on immigrant fertility has been debating whether immigrant fertility adjustment should be explained in a framework of fertility assimilation or in a model of fertility disruption. The assimilation model predicts that immigrant fertility converges to native levels, whereas the disruption model predicts increasing fertility following the disruptive effect of migration itself. With rising population shares of immigrants in western countries,[3] and given ongoing debates of appropriate immigration policies, this is an important issue to investigate. Also, immigrant fertility has direct implications for the labor market involvement of the first generation, and – due to tradeoffs between the demand for child quantity and child quality – indirect effects on the human capital of second generation immigrants.

While almost all fertility adjustment studies investigate the case of immigrants to the United States (using decennial census data) this analysis focuses on migration to Europe. The selection and attraction mechanisms causing migration to Europe may differ considerably from those relevant for the United States, and may affect subsequent immigrant behavior.

In the literature on immigrant fertility adjustment over the duration of stay in the destination country it is accepted that duration and immigration year effects cannot be separately identified on the basis of cross-section data. We argue that the fertility literature, which unanimously controls for years since migration, has applied an inappropriate duration measure: When one is interested in fertility outcomes it is not the total duration of stay which should affect the number of births but the duration of stay in the receiving country which occurs *during a woman's reproductive phase*. In other words, whether a woman who migrated at age 35 has been in the country for 10 or 20 years will hardly make a difference for her completed fertility. What matters is the number of fertile years spent in the receiving country. This issue has been overlooked in the existing literature on fertility. An interesting consequence of this correction in variable definitions is that now cross-section data are sufficient to separately identify the effects of the number of fertile years in the host country and the year of immigration.

The paper proceeds as follows: After a discussion of the literature on models of immigrant fertility adjustment and a review of past findings in Sect. 2, we provide a brief description of our data, which are taken from the German Socioeconomic Panel (GSOEP). Sect. 3 additionally describes our model specification and estimation method. The results are discussed and interpreted in part four of the paper, before we conclude in Sect. 5.

2. The assimilation of immigrant fertility

While many studies have analysed immigrant fertility adjustments, few justify their hypotheses using economic arguments. This is surprising because the economic theory of fertility provides convincing rationales for fertility adjustments after migration (for a survey see Hotz et al. 1997). Couples' demand for children can be modelled as a function of prices and income (Becker 1981): Among the relevant prices are the (potential) wage of the wife, which is frequently approximated by her human capital, the cost of child care, and the cost of fertility regulation. Husbands' earnings are the source of income effects.

The model predicts that the demand for children declines if the opportunity cost of the wife's time, her potential wage, increases. Thus one reason for fertility adjustment after migration may be that potential wages in the destination country differ from women's earnings potential at home. The effects of husbands' income on fertility demand predicted by theory are ambiguous. On the one hand a higher income may increase the demand for child quantity, because the costs of children become affordable. On the other hand higher incomes increase the demand for child quality. Child quality raises the cost per child and thus justifies a negative correlation between income and the demand for children. Again, with different incomes in the origin and host countries, couples may adjust their fertility plans after migration.

This demand focused model of fertility ('Chicago-Columbia model') contrasts with the 'Pennsylvania' model, which also considers supply side factors of fertility determination, in particular a couples' fecundity and the cost of fertility regulation (e.g. Easterlin 1987, or Rosenzweig and Schultz 1985). This perspective provides another justification for the adjustment of immigrant fertility from origin to destination country levels: not only may potential incomes converge to the receiving country's standards, also cost and availability of contraception may differ from those in the country of origin.

Thus economic fertility theory yields three immediate arguments for fertility adjustments of immigrants: Changes in female wages, in male incomes, and the price of fertility regulation. The relevant demographic and economic literature, however, has focused on a separate line of argument in the analysis of immigrant behavior, and juxtaposes two models of fertility adjustment neglecting the arguments presented above (see e.g. Blau 1992, Schoorl 1990, Gorwaney et al. 1990, Kahn 1994, or Ford 1990.).

The assimilation model suggests that couples, who migrate from a high fertility country to a low fertility country, initially follow traditional high fertility patterns, and over time adjust to the lower fertility in the destination country. Therefore it is hypothesized that the difference in completed fertility between natives and immigrants falls, the earlier in a woman's reproductive career migration to the destination country occurs. In contrast, the disruption model stresses that migration itself causes an initial drop in couples' fertility and that, subsequently, fertility will rise again. This model does not explain the level of initial or final immigrant fertility relative to the native population, but argues in terms of the direction of adjustments in period-specific – though not necessarily completed – fertility.

The two models lead to different conclusions with respect to two aspects of immigrant fertility: First, they differ with respect to the direction of short-term fertility adjustment. The assimilation model considers a slow decline in fertility and the disruption model expects an increase in fertility after the disruptive migration event. Second, the migration effect on completed fertility may differ in the two scenarios: Since in the assimilation framework migrants generally have above native level fertility until assimilation is completed, they will have higher levels of completed fertility. This "excess fertility" beyond the native level should decline the more of its fertile years a couple spent in the receiving country (see Fig. 1).

The pattern of completed fertility likely differs in the case of the disruption model. Here at least three scenarios are possible, which are depicted in Fig. 2. First, if – as some U.S. studies suggest (e.g. Jasso and Rosenzweig 1990) – immigrant fertility catches up after a temporary disruption, then completed

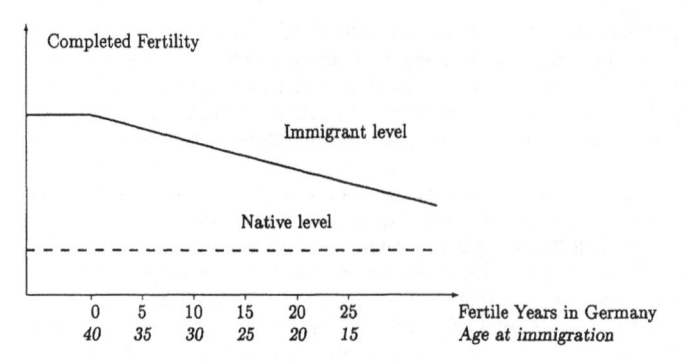

Fig. 1. Completed fertility according to the assimilation hypothesis

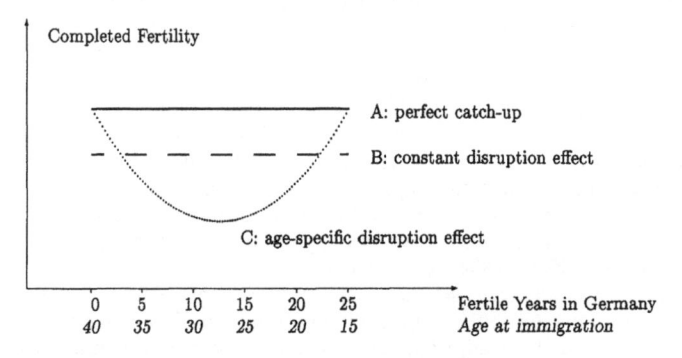

Fig. 2. Completed fertility according to different disruption hypotheses

fertility rates remain unaffected by the migration event and stay at the home country level (scenario A in Fig. 2). Second, couples may never be able to fully catch up for the births lost due to the disruptive migration event. If the disruption effect in terms of the number of lost births is constant across all age groups, it causes a parallel downward shift in completed fertility, independent of the number of fertile years a woman spent in Germany (scenario B in Fig. 2). Third, if couples do not catch up and the number of lost births is highest if migration occurred during the peak years of age-specific fertility, we may observe a U-shaped curve of completed fertility, when plotted against the fertile years spent abroad (scenario C in Fig. 2): Disruption causes smaller losses in the years before and after peak age-specific fertility disruption than in the period of peak fertility, which generally lies between ages 20 and 30.[4] In neither scenario do we expect to see a decline in completed fertility as a function of the time spent in the receiving country.

Therefore a test between the assimilation and disruption model has to evaluate first the total difference in cumulative fertility for natives and immigrants. If immigrants from high fertility countries have below native level cumulative fertility the assimilation model can be rejected. Second, the direction of fertility adjustment can be investigated. If cumulative fertility falls over the entire range of fertile years spent in Germany this is suggestive of assimilation effects. If we observe completed fertility to be constant over the range of fertile years in Germany, we can reject the assimilation hypothesis. While it would be interesting to compare the relative impacts of the assimilation and disruption effects in detail, data limitations force us to evaluate the overall effect of migration on completed fertility.

Generally it appears that the literature on the fertility adjustment of immigrants supports the disruption model more than the assimilation explanation. Comparing observed fertility rates over the last decades (available studies use data from the 1960, 1970, and 1980 census) e.g. Blau (1992) and Jasso and Rosenzweig (1990) are careful to control for the effects of declining fertility in the native U.S. reference population as well as the effect of a changing composition of immigrant origin countries.

Besides the assimilation vs. disruption issue, the literature explicitly analyses the additional effects of (1) different countries of origin, (2) self-selection among immigrants, and (3) emigration bias. Both, Blau (1992) and Jasso and Rosenzweig (1990) find that immigrants from high fertility source countries have higher fertility in the destination country and Kahn (1988) shows the pervading influence of home country fertility. Secondly, relative to their home country population self-selected migrants are more prone to undertake long-term (e.g. human-capital) investments and to have low fertility rates. Blau (1992) shows that immigrant women are among the best educated in their native countries, which indicates high opportunity costs of child bearing. She also provides evidence that immigrants have higher tastes for child quality than natives, suggesting low fertility in the destination country. This taste for child quality is confirmed by Jasso and Rosenzweig (1990) who show that immigrants school their children at a higher rate than natives. Finally, these authors point out that selective emigration of immigrants may cause an upward bias in measured immigrant fertility, since couples with many children are less likely to return to their home country.

Both, Blau (1992) and Jasso and Rosenzweig (1990), conclude that their evidence is consistent with the model of fertility disruption. They do not find assimilation to destination country fertility levels but show that after initially low birth rates immigrants added to their family sizes at faster rates than the native population. This finding is confirmed by Ford (1990) and Kahn (1994). Only Gorwaney et al. (1990) detect disruption effects for immigrants from developed countries but conclude in favor of the assimilation model for immigrants from developing countries.

All of these studies use data from United States (U.S.) censuses and build their analyses on the results of cross-tabulations and least squares regressions. None of the papers discusses whether the period of residence in the United States is the appropriate variable to describe immigrants' exposure to U.S. culture and labor markets for the purpose of describing its effects on fertility. Also, none of these studies chose the count data estimation approach, which is compatible with the positive integer valued outcome measure. Since King (1988) we know that least squares regression may yield inconsistent estimates if applied to count data outcomes. Therefore our analysis extends the existing literature in a number of important dimensions.

While we are not aware of past studies on immigrant fertility adjustment for Germany, a related literature analyses the fertility effect of German unification. Between 1989 and 1994 East German births fell by sixty percent.

Conrad et al. (1996) and Lechner (1998) investigate the East German fertility transition and conclude that fertility takes on West German patterns. They suggest that the strong fertility disruption immediately after unification was only a temporary adjustment phenomenon: Fertility rates of older women suddenly dropped, since their completed fertility already exceeded Western patterns, and young women postponed births adhering to the West German pattern of late first births. Here a situation which looked like disruption masks the first signs of assimilation.

From the above discussion we derive five hypotheses which we test below:

(H1) The higher a woman's (potential) labor market income, the lower her completed fertility.
(H2) The assimilation hypothesis suggests that immigrants' completed fertility exceeds that of natives and that it falls with the number of fertile years spent in Germany.
(H3) The disruption hypothesis with catch-up suggests that immigrants' completed fertility does not vary over the number of fertile years spent in Germany.
(H4) The disruption hypothesis without catch-up suggests that immigrants' completed fertility takes on a U-shaped form over the number of fertile years spent in Germany.
(H5) Country of origin fertility differences are reflected in immigrant fertility.

3. Data, specification, and estimation method

Our data are taken from the 1996 wave of the German Socioeconomic Panel (GSOEP). The GSOEP is a representative survey of households and individuals, administered annually since 1984. It oversamples the guest-worker population in Germany with Turkish, Spanish, Greek, Italian, and what was Yugoslavian origin. The original 1984 sample consisted of about 4,500 native German and 1,400 foreign households with a total of more than 12,000 respondents.

Since guest-worker immigration to Germany commenced in the late 1950s, some of the foreign respondents of the 1996 GSOEP survey are already second generation immigrants, and born in Germany. (The first guest-worker treaty was signed in 1955 with Italy.) To generate a homogenous sample we consider only those female respondents, who are either of German nationality and born in Germany (our native sample), or of foreign nationality and born abroad (the immigrant sample). Additionally, we restrict attention to immigrants from the five oversampled sending countries. Since we are interested only in completed fertility, we selected observations of women age 40 and above, and coded the number of their past births as our dependent variable. After omitting observations with missing values on core variables (such as the immigration year or schooling indicators) our native sample consisted of 1,718 and the immigrant sample of 375 observations.

In the immigrant sample one third of the women are Turkish, 28% originated in former Yugoslavia, 17% each came from Greece and Italy, and 6.5% are of Spanish descent. Table 1 describes the fertility developments in these countries and in Germany over the last seven decades. It is apparent, first, that German fertility up to the 1980s has been below that of the five sending

Fertility assimilation of immigrants

Table 1. International fertility rates

Year	West Germany	Greece	Italy	Spain	Turkey	Ex-Yugoslavia
a) Crude fertility rates						
1930	18	31	27	28	n.a.	32
1940	20	25	24	24	n.a.	25
1950	16	20	19	20	n.a.	n.a.
1960	17	19	18	22	43	24
1965	18	19	18	22	41	24
1970	13	17	17	20	36	18
1975	10	16	15	19	34	18
1982	10	14	11	15	31	15
1985	10	12	10	12	30	16
1989	11	10	10	11	26	14
1993	11	10	10	10	27	n.a.
b) Average completed fertility						
1970/75	1.64	2.32	2.28	2.89	5.04	n.a.
1980/85	1.46	1.96	1.55	1.86	4.10	n.a.
1990/95	1.50	1.47	1.31	1.38	3.45	n.a.
1995/2000	1.30	1.40	1.27	1.23	3.04	n.a.

Note: Crude Fertility Rates: Rounded livebirths per 1000 inhabitants; *Average Completed Fertility:* Hypothetical average number of births per woman based on age-specific fertility in observation period.
Source: Crude Fertility Rates – United Nations Demographic Yearbook, Federal Statistical Office Germany: Statistical Yearbook, World Bank: World Development Report; Average Completed Fertility – Federal Statistical Office Germany: Statistical Yearbook for Foreign Countries 1998.

countries. Second, fertility in Turkey has always been above that of any other country. Third, in all countries fertility declines over time and, finally, since the mid eighties fertility in Greece, Italy, Spain, and Germany has converged at a low level.

These trends are also apparent in the distribution of the dependent variable of our analysis. Table 2 describes our dependent and explanatory variables by subsample. German completed fertility with 1.93 births per woman is below that of the immigrant population with an average of 2.89 births. However, this average across immigrant groups hides substantial nationality differences: The average number of 3.8 births for Turkish women far exceeds the immigrant average. Next in rank are women of Italian and Spanish nationality with 2.8 and 2.5 births, respectively. The women from Greece and from former Yugoslavia in our sample average 2.3 births (these figures are not presented in Table 2).

Fig. 3 gives an impression of the correlation in our data between completed fertility and the number of fertile years an immigrant woman spent in Germany. The overall negative trend is obvious and even clearer when we consider average completed fertility as summarized by fertile year groups in Table 3: The reference fertility of women who spent their entire fertile period abroad (first row) is on average 3.8 children. Women who spent between one and five years of their fertile period in Germany average 3.22 births, those who spent almost all their fertile time in Germany average 2.33 births, much

Table 2. Descriptive statistics

Variable	Description	Native sample	Immigrant sample
Numbirth	Number of births	1.931 (1.353)	2.893 (1.782)
Age	Woman's age ($*10^{-1}$)	5.981 (1.243)	5.243 (0.775)
Pre-fertile-years	Number of years spent in Germany prior to age 15	0 (0)	0.024 (0.416)
Handicap	0/1 woman is handicapped	0.185 (0.388)	0.107 (0.309)
Schooling	Years of schooling ($*10^{-1}$)	1.074 (0.209)	0.885 (0.196)
S_mandatory	0/1 Woman completed mandatory schooling	0.695 (0.461)	0.005 (0.073)
S_advanced	0/1 Woman completed advanced schooling degree	0.299 (0.458)	0.488 (0.501)
V_apprentice	0/1 Woman completed apprenticeship	0.384 (0.486)	0.077 (0.268)
V_advanced	0/1 Woman completed advanced vocational degree	0.239 (0.426)	0.088 (0.284)
German_spoken	Good knowledge of spoken German (coded 0 for native sample)	0 (0)	0.269 (0.444)
Catholic	0/1 Woman is catholic	0.434 (0.496)	0.395 (0.489)
Protestant	0/1 Woman is protestant	0.487 (0.500)	0.005 (0.073)
Other_religion	0/1 Woman is of non-christian religion	0.001 (0.034)	0.333 (0.472)
Catholic*immi	0/1 Woman is catholic and immigrant	0 (0)	0.395 (0.489)
Protestant*immi	0/1 Woman is protestant and immigrant	0 (0)	0.005 (0.073)
Other_religion*immi	0/1 Woman is non-christian and immigrant	0 (0)	0.333 (0.472)
Immigrant	0/1 Woman is an immigrant	0.000 (0.000)	1.000 (0.000)
N_Turkish	0/1 Woman is of Turkish Nationality	0 (0)	0.320 (0.467)
N_Yugoslav	0/1 Woman is of Ex-Yugoslavian Citizenship	0 (0)	0.280 (0.450)
N_Greek	0/1 Woman is of Greek Nationality	0 (0)	0.165 (0.372)
N_Italian	0/1 Woman is of Italian Nationality	0 (0)	0.171 (0.377)
N_Spanish	0/1 Woman is of Spanish Nationality	0 (0)	0.064 (0.245)
Fertile years	Number of fertile years spent in Germany ($*10^{-1}$) (coded 0 for native sample)	0 (0)	1.312 (0.711)
FYG_G0	0 fertile years spent in Germany	0 (0)	0.093 (0.291)
FYG_G1	1–6 fertile years spent in Germany	0 (0)	0.117 (0.322)
FYG_G2	7–9 fertile years spent in Germany	0 (0)	0.101 (0.302)
FYG_G3	10–13 fertile years spent in Germany	0 (0)	0.144 (0.352)

Fertility assimilation of immigrants

Table 2 (continued)

Variable	Description	Native sample	Immigrant sample
FYG_G4	14–17 fertile years spent in Germany	0 (0)	0.192 (0.394)
FYG_G5	18–21 fertile years spent in Germany	0 (0)	0.259 (0.439)
FYG_G6	22–25 fertile years spent in Germany	0 (0)	0.093 (0.291)
Immigrated before 1971	0/1 Immigration before 1971 (coded 0 for native sample)	0 (0)	0.405 (0.492)
Immigrated 1971–79	0/1 Immigration between 1971 and 1979 (coded 0 for native sample)	0 (0)	0.517 (0.500)
Number of observations		1718	375

Note: Standard deviations in parentheses.
Source: German Socioeconomic Panel.

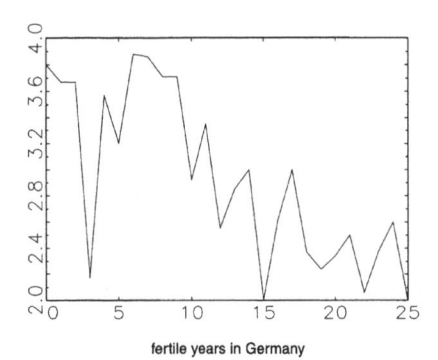

Fig. 3. Average completed fertility by fertile years in Germany
Source: Own calculations based on German Socioeconomic Panel (GSOEP).

closer to the native average of 1.93. Table 3 presents average fertility also by the standard measure of duration in this literature, years since migration. The tabulation by fertile years in Germany shows a smoother development in the average number of births than years since migration, which confounds age and immigration year effects. The high average number of births in the 6–10 year group of fertile years in Germany (3.63 births) arises in part due to the effect of two Turkish outlier observations with 10 births in this group. (Omission of these two observations leads to an average of 3.44 births in this group for the overall sample and of 5.07 in the Turkish sample.)

When comparing the descriptive statistics of the explanatory variables in Table 2 across the two samples we notice a number of differences. First, the average age of the German sample is clearly above that of the immigrant population. Further, immigrant women have on average about two years less education than their native counterparts, where the years of schooling mea-

Table 3. Average completed fertility by alternative 'duration' indicators

	All Immigrants		Turkish		Non Turkish immigrants	
	FYG	YSM	FYG	YSM	FYG	YSM
0	3.80	n.a.	3.14	n.a.	4.24	n.a.
1–5	3.22	2.50	3.64	1.00	2.77	3.25
6–10	3.63	6.50	5.41	4.00	2.31	7.33
11–15	2.73	2.50	3.40	2.33	2.40	2.67
16–20	2.49	3.59	3.19	4.33	2.25	2.63
21–25	2.33	2.97	3.08	3.85	2.16	2.30
26–30	–	2.77	–	4.00	–	2.43
31–35	–	2.48	–	3.25	–	2.35

Note: FYG = fertile years in Germany; YSM = years since migration.
Source: Own calculations based on German Socioeconomic Panel (GSOEP).

sure combines school and vocational training. The difference between the immigrant and native samples is more strongly reflected in the distribution of schooling degrees, where about half of all immigrant women fall in the omitted category of no schooling degree compared to less than one percent of the natives. Whereas only 38% of all native females in our sample have no vocational degree, this holds for 85% of the immigrant women.[5] Based on female opportunity cost of child bearing, these statistics suggest that immigrant families are likely to have higher rates of fertility than natives. The variables describing the women's religious affiliation suggest that natives are much more likely to be either catholic or protestant (jointly 90% of the native sample). In the immigrant sample there are almost no protestants and about one third is in the "other" category, which mostly comprises muslims.

Based on the discussion in Sect. 2, the specification of our empirical model for completed fertility considers four groups of explanatory variables. First, we control for overall demographic effects consisting first of a woman's age, to account for cohort differences in fertility (cf. Table 1). To control for her health the specification controls for her handicap status, assuming that health in 1996 is indicative of health during the reproductive phase. The health effect is not clear a priori: Through biological mechanisms poor health may reduce fertility, but then reduced earnings potentials of those in poor health reduce the opportunity costs of fertility. Clearly, the 1996 health measure is a poor approximation of a woman's health during her fertile period. However, unfortunately a more accurate health indicator is not available. In order to test whether the number of years a woman spent in the destination country prior to her fertile period affects her fertility we additionally control for pre-fertile years spent in Germany before age 15. In order to control for potential immigration year effects, two indicator variables are considered.[6]

Second, we approximate the effect a woman's earnings potential, using as control variables indicators of whether she speaks German well, years of education, schooling (including years of post-secondary education) and vocational training degree indicators, where 'no degree' is the omitted category.

Third, following the fertility literature we control for the effect of religious affiliation on fertility (e.g. Winkelmann 1995).

Finally, we control for women's immigrant status: In the 'immigrant model' we consider only an indicator variable for whether the woman is an immigrant. In a 'nationality model' we evaluate independent nationality effects for the source countries represented in our sample. The effect of fertile years in Germany on completed fertility is captured in three alternative specifications: In our baseline immigrant model we control for fertile year effects fitting a third order polynomial. Then we lift the parametric restriction on the effect of fertile years in Germany and instead control for a set of indicator variables. The third model drops the underlying assumption that different nationalities have identical effects and instead estimates separate third order polynomials for each nationality group.

Given that the dependent variable of our analysis always takes on positive, integer values, count data models are the natural choice for the regression. A problem which we face upon application of the standard Poisson model is that – as in other studies of completed fertility (see e.g. Winkelmann and Zimmermann 1994) – the equidispersion assumption which underlies this estimation approach, is violated in our data. We applied regression-based tests of the equidispersion hypothesis (Cameron and Trivedi 1990) and find clear evidence of underdispersion, i.e. the conditional mean exceeds the conditional variance. In such a situation the Poisson-ML estimator overestimates the standard errors.

To solve this problem, different approaches have been proposed, which are based on special distributions allowing for underdispersion and estimated via maximum likelihood. Examples are the generalized event count model (Winkelmann and Zimmermann 1994), the generalized poisson model (Consul 1989), or the Gamma count data model (Winkelmann 1995). In contrast and following McCullagh and Nelder (1989), we adapt a quasi-likelihood approach to generalize the Poisson model. The method is more general than the above in that it relies directly on the specification of the first two (conditional) moments,

$$E[y_i|X_i] = \lambda_i = \exp(X_i\beta) \tag{1}$$

$$V[y_i|X_i] = \phi * \lambda_i,. \tag{2}$$

where y_i and X_i are the univariate dependent count variable and the vector of regressors respectively, β is the parameter of interest and ϕ is an additional dispersion parameter. On the basis of these two moments a quasi-likelihood estimating equation is derived which is solved to get estimates $\hat{\beta}$ of β. It is important to mention, that these estimates do not depend on ϕ. In a second step estimates for ϕ are obtained as moment estimators

$$\hat{\phi} = \frac{1}{n}\sum_i \frac{(y_i - \exp(X_i\hat{\beta}))^2}{\exp(X_i\hat{\beta})}. \tag{3}$$

With $\hat{\phi}$ in hand reliable standard errors of $\hat{\beta}$ can be calculated (see McCullagh and Nelder 1989). Section four now discusses our estimation results.

4. Estimation results

This section interprets the estimation results with respect to the hypotheses formulated in Sect. 2 above. Table 4 presents the estimation results. Column (1) presents the immigrant model which controls for an immigrant indicator, and a third order polynomial of the number of fertile years an immigrant woman spent in Germany. The hypothesis that a fourth order polynomial significantly improves the goodness of fit over a third order specification was rejected at high levels of significance. Column (2) presents the immigrant model with a categorical representation of the fertile years in Germany effect and the last column describes the estimation results controlling for nationality differences. The data for our native and immigrant samples are pooled in the estimations. In preliminary estimations we tested for differences in coefficient effects between the native and immigrant samples. These tests yielded statistically significant differences only for variables describing religious affiliation. Hence these interaction effects are considered in the final specifications.

For every of the final specifications we performed an underdispersion test (Cameron and Trivedi 1990) which always rejected the hypothesis of equidispersion at the 1% significance level. Since the Poisson model is not appropriate for our data we only report the results from the quasi-likelihood estimation. As in the framework of Poisson regressions, the estimated coefficients can be interpreted as semi-elasticities. (In case of dichotomous explanatory variables an estimated coefficient β_0 corresponds to an $(\exp(\beta_0) - 1) * 100$ percent change in the dependent variable.) Thus e.g. a one unit increase in age causes here an insignificant decrease in completed fertility by 0.7%. Given the scaling of the age variable, the one unit change represents a ten year difference in birth cohorts. The effects of a handicap and of pre-fertile years spent in Germany on completed fertility are small and not significantly different from zero.[7]

The coefficients of the six variables describing women's human capital should be interpreted in view of hypothesis H1, which proposed a negative correlation between a woman's (potential) income and her completed fertility.[8] The hypothesis is confirmed by the estimated coefficients: We find a statistically significant decline in completed fertility by 3.8% for every year of schooling. Whereas the indicators of schooling degree are not statistically significant, having a vocational degree is correlated with lower completed fertility. The only surprising finding is that women with only an apprenticeship degree reduced their births by more than those with an advanced degree. Also confirming H1, those immigrant women, who speak German well, have significantly fewer births than those with limited language capability. The six coefficients of the human capital variables are jointly statistically significant in each of the three estimated specifications.

The controls for religious affiliation are statistically highly significant and indicate for the native sample that catholics and protestants have significantly more births than those of other christian or no religious affiliation. Some immigrant effects differ significantly from those for natives such that the net effects of being catholic or protestant on completed fertility among immigrants is negative and that of being of another religion (mostly reflecting the muslim religion) maintains an overall positive effect, even though it is not statistically significant.

The year of immigration variables indicate that completed fertility over

Fertility assimilation of immigrants

Table 4. Estimation results

Variable	Immigrant model (IM)		Nationality model (NM)
	Polynomial (1)	Categorical (2)	Polynomial (3)
Constant	0.887**	0.884**	0.858**
	(4.994)	(4.976)	(4.836)
Age ($*10^{-1}$)	−0.007	−0.007	−0.006
	(−0.495)	(−0.525)	(−0.460)
Pre-fertile-years	−0.005	0.008	0.025
	(−0.062)	(0.092)	(0.271)
Handicap	−0.015	−0.015	−0.017
	(−0.375)	(−0.378)	(−0.438)
Schooling ($*10^{-1}$)	−0.385**	−0.383**	−0.386**
	(−2.453)	(−2.440)	(−2.473)
S_mandatory	0.047	0.051	0.075
	(0.649)	(0.702)	(1.018)
S_advanced	−0.000	0.004	0.030
	(−0.004)	(0.050)	(0.392)
V_apprentice	−0.167**	−0.168**	−0.168**
	(−3.909)	(−3.930)	(−3.960)
V_advanced	−0.067	−0.068	−0.072
	(−1.073)	(−1.092)	(−1.152)
German_spoken	−0.148*	−0.162**	−0.164**
	(−1.953)	(−2.118)	(−2.030)
Catholic	0.284**	0.284**	0.284**
	(3.860)	(3.863)	(3.881)
Protestant	0.287**	0.288**	0.287**
	(3.916)	(3.920)	(3.938)
Other_religions	0.263	0.268	0.266
	(0.555)	(0.566)	(0.566)
Catholic*immi	−0.298**	−0.302**	−0.396**
	(−2.772)	(−2.811)	(−2.897)
Protestant*immi	−1.916**	−1.908**	−1.860**
	(−2.037)	(−2.026)	(−1.983)
Other_religions*immi	0.060	0.050	0.007
	(0.125)	(0.104)	(0.015)
Immigrated before 1971	0.180	0.181	0.193
	(1.356)	(1.343)	(1.283)
Immigrated 1971–79	0.254**	0.262**	0.253*
	(2.078)	(2.104)	(1.778)
Immigrant	0.471**	–	–
	(3.259)		
FYG/10	0.073	–	–
	(0.225)		
$(FYG/10)^2$	−0.296	–	–
	(−0.903)		
$(FYG/10)^3$	0.087	–	–
	(0.937)		
FYG_G0	–	0.510**	–
		(3.484)	
FYG_G1	–	0.383**	–
		(2.289)	
FYG_G2	–	0.480**	–
		(2.712)	
FYG_G3	–	0.279*	–
		(1.672)	

(*continued overleaf*)

Table 4 (continued)

Variable	Immigrant model (IM)		Nationality model (NM)
	Polynomial (1)	Categorical (2)	Polynomial (3)
FYG_G4	–	0.168 (0.992)	–
FYG_G5	–	0.177 (1.036)	–
FYG_G6	–	0.086 (0.449)	–
N_Turkish	–	–	0.182 (0.747)
N_Italian	–	–	0.912** (3.625)
N_Spanish	–	–	0.851** (2.619)
N_Greek	–	–	0.048 (0.113)
N_Yugoslav	–	–	0.760** (4.119)
ϕ	0.874	0.874	0.863
Number of observations	2093	2093	2093

Note: 1. Approximative *t*-statistics in parentheses.
2. The polynomial nationality model additionally controls for nationality-specific third order polynomials, which are not presented to save space.

immigration cohorts takes on an inverted U-shape. Relative to the most recent immigrants, those who entered in the 1970s experienced significantly more births, whereas the earliest immigrants did not show a significant difference in their fertility. The two immigration year indicators are jointly statistically signficant. As expected, the overall immigrant indicator variable is positive, of large magnitude, and significantly different from zero.

We are most interested in the effects of fertile years in Germany on completed fertility. Since the coefficients of the third order polynomial, which are jointly highly significant, are difficult to interpret by inspection, we plotted the curve of this effect in Fig. 4.[9] The solid line represents the fertile years effect, the dashed lines are 90% pointwise confidence bands. For each fertile year the depicted effect represents the difference between foreign and native fertility, e.g. after 15 fertile years in Germany average immigrant fertility is $(\exp(0.3) - 1) * 100 = 35\%$ above the native level. Fig. 4 contains three interpretable pieces of information: First, over the entire range of fertile years that are possibly spent in Germany the immigrant effect is positive. Based on this we cannot reject the assimilation hypothesis (H2) out of hand. Second, the impact of being an immigrant in Germany (conditional on the other covariates) falls almost over the entire range of fertile years. Finally, immigrant status is correlated with a statistically significant positive effect on completed fertility for immigrants who spent at least nine of their fertile years at home and entered Germany after age 24.[10]

A different test of the fertile year effect can be derived from the second specification, which instead of the third order polynomial controls for a set

Fertility assimilation of immigrants

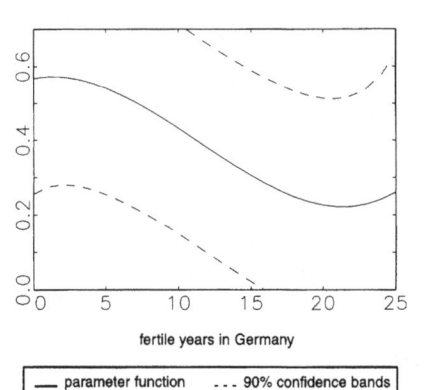

Fig. 4. Impact of being an immigrant as a function of FYG

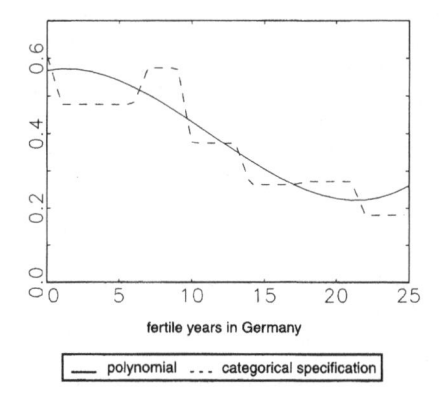

Fig. 5. Impact of being an immigrant according to polynomial and categorical specification as a function of FYG

of categorical variables (column 2 in Table 4). The coefficients of the other explanatory variables are robust to this change in the specification. The seven indicators of fertile years spent in Germany are jointly statistically significant and positive. Fig. 5 plots the estimated effects of fertile years spent in Germany for specifications (1) and (2) of Table 4. While the increase in the step function of categorical effects after the sixth fertile year in Germany is difficult to explain within either of our hypotheses, we find that the increase in completed fertility after year 22 disappears in the results of specification (2).

In order to evaluate hypotheses H2 through H4 posed in Sect. 2 we performed two types of tests. Based on the polynomial specification we tested the hypothesis that a higher number of fertile years spent in Germany yields the same completed fertility compared to zero fertile years spent in Germany. Confirming the depiction in Fig. 4 we were able to reject this hypothesis at the

5% significance level for 13 through 24 fertile years spent in Germany. Based on the categorical specification we tested the hypothesis that the coefficient on a higher number of fertile years spent in Germany yields the same effect as that of zero fertile years spent in Germany. This hypothesis was rejected at the one percent significance level for the indicators reflecting 14 through 25 fertile years spent in Germany.

With respect to our hypotheses formulated above we conclude first that immigrants' completed fertility exceeds that of natives. Second, we find that those who spent more than 13 of their fertile years in Germany, i.e. those who migrate prior to age 28, have significantly fewer births than those coming later in life. So overall H2 cannot be rejected, while the hypothesis of a disruption effect with complete catch-up (H3) is rejected.

Hypothesis H4 proposes a U-shaped pattern in the curve depicted in Figs. 4 through 5. While we cannot reject this hypothesis based on a statistical test, the support for it is limited, and non-existent if we base our judgement on the categorical specification. Even though the analysis does not permit conclusions regarding the existence of disruption effects, it is apparent that cumulative fertility approaches that of the native population "from above", the longer a woman's exposure in Germany during her fertile period. Therefore we conclude with respect to hypothesis H4 above that our evidence favors the assimilation model of fertility adjustment for the sample of immigrants to Germany.

In order to test hypothesis H5, we estimated specification (3) in Table 4, which controlled for nationality-specific third order polynomials of the fertile year effect. While some of the estimated coefficients are sensitive to this change in the specification, the overall conclusions regarding other explanatory variables outlined above do not change. In Table 4 we present the first order nationality effects, which can only be interpreted in conjunction with the other jointly estimated immigrant effects. To simplify the interpretation we plotted the nationality-specific fertile years effect in Figs. 6 through 10. Each of the plots depicts the fertile years effect jointly with the average effects of immigrant status, immigrant religion and immigration year, which has the same interpretation as in Fig. 4 above.

Inspection of these figures yields that the fertility adjustment effect across

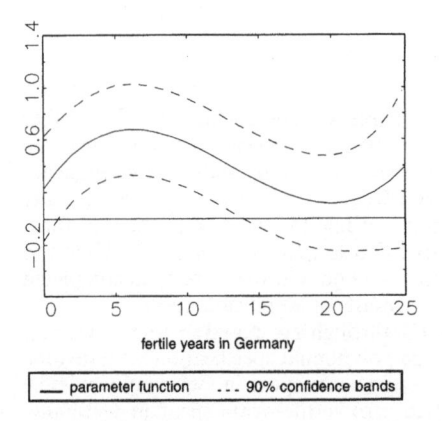

Fig. 6. Impact of being Turkish as a function of FYG according to polynomial specification

Fertility assimilation of immigrants

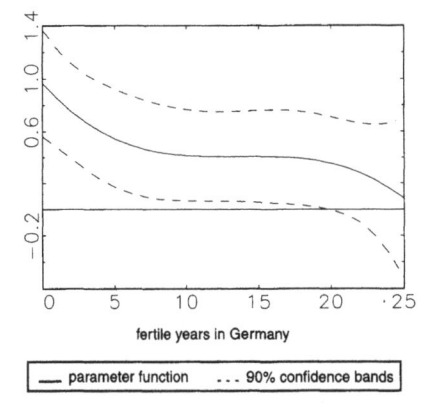

Fig. 7. Impact of being Italian as a function of FYG according to polynomial specification

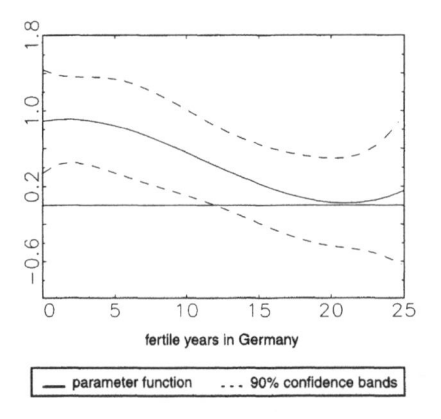

Fig. 8. Impact of being Spanish as a function of FYG according to polynomial specification

fertile years in Germany follows different transition paths for the different origin countries supporting hypothesis five (H5) above. For all but the Greek sample we find significant deviations from native German completed fertility in each of these depictions, even though the exact curves vary across nationalities. The smallest absolute deviation in completed fertility relative to the native sample is found for immigrants of Greek nationality in Fig. 9. The almost flat completed fertility line suggests no assimilation effects for this subsample. The graphs most supportive of assimilation effects are those describing the fertility adjustments of the Italian and Spanish immigrant populations in Figs. 7 and 8. In contrast, immigrants from former Yugoslavia (Fig. 10) almost show a weak U-shaped adjustment and those from Turkey (Fig. 6) do not match any of the posed hypotheses. We do not wish to stress

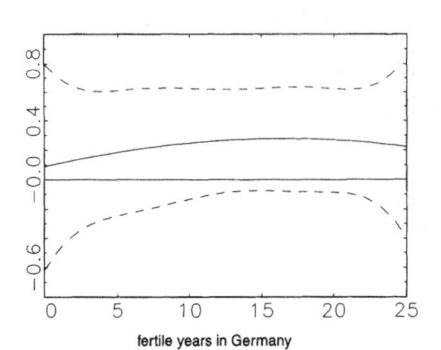

Fig. 9. Impact of being Greek as a function of FYG according to polynomial specification

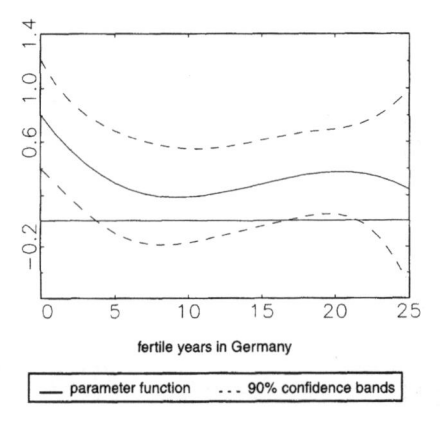

Fig. 10. Impact of being Yugoslavian as a function of FYG according to polynomial specification

these patterns too much, as the parameters are estimated on small samples with e.g. only 24 observations for the case of Spain, or about 60 for Italy and Greece.

In order to determine, whether there are statistically significant country-specific effects we estimated a version of specification (3), where the controls for the interaction effects for Turkish nationals were replaced with overall immigrant effects. (The results are available from authors upon request.) This allows us to test the hypothesis that the effects for single nationalities are identical with the overall immigrant effect. The results yielded significant differences for immigrants from Italy and from former Yugoslavia. Therefore we cannot reject hypothesis H5, which states that there are significant country of origin differences in fertility and fertility assimilation.

5. Conclusions

This study contributes to the literature on fertility adjustment in a number of ways. First, we test the assimilation hypothesis for the case of immigration to Germany. Given that almost the entire literature focuses on the United States and applies the same U.S. population census data, new insights are gained by widening the perspective to the scenario of European immigration. Second, we suggest that a measurement error has pervaded the existing literature. Since the researcher is interested in the effects of living in the destination country on immigrant behavior, years since migration has been utilized as the relevant duration measure. We argue that this is inappropriate for the issue of fertility, where one should be interested in the number of fertile years spent in the destination country. Third, in contrast to former studies, which applied least squares estimators even though the relevant dependent variable is a count, this study applies the appropriate count data estimation technique.

In the United States recent immigrants entered with very low fertility rates but then added to their family sizes at rates beyond those of natives (e.g. Blau 1992, Jasso and Rosenzweig 1990). The increase in immigrant fertility rates over the duration of stay in the host country there is taken as evidence for the disruption and against the assimilation model of fertility adjustment.

Our results suggest that immigrants to Germany enter the country with fertility rates above native levels and that their completed fertility falls the more of their fertile time they spend in Germany. This finding corresponds to the predictions of the assimilation model (H2). We reject the hypothesis that immigrant fertility follows a disruption model with complete catch-up (H3), and have no evidence supporting a disruption effect without complete catch-up (H4). Beyond the fertility adjustment effect, we confirm the prediction of the standard economic model regarding the negative opportunity cost effect of female human capital on total fertility outcomes (H1) and find statistically significant differences in fertility assimilation by country of origin (H5).

We can only speculate as to why prior U.S. studies did not find assimilation effects. If assimilation behavior is in fact driven by economic variables, then the fertility convergence result which we find for Germany, must be explained by the differences in fertility determinants (wages, incomes and cost of contraception) between the countries of origin and destination. These differences must be more pervading for immigrants to Germany, than for immigrants to the United States. In other words, the difference between the Turkish rural standard of living and that in German towns must be more substantial than that between northern Mexico and southern Texas. To the degree that German society is more homogenous than the American society this argument is plausible. Interestingly, the analysis of Dutch immigrants by Schoorl (1990) also yields an assimilation result. A more concrete example of such differences results if we argue that children function as an old-age insurance device. Since guaranteed social security incomes in the United States typically exceed those of immigrants' countries of origin by less than those in Germany, this might explain the different adjustment patterns.

However, the findings may in part be due to the different data and estimation methods. While the U.S. studies use decennially available census evidence we apply a representative micro-level dataset. Our estimation method accounted for the discrete nature of the outcome variable and for its underdispersion. It proofed to be highly appropriate for the research question and we are confident that our results are reliable and provide an interesting addition to the literature on immigrant fertility adjustment.

Endnotes

[1] See e.g. Schmidt 1995, Bauer and Zimmermann 1997, Schoeni 1998, or Chiswick et al. 1997.

[2] See e.g. Baker and Benjamin 1995, Hu 1998, Borjas and Hilton 1996, Riphahn 1998.

[3] The population share of immigrants in Germany grew from 1% in the 1950s to about 10% today; similarly, immigrants made up more than 10% of the 1990 population in countries such as Canada, Australia, or France (Segal 1993).

[4] In the early 1980s age-specific fertility peaked in the agegroup 20–24 in Greece and former Yugoslavia, and in the agegroup 25–29 in Italy and Spain (UN Demographic Yearbook 1991).

[5] The low probability of having exactly the mandatory schooling degree seems surprising and might be due to coding problems with foreign degrees. Since we tested for but did not find statistically significant differences in the effect of these measures on completed fertility for the native and immigrant sample, we are confident that the potential measurement error does not bias our results in important ways.

[6] Whereas the standard assimilation measure 'years since migration' imposes a limitation on cross-section estimation through the linear relationship: immigration year + years since migration = survey year, the relationship in our specification provides more degrees of freedom. In our case the restriction is: immigration year + pre-fertile years in Germany + fertile years spent in Germany + post-fertile years in Germany = year of survey.

[7] Most likely the latter result is due to the small number of women with pre-fertile years in Germany. As an alternative to our assimilation measure we examined whether the sum of pre-fertile and fertile years in the host country yields different results, which was not the case.

[8] While some might argue that the educational attainment of a woman is determined by similar mechanisms as completed fertility and therefore endogenous, we refer to the findings of Heckman et al. (1985) that even concurrent school attendance is not endogenous to observed period-specific fertility. In addition, the completed fertility outcome is observable only after age 40 while typical educational decisions are taken prior to age 20. This limits any potential endogeneity.

[9] The intercept in Fig. 4 is determined by the coefficients of the immigrant indicator, the interacted religion effects and the year of immigration, where the latter variable groups are evaluated at sample means.

[10] The positive slope after the twentysecond fertile year may be due to the parameterization of the fertile year effect. Less than three percent of the immigrant sample have 23 or more fertile years in Germany. Reestimations of the model omitting observations with more than 20 fertile years in Germany yielded the same functional form as obtained with the full sample. This suggests that the positive slope is due to functional form, rather than to higher completed fertility.

References

Baker M, Benjamin D (1995) The Receipt of Transfer Payments by Immigrants to Canada. *Journal of Human Resources* 30(4):650–676

Bauer T, Zimmermann KF (1997) Unemployment and Wages of Ethnic Germans. *Quarterly Review of Economics and Finance* 37(0) special issue: 361–377

Becker GS (1981) *A Treatise on the Family*. Harvard University Press, Cambridge Mass. and London

Ben-Porath Y (1973) Economic Analysis of Fertility in Israel: Point and Counterpoint. *Journal of Political Economy* 81(2):202–233

Blau FD (1992) The Fertility of Immigrant Women: Evidence from High-Fertility Source Countries. In: George JB Freeman RB (eds) *Immigration and the Work Force: Economic Consequences for the United States and Source Areas*. The University of Chicago Press, Chicago and London, pp 93–133

Borjas GJ, Hilton L (1996) Immigration and the Welfare State: Immigrant Participation in Means-Tested Entitlement Programs. *Quarterly Journal of Economics* 111(2):575–604

Cameron AC, Trivedi PK (1990) Regression-Based Tests for Overdispersion in the Poisson Model. *Journal of Econometrics* 46:347–364

Chiswick BR, Cohen Y, Zach T (1997) The Labor Market Status of Immigrants: Effects of the Unemployment Rate at Arrival and Duration of Residence. *Industrial and Labor Relations Review* 50(2):289–303

Conrad C, Lechner M, Werner W (1996) East German Fertility After Unification: Crisis or Adaptation. *Population and Development Review* 22(2):331–358

Consul PC (1989) *Generalized Poisson Distributions: Properties and Applications.* Marcel Dekker, New York

Easterlin RA (1987) Fertility. In: Eatwell J, Milgate M, Newman P (eds) *The New Palgrave. A Dictionary of Economics.* The Macmillan Press Ltd., London, pp 302–308

Ford K (1990) Duration of Residence in the United States and the Fertility of U.S. Immigrants. *International Migration Review* 24 1(89):34–68

Gorwaney N, Van Arsdol MD, Heer DM, Schuerman LA (1990) Variations in Fertility and Earnings Patterns among Immigrants in the United States, 1970–1980: Assimilation or Disruption? *International Migration* 28:451–475

Heckman JJ, Hotz VJ, Walker JR (1985) New Evidence on the Timing and Spacing of Births. *American Economic Review* 75(2):179–184

Hotz VJ, Klerman JA, Willis RJ (1997) The Economics of Fertility in Developed Countries. In: Rosenzweig MR, Stark O (eds) *Handbook of Population and Family Economics.* Vol 1a. Elsevier Publishers, North-Holland, pp 275–347

Hu W (1998) Elderly Immigrants on Welfare. *Journal Human Resources* 33(3):711–741

Jasso G, Rosenzweig MR (1990) The Immigrant's Legacy: Investing in the Next Generation. In: Jasso G, Rosenzweig MR (eds), *The New Chosen People: Immigrants in the United States.* Russell Sage Foundation, New York, pp 382–410

Kahn JR (1988) Immigrant Selectivity and Fertility Adaption in the United States. *Social Forces* 67(1):108–128

Kahn JR (1994) Immigrant and Native Fertility During the 1980s: Adaptation and Expectations for the Future. *International Migration Review* 28(3):501–519

King G (1988) Statistical Models for Political Science Event Counts: Bias in Conventional Procedures and Evidence for the Exponential Poisson Regression Model. *American Journal of Political Science* 32:838–862

Lechner M (1998) Eine Empirische Analyse des Geburtenrückgangs in den Neuen Bundesländern aus der Sicht der Neoklassischen Bevölkerungsökonomie. *Zeitschrift für Wirtschafts- und Sozialwissenschaften* 118(3):463–488

McCullagh P, Nelder JA (1989) *Generalized Linear Models*, 2nd ed. Chapman and Hall, New York

Riphahn RT (1998) Immigrant Participation in the German Welfare Program. *Finanzarchiv* 55(2):163–185

Rosenzweig MR, Schultz TP (1985) The Demand for and Supply of Births: Fertility and its Life Cycle Consequences. *American Economic Review* 75(5):992–105

Schmidt CM (1995) *The Earnings Performance of Migrants in the German Labor Market.* mimeo University of Munich

Schoeni RF (1998) Labor Market Assimilation of Immigrant Women. *Industrial and Labor Relations Review* 51:483–504

Schoorl JJ (1990) Fertility Adaptation of Turkish and Moroccan Women in the Netherlands. *International Migration* 28:477–495

Segal A (1993) *An Atlas of International Migration.* Hans Zell Publishers, London

United Nations (1992) *Demographic Yearbook 1991*, 43rd issue, United Nations Publication, New York

Winkelmann R (1995) Duration Dependence and Dispersion in Count-Data Models. *Journal of Business and Economic Statistics* 13:467–474

Winkelmann R, Zimmermann KF (1994) Count Data Models for Demographic Data. *Mathematical Population Studies* 4:205–221

[22]

New Immigrants' Location Choices: Magnets without Welfare

Neeraj Kaushal, *Columbia University*

The Personal Responsibility and Work Opportunity Reconciliation Act denied legal noncitizens who arrived in the United States after August 1996 access to means-tested federal benefits for the first 5 years. However, using state funds, a number of states restored some of the benefits. I use this state-level policy variation to study whether newly arrived immigrants make location decisions on the basis of benefit eligibility and generosity. I find that safety-net programs have little effect on the location choices of newly arrived low-skilled unmarried immigrant women.

I. Introduction

The Personal Responsibility and Work Opportunity Reconciliation Act (PRWORA) denied legal noncitizens who arrived in the United States after August 1996 access to means-tested federal benefits in the first 5 years of their residency in the country. The legislation was motivated by two main factors: first, there was a growing fear that the U.S. welfare state was attracting low-skilled immigrants who were at risk of becoming a state liability.[1] Second, immigrants' actual dependence on means-tested programs had grown disproportionately large in recent years (Borjas and

---

I thank Josh Angrist, Irwin Garfinkel, Michael Grossman, Ted Joyce, Robert Kaestner, Sanders Korenman, and Cordelia Reimers for their extremely helpful suggestions. Contact the author at nk464@columbia.edu.

[1] Federal law states that availability of public benefits should not serve as an incentive for immigrating to the United States. It maintains that "self-sufficiency" is the basic principle of U.S. immigration law.

[*Journal of Labor Economics*, 2005, vol. 23, no. 1]
© 2005 by The University of Chicago. All rights reserved.
0734-306X/2005/2301-0003$10.00

Hilton 1995). Banning noncitizens from means-tested programs was seen as a way to change these trends and reduce federal expenditure.[2]

The immigrant provisions under PRWORA did not receive full political support from all quarters. Backlash against the original law forced the federal government to restore food stamps and Supplemental Security Income (SSI) to children, elderly, and disabled immigrants. In addition, many states used state funds to restore safety-net programs to poor immigrant families who were denied benefits under federal law: 10 states have created food stamps programs, 15 have substitute Medicaid, 3 have substitute SSI, and 19 have provided funds for the welfare needs of newly arrived immigrants.[3] Of the six traditional immigrant states where three-fourths of all immigrants live, only California provides newly arrived immigrant families access to all four programs.[4] In Illinois and New York, newly arrived immigrants get Medicaid but no other benefits. In Texas, Florida, and New Jersey, newly arrived immigrants get none of these benefits.

One of the objectives of PRWORA was to reduce adverse immigration (inflow of low-skilled immigrants). The objective was based on the belief that immigrants make their location decisions in the United States at least partly on the basis of the generosity of welfare programs. If true, the new law should result in new patterns of immigration, as immigrants would respond by increasingly choosing states where they have access to means-tested programs. The purpose of this article is to test this hypothesis, also known as the "welfare magnet" hypothesis.

To investigate this issue, I study whether access to means-tested programs has affected the location choices of newly arrived legal immigrants. I use data from the Immigration and Naturalization Service (INS) for 1995–96 and 1998–99. The first 2 years measure the location choices of newly arrived immigrants in the period before the policy change. The last 2 years capture the variation in location choices after the new policy was implemented, excluding 1997, the year when most states implemented PRWORA.[5]

---

[2] Denying benefits to legal permanent residents resulted in 44% of the total net savings from PRWORA. That noncitizens lacked the political power to oppose such legislation was an added incentive.

[3] See Zimmerman and Tumlin (1999). Initially, new immigrants were ineligible for Medicaid in New York. A court decision in June 2001, however, declared that policy unconstitutional.

[4] The traditional immigrant states are California, New York, Texas, Florida, Illinois, and New Jersey.

[5] Most states that reinstated benefits did so in a manner that essentially preserved continuity into the PRWORA period. Among those that did not, the most notable is New York, which restored benefits after a 5-year lag in 2001. This may not be of significant concern, as the analysis pertains to 1995–96 and 1998–99.

II. Previous Research

Previous research on the impact of welfare programs on the location choices of immigrants is inconclusive. While Bartel (1989), Buckley (1996), Borjas (1999), and Dodson (2001) find that immigrants are attracted to states with generous welfare policies, Zavodny (1997, 1998) does not find any evidence to this effect. These articles encounter a number of empirical, theoretical, and data-related problems, which my article attempts to address.

Most previous work relies solely on time-series or cross-state variation in welfare benefits to identify the effect of welfare policy on location choice (Bartel 1989; Buckley 1996; Borjas 1999; Dodson 2001). Therefore, macroeconomic variables or differences in state characteristics may be confounded with benefit generosity. An innovation in my article is the use of PRWORA and state responses to set up a natural experiment research design that controls for state and year effects. States that reinstated benefits for immigrants are used as control for states that allowed the PRWORA restrictions to come into force.

I argue that the heterogeneous reactions by state governments toward immigrant provisions in PRWORA could not have been easily predicted. For instance, in 1994, California passed Proposition 187, which banned all social services to illegal immigrants. But California also used state-level funds to provide Medicaid, SSI, cash welfare, and food stamps to post-1996 immigrants, which was unexpected in the light of the state policy changes prior to PRWORA. All of the other five major immigrant states—where close to 45% of immigrants live—decided to deny cash benefits, SSI, and food stamps to post-1996 immigrants, and four of them denied Medicaid to new immigrants.[6] These decisions suggest that immigrant behavior or political power did not influence policy changes, at least in these five states. Besides, although debate over the federal legislation was under way during 1996, state responses to the federal law were relatively sudden and became known only during 1996–97. I use these arguably more exogenous changes in state policies to test the welfare magnet hypothesis. Moreover, the change in policy that I examine represents a more significant variation than that found in previous studies that rely on differences in AFDC (Aid to Families with Dependent Children) cash benefits.

Previous research on the welfare magnet hypothesis also relies on less

---

[6] The following states have substitute TANF programs for newly arrived immigrants during the 5-year federal ban: CA, MA, MD, WA, PA, OR, CT, GA, MN, HI, WI, MO, UT, RI, TN, NE, ME, VT, and WY. New immigrants are eligible for Medicaid in CA, IL, MA, MD, VA, WA, PA, CT, MN, HI, RI, NE, DE, and ME. Since 2001, new immigrants are eligible for Medicaid in New York. The states where new immigrants get food stamps are CA, MA, MD, WA, CO, CT, MN, WI, NE, and ME ; the states where they get SSI are CA, OR, and ME.

than ideal data. Studies by Bartel (1989) and Borjas (1999) do not distinguish legal from illegal immigrants. Welfare law does. All legal immigrants were allowed to receive welfare benefits under AFDC, but illegal immigrants were not. Temporary Aid for Needy Families (TANF) also makes a clear distinction between the two groups. Studies that use census data suffer from the problem of measuring their target groups imprecisely. In their elegant critique of studies of recent immigrants that use census or Current Population Survey (CPS) data, Jasso, Rosenzweig, and Smith (2000, 189) argue, "the samples (Census or CPS data) on which conclusions are drawn may be neither recent nor immigrant."

I avoid this problem by using INS data on newly arrived immigrants, which provide information on all foreigners granted permanent legal status in a certain year.[7] The data set also provides information on the immigrant's year and category of arrival in the United States, which is used to restrict the study to new nonrefugee entrants who are granted permanent residence status in the year of their entry. While it is interesting to study whether immigrants already living in the United States relocate in response to accessibility to means-tested programs, the location choices of new immigrants address a specific policy issue, which is whether denying access to means-tested programs would discourage future immigration of low-skilled people. Since this was a concern that led to the passage of PRWORA, I restrict my analysis to newly arrived immigrants.

Most of the earlier studies on immigrants' location choices have confronted a number of other data problems. One of them concerns how to control for destination characteristics that may be correlated with both welfare policy and immigration pattern. Earlier studies controlled for destination characteristics using a variety of measures, such as state population, mean wage, share of people from the immigrant's country of birth, unemployment rate, taxes, share of manufacturing, and agriculture employment (Jaeger 2000; Dodson 2001). However, several unobserved destination features remain unmeasured. Like Zavodny (1997, 1998), I introduce state fixed effects to control for unobserved time-invariant destination characteristics.

A second issue concerns the cost of immigration. A number of studies use the distance between the capital of the immigrant's country of birth and the population-weighted center of the metropolitan area in the United States where they finally decide to live as a proxy for the cost of immigration (Bartel 1989; Jaeger 2000). However, several country-of-origin- and state-of-destination-specific characteristics may determine the costs and benefits of immigration. In this article, I control for

---

[7] Although not as widely used as the CPS, the INS data set has been used in a number of other studies, such as Buckley (1996), Zavodny (1997, 1998), Jaeger (2000), and Dodson (2001).

these factors by dividing new immigrants into nine categories based on their countries/regions of birth. Separate analysis for each country/region with state fixed effects controls for any country-of-origin- and state-of-destination-specific factors, including costs that may influence the location choices of immigrants.

III. Theoretical Issues

Generally, immigrants leave their country of birth in search of a new abode where they have better work opportunities, higher living standards, and greater political freedom. They search for ethnic enclaves in their acquired homeland to maximize the opportunities and to minimize the psychological and economic costs of relocation.

Mincer (1978) argues that family ties have an important bearing on people's migration decisions. In the case of natives, he argues, family ties deter migration. For new immigrants, family ties in the destination ease the process of relocation by providing access to, or information about, the labor market. In these ethnic enclaves, new immigrants also find cultural and linguistic affinities, which ease the process of relocation but may slow assimilation. Thus, immigrant concentration in a state is an important determinant of the location choices of new immigrants.

Another factor that may explain the location pattern of immigrants is immigration law, which gives overwhelming preference to family-based immigration. The INS gives permanent residence status to foreigners under two categories: numerically unlimited visas for immediate relatives of U.S. citizens (e.g., spouses, minor children, and parents), refugees and asylees, and numerically limited visas. There are three subcategories under the numerically limited group: family sponsored, employment based, and diversity programs. During the 1990s, around 60% of the legal immigrants to the United States fell under the immediate relative of U.S. citizen or family preference category (INS).[8] It can be argued that those immigrants who primarily come to the United States to unite with their family members would live in the same cities as the latter, which may explain some of the clustering.

Finally, new immigrants' access to safety-net programs such as TANF, Medicaid, and food stamps may be a factor in determining their residential choices. Access to safety-net programs provides insurance against poor labor market outcomes.[9] Borjas (1999) has argued that new immigrants

---

[8] The proportion was much higher during the 1980s. The Immigration Act of 1990 more than doubled the quota for employer-sponsored immigrants and reduced the maximum number of visas available to low-skilled immigrants and their families under the employer-sponsored category.

[9] An extreme interpretation of the welfare magnet hypothesis is that if immigrants are denied access to social welfare programs, they would either go back to their countries of birth or stop coming to the United States.

are more likely to make location choices on the basis of these factors than immigrants already living in the United States or natives. New immigrants factor in travel and relocation expenses when they decide to come to the United States. Having incurred these expenses, it is in their best interest to live in states where new immigrants are eligible for means-tested programs. In contrast, resident immigrants have to incur additional relocation and travel expenses if they want to migrate to states that offer generous benefits.

There are, however, a number of factors that may make newly arrived immigrants less responsive to welfare generosity as compared to natives or immigrants already living in the United States. One, newly arrived immigrants may attach greater significance to family or community ties, as these ties ease the relocation process. Generosity of welfare benefits may not be as important to new immigrants in their initial years in the United States. Two, newly arrived immigrants may not have as much knowledge of state-level welfare policies as natives or immigrants already living in the United States and therefore may not be able exploit these policies as effectively.

IV. Econometric Model

The baseline regression model is

$$p_{st} = \alpha + \beta \text{Policy}_{st} + \gamma_t + \delta_s + \varepsilon_{st}, \tag{1}$$

where p_{st} is the proportion of newly arrived immigrants in year t who locate in state s. The variable Policy_{st} is an indicator for whether new immigrants are eligible for means-tested programs (such as TANF, Medicaid, food stamps) in state s in year t. This variable is equal to one for all states prior to federal welfare reform. In the post-PRWORA period, it is equal to one for states that have means-tested programs for newly arrived immigrants and zero for those that do not. The parameters γ_t and δ_s are year and state effects.[10]

The welfare magnet hypothesis is true if β is positive and significantly different from zero. A positive coefficient would indicate that in the post-PRWORA period a relatively larger proportion of new entrants live in states that continue to give newly arrived immigrants access to means-tested

---

[10] I also did the analysis by controlling for a vector of time-varying state-level characteristics, such as real wage of women, unemployment rates with 1- and 2-years' lag, state's share of population, and proportion of recent immigrants living in a state. In this analysis, all time-varying state characteristics were lagged by a year. Introduction of time-varying state controls did not have any effect on the coefficient for policy. This is expected, as most of the controls do not vary by much during the period of investigation. Arguably, many of the controls are endogenous, therefore, the reported results are from an analysis that controls for only state and year effects.

programs as compared to the proportion that did in the pre-PRWORA period.

To estimate the model, I drop one state. Since p_{st} sums to one within a year, one state is redundant. The left-hand-side expression in equation (1) is a multinomial probability. The standard errors should account for multinomial correlation and heteroscedasticity. Year effects partly control for the mechanical empirical correlation between multinomial probabilities. Further, heteroscedasticity-adjusted robust standard errors are reported.

The models described above focus on all new immigrants who arrived in the United States in a certain year. However, low-skilled and poor immigrants, who are at high risk of receiving means-tested benefits, may have a greater incentive to live in states where immigrants are eligible for benefits. Similarly, new entrants who received permanent residence status through their employer may be more constrained in making location choices as compared to other immigrants. For this reason, the estimated value of β may be biased toward zero. Therefore, I estimate equation (1) for various groups of immigrants according to their economic vulnerability and risk of becoming dependent on means-tested programs.

According to the March Current Population Survey, in 1993, 20% of unmarried noncitizen women ages 18–44 years, with 12 or fewer years of education, received TANF. In contrast, only 6.1% of married noncitizen women in the above age group with 12 or fewer years of education received TANF. Welfare use by women with at least some college in the above age group was even lower: 5.9% of unmarried and 1.8% of married noncitizens received cash welfare. The relative risk of Medicaid and food stamps use among various noncitizen groups was quite similar, indicating that low-educated unmarried immigrant women are economically the most vulnerable group and face the highest risk of becoming dependent on means-tested programs, followed by married low-educated and unmarried high-educated immigrant women.[11] Married high-educated immigrant women appear to be at the lowest risk of receiving means-tested benefits. If the welfare magnet hypothesis is correct, I expect to find larger

---

[11] In 1993, among unmarried low-educated noncitizen women, 31.5% had Medicaid coverage, and 33% used food stamps. In contrast, among married low-educated noncitizen women, 17% received Medicaid, and 19% received food stamps; among unmarried noncitizen women with at least some college education, 11% received Medicaid and 13% received food stamps; and among married noncitizen women with at least some college education, 6.3% received Medicaid, and 4.9% received food stamps. The combined CPS data for 1994–2001 also indicates that 25% of the recently arrived noncitizen unmarried women with 12 or fewer years of education had at least one child, as compared to only 11% of unmarried women with at least some college, indicating that a relatively large proportion of recently arrived low-educated unmarried women have dependents.

effects of PRWORA on groups most likely to make use of the benefits associated with such policy.

The INS data do not include information on education. Therefore, I use occupational category as a proxy to define low- and high-skilled women. Specifically, I study the location choices of four groups of newly arrived immigrant women: low-skilled unmarried, low-skilled married, high-skilled unmarried, and high-skilled married.

The location choices of immigrants differ depending on their country of origin, and pooling them may bias the coefficient of interest if there are interactions between country of origin, policy, and other variables. I approach this problem in two ways. First, I run specifications that include country fixed effects and country-state interactions. Second, I allow for country characteristics to affect locational choice in a more unconstrained way by estimating equation (1) by country (or region) of origin. As a check on the inference issue, I also apply a multinomial conditional logit model using individual data, which is described below.

Let P_{ist} be the probability that immigrant i who arrived in the United States in year t will reside in state s. Each immigrant has the option to live in one of the 50 states or the District of Columbia. The probability of choosing a state is

$$P_{ist} = \frac{e^{Z_{st}\delta + e_{ist}}}{\sum_{s=1}^{51} e^{Z_{st}\delta + e_{ist}}}, \qquad (2)$$

with the condition that $\Sigma P_{ist} = 1$ (assuming $e_{ist} \sim$ independently and identically distributed, with Weibull distribution).

In equation (2), Z_{st} is a vector of state welfare policy, state, and year effects (as in eq. [1]). I estimate the conditional logit model using the maximum likelihood procedure in STATA.

In a conditional multinomial logit model, the year of arrival is not a characteristic of choice but a characteristic of the individual. The only way to introduce time effects in this model, therefore, is to interact year dummies with the choices. This means the year effects would have to be interacted with the state dummies, and that would eliminate all the variation in policy.

I introduce time effects in the above model by constraining the year effects to be the same for all choices except for a reference state. In any year, the year dummy is equal to one if an individual goes to one of the 50 states other than the reference state and equals zero if he or she goes to the reference state. So year effects capture trends in the proportion of immigrants who choose to locate in states other than the reference state.[12]

---

[12] For the sake of consistency, the state where most new immigrants from a country/region reside is chosen as the reference state.

If Policy$_{st}$ is a continuous variable, its marginal effect on the probability of residing in a state can be obtained by differentiating P_{st} with respect to Policy$_{st}$ (Greene 1993).

$$\frac{\partial P_{st}}{\partial \text{Policy}_{st}} = \hat{P}_{st}(1 - \hat{P}_{st})\beta, \qquad (3)$$

where $\hat{P}_{st}$ is the predicted probability. Equation (3) implies that there would be as many marginal effects as the number of choices. The primary objective of this analysis is to compare the marginal effects and their standard errors with the corresponding estimates obtained in the ordinary least squares (OLS) analysis. To accomplish that, I compute the marginal effect around the mean probability of choosing a state. In the empirical analysis, I estimate equation (2) using disaggregated country-by-country data.[13]

V. Data

I use INS data on immigrants who arrived in the United States during 1995–96 and 1998–99.[14] The first 2 years capture the location choices of newly arrived immigrants in the period before the policy change. The last 2 years are chosen to capture the variation in location choices after the new policy is implemented, excluding 1997, the year when most states implemented PRWORA.

The INS data set has certain advantages. It contains information on legal immigrants only, which is crucial for this study because illegal immigrants are ineligible to participate in the means-tested programs discussed here. The INS also provides information on all legal immigrants who arrived in the United States in a particular year and not just a sample, such as in the CPS. The INS data also give information on whether an immigrant is a new arrival or has adjusted her visa status from a temporary or illegal resident to a permanent legal resident. The focus of this analysis is new arrivals. Therefore, I confine the analysis to immigrants who received a green card and arrived in the United States in the same year.[15]

---

[13] Computational difficulties involving large size samples make it difficult to do the multinomial analysis on all immigrants stacked across countries. The conditional multinomial logit model involves providing 51 choices to each individual—so each individual appears in the data 51 times. For some samples in the stacked-across-country analysis, this raises the number of observations to 7.6 million.

[14] The data for 1999 are from January to September, which is the latest period for which detailed data used in this analysis are available.

[15] The INS collects individual records at the time of approval for legal permanent residence. It is possible that in some cases, the approval year may differ from the arrival year in the United States. However, such cases get excluded from this study.

The INS data include a number of personal characteristics of immigrants, such as age, sex, and marital status, which are used as control variables and to stratify the samples. As almost 80% of adult TANF beneficiaries are aged 18–45, I restrict the analysis to immigrants in this age group.

The INS data also have a few limitations. For instance, the INS only gives the state of intended residence of new immigrants, which in some cases may differ from their actual residence. However, there is no reason to believe that reporting errors are correlated with welfare reform.[16] In addition, the INS data set does not contain information on the education level of immigrants, but it specifies the present occupation of immigrants granted visas under the employment preference category; for others, it gives the occupation category in the country of last residence. I use occupation category to identify those whose location choices are likely to be affected by social policy and those whose choices are likely to remain unaffected.

Women in the following occupations are classified as "low skilled": homemakers, laborers, service, and unemployed. Women in professional groups such as doctors, nurses, executives, engineers, teachers, or artists are classified as "high skilled." In approximately 6.5% of the cases, the occupation of newly arrived immigrants is not mentioned. These cases are excluded from the analysis that uses information on occupation.[17] During the period of this study, about 4% of the newly arrived immigrant women in age group 18–45 years received green cards through employer sponsorship.[18] Given the relative inflexibility of their residential choice, these women are likely to be less responsive to welfare policies and are excluded from the analysis that stratifies data by occupation. Net of the exclusion, approximately 30% of the sample consists of high-skilled women, and the remaining 70% are low-skilled women.

---

[16] I compared the location pattern of newly arrived immigrants as reflected in the INS data for 1995–96 with the location pattern of foreign-born individuals from the March CPS for 1995–2001. The intended location choices of new entrants appear to resemble the location pattern of previously arrived immigrants by country/region of origin. The CPS data reflect a higher degree of dispersion, which is expected, as the CPS data relate to all foreign-born people, while the INS data are about newly arrived permanent legal residents. The CPS comparison cannot be refined to recently arrived foreign-born individuals, as the CPS sample for newly arrived persons is very small and therefore unreliable.

[17] I had also repeated the analysis by including women whose occupation is unknown in the low-skilled category. The results were unaffected by their inclusion.

[18] Most employers first hire immigrants on temporary work permits and then sponsor them for green cards. Since this study excludes people who adjusted their visa from temporary or illegal to legal permanent resident, only a small proportion of women who entered on employer-sponsored visas are left in the sample.

Distance affects immigration flows through diminished information and increased travel and psychic costs (Schwartz 1973). Further, country/region characteristics may affect location choice for other reasons, such as cultural affinities and social, political, and physical environment. To control for these factors, I stratify the sample according to immigrants' country/region of birth into nine groups consisting of four countries (Mexico, the Philippines, China, and Vietnam) and five regions: Central America; three countries in South Asia—Bangladesh, India, and Pakistan (henceforth referred to as South Asia); four countries in East Europe—Russia, Ukraine, Romania, and Poland (henceforth referred to as Eastern Europe); three countries in South America—Ecuador, Colombia, and Peru (henceforth referred to as South America), and the Caribbean (excluding Haiti and Cuba). Immigrants from Haiti and Cuba are excluded, as they are treated as refugees (Dodson 2001). These nine countries/ regions represent over 65% of all immigrants in the above age group who arrived in the United States during 1995–96, the base years of the study.

I study the impact of state policies with regard to recent immigrants' eligibility for three means-tested programs: Medicaid, TANF, and food stamps. I compute three types of policy variables: whether a state offers TANF benefits to new immigrants, whether it offers any of the above three programs to new immigrants, and the generosity of benefits under these programs. Information reported in Zimmerman and Tumlin (1999) is used to construct the first two policy variables.

The generosity of welfare benefits differs across states. For instance, in 1996, in Alaska, the maximum cash benefit for a family of three was $923 per month, seven-and-a-half times the cash benefit awarded by the least generous state, Mississippi ($120 a month). The location choices of immigrants are likely to be affected by both accessibility and generosity of means-tested programs. A complete specification of the cost-benefit analysis would require constructing a variable based on both generosity and eligibility. Therefore, I also construct the three policy variables according to the benefit level. The maximum TANF/AFDC benefit for a family of three and the maximum food stamps voucher for a family of three are taken from the Background Material on the Committee on Ways and Means, U.S. House of Representatives (http://www.aspe.hhs.gov/2000gb/). Average Medicaid expenditure per recipient is computed from the Health Care Financing Review/2000 Statistical Supplement. All three amounts are added and deflated by the national consumer price index.

VI. Results

Descriptive Analysis

Table 1 presents the location choices of newly arrived legal immigrants during 1995–96, the base years of the study. It confirms the clustering of

Table 1
Location Choices of Newly Arrived Legal Immigrants, by Country of Birth (INS Data on Legal Immigrants Who Arrived in the United States during 1995–96 in Age Group 18–45 Years)

Mexico		Central America		Caribbean		Peru, Colombia, and Ecuador		China		Philippines		Bangladesh, India, and Pakistan		Vietnam		Poland, Romania, Russia, and Ukraine	
State	%	State	%	State	%	State	%	State	%	State	%	State	%	State	%	State	%
CA	41.38	CA	35.25	NY	60.72	NY	37.59	NY	37.54	CA	49.63	NY	26.03	CA	39.52	IL	26.82
TX	31.95	NY	14.36	FL	11.5	NJ	19.41	CA	32.15	HI	11.63	CA	15.76	TX	11.55	NY	23.31
IL	6.21	FL	10.03	NJ	11.26	FL	14.67	MA	3.55	IL	4.36	NJ	10.55	VA	3.81	NJ	9.48
AZ	4.41	TX	8.71	MA	4.45	CA	7.89	NJ	2.68	NY	4.01	IL	8.73	WA	3.47	CA	8.01
NM	2.54	NJ	4.7	CT	2.24	CT	2.56	IL	2.61	NJ	3.78	TX	7.35	FL	3.29	MI	3.9
CO	1.37	VA	3.74	MD	1.69	IL	2.48	MD	1.82	WA	3.77	VA	3.17	PA	2.88	CT	3.26
% in top six states	87.86		76.79		91.86		84.6		80.35		77.18		71.59		64.52		74.78
N	35,761		15,207		35,791		15,258		17,615		30,425		39,351		10,423		17,200

immigrants in a few states. Depending on their country/region of birth, 64%–92% of the newly arrived immigrants located in just six states during 1995–96. The degree of geographic concentration and favorite destinations differed across groups. For instance, 61% of the newly arrived immigrants from the Caribbean located in New York; 50% of Filipinos and 41% of Mexicans in California. Newly arrived immigrants from the South Asian and East European countries studied here were more evenly dispersed.

Geographic proximity to the country/region of birth also seems to have an important bearing on where new immigrants locate. The top six states in which newly arrived immigrants from the Caribbean chose to live during 1995–96 were all on the east coast, while none of the six top destinations for newly arrived immigrants from Mexico was on the east coast. Immigrants from China, the Philippines, East Europe, South America, and South Asia had their favorite destinations both on the east and the west coasts of the country.

Table 1 corroborates that new immigrants have a few favorite destinations in the United States. The question is, are immigrants locating in these states at least partly because of generous means-tested programs? To answer this question, I turn to table 2, which presents the proportion of newly arrived immigrants who chose to locate in states where they had access to at least one of the three means-tested programs (TANF, Medicaid, and food stamps) in the post-PRWORA period.

The figures in table 2 show that for every demographic group, there is an increase in the proportion of newly arrived immigrants who located in states that offered access to at least one of the three means-tested programs. The increase is about 2.7 percentage points for unmarried low-skilled women, the demographic group most at risk of being on welfare, and 2.6 percentage points for married high-skilled women, a group least likely to be on welfare. The changes in location choices are not uniform across immigrants from different countries/regions of birth (cols. 9 and 10). The proportion increased by more than 1 percentage point for four groups, fell by more than 2 percentage points for one, and remained almost unchanged for the remaining four groups (with the percentage point change being less than ±0.6).

This change in the location choices of newly arrived immigrants could be due to welfare reform or due to changes in certain other state characteristics. If it is due to welfare reform, more vulnerable groups who are at high risk of being on welfare, such as low-skilled unmarried women, should be more responsive to the change than high-skilled women. Columns 1–8 of table 2, however, provide mixed evidence in this regard. For instance, while low-skilled Mexican women were around 5–6 percentage points more likely to live in generous welfare states after welfare reform, high-skilled, unmarried Mexican women were 16 percentage points more likely to live in these states in the postreform period, and high-skilled

Table 2
Proportion of Newly Arrived Immigrant Women Living in Generous States (INS Data on Newly Arrived Legal Immigrants in Age Group 18–45 Years, in Percents)

Sample	Unmarried Low-Skilled Women 1995–96	Unmarried Low-Skilled Women 1998–99	Married Low-Skilled Women 1995–96	Married Low-Skilled Women 1998–99	Unmarried High-Skilled Women 1995–96	Unmarried High-Skilled Women 1998–99	Married High-Skilled Women 1995–96	Married High-Skilled Women 1998–99	All Women 1995–96	All Women 1998–99
Mexico	58.10	63.72	53.98	60.43	61.30	77.41	62.58	75.74	55.88	62.64
Central America	57.24	58.88	46.59	48.05	58.85	54.59	43.18	44.70	49.44	50.61
Caribbean	14.77	15.29	11.10	15.75	13.86	15.06	12.42	16.39	12.72	15.60
Peru, Colombia, and Ecuador	21.16	23.70	19.73	26.30	21.99	26.50	26.80	31.39	21.54	26.87
China	50.15	48.81	55.15	53.23	57.95	56.73	61.61	58.76	57.71	55.62
Philippines	81.01	82.92	68.43	68.33	78.65	78.23	70.81	74.50	72.79	72.82
Bangladesh, India, and Pakistan	53.96	52.71	42.57	42.32	48.97	46.67	45.03	46.36	43.51	43.36
Vietnam	71.94	73.85	72.28	72.19	67.54	70.12	70.96	71.38	71.18	71.77
Poland, Romania, Russia, and Ukraine	51.49	52.15	51.95	50.93	50.61	50.87	50.93	51.71	51.16	51.45
Total from all countries	45.61	48.32	46.79	51.85	47.90	48.16	51.28	53.85	47.88	51.74

NOTE.—INS = Immigration and Naturalization Service. Generous states are states that provide post-1996 immigrants access to at least one of the following three programs: Temporary Assistance for Needy Families (TANF), Medicaid, and food stamps. The last row, total from all countries, is for immigrants from all countries and not just the nine countries/regions mentioned above. All samples exclude women who received permanent resident visas under an employment category or as refugees.

Table 3
OLS Estimates of the Effect of Access to Means-Tested Programs on the Location Choices of Newly Arrived Immigrant Women

Sample	Low-Skilled Unmarried Women	Low-Skilled Married Women	High-Skilled Unmarried Women	High-Skilled Married Women
TANF	.001 (.001)	.002 (.002)	.001 (.001)	.001 (.001)
Access to at least one welfare program	.002 (.002)	.003 (.002)	.001 (.001)	.002 (.001)
No. of observations in each regression	200	200	200	200
No. of women in the sample	31,959	149,786	26,295	74,411

NOTE.—OLS = ordinary least squares; TANF = Temporary Assistance for Needy Families. Each cell is from a separate regression. Column headings describe the sample. The dependent variable is the proportion of the sample in year t that chose to reside in state s. Each regression controls for state and time fixed effects. Heteroscedasticity-adjusted standard errors are in parentheses.

married Mexican women were 13 percentage points more likely to live in these states. This also suggests that factors other than PRWORA may be responsible for the changing location patterns of immigrants after welfare reform. Note that in a large number of cases, the variations in location choices were marginal between the two periods.

Multivariate Analysis

Table 3 presents the results of the analysis using ordinary least squares. Each cell in this table is from a different regression. Each regression controls for state and year fixed effects. The top row of this table shows that TANF eligibility raised the probability of residing in a state by a statistically insignificant 0.1–0.2 percentage points for various groups of women. Row 2 presents the effect of eligibility for at least one of the three means-tested programs—TANF, Medicaid, and food stamps, and shows that eligibility increases the probability of going to a state by a statistically insignificant 0.1–0.3 percentage points.

Table 3 suggests that access to PRWORA has had a modest effect on immigrants' locational choices. Further, more vulnerable groups are not more sensitive to TANF accessibility than less vulnerable groups. These regressions do not allow for heterogeneity among immigrants from different countries/regions of birth and therefore may be biased. To remove this bias, I first repeat the analysis by introducing country fixed effects and then do the analysis for each country/region separately. This analysis is restricted to immigrants from the nine country/regions that accounted for 65% of the immigrants who arrived in 1995–96. Table 4 presents the results of the first analysis. It has the same layout as table 3. Each re-

Table 4
OLS Estimates of the Effect of Access to Means-Tested Programs on the Location Choices of Newly Arrived Immigrant Women ($N = 1,800$)

Sample	Low-Skilled Unmarried Women	Low-Skilled Married Women	High-Skilled Unmarried Women	High-Skilled Married Women
Panel 1:				
TANF	.001	.001	.002	.002
	(.003)	(.003)	(.003)	(.002)
Access to at least one program	.001	.002	.001	.002
	(.003)	(.003)	(.003)	(.003)
Panel 2:				
TANF	.001*	.001**	.002**	.002**
	(.001)	(.000)	(.001)	(.001)
Access to at least one program	.001	.002**	.001	.001**
	(.001)	(.001)	(.001)	(.000)

NOTE.—OLS = ordinary least squares; TANF = Temporary Assistance for Needy Families. Each cell is from a separate regression. Column headings describe the sample. The dependent variable is the proportion of the sample in year t that chose to reside in state s. Each regression controls for state, year, and country fixed effects. Estimates in panel 2 also control for country-specific state fixed effects. Heteroscedasticity-adjusted standard errors are in parentheses.
* $p \leq .05$.
** $p \leq .01$.

gression in panel 1 controls for state, year, and country fixed effects. Regressions in panel 2 also have country-state interactions.

The estimated results in row 1, panel 1 of table 4 suggest that TANF eligibility raises the probability of locating in a state by 0.1 to 0.2 percentage points. None of the coefficients is statistically significant. Estimates in row 2 echo the results presented in row 1, that is, accessibility to means-tested programs has a modest and statistically insignificant effect on the location choices of women, irrespective of their marital status and skills. Panel 2 shows that TANF or accessibility to any of the three programs raised the probability of residing in a state by 0.1 to 0.2 percentage points. The results are often statistically significant.

Tables 5 and 6 show the results for the analysis of country/region-specific samples. The presentation is the same as in tables 3 and 4.

Table 5 shows the effect of TANF eligibility on locational choices. It suggests that TANF accessibility has a statistically insignificant effect on the location choices of unskilled unmarried women from all countries/regions except for those from the Philippines. Accessibility to TANF raised the probability that Filipino low-skilled unmarried women would locate in a state by 0.5 percentage points. It also raised the probability that low-skilled married women from Central and South America would locate in a state by 0.3 percentage points. High-skilled women from certain countries/regions, for example, Mexico, Eastern Europe, South America,

Table 5
OLS Estimates of the Effect of TANF on the Location Choices of Newly Arrived Immigrant Women, by Country of Birth

Sample	Low-Skilled Unmarried Women	Low-Skilled Married Women	High-Skilled Unmarried Women	High-Skilled Married Women
Mexico	.002 (.001)	.002 (.002)	.006* (.003)	.005* (.002)
Central America	.002 (.002)	.003* (.001)	−.000 (.002)	.004 (.002)
Caribbean	.001 (.001)	.003 (.002)	.001 (.001)	.003 (.002)
Peru, Colombia, and Ecuador	−.000 (.001)	.003* (.002)	.004* (.002)	.003 (.002)
China	−.001 (.002)	−.001 (.001)	−.001 (.002)	−.001 (.001)
Philippines	.005* (.002)	−.002 (.001)	.001 (.002)	−.000 (.001)
Bangladesh, India, and Pakistan	−.001 (.002)	.000 (.001)	.005 (.003)	.000 (.001)
Vietnam	.000 (.003)	.002 (.001)	.001 (.002)	.003* (.001)
Poland, Romania, Russia, and Ukraine	.006 (.003)	.002 (.002)	.006* (.002)	.003* (.001)

NOTE.—OLS = ordinary least squares; TANF = Temporary Assistance for Needy Families. Each cell is from a separate regression. Column headings describe the sample. The dependent variable is the proportion of the sample in year t that chose to reside in state s. Each regression controls for state and year fixed effects. Heteroscedasticity-adjusted standard errors are in parentheses.
* $p \leq .05$.

and Vietnam, were also more likely to choose states with TANF accessibility. The effect is statistically insignificant in all other cases.

The analysis in table 5 was limited to TANF eligibility. I also want to study whether accessibility to any of the other programs affected the location choices of newly arrived immigrants. To do so, I investigate the effect of eligibility to any of the three means-tested programs on location choices. Table 6 has the results of this analysis.

Table 6 suggests that eligibility to means-tested benefits has a small and statistically insignificant effect on the location choices of low-educated unmarried women from all regions except Mexico and the Philippines. These women were 0.3–0.5 percentage points more likely to locate in states with a substitute TANF program. High-skilled Mexican women, however, were even more likely to locate in states where they were eligible for at least one of the means-tested programs. Estimated results also indicate that married low-skilled women from Mexico, South America, Central America, and Vietnam were more likely to live in states with at least a substitute program. Finally, high-skilled married women from Central

Table 6
OLS Estimates of the Effect of Access to Any Means-Tested Program on the Location Choices of Newly Arrived Immigrant Women, by Country of Birth

Sample	Low-Skilled Unmarried Women	Low-Skilled Married Women	High-Skilled Unmarried Women	High-Skilled Married Women
Mexico	.003*	.004*	.007*	.005*
	(.002)	(.002)	(.003)	(.003)
Central America	.002	.004*	−.001	.004*
	(.002)	(.001)	(.002)	(.002)
Caribbean	.001	.003	.001	.003
	(.001)	(.002)	(.001)	(.002)
Peru, Colombia, and Ecuador	.001	.005**	.003	.004
	(.001)	(.002)	(.002)	(.002)
China	.000	−.001	−.001	−.001
	(.002)	(.001)	(.002)	(.001)
Philippines	.005*	−.001	.000	.001
	(.002)	(.001)	(.002)	(.001)
Bangladesh, India, and Pakistan	.000	.001	−.001	.001
	(.002)	(.001)	(.004)	(.001)
Vietnam	−.001	.002*	.002	.003**
	(.003)	(.001)	(.002)	(.001)
Poland, Romania, Russia, and Ukraine	−.000	−.001	−.001	−.000
	(.003)	(.002)	(.003)	(.002)

Note.—OLS = ordinary least squares. Each cell is from a separate regression. Column headings describe the sample. The dependent variable is the proportion of the sample in year t that chose to reside in state s. Each regression controls for state and year fixed effects. Heteroscedasticity-adjusted standard errors are in parentheses.
* $p \leq .05$.
** $p \leq .01$.

America and Vietnam were also more likely to locate in these states. In all other cases, the estimated effects were statistically insignificant.

To summarize, tables 5 and 6 provide weak evidence in favor of the welfare magnet hypothesis for low-educated unmarried women and partial evidence in favor of the welfare magnet hypothesis with regard to low-skilled married women. The above analysis also provides partial evidence in favor of the hypothesis for high-skilled women, both married and unmarried. The evidence is weakened if we believe that more vulnerable groups from any country/region should be more sensitive to the policy change than less vulnerable groups, as the analysis does not reflect this.

Effects of Eligibility and Generosity of Means-Tested Programs

The analysis so far was about the effect of accessibility to means-tested programs on residential locations. A complete specification of the cost-benefit analysis, however, would require constructing a variable that is based on access and generosity of benefits. I construct a variable benefit according to immigrant eligibility and the benefit amount. Prior to 1997, benefit is equal to the consumer price index (CPI) deflated value of the total monthly benefit under the three programs in period $t - 1$. After the implementation of PRWORA, "benefit" equals zero if a state does not provide for any of the benefits; otherwise, it takes the real value of the benefit of the programs for which new immigrants are eligible. This variable is measured in thousands of dollars. Table 7 presents the results of the analysis using OLS and conditional multinomial logit models.[19]

The analysis using OLS models suggests that a $1,000 increase in real monthly benefit (or 150% increase in the monthly average benefit for the three programs) would raise the probability of low-skilled married women from Central and South America locating in a state by 1.1–1.6 percentage points.[20] In all other cases, benefit generosity has small and statistically insignificant effects on locational choices.

Figures reported in the analysis using conditional logit models are marginal effects with corresponding standard errors. The effect of welfare generosity continues to be modest. A 150% increase in benefit generosity raises the probability of going to a state by 0.8 to 1.3 percentage points for low-skilled women from Central and South America and the Philippines. The analysis also shows that unskilled women from China and South Asia are less likely to go to states with high welfare generosity. Finally, high-skilled women from Mexico, South America, Vietnam, and Eastern Europe are also more likely to locate in states with higher welfare generosity.

To sum up, the country-level analysis based on the linear model rejects the welfare magnet hypothesis for low-skilled unmarried women, the most vulnerable group that is also at high risk of becoming dependent on means-tested programs. For the second most vulnerable group, married low-skilled women, the OLS analysis suggests that only immigrants from Central and South America seem to be more attracted to states with higher benefits. The conditional logit analysis finds mixed effect of welfare generosity on locational choices. Unskilled women from some regions are more likely to locate in high welfare states, and those from other regions are less likely to locate in these states. A similar pattern is observed for high-skilled women, weakening evidence in favor of the welfare magnet hypothesis.

---

[19] I have argued earlier that generosity of benefits is endogenous. Therefore, I also use accessibility to the three programs as instruments for welfare generosity and investigate the effect of benefits on location choices. The instrumental variables (IV) and OLS estimates are quite similar. Therefore, I opt not to present the IV estimates.

[20] The average monthly real benefit for the three programs was $680 during 1995–96, so a $1,000 rise is roughly an increase of 150%.

Table 7
OLS and Conditional Multinomial Logit Estimates of the Effect of Generosity of Means-Tested Programs on the Location Choices of Newly Arrived Immigrant Women, by Country of Birth

	Low-Skilled Unmarried Women		Low-Skilled Married Women		High-Skilled Unmarried Women		High-Skilled Married Women	
Sample	OLS	Conditional Logit	OLS	Conditional Logit	OLS	Conditional Logit	OLS	Conditional Logit
Mexico	.000 (.001)	.004 (.005)	.001 (.001)	.003 (.002)	.003 (.002)	.028* (.013)	.002 (.001)	.011 (.008)
Central America	.012 (.006)	.013** (.004)	.011* (.005)	.012** (.002)	.001 (.005)	.003 (.005)	.007 (.004)	.008 (.004)
Caribbean	.003 (.004)	.003 (.003)	.015 (.009)	.002 (.002)	.006 (.005)	.003 (.004)	.013 (.008)	.002 (.004)
Peru, Colombia, and Ecuador	.001 (.005)	.001 (.004)	.016** (.006)	.011** (.002)	.009 (.005)	.011** (.005)	.011 (.006)	.002 (.004)
China	−.003 (.005)	−.014* (.006)	−.003 (.004)	−.002 (.002)	−.003 (.007)	.004 (.005)	−.005 (.003)	−.005* (.002)
Philippines	.003 (.003)	.008* (.004)	−.000 (.002)	−.000 (.002)	−.002 (.003)	−.005 (.005)	.001 (.002)	.002 (.003)
Bangladesh, India, and Pakistan	−.005 (.004)	−.003 (.004)	.001 (.004)	−.002* (.001)	−.003 (.010)	−.001 (.008)	.001 (.004)	−.001 (.003)
Vietnam	−.002 (.006)	−.000 (.007)	.003 (.002)	.004 (.003)	−.000 (.004)	.000 (.006)	.005 (.002)	.006* (.003)
Poland, Romania, Russia, and Ukraine	.000 (.006)	.006 (.006)	.003 (.003)	.003 (.002)	.010 (.006)	.011** (.003)	.006 (.004)	.006** (.001)

NOTE.—Column headings describe the samples for each country. Figures reported in each cell are from a separate regression. Each regression controls for state and year fixed effects. The reported coefficients are marginal effects, and the corresponding standard errors are in parentheses. For OLS (ordinary least squares) models, standard errors adjust for heteroscedasticity. For the conditional logit models, the marginal effects are computed around the mean probability of choosing a state.
* $p \le .05$.
** $p \le .01$.

VII. Conclusion

The above analysis suggests that changes in immigrants' access to means-tested programs—TANF, Medicaid, and food stamps—had at best a weak effect on the location choices of newly arrived immigrants. Estimates of the effect of access and generosity of social programs on low-skilled unmarried immigrant women's location choices were mostly statistically insignificant and often smaller than estimates for other demographic groups that faced a lower risk of using these programs.

This analysis differs from previous studies that found evidence in support of the welfare magnet hypothesis in at least three ways. First, I study the effect of changes in policies that denied new immigrants access to means-tested programs in a number of states. Earlier papers tested interstate and overtime variations in welfare generosity. Therefore, differences in state characteristics may have been confounded with benefit generosity. An innovation in my article is the use of PRWORA and state responses to set up a natural experiment research design that controls for state and year effects. States that reinstated benefits for immigrants are used as control for states that allowed the PRWORA restrictions to come into force.

Second, to allow for heterogeneity among immigrants from different regions, I use models with country fixed effects and country-state interactions. I also do disaggregated country-level analysis. Finally, I use the INS data that have information on all newly arrived immigrants. Most previous studies used the CPS or census data that do not provide information on the immigration status of foreign-born people. These studies, therefore, do not measure the target population precisely.

The focus of my analysis is newly arrived immigrants. Immigrants who have been living in the country for several years (or resident immigrants) may act differently toward interstate welfare generosity. They may have better knowledge of state welfare policies as compared to newly arrived immigrants and therefore may be more responsive to welfare generosity. If PRWORA altered the location choices of resident immigrants, it may also indirectly affect the location choices of future waves of immigrants. What factors determine the location choices of resident immigrants is an important topic for future research and may have an indirect bearing on how new waves of immigrants would locate in the United States.

References

Bartel, Ann P. 1989. Where do the new U.S. immigrants live? *Journal of Labor Economics* 7, no. 4 (October): 371–91.

Borjas, George J. 1999. Immigration and welfare magnets. *Journal of Labor Economics* 17, no. 4 (October): 607–37.

Borjas, George, and Lynette Hilton. 1995. Immigration and the welfare state: Immigrant participation in means-tested entitlement programs. Working Paper no. 5372, National Bureau of Economic Research, Cambridge, MA.

Buckley, F. H. 1996. The political economy of immigration policies. *International Review of Law and Economics* 16, no. 1:81–99.

Dodson, Marvin E., III. 2001. Welfare generosity and location choices among new United States immigrants. *International Review of Law and Economics* 21 (March): 47–67.

Greene, William H. 1993. *Econometric analysis*. 2nd ed. New York: Macmillan.

Jaeger, David. 2000. Local labor markets, admission categories, and immigrant location choice. Unpublished manuscript, Hunter College, New York.

Jasso, Guillermina, Mark R. Rosenzweig, and James P. Smith. 2000. The changing skill of new immigrants to the United States: Recent trends and their determinants. In *Issues in the economics of immigration*, ed. George Borjas. A National Bureau of Economic Research Conference Report. Chicago: University of Chicago Press.

Mincer, Jacob. 1978. Family migration decisions. *Journal of Political Economy* 86, no. 5 (August): 749–73.

Schwartz, Aba. 1973. Interpreting the effects of distance on migration. *Journal of Political Economy* 81, no. 5 (September–October): 1153–69.

Zavodny, Madeline. 1997. Welfare and the location choices of new immigrants. *Economic Review* (Federal Reserve Bank of Dallas), 2nd quarter: 2–10.

———. 1998. Determinants of recent immigrants' locational choices. *International Migration Review* 33 (December): 1014–30.

Zimmerman, Wendy, and Karen Tumlin. 1999. Patchwork policies: State assistance for immigrants under welfare reform. Occasional Paper no. 24, Urban Institute, Washington, DC.

Immigrant Assimilation and Welfare Participation
Do Immigrants Assimilate Into or Out of Welfare?

Jorgen Hansen
Magnus Lofstrom

ABSTRACT

This paper analyzes differences in welfare utilization between immigrants and natives in Sweden using a large panel data set for the years 1990 to 1996. We find that immigrants use welfare to a greater extent than natives and that differences cannot be explained by observable characteristics. Welfare participation decreases with time spent in Sweden. Refugees assimilate out of welfare at a faster rate than nonrefugee immigrants, but neither group is predicted to reach parity with natives. Increases in unemployment and immigration, as well as the change in the composition of immigrants, contributed to the increase in welfare utilization in Sweden.

I. Introduction

There has been a dramatic increase in the expenditure on social assistance (SA) in Sweden since the early 1980s.[1] According to the National Board of Health and Welfare, total real expenditures between 1983 and 1996 increased form 4.4 billion Swedish kronor (SEK) to 11.9 billion SEK. As we will show, immigration

---

Jorgen Hansen is an assistant professor of economics at Concordia University. Magnus Lofstrom is an assistant professor of economics and political economy at the University of Texas at Dallas. The authors would like to thank two anonymous referees, Thomas Bauer, Anders Bjö;rklund, Don DeVoretz, Lennart Flood, Bjorn Gustaffson, Dan-Olof Rooth, participants at the Canadian Economic Association's annual meeting 2000, the CEPR/TSER workshop at Bar-Ilan University, the Canadian International Labour Network's conference 2000, the European Economic Association's annual meeting 2000, and seminar participants at Gothenburg University, Lund University, SOFI, Simon Fraser University for helpful comments. Financial support from the European Commission (grant SOE2-CT97-03052) and the Swedish Council for Social Research is gratefully acknowledged. The data used in this paper are provided by Statistics Sweden. For information about accessing these data and user restrictions, contact Statistics Sweden at <swestat@scb.se>.
[Submitted February 2000; accepted August 2001]
ISSN 022-166X © 2003 by the Board of Regents of the University of Wisconsin System

1. The term social assistance is used synonymously with public assistance and welfare in this paper.

is central to the increase in welfare costs. For example, by the mid-1990s, expenditures on social assistance for immigrants equaled expenditures for natives, even though immigrants represented only 10–11 percent of the total population. Immigrants are also greatly overrepresented in the welfare population in the United States and Germany (see, for example, Bean, Van Hook, and Glick 1997; Borjas and Trejo 1991; Riphahn 1998).

It is quite clear that the concern about immigrant welfare usage is not specific to Sweden, but is also central to the immigration debates in other countries. For example, concerns about the rising welfare costs in the United States led the Congress to pass The Personal Responsibility and Work Opportunity Reconciliation Act (PRWORA) of 1996, which denies noncitizens who arrived after 1996 the right to receive most types of public assistance. The concerns about immigrant overutilization of public assistance are obvious in Germany as well. Immigrants without permanent residency in Germany may lose the right to stay in the country or may be denied residency extensions if they rely on social assistance.

In Sweden, the main reason for the growth in welfare expenditure is, not surprisingly, an increase in the utilization of SA. In 1983, 7.8 percent of all households received SA. This figure had increased to 10.7 percent by 1996. This represents a quite remarkable increase of more than 37 percent. The rise is especially strong among the immigrant population. In particular, households from refugee countries are overrepresented among the households that receive SA. During the same period, the proportion of immigrants in the Swedish population increased significantly, from 7.6 percent in 1983 to 10.8 percent in 1996. The overrepresentation of immigrants in the welfare population in combination with the increase in immigration can also explain part of the rise in welfare costs.

One important reason for the increase in welfare participation, and the consequent growth in expenditures, is the growth in the unemployment rate in the 1990s in Sweden, which grew from 1.7 percent in 1990 to slightly more than 8 percent in 1996. For immigrants, the labor market deteriorated even more. In 1990, approximately 4 percent of the immigrant population was unemployed. This had increased to 23 percent by 1996. The increase in welfare expenditures in Sweden in the 1990s can partly be explained by the large inflow of immigrants who arrived during this period who were not eligible for unemployment insurance and therefore had to rely on social assistance for their subsistence.

In this paper we try to answer two questions central to the debate of immigrant welfare utilization by using a unique large Swedish panel data set, Longitudinal Individual Data (LINDA). The first question we ask is whether the overrepresentation of immigrants among public assistance receiving households is due to differences in observable characteristics, such as age, family composition and the level of education, or if it is due to unobservable heterogeneity.[2] For example, if the higher immigrant welfare-participation rates are partially caused by differences in educational attainment, then policies directed towards increasing the educational level among immigrants may reduce the fiscal burden of social assistance in the future. However,

---

2. Examples of unobserved heterogeneity leading to differences in welfare-participation rates between immigrants and natives include behavioral differences (for example, dissimilarity in the reservation wage) and differences in the labor markets faced by the two groups (possibly due to discrimination).

if the observed differences in SA utilization depend on differences in preferences, then these types of policies would have a very limited effect, if any effect at all.

The second question deals with the important long term effects of immigration on welfare expenditures. Are immigrants likely to assimilate "into" or "out of" welfare dependency, that is, do immigrants increase or decrease their participation in social assistance with time spent in the host country? If immigrants' participation rates will change with time spent in the new country, the initial, upon arrival, costs of welfare should not be used to infer lifetime welfare costs of immigrants. For example, if immigrants assimilate out of welfare, initial welfare costs will overstate the long-run social assistance expenditures incurred by the immigrant population.

Previous studies of immigrant welfare dependency in the economics literature generally find that immigrants are on average more likely to receive welfare than native-born individuals. However, differences in observable socioeconomic characteristics explain greater participation rates among immigrants than natives in the United States, Australia, and Germany (Blau 1984; Maani 1993; and Riphahn 1998, respectively). Previous studies have also found that time spent in the host country affect participation rates of immigrants. For example, in the United States, Canada, and Germany immigrants appear to increase welfare utilization with time spent in the new country (Borjas and Trejo 1991 and 1993; Borjas and Hilton 1996; Baker and Benjamin 1995; Riphahn 1998). In other words, the existing literature suggests that immigrants assimilate *into* welfare dependency.[3]

The longitudinal data used in this paper provide a clear advantage over the data used in previous studies. Most of the above-mentioned papers utilized cross-sectional data, except for two, Borjas and Hilton (1996) and Riphahn (1998), who used panel data for the United States and Germany, respectively. Borjas and Hilton estimate linear probability models with fixed effects using a relatively short panel based on survey information. Riphahn controls for both unobserved heterogeneity and attrition. However, the data are not a representative sample of immigrants in Germany. Unfortunately, it only includes a small sample of guest workers and no refugees.

In this paper we take advantage of a recently collected large representative panel data set containing information on more than 300,000 individuals annually for the period 1990–96. The data are collected from administrative records implying essentially no attrition and less measurement error than what would be expected in survey data. Another significant advantage is that the longitudinal data set allows us to use methods controlling for unobserved heterogeneity. It is essential to control for unobserved effects since many of the factors determining whether a household receives welfare or not, including the reservation wage and stigma effects from participating in welfare programs, are unobserved by the econometrician.

The key findings in this paper are that immigrants are more likely to participate in the social assistance program than natives even when controlling for observable characteristics, and that immigrants assimilate out of welfare with time spent in the new country. The former of these findings contradicts what has generally been found

---

3. Regarding Baker and Benjamin's (1995) finding that immigrants appear to assimilate into welfare in Canada, Crossley, McDonald, and Worswick (2001) show that these results are sensitive to years included in the sample. As reported below, we do not find the same sensitivity of the results, with respect to survey years, in the Swedish data used here.

previously in the literature. The self-selection of immigrants coming to a relatively generous welfare state is likely to be one of the reasons for this result. We also find that immigrants reduce welfare-participation rates with time spent in the new country. Although refugees display substantially higher participation rates upon arrival compared to nonrefugee immigrants, they assimilate out of welfare much more rapidly than their nonrefugee counterparts. We also find that roughly 50 percent of the observed increase in welfare utilization in Sweden in the 1990s can be attributed to the increases in both unemployment and immigration.

The result, that immigrants assimilate out of welfare, appears to contradict previous findings in regards to the assimilation of immigrants' welfare utilization. However, even after 20 years in the host country we find that both refugee and nonrefugee immigrants show significantly higher social-assistance-participation rates than statistically similar natives—by between 8 and 10 percentage points. These numbers are quite close to the findings of Borjas and Hilton (1996) and Baker and Benjamin (1995). These results suggest that immigrants in a relatively generous welfare state, like Sweden, display similar welfare participation behavior as immigrants in less generous welfare states, like the United States, relative to natives after having spent some time in the new host country.

The paper is organized in the following way. In Sections II and III we give background information about immigration into Sweden and the social assistance program. Section IV describes the data and variables while Section V depicts trends and differences, between immigrants and natives, in welfare participation. In Section VI we test whether differences in welfare utilization can be explained by differences in socioeconomic characteristics. Assimilation issues are also analyzed in this section. Finally, we conclude in Section VII.

II. Historical Background—Immigration into Sweden

The inflow of immigrants to Sweden has undergone a number of changes during the last six decades. Figure 1 shows annual immigration to Sweden from 1940 to 1998, both in terms of actual immigrant inflow and inflow expressed as a proportion of the population in the corresponding year. Overall, annual immigration has amounted to about 0.4 percent of the population, but it was notably higher during 1990s. The proportional inflow is slightly higher than the U.S. experience of the 1990s, but quite similar to the experiences of Canada and Australia. Naturally, the large inflow of immigrants has also changed the composition of the population in Sweden. In 1991, almost 10 percent of the Swedish population was born outside Sweden. This is a relatively high figure compared to the United States (7.9 percent), but is lower than the proportion of foreign-born in Canada (16.1 percent) and Australia (22.3 percent) (SOPEMI 1998).

The reasons people immigrate to Sweden have changed substantially during the post-war period. In principle, we can distinguish between three categories of immigrants, based on the reasons for immigration: economic migrants (due to the recruitment of labor, for example), tied movers (based on family ties) and refugees. In the late 1940s, a large fraction of the immigrants arrived in Sweden as refugees. In the period from 1950 to 1970, however, most immigrants were recruited by the Swedish

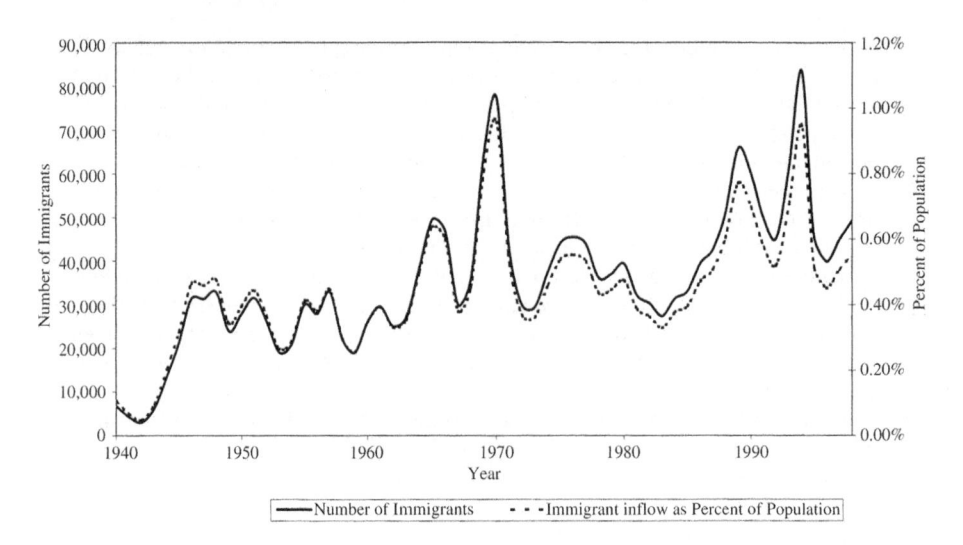

Figure 1
Immigration into Sweden, Annual Inflow and Proportion of Population, 1940–98
Source: Statistics Sweden, Historical Population Development Table, 1999.

industry or arrived because of family ties. Since 1970, the proportion of immigrants arriving as refugees has increased significantly, from less than 10 percent of the immigrant inflow in 1970 to about 70 percent in the early 1990s. In 1994, this proportion dropped from 70 percent to about 50 percent, mostly due to improved conditions in the Balkan countries.

III. Social Assistance in Sweden

The Swedish welfare system is well known internationally for the degree of income security that it provides for its citizens. Recently, this generous system has been the target of a number of reforms, mainly due to the recession that hit Sweden, and many other countries, in the early 1990s.

As an ultimate safety net, people in Sweden are covered by social assistance (SA). In order to be eligible for SA, all other welfare programs, such as unemployment compensation, housing allowance (*bostadsbidrag*), child allowance (*barnbidrag*), maintenance allowance (*underhållsbidrag*), and various pensions, must be exhausted first. The benefit levels vary, both across family types and regions, but are intended to cover expenses essential for a "decent" living.[4] To be eligible for SA benefits, a family must have income and assets below certain specified benefits levels (known as norms). Unit 1998, the norms were determined in each of the 288 municipalities

---

4. For example, in 1994, for a single individual, the norm varied between 1,613 SEK and 4,107 SEK per month across the municipalities. The benefits are meant to cover expenses for so-called necessary consumption, such as food, basic clothing, leisure, health, newspapers, telephone, and fees for TV.

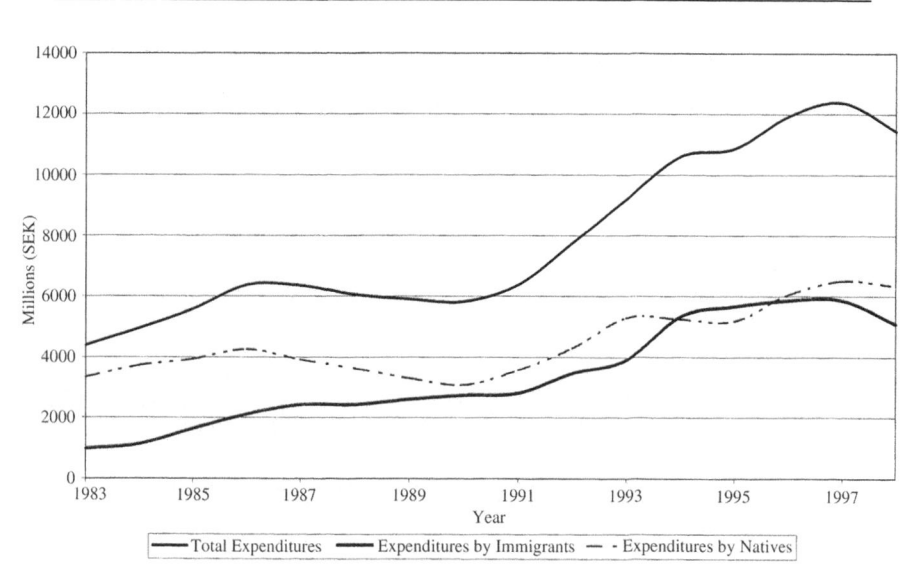

Figure 2
Real Expenditures on Social Assistance in Sweden, 1983–98, in 1996 SEK
Source: National Board of Health and Welfare, Social Assistance, Table 1, 1998.

in Sweden and served as guidelines for the social worker, who decided the actual size of the benefits. SA benefits were paid according to a schedule that set a guaranteed amount for a family of a given size. These benefits were reduced at a 100 percent reduction rate as the family's income rose.

Expenditures on social assistance have increased quite substantially in Sweden during the last 15 years. In Figure 2, we show total expenditures on SA from 1983 to 1998. During the 1980s, total expenditures on welfare increased by more than 30 percent. However, the most rapid increase in expenditures took place in the 1990s. Between 1990 and 1996, welfare costs increased by roughly 100 percent. In 1996, 11.9 billion SEK was spent on social assistance, or approximately 2 percent of all government expenditures.

Figure 2 also divides welfare expenditures separately for native Swedes and immigrants. Clearly, welfare expenditures increased at a much faster pace for immigrants than for native-born Swedes between 1983 and 1998. Throughout the 1990s, immigrants and natives accounted for about the same amount of welfare expenditures. This is quite remarkable given that immigrants represent a 10 percent minority of the population in Sweden.

IV. Data

A. Description of the Data and Sampling Procedures

The data used in this paper are taken from a recently created Swedish longitudinal data set, Longitudinal Individual Data (LINDA). LINDA is a register-based data set and it consists of a large panel of individuals and their household members, which are representative for the population from 1960 to 1996. LINDA is a joint endeavor between the Department of Economics at Uppsala University, The National Social Insurance Board (RFV), Statistics Sweden, and the Ministries of Finance and Labor. The main administrator of the data set is Statistics Sweden. For a more detailed description of the data used here, including the sampling structure, see Edin and Fredriksson (2000).

LINDA contains a 3 percent representative random sample of the Swedish population, corresponding to approximately 300,000 individuals for the period studied here. The sampled population consists of all individuals, including children and elderly persons, who lived in Sweden during a particular year. The sampling procedure used in constructing the panel data set ensures that each cross-section is representative for the population in each year. Attached to LINDA is a nonoverlapping representative random sample of immigrants containing the same variables, and created in the same fashion, as the general sample. The immigrant sample consists of 20 percent of all individuals born abroad. We merged this sample with the general population sample. This generated a sample of the Swedish population in which immigrants are overrepresented. The overrepresentation can be adjusted for by using appropriate methods.

The sample used in this study consists of information from LINDA for the year 1990–96.[5] We excluded all households in which the sampled person is younger than 18 years or older than 65 years. Because welfare participation in Sweden is based on household characteristics and household income, the appropriate unit of observation is the household. A common approach in the literature is to let the household be represented by the household head, meaning that the characteristics of the household coincide with those of the household head. However, we are not able to identify the head of the household in LINDA and instead we let the household be represented by the sampled individual. This means that the value of different observable characteristics, such as age and education, in the subsequent analysis refer to the person in the household that was originally sampled. Furthermore, a household is defined as an immigrant household if the sampled person was born abroad, and as a refugee household if he was born in a refugee country, as defined by the Swedish Immigration Board, or in a sub-Saharan country.[6] If the person representing the household is an immigrant or a refugee, we have information about the year of arrival in Sweden.[7] We also estimated models with a slightly different definition of an immigrant household in which the household was defined to be an immigrant household if *any* household member was an immigrant. This appears to have no impact on the analysis presented below.

---

5. We lack information about welfare use prior to 1990.
6. The countries defined by the Swedish Immigration Board as refugee countries: Ethiopia, Afghanistan, Bulgaria, Bangladesh, Bosnia, Chile, Sri Lanka, Cuba, Iraq, Iran, India, Yugoslavia, China, Croatia, Lebanon, Moldavia, Peru, Pakistan, Poland, Russia, Soviet Union, Romania, Somalia, Syria, Togo, Turkey, Ukraine, Uganda, and Vietnam.
7. All immigrant households included in LINDA, whether defined as refugees or not, have obtained residence permits. This means, for instance, that asylum seekers who have not yet obtained a residence permit are not included in our sample. Furthermore, the data do not allow us to identify the exact year of arrival for immigrants who arrived in 1968 or earlier.

Table 1
Mean Observable Characteristics by Immigrant Status and Welfare Receipt

		Natives		Immigrants			
				Nonrefugee Country		Refugee Country	
	Total	Nonwelfare Recipient	Welfare Recipient	Nonwelfare Recipient	Welfare Recipient	Nonwelfare Recipient	Welfare Recipient
Age	39.91	40.46	32.31	39.31	35.08	35.91	34.54
Years since migration	12.52	N/A	N/A	15.87	13.34	9.63	5.37
Education							
Elementary school	32.40%	31.34%	43.54%	36.29%	47.31%	38.61%	45.97%
High school	57.42%	58.22%	54.65%	51.99%	48.56%	47.93%	44.57%
College	10.19%	10.43%	1.81%	11.73%	4.13%	13.46%	9.46%
Single	53.34%	51.98%	89.47%	51.74%	80.04%	41.79%	55.67%
Number of children	0.59	0.57	0.52	0.71	0.70	0.99	1.01
SA norm	5,961	5,979	4,859	6,137	5,341	6,742	6,353
Unemployment rate	6.04%	6.01%	6.40%	6.04%	6.22%	6.24%	6.81%
Sample size	1,647,390	1,009,780	44,372	304,239	33,125	183,162	72,712

Source: Longitudinal Individual Data for Sweden (LINDA), 1990–96.

B. Variable Definition and Descriptive Statistics

To answer the questions regarding immigrant assimilation and welfare participation raised in the introduction, we estimate models where the dependent variable is a binary variable equal to one if the household received SA for at least one month during the year, and equal to zero otherwise.

The Swedish municipalities provided data on social assistance benefit levels. We were able to assign a social assistance norm, which determines the benefit level, to each household in the sample in 1994 and in 1996. The municipality in which the household resides, as well as the family composition, such as marital status, ages, and number of children, determines the norms. Unfortunately, we have not been able to obtain similar information for the other years. For that reason, we assign the 1994 norms to all years prior to 1995 and the 1996 norms to the years 1995 and 1996.[8] By including the norms into the models, we can obtain estimates of the effects of higher benefit levels on public assistance utilization. To control for local variation in unemployment rates, we include county unemployment rates, obtained from Statistics Sweden's labor force surveys. These are assigned to each household in each year based on the household's region of residence.

In Table 1, we present average characteristics for the household by welfare recipiency for the period 1990 to 1996. In general, we observe that households on welfare are younger, less educated and, to a larger degree, single, as compared to households not on public assistance.[9] For immigrants, we observe that SA recipients have on average been in the country for a shorter period than those households off SA. Interestingly, refugee households have on average higher post-secondary education compared to native Swedish and nonrefugee immigrant households. Moreover, the fraction of college-educated households receiving SA is substantially larger among refugees than among the other two groups.

V. Trends and Differences in Welfare Participation

As Figure 2 shows, real expenditures on welfare increased substantially in Sweden during the 1990s. During this period, there was a substantial increase in the number of households receiving SA. The National Board of Health and Welfare reports that 7.9 percent of all households in Sweden in 1990 received social assistance. By 1996, the participation rate had increased to 10.7 percent. This represents an increase by 35 percent. Furthermore, the average monthly amount received did not change much and increased by slightly less than 5 percent. This suggests that the increase in expenditures is not due to an increase in the generosity of the welfare system.

---

8. To ensure that the findings reported below are not sensitive to the limited availability of municipal welfare benefits rules, we reestimated the models shown in Tables 3 and 4 using a sample restricted to the two years the norm is available for, 1994 and 1996. The results from the restricted sample, available upon request from the authors, are very similar to the ones obtained utilizing the full sample and the conclusions reported in this paper remain the same.

9. Since participation in SA is based on household characteristics, the entries in Table 1 refer to those of the household representative.

Table 2
Welfare Participation by Immigrant Status and Arrival Cohort, 1990 and 1996

	Sample Size		Welfare Participation Rates		
	1990	1996	1990	1996	Difference 1990–96
Natives	147,319	151,096	3.18%	4.68%	1.50
Immigrants					
Nonrefugee country					
All cohorts	30,419	53,648	8.29%	10.15%	1.86
Arrival cohort					
1968–75	19,011	22,557	7.01%	6.64%	−0.38
1976–80	6,200	10,595	8.90%	10.01%	1.10
1981–85	3,405	6,005	11.34%	10.99%	−0.35
1986–90	1,803	8,422	13.92%	13.58%	−0.34
1991–96		6,069		17.85%	
Refugee country					
All cohorts	13,055	53,095	16.49%	31.99%	15.50
Arrival cohort					
1968–75	2,536	3,330	7.85%	9.10%	1.25
1976–80	4,121	6,458	11.65%	11.66%	0.01
1981–85	4,094	6,818	16.17%	16.46%	0.29
1986–90	2,304	16,009	35.24%	30.06%	−5.18
1991–96		20,480		48.80%	

Source: Longitudinal Individual Data for Sweden (LINDA), 1990 and 1996.

Welfare-participation rates have been shown to be different for immigrants and natives in many countries (see, for example, Borjas and Trejo 1991; Maani 1993; Riphahn 1998). Table 2 shows that this is true for Sweden as well.[10] Immigrants from both refugee and nonrefugee countries are more likely to receive social assistance than native-born Swedes. Furthermore, refugees participate to a greater extent in the social assistance program than nonrefugees. The table also shows that the increase in the welfare participation rate over the period 1990–96 was greater for immigrants than it was for natives.

Table 2 also shows substantial differences in welfare participation rates across arrival cohorts. The table suggests that immigrants reduce their social assistance reliance with time spent in Sweden. However, the observed assimilation out of welfare could be due to a decline in the skill level of later cohorts, so-called negative cohort effects. In a series of articles, Borjas (1985 and 1994, for example) has shown

---

10. The immigrant sample used in Table 2 corresponds to 20 percent of the immigrant population for *each* year. This combined with the dramatic increase in immigration into Sweden during the period analyzed explains the large difference in number of immigrant observations in 1990 and 1996.

that such cohort effects can cause overestimated assimilation rates of immigrants. Notwithstanding, Table 2 shows that the welfare utilization rate decreases relative to natives, for *any* given arrival cohort, over the period studied here. The native welfare participation rate increased by 1.5 percentage points from 1990 to 1996. No immigrant arrival cohort displays a greater increase in social assistance utilization rate than 1.25 percentage points over the same period. This indicates that negative cohort effects are not the source of the observed assimilation pattern. Furthermore, this suggests that the increase in immigrant welfare participation does not stem from an increase in immigrants' propensities to participate in the social assistance program, but is instead, at least partially, due to the substantial increase in immigration that Sweden experienced in the 1990s. We will explore the effect of the rise in immigration on the observed increase in welfare participation below.

Immigrant assimilation out of welfare becomes quite clear when the difference in participation rates between immigrants and natives are shown by years since migration, as in Figure 3. Refugees in particular seem to assimilate quickly. Their initial welfare-participation rates are between 40 and 50 percentage points higher than natives. After 10 or 11 years in Sweden, the difference drops to about 10 percentage points. Nonrefugee immigrants also appear to assimilate out of welfare. It should be noted that these comparisons are flawed in several ways. For example, the average age of natives is held roughly constant while the average age of the immigrant population increases with years since migration. Controls for cohort effects are also important to incorporate. Differences between immigrants and natives, or changes in

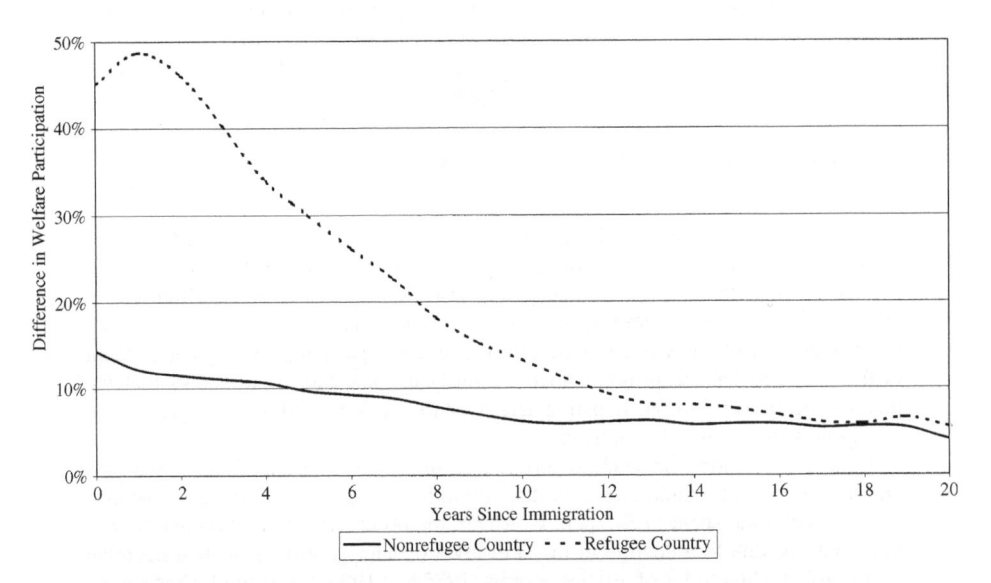

Figure 3
Observed Differences in Welfare Participation, Native-Born Swedes and Immigrants, by Years Since Migration
Source: Longitudinal Individual Data for Sweden (LINDA), 1990 to 1996.

differences over time, in socioeconomic and geographic characteristics may also partly explain the pattern. To accurately analyze assimilation rates, an empirical model needs to be estimated. We now turn our attention to such a model.

VI. Empirical Specification and Results

To analyze welfare utilization we need insight into why households participate in social assistance. Clearly, the labor market conditions household members face will affect the probability that the household will end up on welfare. In other words, the factors we believe will affect employment probabilities also need to be incorporated into our welfare utilization models. It is also quite plausible that immigrants and natives do not face the same labor market conditions. For example, human capital obtained abroad may be viewed differently than human capital acquired in the new country. Indication of this was found in Betts and Lofstrom (2000) for the United States. Another possibility is discrimination against immigrants. It is therefore important to allow the employment factors to affect welfare participation probabilities differently for immigrants and natives. Individuals' preferences and tastes for leisure will also affect the probability of being on welfare through differences in the reservation wages. The so-called stigma effect of receiving welfare payments also depends on individuals' preferences. The individual differences in reservation wages and the potential stigma of being on welfare are inherently unobservable but can be controlled for by using estimation methods that account for differences across individuals, including random or fixed effects.

A. Do Differences in Observable Characteristics Explain Differences in Welfare Participation?

In the introduction we asked whether the overrepresentation of immigrants among welfare-recipient households is due to differences in observable characteristics, to behavioral differences, or to differences in labor market conditions. To answer this, we formulate random-effects probit models of welfare participation.

To be specific, the estimated models can be described as follows. Let

(1) $\quad y_{it}^* = X_{it}\beta + \varepsilon_{it} \qquad \forall\ i = 1, 2, \ldots, n \text{ and } t = 1, 2, \ldots, T_i$

where

(2) $\quad \varepsilon_{it} = \mu_i + v_{it}$

y_{it}^* is a latent variable representing preferences for welfare utilization of household i at time t. X is a vector of socioeconomic and geographic characteristics, including age, educational attainment, marital status, and the number of children. In addition, it contains information about the municipal social assistance norm and the county unemployment rate. The unobserved household specific effect, assumed to be time invariant, is represented by μ_i and v_{it} and is a white-noise error term. We assume that these unobserved stochastic terms have the following properties:

(3) $\quad \mu_i, v_{it} \sim N(0, \Omega)$

with

(4) $\Omega = \begin{bmatrix} \sigma_\mu^2 & 0 \\ 0 & 1 \end{bmatrix}$

This implies that

(5) $\text{Var}(\varepsilon_{it}) = \sigma_\mu^2 + 1$

and

(6) $\text{Corr}(\varepsilon_{it}, \varepsilon_{is}) = \rho = \dfrac{\sigma_\mu^2}{\sigma_\mu^2 + 1}$

We do not observe y^*, but we assume that we can observe the sign of it, and based on that we can formulate the following decision rule:

(7) $y_{it} = 1$ if $y_{it}^* > 0$, and 0 otherwise

where $y_{it} = 1$ represents utilization of SA.

The set of control variables is very similar to what has been used in previous studies for other countries. The vector X also includes three *not* mutually exclusive nativity indicator variables. The following three immigrant dummies are defined: *Immigrant* (equal to one for all immigrants), *Nordic Immigrant* (equal to one for all immigrants from the Nordic countries) and *Refugee Immigrant* (equal to one for all immigrants from the previously defined refugee countries). This implies that the coefficient on the *Immigrant* dummy captures differences between natives and all immigrants while the coefficient on the *Refugee Immigrant* dummy captures differences between nonrefugee immigrants and immigrants from refugee countries. Given this definition of the nativity variables, the disparity between immigrants from refugee countries and natives is the sum of the two estimated coefficients for immigrants and refugees. Similarly, the difference in probability of welfare participation between Nordic immigrants and natives is the sum of the *Immigrant* and *Nordic Immigrant* estimated coefficients. If higher welfare-participation rates among immigrants are simply due to differences in observable characteristics between natives and immigrants, the estimated relevant coefficients on the nativity variables should not be significantly different from zero when these controls are included in the model. The results and marginal effects calculated at the mean of the observables are presented in Table 3.

All immigrants appear to be more likely to participate in the social assistance program even after observable characteristics are controlled for. Model 1 shows the differences in the probability of receiving welfare between the three immigrant categories and natives, adjusting for the national trend over the period. The overall difference between nonrefugee immigrants and natives is 6.9 percentage points. The probability that a Nordic immigrant household participates in the social assistance program appears to be slightly less than a nonrefugee immigrant's household. A refugee household is substantially more likely to be on welfare than a native household; the difference is about 18.6 percentage points.

The results for Model 2 indicate that differences in observable characteristics explain very little of the differences in welfare participation between natives and immigrants. Immigrants from nonrefugee countries are about 6.6 percentage points more likely to receive welfare compared to statistically similar natives. Only 5 percent of the total observed difference is due to differences in observable characteristics. The estimated difference for a refugee household drops by 1.6 percentage points when the observable socioeconomic variables are included in the model. A very small proportion, slightly less than 9 percent, of the higher observed-participation rates of refugees can be explained by differences in age, education, household composition, and geographic location.

Table 2 shows that it is important to allow for differences in welfare utilization between arrival cohorts. To ensure that changes in the composition of immigrants over the period do not explain the large differences even after observables have been controlled for, we reestimated Model 2 in Table 3 with arrival cohort dummies. The results are shown in Table 3 as Model 3. The differences between immigrants and natives remain for all arrival cohorts. It is quite clear that differences in welfare participation between immigrants and natives are not due to differences in socioeconomic characteristics.

Our findings that differences in observable characteristics between immigrants and natives do not explain the higher welfare-participation rates of immigrants differ from the findings for the United States, Canada, Australia, and Germany. The analysis performed here does not tell us whether the differences between immigrants and natives are due to behavioral differences or differences in the labor market opportunities between the two groups.

Two possible reasons may explain the differences in findings across countries. First, the Swedish labor market may view immigrants and their observable characteristics differently from the previously mentioned countries' labor markets. Another possible reason is that immigrants do not randomly choose the destination country. Instead, they may self-select according to preferences, relative expected earnings, and the generosity of the welfare system in the new host country. If so, immigrants may select Sweden partially due to its fairly generous welfare system. It should be noted that our analysis does not allow us to determine the extent to which each possible reason contributes to the discrepancy in findings across countries.

B. Assimilation Into or Out of Welfare?

Our results indicate differences in the welfare utilization between immigrants and natives, even after controlling for observable characteristics. Our next step is to analyze how immigrants' welfare participation behavior changes with time spent in the host country. In doing so, it is important to control for unobserved effects. We do this by estimating a random effects probit model, similar to the one discussed above.

To allow for different effects of observable variables for native Swedish households and immigrant households (both refugee and nonrefugee), we specify an interacted model, where all the observable variables are interacted with indicator variables for immigrants and refugees. However, we impose equal year effects across the three groups in order to identify the assimilation effects. This model is not fully interacted in the sense that we do not interact all the variables with the Nordic immigrant variable. The reason for this is that estimated models including these interactions

Table 3
Random Effects Probit Models of Welfare Participation

Variable	Model 1 Estimated Coefficient	Model 1 Marginal Effect	Model 2 Estimated Coefficient	Model 2 Marginal Effect	Model 3 Estimated Coefficient	Model 3 Marginal Effect
Immigrant	0.9734 (0.0327)	0.0692	0.9758 (0.0328)	0.0656	1.5913 (0.0644)	0.1042
Nordic immigrant	−0.1059 (0.0395)	−0.0075	−0.1390 (0.0404)	−0.0093	−0.0500 (0.0395)	−0.0033
Refugee immigrant	1.6376 (0.0341)	0.1165	1.5519 (0.0344)	0.1044	1.9987 (0.0687)	0.1308
Arrival 1986–90					−0.4497 (0.0743)	−0.0294
Arrival 1981–5					−0.6690 (0.0808)	−0.0438
Arrival 1976–80					−0.7504 (0.0736)	−0.0491
Arrival 1968–75					−1.0144 (0.0691)	−0.0664

Arrival 1986–90*refugee		−0.6586 −0.0431
		(0.0841)
Arrival 1981–5*refugee		−1.3864 −0.0907
		(0.0991)
Arrival 1976–80*refugee		−1.6859 −0.1104
		(0.0937)
Arrival 1968–75*refugee		−1.8215 −0.1192
		(0.1104)
Included controls		
Time fixed effects	Yes	Yes
Individual characteristics	No	Yes
Regional characteristics	No	Yes
County fixed effects	No	Yes
Within-group correlation	0.7723	0.7473 0.7266
Number of observations	405,426	405,426 405,426
Log likelihood	−77,411	−74,133 −72,570

Note: Standard errors appear in parentheses. Data used are from LINDA, 1990–96. Estimates are based on a 25 percent random subsample of the full LINDA sample. P-value of likelihood ratio test for no within-group correlation is less than 0.0001 for all models.

indicated no differences between Nordic immigrants and other nonrefugee immigrants. Hence, we limit interactions to the nativity variables for immigrants and refugee immigrants. However, we allow for different mean effects among Nordic immigrants and other immigrants by including the Nordic immigrant dummy variable. We incorporate information about years since migration to assess whether immigrants assimilate into or out of welfare dependency. We also know from Section II that the composition of immigrants has changed substantially over the last 30 years, and it is therefore important to control for differences in arrival cohorts.

The results from the model described above can be found in Table 4. In the first two columns, we present the results for native Swedes, while Columns 3 and 4 present the differences between immigrants from nonrefugee countries and natives. Finally, the last two columns show the estimated differences between refugees and nonrefugees. Note that to obtain marginal effects for nonrefugee immigrants, it is necessary to add the estimated marginal effects for natives, shown in Column 2, to the effect specific to immigrants, as shown in Column 4. Similarly, to get the marginal effects for immigrants from refugee countries, it is necessary to add the shown effects in Columns 2, 4, and 6.[11]

We focus our discussion on the main parameters affecting assimilation into or out of welfare dependency. In passing, we note that the effects of education and family composition have the expected signs.

An interesting result is that the effect of the social assistance norm is positive and significant, implying that, everything else held constant, welfare-participation rates are higher in municipalities where the norm is relatively high. Immigrants are less sensitive to variation in the benefit levels than natives. In fact, it appears that the social assistance norm has no significant effect on the welfare utilization of both refugee and nonrefugee immigrants. Furthermore, our results indicate that welfare participation is weakly, in terms of statistical significance, positively associated with changes in the local unemployment rate for all three groups.

One of the main purposes of this paper is to study whether immigrants assimilate into or out of welfare dependency. The estimated coefficients for the age and years since migration variables can be used to trace out differences in the probability of welfare recipiency between immigrants and natives by years since migration. It is also necessary to choose values for the other characteristics included in the matrix X. We have chosen 1996 as our baseline year and a household located in one of the major cities. The sample person is a high school graduate who is married with one child. These choices represent the mode for these variables. The predicted differences in welfare participation between immigrants and natives, calculated for the representative household described above, are shown in Figures 4, 5, and 6.

The figures indicate that immigrants assimilate out of welfare with time spent in Sweden. Figure 4 shows that both nonrefugee and refugee households reduce their utilization of welfare, relative to natives with years since migration. In particular, the assimilation process is substantially faster for refugee households. Despite much higher initial participation rates, after 14–15 years refugee households display very similar welfare-participation rates as nonrefugee households. However, it should be

---

11. The reason for defining the immigrant status variables in this way is so that we can easily test for differences across immigrant groups.

noted that neither group appears to reach the participation rates of native households within a 20-year period in Sweden.[12]

In Section II we showed that the composition of immigrants has changed substantially over the last 30 years. It is therefore important to control for arrival cohorts. Figures 5 and 6 show differences in welfare participation between natives and immigrants by arrival cohorts. The trends in Figure 5 indicate quite small differences in the predicted assimilation patterns among arrival cohorts for immigrants from nonrefugee countries. Figure 6 shows a different pattern for refugee households. Our results indicate that the latest arrival cohorts have higher participation rates than all the earlier arrival cohorts of refugee immigrants.

There is a concern that the findings above may be due to nonrandom selective return migration. That is, if those immigrants who are less likely to participate in welfare programs are also the ones who are most likely to stay, our estimates would overstate the decline in welfare participation with time spent in Sweden. However, Edin, LaLonde, and Aslund (2000) also use data extracted from LINDA and find that the immigrants who stay in Sweden are more likely to receive welfare than the ones who leave. Furthermore, they find that return migration among refugees is low and that earnings assimilation of this group is not sensitive to emigration.[13] Based on this, we do not think that our findings are driven by selective return migration.

To ensure that our results are not specific to the random effects assumptions, we also estimated a fixed effects logit model. We were concerned about the assumption made in the random effects model that the household specific error terms are uncorrelated with the observed independent variables. The assimilation results derived from the fixed effects logit model are remarkably similar to the random effects probit results. For that reason and because the effects of the time invariant variables are of interest in a study like this, we only report the above-discussed random effects probit results.

To summarize our results concerning immigrant assimilation in welfare utilization, we find strong support for the hypothesis that immigrant households in Sweden tend to assimilate out of rather than into welfare dependency. This result differs from the results found in the existing literature on the welfare assimilation of immigrants. However, even after 20 years in the host country we find that both refugee and nonrefugee immigrants show significantly higher social-assistance-participation rates than statistically similar natives by between 8 and 10 percentage points. Remarkably, our findings are very similar to those of Borjas and Hilton (1996), using U.S. data, and of Baker and Benjamin (1995), using Canadian data, whose estimates

---

12. The figures show differences in welfare-participation rates, assuming that age at migration is equal to 18. To assess the impact of age at migration, we recreated Figure 4, setting age at migration to 30. Our findings suggest that age at migration has a very minor impact on nonrefugee immigrants' participation behavior. Refugee immigrants, however, display slightly slower assimilation rates the older the immigrant is upon arrival in Sweden. We also estimated models including explicit controls for age at migration and found no differences to the findings reported in the paper.

13. Edin, LaLonde, and Aslund (2000) also find that if an immigrant is to leave Sweden, departure is most likely to take place within the first few years after arrival. Motivated by this finding and the policy in Sweden of giving most refugee immigrants welfare upon arrival in Sweden, we reestimated the model in Table 4 excluding all immigrants who had been in Sweden for fewer than three years. The results show that assimilation patterns are not sensitive to this sample selection.

Table 4
Random Effects Probit Model of Welfare Participation

Variable	Estimated Coefficient	Marginal Effect	Estimated Coefficient (Immigrant Dummy)	Marginal Effect (Immigrant Dummy)	Estimated Coefficient (Refugee Immigrant Dummy)	Marginal Effect (Refugee Immigrant Dummy)
Constant	-4.3198 (0.2416)		2.2770 (0.3268)	0.1533	1.3447 (0.3419)	0.0905
Age	0.0320 (0.0071)	0.0022	-0.0032 (0.0128)	-0.0002	-0.0098 (0.0120)	-0.0007
Age squared/100	-0.0833 (0.0093)	-0.0056	0.0196 (0.0165)	0.0013	0.0637 (0.0155)	0.0043
High school	-0.2287 (0.0256)	-0.0154	0.0296 (0.0440)	0.0020	0.2528 (0.0411)	0.0170
College	-1.2294 (0.0696)	-0.0827	0.1661 (0.1006)	0.0112	0.7707 (0.0891)	0.0519
Single	1.2829 (0.0655)	0.0863	-0.4816 (0.0973)	-0.0324	0.0173 (0.0949)	0.0012
Number of children	-0.0360 (0.0519)	-0.0024	0.1651 (0.0742)	0.0111	0.0269 (0.0646)	0.0018

Single*number of children	0.2245	0.0134	−0.0254	−0.0017
	(0.0260)	(0.0393)	(0.0380)	
SA norm/1000	0.0581	−0.1035	−0.0168	−0.0011
	(0.0233)	(0.0337)	(0.0297)	
Local unemployment rate	0.0161	−0.0083	0.0023	0.0002
	(0.0105)	(0.0075)	(0.0085)	
Nordic immigrant		−0.0286		
		(0.0397)		
Years since migration		−0.0374	−0.1678	−0.0113
		(0.0137)	(0.0112)	
Years since migration^2/100		−0.0216	0.4016	0.0270
		(0.0339)	(0.0428)	
Arrival 1986–90		−0.2718	−0.2441	−0.0164
		(0.0852)	(0.0983)	
Arrival 1981–5		−0.2835	−0.6840	−0.0460
		(0.1260)	(0.1518)	
Arrival 1976–80		−0.1508	−0.9724	−0.0654
		(0.1571)	(0.1938)	
Arrival 1968–75		−0.1254	−1.2386	−0.0834
		(0.1971)	(0.2588)	
Within-group correlation		0.7240		
Log likelihood		−72,019		
Sample size		405,426		

Note: Standard errors appear in parentheses. Data used are from LINDA, 1990–96. Estimates are based on a 25 percent random subsample of the full LINDA sample. Model includes both county and year fixed effects. P-value of likelihood ratio test for no within-group correlation is less than 0.0001.

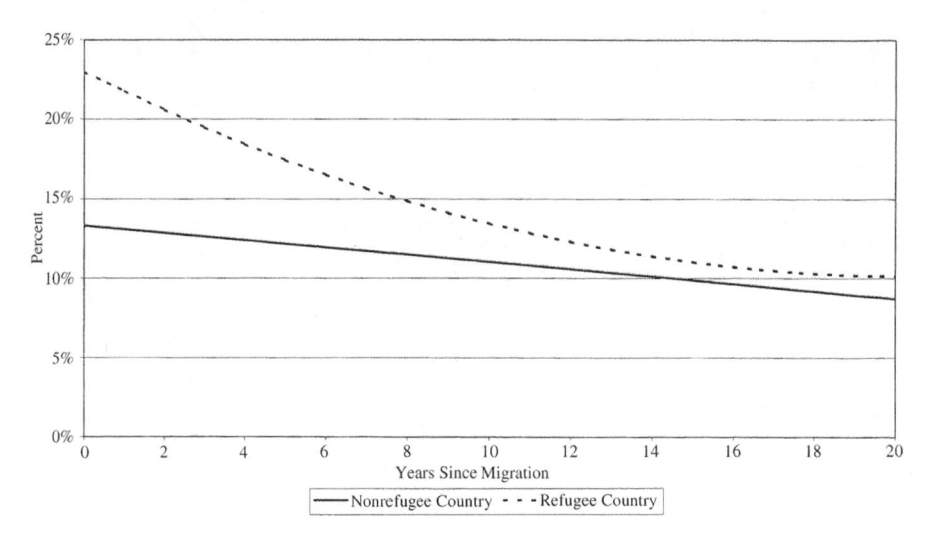

Figure 4
Predicted Differences in Welfare Participation between Native-Born Swedes and Immigrants, by Years Since Migration, Age at Migration = 18, 1996 Baseline
Note: Based on estimates presented in Table 4.

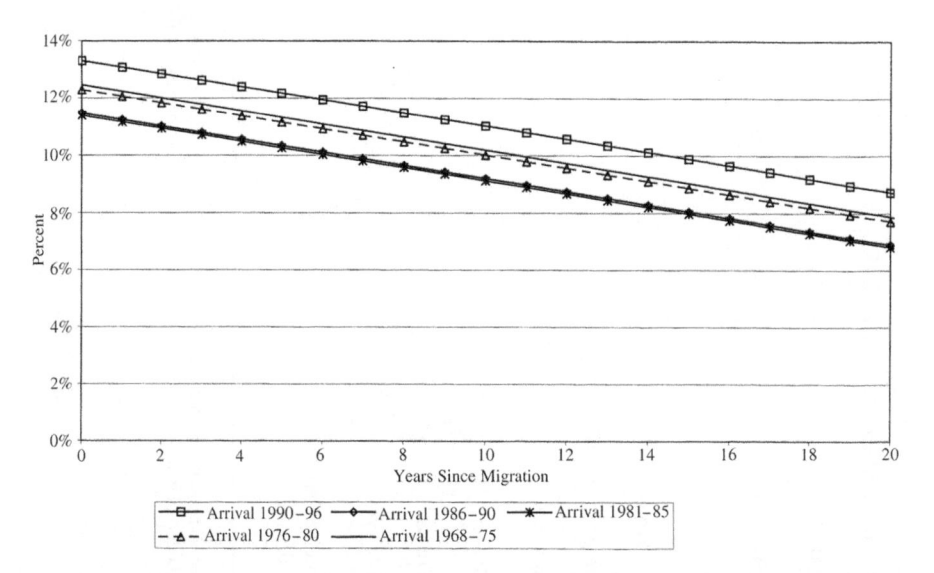

Figure 5
Predicted Differences in Welfare Participation between Native-Born Swedes and Immigrants from Nonrefugee Countries, by Arrival Cohort and Years Since Migration, Age at Migration = 18, 1996 Baseline
Note: Based on estimates presented in Table 4.

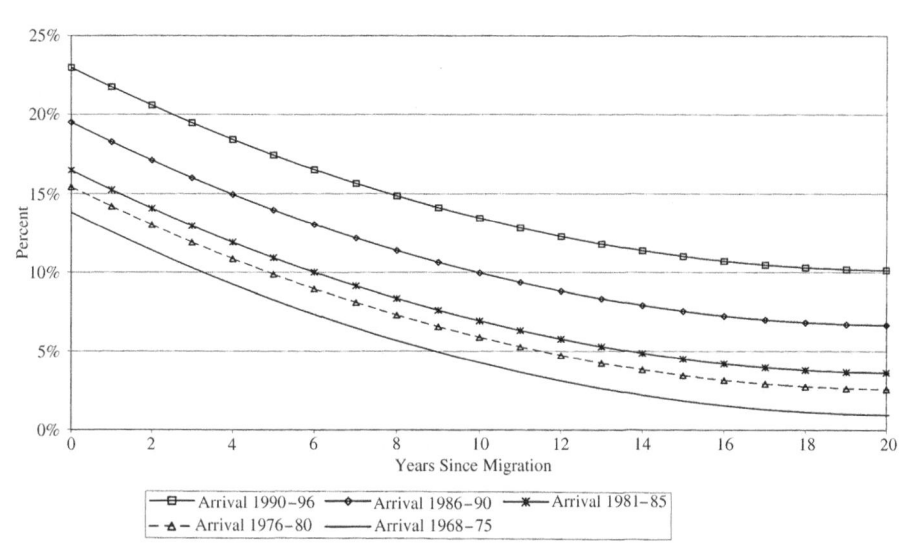

Figure 6
Predicted Differences in Welfare Participation between Native-Born Swedes and Immigrants from Refugee Countries, by Arrival Cohort and Years Since Migration, Age at Migration = 18, 1996 Baseline
Note: Based on estimates presented in Table 4.

imply differences of around 12 and 8 percentage points respectively.[14] This finding suggests that immigrants in a comparatively generous welfare state, like Sweden, display welfare-participation behavior similar to that of immigrants in less generous welfare states, like the United States, relative to natives after having spent some time in the new host country.

The model presented in Table 4 can be used to simulate effects of changes in immigration and unemployment on welfare-participation rates. The findings in this paper suggest that the increase in welfare participation is at least partially due to the increases in both immigration and unemployment, which Sweden experienced in the 1990s. To investigate how much these two factors contributed to the increase in social assistance utilization we predicted four time series of welfare participation. These are shown in Figure 7. Series 1 is derived based on the observed sample means of the included variables and the estimated parameters. Series 2 is derived in the same way, but we hold county unemployment rates constant at the observed 1990 levels. As expected, the deteriorating Swedish labor market is one of the reasons welfare-participation rates increased. However, changes in unemployment rates ex-

---

14. We used the estimated coefficients Borjas and Hilton (1996) report in Table 7 and the ones Baker and Benjamin (1995) report in Table 2 to calculate the predicted differences in participation rates. The predictions were calculated by assuming 20 years since migration for the most recent cohort and age at migration was set equal to 18 years. The models estimated by Benjamin and Baker (1995) do not control for age at migration.

[Figure 7: line chart showing welfare participation from 1990 to 1996, ranging from about 4% to 6%, with four series:
- Series 1: Observed Variation in Unemployment and Immigration
- Series 2: Constant Unemployment
- Series 3: Constant Unemployment and Proportion of Immigrants
- Series 4: Constant Unemployment and Immigration]

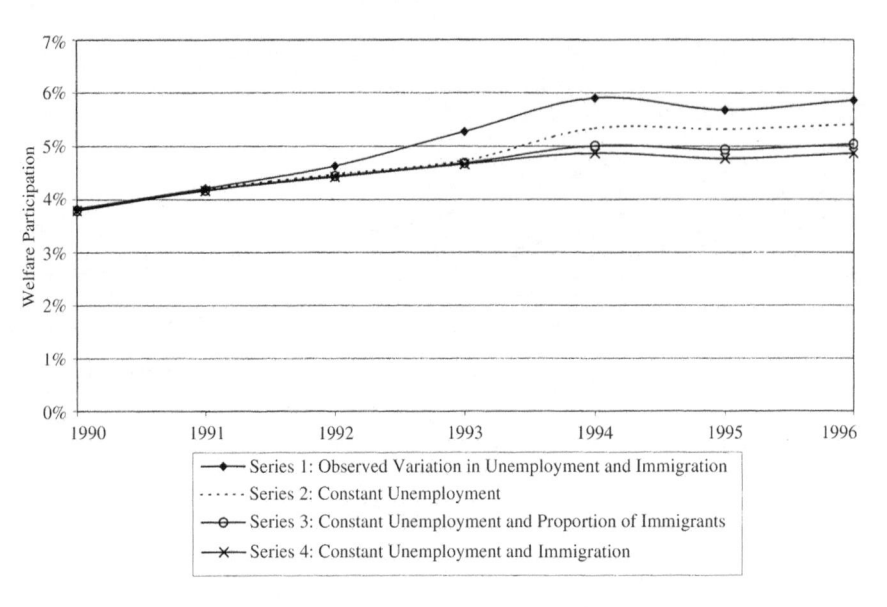

Figure 7
Simulated Welfare-Participation Series, with and without Changes in the County Unemployment Rates, the Proportion and the Composition of Immigrants
Note: Based on estimates presented in Table 4.

plain only about 20 percent of the increase between 1990 and 1996. As discussed above, the increase in immigration may also have contributed to the rise in welfare utilization. In Series 3, we hold constant both the unemployment rates and the proportion of immigrants in the population to the 1990 proportions. The result from this exercise suggests that 40 percent of the increase in welfare utilization rates between 1990 and 1996 stems from these two sources. In other words, the increase in immigration contributed as much to the upward trend as did the higher unemployment rates. In the last series, Series 4, we also hold constant the composition of immigrants. In other words, the proportion of immigrants who are Nordic from nonrefugee and refugee countries is held constant to the 1990 shares. This, too, appears to have had an impact on social assistance utilization. Altogether, the worsened labor market coupled with the increase, and the change, in composition in immigration explains about 50 percent of the higher welfare-participation rates observed in 1996, compared to 1990.[15]

---

15. Our results indicate that changes in unemployment and immigration cannot explain all of the observed increase in welfare participation, but only roughly half of the increase. An obvious question then is, what are some of the other factors that caused the social-assistance-participation rates to increase in the 1990s? Because we control for the generosity of the welfare system by including the welfare norm, in addition to the observation that benefit levels only increased slightly, changes in the social assistance rules are not a likely reason for the unexplained portion of the increase. Cost savings measures implemented due to budget concerns, however, affected other government transfer programs. For example, the unemployment benefits ratio for the largest unemployment insurance program in Sweden (*arbetslöshetskassa*) declined from 90 percent to 75 percent during the period studied here. For a given unemployment rate, the probability

VII. Conclusion and Summary

This paper analyzes differences in the welfare utilization between immigrants and natives in Sweden using a large panel data set, LINDA, for the years 1990 and 1996. Welfare expenditure in Sweden, as with many western countries, increased substantially in the 1990s. Closely linked to the increase in welfare costs in Sweden is an increase in immigration. In this paper we find that immigrants use welfare to a greater extent than natives use it. Furthermore, nonrefugee immigrants utilize social assistance less than refugee immigrants. Differences in welfare participation between immigrants and natives cannot be explained by observable socioeconomic characteristics.

Immigrants appear to reduce their welfare-participation rates with time spent in Sweden in both an absolute sense, as well as relative to natives. Although refugees display substantially higher public-assistance-participation rates upon arrival in Sweden compared with nonrefugee immigrants, they assimilate out of welfare at a faster rate than nonrefugee immigrants. However, it should be noted that neither group is predicted to reach the participation rates of native households within a 20-year period in Sweden. We also find that approximately 50 percent of the observed increase in welfare utilization in Sweden in the 1990s can be attributed to the increases in both unemployment and immigration, as well as to the increase in the proportion of refugees in the immigrant population.

Immigration has been at the heart of welfare debates in many countries in the 1990s. Due to the continued increase in immigration in many countries such as the United States, Germany, and Sweden, this is unlikely to change anytime soon. Given the rapid decrease in welfare utilization of immigrants, particularly refugees, with time spent in the new country, the welfare cost upon arrival should not be used to make long-term prediction of welfare costs caused by immigration. However, immigrants are overrepresented among the welfare population even after observable characteristics are controlled for. This suggests that in future research it is important to analyze why this is the case. One question that arises is: Are immigrants' observable skills not recognized to the same extent as natives' skills in the Swedish labor market or do immigrants have higher reservation wages?

References

Baker, Michael, and Dwayne Benjamin. 1995. "The Receipt of Transfer Payments by Immigrants to Canada." *Journal of Human Resources* 30(4):650–76.

Bean, Frank D., Jennifer V.W. Van Hook, and Jennifer E. Glick. 1997. "Country of Origin, Type of Public Assistance, and Patterns of Welfare Recipiency among U.S. Immigrants and Natives." *Social Science Quarterly* 78(2):432–51.

Betts, Julian R., and Magnus Lofstrom. 2000. "The Educational Attainment of Immigrants: Trends and Implications." In *Issues in the Economics of Immigration*, ed. George J. Borjas, 51–115. Chicago: University of Chicago Press.

---

a household will apply and receive welfare is higher in 1996 than it was in 1990. Hence, the less generous unemployment compensation program is likely to have increased participation in social assistance.

Blau, Francine D. 1984. "The Use of Transfer Payments by Immigrants." *Industrial and Labor Relations Review* 37(2):222–39.

Borjas, George J. 1985. "Assimilation Changes in Cohort Quality and the Earnings of Immigrants." *Journal of Labor Economics* 3(4):463–89.

———. 1994."The Economics of Immigration." *Journal of Economic Literature* (32)4: 1667–717.

Borjas, George J., and Stephen J. Trejo. 1991. "Immigrant Participation in the Welfare System." *Industrial and Labor Relations Review* 44(2):195–211.

———. 1993. "National Origin and Immigrant Welfare Recipiency." *Journal of Public Economics* 50(3):325–44.

Borjas, George J., and Lynette Hilton. 1996. "Immigration and the Welfare State: Immigrant Participation in Means-Tested Entitlement Programs." *Quarterly Journal of Economics* 111(2):575–604.

Crossley, Thomas F., James Ted McDonald, and Christopher Worswick. 2001. "Immigrant Benefit Receipt Revisited: Sensitivity of the Choice of Survey Years and Model Specification." *Journal of Human Resources* 36(2):379–97.

Edin, Per-Anders, and Peter Fredriksson. 2000. "LINDA—Longitudinal Individual Data for Sweden." Working Paper Number 19, Department of Economics. Uppsala, Sweden: Uppsala University.

Edin, Per-Anders, Robert J. LaLonde, and Olof Aslund. 2000. "Emigration of Immigrants and Measures of Immigrants Assimilation: Evidence from Sweden." *Swedish Economic Policy Review* (7)2:163–204.

Maani, Sholeh A. 1993. "Immigrants and the Use of Government Transfer Payments." *Australian Economic Review* 0(104):65–76.

Riphanh, Regina T. 1998. "Immigrant Participation in Social Assistance Programs: Evidence from German Guestworkers." IZA Discussion Paper Series No. 15. Bonn, Germany.

SOPEMI. 1998. *Trends in International Migration*. Paris: Organization for Economic Cooperation and Development.

Educational attainment: analysis by immigrant generation

Barry R. Chiswick *, Noyna DebBurman

Department of Economics (M/C 144), University of Illinois at Chicago, 601 South Morgan Street, Chicago, IL 60607-7121, USA

Received 21 February 2003; accepted 9 September 2003

Abstract

This paper presents a theoretical and empirical analysis of the largely ignored issue of the determinants of the educational attainment of adults by immigrant generation. Using current population survey (CPS) data, differences in educational attainment are analyzed by immigrant generation (first, second, and higher order generations), and among the foreign born by country of birth and age at immigration. Second-generation American adults have the highest level of schooling, exceeding that of the foreign born and of the native born with native-born parents. Teenage immigration is associated with fewer years of schooling compared to those who immigrated at pre-teen or post-teen ages. The gender difference in educational attainment is greatest among the foreign born. Hispanics and Blacks lag behind the non-Hispanic Whites in their educational attainment, with the gap narrowing for higher order immigrant generations among Hispanics, but rising among blacks.
© 2003 Elsevier Ltd. All rights reserved.

JEL classification: I21; J24; J61

Keywords: Demand for schooling; Human capital; Immigrants

1. Introduction

Immigration is a controversial labor and social issue in the United States, with significant impacts on present and future US education. The pattern of immigration in the last few decades coupled with the tendency for ethnic differences in education attainment to persist over subsequent immigrant generations has led to an increasing gap in educational attainment between some of the fastest growing immigrant communities in the United States, and with the native-born population. At the same time, long-term structural changes in the US economy have markedly increased the importance of education, making high-school completion a minimum requirement for any individual to compete successfully in the labor market. Thus, educational institutions in the US today are faced with a two-fold issue: one, to educate a larger and more diverse population and, two, to bridge the gap in educational attainment among the various ethnic groups. Immigration is also poised to strongly impact the future of US education, as immigrants and children of immigrants increasingly account for a larger proportion of school age children, highlighting the need to better understand the educational attainment of immigrants.

This study makes a significant contribution to the immigration literature by conducting a systematic analysis of schooling acquisition by immigrant generation. In addition, this research also examines the effects of country of origin and age at immigration on immigrant education. A growing body of literature on the economic assimilation of immigrants has focused on human capital transfer, human capital investment, and the labor market adjustment of immigrants. Research on immigrant educational attainment is a fairly recent phenomenon. A persistent limitation is that most studies fail to distinguish between the different generations of US residence. Second-generation immigrants (i.e. those born in the US

---
* Corresponding author. Tel.: +1-312-996-2683; fax: +1-312-996-3344.
E-mail address: brchis@uic.edu (B.R. Chiswick).

of one or two immigrant parents) are typically grouped together either with first-generation immigrants (i.e. those who are immigrants themselves) or with native-parentage adults and children (i.e. those who are US born with US born parents).

Several reasons exist why an analysis by immigrant generation is crucial in understanding immigrant educational attainment. First, a continuous influx of immigrants into the US in the past three decades has resulted in a significant proportion of the US population today being comprised of second-generation Americans (i.e. children of immigrants), and this proportion will continue to grow in the foreseeable future. Second, while first-generation immigrants receive little or none of their education in the United States, second-generation immigrants, and native-parentage adults receive all their education in the United States. Third, the second-generation immigrants are a distinct group: they are born in the United States, but unlike native-parentage adults, immigrant influences through their parents play a crucial role in the formation of their human capital. An examination of educational attainment by immigrant generation will enable us to understand if educational differentials decrease with each successive generation, and will help recognize the intergenerational impact of ethnic background on educational outcomes.

For adult immigrants, education typically has two components—schooling completed in the home country prior to immigration, and schooling acquired in the destination country after immigration. Three studies on post-immigration schooling investment of immigrants stand out. Borjas (1982) and Hashmi (1987) have examined the determinants of post-immigration investment in education in the United States, and Chiswick and Miller (1994) have conducted a similar study for Australia.[1] Both of the US based studies have focused on men alone. But while Hashmi examined foreign-born men between 18 and 64 years, who migrated at age 15 and above, Borjas limited his analysis to Hispanic male immigrants between 18 and 64 years. Moreover, a limitation of both of these studies is that the datasets used necessitated that years of schooling in the United States be measured as a residual.[2] Chiswick and Miller's (1994) analysis is more comprehensive since they analyzed the determinants of post-migration investment for all adult (age 25 to 64) immigrants in Australia and used data that provided explicit information on pre- and post-migration schooling.

The goal of this study is to focus on total schooling acquired (a stock concept) by adult immigrants rather than on post-migration investment in schooling (a flow concept). Unlike the earlier US related studies, the research presented here includes both men and women, revealing any existing pattern in gender differences, if they exist. This study also expands on the existing literature specifically through its analysis by immigrant generation, and by age at immigration.

This paper proceeds as follows. Section 2 reviews the literature on immigrant education. Section 3 discusses the theory of human capital investment and the theory of demand for schooling, and uses them as a basis to formulate a theoretical model for studying immigrant schooling attainment. Section 4 describes the October 1995 Current Population Survey, the dataset used for this study, as well as the estimating equations. The estimation results are described in Section 5. Finally, conclusions and policy implications are summarized in the last section.

2. Review of literature

It is easiest to classify the existing literature on immigrant educational attainment into two broad group based on the research methodology and/or discipline. Anthropologists and sociologists have led the major work in this field and form the first group, while in more recent years, economists have also become engaged to form the second group.

Among sociologists and anthropologists, two theories have dominated their research on educational attainment of US immigrants: the cultural discontinuity theory and the cultural ecology theory. Proponents of the cultural discontinuity theory believe that immigrant youth are disadvantaged due to language, cultural, and social interactional conflicts between home and school (Carter & Segura, 1979; Trueba, 1987; Perlmann, 1988). In their studies, they find that immigrant attainment increases with increased duration of stay in the US and more acculturation to American society. On the other hand, cultural-ecological theorists believe that immigrant attainment is affected by a complex interaction of multiple factors, that include motivation to immigrate, perceptions of opportunity, and labor market payoff for attainment (Ogbu, 1978, 1987; Ogbu & Matute-Bianchi, 1986). These latter theorists propose that ethnicity and generation together determine educational attainment. However, more recently, some studies have produced findings that do not always fully agree with one or the

---

[1] A condensed version of Hashmi's 1987 analysis is reported in her later paper, Khan (1997).

[2] The Survey of Income and Education used by both Borjas (1982) and Hashmi (1987), provided information on total years of schooling and pre-immigration schooling, with post-migration schooling estimated as total minus pre-immigration schooling. Hashmi (1987) also used the 1980 Census data and based on the assumption of continuous school attendance from age 6, post-migration schooling was calculated as total years of schooling minus age at migration (which is current age minus years since migration). Such procedures are likely to impart a negative correlation between measured post-migration years of schooling and measured pre-migration schooling.

other of these two theories, nevertheless they represent important advances and are described below.

Several key studies specify that immigrant generation plays an important role in educational attainment and school performance (Portes & Rumbaut, 1990; Rong & Grant, 1992; Kao & Tienda, 1995). Usually, second-generation youth perform better academically (academic achievement was measured by middle school grades and standardized math and reading test scores) than first-generation youth or native born youth. But, first-generation youth who immigrate at very young ages often exhibit educational attainment similar to those attained by the second-generation youth. Most such studies also point out substantial effects of ethnicity on educational attainment (Rong & Grant, 1992; Kao, Tienda, & Schneider, 1996). Asians outperform other groups in attainment (Hirschman & Wong, 1986; Lee & Rong, 1988). Hispanic students, in particular, have lower achievement levels and higher dropout rates, compared to Asians and non-Hispanic whites (Arias, 1986; Velez, 1989). Furthermore, Rong and Grant (1992) examined the combined effects of immigrant generation and ethnicity on educational attainment. Their study found that immigrant generation affects youth educational attainment, but this influence is not consistent across generations and ethnicity.

Although their foray into immigration research has been more recent, economists have made significant contributions focusing on two aspects of educational attainment: one, post-migration schooling of immigrants (Schultz, 1984; Hashmi, 1987; Khan, 1997; Chiswick & Miller, 1994; Chiswick & Sullivan, 1995); and two, patterns of the education attained by immigrants in their country of origin (Funkhouser & Trejo, 1995; Cohen, Zach, & Chiswick, 1997). The key findings that have emerged from the post-migration schooling literature is that age at immigration coupled with duration of residence in the host country is a primary determinant of investment in schooling. Chiswick (1978) indicates that immigrants tend to make their largest human capital investments within the first few years of arriving in the host country. Moreover, as the duration of residence in the US increases, the years of post-migration schooling increases, but at decreasing rate (Chiswick & Miller, 1994; Khan, 1997). Most studies of post-migration investment agree that in English-speaking destinations, foreign-born people from non-English speaking countries invest more in post-migration schooling than the foreign-born from English-speaking countries (Chiswick & Miller, 1994; Khan, 1997; Duleep & Regets, 1999; Cobb-Clark, Connolly, & Worswick, 2000). Furthermore, human capital investments in the destination tend to be lower when the cost of to-and-from migration to the home country is low (Borjas, 1982; Chiswick & Miller, 1994; Duleep & Regets, 1999).

Recently, several new studies have had considerable impact on our understanding of post-migration schooling. Schaafsma and Sweetman (1999) investigated the impact of age at immigration on educational attainment in Canada. They found that educational attainment varies systematically by age at immigration: immigrants arriving when they are between ages 15–18 acquire less total education than those who immigrate at a younger or older age. According to the authors, "adjusting to a new environment near the transition out of high school may have a permanent effect". Furthermore, Gang and Zimmerman (1999) indicated that the gap in educational attainment between immigrants in Germany and their comparable German-born cohort is much smaller in the second-generation compared to the gap in the first-generation, implying that assimilation exists in the acquisition of education. This finding is in line with Schultz (1984) and Betts and Lofstrom (2000), who found that the schooling level of children of immigrants in the US converges toward that of the children of natives.

The studies on patterns of educational attainment indicate that the schooling level of immigrants to the US exceeds the national average (Portes & Rumbaut, 1990). In studying immigrant cohorts, Borjas (1987) described a decline in the schooling level of immigrants in the 1970s, but Cohen, Zach and Chiswick (1997) found that during the 1980s, this trend had stopped and had been reversed.

Despite a growing body of literature on educational attainment, limitations persist. This paper is one of the few attempts in the literature that provides testable hypotheses which relate exclusively to the total schooling acquisition of immigrants at a national level. Moreover, it will extend previous studies by analyzing educational attainment by country of origin, by age at immigration and by immigrant generation.

3. Theory and hypotheses

This study draws on the theory of investment in human capital developed by Schultz (1961) and Becker (1964). Human capital theory assumes that individuals invest in human capital in order to maximize their net wealth. Becker employed the investment framework primarily to analyze educational attainment and the rate of return to education for individuals. Chiswick, 1978, 1979) extended Becker's human capital framework substantially through its application to studying labor market aspects of immigration. This modified human capital model has since been instrumental in analyzing the process of immigrant adjustment in the host-country labor market.

Chiswick (1978) was the first to argue that, for the same number of years of schooling, the ability to convert schooling into earnings might differ between the foreign-born and the native-born. This argument implied that immigrants would be unable to transfer completely the human capital accumulated in their home country to the labor market of the destination country. To analyze this aspect of immigration, Chiswick developed the phrase 'international transferability of skills'. International transferability of skills can be viewed as a function of similarities in the labor markets of the home country and the host country, schooling and language being two important indicators. Schooling has two components — an origin-specific component and an internationally transferable component. The importance of these two components differs by the level and the type of education attained by immigrants. The more general the skills acquired through schooling in the origin, the greater the transferability to the destination and hence the smaller the decline in value of skills upon migration.

The human capital investment framework discussed above is appropriate for testing hypothesis related to different types of human capital investments, such as migration, schooling and on-the-job training. Therefore, this study uses the human capital framework for analyzing educational attainment and school enrollment. Within this framework, attention is focused on factors that affect the demand for schooling, particularly in the context of immigrants.

Becker (1967) developed a model of optimal schooling. The model's underlying assumption is that individuals face a demand schedule, which reflects the marginal rate of return on investments in schooling, and a supply schedule, which reflects the marginal interest cost of obtaining funds to finance the investment in schooling. Optimal investment occurs when the marginal rate of return on investment equals the marginal interest cost of funds. Chiswick (1988) reinterpreted Becker's model in the broader context of racial and ethnic groups. Chiswick argued that group differences in investment in schooling might arise from either differences in demand conditions, or differences in supply conditions, or from their combination. He further maintained that group differences in demand conditions vary more than group differences in the supply conditions, which in turn implies a positive relationship between levels of schooling and rates of return from schooling.

The main hypothesis that emerges from the preceding discussion is that the demand for schooling is determined by economic incentives. An increase in the costs associated with schooling will cause individuals to substitute away from education, while an increase in the benefits from schooling will increase its demand. Based on the above discussion, the theoretical demand for schooling equation for immigrants can be expressed as a function of both pre-immigration conditions and the post-migration experience of immigrants.

Pre-immigration conditions and post-migration experience play vital roles in immigrant schooling investment decisions because they affect the level, and the transferability of skills that immigrants bring with them. While pre-immigration conditions include age at immigration, country of origin, and pre-immigration educational attainment, post-migration experience is associated with immigrant duration in the destination country.

For the foreign-born, total schooling has two components — schooling acquired before, and schooling acquired after migration. Hashmi (1987) and Borjas (1982) have examined post-migration investment in schooling by immigrants in the United States. While their studies represented important advances on the subject, a serious limitation of both the studies was the need to estimate years of schooling in the United States as a residual since such a procedure is likely to impart a negative correlation between measured post-migration years of schooling and measured pre-migration schooling. The datasets used for this study do not provide direct information on the division between pre-immigration schooling and post-migration schooling either. Therefore, based on the assumption of continuous school attendance from age 6, post-migration schooling would have to be calculated as total years of schooling minus age at migration (which is current age minus years since migration). Using this procedure to study post-migration schooling would not resolve any of the bias inherent in the existing studies of Hashmi and Borjas. Hence, this study focuses on total schooling, a relatively unexplored area rather than on post-migration investment in schooling. Moreover, often people first decide on the total level of schooling they will attain, and then decide on the location of their schooling. Consequently, the decision between pre- versus post-migration schooling becomes an endogenous one, which further justifies our study of total schooling.

For adult immigrants, age at arrival affects the costs of and returns from human capital investment. First, the older the age at immigration, the higher the opportunity costs associated with schooling (due to investment in the origin country).[3] Second, the older the age at immigration, the shorter the duration in the host country to receive benefits from investment in destination-specific skills. These factors make migration as well as investment in post-migration schooling more profitable for younger immigrants compared to older immigrants. This profitability in turn, implies that the enrollment in schooling in the destination will fall with age at migration, and holding age constant, with duration in the destination. Consequently, total schooling increases with

---

[3] There are two costs associated with post-migration investment in schooling — the direct cost of schooling in the United States, and the indirect foregone earnings in the country of origin. Testing the effect of age on post-migration education provides an indirect index of the opportunity cost of foregone earnings, and this approach is used in this study.

age at a decreasing rate. While immigration at an early age is considered beneficial, recent evidence also points to a lower return to schooling for those immigrating in their late teens compared to those immigrating at a slightly younger or older age. Country of origin differences among immigrants arise from differences in the propensity for return migration. The higher the propensity for return migration, the lower is the incentive for immigrants to invest in education for themselves or their children that are destination specific. Moreover, the relation (substitute or complement) between pre-immigration and post-immigration schooling influences the total level of schooling attained in the destination country.[4]

Post-migration experience measured by duration in the destination is a particularly important index of the economic adjustment of immigrants. Whether or not an immigrant invests in destination specific schooling depends on some of the factors discussed earlier. However, if post-migration investments are made, they occur in the first few years after immigration and diminish thereafter (Hashmi, 1987). This arises because of three reasons. One, investments that are profitable tend to yield greater returns the earlier they are made. Two, the sooner such investments are made, the lower is the opportunity cost of time since earnings rise with length of stay. Lastly, a delay in investment results in a shorter remaining working life in which to receive benefits from the investment. This investment pattern implies that the total level of schooling attained increases at a decreasing rate with an increased duration in the destination, and that current enrollment rates decrease with duration.

Based on the theoretical model discussed above, the following hypotheses have been developed.

The model of immigrant adjustment based on human capital theory suggests that the economic status of immigrants improves with their duration of stay, i.e. immigrant assimilation in the host country is positively related to length of stay. The assimilation literature focuses on the effect of duration of residence in the destination country on immigrant assimilation in the host country. Implicit in the concept of 'assimilation' is the impact of immigrant generation, if we further distinguish between the native-born who have at least one foreign-born parent (second-generation immigrants) and the native-born who have two native-born parents (native-parentage). Second-generation immigrants will likely out-achieve first-generation immigrants because the former possess more destination specific skills. Second-generation immigrants may out-achieve native-parentage immigrants due to the positive influence of foreign-born parents arising from the selectivity bias in migration, which implies that immigrants tend to be disproportionately high ability or highly motivated people (Chiswick, 1977, 1999).

Hypothesis 1. Among immigrants, educational attainment will differ by immigrant generation. The second-generation of immigrants (children of immigrants) will exhibit higher educational attainment than the first-generation and may receive more schooling than those with native born parents.

Language is an important component affecting transferability of skills since the lower the immigrant's fluency in the destination language, the lower the transferability of the origin country skills. Furthermore, the lower an immigrant's transferability of skills, the greater the incentive to invest in destination specific human capital because of the positive effect that destination country education has on increasing the transferability of origin-country skills.

Hypothesis 2. Among immigrants, educational attainment will differ by country of origin. Immigrants to the US from non-English speaking countries will exhibit a higher demand for investments specific to the US, but will be handicapped by their lesser proficiency in English.

Age at immigration affects labor market outcomes both directly and indirectly. The direct impact of age at immigration on labor market outcomes is easily explained in terms of costs and benefits. A higher age at immigration is associated with a higher opportunity cost of schooling and job training (due to previous investment) coupled with a shorter remaining working life in the destination labor market to receive benefits. The direct impact of age at immigration is due to schooling and labor market experience in the source country not being recognized as equivalent to schooling and experience in the host country. The indirect impact of age at immigration stems from the fact that younger immigrants are more able to adjust to linguistic and cultural challenges associated with migrating to a new country. For example, children have a superior ability to acquire new language skills, and this diminishes with age. Moreover, the complementarity between destination language and other forms of human capital (schooling) also suggests that youth will accrue more benefits from

---

[4] Total schooling acquired may be affected by pre-immigration schooling in two ways. One is the quantity measure of pre-immigration schooling, which is years of schooling completed in the origin. Two, holding quantity constant, the quality of pre-immigration schooling may differ by country of origin. For example, the knowledge acquired through 10 years of schooling in Mexico could be quite different from the same number of years of schooling in Sweden. In general, education systems in some countries are known to be more rigorous than others. While the importance of quality of pre-immigration schooling cannot be denied, it is difficult to obtain data measures of schooling by country-of-origin that would account for such differences, therefore, it is beyond the scope of this work to investigate the qualitative effects of pre-immigration schooling on total schooling, other than through dichotomous country of origin (fixed effects) variables.

undertaking any destination specific investment (Chiswick and Miller, forthcoming). In light of these effects, we can expect post-migration years of schooling (a component of total schooling) to fall with age at immigration.[5]

Hypothesis 3. Educational attainment will vary with age at immigration. Specifically, post–migration educational attainment will tend to fall with age at immigration, and fall at a decreasing rate.

4. Data and estimating equations

The empirical analysis discussed in this paper is based on data from the October 1995 Current Population Survey. The Current Population Survey (CPS) is a monthly survey of about 57,000 households conducted by the Bureau of the Census for the Bureau of Labor Statistics (US Bureau of the Census, 1995). Respondents are interviewed to obtain information about the employment status of each member of the household 15 years of age and older. Each household is interviewed once a month for 4 consecutive months over 1 year, and again for the corresponding time period a year later. Each month new households are added and old ones are dropped and thus part of the sample is changed. The CPS sample is scientifically selected on the basis of area of residence to represent the nation as a whole, individual states, and other specified areas. The unit of observation in the CPS is the household, but the data are collected on each household member.

The basic CPS provides information on employment, unemployment, earnings, hours of work, and other labor force indicators on all household members above 16 years old. Such data are available by a variety of demographic characteristics including age, sex, race, marital status, and educational attainment. In addition to the basic demographic and labor force questions, questions on selected topics (school enrollment, income, employee benefits, and work schedules) are included as supplements to the regular CPS questionnaire in various monthly surveys. These supplemental topics are usually repeated in the same month each year. Information on immigrant year of entry to United States and information on a respondent's parental place of birth is vital to this study. Only the post-1994 CPS surveys provide this information, and the October 1995 CPS was used for this study. The question used for defining the dependent variable, educational attainment was as follows: What is the highest level of school completed or the highest degree received by the person? Sixteen response categories exist: less than 1st grade, grades 1 to 4, two categories for middle school, five categories for high school, four categories for college, and, three categories for graduate school. The remaining variable definitions are provided in Table A1 in the Appendix.

4.1. The sample

The total sample size of the 1995 CPS was 148,392 individuals. For this study, the non-interviewed records from the sample were excluded, reducing the sample size to 134,946 individuals. The study of educational attainment was conducted for all adults between 25 and 64 years. The relevant sample size was 69,746. The population studied was first-generation immigrant adults, second-generation immigrant adults, and native-parentage adults. 'First-generation immigrant adults' were defined as those adults born outside the United States, who immigrated either as children or as adults. 'Second-generation immigrants adults' were defined as those adults born in the US, but having one or both foreign-born parents. 'Native-parentage adults' were defined as those adults born in the US of US-born parents. Adults born in outlying areas of the United States, such as Puerto Rico, as well as adults born of American parents living abroad were excluded from this analysis. Also excluded were adults who have both parents born in Puerto Rico and other US outlying areas. The size of the first-generation adult sample was 7496; that of the second-generation adult sample 4506, and native-parentage adult sample 56,483. Therefore, the pooled sample size was 68,485. The data on period of immigration are for when the person first came to the United States to stay. The visa under which the respondent entered or the motive for migration are not known. It is therefore not possible to identify those first-generation immigrants who entered the United States on student visas.

4.2. The estimating equation

The explanatory variables in the educational attainment equation were of the following types: human capital variables (age, years since immigration), control variables (marital status, south, MSA, black, hispanic, and male), and country of origin variables.

The basic estimating equation for educational attainment was written as:

Educational attainment = $f(\mathbf{H}, \mathbf{D}, \mathbf{G}, \mathbf{C})$.

H is a vector of human capital variables, including age and age at immigration. *Age* is expected to have a positive impact on educational attainment. To test the rate of increase of educational attainment with age, age

---

[5] Another variable that reflects post-migration investment in schooling is the current enrollment status of the immigrant. While the importance of analyzing current enrollment status in a study of educational attainment is recognized, it is beyond the scope of this work.

squared was introduced into the estimating equation.[6] *Years since migration* (YSM) measures the number of years that an immigrant has resided in the host country. *Age at immigration* (AGEIMMIG) captures the impact of immigration at different ages. There are three concepts of age important in the context of the foreign-born: current age of an immigrant, age at the time of immigration, and years since migration. The three age variables are, however, collinear—therefore, given any two of them in the regression, the effect of the third can be calculated.

For ease of interpretation, this study used the variables, AGE, AGE^2, and AGEIMIG, AGEIMIG^2. As an immigrant's length of stay in the US (YSM) increases, his stock of investment in US schooling increases, but at a decreasing rate. Therefore, holding age constant, as age at immigration increases, post-migration educational attainment is expected to fall, but at a decreasing rate. Furthermore, following Schaafsma and Sweetman's (1999) decomposition of age at immigration into several age at immigration classes, in an immigrant earnings analysis for Canada, this study incorporates eight age at immigration dummy variables (e.g. age at immigration: 0 to 4, 5 to 12, and so on) to capture the differing effects of immigration over particular age ranges.

D is a vector of demographic control variables for gender, marital status, and race/ethnicity. Dichotomous variables for being *Black* and *Hispanic* were used to measure the impact of racial disadvantage on educational attainment, *male* was used to control for gender differentials in educational attainment, *married* captures the effect of being married as distinct from other marital statuses. **G** is a vector of geographic variables. Dichotomous variables, *south*, representing south/non-south residence, and *MSA*, representing metropolitan/non-metropolitan residence, controls for the effect of region of residence and urbanization on educational attainment, respectively.

C is a vector of country of origin dummy variables to capture country fixed effects, including the impact of the transferability of skills and motive for migration. Based on the assumption that economic migrants from English speaking developed countries possess highly transferable skills, the benchmark group created for the country of origin analysis was English-speaking developed countries. Other countries were clustered into broad groups to represent economic migrants from certain major non-English speaking countries and also refugee migrants from other countries. When applying the estimating equation to the pooled sample of native-born and foreign-born, native-born was the benchmark in the **C** vector, so a dichotomous variable for the English-speaking countries was added to the equation.

5. Empirical analysis

5.1. Summary statistics

Comparative statistics for all adult (25–64 year old) natives, and first- and second-generation immigrants are summarized in Table 1. An average first-generation immigrant is 41 years of age, has 11.8 years of schooling, and has been in the United States for about 16 years. The average second-generation immigrant is 45 years of age, and has an education level of 13.7 years, in contrast to the native parentage age of 42 years and 13.5 years of schooling. Furthermore, the natives are more southern (38%) than either the first-generation or second-generation (24% each). Compared to 22% of native-parentage living in non-metropolitan areas, only 11% of second generation immigrants and even fewer (5%) first-generation immigrants live in non- metropolitan areas. The first-generation has a large percentage of Hispanics (47%) compared to the second-generation (20%) and native-parentage (3%) adults.

5.2. Regression analysis

This section first discusses the pooled sample of first-generation, second generation, and native-parentage adults. Separate regressions by immigrant generation in the next three sub-sections allow a comparative study of the determinants of educational attainment between the three groups. The first-generation sample also allows us to study educational attainment by different countries of origin, and different ages at immigration.

5.2.1. Pooled sample

Ordinary least square regressions were run using the 1995 CPS data. The dependent variable for the regression equation was years of schooling, referred to as 'educational attainment'. Three different specifications of the equation were considered. The primary explanatory variables used in all three specifications were male, age, age squared, Black, Hispanic, married, south, non-MSA, age at immigration and age at immigration squared. The basic specification (column 1 in Table 2) was a simple model, which used the abovementioned set of demographic and geographic variables as the explanatory variables along with the two immigrant generation variables. The second specification (column 2 in Table 2) added birthplace dummy variables to the set of explanatory variables. The last specification (column 3 in Table 2) deleted the quadratic age at immi-

---

[6] The age variable captures two effects—one, the cohort effect (younger cohorts acquire more education) and two, the life cycle effect (education increases with age in the life cycle). Due to the secular increase in schooling, beyond a certain point the negative cohort effect of an older age dominates the positive life cycle effect.

Table 1
Means and standard deviations of variables, first-generation, second-generation, and native-parentage adults, United States, 1995

Variable	First-generation	Second-generation	Native-parentage
Educational attainment	11.81 (4.24)	13.68 (2.67)	13.46 (2.44)
Male	0.49 (0.50)	0.50 (0.50)	0.49 (0.50)
Age	40.85 (10.65)	44.46 (11.95)	41.71 (10.54)
Black	0.07 (0.26)	0.02 (0.14)	0.13 (0.34)
Hispanic	0.47 (0.50)	0.20 (0.40)	0.03 (0.16)
Married	0.72 (0.45)	0.67 (0.47)	0.67 (0.47)
South	0.24 (0.43)	0.23 (0.42)	0.38 (0.48)
Non-MSA	0.05 (0.22)	0.11 (0.31)	0.22 (0.42)
Age at immigration	24.79 (11.07)	n.a.	n.a.
Sample size	7496	4506	56,483

Source: Current Population Survey, United States Bureau of the Census, October 1995. Variables are as defined in Table A1. n.a., Variable not applicable. Standard deviations are in parentheses.

gration variables, but added age at immigration dummy variables as regressors.

We first discuss the analysis of the pooled sample of native-born and foreign-born population. Focusing on model (1) of the regression for the total pooled population, the positive sign of age coupled with the negative sign of age squared shows an increase in education with age, but at a decreasing rate. The peak occurs at 32.5 years, after which the effect of age on education becomes negative. The age variable captures two effects—one, the cohort effect, which implies that younger cohorts acquire more education, and two, the life cycle effect, which implies that education increases with age in the life cycle within a cohort. Apparently, beyond age 32.5 years, the negative cohort effect dominates the positive life cycle effect.

The effect of foreign birth on educational attainment (irrespective of the country of origin) is given jointly by the coefficients of variable 'first-generation' and the variables on 'age at immigration'.[7] The negative and positive coefficients of age at immigration and age at immigration squared, respectively, indicate that educational attainment decreases with age at immigration, and it decreases at a decreasing rate. Evaluated for different values of age at immigration, the partial effect of being a first-generation immigrant on educational attainment is: 0.52 years for age at immigration = 1, 0.23 years for age at immigration = 5, −0.01 years for age at immigration = 10, −0.47 years for age at immigration = 20, and −0.86 years for age at immigration = 30. Clearly, the effect of foreign-birth (being a first-generation immigrant) on educational attainment depends on age at immigration. Only those immigrating at a very early age will have attainment levels similar to their native counterparts. However, the positive coefficient of second-generation clearly indicates that second-generation immigrants acquire 0.47 years more of total schooling than native-parentage adults.

The remaining coefficients in the estimating equation are all highly significant. Men attain 0.14 years more of education than women. Being black reduces educational attainment by 0.69 years, and being Hispanic decreases educational attainment by a very large 2.59 years. Residence in the southern states or in a non-metropolitan area is associated with a negative impact on educational attainment. Being married is associated with 0.31 more years of education.

The second specification (Table 2, column 2) included the usual explanatory variables plus the country variables representing all countries of origin. The benchmark was native-parentage adults, hence holding all other coefficients constant, the coefficients represent the difference in education between first-generation immigrants from a particular country and native-parentage adults. The coefficients indicate that Africans, South Asians, and North and West Europeans acquire 3 years more education, and Philippines, East Asians, East and Central Europeans and Middle-Easterners about 2 more years compared to all native-parentage adults. Cubans, Chinese and immigrants from English-speaking countries acquire between 1.0 and 1.5 years more of education compared to native-parentage adults. The positive differential is negligible for immigrants from South and Central America.

---

[7] If Education = ... + b_1(first - generation) + b_2(Ageimmig) × (first - generation) + b_3 (Ageimmig)^2 × (first - generation) + ..., then taking derivatives, δ(Education)/δ(first - generation) = b_1 + b_2 (Ageimmig) + b_3 (Ageimmig)^2.

[8] This finding for Southern Europe is consistent with the Miller and Volker (1989) finding for Australia that immigrants from these countries were more focused on their children's education than on their own educational attainment.

Table 2
Regression estimates of pooled sample of first-generation, second-generation, and native-parentage adults, United States, 1995. Dependent variable: Educational attainment

Variable	(1)	(2)[a]	(3)[a]
Constant	11.408 (71.14)	11.500 (73.26)	11.49 (71.55)
Male	0.136 (6.91)	0.149 (7.74)	0.137 (6.98)
Age	0.136 (17.74)	0.129 (17.22)	0.131 (17.14)
Age^2	−0.002 (21.28)	−0.002 (20.82)	−0.002 (20.70)
Black	−0.689 (20.36)	−0.688 (20.56)	−0.688 (20.34)
Hispanic	−2.586 (59.16)	−1.317 (23.69)	−2.548 (58.21)
Married	0.306 (14.14)	0.322 (15.22)	0.306 (14.17)
South	0.278 (12.63)	−0.301 (13.94)	−0.280 (2.76)
Non-MSA	0.810 (34.60)	−0.795 (34.67)	−0.810 (34.62)
Age at immigration (Ageimmig)	−0.058 (6.53)	−0.068 (7.76)	n.e.
Ageimmig^2/100	0.038 (2.45)	0.027 (1.75)	n.e.
First-generation	0.539 (4.48)	n.e.	n.e.
Second-generation	0.472 (11.63)	0.317 (7.95)	0.466 (11.49)
Country-of-origin			
English speaking countries	n.e.	1.580 (11.06)	n.e.
Africa	n.e.	2.970 (10.35)	n.e.
Mexico	n.e.	−2.442 (17.46)	n.e.
Cuba	n.e.	1.339 (6.59)	n.e.
S. and C. America	n.e.	0.401 (2.62)	n.e.
Caribbean	n.e.	−0.261 (1.34)	n.e.
Southern Europe	n.e.	−1.387 (8.33)	n.e.
E. and C. Europe	n.e.	1.973 (13.67)	n.e.
N. and W. Europe	n.e.	3.262 (10.17)	n.e.
Philippines	n.e.	1.910 (11.29)	n.e.
China	n.e.	1.130 (5.72)	n.e.
Vietnam	n.e.	−0.387 (1.79)	n.e.
East Asia	n.e.	2.112 (11.73)	n.e.
South Asia	n.e.	3.371 (17.64)	n.e.
Middle East	n.e.	2.095 (9.51)	n.e.
Other Asia	n.e.	−0.153 (0.77)	n.e.
Remaining countries	n.e.	1.820 (11.29)	n.e.
Age at immigration			
0 to 4	n.e.	n.e.	0.818 (5.54)
5 to 12	n.e.	n.e.	0.431 (4.11)
13 to 19	n.e.	n.e.	−0.960 (12.15)
20 to 24	n.e.	n.e.	−0.751 (11.31)
25 to 29	n.e.	n.e.	−0.401 (5.71)
30 to 34	n.e.	n.e.	−0.693 (8.30)
35 to 44	n.e.	n.e.	−1.039 (11.82)
45 to 64	n.e.	n.e.	−1.713 (13.55)
Adjusted R^2	0.110	0.149	0.112
Sample size	68,485	68,485	68,485

Source: Current Population Survey, United States Bureau of the Census, October 1995. Variables are as defined in Table A1. n.e., Variable not entered. t-statistics are in parentheses.
[a] Benchmark group comprises all native-born adults.

Immigrants from Mexico and Southern Europe have lower levels of educational attainment compared to all native parentage adults. The differential is 2.5 years for Mexicans and 1.4 years for Southern Europeans.[8] The inclusion of the country of origin variables is associated with a change in the estimated impact of the variable Hispanic. For Hispanic, the partial effect changes from −2.59 to −1.32. This change in the magnitude of the Hispanic variable can be attributed to the large negative coefficient of Mexico. Thus a Hispanic from Mexico (as are nearly all Mexican immigrants) would have 3.8 fewer years of schooling, other variables the same, than native parentage non-Hispanic adults.

Specification 3 (column 3 in Table 2) included the usual explanatory variables (without the age at immigration quadratic variables) plus the age at immigration dummy variables. The benchmark was all native-parentage adults, hence the age at immigration coefficients gives the difference in education between foreign-born people from a particular age at immigration group and native-parentage adults. Our analysis indicates that adults immigrating in the 0 to 4 age-group acquire 0.8 years more of education, and those immigrating in the 5 to 12 age-group acquire 0.4 year more years of education compared to the benchmark group. Also relative to all native-parentage adults, first-generation immigrants migrating between ages 13 and 19 acquire 1.03 fewer years of education, those between ages 20 and 24 acquire about 0.8 years less of education, and between ages 25 and 29 acquire 0.41 fewer years of education. For foreign-born adults immigrating after age 30, the differential with their native parentage counterparts gets progressively larger with age.

The quadratic specification on age at immigration using the CPS data simply depicted a negative relation between age at immigration and educational attainment. When plotted graphically, this relationship appears as a smooth downward slope curve (Fig. 1A). The specification with the age at immigration dichotomous variables portrays a more detailed picture. When educational attainment is plotted graphically (Fig. 1B) against the age at immigration categories, we observe a dip at age at immigration 13–19 years and a local peak at 25–29 years. The age at immigration dichotomous variables indicate that educational attainment falls with an increase in age at immigration. However, it also captures an additional effect not obvious from the quadratic specification results, that is, immigrating during the secondary school years is associated with a greater disadvantage than if the immigration took place a few years earlier or later.

5.2.2. First-generation sample

This section discusses the results for the sample of 7496 first-generation adults between 25 and 64 years old. Table 3 presents the means and standard deviations of educational attainment and age at immigration by country of origin. As column 1 indicates, approximately 9% of immigrants are from English-speaking countries (United Kingdom, England, Australia, New Zealand, British West Indies). The dominant immigrant source country is Mexico (22%), followed by South and Central America (12%), East and Central Europe (9%), Philippines (6%), and Southern Europe and East Asia (5%). The remaining country-groups constitute 1–4% each.

Column 2 in Table 3 indicates that immigrants from

A. Quadratic specification of age-at-immigration variable

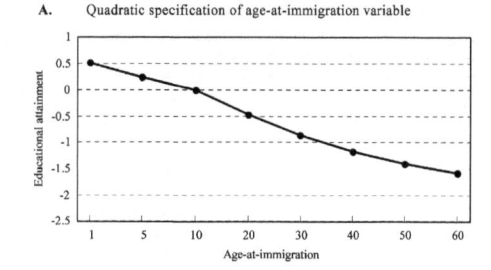

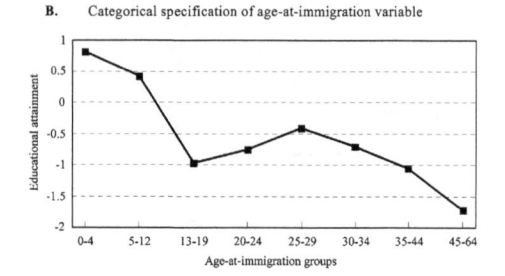

B. Categorical specification of age-at-immigration variable

Fig. 1. Effect of age at immigration on educational attainment. Source: Based on regression results from Table 2, columns 1 and 3.

South Asia, Africa, and North and West Europe have the highest level of schooling (15 years), followed by those from East Asia, Middle East, Philippines, China, and, East and Central Europe (14 years), North and West Europe, and English-speaking countries (13 years), followed by those from Cuba, Caribbean, Southern Europe, South and Central America and Other Asia (11 years). Immigrants from Mexico have the lowest level of education (9 years). The mean values of age at immigration (Table 3, column 3) by country of origin group reflects the fact that immigrants from Southern Europe, and North and West Europe, Cuba and Mexico tend to migrate at a much younger age (20–24 years) compared to those from East Asia, Vietnam and China (28–31 years) who are disproportionately refugees. The other country groups lie between the two extremes.

Table 4 presents the means and standard deviations of educational attainment by different age at immigration groups. Immigrants who migrate prior to their teenage years have schooling levels very close to the native-born. While the native-born have a mean schooling level of 13.5 years, those immigrating between 0 and 4 years acquire an average 13.7 years of schooling, with the 5–12 year group following very closely at 13 years. The 13–19 age group attains an average of 11.2 years of schooling, which is lower than any group immigrating between 20 and 44. Moreover, those migrating between

Table 3
Summary statistics of selected variables, by country of origin, first-generation adults, United States, 1995

Country of origin	Sample size	Educational attainment	Age at immigration
English-speaking countries	720 (9.61)[a]	13.73 (2.68)[b]	23.70 (11.66)[b]
Africa	94 (1.25)	14.98 (3.26)	26.66 (8.54)
Mexico	1650 (22.01)	8.66 (3.83)	22.79 (9.94)
Cuba	233 (3.11)	11.96 (3.35)	24.04 (13.10)
S. and C. America	890 (11.87)	11.58 (3.87)	25.54 (9.97)
Caribbean	287 (3.83)	11.06 (3.72)	26.44 (8.94)
Southern Europe	360 (4.80)	11.64 (4.16)	20.26 (11.158)
E. and C. Europe	698 (9.31)	14.10 (2.96)	27.22 (13.82)
N. and W. Europe	70 (0.93)	15.31 (2.31)	22.70 (8.74)
Philippines	438 (5.84)	14.11 (2.82)	26.78 (11.28)
China	259 (3.46)	13.60 (4.37)	30.61 (11.67)
Vietnam	191 (2.55)	11.99 (4.17)	29.18 (13.06)
East Asia	363 (4.84)	14.43 (2.64)	27.73 (10.42)
South Asia	307 (4.10)	15.57 (3.04)	26.74 (7.86)
Middle East	183 (2.44)	14.33 (3.62)	25.58 (10.14)
Other Asia	252 (3.36)	11.71 (4.52)	26.10 (10.42)
Remaining countries	501 (6.68)	13.97 (3.17)	25.87 (10.77)
Total	7496 (100.00)	11.82 (4.23)	24.79 (11.07)

Source: Current Population Survey, United States Bureau of the Census, October 1995. Variables are as defined in Table A1.
[a] Percent foreign-born are in parentheses.
[b] Standard deviations are in parentheses.

Table 4
Summary statistics of educational attainment, by age at immigration, first generation adults, United States, 1995

Age at immigration	Sample size	Educational attainment
0 to 4	305 (4.07)[a]	13.71 (2.69)[b]
5 to 12	620 (8.27)	13.04 (3.08)
13 to 19	1172 (15.64)	11.19 (3.96)
20 to 24	1656 (22.09)	11.55 (4.15)
25 to 29	1436 (19.16)	12.15 (4.43)
30 to 34	994 (13.26)	11.91 (4.44)
35 to 44	889 (11.86)	11.52 (4.62)
45 to 64	424 (5.65)	10.69 (4.95)
Total	7496 (100.00)	11.82 (4.23)

Source: Current Population Survey, United States Bureau of the Census, October 1995. Variables are as defined in Table A1.
[a] Percent in age at immigration group in parentheses.
[b] Standard deviations are in parentheses.

25 and 29 have a slightly higher average (12.2 years) compared to the age-group prior to (11.6 years) or age-group after (11.9 years) them. Educational attainment is lowest for those immigrating after age 45, reflecting the worldwide secular rise in schooling.

Ordinary least squares regression results for the first-generation immigrant sample are summarized in Table 5. Three different specifications corresponding to specification 1, 2, and 3 of the pooled sample are considered for the first-generation sample. The basic specification indicates that educational attainment increases with age until age 29, after which it starts declining due to younger cohorts receiving more schooling. The negative sign of age at immigration together with the positive sign of age at immigration squared implies that as age at immigration increases, educational attainment falls, but at a decreasing rate. Evaluated for different values of age at immigration, the partial effect of age at immigration on educational attainment is: −0.05 years for age at immigration = 1, −0.05 years for age at immigration = 10, −0.04 years for age at immigration = 20, −0.04 years for age at immigration = 30, and −0.03 years

Table 5
Regression estimates of first-generation adults, United States, 1995. Dependent variable: Educational attainment

Variable	(1)	(2)[a]	(3)[b]
Constant	12.97 (18.88)	14.37 (21.92)	12.78 (17.65)
Male	0.462 (5.43)	0.520 (6.54)	0.469 (5.53)
Age	0.111 (3.29)	0.062 (1.98)	0.075 (2.18)
Age^2	−0.002 (4.29)	−0.001 (3.19)	−0.001 (3.22)
Black	−0.328 (1.97)	−0.284 (1.59)	−0.317 (1.90)
Hispanic	−3.879 (42.99)	−1.086 (5.56)	−3.817 (42.21)
Married	0.043 (0.44)	0.162 (1.79)	0.048 (0.49)
South	0.312 (2.87)	0.033 (0.32)	0.287 (2.64)
Non-MSA	−0.700 (4.00)	−0.465 (2.83)	−0.702 (4.02)
Age at immigration (Ageimmig)	−0.053 (4.11)	−0.068 (5.56)	n.e.
Ageimmig^2/100	0.028 (1.19)	0.038 (1.74)	n.e.
Country-of-origin			
Africa	n.e.	1.223 (3.24)	n.e.
Mexico	n.e.	−4.217 (17.41)	n.e.
Cuba	n.e.	−0.498 (1.55)	n.e.
S. and C. America	n.e.	−1.320 (5.70)	n.e.
Caribbean	n.e.	−1.988 (7.65)	n.e.
Southern Europe	n.e.	−2.731 (11.88)	n.e.
E. and C. Europe	n.e.	0.589 (3.07)	n.e.
N. and W. Europe	n.e.	1.739 (4.04)	n.e.
Philippines	n.e.	0.497 (2.30)	n.e.
China	n.e.	−0.334 (1.29)	n.e.
Vietnam	n.e.	−1.924 (6.70)	n.e.
East Asia	n.e.	0.654 (2.84)	n.e.
South Asia	n.e.	1.872 (7.68)	n.e.
Middle East	n.e.	0.586 (2.02)	n.e.
Other Asia	n.e.	−1.667 (6.44)	n.e.
Remaining countries	n.e.	0.281 (1.39)	n.e.
Age at immigration			
0 to 4	n.e.	n.e.	1.119 (4.83)
5 to 12	n.e.	n.e.	0.826 (4.67)
13 to 19	n.e.	n.e.	−0.404 (2.77)
20 to 24	n.e.	n.e.	−0.306 (2.30)
30 to 34	n.e.	n.e.	−0.229 (1.50)
35 to 44	n.e.	n.e.	−0.605 (3.72)
45 to 64	n.e.	n.e.	−1.287 (5.82)
Adjusted R^2	0.215	0.322	0.218
Sample size	7496	7496	7496

Source: Current Population Survey, United States Bureau of the Census, October 1995. Variables are as defined in Table A1. n.e., Variable not entered. *t*-statistics are in parentheses.
[a] Benchmark group is all foreign-born adults from English-speaking countries.
[b] Benchmark group is all foreign-born adults who immigrated between ages 25 to 29.

for age at immigration = 40. Not all the remaining coefficients are significant.

Foreign-born men acquire about 0.46 years more schooling compared to foreign-born women. Residence in southern states increases educational attainment among the foreign-born by 0.31 years, while a non-metropolitan residence decreases educational attainment by 0.70 years. Being Hispanic has a highly significant negative effect on educational attainment (3.88 years).

The next specification (Table 5, column 2) introduced the country of origin regressors. In analyzing the first-generation sample, the benchmark group was the English-speaking foreign countries. Therefore, the coefficient of the country variables is interpreted as the difference in years of schooling between first-generation immigrants from a particular country group and first-generation immigrants from English-speaking countries. Immigrants from Africa, Philippines, East and South Asia, Middle East, and Europe (except southern) show higher levels of educational attainment than those from the English speaking countries. Immigrants from South and Central America, the Caribbean, Vietnam, Southern Europe and Mexico show lower levels of educational attainment than English speaking countries. Mexicans have the largest differential (4.2 years), followed by Southern Europe (3 years), and the remaining country-groups have less than 1-year differential. The differential for Hispanics goes down from a highly significant −3.88 to a much less significant −1.09, but the negative effect of Hispanic on educational attainment is clearly captured by the significant, large negative coefficient for Mexico. Hispanics born in Mexico have 5.3 years of schooling less than those from the English-speaking countries.

The last specification (Table 5, column 3) includes the usual explanatory variables plus the age at immigration dummy variables. In analyzing the first-generation sample, the benchmark age at immigration was the 25–29 age group. Our analysis indicates that adults who immigrated between the ages of 0 to 4 acquire 1.1 more years of schooling, and those who migrated between age 5 and 12 acquire 0.8 more years of schooling compared to the benchmark group, those who immigrated between ages 25 and 29. Adults immigrating in the 13–19 and 20–24 age groups and those who immigrated at age 30 and older have less schooling than the ages 25–29 years group. The differential is less than one-half of a year, except for the oldest group (age 45–64 at immigration). In summary, the 13–19 group and 20–24 group acquire lower education compared to the 25–29 age-group, as do immigrants with older age at arrival. Moreover, the total years of schooling declines progressively in relation to the benchmark group for those immigrating after age 34.

The summary statistics discussed in Table 1 indicated a large proportion of the first-generation sample to be Hispanic. To test if the Hispanic sample dominates the results derived from our analysis of the foreign-born sample, the basic specification (only demographic and geographic variables) and the specification with age at immigration dummies were run separately on the Hispanic sample and the non-Hispanic sample (see Table 6). The regression coefficients in the Hispanic sample differ from the coefficients in the non-Hispanic sample.

While being black increased educational attainment by 2.5 years among Hispanics, being black reduced educational attainment by 0.8 years among non-Hispanics (Table 6). The black/non-black differential in schooling attainment between the Hispanic and non-Hispanic samples is perhaps explained by the fact that black Hispanics originate primarily from the Caribbean or Central America, and not from Mexico.

Being married does not have a significant effect in the Hispanic sample, but has a positive effect on educational attainment for the non-Hispanic sample.

Another major difference noted between the Hispanic and non-Hispanic sample is the effect of age at immigration. The Hispanic sample clearly depicts that educational attainment decreases with age at immigration at an increasing rate, but for the non-Hispanic sample, the age at immigration variable is insignificant. What emerges from the age at immigration dummies is that among Hispanics, child immigrants (those immigrating prior to age 12) acquire 2.5 to 3 years more education than adult immigrants. However, among non-Hispanics, those immigrating at 25–29 acquire more education than those immigrating at earlier years. Among non-Hispanics, but not among Hispanics, there is a very large negative effect of immigrating in the 13–19 age-group.

5.2.3. Comparative study of first-generation, second-generation and native-parentage adults

Regressions estimated separately for the first-generation immigrants, second-generation immigrants, and native-parentage adults are presented in Table 7. While educational attainment increases to age 37, and declines thereafter, for both second-generation immigrants and native-parentage; first-generation immigrants reach their peak much earlier at age 28. One noteworthy factor is the variation in the Hispanic/non-Hispanic differential in educational attainment across the three groups of study. The Hispanic/non-Hispanic differential is most pronounced in the first-generation (3.9 years), followed by the second-generation (1.7 years), and the native-parentage group (1.3 years).

In order to study the effect of foreign-parentage on educational attainment, we consider the sample of all native-born adults (i.e. second-generation and native-parentage adults). We introduced three variables (mother only foreign-born, father only foreign-born, and both parents foreign-born) into the basic regression specification. The benchmark is both parents being native-born.

Our results indicate that having either parent foreign-born or both parents foreign-born has a positive effect on educational attainment. Compared to the native parentage, a foreign-born mother is associated with 0.4 years more schooling, a foreign-born father with 0.34 more years, but if both are foreign-born only 0.21 more years. This result agrees with the Schultz (1984) finding that if both parents are foreign-born, duration of residence in the United States is associated with increased levels of schooling. Also if immigrants are favorably self-selected and more able (Chiswick, 1977, 1999), it suggests that they are more inclined to invest in their children's schooling than native-born parents. Therefore, it is not surprising that second-generation immigrants (who by definition have at least one foreign-born parent) acquire more schooling than their native-born counterparts.

6. Conclusions

Given the importance of immigrants in the US workforce and increasing awareness of the critical role of edu-

Table 6
Regression estimates of first-generation adults by Hispanic/non-Hispanic origin, United States, 1995. Dependent variable: Educational attainment

Variable	Hispanic (1)	Hispanic (2)	Non-Hispanic (1)	Non-Hispanic (2)
Constant	11.807 (10.03)	9/678 (7.84)	11.821 (14.21)	12.176 (13.85)
Male	0.020 (0.13)	0.056 (0.38)	0.756 (7.46)	0.755 (7.45)
Age	0.066 (1.12)	0.016 (0.27)	0.122 (3.03)	0.113 (2.69)
Age^2	−0.079 (1.13)	−0.030 (0.42)	−0.002 (4.24)	−0.002 (3.84)
Black	2.516 (5.50)	2.432 (5.33)	−0.821 (4.80)	−0.796 (4.66)
Married	−0.274 (1.70)	−0.256 (1.59)	0.261 (2.20)	0.246 (2.07)
South	0.280 (1.63)	0.224 (1.31)	0.331 (2.38)	0.317 (2.27)
Non-MSA	−1.197 (4.20)	−1.221 (4.30)	−0.257 (1.18)	−0.235 (1.08)
Age at immigration (Ageimmig)	−0.184 (7.27)	n.e.	0.009 (0.59)	n.e.
$Ageimmig^2/100$	0.002 (4.06)	n.e.	−0.056 (2.15)	n.e.
Age at immigration				
0 to 4	n.e.	3.092 (6.96)	n.e.	0.148 (0.56)
5 to 12	n.e.	2.402 (7.84)	n.e.	−0.103 (0.49)
13 to 19	n.e.	0.133 (0.56)	n.e.	−0.641 (3.46)
20 to 24	n.e.	−0.013 (0.06)	n.e.	−0.368 (2.31)
30 to 34	n.e.	−0.243 (0.89)	n.e.	0.352 (1.97)
35 to 44	n.e.	−0.469 (1.49)	n.e.	0.782 (4.24)
45 to 64	n.e.	−1.509 (3.34)	n.e.	−1.338 (5.46)
Adjusted R^2	0.061	0.068	0.057	0.061
Sample size	2858	2858	4638	4638

Source: Current Population Survey, United States Bureau of the Census, October 1995. Note: Variables are as defined in Table A1. n.e., Variable not entered. *t*-statistics are in parentheses.

Table 7
Regression estimates of first-generation, second-generation, and native-parentage adults, United States, 1995. Dependent variable: Educational attainment

Variable	First-generation	Second-generation	Native-parentage	All native-born
Constant	12.97 (18.88)	11.775 (19.93)	11.35 (69.54)	11.32 (72.03)
Male	0.462 (5.43)	0.250 (3.32)	0.091 (4.56)	0.103 (5.34)
Age	0.111 (3.29)	0.136 (4.94)	0.136 (17.43)	0.137 (18.34)
Age^2	−0.002 (4.29)	−0.002 (6.45)	−0.002 (20.55)	−0.002 (21.79)
Black	−0.328 (1.97)	−0.365 (1.29)	−0.709 (21.55)	−0.707 (21.58)
Hispanic	−3.879 (42.99)	−1.650 (14.66)	−1.254 (18.35)	−1.333 (23.28)
Married	0.043 (0.44)	0.432 (5.26)	0.333 (15.25)	0.339 (16.06)
South	0.312 (2.87)	−0.012 (0.12)	−0.343 (15.82)	−0.328 (15.43)
MSA	−0.700 (4.00)	0.880 (8.30)	0804 (35.70)	0.809 (36.65)
Age at immigration	−0.053 (4.11)	n.e.	n.e.	n.e.
$Ageimig^2/100$	0.028 (1.19)	n.e.	n.e.	n.e.
Mother foreign-born	n.e.	n.e.	n.e.	0.400 (5.91)
Father foreign-born	n.e.	n.e.	n.e.	0.342 (5.64)
Both parents foreign-born	n.e.	n.e.	n.e.	0.212 (3.47)
Adjusted R^2	0.215	0.095	0.062	0.065
Sample size	7496	4506	56,483	60,989

Source: Current Population Survey, United States Bureau of the Census, October 1995. Variables are as defined in Table A1. n.e., Variable not entered. *t*-statistics are in parentheses.

cation in labor market success, this study sought to investigate the determinants of the educational attainment of immigrants and the US-born children of immigrants. This paper contributes to the existing literature on education by examining the educational aspect of the assimilation process of immigrants, through the separate investigation by first-generation and second-generation immigrants, and analyses among immigrants by age at immigration, and country of origin.

Based on the regression estimates, this paper's major finding is that educational attainment differs significantly among the three immigrant generations. Second-generation Americans acquire about half a year more schooling than their native-parentage counterparts. Other explanatory variables (age, gender, marital status) held constant, those who immigrate at a very young age (up to age 4) acquire 0.35 years more schooling than second-generation, and 0.81 years more schooling than native-parentage adults. However, migration from age 5 up to age 19 is associated with less schooling than second-generation immigrants, and immigration from age 13 up to age 19 is associated with fewer years of schooling even relative to native-parentage adults. Immigration in the teenage years (ages 13–19) appears to convey the greatest disadvantage. Those who migrate late in their twenties (age 25–29) complete more schooling (about half a year) than those migrating in their teen years. However, the attainment level drops significantly, and progressively with age at immigration beyond 30. Thus the empirical analysis supports the hypothesis regarding the negative effect of age at immigration on post-migration investment in schooling, but the estimated relationship is complex, with a big dip among those who immigrate as teenagers.

Another major finding is the substantial heterogeneity that exists among immigrants depending on their country of origin. Immigrants from Africa, South and East Asia, Philippines, and North and Western Europe obtain 1.0 to 1.5 years more schooling in comparison to their counterparts born in the US or immigrants from English-speaking countries. Mexicans and Southern Europeans, on the other hand, acquire less schooling relative to the native-born adults, as well as immigrants from English-speaking countries. Mexicans lag behind their US-born, and their English-speaking birthplace immigrant counterparts by about 4 years. The lower education of Mexican immigrants can be attributed to the nature of migration from Mexico to the United States, a large percentage being illegal immigrants who have less economic incentive to invest in human capital. Additionally, given the close proximity of Mexico to the United States, costs of to-and-fro migration are very low, and this factor leads to a weaker incentive to invest in both origin-specific and destination-specific skills.

The analysis also indicates that being black, and more so being Hispanic, is associated with lower levels of education compared to non-Hispanic whites and Asians for immigrants, second-generation Americans and native-parentage adults. The black/non-black differential is less than a year (0.7 years), but the Hispanic/non-Hispanic differential is about 2.5 years. While the Hispanic/non-Hispanic differential is less pronounced with each subsequent generation, the black/non-black differential persists, and in fact, is greatest in the native-parentage generation.

There are also gender differentials. Immigrant women acquire about half a year less schooling than immigrant men. This differential narrows with each successive generation.

The policy implications of our findings are significant, particularly for the minority groups studied. It would seem appropriate to enact appropriate immigration, assimilation and education policies not only to prevent the existing educational gap from widening any further, but also to narrow the existing gap.

Two kinds of policy can be used to influence the education levels of the immigrant population. First, immigration policy can be used to reduce the existing gap among various ethnic groups by restricting immigration among adults to those with some specified minimum level of schooling. Second, assimilation policy can be used to help immigrants, adults as well as children, assimilate into the host country, particularly in overcoming language and education barriers. The analysis indicates that racial/ethnic differences are most prominent in the first-generation among Hispanics. For example, assimilation policy involving increased commitment to the education of immigrants though emphasis on the acquisition of English language skills can play a major role in facilitating the adjustment and progress of Hispanic immigrant children whose parents typically have little education and/or do not speak English.

Appendix

Educational attainment: The following categories were used for defining the number of years of schooling completed by the respondent: "no school completed or completed less than or equal to 4th grade", 2.5 years; "completed between 5th and 8th grade", 7 years; "completed 9th grade", 9 years; "completed 10th grade", 10 years; "completed 11th grade", 11 years; "completed 12th grade with or without diploma, or completed GED", 12 years; "some college, no degree, or associate degree", 14 years; "Bachelors degree", 16 years; "Masters degree", 17.5 years; "Professional degree", 18 years; "Doctorate degree", 20 years.

YSM: The CPS provides categorical information on year of immigration to the US. The CPS calculations used 1995 as the base year. The year of entry information is converted into a continuous measure (YSM) using the

Table A1
Definition of variables

Variables	Code	Description
Dependent variable:	Educational attainment	Highest level of education (20 categories)*
Explanatory variables:		
Gender variable	Male	Dichotomous variables are equal to unity for indicated characteristic; otherwise they are zero
Age variables	Age	Age in years
	Age²	Age squared
	YSM	Years since migration*
	YSM²	Years since migration squared
	Ageimmig	Age at immigration
	Ageimmig²	Age at immigration squared
Race/ethnicity	Black Hispanic	Dichotomous variables are equal to unity for indicated characteristic; otherwise they are zero
Foreign-born	Forborn	Dichotomous variables are equal to unity for indicated characteristic; otherwise they are zero; derived from CPS variable on place of birth recode
Region/size of place	South Rural	Dichotomous variables are equal to unity for indicated characteristic; otherwise they are zero
Marital status	Married	Dichotomous variables are equal to unity for indicated characteristic; otherwise they are zero
Age at immigration variables*	0 to 4	Dichotomous variables are equal to unity for indicated characteristic; otherwise they are zero
	5 to 12	
	13 to 19	
	20 to 24	
	25 to 29	
	30 to 34	
	35 to 44	
	45 to 64	
Country-of-origin variables*	Africa	Dichotomous variables are equal to unity for indicated characteristic; otherwise they are zero
	Mexico	
	Cuba	
	S. and C. America*	
	Caribbean*	
	Southern Europe*	
	E. and C. Europe*	
	N. and W. Europe*	
	Philippines	
	China	
	Vietnam	
	East Asia*	
	South Asia*	
	Middle East*	
	Other Asia*	
	English-speaking countries*	
	Remaining countries*	

(continued on next page)

Table A1 (continued)

Variables	Code	Description
Immigrant generation variables	First-generation Second generation Mother foreign-born Father foreign-born Both parents foreign-born	Dichotomous variables are equal to unity for indicated characteristic; otherwise they are zero

* See appendix notes

following values: "1992–1995", 1.75 years; "1990–1991", 4.25 years; "1988–1989", 6.25 years; "1986–1987", 8.25 years; "1984–1985", 10.25 years; "1982–1983", 12.25 years; "1980–1981", 14.25 years; "1975–1979", 17.75; "1970–1974", 22.75: "1965–1969", 27.75; "1960–1964", 32.75; "1950–1959", 40.25; "Before 1950", 54.75.

Age at immigration: Ageimmig is calculated by subtracting YSM from current age. Thus ageimmig = YSM − Age. YSM is calculated as explained above. This approximation, however, results in some negative values for 'ageimmig', but only for the two earliest periods (1950–1959 and pre-1950). For example, a 34-year-old, who migrated in 1957 (at the age of 1), has his YSM approximated as 35.5 and hence gets a −1.25 value for ageimmig. It is reasonable to assume that all the adults who get a negative calculated ageimmig probably immigrated at a very young age, therefore they are assigned a value of zero. Categorical age at immigration (dichotomous) variables were computed from the continuous variable.

Country of origin variables: The country dummy variables are self-explanatory except for those discussed below.

Southern Europe includes Albania, Italy, Malta, Monaco, Portugal, Madeira Island, Spain, Vatican City, Yugoslavia.

East and Central Europe includes Austria, Belgium, Czechoslovakia, Denmark, Germany (East and West), Berlin (East and West), Liechtenstein, Luxembourg, Netherlands, Switzerland, Hungary, Poland, Romania, former USSR, Baltic States, Estonia, Latvia, Lithuania.

North and West Europe includes Faroe Islands, Jan Mayen, Finland, Iceland, Norway, Sweden, Svalbard, Lapland, Andorra, France, Guernsey, Jersey, Azores Islands, Madeira Islands.

South Asia includes Afghanistan, Bangladesh, Bhutan, Burma, India, Pakistan, Sri Lanka, Nepal.

East Asia includes Japan, Korea, Macau, Mongolia, Taiwan.

Other Asia (primarily South-east Asia) includes Brunei, Cambodia, Hong Kong, Indonesia, Laos, Malaysia, Singapore, Thailand, Indochina.

Middle East includes Bahrain, Cyprus, Iran, Iraq, Israel, Jordan, Kuwait, Lebanon, Quatar, Saudi Arabia, Syria, Turkey, United Arab Emirates, Yemen, Mesopotamia, Palestine, Persian Gulf States, West Bank.

English-speaking countries includes United Kingdom, England, Ireland, Scotland, Wales, Canada, Australia, New Zealand; English-speaking parts of Caribbean islands (Bahamas, British Virgin Islands, Jamaica, British West Indies).

Remaining countries includes all countries not included in the country dummies, the major composition being Oceania (except Australia and New Zealand).

Source: Current Population Survey, United States Bureau of the Census, October 1995.

References

Arias, B. M. (1986). The context of education for hispanic students: an overview. *American Journal of Education*, 95, 26–57.

Becker, G. S. (1964). *Human capital: a theoretical and empirical analysis, with special reference to education*, 2nd edn. New York: National Bureau of Economic Research, Columbia University Press.

Becker, G.S. (1967). Human capital and the personal distribution of income, Wyotinsky Lecture, No. 1, Ann Arbor: University of Michigan.

Betts, J. R., & Lofstrom, M. (2000). The educational attainment of immigrants: trends and implications. In G. J. Borjas (Ed.), *Issues in the Economics of Immigration* (pp. 51–117). University of Chicago Press.

Borjas, G. J. (1982). The earnings of male hispanic immigrants in the United States. *Industrial and Labor Relations Review*, 35(3), 343–353 April.

Borjas, G. J. (1987). Self-selection and the earnings of immigrants. *American Economic Review*, 77(4), 531–553.

Carter, T. P., & Segura, R. D. (1979). *Mexican Americans in school: A decade of change*. New York: College Entrance Examination Board.

Chiswick, B. R. (1977). Sons of immigrants: Are they at an earnings disadvantage? *American Economic Association, Papers and Proceedings*, 67(1), 376–380 February.

Chiswick, B. R. (1978). The effect of Americanization on the earnings of foreign-born men. *Journal of Political Economy*, 86(5), 897–922 October.

Chiswick, B. R. (1979). The economic progress of immigrants: Some apparently universal patterns. In W. Fellner (Ed.), *Contemporary Economic Problems* (pp. 359–399). Washington: American Enterprise Institute for Public Policy Research.

Chiswick, B. R. (1988). Differences in education and earnings across racial and ethnic groups: tastes, discrimination, and investments in child quality. *Quarterly Journal of Economics*, 103(3), 571–597.

Chiswick, B. R. (1999). Are immigrants favorably self-selected? *American Economic Review*, 89(2), 181–185.

Chiswick, B. R., & Miller, P. W. (1994). The determinants of post-immigration investments in education. *Economics of Education Review*, 13(2), 163–177.

Chiswick, B. R., & Sullivan, T. A. (1995). The new immigrants. In R. Farley (Ed.), *State of the Union: America in the 1990s* (pp. 211–270). New York: Russell Sage Foundation.

Cobb-Clark, D., Connolly, M.D., & Worswick, C. (2000). The job search and education investments of immigrant families. Research School of the Social Sciences, Australian University, unpublished Paper.

Cohen, Y., Zach, T., & Chiswick, B. R. (1997). The educational attainment of immigrants: changes over time. *Quarterly Review of Economics and Finance*, 37, 229–243 Special Issue.

Duleep, H., & Regets, M. C. (1999). Immigrants and human-capital investment. *American Economic Review*, 89(2), 186–191.

Funkhouser, E., & Trejo, S. J. (1995). The labor market skills of recent immigrants: evidence from the CPS. *Industrial and Labor Relations Review, 48*(4), 792–811.

Gang, I.N., Zimmerman, K.F. (1999). Is child like parent? Educational attainment and ethnic origin. Center for Economic Policy Research, Discussion Paper No. 57.

Hashmi, A. (1987). Post-migration investment in education by immigrants in the United States. PhD dissertation, University of Illinois at Chicago.

Hirschman, C., & Wong, M. G. (1986). The extraordinary educational attainment of Asian Americans: a search for historical evidence and explanations. *Social Forces, 65*(1), 1–27.

Kao, G., & Tienda, M. (1995). Optimism and achievement: The educational performance of immigrant youth. *Social Science Quarterly, 76*(1), 1–19.

Kao, G., Tienda, M., & Schneider, B. (1996). Racial and ethnic variation in academic performance research. *Sociology of Education and Socialization, 11*, 263–297.

Khan, A. H. (1997). Post-migration investment in education by immigrants in the United States. *Quarterly Review of Economics and Finance, 37*, 285–313 Special Issue.

Lee, E. S., & Rong, X. (1988). The educational and economic achievement of Asian Americans. *Elementary School Journal, 88*(5), 545–560.

Miller, P. W., & Volker, P. A. (1989). Socioeconomic influences on educational attainment. *Australian Journal of Statistics, Special volume 31A, Youth Employment and Unemployment, August*, 47–70.

Ogbu, J. U. (1978). *Minority education and caste: the American system in cross-cultural perspective*. New York: Academic Press.

Ogbu, J. U. (1987). Variability in minority school performance: A problem in search of an explanation. *Anthropology and Education Quarterly, 18*(4), 313–334.

Ogbu, J. U., & Matute-Bianchi, M. E. (1986). Understanding sociocultural factors: Knowledge, identity, and school adjustment. In *Beyond Language: Social and Cultural Factors in Schooling Language Minority Students* (pp. 73–142). Los Angeles: Office of Bilingual Bicultural Education.

Perlmann, J. (1988). *Ethnic differences*. Cambridge: Cambridge University Press.

Portes, A., & Rumbaut, R. G. (1990). *Immigrant America*. Berkeley: University of California Press.

Rong, X., & Grant, L. (1992). Ethnicity, generation, and school attainment of Asians, Hispanics and Non-Hispanic Whites. *The Sociological Quarterly, 33*(4), 625–636.

Schaafsma, J., & Sweetman, A. (1999). Immigrant earnings: Age at immigration matters. *Canadian Journal of Economics, 34*(4), 1066–1099.

Schultz, T. P. (1984). The schooling and health of children of US immigrants and natives. *Research in Population Economics, 5*, 251–288.

Schultz, T. W. (1961). Investment in human capital. *American Economic Review, 51*(1), 1–17.

Trueba, H. (1987). *Success or failure? Learning and the language minority student*. Cambridge, MA: Newbury House.

US Bureau of the Census. (1995). School enrollment supplement: Technical documentation. Washington, DC, October.

Velez, W. (1989). High school attrition among Hispanic and Non-Hispanic White youths. *Sociology of Education, 62*(2), 119–133.

[25]

The economic determinants of ethnic assimilation

Carmel U. Chiswick

Received: 20 July 2006 / Accepted: 11 January 2008 /
Published online: 7 May 2008
© Springer-Verlag 2008

Abstract A human capital model is developed that distinguishes between ethnic-specific skills (applicable only to a specific indigenous or immigrant group) and shared or general skills. An important determinant of assimilation is the extent to which these two forms of human capital are complements, thus promoting both assimilation and ethnic persistence, or anti-complements, promoting either assimilation or ethnic retention but not both. Implications of the model are developed for various applications including intermarriage, the effects of group size, language and religion as a basis for ethnic mergers, and the transfer society as a potential barrier to assimilation.

Keywords Ethnicity · Human Capital · Ethnic Intermarriage

JEL Classification J15 · J24 · Z13

1 Introduction

The relevance of ethnicity for economic analysis derives from the fact that ethnic groups differ in their consumption patterns and in their supply of resources to the economy at large. Some of these differences are relatively minor, accounting for less variation in supply and demand than individual differences in tastes and preferences.

Responsible editor: Klaus F. Zimmermann

C. U. Chiswick (✉)
Department of Economics (m/c 144), University of Illinois at Chicago, 601 S. Morgan Street, Chicago, IL 60607-7121, USA
e-mail: cchis@uic.edu

C. U. Chiswick
IZA, Bonn, Germany

Others have effects on markets—and on the institutional basis of the economy—that can be both pronounced and persistent. By exploring the economic determinants of ethnic assimilation, this paper also develops implications for the persistence of differences among ethnic groups and some implications of these differences for society as a whole.

Ethnic group members develop consumption patterns within the community specific to the group and not shared by other members of the larger society. Ethnicity-specific goods and services (referred to as "ethnic goods") may include food and clothing items, religion, music, or ethnic newspapers, radio, and TV stations (Chiswick and Miller 2005). Human capital related to these consumption patterns may also be ethnic-specific. Important examples of ethnic human capital are skills related to ethnic languages and religions, as well as gender and age roles. Much of this human capital is formed within the family and community, often fairly early in life, and affects the way in which people relate to the larger society in which the ethnic group is embedded. The process of ethnic human capital formation (referred to here as "ethnic education") may itself be group-specific, a possibility that will be explored later in this paper.

Ethnic differences in consumption and labor supply also induce differences in patterns of investment in general human capital, resulting in cases of occupational "specialization" within ethnic groups and to dramatic differences in schooling levels between "successful" and "disadvantaged" ethnic groups (Chiswick 1988; Borjas 1992, 1995; Lehrer 2004). These in turn influence ethnic differences relating to more intimate matters such as health and medical care, marriage patterns, fertility rates, and family life. To a large extent, it is these differences that give an ethnic group visibility and contribute to its image within the larger society.

The analysis developed in this paper begins with the assumption that each individual belongs unambiguously to one and only one ethnic group.[1] For simplicity, there are only two distinctive ethnicities within a larger society that they both share.[2] Individuals face tradeoffs between goods that are shared (i.e., demanded by persons of both ethnicities) and those that are specific to their own ethnic group. Similarly, they allocate their education budgets between shared and ethnic-specific human capital. Part II develops this model and uses it to distinguish between two concepts of ethnic assimilation. Part III applies the model to various issues related to assimilation, including inter-ethnic marriage patterns, group size effects, and ethnic conflict. Part IV concludes with a discussion of implications for social and economic policy aimed at fostering the assimilation of ethnic groups.

---

[1] In some usage, an ethnic group is defined residually after controlling for such characteristics as race, religion, or place of origin. This study uses the term broadly to include groups defined by these characteristics as well. For simplicity, these characteristics are assumed to be unambiguous and well known, so that every member of the population knows the ethnicity of every other member.

[2] Individuals who distance themselves from ethnic particularism may view themselves as having no ethnicity. Typically, however, people who share this viewpoint develop their own social structures and thus create the equivalent of a more or less new ethnicity. The fact that these people have origins in different ethnic groups is not relevant for the distinction between ethnic-specific and shared types of human capital.

Springer

2 An economic model of ethnic identity

Membership in an ethnic group is understood to be a "good" in the sense that it is desirable but not costless. That is, identification with the group provides benefits both tangible and intangible but requires diversion of scarce resources from other uses. Although ethnicity cannot be purchased directly, it is best thought of as a z-good produced by combining ethnic goods and services (e.g., ethnic clothing, food, entertainment, charities, and club memberships) and time expenditures on group-specific activities.[3] Each ethnic group is part of the larger society, and each has a group-specific ethnic z-good, E, that effectively defines its identity.

2.1 The ethnic consumer

Utility-maximizing consumers allocate their time between ethnic and general activities. The problem can be expressed as:

$$\text{Max } U(E, Y) \quad \text{subject to} \quad L_E + L_Y + L_S = L^* \tag{1}$$

where

E Ethnicity-specific goods and services
Y All other (shared) goods and services
L_E Time spent in ethnic-specific activities
L_Y Time spent in general activities
L_S Total time spent in human capital formation

and L^* is the total time available for all purposes.

Human capital may or may not be work-related, referring rather more generally to the skills and experiences relevant for producing the consumption goods, E and Y. It is useful to distinguish between ethnic human capital, the skills and experiences specific to E production thus useful only for members of that ethnic group, and shared human capital, the skills and experiences that raise productivity for Y production and are thus useful to members of all groups. For example, ethnic human capital, H_E, might include a group-specific ethnic language, religion, or customs affecting family relationships, while human capital shared by all ethnic groups, H_Y, would include the common language and labor market skills useful for everyone without regard to ethnicity.

Ignoring for simplicity the role of purchased goods and services, let the two consumption goods, Y and E, be self-produced with human capital specific to each activity:

$$E = g(h_E L_E) \tag{2}$$

$$Y = f(h_Y L_Y) \tag{3}$$

where h_E level (quality) of ethnic human capital
and h_Y level (quality) of general human capital.

---
[3] For a discussion of ethnic goods, see Chiswick and Miller 2005. The ethnic good concept permits a generalization of the model of religious groups presented in Chiswick 2006.

In this specification, the total amount of human capital, $H_E \equiv h_E L_E$ or $H_Y \equiv h_Y L_Y$, respectively, is the sole input for producing the corresponding consumption good. Each ethnic group is thus characterized by its own group-specific human capital.

In the present analysis, the term "ethnic education" refers to any investment in ethnic-specific human capital, a skill-formation process that enhances the productivity of resources deployed within the group (i.e., for making the ethnic z-good) but not productivity in the general labor market or in general consumption activities. Ethnic education in this sense begins early in childhood with ethnic-specific parenting styles and family customs, later expanding to include socialization within the ethnic community and more or less formal training in group-specific skills. The rate of return to ethnic education depends not only on individual preferences (a lifestyle choice) but also on the production function for ethnic experience.

Each type of human capital is the output of an educational process with its own production function, the main input to which is the student's time. These can be written inversely as cost functions, expressing the time cost of education as a function of the level of skill to be acquired.

$$L_S = L_{YS} + L_{ES} \tag{4}$$

$$L_{YS} = \varphi(h_Y)/\alpha \quad \varphi', \varphi'' > 0 \tag{5}$$

$$L_{ES} = [\gamma(h_E) - \omega\, h_Y\, h_E]/\alpha \quad \gamma', \gamma'' > 0 \tag{6}$$

where L_{YS} time spent in general (shared) learning activities
and L_{ES} time spent in ethnic-specific learning activities.

The efficiency parameter $\alpha > 0$ in Eqs. 5 and 6 is an individual-specific positive constant that captures differences in learning abilities, with $\alpha > 1$ for a high ability student (who can acquire a given level of skill in less time) and $\alpha < 1$ for a low-ability student. The constant parameter ω is group-specific and indicates the degree to which the acquisition of general human capital imposes an external effect on ethnicity-specific education. For example, if $\omega > 0$ a greater level of general human capital (h_Y) would make it less costly to acquire any given level of ethnic education (h_E), while if $\omega < 0$ the opposite would be true.[4]

The consumer's problem is solved by maximizing the Lagrangian function:

$$\pounds = U(g(h_E L_E), f(h_Y L_Y))$$
$$- \lambda \{L_E + L_Y + +[\gamma(h_E) + \varphi(h_Y) - \omega\, h_Y h_E]/a - L^*\} \tag{7}$$

---

[4] A similar externality with respect to the general education process is ignored here for the sake of simplicity. If the term $\omega^* h_Y h_E/\alpha$ were to be subtracted from the right-hand side of Eq. 5, the only effect on Eq. 7 would be to replace the constant parameter ω with $(\omega + \omega^*)$. The following equations would have to be adjusted accordingly, but there would be no substantive difference in their interpretation.

where Eqs. 4, 5, and 6 have been substituted into the time constraint to eliminate the schooling time variables. The first-order conditions can be solved to yield

$$U_{gg}'h_E = U_{ff}'h_Y \tag{8}$$

$$L_E/h_E = [\gamma' - \omega\, h_Y]/\alpha \tag{9}$$

$$L_Y/h_Y = [\varphi' - \omega\, h_E]/\alpha \tag{10}$$

$$L^* = L_E + L_Y + [\gamma(h_E) + \varphi(h_Y) - \omega\, h_Y\, h_E]/\alpha \tag{11}$$

Equation 8 equates the marginal rate of substition in consumption between ethnic-specific and common (shared) uses of time to -1, the slope of the time budget line, requiring that the marginal value of time be the same in both consumption activities. Equations 9 and 10 equate the slopes of the human capital quantity–quality isoquants, L_E/h_E and L_Y/h_Y respectively, to the marginal cost of the corresponding type of education. These conditions allocate time to each type of education up to the point where its marginal value in human capital formation is the same as the opportunity cost of that time in consumption activities. Equation 11 restates the overall time constraint for all activites.

Solving Eqs. 9 and 10 for h_E and h_Y, respectively, substituting the result into Eq. 8 and rearranging terms yields:

$$\frac{U_{gg}'L_E}{U_{ff}'L_Y} = \left[\frac{\gamma' - \omega h_Y}{\varphi' - \omega h_E}\right] \tag{12}$$

The expression on the left-hand side of Eq. 12 is the marginal rate of substitution in consumption between h_E and h_Y, the slope of an indifference curve between levels of the two types of education. The right-hand side is the slope of a production possibility frontier (PPF) between h_E and h_Y.

Individuals face a family of PPF curves defined by $L_S = [\gamma + \varphi - \omega h_Y h_E]/\alpha$, each corresponding to a fixed level of resources—i.e., to a fixed value of L_S—devoted to general and ethnic training combined. A group of people with identical indifference curves and the same value of L_S may also be thought of as facing a family of PPF curves, as the amount of human capital attainable with a given amount of resources is positively related to the ability parameter α. Variations in α may thus be viewed as generating a positively sloped expansion path (for both h_Y and h_E normal) along which individuals with similar tastes but different abilities are ranged. For any given combination of h_Y and h_E, however, Eq. 12 shows that the slope of the PPF is independent of α and thus the same for all members of the group.

Equations 9 and 10 may also be solved for L_E and L_Y respectively, the results substituted into Eq. 11, and the terms rearranged to obtain:

$$L^* = [h_E\gamma' + h_Y\varphi' + \gamma + \varphi - 3\omega h_E h_Y]/\alpha \tag{13}$$

Thus, the education production functions can be used to convert the overall time constraint into an expression that is solely a function of skill levels, h_E and h_Y, the ability parameter α, and the externality parameter ω. Like the PPF, this time-constrained opportunity set is larger for high-ability individuals, but its slope is independent of α and thus the same for all group members.[5]

The overall solution to the consumer's problem occurs at the point where the individual's expansion path crosses the time constraint of Eq. 13 associated with the appropriate value of α. This point uniquely determines the optimal combination h_E and h_Y, whose values may then be substituted into Eqs. 9 and 10 to obtain the optimal allocation of consumption time and into Eqs. 5 and 6 to obtain the optimal time devoted to each type of education. Although consumers focus their attention on the time allocation problem, the focus in this paper will be on the educational outcomes uniquely associated with consumers' decisions.

The key parameter in the model developed in this paper is ω, an indicator of cultural tension between the ethnic group and the shared environment. When ω is positive, the two kinds of human capital are acquired by means of complementary learning processes: The greater the level of h_E embodied in a person, the more efficiently he can learn general skills, and the greater the level of shared human capital, the more efficiently he can acquire ethnic-specific skills. The opposite is true when ω is negative, indicating that high levels of ethnic human capital (hence attachment to the ethnic communmity) make it more difficult to acquire general skills and vice versa. The parameter ω will thus differ across ethnic groups to a degree that depends on the relationship between each group's culture relative to the shared culture of the larger society.

Figure 1 illustrates the consumer's decision and its sensitivity to the group-specific parameter ω. The indifference map between ethnic-specific skills (on the horizontal axis) and shared skills (on the vertical axis) has been drawn to represent an individual with a strong preference for the ethnic good.[6] Three possible PPFs have been drawn, all using the same total resources and thus with endpoints at A and B. The PPF corresponding to a group where ethnic education and general education are mutually independent (i.e., where $\omega=0$) has been emphasized with a dark curve. In this case, the optimal combination of human capital would be at point C, and the expansion path is indicated by a similarly dark line.[7]

For purposes of comparison, Fig. 1 shows how different PPF curves would affect outcomes for the same individual with a strong preference for ethnic consumption. The PPF corresponding to positive externalities in the education process ($\omega>0$) is tangent to the indifference map at point D, on a higher indifference curve than C and characterized by greater investments in both types of human capital but with relatively more h_Y than in the mutually independent case. In contrast, the optimal investment if there are negative externalities between the two educational processes ($\omega<0$) is at point E, on a lower indifference curve and with greater specialization in

---

[5] A sufficient (but not necessary) condition for this slope to be negative is $\omega \leq 0$, meaning that the external effects of general education on ethnic education (and vice versa) are non-positive.

[6] For an interesting empirical exercise in measuring these axes for people in Germany, see Constant et al. (2006) and Constant and Zimmermann (2008). A promising approach to measurement elsewhere is suggested in Jasso et al. (2006).

[7] The expansion path connects the tangencies between the indifference map and a family of PPF curves for which $\omega=0$, only one of which is shown in Fig. 1.

Fig. 1 Strong preference for ethnic goods

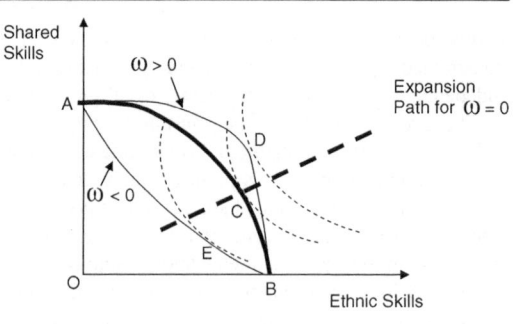

[Figure 1: Graph with axes "Shared Skills" (vertical) and "Ethnic Skills" (horizontal), showing curves labeled $\omega > 0$, $\omega < 0$, points A, D, C, E, B, O, and "Expansion Path for $\omega = 0$"]

ethnic human capital. Although not shown on this graph, the expansion path passing through E is to the right and less steep than the path through C, while the one passing through D is to its left and more steep.

2.2 The ethnic group

By definition, an ethnic group is the set of all consumers who consume its ethnic-specific good E, and all consumers in a given ethnic group face the same family of PPF curves and time constraints. Individual consumers vary in their tastes and preferences for the ethnic good, however, as well as in the efficiency with which they acquire new human capital. Thus, each person's human capital expansion path is individually determined, as is the optimal point on that path. To analyze the implications of these individual decisions for the ethnic community as a group and for the larger society in which it is embedded, each member of the group is assumed to make a decision based on a common family of PPF curves but an expansion path determined by his or her own indifference map and learning ability.

Figure 2a illustrates the case of an ethnic community with positive ω, indicating that the two learning processes are mutually complementary so that its PPF curves will be bowed outward (i.e., its convexity will be high), and Fig. 2b illustrates the case of negative externalities where ω is negative and large in magnitude. In both graphs, the dotted-line expansion path corresponds to the indifference map of persons with a strong preference for the ethnic good, shown in Fig. 1 as having a tangency to a PPF at points D (for Fig. 2a) or E (for Fig. 2b). The solid-line expansion path corresponds to the indifference map of people with weak preferences for the ethnic good or strong preferences for the consumption basket shared by all groups. Those with more balanced preferences will have expansion paths somewhere between these two extremes.

People locate themselves along their respective expansion paths according to their educational abilities. In Fig. 2, a shaded oval area around each of the two extreme expansion paths is intended to suggest a scatter of outcomes for group members with similar (but not identical) preferences. Not indicated in the graph is the scatter of outcomes for people in between these two extremes. Figure 2a illustrates the case of a group with very high value of ω, where extreme differences in preferences nevertheless yield similar outcomes so that the in-between area is small and the group is fairly homogeneous. Figure 2b illustrates the case where ω is very low

Fig. 2 Derived demand for ethnic Human capital. **a** positive externalities: $\omega>0$. **b** negative externalities $\omega<0$

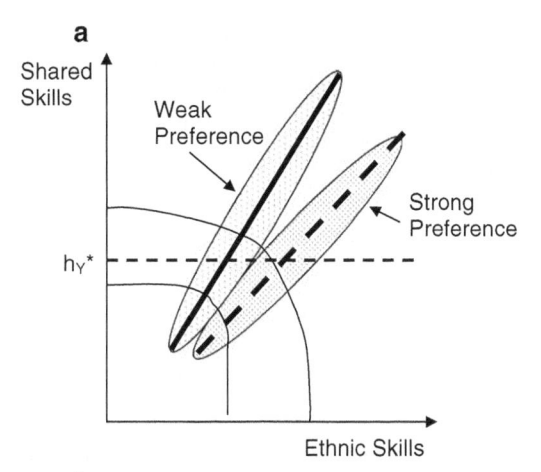

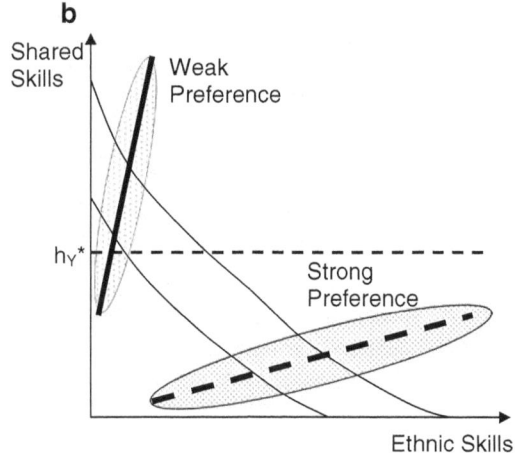

(highly negative), where a balanced human capital portfolio is fairly costly. People with balanced preferences would have outcomes within this region, but the tendency would be for the scatter of outcomes to thin out as it approaches the center and to concentrate at lower levels of human capital. The scatter of points for groups with moderate values of ω would have more members in the area between these two extremes.

2.3 Ethnic identity and assimilation

The concept of ethnic assimilation is socially determined and depends importantly on the shared culture of the larger society. Two extreme cases will be considered in this paper, referred to briefly as "pluralistic" and "monolithic," respectively. As its name suggests, a pluralistic society is one in which multiple ethnic groups coexist within a larger social framework that they all share. In this context, an ethnic group is considered to be assimilated whenever its members accept the values, attitudes, and norms of the shared culture and participate more or less actively in its economic and social life. In contrast, a monolithic society is one where everyone is expected to conform to a shared ideal, typically associated with the ethnic culture of one or more specific groups. In this context, a group is not viewed as assimilated until its members adopt the dominant ethnicity and the minority group effectively disappears.

2.3.1 Acculturation in a pluralistic society

Groups in a pluralistic society assimilate with respect to each other when they share values, goals, and activities, giving their members an incentive to invest in a common set of human capital attributes. That is, the greater the level of shared human capital embodied in a person, h_Y, the more he or she has in common with members of other ethnic groups and hence, by definition, the greater the degree of acculturation.[8] For simplicity, suppose there is some threshold level of shared human capital, h_Y^*, beyond which an individual may be characterized as acculturated. By the same token, a group may be characterized as assimilated into the shared culture of a society if a large proportion of its members are acculturated because they embody at least h_Y^* amount of shared human capital.

Figure 2a and b illustrate this threshold with a horizontal line at h_Y^*. The portion of the shaded ovals above this line represent people who are assimilated in this sense, sharing the values, attitudes, experiences, and knowledge common to all ethnic groups in the larger society. The portion below this line represent the unacculturated, people who do not share much human capital with the mainstream society and are thus perceived, by themselves and by others, as outsiders.

By this definition, assimilation need not mean homogeneity, for only the amount of shared human capital, h_Y, is relevant for determining participation in a shared culture. The amount of ethnic-specific human capital, h_E, is an important determinant of his or her ethnic identity and hence participation in an ethnic community, but it does not affect the extent to which an individual participates in the larger society.

Again for simplicity, suppose there is some threshold level of ethnic human capital, h_E^*, required for a person to have a clear association with a particular ethnic group. Persons with more than this amount of h_E identify with the ethnic community and would lose the value of their ethnic human capital if they were to exit. Those with less than h_E^* have little attachment to the community and would incur little cost if they were to leave. While members of the latter group are sometimes described as "assimilated" because of their low ethnic identity, they may or may not be active participants in the society's shared culture.

---

[8] Note that this definition applies symmetrically to all groups, including those described as "dominant" because of their large size or cultural influence.

The relationship between ethnic identity and assimilation is best seen by considering both definitions simultaneously, as illustrated in Fig. 3 by the division into four quadrants. The axes and the shaded ovals duplicate those in Fig. 2a and b, respectively. Individuals whose education choices places them to the right of the vertical line at h_E^*, in quadrants I or II, have strong ethnic identities, while those in quadrants III or IV, to the left of this line, do not. The people in quadrants I and IV embody more shared human capital than h_Y^* and are thus assimilated in the sense that they share the same values, attitudes, experiences, and knowledge as the members of other ethnic groups in the larger society. Those in quadrants II and III are below the threshold value of h_Y^* and are in this sense "outside" the shared culture. People in quadrant II are "outsiders" because they identify with an ethnic

Fig. 3 Propensity to assimilate. **a** positive externalities: $\omega > 0$. **b** negative externalities: $\omega < 0$

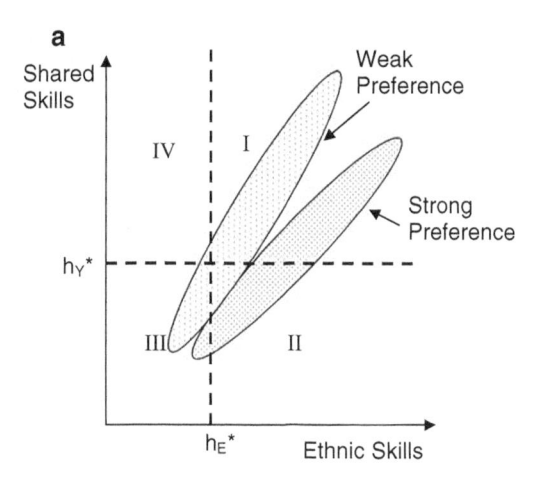

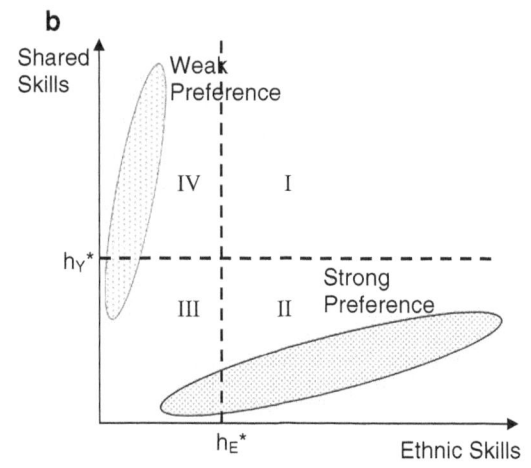

group that does not share the society's common values. Those in quadrant III constitute a marginalized underclass that participates in neither the common culture nor an ethnic subculture.

A taxonomy distinguishing between "assimilation" and the "integration" of ethnic groups into the mainstream of society has been suggested elsewhere (Constant et al. 2006; Constant and Zimmermann 2008).[9] People in quadrant I, with high levels of general human capital although their consumption patterns continue to include ethnic goods and hence a demand for ethnic-specific human capital, are said to be "integrated" into the larger society. Together they form an "integrated" ethnic community, in contrast to the people in quadrant II who constitute a "separated" ethnic community. The term "assimilated" is reserved for the people in quadrant IV who have little ethnic human capital and hence low productivity in ethnicity-specific consumption patterns but otherwise participate in the general society.[10] In this respect, they differ from the "marginalized" people in quadrant III who are at best loosely attached to society at large and to their own ethnic group.

People in quadrant IV are assimilated, and those in quadrant II are unassimilated (separatist), with respect to any society, whether pluralistic or monolithic. As Fig. 3b suggests, these quadrants dominate in groups for which ethnic education is most anti-complementary with respect to general education, inducing people to specialize in either ethnic or shared human capital. Those who choose the ethnic-specific investment path have low levels of h_Y and thus tend to be socially—and perhaps also geographically—separated from the mainstream. Group members who choose the shared-human-capital investment path tend to fall in quadrant IV, where low levels of ethnic human capital reduce the priority placed on ethnic lifestyles and high levels of shared human capital provide a common bond with persons of other ethnicities whose priorities are similar.

Figure 3a illustrates the propensity to assimilate for groups in which ethnic-specific and general educations are mutually complementary. This complementarity in education raises the incentive to invest in both kinds of human capital, inducing outcomes in which most members are likely to be in quadrant I and a less-educated minority in quadrant III. The group would thus be dominated by productive and culturally assimilated members of the larger society who also have a strong ethnic identity and are likely to participate in the ethnic community. Members who assimilate in the sense of reduced ethnic identity would tend to have low levels of shared human capital and hence would also find it difficult to participate fully in the larger society.

---

[9] These papers focus on measuring the degree of ethnic assimilation rather than an analysis of its determinants, but their classification of ethnic groups for this purpose is much the same as the four quadrants illustrated in Fig. 3 of the present paper.

[10] In common parlance, the term "assimilation" often combines both concepts. For example, American Jewry in the early twentieth century was an immigrant community that viewed assimilation as a highly desirable goal, but in the late twentieth century was more likely to view it as a serious problem. The earlier community understood assimilation as a movement from quadrant II into quadrant I, investing heavily in h_Y often at the expense of investments in h_E. The later generation was centered in quadrant I but included many people in quadrant IV whose connections to the Jewish community were weak or ambivalent. While both communities used the term "assimilation," the earlier period used it in its broader sense (quadrants I and IV) while the narrower usage (quadrant IV) is implied during the later period.

2.3.2 Assimilation in a monolithic society

In a society whose shared culture emphasizes the benefits of homogeneity, ethnic particularism is discouraged, and assimilation is defined as a decision to identify with the mainstream "shared" society. The decision to switch ethnicity to join the mainstream, whether informally or through some sort of formal conversion process, requires that the benefits of switching outweigh the cost. In this respect, it is analogous to migration: The higher the stock of non-transferable ethnic skills, the higher the cost of switching and greater the gain required to compensate for the loss associated with changing groups.

If the largest cost of joining the mainstream is determined by the loss of non-transferable ethnic human capital, the vertical line at h_E^* in Fig. 3 can be interpreted as the borderline dividing the ethnic group between leavers and stayers. People with human capital endowments to the right of this line have high levels of ethnic attachment and high costs of leaving the group, while those to the left of this line have low levels of ethnic human capital and hence a low cost of exit from the group.[11]

Figure 3a suggests that members of successful ethnic groups with high positive values of ω are unlikely to assimilate in this sense and that members of those groups who choose to switch affiliation are likely to be the least educated within the community. In contrast, for groups with large negative values of ω, illustrated by Fig. 3b, the ethnic community will be divided into those that choose to assimilate by joining the mainstream (in the vertical oval mostly to the left of h_E^*) and strongly identified ethnics who resist assimilation (in the horizontal oval that is mostly below h_Y^*). In a society that places a high value on ethnic homogeneity, high levels of group-specific human capital associated with religion, language, or family life that reinforce clear group boundaries may thus serve as a de facto barrier to assimilation even if the ethnic group itself does not actively discourage its members from switching.

3 Applications and extensions

The model developed above can be applied to a variety of issues associated with the assimilation of ethnic groups with respect to the larger society or with respect to each other. In doing so, it is often necessary to relax one or more of the restrictions assumed in the previous section for the sake of simplicity. This section considers four such issues. Section 3.1 discusses the relationship between ethnic intermarriage and assimilation. Section 3.2 discusses the effects of ethnic group size on assimilation. Section 3.3 considers the possible endogeneity effect that can occur when two or more minority ethnic groups merge with each other, and Section 3.4

---

[11] The rate of return to changing one's ethnic identity is the net present value of the gain in utility divided by the net present value of the cost of switching. If everyone faces the same prospects of gain and the same cost function for acquiring human capital specific to the new ethnicity, all differences in rates of return arise from individual differences in learning ability, α, and in the amount of ethnic human capital h_E specific to the origin group.

considers the conflict that arises when ethnic groups jockey for economic or political power within the larger society. In each case, the basic human capital model is applied with appropriate modifications (if any).

3.1 Assimilation by ethnic intermarriage

Low levels of ethnic human capital would facilitate movement by individuals across ethnic boundaries, whether purposeful (by conversion or intermarriage) or inadvertently as a byproduct of other consumption decisions. To the extent that such movements result in assimilated families with relatives who are ethnically identified, they may lead ipso facto to a blurring of the social boundaries by which ethnic groups are distinguished from the mainstream and from each other. Vague boundaries in turn facilitate further blending of ethnic identities as they reduce the cost of switching into the relatively homogeneous mainstream. To the extent that ethnic intermarriage occurs in such a society, it can be understood as both a cause and a symptom of ethnic assimilation.

Viewing ethnic intermarriage as symptomatic of assimilation requires the narrower definition (i.e., quadrant IV) most often associated with an assumption that the society has homogeneity as its ideal. In a pluralistic society, intermarriage may be associated with the merging of ethnic identities (as, for example, when people of English and Scottish descent become Anglo-Americans, or when people of Pakistani and Moroccan origin become Moslem-Americans), but it is generally irrelevant as an indicator of assimilation into the larger society. In a society that places a premium on homogeneity, however, intermarriage is closely associated with assimilation into the dominant mainstream group, with the weakening of ethnic ties, and with the eventual disappearance of the ethnic group. With this caveat in mind, the model developed above has implications for the economics of intermarriage as a vehicle for ethnic assimilation.

Marital compatibility is generally greatest for people with similar levels and types of human capital (Lehrer and Chiswick 1993; Lehrer 1996, 1998; Becker 1981). The optimal marital sort would thus tend to pair people who are close to each other with respect to both h_Y and h_E. People who closely identify with an ethnic group because they have $h_E > h_E^*$ would prefer partners of the same ethnicity, those who are assimilated into the shared culture because they have $h_Y > h_Y^*$ would prefer partners who are similarly acculturated, and those whose human capital falls below these thresholds are likely to marry each other.

To see the implications of this for intermarriage between members of different ethnic groups, Fig. 4 illustrates the situation for the simplest case where two ethnicities coexist in the same society.[12] The portions of Fig. 4a and b to the right of their respective origins, with horizontal axes that measure ethnic skills of Group A, are a duplicate of Fig. 3a and b. The portions to the left of the origin measure the ethnic skills of Group B from right to left, but otherwise they also duplicate Fig. 3a and b, respectively. While it is not necessary (or even likely) that two ethnic groups

---

[12] This analysis implicitly assumes that the content of ethnic education for the two groups is mutually compatible or at least neutral (i.e., does not generate hostility) with respect to each other.

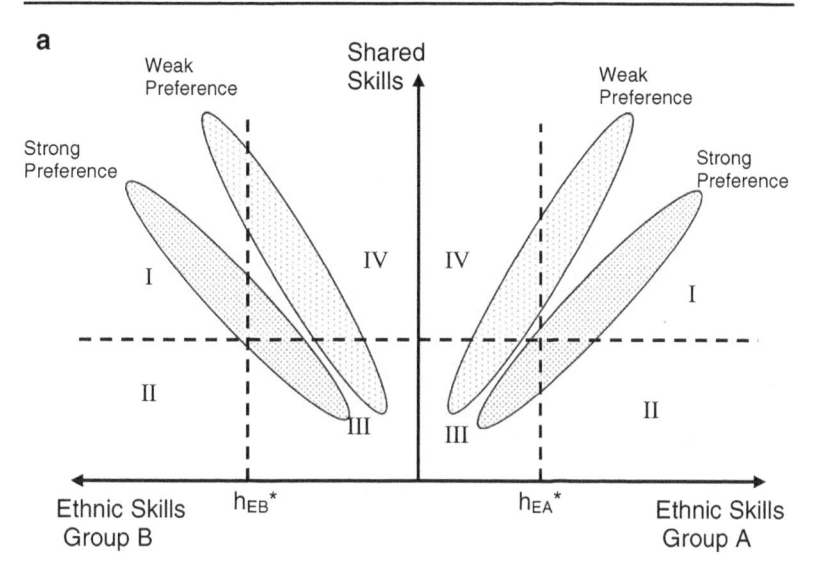

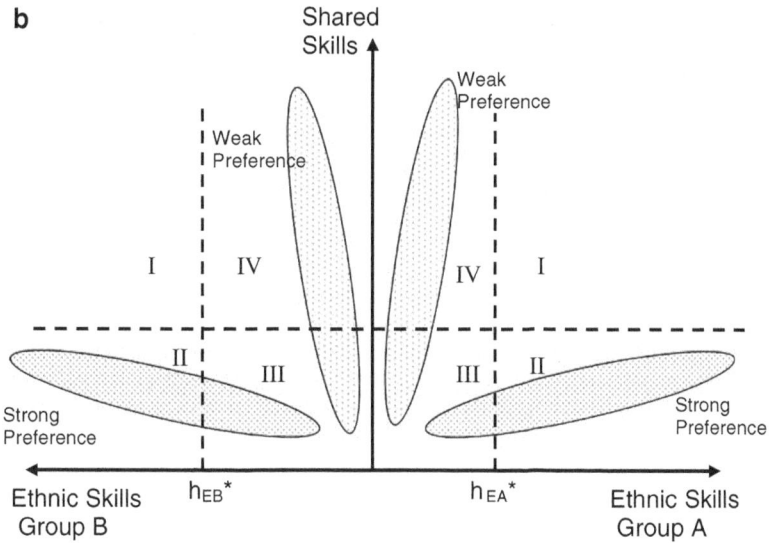

Fig. 4 Two ethnic groups with externalities. **a** positive externalities: $\omega > 0$. **b** negative externalities: $\omega < 0$

would have the same production functions for ethnic human capital, the present discussion is sufficiently general to permit abstraction from such differences.

Because people with high levels of ethnic human capital are most likely to seek marriage partners with similarly high levels of h_E, the propensity for intergroup marriage is low for people in quadrants I and II of either group. The propensity for ethnic intermarriage is greater for people in quadrants III and IV in part because they have low productivity in ethnic consumption and in part because their rate of return to switching groups is higher than that of people with more ethnic-specific human capital. It may even be that alienation from their respective ethnic communities provides a common bond for people on either side of the vertical axis but close to it, thus further increasing the likelihood of intermarriage.

Figure 4a illustrates the case where ethnic and general educations are mutually complementary, providing incentives to invest in both kinds of human capital. People with large investments in human capital would tend to have relatively high levels of ethnic and shared human capital and thus be less likely to seek partners outside the group. Ethnic intermarriage is more likely to occur among the less educated, who are also more likely to include persons with weak preferences for the ethnic good. At all levels of education, however, members with different preferences (and thus in different shaded ovals) have similar combinations of h_E and h_Y and thus can form stable marriages with each other.

In contrast, differences in preferences are extremely important for marital propensities in Fig. 4b, where it is much less likely that people of the same ethnicity but with different preferences would match themselves with each other. When ethnic and general educations are anti-complementary (i.e., when each generates negative externalities for the other), people face reduced incentives to invest in human capital and tend toward specialization in one or the other type. In Fig. 4b, the only people with a strong incentive to seek partners within the group are those with strong preferences for the ethnic good and heavy investments in ethnic human capital. In contrast, persons with weak preference for the ethnic good (or a strong preference for the shared good) are close to the vertical axis (most likely in quadrant IV) and thus unlikely to seek marital partners among those in quadrant II. People with low levels of h_E may marry each other or they may match themselves with partners of a different ethnic origin but with similarly low levels of their respective ethnic human capital.

The configurations illustrated in Fig. 4a and b are symmetrical in that the general human capital is equally complementary with the ethnic human capital of the two groups. This need not be the case. For example, the human capital shared by everyone might be highly complementary to the ethnic human capital for Group A but anti-complementary to that of Group B. In this case, the graph to the right of the vertical axis would look like the corresponding portion of Fig. 4a and the graph to the left of the axis would look like Fig. 4b. People in Group A with low ethnic attachment would also have low levels of h_Y, but people with low levels of attachment to Group B would have high levels of h_Y. Ethnic intermarriage is thus much less likely to occur between these groups even among people who are assimilated.

3.2 Group size effects

An important asymmetry occurs when the two ethnic groups differ in the size of their respective populations. Suppose the two ethnic groups in Fig. 4 were identical in every respect except that Group A is ten times larger than Group B. Then, each quadrant would have ten people in Group A for every person in Group B. In the extreme case where Group B experiences a 100% intermarriage rate, the intermarriage rate for Group A could never exceed 10%. Even if the propensity to intermarry were the same for both groups, in the sense illustrated by the symmetry in Fig. 4, the probability that people in quadrants III and IV of one group could find a match from the other would be very high for members of Group B but very low for members of Group A. Thus, the observed intermarriage rate would be much higher for group B than for group A and would have very different implications for their respective ethnic communities.

Within a single ethnic group, the relative number of people within each set of preferences may also have implications for intermarriage rates.[13] Suppose, for example, that 75% of the people in Fig. 4b are in the high-ethnicity quadrant II and only 15% in quadrant IV, with the other 10% loosely scattered in the other two quadrants. Suppose further that the threshold level of education h_Y^* corresponds to graduation from high school. This group would be characterized as low-achieving because the large majority of its members have less than h_Y^*. The "exceptional" group members who are high school graduates would be found in quadrant IV and would be likely to marry outside the group not only because their ethnic identity is weak but also because their numbers are few.

Now suppose these numbers were reversed, with 15% of the people in the high-ethnicity, low-education quadrant II and 75% in the high-education, low-ethnicity quadrant IV. Then the group might be perceived as assimilated, with an "exceptional" minority preserving the ethnic heritage. Persons in the disadvantaged minority subgroup can be expected to marry each other and so have a low out-marriage rate. Those in the assimilated majority might be open to ethnic intermarriage, but they also have a large pool of potential partners in the same ethnic subgroup. Ethnic out-marriage would be socially acceptable—even welcomed—within the assimilated high-education subgroup, but its intermarriage rate is not predictable.

This simple example illustrates several hypotheses linking education levels and ethnic intermarriage rates. For ethnic groups characterized by high levels of general education and strong ethnic identity, out-marriage rates would tend to be higher among the less-educated minority. For groups with high levels of general education and weak ethnic identity, out-marriage rates would tend to be higher the smaller the size of the group. For groups with strong ethnic identity and low levels of general education, out-marriage rates would be higher among the well-educated minority.

The association between ethnic intermarriage rates and assimilation is thus observable only in certain special cases. It can be expected in a society that places a high value on ethnic homogeneity, where ethnicity-specific human capital is ipso facto anti-complementary to the shared human capital of the larger society. It can also be expected in a pluralistic society if the ethnic group is a small minority whose membership includes people who are marginally attached to the group. Assimilation is much less likely to be associated with inter-ethnic marriages for large groups in a

---

[13] Size is much less important for a group illustrated by Fig. 4a, where people in different ovals may marry each other and where the "exceptional" members with high out-marriage rates would tend to be relatively few and among the least educated.

pluralistic society or for groups that differ greatly in their investment in shared human capital.

The size of an ethnic group also has an indirect effect on intermarriage rates because of economies of scale in the production and consumption of ethnic goods. Investment in language skills are clearly more productive the larger the pool of people speaking the same language, and the more people who speak an ethnic language, the greater the incentive to express oneself in it and hence the more extensive the literature that emerges. Human capital formation in childhood is more effective if all members of the family share the same ethnicity, and the cost is further reduced when family life is embedded in an ethnic community with its larger stock of human capital and attendant social institutions. The utility-generating productivity of a group's ethnic human capital is thus amplified when there are many consumers with high levels of the human capital specific to the same ethnicity.

Because shared experiences and goals are the bases for many voluntary social organizations, ethnic groups often exhibit characteristics typical of membership societies or clubs. Of particular interest here is the mutual complementarity among members of various forms of participation. Each individual finds the utility-generating productivity of resources devoted to ethnic consumption to be enhanced by the active participation of other group members or, conversely, finds the benefits of participation to be lower in a group where other members are apathetic. This generates "bandwagon" effects that can be either positive or negative.[14]

3.3 Ethnic mergers

The assumption until now has been that each individual acquires human capital specific to one and only one ethnicity and that ethnic human capital has little between-group transferability. This assumption can now be relaxed. Even people who identify strongly with one ethnic group may learn about (or acquire human capital specific to) another. In societies with multiple ethnic groups, two groups may have some ethnic human capital in common (e.g., language or religion) although it is not shared by everyone in the larger society.

To illustrate the new possibilities, each of the two-dimensional graphs in Fig. 4 can be folded 90° along its vertical axis to make a third dimension, with one of its axes labeled Ethnic Skills Group A and the other labeled Ethnic Skills Group B. Individuals who specialize in the human capital of their own ethnic group would still be found near one of these axes (and hence near the ovals illustrated in Fig. 4), but those who acquire some human capital specific to the other group would be represented by a point somewhere in this third dimension. In the extreme case, where the two types of ethnic human capital are mutually compatible (complementary) and people from both groups tend towards the central area in this plane, the groups may effectively assimilate with respect to each other and form a combined ethnicity.

In general, the greater the ethnic specificity of family-related human capital, the greater the incentive to choose a marriage partner from within the group (Chiswick

---

[14] For some interesting applications of this phenomenon, see Iannaccone (1992), Chiswick and Chiswick (2000), and Kahanec (2006).

and Lehrer 1991; Lehrer and Chiswick 1993). For ethnic groups that differ with respect to parenting skills and family relationships, intermarriage is most likely to occur among people who are not planning to have children or are otherwise distant from close relatives. If ethnic differences have little bearing on childrearing skills and family experiences, intermarriage is less difficult and thus more likely. Ethnic group boundaries are further blurred when marital partners from different groups raise children with ambiguous affiliations, whether they belong to both groups or to neither. Intermarriage is thus both a symptom and a cause of assimilation.

This suggests an important relationship between religion, language, and ethnicity that tends to link the two aspects of group identity. Passing on an ethnic language and the formation of religious human capital during childhood and youth are important functions of the family and community. If these types of human capital are transferable across ethnic groups that share the same language and/or religion, an ethnic intermarriage would be less costly between them than between groups speaking a different language or practicing another religion. In practice, the linguistic barrier to intermarriage can be overcome because members of all ethnic groups share the common language of the larger society.[15] The children of such intermarriages typically learn only the common language, with the long-run implication for ethnic languages to fade out. Finding a shared religion is more difficult, so ethnic intermarriages are less likely to cross religious boundaries; the long-run tendency would be for intermarriage to blur ethnic distinctions within religious groups so that ethnicity and religion become identified with each other.

3.4 Ethnic conflict

When one ethnic group is "dominant," whether because of its relative size, its economic influence, or its political power (history), the distinction between general and ethnic human capital for that group is not always clear. Its situation would be the one illustrated by Fig. 3a, where the formation of general skills and ethnic skills are so highly correlated that, for practical purposes, the distinction between the two is blurred. Members of the dominant ethnicity would have a clear economic advantage over the members of other ethnic groups. There is also a tendency for the dominant group to be described as "mainstream" and for assimilation to be perceived as investment in its ethnicity-specific human capital.

Although this confusion is common in many countries, it generates a number of problems that may retard the assimilation of minority groups. For example, it increases the likelihood that a minority ethnic group faces the kind of negative externalities illustrated by Fig. 3b. Suppose, for example, that ethnic Germans are the dominant group in Germany and that members of this group invest heavily in knowledge about science (a general skill) and German customs regarding marriage and family life (ethnic skills). Scientists would be observed to follow these customs, and a spurious causal relationship might be inferred. This would make it more difficult for members of, say, a Turkish minority in Germany to invest in a science

---

[15] This condition is less likely to be met by immigrants than by their native-born children, although immigrants in small immigrant communities have a stronger incentive to learn the language of the larger society and thus are more likely to intermarry.

education, for they might think that by doing so they would be exchanging their Turkish family lifestyle for a German one, effectively switching from one ethnic group to another. Confounding the ethnic human capital of a dominant group with general human capital is thus a potential source of ethnic tension that may retard assimilation.

Economic agents have two basic strategies for expanding their opportunities for consumption, by raising productivity or by seeking to transfer to themselves (whether by taxation, fiat, theft, or extortion) the rents earned by other agents (Anderson and Hill 1989). In the "production" economy, free markets maximize aggregate consumption and cause the income distribution to be Pareto optimal. In the "transfer" economy, this is not the case, for even when transfers are limited to scarcity rents (in which case they would not change the level or allocation of existing resources), they represent a reduction in capital formation and hence a deadweight loss in aggregate production.

Any ethnic group with a high positive value of ω will have many members with high levels of both h_Y and h_E who are successful participants in production activities. Many different productive skills are encompassed in the concept of h_Y, and there is a tendency for group members to cluster in occupations for which their ethnic human capital is especially complementary. Even if they do not dominate the labor supply for a particular occupation, the advantage in skill acquisition that attracts them implies a scarcity rent that tends to be higher than that of co-workers from different ethnicities.

In contrast, when ω is negative, strongly attached members of an ethnic group tend to be low-earning, isolated socially and perhaps also geographically from other ethnic groups with whom they share little human capital. The combination of isolation and disadvantage can foster a sense of grievance, but more importantly, it raises the return to rent-seeking behavior relative to production activities. Ethnic differences in scarcity rents provide economic incentives to participate in the "transfer" economy, where laws or other arrangements are designed to benefit one ethnic group at the expense of others. The incentives to support such an economy are positively related to ethnic-group differences in the levels of economic rent and inversely related the cost of enforcing the transfer.

Ethnic groups differ in their attitudes toward rent seeking as an acceptable alternative to production, as well as in their power to enforce such exchanges, and they vary accordingly in their support for these strategies. A transfer can be ethnic-based either explicitly, as in affirmative-action programs, or implicitly, as in large-family subsidies whose benefits fall disproportionately on a few groups. Where such ethnic-based transfer strategies are viable, they constitute a clear incentive for groups to resist assimilation into the shared mainstream (Epstein 2006). As with any other economic activity, the efficiency of rent seeking can be enhanced by an increase in the relevant skills. Unlike production skills, which are potentially shared by all groups, rent-seeking skills can be focused on group-specific goals. When this is the case, a relatively high investment in such group-specific transfer skills would provide an economic incentive to resist assimilation.

Although the notion of a "mainstream" or dominant ethnic group is fairly common, the specific group that defines the mainstream can change over time or from one region to the next even within a single country. Ethnic dominance in this context is endogenous, and jockeying for that status can be a source of ethnic conflict. The modern era has added a new dimension to the transfer society and hence a new economic impetus for ethnic conflict. Even as high productivity raises the stakes by increasing aggregate income, public-sector provision of services provides an institutional structure that facilitates extensive income transfers. Thus, control of a national government is a prize worthy of considerable sacrifice, and many ethnic groups have chosen to divert resources to that end. This suggests that it is no coincidence that economic development in the nineteenth and twentieth century has been accompanied by the emergence of particularly powerful nationalist movements on the part of many ethnic groups for whom sovereignty was not previously an issue.

Rent-seeking skills would be especially valuable in countries where transfers have been relatively more important than production as a source of income, whether because productivity is low (as in some less-developed countries) or because transfers are especially large (as in the former Soviet Union) or both. Thus, it may be no coincidence that some of the most virulent ethnic violence of our time occurs in countries with low levels of modern human capital or a history of inefficiency in production. Economically induced ethnic violence may be self-limiting, if only because it dissipates the very rents that serve as its reward.[16] Yet, it also can be very destructive and have immiserating long-run effects on the economy as a whole.

4 Conclusion and policy implications

The focus of this paper has been on understanding economic forces that support the assimilation of ethnic groups into a larger society. A microeconomic model of investment in ethnic human capital served as the basis for modeling the determinants of ethnic identity and the relationship between the ethnic group and the general society. This relationship provided a context for defining assimilation in two different ways, depending on whether the general society is pluralistic or monolithic with respect to its ethnic ideals. The likelihood that an ethnic group would assimilate was shown to be sensitive to the degree to which investment in its ethnic human capital complements investments in general (shared) forms of human capital.

The degree of complementarity or anti-complementarity was shown to have important implications not only for persistence of the ethnic group but also for such ethnic-group differences in general investments as educational attainment and demographic behavior. The model was applied to an analysis of inter-ethnic marriages, often considered a symptom of assimilation. This association was shown to be important when the ethnic group is small relative to the general society, when investment in the group's ethnic human capital is anti-complementary to investments in general human capital, and when the general society has homogeneity as an ideal. Assimilation is less likely to associate with intermarriage for relatively large ethnic groups, for groups with a high degree of complementarity between investments in ethnic and general human capital, or for groups in a pluralistic society.

---

[16] The image of a "cash cow"—yielding a steady flow of income with no diminution of capital—meets the fable of the "goose that lays a golden egg"—a source of easy income only as long as it remains intact.

Some of the model's assumptions were relaxed to allow consideration of factors associated with the endogeneity of ethnic identification over time and space. In some cases, groups with ethnic human capital that is mutually complementary may merge to form a larger ethnic community that can benefit from economies of scale and positive bandwagon effects. For example, second- and third-generation immigrant groups with a common religion often merge to form a single ethnic identity based on religion rather than country of origin. In other cases, between-group differences in the nature of ethnic human capital may generate differences in general skills and hence in scarcity rents earned by group members. When these differences are large, they provide an incentive for low-rent groups to extract income transfers from high-rent groups, a process that typically involves some degree of ethnic conflict and serves as a disincentive to assimilation.

The model developed in this paper suggests several different approaches to achieving assimilationist goals. First, and perhaps most importantly, it suggests that ethnic identity per se is neither undesirable nor a barrier to the assimilation of individuals into the larger society. In a pluralistic society, the goal of assimilation is not to erode all ethnic distinctions, but rather to enhance the common culture and economic opportunities shared by all groups. Adaptations of the shared culture that increase its compatibility with a particular ethnic group would also have the effect of raising that group's externality parameter, ω, and thus encourage its members to invest in the shared human capital that constitutes assimilation. Policies that welcome ethnic diversity within the larger society without encouraging separation would have this effect. A policy of multiculturalism would fit this description as long as it is genuinely inclusive, but multicultural policies that elevate some groups (e.g., "disadvantaged" relative to "advantaged") or that subsidize the acquisition of ethnic human capital relative to general human capital would not have the desired effect.

Within an ethnic group, any adaptations that raise positive externalities between ethnic-specific and general education, ω, would have the effect of increasing assimilation without loss of ethnic identity (integration). If the PPF for the acquisition of these two types of skill is concave to the origin, this will bow it out even further and thus have the effect of strengthening ethnic identity as well. If the externalities are negative and sufficiently large, cultural adaptations that make ethnic skills more compatible with the larger society (i.e., that make ω less negative) encourage more members to assimilate, but they also reduce the likelihood that assimilated members will leave the group. For such groups, the challenge is to find adaptations to the ethnic culture that reduce negative externalities without sacrificing the ethnic identity that gives the group its special character.

Apart from these changes in human capital, economic policies that encourage inter-ethnic rent-seeking rivalries will retard assimilation and should be avoided. Any transfer society based on group differences would ipso facto generate such rivalries. Whether income transfers are implemented by a public tax-transfer system or by voluntary charity, a "disadvantaged" ethnic group with a large proportion of transfer recipients may develop institutions that implicitly support low levels of assimilation and encourage "disadvantaged" status. The challenge is to design transfers that are neutral with respect to group membership to avoid the unintended consequence of erecting barriers to assimilation.

Acknowledgment This paper has evolved over several years during which it has benefited from interactions with many people. An earlier version was presented at the Second Annual Migrant Ethnicity Meeting (IZA) and at the 2006 Annual Meeting of the European Society for Population Economics (ESPE), and a much earlier version at the Twelfth International History Congress, all of which were sources of helpful suggestions. The author is especially grateful to Barry R. Chiswick, Alan Olmstead, Timothy Hatton, Guillermina Jasso, and some anonymous referees for their encouragement and comments. The author, however, takes full responsibility for the contents of this paper.

References

Anderson T, Hill PJ (1989) The birth of a transfer society. University Press of America, Lanham, MD, USA

Becker GS (1981) A treatise on the family. Harvard University Press, Cambridge, MA, USA

Borjas GJ (1992) Ethnic capital and intergenerational mobility. Q J Econ 107(1):123–150

Borjas GJ (1995) Ethnicity, neighborhoods, and human capital externalities. Am Econ Rev 85:365–390

Chiswick BR (1988) Differences in education and earnings across racial and ethnic groups: tastes, discrimination, and investments in child quality. Q J Econ 103:571–597

Chiswick CU (2006) An economic perspective on religious education: complements and substitutes in a human capital portfolio. Res Labor Econ 24:449–467

Chiswick CU, Lehrer EL (1991) Religious intermarriage: an economic perspective. Contemp Jew 12:21–34

Chiswick BR, Chiswick CU (2000) The cost of living Jewishly and Jewish Continuity. Contemp Jew 21:78–90

Chiswick BR, Miller PW (2005) Do enclaves matter in immigrant adjustment? City and Community 4(1):5–35

Constant A, Zimmermann KF (2008) Measuring ethnic identity and its impact on economic behavior. J Eur Econ Assoc (in press).

Constant A, Gataullina L, Zimmermann KF (2006) Ethnosizing Immigrants. IZA Discussion Paper DP2040

Epstein GS (2006) Migrants, ethnicity and employment. Unpublished manuscript, 29

Iannaccone LR (1992) Sacrifice and stigma: reducing free-riding in cults, communes, and other collectives. J Polit Econ 100(2):271–291

Jasso G, Massey DS, Rosenzweig M, Smith JP (2006) Interethnic marriage, citizenship, and measurement of ethnicity. IZA Discussion paper 2212

Kahanec M (2006) Ethnic specialization and earnings inequality: why being a minority hurts but being a big minority hurts more. IZA Discussion paper DP2050

Lehrer EL (1996) The determinants of marital stability: a comparative analysis of first and higher order marriages. Res Popul Econ 8:91–121

Lehrer EL (1998) Religious Intermarriage in the United States: Determinants and Trends. Soc Sci Res 27:245–263

Lehrer EL (2004) Religion as a determinant of economic and demographic behavior in the United States. Popul Dev Rev 30:707–726

Lehrer EL, Chiswick CU (1993) Religion as a determinant of marital stability. Demography 30(3):385–404

Ethnosizing immigrants

Amelie F. Constant [a], Liliya Gataullina [b], Klaus F. Zimmermann [c],*

[a] *DIW DC, Georgetown University, and IZA, Germany*
[b] *IZA, Germany*
[c] *Bonn University, IZA, and DIW Berlin, Germany*

ARTICLE INFO

Article history:
Received 24 March 2006
Received in revised form 3 October 2008
Accepted 8 October 2008
Available online 17 October 2008

JEL classification:
F22
J15
J16
Z10

Keywords:
Ethnicity
Ethnic identity
Acculturation
Migrant assimilation
Migrant integration

ABSTRACT

The *ethnosizer*, a new measure of the intensity of a person's ethnic identity, is proposed using information on language, culture, societal interaction, history of migration, and ethnic self-identification. A two-dimensional version classifies immigrants into four states: integration, assimilation, separation and marginalization. Results based on the German Socio-economic Panel for 2001 are as follows. Young migrants are assimilated or integrated the most. While Muslims and Christians do not integrate, both assimilate the best. Immigrants with college in the home country separate less. Having some schooling is worse than no schooling for integration and assimilation. While ex-Yugoslavs assimilate more, Greeks, Italians and Spaniards are no different than Turks.

© 2008 Elsevier B.V. All rights reserved.

1. Introduction

The notion of migrant ethnicity is attracting a growing interest in economic research. Migration theories that treat immigrants as a homogeneous group are becoming less relevant in the presence of ethnically and culturally diverse populations. Strong ethnic differences are found in labor market preferences and behavior (Piche et al., 2002; Dana, 1997; Constant and Zimmermann, 2005), in wages and income (Zorlu, 2003; Neuman and Oaxaca, 2005; Mason, 2004), as well as in schooling performance (Betts and Fairlie, 2001; Smith, 2004). Research on migrant ethnicity is becoming a significant part in the growing literature on the effects of culture on economic outcomes (Guiso et al., 2006). Contributions on the significance of immigrants' ethnic diversity share the 'primordial' understanding of ethnicity as a lineage, a cultural inheritance or a "common ancestry based on shared individual characteristics and/or shared sociocultural experiences" gained at birth and marking the individual for life (Ruble, 1989, p. 401; Dashevsky, 1976).

In the past, ethnicity has often been treated as a permanent and static social characteristic of an individual, measured in terms of country of origin, nationality, citizenship or race. This static understanding of ethnicity does not allow accounting for an individual's sense of belonging and commitment to the group of people who share a common ancestry and culture

---

* Corresponding author at: IZA, P.O. Box 7240, D-53072 Bonn, Germany. Tel.: +49 228 3894 200; fax: +49 228 3894 210.
E-mail address: Zimmermann@iza.org (K.F. Zimmermann).

0167-2681/$ – see front matter © 2008 Elsevier B.V. All rights reserved.
doi:10.1016/j.jebo.2008.10.005

while they are in a heterogeneous host society. For example, ascribing or classifying an immigrant as Turk based solely on citizenship, nationality, or Turkish parenthood loses crucial information on how much culturally, socially and psychologically committed to the Turkish ancestry and values this immigrant is.

To convey the inner feelings of belonging, commitment and overall attitude to the culture and society of origin, an alternative 'individualist' notion of *ethnic identity* has been generated and used in anthropology, psychology, sociology, economics and marketing. Ethnic identity is "developed, displayed, manipulated, or ignored in accordance with the demands of a particular situation" (Royce quoted in Ruble, 1989, p. 401). There is a general agreement that when compared to the 'primordial' understanding of ethnicity, ethnic identity as a changing characteristic is a better measurement of the internal transformations in personal beliefs and commitments to values and culture inherited from the ancestry. Research documents, it is ethnic identity rather than the ethnicity of immigrants that defines their social, psychological (Hazuda et al., 1988; Phinney, 1990, 1992, 1996), economic (Mason, 2004) and consumer behavior (Hirshman, 1981; Ogden et al., 2004; Webster, 1990–1991; Laroche et al., 2005).

The general theoretical framework developed by Akerlof and Kranton (2000) connects identity with different social categories and shows how individuals in those affiliations should behave. The choice of an individual to be a particular type of person then becomes a powerful economic decision with substantial changes in the conclusions in comparison with traditional economic analysis. Bénabou and Tirole (2007) model a broad class of beliefs of individuals including their identity which people value and invest in. They also study endogenously arising self-serving beliefs linked to pride, dignity or wishful thinking. While there is a large potential of these frameworks for the analysis of ethnicity, they have not been further applied to that issue.

There are, however, a number of theoretical studies that develop economic theories of ethnic identity and explicitly explore their implications for economic behavior. Kuran (1998) has created a theory of reputational cascades that explains the evolution of behavioral ethnic codes that individuals follow to preserve social acceptance. The speed of acting ethnic is chosen under the influences of social pressures that the individuals themselves create and sustain. It is fostered by interdependencies among individual incentives that crucially affect personal choices. This theory can explain why similar societies may show very different levels of ethnic activity. Darity et al. (2006) provide a long-term theory of racial (or ethnic) identification formation. Their evolutionary game theory model may result in equilibrium where all persons follow an individualist identity strategy, another where all persons pursue a racialist (or ethnic) identity strategy, or a mixture of both. Consequently, race or ethnicity may be more or less significant for both market and non-market social interactions. A positive impact of racial identity on economic outcomes, that is, the productivity of social interactions, is the cornerstone of the theory. This also explains the persistence of racial or ethnic privileges in market economies.

Fearon and Laitin (2000) argue that ethnic identities are socially constructed, either by individual actions or by supra-individual discourses of ethnicity. They also may take the form of oppositional identities, which imply a rejection of the dominant, typically white behavioral norms (Austen-Smith and Fryer, 2005; Battu et al., 2007). Cutler et al. (1999) show that the end of legal barriers enforcing segregation in location choices in the US has been replaced by decentralized racism, where whites pay more than blacks for housing in predominantly white areas. Bisin et al. (2006) find that in line with their theoretical analysis, identity with and socialization to an ethnic minority are more pronounced in mixed than in segregated neighborhoods.

Our research in this paper concentrates on the study and measurement of ethnic identity, while it also values and uses the notion of ethnicity. We treat ethnic identity and ethnicity as two distinct, but closely related concepts. While ethnic identity can change, adapt, and evolve after arrival, ethnicity remains a permanent characteristic of the country of origin. We assume that ethnic identity becomes particularly meaningful and relevant after migration. In a globalizing world, ethnic identity can be an issue for people even in their country of origin, but at home there is not as much of a challenge to the commitment and sense of belonging to the values and culture inherited upon birth from one's parents. The real challenge typically appears after arrival in the host county when pre- and post-migration cultures, customs, and habitudes clash. As immigrants are now exposed to a dissimilar ethnicity, different levels of self-identification and feelings of belonging (either to the culture and values of ancestry or to the host society) develop. We examine various states of post-migration ethnic identity by individual characteristics, which cannot be affected by the act of migration. Once a person migrates, the ambivalence and the struggle of cultures begin.

The potential value of measuring ethnic identity is high. We know from various studies on the determinants of socio-economic outcomes such as education, income and work participation that country of origin or race dummies explain a significant part of such behavior. But such dummies measure ethnic or racial origin and not ethnic or racial identity and can be rather misleading. Migrants may neither look nor feel ethnic, or they may affiliate less or more with the culture of the host country. Mason establishes a stable identity formation among Mexican-Americans and other Hispanics. He shows that these ethnicities are able to increase their income substantially through acculturating into a non-Hispanic white racial identity. We will provide additional empirical evidence that ethnic identity actually interacts with such socio-economic outcomes.

How can we measure the intensity of the ethnic identity of a migrant? How ethnic is an immigrant, and where does this position the individual in the ethnic identity quadrant? Are people of certain age, gender, education, and religion more likely to maintain a strong commitment to the origin (or be more ethnic) after migration? Does ethnic origin affect the ethnic identity of migrating individuals differentially? While the focus of most of the previous economic literature is on theoretical analysis, we concentrate on the measurement and analysis of the empirical determinants. By combining information on language, culture, societal interaction, history of migration, and ethnic self-identification, we are able to provide a measure of ethnic identity, the *ethnosizer*. It enables us to classify immigrants into four states: integration, assimilation, separation and marginalization. We identify the societal sources of these regimes and suggest a basis for testing the various economic theories of ethnic identity.

In Section 2 we explain our concepts of measuring ethnic identity and of constructing the *ethnosizer*. Section 3 presents the data set used and discusses the variables in our analysis and their descriptive performance. Section 4 investigates the empirical behavior of the derived measures of ethnic identity and examines their determinants econometrically. Section 5 contains a summary and concludes.

2. Measuring ethnic identity

While a general understanding of flexible ethnic identity is shared among many social scientists, there is still no consensus on all the elements that compose ethnic identity. Among the suggested and widely used key elements of ethnic identity are the subjective expression of one's commitment to, sense of belonging to, or self-identification with the culture, values, and beliefs of a specific ethnic group and social life (Masuda et al., 1970; Tzuriel and Klein, 1977; Makabe, 1979; Unger et al., 2002). Most frequently employed are cultural elements such as language, religion, media and food preferences, celebrated holidays and behavior (Phinney, 1990, 1992; Unger et al., 2002; Laroche et al., 2005). A combination of these elements with heavy emphasis on culture has been used to develop measurements of ethnic identity, which are either specific to a certain ethnic group of individuals (Kwan and Sodowsky, 1997; Nguyen and von Eye, 2002), or are generally applicable to ethnically diverse samples of immigrants (Phinney, 1990, 1992; Laroche et al., 2005).

In this paper we develop a more general approach to ethnic identity, recognizing that while there may be some general commonalities among individuals of the same ethnicity, the individuality, personality, distinctiveness, and character of a person in an ethnic group prevails, can differ from one person to another, and can alter and evolve in different directions. We agree with Phinney (1990, p. 507) that "there are elements that are both common across groups and unique to ethnic identity for any group". We assume that the uniqueness of each ethnic group is captured by the ethnicity of the individual. Ethnic identity is how individuals perceive themselves within an environment as they categorize and compare themselves to others of the same or different ethnicity. It is the closeness or distance one feels from one's own ethnicity or from other ethnicities as one tries to fit into the society. As such, it can differ among immigrants of the same origin or be comparable among immigrants of different ethnic backgrounds. We consider the generality of ethnic identity to be one of the most important characteristics of our conception of identity because it makes it possible to compare immigrants within an ethnic group, and to draw parallels between representatives of different ethnicities. To operationalize and measure the general concept of ethnic identity, we employ five groups of quantifiable attributes, frequently used in previous research on the measurement of this type of concepts: (i) linguistic, (ii) visible cultural elements, (iii) ethnic self-identification, (iv) ethnic networks, and (v) migration history. Note that we choose these five groups because, while all five of the selected attributes are relevant, they are not specific to any ethnic group.

Social scientists approach various factors of ethnic identity from different angles. Some define ethnic identity in terms of immigrants' origins (Laroche et al.). Others look at ethnic identity from the host culture perspective, and measure it as the level of commitment to the host society and its values (Makabe, 1979; Ullah, 1985). Yet, a third group of researchers expresses the ethnic identity of immigrants as both an attachment to the culture or society of origin and devotion to the host country (Montgomery, 1992; Unger et al., 2002; Nguyen and von Eye, 2002). Similar to the latter group, in this paper we recognize that maintaining or losing one's own culture and self-identification with the origin is very closely related to gaining the culture of and self-identifying with the host society.

We, therefore, define ethnic identity as the balance between commitment to, affinity, or self-identification with the culture, norms, and society of origin and commitment to or self-identification with the host culture and society achieved by an individual after migration. In our definition we do not restrict ethnic identity to any specific type of the relationship between commitment to the origin and commitment to the host country. For simplicity of the outline, we conjecture that an immigrant moves along a plane formed by two positive vectors normalized from 0 to 1, with 1 representing maximum commitment. On the horizontal axis we measure commitment to and self-identification with the country of origin, and on the vertical axis we measure commitment to and self-identification with the host country. This two-dimensional model allows for several permutations between commitments to one or the other country in any possible combination.

Fig. 1 illustrates this concept to a special case. In this one-dimensional but continuous model one assumes a one-to-one correspondence or a zero-sum game. That is, at any time, the commitments are linearly dependent and mutually exclusive, and they sum up to one. Consequently, the more an individual commits to and feels for one country, the less he or she commits to and feels for the other country. This linear representation is depicted by a movement along the diagonal (1,0) to (0,1). We call this measurement of ethnic identity, the one-dimensional *ethnosizer*. Immigrants with maximum commitment only to the origin, point (1,0), are 'ethnic' because they did not alter their ethnic identity and affinity with the country of origin after they migrated and changed country of residence. On the vertical axis, as immigrants move from 0 to 1, they lose commitment to values and beliefs of the country of origin, and they identify all the more with the host country. They achieve a maximum bond with and commitment to the host society at point (0,1). We assume that immigrants who are at this coordinate achieve an ethnic identification that is similar to that of natives. Specifically, point (0,1) denotes a sameness, full adaptation of, strong bond with, and total identification with the culture of the host country. Such a linearity of the relationship between the commitments to two societies is comfortable for empirical research because it allows measuring

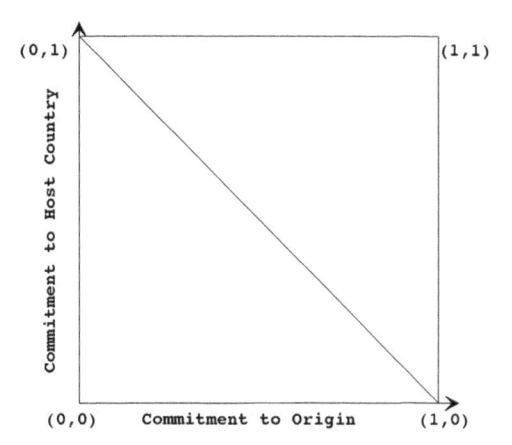

Fig. 1. The *ethnosizer* as a one-dimensional understanding of ethnic identity.

the immigrants' ethnic identity even when information on the commitment is available only for one country. Implicitly, this is the idea of immigrant assimilation in economic research.

However, individuals may exhibit strong association with and commitment to both the culture of ancestry and the host culture.[1] The two-dimensional model of the measurement of ethnic identity suggests that commitments to two different societies can coexist and influence each other in several ways. In other words, the level of dedication to the origin does not preclude the degree of the immigrants' commitment to the host society. This assumption recognizes that an immigrant who strongly identifies with the culture and values of his or her ancestry may or may not have a strong involvement with the dominant culture. Similarly, an immigrant with a strong affinity to the values and beliefs of the host country may or may not totally identify with the culture of ancestry. At the same time, immigrants may also be completely detached from the home or host countries. Our two-dimensional *ethnosizer* allows for this case as well.

The two-dimensional model of measuring ethnic identity helps to define the size of dedication to both the origin and the host cultures. We call the measurement of this ethnic identity the two-dimensional *ethnosizer*. As illustrated in Fig. 2, there are four states of ethnic identity, differentiated by the strength of cultural and social commitments. Quadrants A, I, M, and S correspond to *Assimilation* (A), a strong identification with the host culture and society, coupled with a firm conformity to the norms, values, and codes of conduct, and a weak identification with the ancestry; *Integration* (I), achieved when an individual combines, incorporates, and exhibits both strong dedication to the origin and commitment and conformity to the host society; *Marginalization* (M), a weak dedication to or strong detachment from either the dominant culture or the culture of origin; and *Separation* (S), an exclusive commitment to the culture of origin even after years of emigration, paired with weak involvement in the host culture and country realities. Starting at point (1,0), a migrant can undergo a more complicated journey through the various states, leaving separation towards integration, assimilation or marginalization, or remaining separated all measured by the two-dimensional *ethnosizer*.

Our two-dimensional understanding and measurement of ethnic identity is similar to Thurnwald's (1932) four rhythms of acculturation and Berry's (1980) definition of acculturation. In Fig. 2 we illustrate our rationale of the two-dimensional *ethnosizer* similar to Berry et al. (1989). However, we do not define the exact relationship between the exhibited involvement with the culture or origin and the culture of the host society in our understanding of ethnic identity.

To summarize, ethnicity denotes what people are since they are born in their home country. Ethnic identity denotes a complex construct and is defined as the fluid balance between commitment to or self-identification with the culture, values, and society of the origin and commitment to or self-identification with the host culture and society, achieved by an individual after migration. Whereas ethnicity is a permanent characteristic, ethnic identity is dynamic and may evolve in several directions. We are interested in measuring the intensity of ethnic identity of migrants after immigration. We define the instrument of the measurement of ethnic identity, the *ethnosizer*, and detail its construction in the next section. The objective is to parameterize the *ethnosizer* and estimate these parameters for the one-dimensional and two-dimensional

---

[1] Modern technologies have made attachments to multiple ethnic groups easier. Thanks to modern communications and improvements in the transportation system, it is now possible to live in one place and keep in steady and close contact with another. Attachments can also vary according to context. Turks in Germany identify with Turkish football teams, but they fervently support German teams in tournaments without Turkish teams. On matters of health they, by and large, trust the German health system relatively more and have come to expect German standards of medical excellence.

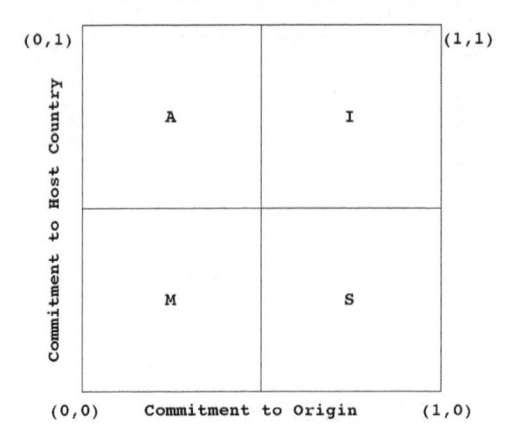

Fig. 2. The *ethnosizer* as a two-dimensional measurement of the size of ethnic identity.

variants using individual data from migrants of different ethnicities. We also define the verb *ethnosize* as containing a higher quantity of commitment to, devotion to, or self-identification with one's own ethnicity.

3. Data set and variable description

3.1. The sample

Our empirical analysis uses data from the German Socio-economic Panel (GSOEP), a nationally representative dataset collected annually since 1984 (SOEP Group, 2001). Patterned after the PSID, the GSOEP is a well-designed survey with a long-term proven record of reliable answers and a reputation as one of the best household surveys in the world. The GSOEP takes strict measures of confidentiality and guards the anonymity of participants in all research output. The 2000, 2001 and 2002 waves contain all relevant information needed for the measurement of ethnic identity. We therefore limit our sample to respondents who participated in all three waves, while we choose the year of 2001 as the base year of observation. That is, if information is not available in 2001, we use information from the years 2000 or 2002. Many of the questions from the GSOEP 2000–2002 that are relevant to our research interests were asked only to those immigrants whose citizenship is not German. Consequently, we limit our sample to non-German nationals only. We also exclude from our sample the German-born immigrants since we want to focus on the adjustment effects among (first-generation) immigrants. All in all, our sample consists of 1400 individuals; since some variables have missing values regressions are based on smaller samples.

In Table 1 we present the summary statistics of our sample. On average, there are slightly fewer women (49 percent), and the age of the respondents varies between 18 and 84 with the average being 45 years. Over a third of the immigrants in the sample are Muslims, and about another third Catholic. Most immigrants have either vocational or secondary education in their home countries. Over 46 percent of the sample did not receive adequate education in the country of origin, which could partially be explained by the young average age (about 22 years) at the time of immigration. About 8 percent of immigrants have obtained a college degree in the country of origin.

The selected sample is representative of all major ethnic groups of immigrants who live in Germany, namely Turks, Greeks, Italians, Spaniards, and people from the former Yugoslavia. We classify immigrants by ethnicity according to their country of origin. Turks form the largest ethnic group (34.8 percent) followed by ex-Yugoslavs (18.2 percent), Italians (15.3 percent), Greeks (8.5 percent) and Spaniards (3.6 percent). Immigrants from other ethnicities are 20 percent of our sample.

3.2. Construction of the dependent variables

In this section we explain the practical construction of the one- and two-dimensional measures of ethnic identity, the *ethnosizer*, that we suggested in Section 2. We form the *ethnosizer* by combining and weighing together five essential elements of personal devotion to the German culture and society and to the culture and society of origin: (i) language, (ii) culture, (iii) ethnic self-identification, (iv) ethnic interaction, and (v) migration history. We identify questions that transmit information on these salient components of ethnic identity. Table 2 presents the specific variables used for the measures for each classification by factor group in both models.

A potential problem is that ethnic attachment can be feigned, and the respondent may be playing to the interviewer. This might be especially true for ethnic self-identification, where individuals are asked whether they feel German or how closely

Table 1
Descriptive sample statistics.

Variables	Mean	Standard deviation
Female	0.491	0.500
Age	45.062	13.956
Age at entry	22.587	11.034
Religion		
Muslim	0.341	0.474
Catholic	0.308	0.462
Other Christian	0.180	0.384
Other religions	0.123	0.328
Non-religious	0.151	0.358
Schooling		
Have at least college in the home country	0.079	0.270
Have vocational training in the home country	0.291	0.454
Have completed schooling in the home country	0.340	0.474
Have incomplete schooling in the home country	0.161	0.368
Have no education degree from the home country	0.300	0.458
Ethnicity		
Turkish	0.348	0.476
Ex-Yugoslav	0.182	0.386
Greek	0.085	0.279
Italian	0.153	0.360
Spanish	0.036	0.187
Other	0.196	0.397
Ethnosizers		
One-dimensional *ethnosizer*	0.548	0.186
Integration	1.191	0.999
Assimilation	1.080	1.083
Separation	1.871	1.388
Marginalization	0.859	0.890

they are still attached to the country of origin.[2] However, this question was asked a number of times to the same individuals since 1984, the year the GSOEP started. Our *ethnosizer* also uses a number of additional questions on the same items from this survey, and averages their outcomes so that a potential reporting bias in some questions is balanced.

In calculating the one-dimensional *ethnosizer*, we weigh the sub-indices for the five variable groups equally. The sub-indices standardize the available information and proxy the ethnic identity of the individual from a different perspective. They are suggested to contain equally valuable information. For the one-dimensional *ethnosizer*, we also analyse the indices separately. For the two-dimensional *ethnosizer*, we summarize directly all individual data points for the five variable groups equally.

According to the one-dimensional model, the information summarized in column 1 of Table 2 about the attachment to the host country is also sufficient to define the immigrants' commitment to their origin and, therefore, to estimate their ethnic identity. We assigned a value to all alternative answers that a respondent was offered to choose from in replying to each stated question. That is, '1' corresponds to an answer indicating the least commitment to the German culture and '0' to an answer demonstrating the highest commitment to the German culture. An individual who indicates a 'very good' knowledge of spoken German, for example, receives the value of zero on this particular question. Following the same logic, the value of 'good' knowledge of German scores 0.25, 'fair' knowledge of German scores 0.5, 'poor' knowledge of German scores 0.75, and 'none at all' knowledge of German scores 1. In the linear model, the person who receives 1 demonstrates the most linguistic identification with the origin and is linguistically ethnic. On the other hand, an individual who scores zero on the same question is linguistically identical to a native German and has lost all ethnic identification with the language of origin. A similar procedure was performed on all other variables from the five components.

From the mean value of answers that a respondent gave to the questions from each category of factors, we generate the following five variables: *Language*, the mean assigned value of the respondents' answers to the questions on the language use category; *Cultural elements*, the mean assigned value of answers to the questions on the visible cultural elements category; *Interaction*, the mean assigned value of answers to the questions on the ethnic interaction and social relatedness category; *Self-identification*, the mean assigned value of answers to the questions on the ethnic self-identification category; and *Migration history*, the mean assigned value of answers to the questions on the category migration history.

---

[2] The questions are (1) 'Feel German:' "To what extent do you view yourself as a German?", and (2) 'Feel connected to the country of origin:' "To what extent do you feel that you belong to the culture of the country where you or your family comes from?" Potential answers are "completely, for the most part, in some respects, hardly, or not at all".

Table 2
Five elements of ethnic identity that compose the *ethnosizer*.

One-dimensional model	Two-dimensional model
(1) Based on Germany alone	(2) Based on both countries
Language	*Language*
Own opinion of spoken German	Own opinion of spoken German
Own opinion of written German	Own opinion of written German
Language mostly used in Germany	Own opinion of spoken language of origin
	Own opinion of written language of origin
Culture	*Culture*
Preferred media	Preferred media
Preferred music	
Cooked meals	
Ethnic self-identification	*Ethnic self-identification*
Self-identify as German	Self-identify as German
	Self-identify with the country of origin
Ethnic interaction	*Ethnic interaction*
Ancestry of three closest friends and relatives	Ancestry of three closest friends and relatives
Paid visits to Germans during the last year	
Received visits from Germans during the last year	
Remit to family abroad	
German spouse	
Migration history	*Migration history*
Wish to remain in Germany permanently	Intend to apply for German Citizenship if can have dual
Take trips to the country of origin	Want to return to the country of origin

The one-dimensional *ethnosizer* is the mean assigned value of answers to the questions from all five categories. The variables language, cultural elements, interaction, self-identification and migration history are mini-scales, sizing the ethnic identity of immigrants by a specific factor of ethnic identity. The one-dimensional *ethnosizer*, however, can be viewed as a super-scale, sizing the ethnic identity of individuals using all factors of this concept. All five scales measure ethnic identity as a continuous variable bounded to an interval between 0 and 1. The closer the value of the measured ethnic identity is to zero, the less commitment to the origin it indicates, and the closer it is to 1, the less the immigrant's devotion and commitment to the host society is.

However, the linear model can be seen as too restrictive or simplistic. For example, some people identify linguistically with multiple languages. This is quite natural: Europeans, unlike Americans, grow up in multilingual environments and become fluent in more than one language. By the same token, an immigrant who is fluent in German need not have lost identification with the ancestral language. To measure this two-dimensional nature of reality, a multi-dimensional framework is appropriate. In this paper we concentrate on the two-dimensional generalization only.

To measure ethnic identity by the two-dimensional *ethnosizer*, we need information on commitments to both the host and home societies and cultures. We identified questions that help us compare a personal devotion to German culture and society with the commitment to the culture and people of origin. In most cases we paired each variable indicating commitment to German culture with a variable measuring a similar aspect of commitment to the culture of origin. The pairing was not required for the variable in the 'cultural elements' factor group because the construction of the variable alone allowed evaluating the strength of commitment to the German media and the media from the country of origin. Column 2 of Table 2 displays the list of variables used to measure ethnic identity in the two-dimensional model.

Following our rationale depicted in Fig. 2, we identify the status of the immigrants' ethnic identity by each group of elements. A respondent with a 'very good' or 'good' command of both German and the language of origin is classified as linguistically integrated; a respondent with 'good' command of German and 'bad' or 'no command' of the language of origin is considered linguistically assimilated; a respondent with 'very good' or 'good' command of the language of origin, and 'fair' or 'worse' command of German is labeled linguistically separated; and, finally, a person with a 'bad' command of both languages is classified as linguistically marginalized. Similarly, people who equally prefer the German media and the media of their country of origin are culturally integrated; those who are involved only in the German media are culturally assimilated, the readers of media only from the country of origin are culturally separated, and those who do not read any media are culturally marginalized. We performed the same operation of transformation and classification on the variables of preferences in ethnic interaction, self-identification, and migration history.

Classifying immigrants as strictly integrated, assimilated, separated or marginalized in all five components can be delusive. A person can be culturally and linguistically integrated into the German society, but may still have no friends in Germany or strongly identify with the home country. In fact, in our sample there are only very few immigrants who are identified as assimilated or separated in all five factor groups of ethnic identity and no one at all who is identified as integrated or marginalized in all factor groups. In most cases the respondents' content of ethnic identity varies across the factor groups, which is why the measure is scientifically valuable.

Table 3
Distribution of the one- and two-dimensional *ethnosizers* by ethnicity, gender, and religion.

	One-dimensional	Two-dimensional			
	Ethnosizer	Integration	Assimilation	Separation	Marginalization
Ethnicity					
Turkish	0.639 (0.007)	1.032 (0.046)	0.779 (0.045)	2.293 (0.063)	0.896 (0.043)
Ex-Yugoslav	0.523 (0.010)	1.219 (0.062)	1.107 (0.065)	1.756 (0.083)	0.917 (0.059)
Greek	0.573 (0.015)	1.121 (0.095)	0.897 (0.083)	2.069 (0.132)	0.914 (0.083)
Italian	0.540 (0.012)	1.163 (0.064)	1.077 (0.080)	1.894 (0.095)	0.865 (0.064)
Spanish	0.529 (0.026)	1.388 (0.162)	1.122 (0.145)	1.776 (0.213)	0.714 (0.109)
Other	0.410 (0.010)	1.471 (0.062)	1.681 (0.069)	1.117 (0.070)	0.732 (0.049)
Religion					
Muslim	0.623 (0.008)	0.929 (0.044)	0.862 (0.047)	2.262 (0.064)	0.946 (0.043)
Catholic	0.497 (0.009)	1.245 (0.046)	1.295 (0.058)	1.634 (0.067)	0.826 (0.043)
Other Christian	0.523 (0.011)	1.255 (0.066)	1.119 (0.067)	1.761 (0.087)	0.864 (0.054)
Other religion	0.511 (0.014)	1.538 (0.084)	1.138 (0.081)	1.538 (0.098)	0.788 (0.068)
No religion	0.500 (0.013)	1.585 (0.078)	1.169 (0.072)	1.518 (0.092)	0.728 (0.062)
Gender					
Female	0.561 (0.007)	1.151 (0.040)	1.030 (0.041)	1.918 (0.055)	0.901 (0.036)
Male	0.536 (0.007)	1.229 (0.038)	1.127 (0.042)	1.827 (0.053)	0.818 (0.033)
Mean	0.548 (0.005)	1.191 (0.027)	1.080 (0.030)	1.871 (0.038)	0.859 (0.024)

Note: Standard errors in parentheses.

With our technique, it is also possible to discuss the status of ethnic identity in comparative terms. For example, if respondent A is identified as assimilated in terms of language, culture, and self-identification and respondent B is identified as assimilated only in terms of self-identification, then respondent A is generally more assimilated than respondent B. If, on the other hand, respondent B is identified as separated in more factor groups than respondent A, he or she could be considered as more separated than respondent A. Therefore, we generate the following four dependent variables that measure the ethnic identity of immigrants: (i) *integration* is the number of times that each respondent is identified as 'integrated' in all five factors groups of ethnic identity, (ii) *assimilation* is the number of times that each respondent is identified as 'assimilated' in all five factor groups, (iii) *separation* is the number of times that each respondent is identified as 'separated' in all five groups, and (iv) *marginalization* is the number of times that each respondent is identified as 'marginalized' in all five groups. Each of these four variables can take a value between 0 and 5, and for each immigrant they sum up to five.

The descriptive statistics in Table 1 reflect some interesting patterns of our one- and two-dimensional *ethnosizers*. Based on the mean value of the one-dimensional *ethnosizer* (0.548), the immigrants in our sample demonstrate about the same commitment to the culture of the host society as to the culture of origin with a marginal advantage for the home society. However, the average immigrant in our sample demonstrates stronger separation (1.9) than integration (1.2), assimilation (1.1) or marginalization (0.9). According to these four states (the two-dimensional *ethnosizer*), immigrants in Germany demonstrate a stronger commitment to the culture and society of origin than to the host country. While these observations are somewhat conflicting at first sight, they are the direct consequence of the differences in the dimension of observation and the depths of measurement. Not surprisingly, the one-dimensional *ethnosizer* overestimates the adaptation and acculturation of immigrants to the host country.

Our one- and two-dimensional measures of ethnic identity condense information on language, culture, ethnic self-identification, ethnic interaction and migration history. This information is collected typically some time after the immigrant has entered the country and has been exposed to adjustment challenges. We, therefore, treat education in the home country as a pre-determined and exogenous production factor of ethnic identity towards the home and the host country. Education and work participation in the host country, however, is potentially jointly endogenous with ethnic identity at the time of measurement and, hence, should be excluded from a set of potential regressors provided that there are no particular good reasons to do otherwise.

To establish a rough understanding to what extent ethnicity correlates with socio-economic outcomes, we have calculated the correlation coefficients between the integration, assimilation, separation and marginalization measures and total years of education in the home and host country, with a dummy to work and with income (and a reduced sample of those working only). The expected tendency shows up, namely that integration and assimilation are positively correlated with success, and separation and marginalization are negatively correlated.

3.3. Distribution of the measurements of ethnic identity

Table 3 presents the mean distribution of our key measurements of ethnic identity by ethnicity, religion and gender. On average, immigrants of any ethnic or religious group are more likely to exhibit commitment either to the German culture and society or to the society and culture of the origin than not exhibit any commitment at all. Marginalization is a weak phenomenon among immigrants in Germany. The average ethnic, religious, or gender group demonstrates marginalization in less than one factor of ethnic identity.

Turkish immigrants exhibit the strongest identification with their origin and the weakest identification with the German culture and society in both the one- and two-dimensional models of ethnic identity. Individuals of Turkish ethnicity are the only ethnic group of immigrants in our sample whose mean score on the *ethnosizer* is largely higher than the sample average score. This indicates that Turks have more commitment to the country of origin or less than average devotion to the German culture. Moreover, on average, Turkish immigrants manifest the lowest level of either integration or assimilation and the highest level of separation among all ethnic groups. This can be interpreted as the Turks' strong commitment to the culture of ancestry and weak devotion to German society.

To the contrary, Spanish immigrants demonstrate the strongest average commitment to the German culture and society among all other major groups of immigrants in Germany. Together with the ex-Yugoslavs, Spanish respondents score the lowest on the *ethnosizer* and therefore are, on average, less ethnic than most other major immigrant groups in Germany. They also exhibit the highest integration and assimilation scores and the lowest marginalization and separation from the German society. Note that all other ethnicities together score the lowest among all immigrants on the *ethnosizer*, the highest on assimilation and integration and the lowest on separation.

Table 3 also indicates that Muslims in our study have a pattern of cultural and social commitment that is very similar to the pattern of cultural and social devotion of Turks, while the Catholics' pattern of cultural devotion resembles that of Spaniards. For instance, Muslims score, on average, as high on the *ethnosizer* as Turks do. Also, Muslims demonstrate as strong of a separation as individuals of Turkish ethnicity but slightly stronger assimilation and much lower integration than them. Similar to Spaniards, Catholics score low on the *ethnosizer*, exhibiting stronger integration and assimilation and lower separation than Muslims do. Because many Turks are Muslims and many Spaniards are Catholic, the question which is relevant here (and which we will answer in our further statistical analyses) is whether it is the ethnicity of immigrants or their religion that defines the cultural and social commitment to the origin and to the host society.[3]

Lastly, we find that immigrant women are, on average, slightly more committed to the culture and society of the country of origin than men are. As Table 3 shows, the average immigrant woman not only is a little bit more ethnic, but also demonstrates less integration and assimilation and more separation and marginalization than the average immigrant man. Work habits may contribute to this finding. Ethnic identity and work preferences are generated jointly. However, those women who are pulled into work can integrate and assimilate better since work makes such adjustments easier due to the special exposure it provides. Given the low incentives for women to work in Germany, they should be attached closer to the home culture than men.

4. Quantifying ethnic identity

4.1. The one-dimensional ethnosizer

We now turn to the econometric investigation of our measures of ethnic identity. Table 4 contains the ordinary least squares (OLS) regression results[4] of the one-dimensional *ethnosizer* and its components, namely language, culture, social interaction, migration history, and self-identification. This exercise shows how ethnosized immigrants are according to their characteristics. Recall that while the *ethnosizer* indicates stronger commitment to the origin, the individual components in columns 1-5 are constructed with information on Germany alone. A higher value in language, for example, shows a lower commitment to the German language and is interpreted as being more linguistically ethnic. Note that the reference individual is a non-religious, male, Turk with no education in the home country. Column 6 shows that, overall, the expressed affiliation and affinity of immigrants with the home country increases with age and is smaller the older a person is upon arrival in Germany. Put differently, for each additional year one arrives older, the ethnic identity towards the home country is larger, albeit at a decreasing rate. Females and those with complete or incomplete schooling in the home country remain more ethnically attached than the reference group, while Catholics are less. Interestingly, immigrants with college education from the home country are less ethnosized. Controlling for all regression determinants (especially religion), we find that Italians, Spaniards, Greeks, ex-Yugoslavs and immigrants of other ethnicities are significantly less ethnosized than Turks.

The analysis on the components of the *ethnosizer* exhibits a much more complex picture. The affiliation with German as the adopted language and the relative use of the language of ethnic origin is of central concern in scientific research and in the political debate since language proficiency is positively associated with labor market success (Chiswick, 1991; Chiswick and Miller, 1996; Esser, 2006). With the exception of a few variables, column 1 of Table 4 basically mimics the findings of the general one-dimensional *ethnosizer*, although the estimated significant parameters are mostly larger in absolute terms.

---

[3] There is substantial independent variation for the ethnicity and religion variables. As exhibited in Table 1, the categories for religion are Catholic, Other Christian, Muslim, Other Religion, and Non-religious. While Greeks, Italians and Spaniards are predominantly Christians (Greek Christians are largely non-Catholics), only about three quarters of the Turks in the sample are Muslims and about 4 percent are Christians; about 30 percent of the ex-Yugoslavs are Muslims and about 60 percent are Christians; 2 percent of the Greeks are Muslims.

[4] We present here and in the sequel only OLS regressions since these findings are pretty consistent with the more complex logit and limited-dependent variable models we examined.

Table 4
OLS estimates of one-dimensional measurements of ethnic identity.

Variables	Language (1)	Culture (2)	Social interaction (3)	Migration history (4)	Self-identification (5)	Ethnosizer (6)
Constant	0.388** (2.16)	0.544*** (4.05)	0.688*** (3.38)	0.942*** (4.06)	0.654*** (3.19)	0.643*** (5.37)
Age	−0.014 (−1.14)	−0.007 (−0.78)	−0.004 (−0.27)	−0.023 (−1.51)	−0.012 (−0.85)	−0.012 (−1.48)
Age squared	0.0002 (0.93)	0.0001 (0.66)	−5.84e−07 (−0.00)	0.001** (2.21)	0.0003 (0.87)	0.0003 (1.58)
Age cubic	−1.70e−06 (−0.94)	−8.26e−07 (−0.61)	3.79e−07 (0.18)	−6.22e−06*** (−2.66)	−2.34e−06 (−1.13)	−2.14e−06* (−1.78)
Age at entry	0.020*** (10.10)	0.010*** (6.50)	0.005** (2.11)	0.001 (0.21)	0.009*** (4.19)	0.009*** (6.72)
Age at entry squared	−0.0001*** (−3.69)	−0.0001*** (−3.25)	−4.30e−06 (−0.11)	−0.0001 (−1.29)	−0.00002 (−0.48)	−0.0001** (−2.54)
Female	0.054*** (4.27)	0.045*** (4.70)	0.001 (0.05)	0.007 (0.45)	0.025* (1.74)	0.026*** (3.12)
Muslim	0.064** (2.13)	0.069*** (3.05)	−0.019 (−0.55)	−0.173*** (−4.43)	0.029 (0.84)	−0.006 (−0.29)
Catholic	−0.017 (−0.55)	−0.024 (−1.06)	−0.101*** (−2.92)	−0.058 (−1.48)	−0.044 (−1.26)	−0.049** (−2.40)
Other Christian	−0.014 (−0.45)	0.007 (0.31)	−0.069* (−1.91)	−0.091** (−2.23)	0.007 (0.20)	−0.032 (−1.51)
Other religion	−0.009 (−0.28)	−0.008 (−0.36)	−0.063* (−1.73)	−0.082* (−1.98)	−0.012 (−0.33)	−0.035 (−1.63)
College and higher education in the home country	−0.018 (−0.70)	0.020 (1.02)	−0.058* (−1.96)	−0.075** (−2.25)	−0.064** (−2.17)	−0.039** (−2.26)
Vocational training in the home country	−0.037** (−2.28)	−0.022* (−1.76)	0.011 (0.57)	0.019 (0.91)	0.006 (0.33)	−0.005 (−0.42)
Complete schooling in the home country	0.095*** (6.39)	0.034*** (3.09)	0.037** (2.20)	0.016 (0.84)	0.024 (1.39)	0.041*** (4.16)
Incomplete schooling in the home country	0.119*** (6.19)	0.046*** (3.21)	0.108*** (4.94)	0.051** (2.07)	0.037* (1.69)	0.072*** (5.63)
Ex-Yugoslav	−0.115*** (−5.35)	−0.151*** (−9.38)	−0.079*** (−3.20)	−0.127*** (−4.56)	−0.107*** (−4.33)	−0.116*** (−8.05)
Greek	−0.040 (−1.28)	−0.061*** (−2.58)	−0.080** (−2.24)	0.022 (0.54)	−0.047 (−1.30)	−0.041* (−1.96)
Italian	−0.010 (−0.36)	−0.056*** (−2.69)	−0.080** (−2.54)	−0.096*** (−2.68)	−0.020 (−0.62)	−0.052*** (−2.83)
Spanish	−0.066* (−1.68)	−0.114*** (−3.85)	−0.144*** (−3.20)	0.00004 (0.00)	0.033 (0.73)	−0.058** (−2.20)
Other ethnicity	−0.307*** (−12.70)	−0.265*** (−14.63)	−0.315*** (−11.46)	−0.171*** (−5.46)	−0.163*** (−5.90)	−0.244*** (−15.12)
Adjusted R^2	0.399	0.373	0.229	0.095	0.112	0.349
Number of observations				1300		

Note: t-ratios in parentheses. The reference individual is a non-religious, male, Turk with no education in the home country. Dependent variables are coded as highest value corresponds to lowest commitment to Germany or highest commitment to the origin.
* Significant at 10 percent (two-tail test).
** Significant at 5 percent (two-tail test).
*** Significant at 1 percent (two-tail test).

Muslim religion is a significant contributor to identifying with one's own ethnicity and increases one's linguistic ethnic identity. Pre-migration education shows interesting results. Vocational training in the home country leads to stronger affiliation with the German language, but some or complete schooling in the home country makes immigrants more linguistically ethnic. We find that Italians, Spaniards and Greeks are no linguistically different than Turks, while ex-Yugoslavs, Spaniards and other ethnicities are less linguistically ethnic and identify with the German language more than Turks.

The cultural ethnic identity findings in column 2 of Table 4 display a structure similar to language. One exception is the parameter estimates on all ethnicity dummies indicating that, compared to Turks, other immigrants are less culturally ethnic and identify more with the German culture.

Exposure to German nationals and people of the own ethnic group (interaction) is analysed in column 3 of Table 4. Note that Catholics, other Christians and other religions interact more with Germans in comparison to non-religious individuals and Muslims. Low levels of education in the home country result in a stronger attachment to and socializing with individuals from their own ethnicity, but college education produces the opposite effect. Other things equal, we find again that all ethnicities are significantly less ethnic in their social interaction with people than Turks.

The migration history column (column 4 of Table 4) measures attachments to the home country and nationality. The attachment to the home country increases with age and incomplete schooling, while it decreases among Muslims, other Christians, other religions and with college and higher education in the home country. Ex-Yugoslavs, Italians and all other ethnicities have a stronger attachment to the host country than Turks; meaning that they wish to remain in Germany.

The individual self-expression of ethnic identity finally provides once again a somewhat similar picture to the general *ethnosizer*. As the estimates in column 5 of Table 4 suggest, the individual affiliation of migrants with the host country is smaller the older a person is upon arrival in Germany. Women self-identify with Germans significantly less than men. Interestingly, when it comes to self-identification, no religion plays a significant role. Those with incomplete schooling in the home country remain significantly more ethnic in their self-identification than the reference group. A college degree helps immigrants significantly self-identify with Germans than no degree at all. While Spaniards, Italians and Greeks are no different than Turks, ex-Yugoslavs and immigrants from other ethnicities are self-identifying less with their heritage and culture of origin.

Across all indicators, this analysis provides rough predictions of ethnic integration into the host country's ethnicity: the attachment is smaller among females, those with higher age at entry and among those with incomplete or complete schooling. It is larger among Catholics and the college-educated. Muslims are culturally and linguistically attached to their origin, but exhibit a more German-oriented migration history which results in an overall effect of zero for the general one-dimensional *ethnosizer*. Most parameter estimates for the ethnic groups are statistically significant, and when so, they are negative. This implies that all ethnicities are significantly less ethnic than Turks, the reference group.

4.2. The two-dimensional ethnosizer

We now move over to the analysis of our two-dimensional model of ethnic identity. This approach enables us to differentiate between integration, assimilation, separation and marginalization of the ethnic groups. Recall that here individuals can identify with more than one country and culture. Regression results are again OLS estimates and presented in Table 5. As before, the reference individual is a male, non-religious, Turk with no education in the home country. Age at entry matters: it decreases the scores for integration and assimilation and increases the scores for separation and marginalization; the effect is linear for integration only, while it is moderated with higher age at entry in the other three cases. Age, in general, does not affect the strength of integration or assimilation at all, but it is negatively associated with separation and positively connected with marginalization. Taken together, they imply that younger immigrants upon arrival are more likely to assimilate or integrate than older ones, and this does not change with duration of residence. The older individuals are upon arrival, the less probable is separation and the more probable is marginalization at the time of entry; while after that age affects marginalization positively (albeit at a decreasing rate), separation becomes less probable with rising age. Females are no different than males in all three states of the two-dimensional *ethnosizer* except in assimilation, suggesting that women are less assimilated than men.

As it turns out, religion is a decisive indicator for the evolution of two states of ethnic identity in the two-dimensional model. Muslims are less likely to integrate and more often marginalized than non-religious immigrants; they are however more likely to assimilate. Catholics are also integrating less than non-religious individuals, but they are strongly more assimilated and less separated than the reference group. Other Christians also exhibit less integration and more assimilation in comparison to non-religious individuals. Immigrants in other religions separate less and marginalize more. If assimilation is the central goal, then Muslims, Catholics or other Christians are the preferred groups; if integration is the required level of performance, then non-religious individuals outperform all others.

Pre-migration education exhibits a differentiated impact on the evolution of ethnic identity of immigrants. Complete or incomplete schooling before emigration leads to higher levels of separation; the effect is stronger with incomplete schooling than with complete schooling, both in comparison to no education. While complete schooling leads to lower levels of integration and assimilation, incomplete schooling has stronger negative effects. College and higher education in the home country make a significant difference only in the separation levels; those individuals are less prone to separate from the host country than those with no education. Vocational training plays a role in marginalization only. Namely, immigrants with vocational training are less likely to marginalize in Germany that those with no such education.

Table 5
OLS estimates of two-dimensional measurements of ethnic identity.

	Integration (1)	Assimilation (2)	Separation (3)	Marginalization (4)
Constant	1.090 (1.44)	1.709** (2.24)	3.363*** (3.44)	−1.162 (−1.63)
Age	0.058 (1.14)	−0.002 (−0.05)	−0.169*** (−2.58)	0.114** (2.38)
Age squared	−0.001 (−0.85)	0.0001 (0.05)	0.004*** (2.67)	−0.003*** (−2.82)
Age cubic	4.76e-06 (0.63)	−1.60e-07 (−0.02)	−0.00003*** (−2.90)	0.00002*** (3.33)
Age at entry	−0.030*** (−3.64)	−0.064*** (−7.69)	0.074*** (6.94)	0.020** (2.56)
Age at entry squared	0.0001 (0.99)	0.001*** (4.95)	−0.001*** (−2.82)	−0.0003** (−2.48)
Female	−0.043 (−0.81)	−0.121** (−2.26)	0.084 (1.22)	0.081 (1.61)
Muslim	−0.562*** (−4.33)	0.228* (1.74)	−0.034 (−0.20)	0.368*** (3.00)
Catholic	−0.340*** (−2.60)	0.458*** (3.48)	−0.279* (−1.65)	0.161 (1.31)
Other Christian	−0.252* (−1.87)	0.267** (1.96)	−0.208 (−1.19)	0.193 (1.51)
Other religion	−0.098 (−0.71)	0.179 (1.29)	−0.307* (−1.73)	0.226* (1.75)
College and higher education in the home country	0.143 (1.32)	0.092 (0.84)	−0.396*** (−2.82)	0.161 (1.57)
Vocational training in the home country	0.065 (0.94)	0.048 (0.69)	0.067 (0.75)	−0.180*** (−2.76)
Complete schooling in the home country	−0.169*** (−2.70)	−0.268*** (−4.25)	0.449*** (5.53)	−0.011 (−0.18)
Incomplete schooling in the home country	−0.405*** (−5.02)	−0.390*** (−4.79)	0.682*** (6.54)	0.112 (1.48)
Ex-Yugoslav	0.107 (1.18)	0.335*** (3.67)	−0.584*** (−4.99)	0.143* (1.67)
Greek	−0.172 (−1.31)	0.033 (0.25)	0.017 (0.10)	0.122 (0.98)
Italian	−0.094 (−0.80)	0.063 (0.54)	−0.085 (−0.57)	0.116 (1.06)
Spanish	0.086 (0.52)	0.062 (0.37)	−0.126 (−0.59)	−0.022 (−0.14)
Other ethnicity	0.312*** (3.03)	0.963*** (9.28)	−1.330*** (−10.00)	0.055 (0.56)
Adjusted R^2	0.137	0.230	0.262	0.055
Number of observations		1269		

Note: t-ratios in parentheses. The reference individual is a non-religious, male, Turk with no education in the home country.
* Significant at 10 percent (two-tail test).
** Significant at 5 percent (two-tail test).
*** Significant at 1 percent (two-tail test).

The effects of ethnicity are covered by parameters for country of origin dummies, which need to be interpreted with respect to the Turkish reference group. People from the former Yugoslavia seem to go to extremes. While they are more likely to assimilate and less likely to separate, they are also more likely to marginalize. Greeks, Italians and Spaniards are similar to Turks in their ethnic identity struggle in all four states of the *ethnosizer*. Lastly, immigrants from other ethnicities manage to be more integrated and assimilated and less separated than Turks.

While we have found that religion is a decisive production factor in the process of ethnic adjustment and identification, the country of origin dummies suggest small but considerable differences in ethnic identity according to nationality and ancestry. This implies that ethnicity measured by country of origin cannot be reduced to religious factors. Expressed differently, religion has an independent impact on an individual's ability to adjust into another ethnicity, and this might be related either to the particular characteristics of the religion or to its closeness to the dominant religion in the host country.

5. Summary and conclusions

In this paper we investigate migrant ethnicity and the evolution of ethnic identity during residence in the host country. To operationalize ethnic identity we establish five groups of essential elements that can best capture the salient features of ethnic identity: language use, cultural aspects, ethnic networks, migration history, and ethnic self-identification. Using these factor groups, we start with a linear continuous representation of ethnic identity measuring devotion to the host society and commitment to the origin on a scale from zero to one. This zero-sum concept of ethnic identity we call the one-dimensional *ethnosizer*. A two-dimensional *ethnosizer* allows us to capture four possibilities of different commitments to the host and home cultures. Therefore, we distinguish between integration, assimilation, separation and marginalization of migrant ethnic identity in a more realistic setting. Using data from the German Socio-economic Panel, we then calibrate the various measures and investigate their relationship to age, age at entry, religion, educational levels, and ethnic origin.

The first round of analyses is based on the one-dimensional *ethnosizer*. Here, we find that immigrant women manifest a closer bond to their native ethnic identity than men, and this is caused by a low attachment to Germany concerning language use, cultural aspects and ethnic self-identification. Catholics adapt stronger to the ethnic identity of the host country, mainly because of their German social interactions. While Muslims remain strongly more linguistically and culturally ethnic, they are less ethnic in their migration history and want to stay in Germany permanently. Other Christians and immigrants of other religions also form an ethnic identity closer to Germans in their interactions and migration history. Completed and incomplete schooling in the home country keeps migrants more ethnic and inflexible towards adjustment. College and higher education in the home country lead to a stronger interaction with Germans, a larger willingness to stay in Germany and a deeper self-identification with the host country. The highly educated are overall less ethnic as they have a negative statistically significant effect on the general one-dimensional *ethnosizer*. All ethnicities are less ethnosized than Turks, who have a strong Turkish ethnic identity. This is also true for the culture, social interaction with co-ethnics and migration history elements.

In the two-dimensional *ethnosizer*, young migrants at arrival are integrated or assimilated the best, while they marginalize the least and are more probable to separate. Women are only different than men in their assimilation scores, meaning that they assimilate or become the same as Germans less than men. When it comes to integration, that is, keeping and valuing both cultures, religion is important. Muslims, Catholics, and other Christians do not integrate, but assimilate well in comparison to non-religious individuals. Muslim immigrants also score high on marginalization in comparison to non-religious individuals followed by the other religions. Catholics separate less than the non-religious followed by other religions. Immigrants with a college degree or higher education in the home country separate less than those with no education. School education, whether complete or incomplete, is more harmful for the process of integration or assimilation than no education in the home country; it also leads to more separation. Vocational training in the home country mitigates marginalization. The ethnicity of the individuals, measured by dummy variables of the countries of origin, remains statistically different from zero in some cases with an interesting pattern. Ex-Yugoslavs assimilate more and separate less than Turks, but they also marginalize more. While Greeks, Spaniards and Italians are no different than Turks, people from other ethnicities integrate and assimilate more; they also separate less than Turks.

Since the provision of data and reliable measures are important to investigate the validity of the developed theories, the paper could complement and stimulate the existing strands of the literature. The *ethnosizer* can contribute to testing various influential arguments in sophisticated ways. For instance, it is able to measure the social categories or multiple identities of Akerlof and Kranton, examine how individuals sort themselves into those categories, and determine how such choices affect economic performance. The *ethnosizer* may further provide evidence of multiple equilibria with respect to levels and types of ethnic activity as in Kuran, who describes situations of low and massive ethnifications. This suggests ways to explore why ex-Yugoslavs go to extremes, as in the data set presented in the paper, where they assimilate and marginalize more at the same time than most of the other ethnicities. Similarly, it might provide insights into why other ethnicities may be more integrated and more assimilated than the Turks. It is also possible to study why socialization would be more pronounced in mixed neighborhoods than in segregated neighborhoods, an issue that was put forward by Bisin et al. We hope that the *ethnosizer* will help to generate an exciting agenda of further research.

Acknowledgements

This is a substantially revised version of our March 2006 IZA Discussion Paper No. 2040. Financial support from Volkswagen Foundation for the IZA project on "The Economics and Persistence of Migrant Ethnicity" is gratefully acknowledged. We wish to thank the IZA-Volkswagen Ethnicity Research Team, participants from the March 2006 Annual Meeting of the Population Association of America in Los Angeles, a Research Seminar at the Center for Comparative Immigration Studies of the University of California, San Diego, in April 2006, the Eleventh Annual Meeting of the Society of Labor Economists in May 2006, the Second IZA Migrant Ethnicity Meeting in May 2006, and two anonymous referees for very valuable comments and suggestions.

References

Akerlof, G.A., Kranton, R.E., 2000. Economics and identity. Quarterly Journal of Economics 115, 715–753.
Austen-Smith, D., Fryer Jr., R.G., 2005. An economic analysis of "Acting White". Quarterly Journal of Economics 120, 551–583.
Battu, H., Mwale, M., Zenou, Y., 2007. Oppositional identities and the labor market. Journal of Population Economics 20, 643–667.
Bénabou, R., Tirole, J., 2007. Identity, dignity and taboos: Beliefs as assets. IZA Discussion Paper No. 2583.
Berry, J., 1980. Acculturation as varieties of adaptation. In: Padilla, A.M. (Ed.), Acculturation: Theory, Models and Some New Findings. Westview, Boulder, CO, pp. 9–25.
Berry, J., Kim, U., Power, S., Young, M., Bujaki, M., 1989. Acculturation attitudes in plural societies. Applied Psychology: An International Review 38, 185–206.
Betts, J., Fairlie, R., 2001. Explaining ethnic, racial and immigrant differences in private school attendance. Journal of Urban Economics 50, 26–51.
Bisin, A., Patacchini, E., Verdier, T., Zenou, Y., 2006. 'Bend it like Beckham': identity, socialization and assimilation. CEPR Discussion Paper No. 5662.
Chiswick, B.R., 1991. Speaking, reading and earnings among low-skilled immigrants. Journal of Labor Economics 9, 149–170.
Chiswick, B.R., Miller, P.W., 1996. Ethnic networks and language proficiency among immigrants. Journal of Population Economics 9, 19–35.
Constant, A., Zimmermann, K.F., 2005. Legal status at entry, economic performance, and self-employment proclivity: a bi-national study of immigrants. IZA Discussion Paper No. 1910.
Cutler, D.M., Glaeser, E.L., Vigdor, J.L., 1999. The rise and decline of the American ghetto. The Journal of Political Economy 107, 455–506.
Dana, L.P., 1997. The origins of self-employment in ethno-cultural communities: distinguishing between orthodox entrepreneurship and reactionary enterprise. Canadian Journal of Administrative Sciences 14, 52–68.
Darity, W.A., Mason, P.L., Stewart, J.B., 2006. The economics of identity: the origin and persistence of racial identity norms. Journal of Economic Behavior and Organization 60, 283–305.
Dashevsky, A., 1976. Ethnic Identity in Society. Rand McNally, Chicago.
Esser, H., 2006. Migration, Sprache und Integration. AKI Forschungsbilanz 4. Mimeo, Science Center Berlin.
Fearon, J.D., Laitin, D.D., 2000. Violence and the social construction of ethnic identity. International Organization 54, 845–877.
Guiso, L., Sapienza, P., Zingales, L., 2006. Does culture affect economic outcomes? Journal of Economic Perspectives 20, 23–48.
Hazuda, H., Haffner, S., Stern, M., Eifler, C., 1988. Effects of acculturation and socioeconomic status on obesity and diabetes in Mexican Americans. American Journal of Epidemiology 128, 1289–1301.
Hirshman, E., 1981. American Jewish ethnicity: its relationship to some selected aspects of consumer behavior. Journal of Marketing 45, 102–110.
Kuran, T., 1998. Ethnic norms and their transformation through reputational cascades. Journal of Legal Studies 27, 623–659.
Kwan, K.L., Sodowsky, G., 1997. Internal and external ethnic identity and their correlates: a study of Chinese American immigrants. Journal of Multicultural Counseling and Development 25, 51–67.
Laroche, M., Kim, Ch., Tomiuk, M., Belisle, D., 2005. Similarities in Italian and Greek multidimensional ethnic identity: some implications for food consumption. Canadian Journal of Administrative Sciences 22, 143–167.
Makabe, T., 1979. Ethnic identity scale and social mobility: the case of Nisei in Toronto. The Canadian Review of Sociology and Anthropology 16, 136–145.

Mason, P.L., 2004. Annual income, hourly wages, and identity among Mexican-Americans and other Latinos. Industrial Relations 43, 817–834.
Masuda, M., Matsumoto, G., Meredith, G., 1970. Ethnic identity in three generations of Japanese Americans. Journal of Social Psychology 81, 199–207.
Montgomery, G., 1992. Comfort with acculturation status among students from South Texas. Hispanic Journal of Behavioral Sciences 14, 201–223.
Neuman, S., Oaxaca, R.L., 2005. Wage differentials in the 1990s in Israel: endowments, discrimination, and selectivity. International Journal of Manpower 26, 217–236.
Nguyen, H.H., von Eye, A., 2002. Validating an acculturation scale for Vietnamese adolescents (ASVA): a bidimensional perspective. International Journal for Behavioral Development 26, 202–213.
Ogden, D., Ogden, J., Schau, H., 2004. Exploring the impact of culture and acculturation on consumer purchase decisions: toward a microcultural perspective. Academy of Marketing Science Review [Online] 8. See http://www.amsreview.org/articles/ogden03-2004.pdf (accessed on September 13, 2008).
Phinney, J., 1990. Ethnic identity in adolescents and adults: review of research. Psychological Bulletin 180, 499–514.
Phinney, J., 1992. The multigroup ethnic identity measure: a new scale for use with diverse groups. Journal of Adolescent Research 7, 156–176.
Phinney, J., 1996. When we talk about American ethnic groups, what do we mean? American Psychologist 51, 918–927.
Piche, V., Renaud, J., Gingras, L., Shapiro, D., 2002. Economic integration of new immigrants in the Montreal labor market: a longitudinal approach. Population (English Edition, 2002) 57, 57–82.
Ruble, B., 1989. Ethnicity and Soviet cities. Soviet Studies 41, 401–414.
Smith, J.P., 2004. Immigrants and their schooling. The Center for Comparative Immigration Studies, Working Paper 108.
SOEP Group, 2001. The German Socio-Economic Panel (GSOEP) after more than 15 years—overview. In: Holst, E., Lillard, D.R., DiPrete, T.A. (Eds.), Proceedings of the 2000 Fourth International Conference of German Socio-Economic Panel Study Users (GSOEP 2000), Vier-teljahrshefte zur Wirtschaftsforschung (Quarterly Journal of Economic Research) 70, 7–14.
Thurnwald, R., 1932. The psychology of acculturation. American Anthropologists 34, 557–569.
Tzuriel, D., Klein, M., 1977. Ego identity: effects of ethnocentrism, ethnic identification, and cognitive complexity in Israeli, oriental and western ethnic groups. Psychological Reports 40, 1099–1110.
Ullah, P., 1985. Second generation Irish youth: identity and ethnicity. New Community 12, 310–320.
Unger, J., Gallaher, P., Shakib, S., Ritt-Olson, A., Palmer, P., Johnson, C., 2002. The AHISMA acculturation scale: a new measure of acculturation for adolescents in a multicultural society. Journal of Early Adolescence 23, 225–251.
Webster, C., 1990–1991. Attitudes toward marketing practices: the effects of ethnic identification. Journal of Applied Business Research 7, 107–116.
Zorlu, A., 2003. Do ethnicity and sex matter in pay? Analyses of 8 ethnic groups in the Dutch labor market. NIMA, Working Paper Series No. 21.